VIKING BRITAIN

THOMAS WILLIAMS

VIKING BRITAIN

AN EXPLORATION

**WILLIAM
COLLINS**

William Collins
An imprint of HarperCollins*Publishers*
1 London Bridge Street
London SE1 9GF

www.WilliamCollinsBooks.com

First published in Great Britain in 2017 by William Collins

1

A catalogue record for this book is
available from the British Library

ISBN 978-0-00-817193-3

Maps by Martin Brown

Printed and bound by
CPI Group (UK) Ltd, Croydon, CR0 4YY

MIX
Paper from
responsible sources
FSC
www.fsc.org   FSC™ C007454

This book is produced from independently certified FSC paper
to ensure responsible forest management

For more information visit: www.harpercollins.co.uk/green

FOR Z

Storms break on stone-strewn slopes,
Snows falling, the ground enfettered,
the howling of winter. Then darkness awakens,
deepens the night-shadow, sends from the north
a harsh hail-harrying bringing terror to men.

The Wanderer (tenth century)[1]

CONTENTS

BRITAIN
c. 800 AD

ATLANTIC
OCEAN

PICTAVIA

DÁL RIATA

ALT CLUD

NORTH
SEA

NORTHUMBRIA

IRISH SEA

GWYNEDD

MERCIA

POWYS

EAST
ANGLIA

DYFED

GWENT

ESSEX

WESSEX

KENT

SUSSEX

CORNWALL

ENGLISH CHANNEL

BRITAIN
C. 1000 AD

EARLDOM OF ORKNEY

SCOTLAND

MAN AND THE ISLES

STRATHCLYDE

ATLANTIC
OCEAN

NORTH
SEA

IRISH SEA

GWYNEDD

DEHEUBARTH

MORGANNWG

ENGLAND

ENGLISH CHANNEL

PLACES IN
BRITAIN
REFERRED TO IN
THE TEXT

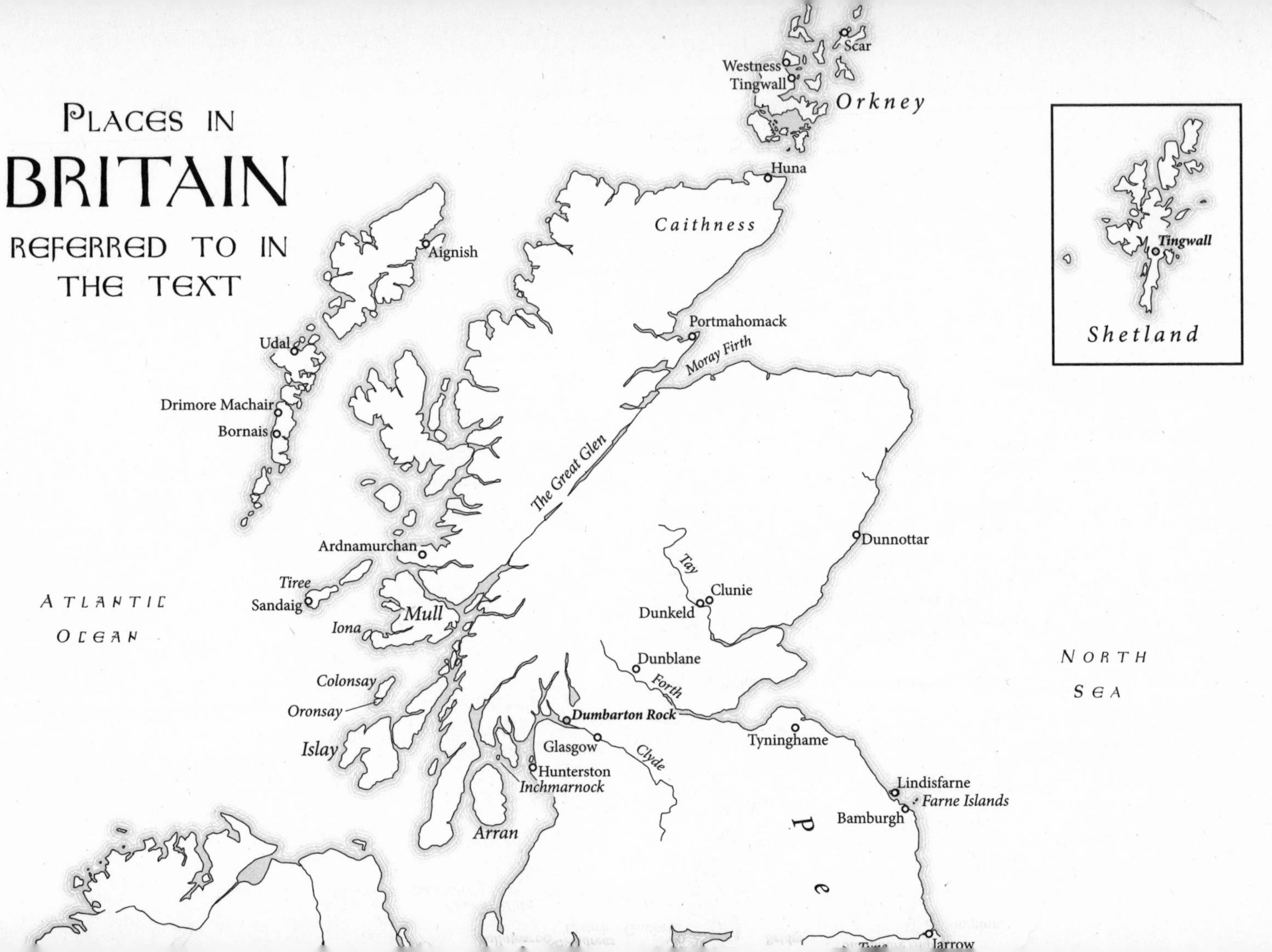

Shetland

Tingwall

NORTH SEA

Orkney

Scar

Westness
Tingwall

Huna

Caithness

Portmahomack

Moray Firth

The Great Glen

Aignish

Ardnamurchan

Mull

Iona

Tree
Sandaig

Drimore Machair
Udal

Bornais

Colonsay

Oronsay

Islay

ATLANTIC OCEAN

Tay

Clunie
Dunkeld

Dunblane

Forth

Dumbarton Rock

Glasgow
Hunterston
Inchmarnock

Arran

Dunnottar

Lindisfarne
Farne Islands

Bamburgh

Jarrow

Tyninghame

P   e

Clyde

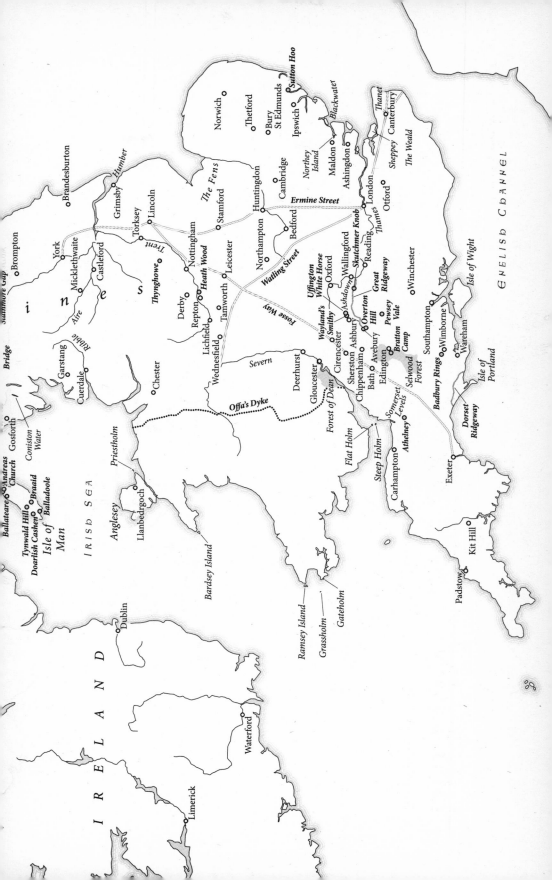

PREFACE

I n 2013–14 I was the project curator for the exhibition *Vikings: Life and Legend* at the British Museum. One of the first reviews, published in a major national newspaper, offered the following critique:[1]

> There's no stage-setting. No gory recreation of the Lindisfarne raid, say, to get us in the mood [...] I felt like crying. Where were the swords? And if I was ready to bawl, what does this exhibition offer its younger visitors? It can't claim not to be for them. You can't put on an exhibition called Vikings without expecting some kids. The only way this exhibition could sound more child-friendly would be if it was called Vikings and Dinosaurs. But the austerely beautiful cases of brooches and golden rings and amber offer very little to fans of *Horrible Histories*.[1]

Leaving aside the issue of whether sensationalizing historical violence for the entertainment of children is ever appropriate (how about a 'gory recreation' of the Srebrenica massacre?), what these comments really reveal is an uncritical assumption that the Vikings have their proper place as players in a hilarious historical Grand Guignol, alongside head-chopping at the Tower of London. The Vikings, it seems to say, are a cheerful, bloody diversion for the kids on a wet bank-holiday afternoon, not a proper historical phenomenon. The indignation that springs from not having had these prejudices confirmed is palpable. Brooches? Women? Trade? BORING! Vikings are big men with swords, crushing skulls left, right and centre: the barbarian archetype writ large and red.

It occurred to me at the time that nobody would treat Roman history in this way. It is unthinkable, for example, that any art critic would yearn for lurid re-enactments of Roman soldiers cheerfully raping and murdering British women and children – least of all within the austere neo-classical precincts of the British Museum. The Romans, it is instinctively felt, are refined, have gravitas. They benefit from a cultural snobbery with extraordinarily deep roots (ultimately fastened in the smug imperial propaganda of the Romans themselves). Roman Britain, in particular, is widely presented in a solidly respectable way – epitomized in tiresome tropes of roof tiles and under-floor heating, good roads and urban planning, fine wine and fancy tableware. It is a period that can serve as an acceptable backstory to who we are and where we come from, a people 'just like us', who went to parties and wrote letters and had jobs. *Romanitas* – Romanness – means 'civilization'.

Few think of the age of the Vikings in those terms. Like other romantic curios they have been fetishized and infantilized, set apart from wider history alongside pirates, gladiators, knights-in-armour and, I suppose, dinosaurs. The Vikings are presented as cartoon savages who had a short-lived cameo rampaging around in the gloomy interlude between the end of Roman Britain and the Norman Conquest. It does them a grave disservice.

Between the conventional beginning of the Viking Age in the late eighth century and its close in the eleventh, Scandinavian people and culture were involved with Britain to a degree that left a permanent impression on these islands. They came to trade and plunder and, ultimately, to settle, to colonize and to rule. It is a story of often epic proportions, thronged with characters whose names and deeds still fire the blood and stir the imagination – Svein Forkbeard and Edmund Ironside, Ivar the Boneless and Alfred the Great, Erik

Bloodaxe and Edgar the Pacifier – a story of war and upheaval. It is also, however, the story of how the people of the British Isles came to reorient themselves in a new and interconnected world, where new technologies for travel and communication brought ideas and customs into sometimes explosive contact, but which also fostered the development of towns and trade, forged new identities and gave birth to England and Scotland as unified nations for the first time. By the time of the Norman Conquest, most of Britain might justifiably be described as 'Viking' to varying degrees, and in language, literature, place-names and folklore the presence of Scandinavian settlers can still be felt throughout the British Isles, with repercussions for all those places that British culture and colonization have subsequently touched.

The Vikings have also retained their influence as a powerful cultural force in the modern world, and representations of the Viking Age in art, music and literature have had a profound impact on the western imagination. Indeed, much of what we imagine when we think of this period in British history – even the word 'Viking' itself – grew from political, literary and artistic currents that swelled in the nineteenth and early twentieth centuries. Here, too, a 'Viking Britain' came alive and, to the likes of William Morris and J. R. R. Tolkien, this was a place that seemed to lurk unseen just at the borders of their rapidly modernizing world. It was there not only in the writings and monuments that time had preserved, but also (and perhaps especially) in the elements themselves – the grey sea, the north wind and the very bones of the earth. In travel, art and literature, landscape became a way to commune with the people of the Viking Age – people who had seen the same red sun rising, felt the same cold wind on their necks, touched the same fissures in the smooth grey rock. This has in turn become a way to explore the mentality and world-view of a people with an intimate and profoundly imaginative relationship with the environment. For people living in the latter centuries of the first millennium, the landscape was teeming with unseen inhabitants and riddled with gateways to other worlds. Pits and ditches, barrows and ruins, mountains, rivers and forests: all could be home to the dead, the divine and the diabolical, haunted by monsters and gods.

Telling the story of the Vikings in Britain is therefore not a straightforward undertaking – it is the tale of a people who were not a people, who came to lands that were not yet nations. The historical record is patchy, the archaeology equivocal. Even the very words we use – 'Viking' most of all – slither away from easy definition. It is, moreover, the story not only of the three centuries leading up to (and overlapping) the Norman Conquest, but also of how that time has been remembered, recycled and reimagined by successive generations. It is, as earlier generations seem better to have appreciated, a world that is still tangible. The sense that the past is present in the landscape – that there is another world hovering just out of sight – has receded in step with modernity's alienation from the land. Against the advance of technology, urbanization and globalization, our imaginative connection to landscape continues to fight the long defeat. The land, water and sky have largely been disenchanted of the past, just as they were disenchanted of their elves and spirits during the enlightenment and industrial revolution. But the past can never be wholly erased, and the rivers, hills, woods and stones of Britain remain deeply imprinted with memories of the Vikings and their world.

It is a legacy that runs far beyond the confines of Britain itself. From the seventeenth century to the present, the English-speaking diaspora – of people, ideas, systems, values, laws and language – has had a transformative impact on the world, firstly through the expansion of Britain's Empire, and latterly through the ongoing dominance and global reach of North American culture and economic power. The memory of the Vikings may only be one small cell in the vast genome of Anglophone identity, but it is a tenacious and enduring one. Sometimes it appears overtly, in the simplified and bowdlerized versions of Norse myths and Viking stereotypes that penetrate popular culture, whether through the pages of comic books, the iconography of football teams or the covers of heavy-metal albums. But it also runs in deeper channels of thought and language, the serpentine ships that travel the dark rivers of the subconscious mind, a half-seen shadow of grim gods and thudding oars and dark pine forests wreathed in mist.

The chapters that follow tell the tale of the Vikings in Britain as a broadly chronological narrative. At times the story diverges as events begin to unfold simultaneously across Britain, but I have largely endeavoured to keep the overall momentum moving forward as much as possible. At the same time, however, this is also a book about ideas, objects and places. Through the physical remains and landscapes that the Vikings fashioned and walked – their runestones and ship burials, settlements and battlefields – it is possible to reach beyond the bare rehearsal of names and dates to explore the way that people in Viking Age Britain thought about their world and their place within it, and the way they have been remembered in the centuries since their passing: the stories they told and the tales they inspired, their fears, their fantasies, and the dooms they aspired to. Several themes recur throughout this book – in particular what being a 'Viking' really meant, how attitudes and identities changed over time, and what that meant for the ethnic evolution of the people of Britain – but in a general sense this book is about illuminating an influence on British history that has been profound and enduring, one that has shaped languages, culture and the historical trajectory of the British Isles and beyond for hundreds of years. In a small way, I hope, this book may help to restore to the Vikings some of the dignity that they have too often been denied.

There are, it must be acknowledged, some difficulties that attend the writing of a chronological history of this period; some parts of Britain – England especially – receive more detailed treatment than others, and not all of the evidence is discussed at equal length. In many cases this reflects the availability of source material: both the lack of it and – less often – its abundance. A complete inventory of all Viking-period archaeology found on the Isle of Man would run to many hundreds of pages; a compendium of all the contemporary written references to Viking activity in the same place would fit on the back of a small envelope. Frequently, however, the question of what to cover and what to leave out has been decided by me, and I make no apology for this: it reflects the fact that this book is a personal, at times perhaps idiosyncratic, exploration of the subject. It is intended to be neither definitive nor comprehensive – it cannot hope to be either, not within the covers of a book as slim as this. For all of the detailed regional surveys and the surfeit of books (of wildly varying quality) on the Vikings as a whole, a truly definitive compendium of evidence for the Vikings in Britain remains to be written: it would be a mammoth undertaking, probably running to multiple volumes. It would also, more than likely, be made less than definitive within days of its publication, as new data – much of it gathered by metal-detectorists – continues to roll in, week after week, and spectacular finds are made with some regularity.[2] At the same time, major research projects continue to transform our perception of Viking Age societies, their interactions and their evolutions; this too is unlikely to stop any time soon.[3]

This book has not been written with an academic audience in mind, but I am nevertheless deeply conscious of the need to provide signposts for the reader to the sources of the material from which this narrative has been constructed. Although it would be unnecessarily distracting to provide full scholarly citations, some textual references are necessary for the reader's orientation and to acknowledge sources that I have cited directly. I have chosen, in the main, to restrict these citations to primary written sources and archaeological reports – that is, to evidence rather than interpretation. However, where the work of individual scholars is referred to directly, or where a particular argument or line of reasoning is consciously derived from the work of others, I have also provided the appropriate citations. For brevity, a full citation is only provided the first time a work is referred to in the notes; thereafter, works are referred to by their author (or editor) and abbreviated title only. Primary sources that are referred to frequently have been abbreviated, and a full list of the abbreviations used and a full citation to the edition(s) relied upon in each case are provided in the endmatter. Where primary sources have been quoted in the text and the translation is my own, the citation in the Notes refers to an original language edition of the source in question. Where a translated edition of a source has been quoted, the citation in the Notes directs the reader to the translated edition relied upon. Exceptions are indicated in the Notes. A short summary of relevant further reading can be found at the end of this book. This is intended to direct the reader to the most accessible and up-to-date treatments and is intended only as a starting point to the vast literature that touches on the Vikings – in Britain and in wider perspective.

Acknowledgements

The ideas and opinions expressed in this book are – even where I believe them to be my own – indebted to a huge number of historians, archaeologists, linguists, numismatists, scientists and others, whose work I have read or with whom I have had the privilege of working, whether as a student, a colleague or a friend. Those people will know who they are, and may well recognize their own fingerprints on my thought-processes. Particular thanks are due to Gareth Williams (no relation), my colleague at the British Museum, and a man to whom I owe a great personal and intellectual debt. Neil Price at the University of Uppsala did me the honour of reading the entire book in draft. His comments have been both hugely encouraging and unerringly pertinent. My editors, Arabella Pike and Peter James, deserve many thanks indeed. Their ministrations – and, in the case of the former, great forbearance – have helped to ensure that the best possible version of this book was ultimately realized. My agents, Julian Alexander and Ben Clarke at LAW, also deserve fulsome thanks for their support and tireless efforts on my behalf. Tom Holland requires a special mention: if it had not been for a good-natured intervention on his part, my introduction to the aforementioned gentlemen would never have been effected, and this book may not have come into being at all.

My father, Geoffrey Williams, read every word of the manuscript as the chapters were produced and watched its slow gestation over many months. My discussions with him, and the innumerable errors identified and improvements suggested, have undoubtedly made this a better book. My mother, Gilli, produced (at exceptionally short notice and with remarkable facility) several of the fabulous line drawings in this book. For all of the help that both my parents have provided, as well as their unwavering love and support, my gratitude is profound.

And finally my wife, Zeena, has had to contend with an intrusive Viking presence in her life for longer now than she probably ever imagined. But she has weathered the storm and borne me up whenever I felt that I might sink. Nothing would have been possible without her. She is the best.

I cannot stress enough, however, that none of the people I have mentioned above can in any way be held responsible for my wilder flights of imagination, or for any errors that have made it into print: these are all my own.

A Note on Names

There is a bewildering amount of variation in the rendering of personal names across this period, with the same name frequently appearing in wildly different spellings depending on the language of the written source in which it appears. As a rule of thumb, I have preferred to use the most contemporary and ethno-linguistically appropriate versions wherever possible. I have, however, made frequent exception wherever normalized modern spellings of names are likely to be more familiar to the reader: hence 'Olaf', rather than *Oláfr*; 'Eric', rather than *Eiríkr*; 'Odin', rather than *Oðinn*. Where variant forms are used (especially in quotations), I have provided the more familiar form in square brackets. Given the complexities and ambiguities of Viking Age onomastics, it is entirely likely that some inconsistencies remain: my apologies in advance if this is so.

In the text and Notes, 'ON' denotes Old Norse, 'OE' Old English and 'ModE' Modern English.

1

OUTSIDERS FROM ACROSS THE WATER

When the watchman on the wall, the Shieldings' lookout
whose job it was to guard the sea-cliffs,
saw shields glittering on the gangplank
and battle-equipment being unloaded
he had to find out who and what they were. So he rode to the shore,
this horseman of Hrothgar's, and challenged them
in formal terms, flourishing his spear.

Beowulf[1]

I n the days of King Beorhtric of Wessex (786–802), 'there came for the first time three ships of Northmen from Hordaland',[2] and 'they landed in the island which is called Portland'.[3] '[T]he king's reeve, who was then in the town called Dorchester, leapt on his horse, sped to the harbour with a few men (for he thought they were merchants rather than marauders), and admonishing them [the Northmen] in an authoritative manner, gave orders that they should be driven to the royal town. And he and his companions were killed by them on the spot. The name of the reeve was Beaduheard.'[4]

'Those were the first ships of Danish men which came to the land of the English.'[5]

*

Looking south from the summit of the barrow, the land feels like it is slipping away, yielding itself to the ineffable splendour of the ocean. Away in the distance the dark bulk of Portland languishes, a last defiant redoubt set in the glittering sea. The world is wide here, the coast of England laid out in broad wings to east and west; on a bright clear day – the ozone hollowing out the sinuses – you feel weightless, as if you could step from the top of that mound and be lifted into the firmament, soar into that white light obliterating the edges of land, sea and sky, tumbling in the breeze.

The mound is known, for reasons now lost, as Culliford Tree. It is a tumulus, a Bronze Age burial mound – one of five running east to west – that had stood on the Dorset chalk for more than 2,000 years before it received a name in the English tongue. Like breakwaters in the surf, the mounds and their ancient dead have endured the battering tides of time, forcing history to shape itself around them. At some point after it was named, the barrow became the meeting place of Culliford Tree Hundred, the administrative district of which Portland formed part at the time of the Domesday Survey in 1086. It had probably served this purpose for hundreds of years prior to William the Conqueror's great national audit and by the end of the eighth century it was almost certainly a significant regional meeting place. It was in this place and in others like it that royal officials enacted the king's will and delivered his justice, adjudicating disputes and pronouncing verdicts which could include fines, mutilation and death. From the summit of the barrow, the landscape reveals itself to the watcher – a place from which the land could be claimed, authority enacted in the act of seeing.

On that day at the end of the eighth century when three ships came unasked to Portland, the man riding down to Portland strand might well have paused and looked back over his shoulder, looked for Culliford Tree. He might have sought comfort from the distant mound on the horizon – a dark beacon of antiquity and earth-fast custom, a symbol of territory and authority, of land and legitimacy. This man, Beaduheard, would have known that the barrow watched over him, lending him the power in the land, confirming the prerogatives of his office. He was reeve to the king of Wessex, Beorhtric, and as such he exercised the king's delegated authority. Reeves represented the king in towns, ports and sometimes across whole shires; the modern and medieval word 'sheriff' has its origin in these 'shire-reeves'. Beaduheard, therefore, was an important man – responsible, perhaps, for local government in Dorchester and the surrounding countryside, a man used to getting his own way.

Beaduheard arrives on Portland to find a group of travellers arrayed on the beach, their ships drawn up behind them, their backs to the sea. They are wary – frightened even. They are strangers in a strange land, conditioned perhaps to expect a frosty welcome. Beaduheard dismounts from his horse to receive them, others following his lead, shingle crunching beneath leather-shod feet. Words are exchanged but their meaning is lost – whatever mutual words they understood failing in the tension of the moment, drowned by the crashing of the waves. But Beaduheard is no diplomat, and the tenor of his words is clear enough. He 'admonishes' the newcomers in an 'authoritative manner', he attempts to 'drive them' to the king's residence ('against their will' as the chronicle of John of Worcester adds).[6] He knows his duty, and he knows the law.

The West Saxon edicts that are closest in date to these events are the laws of King Ine (r. 688–726). Clause 20 gives a sense of the sort of welcome that the unfortunate wanderer could expect in eighth-century Wessex: 'If a man from afar, or a stranger, goes through the woods off the highway and neither calls out nor blows a horn, he may be considered a thief, to be slain or to be redeemed [by paying his *wergild* ("man-price")]'.[7] Britain's most southerly realm offered cold comfort to the lost.

In the Old English poem *Beowulf* – composed at some point between the early eighth and the early eleventh century – there can be found, expressed in the Reeve's own West Saxon tongue, a form of words that we might imagine Beaduheard speaking in his final hours: an echo of a lived experience.[8]

'What kind of men are you who arrive
rigged out for combat in coats of mail,
sailing here over the sea-lanes
in your steep-hulled boat? [...]

Never before has a force under arms
disembarked so openly – not bothering to ask
if the sentries allowed them safe passage
or the clan had consented [...]

So now, before you fare inland
as interlopers, I have to be informed
about who you are and where you hail from.
Outsiders from across the water,
I say it again: the sooner you tell
where you come from and why, the better.'[9]

In the poem, these words are spoken by the Danish coastguard to the eponymous hero and his men as they arrive from the realm of the Geats (southern Sweden) to lend their aid to Hrothgar, the Danish king. They are formalities, to be understood both by questioner and visitor: the back-and-forth ritual of arrival.

In the real-life counterpart to this scene, however, the newcomers on the Portland beach chose not to participate, not to play the game. Perhaps they did not know the rules.

The travellers, berated in a foreign tongue by an aggressive stranger, are frightened and frustrated – the instinct to fight or flee like a high-pitched whine, raised to intolerable pitch. In the heavy moments that follow, the confrontation develops the hypertension of a shoot-out: a bead of sweat running down the back of a sun-burnt neck, eyes darting left and right as time slows to dream-pace, measured out by the metronomic crashing of the surf. Perhaps a hand flickers towards a sword hilt; perhaps a horse stamps, a cloak billows, a gull shrieks ... When the spell finally breaks the violence seems inevitable – preordained – as if only death can bring the world back into balance.

In the end, all that is left, in place of Beowulf's polite and formal replies, are huddled corpses on the strand, their blood swallowed between stones.

The arrival of these Northmen in Portland – the carbuncle that sprouts from Dorset into the English Channel – established the leit-motifs for Britain's early interactions with its northern neighbours: unanswered questions and sudden brutality, the fluid identity of the merchant-marauder, the collision of cultures at the margins of the land. For almost three centuries, seaborne marauders would return again and again – sometimes like the inevitable attrition of the tides, dissolving the most vulnerable shores one wave at a time, at others like a mighty storm that smashes sea-walls and wreaks devastation before expending itself exhausted. Sometimes it would seem more like the inexorable flood of a climate apocalypse, the waters rising and rising without respite, washing deep inland and bursting river banks deep in the interior of the land. Everywhere the crimson tide flowed and pounded, the history of these islands would be changed for ever, new channels and shapes scoured and moulded in the clay of British history.

The island that the crew of those three ships blundered into in the reign of King Beorhtric was still far from settling into its famil-iar modern grooves. Scotland, Wales and England did not exist, and the shifting patchwork of petty kingdoms that made up the political geography of Britain was fractured along cultural, linguistic, reli-gious, geographical and historical lines. Major fault-lines divided those parts of Britain that had once been exposed to intensive Roman colonization from those which had not, those which adhered to Roman and which to Irish forms of Christian liturgy, those who believed their ancestors were British from those who looked to a homeland in Ireland or across the North Sea. Landscape sundered highland zones from lowland zones; language divided speakers of Celtic languages from those who used a Germanic tongue; the sea brought an influx of foreign goods and ideas to some, while shutting others out.

The map of Britain at the end of the eighth century had developed slowly from conditions arising from the decline of the Roman Empire during the fourth century. In Britain, the removal of direct Roman administration and military defence around the year 400 coincided with changes to the cultural orientation of communities along Britain's eastern seaboard. Increasingly, their centre of gravity shifted from the Mediterranean world to the North Sea. Part of the reason for this was political and economic, but migration also played a major role. People from what is now northern Germany, southern Scandinavia and the Low Countries had been moving into eastern areas of Britain – particularly Kent, East Anglia and England north of the Humber – from at least the early fifth century. The numbers involved, and the nature of the migration, remains fiercely contested, but the impact was undeniable and dramatic.

By the early eighth century, the northern monk Bede was able to write with confidence about an 'English-speaking people' who were distinct from the native British. The key distinguishing characteristic of this group – as implied by Bede's phrase – was their tongue. These were people who spoke a different language from both Romano-British elites (for whom Latin was the ubiquitous written language) and the 'indigenous' Britons, who spoke varying forms of a Celtic language known as Common or Old Brittonic (or Brythonic). The newcomers, however, spoke a Germanic language known to modern scholars as 'Old English' (or, more rarely these days, as 'Anglo-Saxon') which was closely related to the languages spoken in the regions from which migrants across the North Sea had come.

While doubts hover over a great deal of Bede's narrative, and particularly his migration and conquest narratives (much of which is an elaboration of a vague, tendentious and ideologically motivated sermon written by the British monk Gildas in the sixth century),[10] the impact of the English language is not in doubt. Place-names and early vernacular written records attest that English became dominant and widespread at a remarkably early date. Moreover, these English-speakers (whatever their genetic ancestry) had, by Bede's day, become culturally and linguistically dominant in most of lowland Britain, forming a tapestry of greater and lesser kingdoms which had grown out of an inconsistent pattern of tribal groupings and late Roman administrative districts.

The most northerly of these English-speaking realms was Northumbria – literally the land north of the River Humber. By the late eighth century this kingdom covered a huge swathe of northern Britain, from the Humber to the Forth, cobbled together from a number of former British territories: Deira, Bernicia, Gododdin, Rheged and Elmet. For over a century, Northumbria had represented a high point of post-Roman achievement in scholarship and artistic culture, driven from major centres of learning such as Wearmouth-Jarrow (where Bede wrote, among much else, his *Ecclesiastical History of the English People*) and the island monastery of Lindisfarne. This extraordinary cultural flowering was also remarkable for its fusion of British, Irish, Anglo-Saxon and Mediterranean influences. The Lindisfarne Gospels – an illuminated manuscript of breathtaking beauty and craftsmanship – exemplifies the splendour, ingenuity and spontaneity of this northern renaissance, its famous 'carpet pages' weaving Celtic, Germanic and Coptic Christian themes into mind-bending symphonies of colour and cultural synthesis.

However, despite the cultural refinement and territorial muscle, Northumbria had been growing weaker throughout the eighth century, undermined by the incessant feuding of its aristocracy and the instability of its royal house. In 790, for example, around the time that the Northmen had arrived in Portland, King Osred II was deposed after only a year on the throne, forcibly tonsured and exiled from his kingdom. His replacement, Æthelred I, seems to have had powerful friends. It is likely that the coup was carried out with the support of Northumbria's large and belligerent southern neighbour: the kingdom of Mercia.

Covering most of the English midlands from approximately the modern Welsh border in the west to the borders of East Anglia in the east, and from the Thames valley in the south to the Humber and the Wirral in the north, Mercia dominated southern Britain and reached the apogee of its political dominance under King Offa (r. 757–96). In the last decade of the eighth century, Offa was at the height of his powers. From his power-base in the Staffordshire heartlands around Tamworth, Lichfield and Repton, the king exercised not only direct rule over Mercia, but political and military control over the neighbouring kingdoms of East Anglia, Essex, Kent, Sussex and Wessex. The greatest surviving monument of his reign is the massive defensive earthwork marking the western boundary of Mercia: Offa's Dyke. The scale of this engineering project is testament to the extent of the king's power and ambition, not to mention his ability to coerce his subjects into undertaking state-wide projects.[11] Offan statecraft was of the Corleone school of governance. When, for example, King Æthelberht of East Anglia attempted to assert a measure of independence (briefly minting his own coins), 'Offa ordered King Æthelberht's head to be struck off.' This sort of gangland authority was closely tied to the personal charisma of the king and, as it turned out, the Mercian supremacy unravelled shortly after Offa's death in 796.[12]

The decapitation of King Æthelberht wasn't enough to bring the kingdom of East Anglia to an end. Comprising at its core the ancient counties of Norfolk and Suffolk (the 'north folk' and the 'south folk' in Old English), the kingdom had, at the beginning of the seventh century, been an important power-broker. East Anglia had once boasted links to Scandinavia, the rest of continental Europe and beyond, and nothing better exemplifies the kingdom's cosmopolitan splendour than the great ship burial at Sutton Hoo near Woodbridge in Suffolk. The famous mustachioed helmet found at Sutton Hoo is the ubiquitous icon of the Anglo-Saxon age, an object which in its style, iconography and manufacture has its closest parallels among the grave goods buried with the military elite of southern Sweden. But the burial also contained – among other objects – silverware from the Byzantine Empire (the surviving eastern part of the Roman Empire, centred on Constantinople – modern Istanbul), coins from Merovingian Gaul (which comprised parts of France, Germany and the Low Countries) and weapons and jewellery embellished with garnets imported from India. Although East Anglia would never again achieve the influence it commanded in this glittering seventh-century heyday, it nevertheless maintained its independence long into the ninth century.[13]

The smaller kingdoms which had lain under Mercian domination during Offa's reign were, however, destined ultimately to becoming defunct as independent concerns. The royal dynasty of the East Saxons (with its core in Essex) and those of the South Saxons (Sussex) and Kent either disappeared or had been demoted to junior aristocratic rank by the early ninth century. The killer blow in each case was delivered not by Mercia but by another resurgent player in the English-speaking community: Wessex – the kingdom of the West Saxons.

Wessex had experienced a torrid eighth century. With its heartlands in Hampshire and Dorset, Wessex was an assertive force in southern Britain, extending north across Somerset, Wiltshire and Berkshire, and eating steadily westwards into Devon. During its heyday in the reign of King Ine (r. 688–726), West Saxon authority had also extended across Surrey and Sussex in the east. But more than sixty years of attritional warfare with the Mercians to the north had eroded its territories south of the Thames, created a militarized zone across the chalk uplands of Wiltshire and Berkshire and seen control of Sussex lost to Offa's Mercia. In 786, the pugnacious West Saxon ruler Cynewulf was killed in a power-struggle and the man who emerged as king, Beorhtric, was, it seems, Offa's man. The impression of Wessex in these years is of a beaten-down kingdom, exhausted by war and resigned to its subordinate status in Offa's new order. The man who would pick up the banner of West Saxon kingship from Beorhtric, however, was of a markedly different stamp. King Ecgberht (r. 802–39) would take the West Saxon king-dom to the peak of its power and prestige, overwhelming its smaller neighbours, restoring the pride and reputation of its royal house, and ultimately providing the self-confidence that future kings would need in the dark days that lay ahead. But all this was in the future. When the Northmen arrived on Portland, Wessex yet remained a weakened client state of the Mercian supremacy.

Although English kingdoms had been, and continued to be, dominant in lowland Britain, they were never the whole story, and in parts of Britain – notably the highlands and islands of what is now Scotland, Cumbria and the valley of the Clyde, the lands west of Offa's Dyke and the Cornish peninsula – a number of kingdoms of mixed provenance maintained distinct identities, languages, reli-gious practices and cultural norms. Cornwall, beyond the south-western marches of Wessex, had been only lightly touched by direct Roman rule. At the western end of the kingdom of Dumnonia (Devon and Cornwall), the region had developed a distinctive culture that blended British and Irish influences and maintained maritime links with both Brittany and the Byzantine Empire. While Devon, the eastern part of Dumnonia, became subsumed by Wessex over the course of the eighth century – becoming thoroughly Anglicized in the process – Cornwall, for the time being, retained its independence.

Further north, the kingdoms of what is now Wales present an altogether more complex picture, and posed a greater challenge for their Mercian neighbours to the east. The scale of the threat is represented by the magnitude of the effort made by Offa, and perhaps his predecessors, to contain it (through the construction of the dyke), and a range of sources make clear that border raids into Mercian territory (and vice versa) were endemic.[14] The Celtic-speaking people of what is now Wales were no more unified, however, than their Anglophone rivals. The four main kingdoms, as established by at least 850, were Gwynedd (in the north and north-west), Dyfed (in the south-west), Gwent (in the south-east) and Powys (in the eastern and central regions). All of these, in one way or another, were based on the former Roman *civitates* of western Britain, themselves based on old Iron Age tribal groupings.[15] This, it must be admitted, is to simplify a complex and volatile pattern of tribal confederations, but it is evident that ruling Welsh elites clung to an idea of *Romanitas* even as it drifted ever further into the past. Latin and bilingual inscriptions on standing stones (stones deliberately erected as upright monuments) throughout Wales (and elsewhere in former Roman Britain) reveal a self-consciously Latinate identity that lasted into the ninth century and beyond. The bitter irony was that it was the heathen interlopers – the Anglo-Saxons – who, having adopted an explicitly Roman model of Christianity, would ultimately align themselves with the new mainstream culture of 'Latin' Europe; the British, despite having kept alive a vibrant, if idiosyncratic, Christian faith alongside the memory of their imperial heritage, were increasingly cast as the barbarians in this changing European landscape.[16]

The British kingdoms of Wales and Cornwall were by no means the only representatives of Brittonic-speaking culture to survive the Anglo-Saxon cultural takeover. Though some (such as Rheged, Gododdin and Elmet) had perished in the expansion of Northumbria, the British kingdom of Alt Clud ('the rock of the Clyde') still held out in the region bordering the Clyde. A shadowy kingdom of obscure origin, Alt Clud had its fortress capital at Dumbarton Rock. The kingdom had spent most of the eighth century fending off the unwelcome advances of its neighbours, and in 780 was burned (by whom, or why, is not known). One of the possible culprits was Alt Clud's neighbour to the north-east, the substantial and periodically powerful kingdom of the Picts (sometimes referred to as 'Pictavia'), a realm that had its heartland in northern and eastern Scotland, and which seems to have held sway (at least culturally) over the Orkney and Shetland islands. The most visible and dramatic monuments to Pictish culture are the symbol stones – slabs carved with images of beasts and enigmatic symbols that are most often interpreted as representations of the names of kings and aristocrats. By the eighth century, many of these objects displayed ostentatiously Christian iconography, and it is clear that Christianity had by that time become associated with expressions of power and status: a monastery at Portmahomack, on the Tarbat peninsula in Easter Ross, had been established as early as the sixth century, possibly with royal patronage.[17]

Pictish power was by no means unchallenged in northern Britain. The kingdom's main rivals were Northumbria, whose borders extended to the Forth, and whose armies it had repeatedly beaten back during the earlier part of the century, and the kingdom of Dál Riata, a Gaelic-speaking polity spanning the Irish Sea to include Argyll, Lochaber and the north-eastern part of Ulster. Dál Riata had its power-base at Dunadd near Kilmartin, an imposing hill-fort where its kings were believed to have been inaugurated – the impression of a foot, worn into the living rock, may have played a key role in the rituals that were enacted there. By the end of the eighth century, however, Dál Riata was coming under Pictish domination. In 736 Dunadd had been captured by the Pictish king Oengus (he underscored his dominance by dragging the sons of the Dál Riatan king back to Pictavia in chains), and by 811 Dál Riata was being ruled directly by the Pictish king Constantine (r. 789–820). By then, however, a new power was rising, and the Viking impact in northern Britain would have profound consequences for all of its regional players.

There is more that might be said. Ireland, the Isle of Man and the Irish monastic colonies of the Western Isles – Iona chief among them – are all stitched tightly into the events that followed the advent of the Northmen. Nor can the story of the Vikings in Britain be told without some reference to events in continental Europe. Nevertheless, the foregoing paragraphs sketch – in broad outline – the most important contours of British political geography at the time that three strange ships pitched up on the beach at Portland. Though nobody could have known it then, the death of Beaduheard marked the beginning of a series of cataclysmic upheavals that changed Britain for ever. Many of the places mentioned above will be revisited in the chapters that follow; many of the kingdoms will fall.

But before that story can be told, we must return to that beach in Portland, the dark sails receding into the distance. We watch them go, and the coastguard's questions replay in our minds, too late now for any hope of an answer: 'Outsiders from across the water [...] the sooner you tell where you come from and why, the better.'[18]

There is no written source that tells these events in the words of the Vikings themselves. For the most part, the people of Scandinavia did not record their history in written form until long after the Viking Age is usually considered to have closed. The sagas and histories, produced in Norway and especially in Iceland, are products of the late twelfth century and later – sometimes much later. To say that the Vikings were illiterate is strictly false, however. As will be seen, they made use of their own runic script for inscriptions marking ownership or memorializing the dead. Moreover, poems composed during the Viking Age survived orally to be written down in later centuries. Nevertheless, very little of the Viking voice survives, and certainly nothing that will explain the identities, motivations and origins of those first violent pioneers. In the face of this Scandinavian silence we must turn and consider who the people of early medieval Britain thought these strangers were, where they had come from and what had driven them on to British shores.

The written sources for the Viking Age in Britain are not a straightforward guide to contemporary events. These were documents written for specific purposes, in different times and in different places, each one reflecting the views of the people who compiled or commissioned them. As such, they are partial and biased, limited by the range of knowledge which their authors possessed, though not by their imaginations. By far the most important sources for this period are the various manuscripts of the *Anglo-Saxon Chronicle*. The first, and oldest, of these manuscripts is normally referred to as the A text or, sometimes, as the 'Winchester Chronicle'. It was put together in the late ninth century – probably in the 890s

– as part of the intellectual scene that surrounded the court of King Alfred in Wessex. All later historians and chroniclers of the Middle Ages, including the other texts of the *Anglo-Saxon Chronicle*, rely on the A text to some degree.

The earliest record of the Viking arrival on Portland is found in the A text, and was therefore written down a century later than the events it describes. Although this *Chronicle* almost certainly contains real traditions and material from older sources, none of these survive for us to make a comparison. The suspicion therefore remains that the view of history which the *Chronicle* presents is coloured by a bleak century of Scandinavian plunder, conquest and colonization. In particular, one might justly raise an eyebrow at the chronicler's assertion that these 'were the first ships of Danish men which came to the land of the English [*Angelcynnes lond*]': quite apart from the vexed question of what exactly the chronicler meant by '*Angelcynnes lond*', one might well question how, 100 years later and from the perspective of Britain's most southerly realm, such knowledge could possibly have been possessed.[19]

The A text tells us, in no uncertain terms, that the newcomers were 'Danish' (*denisc*). While this might seem, on the face of things, to be a useful statement of origins, it is not at all certain whether that which seemed 'danish' to Anglo-Saxon eyes would necessarily appear 'Danish' to our own. As will be seen, the term *denisc* (along with other generic terms used throughout Britain) in fact came to be applied indiscriminately to people and things held to have emanated from the North. Far more promising is the statement that the newcomers were 'Northmen' (Norðmanna) from Hordaland (Hereðalande), now a county of western Norway centred on Bergen. Alas, this is surprisingly (and suspiciously) specific. The earliest record of this notice is found, not in the A text, but in the so-called 'northern recension' of the *Anglo-Saxon Chronicle*, and can be dated no earlier than the mid-eleventh century – at least 250 years after the incident at Portland. This reference may shed more light on the origin of eleventh-century Scandinavian settlers in Northumbria than it does on events in late eighth-century Wessex.[20]

In other words, the sources – so promising at first reading – really only tell us that the newcomers were foreigners, probably from somewhere across the North Sea. It is certain, however, that the people of Britain thought *something* when they encountered strangers on their beaches and imagined the worlds from which they had come. Understanding what that something might have been – what it meant – is bound up with how the people of early medieval Britain understood their own world, and their place within it.

2

HEART OF DARKNESS

Then the Lord said unto me, Out of the north an evil shall break
forth upon all the inhabitants of the land.

JEREMIAH 1:15[1]

northwards lies the road to hell

SNORRI STURLUSON, *Gylfaginning* (early thirteenth century)[2]

Ærest of swin forda upp andlang broces to ceolnes wyllan …

('Go first up from the swine ford and along the brook to *ceolnes*
[Ceolwine's?] well')[3]

At the river's edge you pass a churl driving his pigs across the muddy
ford, hairy oinkers on their way to the wood pasture, eager to rootle
among *wyrttruma* ('woody roots') for acorns and beech mast; the
animal scent of sweat and pig shit, crumbly clods of dried mud
dropping from bristly bottoms. It is damp down here, soggy. Water
seeps into your shoes (stitched leather – hardly watertight) as you
turn to the north, away from the ford. Perhaps you slip a little on the
muddy path that runs beside the brook and stub a toe on a stone

– the dull throbbing adding injury to numbness in your cold feet; at least there are no midges (*mycgas*) at this time of year. You pause and place a bright glass bead on the flat mossy stone beside the spring where the brook wells up – you have heard from the monks how, long ago, a pilgrim called Ceolwine struck his ash staff on the stone and a rush of cold water sprang up to slake his thirst: a miracle they said. But an old man in the village told you this was rubbish: his grandfather had been a boy when the old gods still lived here and the folk made sacrifice, mounting the heads on ash poles and throwing the bones into the water; now their corpses haunt the marshy edgelands: 'you can hear them coming when the light fails boy: drip … drip … drip …'

Probably best to leave a gift either way.

*andlang hege ræwe to luttes crundele · þanon to grafes owisce ·
Andlang owisce to wege …*

('along the hedgerow to luttes [Lutt's?] pit and then on to the eaves of the grove; along the eaves to the road')

Reaching the hedgerow is a welcome relief: the land slopes slightly away from the brook here, the earth becomes firmer. As you walk alongside the broad band of bramble and blackthorn, you can hear the rustling of foraging birds: a blackbird (*ōsle*) probably, or a finch (*finc*). A streak of brown – a mouse (*mūs*), or a shrew (*screāwa*) perhaps – shoots across the path ahead and disappears rustling into the undergrowth: all are hunting for the last berries of autumn.[4] It is November (*Blōt-mōnaþ*: 'the month of sacrifice'), and the scent of damp earth mingles with the vinegar notes of rotten apples. You hurry past Lutt's pit – part stone quarry, part sepulchre (the word, *crundel*, is ambiguous): you have heard stories about this place too, but you would rather not dwell on them now, not until you are clear of the dark overhanging woods. You know you're being a baby – this is managed woodland after all – but you're glad when you reach the road all the same.

... Andlang weges to æles beorge · nyþer on aler cumb · Andlang aler cumbes ut on afene · Andlang afene eft on swin ford.

('along the road to æles [Ælle's?] barrow and down to alder-tree valley; along alder-tree valley and out to the Avon; along the Avon to the swine ford.')

From here it is an easier stroll on the compacted earth, compressed by the tread of generations of men and beasts. You need to watch where you're going, mind – sometimes dips in the path have allowed the rain water to gather. Here the plunge of heavy hoofs, and the ruts riven by the ox-wains, have churned the path into patches of slimy mud – you dance your way with giant steps, and try to keep to the green stripe that marks the middle of the track. When you eventually look up, you give an involuntary start: massing against the westering sky, the dark bulk of Ælle's barrow looms. The atmosphere thickens. This is a place of power; everyone knows it ... even the monks, though they pretend it's all just superstition: heathen folly, you've heard them call it, although not in front of the reeve – he'll tell anyone who listens that his ancestor is buried under that mound, sleeping until the day his people call upon his aid in battle. It's not so different, now you think of it, to the stories the monks tell: of long-dead saints who return to help the living ... Lost in thought you stroll through the alder trees and back down the valley, arriving at the river as the light begins to fail.

Standing on the banks you watch the ghost-white spectre of a swan glide past, the curve of its neck rising from its breast as the prow of a ship rises from its keel, carving the placid water, silent in its grace.

The fragments of Old English, translated above, are from what is known as a boundary clause, a description of the edges of a parcel of land. This one describes an area at North Stoke in Somerset. It was written down and added to a charter documenting a grant of land made by the West Saxon king Cynewulf (r. 757–86), Beorhtric's predecessor. Like many such clauses, it is written in English – the common tongue – but it is inserted into a document otherwise drafted in Latin, the officialese of ecclesiastical administrators. The implication is clear enough: while Latin was appropriate for the legal formulae of witness lists and the stern religious injunctions against violating the terms of the charter, the description of the land came straight from lived experience – from the mnemonic commitment of landscape to oral narrative.

A boundary clause circumscribes a place known at an intimately local level, swaddling a parcel of land with animals, plants and the bumps and wrinkles of the soil. In some cases these bounds can still be followed in the perimeters of modern parishes, and the 'beating of the bounds' – a communal ritual of remembering in which the bounds are not only walked, but the landmarks physically struck by the participants – has in some places endured to the present day. These texts provide more than a simple insight into local administrative geography, however. They show us a way of understanding the world, not with the false objectivity of the map-reader looking down from above, but as an actor and participant within it. Names and monuments emerge by the wayside: no one knows any more who this Ceolwine was or what he meant to the stream that bore his name; none can say what crawling things or shadow walkers (*scea-dugangan*) might have emerged from Lutt's pit or Ælle's barrow in dark Anglo-Saxon dreams. What is beyond doubt is that places like these, all over England, were the punctuation points in the stories that rural communities told about their world: more than how to get from A to B (or, in the case of boundary clauses, how to get from A back to A), these were the tapestries of lived existence that were woven both in words and in the physical actions of human beings moving and interacting with the world around them.[5]

In a modern context, geographical knowledge tends to be represented in forms which are relatively static. We think of masses of land and water viewed from space, the contours of mountains, the

reflective spatter of lakes, the ragged torn coastline of Norway –
remembered by Slartibartfast in the *Hitchhiker's Guide to the Galaxy*
for its 'lovely crinkly edges'.[6] We also think of neatly inked political
boundaries, the nation states limned in pink and powder blue, or of
roads and railways scored decisively across the page. These types of
knowledge are essentially cartographical, known to us through
abstracted, two-dimensional images. Whether carried in the imagination, drawn by hand or photographed from space, the map is the
dominant means by which we understand our relationship to the
physical world. And yet, in myriad ways, it is fundamentally flawed
– made all the more misleading by the sense of omniscience it
instils: maps, we feel, make gods of us. It takes only a little scratching to find the bloodstains under the cartographer's pastel palette.
Enduring fault-lines of religion, language and politics are obscured;
ancient pathways fade from view. Distances are rendered down to
straight lines through empty space, continents grotesquely
contorted through the amputation of their third dimension. The
senses are cauterized: map-world is a place for the eyes alone. That
we instinctively feel this sensory loss can be judged by the compul-
sive desire to run frustrated fingertips over the smooth surfaces of
maps and globes, subconsciously seeking the missing textures of
the earth.[7]

How inadequate – how *anaemic* – this would have seemed to
Beaduheard's contemporaries, steeped in a geography that was
personal, local, storied. For early medieval Britons, geographical
knowledge was more than just a series of routes and landmarks; it
was a series of signs and symbols that plumbed time, mythology
and identity – moving through ancient landscapes could mean
travelling backwards in time, while ancestral mythologies transported people to far-off realms.

Maps were not unknown, but their circulation was restricted to
a handful of learned men and fulfilled very different purposes from
their modern counterparts. A common form was the T-O map – a
schematic diagram, or 'ideogram', that divided the world into three
unequal segments: Asia (the top half of the circle), Africa (the

bottom right quarter) and Europe (the bottom left). Jerusalem lay at the centre. The image was in part a means of concentrating the mind on the totality of God's creation, its symmetry and its unity. By superimposing the letters T and O on to its form, it also incorporated the initials of the words *terra orbis* (orb of the world; the globe) into the design. Needless to say, it was of limited utility to the disorientated traveller. Like boundary clauses, early maps and the base of knowledge from which they were derived were essentially concerned with circumscription – the gathering of what was known into (usually circular) plans, forming an 'inside' and an 'out there'. In the Greek and Roman worlds this had symbolized the distinction between civilization and *barbaricum*; in the Christian epoch 'inside' indicated, if not exactly Christendom, then the totality of that portion of the earth which lay within the orbit of potential salvation. Later medieval maps – such as the Hereford Mappa Mundi – depict Christ standing behind the world, literally embracing creation.[8]

That which lay beyond these borders was, in this conception, more dreadful than mere *terra incognita*. It was the abyss – the world beyond God.

A sense of how fearsome this outer world could seem is evident in Old English poetry and the cosmology it reflects: the Old English poetic retelling of Genesis, for example, paints the earth as a golden hall surrounded by a sea of darkness – the void a place of mist and sorrow beyond the light of God.[9] Other poems refine this image: the cold seas of *The Wanderer* and *The Seafarer* reflect both physical and spiritual desolation. It is *Beowulf*, however, that really drives this fear home:

> Grendel was the grim ghoul named,
> Famous edge-marcher, who held the moors
> The fen and fastness ...[10]

The first part of *Beowulf* tells the story of how the eponymous hero came to Denmark from his home in the land of the Geats, drawn by tales of a monster – named Grendel – who for many years had menaced the hall – Heorot – of the Danish king Hrothgar. Beowulf defeats the monster, tearing off his arm and sending him fleeing back to die in his fenland home. But the real power and tension in this part of the poem follows the monster. Grendel is the border-walker, the dweller in shadow, the descendant of Cain and an avatar of jealous alienation. He is of the world 'outside' – *fifelcynnes eard*, literally 'monster-world' – and it is with horrible fascination that the poet follows him 'down over mist-slopes', creeping through the darkness, coming with the fog, greedy hands pushing at the hall door.[11]

'Heorot' literally means 'hart' (a male deer), but the word is derived from the same root as the Old English *heorte*, a word which means 'heart' in all its literal and figurative senses; and in *Beowulf* the hall is, indeed, the beating heart of human culture – a symbol of warmth and light, safety and security, community and the affirmation of bonds: it is fortress, pub and family home wrapped into one. The violation of that safety and sanctity is what gives the poem a psychological edge that cuts easily across the centuries – Grendel is the home-invader, the wolf in the fold, striking deep at the vitals of society.

In fact, Grendel and his kin are described in explicitly lupine terms by the *Beowulf* poet, a distinction they share with other malefactors of the Anglo-Saxon world. The term *wearg* (the origin of Tolkien's 'warg') meant both 'wolf' and 'criminal', and the label *wulvesheofod* ('wolf's head') was, by the eleventh century, used to define outlaw status. The Vikings who appear in the poetic account of the battle of Maldon in 991 are 'slaughter-wolves' (*waelwulfas*). These groups – monsters, criminals, outlaws, Vikings – posed threats to the ordered world represented by the hall: they were the wolves beyond the border, the slaughterers, raveners, stealers of property, of livestock, of children. In a world where terrors could be made horribly and suddenly real, it is small wonder that Ine's laws should have been so unforgiving to the outlander.[12]

Of all the compass points from which terror might emanate, there was one which held the greatest dread. This was not just because the sea had repeatedly disgorged boatloads of child-snatchers and hall-burners from precisely this direction, nor indeed because empirical observation demonstrated that this was the horizon over which the most wretched weather tended to hurtle, but because the Anglo-Saxons already knew full well that it was here that Satan had set his throne.

This was the medieval world's heart of darkness: the North.

Behind are the familiar paths and places of home, the songs in the hall, the fire, the harp. Out here there is only the dark, only the cold, only the biting north wind that screams over the barren hillsides. Rocky paths lie ahead, thin winding ways where death leers blackly from the fells below. A mist closes in, a wolf howls … Down through the mist-bands, a glimmer of light flickers – ghostly, ethereal, unnatural: a sheen of dark water, witch-fires burning on its surface. Beyond the water a bleak forest looms, glowering from gloomy cliffs. Branches encrusted with rime and hoarfrost drag skeletal fingers through the frigid air; roots like serpents quest over slimy banks towards the rotting stagnant tarn. In the reeking water nameless things writhe and wriggle. Monsters dwell here – among the 'wolf-slopes, windy headlands, dangerous fen-tracts'.[13] To go further would be to risk soul and sanity: here the laws of nature are perverted and upended – the burning black water rushes upwards towards the heavens and gouts of ice and flame entwine. From the sky comes a deadly hail, lashing from the roiling clouds, and amid the black mist comes the beating of wings in the darkness, like clouds of leathery moths searching for prey to pluck into the storm-wracked heavens. Further northwards, and deeper down, lies the abyss itself: sometimes a foul cavern beneath the waves, infested with serpents and other filthy wriggling things, sometimes a grim bastion wreathed in smoke and fume, 'evil spirits running about amid the black caverns and gloomy abysses'.[14]

Other than the T-O ideograms, very few maps date to the eighth century or earlier, and the northern world is all but absent from them. It seems that, at the beginning of the Viking Age, what learned British monks knew of classical scholarship implied that Britain was, itself, at the ends of the earth: about lands further north, classical and Christian learning was vague, and it is uncertain how much of this knowledge was even accessible to British monks. The image they would have had was one of vaguely drawn islands floating in sluggish seas: of the isle of Thule and the land of the Hyperboreans (the dwellers 'beyond the north wind'), of men with bestial bodies and others with the heads of dogs – a dwelling place of monsters.[15] In this, it was not unlike any of the unknown regions of the earth, but the theme of the North as a specifically satanic realm also manifested itself in the literature of medieval Britain. Often this can be found in ways clearly derived from biblical narratives, but at others it appeared in vivid and idiosyncratic form.

In the tale of St Guthlac, written at the monastery of Crowland in Lincolnshire in the 730s by a monk called Felix, the treatment meted out by a demonic horde to the unfortunate anchorite is described in vivid terms. After a relentless campaign of physical and psychological punishment,

> they began to drag him through the cloudy stretches of the
> freezing skies to the sound of the horrid beating of their wings.
> Now when he had reached the lofty summit of the sky, then,
> horrible to relate, lo! the region of the northern heavens seemed
> to grow dark with gloomy mists and black clouds. For there
> could be seen coming thence to meet them, innumerable
> squadrons of foul spirits. Thus with all their forces joined in
> one, they turned their way with immense uproar into thin air,
> and carried the afore-named servant of Christ, Guthlac, to the
> accursed jaws of hell.[16]

Nor is this the only northern tradition to riff on the biblical theme of the diabolical North. The vision of St Paul, as told in late Anglo-Saxon England, recounts that 'St Paul was looking at the northern part of this world, where all the waters go down, and he saw there above the water a certain grey rock, and there had grown north of that rock very frosty woods, and there were dark mists, and under that rock was a dwelling place of water-monsters and wolves; and he saw that on that cliff there hung in those icy woods many black souls, tied by their hands, and their foes, in the guise of water-monsters, were gripping them like greedy wolves, and the water was black ...'[17]

That these ideas had deep roots in the northern psyche is implied by striking similarities between this description of the monster-haunted North and the *Beowulf* poet's description of the home of Grendel and his mother. The two descriptions are almost certainly related.

Though no comparable tales survive from the Celtic-speaking areas of Britain, the Irish life of St Brendan – written in the seventh century – describes boiling northern seas and an island of flame and tormented howling: 'the confines of Hell' as the saint puts it.[18] Even the people of Scandinavia themselves knew that *niðr ok norðr liggr Helvegr* ('netherwards and northwards lies the road to hell').[19] The word 'hell' itself has no Latin-Christian origin. It is older than that, reflecting fragments of a shared vision that haunted the darker dreams of the Anglo-Saxons and their contemporaries: a nightmare North of the early medieval imagination.

The human inhabitants of this world, if known at all, would have been distinguished for their heathenism – their rejection of Christian norms and values, their bloodletting and their weird rites. It would have been natural to imagine them, to use the historian Eric Christiansen's memorable phrase, as 'robot agents of Satan's foreign policy', flesh and blood avatars of the monster-world beyond the pale.[20]

When the men of the North next appeared in the written record, in all their dreadful pomp and fury, they more than lived up to the fevered imaginings of their victims. In 793, the North disgorged its innards in lurid tones, and chroniclers responded with imagery that came easily:

> In this year dire fore-bodings came over Northumbria and miserably terrified the people: there were immense whirlwinds and flashes of lightning, and fiery dragons were seen flying aloft. Those signs were soon followed by a great hunger, and a little after that in the same year, on 8 June, the harrying of heathen men wretchedly destroyed God's church on Lindisfarne, with plunder and slaughter.[21]

Of all the religious centres of northern Europe, there were few that could rival the cultural muscle of the island priory of Lindisfarne. Its peripheral location, tied to the Northumbrian coast by the narrow umbilical cord of its tidal causeway, belied the wealth and status that it had accrued since its foundation in the early seventh century. Much of this flowed from the stories told of its most famous bishop, Cuthbert (*c.* 634–87). Cuthbert – a monk originally from Melrose who had later been appointed prior of the community at Lindisfarne – was elevated to bishop in March 685. For perhaps as long as nine years, Cuthbert lived in self-imposed exile from Lindisfarne as a hermit on Inner Farne, a wildly bleak outcrop of grey granite stacks, jutting gloomily from the sea.[22] It was a life of hardship, solitude and self-denial modelled on the penitential attitudes of the desert fathers – St Anthony in particular. His elevation to bishop did little to change his temperament – by 687 he had returned to his hermitage, determined to live out his last in solitude.

On Inner Farne, Cuthbert – like St Anthony – encountered devils in the wilderness. The accounts of his struggles are brief – he fought them with 'the helmet of salvation, the shield of faith and the sword of spirit which is the word of God' – and the vanquished demons are left to the imagination.[23] But it is perhaps justifiable to imagine them in the same way that Felix depicted the diabolical horde that appeared in his life of St Guthlac:

they were ferocious in appearance, terrible in shape with great heads, long necks, thin faces, yellow complexions, filthy beards, shaggy ears, wild foreheads, fierce eyes, foul mouths, horses' teeth, throats vomiting flames, twisted jaws, thick lips, strident voices, singed hair, fat cheeks, pigeon breasts, scabby thighs, knotty knees, crooked legs, swollen ankles, splay feet, spreading mouths, raucous cries [...] they grew so terrible to hear with their mighty shriekings that they filled almost the whole intervening space between earth and heaven with their discordant bellowings.[24]

The effect is cumulative. What starts out as absurd – comical even (shaggy ears? wild foreheads?) – becomes ever more grotesque and horrible, one perversion heaped on top of another, until the vision devolves into a squamous mass of deformed, unnatural depravity. If this is what early medieval people saw when they dreamt of wild places, then their dreams must have been dark indeed.

Whatever Cuthbert saw or did not see on Inner Farne, he conquered his little wilderness, living out the brief remainder of his life in self-imposed exile: eating, sleeping, fasting, praying. It is easy to picture him, like the figure in Caspar David Friedrich's famous painting, gazing sadly at the cold grey ocean that embraces him: a last outpost of human life, wearily defiant before the uncaring gulf and his own mortality.

When he died, Cuthbert's body was taken by boat to Lindisfarne. A great crowd received it, psalms were sung, and it was carried to the Church of St Peter and buried in a stone coffin beside the altar. Miracles were reported and he was canonized, his tomb becoming a place of pilgrimage. When, eleven years later, his resting place was deemed inadequate, he was exhumed for translation to a more exalted shrine. His body was apparently found uncorrupted, as pristine as the day he had passed away. The story only confirmed his sanctity and his legend spread, the monastery growing in size and wealth, its scriptoria producing illuminated gospels which – like the Lindisfarne Gospels (commissioned to ornament

Cuthbert's shrine-tomb) – are some of the greatest treasures of their age.

We might be justified in imagining that, for later generations of monks, the monastic life became rather more comfortable than Cuthbert and his forebears would have approved of. By the time of the raid on Lindisfarne, contemporaries – as we shall see – had already begun to voice their opinion on these matters, and it is likely that there really was a drop in standards in the century after Cuthbert's death; or, rather, that the monks gained access to temptations that their forebears had not enjoyed. Even so, the same cold sea would have lapped at their heels and the stories of the devils of Inner Farne would have been told again and again. For the monks living out their lives on the edge of the world, the sea would have been omnipresent – a wide and brooding, raging wilderness stretching out to eternity. Empty, but alive.

When the Vikings came it must have seemed to the monks as though something dreadful had finally stirred from its century-long slumber. What horrors did their bleary eyes see rushing up the moonlit shore, what gargoyles leered from the prows of the great black leviathans looming at the edge of the shadowed water? Did they see devils in the shadows – lit red in the glare of blazing torches? Were they 'ferocious in appearance' and 'terrible to hear with their mighty shriekings'? Did they possess 'filthy beards' and 'fierce eyes', 'foul mouths' and 'strident voices'?

Against the blood-red glare cast by fire, the dragon-headed prows of the ships stand in silhouette, grim spectators of the unfolding chaos. Like oars striking water, the axes rise and fall, biting into timber, bone and flesh; blood splatters across blankets and altar-cloths, burgundy smears in firelight. Brightly coloured shards of ruined gospels flutter among glowing embers, like butterflies and fireflies dancing together in the thermal draughts. A sea-cold breeze whips off the water, lifting the iron tang of blood and metal with the brine, the stink of death and burning carried deep into the land.

The attack on Lindisfarne in 793 has become the iconic moment that defines the engagement of Britain's inhabitants with their neighbours across the North Sea. A sudden seaborne assault on a renowned centre of Christian learning, it was an event that sent shockwaves through Europe. From the court of Charlemagne across the Channel, the English cleric Alcuin wrote a series of letters to his brethren in England in response to this unprecedented tragedy. To him, a terror from the North should have been foreseen, particularly in the light of 'the bloody rain, which [...] we saw fall menacingly on the north side' of St Peter's Church in York 'though the sky was serene'. Therefore one should not be surprised, he adds, 'that from the north there will come upon our nation retribution in blood, which can be seen to have started with this attack'.[25]

A sense of the psychological impact these raids had in the communities they visited can be found in one of the more unsettling objects to have survived them. A carved stone – cracked at its base, rounded at its top – was discovered on Lindisfarne and first mentioned in the 1920s. It numbers among more than fifty tombstones – many of them decorated with Anglo-Saxon carvings and inscribed with names – that have been unearthed on the island. This one, however, is unique. On one side, figures are depicted gesturing towards the sun and moon which ride the sky together on either side of an empty cross. It is an image evoking the passage of time, the transition of day into night, mediated by the risen Christ – a reminder of the judgement to come when night finally falls over the earth.

On the other side of the stone are depicted seven men, all facing forward, their arms raised. Weapons are held aloft by five of them

– three swords and two axes – and their clothing is distinctive. If the stone is taken as a whole, it seems to be a representation of the apocalypse, the armed men perhaps a representation of the wrath of God in corporeal form – a form that English monks would recognize. As we shall see, ecclesiastical commentators found it easy enough to imagine the Vikings as an instrument of divine justice. The stone was probably carved in the late ninth century, and there is no way of knowing whether these armed men are intended to depict Vikings rather than any other armed group, but it is hard to dispel the feeling that the trauma inflicted in Lindisfarne left psychological scars that would trouble the imaginations of generations of monks, colouring their apocalyptic visions.[26]

Lindisfarne was the first raid of this type to be recorded, but it was by no means the last. The years around the turn of the ninth century saw waterborne raiders attacking and pillaging poorly defended monasteries and settlements all around northern Britain and Ireland, as well as elsewhere in continental Europe, and for those on the receiving end it must have been a dreadful experience – made all the more terrifying by the primal horror that a heathen assault inspired.

Alcuin's words, very often ripped from their context, are found at the beginning of many treatments of the Viking Age: 'the pagans have desecrated God's sanctuary,' he lamented in his letter to Bishop Higbald of Lindisfarne, 'shed the blood of saints around the altar, laid waste the house of our hope and trampled the bodies of the saints like dung in the street'. One has to wonder whether Higbald and the monks needed reminding. Indeed, one could easily forgive the torrent of Anglo-Saxon invective that we might imagine issuing from the good bishop's lips upon reading the rest of Alcuin's letter, for it is not – as one might think appropriate – a warm-hearted missive expressing sorrow, solidarity and offers of practical assistance. It is, instead, a lecture on the assumed defects of Higbald's authority and the sub-par behaviour of his monks: they are accused of having asked for it through their drunkenness, vanity, lewdness, degeneracy and – most unfairly of all – lack of manliness ('you who survive, stand like men').[27]

In a similar letter to King Ethelred of Northumbria, Alcuin wrote the words which have led many to imagine the heathen storm breaking on the shores of Britain like lightning from a clear sky:

Lo, it is nearly 350 years that we and our fathers have inhabited this most lovely land, and never before has such terror appeared in Britain as we have now suffered from a pagan race, nor was it thought that such an inroad from the sea could be made. Behold, the church of St. Cuthbert spattered with the blood of the priests of God, despoiled of all its ornaments ...[28]

Once again the expat cleric used the opportunity to castigate the monks, this time for wishing to 'resemble the pagans' in their 'trimming of beard and hair'. With this stern intervention into the hairdressing habits of his former colleagues, however, Alcuin inadvertently alerts us to something potentially more significant than Northumbrian fashion trends, something which challenges and complicates the image of the North as a hellish realm and its peoples as the devil's imps.

While learned attitudes to the North seem certainly to have emphasized the diabolic qualities of its inhabitants, comments such as Alcuin's imply a measure of contact and even, in some cases, admiration or nostalgia for the Scandinavian world and its denizens: a contradiction at the heart of Anglo-Saxon ideas about the wider northern world. On a simplistic level, in order to copy heathen haircuts, the monks must have been exposed to and favourably impressed by them – and presumably not when ducking a swinging axe. It seems highly probable, if not yet provable, that Scandinavian traders had become a feature at some of the new trading settlements of eighth-century England (as well as, perhaps, in the Northern Isles and Pictish Scotland as well).[29]

It is certainly the case that the Viking Age emerged against a background of increasingly sophisticated European trade. A new type of specialized trading settlement had grown up around the North Sea during the eighth century, exploiting and facilitating long-distance trade. These settlements – known to historians and archaeologists as 'emporia' – included Southampton (Hamwic), London (Lundenwic), Ipswich (Gipeswic) and York (Eoforwic) in England, as well as trading settlements at Quentovic (France), Dorestad (Netherlands), Hedeby and Ribe (Denmark), Birka (Sweden) and Kaupang (Norway) among others. It seems inconceivable that every exchange of goods between Britain and Scandinavia in the eighth century was conducted through continental middlemen.

Whatever the realities of direct trading relationships in the decades leading up to the earliest Viking raids, archaeology suggests that contacts across the North Sea in the preceding centuries had been close. A famous example (referred to in the preceding chapter) serves to illustrate the point. The great masked helmet (the Old English word, rather wonderfully, is *grimhelm*) that was excavated from the boat grave found beneath Mound 1 at Sutton Hoo in Suffolk finds its closest parallels in the highly elaborate boat graves from the cemeteries at Vendel and, later, Valsgärde in Sweden; the parallels, in both the style of artefacts and the manner of their burial, demonstrate elements of a cultural identity that spanned the North Sea. This, and a great deal of other evidence (not least the transformation of lowland Britain from a Romano-British-speaking population to one which used the western Germanic 'Old English' language), broadly supports the stories which the Anglo-Saxons told about their own origins.[30] On this point, the Northumbrian monk and scholar Bede – writing at Jarrow in the early eighth century – was quite explicit:

In the year of our Lord 449 [...] the Angles or Saxons came to Britain at the invitation of King Vortigern in three long-ships [...] They [...] sent back news of their success to their homeland, adding that the country was fertile and the Britons cowardly [...] These new-comers were from the three most formidable races of Germany, the Saxons, Angles, and Jutes.[31]

The first group, the Saxons, came from a region identified by Bede as 'Old Saxony' – now north-west Germany. The Angles and the Jutes originated in the Jutland peninsula, occupying land which, by the time Bede was writing, lay within the kingdom of the Danes. Quite how true this story is remains unknowable (though it is certain that significant migration from the continent did occur). But what is critical is that the Anglo-Saxons themselves believed it to be true.[32]

By Bede's day, the 'Anglo-Saxons' had been in Britain for the best part of 300 years (by his reckoning), and had been Christian, in most cases, for several generations. By the late eighth century, they had formed a number of independent kingdoms, each with its own cultural and geographical peculiarities. Nevertheless, the tribes from whom they claimed descent were (and, in the late eighth century, remained) pagan peoples, part of a wider northern European heritage that had stood beyond the limits of Rome's continental frontiers. As receivers of that heritage, the Anglo-Saxons were torch-carriers for traditions, tales, words and images from a legendary world. That world, though its shapes and contours grew ever more indistinct, yet blazed brightly in the imaginations of poets and storytellers. The earliest genealogical lists of Anglo-Saxon royal houses typically extend via Woden, the pagan deity equivalent to Odin (ON Óðinn) in Old Norse mythology, through Finn (a legendary Frisian king) to Geat, the eponymous ancestor of Beowulf's own Scandinavian tribe.

Even a century of Viking attacks failed to dampen enthusiasm amongst the Anglo-Saxons for their northern heritage. By the end of the ninth century, royal genealogies had expanded to include Bældæg (the Old Norse god Balder), Scyld (the legendary progenitor of the Danes) and possibly Beowulf the Geat himself.[33] Negotiating the evidence for the ways in which the Anglo-Saxons identified with this heritage is complex and sometimes bewildering.

Much of what remains is reduced to the blank names of kings and heroes – names which must once have conjured great arcs of narrative, laced with the myths of the pre-Christian past, but whose owners now stand mute guard at the entrance to pathways which can never now be trod.

The perpetuation of this fascination with the ancestral North did not, however, go unchallenged. Writing in around the year 800, our friend Alcuin was so incensed by this sort of thing that, in a letter to another Anglo-Saxon bishop, he demanded to know 'what has Ingeld to do with Christ?' We know only a single anecdote about Ingeld, king of the Heathobards – a gloomy story about how he burned Hrothgar's hall, Heorot, and was thereafter a target of the Danish king's vengeance. The story is alluded to in *Beowulf* and mentioned in passing in another Old English poem, *Widsith*. Alcuin's reference to Ingeld pops up in a passage in which he lambasts his fellow ecclesiasts for listening to music and 'inappropriate' stories at dinner-time and for laughing in the courtyards (he presumably didn't get invited to many parties). It is of particular interest, however, because it suggests that even in what should have been a thoroughly Christian environment, the old stories were still popular – and this at a time when, in Alcuin's own words, the 'bodies of the saints were being trampled like dung' by the living descendants of Hrothgar and his kin.[34]

Rather less is known about attitudes to the ancestral North in other parts of Britain. One tradition, reported by Bede, held that the Picts – the people inhabiting the highland and island regions of what is now Scotland – had originated in 'Scythia'. This land had been believed by classical authorities to have existed in an ill-defined region somewhere, seemingly, in northern Eurasia. Whether the Picts themselves believed this to be true – and if they did, what they thought of it – is less than clear. The Welsh, on the other hand, had their own distinct boreal traditions: to them, Hen Ogledd ('the Old North') referred to those parts of Britain from which their ancestors had been ejected by Anglo-Saxon incomers in the sixth and seventh centuries. It was an altogether more insular sense of northernness, and can only have compounded the sense that northern lands beyond the sea were a place whence nothing much good ever came.[35]

Among the English-speaking peoples, however, we are left with an apparent paradox – a set of attitudes to the North that painted it as both shining ancestral homeland and infernal monster-infested wasteland, its inhabitants as both cousins and aliens. As a result, the Viking has emerged as a Janus-faced figure, constantly at war with himself in our imaginations: poet or plunderer, merchant or marauder, berserker or boat-builder, kinsman or kin-of-Cain. The reconciliation of these themes and the resolution of these identities is in large measure the story of Viking Britain. It is a process of negotiation that continues to this day, and begins with the fundamental question of who we understand the Vikings to be.

3

MOTHER NORTH

Huge warriors with golden beards and savage eyes sat or lounged on
the rude benches, strode about the hall, or sprawled full length on the
floor. They drank mightily from foaming horns and leathern jacks,
and gorged themselves on great pieces of rye bread, and huge chunks
of meat they cut with their daggers from whole roasted joints […]
All the world was their prey to pick and choose, to take and spare
as it pleased their barbaric fancies.

ROBERT E. HOWARD, 'The Dark Man' (1931)[1]

When I was growing up, my idea of what a 'Viking' should be
was not, I presume, very different from that imagined by
anyone else of my generation.

My grandmother – who lived in Glastonbury, Somerset – was a
full-time carer and companion to a (to my young eyes) elderly disabled gentleman whom I knew only, and affectionately, as 'Venge'. An
Italian by birth, who in truth luxuriated in the name Bonaventura
Mandara, Venge was an exceptionally kind and gentle man, with a
love of brandy, cigars, cards and horse-racing: he was, in other words,
a jolly fine fellow. He would often encourage me, sprog that I was, to
clamber on to his bad leg (always propped up horizontally in front
of him, encased in a steel and leather contraption that both frightened and fascinated) and read me the cartoon strips from the back
of his newspaper. Only one of these left any kind of impression.

Hägar the Horrible – a comic strip drawn by the American cartoonist Dik Browne – was probably my first encounter with a Viking. The eponymous Hägar fulfilled all the stereotypes: an unruly faceful of red beard, an unashamedly horned helmet, a flagon of foaming ale, an aversion to bathing. In essence he remains the classic 'Viking as barbarian', essentially indistinguishable from the cartoon caveman. That was fine with me. Hägar and his frequent anachronistic assaults on large medieval stone castles fitted easily into early childhood visits to Glastonbury spent rampaging around the ruins of the medieval abbey and staring through the windows of King Arthur themed crystal shops.

When I was a little older, I remember being taught about the Vikings – the only time I ever encountered the subject in compulsory education. I must have been about eight, and although perhaps not best equipped to appreciate the significance of what I was learning, I remembered that lesson when all else had faded away. The thing that stuck, the one key message that lodged most firmly in my brain, was that no Viking ever wore, possessed – or perhaps even imagined – a horned helmet.

The absence of horns on Viking helmets invariably comes as a blow to those who aren't prepared for it. Many is the occasion on which I have been obliged to plunge in this particular knife; it is remarkable to witness, in fully grown adults (in fact, especially in adults), the visible shrinking of the spirit that accompanies the unexpected death of an image formed in childhood. There may well be, and I apologize for it, readers of this book who are right now experiencing the bewildering combination of anger and disbelief that accompanies the detonation of this fact-bomb.

To a small boy weaned on *Hägar the Horrible* the news was, well, horrible. I still remember the frustration of it all – if the Vikings didn't have horned helmets, why had I been lied to? Thankfully my young mind was still fertile enough to bounce back from this mental napalm. The blow was also softened slightly by the discovery that the helmets they did wear were *almost* as cool (or so I tried to convince myself) as their cornigerous surrogates. The evidence for helmets of any kind, however, is slim. Aside from scattered fragments, only one complete Scandinavian helmet of the Viking Age has ever been found. This is the famous Gjermundbu helmet (named after the place in Norway where it was buried, along with its owner), an arresting object defined by the sinister half-facemask that was intended to protect the eyes and nose. Its owl-like visage – cold, impassive and predatory – was the face presented by at least one Norwegian warrior in his battle-cladding.[2]

Outside Scandinavia, other helmets have been found in graves that may, on the strength of their form or contents, have been the burial places of Vikings – or, at least, of people with a cultural affinity to Scandinavia. But none of these – most of which have been found in what is now Russia and Ukraine – is distinct from the material culture of the (non-Viking) local populations. Are these Viking helmets? If the only qualification is that a person of Scandinavian extraction might once have put one of these things on his head then the answer must be yes. But these helmets are radically different to the Gjermundbu helmet: open faced, conical, distinctly eastern – and worn by all sorts of other people who were definitely not Vikings. So perhaps these were just helmets that some Vikings happened to wear – not 'Viking' helmets at all. Perhaps these were no more 'Viking' helmets than the Volga salmon they ate for dinner was 'Viking' fish. But, of course, that is equally true of the Gjermundbu helmet as well – simply putting it on didn't make the wearer a Viking, and we can't even be certain (no matter how probable it may be) that it was made by, or even worn by, someone born and bred in Scandinavia. As we shall see, material culture can be a most treacherous guide to ethnicity.

The problems lie both in the semantics (the word 'Viking') and in the underlying premise that 'the Vikings' were a 'people' whose characteristics can be listed like a Top Trump card or tabulated like a character-class in a role-playing game. It is fair to say that Vikings, in this sense at least, never existed.

Most modern academics have an uneasy relationship with the term 'Viking', and reject the idea that it can be used as an ethnic label. Its original meaning is disputed. It could mean people who hung around in bays getting up to no good (from ON *vik*, meaning 'bay or inlet') or perhaps people who frequently showed up at trading settlements (from OE *wics*); there are, also, other possibilities. However, its original derivation is largely irrelevant – what is important is what people thought they meant by it when (and if) they used the word. As a common noun (in its Old Norse and Old English forms Vikingr and Wicing respectively), the word was used rarely during the Viking Age and was applied only to a minority, not all of whom were Scandinavians. In Old Norse poetry composed in praise of Viking kings (known as skaldic verse), much of which dates to the Viking period, the word was as likely to be applied to the enemies of Scandinavian kings as to home-grown marauders. Indeed, one of the rare English uses of the term is found in Archbishop Wulfstan's lament, *c.* 1014, that slaves were running away from their English lords to become 'Vikings'.[3] Who the Vikings were, therefore, could be a relative concept. It was never an ethnic category, and in most cases it seems to have been used disapprovingly, suggesting that 'Vikings' could prove as much a menace to Scandinavians as to their victims elsewhere.[4]

Runestones – memorials to the dead erected during the Viking Age and inscribed in the runic alphabet that was used to render the Old Norse language in written form – also record a number of instances of the word. In most of these cases the word appears as a personal name, and this phenomenon is known from Viking Age Britain as well: a man called 'Wicing' was minting coins in Lydford (Devon) on behalf of King Cnut in the eleventh century.[5] The implication is that the term 'Viking' wasn't necessarily negative, and although we can't know for certain if these were names given at birth, it accords well with a society in which individuals revelled in tough-guy epithets.[6] Indeed, the abstract form of the noun (ON *viking*), particularly as encountered in later Icelandic literature, meant a seaborne mission involving adventure, violence, plunder and risk, and was a normal and honourable means by which a man might make his name.

The poetry of the tenth-century Icelander Egil Skallagrimsson – contained in the thirteenth-century saga of his life – sums up, in words which just might originate with Egil himself, a view of the indulgent nature of Viking parenting:

My mother said to me
That they would buy for me
A ship and lovely oars
To go away with Vikings,
Standing in the stern,
Steering the glorious ship,
Then putting into ports,
Killing a man or two.[7]

In this sense, 'Viking' was fundamentally something that one *did* or was a part of, and there is very limited evidence that the word was used in this way during the Viking Age. A runestone erected by a mother in Vastergotland (Sweden) implies that to engage in 'Viking' activity (in this case in the west – that is, in Britain and Ireland) could be considered praiseworthy: 'Tóla placed this stone in memory of Geirr, her son, a very good valiant man. He died on a Viking raid on the western route.'[8]

However, there seems to have been an expectation that a man (it was almost certainly an overwhelmingly – if perhaps not exclusively – male occupation) would, at some point, settle down. Supported by the wealth accrued during his Viking days, he might set himself up as a farmer and landowner, the head of a family, with a good reputation among his peers. He might take on some public duties at legal gatherings, and he would use his wealth to patronize poets and craftsmen and perhaps even organize trading expeditions. He would become, in other words, respectable. Inevitably, however, there were always individuals who were sufficiently bloodthirsty, marginalized, restless, irresponsible, fame-hungry, greedy or outcast to make the Viking lifestyle a permanent occupation – these outsiders would have been among those who self-identified as Vikings, and it is for these people that the disapproval of Scandinavian skalds seems to have been reserved. This distinction between being and doing was perhaps a little like the different attitudes that a young person might encounter if he or she were to state an ambition to become 'a traveller' rather than merely to 'go travelling'.

All of which is rendered somewhat irrelevant by the unavoidable observation that hardly anybody was ever called a Viking during the Viking Age itself: they were referred to across Europe and beyond as Danes, Dark Heathens, Dark Foreigners, Fair Foreigners, Foreign Irish, Gentiles, Northmen, Pirates, Pagans, Rūs, Scythians and Varangians, but hardly ever – in Old English – as Vikings (*wicings*). As we have seen, the *Anglo-Saxon Chronicle* tends most frequently to speak of 'Danes', despite considerable evidence to indicate that many of the Vikings who found themselves in Britain came from all over the northern world: various Viking leaders can be shown to have had Norwegian origins, runestones commemorate the death of Swedish Vikings in Britain, and even the Viking dead themselves, through analysis of the oxygen isotopes in their teeth, can be shown to have grown up as far afield as Estonia, Belarus and high latitudes beyond the Arctic circle.

The early English had form when it came to conflating complex cultural phenomena into a homogeneous 'them' – the diverse inhabitants of much of Celtic-speaking Britain had been labelled *wealas* ('foreigners', whence the modern 'Welsh') and treated as a largely undifferentiated rabble since at least Bede's day. Likewise, 'Danish' seems to have become a convenient catch-all term for people who predominantly spoke Old Norse, wherever they actually came from.[9]

One might expect that modern historians would have long ago developed more subtle approaches to complex issues of identity and cultural affiliation. And yet, until relatively recently, it was widely assumed that past 'peoples' could be identified as essentially unchanging racial blocs with cultural traits that were stable, heritable and identifiable through language, behaviour, skull-size and material culture. This 'culture-historical paradigm', accompanied by racist bricolage of varying offensive shades, was driven by the twin engines of misapplied Darwinist logic and the German revolution in philology (which had demonstrated the interconnections between Indo-European languages and the mechanics of linguistic development). Social, cultural and racial development was soon seen to be as predictable as vowel mutation and as inexorable as evolution.[10] It was only during the second half of the twentieth century that these views began to change and mainstream academia started thinking more critically about past ethnicity.[11]

It is no coincidence that in Anglophone scholarship this shift coincided with the loss of Britain's Empire and the country's diminution as a global power. The culture-historical model shared many features with the system of racial classification that had been used by academics and administrators to reinforce the discriminatory structures of the British Empire – and in particular the position of white English men at the pinnacle of the world order they had invented. It was a classic circular argument – the fact of Empire proved the superiority of the British, the innate genius of whom had made British global supremacy inevitable. At the time, the obvious implication was that the greatness of Britain had been present in the genes; for, if cultural traits were – like DNA – handed down the generations, then surely the seeds of that greatness lay in the blood of mighty ancestors. And, of course, they found greatness in abundance: in the Romans whose civilization prefigured their own Empire, in the Anglo-Saxons whose Germanic origins had (in their minds) brought law, democracy, freedom and a distinctively 'English' Christianity to Britain, and, increasingly, in the Vikings.[12]

As the nineteenth-century children's author R. M. Ballantyne wrote in 1869, 'much of what is good and true in our laws and social customs, much of what is manly and vigorous in the British Constitution, and much of our intense love of freedom and fair play, is due to the pith, pluck and enterprise, and sense of justice that dwelt in the breasts of the rugged old sea-kings of Norway!' A stirring message for the Empire's future administrators.[13]

The British Empire was in essence a maritime concern. From Francis Drake to Horatio Nelson its greatest heroes and progenitors had been seamen. Even Alfred, the ninth-century king of Wessex, was fêted (on the strength of very little evidence indeed) as the founder of the English navy.[14] The Vikings, as a seafaring people, seemed to embody and prefigure all the greatest traits and achievements of the British: the spirit of commerce and adventure, the cutting-edge maritime technology, the suicidal bravery on land and sea, the discovery and settlement of new and exotic lands, the rattling of sabres in the faces of savage natives – even the cheerful pillaging of Catholic Europe with a gusto of which Drake would have been proud. The thought that these qualities had been reproduced in the British – not only by the example but in the very blood of the Vikings – was a tremendously exciting one in the intellectual climate of the late nineteenth and early twentieth centuries. Here was a myth of origins that did not rely on the Mediterranean parallels and exempla that had been the staples of classical education since the Renaissance; the Old North was real and palpable in the cold salt spray of home waters, and the roar of Boreas carried the family ghosts with it.

So, out of half-digested Icelandic sagas, Wagnerian wardrobe cast-offs, classical ideas of barbarian virtue and a good dose of romantic nationalism, the classic image of the Viking was born: blond and bare-chested, lusty and bold, a noble savage for the north

European soul. This, incidentally, was also the crucible in which the horned helmet was forged, a fantasy propagated and popularized through book illustrations. Thomas Heath Robinson's illustrations for the English retelling of Frithiof's Saga, published in 1912, have a lot to answer for in this respect, and Arthur Rackham's drawings accompanying the translated libretto of Wagner's *Ring* cycle didn't help either; even though the *Ring* wasn't 'about' Vikings, the valkyries, gods, dwarves and other paraphernalia of Norse myth placed it in the same milieu. Most importantly of all, it was in the latter part of the nineteenth century that the word 'Viking' came popularly to be applied to these people, their culture and their age.[15]

In the light of modern attitudes towards Britain's imperial project, it is now hard to view the enthusiasm of men like Ballantyne without cynicism. The approving comparisons made by men of the nineteenth century between themselves and their Viking forebears now carry a grim irony. Shackles and collars have been excavated from major Viking commercial centres at Dublin and elsewhere along the trade routes to the slave-markets of central Asia; they are functionally and technologically identical to those used in the African slave-trade that underpinned much of Britain's vast imperial wealth. The greed, brutality and callous disregard for the art and culture of others that the British were periodically to display across the globe were aptly prefigured in the rapacious Viking lust for silver, slaves and tribute. The qualities that some in the past saw as 'manly vigour' might very well strike us today as psychopathic tendencies – whether manifested in the eleventh-century Norwegian king Harald Hard-ruler or the nineteenth- and twentieth-century British general Horatio Herbert Kitchener. And, as Britain's Empire unravelled in the decades following the Second World War, misty-eyed nationalist eulogies to the North became ever more absurd, and comparisons with the recently humiliated Nordic countries increasingly unwelcome.

The marchers move with a practised military discipline, boots polished to a high shine, brass buttons gleaming. At the front march the Rikshird (the State Troopers) in navy blue, followed by the Kvinnehird (the women's brigades) and the various youth groups gathered together under the banner of the Nasjonal Samling Ungdomsfylking ('National Unity Youth Front'). Everywhere there are shining eyes and waving banners, gold crosses on red fields, eagles and swords. They move like an army, down from the plain little whitewashed church towards the barrow cemetery. The hump-backed mounds rise and plunge in the grass, like leviathans playing in the shallows of Oslo fjord, the glittering waters spreading out to the east.

A pouchy-looking fellow, with limp sand-coloured hair and slightly bulgy eyes, is standing at a podium. As he begins to speak, the faces of the young men and women assembled before him look up in rapture, glowing with the promise of a golden dawn.

'Norwegian women, Norwegian men. Today, we are gathered in a historic place, at a historic time in the lives of our people … It was from here, where the Yngling dynasty has its graveyard, that – with thought and deed acting in concert – Norway became united [...] Was it not the Viking kings, the Ynglings resting here, the strong Nordic men, who one thousand years ago drove forward the will of the Norwegian people [...]?'[16]

The speaker was Vidkun Quisling, leader of the puppet regime that governed Norway under close supervision from Nazi Germany between 1942 and 1945, and chairman of the Norwegian fascist movement Nasjonal Samling ('National Unity'). Between 1935 and 1944, Nasjonal Samling held meetings during the Pentecost holiday at the Borre national park in Vestfold, near Oslo.[17] The park is the setting for a cemetery of forty surviving grave-mounds, the largest of which are 23 feet tall and up to 150 feet in diameter. In 1852, one of the mounds was demolished by the Norwegian Public Roads Administration for the purpose of gravel extraction. In the process, the remains of an elaborate Viking Age ship burial were discovered. Although the excavations were botched and most of the evidence of the ship itself was lost, the treasures that were found accompanying the burial were spectacular. Gilt-bronze bridle fittings, with their knot-work and zoomorphic decorations, gave rise to the definition of a new Viking art-form: the 'Borre' style.[18] These were some of the first artefacts that allowed Norwegians to imagine the splendour of Viking Age power, and historians eagerly took up the Borre site as emblematic of national origins – a powerful symbol in the period around 1905 when the independent kingdom of Norway formally came into being after more than 500 years of political and dynastic union with Denmark and (latterly) Sweden. In 1915, Professor Anton Wilhelm Brøgger sensationally claimed that the ship burial was the grave of Halfdan the Black, father of Harald Finehair (*c.* 850–*c.* 932) – the man credited as the first king of a unified Norway. This built on medieval traditions that considered the Borre mounds to be the cemetery of the legendary Yngling dynasty, from which Halfdan and Harald ultimately sprang.

These elaborate confections of folklore and invented tradition have disintegrated under scrutiny in recent decades. But, in the political climate of post-independence Norway at the beginning of the twentieth century, a national myth of such potency went unchallenged. In 1932, with Brøgger as its indefatigable cheerleader, Borre became Norway's first national park – a sacred site, as he saw it, in the birth of Norwegian nationhood.[19]

These were the myths that Quisling, and men like him, eagerly embraced. Borre was not the only Viking Age site that Nasjonal Samling commandeered for their propaganda – they also met at the iconic battle-sites of Stiklestad and Hafrsfjord where Quisling told his audience (wrongly), 'Norwegian kings sat on Scotland's throne and for almost four hundred years Norwegian kings ruled Ireland,' pointing out too (and stretching the truth almost as much) that 'Ganger Rolf [Rollo], who was a king of Norwegian birth [he wasn't], founded a kingdom in Normandy [he didn't] which was so powerful that it conquered England [150 years later].' The promotion of the archetypal Viking image – the aggression, the expansionism, the machismo – became a powerful recruiting tool for the Nazis and their fascist allies. Numerous propaganda images (the majority produced by the Norwegian artist Harald Damsleth) featured lantern-jawed Nordic types riding the decks of dragon-prowed long-ships, alongside more sophisticated and esoteric uses of runic scripts and mythological allusions. These fostered a spurious sense of continuity between the Viking Age and the National Socialist project. The deep roots and time-hallowed legitimacy that these symbols implied lent the ultra-modern ideology of racist nationalism a gravitas that helped it to transcend its inherent novelty and absurdity.[20]

It was the latter quality that fascist movements in Britain never quite managed to escape: P. G. Wodehouse's brilliant lampoon of the British politician Oswald Mosley and his British Union of Fascists, or 'Blackshirts' (with Roderick Spode's 'Blackshorts'), proved that the British capacity to laugh at anything was a useful barricade against the pompous po-facedness of fascist demagoguery.[21] But the ultimate failure of British fascism is perhaps also testament to the fact that, by the mid-twentieth century, the medieval (including the Viking) past – so relentlessly plundered by nationalist movements across Europe – had already been integrated into British national culture in forms which were harder to bend into totalitarian shape. Nevertheless, the degree to which the Nazis successfully co-opted the image of the Vikings into National Socialist propaganda can be measured in the long-term and widespread contamination of northern European heritage. J. R. R. Tolkien's deeply held loathing for 'that ruddy little ignoramus' Adolf Hitler rested in no small part on his recognition of the damage done by 'Ruining, perverting, misapplying, and making forever accursed, that noble northern spirit, a supreme contribution to Europe, which I have ever loved, and tried to present in its true light'.[22]

It remains the case today that too warm an enthusiasm for the 'Germanic' past can raise suspicions (often justified) of unsavoury politics: the subject remains a fecund repository for the imagery of racist propaganda. This taint is one of the quietest, most tenacious and most ironic legacies of the Third Reich.[23]

This squeamishness about the Vikings and their world would lead ultimately to a thorough reappraisal of the Viking Age in the decades following the Second World War. Pioneered by the British archaeologist Peter Sawyer, revisionist histories sought to downplay the lurid violence and warrior ethics of the Vikings, emphasizing instead their artistic, technological and mercantile achievements.[24] There is no doubt that it was a necessary corrective, rebalancing the Viking image and dispelling a plethora of myths and falsehoods that had stood unchallenged since the Middle Ages. However, far from liberating the Vikings from nationalist captivity, the new narratives provided a fresh palette with which revivalists and nationalists could embellish what had previously been a relatively two-dimensional image. Viking ancestors became pioneers without equal, craftsmen and poets, engineers and statesmen – as well as remaining the warriors and conquerors they had always been. All of which was true of course, at least of some individuals at certain times and in different places. But the desire to demystify the Viking Age also brought in train a new myth: that the Vikings – with their storytelling and home-making, their pragmatism, their games and their shoe-menders – were essentially the same as we are, but fitter, stronger, clearer of purpose, uncorrupted by modernity. Peering into the Viking world, some have found a mirror reflecting back all that they would wish themselves and the modern world to be: simple, undiluted, purified ...

But, as we shall see, the Vikings *were* strange. They were strange to their contemporaries and they should be strange to us too. Theirs was a world in which slaves were raped, murdered and burned alongside the decomposing corpses of their dead owners, a world where men with filed teeth bartered captive monks for Islamic coins, where white-faced women smeared their bodies in fat and human ash and traversed the spirit world in animal form: it is not the template for a brave new world that I, for one, would choose. Thus 'the Vikings', to us now and to their contemporaries in their own time, could represent something both familiar and alien: they could be weird and remote, monstrous even, but also bound tightly into narratives of who the English-speaking peoples have felt themselves – wanted themselves – to be. It is a complex and enduring problem, and shifting emphases in the presentation of the Vikings and their homelands, from the eighth century to the present day, illuminate the preoccupations of the modern psyche just as much as they do the realities of the Viking Age itself.[25]

All of which is to say that the whole idea of the 'Viking' needs to be handled with care. As it is used in a modern sense (and in this book), the word is largely employed as a term of convenience. It is used to define a period, the seaborne warriors whose activities characterized that period, and the shared cultural connections, ideas and art-styles (mostly, but not exclusively, of Scandinavian origin) that both bound people together and spawned new identities. It is important to recognize that – like the reality of all human life – what we mean by the term is chaotic, contestable and imprecise, resisting easy definition. How that chaos is, and has been, negotiated is in part what this book is about. And thinking about it is important, because the stereotypes can be deadly.

In the 1940s, hundreds of young Norwegian men, stirred by images of their 'Viking' heritage and convinced by nationalist propaganda of the threat from Russian Bolshevism, signed up for the 'Norwegian Legion'. They were promised that they would be fighting in the interests of a free and independent Norway. Instead they found themselves, barely out of training, ordered by German officers into the meat-grinder of Hitler's Eastern Front. A hundred and eighty of them (around 20 per cent) were killed before the legion was acrimoniously disbanded. Those few who remained committed to the Nazi cause were integrated into the SS Nordland Division, a force of mainly Scandinavian volunteers which had

Norwegian propaganda for the SS

formerly constituted a part of the SS Wiking Division. These were the men who were inspired by the Viking-themed propaganda images churned out by the Reich and who had listened misty-eyed to Quisling's fantasies in the supposed burial ground of Halfdan the Black. The men of SS Nordland, convinced of the superiority of their Viking blood, would go on to commit atrocities in eastern Europe which were equal to the crimes of any of their Nazi peers.[26]

4

SHORES
IN FLAMES

Bitter is the wind tonight,
it stirs up the white-waved sea.
I do not fear the coursing of the Irish sea
by the fierce warriors of Lothlind [Vikings].

Irish monk (ninth century)[1]

If the raid on Lindisfarne in 793 remains the apocalyptic touchstone for the Viking Age in Britain, it was only the first of many similar attacks that were to rage up and down the coastlines of Britain and Ireland in the years around 800. Viking raiders struck at Iona in the Western Isles in 795, at Jarrow (former home to the monastic scholar Bede) in 796, at Hartness and Tynemouth in 800, at Iona again in 802 and 806.[2] The earliest raids in Ireland fell in 795 on Rathlin Island, Co. Antrim (almost certainly the same group that had already hit Iona in that year), at St Patrick's Isle (Co. Dublin) in 798 and at Inishmurray (Co. Sligo) in 798 and 807.[3] The record is patchy and incomplete; but what is certain is that people died and people suffered. There is not much direct evidence of the impact of these early Viking raids, no clear indication of the human cost exacted – of the people, possessions and lives that were snatched away. But there are traces – objects and remains that give terror and plunder a weight and substance that even the purplest of ecclesiastical prose fails to convey. It is here, in the material traces

51

of the Viking Age – in stone and bone and metal – that something of the original purpose and the impact of the Vikings in Britain can be seen.

A grim and bearded head lies within the collection of the British Museum.[4] It is small, made of bronze and dated to the eighth century – a piece of Scottish, Irish or Northumbrian workmanship. It was probably intended to depict the face of a saint (it is strikingly similar to the depiction of St Mark in the Lichfield Gospels). Discovered near Furness Abbey in Cumbria (a region, as we shall see, of later Scandinavian settlement), the head has been adapted as a weight in a manner typical of Viking traders. Stuffed with lead, it has been turned to a new use in the hands of owners more concerned with personalizing their belongings than with piety. The little head, severed from its body, hacked from whatever piece of ecclesiastical treasure it had once been intended to decorate, is a reminder of the material consequences of Viking raids – of the treasured possessions that were broken and stolen, the human heads that were detached from their bodies, of the people taken away from their homes and disposed of far away.

Direct evidence for the sort of violence recorded by monastic writers is rare and often equivocal; a number of skeletons excavated from the ditch of an enclosed settlement at Llanbedrgoch on Anglesey, for example, were long believed to be local victims of Viking raiding until chemical analysis of the remains revealed several of them to have grown up in Scandinavia: not, in itself, any reason to believe that they were not the victims of raiding, but enough to complicate the narrative considerably.[5] In only one place in Britain – at the former monastery at Portmahomack in Scotland – has good evidence for the violence of Viking raiding been uncovered; it is a place, moreover, that is not mentioned in any written source that has survived from the Viking Age.

*

'The further north you go in the island of Britain, the more beautiful the scenery becomes, the hills wilder, the skies wider, the air
clearer, the seas closer. Even for those not born in Scotland, you feel
as if you are driving towards your beginnings.'[6] This is how Professor
Martin Carver described his journey to Portmahomack. The small
fishing settlement lies at the north-eastern tip of the Tarbat peninsula: a finger of land that points emphatically north-east, separating
the Moray and Dornoch Firths. It is the shard of crust marking the
end of the Great Glen, the weirdly rectilinear fracture that shears a
diagonal fissure through Scotland, scoring a damp line that puddles
along its length into Loch Ness and Loch Linnhe before dispersing
into the Firth of Lorne. There is a sense up here, as elsewhere in the
far north of Britain, of land dissolving at the margins, like the edge
of pack ice giving way to the ocean, splintering and drifting into
ragged and provisional forms. To travel there is to a find a place –
not of journeys ending – but of transitions and embarkations: a
terminus, rather than a homecoming.

The monastery that Carver discovered at Portmahomack was
revealed in a series of archaeological investigations between 1994
and 2007. It is, just for the fact of its existence, a supremely significant addition to our knowledge of the early medieval north. No
record of it exists in any written source, and it is – so far – the only
monastery discovered within the notional bounds of the Pictish
kingdom; indeed, it lies close to its heart. At the height of its wealth
and productivity in the eighth century, the monastery was producing prodigious quantities of vellum for the production of manuscripts as well as high-quality liturgical metalwork such as chalices
and pyxes (containers for holding the consecrated bread used in
the Eucharist). There was obviously a limit to the number of such
objects (particularly of the latter sort) that a single church required,
and so the workshops probably served newer, start-up monasteries
elsewhere in Pictland and perhaps beyond. It is precisely this sort
of wealth and activity that drew attention to Portmahomack and
probably sealed its fate. For at that time, and in that place, the
attention of outsiders was something that no one would have

wanted to attract; at some point around the year 800, the monastery burned.

The parts nearest the sea went first, the blaze ripping through the workshops of the vellum-makers, immolating timber, straw and heather. The severity of the fire can be judged by the condition of stone fragments, cracked and reddened in the heat of the burning. Carver's team discovered that most of these stones, strewn on top of the fire, had been part of a great cross-slab (a flat rectangle with a cross carved upon it in relief). The stone, which had originally stood at the edge of the monastic graveyard, had been toppled and obliterated – pulverized with a calculated malice more reminiscent of the violence done by Islamic fundamentalists to ancient artefacts than of any casual vandalism. This was destruction with a purpose – the work of people with motive and intent, who had an understanding (whatever that was) of what such a monument stood for. It was not the only one: other stone cross-slabs (at least one, probably three) were broken down and shattered on this site.[7]

A famous example of the sort of thing that was broken at Portmahomack can be seen just 5 miles away at Hilton of Cadboll. The stone that stands near the chapel there is an imposing monument, nearly 8 feet tall and 4½ feet wide, heavy and overbearing. The images that decorate its surface – like those discernible among the fragments from Portmahomack – are stunning in their quality and execution, renderings in stone of the types of imagery more familiar from illuminated manuscripts like the Book of Kells. It is a replica, the original stone having been moved from here in the mid-1800s and ultimately finding its way to the National Museum of Scotland in Edinburgh.[8] The imagery that survives on the original monument is almost all on one side. Scenes of aristocratic life – hunting dogs and a deer run to ground, mounted men with spears and others blowing horns, a woman riding side-saddle – are surrounded by a frame of twisting vines and interlacing animals. Surmounting it all are the idiosyncratic hieroglyphs known as 'Pictish symbols' – in this case the 'crescent and V rod' and the 'double-disc and Z rod', as well as the 'comb and mirror', tucked into

The Hilton at Cadboll stone

the corner of the figurative hunting scene. Nobody really knows what these symbols represent, but they certainly had their origins in a distant past. The best guess at present is that they signify the names, and perhaps ranks or affiliations, of Pictish aristocrats.[9]

Missing from the original Hilton of Cadboll stone is the feature that, at the time of its making, would have been its definitive attribute: the huge and elaborate cross that once decorated its eastern side (a reconstruction of this cross can now be seen on the replica, sculpted by Barry Grove). This cross was deliberately defaced, methodically, carefully and totally; but not by Vikings. In 1667, or a little later, the redressed stone was inscribed with a memorial to one Alexander Duff and his three wives (one assumes that these were consecutive, rather than concurrent, relationships). In the febrile religious climate of seventeenth-century Scotland, it seems possible that the ostentation of this cross was enough to make it a target for iconoclasts. No one knows whether it originally carried an image of the crucified Christ; if it did it would have been even more offensive to Protestant sensibilities – nothing says 'Popish' quite like an enormous ornamental crucifix embellished with vine scrolls and animal interlace. At the very least it was clearly not considered worth preserving such an object, pregnant as it was with associations that ran counter to prevailing cultural, political and religious norms.[10]

In 1640, the Aberdeen Assembly (the General Assembly of the Church of Scotland) determined that 'in divers places of the Kingdome, and especially in the North parts of the Same, many Idolatrous Monuments, erected and made for Religious worship are yet extant' and should be 'taken down, demolished and destroyed, and that with all convenient diligence'. Such stones, in other words, in the seventeenth century, were inescapable reminders of a regional, native identity that was partly defined and sustained by its religious affiliations. For the men of the Aberdeen Assembly, such reminders were intolerable – on religious grounds, certainly, but perhaps also as memorials to an aristocratic, kin-centric and local way of life, deep-rooted and old-fangled things that lay far beyond the systems and controls of civic assemblies, national government and kirk. At the time of their making, however, these stones were billboards proclaiming the political and cultural dominance of the prevailing local dynasties, and clearly could be no less provocative. Around the year 800, not long after the monuments at Portmahomack and Hilton of Cadboll were erected, a new power was plying the coastal waters of Pictland. This power, founded in raw military strength and impressive maritime technology, was unimpressed by the strictures, injunctions and symbols of the British Christianity it encountered. Moreover, it had a vested interest in challenging the strident Pictish identity that those stones gave voice to. It was a power determined to frame the landscape in its own terms, without reference to local landmarks and the bigwigs who had built them. For Viking warlords – seeking, perhaps, to consolidate their spheres of influence – the Pictish monuments of Portmahomack may have represented an intolerable challenge to their mastery of the northern oceans. This perhaps was the reason why they suffered so badly.[11]

It was not, of course, only the stones that suffered. Although it is the damage done to buildings and to things that endures in the archaeological record, and although it is the irretrievable loss of cultural heritage that grieves the historian most acutely, for the monks who were present at the monastery on the day it burned there were corporal and existential issues at stake. Excavation of the monastic cemetery revealed the skeletons of three men who had suffered extreme personal violence. One of them (number 158 in the excavations report) was struck in the face with a sword, a wound which cleaved through his flesh and into the bones of his skull. Somehow he survived to die another day. Another monk, number 152, received three blows to the head with a heavy bladed weapon. He was less fortunate than his brother. 'As two of the cuts were on the back of the head,' Carver explains, 'it is likely that the assailant attacked from behind. Given that one of the fractures was on the crown of the head, the individual may have been below the assailant at one point (e.g. kneeling). As injuries with larger weapons are more likely to produce terminal fractures, it is possible that a weapon such as a large sword may have been used to produce these fractures.'[12]

Here are the Vikings we think we know – hacking apart the head of a fleeing monk, shearing open his skull from behind as he drops to his knees. Did he stumble in his flight – driven by the burning terror that had spewed up out of the ocean? Or did he drop to his knees in prayer, facing death as a martyr with the *Pater Noster* on his lips? This we cannot know. What we can say with certainty, however, is that someone cared enough about him in death to remove his bloody corpse from the smoking ruins and inter it with dignity within the confines of the monastic cemetery. These were hardly likely to be the actions of his killers. They, presumably, were long gone, in ships laden with silver chalices and the gilded covers of holy manuscripts, their precious painted vellum leaves left to burn in the smouldering wreckage or used to stoke the camp-fires at their next stop along the coast. Not that the Vikings would leave this corner of Britain alone. There were other islands, and other sources of wealth, to be won.[13]

The island of Inchmarnock, lying off the Scottish coast among the other islands of the Clyde, is not much of anything really, not now at any rate: a smear of wooded hillside between the coast of Bute and the Kintyre peninsula, a few fields caught napping when the tide came in too fast. These days it is privately owned by Lord Smith of Kelvin, who breeds highland cattle on the island; there are no other human residents.[14] Twelve hundred years ago, however, Inchmarnock was thriving. Excavation in and around the medieval ruins of St Marnock's church has revealed evidence of early medieval metalworking, and – most significantly – of what has been interpreted as a monastic schoolhouse. Dozens of fragments of slate, scratched with graffiti, patterns and text, seem to be the work of students, copying or practising writing and carving: a longer Latin text in a neat insular minuscule is perhaps an exemplum – passed around for copying – and fragments of cross-slab monuments imply the ultimate intended expression of the artistic skills being taught here.

One can imagine a clutch of young boys, seated cross-legged on a hard earth floor, stifling their yawns as an older monk tries patiently to explain the importance of making sure their half-uncials are all the same height. A little way from the main group, one boy sits apart. He doesn't join in with the covert attempts of the others to turn their practice slates into gaming boards,[15] or to flick pebbles at the brother's back when he gets up to go for a piss. Instead he silently persists in his own project, scratching at the lump of grey schist he keeps tight in his left hand, pressing down hard, his muscles taut. He hasn't been long on the island – he came with some older monks from Iona; something had happened there, apparently, but the other boys weren't told what. The new boy won't speak, and the monks won't tell them. 'Just keep on eye on the sea,' they say, 'just watch the sea.'

Among the slates found on Inchmarnock, one stands out as utterly unlike anything else found there.[16] It depicts four figures, all in profile, facing to the right as if moving together resolutely in the same direction. Three of them – only one of which is complete (the upper-right portion of the image has broken away and is presumably lost, or perhaps still somewhere under the surface of Inchmarnock or in the foundations of its ruinous buildings) – appear to be armed men dressed in mail shirts, the cross-hatching on their legs perhaps indicating the tight wrappings that were worn to gather the loose material of fabric trousers. They surround the image of a ship, its multitude of oars giving it the appearance of an unpleasant, scuttling invertebrate. The central figure in particular dominates the composition – large and commanding, a shock of long hair streaming from his bristly, oversized head. He leans forward slightly, propulsive and determined, in total contrast to the pathetic figure behind him. Stunted and unfinished, his head is barely outlined – just a jumble of lines; he is indeterminate, without identity: a nobody, a blank. What gives him purpose is the object attached to him, shackled to him in fact, hanging from an arm that pushes forward, reaching out. There is something terribly poignant about the gesture – drawn so clearly, where the face is absent, the fingers delineated and the hand open. It is on the object, however, that interpretation of the image turns. It could be a lock or a manacle; several such objects have been discovered in Ireland and around the Baltic. The object seems to be chained to the body of the figure in some way, and perhaps to the waist of the warlike central figure as well. Lines extending from the shoulder of the latter figure also seem to imply a captive being dragged into bondage – dragged, perhaps, to the waiting ship and a long journey east.[17]

If the object is not a manacle, it is most probably a depiction of a portable reliquary shrine. These little house-shaped objects are a familiar component of ecclesiastical culture around the Irish Sea; containing the relics of a saint, they would have functioned both as containers for holy objects and as portable focal points for devotion. As such, they were often highly decorative and valuable. Surviving examples, like the Scottish Monymusk reliquary, give an indication of the craft and precious materials with which such treasures were invested. As such, they made tempting targets for robbers – especially robbers with scant regard for Christian sensibilities. Substantial quantities of ecclesiastical metalwork, including house shrines, from northern Britain and Ireland in particular, have been found in Scandinavian graves and settlements – often adapted for use in new ways. A casket of exactly this type, manufactured in the eighth century in Ireland or western Scotland, was discovered in Norway, eventually entering the royal collections of the Danish–Norwegian royal family and from there into the collections of the National Museum of Denmark. It is empty, long having lost the relics it was built to house, but on its base is scratched an inscription in Old Norse, the letters formed in the distinctive runic alphabet used in south-west Norway and in the later Norse colony of Isle of Man: 'Rannveig owns this casket.'[18]

The noise is deafening. The sail cloth beats and rumbles like barrels tumbling over cliffs, and the ship's timbers scream in the rending hands of wind and water; above it all comes the shrieking gale, the thousand voices that howl together, raging and vengeful as they pour unending out of the blackening sky, riding on the salty arrows of the storm. He fights to bring the sail in, to stop the oar holes, to secure the provisions. He thinks he can hear the howling – the wolf that will swallow the sun; he thinks he can feel the thrashing of coils – the serpent that encircles the earth; he thinks he can see the shadow of the ship, *Naglfar*, built from the fingernails and toenails of the dead.[19] His right hand reaches up and grips the hammer that hangs around his neck. He forces his thoughts homeward, to the bright hearth and the cows in the byre. He thinks of his boys playing on the hillside, and the carvings around the hall door; he thinks of his wife, sitting by the fireside, her head bowed, weeping. Suddenly the storm is dying, the rain reducing to great globs of water that strike hard but sparingly, the rage of the wind expended, quietened now to a whispered lament. A ray of sunlight breaks through the fortress of black clouds in the east, a golden glimmer spreading on dark water. An arch begins to form, building itself from the ether into a bridge of colour linking the heavens with the earth. He smiles: it is a good omen. Bending down to open the chest that serves as a rowing bench, he begins to rummage among the clinking metal objects within. Eventually he produces a house-shaped box. It is small but exquisite, gleaming with gilt bronze. He wipes a ruddy-brown stain from the lid with a corner of his cloak and opens it up, peering inside and grunting. Standing, he upends it over the edge of the boat and towards the disgruntled water, shaking its contents into the breeze. Scraps of fabric, little brown bones, a fragment of wood, tumble into the slate-grey sea and are swallowed in darkness. He closes the box again, turning it in his big, scarred hands, the fugitive light glinting from its golden edges; he thinks of his wife, sitting by the fireside, the casket in her lap; she looks up, and she smiles.

Rannveig is a woman's name, and there is every possibility that the casket that bears it was brought back from a successful campaign of raiding in the west, its holy contents dumped without ceremony, repurposed as a lavish gift from a father, husband or suitor. An Irish annal of 824 describes the fate that befell the bits and pieces that had once been or belonged to St Comgall: 'Bangor at Airte was sacked by heathens; its oratory was destroyed and the relics of Comgall were shaken from their shrine.'[20]

Of course, Rannveig might well have acquired such an object by other means before marking her ownership in writing; Viking women were not dependent on men for their status and possessions.[21] But it is hard to imagine how such an object could have been liberated from its keepers and divested of its holy cargo without the application or threat of violence, and this – in the overwhelming majority of cases – was the preserve of men.

It may well be, therefore, that the Inchmarnock stone depicts the abduction of valuables both human and material, shackled together, shrine and guardian hauled off into bondage as one. The drawing was made – on the basis of its context and the style of the lettering found on its reverse side – around the year 800, the same time that the monastery of Portmahomack burned. It seems highly likely, given what else we know of events in that region in those years, that Viking raids on Iona and the coast of Ireland, as well as further away to the west, furnished the imagery and impetus for someone to scratch this odd graffito on to stone. With its menacing ship and exaggerated, trollish warriors, it calls to mind those heartbreaking drawings produced by the child survivors of wars and atrocities – crude images in which men, their weapons and their vehicles loom huge and all powerful, the visual manifestation of unhealable mental scars. As always, of course, there are competing interpretations (as with the apocalyptic gravestone at Lindisfarne, we can never know for sure what this scene was intended to convey), but it is easy to see how the arrival of murderous waterborne marauders could have jolted those on the receiving end into novel spasms of creativity.[22]

Thus we come to perhaps the most lucrative and plentiful source of wealth that the Viking raiders targeted – plunder that leaves little trace in the archaeological record, but which defined the activities of people from the north in the eye of those they encountered. In the early tenth century, the Arab traveller Ahmad ibn Rusta described the activities of Vikings in eastern Europe (the Rūs). He explained how they raided their neighbours, 'sailing in their ships until they come upon them. They take them captive and sell them in Kharazān and Bulkār (Bulghār) [...] They treat their slaves well and dress them suitably, because for them they are an article of trade.'[23] Being treated well, however, was – for a slave – a relative concept. For women and girls, the experience was as horrific as could be expected, and frequently far worse. Another Arab writer, Ahmad ibn Fadlan, describes his encounters with a group of Rūs travellers, making their way from the north along the Volga towards the markets of central Asia and the Middle East. In an extended description of the funeral of the Rūs chief, ibn Fadlan describes how a slave girl – owned in life by the dead man – 'volunteered' to die and accompany him to the grave. After a lengthy ritual, the girl was stupefied with alcohol, repeatedly raped, stabbed with a dagger and strangled with a cord. Once dead, she was burned upon the funeral pyre with the dead man, his horses and his hounds.[24]

These accounts are from the east, where the Viking trade routes came into contact with the Abbasid Caliphate, the Byzantine Empire and the flowing riches of the Silk Road.[25] But the goods they brought to trade were harvested far away; all and any of the people who could be preyed upon by sea might find themselves shackled and transported. Descriptions of the seizure of people are common-place – particularly in the Irish chronicles. The year 821, for exam-ple, saw the 'plundering of Etar [Howth in Dublin] by heathens; from there they carried off a great number of women'. Ten years later, in 831, 'heathens won a battle in Aignecha against the commu-nity of Armagh, so that very many were taken prisoner by them'. In 836 came 'the first plunder taken from Southern Brega by the heathens [...] and they slew many and took off very many captive'.[26]

Monks may have been of less value as sex-slaves, and men were probably valued primarily as manual labour, often carried back to Scandinavia to work the farms of landowners where they, as well as female slaves, would have been expected to undertake the hardest and foulest work. Recent research has even suggested the institu-tion of slave 'plantations' in parts of Scandinavia, where imported workers were housed in cramped conditions and forced to mass-produce textiles for the export market.[27] There they were known in Old Norse as þrælar ('thralls'), a word which survives in modern English with something close to its original meaning (to be in 'thrall' to something is to be captivated by it). The low regard in which these unfortunate folk were held can be gauged by a poem, written down – in the only surviving version – in the thirteenth or fourteenth century, but probably preserving a much older text and ideas.[28] It describes the mythologized origins of social castes in Scandinavia and lists the sort of pejorative names and menial tasks thought suitable for the children of a thrall ('slave'; ON *þræll*) or thrall-woman (ON *þír*):

> I think their names were Big-mouth and Byreboy,
> Stomp and Stick-boy, Shagger and Stink,
> Stumpy and Fatso, Backward and Grizzled,
> Bent-back and Brawny; they set up farms,
> shovelled shit on the fields, worked with pigs,
> guarded goats and dug the turf.
>
> Their daughters were Dumpy and Frumpy,
> Swollen-calves and Crooked-nose,
> Screamer and Serving-girl, Chatterbox,
> Tatty-coat and Cranelegs;
> from them have come the generations of slaves.[29]

Slavery was an institution across Europe, as it had been in the days of the Roman Empire, and persisted into the Norman period. In 1086, some 10 per cent of the English population was recognized as being unfree, and Anglo-Saxon slave-owners had the power of life and death over their slaves until the late ninth century.[30] The capture of defeated enemies was also a feature of inter-kingdom warfare in both Britain and Ireland before and during the Viking Age. In 836 (the same year that Vikings took captives from Brega), Fedelmid mac Crimthainn, king of Munster, attacked the oratory at Kildare 'with battle and weapons', taking the abbot Forindan and his congregation captive: they were shown, according to the chronicler, 'no consideration'.[31]

What was different about the Viking slave-trade was its integration into long-distance commercial networks that connected the

Irish and North Seas with the Baltic, Black, Caspian and Mediterranean Seas. No longer could slaves taken in Britain and Ireland expect to remain within a reasonable radius of their erstwhile homes, surrounded by people who differed from them little in speech or custom, and who respected social and cultural norms that were mutually understood. Instead they faced the possibility – if they weren't shipped directly to Scandinavia or to more local Viking colonies – of being transported like livestock over vast distances, to be sold in the markets of Samarkand or Baghdad, or – perhaps – to meet a horrific death on the banks of the River Volga. If they survived that journey and made it to market, they may well have found themselves, prodded and manhandled, forced to watch as their price in silver was carefully measured out – the scales tipping with the heft of weights, gleaming with ornaments ripped from the books and treasures that had once adorned their homes and churches.

5

BEYOND THE
NORTH WAVES

What is a woman that you forsake her,
And the hearth-fire and the home-acre,
To go with the old grey Widow-maker?

RUDYARD KIPLING, 'Harp Song of the Dane Woman' (1906)[1]

Explaining the beginnings of the Viking Age is to enter into difficult and contentious territory. We can observe the Vikings' arrival in the written sources, and glimpse what they wanted and how they went about getting it. But to question why people from northern Europe suddenly began to risk their lives on the wide ocean and brave the unknown dangers of foreign lands is another matter. To make progress on this front requires consideration of where the Vikings came from – not just geographically, though this is important for understanding the economic and political pressures that affected them, but also culturally. The structure of society in the pagan north, the shared values and beliefs – these were critical factors in pushing people towards the 'Viking' way. Ultimately, these are questions to which there can be no firm answers, only sugges-tions and reconstructions and ideas placed in the minds of people we cannot hope to know, but by doing so we can perhaps inch a little closer to understanding what made the Vikings tick.

Despite the very limited information provided by the written sources, it is clear that the people who were raiding Britain at the turn of the eighth century came from somewhere in the 'Danish'-speaking (that is, Old Norse-speaking) north-east and – most importantly from the perspective of Christian writers – were heathens. In the year 800, the Baltic was a pagan lake. The people who had turned their attention to Britain came from the west of this region – from what is now Denmark, Norway and Sweden – but all of the neighbouring lands to the east were also inhabited by pagan peoples, by Baltic and Slavic tribes in (moving clockwise around the Baltic coast) modern Finland, Russia, Estonia, Latvia, Lithuania, Russia (again), Poland and Germany. It would be wrong to draw very firm distinctions or borders between these groups – as in Britain, it is better to try to forget everything we know about the way that the storms of history have left their tide lines on the map. The formation of modern north-eastern Europe – its political geography and its religious and ethno-linguistic fault-lines – has been the result of more than a millennium of often catastrophic upheaval that lasted well into the second half of the twentieth century. The people who formed Viking raiding parties could have been (and in later centuries demonstrably were) drawn from all over this wider region.[2]

To the south and west was the Carolingian Empire, a great swathe of Europe – corresponding to most of modern France, northern Italy, western Germany and the Low Countries – united under a Frankish king (the Franks were a Germanic tribe who had begun to settle the Roman province of Gaul in the fifth century and who give their name to the modern nation of France). That king, in the same year, had been crowned emperor of the Romans by Pope Leo IX, a title that confirmed him as the sanctioned champion of an aggressive Christianity and the successor to the authority of the long-defunct Roman Empire in the west (the eastern, or Byzantine, Empire, centred on Constantinople – modern Istanbul – remained a going concern). That king would come to be known as 'Karolus Magnus': 'Charles the Great', or Charlemagne. By the time he received the imperial crown, Charlemagne had already redrawn the boundaries of Christendom in western Europe. In particular, a series of bloody campaigns against the pagan Saxons of northern Germany – effectively completed in 797, though revolts continued until 804 – had brought the boundaries of Frankish Christian Europe into contact with the pagan Scandinavian and Slavic tribes of the Jutland peninsula and western Baltic littoral. These wars had been exceptional for their combination of extreme brutality with religious zeal. In 772 Charlemagne ordered the destruction of the Irminsul, a holy tree or pillar central to Saxon worship.

Ten years later, in a particularly notorious incident, he had 4,500 Saxon prisoners beheaded on the banks of the River Weser near the town of Verden, apparently in retribution for their involvement in a revolt against Frankish domination. This was followed by laws that made death the penalty for refusing baptism.[3] The violence of Charlemagne's Christian mission prefigured the Crusades by three centuries.

Whatever the precise nature of the religious beliefs of the Saxons, it is likely – as we shall see – that they were shared, at least in part or in outline, by their neighbours to the north in what is now Denmark. Indeed, an inconsistent but interconnected network of beliefs, stories and rituals extended from the borders of the Frankish world throughout the Baltic world, linking together people of markedly different linguistic and cultural backgrounds through broadly compatible world-views and systems of social hierarchy. It is certain that Charlemagne's bellicose Christian foreign policy would have sent ripples of alarm shuddering out across the Baltic. Kings, chieftains, priests and priestesses would have wondered how long it would be before their traditional way of life and their political independence would be snuffed out beneath the hooves of Frankish horsemen, how soon they would see their timber halls burning and their sacred groves falling beneath the axes of Christian missionaries.[4]

This fear and uncertainty prompted a range of reactions. Some, like the Slavic Obodrites, did a deal with the superpower to their west, accepting Charlemagne as nominal overlord, providing the Empire with military aid and, in return, maintaining a level of political and religious freedom. They did this, admittedly, under duress: Charlemagne had invaded their territory and taken hostages. The Danes, for their part, provided shelter to Charlemagne's enemies and took steps to defend their landward border with Saxony by reinforcing the ditch and rampart structure – the Danevirke (literally the 'Dane-work') – that divided Germania from the Jutland peninsula.[5] As Charlemagne's conquests in Saxony became established geopolitical facts, Danish kings increasingly found themselves having to deal directly with Frankish power.

In 804, the Danish king Godfred arrived with his fleet and 'the entire cavalry of his kingdom' at Hedeby (Schleswig) on the Danish border.[6] It was a show of strength and, after a diplomatic exchange with the emperor, he departed – feeling, presumably, that he had roared loudly enough to convince his Frankish neighbours that the Danes were not to be trifled with. In 808, however, he apparently changed his mind, this time crossing with his army into Obodrite territory to the south-east, sacking a number of Slav settlements and burning the coastal trading settlement at Reric. The Obodrite inhabitants of the town, on the Baltic coast east of Jutland (close to the modern German town of Wismar), may have been accustomed to paying tribute to the Danish king. If so, the alliance with Charlemagne put an end to that, and also gave the Frankish Empire a friendly port on the Baltic. It was probably for both these reasons that Godfred, after destroying the town, deported its traders to Hedeby, placing them – and their tax revenues – firmly within his own sphere of control.[7]

Charlemagne hardly leapt to the defence of his allies. The *Frankish Royal Annals* describe how he sent his son Charles to wait at the banks of the Elbe to make sure that no one entered Saxon territory; the Obodrites were left to their fate. Once the Danish army had withdrawn, the Franko-Saxon army crossed the river and burned the fields of those Slavic tribes who had allied themselves with the Danes (and who had probably done so in order to avoid similar treatment from the Danish king; this has ever been the fate of small tribal communities – the weakest always suffer the most).

Some fairly empty diplomacy followed in 809 – conducted, so it would seem, to give both sides an excuse to shore up the loyalty of their various Slavic allies. Godfred, however, had not finished baiting the Empire.

In the summer of 810, Charlemagne was at the great palace complex he had commissioned at Aachen (now in Germany), the new capital of his hard-won realm. The cathedral at Aachen still incorporates a building – the Palatine Chapel – built as part of the original palace in the 790s by the architect Odo of Metz. The extraordinary scale and lavish attention to detail of the building, with its many-coloured marble floors and tiers of rounded portals – the eight sides of the central vestibule surrounded by the sixteen-sided outer perimeter – are the monumental vestiges of the staggering wealth and imperial grandeur of Carolingian power at its apogee. Gleaming white stone, green porphyry and blood-red Egyptian granite, frescos and mosaics, marble and bronze – the remains of great civilizations of the past were being gathered together, literally building a new empire.[8]

In 787, Pope Hadrian I wrote to Charlemagne agreeing to let him take from Ravenna 'mosaic and marble and other materials both from the floors and the walls', and the emperor's biographer – Einhard – describes him having marbles and sculptures brought from Rome and Ravenna to adorn the palace at Aachen.[9] The most startling of all the surviving fixtures of the Palatine Chapel, however, is the throne. Raised on a dais of six steps, the simple and unadorned seat exudes a living presence from the vaulted shadows. Though it has been sat upon by thirty-one German kings since Charlemagne's day, it is indissoluble from the memory of its first master, the first Holy Roman Emperor. It is easy to indulge the imagination by picturing the great ruler brooding here amid the magnificence of his rule, chin resting on one hand as he gazed on the holy altar to the east, considering the price of power and the promise of salvation.

In June 810 Charlemagne's eldest daughter, Hruodtrude, died and the emperor may well have found himself in sombre and reflective mood; whether he ever burst from his throne in rage or retreated to it in search of holy guidance can never be known, but the events that followed can have done little to improve his mood:

> he received the news that a fleet of two hundred ships from Denmark had landed in Frisia, that all the islands off the coast of Frisia had been ravaged, that the army had already landed and fought three battles against the Frisians, that the victorious Danes had imposed a tribute on the vanquished, that already one hundred pounds of silver had been paid as tribute by the Frisians, and that King Godofrid [Godfred] was at home.[10]

The chronicler, evidently concerned that his Frankish readership would find this all rather hard to swallow, felt compelled to affirm that 'that, in fact, is how things stood'. As if this were not bad enough, the elephant which Charlemagne had been given by Harun al-Rashid, caliph of Baghdad, died suddenly soon afterwards: a bad summer indeed.

Charlemagne, of course, was not prepared to let Godfred's belligerence stand. He began to raise an army and would no doubt have pursued his opponent with all of his customary zeal, had not the Danish king died as suddenly as the elephant, apparently murdered by his own people (who would, understandably, have been worried that their king's pathological warmongering was leading them into the teeth of Charlemagne's war machine; before his death, Godfred had reportedly boasted that he was looking forward to fighting the emperor in open battle). What the *Annals* fail to conceal, however, is the extent to which the Frankish Empire had been rattled; Godfred, one might say, had given even Karolus Magnus the willies.

This may all seem like something of a digression: what, one might ask, do the border wars of Frankish kings have to do with the story of Viking Britain? But the story of Godfred and his dealings with the emperor brings a number of issues into perspective. Firstly, it highlights the critical point that, at precisely the same time as the first Viking raids in Britain were taking place, continental Europe was dominated by a mighty superpower at the height of its strength. Charlemagne's Empire was economically and militarily superior to any other regional power, and its presence fundamentally affected the way in which rulers dwelling in its shadow (including Anglo-Saxon kings) could operate. New avenues for raiding may well have become markedly more appealing than once they had been. Secondly, it highlights the political and economic importance of towns and trade and the maritime technology by which these could be exploited, defended and harassed. Places like Reric, Hedeby and the coastal settlements of Frisia formed part of a much larger network. Such networks, and the opportunities for long-distance trade they presented, opened new frontiers for the most ruthless and entrepreneurial individuals – particularly those with access to effective maritime technology.[11]

Finally, the belligerent career of Godfred indicates that by the late eighth and early ninth century there were individuals in parts of Scandinavia who were able to wield resources and military power that had the potential, at the very least, to disrupt and dismay their most powerful neighbours. They were, moreover, human beings (not merely the demonic hordes of clerical imagination) – people who dealt in the pragmatic realities of early medieval politics and trade. They were people with aspirations towards lordship and power on an increasingly grand scale; and, to achieve and maintain it, they would need the trappings, the wealth, the loyalty and the prestige that society demanded of them.

At over 260 feet in length, the house at Borg on Vestvågøy is – by any standard – a massive structure. Dark, squat and muscular, the great hall holds fast to the Norwegian soil, its eaves reaching almost to the ground. It is a dwelling of the earth, rooted in the soil, rising from it like the gently arching back of some giant slumbering beast. In winter, if the snows come – despite the latitude, the Gulf Stream keeps the Lofoten Islands relatively warm – it is given back to the landscape: one more gentle mound among undulating drifts of white – betrayed, perhaps, only by the thin drift of wood smoke that rises from the roof-spine. And though massive, it represents an utterly different expression of power from that expressed by Charlemagne's palace at Aachen. Where the Palatine Chapel soars, tiers of columns and arches reaching upward to heaven, the long-house at Borg spreads in the horizontal, hugging the skyline, long, low and narrow (only around 30 feet wide). Aachen is an expression of a cosmopolitan outlook, its stylistic cues taken from the architecture of Rome and Byzantium, its fixtures literally transplanted from elsewhere – signifiers of a pan-continental imperialism, rendered in imported stone. Borg, on the other hand, is a creature of the vernacular. Its form – the long, bow-sided plan and gently curving roof-line – is peculiar to early Scandinavian architecture, an evocation perhaps of the curving keels of the ships which defined northern life. More fundamentally, the hall itself is built from the very tissue of the land: the trees that were felled to raise its skeleton, the turf blocks that were cut and stacked to flesh it and to bind it to the earth. The hall is fashioned from its environment, moulded into a new form, clinging to the shores of a sheltered tidal estuary (Inner Pollen), the glittering peaks of Himmeltinden and Ristinden looming to the west.

The traveller rides from his ship on the lakeside, up, past outbuildings and over fields, to the great house hunkered in the snow, atop the low hill before the mountains. There are four doors along its eastern side, but the southernmost entrance is grander than the others, with its pillars and lintel carved with the images of writhing creatures, biting and twisting and gripping each other in a tangle of sinuous limbs and gaping mouths. The traveller dismounts and a thrall-boy appears from another door; he runs to take the reins of the horse, leading it away towards the north-easterly end of the building. The traveller follows for a few steps, catching the soft shuffle of heavy feet inside, a low whinny, the hot stench of dung and warm animal bodies. Cattle and horses, pungent and comforting: a homely smell. He smiles and turns back to the carved portal, ducks his head and passes through.

Inside the cold violet of the Lofoten dusk gives way to a deep orange glow of firelight, bouncing from tapestries and the rich umber of the timber walls. The flames cast shadows that set the carved beasts wriggling on the pillars that run in two aisles down the length of the building. Between them the long hearth lies sunken in the floor, flames licking up to light the rafters, heat filling the hall that extends to the right of the door. There are older men seated at benches along the sides of the hall, and they rise as he enters, bringing the wide world indoors, shaking the smell of winter from his cloak.

The long-house, as experienced today, is a reconstruction of the building as it may have looked between the early eighth century when it was constructed (on the site of an earlier, sixth-century building), and the mid-tenth century when it was demolished. The original hall lay a few hundred yards to the east; the position of its timber pillars, long since rotted away, are marked now with modern posts, its outline clearly visible from the air. At 270 feet in length, the building was 30 feet longer than Westminster Hall. Unlike that great sepulchral eleventh-century chamber, however, the hall at Borg was the social hub of a whole farming community, and saw all of life swirling through its portals. Archaeological investigation of the site suggests that the building was divided into five rooms. The largest of these – at the north-east end of the building – was a cattle byre and stable-block, a home to precious animals over the cold, dark winter months and a source of living warmth to the human inhabitants of the building. Perhaps for obvious reasons, the slope on which the building stands drops away to the north-east, meaning that the north-east end of the building lies around 5 feet lower than the part of the building that contained the domestic and human-centred areas – nobody wants a river of shit pouring through their living room all winter.[12]

Objects found in the rest of the building give clues to the various uses to which the apparently communal spaces were put: whetstones and spindle whorls, sword fragments, iron tools and arrow heads indicate the sorts of activities that men and women would have undertaken from and in the building – weaving, hunting, farming and preparations for the possibility of violence. There were also a number of what are known in archaeological circles as *gullgubber* – thin gold foils struck with images that are most commonly believed to depict mythological scenes – leading to the suggestion that the communal activities that took place here included religious or ritual functions as well as social and practical ones.[13] The evidence seems to suggest that, unlike the hierarchical and authoritarian structures of the Christian Church, with its professional priesthood and purpose-built temples, Viking religion – at least at the beginning of the Viking Age – was personal and domestic. It is probable that, at places like Borg and elsewhere (such as Lejre in Denmark or Gamla Uppsala in Sweden), the principal heads of individual estates would have adopted the role of cult leader alongside their more prosaic responsibilities, perhaps taking the lead in making sacrifices of animals (*blót*) and in depositing the valuables that have been discovered in earth and water in these places. *Gullgubber*, precious objects already invested with mythic symbolism, would have made appropriate offerings.[14]

It has been suggested, with varying degrees of emphasis, that religion played a role in the violence doled out to churches, monasteries and Christian communities – that the Vikings, aware of the impending threat posed by aggressive Christian nations, turned on the most visible and accessible symbols of this religion in a sort of pre-emptive strike (or not so pre-emptive if, as one might argue, Charlemagne's Saxon wars were regarded as the first demonstration of what awaited all their pagan neighbours). In such a war of cultural self-preservation, it would have mattered little whether the churches and monasteries were situated in Frankia or in Britain. The symbols were the same, and thus – it is argued – the political identity of their creators would have been regarded as part of a homogeneous bloc, a united threat to tribal culture and independence. Indeed, such was Charlemagne's power that the whole of Christian Europe, Britain included, can in some respects be seen as lying within a Frankish sphere of influence.[15] It is hard to imagine how the events of the late eighth and early ninth century could have failed to leave a deep and negative impression on communities around the Baltic, particularly about the nature of Christian faith and the character of its practitioners – violence, terror and subjugation would have seemed the inescapable outriders of the cross.

The destruction of the cross-slabs at Portmahomack can, from this perspective, be seen as evidence for an ideological component to Viking raiding. Just as a raiding army might harass the lands and dependants of an enemy king in order to force a confrontation, the Vikings – it could be argued – were directly and deliberately targeting the houses of God and his personnel. It is, it must be said, easy to get carried away with the idea that the Viking Age began as a pagan religious war. But as even the most frequently cited exponent of this thesis – Bjørn Myhre – has pointed out, Christianity should be seen in the light not just of its spiritual content but of the political affiliations it affirmed.[16] For Charlemagne, as for many other European monarchs, Christianity represented a powerful toolkit of symbols, hierarchies and rituals through which he could emulate the political and military achievements of the Emperor Constantine and, by extension, Roman imperial power as a whole; simple soul-food it was not. Cultural vandalism directed by pagans towards those same symbols (if that is what Carver uncovered at Portmahomack) might therefore be better interpreted as a statement of defiance against rampant Frankish imperialism – not anything 'anti-Christian' in the strictly religious sense.

However, what seems to have been much more important than any of this was the acquisition of wealth. This term is a little abstract – in modern culture 'wealth' tends to be measured by fairly crude standards: the amount of money in a bank account, the relative value of share prices, projected tax receipts, quantity and quality of property, land, assets.[17] 'Wealth' in the early Viking Age, however, can be seen as a rather more expansive concept. Luxury goods – such as the English and Frankish glassware also discovered at Borg – were highly prized for their intrinsic quality and usefulness, and ownership of them was, as now, one index of achievement. But such assets also performed key social functions, and their ownership hinted at broader networks or the potential to forge them. In the early Middle Ages, gift-giving between lords and their retainers (as well as between rulers) was the basic agent of social cohesion and a measure of relative political substance; in return for weapons, jewellery and luxury items (and the expectation of more), men would pledge loyalty to their lords as warriors. This relationship was the fundamental basis of the war-band, and bonds thus forged were subsequently invested with and cemented by solemn oaths and a code of heroic ethics.

The system was very similar in Britain and had endured for centuries: the Old Welsh poem *Y Gododdin* (describing events of the fifth century, but written any time between the sixth and thirteenth centuries), for example, describes the operation of a war-band of this nature – its constituents paid in advance for their loyalty and support in battle with mountains of food and rivers of booze.[18] In Old English and Old Norse poetry, however, this relationship had developed into a material exchange, driven in part by the desirability of the goods being produced in Frankish and, to a lesser extent, Anglo-Saxon workshops. By the Viking Age this had crystallized into a general expectation of the role of a monarch, expressed most succinctly in Old English maxims ('the king belongs in his hall, sharing out rings'),[19] but also repeated through a mind-boggling number of 'kennings' in skaldic verse – an economical means by which to emphasize the virtue of any given ruler:

'lofty ring-strewer'; 'thrower of gold'; 'eager, wolf-gracious bestower of friendly gifts' …[20]

The ownership of precious objects was thus a symbol of the quality of one's social connections – not merely personal riches, but a visible symbol of the patronage of a powerful lord; perhaps even, ultimately, signifying the potential to dole out gifts to one's own dependants. The ability of important individuals to acquire prestigious objects was, therefore, an absolute prerequisite to the exercise of power, and generosity was seen as one of the two fundamental pillars of exemplary lordship. The other pillar, however, perhaps less immediately appealing to modern sensibilities, was the ability to provide an unending diet of human corpses to satisfy the sanguine cravings of wolves, ravens and eagles.[21] The king or warlord who could demonstrate himself to be both open- and bloody-handed was likely to cement his reputation – ideally in verse – and the ownership of portable wealth spoke to both of these qualities.

Happily, these two traits dovetailed neatly. It is quite obvious how a Viking warlord, seeking to improve both his reputation and the size of his war-band, could kill two birds with one stone by violently extracting wealth from foreign shores and doling it out among his followers. Such a socio-economic system, however, has its drawbacks. Though its mechanisms are straightforward, its demands necessarily mushroom: increasing war-bands require increased resources, increased resources require larger and more frequent raids, larger and more frequent raids require larger war-bands, and so on.[22]

Of course, there are other ways of acquiring portable wealth, and it seems that Scandinavian traders were pioneers in exploiting the trade networks that had developed around the North Sea during the eighth century. We have seen already the keen interest that Godfred took in securing access to Baltic and North Sea trade, but there is no reason to separate the acquisition of goods through trade from the violence enacted elsewhere. Books, exhibitions and school textbooks often make a great deal of the characterization of

Vikings as either 'raiders' or 'traders', with the public encouraged to view the Vikings through one or other of these lenses. This irritating meme is, in essence, a product of the academic debates of the 1970s and 1980s – debates which, while important at the time, have tended to perpetuate the wrong sorts of questions. It is obvious, of course, that raiding and trading were never mutually exclusive phenomena; the Viking slave-trade is the most obvious manifestation of this false dichotomy. The burning, killing and plundering that accompanied Viking activity around the coasts of Britain and Ireland were carried out by the same individuals who might have been found weeks later hawking their captives in the Hedeby slave-market or peddling bits of plundered church furniture in the bazaars of central Asia. Nevertheless, the evidence for peaceful trading is plentiful, and Scandinavian traders must have been a familiar sight at major emporia like Ipswich, York and Southampton. Indeed, it is probably as a result of such trading expeditions that Scandinavians came to be aware of the wealth of Anglo-Saxon kingdoms, the geography of the British coastland and the location of monasteries and the wealth they housed. It also, presumably, allowed for an insight into local political fault-lines that ambitious men might hope to exploit.[23]

None of this can really diminish the possibility that the earliest raids were the outcome of individual initiative, with their subsequent popularity among Scandinavian seafarers a reflection of the ease and profitability with which monasteries could be divested of their valuables. This comes close to a Victorian view of Viking derring-do, a tendency to explain the Viking Age by the hot-blooded 'pith and pluck' of Nordic men that drove them to adventure. But it cannot be denied that human agency would have had a disproportionate impact in an age when populations were small, and when stories of young men returning from overseas, their boats sitting low in the water with treasure and slaves, would have spread fast and far. To the farming communities of Norway, stretched out along the narrow strip of cultivable land, eager for the social and economic capital to resist political pressure from the south, such apparently easy wealth would have seemed to present opportunities on a scale previously undreamt of. There is unlikely to have been a shortage of volunteers for future expeditions, or a dearth of ambitious chieftains planning new adventures. Perhaps the lord of Borg was one of them.

6

THE GATHERING STORM

… The bird cries,
grey-coat screams, battle-wood resounds,
shield to spear-shaft replies. Now shines the moon
drifting into dimness. Now deeds of woe arise
that will propel this peoples' malice.
But awake now, warriors of mine,
Seize thy linden-shields, dwell on courage,
Fight at the front, be fierce and bold!

The Fight at Finnsburg[1]

Although Viking raids would continue to afflict Ireland with almost absurd frequency throughout the 820s and 830s, there is a gap of twenty-nine years after the third raid on Iona in 806 before a Viking raid is again recorded in Britain.[2]

For historians, knowing what was to come, this can seem like a trivial span of time, a brief hiatus before the hammer would fall with all its force. But for people living at the time it would have seemed very different; they did not know that they were living in the 'Viking Age'.[3] Many of those who were aware of the attacks on Lindisfarne, Jarrow and Iona, including some of the survivors, would have lived out the rest of their lives with the impression that this diabolical onslaught had burned itself out – passing, perhaps, like the fiery whirlwinds and bloody rain that had presaged its arrival. Indeed, for more than a generation after the appearance of the first Vikings in the written record, the overwhelming fear – in southern Britain at least – would have been that, if violence were to come, it would come from people who spoke familiar (if not shared) languages, who lived similar lives in recognizable landscapes and who worshipped the same god in broadly compatible ways.

In 798, for example, King Ceolwulf (newly king of Mercia after Offa's death in 796) ravaged Kent and captured its king, Eadberht. Eadberht was dragged to Mercia in chains where he had his eyes gouged out and his hands cut off.[4] In 815, King Ecgberht of Wessex raided the 'west welsh' (that is, the Cornish) from 'east to west'.[5] Ten years later, the same king defeated the Mercians at a place called Ellendun (now somewhere underneath the western suburbs of Swindon), 'and a great slaughter was made there'.[6] A fragment of poetry recalls that 'Ellendun's stream ran red with blood, was stuffed up with corpses, filled with stink'.[7] In the same year King Beornwulf of Mercia was killed by the East Angles (it was a bad year for the Mercians). These violent convulsions all took place during a period that saw a steady shift in the centre of political gravity in southern Britain, focusing power around the kingdom of Wessex at the expense of Mercia and some of the smaller southern realms. In this reorientation – which would have huge repercussions later on – the Vikings were of little consequence. In the early ninth-century brutality league they would have struggled to make the play-offs.

Ultimately, however, this state of affairs did not hold. The first black clouds reappeared in 835, when 'heathen men' raided across the Isle of Sheppey, but even darker days lay ahead. In 836, a fleet of thirty-five ships (one version of the *Anglo-Saxon Chronicle* says twenty-five) arrived at Carhampton on the Somerset coast, and the formidable King Ecgberht – bane of Mercians and Cornishmen – was there to face them. The fighting that ensued was the first setpiece battle (that we know of) that pitched a Viking army against British foes. Once again, and not for the last time, the *Chronicle* provides the gloomy observation that 'a great slaughter was made there', and from what little else is known about it, it seems indeed to have been a grim day's work. If the number of ships is taken at face value, a Viking army numbering 1,500 men would be a conservative estimate, and it is probably fair to assume a similar number assembled to fight them. Three thousand men engaged in brutal hand-to-hand fighting with axe and sword would have made for a terrifying spectacle.[8]

Although Anglo-Saxon chroniclers reveal little about the realities of early medieval battle, their poets were less reticent:

The horror of battle materialized. There was cracking of shields, attacking of warriors, cruel sword-chopping and troops dropping when first they faced a volley of arrows. Into that doomed crowd, over the yellow targe and into their enemies' midst, the fierce and bloody antagonists launched showers of darts, spears, the serpents of battle, by the strength of their fingers. Relentless of purpose onwards they trod; eagerly they advanced. They broke down the shield barrier, drove in their swords and thrust onwards, hardened to battle.[9]

The opposing armies would have faced up to one another in close formation, huddling together so that each man might benefit from the protection afforded by the large, round timber shield held by the man to his right. The defensive barrier thus created – a sort of clinker-built fence of human-held timbers – is known by poetic convention in Old English and Old Norse poetry as the 'shield-wall'. Its importance as a military concept has probably been over-stressed by modern historians – it was a product of fear and necessity as much as it was ever a formalized battlefield tactic, its description in poetry a function of conventional semantics (like other evocative constructs such as *wíhagen*, 'war-hedge') – but there is no doubt that an army arranged this way presented a formidable face to the enemy. The shields would have been brightly painted, probably carrying religious symbols or depictions of beasts designed to intimidate enemies and provide courage to those who sheltered behind them. Ninth-century examples, excavated in Norway with their timber still surviving, are around 3 feet in diameter and painted black or yellow. Rimmed with iron, these shields were augmented with a large semi-circular metal boss riveted to the centre. This protected the hand (which gripped the handle attached behind it), but could also blunt the edges of misplaced weapon-strikes or smash the face of an enemy once the shield-wall had broken down into the series of individual duels and knots of vicious combat that the battle would inevitably devolve into.[10]

The smashing of one's own face was, obviously, something to be avoided wherever possible. Helmets, like the one discovered at Gjermundbu, were probably more common than their rarity in the archaeological record might imply; the simple psychology of self-preservation would suggest that some sort of head and face protection would be desirable. An Anglo-Saxon helmet, found during the Coppergate excavations in York in the late 1970s, suggests the sort of thing that might have been available to the wealthiest warriors. Although it would have been old fashioned by the 830s (it was probably made in the third quarter of the eighth century), it seems to have remained in use until the first half of the ninth century. Old fashioned it may have been, but it was of exceptional craftsman-ship and quality – not least the creatures that are woven into an intricate lattice in the decoration of the brazen nose-guard, and the eyebrows terminating in the heads of fanged serpentine creatures. The equipment of warriors in this period would have been far from homogeneous, and military gifts and heirlooms could be prized symbols of lineage, affiliation and religious persuasion. The Coppergate helmet carries an inscription on the brass crest that runs over the top of the helmet, an invocation to commend protection of its wearer – a man named Oshere – to the care of the saints.[11] The inscription enhanced the helmet's protective capabilities, transform-ing it into a magical item that conferred mystical as well as physical protection: a reminder that, to the warriors of the Viking Age, super-natural forces could play a critical role on the battlefield: 'IN NOMINE DNI NOSTRI IHV SCS SPS DI ET OMNIBUS DECEMUS AMEN OSHERE XPI' ('In the name of our Lord Jesus Christ and of the Spirit of God, let us offer up Oshere to All Saints. Amen').[12]

Other helmet fragments, like an eyepiece discovered at Gevninge on Zealand (Denmark) and dated to the cusp of the Viking Age, imply that the finest helmets might still have resembled those recovered from the Vendel, Valsgärde and Sutton Hoo cemeteries. These objects, with their full-face coverings of mask or mail, their swooping dragons and coiling serpents, their images of riders and spear-shakers, are objects to inspire awe and terror in equal measure. They rise up darkly from an age of legend, conjuring images of heroes and kings – dripping with antiquity and the glamour of mighty forebears. If helmets like these did indeed appear on the battlefields of the Viking Age, it would have seemed to contemporaries as though the ghosts of the mighty dead strode among them still, time collapsing amid the blood and chaos of battle, the eternal raven wheeling overhead.[13]

Several high-ranking West Saxons fell in the fighting at Carhampton: the ealdormen Duda and Osmod (ealdormen were senior nobles, subordinate to the king and often in charge of a shire or, later, groups of shires) and the bishops Herefrith and Wigthegn. They were surely the tip of a bloody iceberg, but the *Anglo-Saxon Chronicle* was never much concerned with the deaths (or the lives) of the average warrior. Of their enemies we know even less. All we are told, in a phrase that would roll out with grim regularity on the parchment leaves of the *Anglo-Saxon Chronicle*, is that *þa Deniscan ahton wælstowe geweald*: 'the Danes had possession of the place of slaughter'. In other words, they were victorious.[14]

The attack at Carhampton was a major incident, and it represented a sea-change in how Viking raiders related to the people of Britain. No longer content with the small-scale smash-and-grab raids which had defined Viking activity in the early ninth century (and which had picked up again in Ireland and Frankia from the 820s), the Vikings who attacked Carhampton seem to have done so with a heightened sense of what might be achieved through violence. A settlement of some importance, with archaeological traces dating from the fifth to the eighth centuries, Carhampton seems also to have been the site of an early monastic church

– associated with the Celtic saint Carantoc. It may, therefore, have been a place of pilgrimage and a major centre of wealth, and in this it would fit the pattern of the targets of earlier Viking attacks, both in Britain and abroad.[15]

However, Carhampton was also the site of a royal estate (it is included in the will of Ecgberht's grandson, Alfred, drawn up sixty years later) and was later the administrative centre for the hundred in which it sits – all of which suggests that it was an important political centre. This might, in part, explain why King Ecgberht himself was there to deal with the Viking threat – for if a king couldn't hold his own, how could he be expected to defend an entire kingdom? His failure to do so in this case may well have emboldened the people who had sailed against him. Victory against the fearsome king of Wessex can only have awakened Viking warlords to their ability not only to wrest wealth from hapless coastal communities, but also, through sheer force of arms, to win glory, fame and – perhaps – power and dominion of their own.

In 838, King Ecgberht brought his army to Hengestdun, now known as Kit Hill in Cornwall. He had come to head off a new threat to his growing hegemony – an army of Cornishmen and their 'Danish' allies who had marched east to contest with the West Saxon king for control of their borders and to make a stand against his increasingly domineering approach to the south-west. The battle that ensued was significant, not so much because of its outcome, but because – for the first time that we know of – a Viking army had chosen to involve itself in the internal politics of Britain, making common cause with the Cornish to fight against the West Saxon king.

It is not known why the Vikings chose such involvement. Perhaps they fought as mercenaries, seeking a share in the spoils, or perhaps they had been promised land or trading rights in whatever new arrangement could be wrested from the English king. Whatever the reason, it was a sign of things to come: over the course of the ninth century, Viking war-bands would increasingly use their military muscle to redraw the map of Britain. On this occasion it came to naught. Ecgberht, as we have seen, was not a king to be trifled with (his heavy-handed treatment of the Cornish in the 820s had perhaps gone some way to inspiring the events of 838). When the king 'heard of that [the alliance between the Vikings and the Cornish], he then went there with his army and fought against them at Hengestdun, and put both the Britons and the Danes to flight'.[16]

Rising to the impressive height of 1,096 feet, Kit Hill dominates the valley of the Tamar from which it rises, standing aloof from its comrades that huddle together in the uplands of Bodmin Moor. Up here you can see for miles. From Bodmin to Dartmoor to Plymouth Sound, a vast swathe of Britain's south-western peninsula opens itself to the eye: rime-scoured boulders and ancient field boundaries, rough delvings and crook-backed pollards, the scars of a tussle between the tough, wilful landscape and its human wranglers that has been fought over millennia. To the south the sea glints in a cleft cut into the horizon by the broad silver band that snakes through green pastures on its way from the hills. It is no doubt the combination of its commanding position and its accessibility by sea and river that gave this place the strategic importance that it seems to have had in the ninth century; whoever held this place could, with good reason, consider himself master of the Cornish borders.

The significance of the formative battle that was fought here was not lost on early English antiquarians. Of the many earthworks and monuments that litter the sides and summit of Kit Hill, one of the most prominent is a five-sided enclosure of low walls, with bastions at four of the five intersections. It looks like the shaggy remains of a fortress. This curious structure was long interpreted as a Civil War-era fortress (1642–51) on the strength of compelling similarities with the plans of other, better-documented forts around England. However, appearances were deceptive. On 27 June 1800, Sir John Call, who owned the adjacent estate and manor at Whiteford, wrote in his will that he desired a 'tomb of Cornish granate [sic] alias Moorstone' to be made on top of Hingsdon Down or Kit Hill 'within or adjoining to the Inclosure of the Castle I have built there'.[17]

'[T]he late Sir John', William Betham explained in the fourth volume of his *Baronetage of England* (1801–5), 'erected something like an old Saxon castle on the summit, with large stones of granite found there in great plenty.' It seems likely that this peculiar endeavour (though not untypical of the folly-building extravagances of his peers) was intended to evoke the battle that was fought there in 838 – a battle of which he seems to have been dimly aware: 'a Battle was undoubtedly fought at the bottom of that hill some time between the 7th and 8th century [fought in 838, it was in neither of these centuries]'. It is perhaps surprising that Sir John should have been so sketchy about the details – he was, from 1785, a fellow of the Society of Antiquaries, the learned society set up in 1707 to cater for the growing interest of certain well-heeled gentlemen in the physical evidence of the past. In its early days, the Society seems to have been largely a drinking club for like-minded men of a particular sort, and there were no formal entry requirements. Sir John, for example, seems to have been admitted on the strength of some interesting lithographs he had picked up in India. He had worked there as a military engineer, planning the fortifications at Madras – this, of course, being the reason for his 'Saxon fort' looking more like a typical post-medieval redoubt than the Anglo-Saxon stronghold he intended.[18]

When I visited Kit Hill with my wife and parents, it was a disconcerting experience. Thick banks of dreary mist swamped the landscape and shut down visibility to 20 feet in every direction. I felt as though, rather than standing at the summit of a massive Precambrian abscess on the sedimentary bedrock, we had been washed up on the shores of some weird fog-bound island, its coarse cliff-top vegetation concealing innumerable pits and fissures from which some Cornish Caliban could spring at any moment. The atmosphere was distinctly alien – a landscape stripped of all familiarity; even the cagoule-clad ramblers seemed vaguely sinister. At the highest point a great masonry tower rises through the white shrouds of clinging ether like a star-gazer's tower, the haunt of some Prospero, rising – to use Mervyn Peake's immortal words – 'like a mutilated finger [...] pointed blasphemously at heaven'.[19] Or, perhaps, like the funnel of some fantastical steamship, ploughing onwards through fog-bound oceans, on its way to a lost world.

This tower is, indeed, a chimney, unusually ornamental for its purpose. An obsolete monument to the industrial mining operations of the second half of the nineteenth century, it once exhaled the by-products of the steam engine which pumped water from the deep delvings below. Mining took place on Kit Hill from the Middle Ages until the early twentieth century, and the seemingly random gouges in the upper slopes are memorials to the earliest, open-mining phases of this activity. In subsequent centuries, workings grew deeper and more elaborate, as miners began seeking out the veins of tin and copper that had seeped into fissures in the granite in some unimaginably ancient epoch, and now the hill is riddled with shafts and tunnels, their lethal openings hidden amid gorse and bracken. These borings reached their climax in the 1880s with the Excelsior Tunnel, an 800-yard gallery driven horizontally into the side of the hill, like the passage to some improbably vast tomb. It was, in fact, constructed to mine the deepest lodes, and was extended on a few occasions in the early twentieth century. In 1959–60, however, the tunnel was taken over by the UK Atomic Energy Authority for bomb testing. Despite rumours to the contrary, these tests never involved any nuclear material, although – despite modern radiation tests confirming the Ministry of Defence's assurances – rumours to the contrary inevitably persist.[20]

In the ninth century, Kit Hill was known for other reasons and, as we have seen, by a different name – Hengestdun, the hill of Hengest – and a wisp of its memory still clings to its lower eastward slopes in the tautological place-name Hingsdon Down ('don' and 'down' both derive from OE *dun*, meaning 'hill').[21] The name is important. Hengest would have had a dual meaning in Old English. It means 'stallion'. But it was also the name of the legendary founding father of the English-speaking people – one half of the alliterative duo who, according to Bede, arrived in three ships from across the North Sea in the mid-fifth century. Landing in Kent, Hengest and his brother Horsa (and later his son Æsc) defeated the unfortunate Vortigern and his sons and began the process of clearing out the degenerate Romano-British order, founding the royal house of Kent in the process.

The story raises all sorts of red flags. The idea of a duo named 'Stallion' and 'Horse' paving the way, through the might of their arms, for a whole new set of nations, has 'foundation myth' written all over it (despite its continued acceptance as fact in some quarters). It may well be that Hengest and Horsa were, originally, a pair of pre-Christian deities who were turned from gods into human ancestors by Christian writers and given prominent roles in the authorized version of English origins. Whatever the reality, it is clear that the name had a great deal of potency attached to it by the ninth century.[22]

Early medieval battles were often fought at places associated with the names of gods and heroes, some of them burial mounds, others – like Hengestdun – massive hills that might have been imagined in some way to house the oversized remains of superhuman occupants. These were places where the past dwelt and where the memories of mighty warriors could be imagined to confer an aura of legitimacy, rootedness and martial prowess on those who fought in their shadow. These were also, conversely, places where ancient English claims could be challenged and new (or older) associations of landscape inscribed or resurrected – places where symbolic blows could be struck in the struggle for hegemony.[23] It must be partly for these reasons (as well as for its strategic significance) that when the Cornish wished to challenge the supremacy of the West Saxon dynasty, it was here that they came to meet King Ecgberht in battle.

The defeat of the Cornish cemented West Saxon authority over the south-west, but it did little to deter future Viking war-bands from chancing their arm in Britain. For the rest of the century, a rising tide of violence was directed towards the Anglo-Saxon kingdoms. Some of them were raids, directed – just as they always had been – towards concentrations of wealth. However, the battles of Ecgberht's reign, fought at places of symbolic significance like Carhampton and Hengestdun, signalled a shift in the level of engagement that the Vikings displayed towards their adversaries. From this point onwards, Viking armies were to display an increasingly sophisticated understanding of how power was articulated within the kingdoms of Britain, exploiting, undermining and appropriating the political and physical landscape until they themselves became an integral part of it.

7

DRAGON-SLAYERS

This is a very old story: the Danes who used to fight with the
English in King Alfred's time knew this story. They have carved on
the rocks pictures of some of the things that happen in the tale, and
those carvings may still be seen. Because it is so old and so beautiful
the story is told here again, but it has a sad ending – indeed it is
all sad, and all about fighting and killing, as might be expected
from the Danes.

ANDREW LANG, 'The Story of Sigurd' (1890)[1]

In 850, the *Anglo-Saxon Chronicle* reports, 'heathen men stayed
over the winter for the first time'. Although this notice passes
without commentary in the *Chronicle*, dropped in almost as though
it were an afterthought, the over-wintering of the heathens was the
breath of wind that carried off the first leaves of autumn from the
old Anglo-Saxon kingdoms. It was the harbinger of a storm that
would not only strip those old oaks bare, but tear many of them up
by their roots.[2]

Viking attacks had been increasing in volume and severity since
the 830s, particularly in Wessex and the south-east. Between 840
and 853, this part of Britain was attacked at least fifteen times, and
an attack is also recorded as taking place in Northumbria in 844 –
resulting, disastrously, in the death of the king and his heir.[3] The
first raids on Lundenwic (London) occurred in 842 and 851,[4] and

there were attacks on Southampton and Portland (840), Romney Marshes (841), Rochester (842), Carhampton again (843) and Canterbury (851).[5] Many of these seem to have started off as raids with, presumably, economic motives, and most seem not to have encountered serious resistance. On occasion, however, Viking raiding armies were intercepted by shire levies raised by local leaders or by the king, resulting in pitched battles in which Viking armies often took a serious mauling.

At the mouth of the River Parrett in 848, the men of Dorset and Somerset – led by their respective ealdormen, Osric and Eanwulf, and Ealhstan, bishop of Sherborne – 'made a great slaughter' of a Viking war-band.[6] The Vikings were defeated again in 850 at a place called Wicga's Barrow by Ealdorman Ceorl and the men of Devon,[7] and in the following year King Æthelwulf of Wessex and his son Æthelbald routed the Viking army at a place called Aclea where they 'made the greatest slaughter of a heathen horde that we have ever heard tell of'.[8] Achieving a crushing victory over his heathen foes would have brought the king great personal satisfaction. In 843 he had gone to Carhampton with the intention of defeating a Viking army at the very place where humiliation had befallen his father, Ecgberht, in 836. But at the second battle of Carhampton, Æthelwulf too had been outfought. The victory at Aclea in 851, therefore, avenged both his own and his father's shame, ending it the way that Anglo-Saxon feuds had always traditionally been settled: in blood.[9]

After this robust West Saxon response, Viking war-bands seem to have become wary of assaulting Wessex directly, with raids in southern Britain confined to Kent for the rest of the decade. But the Viking winter camps of 850 – or at least the concept of such camps – were never abandoned. It became possible for Viking armies to mount raids throughout the year, as seems to have been the case in the early 850s, and by living off the land they could keep large numbers of warriors permanently in arms. Reinforcements from overseas could join them unimpeded, and the numbers of men and the size of their fleets could therefore grow unchecked. Unlike the Anglo-Saxon warriors they faced, there was no imperative for them to return to their fields for the harvest, or – like their compatriots in Scandinavia – to stay at home when North Sea storms kept their ships moored over the winter.[10]

Conflict between Anglo-Saxon kingdoms had always been, to a certain extent, a ritualized activity. The phrase 'ritual war' is an unfortunate one, implying something lacking in severity (what one anthropologist has compared to 'over-enthusiastic football'),[11] and in truth there is no reason to believe that Anglo-Saxon battles were not brutal and serious affairs. But they rarely resulted in lasting political change. Warfare seems generally to have followed a traditional pattern that was mutually understood, and battles – as we have seen – were often fought at places that held a mutual significance. Conflict was also limited by the natural constraints of the agricultural year. Campaigns took place during summer, before the harvest, while the weather was at its best and the roads were most passable; fortifications were seldom used, the Anglo-Saxons seeming to have preferred to face their enemies in the open, an opportunity – whether in victory or defeat – to carve out a legend that would be worth remembering.[12]

The Vikings, however, seemed – in the beginning at least – to be breaking all of these rules.[13] They had no respect for the traditional patchwork of allegiances and loyalties, the ancient boundaries or the conventions of war. They were perfectly happy to dig themselves in to fortified harbour-sites on major rivers, and their focus on portable food and wealth meant that much of their violence fell on settlements, monasteries and royal halls. They avoided pitched battles where they could and were able – thanks to their ships – to strike quickly and quietly into the very heart of Britain, regardless of the state of the roads. Places that had been far from any border now found themselves, as a result of a coastal or riverine position, exposed to war in a way that they had not been in the past.[14]

'They have no cultivated fields,' one contemporary Islamic writer observed of the Rūs he encountered travelling through eastern Europe and central Asia. Instead, he went on, 'they live by pillaging the land of the Saqāliba'.[15] These (the Rūs) were men who had chosen a different path to prosperity, and their harvest lay before them, to be reaped on the battlefield: 'When a son is born,' the same writer elaborated, 'the father throws a naked sword before him and says: "I leave you no inheritance. All you possess is what you can gain with this sword."'[16]

Entrepreneurial values like these, arising in a society that praised highly the fruits of memorable feats of violence and bravery, bred dangerous men with a single-minded determination to get rich quick or die trying. They were not going home to stack hay and muck out pigs, at least not empty-handed. And this meant – for the kingdoms of Anglo-Saxon England – a threat unlike any they had previously had to face.

In 866 an army appeared in East Anglia that was described in the *Anglo-Saxon Chronicle* as a *micel hæðen here* – 'great heathen horde'. *Here* is a difficult word to translate. It is clear that, in general terms, it meant army – the numerous 'herepaths' and 'herefords' that can be found among the place-names of England testify to its common usage in describing militarized infrastructure. However, the word normally used of Anglo-Saxon armies in this period is *fyrd*, and presumably *here* originally had other connotations. A clue to what these were can be found in the laws of King Ine, which explain how *þeofas* ('thieves') appropriately describes a group of up to seven individuals and *hloð* ('band') a group of more than seven but fewer than thirty-five. Any more marauders than this should, according to the laws, be called a *here*. A *here* therefore, in this context, was just a large group of thieves all working together – as good a defini-tion as any for a Viking army operating unlawfully within the bounds of an Anglo-Saxon kingdom, without regard to life, prop-erty or the king's laws.[17]

What is less debatable is that this particular *here* was *hæðen*, and that it was *micel*. Although numbers are problematic (as Ine's laws make clear, a *here* need have been no bigger than three dozen – the number needed to crew a single vessel the size of the ship discovered at Gokstad, near Oslo in Norway), the Viking forces that had menaced Carhampton had, on both occasions, numbered perhaps as many as 1,500 men – enough to defeat West Saxon royal armies on two separate occasions. It is probably safe to assume that the 'great heathen horde' was considerably bigger; as we shall see – archaeological traces of Viking camps of this period in Britain imply sizeable groupings.[18]

What happened next is not altogether clear, but it seems that the *micel hæðen here*, having taken horses from the East Anglians, rode north. Once out of East Anglia, they may have used Ermine Street – the 'Great North Road' – that climbs the country between the Pennines and the Fens, linking London with York. It seems likely, though the sources do not tell us this, that the Viking fleet shadowed the progress of the mounted army as it made its way north, carrying supplies and reinforcements and providing the means for a quick getaway if things turned out badly. Certainly this would have allowed the land-based force to travel faster and more lightly than would otherwise have been possible, while at the same time removing the constraint on manpower that a purely amphibious offensive would have entailed.[19]

Out in the countryside, the inhabitants of the timbered hamlets and farmsteads would have been woken, if they were lucky, by dark news riding hard up the Great North Road: they would have grabbed what they could and fled, the Viking army sweeping through deserted settlements, taking the wheat and slaughtering the livestock, ransacking the church and burning the homes. The horde swept into Northumbria, a sudden blitzkrieg that took the kingdom off guard. Before any resistance could be mustered, the Vikings were already within the walls of Eoforwic (York), the heart of Northumbrian power and the seat of the second most important ecclesiastical diocese in Britain.

*

By the mid-ninth century, Northumbria was no longer the beacon of Christian learning and sainted warrior kings that it had once been; the lustre of its golden age had dulled considerably by the time of the first raids on Lindisfarne and Jarrow. Civil wars and endemic feuding had weakened the kingdom, and Viking attacks had taken a toll on its ruling class, killing its king in 843 and disrupting the succession. And, although the kingdom was by no means a spent force, there can be little doubt that the sacking of its monasteries – international powerhouses of wealth, learning and industry – had been a setback to Northumbrian culture and economy, disrupting trade and creating the insecurity in which political fragmentation was ever more likely.[20]

Northumbria's rivals seem to have sensed its weakness. In 828, Ecgberht of Wessex had led a huge army to Dore (literally 'door' or 'narrow pass'), part of a continuum of features that marked the northern borders of Mercia.[21] The result of the meeting at Dore was that Ecgberht received the 'submission and concord' of the Northumbrians, and was recognized (in the Wessex-produced *Anglo-Saxon Chronicle* at least) as 'Bretwalda' – overlord of Britain.[22] Forty years on and the situation had not improved; the Northumbrian king, Osberht, had been deposed in favour of a rival named Ælle, of whom very little is known, other than that – from the perspective of later chroniclers – he was an 'unnatural king' (that is, he was perceived as a tyrant without a legitimate claim to the throne).[23] It is unlikely, given the precedent of Northumbrian politics over the previous century, that this had been a peaceful transition of power, and it is probable that murders and civil war had taken a toll on the aristocracy and the fighting capacity of the kingdom. It may have been, in some respects at least, a weakened state, unprepared to face a ruthless and opportunistic enemy seeking to take advantage.[24]

The Viking capture of York in 866 seems initially to have stunned the Northumbrians into inaction, and it took months for them to organize a response. Part of the delay was probably diplomatic, for when an Anglo-Saxon army was eventually gathered, both the rival claimants to the Northumbrian throne were present. The idea, presumably, was to set differences aside until the existential threat had been overcome. For Ælle and Osberht, however, the reassuring familiarity of their former enmity was gone for ever.

The Anglo-Saxon counter-attack on York was, at first, dramatically successful. The old Roman walls, reduced in height but still largely intact, had been reinforced with wooden ramparts by the ninth century. Nevertheless, it seems the Northumbrian forces were able to break into the city with little difficulty. The exuberance of this head-on assault, however, seems to have been the undoing of the Northumbrians; having smashed their way in, they swiftly found themselves trapped inside the city. Surrounded and outnumbered, with no means of retreat, the vanguard was annihilated.

No one knows what happened within the walls of York in 867. But the remnants of the Northumbrian army must have looked on in horror as the Viking army emerged from a city that remained resolutely in their grip. Perhaps the Vikings jeered at the survivors, or hurled foul abuse; perhaps they bared their arses or displayed the severed heads of fallen Northumbrians on the points of their spears.[25] Whatever the case, Northumbrian resistance was broken. Fighting continued, but by the end of the day 'an immense slaughter' had been made of the Northumbrian army, and both Ælle and Osberht were dead.[26]

The capture of York left a deep impression. The story of its fall and the events that led to it and flowed from it were told and retold over the centuries, the form the story took in the Old Norse saga literature of the Middle Ages colouring the way in which the historical events – and the conduct of the Vikings in general – have been perceived. By way of backstory to the capture of York, the sagas offer up the character Ragnar Loðbrók, the supposed father of the leaders of the *micel here*. Ragnar Loðbrók – which is to say, Ragnar Hairy-pants (ON *brók* is from the same Germanic root as the

English word 'breeches') – is of indeterminate historicity, and his exploits, as recounted in several sagas and a twelfth-century history written by the Danish cleric Saxo Grammaticus, tend towards the implausible.[27] His deeds, and his death, were used to frame an epic story of revenge and super-human prowess, a tale that flowed from deep seams of myth.

It all begins with the tale of how Ragnar gained his nickname. What follows is my version of the story, rationalized from the various sources in which it is told, embellished a little, but still leaky with plot-holes.

Jarl Herruð of Gautland[28] (the land of the Geats, in southern Sweden) had a daughter named Þóra; she was the most beautiful woman of whom any had heard tell. Her father had made for her a fenced hideaway in which she dwelt. One day, the Jarl gave to his daughter a small serpent – a baby – and she kept the snake in a box of ashes upon a mound of gold. But babies, as they are wont to do, grow bigger, and so it was with the snake.[29] Larger and larger the serpent grew, and the gold multiplied beneath it, until the serpent was so big that it coiled around Þóra's dwelling, its tail eventually meeting with its head, lying upon a huge heap of treasure. None could approach it, so fierce and deadly had it grown, and every day it devoured a whole ox – no doubt to the great upset and impoverishment of the folk thereabouts. Jarl Herruð could see that this state of affairs could not continue, and let it be known that whosoever would rid him of this menace could take his daughter as wife and claim all the gold that lay beneath the serpent's belly. When this news reached Ragnar, the son of Hring, king of Denmark and Sweden, he determined to slay the monster and win for himself the fame, riches and marriage that Herruð had promised. In preparation he fashioned for himself a suit of shaggy clothes of fur and wool. These he boiled and soaked in tar and dipped in sand to harden them (though others say that he drenched them in water and froze them in the snow until they were ice-clad: a glittering suit of crystalline armour, jagged and deadly). Thus attired, Ragnar took up his shield, spear and sword and sought the beast.

When Ragnar reached the lair of the serpent, it was quickly roused against him. Rearing up to a fearsome height, it hung in the air above its challenger, swaying ominously from side to side, fangs bared and dripping with venom. Suddenly, it vomited its poison, but the foul bile was futile against the strange armour Ragnar wore. Enraged, the serpent darted forward, an emerald blur, its great jaws gaping wide, seeking to rend and tear. But Ragnar held his shield steady in front of him and rushed forward to meet the creature, thrusting with his spear. The jaws of the snake closed uselessly around the iron-banded shield, gouging at the wooden boards, snapping on the metal boss; but the spear struck home, biting into the serpent's neck and through its spine into the ground beyond. The thrashing of the beast in its death-agony shook the earth and made the pillars of Þóra's hall tremble like the forest trees when the storms come. But Ragnar was unafraid; he drew his sword and raised it high, before bringing it down with all his strength, hacking through the sinewy neck and striking the serpent's head from its body. The maimed coils flung themselves from left to right, the tail beating on the ground, black blood pouring on to the earth. When at last it lay still, and Ragnar was sure the beast was dead, he departed. But he carried away only the shaft of his spear and left behind the spear-head where it stood, still upright, pinning the head of the serpent to the soil.

The next day, Jarl Herruð marvelled at the carnage that had been wrought and listened to his daughter's tale. She suggested that he call a great assembly – a *thing* – to which all men should be commanded to attend. In this way, she thought, the man whose spear-shaft matched the spear-head that had been left in the ground would be discovered, and the mystery of the hairy slayer solved. On Herruð's orders this was duly done, and – on the appointed day – Ragnar arrived at the gathering, clad as before in his strange suit of shaggy clothes. He stood apart from the other men at the edge of the *thing* and watched as each hopeful suitor – many of them great earls and powerful warlords, clad in fine embroidered cloaks of bright colours and with silver rings jangling on their arms – came and tried to fit his spear-head to their spear-shafts. None of them, of course, could make the spear-head fit. At last it was Ragnar's turn and he stepped from the shadows, still stinking with the serpent's gore and venom. There was a murmuring among the disappointed suitors: how dare this foul-smelling vagrant think to claim such a fair prize? Ragnar cared not: he duly presented his spear-shaft. Þóra lifted the spear-head and slipped it on to the end: it fitted – of course it did – and a gasp went up from the assembled throng. But then Ragnar pushed the fur hood from his head, and suddenly all could see that it was the son of King Hring who was the serpent-slayer. The embarrassed silence lasted for long seconds, but it was broken by Herruð, who let out a great bellow of mirth: 'My son-in-law shall you be, Ragnar Hringsson, but all shall know you now as "Hairy-pants"!' At this, all those who were gathered fell about laughing, and Herruð commanded that the *thing* become a wedding feast. Ragnar and Þóra were duly married, and with her by his side, Ragnar in time returned home to rule his father's realm as king.

The plot-holes are inevitable really, as all of the surviving versions have their internal inconsistencies and none of them agree. Saxo's version, for instance, has Þóra receiving a clutch of snake-babies that grow up to rampage around the countryside wreaking havoc. But that the story is an old one is confirmed by the fact that the tale seems already to have been well established by the twelfth century, appearing not only in Saxo's *Gesta Danorum*, but also in the first lines of a poem called *Krákumál* – purportedly Ragnar's death-poem, but written long after his death:

We struck with our swords!
So long ago, it was:
we had gone to Gautland
for the *ground-wolf*'s slaughter.
Then we won fair Thora;
thus the warriors named me
Loðbrók, when I laid that
heather-eel low in battle,
ended the *earth-coil*'s life
with inlaid shining steel.[30]

Krákumál makes use of a number of kennings to describe the serpent: 'ground-wolf'; 'heather-eel'; 'earth-coil'. All describe the same thing: a writhing snake-like beast of monstrous size – a *wyrm* in Old English, *ormr* in Old Norse – a thing of soil, and ground-dwelling. Although these verses perform a subtle linguistic dance around the issue, we understand intuitively the true nature of the monster. It is the creature that has haunted the imaginations of human civilizations from the moment they were able to express themselves: the oldest terror of all. Dragon.

The Geats of Gautland had already suffered their share of dragons in the literature of northern Europe. *Beowulf* famously concludes with the hero's fight – as king of the Geats – against a beast far more terrible than the earth-bound *wyrm* that Ragnar faced. Beowulf's dragon is airborne and fire-spewing, like those which presaged the arrival of the Vikings at Lindisfarne, a harbinger of apocalyptic devastation:

The dragon began to belch out flames
and burn bright homesteads; there was a hot glow
that scared everyone, for the vile sky-winger
would leave nothing alive in his wake.
Everywhere the havoc he wrought was in evidence.
Far and near, the Geat nation
bore the brunt of his brutal assaults

and virulent hate. Then back to the hoard
he would dart before daybreak, to hide in his den[31]

Nevertheless, like others of his kin, this dragon is also at heart an earth-dweller: the 'harrower of the dark [...] who hunts out barrows [...] driven to hunt out hoards underground, to guard heathen gold through age-long vigils'.[32] This gold-hoarding habit of dragons is a common theme and was regarded as self-evident in Anglo-Saxon verse – the gnomic poem *Maxims II* presents the idea that the 'Dragon must dwell in the barrow, cunning, proud of its treasures' as a fact equivalent to the truth that 'fish must dwell in water'.[33]

The dragon's jealous and possessive attitude towards hoarded treasure seems to have operated in both Old English and Old Norse literature as a symbol of the pernicious and destructive vice of avarice, to be contrasted directly (as it is in *Maxims II*) with the dictum that 'the king belongs in his hall, dealing out rings'. The gold-hoarding serpent was thus – as well as being an embodiment of flaming Armageddon – a more subtle nemesis of ordered life, a poison gnawing at the roots of society, breaking the bonds that held people together; it was the duty of heroes and kings to fight them, even if the entropic forces they represented could never be truly defeated.[34]

These characteristics of the monstrous serpent were well represented in the most epic streams of Norse mythology. Niðhöggr ('spite-striker') and Jörmungandr ('mighty-wand', aka Midgarðsormr – lit. 'Middle-earth-serpent') were creatures of another order of magnitude altogether. The former gnawed at the roots of the world tree, literally undermining the pillar of creation. In the end of days Niðhöggr would, it was foretold, herald the doom of the world:

Then there comes there the dark dragon flying,
the glittering snake up from Moon-wane hills,
it bears in its wings – and flies over the plain –
dead bodies: Spite-striker [Niðhöggr]; now she must sink.[35]

Jörmungandr – the world-serpent – was a being of yet more profound cosmological significance: he was the mighty *wyrm* whose body encircled the mortal realm, separating the human world from chaos. He, too, would break his bonds at the end, when the denizens of Utgarð (the 'out-world') would thrust the world into oblivion at *Ragnarök* – the 'doom of the gods'. To contend with such a menace, no mortal champion would suffice: Thor the Thunderer, protector of gods and men, would be the one to shoulder the futile burden; his many contests with the world-serpent were told in tales that travelled far and wide across the Viking world.

Although mention of more 'mundane' dragons in Old Norse literature is fairly common, serpents of Beowulfian splendour are, to quote Tolkien once again, 'as rare as they are dire'.[36] The template for them all, however – the ur-dragon – is Fáfnir, the creature slain in one of the most important cycles of Old Norse hero-tales by Sigurd the Völsung – the godfather of all dragon-slayers. The tale begins as follows:

When Otr, while swimming in the guise of (no surprise) an otter, was killed by the god Loki, recompense was paid in treasure to his father, Hreidmar, and his brothers, Regin and Fáfnir. The treasure, however, as treasure often does in such stories, worked an evil spell upon the brothers, partly as a result of a cursed ring that Odin had added to the treasure hoard at the last moment. The brothers conspired and murdered their father, but Fáfnir betrayed his brother and stole the treasure for himself. He fled with it to a place called Gnitaheiðr, where he became transformed into a dreadful serpent, there to guard his hoard jealously. Regin, meanwhile, plotted his vengeance, becoming skilled in smithcraft and adopting a young man named Sigurd as his protégé. In time Regin forged a deadly sword, which he called Gram, and set Sigurd on the quest to which his life hitherto had led. Sigurd went to Gnitaheiðr and dug a hole for himself, waiting for Fáfnir to slither overhead. The dragon duly returned and Sigurd drove the sword upwards through the serpent's body.

Fáfnir took a long time to die, and conversed long with his murderer, but die he eventually did, and – as Regin had instructed him – Sigurd cut out the dragon's heart and began to roast it on a stick over the fire in order that he should serve it up to his master. Anxious not to deliver undercooked organs, Sigurd tested the meat with his fingers, burning his thumb. He stuck the thumb into his mouth and tasted the dragon's blood that was smeared there. Instantly, Sigurd gained the ability to understand the speech of birds. Seven such creatures, so it transpired, were conversing in the trees above him and were taunting him for his apparent stupidity, explaining that Regin had tricked and used him to enact this vengeance, and that he intended to claim the dragon's treasure all for himself. On hearing this, Sigurd promptly sought out Regin, and lopped off his head with Gram, the sword Regin himself had forged.[37]

That is the end of the dragon-slaying part of the tale, though it is not by any means the end of the Sigurd legend. This segment, and the convoluted story of thwarted love and vengeance between kinsfolk that follows, was told and retold throughout the Middle Ages, finding epic form in the thirteenth century in the Old High German *Nibelungenlied* and the Old Norse *Völsunga saga*, medieval poems that would ultimately inspire Richard Wagner's *Der Ring des Nibelungen*, a series of operas – *Das Rheingold*, *Die Walküre*, *Siegfried* and *Götterdämmerung* – first performed as a cycle in 1876. The original costume designs for these operas, by Carl Emil Doepler, alongside Arthur Rackham's illustrations for the English-language version of Wagner's libretti, would prove to be enormously influential for Victorian imaginings of Norse mythological themes; Thoma's winged helmets and bronze bustiers set a template for how Wotan (Odin) and his valkyries should be presented that has proved remarkably resilient.[38]

The Völsung legend, however, would also find its way into the British (and global) psyche through a less overt but equally influential route. In the closing years of the nineteenth century, a small boy living with his mother in a village close to the outskirts of industrial

Birmingham made a discovery. Towards the end of the *Red Fairy Book*, the second of British writer and critic Andrew Lang's compendia of fairy-tales, a young J. R. R. Tolkien found 'The Story of Sigurd'. It affected him deeply. 'I desired dragons with a profound desire,' he recalled in 1939; '... the world that contained even the imagination of Fafnir was richer and more beautiful, at whatever cost of peril.' It would have a seismic effect on his imagination, shaping a lifelong enthusiasm.[39]

In 1914, having won the undergraduate Skeat Prize for English at Exeter College, Oxford, Tolkien would use his winnings to purchase the 1870 translation of *Völsunga saga* produced by the great artist, writer, craft pioneer and medievalist William Morris (who was also an important figure in the nineteenth-century Viking revival) and his friend the Icelandic scholar Eiríkr Magnússon.[40] In tone, plot and subject matter, the legend of Sigurd would inspire a great deal of Tolkien's oeuvre: both directly, in a poem that he wrote in the traditional English alliterative metre (published posthumously as *The Legend of Sigurd and Gudrún*) and indirectly, in myriad elements of his tales of Middle-Earth: from the slaying of the dragon Glaurung by the hero Turin Turambar (like Sigurd, from beneath) in *The Silmarillion*, to the gold-madness of Thorin Oakenshield in *The Hobbit* and, of course, the cursed ring that defined *The Lord of the Rings* trilogy.[41]

William Morris, for his part, also produced his own epic retelling of the Sigurd story that was separate from the translation undertaken with Eiríkr Magnússon. Now largely forgotten, the 10,000 lines of rhyming hexameters that comprised *The Story of Sigurd the Volsung and the Fall of the Niblungs* (1876) was once an object of high praise, and its author considered it his finest poetic achievement. George Bernard Shaw, for one, was filled with enthusiasm, gushing that with *Sigurd the Volsung* Morris had 'achieved the summit of his professional destiny by writing the greatest epic since Homer'. According to Shaw, Morris 'was quite aware of the greatness of this work, and used to recite passages from it, marking its swing by rocking from one foot to another like an elephant. After one of these recitations he sat down beside me. I said "This is the stuff for me; there is nothing like it."[42]

In the longer term, *The Story of Sigurd the Volsung* suffered from the inevitable comparisons that were drawn between it and Richard Wagner's monumental work on the same theme. The four operas of the *Ring* cycle were first performed together at Bayreuth in 1876, the same year that Morris' poem was published, and caused a sensation in Europe. It was not a comparison that Morris would have welcomed. His own opinion of Wagner's work, indeed, of opera in general, was not a charitable one: 'I look upon it as nothing short of desecration to bring such a tremendous and world-wide subject under the gas-lights of an opera; the most degraded and rococo of all forms of art – the idea of a sandy-haired German tenor tweedledeeing over the unspeakable woes of Sigurd, which even the simplest words are not typical enough to express!'[43] This is probably unfair to Wagner who, after all, had his own axes to grind about the state of theatrical music. But Morris, by almost any sane measure, is a more sympathetic character than the great German maestro, so I hesitate to intervene in the latter's defence.

Thus the Sigurd narrative has been – and continues to be – an incredibly potent force in shaping our conceptions of northern mythology and the tone and texture of modern fantasy. This potency, however, arises from and builds on the defining role this legend played in the world-view of northern peoples from an exceptionally early date. As the archetype for many other human dragon-slaying heroes, Beowulf and Ragnar included, Sigurd represented an important and popular figure of early medieval folk culture.[44] Images of the hero stabbing the dragon in its soft underbelly – alongside other scenes from the tale – have been found as far afield as Tatarstan.[45] The most famous depictions are found cut into standing stones in eastern Sweden, with particularly striking examples at Ramsund and Gök in Södermanland. In these carvings, the body of the serpent coils in an oval loop around the stone, an attenuated ribbon that carries an inscription incised in runes – a message to commemorate the dead. This is commonplace on the

Viking Age runestones of Scandinavia – as though the names conveyed by the runes could somehow shimmer into serpentine life, to be carried into immortality on the backs of dragons. But in these examples, down below the runes, an intrusive figure lurks, his sword jutting upwards, piercing the body of the *wyrm*: here is Sigurðr Fánisbani – Sigurd Fáfnir's Bane – striking the heroic, cowardly blow that defines him.[46]

Sigurd imagery also found its way to Britain during the Viking Age: four Christian runestones erected on the Isle of Man by communities of Viking origin display imagery from the Sigurd legend, and an iconographic scheme that depicts the roasting of Fáfnir's heart and Sigurd sucking his thumb was carved into a standing cross at Halton in Lancashire.[47] One of the Manx stones contains a rare detail, found in only a handful of other depictions of the story. This is the image of Gunnar in the snake-pit; a scene from later in the story – pithily summarized in the thirteenth-century *Völsunga saga*. Gunnar, who with his brother Högni had murdered Sigurd in order to claim the treasure for themselves, fell foul of their brother-in-law, Attila the Hun, who – having invited them over for dinner – had Högni's heart cut out and Gunnar thrown into a pit of snakes. The latter brother was able to fend off death for a short while by playing a harp with his feet: all of the snakes fell asleep, except for one, which delivered the fatal bite.

Ragnar Loðbrók was in many respects a reinvention of his drag-on-slaying antecedent Sigurd; it was even said (with cavalier regard for chronology) that Ragnar's second wife, Aslaug, was the daughter of Sigurd himself (with the valkyrie Brynhildr). Ragnar and Aslaug even had a son they named 'Sigurd', a young man who, it was said, had the image of a snake biting its own tail swirling in his iris: for obvious reasons he became known as Sigurd 'snake-in-the-eye' (*ormr í auga*).[48]

Ragnar may never have existed, and if he did, almost nothing we are told of his life in the sagas is true. His death, as recorded in the sagas and in *Krákumál*, is pure fantasy. He was said to have died languishing at the bottom of a snake-pit – consigned to this improbable death by Ælle, one of the two kings of Northumbria killed by the *micel here* in 867. (The similarity to the treatment of Gunnar in *Völsunga saga* is obvious and probably deliberate.) What is clear, however, is that when Scandinavians of the later Middle Ages came to write about the deeds of Ragnar and his sons they saw them in the light of the most heroic figure of all: Sigurd the dragon-slayer himself. This alone should tell us something about the high regard and wide-ranging fame that attended the reputations of the men who took York in 867. But what is also clear is that it was felt necessary to provide some sort of explanation for the Viking invasions of Britain in the 860s, a compelling origin tale to explain what happened, to justify all the violence and the bloodshed, to explain the appalling deeds and doings of a cast of individuals who (or some of whom at least) have a far better claim to historicity than their supposed father.[49]

8

EAGLES
OF BLOOD

Do you know how to cut? Do you know how to read?
Do you know how to stain? Do you know how to test?
Do you know how to invoke? Do you know how to sacrifice?
Do you know how to dispatch? Do you know how to slaughter?

Hávamál[1]

Björn Ironside, Halfdan Whiteshirt,[2] Ubbe, Sigurd Snake-in-the-Eye and Ivar the Boneless.

The recitation of their names has a poetry about it, like the ritual summoning of Viking ghosts. Most of these individuals – if not all of them – were, unlike their supposed father, real people. Of the five, three of them – Ubbe, Halfdan and Ivar – had a major role to play in Britain during the ninth century. In the stories that were written about them in later centuries, the relationship with their father, Ragnar Loðbrók, was crucial – not least in establishing a motive for their violent intrusion into England.

The vengeance that they (and Ivar in particular) were believed to have wrought on King Ælle for supposedly dumping their dad into a snake-pit has been held up for centuries as the epitome of Viking savagery and pagan cruelty. 'Ivar and the brothers', so the story is told in *Ragnarssona þáttr* ('The Tale of Ragnar's Sons', written *c.* 1300), 'had the eagle cut in Ella's back, then all his ribs severed from the backbone with a sword, so that his lungs were pulled out'.[3]

This grotesque performance has become known as the 'blood-eagle'. Saxo Grammaticus, writing at least a hundred years earlier than the author of this account (though still 300 years after the event) gives a version of something similar, but his description is 'milder' in that the outline of an eagle is simply incised into Ælle's back; no messing around with ribs and lungs flapping about all over the place (although Saxo does introduce some literal salt into the wound: 'Not satisfied with imprinting a wound on him, they salted the mangled flesh').[4] More pressing than the disagreement between these sources, however, is the fact that the only contemporary account of Ælle's death implies that it occurred during the Northumbrian attempt to recapture York in 867. Even if we imagine this unpleasant spectacle taking place in the immediate aftermath of victory, one might expect that something so outlandish would have received a passing mention, even in a document as famously laconic as the *Anglo-Saxon Chronicle*.

The earliest Old Norse reference to the killing of King Ælle comes in verse form. In a stanza of one of several skaldic poems composed in praise of King Cnut in the eleventh century (known collectively as *Knútsdrápur*), the poet Sigvatr Þórðarson wrote:

Ok Ellu bak,
At lét hinn's sat,
Ívarr, ara,
Iorví, skorit.[5]

Translated literally, this turns out as:

And Ella's back,
at had the one who dwelt,
Ivarr, with eagle,
York, cut.[6]

To say that skaldic verse is an economical art-form would be something of an understatement, and the particular form that the *Knútsdrápur* took (a metre known as *tøglag*) was particularly compressed. Most pertinently, the relationship of the elements within the stanza is as ambiguous in Old Norse as it is in modern English. It *can* be translated as 'Ivar, who dwelt at York, had an eagle cut into Ælle's back' – the implication being that Ivar cut the *image* of an eagle into Ælle's back. This seems to have been how medieval writers understood it, and modern historians have tended to accept the interpretation of Saxo and the saga-writers.

However, the verse could equally well mean 'Ivar, who dwelt at York, caused an eagle to cut Ælle's back'.[7] Or, if one is to fill in the subtext: 'Ivar, having captured York, defeated and killed King Ælle: which meant, to everyone's general satisfaction, that eagles were able to gouge the flesh of his corpse as it lay face down and naked in the mud: hooray for Ivar, feaster of eagles!' This, the reader may remember, is very much the sort of thing that Viking aristocrats enjoyed being praised for. Good kings were those who could claim particular success in turning their enemies into fleshy morsels for raptors and carrion creatures (especially the wolf, raven and eagle). In other words, it is utterly conventional, and precisely the sort of thing we should expect a skaldic poet to come out with.[8]

The elaborate and inconsistent descriptions of gory rituals contained in Saxo's history and in the sagas seem, when seen in this light, to have been the product of a medieval misunderstanding, one which has been compounded by a tendency among modern translators to approach the poetry through the prism of those later embroideries.

The supposed 'rite of the blood-eagle' seems, therefore, to be a myth of Viking barbarity conjured up in later centuries by antiquarians enthralled by the exoticism of their forebears and titillated by their gory antics. As the late Roberta Frank, the incomparable scholar of Germanic languages and literature, put it: 'Medieval men of letters, like their modern counterparts, could sometimes be over-eager to recover the colourful rites and leafy folk beliefs of their pagan ancestors.'[9] This should not be allowed to obscure the fact that the pagan people of northern Europe did indeed engage in practices which – from our perspective – appear horrific and bloodthirsty.

In a famous passage in his *Gesta Hammaburgensis ecclesie pontificum* ('Deeds of the Bishops of the Church of Hamburg-Bremen'), the eleventh-century German chronicler Adam of Bremen decided to give an account of what he called 'the superstition of the Swedes'. After an extraordinary (and frankly somewhat unlikely) description of a temple at Uppsala, he goes on to explain that:

> each of their gods have appointed priests to offer up the
> sacrifices of the people [...] The sacrifice proceeds as follows:
> nine males of every living creature are offered up, and it is
> customary to placate the gods with their blood: their corpses
> are hung in the grove next to the temple. That grove is so sacred
> to the heathens that every single tree is considered to be divine,
> thanks to the death or rotting carcass of the sacrificed; they
> hang dogs and horses there alongside men.[10]

There are plenty of details in Adam's account that provoke sceptical beard-stroking – the grandiose scale of the temple and its associated rituals, as well as the obvious Christian agenda of the author, are paramount among these.[11] But even if the details are dubious – indeed, even if there never was a temple at Uppsala[12] – evidence from elsewhere in the Viking world suggests that sacrifice, perhaps including human sacrifice, was very much a part of pre-Christian religion in the north. In 1984, remodelling of Frösö Church in Jämtland, Sweden, led to an archaeological investigation of the chancel. Beneath the altar, the excavators discovered the stump of a birch tree, cut down before the church was built. In the dark earth surrounding the tree were found the bones of animals – cattle, goat, sheep, pig, horse, dog, chicken, grouse, squirrel, deer, elk and bear – scattered in profusion, disarticulated, broken and cut. The remains of humans were also found: two adults (possibly more) and two children – one between three and five years old, the other a baby of less than six months. All of the bones, human and animal, can be dated broadly to the Viking Age. The evidence from Frösö strongly suggests that the tree was a focal point for sacrificial offerings, and it is possible that humans and animals (or parts of animals) were hung from branches – in a manner similar to that described by Adam of Bremen – until they were cut down and buried, or rotted and fell to the earth below.[13]

Other images and texts from the Viking Age seem to corroborate Adam of Bremen's tale – at least in part. Ibn Fadlān explained that, in gratitude for supernatural intervention and assistance, animals were slaughtered and their remains offered to the idol. The offerer 'hangs the heads of sheep or cows on the wooden stakes which have been driven into the ground'.[14] Ibrâhîm ibn Ya'qûb al-Ṭurṭûshî, a Jewish merchant from Islamic Spain, reported that in Hedeby, 'When a man kills a sacrificial animal, whether it be an ox, ram, goat, or pig, he hangs it on a pole outside his house so that people will know that he has made a sacrifice in honour of the god.'[15] It must have made for a grisly street scene.

A fragment of tapestry, woven in the ninth century, was preserved in a ship burial at Oseberg near Oslo in Norway. It seems to depict a strange tree laden with corpse-fruit while a procession of wagons, horses, women and warriors passes beneath it. Finally, the famous Stora Hammars picture stone from Gotland appears to show something more elaborate: a small figure lies face down on a small structure. Behind, to the right, stands a bearded man, leaning forward, wielding a spear. Behind him and above him, two large birds are depicted – ravens, perhaps. To the left of the scene an armed man hangs from a tree, to the right a crowd wave their weapons in the air.[16] No one knows what this scene is intended to convey (a mythological scene, a legendary narrative, a depiction of contemporary practices?), but the impression of blood-ritual is unmistakable and a connection to the cult of the god Odin entirely plausible.

One of the most evocative of medieval embellishments was that which transformed the supposed rite of the blood-eagle from a sadistic and vengeful act into a religious ritual. This notion of cultic sacrifice has its origins in the only other saga account of the practice – a description in the thirteenth-century *Orkneyinga saga* which insists that Halfdan Long-leg (a son of the ninth-century Norwegian king Harald Finehair) 'had his ribs cut from the spine with a sword and the lungs pulled out through the slits in his back' by Einar, Earl of Orkney, who 'dedicated the victim to Odin as a victory offering'.[17] The saga is deeply flawed as a guide to historical events, its grisly details as unreliable as the sources discussed above. In one detail, however, the saga may preserve a real aspect of the relationship between death and ritual during the Viking Age: an association with the lore and cult of Odin, Lord of the Hanged (Hangadrottinn).

There is no escaping the fact that Odin, as we know him from Old Norse poetry, as well as from later medieval writings, is a troubling and sinister deity. Among the most ominous of the huge number of names by which he was known are Valföðr ('father of the slain'), Skollvaldr ('lord of treachery'), Hjarrandi ('screamer'), Grímnir ('the hooded one'), Hildolfr ('battle-wolf'), Bölverkr ('evil worker'), Draugadróttinn ('lord of the undead'), Hengikeptr ('hang-jaw') …[18] His portfolio is a broad one: magic, warfare, rune-craft, fate, poetry, prophecy, dissimulation, power and death seem to have been considered his main areas of interest. Odin's multifaceted nature makes him a difficult god to characterize. But in all his guises there runs a skein of darkness, an intimacy with death that hangs off him like a cloak of shadow that obscures and obfuscates – a dark and tattered mantle.

Odin's association with bloody rituals is bound up with the god's repeated acts of self-sacrifice in the pursuit of hidden or forbidden wisdom. His one empty eye socket – the god's most unambiguous distinguishing feature – was the result of his thirst for a draught from the well of Mímir, the fountain of wisdom and intellect presided over by its eponymous guardian. To gain access to the well, Odin plucked out his own eye and gave it to the waters – an exchange of sight for insight.[19] When Mímir the guardian died, decapitated during a war between the gods, Odin took possession of the severed head. He carved runes into it, spoke charms over it. Ever after it would speak with him, whispering him secrets, telling of other worlds. Here is Odin the necromancer, conversant with corpses.

The knowledge of runes and charms came about as the result of an even greater sacrifice – the god's dedication of himself to himself:

I know that I hung on that windy tree,
spear-wounded, nine full nights,
given to Odin, myself to myself,
on that tree that rose from roots
that no man ever knows.

They gave me neither bread, nor drink from horn,
I peered down below.
I clutched the runes, screaming I grabbed them,
and then sank back.[20]

The tree from which Odin was hung is probably to be identified with the world tree, Yggdrasil. The spear with which he was wounded is probably his own dwarf-forged spear, Gungnir. Unlike the loss of his eye, given as surety to a third party, this was a more profound sacrifice – one which acknowledged Odin himself as the highest power to which an offering could be made, himself to himself, an ordeal of transcendental suffering – the primal bargain of power for pain.

The initial Viking capture of York came towards the end of 866, and the calamitous Northumbrian counter-attack didn't materialize until March of 867.[21] The delay meant that the Vikings were probably able to celebrate their victory in synchronicity with the mid-winter festival, a time of drinking, feasting and sacrifices known, in Old Norse, as *jol* – or, as we know it, Yule. As is so often the case, we only have much later writers to rely on for any sense of what this festival involved. And, almost as predictably, it is the Icelander Snorri Sturluson in his great historical cycle *Heimskringla* who provides the detail. This comes, firstly, in *Ynglinga saga*, where he explains that sacrifices were made at mid-winter for a good harvest (a provision which makes sense if one imagines mid-winter as marking the rebirth of the sun – the start of the solar year – and the beginning of a new cycle of growth),[22] and, secondly, in *Hakonar saga góða* (the saga of Hákon the Good). Hákon (King of Norway between 934 and 961) is principally remembered for his role in promoting Christianity in Norway, and one of the ways he apparently tried to achieve this was by aligning the Yule festival with the dates of Christmas. As Snorri explains, 'previously observance of Yule began on midwinter night (12th January), and continued for three nights'. He goes on:

It was an ancient custom, when a ritual feast was to take place, that all the farmers should attend where the temple was and bring there their own supplies for them to use while the banquet lasted. At this banquet everyone had to take part in the ale-drinking. All kinds of domestic animals were slaughtered there, including horses, and all the blood that came from them was called *hlaut* ('lot'), and what the blood was contained in, *hlaut*-bowls, and *hlaut*-twigs, these were fashioned like holy water sprinklers; with these the altars were to be reddened all over, and also the walls of the temple outside and inside and the people also were sprinkled, while the meat was to be cooked for a feast. There would be fires down the middle of the floor in the temple with cauldrons over them. The toasts were handed across the fire, and the one who was holding the banquet and who was the chief person there, he had to dedicate the toast and all the ritual food; first would be Odin's toast – that was drunk to victory and to the power of the king – and then Njǫrð's toast and Freyr's toast for prosperity and peace. Then after that it was common for many people to drink the *bragafull* ('chieftain's toast'). People also drank toasts to their kinsmen, those who had been buried in mounds, and these were called *minni* ('memorial toasts').[23]

Although this description is generic – it could apply to any festival – the fact that it follows Snorri's reference to Yule implies that he expects it to be read in that context. Much of it evokes a familiar yuletide scene – families gathered together around the fire, plenty of booze and roasted meat, companionable glasses raised to family and absent friends, to peace and good fortune. From a modern perspective, however, this cheerful tableau of comfort and joy is somewhat compromised by the torrent of gore applied liberally to walls, floors and guests. Still, if we believe Snorri (and his description is disarmingly artless and non-judgemental), this is the sort of scene that we can imagine Ivar, Ubbe and Halfdan enjoying over the York festive period during the winter of 866/7.

Snorri Sturluson, as imagined by the
artist Christian Krohg in 1899

After consolidating their initial victory by defeating and killing Osberht and Ælle, the Viking army was soon making provision to move on. By the end of 867, the great heathen horde was in Mercia, bedding down for another winter and, perhaps, a new round of Yule sacrifice. This, understandably, was not to the liking of the Mercian king, Burhred, though there seems little he could do about it. He was compelled to send south – to Wessex – and request the assistance of his brother-in-law, King Æthelred (Burhred had married Æthelswith, the daughter of the old West Saxon king Æthelwulf in 853). The following year, 868, the West Saxons, led in person by Æthelred and his brother Alfred, joined forces with the Mercians and advanced on Nottingham where the Viking army, 'protected by the defences of the fortress, would not give battle'.[24] This was probably not what the English had expected; pitched battles – not sieges – had long been the preferred Anglo-Saxon way of war. This new-fangled use of fortifications set an unwelcome precedent.

We don't know a great deal about the realities of siege warfare during the early medieval period, and what we do know is often derived from continental contexts where continuity with late Roman military strategy and technology was arguably stronger. Even so, offensive strategies against fortified positions were, in the words of one distinguished historian of early medieval military affairs, 'usually conducted with a minimum of finesse'.[25] In the ancient world, siege technology had been impressive. A great Assyrian relief carving produced in the early seventh century BC depicts the capture of the walled Hebrew city of Lachish in 701 BC by the Assyrian king Sennacherib. That siege, which took place 1,500 years before the Viking Age, involved massed archers, scaling ladders, siege towers and battering rams – the latter encased in a contraption with more than a passing resemblance to a tank.[26] Compare this to the images depicted in relief on the early eighth-century AD 'Franks' casket, a remarkable whalebone box crafted in Northumbria and now housed (apart from a single panel in the Bargello Museum in Florence) at the British Museum. On its lid, a single archer is depicted defending a fortified enclosure, firing arrows from the only point of egress – presumably the door. Ranged against him is a motley band which, compared to the mighty hordes of Sennacherib, seems woefully underprepared for the task in hand (although, to be fair, the scale of the undertaking hardly appears comparable).

Techniques of siege warfare seem to have been rudimentary at best. In the absence of any evidence in Britain for siege engines, the assumption has to be that assaults were typically conducted using the 'direct approach'; such seems to be the implication of the few indications that survive.[27] In 757, an internecine feud within Wessex resolved itself in a kerfuffle at the royal hall at Meretun (unidentified). The episode concluded with fighting that took place 'around the gates', until a faction loyal to the (slain) king, Cynewulf, 'forced their way in' and did for the would-be usurper, Cyneheard. In 917, when Æthelflæd, 'the lady of the Mercians', captured Derby from the Vikings, 'four of her thegns [lesser Anglo-Saxon noblemen], who were dear to her, were slain within the gates', implying that – 150 years later – barrelling through the front door was still the principal method for gaining access to fortified places.[28] These are the occasions on which such tactics worked: when they went wrong – as at York in 867 – they could be catastrophic. More often than not, however, the sieges reported in the *Anglo-Saxon Chronicle* seem to have ended in something rather more bathetic. Engagements of this nature probably resembled the first attempt on the French castle in *Monty Python and the Holy Grail*: a futile charge, a pelting with a range of unpleasant objects, and an ignominious retreat.

Of course, we don't know for sure that the siege of Nottingham was quite as calamitous as all that. Nevertheless, it does seem to have been a bit of a damp squib. 'There occurred no serious fighting there,' the *Anglo-Saxon Chronicle* offers, rather feebly. John of Worcester adds limply, 'the Christians were not able to breach the wall'.[29] In the end, the Mercians 'made peace' with the Viking army; in other words, with no end to the stand-off in sight, and the troops grumbling about their fields and families, the English bought the Vikings off.

All parties went their separate ways – the Vikings back to York, Æthelred and Alfred back to Wessex (presumably). The whole affair has the appearance, if not of cock-up, then certainly of anti-climax. Nevertheless, the episode is significant for several reasons: firstly, it demonstrated how weak Mercia had become since its heyday a hundred years earlier. Not only had Burhred failed to deal with the Viking threat, but he had been forced to turn to his brother-in-law (and, probably, nominal overlord) to dig him out of the hole – unsuccessfully, as it turned out.[30] Secondly, it highlighted the willingness, as we have seen, of the Vikings to make use of fortifications in a way which left their enemies off-balance and struggling for military solutions. Finally, and related to the last point, it points to the strategic choice to which Anglo-Saxon kings would resort over and over again when faced with this sort of Viking aggression: they reached for their metaphorical chequebooks, rather than their swords, frequently with – predictably – disastrous consequences.

Burhred was not the first to pay the Vikings to go away. The East Anglian king, Edmund, seems to have done much the same when the *micel here* turned up on his doorstep in 866; the horses and provisions they had taken in his kingdom in 865 were almost certainly rendered up by the East Anglians in order that they might avoid any further unpleasantness, instead passing the bad news on to their northern neighbours. If that had been Edmund's hope, then it proved to be a forlorn one.

Here is how the *Anglo-Saxon Chronicle* puts it: '870: [In this year] the *here* rode over Mercia into East Anglia and took up winter settlement at Thetford. And that winter King Edmund fought with them, and the Danes took the victory, and slew the king and took all the land.'[31] This brief notice, a mere thirty-five words, represents effectively everything that is known of the Viking conquest of East Anglia: no battle, no deed of heroism or cruelty, no desperate resistance or punitive vengeance has survived to be passed on to us. All we know is that, 450 years after the Anglian settlement of eastern England, 300 since the South folk and the North folk had recognized a single king to rule over them, 250 since the occupant of Mound 1 had been laid to rest at Sutton Hoo in a ship filled with the treasures of the age, and only 40 since the East Anglian king Æthelstan had slain two Mercian kings in battle,[32] Anglo-Saxon East Anglia had fallen to new rulers.

Like the capture of York and the death of King Ælle, however, the conquest of East Anglia and, particularly, the killing of King Edmund were to leave a lasting imprint on the early medieval imagination, eventually developing a significance that would reverberate through the centuries. And, as with Ælle, this would hinge almost entirely on the way that Edmund's death was later reported.

The first – and fullest – account of Edmund's death, the *Passio Sancti Eadmundi*, was written in Latin during the second half of the tenth century by a man called Abbo, a Frankish Benedictine monk from the Abbey of Fleury (in modern France). Probably aware that the century-long gap between Edmund's death and his account might raise issues of credibility, Abbo was particular about establishing the provenance of his tale. He claimed that he had heard it from Archbishop Dunstan, who had himself heard it told to King Athelstan (of Wessex) by an ancient who had served as King Edmund's armour-bearer. Believe that if you will – there is no way to prove it either way. Suffice it to say, however, that there are aspects of Edmund's death (and subsequent undeath) that present certain difficulties.

Abbo starts, in time-honoured fashion, to establish some familiar tropes (I quote at length to give a flavour of his idiosyncratic waffle). He reminds us:

> that from the north comes all that is evil, as those have had too good cause to know, who through the spite of fortune and the fall of the die have experienced the barbarity of the races of the north. These, it is certain, are so cruel by the ferocity of their nature, as to be incapable of feeling for the ills of mankind; as is shown by the fact that some of their tribes use human flesh for food, and from the circumstance are known by the Greek name

Anthropophagists. Nations of this kind abound in great numbers in Scythia, near the Hyperborean Mountains, and are destined, as we read, more than all other races, to follow Antichrist, and to batten without compunction on the agonies of men who refuse to bear on their foreheads the mark of the beast.[33]

Vikings, Abbo wants us to understand, are a very bad thing.

He continues, in this wonderfully circumlocutious way, to elaborate the arrival of Ivar ('a tyrant who from sheer love of cruelty had given orders for the massacre of the innocent') and Ubbe ('his associate in cruelty') in East Anglia and the hideous and horrible atrocities they carried out there. All of which is mere preamble to the real point of Abbo's story – the description of the gruesome and absurdly sadistic killing of King Edmund, drawn out in lingering, almost eroticized, prose. Edmund, stoic in his refusal to fight, was bound in chains, mocked, beaten and tied to a tree. He was lashed and tortured, 'but unceasingly called on Christ with broken voice'. Irritated by this, the Vikings 'as if practising at a target' discharged a forest of arrows into the hapless king until he resembled 'a prickly hedgehog' (*asper herecius*). Somehow, this was not enough to finish off the defiant Edmund, or even to silence him (his people may have wished that he had shown the same backbone on the battlefield). This was apparently the final straw for Ivar. Edmund, barely able to stand, 'his ribs laid bare by numberless gashes', prepared for the killing blow: 'while the words of prayer were still on his lips, the executioner, sword in hand, deprived the king of life, striking off his head with a single blow'.[34]

In the past, some historians have attempted to argue that Abbo's lurid descriptions are an essentially accurate illustration of a ritualized killing, a garbled retelling of the sacrificial rite of the blood-eagle. This is manifestly absurd. For one thing, the *Passio Sancti Eadmundi* should be judged precisely as it is titled. It is a *Passio* (a 'passion'), a story modelled on the Passion of Christ, a martyrdom story explicitly intended to elicit empathy and sympathy from its audience for its anguished protagonist – an overwrought exhortation for reader or listener to wallow in second-hand suffering, to facilitate mental excoriation in order that the audience can better comprehend the corporal self-sacrifice that God inexplicably demands from his most devout followers. It is also, of course, modelled explicitly on the sufferings of Christ and of St Sebastian, that other famous Christian pin-cushion. Abbo is not trying to fool us. 'In his agony', he patiently explains, Edmund resembled 'the illustrious martyr Sebastian'. To argue that the *Passio* is a description of an offering of royal blood to Odin, with Ivar officiating as fanatic pagan priest,[35] betrays a gross misunderstanding of the conventions of martyrological literature, as well as a failure properly to challenge the dubious provenance of the tale.

Other details more fundamentally undermine the *Passio*'s credibility. After the killing, Edmund's severed head was taken into the woods and thrown into a bramble patch. Dismayed, those loyal to the dead king resolved to find it and bring it back for burial alongside the rest of his remains (which, Abbo delights in reminding us, were 'bristling with grievous arrows, and lacerated to the very marrow by the acutest tortures'). However, not even decapitation could stop Edmund from babbling:

> The head of the holy king, far removed from the body to which it belonged, broke into utterance without assistance from the vocal chords, or aid from the arteries proceeding from the heart. A number of the party, like corpse-searchers, were gradually examining the out-of-the-way parts of the wood, and when the moment had arrived at which the sound of the voice could be heard, the head, in response to the calls of the search-party mutually encouraging one another, and as comrade to comrade crying alternately 'Where are you?' indicated the place where it lay by exclaiming in their native tongue, Here! Here! Here! In Latin the same meaning would be rendered by Hic! Hic! Hic! And the head never ceased to repeat this exclamation, till all were drawn to it. The chords of the dead man's tongue

vibrated within the passages of the jaws, thus displaying the miraculous power of Him who was born of the Word and endowed the braying ass with human speech.[36]

The search party duly discovered the garrulous head in the bushes, where it was being guarded by a monstrous wolf. 'Lifting up, therefore, with concordant devotion the pearl of inestimable price which they had discovered, and shedding floods of tears for joy, they brought back the head to its body.'[37] They were accompanied by the wolf, who – having seen the head safely entombed – wandered placidly back into the forest.

The *Passio* was, transparently, a carefully crafted piece of promotional literature – a puff piece for an ineffective king, elevated to sainthood on account of his death at the hands of an ungodly horde. The cult of St Edmund developed in East Anglia remarkably quickly after his death, but it was Abbo's writings that really got it off the ground. Shortly after it was written it was translated into Old English (in a mercifully abridged – and far more elegant – form) by the prolific writer and abbot of Cerne, Ælfric of Eynsham. With new-found interest beyond East Anglia, and a compelling myth with which to sell it, the cult grew during the latter half of the tenth century and into the eleventh. By the reign of Cnut, the shrine of the saint-king was receiving significant investment and royal patronage. Enthusiasm for the saintly Edmund continued beyond the Norman Conquest and grew throughout the Middle Ages: Edward I's younger brother (1245–96) was named after him, and St Edmund also appears on the Wilton diptych as a patron and guardian of the angel-faced Richard II (r. 1377–99), alongside John the Baptist and Edward the Confessor. Although his prominence declined after the adoption of St George as the patron of Edward III's Order of the Garter in 1348, Edmund's tomb-shrine ceased to be a major place of pilgrimage only when it was destroyed in 1539 during the reign of Henry VIII. Nevertheless, the town and the abbey which housed it still bear his name – Bury St Edmunds: the *burh* ('stronghold') of St Edmund.[38]

Edmund's story reminds us that the Christian Anglo-Saxons had their own notions of sacrifice, their own notion of the power of holy blood. And of course, like the Vikings, Christians had their own corpse-god, and their own spiritual mysteries to unravel. Like Odin, Christ had also hung upon a windy tree (in Old English, *treow*, 'tree', was a ubiquitous simile for 'cross'), pierced in the side by a spear. And, like Odin's auto-sacrifice, Christ's semi-permanent death on the cross was also – in its own confusing way – an offering of self to self: the sacrifice of a son by a father, both of whom were indivisible parts of a triple-faceted deity.[39] These similarities are unlikely to be coincidental. The story of Odin's sacrifice may well have been influenced by Christian theology (bearing in mind that all the written sources pertaining to the god date – in the form they survive – from the Christian era). Conversely, both stories, Christian and pagan, may have derived some of their content and their cultural capital from yet more ancient mythic stock. What is certain, however, is that the Vikings shared a range of fundamental religious, moral and supernatural ideas with the Christian Anglo-Saxons with whom they came into contact, not least concerning the transcendental value of self-sacrifice. They saw it in the stories of their god, and they also found it in the way that human beings met their own ends.

9

WAYLAND'S BONES

From hence he little Chawsey seeth, and hastneth for to see
Faire Reading towne, a place of name, where Cloths ywoven be.
This shewes our Aelfrids victorie, what time Begsceg was slaine
With other Danes, whose carcasses lay trampled on the plaine ...

WILLIAM CAMDEN, *Britannia* (1607)[1]

We are treading on heroes. It is sacred ground for Englishmen, more
sacred than all but one or two fields where their bones lie whitening.
For this is the actual place where our Alfred won his great battle, the
battle of Ashdown ('Æscendum' in the chroniclers), which broke the
Danish power and made England a Christian land.

THOMAS HUGHES, *Tom Brown's School Days* (1857)[2]

'Probe with bayonets,' Lenin is famously supposed to have
advised. 'If you encounter steel, withdraw. If you encounter
mush, continue.'[3] If the Vikings in England had a strategy in the
years that followed the death of King Edmund, this may have been
it. Northumbria and East Anglia had fallen, Mercia revealed as
decidedly soft. Only Wessex was yet to be properly tested, and the
micel here was preparing to thrust the bayonet.

In 870, a Viking army struck suddenly up the Thames valley and
seized the settlement known as Readingum (Reading) at the

confluence of the Thames and Kennet rivers. It was mid-winter, and Reading may have been a tempting target, a depot, perhaps, for provisions gathered against the season. Local resistance, however, did not collapse entirely. Soon after the Vikings had captured Reading, a Viking raiding party – presumably foraging for supplies – managed to fall foul of the Berkshire levy, led by their ealdorman, Æthelwulf. A Viking *jarl*, Sidroc, was killed in the fighting. The engagement was fought just west of Reading, at a place called Englafeld (somewhere near the small village of Englefield, Berkshire, about a mile south of the M4). It was, in all likelihood, a minor skirmish, fought between a provincial militia and a small band of raiders (who had probably expected little resistance from the terri-fied peasantry). Nevertheless, it was the first time – so far as we are aware – that the *micel here* had suffered any sort of reverse in England since its arrival in 866. It was the first time that the bayonet had struck anything like steel.

The Vikings withdrew to their foothold in Reading, and began to prepare for the inevitable West Saxon counter-offensive. They constructed a rampart to join the two rivers, creating a fortress assailable only from the west, and waited for the Anglo-Saxon army to arrive.[4]

The West Saxon king, Æthelred, and his brother, Alfred, had already had experience of facing a dug-in Viking army when they had failed to dislodge the force that had captured Nottingham in 868. This time, however, they were defending their own kingdom. Arriving at Reading, they once again decided to pursue the direct approach, 'hacking and cutting down all the Vikings whom they had found outside' until they reached the gates of the stronghold. The assault on Wessex might have turned out rather differently if the Vikings had trusted to their ramparts, sitting it out until the West Saxons had been forced – as at Nottingham – to cut some sort of deal. However, for whatever reason, the Vikings chose not to wait it out. Perhaps they did not have sufficient supplies to endure a siege (Æthelwulf's victory at Englefield may have undermined efforts to acquire adequate provisions) or perhaps the fortifications – which must have been constructed at speed – were insufficient to inspire any feelings of security. Whatever the reason, the Vikings, trapped and with no means of retreat, decided to go on the offensive: 'like wolves they burst out of all the gates and joined battle with all their might'.[5] Fighting was fierce, and 'a great slaughter was made on both sides',[6] but in the end, 'alas, the Christians eventually turned their backs, and the Vikings won the victory'.[7]

The battle at Reading, from a West Saxon perspective, was a fiasco. Ealdorman Æthelwulf, the hero of Englefield, died in the fighting, and the royal house had been defeated and humiliated. There were, however, three feeble rays of light that broke through the dark cloud that was now hanging over Wessex – though it is doubtful whether anyone could perceive them at the time. Firstly, the king and his brother had survived the debacle. Had they not, it is likely that the kingdom would have collapsed as quickly as East Anglia and Northumbria had. Secondly, Æthelwulf had proven that the Vikings of the *micel here* could be beaten, a reminder that West Saxon armies – as recently as the 850s – had punished Viking intruders in the past. Finally, the *micel here* was no longer quite so *micel* as it had been.

The juggernaut that had rolled over Northumbria, Mercia and East Anglia with such contemptuous ease in the 860s was now, almost certainly, beginning to fragment. It is likely that sizeable contingents remained in Northumbria and East Anglia to retain their grip over the local populations, even as their more entrepre-neurial comrades turned west – after all, supply lines needed to be established and maintained, ships guarded and provisions gathered, new recruits absorbed, equipment repaired, camps and fortifica-tions constructed. Although the written sources reveal very little of these processes, archaeology is beginning to provide enormous quantities of new data regarding the way in which these armies operated in England; nevertheless, we are still largely in the dark about the personnel and make-up of the army that invaded Wessex. It appears, however, that of the sons of Ragnar Loðbrók only Halfdan accompanied the army that advanced from Reading. He was one of two 'kings', along with another chieftain named Bacsecg, whom the English sources refer to by name.

None of this would have provided much comfort to King Æthelred as he led his beaten and demoralized army away from the confluence of the Kennet and the Thames. They travelled along the river, the Viking army in close pursuit, into the marshlands that sprawled along the river banks. The Anglo-Norman poet-chronicler Geoffrey Gaimar, writing in Norman French in the 1130s, provides considerable – if slightly confusing – detail about the direction of the West Saxon army's flight. According to Geoffrey, they went (somewhat counter-intuitively) east – away from the West Saxon heartlands. 'Æthelred and Alfred were driven back to Whistley [Wiscelet],' Gaimar explains, 'a ford in the direction of Windsor [Windesoures] across an expanse of water in a marsh. This is where one of the Danish armies turned back to, but they were not aware of the ford over the river here. The ford to which the Danes withdrew was Twyford [Thuiforde], as it has always been called, and this is how the English escaped, but not without suffering many casualties and mortalities.'[8]

It was deep winter. Forced to take the most difficult way, armoured men would have struggled through the sucking mud of frigid swollen bogs, their shields and weapons discarded as freezing mist and brackish water saturated woollen clothes and leather shoes. The weakest would have come quickly to grief – those who dropped behind, wounded or exhausted, left to drown in the mud or be speared like eels, wriggling in the shallows. For the battered survivors, although the northward crossing of the river would have meant a brief respite from the threat of imminent death, there would have been little opportunity to catch their breath. Only four days after the flight from Reading, Alfred and Æthelred would be forced to fight the Viking army again, at a place called Ashdown (Æscesdun).

The main source for the battle – and for Alfred's career in general – is the *Vita Ælfredi regis Angul Saxonum* (the 'Life of Alfred king of the Anglo-Saxons'), written by Asser, bishop of Sherborne, a

Welsh monk, originally from the community of St David's in Dyfed (Wales), who was invited to join the learned circle that surrounded King Alfred in the 880s. The life was written in 893, and shares much of its detail with the *Anglo-Saxon Chronicle*, the earliest version of which (the A recension, or 'Winchester Chronicle') was also written in the 890s in the court of King Alfred. They were, therefore, products of the same time and place and written under the patronage of the same individual: Alfred (King Alfred, as he was by the time they were written). We should then expect them to have been based on first-hand knowledge when dealing with events from Alfred's life, to be accurate and specific when making reference to named places, to share the same West Saxon biases and positive attitude towards their patron, and to agree on most fundamental details. In general these expectations are met. Both sources identify the location of the battle as a place called Ashdown. The fighting took place '*on Æscesdune*' according to the *Anglo-Saxon Chronicle* and Asser gives the same English name, adding helpfully, '*quod Latine "mons fraxini" interpretatur*' ('which in Latin means "hill of the ash-tree"'). The good bishop was in this, as in much else, exceptionally well informed.[9]

His description of the conflict itself is remarkable – the fullest contemporary description of an early medieval battle before 1066:

> the Vikings, splitting up into two divisions, organized shield-walls of equal size (for they then had two kings and a large number of earls), assigning the core of the army to the two kings and the rest to all the earls. When the Christians saw this, they too split up the army into two divisions in exactly the same way, and established shield-walls no less keenly. But as I have heard from truthful authorities who saw it, Alfred and his men reached the battlefield sooner and in better order: for his brother, King Æthelred, was still in his tent at prayer, hearing Mass and declaring firmly that he would not leave that place alive before the priest had finished Mass, and that he would not forsake divine service for that of men; and he did what he said.

The faith of the Christian king counted for much with the Lord, as shall be shown more clearly in what follows.

But Alfred could only wait so long, and eventually – while Æthelred 'was lingering still longer in prayer' – Alfred was forced to take matters into his own hands: 'acting courageously, like a wild boar, supported by divine counsel and strengthened by divine help, when he had closed up the shield-wall in proper order, he moved his army without delay against the enemy.'

The fighting took place around a 'small and solitary thorn-tree' (which Asser noted, 'I have seen for myself with my own eyes'):

> the opposing armies clashed violently, with loud shouting from all, one side acting wrongfully and the other side set to fight for life, loved ones and country. When both sides had been fighting to and fro, resolutely and exceedingly ferociously, for quite a long time, the Vikings (by divine judgement) were unable to withstand the Christian onslaught any longer; and when a great part of their forces had fallen, they took to ignominious flight. One of the two Viking kings and five earls were cut down in that place, and many thousands on the Viking side were slain there too – or rather, over the whole broad expanse of Ashdown, scattered everywhere, far and wide: so King Bacsecg was killed, and Earl Sidroc the Old, Earl Sidroc the Younger, Earl Osbern, Earl Fræna and Earl Harold; and the entire Viking army was put to flight, right on until nightfall and into the following day, until such time as they reached the stronghold from which they had come. The Christians followed them till nightfall, cutting them down on all sides.[10]

These were the first links to be forged in the armour of Alfred's formidable later reputation, and they were cunningly wrought. But despite the length and apparent detail of the account, Asser's narrative differs markedly from other key sources in one critical area – the role of the king.

Reading Asser's account, one would be forgiven for thinking that Æthelred did not show up for the fight at all, spending the whole battle mumbling his paternosters in pious ineffectitude. And yet the *Anglo-Saxon Chronicle* is clear: 'Æthelred fought against the kings' force, and there the king Bagsecg was killed.' Later historians of the twelfth century supplied even more detail. William of Malmesbury (d. 1143) gives the firm impression that it was Æthelred's late intervention that saved the day for the West Saxons. By downplaying Æthelred's military role, Asser was deliberately emphasizing Alfred's exceptional martial skill, fortitude and porcine courage at Æthelred's expense; he had, however, managed to do so while still emphasizing the former king's laudable piety – this, Asser asserts, was also key to victory ('it counted for much with the Lord'), by ensuring that Alfred was able to act with holy sanction, direction and support – a conduit for the stern judgement of the Lord on a pagan people. Getting this balance right was difficult, and politically sensitive.

By the time Asser was writing his account, in the 890s, Alfred had become king of Wessex. He had succeeded after Æthelred's death in 871, a few months after the battle of Ashdown. Alfred, like his brother, derived his claim on the West Saxon throne from his father – King Æthelwulf – reinforced by the important role he had played as right-hand man to his brother, King Æthelred. Alfred, therefore, had an interest in upholding the legitimacy of the West Saxon dynasty and the previous incumbents of its throne. So Asser was careful to stress King Æthelred's efficacious religiosity and the divine aura this conferred on the West Saxon crown. The 'solitary thorn-tree' around which the battle was fought was also probably intended to make the same point. Trees symbolized the cross in Anglo-Saxon thought, and the thorn tree – in providing the material from which Christ's mocking 'crown of thorns' was made – had particular significance; whether or not there really was such a tree at Ashdown, Asser's reference to it was clearly intended to double down on the idea that the appropriate divine powers had been invested in the battle.

Bothering God, however, was only part of the job description for an early medieval king, albeit an important part. Kings also needed, perhaps more than anything else, to be effective war-leaders: virile protectors of their lands, treasures and people. The subtext of Asser's narrative, therefore, carried a subtle but clear message: Æthelred may have had the ear of the Lord, but Alfred was his strong right arm; and that, ultimately, was what counted.

No one knows for certain where the battle of Ashdown was fought. It is known *roughly* where – somewhere on the high chalk uplands of the Berkshire downs – but the specific place is supposedly lost.[11]

Until the early twentieth century, it was generally believed that the battle was fought near a village called Ashbury, now in Oxfordshire but formerly in Berkshire (prior to the 1974 county boundary changes). An earthwork near the village was already known as 'Alfred's Castle' in 1738, and the association could conceivably be older.[12] The connection between this part of the downs and Alfred's battles against the Vikings was fixed in the imagination by a belief that the White Horse of Uffington, the massive equine figure carved into the chalk roughly 2 miles to the east of Ashbury, probably Iron Age, was originally fashioned as an Anglo-Saxon monument to victory.[13] Despite being utterly fallacious, this notion was popularized by Thomas Hughes in his wildly successful novel of 1857, *Tom Brown's School Days*. Hughes imagined that after his victory 'the pious king [Alfred, Æthelred having been quietly ejected from the story], that there might never be wanting a sign and a memorial to the countryside, carved out on the northern side of the chalk hill, under the camp, where it is almost precipitous, the great Saxon white horse which he who will may see from the railway, and which gives its name to the vale over which it has looked these thousand years and more'.[14]

You can still see the White Horse from the railway today, galloping along the southern rim of the vale that takes its name. Those who have frequently 'travelled down the Great Western Railway as far as Swindon' (as I have done and Thomas Hughes evidently also did) will, if they 'did so with their eyes open, have been aware, soon after leaving the Didcot station, of a fine range of chalk hills running parallel with the railway on the left-hand side as you go down and distant some two or three miles, more or less, from the line'.[15] The White Horse has galloped across those chalk hills since long before any Viking or Anglo-Saxon pondered its perplexing outline against the upland grasses.

Ashbury's fall from favour as the location of the battle of Ashdown is largely attributable to the work of the renowned place-name scholar Margaret Gelling and her demonstration that Æscesdun (Ashdown) could not convincingly be associated with any single place. She drew attention to the indisputable fact that, from at least the tenth century, the term 'Ashdown' was used to refer to the whole of the Berkshire downs.[16] This is highly unusual: as Gelling admitted, no other tree-hill compound place-name is used to describe such a wide area. Nonetheless, the evidence that the term was used in this way is entirely sound. However, it seems to me likely, in the context of descriptions of the battle of Ashdown, that Asser and the *Anglo-Saxon Chronicle* intended the place-name to have a specific geographical meaning.

One reason for this is that in no other instance does Asser or the anonymous Anglo-Saxon chronicler fail to identify with precision the location of a battle fought by Alfred. Moreover, on each occasion they associate Alfred's battles with royal estate-centres. There are many reasons why this might be so: for example, royal halls may well have served as muster-points and supply depots for West Saxon armies, and the practical exigencies of campaigning meant that battles were often fought at or close by them.[17] But Alfred's interest in promoting flattering accounts of his reign, alongside his promotion of literacy (it was, after all, no good commissioning biographies and chronicles if nobody could read), is suggestive of the king's concern with shaping his own legacy – a desire to propagate his legend through the work of Asser and the chronicler. It may be that, faced with a largely illiterate populace, Alfred's circle set about deliberately linking the king's most memorable achievements with well-known places – particularly those which already had royal associations. In that way, Alfred's legend could be insinuated into the very fabric of his kingdom, the list of place-names a mnemonic tally of his martial exploits, stitched into the landscape.

It should follow that if a *specific* place known as Æscesdun, particularly one known to have been in royal hands around the time of the battle, could be located within four days' march from Reading, it would have a sound prima facie claim to being close to the site of the famous battle. Judged against these criteria, Ashbury – the traditional location of the battle – has a compelling claim.

The village is referred to in a charter of 840 which describes the grant of land at Ashdown (Asshedoune) from King Æthelwulf (Alfred's and Æthelred's father) to a man named Duda. The charter is headed with the place-name 'Aysheburi' (Ashbury), implying that Ashbury was known to be the centre of an estate in which land at Ashdown was located.[18] Over a hundred years later, in 947, the West Saxon crown was again giving away land at Ashdown (Aysshedun); in this charter, land was given by King Eadred to a chap called Edric which this time included a manor '*quod nunc vocatur Aysshebury*' ('which is now called Ashbury'). This charter also contains an Old English boundary clause, which described the perimeter of the parish of Ashbury, or at least its western half.[19] Taken together, these two documents tell us that, when used in a legal sense, the term Ashdown was understood to refer to a specific area of the Berkshire countryside surrounding the manor of Ashbury (which later gave its name to the modern parish); and that Ashbury was an estate in West Saxon royal ownership by 840, and remained so until 947 when the manor was transferred to a nobleman called Edric. Given their knowledge of West Saxon toponomy, tendency towards specificity, and interest in crafting Alfred's legend in explicable, geographical terms, it seems more than likely that, when Alfred's writers used the term Ashdown, it was Ashbury in particular that they meant.

A ninth-century gravestone from the monastery at Lindisfarne depicts the onslaught of armed men

The late-tenth-century Gjermundbu helmet, the only complete Viking Age helmet ever found in Scandinavia

A lead weight, adapted from a piece of ecclesiastical metalwork

0   5 cm

The Inchmarnock 'hostage stone'; a graffito that appears to depict a slave-raid in progress

The reconstructed Viking Age long-house at Borg, Lofoten (Norway)

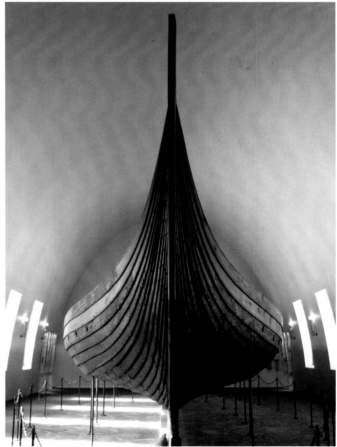

The Gokstad Ship, built *c*.890, now housed in Oslo

Opposite: This image, from a twelfth-century life of St Edmund, depicts Ivar and Ubbe setting sail for England

The Coppergate Helmet, a Northumbrian helmet forged between 750 and 775

Sigurd pierces the body of the dragon Fáfnir from beneath on a runestone from Ramsund, Södermanland (Sweden)

Wayland's Smithy in *c.*1900, before restoration of the barrow took place in the 1960s

When the Somerset levels flood, the early medieval landscape is briefly restored. The village of East Lyng is to the left, attached to the Isle of Athelney, the strip of green extending diagonally up and right from the centre of the photograph

Opposite: A reconstruction of the Viking camp at Repton

An Anglo-Saxon font, carved in the ninth century, at Deerhurst in Gloucestershire

The early medieval crypt of St Wystan's Church at Repton

A reconstruction of the Viking camp at Torksey

COMPOST
CREATIVE

Early medieval battle-sites frequently have a number of other characteristics in common. Established meeting places are one, and Ashbury is close to the meeting place of the defunct Hildeslaw hundred.[20] Proximity to major roads is another, and many battles were fought along the Wessex Ridgeway that passes to the south-east of the village.[21] But the most evocative feature of the places where men came to fight and die in early medieval Britain, in Wessex at any rate, was the presence of prehistoric monuments. Alfred's Castle, the Bronze Age univallate hill-fort that lies to the north-west of the Ridgeway, has been mentioned already. But there are other, older monuments in this landscape, and one in particular – brooding on the high chalk – that would have worked a dark spell on the West Saxon imagination.

My wife and I came to Ashbury in late afternoon, the sun already beginning to signal its long retreat. We sat for a few minutes in our defiantly out-of-place Nissan Micra, eating cheese rolls and sipping coffee. If you were to ask Google about Ashbury, you would be presented with images of the quintessential English village: the Christmas-card-perfect Norman church, sixteenth-century public house and half-timbered buildings, thatched cottages surrounding the village green. It is the sort of place where it's all too easy to imagine John Nettles bimbling about, investigating the death of a parson in the vicarage potting shed. English rural settlements aren't really like that, of course, not entirely – except, perhaps, here and there in the swamp of affluence that pools along the Thames valley corridor, from Richmond in the east to Cirencester in the west. In this attractive stripe of southern Britain, the combination of influential Tory constituencies, a convenient commuter route to Paddington, coachloads of Japanese tourists and a surfeit of substantial pensions combine to provide the conditions and incentives that make places like Witney and Bibury so improbably manicured and photogenic. Most English villages, however, away from their village greens, are not so neat and tidy: plastic bus shelters with their small rusty waste-bins and resolutely brutalist lamp-posts, rusting corrugated-iron lean-tos and discarded tarpaulins, unlovely post-war architecture spilling into the surrounding countryside – most villages and small towns in the UK boast their own tatty hinterlands, miniature frontiers where human habitation gives out untidily into the woods and farmland beyond. It's always been that way, the lived-in contingency that blurs the boundaries between private, public and wild space.

The lay-by where we sat with our Thermos was at the edge of the village: a yellow grit silo, a bollard, gardens and concrete houses stuttering out into farmland. We got out of the car and began to walk, up a footpath towards the east, climbing the chalk ridge. I can't remember what we were arguing about – we were both tired; a misunderstanding about a buzzard I think, or something to do with sheep ... maybe both. I know that I broke my umbrella in a fit of pique – the spike was stuck in the earth when I kicked it, and it bent beyond repair. I had to carry the useless thing around with me for the next hour as a badge of shame. It was forgotten though, when we got to the top of the chalk and started along the Ridgeway. The afternoon was beginning to thicken. Darkness was a way off yet, but the atmosphere was changing, deepening; the shadows between the trees were blacker, distances subtly distorted. We arrived at the monument suddenly, and silence fell like a heavy shutter; the dark bulk of the orthostats caught the low oblique sunlight that spilled in ribbons through the beech trees. A mist was rising in the valley behind us.

The Neolithic chambered tomb, constructed around 5,500 years ago, wouldn't have looked to Alfred as it appears to us now. Its modern arrangement is a restoration of something approximating its original (or, rather, final) appearance. The four huge sarsen stones that dominate the southern end of the long-barrow were set upright after excavations carried out in the early 1960s by the archaeologists Stuart Piggott and Richard Atkinson; there were originally six of them, silent guardians flanking the dark burrow of an entrance – a portal, unmistakably, to another world.[22] Photographs taken in the early twentieth century show the monument as it looked before any restoration had taken place: a tumble of overgrown stones, wilder and weirder – if a little less grandiose – than it appears now. This, or something close to it, would have been how the people of early medieval Britain encountered the monument.[23] What the Romano-British called it, we do not know. Speakers of English, however, had called it *welandes smiððan* – Wayland's Smithy – from the middle of the tenth century, and probably long before.[24]

The association between this tomb and the work of a legendary smith endured for a staggeringly long time. In an eccentric letter of 1738 to one Dr Mead, Francis Wise, keeper of the Oxford University archives, repeated the legend of Wayland's Smithy that he had heard from 'the country people': 'At this place lived formerly an invisible Smith, and if a traveller's Horse had lost a Shoe upon the road, he had no more to do than to bring the Horse to this place with a piece of money, and leaving both there for some little time, he might come again and find the money gone, but the Horse new shod.'[25] If Wise's account does genuinely preserve a folk tradition attached to the long-barrow (rather than a flight of Francis' admittedly over-stimulated imagination), it would suggest that stories of Wayland had continued to circulate in the Berkshire hills for at least eight centuries.[26]

Alfred knew who Wayland was. In the Old English translation of Boethius' *De consolatione philosophiae* – usually attributed to Alfred's court, and perhaps to Alfred himself – the phrase '*Ubi nunc fidelis ossa Fabricii manent?*' ('Where now lie the bones of faithful Fabricius?') is translated as '*Hwaet synt nu þæs foremeran* ['and'] *þæs wisan goldsmiðes ban Welondes?*' ('Where now are the bones of the wise and famous goldsmith Weland [Wayland]?').[27] They weren't in Ashbury, that's for sure, although archaeologists did find plenty of bones in the barrow when they excavated it.[28] But the Anglo-Saxons hadn't called it *welandes beorg* or *welandes hlæwe* (Wayland's Barrow) – they had called it a smithy, and such – in their imaginations – it presumably was, the workshop of a craftsman both famous and wise: 'Wise, I said, because the craftsman can never lose his craft nor can it be taken easily from him – no more than the sun may be shifted from its place. Where are the bones of Weland now, or who knows now where they were?'

It is interesting that the Boethius translator should pause and digress on the value of craft at this point in *De consolatione*. The passage into which Wayland was inserted is a meditation on the transience of mortal life and the futility of earthly fame in the face of death and the passing of generations – topics which, as we have seen, appear to have weighed heavily on the Anglo-Saxon imagination. But Alfred seems also to have been uncommonly fixated by his own legacy, with crafting a kingdom that would outlive him. Indeed, the word 'craft' (OE *cræft*) has been recognized as one of the most important in Alfredian literature, invested with connotations not merely of skill but also of virtue, and other works attributed to Alfred are replete with the imagery of construction and labour: his version of St Augustine's soliloquies, for example, frames the gathering of knowledge as a great building project, detailing the collection of timbers and materials to construct a new and better world and the skill involved in their assembly.[29] The metaphor was matched in the physical construction of towns and ships that would occupy his later reign and those of his children and grandchildren. Alfred, in other words, seems to have been determined to challenge – through craft, fame and wisdom – the fatalistic pessimism of Boethius.

Wayland, however – the craftsman whose skill was as everlasting as the sun – was an uncomfortable avatar to invoke. Old English poetry makes a few references to him. *Beowulf* refers approvingly to a Wayland-forged mail-shirt, and the poem *Deor* – one of the oldest in the canon – gives voice to the tale of Wayland in a highly abridged and allusive, but relatively complete, form.[30] The most complete account of the myth, however, is found in Old Norse verse – a poem called *Völundarkvida* ('the song of Völund [Wayland]') – demonstrating that Wayland was an entity whose tale, like so much else, was shared across the North Sea. It is a thoroughly unpleasant story, which culminates in the eponymous hero – who had been captured and hamstrung by the wicked King Nídud (OE Nithhad) – raping and impregnating the king's daughter, murdering his sons, fashioning cups from their skulls, jewels from their eyes and brooches from their teeth (which he presents to their oblivious parents), and then escaping on the wing like some vengeful Nordic Daedalus. At least one scene from the legend decorates the Frankish casket: a bearded figure holds out a cup he has forged, a mysterious object gripped in a pair of tongs in his other hand. Below the work-bench a headless body lies. As *Völundarkvida* has Wayland explain to the horrified Nídud:

'Go to the smithy that you set up:
there you'll find bellows spattered with blood;
I cut off the heads of those small cubs,
and in the mud beneath the anvil I laid their limbs.'[31]

This is not the workshop of the benevolent, elvish tinker imagined by the folk of eighteenth-century Berkshire. Perhaps it was the sight of Neolithic bones protruding from the earth that suggested to the Anglo-Saxon mind the association of the long-barrow with Wayland. It was a dark place, a bloody place – sown with corpses, seeded with bones.

The story of Wayland hints at a tension in the Anglo-Saxon psyche. It reminds us that while Asser paints the Viking wars as a binary struggle between godless heathen and the Christian warriors of Wessex, older and darker things yet lurked in the Anglo-Saxon mind – skeletons in the closet. Alfred and his circle wanted to leave the impression that they were building a new world, a world of craft and learning and Christian enlightenment. But somewhere, down in the mud beneath the anvil, down among the roots of Alfred's new England, the bones of Wayland still lay – a pagan past that the English had never properly come to terms with: a past with its roots in the old North, in stories of rape and mutilation, transmutation and supernatural flight, of vengeance and violence.

The archaeologist Neil Price has suggested that the Anglo-Saxons reacted in such a visceral way to the heathen Vikings appearing suddenly in their midst not only because of their violence and their paganism, but also because of a dreadful familiarity – a familiarity born of an ancient kinship and a shared web of stories and ways of seeing:

> The Anglo-Saxons [...] knew that this Viking world-view was not so far removed from what theirs had been not so long before, and maybe, under the surface, still was [...] The Vikings were not only conventionally terrifying, they were a dark mirror held up to the image of what the English needed to believe themselves to be.[32]

The Anglo-Saxons, looking into that mirror, saw things that they preferred not to confront – felt as though they stood unsteadily on the brink of the howling abyss of pagan savagery from which they had lately hauled themselves. The Vikings were, therefore, in Freudian terms, *unheimlich* ('uncanny'). They were that which 'ought to have remained secret and hidden but has come to light', a manifestation of 'something which is familiar and old established in the mind and which has become alienated from it'.[33] Freud's concept of the *unheimlich* has been productively employed to explain the potency in supernatural horror of the dislocation of the familiar and the mundane – the chair that moves in the empty room, the child that begins speaking in tongues ... It has also been invoked to explain the frisson of archaeology, the uncovering of that which should remain hidden. The frequent recourse to archaeological themes by the writers of weird literature – M. R. James, H. P. Lovecraft, Robert E. Howard, Clark Ashton Smith, Arthur Machen, Algernon Blackwood – stands testament to the thrill and horror of uncovering unspeakable hidden knowledge, places and things. But, for the Anglo-Saxons, the 'uncanny' had a horrible and malevolent reality, marauding across the countryside with axe and flame. The lost English homeland – 'emptied of its people', as Bede had believed, at the time of the fabled Anglo-Saxon migrations – had shown itself to be far from depleted. This lost world, romanticized in fireside tales where the monsters were remote and the heathen gods glossed with Christian ethics, was spewing forth a revenant nation, reaching out a rotting hand to drag the English screaming back into the mire.

The Anglo-Saxons may have thought they had escaped their past. But now their sundered kinsmen, their gods and their beliefs were rising up out of the darkness, borne on black tides from a world beyond the pale.

Ashdown may have been a major victory for the West Saxons, but it was hardly a decisive one – the exception rather than the rule. Probably this is why Asser made such a big deal of it: the years that followed marked a pretty desperate start to Alfred's reign as king.

In 871, Æthelred and Alfred fought the Viking army at Basengum (probably Old Basing in Hampshire). They were defeated. Later in the year they fought again at the unidentified Meretun; despite putting up a stiff fight, they were defeated again with serious casualties (including Heahmund, bishop of Sherborne). After Æthelred's death later that year, Alfred fought the Vikings again at Wilton (Wiltshire). The Vikings, once again, 'had possession of the place of slaughter'.[34] Exhausted by the fighting (the *Anglo-Saxon Chronicle* notes that there had been nine *folcgefeoht* – literally, 'folk-fights', probably battles involving shire levies from across Wessex, rather than single local militias – as well as innumerable raids and skirmishes), and presumably demoralized by the succession of losses, the West Saxons agreed terms in 871. The Viking army, led by Halfdan, retreated – first to Reading and then to London.[35]

Once again, the Vikings had been bought off by their victims.

10

REAL MEN

A Geat woman too sang out in grief;
with hair bound up, she unburdened herself
of her worst fears, a wild litany
of nightmare and lament: her nation invaded,
enemies on the rampage, bodies in piles,
slavery and abasement. Heaven swallowed the smoke.

Beowulf

The sun is low, striking sharply against the earthen furrows, deepening them to chasms of peaty black between golden brown ribs of soil. The oxen have stopped at the edge of the water meadow; they stare listlessly ahead, snorting white clouds of spectral vapour into the frigid air. Steam rises from their great ruddy backs. The man stands by the plough, ready to move the animals and reharness them, ready for the return journey back up the next strip of land, back towards the village and a welcome fire. It is winter, and the river has flooded the water meadow, waterlogging it, leaving no trace of the rampaging cowslip and cranesbill that will saturate the field with colour in the spring. Now the silver water lies pale under skeleton trees, their roots breaking the surface like tentacles. Alder and goat-willow screen the water. Later in the winter the villagers will cut

144

withies for poles and baskets, but for now the willow pollards march beside the river with their misshapen bodies and wild upright hair: a throng of trolls mustering on the river bank. Beyond them the sun is raising the ghost of a fog. There is a sudden plop, perhaps an otter taking to the water, then a sudden rush of wings – a thrush startled into flight, the clumsy crash of a wood pigeon. There is something out there, a presence on the river. The man squints, trying to squeeze his vision between the withies, into the silver twilight between the trees. He sees nothing, just the gathering mist, but a sound comes. A gentle swish of oars and, buried in it, a low pulse like a muffled heartbeat. He can feel sweat beginning to bead at the back of his head, prickling on his top lip, like insects crawling at the roots of his hair. Something is coming – something big – real and tangible, gliding into the November sunlight: sightless eye, immobile jaws gaping, a monster of oak carving through the land. And then it is gone, back into the mist.

The image of the Viking ship in full sail on the open sea, emerging blackly on the wide horizon, is a reasonably familiar one. Less commonly pictured in the mind's eye is the glimpse of the carved bestial prow glimpsed through the trees on a quiet river bank. Yet it was the exploitation of England's river routes – made possible by their light and shallow-draughted ships – that provided Viking armies with a means of swift and efficient movement through Britain's interior that vastly increased the range of their attacks and the extent to which they were able to destabilize Anglo-Saxon kingdoms in the second half of the ninth century.

There are few places in Britain that are further from the sea than Repton in Derbyshire, a quiet, pretty village of smart Georgian and Victorian houses and shopfronts, running in a ribbon of red brick away from the southern bank of the River Trent. Repton is further now from the river than it was a thousand years ago when it lay at the heart of the kingdom of Mercia, but the Trent is still capable of flexing its muscles in the faces of the villagers. In 2012, flood waters swamped the fields that fill the plain to the north of the village, between the river's old bed and its new route skirting the southern edge of neighbouring Willington. A wide band of English countryside, almost three-quarters of a mile across in places, was transformed into a gloomy dystopian landscape, spindly bare trees and bedraggled hedgerows standing proud of the brown and brackish water, watched over by bleak concrete ramparts – the monstrous cooling towers of Willington power station.

The rising water stopped mercifully short of Repton itself; although the sports fields of Repton School were submerged, the swollen river's creep was checked at the perimeter of St Wystan's churchyard by the banks of the stream – the Old Trent Water – that still follows the ninth-century course of the river. When Repton Abbey was founded as a double-monastery (a monastery with a twin community of monks and nuns) in the seventh century, the rising ground to the south had probably ensured that the community was safe from all but the most extreme flooding, despite the river running perilously close. It was here that a young, bellicose nobleman called Guthlac had come to take monastic vows in the late seventh century, before embarking on a new career as a spiritually obstinate, demon-defying fenland hermit. It was evidently a secure and amenable environment, allowing the monastery to become the recipient of considerable investment in subsequent centuries. The Church of St Wystan as it appears today is mostly the product of the thirteenth and fourteenth centuries, but hidden beneath the high medieval gothic spires can be still be found the crypt of the Mercian church, built in the early eighth century.

It is quite extraordinary, the physicality of the atmosphere in this small and dingy subterranean cube. John Betjeman described the space as 'holy air encased in stone', a turn of phrase which perfectly encapsulates the curious sense of *substance* that one encounters on descending into the gloom, the shadowed vault supported on four candy-twist columns, like rustic Tudor chimney pots. It is a place rank with religion, the air thickened by the ineffable weight of antiquity and prayer, as though something has been trapped down here, entombed for centuries. This aura is compounded, perhaps conjured, by the knowledge that this crypt served as – may indeed have been built for – the bones of Mercian kings. The first of these (and the one for whom it may have been constructed) was King Æthelbald, who was interred in the crypt in 757. His bones were later joined by those of King Wiglaf (died *c*. 839) and Wiglaf's grandson Wystan who, though he declined to take the crown in favour of a religious life, was nevertheless done in by his relations in 849.

As John of Worcester reported it, Wystan – or St Wystan as he became in death – 'was carried to a monastery which was famous in that age called Repton, and buried in the tomb of his grandfather king Wiglaf. Miracles from heaven were not wanting in testimony of his martyrdom; for a column of light shot up to heaven from the spot where the innocent saint was murdered, and remained visible to the inhabitants of that place for thirty days.'[1]

Twenty-four years later, the men and women living in the precincts of the church that still bears his name may well have wished that Wystan's left-over parts could have produced some new and impressive miracle – preferably, this time, something with a more practical application. For the river had finally proved a risk to the religious community and the relics of the saints and kings it curated; in the winter of 873/4, however, it was not the water that threatened to sweep Repton away, but the deadly flotsam that it bore.

When the Vikings left Wessex in 872 after making terms with Alfred, they first found their way to London where, the *Anglo-Saxon Chronicle* recounts, the Mercians 'made peace with them'.[2] The Viking army spent another winter there before moving on, travelling to Lindsey (a region within what is now Lincolnshire) in 873 and establishing a new camp at Torksey, 10 miles north-west of

Lincoln. The Mercians, once again, 'made peace'.[3] If the Viking bayonet was probing for steel, it was finding little of it. When spring came, the *micel here* was on the move again. From Torksey the River Trent offered an inviting artery that led straight to the heart of the Mercian kingdom. The sources tell us very little – even by their own stingy standards – but the impression given is of a swift and surgical intervention that brought the once glorious kingdom to its knees at a single stroke: 'the horde went from Lindsey to Repton and took winter-quarters there, and drove King Burhred across the sea [...] and occupied that land'.[4]

In the *Anglo-Saxon Chronicle*, Burhred comes across as a hapless king: thrice he had come to terms with the Viking great army (in 868, 871 and 872), only to find himself ejected from his kingdom, and his people subjugated with humiliating ease (he died in Rome, and was buried at St Mary's Church in the city's English Quarter).[5] The contrast with the way that Viking progress in Wessex was described should be obvious: there the Viking army is depicted as encountering resistance at every step, suffering defeats at Englefield and Ashdown and grinding out hard-won victories elsewhere (although we should remember that Alfred had also, in 871, paid the Vikings to go away).

It is tempting to read the sources at face value, and to see the West Saxons as the defiant epitome of the bulldog mentality, a striking contrast to the flaccid appeasement practised by the Mercians: Alfred playing Churchill to Burhred's Chamberlain. To do so, however, is to be corralled by channels of thought dug by Alfred's own propagandists. There is simply no way of knowing how hard the Mercians fought to preserve their kingdom and eject the Viking menace. As we shall see, at least one Viking warrior came to grief on Mercian soil.

The subtle disparagement of their Mercian neighbours that we can perceive in the West Saxon sources served Alfred's political ends. By the latter part of his reign, when these documents were compiled, Alfred was increasingly concerned with claiming a hegemony than extended far beyond Wessex. His own military reputation (which was patchy at best before the late 870s) was bolstered by having his contemporary monarchs painted as battle-shirking weaklings. More importantly, by painting the last independent kings of Mercia as weak, ineffective and lacking credibility, the claims of Alfred and those of his offspring to rule in Mercia appeared more legitimate than they otherwise might have done.

At some point, not long after Repton was taken under new management, a ditch and rampart were dug, closing off an area to the north of the church and forming a D-shape against the river bank – a space providing unimpeded access for ships to moor but offering landward protection, the direction from which danger was most likely to arrive. The church building itself was incorporated into the defensive circuit, a masonry gate-house through which access could be controlled. Instead of Mercian royalty, monks and devout pilgrims, Viking warriors now breathed the holy air of St Wystan's crypt. At around the same time, the first of a number of graves were dug around the church, many of them decidedly unconventional for ninth-century Mercia.[6] One man was buried with a gold ring on his finger and five silver pennies, all of which can be dated to the mid-870s; his grave, which lay adjacent to the church wall, was cut through a layer of burnt stone and charcoal – an indication that the church had been severely damaged, broken rubble and burnt timber strewn where they had fallen after the upper parts of the building had burned. As at Portmahomack, a monolithic stone cross was shattered and discarded, its fragments buried in a pit to the east of the chancel.

The most famous of these burials is Grave 511. Like several others, the man in this grave was buried with weapons – in this case a sword and knife. He had died, it would appear, unpleasantly. Following a blow to the head, he had suffered a deep cut to the left femur where it connected to the pelvis – probably from a sword or axe. The blow was administered when the victim was already on the ground, and it would have severed the femoral artery resulting in massive blood loss; it would also have deprived him of the soft parts that had once dangled between his legs. In an apparent attempt to compensate for this loss, those who buried him placed the tusk of a boar in the appropriate position. And, if any doubt were to remain about the cultural affiliations of the deceased, this man had been laid in the grave with, among other objects and pieces of metal-work, the hammer of Thor about his neck.

Odin and Thor were the most popular and powerful gods of the Norse pantheon, but in many ways they were diametrically opposed to each other in character. Where Odin was subtle and sinister, the patron of poets, sorcerers and kings, Thor presented a less compli-cated personality. He was a proponent of what we might call the direct approach – more action, fewer words; less brain, more fist. He is often (as we see him in the stories that survive of him) a bit of an oaf. Most of these tales features the god smashing things up, shouting, getting drunk, breaking things and hitting people. He is a 'mannish' god – a god of farmers, fishermen and fighters (as the runologist R. I. Page put it, 'the everyday Viking […] the man-in-the-fiord').[7] He is precisely the sort of god we would expect to feel particularly embarrassed about a misplaced member, and whose devotees might have felt the need to make showy compensation for their comrade's missing man-parts.

In the *Prose Edda*, a medieval primer on Norse mythology and one of the most valuable sources for pre-Christian belief in Scandinavia, Snorri provides a potted outline of the god's key attributes:

Thor […] is the strongest of all gods and men […] [He] has two male goats called Tannigost [Tooth Gnasher] and Tannigrisnir [Snarl Tooth]. He also owns the chariot that they draw, and for this reason he is called Thor the Charioteer. He […] has three choice possessions. One is the hammer Mjollnir. Frost giants and mountain giants recognize it when it is raised in the air, which is not surprising as it has cracked many a skull among their fathers and kinsmen. His second great treasure is his Megingjard [Belt of Strength]. When he buckles it on, his divine strength doubles. His third possession, the gloves of iron, are also a great treasure. He cannot be without these when he grips the hammer's shaft.[8]

The story that best sums up Thor's character is recounted in the eddic poem *Þrymskviða* ('the Song of Thrym'). Unlike the dark and difficult texts with which it was compiled in the Codex Regius (poems, for example, like *Völuspá* and *Grímnismál*), *Þrymskviða* is a fairly light-hearted romp. Nevertheless, like all good satire, it gets to the heart of the matter (in this case Thor's character) with pointed efficiency. It runs thus: Thor woke up one morning to find his magical hammer, Mjölnir, missing. Loki, the trickster god, was deputed to find out where it was and flew to the hall of the giant, Thrym. Thrym admitted to having stolen it and claimed to have hidden it 'eight leagues under the earth', adding that 'No one shall have it back again unless he brings me Freyja as bride.'[9] On receiving this news, Thor was keen to take the giant up on the bargain ('these were the first words he found to say: "Freyja, put on your bridal veil"'). Freyja, unsurprisingly, was less enthusiastic ('Freyja was enraged, and gave a snort, so that the gods' hall trembled, and the great Brísings' neck-ring tumbled: "You'd think I'd become the maddest for men if I drove with you to Giants' Domain [Jötunheimr]"').
 Eventually, the god Heimdall came up with a cunning plan:

'Let us put Thor in the bridal veil,
let him wear the great Brísings' neck-ring!

Let us have keys jangling beneath him,
And women's clothes falling round his knees,
and broad gem-stones sitting on his chest,
let us top out his head with style.'

Then Thor spoke, the strapping god:
'The gods will call me a cock-craver,
if I let myself be put in a bridal veil.'[10]

Thor's protests notwithstanding, Heimdall's scheme was put into action. Thrym, evidently not the brightest of characters, was easily bamboozled by the cunning disguise; nevertheless, his suspicions were eventually aroused by his bride-to-be's table habits: 'Freyja' (Thor) packed away a whole ox, eight salmon, all the food laid out for the women and three casks of mead. Loki (in the guise of a maidservant) was forced to claim that the false bride had not eaten for eight days because of her excitement at the approaching nuptials (Loki, unlike Thor, apparently had no qualms about cross-dressing). Finally the moment of the wedding ceremony arrived, and Thrym called for the hammer Mjölnir to be brought forth to hallow the union. Thor needed no more encouragement than this: his heart 'laughed in his chest' as he grasped the hammer and set about venting his anger and humiliation:

Thrym, lord of ogres, was the first one he felled,
before battering all of the giant-race.[11]

Þrymskviða is a tale that, at least in its received form, postdates the Viking Age – possibly by some margin (the manuscript in which it is found – the Codex Regius – was compiled in the latter part of the thirteenth century). The poem may have been intended to parody the absurdities of past beliefs; perhaps transforming the mighty Thor into a berserk Widow Twanky was one way to tame the unsettling residue of a none-too-distant pagan heritage.[12] Nevertheless, several themes in the poem resonate with much of what else we know or is implied about Viking attitudes to sexuality and Thor's place in the pantheon.

The term which Andy Orchard, regius Professor of Anglo-Saxon at Oxford University, provocatively translated as 'cock-craver' is the Old Norse word argr, which is normally (and euphemistically) rendered as 'unmanly'.[13] In reality, *argr* (and its cognate form *ragr*) was an insult which, when directed at both men and women, implied some sort of unusual enthusiasm for being penetrated. When directed at a woman, therefore, it suggested promiscuity; when directed at a man it ascribed a passive homosexuality. It was a particularly rude charge to level at one's (male) counterparts, and to insult someone in these terms could constitute a potentially lethal slight. The earliest Icelandic law codes are clear that no intervention or recompense could be expected if those bandying unsubstantiated slanders came to violent grief as a result of their impertinences.

The Norwegian Gulathing law was specific about what constituted the worst sorts of insult:

Concerning terms of abuse or insult. There are words which are considered terms of abuse. Item one: if a man say of another man that he has borne a child. Item two: if a man say of another man that he has been homosexually used [*sannsorðenn*]. Item three: if a man compare another man to a mare, or call him a bitch or a harlot, or compare him to any animal which bears young.[14]

This, however, wasn't a moral abhorrence of homosexuality in the sense that the Christian Church would later seek to formulate it, and the law codes and sagas – all of which date to the post-conversion epoch – have to be read carefully in this light. What, instead, the Vikings seemed to find upsetting was the feminized role of the *ragr-mann* (gently translated: 'unmanly-man'). Indeed, using men for sex – particularly in a punitive way – seems to have incurred no moral judgement. To bugger one's enemies was a manly way to humiliate a vanquished foe: the latter, by contrast, would then be considered *argr/ragr*, *rassragr* ('arse-*argr*'), *stroðinn* or *sorðinn* ('sodomized') or *sansorðinn* ('demonstrably sodomized').[15]

The problem, it seems, was not so much being gay as being thought to be 'unmanly' in some way. Indeed, other typically female behaviour could also attract accusations of *ergi* (unmanliness), suggesting that it was the adoption of inappropriate gender roles that Vikings objected to, rather than homosexual liaisons per se.[16] Even the gods could be susceptible to these imputations – Loki, in the most extreme example, gave birth to Odin's eight-legged horse Sleipnir after an intimate moment with the frost-giant's stallion Svaðilfari ('Unlucky Traveller'); Loki was in the guise of a mare at the time. Odin too, though more indirectly, was labelled *argr* because he practised a form of sorcery – *seiðr* – that was explicitly considered the preserve of women. As Loki pointed out:

> 'It's said you played the witch on Sámsey,
> beat the drum like a lady-prophet;
> in the guise of a wizard you wandered the world:
> that signals to me a cock-craver.'[17]

This, however, is a very specific image of effeminacy, and one to which we shall return. The picture it conjures (Loki's crude insult aside) is an indefinably eerie one – another thread in the weft of Odin's surpassing weirdness.

It is this fear of effeminacy (or, rather, the fear of being seen as effeminate) that Thor expresses in *Þrymskviða*. In the end, he is forced to erase the threat to his manhood in the only way a deity with limited subtlety of mind could manage: by beating all and sundry to a pulp. This image of Thor fits easily into our conception of this god of warriors and working men, an unreconstructed he-man who responded to danger, irritation and humiliation with brute force – problem-solving with a hammer. Certainly, the cult of Thor seems to have become extremely popular in the late Viking Age. By the time Adam of Bremen was describing the temple at Uppsala, Thor was regarded – from a Christian perspective anyway – as the major deity. Hundreds of Thor's-hammer pendants and rings (from which small hammers and other amulets were suspended) have been found throughout the Viking world, from Iceland and Ireland to Poland and Russia – many, though by no means all, in graves.[18]

And yet, despite all this, when we start to probe the details of the cult of Thor a surprisingly complex picture begins to emerge. For one thing, the vast majority of individual Thor's-hammer pendants found in graves (as opposed to the rings and the disassociated finds) are found in the graves of women.[19] This fact alone is enough to suggest that there was more to the invocation of the god than the doom-brained muscle-cult we may have been led to expect by sources like Þrymskviða. Moreover, runic inscriptions invoking Thor's blessing of monuments implies that his role could be imagined as a broader responsibility to preserve and protect those things that people held valuable.[20] His hammer could even (if Þrymskviða can be trusted) be used symbolically to seal a marriage ceremony.[21]

Grave 511 at Repton, with its Thor's-hammer pendant, is therefore a reminder of the heathenism of the Vikings who comprised the *micel here*, and allows us to begin to imagine the social mores and attitudes of the people who found themselves here in the winter of 873/4. But the presence of the boar's tusk and the humerus of a jackdaw among the grave goods suggests that, woven into the machismo of the Viking way of life, were ideas and attitudes that remain alien to us, and whose significance is irrevocably lost. The part of the Repton excavations that makes this latter point most dramatically, however, is another grave – this time a mass grave – that remains as strange, unique and compelling as it was when it was first broken open in 1686. In an account given to the antiquarian researcher Dr Simon Degge in 1727, a man called Thomas Walker described how he had dug into a large mound that stood west of St Wystan's Church:

About Forty Years since cutting Hillocks, near the Surface he met with an old Stone Wall, when clearing farther he found it to be a square Enclosure of Fifteen Foot: It had been covered, but the Top was decayed and fallen in, being only supported by wooden Joyces. In this he found a Stone Coffin, and with Difficulty removing the Cover, saw a *Skeleton* of a *Humane Body Nine Foot* long, and round it lay *One Hundred* Humane Skeletons, with their feet pointing to the Stone Coffin. They seem'd to be of the ordinary Size.[22]

Walker went on to confess that 'The Head of the great Skeleton he gave to Mr. Bowers, Master of the Free-school.' Dr Degge made further enquiries with the son of the aforementioned Mr Bowers, who said at the time that 'he remembers the Skull in his Father's Closet, and that he had often heard his Father mention this Gigantic Corps ...'[23]

Wonderful as this all is, we would be right to be sceptical, and a later generation of fascinated antiquarians were determined to prove the case one way or another. Excavations in 1789 and 1914 followed, the former – despite finding the Gigantic Corps absent – confirmed the presence of 'vast quantities of human bones'.[24] It wasn't until the 1980s, however, that a systematic programme of excavation was undertaken. The results of that campaign revealed one of the most shocking and enigmatic burials ever excavated in the British Isles.

The mound had been constructed over a twin-celled stone build-ing dated to the seventh or eighth century, undoubtedly part of the religious complex on the site. Prior to its final repurposing it had been used as a workshop, although it may originally have been built as a chapel or mortuary. To construct the mound, the walls of the building had been dismantled to ground level, leaving only the subterranean part of the building in situ. The floor of the eastern cell was covered with a layer of red marl, and a stone cist had been erected in the centre. All traces of the body which this contained, as described to Dr Degge, had disappeared – as had most evidence for the cist itself (unsurprising, given the repeated, and mostly inex-pert, prior interventions). What did survive, however, were the other bones: 1,686 of them to be precise, the disarticulated remains of 264 people, strewn about in charnel chaos, a disordered land-scape of death. Among the bones, objects were discovered – a Scandinavian-style axe-head, sword fragments, two long single-bladed knives (seaxes), a key and a range of decorative fragments of metalwork dating to the seventh or eighth centuries. Amid all this were five silver coins, four of them dated to 872, one of them to 873/4. These last artefacts were a critical, and astoundingly fortui-tous, discovery, for they dated the construction of this extraordi-nary monument, with exceptional precision, to the period when Repton was under occupation by the Viking *micel here*.

Although the scene uncovered by the excavators was one of morbid disarray, this was all as a result of the rough treatment the burial had received at the hands of Thomas Walker and his ilk. It soon became apparent that the bones had originally been carefully sorted by length and stacked neatly around the central grave. Moreover, most of the small bones (hands, feet, vertebrae) were absent, suggesting that the skeletons had been moved, reinterred in the mound after an initial period of burial elsewhere – long enough, it would seem, to ensure that the remains were free from fleshy parts. Carbon dating of a small sample brought back a range of dates between the seventh and the ninth centuries, and the general absence of trauma to the bones complicates an interpretation of these skeletons as the remains of battle-damaged Vikings of the *micel here* or their victims.

Debate continues about who they were and why they were interred in this way, and ongoing analysis seeks to clarify their origins. It may be – as the excavators believed – that some of the bones are Scandinavian, the remains of the followers of some great lord gathered up to lay beside him in death. On the other hand, it may be that some of the disarticulated bones are the remains of Mercian monks, nuns and aristocrats whose bones were disturbed by the digging of the ditch and the clearing of the mausolea.[25] It may even be the case that the bones of the Mercian kings – Æthelbald and Wiglaf – were jumbled in among them, as well as, perhaps, the holy remains of St Wystan himself:[26] the carefully conserved relics of a proud nation, reduced to morbid trophies in a ghoulish heathen catacomb.

Who, then, was the missing occupant, the *'Humane Body Nine Foot* long' who had once been laid in the central grave in such grim splendour? Although we can be pretty certain that his or her physical stature was exaggerated, this was clearly the grave of an important individual, afforded a rare and imposing memorial. We know with more certainty who it was not. The movements of the Viking leaders Halfdan and Ubbe are mentioned in the years following the over-wintering at Repton; other leaders of the army – Guthrum, Oscetel and Anwend – led a part of the army to Cambridge in 874 and were also clearly still alive. Bacsecg was killed at Ashdown in 871, and it seems unlikely that even the most devoted of followers would have been prepared to carry a ripe corpse around England for three years. There is only one other Viking warlord active in England whose name we know, but whose fate and movements in the years after 870 are uncertain. The evidence is contradictory, but the excavators make a good case that the mound at Repton was raised for Ivar the Boneless.[27]

Two and a half miles west and slightly south of Repton, on high ground overlooking the valley of the Trent, yet more mounds were being raised to the dead in the years following 873. The cemetery at Heath Wood comprised fifty-nine barrows, hillocks of earth that once stood on open heathland – like the workings of an army of giant moles. These were monuments that marked the places where the ashen remnants of the dead had been interred, fifty-nine memorials to occasions when the earth of Derbyshire had been dug and reformed to cover the cremated fragments of human beings and animals, swords and shields, buckles and spurs, nails, pins and melted treasures. These were the graves of pagan people whose community practised a rite of burial long abandoned by the Christian English, laying out the dead upon a funeral pyre, draped with jewellery or girded with weapons, surrounded by sacrificial offerings, immolated.

Snorri explained that 'Óðinn […] ordained that all dead people must be burned and that their possessions should be laid on a pyre with them. He said that everyone should come to Valhǫll with such wealth as he had on his pyre, and that each would also have the benefit of whatever he himself had buried in the earth. But the ashes were to be taken out to sea or buried down in the earth, and mounds were to be built as memorials to great men.'[28] Although we would be right to be dubious of the specificity with which Snorri describes the thoughts and motivations of people who lived hundreds of years before his own time, his words nevertheless resonate not only with the archaeology, but with other more contemporary accounts. Here once more is ibn Fadlan, describing the funeral of a Rūs chieftain:

> They dressed him [the dead man] in trousers, socks, boots, a tunic and a brocade caftan with gold buttons. On his head they placed a brocade cap covered with sable. Then they bore him into the pavilion on the boat and sat him on the mattress, supported by cushions. Then they brought *nabīdh* [alcoholic drink], fruits and basil which they placed near him. Next they carried in bread, meat and onions which they laid before him.
>
> After that they brought in a dog, which they cut in two and threw into the boat. Then they placed his weapons beside him. Next they took two horses and made them run until they were in lather, before hacking them to pieces with swords and throwing their flesh on to the boat. Then they brought two cows, which they also cut into pieces and threw on to the boat. Finally they brought a cock and hen, killed them and threw them on to the boat as well.[29]

After a lengthy ritual, the slave-girl was finally killed, having been laid beside the dead man:

Then people came with wood and logs to burn, each holding a piece of wood alight at one end, which they threw on to the wood [that was piled below the boat]. The fire enveloped the wood, then the boat, then the tent, the man, the girl and all that there was on the boat. A violent and frightening wind began to blow, the flames grew in strength and the heat of the fire intensified.[30]

This was a grand funeral for a great man. The burning of boats, like their burial, was probably uncommon,[31] but the broad outlines of the pomp and sacrifice – and their explanation – would have been familiar across the Viking world. As they stood on the banks of the river watching the burning, one of the Rūs party spoke to ibn Fadlan's interpreter. 'You Arabs are fools!' he apparently exclaimed. 'Why is that?' ibn Fadlan politely enquired through his interlocutor. 'Because you put the men you love most, and the most noble among you, into the earth, and the earth and the worms and insects eat them. But we burn them in the fire in an instant, so that at once and without delay they enter Paradise.'[32]

The rites practised at Heath Wood may have replicated – albeit on a smaller scale – the scenes witnessed by ibn Fadlan on the Volga; similar funerals are also known to have taken place in Scandinavia – Norway and Sweden especially – during the Viking Age.[33] Nevertheless, in England, obviously 'Viking' burials are rare discoveries. Despite the development of new Scandinavian-inflected identities and socio-economic change that occurred in the decades following the 870s, the graves at Heath Wood and Repton remain the only places where good evidence exists for a whole community behaving in a way that was significantly divergent, obviously heathen. These were the people of the *micel here*, and here – for the first time – they were putting their roots into English soil. They would run deep: although their funerals would become less distinctive – less visible in the archaeological record – Viking sculpture, found at Repton, attests to a more than transient Scandinavian presence in this part of Britain. And, in time (or perhaps straight away), Old Norse names were bestowed on the neighbouring villages, names which speak eloquently of perceived ethnic difference in the first phases of Viking settlement. They are still the names these villages bear today: Ingleby – the 'farm of the English'; Bretby – the 'farm of the Britons'.

In 874, according to the *Anglo-Saxon Chronicle*, the great Viking army that had first arrived in England in 865 broke apart, never again to operate as a unified force in England. (Perhaps the death of whoever lay in the Repton mound snapped the last thread of unifying authority binding together the confederation of chieftains and warlords that made up the *micel here*. Perhaps the raising of that mound to their fallen leader was a last symbolic act of triumph and remembrance – the interment of a Viking hero at the symbolic heart of England's once mightiest realm, left to slumber on among the skulls of conquered kings.) Guthrum and the others went east. Halfdan, however, went back to Northumbria to assert some measure of authority in the northern part of that kingdom. He wasted no time in getting on with the traditional occupations of Northumbrian rulers by harassing the Picts and Strathclyde Britons ranged along his northern and western borders. What was recorded under the year 876, however, was much more significant. The *Anglo-Saxon Chronicle*, in one of the most understated but consequential remarks in the recorded history of early medieval Britain, notes that 'Halfdan divided up the land of Northumbria,' and his people 'were ploughing and supporting themselves'.[34]

By 875, the land was changing – utterly and irrevocably. And not merely in the terminal collapse of age-old kingdoms; the Vikings had insinuated themselves into the very marrow of England. The soil was being ploughed by Viking hands, and their dead were laid to rest in it. The earth was being worked and mounds raised; even the bones of the English dead, perhaps even their kings, were now being co-opted into the graves of warriors born in Denmark, Norway or beyond. In every part of these islands, the children of Viking men were being born to native mothers. And, perhaps most profound of all, the names of things had begun to change: places that had borne English names for 400 years or more were shedding them as a new lexicon established itself in the wake of settlement: Norse words, Viking words. This was no longer a harrying, nor even a simple conquest, the exchange of one ruling dynasty for another. This was colonization, with all the cultural, linguistic, geographical and political upheaval such a process brings in train. Its impact can still be felt today.

11

THE RETURN
OF THE KING

And naught was left King Alfred
But shameful tears of rage,
In the island in the river
In the end of all his age.

In the island in the river
He was broken to his knee:
And he read, writ with an iron pen,
That God had wearied of Wessex men
And given their country, field and fen,
To the devils of the sea.

G. K. CHESTERTON, *The Ballad of the White Horse* (1911)[1]

In March 878, seeking refuge, King Alfred came to Athelney, a hidden spit of land, rising gently from the bleak expanse of the Somerset Levels.

He had led his battered court to this remote place in the short dark days of January and February, 'leading a restless life in great distress amid the woody and marshy places of Somerset'.[2] The language of the *Anglo-Saxon Chronicle*, with its woods (*wuda*) and moor-fastnesses (*mór-fæstenas*), recalls the monster-haunted wildernesses of *Beowulf* and *St Guthlac*, drawing, with allusive economy, a world at the margins of human life – a place of estrangement and shadow-life. Asser tells us that the king 'had nothing to live on except what he could forage by frequent raids, either secretly or even openly, from the Vikings as well as from the Christians who had submitted to the Vikings' authority'. Alfred was a king turned *wulvesheofod* ('wolf's head'), his tenure in the wilderness an inversion of the order of Anglo-Saxon life. Alfred, like Grendel, had become the *sceadugenga* – the 'shadow-walker' – the wolf beyond the border 'who held the moors, the fen and fastness ...'[3]

These days, Athelney is a nondescript lump of ground, surrounded by the flat fields of the Somerset countryside. But when the flood tides come – as they did in with devastating effect in 2012 and 2014 – we can see it again as Alfred saw it: white sky and white water, the sheet of pale gauze split by the black fingers of the trees, torn by sprays of rushes, limbs of willow lightly touched with sickly green, catkins swinging like a thousand tiny sacrifices. Off in the distance a heron hauls itself skyward, spreading wide black pinions, beating a lazy saurian path across the Levels. The other birds carry on their business, snipe and curlew boring surgical holes into the shallows. The plop of a diving frog adds percussion to the throaty chorus of his fellows, lusty young bulls emerging bleary-eyed from their winter beds, seeking out mates to tangle with in the mud.

Later in his life, Alfred would invest in Athelney by founding a monastery there, perhaps in gratitude and recognition for the role it had played in his career, or perhaps as part of his campaign of self-mythologization. 'Æthelingaeg' is how Asser spells it, though the manuscripts of the *Anglo-Saxon Chronicle* present various different iterations. It means 'isle of princes' (Æðeling 'prince' + *eíg* 'island'), an auspicious name for a royal refuge and one which we might suspect was bestowed only after it had played its part in Alfred's story. He would also establish a stronghold there, a 'formidable fortress of elegant workmanship' connected to the island by a causeway, the genesis of the modern village of East Lyng.[4] But at the time he came there in 878 it was an isolated place – cut off amid the swollen waters of the Levels, an island, 'surrounded' as Asser explained 'by swampy, impassable and extensive marshland and groundwater on every side'.[5]

In 878, Athelney was a place where Alfred could hide from his Viking enemies and plan his attacks against them – attacking them 'relentlessly and tirelessly'.[6] It would briefly become for him the seat of a guerrilla government in exile, of a king without a kingdom, an Avalon unto which the king would pass and where he would be reborn.

It had taken several years for the situation in Wessex to reach this sorry pass. By 875, Northumbria and East Anglia had fallen to Viking armies, and Mercia was riven by faction and war, its ancestral tombs ransacked and defiled. Only Wessex had weathered the Viking storm and remained intact: the military resolve of Alfred and his people had delivered four years of peace. That peace, however, was now over and in 875 the king's warriors fought (and won) a maritime skirmish with a raiding fleet. One Viking ship was captured and six (Asser says five) were driven off. This, however, was only the opening move in a new war for the West Saxon kingdom.[7]

In 876, the army that had been led to Cambridge from Repton by Guthrum, Oscetel and Anwend moved suddenly into Wessex and occupied Wareham, a fortified convent in Dorset. Crisis seemed initially to have been averted through negotiation – hostages were exchanged and the Viking army swore holy and binding oaths – but it transpired that this Viking force had no particular intention of leaving Wessex. The army slipped away from Wareham by night, executing the hostages granted by Alfred (we can imagine that the Vikings held by the West Saxon army suffered a similar fate in return) and moved on to occupy Exeter in Devon. Alfred gave them good chase, but once again the limitations of early medieval siegecraft sucked all the momentum from the campaign: the king 'could not overtake them before they were in the fortress where they could not be overpowered'.[8] Had it not been for the weather, things might have looked bleak for Wessex – 120 Viking ships were lost in a storm near Swanage, preventing them from linking up with their comrades at Exeter.[9] The result, yet again, was a stalemate, and once more hostages were exchanged (none of whom can have felt very optimistic about his future) and oaths sworn; this time, perhaps sapped of confidence as a result of the failure of their planned pincer-movement, the Viking army did indeed withdraw. They went, in fact, to Mercia, where they formally carved up Ceolwulf's kingdom, leaving the latter a rump part, and saw out the winter in Gloucester.[10]

This occurred in 877, and we know nothing of what befell Ceolwulf and his subjects in that, presumably depressing, period. It is likely, however, that the time spent in Mercia was used by the Viking army to consolidate their land-taking and to gather reinforcements. Soon after Twelfth Night (7 January) in the deep winter of early 878, the Viking army rode south into Wessex, to the royal estate at Chippenham in Wiltshire. They probably came via Cirencester, joining the Fosse Way and cutting through southern Gloucestershire like a dagger, before turning to the south-east. No early sources record whether Alfred was himself present at Chippenham, or whether he fought the Vikings there. All we are told (to give Asser's version) is that 'By strength of arms they forced many men of that race [West Saxons] to sail overseas, through both poverty and fear, and very nearly all the inhabitants of that region submitted to their authority.'[11]

Chippenham was occupied by Guthrum's army and Alfred began his period of exile in the wilderness. It was approximately ninety years since the first recorded Viking raids on England had taken place; in that short time, every one of the Anglo-Saxon kingdoms had been broken.

*

In later days in was said that St Cuthbert appeared in a vision to Alfred on Athelney. The speech that the king received was the stuff to put fire in the belly of any dynastic ruler: 'God will have delivered to you your enemies and all their land, and hereditary rule to you and to your sons and to your sons' sons. Be faithful to me and my people because to you and your sons was given all of Albion. Be just, because you have been chosen as king of all Britain.'[12] The story was added to the Alfred myth after the king's death, in either the mid-tenth or mid-eleventh century,[13] and Asser makes no mention of it. It seems likely to have been a tale spun during the reign of Alfred's grandson to prop up his political ambitions and solidify the standing of the cult of St Cuthbert. Nevertheless, had Cuthbert been looking down from his cloud in the 870s, he would have seen plenty of things which might have given him cause to visit destruction on the Vikings – not least the disturbance of his incorruptible slumber. The sack of his former monastery at Lindisfarne in 793 was, by then, a story from another age, but the arrival of the *micel here* in Northumbria was another matter. Heathen warlords were now in positions of power across the north, their people settling and dividing up the land. The reappearance of Halfdan on the Tyne in 875, 'devastating everything and sinning cruelly against St Cuthbert',[14] seems to have been what galvanized the monks to remove Cuthbert's precious bones from their resting place on Lindisfarne. According to the *Historia de Sancto Cuthberto*, so began seven years of wandering for Cuthbert's corporeal remnants, a terrestrial Odyssey of northern Britain designed, perhaps, to spare these relics the indignities that had befallen the dead of Repton. They finally came to rest at Chester-le-Street where they remained until 995, when they were disturbed once more.

If it was not Cuthbert's discorporate exhortations, it may be that something else galvanized Alfred to action. Perhaps it was the news that Odda, ealdorman of Somerset, had destroyed a Viking army that had arrived with twenty-three ships in Devon. His victory came at an unidentified hill-fort called 'Cynwit'.[15] In the fighting, the Viking leader Ubbe, slayer of King Edmund, son of Ragnar Loðbrók and brother to Halfdan and Ivar the Boneless, was killed.[16] Moreover, the *Anglo-Saxon Chronicle* notes, 'ðær wæs se guðfana genumen þe hie hræfn heton' ('there was taken the banner that they called Raven').[17] A later gloss on this passage adds that the banner had been woven by three sisters, the daughters of Ragnar Loðbrók, in a single day: when the banner caught the breeze and the raven's wings flapped, then victory in battle was assured; if it hung lifeless, defeat was in the offing.[18] There is a great deal that might be said about ravens and banners, weird sisters and weaving, and their place on the Viking Age battlefield. For now, however, it is sufficient to note that the seizure of such a banner would have been a considerable morale boost to the West Saxons. Although the defeat of Ubbe at Cynwit may have left Guthrum's army in a more vulnerable position than either he or his enemies had expected, its most important consequence may have been to demonstrate to the West Saxons and to Alfred that the Vikings could be beaten, that God was on the side of the English, and that his assistance – whether mediated through St Cuthbert or not – was more than a match for any heathen battle magic.

Whatever the catalyst, Alfred began to prepare. Messengers must have gone from Athelney to the ealdormen and thegns that remained loyal to him, into the shires to spread the word that the king was preparing to fight. We know that the shires had a well-developed system of hundred and shire assembly places, many of which would have been in use in Alfred's day and probably for long ages before. It is likely that these formed the hubs for military assembly, and that to them, all over Wessex, armed men would have made their way when they received the call of their reeve, ealdorman or king. So little is known, however, of the precise mechanisms by which a West Saxon army assembled – let alone in strange circumstances like those of 878 – that any attempt to reconstruct the movements or constituents of Alfred's army, beyond what Asser and the *Anglo-Saxon Chronicle* reveal, can only ever be informed speculation; indeed, the subject of how armies were raised in Anglo-Saxon England has long been a subject of intense academic scrutiny and debate.[19]

But we can imagine the little beginnings, the woman watching anxiously as the reeve's messenger rides hard away, mud splattering up from the puddles of spring rain; the grave expression on her husband's face as he walks back towards the house; the old sword he gives to his eldest son, still just a boy, to defend the farm when he is gone. We can imagine the tears and the parting, the lonely trudge past familiar fields, a spear over one shoulder, a sack over the other. On towards the hall of the thegn, to meet with other freemen of the hundred; he knows these men, has drunk with them, played games with them as a boy, one is his brother-in-law. They embrace each other and renew their friendships, ask after children and lands and livestock, tell bawdy jokes, ask dirty riddles;[20] but they don't stay long. They are nervous, though companionship helps them hide it. They need to keep moving, a small band now, singing the old songs as they go, songs of Wayland, Finn and Hengest.[21]

There are others on the road, little knots of armed men, some on horseback, others on foot, some in fine armour handed down from their grandfathers, garnets glittering on sword belts, gold on their horse bridles, others with little more than a padded jacket and a rusty spear. They make their way over hills and by herepath, through forests and over moors, by swift-running brooks and stagnant meres, coming together at the barrows and trees, the old stones and muddy fords – the ancient meeting places of Wessex. First the hundred, where local men were met and accounted for and news distributed, the king's summons made plain. Then they are back on the road, a war-band now, heading for the shire-moot, to join the reeve or ealdorman – to form the *fyrd* ('levied army'). As they go, further now from home, they begin to see tongues of flame shooting up from the hillsides, like the breath of dragons in the dusk: at first they think of burning villages, the harrying of Danes, before they recognize the signal fires, beacons calling the men to battle.[22]

When morning comes they see the camp spread out before them, the ealdorman's war banner fluttering, gold thread glittering in the sun. But there is no time to rest and swap stories, to renew old acquaintances. News has reached them that the king is on the move.

Presently, in the seventh week after Easter he [Alfred] rode to Egbert's Stone, which is in the eastern part of Selwood Forest (*sylva magna* ['great wood'] in Latin, and *Coit Maur* in Welsh); and there all the inhabitants of Somerset and Wiltshire and all the inhabitants of Hampshire – those who had not sailed overseas for fear of the Vikings – joined up with him. When they saw the king, receiving him (not surprisingly) as if one restored to life after suffering such great tribulations, they were filled with immense joy. They made camp there for one night. At the break of the following dawn the king struck camp and came to a place called Iley [*ASC: Iglea*, 'island wood'], and made camp there for one night.

When the next morning dawned he moved his forces and came to a place called Edington, and fighting fiercely with a compact shield-wall against the entire Viking army, he persevered resolutely for a long time; at length he gained the victory through God's will.[23]

Walking on the northern rim of Salisbury Plain feels like clinging to the edge of the world – the land drops away 300 feet below the earthen banks of the fortress that crown the hillside like a circlet of turf-grown soil. The ramparts belong to Bratton Camp, a massive Iron Age hill-fort that encloses the long, mutilated hogback of a Neolithic long-barrow at its centre. Walking the perimeter, the wind rips across man-made canyons, forcing the breath back down my throat. I find that I am leaning at almost 45 degrees into the gale, and am suddenly, uncomfortably, aware of the fathoms of empty space to my right, a vast ocean of air; the plain sweeps to the north, a swathe of open country laid bare for leagues. I briefly see myself tossed like a leaf, spinning into oblivion – just another piece of organic matter on the breeze. My gut flips at the sudden feeling of vulnerability, and I begin to tack back towards the long-barrow; the sharp smell of sheep shit hits me in the nose. As I get closer to the mound an old ram with a sad face stares at me reproachfully. I ignore him, and some of his ewes go bouncing off from their grazing patch on top of the barrow, scattering in dim-witted panic.

From up here the strategic significance of the place is obvious, and it is likely that Bratton Camp was once a look-out post. The name of the ground that slopes off to the south of the hill-fort is 'Warden Hill', a swell of upland that runs hard up against the bedyked confines of the hill-fort. The name 'Warden' may very well be a development from the Old English *weard* ('watch') and *dun* ('hill'). From here one can look across to the east, around 2½ miles along the line of the chalk ridge, to Tottenham Wood, the site of another Neolithic long-barrow. There are lots of English place-names with elements like 'tut', 'toot' or 'totten' forming part of them; though often difficult to interpret, many may originate in Old English constructions like *tote-hām* or *tōten-hām* meaning 'house near the look-out station' or 'house of the watchman'.[24] Both Bratton Camp and Tottenham Wood boast commanding views over the low countryside to the north, casting a watchful gaze from the rim of the plateau; down below, 2 to 3 miles from both putative look-out sites, is the meeting place of Whorwellsdown Hundred at Crosswelldown Farm.[25]

Looking south from the farm, Salisbury Plain rises up like a great green cliff edge, the low sun casting its man-made terraces and earthen banks into horizontal bands of undulate chromatism, like a great green tsunami surging northwards to consume the plain. Riding on that crest, both Bratton Camp and Tottenham Wood are clearly visible from the old hundred meeting place – three landmarks, each one visible to and from the others, enclosing the landscape in a triangle of watchfulness. Between them, hugging the base of the escarpment are the villages of Bratton and Edington, the latter a place that takes its name from the bleak hillside that looms over it: Eþandun – 'the barren hill'.

Centuries before Alfred led his armies here, before the West Saxons had become Christians, they had brought their dead to Bratton Camp, to cut their graves into the ancient barrows, to lay them down among the more ancient spirits of the land. Three early

Anglo-Saxon burials, revealed by nineteenth-century excavators, were dug into the long-barrow, and even earlier excavations uncovered the remains of a warrior buried with axe and sword, interred in the top of a Bronze Age round barrow that stood at the southern entrance to the camp.[26] Most thought provoking of all, perhaps, was the evidence of a cremation platform discovered at the long-barrow – the remains of a pyre where the pagan West Saxons had once burned their dead.[27] Up here, up on the heights, the smoke and the flames would have been seen for miles.

The theatre of such events would have impressed themselves on the imagination in ways that would not have been easy to forget, passing into folklore. *Beowulf*, as so often, evokes the majesty and spectacle of the ritual in ways which charcoal and fragments of burnt iron cannot:

> The Geat people built a pyre for Beowulf,
> stacked and decked it until it stood foursquare,
> hung with helmets, heavy war-shields
> and shining armour, just as he had ordered.
> Then his warriors laid him in the middle of it,
> mourning a lord far-famed and beloved.
> On a height they kindled the hugest of all
> funeral fires; fumes of woodsmoke
> billowed darkly up, the blaze roared
> and drowned out their weeping, wind died down
> and flames wrought havoc in the hot bone-house,
> burning it to the core. They were disconsolate
> and wailed aloud for their lord's decease.[28]

One can only speculate how long the memory of the ancestors burned and buried here would have lingered in the collective memory, what associations this landscape may have held for Alfred and his contemporaries; but it is hard to believe, even if the ancient funerals were forgotten, that the monumental remains of Bratton Camp and the numerous barrows of the chalk ridge did not exert a pull on the West Saxon imagination. The names of the long-bar-rows at Bratton Camp and Tottenham Wood – if they ever boasted them – are lost. But, given the evidence of Anglo-Saxon boundary clauses elsewhere, it is highly probable that names or legendary material of some type had accumulated at these monuments by the late ninth century. Places like these were deliberately sought out as venues for battle or military assembly – it was surely deliberate, for example, that Alfred should have chosen to muster his army at Egbert's Stone before moving on to Iley Oak and Edington; it was Ecgberht (Egbert), Alfred's grandfather, who had returned Wessex to pre-eminence among the Anglo-Saxon realms – a military hero whose memory was an appropriate one to invoke ahead of a battle that would determine the fate of his own dynasty and the future course of British history.[29]

There are other reasons why Edington might have been impor-tant to Alfred and why he led his army here. His father, Æthelwulf, had come here in the 850s, the place-name Edington appearing as the place of ratification for a charter granting land in Devon to a deacon called Eadberht.[30] Alfred himself later bequeathed the estate at Edington to his wife, Ealhswith, along with estates at Wantage and Lambourn. (It is tempting to see in this bequest an acknowl-edgement of the importance of Edington to Alfred's sense of himself – Wantage was the place of his birth, Edington of his greatest victory.) The place remained in royal hands until long afterwards. In the tenth century, royal grants of land at Edington were made to Romsey Abbey.[31] It seems certain, therefore, that Edington was a royal estate centre before and after the battle that was fought there. Although nothing confirming a royal residence has yet been discov-ered, an early medieval spindle whorl has been found in the envi-rons of the village,[32] perhaps implying a settlement of some sort, and the remains of a royal hall may yet lie beneath the modern settlement. This in itself would be enough to explain why this place was chosen as the theatre of battle; a powerful symbol of royal authority, its occupation by either side sent a clear message to the rest of Wessex. However, when taken in combination with the evidence of a resonance both deeper and wider – ancient graves and even older monuments, military assemblies and strategic oversight, and the great geological rift in the land – it seems clear that Edington was a powerful and a fearsome place.

In *Alarms and Discursions*, a compendium of short works published by G. K. Chesterton in 1910, the writer and critic described his own experiences exploring this landscape.

the other day under a wild sunset and moonrise I passed the place which is best reputed as Ethandune, a high, grim upland, partly bare and partly shaggy; like that savage and sacred spot in those great imaginative lines about the demon lover and the waning moon. The darkness, the red wreck of sunset, the yellow and lurid moon, the long fantastic shadows, actually created that sense of monstrous incident which is the dramatic side of landscape. The bare grey slopes seemed to rush downhill like routed hosts; the dark clouds drove across like riven banners; and the moon was like a golden dragon, like the Golden Dragon of Wessex.

As we crossed a tilt of the torn heath I saw suddenly between myself and the moon a black shapeless pile higher than a house. The atmosphere was so intense that I really thought of a pile of dead Danes, with some phantom conqueror on the top of it [...] this was a barrow older than Alfred, older than the Romans, older perhaps than the Britons; and no man knew whether it was a wall or a trophy or a tomb [...] it gave me a queer emotion to think that, sword in hand, as the Danes poured with the torrents of their blood down to Chippenham, the great king may have lifted up his head and looked at that oppressive shape, suggestive of something and yet suggestive of nothing; may have looked at it as we did, and understood it as little as we.[33]

I don't think that Chesterton was right about Alfred. I think the king knew full well the significance of Edington and its environs: its Bronze Age and Neolithic graves were reused by Alfred's own Saxon ancestors as a burial ground, his royal hall was sited in their shadow. But what Chesterton clearly understood, and was able to express so powerfully, was the sheer drama, the physical presence and the intrusive – almost overpowering – impact of the environment on the imagination. His words are a reminder that landscape has the power to conjure visions and summon the dead back to life, to superimpose the supernatural on the real world and bring history into a concurrent dialogue with the present. What we feel in a given environment – the angle of the rain, the colour of the sky, the 'tilt of the torn heath' – can connect us to the ancient past through a sense of shared feeling and experience. Moreover, these were feelings and emotions that were more potent, more powerful, in Alfred's day than they were in Chesterton's or remain, indeed, in ours.

The Victorians loved Alfred. For the whole of the nineteenth century, and until – at least – the outbreak of the First World War, the Anglophone world (and white English males in particular) had a mania for crediting the West Saxon king with inventing almost everything that people in those days thought was a good idea – from Oxford University to the Royal Navy and from the British Parliament (and its colonial offspring) to the British Empire itself.[34] He was a paragon of chivalry, of learning and wisdom, a Solomon-like figure, imbued with vast reserves of energy and prowess – a reformer of laws and, simultaneously, a conservative upholder of ancient traditions, a defender of the faith and a master of self-restraint, a scholar, a builder, a man of the people, a sufferer, a redeemer, a mighty warrior and 'the ideal Englishman [...] the embodiment of our civilization'.[35] He was, in the words of the great historian of the Norman Conquest, E. A. Freeman, nothing less than the 'the most perfect character in history'.[36]

To illuminate all of the extraordinary contortions, elisions, exaggerations, falsifications, misunderstandings, credulity, hyperbole, political expediency and mischief that collided in the creation of this absurdly hypertrophic idea of kingship would take us on a long detour from our intended destination.[37] However, even though Alfred's greatest achievement may have been the skill with which he publicized his achievements, like most myths his greatness is rooted in a certain amount of truth: for none of it – neither deserved fame nor inflated hero-cult – would have accrued to Alfred had he not found the wherewithal to fight himself out of the corner into which he had been painted in the spring of 878. Even with the knowledge that our view of Alfred derives from the 'authorized' version of his life, the mythic quality of its resurrection narrative lends something truly epic, cinematic in its emotional charge, to the return of the king.

In Alfred's victory over Guthrum at Edington there is something of what Tolkien called 'eucatastrophe', the cathartic joy of a victory attained, against expectation, in the face of horror and despair. In his view, the archetypal eucatastrophe was found in the death and resurrection of Christ, a story that obtained its extraordinary power from its status as what Tolkien called 'true myth' – the entwining, as he saw it, of the strands of history and fairy-tale into the defining cable of truth running through the centre of human experience.[38] It was this that caused him to insist – most famously to C. S. Lewis in discussions which ultimately caused the latter to reject the atheism of his youth – that myths, of all kinds (but 'northern' myths in particular), were not lies: they were echoes of mankind's understanding of the one true myth that shaped all of humanity's creative endeavour. To some degree this was a self-justificatory argument: Tolkien was ever anxious to reconcile his love of myth and fairy-tale – and his own lifelong creation of them – with a profoundly held Catholic faith.[39]

In essence, however, these were not original thoughts, even if Professor Tolkien expressed them in ways which have retained a rare power. G. K. Chesterton himself had made very similar arguments in a public spat with the atheist and political activist Robert Blatchford in 1904.[40] Chesterton had also recognized the mythic potency of Alfred, composing the weird but remarkable *Ballad of the White Horse* in 1911, one year after his disquisition on the floating shade of 'Ethandune'. The *Ballad* comprises 2,684 lines of epic verse that tell the story of the king's return from Athelney to triumph at Edington.[41] It has been described as the high water mark

Alfred the hero, as envisioned by Morris Meredith Williams in 1913

of Victorian Alfredianism, as well as its effective epitaph,[42] and it is hard not to see, in the power it draws from landscape and mythic archetype, a prefiguring of Tolkien's oeuvre – even though the professor, while admiring the 'brilliant smash and glitter' of its language, was characteristically scathing about its merits overall (another demonstration of his tendency to attack more harshly those things which disappointed him than those that simply didn't interest him: 'not as good as I thought […] the ending is absurd […] G.K.C. knew nothing whatever about the "North", heathen or Christian').[43]

In the *Ballad*, the action of the battle is transposed to the landscape around the Uffington White Horse – a location which, as we have seen, is much more likely to have been the location of Alfred's battle at Ashdown. But the *Ballad* is not about historical reality; the poem is filled with fictional details and improbable symbolism, designed to emphasize Alfred's Christlike journey from 'death' in exile, to resurrection and apotheosis. It recognizes – or, rather, seeks to revive and recast – the story of these few weeks in 878 as the creation not only of Alfred's personal myth, but of the nation itself, of 'Englishness' and, by extension, of 'Britishness' in its Anglocentric imperial iteration, born in a single moment of transcendent bloodshed that washed away the regional differences and ethnic animus of centuries. Chesterton's three central protagonists, Alfred aside, were an Anglo-Saxon, a Briton and, most anachronistically of all, a Roman – three heroic avatars of what he evidently regarded as the progenitive peoples of (southern) Britain. In his view the Vikings were not part of this heritage:

> The Northmen came about our land
> A Christless chivalry:
> Who knew not of the arch or pen,
> Great, beautiful half-witted men
> From the sunrise and the sea.

Misshapen ships stood on the deep
Full of strange gold and fire,
And hairy men, as huge as sin
With horned heads, came wading in
Through the long, low sea-mire.

Our towns were shaken of tall kings
With scarlet beards like blood:
The world turned empty where they trod,
They took the kindly cross of God
And cut it up for wood.

Chesterton's 'Northmen' are dead-eyed, dim-witted barbarians – vital and potent, but a force of nature unfeeling as the storm-wind. They are the primal and impersonal tide against which the quality of Alfred's humanity could be measured, a mute anvil upon which the gilt mantle of his greatness could be hammered out and the shape of the English nation forged. Of such stuff is national mythology built, and Alfred and his descendants themselves ensured that the events of 878 would be remembered in this light.

But, of course, nothing is ever so simple.

12

THE GODFATHER

And there came to his chrism-loosing
Lords of all lands afar,
And a line was drawn north-westerly
That set King Egbert's empire free,
Giving all lands by the northern sea
To the sons of the northern star.

G. K. CHESTERTON, *The Ballad of the White Horse* (1911)[1]

The priest is too close – the kneeling warrior can see the pores of the man's skin, the wiry hairs that project from his nostrils. The breath comes suddenly, short and sharp amid the low rhythmic babble of unfamiliar words, like the wheeze of a thrall who has spent too long tending the hearth-fire; it is hot and musty, the smell of old wine skins. The kneeling man flinches, a scarred hand flickering to the sword hilt that he knows – all too uncomfortably – is not at his hip. He turns sharply to the side, eyebrows raised. The young man to his right whispers back in the Norse tongue: 'He is driving away evil, so that Christ can enter.' The warrior tenses and narrows his eyes. '*Bolverkr*,' he mutters under his breath, but the priest ignores him and carries on regardless. Salt is placed in the kneeler's hand, and then, suddenly, the priest grasps his nostrils (to remind him, the translator whispers, to stay steadfast while he is still breathing).

The Latin is incessant, hypnotic. Occasionally the warrior nods, or grunts an assent when the translator prompts him, but for the most part he fixes his eyes on the serpent that sprouts from the top of the bishop's staff, imagines it moving, coiling into life, the forked tongue lashing out, hissing … Perhaps, he thinks to himself, this priest is a *seiðmaðr* – a sorcerer. A brief shudder animates the bare flesh of his torso. '*Argr*,' he mouths the word silently, glaring at the bishop with new hostility. But suddenly there is oil being painted on his skin – a cross joining his nipples and running down his breastbone, daubs on his shoulders – and then, before he has a chance to understand what is happening, he is on his feet and King Alfred is beside him, leading him towards a great stone basin, carved all around with spirals and rolling scrolls of foliage, brightly painted.[2] Guthrum gazes into the water that fills it, uncomprehending. The bishop's hand is on his head, pushing him towards the surface – a black mirror in which shards of candlelight dart. He can see his own features looking back, shadowy, his eyes hollowed into pits. Fear begins to twist his guts. He resists, looking to the king, who nods reassuringly.

And then his head is in the water, and all the sound of the chanting and the Latin babble is gone – just a hollow swirl in his ears, and darkness. He rises quickly, water running into his eyes, and he shakes his head like a dog springing from a pool, spray flying from his beard. But as he tries to regain his balance, he is pushed immediately back into the water. For a moment he wonders if he will drown. And then, once again, he is back, choking in the candle-smoke and the fug of incense. Guthrum barely registers the white robe that is hung upon him, or the oil that is tipped over his head; a white cloth is bound around his brow. A conversation is taking place in English between Alfred and the bishop. He doesn't understand it all, but he picks out a name, a name repeated several times as they stare at him: Æthelstan.

After Edington, the Viking army was driven in flight to its encampment (probably at Chippenham). The Vikings were forced to make peace with Alfred, agreeing to vacate West Saxon territory – a promise cemented with hostages and 'great oaths'. It may have been the totality of Alfred's victory that meant that the negotiated peace was less conditional than similar agreements had been in the past. Asser specifically noted that while 'the king should take as many chosen hostages as he wanted' from the Viking army, he would 'give none to them' – the emphasis on Alfred's ability to choose his hostages suggesting that the West Saxons were free to select high-ranking or otherwise valuable individuals from among the Viking ranks. This, apparently, was unprecedented: 'never before, indeed, had they made peace with anyone on such terms'.[3]

Most dramatic of all the gestures made, however, was an agreement that Guthrum, the erstwhile invader of Wessex, would renounce his heathen beliefs and become a Christian. This was a radical proposition – the religious affiliation of a Viking leader in Britain had never before been on the negotiating table – and there must have been many at the time who doubted the intentions of the Viking leadership. Solemn oaths had been made before and broken, hostages sacrificed. So it may have occasioned some surprise when, three weeks later, Guthrum and twenty-nine other senior members of his army presented themselves to Alfred at Aller (3 miles east of Athelney) for baptism.

How deeply Guthrum understood the ritual and symbolism of the baptismal liturgy can never be known – the evocation above is imaginative, based on explanations of the rite written by Alcuin in a letter of the late eighth century – and it is possible that he was a far better-prepared catechumen than I have made him out to be.[4] He had certainly been in contact with Christians – indeed, he probably had several in his army already. But it seems unlikely that the deeper religious symbolism would have meant much to him, and it is an open question how much English – let alone Latin – he would have understood.

The politics, however, would have been crystal clear. Asser and the *Anglo-Saxon Chronicle* explain that Alfred stood as Guthrum's godfather and 'raised him' in Asser's words 'from the holy font of baptism'. In the process, a new name was bestowed upon him, one of unimpeachable Anglo-Saxon probity: Æthelstan. This was an interesting choice for a number of reasons. There had been a King Æthelstan of East Anglia, in the first half of the ninth century, and this may be significant given the territory over which Guthrum would come to rule. But Æthelstan was also the name of Alfred's own eldest brother – the first-born son of King Æthelwulf of Wessex. Æthelwulf had been dynastically fortunate in that his first wife, Osburh, had been exceptionally prone to producing sons. It is an extraordinary fact that every single one of them – five in total – ruled as kings (and their only daughter, Æthelswith, had been queen to the luckless Burhred of Mercia): Æthelbald, king of Wessex (858–60); Æthelberht, king of Wessex (860–5) and Kent (855–66); Æthelred, king of Wessex and Kent (865–71); and, of course, Alfred himself (871–99). Æthelstan, the eldest, had been king of Kent, a junior role while his father reigned as king of Wessex, from 839 until some point in the early 850s when he died.

It had been customary since the reign of Ecgberht for kings of Kent to be members of the West Saxon royal house, sometimes unifying the crowns of Wessex and Kent in the person of a single individual, and sometimes delegating authority to a younger son or brother. By Alfred's reign, this practice was beginning to fizzle out, royal power in Kent becoming part of the standard portfolio of the West Saxon king.[5] In any case, Alfred had no sons (of an appropriate age) or little brothers to placate or promote by offering them inferior kingships (his nephew was altogether another matter, as we shall see). He would, however, have remained well aware of how useful it could be to have a grateful junior kinsman on the throne of a subordinate neighbouring kingdom.

Guthrum, clearly, was no blood relative to Alfred, but kinship could be established in other ways. By standing as Guthrum's godfather, and bestowing on him his new, Christian, name, Alfred was establishing a claim to symbolic paternity. When Guthrum became Æthelstan he had also become Alfred's 'son'. A relationship had been created between the two men that mingled the loyalties of close kinship with the power dynamics of family hierarchy. Assuming, as seems most likely, that it was Alfred who chose the name 'Æthelstan', the choice may have been deliberately intended to cast the relationship between Alfred and Guthrum in the same light as that which had existed between Alfred's father Æthelwulf and his eldest brother Æthelstan: the latter the nominal ruler of a subservient client kingdom, the former the hegemonic West Saxon king, in whose gift lay the thrones of lesser realms.

If the political theatre of Guthrum's baptism were not enough to underscore Alfred's intentions for the post-Edington power dynamic, Guthrum acknowledged Alfred's superior lordship in other ways as well. Alfred had sealed the baptism celebrations by showering Guthrum and his men 'with many excellent treasures'.[6] According to well-established social etiquette, the receiver of gifts – particularly if he had little to offer of commensurate value – was placed in a subservient role. Guthrum, from a West Saxon perspective at any rate, became Alfred's man the moment he took Alfred's gifts.

What, we might ask, were Alfred and Guthrum hoping to achieve by all of this? Perhaps Alfred imagined that – at some stage – he would hold, as Guthrum–Æthelstan's 'father' and overlord, a controlling interest in whatever territory the newly Christian Viking came to rule. If Alfred was thinking along these lines, it suggests that he had reason to expect this outcome. What had the West Saxon king promised to Guthrum? What was it that had brought him to baptism, had convinced him to accept such a one-sided peace deal, to honour the terms of it so faithfully?

In 879, the Viking army moved from Chippenham to Cirencester, where it remained for a year. During this time, a new army of Vikings arrived from overseas, sailing up the Thames with – according to Asser – the intention of linking up with Guthrum's forces upstream. The newcomers made camp at Fulham and dug themselves in. It must have been a tense few months for Alfred and the West Saxons, poised between two Viking armies hovering on the Thames. But winter came, and winter went, and nobody moved. Guthrum, it seems, was mindful of his accord with Alfred and the benefits that his patronage might confer. Whatever the reasoning, it was enough to overcome any temptation to make common cause with these newcomers. In 880 the new Viking army left Fulham and crossed the Channel, wreaking a trail of havoc across France and the Low Countries. Guthrum's forces, meanwhile, decamped from Cirencester and made their way to East Anglia.

When they arrived there, just as Halfdan and his people had earlier done in Northumbria, they 'settled that land, and divided it up'.[7] The next we hear of Guthrum–Æthelstan, he is introduced as a king. Perhaps it was this that Alfred had offered in 878, the prize that had lured the heathen Viking to the baptismal waters; perhaps Alfred, the most powerful Anglo-Saxon king left in Britain, had offered his backing and blessing for Guthrum to claim the East Anglian throne for himself.

We know very little about Guthrum's East Anglian regime, the kingdom over which he ruled for a decade until his death in 890. But what does stand out is how swiftly he seems to have come to terms with the new realities and adapted to them. In the early 880s, new coins were being produced in East Anglia. Like most English coins of the period, they bore the name of the king on one side (the obverse) and, usually, the name of the mint and the moneyer on the other (the reverse). A great many of these coins bore the name of King Alfred, despite the evidence indicating that they had been struck outside Wessex.[8] Wholesale imitation of the coins of other rulers is fairly commonplace among new regimes seeking to establish their own legitimacy, and so it is altogether unsurprising that Guthrum should have taken this approach in getting his own coinage up and running (his moneyers also copied some continental coin types). The coins do, however, give us an indication of how the world looked from the perspective of Guthrum's subjects, and how the new king began to adapt to their expectations: it was Alfred's name that was likely to reassure his subjects that the coinage was legitimate, and Alfred's coinage that was recognized and respected as a means of economic exchange. Equally revealing is the fact that, when Guthrum's name *did* appear on the East Anglian coinage, it appeared as (still copying the design of West Saxon coinage) 'EÐELSTAN REX' – 'King *Æthelstan*'.

Money is power. Although it is (almost) always an abstracted and symbolic proxy for value, whether it is piles of banknotes or figures moving up and down on digital indices, we understand intuitively that money is bound up tightly with the expression of authority and status. Physical currency embodies and promotes its relationship to state power through the images with which it is encoded, and these convey a host of ideas about the stability of the state, the core symbols of national pride and identity, the strength of the economy, the values of the authority that produces it. Periodic controversy over the personnel selected to decorate modern banknotes demonstrates how important we still feel this to be.

The people of the Viking Age – and the Vikings in particular – often valued coins for their weight as bullion, rather than their face value. But the symbolic qualities of coinage were as readily understood then as they are now. The very power to cause a coinage to be made was a statement in itself – it indicated a willingness, and an ability, to intervene in the means of exchange between people and to regulate the flow of precious metal. It also signalled a desire to engage in behaviours which spoke of elevated political power: all of the coinage of the early medieval period was modelled, to some degree, on the coins produced by Rome, adopted and adapted by the great successor kingdoms that had followed the Empire's demise in the west. Simply having a coinage minted under one's own name was to stake a claim on the legendary and exalted status of Caesar. To mint coins was also to adopt one of the outward trappings of an elite club whose members could consider themselves the heirs of

Rome – the Christian kings of western Europe. This was probably heady stuff for a Viking warlord like Guthrum.

In late 877 he had been one warlord among many, just another Viking chancer plying his bloody business among the surprisingly spongy kingdoms of Britain; by 879 he was the acknowledged king of an ancient realm, baptized by a king anointed by the pope. Of course, being a member of this club also demanded overt Christianity as a condition of membership, and by using his baptismal name (on a coinage also marked with crosses) Guthrum (as Æthelstan) was making sure this message was distributed as widely as possible. Coins were a particularly useful propaganda tool in this regard: nobody could forget who the king was, not when his name was stamped on every new silver penny.[9]

In any case, finding himself the ruler of a kingdom in which the majority of the population were Christian and Anglo-Saxon, Guthrum didn't need to be a Viking Machiavelli to recognize that it would be politic to promote himself as both of these things: if he wanted to be accepted as a legitimate Christian East Anglian king, he would need to *be* a Christian East Anglian. The thoroughness with which new Viking rulers adopted the outward trappings of their adopted kingdom was manifested with the most spectacular irony during the decade after Guthrum's death. In the mid- to late 890s, a new coin was designed and produced that bore the legend 'SC EADMVND REX A' (*Sanctus Eadmund Rex Anglorum*): 'St Edmund, King of the [East] Angles'. Less than a generation after Ivar and Ubbe – the Viking leaders of the *micel here* – had deprived the last native king of East Anglia of his garrulous head, his memory was being celebrated and his cult promoted by the new Anglo-Viking regime.

This wasn't a phenomenon confined to East Anglia. In all of the regions that had fallen under Viking dominance, efforts were under way to create models of authority and cultural compromise that were as indebted to the Anglo-Saxon past as they were to Viking novelty. This was a new world, broken and remade over twenty years of war. But what emerged was not a neatly bifurcated England, split between an Anglo-Saxon south and a Viking north. It was more complicated than that, its identities less clear cut, its politics more tangled, its trajectory uncertain.

> This is the peace which King Alfred and King Guthrum and the councillors of all the English race [*ealles Angelcynnes witan*] and the people who are in East Anglia have all agreed on and confirmed with oaths, for themselves and for all their subjects, both for the living and for the unborn, who care to have God's favour or ours,
>   1. First concerning our boundaries: up the Thames, and then up the Lea, and along the Lea to its source, then in a straight line to Bedford, then up the Ouse to Watling Street.[10]

This is how the treaty of Alfred and Guthrum opens. It was made, not in the immediate aftermath of the battle of Edington, but probably at some point between 886 when Alfred took control of London and 890 when Guthrum died.[11] Its first clause is often described as the earliest definition of the southern boundary of what came to be known as the 'Danelaw' – that part of Britain in which Danish laws and customs prevailed from the end of the ninth century. Traditional maps of Viking settlement use this glorified boundary clause to ink a border on to the map of Britain, plotting a great wobbly diagonal from London to somewhere near Wroxeter. The overall implication of such maps is clear enough, even while scholarship demurs: this was a frontier, and beyond it the English-speaking people of Britain had passed into the clutches of a foreign people, to choke under the Danish yoke until liberation came from the south.

But the 'Danelaw', at least in that sense, never existed; there was no great Viking realm stretching from the Thames to the Tyne. For one thing, the treaty of Alfred and Guthrum makes no mention of any such entity. Indeed, the term 'Danelaw' wasn't recorded until the early eleventh century.[12] What the treaty seems primarily concerned with is defining the extent of Alfred's – rather than Guthrum's – practical authority. Firstly, it implicitly recognizes

Alfred's status as the de facto ruler of all those lands that Viking armies had failed to overrun permanently, while Guthrum (Æthelstan), notably described now as 'king', is associated only with the people of East Anglia, the kingdom to which he had taken his army in 880.

Most of the rest of Britain is abandoned to an undefined sphere of influence, the only clear characteristic of which seems to be that this influence did not belong to Alfred. This was nothing new: East Anglia, Mercia and Northumbria (let alone anything further west or north) had never been part of Wessex and had only briefly (and intermittently) fallen under West Saxon influence. They were, however, all areas into which Viking armies had already intruded and assumed a degree of political control. On the other hand, most of the lands south of the treaty border were regions where West Saxon dominance had been acknowledged for decades.

Most, that is, but not all. Mercia, its native rulers broken and dispossessed, had received rough treatment throughout the 870s. Now, by the terms of the treaty drawn up by Alfred and Guthrum, it was carved up with impunity, divided along a diagonal axis, its south-western territories passing into the care of an expanded, 'Greater' Wessex. In practical charge of the Mercian rump at this time was a man named Æthelred. It seems that he had succeeded Ceolwulf as the ruler of (unoccupied) Mercia, but unlike his predecessor was rarely referred to as king. (The Welsh on his western border, whom he mercilessly harassed during the 880s, considered him to be such, but their opinion counted for little in Wessex.)

Instead, Æthelred was generally referred to as 'ealdorman' in West Saxon sources, or else was given the suitably vague title 'lord of the Mercians'. By 883 he had acknowledged his subservience to Alfred, and in 886 was given delegated authority in London, a new West Saxon acquisition that had also once been subject to the Mercian kings (being granted authority over something which had historically been a possession was a particularly direct demonstration of dispossession and reduced status – a bit like a neighbour annexing part of your garden, and then giving you the job of looking after it). He was subsequently married to Alfred's daughter Æthelflæd (becoming, in an echo of the deal with Guthrum, Alfred's 'son' as well as his political subordinate). Whatever ambitions Æthelred may once have had to revive the fortunes of an autonomous Mercia were being rapidly squished by West Saxon power and tied up in clever dynastic entanglements: absorbed by the Alfredian blob.

And so we should recognize that the treaty was never intended to delimit a *Viking* sphere of influence: not one inch of the land that formed the 'Danelaw' was Alfred's to give, and none of it could have been taken away by him even if he had wanted to. It was, rather, a treaty that enlisted the aid of Alfred's godson, Guthrum, in the formalization of West Saxon territorial claims that now included half of Mercia as well as all of the land south of the Thames: a land charter for a Greater Wessex. Alfred would spend the remainder of his reign crafting that nation into something new – an inclusive national identity, expressed most obviously in the formulation of an unprecedented royal style. No longer would Alfred be described, like his predecessors, only as *rex Westsaxonum* or *rex Occidentalium Saxonum* ('king of the West Saxons'); instead, from the 880s onward, he would increasingly be known instead as *rex Anglorum et Saxonum*, or, as Asser has it, *Ælfred Angul-Saxonum rex*: 'Alfred, king of the Anglo-Saxons'.

A sense of what Alfred was hoping to encapsulate is articulated in the *Anglo-Saxon Chronicle* entry detailing Alfred's occupation of London in 886: 'and to him turned all of the English that were not in thrall to Danish men'.[13] Alfred, it is clear, now saw himself as king of all the 'English' – an idea also present in the first lines of the Alfred–Guthrum treaty with its invocation of 'councillors of all the English race [*ealles Angelcynnes witan*]'. The *Angelcynn* – the 'English-kin' – was an elastic description that would allow him and his dynasty to promote a claim to natural lordship over everyone and anyone who was not considered 'Danish' in the former English-speaking kingdoms of Britain. Indeed, in its most grandiose expression, it went even further, encompassing 'all the Christians of the island of Britain'.[14] Clearly, its formulation was politically expedient, creating an artificial homogeneity among the people Alfred now claimed to govern, papering over the annexation of western Mercia and allowing remarkable leeway for future territorial aggrandizement. But it also created something as powerful as it was illusory, an idea that would refuse to go away: it created the idea of a single English people and, by extension, the idea of a natural and contiguous homeland that could be – should be – subject to the authority of a single king. Far from establishing a coherent 'Danish' realm in Britain, the Viking wars and the agreements of Alfred and Guthrum that followed had produced something far more enduring. Alfred and the Vikings had invented England.[15]

This, of course, was just a little England. In the 890s, it comprised only the rump of Mercia and the land south of the Thames. But, in this act of rebranding, Alfred had created a remarkably durable, and elastic, identity. This identity allowed Alfred's descendants to promote the idea (and perhaps they even believed it themselves) that every act of aggression and territorial expansion directed northwards was a 'liberation' of the English rather than the imperial conquest it really was. The translation of Bede's *Ecclesiastical History of the English People* into Old English around the same time can be seen as part of this project – a new emphasis placed by the West Saxon court on shared history, rather than regional differences. Of course, for this to work it was essential that 'Englishness' could be easily and straightforwardly differentiated from anything else. And it is in this context that we should see the creation of the 'Dane' as the catch-all category for 'foreign johnny', bandied about with great liberality and very little specificity in the pages of the *Anglo-Saxon Chronicle*.[16]

Chesterton saw the battle of Edington as a contest for the soul of England, waged between the noble indigenous peoples of Britain and the dead-eyed Viking alien. This, clearly, is also how Alfred,

Asser and the Anglo-Saxon chronicler wanted us to see it – a watershed for the creation of a unified English community. But this was almost certainly not how the battle was seen by the people who fought in it. Alfred's army was led by the ealdormen of the West Saxon shires, but the origins of the personnel who fought for the king are entirely unknown. About Guthrum's army there can be even less certainty, and it is likely that a part of it (perhaps even a large part of it) was comprised, not of people born overseas, but of Mercians, East Anglians and others of British birth. From a West Saxon perspective such people would still have been Vikings – 'Danes' as the *Anglo-Saxon Chronicle* saw them – despite being just as 'British' as those they fought.

This, indeed, may have been the case from a relatively early date throughout Britain. Although we know that the *micel here* did receive outside reinforcements – the 'great summer-fleet' (*micel sumorlida*) that arrived during 870 from overseas and attached itself to the band fighting Alfred and Æthelred in Wessex is a case in point[17] – it is not at all certain that these were adequate to compensate for the casualties incurred over long campaigns, or for the attrition caused by those Vikings who may have cut their losses and returned home to farm and family. It seems likely, therefore, that some 'Vikings' must have had more local origins,[18] and it is not hard to imagine the mechanisms that might have enabled an itinerant army to attract willing recruits. In the first place, there would always have been lordless men, outlaws and exiles, runaway slaves and disinherited sons, all too eager to join a successful war-band and gain a share in the spoils of war. It was still a problem a century and a half later, when Archbishop Wulfstan of York lamented that 'it happens that a slave escapes from his lord and leaves Christendom to become a Viking [*wicing* – a rare contemporary use of the word in Old English]'.[19] If this was happening in the eleventh century, there is little reason to suppose that it was not happening in the ninth.[20]

It is also important to remember that warfare between the Anglo-Saxon kingdoms and their neighbours had long been endemic.

Although the nature of warfare may have changed, to a young Anglo-Saxon warrior with a lust for treasure and adventure, joining a Viking raiding army on a campaign in some other part of Britain would not have seemed too dissimilar to the expeditions mounted by men of his father's or grandfather's generation. Moreover, it is also likely that – in those regions where Viking warlords had established more formal political control – men who had always owed military service of some sort would have continued to feel that their allegiances were local rather than ethnic; such men were likely to have had few qualms about following a 'foreign' king in raids on their neighbours, perpetuating traditions of insular animosity dating back centuries. This tendency would have been magnified if new rulers promised plunder, advancement and security for farms and families – even more so, if they were bright enough to see the value in embracing an English name and the religion of their subjects.

But it was not only the English of the 'Danelaw' who could become Vikings in West Saxon eyes. The fifth and final clause of the treaty of Alfred and Guthrum makes it clear that the possibility of members of Alfred's new *Angelcynn* skipping off to join the 'Danes' was viewed as a real problem: 'And we agreed on the day when the oaths were sworn that no slaves or freemen might go over to the [Danish] army without permission, any more than any of theirs to us.'[21] Indeed, the danger of Alfred's subjects renouncing their West Saxon loyalties may lie behind Alfred's treatment of the Wiltshire ealdorman Wulfhere, who was stripped of his lands for 'leaving without permission';[22] it was not just those at the bottom of society who could be considered an Anglo-Saxon in the morning and a 'Dane' by the afternoon. And if further proof of the flimsiness of these ethnic labels were required, West Saxon dynastic politics would eventually deliver it – in spectacular fashion – on Alfred's death.

13

ROGUE TRADERS

It was a scene of strange incongruity, for in contrast with these
barbaric men and their rough songs and shouts, the walls were hung
with rare spoils that betokened civilized workmanship. Fine tapestries
that Norman women had worked; richly chased weapons that princes
of France and Spain had wielded; armour and silken garments from
Byzantium and the Orient – for the dragon ships ranged far.

ROBERT E. HOWARD, 'The Dark Man' (1931)[1]

In his appraisal of Alfred's later years, Bishop Asser was at pains to
stress the frustrating lengths to which the king had gone in his
efforts to galvanize his subjects into undertaking works for the good
of the realm. It is fairly clear, however, from the bishop's tone in this
part of his biography that Alfred had encountered real difficulty in
convincing his people that they wanted to spend (or wanted their
slaves to spend) their afternoons digging ditches, or raising pali-
sades, or whatever other toil the local reeve had been tasked with
delegating. Indeed, when we hear the list of labours that the king
required of his people ('cities and towns to be rebuilt [...] others to
be constructed where previously there were none'; 'treasures incom-
parably fashioned in gold and silver at his instigation'; 'royal halls
and chambers marvellously constructed of stone and wood'; 'royal
residences of masonry, moved from their old position and splen-
didly reconstructed at more appropriate places by his royal

command'), it is no wonder that 'gently instructing' and 'cajoling' soon gave way to 'commanding, and (in the end, when his patience was exhausted) [...] sharply chastising those who were disobedient' and 'despising popular stupidity and stubbornness in every way'.[2]

Evidently, however, all this chastising and despising wasn't always enough, and the king sometimes needed outside intervention in order to convince his subjects of the wisdom of his building programmes. When, according to Asser, Alfred's efforts failed to yield the desired results, and 'enemy forces burst in by land or sea (or, as frequently happens, by both!)',[3] it merely served to teach the people of Greater Wessex a valuable lesson about the unimpeachable wisdom of their king. His wretched subjects 'having lost their fathers, spouses, children, servants, slaves, handmaidens, the fruits of their labours and all their possessions' were probably wasting their time if they thought they could expect much compassion from their spiritual and political leaders: Asser was clear about where to place the blame. The laziness, stubbornness, ineptitude and ingratitude of the people had, in the bishop's eyes, brought affliction down upon their own heads.[4] And, as he approvingly noted, at least those who had 'negligently scorned the royal commands' now 'loudly applaud the king's foresight and promise to do what they had previously refused – that is, with respect to constructing fortresses and to the other things of general advantage to the whole kingdom'.[5]

This is all, of course, the authorized version of events, a narrative constructed to serve the interests of the king. The reality seems to be that Alfred was indeed making practical and long-term changes to the way in which the defence of his kingdom was organized and was also trying hard to overcome resistance to his innovations; it is equally clear, however, that on both counts the king's efforts sometimes failed. (The temptation to blame everyone else for the bungling of executive orders can often be an appealing strategy for a regime and its apologists.) Overwhelmingly, however, whatever the success rates of his projects and the obstacles encountered, what comes across most strongly from Asser's account is the scale of Alfred's ambition: he saw a kingdom ennobled by learning and literacy, adorned with towns and palaces of stone, glittering with treasures of silver and gold. And he wanted to be remembered for it: Asser's biography alone is enough to tell us that Alfred was a man who keenly felt the weight of his own destiny and the desire to preserve its memory.

When he was a small boy, Alfred had travelled to Rome as part of a diplomatic mission, possibly accompanied by his father, possibly by others.[6] While he was there he met the pope who, according to the *Anglo-Saxon Chronicle*, 'hallowed him as king, and took him as his spiritual son'.[7] The questions of when Alfred travelled, who went with him, which pope he met (Leo or Benedict?) and what, precisely, happened when he did, have long been matters of scholarly debate. It is obvious that, from the perspective of West Saxon writers of the 890s, the idea that Alfred was marked for future kingly greatness at such an early age by the heir of St Peter would have been an attractive one to emphasize. It would be wrong, therefore, to take it too seriously – Alfred, after all, still had three older brothers at this stage of his career. However, no matter how faulty his memory and whatever ideas might have been put into the king's head over the years since his meeting with the pope, it would be wrong to assume that Alfred himself did not believe that *something* transcendent, something numinous, had touched him in the holy city. It is likely, indeed, that his experience of Rome affected him deeply.

Imagine the impression it must have left on a boy of five (or eight) whose knowledge of royal and holy splendour began and ended with his father's weather-beaten timber halls and stocky Saxon churches like Winchester Old Minster – impressive, no doubt, in their proper context, but cattle-sheds in comparison with the Pantheon (into which the Old Minster would have fitted several times over) or the mosaic-embellished Basilica of Santa Prassede (completed in the early 820s), let alone the Colosseum, its white marble carcass gleaming in ruinous splendour beneath the Mediterranean sun. If one adds to this the liturgical mystery and material splendour, the carefully cultivated sense of immanent divinity and imperial patrimony that the papacy was uniquely placed to deploy, it becomes difficult to see how the furniture of any sensitive and intelligent young mind could fail to be radically and permanently rearranged. Alfred may well have grown up feeling himself selected for a higher destiny and touched by God, and perhaps some of this lay behind the king's ambitions in education, building works and administrative and military organization: he had seen first hand the legacies that empire could leave, and the role of the divine in animating and motivating their revival.[8] Whatever else, it must have left him with memories – the magical, nostalgia-soaked images of childhood, of an eternal city, shining white and gold, under a sky of endless blue.

One of the most obvious ways in which Alfred's zeal for *Romanitas* manifested itself was in the choice of the 'cities and towns to be rebuilt' and the manner in which 'others [were] to be constructed where previously there were none'.[9] The *urbes* and *oppida* of Roman Britain, long left to wrack and ruin, began to be restored across the West Saxon realm: Bath, Exeter, Winchester and the City of London were slowly restored to the heart of political, economic and social life, their walls repaired, their centres redeveloped. Elsewhere – at Wallingford for example – new proto-urban centres were laid out on a grid that recalled the regular cruciform street plans of Roman towns. Some of the targets for development had already been important places prior to this new phase of consolidation: Malmesbury had been a monastery since the seventh century, Wareham the location of a major church (a minster) and the resting place of King Beorhtric of Wessex, the king whose reign had ushered in the Viking Age in Britain.

But, however motivated Alfred may have been by dreams of civilization (literally, 'city-dwelling'), there is no doubt that the immediate catalyst for this burst of energy was the need to boost the defences of the realm. We have already seen how hard it was in this period of rudimentary siegecraft to dislodge an enemy who had dug himself in – Alfred had experienced this to his own cost at Nottingham, Reading and Exeter – and the need to protect winter stores, people, livestock, property and production had been demonstrated time and time again from the late eighth century onward. Alfred, so it would seem, was not a man to let lessons go unlearned: his would be a kingdom well organized and well fortified, prepared for anything that might threaten it.

At some point between the 880s and the early tenth century, a document was produced, known now as the *Burghal Hidage*.[10] It is a list of around thirty defensible settlements – 'burhs' in Old English (the root of the word 'borough' and the element 'bury' in the names of so many English towns) – of varying origin. Some of them, like Wallingford, were built from scratch; others reused the masonry circuits of dilapidated Roman towns or the earthworks of Iron Age hill-forts, places which had often been neglected for centuries as settlements, but which had retained a powerful grip on the Anglo-Saxon imagination as meeting places, battlefields and the subject of poetry and legend. The purpose of the *Burghal Hidage* was to assess the amount of military manpower required to garrison and maintain each burh according to the length of its defensive circuit and the amount of land from which that manpower could be drawn.[11] More than forts, but not yet true towns, the burhs seem to have been conceived piecemeal in the later years of Alfred's reign and the early years of his son Edward the Elder's in response to the continuing threat of Viking attack from within and without Britain, with the existential threat the *micel here* had posed still fresh in the collective memory. It was, in its primary purpose, a military solution to a specific set of circumstances, a successful one – as Alfred's later reign bore out – and one that his son Edward and daughter Æthelflæd (the lady of the Mercians) continued to roll out in the course of their own bellicose careers.[12]

But burhs also proved to offer a remarkably durable model for imposing, organizing and protecting essential aspects of state governance (such as the minting of coins) in the localities where they were laid out or renewed, as well as providing hubs for manufacture and commerce – places where the inhabitants of the dispersed rural hinterland could exchange agricultural produce for manufactured goods. In this respect, they took over some of the functions that had previously been reserved to monasteries and royal or aristocratic estate centres. As a result, the burhs of the late ninth and early tenth centuries were swiftly on their way to becoming true towns, and though some failed to develop (Eashing, Chisbury, Sashes, the unidentified Eorpeburnan),[13] others were to become (and many still remain) the principal urban centres of the English realm.[14]

In fairness to the rest of Anglo-Saxon England, Alfred and his descendants probably receive too much of the credit for these innovations in urban planning: Mercia seems to have had burhs of its own – at Winchcombe, Hereford and Tamworth.[15] York clearly had defences in 865 (for all the good they did); Thetford, Lincoln and other settlements of East Anglia and the east midlands may or may not have been significantly developed before they fell into Viking hands in the 870s; trading settlements at London, Southampton, Ipswich, Canterbury and York had been in business since the eighth century. But the network of West Saxon burhs was still the most extensive, coherent and ambitious system of planned development in Britain since Roman times, and there can be little doubt that it was principally Viking aggression that had hastened the agglomeration of administrative, ecclesiastical, economic and military functions.

The Vikings, it can be argued, were responsible not just for creating the conditions that gave rise to the nascent English state, but also for the birth of towns and cities, even (or especially) in the parts of southern England that they had never conquered and colonized. They were not, however, merely the unwitting agents of change, catalysts in a chemical reaction in which they themselves remained stable and unaltered. They were, on the contrary, deeply implicated in these changes from the beginning, shaping the outcomes of the socio-economic revolution that their presence had started, their own identities mutating and fusing in the process. The maritime technology and international trading connections that the Vikings brought to Britain were, in this regard, fundamental. So too was the example that they set for the growth of towns. For when Alfred and Edward cast around for the models that their burhs might take, it was not only a dream of Rome that animated the will: closer, more practical, more familiar models already lay close at hand. For the Vikings, from the moment they first stayed over the winter, had been pioneers of the densely settled, bounded and defensible, commercial and administrative hub.

Viking camps had provided a way of life to their inhabitants since the first over-wintering of Viking raiding armies in Britain in the mid-800s. These camps were temporary – at least at first – often adapting structures and defences that were already present (the enclosure at Repton and the camp at Reading are famous examples). But archaeologically the most revealing material in Britain has come from other sites: from Torksey in Lincolnshire and another undisclosed site in north Yorkshire.[16] In Ireland, these Viking winter camps were known as *longphuirt* (singular *longphort*), and several of these camps mutated over time into true urban settlements, the nuclei of what are still Ireland's most populous towns: Dublin, Waterford, Wexford, Limerick and Cork.[17] In England there is little evidence that any camp developed in this way, and when Viking armies turned to permanent settlement it was in places that had at least some pre-existing infrastructure. Nevertheless, the habits developed in places like these – the close-order living, the reliance on local rural communities for food and resources (rather than farming the land directly), the self-sufficiency in craft and manufacture, the provision for shipping, the market economy – translated easily to urban life.

At Torksey, for example, where the *micel here* ensconced itself on a low bluff beside the River Trent over the winter of 872/3, a site of around 65 acres has been discovered through the combined efforts of amateur metal detectorists and professional archaeologists – a sprawling encampment where a large army once lived and transacted its business. And 'business' is the right word, for among the gaming pieces that once marched across wooden boards, only to be lost, perhaps, in the upheaval of the arguments they inspired in drunk and enervated fighting men, were found the tools of craft and industry and the mechanisms of trade. Weaving and smelting, sewing and leatherworking, fishing and woodworking – even the production of imitative coins; this was the self-sustaining business of a proto-town, whose inhabitants were busy with repairs and the provision of essentials: weapons and clothing, ship repairs and sail-cloth, food and tools. And then there are the weights and scales, the coins and the bullion.

More than 350 coins were found at Torksey, including silver pennies of the 860s and 870s struck in England and a large number of copper-alloy 'stycas', a low-value and rather unglamorous Northumbrian coinage of the pre-Viking period. It is these coins that, in great measure, enabled archaeologists to date and identify the encampment as belonging to the *micel here*'s stop at Torksey in 872/3. Crucially, however, it was not only English coins that were discovered. The ground gave up 123 Arabic dirhams, many of them cut into smaller pieces, coins that had once exchanged hands in the streets of Merv (Turkmenistan) or Wasit (Iraq), left to seed the Lincolnshire soil. The dates of these coins, the youngest of which were struck in the late 860s, support the dating of the encampment. But the presence of the fragmentary dirhams is interesting in a number of other ways. Islamic silver coins flowed into Scandinavia in great numbers during the ninth century, travelling up the Russian river-systems towards the Baltic in return for the slaves, furs and amber that poured south. It was this trade that Arab travellers like ibn Fadlan were witnessing when they wrote their accounts of the exotic barbarians they met on the banks of the Volga and elsewhere. The fact that the *micel here* was carrying this coinage in volume, and that some of them were struck later than the arrival of the *micel here* in England, suggests that Viking armies in England remained connected to these sources of silver, even as they kicked their heels on the banks of the Trent. For these venture capitalists of the Viking

Age, the rivers of England and Russia, the sea-roads of the North Sea and the Caspian, were all just byways of one great interconnected network: a world-wide web of slaves and silver.

The fact, however, that the coins were cut into smaller pieces indicates something else significant. For most of the Viking Age, even when Viking rulers were producing coins of their own, a system of economics prevailed across areas of Viking influence that valued precious metal (primarily silver, but also gold and copper alloys) by weight alone. In such a system, silver coins were valuable not so much because they were 'money' but because they represented portable units of precious metal that could be easily melted down and re-formed into other shapes and sizes (as arm-rings, say, or ingots), or broken up into smaller bits as the need arose. And it was not only coins that were tossed into the crucible. Regardless of whether the labour and smithcraft was invested by Anglo-Saxon, Irish or Scandinavian artisans, no work of delicate artistry or imaginative skill, no filigree or niello, enamel or inlay, wire work or beading was safe when the weight of the metal was what mattered: all was there to be melted down or chopped into bits. 'Hack-silver' and, more rarely, 'hack-gold' are commonly found in Viking hoards and settlement sites; both were found at Torksey. Such fragments represent the loose change of a bullion economy, the shrapnel required to top up a large amount or to exchange for lower-value goods. Also present at Torksey are ingots, the result of the melting and re-forming of coins and other objects into bars of precious metal that were easily transported and stored. These provided the raw material for creating new objects, or as convenient building-blocks to be weighed out in a transaction.

The technology of such transactions was also there at Torksey. Dozens of weights were found, many of the 'cubo-octahedral' and 'oblate-spheroid' types that copied the design and weight standards of those encountered in the Islamic world. The latter are colloquially known as 'barrel weights'. The former, with six square and eight triangular faces (imagine a cube with the corners filed down to flat triangular planes), each decorated with a varying number of incised dots, are often known – for obvious reasons – as 'dice weights'. These designs were a visual marker of reliability and, thanks to their incised decoration and distinctive shapes, hard to tamper with.[18] Finally, of course, scales were required, to weigh out silver, to calibrate weights, to measure out loose commodities such as amber, jet, beads or grain. Fragments of a simple balance were recovered from Torksey, but beautifully preserved examples have been found at centres of Viking commerce across the northern world.[19]

Consider, for a moment, what this evidence for trade – at a temporary military encampment unexpectedly thrown up in the Lincolnshire countryside – implies about interactions between Viking armies and local populations. Certainly it suggests that local people were willing to enter into a trading relationship with the *micel here* – the Viking army cannot have been dealing with anyone else, and interaction was probably frequent and associations increasingly familiar. That does not mean, however, that those relationships were symmetrical or respectful ones: trade is not always a happy transaction of goods and services, a mutually beneficial exercise in cultural interchange. It is undeniable that trade has, historically, been one of the greatest drivers of technological innovation, improvements in living standards and the spread of knowledge and ideas. But this is far from being a complete picture: diseases spread faster than knowledge, technology kills as readily as it cures, not all ideas are worth sharing. The history of mercantile adventure, moreover, presents a spectacularly corrupt and bloody carcass: from the infernal horrors of the Belgian Congo to the moral abortion of the Opium Wars, from the mercantile tyranny of the East India Company to the brutality of Amazonian rubber barons, trade has often gone hand in hand with greed, violence and injustice.

It is this tension that makes the signature 'debate' of Viking studies – 'raiders or traders?' – so wearisome and irritating. For what could a Viking army camped on the Trent have had that the local people might have been tempted to buy? The treasures looted from local churches perhaps? The livestock driven from their fields? The grain they had stored against the winter? Their friends? Their families? An account of a Viking army campaigning in France (also during the later ninth century) recorded that they struck camp on an island in the Loire: there they 'held crowds of prisoners in chains', and launched mounted raids to devastate the surrounding countryside. The *Anglo-Saxon Chronicle* makes it plain that Viking camps in Britain disgorged similar raiding parties (it was just such a raid that fell foul of Ealdorman Æthelwulf and the Berkshire *fyrd* in 870). Such raids would have been necessary to provision a large force over winter; but the potential for profiteering from the cruelties inflicted on the locals was ever present. Imagine the misery of a people forced to trade their winter food supplies for their beaten and abused husbands, wives and children, think of them watching blankly as some barbarian measured out the lives of their kin in grain – scales stacked with corn, blood for barley, pigs for people: desperate efforts, in Asser's words, to 'redeem those captured from a hateful captivity'.[20]

Nor was it only human lives that were bartered in this way.

Ealdorman Ælfred and his wife wander through the camp, their cloaks splattered with mud as they stumble on the uneven ground, tripping on tent pegs, skirting the camp-fires. The air thrums with hammers on iron, axes in wood. Away in the distance a wooden pen holds prisoners, shackled and beaten, staring vacantly towards a place that no one else can see. Ælfred and Werburg try not to look at them, terrified of meeting a familiar gaze. As they walk, their own vulnerability radiates from them, turning every foreign word to an insult, distant laughter to cruel jeers. Suddenly, they find the way blocked by a pair of big men, rising suddenly from the low table where they had been seated, pushing dome-shaped pieces of whalebone across a wooden board. They seem to Werburg to leer with undisguised intent, their thoughts as plain as if they had dropped their trousers. Ælfred stammers and waves his hands and eventually they are pointed towards a nearby tent.

Inside, a fat man sits behind a table strewn with silver coins and bullion. Ælfred speaks a little, haltingly, stuttering the words, and a smirking translator – a Northumbrian from his accent – repeats them in Old Norse. A pudgy hand reaches out, to grab the bag of coins that Ælfred offers, spilling them swiftly on to the table. They are gold – coins made long ago, fashioned by the bishops and the old kings of Kent. Surprised, the Viking takes one up and bites down upon it, bends it in his teeth. In the Viking's grimace Ælfred spots the dark grooves that score the man's teeth, blue bands of self-inflicted mutilation; he shudders.[21] The Viking draws a knife and picks up more coins, the point picking and scratching at their surfaces with deft movements born of long practice, like a man gouging the stones from cherries.[22] He grunts, and shovels them on to the pan of a set of scales that hang suspended from a post beside the table. Slowly he places little barrel-shaped weights on to the other side. After a while he looks up, says a few words in Norse. 'Not enough,' the translator sneers.

The tension in the tent rises. The Viking narrows his eyes, looks hard at Werburg and hauls himself upright, reaching out towards her breast. She starts away, Ælfred's hand moving instinctively to his sword hilt. The sound of a weapon unsheathing near the tent door freezes them both, and the hand that had paused in mid-air continues its progress towards the ealdorman's wife, closing around the circular silver brooch she wears on her chest, ripping it suddenly from the fabric. He turns it over in his hands, a silver disc, chased with images of running deer and hounds, the detail limned in black. He tosses it on to the table and the knife comes down, point into the wood and the handle hammered down hard. The brooch splits in one movement, the silver sheared through like hard cheese. The Viking adds half of the brooch to another set of scales, adding weights until he grunts in satisfaction. He bends over to root around in a pile of objects on the floor, retrieving a pile of manuscript pages, tied up in string. Rising red-faced, he tosses them to Ælfred who catches them clumsily, and the couple turn to leave. 'Wait,' comes the voice of the translator. 'Doesn't the lady want her brooch back?'

And they turn, a mangled lump of silver held up in the grinning Viking's fist.

The *Stockholm Codex Aureus* ('the Golden Book') is a copy of the gospels in Latin. The manuscript is a work of art probably produced in Canterbury during the eighth century, glimmering gilded letters and spiral illuminations recalling other famous treasures of the early Anglo-Saxon Church.[23] In the mid-ninth century, however, around a century after the labours of its creators – Ceolhard, Ealhhun, Niclas and Wulfhelm the goldsmith – had come to an end, a new inscription was added:

> + *In the name of our Lord Jesus Christ.* I, Ealdorman Ælfred, and my wife Werburg procured these books from the heathen invading army with our own money; the purchase was made with pure gold. And we did that for the love of God and for the benefit of our souls, and because neither of us wanted these holy works to remain any longer in heathen hands. And now we wish to present them to Christ Church [Canterbury] to God's praise and glory and honour, and as thanksgiving for his sufferings, and for the use of the religious community which glorifies God daily in Christ Church; in order that they should be read aloud every month for Ælfred and for Werburg and for Alhthryth, for the eternal salvation of their souls, as long as God decrees that Christianity should survive in that place. And also I, Ealdorman Ælfred, and Werburg beg and entreat in the name of Almighty God and of all his saints that no man should

be so presumptuous as to give away or remove these holy works
from Christ Church as long as Christianity survives there.

Ælfred
Werburg
Alhthryth *their daughter*[24]

The *Stockholm Codex Aureus* was bought back by Ælfred around
the time that the first Viking camps are recorded in the *Anglo-Saxon
Chronicle* (the first was established at Thanet in 850 – not, we might
note, very far away from Ælfred's own shire of Surrey, or from the
place – Canterbury – at which the book was probably made and to
which it was returned). Of course, we have no idea how this transaction really played out, but it is extraordinary evidence: both for
the reality of the Viking acquisition of holy treasures (almost
certainly through violence or menaces) and for the fact that Viking
armies were trading with local people from the moment they
started to maintain a longer-term presence in Britain (if not before).

For all that Viking winter camps like Torksey were superficially
'urban', they would not – in any known case – develop into lasting
towns in England. They may have established some of the habits of
urban living, may even have given pointers to West Saxon kings
about the value of defensible multi-purpose settlements, but they
were doomed to be short lived. In little over a generation, however,
Scandinavian settlers – whose constituents hailed from overwhelmingly rural communities – had become strongly identified with the
control of places which developed, unequivocally, into 'proper'
towns, many of which have yielded little or no evidence of prior
Anglo-Saxon occupation, and certainly none on a scale or density
comparable to the truly urban environments they became.[25] At
Thetford, Cambridge, Huntingdon, Bedford, Northampton,
Stamford, Leicester, Derby, Nottingham, Lincoln and York,

metropolitan life was suddenly beginning to bloom from the withered remnants of defunct Roman garrison forts and old Mercian estate centres, even as the wonky gridirons of the West Saxon burh were being stamped down on to the landscape in a creeping northward expansion.

The interwoven causes and effects of the economic growth that followed the Viking irruption can be difficult to disentangle: the relative weight that is ascribed to the West Saxon state versus Viking entrepreneurship – to determined planning and top-down reforms of currency, law and administration versus the free-wheeling enterprise of an unregulated merchant-warrior class – is, to a certain degree, a matter of preference, subject specialism and, perhaps, personal politics. We certainly shouldn't discount the impact of the new trading connections that Viking armies brought with them, or the redistribution of wealth that their activities had entailed: think of all that Islamic silver, flowing from the Baltic as the human cargo travelled east; imagine the chalices and processional crosses 'liberated' from the treasure houses of the Church, melted into ingots. It must all have provided quite the economic boost.

Unwelcome interactions like the one that Ælfred and Werburg experienced may well have continued to be a feature of British life for some time after the period of Viking settlement began in England. Within the 'Danelaw', however, it is likely that as communities gradually became more integrated and Viking armies more permanently settled, trading relationships would have grown less exploitative, the differences between newcomers and settled communities less sharply delineated. Regional identities, often definitive in this period, would have rapidly swallowed ethnic distinctions as fashions and languages merged and cultural practices homogenized. People whose families had previously thought of themselves as East Anglians or Northumbrians would doubtless have continued to do so. But in eastern Mercia, in the absence of clear royal authority, narrower loyalties would have risen in importance. Mixed communities of Scandinavians and Anglo-Saxons would probably have identified primarily with local places around which the economic aspects of their lives revolved, and to which they increasingly looked for political, spiritual and military leadership, and the same may have been true in parts of East Anglia and Northumbria.[26] This must be partly conjectural, and the evidence – as ever – is thin. But what evidence there is certainly points in this direction, not least the speed with which 'Danish' authority ultimately collapsed in the face of a concerted campaign from the politically unified kingdom to the south.

14

DANELAW

'I will offer thee another course of law, that we go on the holm here at
the Thing, and let him have the property who has the victory.' That
was also the law which Egil spake, and a custom of old, that every
man had the right to challenge another to holmgang, whether he
would defend himself or pursue his foe.

SNORRI STURLUSON(?), *Egil's Saga* (thirteenth century)[1]

Cuthrum–Æthelstan died in 890 and was remembered with
something approaching fondness in the *Anglo-Saxon
Chronicle*.[2] Although Viking raids on Wessex had continued
throughout the 880s, and tensions had occasionally flared around
the East Anglian borders, there had been no serious trouble for
Alfred to contend with.[3] This all changed after Guthrum's death,
and Alfred spent several years of the final decade of his own life,
alongside his adult son Edward, engaged in conflict with new waves
of Viking raiders, the most dangerous of whom were a group led by
a warlord called Hæsten, who arrived – fresh from harassing the
Frankish kingdoms – in 892 and gathered fighters from East Anglia
and Northumbria. Once again, Alfred's kingdom was in grave
danger, with Viking armies roaming from Essex to the Severn, and
from the Sussex coast to Chester.[4] But ultimately the Alfred of the
890s was too experienced a warlord to suffer again the indignities
of 878. By 896, the worst of this fresh wave of violence was over,

partly thanks to the king's programme of fortress building and military reforms. Hæsten's army dispersed – some to East Anglia and Northumbria, others back across the Channel – and the Anglo-Saxon chronicler, sounding more than ever like Marvin the Paranoid Android, was able to celebrate the news that 'The raiding-horde, thank God, had not totally and utterly crushed the English.' (The chronicler added, however, as though concerned that this sounded a trifle too upbeat, that 'they were greatly more crushed in those three years with pestilence amongst cattle and men.')[5]

Alfred died in 899. In the course of his lifetime he had seen Britain irrevocably transformed, and he ended his days as the king of a realm defined in ways that his predecessors could never have imagined. His obituary in the *Anglo-Saxon Chronicle* described him as 'king over all the English race except that part which was under Danish control,'[6] a neat summation of the shift which had occurred during his reign – a delimitation of authority which was primarily ethnic rather than territorial. And yet the degree to which those ethnic constructs remained mutable and contestable was dramatically exposed on the king's death.

Alfred was, as we might expect, succeeded by his son Edward, known to posterity as 'the Elder'.[7] Not everyone, however, was happy to see Edward ascend to the throne. Alfred's nephew, Æthelwold, did rather poorly out of Alfred's will, and was evidently disgruntled by the manner in which he had been passed over.[8] The younger (and probably the only surviving) son of Alfred's elder brother, King Æthelred (the man who had prayed so vigorously at the battle of Ashdown in 871), Æthelwold had a decent claim to the West Saxon throne. Instead he had been left with three estates in Surrey, far from the centre of West Saxon power – much less than what even Alfred's obscure kinsman Osferth was to receive.[9] In any case, whatever the rights and wrongs of his grievance, his actions articulated the strength of it without room for ambiguity. With Alfred's body barely cold, he seized the royal manor at Twynham (now Christchurch, Dorset) and then rode to Wimborne (also Dorset), to the burial place of his father King Æthelred, where

– alive to the threat that Edward posed – he 'barricaded all the gates against him, and said that he would live there or die there'.[10]

Edward, for his part, took an army to Badbury Rings, the massive Neolithic hill-fort that dominates the landscape of east Dorset. As political theatre these were striking choices. Whereas Æthelwold had laid claim to his father's resting place, no doubt in an attempt to send a message that emphasized his dynastic claims, Edward's choice of Badbury Rings drew on older and deeper wells of political legitimacy. Whether or not the Anglo-Saxons identified this place (as later generations would) with Mount Badon – the location of the legendary victory of the Britons over the Saxons in the sixth century[11] – the massive earthworks would have spoken in primal terms of power that welled up from another age, the vast earthen ramparts the work of supernatural builders and the mighty kings of old. Not only that, but Badbury was also the hundred meeting place of the district in which it stood: by using it as his fortress, Edward was raising his standard not merely on his dynastic claims, but on an ancient and embedded sense of community, territory and antiquity.

Whether it was this or more pragmatic concerns that eroded Æthelwold's resolve, it swiftly transpired that his nerve was less robust than his rhetoric. Taking with him a nun he had extracted from the convent at Wimborne (whether or not she was a willing accomplice, we shall never know), Æthelwold 'rode away under cover of night and sought out the raiding army in Northumbria',[12] where 'they received him as king and submitted to him'.[13] The *Annals of St Neots*, a later chronicle based (probably) on a lost manuscript of the *Anglo-Saxon Chronicle*, puts this extraordinary moment in even more surprising terms. There Æthelwold, son of Æthelred, son of Æthelwulf, son of Ecgberht, scion of the house of Wessex, is described as *rex paganorum* and *rex danorum*: 'King of the Pagans; King of the Danes'.[14]

*

Æthelwold has been described as one of the "'Nearly Men" of early medieval Europe'.[15] During the five years that followed his nocturnal flight from Wessex in 899, the ætheling's flame flared brightly, a brief consuming fire. In that flickering red light we can see the dreams of deeds undone, of destiny unfulfilled – a Viking England united by a man thrice begotten of West Saxon kings, trampling the wreckage of his father's realm at the head of a great Anglo-Viking horde. It would not come to pass; Æthelwold's flame would be extinguished in the leeching damp of the East Anglian Fens.

In 902, Æthelwold brought a fleet to Essex and caused the submission of the East Saxon kingdom. Quite where he had come from, whom he had convinced of his regal standing and why they had acquiesced so readily is unknown, but it may be that he managed to convince a substantial faction in the 'Danelaw' that his claim to the West Saxon throne – and the divided loyalties of its aristocracy – meant that the conquest of Wessex was once again a realistic prospect. The submission of Essex would have been a blow to King Edward: Essex had long formed a buffer zone between West Saxon and East Anglian control. Later in 902, Æthelwold made his move, bringing an army out of East Anglia and advancing into English Mercia, raiding and burning as he went, before crossing the Thames at Cricklade in Wiltshire and plundering the region around Braydon. This was a raid, not an attempt at conquest, and Æthelwold swiftly led his army (laden down 'with all that they could grab'),[16] back to East Anglia. But the fact that he had penetrated so far into Wessex unopposed had sent an unmistakable message to his cousin Edward. The reciprocal raid came immediately. Edward raised an army and chased Æthelwold into East Anglia, ravaging territory from the Devil's Dyke (Cambridgeshire) to the River Wissey and the Fens (Norfolk). Edward, however, like Æthelwold, seems to have had little appetite for battle and ordered a retreat. For reasons that remain obscure, however, the men of Kent disobeyed their king and remained in East Anglia.

A measure of Edward's mounting panic (or, perhaps, of his determination to explain what may have been a monumental blunder) is conveyed by the *Anglo-Saxon Chronicle*'s insistence that he dispatched no fewer than seven messengers in his desperation to recall the Kentish contingent. It was to no avail. Æthelwold's armies surrounded the Kentish force at a place called 'the Holm' and a savage battle was fought. The most evocative description was provided by the West Saxon ealdorman Æthelweard, who wrote a chronicle in Latin at some point towards the end of the tenth century:

> They clashed shields, brandished swords, and in either hand the spear was much shaken. And there fell Ealdorman Sigewulf, and Sigehelm, and a part of the Kentish gentry nearly all-inclusive; and Haruc, king of the barbarians, was there let down to the lower world. Two princes of the English, soft of beard, then left the air they breathed ever before, and entered a strange region below the waves of Acheron, and so did much of the nobility on either side. In the end the barbarians were victors, and held the field with exultation.[17]

It was clearly a disaster for the men of Kent, although quite how exultant the barbarians can really have been, considering the apparently ghastly death toll and the demise of their king, is open to question. The 'Haruc' mentioned by Æthelweard was Eohric, king (it is generally assumed) of East Anglia. Perhaps more significant, however, was the detail supplied by the *Anglo-Saxon Chronicle* in its rather more sober (and contemporary) account of the battle: Æthelwold was killed in the fighting.[18]

The Fens – with their vast skies and level horizons, their dykes and waterways, bogs and meres – are an unfriendly environment to those unfamiliar with them: disorientating and alien. At their wildest they can feel like a remnant of a forgotten world, when mammoth and aurochs wandered the wide plains of Doggerland, the lost land that once connected East Anglia with continental Europe – our own Stone Age Atlantis, drowned beneath the North Sea. The Fens are an unending sea of sedges and peat beds – a paradise, as the Somerset Levels once were, for insects and wading birds, amphibians and water mammals. Like the Levels, the Fens were mostly drained long ago and only 1 per cent of the original wetlands, at places like Lakenheath (Suffolk) and Wicken Fen (Cambridgeshire), still survive.[19] This is enough, however, for us to imagine how the region appeared to those who fought and died here a thousand years ago. It would have been an appalling place for a battle, particularly for those who did not know the lie of the land; when lines broke, desperate men would have lost the security of dry land, flummoxed by the blankness of the Fens, floundering into the mire, choking their lives out in the sucking peat bogs.

The name of the place where the battle was supposedly fought – 'the Holme' – is Old Norse in origin, from *holmr* ('small islet', or 'area of dry land set in wetland'). In the midst of the Fens, the meaning is obvious: any raised area of dry land can feel like an island rising from the reed beds. Although *holmr* is a relatively common topographical term in England (with around fifty examples around the country), most of these apply to small, isolated places, and there is no other battlefield of the early Middle Ages in England that is identified with this place-name element.[20] The term, however, had a particular significance in Old Norse literature, where it referred to the idealized location of a type of quasi-judicial knockabout known as the *hólmgang* (lit. 'island-going'), a form of arbitration-by-combat, a settling of differences through formalized and circumscribed violence.

Several accounts describe duels and *hólmgang* fought in Britain. *Flóamanna saga*, for example, tells the tale of the Icelander Thorgils who fought a *hólmgang* in Caithness on behalf of Olaf, the local *jarl*. The most elaborate description of the *hólmgang* ritual is contained in *Kormáks saga*, a thirteenth-century account of the life of the Hiberno-Icelandic skald Kormákr Ögmundarson. The saga describes a weird and highly ritualized event, revealing how it was the 'the law of the *hólmgang*' that a hide should be spread on the ground, 'with loops at its corners. Into these should be driven certain pins with heads to them, called *tjosnur*. He who made it ready should go to the pins in such a manner that he could see sky between his legs, holding the lobes of his ears and speaking the forewords used in the rite called "The Sacrifice of the *tjosnur*". Once this was done, 'Three squares should be marked round the hide, each one foot broad. At the outermost corners of the squares should be four poles, called hazels; when this is done, it is a hazelled field.'

Only after these bewildering preparations had been accomplished could the combat commence:

> Each man should have three shields, and when they were cut up
> he must get upon the hide if he had given way from it before,
> and guard himself with his weapons alone thereafter. He who
> had been challenged should strike the first stroke. If one was
> wounded so that blood fell upon the hide, he should fight no
> longer. If either set one foot outside the hazel poles 'he went on
> his heel', they said; but he 'ran' if both feet were outside. His
> own man was to hold the shield before each of the fighters. The
> one who was wounded should pay three marks of silver to be
> set free.[21]

In reality there is nothing contemporary to suggest that this sort of ritual duel was actually a Viking Age practice, or – if it was – that it was as formal as accounts like the one in *Kormáks saga* describe.

Nevertheless, a number of similar accounts in other sagas, as well as a definition in the *Hednalagen* ('the heathen law'), a fragment of Swedish law written down *c.* 1200 which specifies the conditions under which the *hólmgang* should occur, present a compelling picture.[22] It is possible that, in the militarized and Viking-inflected culture of tenth-century East Anglia, battle could be seen as *hólmgang* on an epic scale – particularly if that battle was considered to be arbitrating a dispute between kinsmen. In this light, the battle of the Holme may have acquired its name as a result of the importation not only of the Old Norse lexicon, but of Old Norse cultural practices as well. And while it was almost certainly not seen in ritualistic terms by those unfortunate enough to fight there, it is entirely likely that it was remembered in those terms afterwards.

It would certainly be no surprise to find that Scandinavian legal concepts were beginning to drift into British syntax and toponymy: everywhere the Vikings had settled in Britain, they were bringing their systems of law and administration with them.

In the wider Viking world, the places set aside for ritual combat seem often to have been located in areas designated for legal or administrative assembly of other kinds. For example, *hólmgang* that took place after deliberations at the Icelandic 'parliament' – the Althing – were fought on an island (ON *holmr*) in the Axewater, the river that cuts through Thingvellir (ON Þingvöllr, 'the assembly plain'), gushing over the rim of the great tectonic rift and surging into white thunder at Öxarárfoss ('Axe-water-fall').[23]

William Morris, visiting Iceland in 1871, recorded his impressions of his arrival at this extraordinary place. The spontaneity of his language reflects the immediacy of the emotional response:

As we ride along (over the lava now) we come opposite to a flat-topped hill some way down the lava stream, and just below it opens a huge black chasm, that runs straight away south toward the lake, a great double-walled dyke, but with its walls tumbled and ruined a good deal in places: the hill is Hrafnabjörg (Raven Burg), and the chasm Hrafnagjá (Raven Rift). But as we turn west we can see, a long way off across the grey plain, a straight black line running from the foot of the Armannsfell right into the lake, which we can see again hence, and some way up from the lake a white line cuts the black one across. The black and the white line are the Almannagjá (Great Rift) and the Öxará (Axe Water) tumbling over it. Once again that thin thread of insight and imagination, which comes so seldom to us, and is such joy when it comes, did not fail me at this first sight of the greatest marvel and most storied place of Iceland.[24]

Thingvellir is rightly famous; it sits amid an alien world, a landscape unlike any other on earth. Like many parts of Iceland, it feels as though it sits at the beginning and ending of time – a place rent and moulded by the primeval forces that stand behind the world, where the 'sun turns black, land sinks into sea; the bright stars scatter from the sky. Flame flickers up against the world-tree; fire flies high against heaven itself.'[25] As has been long remarked, it is easy to see how the crushing waterfalls and grinding glaciers, hot geysers and livid lava flows, and the spectral green corona of the aurora borealis, could have shaped the elemental tenor of the myths that were first given literary form in this unforgiving outpost of the northern world.

The primordial nature of this environment is part of what makes Thingvellir seem such a suitable cradle for the earliest European experiment in representative republican government.[26] One of the most evocative images of the place remains a painting by the English antiquarian W. G. Collingwood, at once a highly observant portrait of the tortured lithics of the primeval geology – the 'curdled lava flows' (to borrow a Morrisian expression) – and an unusually convincing (for its time) reconstruction of the bustle of an Althing in session. Morris, like Collingwood and many more of his Victorian peers, was fascinated by the aspects of representative and communal government that such assemblies embodied. For Morris, the 'doom-rings' and 'thing-steads' of the sagas seem to have helped him to bridge the intellectual chasm that lay between his romantic old-northernism and the metropolitan socialism by which he was so energized in later life.[27]

Things (ON þing) had been a ubiquitous element of the legal, political and administrative culture of Scandinavia long before the settlement of Iceland in the mid-ninth century, and not all things were great national gatherings like those at Thingvellir. From what we can tell, mostly from later medieval sources, most were regional or local comings-together of heads of families, wealthy farmers, warlords and aristocrats, sometimes under the auspices of a king or jarl. Laws were made and disseminated at these gatherings, and

A thing in progress

arbitration was entered into when disputes arose. Criminal matters were also heard and judgements handed down in accordance with the settled laws of the jurisdiction in which the *thing* was held. These laws – with some exceptions – were not written down. This does not mean that they were vague or flimsy or made up on the hoof; quite the opposite. The laws were traditional and cumulative and, like modern legal practice, freighted with precedent and spiced with occasional innovation: maintaining the laws was integral to the life of a community and rich with ancestral tradition and ancient lore. The burden of keeping this knowledge intact rested primarily on the *ars memoriae*, as practised by a single individual – the *lǫgsǫgumaðr*, the 'law-speaker'.[28]

There are a number of place-names in Britain that incorporate the Old Norse *þing* element, most commonly in combination with *vǫllr* 'plain' (that is, 'the assembly plain' – the same origin as Thingvellir): Tinwald in Dumfries, Dingwall in Ross and Cromarty, Tinwhil on Skye, Tiongal on Lewis (now unlocatable), Tingwall in Orkney, Tingwall in Shetland, Tynwald on the Isle of Man, Thingwall in Lancashire and Thingwall in the Wirral. There are also Thingoe (Suffolk), Thinghou (Lincolnshire) and Thynghowe in

Sherwood Forest, Nottinghamshire (all from ON *þing haugr*, 'assembly mound').[29]

Some of these sites remained in use for centuries. Thynghowe in Sherwood Forest was discovered by amateur historians Stuart C. Reddish and Lynda Mallett who, in 2005–6, came into possession of a document dating to 1816 that described the perambulation of the bounds of the Lordship of Warsop. The local people involved in this expedition gathered at a mound known as Hanger Hill to drink beer and eat cheese and have what sounds like a jolly good time; they did so, apparently, 'according to ancient custom'. Further research revealed that the name Hanger Hill had replaced the old name – Thynghowe – in the seventeenth century. Subsequent exploration of the site revealed parish boundary markers tumbled and choked by undergrowth – ancient standing stones and a Viking meeting place lost to memory, swallowed by the forest for a thousand years.

At Tingwall in Shetland, assemblies were held on an island (a *holm*, in the Old Norse-derived dialect of the islands) in the loch that drives inland from the west. It is an extraordinary place, the hills rising gently on all sides around the water, a sublime natural amphitheatre that cups the setting sun. An account written by a visitor called John Brand, dating to 1701, describes how 'three or four great Stones are to be seen, upon which the Judge, Clerk and other Officers of the Court did sit'. The rest of the assembly gathered on the grassy banks 'at some distance from the Holm on the side of the Loch'. When their cases were to be heard, individuals were called to the island and each crossed the water by a stone causeway 'who when heard, returned the same way he came'.[30] The earliest records of its use date to around 1300, but it is likely that the place was an assembly site from the earliest days of Scandinavian settlement on Shetland.

Tynwald, on the Isle of Man, is the one place in Britain where the Viking past continues to shape the performance – if not the content – of modern law-making. Every year, on 5 July, a representative of the British crown attends a ceremony at Tynwald Hill – the enormous stepped mound, 80 feet in diameter at the base, heavily modified and landscaped over the centuries, that still plays an important role in the tiny devolved government's legislative rituals. There he ascends to declaim the previous year's enacted legislation in English and Manx Gaelic (but not, alas, in Old Norse).[31]

It may be that not all of the *thing* sites in Britain were *new* meeting places established by Vikings in the ninth century; some may have been old local and regional meeting places that came to be known by names and terms introduced by Scandinavian settlers. The same is likely true of the terminology that came to be applied to territorial units in parts of the 'Danelaw'; whereas Anglo-Saxon territories were divided into parcels of land called 'hundreds', by the time of the Domesday Book (1086), these territorial units

Þorgnýr the law-speaker holds forth

were known in large areas of north and west Yorkshire, Nottinghamshire and Lincolnshire as 'wapentakes', from the Old Norse *vápnatak* ('weapon-taking'). The term indicates how weap-on-bearing had a direct link to political participation in Viking society. To attend a 'weapon-taking', one obviously had to have weapons to take; the costlier and more elaborate these were, the better to show off one's wealth and status in a highly public forum.

A sense of what weapon-taking was all about can be found in a handful of sources (most of which, in what becomes a tedious refrain for both author and reader, date to long after the Viking Age itself, and are therefore of questionable reliability). The following vignette from *Óláfs saga Helga*, for example, gives an impression of how the intimidating atmosphere of a weapon-bearing assembly could be used to influence authority. Here the venerable Þorgnýr the law-speaker tells the Swedish king how things stand:

'Should you be unwilling to accept what we demand, then we shall mount an attack against you and kill you and not put up with hostility and lawlessness from you. This is what our forefathers before us have done. They threw five kings into a bog at Múlaþing who had become completely full of arrogance like you with us. Say now straight away which choice you wish to take.'

Then the people immediately made a clashing of weapons and a great din.

The king of the Svear to whom this intemperate diatribe was addressed, evidently not fancying his chances, swiftly agreed to 'let the farmers have their way [...] in everything they wanted'.[32]

Such a scene, however improbable we may find the limpness of the Swedish king's authority, evokes in ways otherwise inaccessible how political assembly in a highly militarized society might have felt; it is no wonder that rules of ritual combat should have developed in connection with such events – the potential for violence must have ever simmered at the surface. But, in their essence, such assemblies acted as a means by which royal and aristocratic authority could achieve public legitimacy, a spear-shaking mandate from the warrior class.

After the death of Æthelwold at the battle of the Holme, the early reign of Edward the Elder proved relatively uneventful, although it was clear that tensions between Wessex and the 'Danish' north and east continued to run high; in 906 it was apparently felt necessary to confirm a peace between King Edward and the East Anglians and Northumbrians – with eastern Mercia remaining a contested region. (Indeed, it is utterly unclear who exactly *was* in effective control of this part of eastern Mercia during the four decades between 870 and 910. Coins minted in the name of an 'Earl Sitric' ('SITRIC COMES') at Shelford ('SCELFOR') in Cambridgeshire suggest that effective authority did not necessarily emanate from kings alone, as in fact continued to be the case in Norway. And, as we shall see, when the towns of the 'Danelaw' made peace, they tended to do so one by one, often with named *jarls* offering their submission along with the local communities in which they presumably had some standing.)

The peace of 906 – like so many before – did not hold, although this time it was Edward's kingdom that was the aggressor. In 909, men from Wessex and Mercia 'raided the northern horde very greatly, both men and every kind of property, and killed many of those Danish men, and were inside there [Northumbria] for five weeks.[33] It is not surprising that the Northumbrians sought retaliation the following year, though the Anglo-Saxon chronicler seems unduly put out by their refusal to see sense, remarking with a slightly indignant tone that 'the-horde in Northumbria broke the peace, and scorned every peace which King Edward and his councillors offered them.[34] They would have been better advised to take Edward up on his offer.

The campaign started well enough for the Northumbrians. They seem to have wrongfooted King Edward, who had assembled a fleet of a hundred ships, perhaps imagining a waterborne assault in the south; when the Northumbrians started marauding across Mercia, Edward was stuck on a boat off the Kentish coast. But it is clear that, by this stage, the military and defensive innovations that had been implemented by Alfred and continued by Edward were in good working order. It was possible, in a way in which in the past it seems not to have been, for Edward to command (presumably from some distance away) the armies of Wessex and Mercia to rouse themselves swiftly and move against the invaders.[35] Even so, it was nearly too late; the raiding army had already had plenty of time to plunder western Mercia, with doubtless unpleasant consequences for its inhabitants. This, however, may ultimately have been their undoing, for, as they headed back home, 'rejoicing in rich spoil' as the chronicler Æthelweard put it, they became bogged down:

> crossing to the east side of the river Severn over a *pons* to give the Latin spelling, which is called Bridgnorth [Cuatbricge] by the common people. Suddenly squadrons of both Mercians and West Saxons, having formed battle-order, moved against the opposing force. They joined battle without protracted delay on the field of Wednesfield [Vuodnesfelda, 'Woden's Field'];[36] the English enjoyed the blessing of victory; the army of the Danes fled, overcome by armed force. These events are recounted as done on the fifth day of the month of August. There fell three of their kings in that same 'storm' [*turbine*] (or 'battle' [*certamine*] would be the right thing to say), that is to say Healfdene and Eywysl, and Inwær also hastened to the hall of the infernal one [*ad aulam properauit inferni*], and so did senior chiefs of theirs, both jarls and other noblemen.[37]

The three 'kings' whom Æthelweard delights in dispatching to Old Nick are better known by the Anglicized names Halfdan, Eowils and Ingvar; none of them is known from other sources, and no coins (that we know of) were minted in their names. If they truly were somehow joint kings of Northumbria, they have left a remarkably light historical footprint; it may well be that they were simply warlords of a lesser degree (the English sources seem often to exaggerate the quantity of royal blood that was spilled on the edges of Saxon swords). But it is also possible that they were related to the dynasty known in Irish sources as the Uí Ímair – the descendants of Ivar – a Viking clan that had made it big in Ireland and whose founder was the same Ivar the Boneless who, with his brothers, had wreaked such havoc among the kingdoms of Anglo-Saxon England.[38] (Whether or not this is so, it is almost certainly the case that – as we shall see – an influx of Vikings from the Irish Sea had begun to make their presence felt in Northumbria at the beginning of the tenth century, refugees from their expulsion from Dublin in 902.[39])

Whatever the political realities within Northumbria, the battle of Wednesfield (more commonly known as the battle of Tettenhall) marked a watershed.[40] From that moment on, the armies of the 'Danelaw' would never again threaten the peace of southern Britain. Instead, in little over fifteen years, the kings of Wessex would establish themselves as the masters of all England; in time they would be counted the overlords of much of the rest of Britain as well. The details of the campaigns which Edward and his sister Æthelflæd waged against those parts of England that lay beyond the boundary their father had drawn with Guthrum–Æthelstan are known primarily from the accounts provided in the *Anglo-Saxon Chronicle*, including the regional addendum known as the *Mercian Register*.[41] The bald sequence of events these sources present is stark and authoritarian, a drumbeat of inexorable military dominance and fortress building. To string it all together with connective tissue and verbiage would be prolix. I present it here, therefore, in outline – a summary of the history as reported – with the caveat that, as ever, this was how the West Saxons wanted us to remember it: the glorious, inevitable march towards English unity and nationhood – the red ink spilled, a slow pink stain spreading across the map.

In 910, Æthelflæd, the daughter of King Alfred, sister of King Edward and wife of Æthelred, lord of the Mercians, had a fortress built at Bremesbyrig (unidentified, probably in Gloucestershire). In the following year, her husband Æthelred died. Although Æthelflæd assumed most of his authority in Mercia, Edward claimed lordship in Oxford (Oxfordshire) and London. In 912, King Edward constructed two forts at Hertford (Hertfordshire), and one at Witham (Essex), 'and a large portion of the folk who were earlier in the power of Danish men submitted to him'.[42] In 914, armies from Hereford (Herefordshire) and Gloucester (Gloucestershire) defeated a Viking raiding army from Brittany. King Edward ordered defences to be set along the south bank of the River Severn, which stymied Viking raids at Porlock and Watchet (Somerset). The king also constructed twin fortifications at Buckingham (Buckinghamshire), and Jarl Thurcytel and the chief men of Bedford (Bedfordshire) and Northampton (Northamptonshire) pledged their loyalty to the king. In 915, Edward occupied Bedford and constructed a fortress there, while his sister Æthelflæd built strong-holds at Chirbury (Shropshire), Weardbyrig (possibly Warbury, Cheshire) and Runcorn (Cheshire). The following year, in 916, the king constructed a stronghold at Maldon (Essex) and 'facilitated' the emigration of Jarl Thurcytel to the continent.

Everyone seems to have been busy in 917. Edward ordered the construction of strongholds at Towcester (Northamptonshire) and Wigingamere (unidentified, possibly Newport, Essex).[43] Viking raids from Northampton, Leicester (Leicestershire) 'and north of there' tried, but failed, to break down the stronghold at Towcester. At the same time, a Viking army from East Anglia built its own fortress at Tempsford (Bedfordshire) and then marched on Bedford, only to be routed by the Bedford militia. Another Viking army from East Anglia besieged Wigingamere, but was unable to capture it and retreated. King Edward's army was, once again, more successful, destroying the Viking fort at Tempsford, killing their king (whoever this may have been), as well as Jarl Toglos and his son, Jarl Manna. Another army raised by Edward from Sussex, Essex and Kent then captured Colchester (Essex), slaughtering the defenders. In response, a Viking army attempted to capture Maldon, but was repelled by the defenders who – with reinforcements – destroyed and routed the erstwhile besiegers.

Presumably demoralized by the way things were going, Jarl Thurferth and his followers, 'together with all the raiding-army which belonged to Northampton, as far north as the Welland', submitted to the authority of King Edward.[44] Taking advantage of this success, Edward restored the defences of Huntingdon (Cambridgeshire), and the local people submitted to his authority. There was more submitting to come: after King Edward had restored the defences at Colchester, the people of Essex and East Anglia swore loyalty to him, and the Viking army at Cambridge (Cambridgeshire) voluntarily adopted King Edward 'as their lord and protector'.[45] To round the year off, Æthelflæd captured Derby (Derbyshire).

In 918 King Edward built a stronghold on the south side of the river at Stamford (Lincolnshire), and the people inhabiting the stronghold on the north bank submitted to the king. Æthelflæd gained the submission of Leicester, but died later that year. Edward did not hesitate to secure his authority over the whole of Mercia, and 'all the race of the Welsh, sought him as their lord'.[46] The king next captured Nottingham (Nottinghamshire) and reinforced its defences, and 'all the people that were settled in the land of Mercia, both Danish and English, turned to him'.[47] In 919 the king ordered a fortress to be built at Thelwall (Cheshire), and in 920 caused forti-fications to be built at Nottingham and Bakewell (Derbyshire). This was apparently the final straw: 'And then the king of Scots and all the nation of Scots chose him as father and lord; and [so did] Ragnald and Eadwulf's sons and all those who live in Northumbria, both English and Danish and Norwegians and others; and also the king of the Strathclyde Britons and all the Strathclyde Britons.' For the rest of Britain, enough had finally proved to be enough.

By 920, Edward, king of Wessex, had become – or wished to be perceived as – not only king of all the English south of the Humber, but the overlord of almost everyone who lived beyond it to the north. This went beyond even the claims of Edward's great-grandfather Ecgberht, who had asserted his overlordship of Northumbria in 828. (Perhaps it was an attempt to make good on Alfred's absurd claim to rule over 'all the Christians of the island of Britain'.[48]) However, while there is no doubt that Edward had achieved for his kingdom and his dynasty an unprecedented degree of *imperium* within Britain, quite how realistic the claims of 920 really were remains uncertain; after all, the world to the north of the Mercian border had changed out of all recognition since Ecgberht's time.

15

LAKELAND SAGAS

Coniston Water it is called by the public now-a-days, but its proper
name is Thurston Water. So it is written in all old documents, maps,
and books up to the modern tourist period. In the deed of
1196 setting forth the boundaries of Furness Fells it is called
Thorstancs Watter, and in lawyer's Latin Tiirstini Watra, which
proves that the lake got its title from some early owner whose
Norse name was Thorstein.

W. G. COLLINGWOOD, *The Book of Coniston* (1897)[1]

It is incontrovertible that large parts of Britain were settled by
Scandinavians; the evidence, when taken as a whole, is overwhelming. Nevertheless, not one of the specific questions that one
might wish to pose – how did this settlement happen and where
precisely was it densest; did it start suddenly or gradually; was it
continuous or sporadic; how many people were involved and where
did they come from and were there women and children among
them as well as men? – can be answered satisfactorily.

That does not mean that the subject has been neglected. As one
scholarly duo put it, 'there is in this area such a weight of scholarly
tradition that everything seems to have been said, and firmly
objected to, before'.[2] This is inevitable in cases such as these, where
the evidence itself is weak and contradictory. Consider, for example, the state of archaeological knowledge regarding rural

settlement in Northumbria: the two most frequently mentioned sites that supposedly display evidence of Scandinavian influence in their design and layout are Simy Folds (Co. Durham) and Ribblehead (north Yorkshire). Among a handful of other Scandinavian features, the buildings excavated at both places seem originally to have been furnished with stone benches that ran along the interior walls, features characteristic of the architecture of Viking colonies in the north Atlantic.[3] The size of the Ribblehead farm building also sets it apart from other English buildings of the period, as does its construction method: it has been described as 'a house which undertakes in stone and timber what elsewhere, i.e. in lowland England, was an earthfast timber form'.[4] Such stone-founded homes bear more resemblance to the Viking long-houses of Orkney and Shetland than to the timber halls of Wessex. Even these weak indicators, however, are compromised by the unfortunate fact that we know very little about *pre*-Viking architecture in northern England, and arguments about size, or layout, or building materials are therefore predicated on an absence of evidence; we just don't know for sure how to tell a 'Viking' house from an 'Anglo-Saxon' house.

Instead, scholarly efforts to pinpoint the extent of Viking settlement have turned on place-names and personal names, language and dialect. We have already seen how elements of Scandinavian legal and administrative terminology were imported into parts of Britain, and in certain English regions the vocabulary of the land feels thick with the Viking past, the countryside rumbling away in Old Norse, or at least with a strong accent. These words and names fall heavily like iron on stone, their sharp cadences catching the glimmer of a low northern sun, salt spray jagging off them on the back of a cold wind: 'Garstang' in Lancashire (ON *geirr* + ON *stǫng*, 'spear-post'); 'Grimsby' in Lincolnshire (ON *grims* + ON *bȳ*, 'Grimr's farm'); Micklethwaite in Yorkshire and Cumbria (ON *mikill* + ON *þveit*, 'great clearing'). These are entirely Old Norse words, displacing whatever had preceded them, renaming the land, reimagining the landscape. Elsewhere, however, the Old Norse words are grafted on to an Old English stock – 'Grimstons', for example, abound in the corpus of English place-names (ON *grims* + OE *tūn*, 'Grimr's settlement'), alongside more exotic formulations like 'Brandesburton' (ON *brands* + OE *burh* + OE *tūn*, 'Brandr's fortified settlement'). In addition, the Norse tongue bled into the everyday words which people, especially in the north, still use to frame the world around them: fell (ON *fjall*), beck (ON *bekkr*), tarn (ON *tjarn*), gill (ON *gjel*) …

When Old Norse place-names are plotted on to a map of Britain, they present a pleasing picture, clustering with varying intensity across all the regions where the historical record leads us to expect them, even respecting (more or less) the border of Alfred's treaty with Guthrum. However, satisfying though this may be, it does little beyond apparently confirming that Old Norse-speakers did, indeed, inhabit parts of England at some point in the past. And the closer one looks, more questions than answers arise. Why, for example, are there apparently so many more Old Norse place-name elements in Norfolk than in Suffolk? What is the significance of hybrid place-names as opposed to 'pure' Old Norse ones? Why do the most significant places (by and large) retain their English names? What impact have other, post-Viking, changes to landownership and language had over the 1,100 years since the first Viking settlers arrived? How many Norse-speakers would it have taken to effect linguistic change on this scale and in this way? Did the changes come early (in the ninth century) or accrue over time? Did these Norse-speakers come from Denmark, or from Norway, or from some other outpost of the Viking diaspora – Ireland perhaps or the north Atlantic?

And so it goes on, without any real resolution, the arguments highly technical and the conclusions provisional.[5] The best that can perhaps be said is that, from the late ninth century onwards, changes wrought through migration were affecting the way people spoke and the way they thought – the world shaped and reshaped by words, mental maps reordered in irrevocable ways. These changes can have been effected only by a sizeable number of Norse-speaking immigrants, though the socially dominant position of these migrants may have meant that their language had an impact that was disproportionate to their number.

Cultural changes are evident across the north and east of England. Among the well-to-do community of moneyers who were responsible for minting coins in 'Danelaw' towns during the late tenth and early eleventh centuries, Scandinavian names had become common, if not ubiquitous.[6] In places like Thetford, Lincoln and Norwich they were a minority, the Ascetels and Ulfcetels, Grims and Thorsteins still outnumbered by the Ælfwines, Eadgars and Leofrics. In York, however, the picture was reversed, with Norse names equalling if not outnumbering the English. These changes did not only affect moneyers, and were long-lasting. Less than a century later, in 1086, the Domesday survey for Lincolnshire recorded 240 names of which 140 were Scandinavian.[7] This doesn't mean, of course, that by 1086 three-fifths of the Lincolnshire population were descended from ninth-century Viking settlers, any more than the (relative) abundance of Scandinavian and Scandinavian-inspired jewellery found in that county (and in East Anglia) signifies large-scale migration.[8] Both names and jewellery, however, do strongly suggest that in cultural terms life in those parts of Britain had taken a Viking turn. Affinity for a transmarine North Sea identity was becoming more fashionable from the turn of the tenth century than it had been at any point since the age of Sutton Hoo in the early seventh century, and was arguably edging out (though certainly not extinguishing) other forms of cultural expression.

These trends didn't last for ever, but they were surprisingly durable. The Norman Conquest of 1066 ultimately reorientated English culture decisively, and by the late twelfth century moneyers across England mostly had names like Hugo, Robert, Walter or William. But even as late as the 1180s, during the reign of Henry II (the first Plantagenet monarch), there were moneyers named Rafn, Svein and Thorstein working at Lincoln, and there was still a 'Turkill' (Thorkell) minting coins in York during the reign of Richard I the

Lionheart (r. 1189–99). Although the vogue for Norse names would ultimately die out, there were other changes that could never be undone. As the English language – rapacious omnivore that it is – ruthlessly harvested and absorbed the Scandinavian speech that was introduced to England, it was irrevocably changed by it. Old Norse words in English are not confined to those that we might consider proper to 'Vikings' ('berserk', 'ransack' and 'skull', for example, are all words of impeccable Old Norse provenance), but even fundamental linguistic building-blocks like the pronouns 'their' and 'they', and outrageously mundane words like 'husband', 'egg' and 'window', are rooted in the speech of Scandinavian immigrants.[9]

This northern onomasticon was thrilling to an early generation of antiquarians, in particular the place-names that compounded still tangible features of the landscape with Scandinavian personal names. During the nineteenth century, surveys were conducted and beautiful hand-inked maps plotted that conjured the ghosts of the Norse-speaking country-folk, summoning them to reclaim the familiar lakes, farms and fells.[10] Some of these antiquarians, like W. G. Collingwood and Charles Arundel Parker, spun sagas of their own out of the place-names with which they were most familiar, the Cumbrian Lake District becoming a subject of particularly intense study and fascination. Tales like Parker's *The Story of Shelagh, Olaf Cuaran's Daughter* (1909) and Collingwood's *Thorstein of the Mere* (1895) and *The Bondwoman* (1896) are practically forgotten today, the stilted tenor of late Victorian narrative militating against their enduring popularity, but they are fascinating for what they reveal about the intellectual climate in which they were written – as enthusiasm for the Viking past developed in the latter decades of the nineteenth century. For what is so striking about writers like Collingwood is their willingness to marry their romantic attachment to the places, languages and objects of the Viking Age past to the pioneering academic study of them. It was scholarship as both art and science – the attempt to conjure the wonder of a lost world back into existence through the combination of patient study and literary and artistic invocation.[11]

Collingwood, who had been intimately acquainted with the Lake District from an early age (he was born in Liverpool), came to live at Gillhead (Lake Windermere) in 1883. But he had been, and

Frontispiece to *Thorstein of the Mere*

remained, closely associated with Coniston; from 1880 he worked as personal assistant to John Ruskin during the long twilight of the latter's life – twenty years during which the great man's powers inexorably dimmed, his mental health failing, his beard growing longer and whiter as his relevance diminished. It was, in Collingwood's own words, a 'very pleasant servitude', often staying one night a week at Ruskin's home, Brantwood, overlooking Coniston Water, the Old Man looming on the far shore. But there can be little doubt of the emotional and practical demands that Ruskin placed on the younger man's shoulders. 'Nobody knows how awful these times are,' he would write of Ruskin's mental degeneration (in 1889, the year before the latter's death).[12] The bond between the two men was a strong one. When Ruskin died, Collingwood designed Ruskin's gravestone (the Ruskin Cross), which stands in the graveyard of St Andrew's Church in Coniston, its elaborate neo-Anglo-Saxon stylings perhaps a more fitting legacy to Collingwood's own life's work than to that of his celebrated patron. Collingwood's own gravestone stands just feet away, modest and plain by comparison, deferential even in death. It is poignant that a man of his talents should be remembered in this way, struggling to break free from a persona as overwhelming as Ruskin's – a young, glittering star, shackled to the orbit of a grotesquely swollen giant, obliterated by the embrace of its sickly dying light.[13]

After Ruskin's death, Collingwood produced a great deal of valuable work; the bibliography of his works – running to seven pages in Matthew Townend's definitive study – speaks for itself. Several of these represented major breakthroughs for early medieval scholarship. His *Northumbrian Crosses of the Pre-Norman Age* (1927), for example – with its meticulously hand-drawn contents, catalogued and described with a breathtaking precision and care born of love – is described by Townend as 'a triumph, a great scholarly achievement, and one that has been enormously influential in the subsequent study of pre-Conquest sculpture.'[14] This was, in many ways, the culmination of Collingwood's antiquarian career – a mature work, published five years before his death in 1932. More remarkable, in some ways, is his much earlier book *Scandinavian Britain*, published in 1908 by the Society for Promoting Christian Knowledge. It has sat on my desk throughout the writing of this book, a reminder that I walk on paths trodden before by others, whose efforts to clear away the brambles and the boulders has made my journey much easier than theirs.[15]

Scandinavian Britain was a book years ahead of its time, a fact acknowledged by some[16] but certainly forgotten by most. Its seamless combination of philology, history and archaeology was a pioneering foray into what we would now call inter-disciplinary study, the attempt to liberate evidence from narrow silos and force them to communicate in conjuring an image of the past. There is deep irony in this: what came naturally to Collingwood, the very quality that makes his writing so easy and unforced and his scholarship so lightly worn, has become a subject of protracted theoretical debate and (sometimes heated) argument; I am sure he would have read much modern historical and archaeological theory with bewilderment.[17] For Collingwood, as for many scholars before the creeping professionalization and specialization of the later twentieth century, it would have been entirely natural to muster all of the evidence for the Viking Age that he could access, deploying it on its own merits, without prejudice.

As a result, many of Collingwood's specific conclusions, as well as the overall tenor of his treatment, remain startlingly modern, not least his recognition that Viking identities were surprisingly adaptable to the cultural climates into which they plunged. More obviously dated, though in no way to its detriment, is the physical quality of the first edition – a fine example of early twentieth-century publishing, with its beautiful gilt lettering and a finely drawn fold-out map. This sort of attention to detail was to be a hallmark of the work with which Collingwood was associated, and more often than not it was his own hand that supplied the maps and illustrations: he was a highly skilled draughtsman, and brought his pen to bear on the sculpture of the north, producing some of the earliest accurate surveys of what we might now call Anglo-Scandinavian sculptural style. But he was also more than equal to the task of illuminating fictional and mythological work with lively borders and marginalia, maps and frontispieces – enlivening his scholarly output with artistry, and grounding his imaginative work with observational rigour.

My great-great-great-great-uncle, G. W. Kitchin (1827–1912), had also, like Ruskin, once lived at Brantwood – indeed he was the occupant who vacated the premises immediately ahead of Ruskin's tenure. The two men had a relationship of sorts, Kitchin having once written a long essay entitled 'Ruskin at Oxford' (one of an improbable number of accomplishments and distinctions).[18] Kitchin spent his time at Brantwood in the early 1870s in the employ of the Clarendon Press, proofing the pages of the mighty Cleasby–Vigfusson English–Icelandic dictionary, a monumental work of scholarship which remains a definitive foundation of the study of Icelandic and Old Norse in English. Indeed, Kitchin had been instrumental in supporting Vigfusson's labours during his time at Oxford in the late 1860s.[19] His interest was active and engaged – while working on the proofs he consulted the local antiquarian Thomas Ellwood about the Old Norse antecedents of Cumbrian dialect words – and later he wrote to Ellwood from Denmark (Kitchin's wife Alice was a friend of Queen Alexandra) with the rather outlandish claim that 'a countryman from here [Denmark] and a countryman from that neighbourhood [the Lake District] would, if speaking their respective dialects, be almost able to mutually understand one another'.[20] (One wonders whether, given the rarefied circles in which he moved, Kitchin had all that many conversations with 'countrymen' of either persuasion.)

Some of this interest doubtless originated in his ancestry. His father, Isaac, came from a family of Cumberland 'Statesmen', a class of yeoman-farmers that he praised for 'their independence, their sturdy battle with nature, their simplicity and traditional loyalty'.[21] Kitchin regarded these 'Statesmen' – independent peasant farmers – as parallels to a Norse (or Swiss) 'type', fiercely protective of their freedoms and their rights.[22] They were, in other words, the models

for Collingwood's conception of the free Norse farmers who popu-
lated fictional works like *Thorstein of the Mere* and, indeed,
Collingwood drew direct parallels between these 'Statesmen' and
the free farmers (*bóndi*) of Old Norse saga literature. It was a
simplistic idea – though a common enough sort of notion in those
days – and an appealing one, particularly for antiquarians working
in a predominantly local milieu. In its crudest iterations it was articulated in clumsy racial stereotypes offered up as evidence for the
longevity of Viking influence. For example, the cleric, writer and
conservationist Hardwicke Rawnsley (1851–1920) felt that to 'look
at the blue eyes and the fine cut profile and heavy jaws, and large
limbs and long arms of the shepherds and farm folk of the dales' is
to 'feel that just such were the Norse sea-rangers'.[23]

This sort of thing would be laughable if such ideas had not been
manipulated to maleficent ends throughout the twentieth century.
Nevertheless, biological descent as an indicator of population movements has, indeed, come to be a viable tool of modern research.
South of Cumbria, along the Irish Sea coastline of the Wirral and
West Lancashire, maybe half of the male population whose ancestors can be shown to have been present in the region before 1600
have Scandinavian markers in their DNA.[24] What such research
cannot show, however, is when or how this genetic material entered
a population or the number of *individuals* from which it ultimately
derives. It is also selective, ignoring the very many other biological
markers that are prevalent in particular communities. More importantly, such research is possible only when it is carried out with
relatively large sample sizes, ensuring that results are statistically
significant and can be compared meaningfully with other populations. When used in this way, it has the potential to reveal something about the scale of past migrations, even if it remains something
of a blunt instrument. Without care, however, it can easily be
manipulated to resemble racial bluster – a means to prove (or
disprove) a biological connection to a past invested with moral
quality or desirable antique glamour: a superiority of the blood.

*

It was turning dark when we arrived in Coniston, and it had just started to rain. We missed the turning. We stopped. I consulted the directions to the cottage provided by the letting company. Turning around we drove back along the darkening street – unfamiliar shop-fronts and strangers in cagoules, wet dogs, impatient local drivers; the rain came down harder. Finally we found it; headlamps catching on the words 'private road', we crossed the cattle grid, feeling the first sickening lurches as the car slumped into the ruts and divots of the unmade road. I started to feel nervous. Safely tucked behind my desk I hadn't thought much about the words 'dirt track'. It had conjured images of a hundred yards of farm track, muddy and bumpy but with a picturesque stripe of greensward rippling down the centre, a touch of bucolic wilderness to signal that the modern world was at our backs – nothing that could threaten defeat.

As we drove on, the gradient increased, until it was clear that the road was taking us into the fells. It soon became apparent that the road was not a road at all. For substantial stretches, the granite bedrock was laid bare beneath us, the bones of the mountain rubbed raw, defleshed by wheels and walkers; and then there were the pools of scree, the carpet of broken slates that poured down from the mountain like a petrified river, the blood of a giant loosed to cover its wounded flanks. I don't really know why we stopped; I think the will just ebbed away. It was the sudden knowledge of having been beaten, the sudden clarity of failure after the adrenaline of panic dies away. But now the car wouldn't move, its sad wheels spinning feebly in the wet sandy gravel. There we were, for a moment, cling-ing like an iridescent beetle to the foothills of the Coniston Old Man, both of us silent, minds blank, despair seeping in.

If three returning walkers hadn't suddenly appeared in the road behind us, all willing to help push the car and endure a muddy splattering and the funk of a tortured clutch, I don't know what would have happened. But they did, and they were, and after a few miserable minutes of grunting and shoving, we were on our way. Finally, tired and dejected, we made it to our lodgings, overlooking the copper mines and the ribbon of silver water that tumbled from the peaks. But up above, glowering down at us, the Old Man was watching. There was no mistaking it. We had been warned.

Almost as soon as we arrived, my wife was struck down with flu. Shuttered in the upstairs room of the cottage, she was not to move beyond the front door until the grim day arrived when she was compelled to drive us both home again. For the rest of the week I watched, increasingly irritated, as a succession of inappropriate hatchbacks bounded up the valley with abandon. On foot I visited the Ruskin Museum, founded by Collingwood in 1901, and the Ruskin Cross, designed by Collingwood in 1900. And every after-noon I sat in the window to write. But always the Old Man was out there watching me, glaring down unmoving, ever changing. I had to climb him. It was inevitable.

'Our first walk is naturally to climb the Coniston Old Man,' declares Collingwood in *The Book of Coniston*: 'It is quite worth while making the ascent on a cloudy day. The loss of the panorama is amply compensated by the increased grandeur of the effects of gloom and mystery on the higher crags.'[25] Everywhere there are delvings and workings, spoil heaps and tunnels, culverts and rush-ing water. Even as I climb, it feels as though the summit recedes, the distances stretching and distorting; the landscape giving up its form grudgingly, revealing its folds and contours one at a time – pain-fully, slowly. I move up under the black-slate crag, the silver-mer-cury water marbling the grey with an endless roar, tumbling down from Low Water above; then up and over the springing turf, past boulders that stud the hillsides, scattered like seeds from the hands of giants, down from Raven's Tor. Suddenly I am up to the rim of Levers Water, the wide cool tarn spreading beneath hunched knots of rock. I skirt the water round to the left and start to climb again. He's always ahead of me, Collingwood, wiry legs poking out from his shorts, a ghost at the bend in the path, always out of reach. A phantom. I picture him like a mountain goat, like the shaggy upland sheep that bound, with terrifying sureness of foot, up and down the mountain paths – a spry old fellow with a bright gleam in his eye, too quick to catch.

'It is here, on a cloudy day when the tops are covered, that the finest impressions of mountain gloom may be found; under the cloud and the precipices a dark green tarn, savage rocks, and tumbling streams; and out, beyond, the tossing sea of mountain forms.'[26]

On the summit ridge, everything changes. Shifting clouds smother the contours, bleaching the landscape, masking the drop. Surrounding peaks loom out of the vapours, hulking leviathans wreathed in mist, no longer chained to the world below but free to crash like icebergs through the fog. The path ahead is bleak and otherworldly, heaped cairns along the path speak of the dead, the horizontal trails of cloud like angry shades, screaming over the mountaintop, voices joined with the howling wind that screams across the peak. Black carrion shapes hover in this twilight kingdom, their wings thrum like propellers overhead.

'The view on a clear day commands Ingleborough to the east, Snowdon to the south, the Isle of Man to the west, and to the north, Scafell and Bowfell, Glaramara and Skiddaw, Blencathra and Helvellyn: and beneath these all the country spread out like a raised model, with toy hills and lakes and villages.'[27]

And then suddenly it clears, and the ghosts are gone. I can see Coniston Water laid out below me, and the fells rising in ranks behind me. And away on the far banks of Coniston Water I can see the house, mere flotsam below the tree line, where Ruskin and Collingwood worked and Kitchin once sat, leafing through proofs from the Clarendon Press; and I know that all of them, every day they were there, raised their eyes from their work to look, up through the great study window, to gaze at the Old Man, unmoving, ever changing, and found me gazing back at them across the water.

16

A NEW WAY

Then, it is well known, good men of the old sort, who could not
abide to see new laws made and old laws undone, took to their
ships and sailed away west. Some of them landed in Iceland;
some went to Orkney, and others wandered about the coasts of
the Irish Sea to find a home; and wherever they could find
shelter and safety, there they settled.

W. G. COLLINGWOOD, *Thorstein of the Mere* (1895)[1]

In *Thorstein of the Mere*, Collingwood gives the account just
quoted in the epigraph of this chapter describing how the eponymous hero's grandfather arrived in Britain – one among the many
Norwegian émigrés supposedly fleeing the autocratic tendencies of
King Haraldr Hárfagri – Harald Finehair (r. *c.* 872–*c.* 932). In
contemporary sources, the extent of Harald's rule and the details of
his life are murky and contradictory in the extreme.[2] In the saga
tradition of the twelfth century and later, by contrast, Harald plays
a pivotal role. He is credited as being the first king to unify the
Norwegian kingdom and thus providing the catalyst for an expansion of Norwegian emigration across the north Atlantic and into
the Irish Sea. The result of this, so the founding mythology runs,
was the establishment of independent colonies on Orkney, Shetland,
Faroe and Iceland, and down the west coast of Scotland towards the
Irish Sea – Viking statelets ruled by (depending on one's view of the

situation) freedom-loving pioneers or belligerent fugitives and outlaws, petty pirate kingdoms of the northern oceans.[3] Indeed, *Orkneyinga saga* describes Harald mounting expeditions to the Northern and Western Isles and the Isle of Man 'to teach a lesson to certain vikings he could no longer tolerate', winning territory for the Norwegian crown in the process.

This version of events is most likely reflective (and supportive) of Norwegian territorial claims of *c.* 1200 when *Orkneyinga saga* was written, rather than an accurate account of what happened some 300 years earlier. The myth of Harald Finehair presents us with a classic example of how complex processes of emigration, cultural compromise and political consolidation could crystallize in legend around particular resonant figures at a much later date.[4] Nevertheless, the extent of Scandinavian influence around the seaways of Britain cannot be disputed. Place-name evidence makes this plain, even if the apparently straightforward patterns we observe mask gaping holes in our understanding of the processes that gave rise to them. Consider, for example, the presence of Irish personal names, Gaelic place-name elements and characteristically Celtic word morphology mixed up with Old Norse in the place-names of north-west England.[5] This could signify the presence of Gaelic- or Brittonic-speaking populations that were later overlaid by, or became subject to, or became influenced by Norse-speaking migrants – a possibility apparently strengthened by Old Norse place-names that seem to single out the presence of Gaelic-speakers in the landscape (for example, Ireby, 'farm of the Irish', in Cumbria). On the other hand it might indicate that some of the migrants themselves were of mixed Norse–Gaelic heritage. Such identities were indeed developing across this zone of cultural interchange.

Nor can the interconnectedness of this maritime world be denied – a world where the sea was a highway that led between strands and inlets, headlands and islets, storms and tides; a world where political authority could often only be provisional and where local chieftains and disparate peoples forged and broke alliances and moulded new identities that shifted and mutated with the ocean currents, or tore like clouds in the wide western sky. We can see this in the violence and insecurity implied by the Viking Age promontory forts of the Isle of Man or the defended settlement at Llanbedrgoch (Anglesey), where the skeletons of four men of Scandinavian origin and one woman were found buried in a ditch, a reminder of the brittleness of life lived on the margins of a world seething with violent profiteering, slave-trafficking and silver. Hoards of coins, arm-rings and bullion, stowed in the earth on Man and Anglesey, speak of the trade that flowed back and forth across the Irish Sea and up and down Britain's western coasts, controlled by the people who built long-houses in the Hebrides at Udal on North Uist and Drimore Machair and Bornais on South Uist, at Braaid and Doarlish Cashen on Man. The same people, possessed of a buccaneering spirit of enterprise, bloody-handed entrepreneurs, ploughed the coastal waters naming the landmarks they passed in their own tongue, the essential vocabulary of a seafaring people; headlands and promontories, islands and bays: Aignish (ON *egg-nes*, 'ridge headland', Wester Ross); Skipnes (ON *skip-nes*, 'ship headland', Coll); Sandaig (*sand-vík*, 'sandy bay', Tiree); Gateholm, Grassholm, Priestholm (all Welsh coast), Steep Holm, Flat Holm (both Bristol Channel), all compounds with ON *holmr* ('islet'); Anglesey, Bardsey, Ramsey – all with ON-*ey* ('island').

At the end of the eighth century, when the first Viking raids fell on the islands of the north, the territories that comprised northern Britain and the Irish Sea made up a diverse and heterogeneous world. There were the ethnically and linguistically British kingdoms of Wales, and the mysterious kingdom of Alt Clud in the region around the Clyde; there was the Gaelic kingdom of Dál Riata, centred on Argyll and the southern Hebrides, and the Pictish kingdom that dominated the highlands and Northern Isles. Of the Isles of Man and Anglesey very little is known, but both seem to have played an important role in trade and travel around the Irish Sea, with mixed Irish, British and perhaps even English populations, some of which were probably transient.[6] Finally, there was the Northumbrian realm, extending to the Forth in the north and west across the Pennines to contest in power with the British-speaking peoples of Wales and Alt Clud.

By the early tenth century, however, after over a century of raiding, disruption, colonization and war, the Pictish kingdom was gone; so too was Alt Clud, at least in its original iteration, its capital of Dumbarton mouldering in ruin on the rock of the Clyde. Dál Riata was no more, its islands overrun, its identity lost. Northumbria was in the hands of Viking kings, and warlords of Scandinavian descent ruled the islands and sea-lanes from the Shetland strands to the Bristol Channel; even the relics of St Columba had been evacuated from Iona 'to escape the foreigners [*Gaill*]'.[7] When, in 920, Edward the Elder raised his claim as overlord of the Scots, the Northumbrians ('English, Norwegian and Danish') and the Strathclyde Britons (who presumably included many of the former people of Alt Clud), the north had already become a graveyard of lost realms, the course of its history decisively rerouted.

But, as in England, it was out of this chaos and dissolution that new kingdoms and new identities would ultimately arise. Enduring Norse lordships in the Isle of Man and the Hebrides, and in Orkney, Shetland and Caithness, would last as political entities long into the Middle Ages, their distinctive cultural footprints still visible in the present day. Most enduring of all, however, was the reconfiguration of the broken polities of mainland Scotland, the mosaic reassembled from the jumble of tesserae left behind when the Viking tides relented. The colours were the same, but they were combined to make new shapes, and new pictures: what emerged was a kingdom of Alba – the kingdom of the Scots – a 'Scot-land' to mirror the 'Angle-land' coagulating to the south. Unlike England, however, the lack of a detailed historical record of the events that triggered and shaped these upheavals (even one as flawed as the *Anglo-Saxon Chronicle* and its derivatives) means that scholars are forced to rely more heavily on a patchwork of evidence, including the fragmentary written sources that do survive, and the much larger corpus of archaeological evidence which – though it can tell us an enormous amount about how, where and to what degree Scandinavian culture penetrated and altered the pre-existing communities it encountered – is often equivocal on matters of chronology and causation. Nevertheless, it is still possible to paint an impressionistic picture of what happened over the course of the ninth and early tenth centuries in these northern regions, even if it is painted with a fairly broad brush.

Raids around Britain's northern shores had been occurring from the end of the eighth century onwards, but 839 is the earliest date that we have for an event with significant political ramifications. The *Annals of Ulster* state that the 'heathen [*gennti*] won a battle against the men of Fortriu in which Euganan son of Óengus and Bran son of Óengus and Áed son of Boanta and an almost uncountable number of others fell'.[8] Fortriu is the name given in Irish chronicles for the north-eastern part of what is now mainland Scotland, the region surrounding the Moray Firth – the great violent V-shaped gash that opens the Great Glen to the cold swells of the North Sea. It is a Gaelic rendering of the Roman tribal name Verturiones, and remained the heart of the Pictish kingdom.[9] The ill-starred Euganan (or, to give him his Pictish spelling, 'Wen'), was the Pictish king and Bran was his brother; Áed was king of Dál Riata, apparently at this point allied to the Picts and probably the junior partner in an unequal relationship.[10] Nobody knows who these particular heathens were, nor where the battle took place. Its aftermath is a void of knowledge, the fate and identity of the victors opaque. We can infer, of course, that it was an unhappy day for the supporters of King Wen et al., but that is all. Such are the limits of the historical record in this period, however, that the fact that it was recorded at all argues strongly for its unusual significance. It may even have been, in the words of one of the principal modern historians of the early medieval north, 'one of the most decisive and important battles in British history'.[11]

One reason for this significance is that, like the Viking assaults on Northumbria and East Anglia, the intervention of a raiding army had brought the curtain down on a native dynasty with total, irreversible finality. With the death of Wen and his brother, the line of Wrguist – the family that had risen to the Pictish throne with Onuist I in 732 – was broken. The next king to rule in Pictavia about whom anything is known was of a different ilk. Cinaed son of Alpín (better known to history as Kenneth McAlpin) is popularly imagined as a Gaelic Scot of Dál Riata who conquered the Picts and, in the process, founded the Scottish kingdom. This is a legend, however, with little to support it. Although it is true that he was king in Dál Riata 'two years before he came to Pictavia', Cinaed was probably a Pict.[12] Nevertheless, his reign did mark the beginning of the increasing political and cultural amalgamation of Picts and Gaels. It also, however, coincided with devastating incursions from land and from sea, from foreigners and from neighbours.

At some point during Cinaed's reign (839–58), the Britons of Alt Clud struck back at their erstwhile overlords, burning the Pictish settlement at Dunblane. This was not the end of Cinaed's troubles: also during his reign Vikings 'wasted Pictavia to Clunie and Dunkeld' (probably striking from the mouth of the River Tay).[13] It was in the west, however, that the most fundamental damage was being done. In 847, 'the Northmen', according to the Frankish *Annals of St-Bertin*, 'got control of the islands all around Ireland, and stayed there without encountering any resistance from anyone'.[14] These territories probably comprised (among others) the islands of Tiree, Mull, Islay and Arran and the Kintyre peninsula (as well as, perhaps, the Isle of Man), places which made up the entire seaward side of the Dál Riatan realm; their loss would have broken whatever connections the Gaelic kingdom still maintained across the Irish Sea, leaving the rump that remained little choice but to move towards ever-closer union with the Picts.

In 865 or 866 a Viking named Olaf ('Amlaíb', as rendered in Irish chronicles) arrived in the kingdom of the Picts. He is described in

Irish sources as the son of the king of Laithlind, although since nobody knows what or where 'Laithlind' was supposed to be (other than being somewhere that Vikings emanated from) the information we have is – once again – not entirely helpful. Olaf had been causing chaos in Ireland since the early 850s, and in the reign of King Constantín (Cinaed's nephew), he laid waste to the Pictish kingdom, occupying it for ten weeks 'with his heathens'.[15] Worse, however, was in store for the resurgent Britons of Alt Clud. In 839 they had got stuck into the Picts by burning Dunbar. In 870, however, their own time had come: '*Arx Alt Clud a gentilibus fracta est*,' the Welsh annals report, 'the fortress of Alt Clud was broken by heathens'.[16] The *Annals of Ulster* elaborate, recording that 'Olaf and Ivar, two kings of the Northmen [...] besieged that fortress [Alt Clud] and at the end of four months they destroyed and ransacked it'.[17] This was the end for the fortress on Dumbarton Rock; it fell out of use and was mentioned no more. Two years later, Irish chronicles refer – for the first time – to the Britons of Strathclyde, a new political entity already beginning to pupate.

For Olaf's friend Ivar, the breaking of ancient kingdoms had become something of a speciality. We have met this man before: the previous year he had been in East Anglia with his brother Ubbe, separating King Edmund's talkative head from the rest of him. It is possible that he dragged a number of Anglian slaves with him when he sailed north, for in the following year Olaf and Ivar 'returned to Dublin from Britain with two hundred ships, bringing away with them in captivity to Ireland a great prey of English, and Britons and Picts'.[18] Olaf died at Constantín's hands in, probably, 872.[19] In the following year, the Irish chronicles record that 'Ímar [Ivar], king of the *Nordmanni* [Northmen] of all Ireland and Britain, completed his life'.[20] And what a life it had been. Ivar, over the course of his career, had presided over the collapse of Alt Clud, Northumbria and East Anglia, plied his bloody business across Mercia and the kingdoms of Ireland and – probably – all across the other northern realms as well. Whether he was really a 'king' in any sense we would now recognize is immaterial – he had done enough to match the

The eighth-century *Stockholm Codex Aureus*. Comments by ealdorman Ælfred were added in the ninth century above, below and to the right of the illuminated letters

Tingwall: an assembly site on Mainland, Shetland

A hogback stone, carved in the tenth century, from Govan Old Church, Glasgow

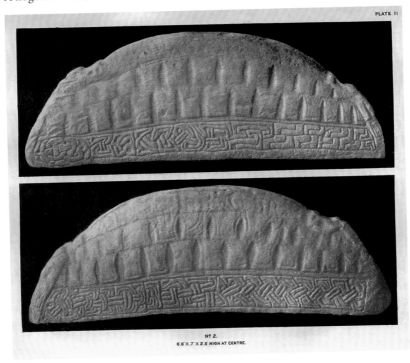

PLATE II

N.º 2.
6.6' X .7 X 2.5' HIGH AT CENTRE.

The whalebone plaque from the tenth-century boat burial at Scar, Orkney

Thorwald's Cross, at Andreas Parish on the Isle of Man, depicts – on one side – Odin swallowed by the wolf Fenrir at *Ragnarök*. The other side displays an apparently Christian scene

The Cuerdale Hoard: 90 pounds of buried treasure (only a fraction of the total is shown in this image)

Coins of Viking rulers in England (obverse at top, reverse at bottom). From left to right: Guthrum-Æthelstan of East Anglia (reigned c.880–90), Siefred of Northumbria (reigned c.894–8), Olaf Guthfrithsson of Northumbria (r. 939–41), Sihtric II of Northumbria (reigned c.942–3), Eric 'Bloodaxe' of Northumbria (r. 947–8 and 952–4)

Reconstruction of tenth-century dwellings at Coppergate, York

Northey Island, Essex: a Viking army crossed the causeway (upper right) to fight the Battle of Maldon in 991

The Sanctuary
monument at Overton
Hill, Wiltshire, erected
around 2000 BC, as
drawn by William
Stukeley in 1723

'Áli had this stone
raised in memory
of himself. He took
Knútr's payment in
England. May God
help his spirit': so runs
the inscription on this
runestone in Väsby,
Uppland (Sweden)

'Ginna and Toki had this stone set up' reads the runic inscription on this stone, found in 1852 in the graveyard of St Paul's Cathedral, London

A mass grave of over fifty decapitated men, most of them originally from Scandinavia, found near Weymouth in Dorset in 2011

Cnut and his queen, Emma (Ælfgifu), depicted in the pages of the eleventh-century *Winchester Liber Vitae*

achievements of any number of anointed monarchs – and the 'dynasty of Ivar', the 'Uí Ímair' as they came to be known in Irish sources, were major players across northern and western Britain and Ireland for generations.[21]

The former industrial shipyards of the Clyde are not the first place one might think to look for the remnants of an early medieval kingdom. Since the decline of Britain's shipbuilding industry, starting in the 1950s, Govan has consistently been one of the poorest parts of the United Kingdom: as silence fell on the shipyards of Clydebank, social and economic problems multiplied in Glasgow's brutalist housing estates, exacerbated by disastrous civic planning policies. Today Govan scores below the Glasgow average for employment, educational attainment and life expectancy; it scores more highly for alcohol-related deaths and the proportions (31.5 and 28 per cent respectively in 2016) of people claiming out-of-work benefits and those considered to be 'income deprived'.[22] To put this into perspective, the overall Glasgow figures for poverty and life expectancy are among the worst in the UK.[23] 'It is as if', declared *The Economist* in 2012, 'a malign vapour rises from the Clyde at night and settles in the lungs of sleeping Glaswegians.'[24] But it was the river that made Govan the greatest shipbuilding powerhouse of the British Empire – in 1900 Govan built a fifth of all new global shipping[25] – and it was the river that turned it into the centre of a durable, and powerful, kingdom of the early medieval world.

I have twice visited Govan Old Church. The first time, as a young PhD student, I was on a field trip organized by the Early Medieval Archaeology Student Symposium (EMASS). I was in Glasgow to give my first ever academic paper, an occasion I had made unnecessarily difficult for myself by consuming prodigious quantities of beer and deep-fried black pudding the night before. I have a dim, and faintly embarrassing, recollection of earnestly lecturing a fellow (Scottish) student on the defects of Scottish nationalism while swaying on a street corner outside a Glaswegian chip shop. My second opportunity to visit the Old Church was undertaken with a group of journalists and others from the British Museum – part of a press trip ahead of the Vikings exhibition of 2014, just before the referendum on Scottish independence.

The church is remarkable for both the antiquity of the setting and the continuity of worship (the current church, dedicated in 1888, is the fourth on this site – there has been a church here since the fifth century), but also for the remarkable collection of early medieval sculpture that is housed within. Such is the quality and quantity of the stonework produced at Govan Old Church that it is now believed likely that the churchyard here was a royal mausoleum for the kingdom of Strathclyde, the successor to the obsolete kingdom of Alt Clud. How this kingdom came into existence, and the ethnic and political dynamics that drove it in its earliest phases are deeply obscure, but there is one clue to what may have been a component of the make-up of this phoenix rising: a rare collection of distinctively Scandinavian-influenced monuments. We had come to see hogbacks.

Hogbacks are most probably gravestones.[26] Not the familiar upright sort, those ubiquitous bedheads for the dead, but more like tomb covers – monuments that once lay lengthwise over the buried corpse below them, perhaps with a standing cross at head or feet.[27] But, unlike recumbent grave slabs and rectangular tombs, hogbacks are, as their name suggests, curvilinear stone edifices, hump-backed and rounded. They are found across the north of England – mostly in Cumbria and Yorkshire – and in Scotland with a famous cluster (five in total) at Govan Old Church. They are curious objects. Examples from Yorkshire, like the ones at St Thomas', Brompton (near Northallerton), are the most endearing, with three-dimensional sculpted bears that cuddle on to the ends of the stones. Most of them are decorated with ropes and cables of Viking-style knots and ring-work, chains of loops and braids incised into the stone. Most, too, have characteristic tegulations that pattern the upper part of the sculpture – overlapping tile-shapes that mean that

Hogbacks at St Thomas', Brompton (drawn by W. G. Collingwood)

hogbacks often resemble armadillos, nervous armoured beasts which might at any minute scuttle off into the shadows when you're not looking (indeed, the animalistic qualities of these objects were not lost on one Govan sculptor, who added an eye and flipper-like feet to his carving, turning it into something that resembles some sort of antediluvian amphibian).

It is the impression of a tiled roof that has led scholars to the understanding that these objects were intended to resemble houses. The Irish and the various peoples of Britain had long traditions of monumental carvings in stone – of crosses in particular – and house-shaped shrines of the type we have encountered before (as Viking loot) were reproduced in stone as tomb covers and as adornments for standing crosses like the early tenth-century Muiredach Cross in Co. Louth, Ireland. But the houses that the hogbacks are modelled on are manifestly unlike these prototypes; they are shingle-roofed and curving like an upturned keel, like the gently bowing roof-lines of the wooden Viking long-house. As we shall see, the

251

idea of the hall as a home for the dead was a powerful concept in the pre-Christian thought-world of the Vikings, and it is certain that such imagery did not vanish from the imagination with any speed. It is, therefore, entirely understandable why Scandinavian settlers on the Clyde would choose this idea to commemorate the dead, even after their conversion to Christianity (which the presence of these stones at an ancient ecclesiastical centre implies). But the result of this impulse was the creation of something unique – a new form of artistic expression that shows how these new communities chose to communicate their sense of themselves to the world around them.

And so, here in Govan, the contradictions of Scottish nationalism feel magnified; few places – from a southerner's perspective – are so unambiguously 'Scottish' as Glasgow. But in the incongruous setting of a strangely severe and massive Victorian neo-gothic church, one can find oneself surrounded by the stonecraft of a people who (if they included a substantial proportion of the surviving Britons of Alt Clud) probably spoke a language closer to Welsh than Gaelic, but among whom dwelt a number of others whose cultural affinities lay with a Scandinavian-infused world, a hybridized Norse–Gaelic culture that was establishing itself all around the Irish Sea. These were people whose own identities were in flux. Hogbacks show us these new identities at the point of their renegotiation. Here were people who saw and embraced traditions of stone carving and house-shaped reliquaries and grave-markers erected in churchyard enclosures and chose these traditions for themselves. But at the same time they were determined to do things in their own way, using their own art-styles, referencing the building styles that were familiar to them. Across northern Britain – from Yorkshire to Cumbria to Clydebank – they were crafting an identity that was distinct: distinct from the communities into which they had intruded, but also from the communities from which they had drifted. Nothing even resembling a hogback exists in Scandinavia.

A classic illustration of what this process meant in cultural terms is found in the transformations that overtook what had hitherto been conservative and ubiquitous accessories. Penannular brooches (open rings that hinge on a long pin, used to secure a cloak at the breast) had for centuries been a typical element of male and female dress in Ireland and the far north and west of Britain. These objects were to play a conspicuous role in defining and reframing identity in the Viking-infused maritime fringes of the west. As tastes and fashions changed with the influx of new people, these brooches swelled to grotesque size as their silver content increased, their bulbous terminals and flat planes chased with decorative interlace and the gaping maws of twisted Viking creatures, or elaborated into thistle-like knobs that announced a new identity taking root. A hoard of such objects, probably gathered together for their weight-value as silver bullion, was recovered from Flusco Pike on Newbiggin Moor near Penrith (Cumbria) over a period of almost two centuries; the first brooch was found in 1795, the second in 1830 and the rest in 1989.[28] The largest of them – the brooch found in 1830 – has a pin that is *c.* 20½ inches in length. There is no way that this can have been a practical object (there are better ways, after all, of fastening a cloak than by using a silver spike weighing a pound and a half). Such objects were intended to communicate the status of their owners, as well as providing a means to carry portable wealth, a vulgar display of power in a society where silver was the crude measure of success.

But perhaps the most direct evidence for this sort of cultural transformation and synthesis can be found in a modification made to an object known, after the place of its finding, as the Hunterston Brooch.[29] Hunterston is over the water from Great Cumbrae where the Firth of Clyde, having turned to the south, broadens out into wider waters around the Isle of Arran. It is not far from Govan, but it is closer to the southern Hebrides – the islands that the *Annals of St-Bertin* described as falling to Viking settlers in the middle of the ninth century. This pre-Viking penannular brooch is, by any standard, an exquisitely wrought piece of jewellery, a Dál Riatan work of art made in around 700, studded with amber gems and wriggling with golden filigree. Any owner of such an object would have fancied himself or herself as quite the business. We do not know for whom or by whom it was originally fashioned, but we do know the name of someone, two centuries after it was made, who owned it. And we know because the name of its owner was written on the back, scratched into the silver: 'Melbrigda owns this brooch'. Melbrigda is an impeccably Gaelic name and thus not, in itself, surprising. What makes this truly significant is the way in which Melbrigda chose to express his ownership: for the language he used was not Irish, nor even Latin, but Old Norse, and the characters that he scratched were Viking runes.

This, then, was the birth of a new people, a new tick-box on the ethnicity forms of the early tenth century. Call it what you will, Anglo-Danish or Hiberno-Norse, Anglo-Scandinavian, even Cambro-Norse, the implication is the same: British (and Irish) Vikings had become distinct from their Scandinavian counterparts.[30] And as the example of the hogbacks demonstrates, the way people buried their dead can tell us a lot about how they – or, more accurately, the people who cared for them in life – imagined their place in their world, their connections and their sense of self.

As the ninth century drew to a close, the successors of Cinaed son of Alpín continued to experience pressure brought to bear by Viking raiding armies. We see it only dimly, in the half-light cast by the sporadic notices of chroniclers who were often writing at some remove from the events they laconically describe. At some point during the eleven years after 899, it is recorded that Pictavia was 'wasted' by Vikings, and in 900 Domnall, son of Constantín I, was slain at Dunnottar 'by the heathens'.[31] The notice of his death is a major turning point in British history, for it marks the moment when the kingdom of the Picts slips for ever into the shadows: 'Domnall son of Constantín,' the Irish chronicles relay, 'king of Alba, dies.'[32] Thus a new kingdom was born, quietly and without fanfare. A century after the Viking Age had begun, not a single political entity of what is now Scotland remained radically unaltered: Alt Clud, Dál Riata, the kingdom of the Picts were all gone, to be replaced by an ill-defined kingdom of Strathclyde, a new kingdom of Alba and a wide coastal belt of more or less intensive Scandinavian settlement and political dominance. The new king of Alba, Constantín II, would reign for forty years. The political and cultural changes that occurred over this period would make permanent this burgeoning sense of nationhood, sharpening its identity, hardening its borders and bringing it – inevitably – into conflict with the Viking-infused powers to the south.[33]

17

THE PAGAN WINTER

axe-age, sword-axe, shields are sundered;
wind-age, wolf-age, before the world crumbles:
no man shall spare another

Völuspá[1]

She walks away from the fire, eyes glassy, empty as ozone, walking slowly towards the west, into the weak sun and the wind and the cold sea spray and the rain, away from the world. Bare white feet press the black soil and broken turf, climbing the mound, dark and damp – an unhealed wound. The old woman is singing, a cracked calling, like the gulls.

The grave lies open, and she kneels. Thunder breaks out; ash on linden. And harsh voices, men's voices; a dog barks, a horse screams.

And screams.

Below the ashes the sleeper sleeps on, sword under soil, spear under stone. Blood steeps the earth, stains the white sand. Ashes close the mound.

Above it all a pillar stands, cut from wood, one eye watching,
Facing the sea.

At some point in the tenth century, a man was buried at Ballateare on the Isle of Man.[2] We don't know where he came from, or who his ancestors were, only that he was buried in the manner of the heathen, like a Viking. Dressed in a cloak fastened with a ringed pin, he was laid in a coffin at the bottom of a deep grave. By his side was a sword, its hilt decorated with inlay of silver and copper. It had been broken and replaced in its scabbard. At his feet was a spear. It too had been broken. Around his neck a knife was hung, and a shield placed upon his body. Then the coffin was closed. Spears were placed upon the coffin, their points pointing towards his feet, and the grave was filled with white sand. Above the sand a mound was raised, cut blocks of turf stacked one on top of the other. Later a grave was dug in the top of the mound. A woman was buried there, face down, arms above her head; the top of her head sliced off with a sword. Nothing accompanied her in the grave, but the mound was sealed with the burnt remains of a horse, a dog, a sheep and an ox. A pillar was raised on top.[3] No one can say what the nature of this pillar was. It may have been an elaborate beast-headed carving like one of the five enigmatic objects buried with the Norwegian Oseberg ship,[4] or something like the 'great wooden post stuck in the ground with a face like that of a man' that ibn Fadlan described among the Rūs.[5] However, the presence at Ballateare of what appear to be sacrificial remains chimes with references to the use of wooden posts in the context of other sacrificial offerings.

The ritualized killing of a slave in order that she might accompany her owner in death has been described already, and the Ballateare grave, along with a number of Scandinavian burials, has long been held up as evidence for the killing of humans (as well as animals) in the rituals surrounding the burial of 'Viking' elites.[6] This interpretation of the evidence is not universally accepted, and there are a number of other possible explanations. The most interesting, but the hardest to prove, is the idea that the woman had died before the blow to the head, and that this had been administered after death in order to release the evil spirits trapped inside.[7] It is also possible that the woman buried here was the victim of a judicial killing – that is, an execution – rather than a sacrifice, although whether this is a substantive distinction is moot. The association of the graves of criminals with prehistoric monuments, including burial mounds, is well established in Anglo-Saxon England.[8] Such burials are often characterized by the unusual position of the body – often buried face down – as well as by evidence of severe corporal trauma. Sometimes it seems (again, in England) that posts were erected to display parts of the victim, especially the head (the OE phrase *heofod stoccan* – 'head stakes' – occurs sixteen times in English charters).[9] However, the cremated remains of animals that were interred above the woman's body at Ballateare imply that her burial was part of an event that involved multiple killings and burials – of animals as well as a human being. Whether or not this woman died to feed the grave, the evidence for elaborate death-theatre is strong and entirely in keeping with the multifarious rites that crowd the mortuary record in the Viking 'homelands'.[10]

One might get the impression, if this were the only sort of evidence we had, that the role of women in the pagan Viking world was an unhappy one, where a likely fate was to be murdered and thrown face down into the grave of a male warrior, one more possession among the other icons of dominance and machismo with which such individuals were wont to be interred. For some women, slaves in particular, such may well have been their fate; but it is also true that such burials are rare and that the evidence for the treatment of women in death was as varied, as enigmatic and often as spectacular as the burial of any male warrior of the age. In fact, the most famous and splendid Viking burial ever discovered – the famous ship burial excavated at Oseberg near Oslo in 1904–5 – contained the bodies of two women, one elderly and the other in late middle age. The ship itself is one of the greatest treasures of the Viking Age, a vessel 70 feet in length, its prow crawling with creatures carved in an interwoven chain of sinuous movement. It dominated the burial, forming the stage on which the dramaturgy of death was performed and the framework for the earthen mound which eventually submerged it.[11] To see beyond it, however, is to be staggered by what the rest of this mighty tomb once concealed. There is no adequate way to convey in words the quality of the objects that were placed in the grave, their weird beauty, the strange carved faces that peer from the sides of the wooden wagon, or the elaborate three-dimensional beast-head pillars that served no purpose that any scholar has been able convincingly to propose.

But the quantity! This is easier to indicate. I reproduce below the inventory published by the Norwegian Museum of Cultural History:

2 women; 2 cows; 15 horses; 6 dogs; 1 ship; oars; rope; rigging equipment; remnants of sails; 1 hand bailer; 1 anchor; 1 cart; 3 ornate sleighs; 1 work sleigh; 2 tents; 1 framework for a 'booth', with walls of textile; 3 long combs; 7 glass beads, 4 with gold inlay; 2 pairs of shoes; 1 small leather pouch containing cannabis; several dresses and other garments; feather mattress; bedlinen; 2 pieces of flint; 5 animal head posts; 4 rattles; 1 piece of wood, arrow-shaped, approx. 40cm long; 1 round pole with a runic inscription, approx. 2.40m long; 1 leather band, knotted like a tie; 1 burial chamber; 1 approx. 1m long wooden pipe; 1 chair; 6 beds; 1 stool; 2 oil-burning lamps; 1 bast mat; 3 large chests; several smaller chests, boxes and round wooden containers with a lid, used mainly for storing food; 3 large barrels; 1 woven basket; 1 wooden bucket with brass fittings; 1 wooden bucket with a 'buddha' figure; 1 small staved bucket made of yew wood; 3 iron pots; 1 pot stand; several stirring sticks and wooden spoons; 5 ladles; 1 frying pan; 1 approx. 2m long trough; 1 earthenware basin; 3 small troughs; 7 wooden bowls; 4 wooden platters; 10 ordinary buckets (one containing blueberries); 2 work axes; 3 knives; 1 quern-stone; bread dough; plums; apples; blueberries; various woollen, linen and silk textiles; 1 large tapestry; 5 different weaving looms; 1 tablet weaving loom; 1 manual spindle and distaff; various small tools for spinning and textile work; 1 device for winding wool; 2 yarn reels; 2 linen smoothers; 1 smoothing iron; 3 wooden needles; 1

pair of iron scissors; 2 washing paddles; 1 round wooden container with a lid, used mainly for storing food; 5 balls of wool; 1 weaving reed; piece of wax; 3 small wooden bowls; 1 small quartz stone; 3 pyrite crystals; 2 slate whetstones; 1 knife handle; 1 bone comb; 1 small wooden bowl; 18 spades (probably belonged to the grave robbers); 1 dung fork; 3 grub hoes; 2 whetstones; 2 awls; 3–5 caskets; 5 wooden pins used to drape things; 1 horsewhip; 1 saddle; various kinds of harness fittings; 5 winter horse shoes of iron; several small wooden pegs for tethering horses; several dog chains of iron; mounts for several dog collars.[12]

An attentive reader of this list may notice a striking absence. There is nothing, at all, of silver or gold, no jewellery, no gemstones, no amber beads or brooches, no pendants, coins or neck-rings, no gilded bridle mounts or hammered bracteates: none of the things, in short, that characterize other high-status Scandinavian graves, male and female, of similar and earlier antiquity. They will also have noted the presence of '18 spades [which] probably belonged to the grave robbers'.[13] These were not modern spades; the mound was disturbed long ago – not long, in fact, after it was closed – and the absence of precious metal objects is probably attributable to this ancient tomb-raiding. (Exactly why the grave was disturbed remains a matter for debate – the scale of the excavation required would have been difficult to manage covertly and may have been sanctioned in some way. Illicit grave-robbing was, in any case, a risky business. Later generations of Norse-speakers were fascinated by the trouble that opened graves could bring down on the heads of intruders – witting or unwitting.) The extraordinary inventory of finds from the Oseberg burial thus represents the left-overs, the picked carcass – the stuff that was too cruddy or too bulky to bother with. In its pristine condition, the burial chamber of the Oseberg grave must have been an astonishing sight, its principal occupant a Nefertiti of the North Sea littoral, buried in a grave to make Sutton Hoo look like Sutton 'whatever'.

Viking ship burials are known from Britain, though nothing on this scale. Nevertheless, whenever a community chose to treat its dead in this way it represented a very public and conspicuous disposal of wealth: a bit like burying a loved one in a car. Anyone so buried, however modest it may seem relative to the Oseberg burial, was being honoured as an important player within the community. One such man was excavated at Ardnamurchan (Scotland) in 2011; his was the first complete boat burial ever to be found on the British mainland. He was buried with sword, axe, spear and shield, laid out in a boat 16 feet in length; in death, he presents the image of a wealthy and powerful pagan warrior, a warlord of the ocean's edge, equipped to pursue a life of adventure on the dark waters of the hereafter. Other male boat burials have been found in the isles (at Colonsay, Oronsay and Orkney, and on the Isle of Man) and fragments of a boat grave – now lost – were found in 1935 at the site of the Huna Hotel in Caithness.[14] At Westness cemetery on Rousay, Orkney, for example, two boat burials were excavated in the 1960s, and the boat graves of men have been found on Man at Balladoole and Knock-e-Dooney. In each case, the boats in which they were interred measured in the region of 13 to 16 feet – the size of the small oared boats that were interred as secondary grave goods in the burial mound of the Gokstad ship in Norway.[15]

It was not only men, however, who were afforded these extravagant death rituals in Britain. At Scar on Orkney a woman in her seventies – a fabulously advanced age for the time – was buried in a boat 25 feet long, alongside a man in his mid-thirties and a child.[16] A whalebone 'plaque', a flat board of roughly rectangular shape, with a simple rope-like pattern cut into it at the borders and decorative roundels incised into its surface, was set at her feet. At one end, the shape of the board has been carved away to fashion the profile of two bestial heads on sinuous necks, spiralling to confront one another – teeth bared and tongues lolling. It is an iconic image of the Viking Age, but no one knows what objects like this were used for (a similar example can be found in the collection of the British Museum, excavated from another female boat burial in

Norway). They were, however, possessions that not every woman in society could expect to be buried with. Possibly they were emblems of status, a symbol of the magical and religious powers that women in Viking society could wield. The other objects in the grave included the paraphernalia of weaving – spindle whorls and weaving sword, needle-case and shears. The processes and symbolism of weaving were far from mundane – they could, for some Viking women, provide the tools and imagery for hidden and terrible powers.

What is perhaps most important about overtly unChristian burial traditions like these is that they were drawing their material vocabulary from the practices of Viking Age Scandinavia: these were the graves of people and of communities who still felt themselves connected to a homeland from which they had been divorced, and their behaviour implies a desire to maintain a cultural link across space and time. The people who buried their matriarch at Scar were inserting her corpse into a tradition that included the women of the Oseberg burial, claiming for her a shared identity and tapestry of beliefs (the Oseberg burial also contained, on a lavish scale, a battery of equipment related to weaving and textile production). The same can be said of all the 'pagan' Viking graves of Britain – the mound at Ballateare and the cemetery at Westness, the barrow graves of Cumbria and the cremated remains of Heath Wood near Repton among many others.

As the hogbacks demonstrate, however, this conservatism was not to last. From almost the moment they arrived in Britain, new beliefs were shaping the way that the Vikings treated the dead and imagined the afterlife, and evolving identities and political realities were refashioning the way that British 'Vikings' found their place in the world. The old ways were dying fast.

First the snows will come, driving hard from all points of the compass; biting winds, shrill and screeching, bringing the cold that cuts. Thrice the winter comes, three times with no relenting; no spring will come, no summer to follow, winter upon winter, the land swallowed by ice unending. The green shoots will die under the frost, the skeleton trees creaking beneath the weight of snow – the world will fall dim and silent, shadowed in perpetual twilight. 'Fimbulvetr' they will call it, the 'great winter', and few will survive its corpse-grip. Those who do will wish that they had died.

Riding on the back of the ice-wind, sweeping down paths of famine and despair, war will sweep the ice-bound world, violence shattering families, severing oaths – 'brothers will struggle and slaughter each other, and sisters' sons spoil kinship's bonds'. So the prophecy runs. And as the axes rise and fall and all the blood of the earth is emptied out on to virgin snows, a howling will be heard away in the east.

Gods and elves will lament and hold council as their doom unfolds. Yggdrasil, the world tree, will shake and an uproar rumble from Jötunheimr; the dwarves will mutter before their doors of stone. For the time now is short before all bonds are broken, and the wolves of Fenrir's line, the troll-wives' brood, will break free from the Iron Wood and run from the east. And they will swallow down the sun and swallow down the moon, and the heavens will be fouled with blood.

Then the Gjallarhorn will sound, the breath of Heimdallr, watchman of the gods, echoing across the worlds, its blast echoing from the mountains. It shall awaken the gods and the *einherjar* – the glorious dead – and they will assemble and make themselves ready for the final battle, Odin speaking with Mímir's head for final words of counsel. For their foes shall have already arrived and will stand arrayed in dreadful splendour upon the battle plain, the field that runs for a hundred leagues in all directions – a bleak and boundless tundra.

There shall come Loki, father of lies, freed from an age of torments; and with him will stand his terrible children: Fenrir, the wolf, his mouth gaping wide enough to swallow the world, fire spewing from his eyes; and Jormungandr, the world serpent, shall haul his foul coils on to the land, writhing and thrashing, venom gushing. To this place, too, shall the giant Hrym come, he will steer the ship of dead men's nails to this place of reckonings, leading the frost giants on to the battle plain. Last to arrive will be the sons of Muspell, the flaming hordes marshalled by Surt, demon of fire, his shining sword setting all ablaze beneath the riven sky.

And Odin will ride to meet them at the head of his host, gripping the spear, Gungnir, forged by the sons of Ivaldi; and he will wear a helmet of gold and a coat of mail. Thor will be with him and Frey and Tyr and Heimdall, and all those heroes who died in battle and were chosen.

And all will fall.

This was how the Vikings imagined the world would end,[17] shattered in the madness of battle, poured out in the blood of the gods on Vigrid – the 'battle plain'. It would die with the thrashing coils of the serpent, the sun devoured, the earth burned away – choked out in torrents of ice and fire, the way it had begun. The story of *Ragnarök* – the 'doom of the gods' – is recorded in two complete versions, the eddic poem *Völuspá* and a prose account compiled by Snorri Sturluson in the mythological handbook *Gylfaginning*, for which *Völuspá* was the primary source. *Völuspá* means 'the prophecy of the *völva*' – the seeress. It is a prophetic poem delivered to Odin, a telling of the great arc of mythic time, from the world's beginnings in the void to its breaking at *Ragnarök* and its subsequent rebirth. It is the ultimate encapsulation of the knowledge that Odin seeks, the knowledge for which he has sacrificed himself to himself, for which he has given his eye and taken the head of Mímir. It offers cold comfort.

Odin will ride into the jaws of Fenrir and do battle with the wolf; he will face it alone, and that will be the end of him, the All-Father swallowed into the maw of death. Thor will ride beside him, but no help will come from that quarter. Thor will be locked in deadly conflict with Jormungandr and, though he will slay the *wyrm*, he will be poisoned by its venom – staggering nine steps before he too will fall. Frey will die also, cut down by Surt's flaming sword. Tyr, the one-handed god, will go down to Garm – the hound who howls before hell's mouth – and Heimdall and Loki will slay each other.

The ideas contained in *Völuspá*, and rationalized and repeated by Snorri, cannot be attributed with any confidence to the Viking Age itself, but allusions to, and scenes from, the story of *Ragnarök* are found in other poems and fragments.[18] Of these, two of the most dramatic are found carved in Britain, shards of the pagan Viking end of days, frozen in immortal rock.

Thirty-one runestones stand on the Isle of Man, the largest number in any place outside Scandinavia. Like their cousins, they are memorials to the dead (although at least one was erected to salve the soul of a living man) and are defined by the runic carvings – inscribed in the Norse language – that record the names of those lost and those remaining, and the people who raised the stones. (Some also carry inscriptions in Ogham, the vertical Celtic alphabet of hatch-marks used in Ireland and western Britain – a sure sign of a culturally and linguistically mixed population.)[19] They make up roughly a third of all the carved stones of Man, an impressive corpus of sculpture bearing the combined influence of Irish stoneworking traditions and Scandinavian art-styles. They are, stylistically, quite dissimilar to the runestone tradition of the

Viking 'homelands' and are primarily cruciform objects – either high standing crosses, or cross-incised slabs akin to the Christian symbol stones of Pictavia.[20] The inscriptions they carry are, for the most part, fairly mundane, although they do provide a thrilling glimpse of the individuals who peopled Viking Age Man, even if the light that the inscriptions cast on these people is but a fleeting glimmer in the dark.

'Þorleifr the Neck raised this cross in memory of Fiak, his son, Hafr›s brother's son,' runs the inscription on the tenth-century standing cross at Braddan Church;[21] 'Sandulfr the Black erected this cross in memory of Arinbjǫrg his wife …' runs another at Andreas Church.[22] Some, like Þorleifr's, hint at premature tragedy ('Áleifr [...] raised this cross in memory of Ulfr, his son'),[23] another acknowledges a guilty conscience ('Melbrigði [incidentally, the same Celtic name (albeit spelled differently) as that scratched into the back of the Hunterston Brooch], the son of Aðakán the Smith, raised this cross for his sin …') but concludes with the prideful boast of the rune-carver ('but Gautr made this and all in Man').[24] Sometimes they hint at familial drama and community tensions. A person who identified himself as 'Mallymkun' raised a cross in memory of 'Malmury', his foster-mother. He ends with the sour observation that '[it] is better to leave a good foster-son than a wretched son'. A thousand years later, the rancour still festers in the stone. Other thoughts are snapped off by time and left hanging: 'Oddr raised this cross in memory of Frakki, his father, but …'[25] But what? It is most likely that the missing runes revealed the name of the carver ('but [so-and-so] cut/made this' is a typical formula), but it is impossible to rule out a more personal aside: '… but Hrosketill betrayed the faith of his sworn confederate',[26] runs the truncated inscription on another stone at Braddan Church. Alas, what Hrosketill did – or to whom, or even for what purpose the stone was raised – is lost for ever.

The most famous of the Manx runestones is the fragment of a monument known as 'Thorwald's Cross', found at Andreas Church. It is a slab-type runestone, with its surviving inscription 'Þorvaldr raised [this] cross' running down one edge, and a decorative cross on each face, embellished with characteristically Scandinavian ring-chain carvings. In the case of this particular runestone, however, the simple Christian message is complicated by the subject matter to which the carver chose to turn his chisel. On one side of what remains of the stone, cut in relief on the bottom right-hand quadrant left vacant by the cross, is the image of a male, bearded figure with a large bird perched upon his shoulder. A spear is in his hand, its point downwards, thrusting towards the open jaws of a wolf – a wolf that is in the process of devouring him, his right leg disappearing down the lupine gullet. There can be little doubt that this is a depiction of Odin, Gungnir in hand and raven on his shoulder,[27] swallowed by the wolf.

Across the sea from Man, at Gosforth in Cumbria, a tall cross stands in the churchyard of St Mary's, 15 feet of slender masonry with pea-green lichen clinging like sea-scum to the ruddy Cumbrian stone. It seems odd and incongruous, standing there amid the dour eighteenth-century tombstones – like some strange Atlantean pillar recovered from the ocean floor and hauled upright, flotsam from another world. Its carvings are in surprisingly good condition, given the millennium during which it has stood against the elements. The lichen is less ancient than the carvings it obscures. In 1881, Dr Charles Arundel Parker – the obstetrician and part-time antiquarian – and his friend the Rev. W. S. Calverley came to Gosforth 'one dull wet day in the late autumn', when, the two gentlemen had determined, 'the continuous damp and rain of the previous weeks would have softened the lichens which had filled every sculptured hollow'. Happily for them and the condition of their frockcoats, these were days when menial labour was easily to be had. These two learned fellows stood in the churchyard while Dr Parker's coachman, 'up aloft, with a dash of a wet brush to the right and to the left hand scattered the softened mosses'.[28] What he revealed were the triquetrae (interlacing triple-arches) that decorated the cross-head, the final details to be revealed and recorded of a monument that boasts the most comprehensive iconographic depiction of Norse mythology dating to the Viking Age anywhere in Europe.

Many of the scenes that cover the four faces of the shaft of the Gosforth Cross remain open to interpretation, but two in particular stand out. One is the torment of Loki, the punishment inflicted for his part in the death of Baldr and the pivotal event of the mythic cycle that ends with *Ragnarök*. We see him bound in an ovoid cell, a pathetic trussed creature, while his wife Sigyn bends over him to catch the venom that drips from the serpent pressing its diamond head into his face. The other is the depiction of a figure, striding purposefully into the gaping mouth of a beast, one foot upon the lower jaw, one hand reaching to grip the upper, a spear held in the other. Snorri provides the key that enables us to identify this figure as Vidar, son of Odin: 'Vidar will stride forward and thrust one of his feet into the lower jaw of the wolf [...] With one hand he takes hold of the wolf's upper jaw and rips apart its mouth, and this will be the wolf's death.'[29] This is the end of the wolf, Fenrir, but it is not the end of the world. That comes with the final blackening of the heavens and the burning of Yggdrasil, the sinking of the earth into the sea – a return to the primeval void.

In all tellings of the *Ragnarök* story, however, there is a final act, a light to guide us through the darkness. In *Völuspá* it is told with heartbreaking simplicity, the heathen *völva*'s vision of a far green country – a promised land to come:

> She sees rising up a second time
> the earth from the ocean, ever-green;
> the cataracts tumble, an eagle flies above,
> hunting fish along the fell.[30]

There are aspects of this unfolding vision that feel familiar – the 'hall standing, more beautiful than the sun, better than gold', where 'virtuous folk shall live' and 'enjoy pleasure the live-long day' and, in one version of *Völuspá*, the sudden appearance of 'the mighty one down from above, the strong one, who governs everything',[31]

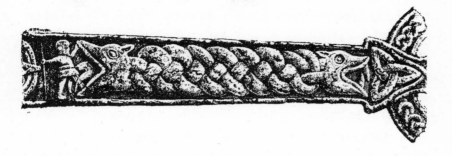

Vidar and Fenrir on the Gosforth Cross

the arrival – as one scholar describes it – 'of Christ in majesty, descending to the earth after the rule of the pagan gods has come to an end'.[32] This Christian coda to the pagan end of days is there at Gosforth as well, more explicitly perhaps than anywhere else. Immediately below the depiction of Vidar's grisly dispatch of Fenrir is a depiction of the crucifixion, the redemptive fulcrum of human history – the event which, in Christian cosmology, ensured safe harbour for the souls of those who embraced its message. It is the symbol of the promise of eternal life, the seal that guarantees that a new world shall rise from the ocean.

It is a supreme irony that the very monuments at Andreas Church and Gosforth which seem to confirm the pagan beliefs written down in a later age also bear witness to their dwindling, their co-option into a new world-view. The old stories were not yet dead at the time these monuments were made, and many of them would never die, living on through the versions written down 300 years after being alluded to in stone. But by this time the stories were no longer (if they ever were) an oppositional belief system, a Viking 'religion' to rival the teachings of the gospel. They were, instead, passing into folklore, becoming tales that could be told without threatening the Christian world-view, complementing it perhaps, explanatory metaphors for the new narratives that were percolating through mixed and immigrant communities. We might imagine that it would, initially, have been easy for a people accustomed to many gods to add another to the throng (or many others – the trinity and the multitudes of saints and angels would doubtless have appeared indistinguishable at first from the gods, ghosts and elves of native belief). Over time, the exclusive nature of the Christian god would have gradually asserted itself, but it cannot have been clear at the beginning. The crosses at Gosforth and Andreas Church can therefore be interpreted in different ways as the products of an incomplete conversion – made for or by people for whom, at the time, Christianity was just an additional set of images and stories to add to the mythological cauldron.

On the other hand, perhaps, these were erudite attempts to juxtapose Christian and pagan images – a means of instructing new converts on the essentials of the Christian faith. For example, although the scene on the reverse of Thorwald's Cross has not been securely interpreted, there is little doubt of its Christian intent: a man wielding a huge cross and a book tramples on a serpent while another Christian symbol, a fish, hovers near by: a triple whammy of Christian symbology. There is room for a little ambiguity here – crosses can easily be mistaken for hammers (indeed, some Thor's-hammer pendants may actually have been intended as crosses, and some deliberately combine cross and hammer on the same object),[33] and Thor was famous as both a fisherman and a fighter of serpents. One thing he was not, however, was bookish, and it is this more than anything else that gives the Christian game away. Although we cannot know for sure, it may be that the missing 'panels' of the complete cross depicted complementary images from pagan and Christian mythology – a sort of pictorial instruction manual to Christianity, the build-it-yourself guide to getting religion with the old myths deployed as the key.

I prefer, however, to see all of this in a different light, to see the *Ragnarök* story as an expression of a melancholy self-awareness, the creative and emotionally profound product of people who could feel the old world slipping away, a poetic response in words and stone to the twilight of an ancient way of life, a twilight of their gods. The *Ragnarök* story brims with sadness and nostalgia, a pagan vision of the future that was alive to the impending extinction of its own world-view in an increasingly homogenized Europe. It is a complex and intellectually involved interplay of hope and defeat, defiance and resignation, an acknowledgement – a recapitulation – of what was already slipping away and a yearning for a new and better world around the corner. For the Viking communities of Britain, that hope lay in the new identities and new ways of being that were being adopted and adapted in different ways across the islands. As the tenth century progressed, old affinities and beliefs began to break down as new political and cultural realities asserted themselves. What it meant to be a 'Viking' in Britain was changing rapidly.[34]

18

THE GREAT WAR

Long was prophesied the time when they will come,
rulers by right of descent taking their possession,
men of the North in a place of honour around them;
in the centre of their van they will advance. [...]
There will be spear-thrusts, a fierce flood.
No friend will spare the body of his enemy.
There will be heads split open, without brains.
There will be women widowed and horses riderless.
There will be terrible wailing before the rush of warriors,
and a multitude wounded by hand before the hosts part.

Armes Prydein Vawr (tenth century)[1]

When, in 920, Edward the Elder finally received the submission of the north, Northumbria had been subject to Viking conquest, settlement and rule for half a century. In the years that followed the capture of York by the *micel here* in 866, power in Northumbria appears to have been shared in an untidy fashion among a number of groups, competing or cooperating as circumstances dictated. There were native Northumbrian rulers (Ecgbert I, Ricsige, Ecgbert II), as well as a separate dynasty that retained a power-base at Bamburgh in the north of the kingdom. Then there were the bishops of Northumbria – at Lindisfarne and York – and also, probably, those leaders of the *micel here* who had not gone south with the army to Mercia, East Anglia or Wessex. In 874, however, a new 'big beast' reappeared on the scene: Halfdan, supposed son of Ragnar Loðbrók, and one of the leaders of the army that had captured York in 866, came north from the capture of Repton with an army.[2] He camped on the Tyne, overrunning northern Northumbria before raiding and briefly occupying Pictavia (during the reign of Cinaed's son, Constantín I) and attacking the new kingdom of Strathclyde.[3]

From this point onwards, and particularly from 876 when the *Anglo-Saxon Chronicle* records that Halfdan began to 'share out the land' of Northumbria, men with Scandinavian names began to be recognized as the prime movers in the kingdom, particularly in those territories centred on York.[4] The years that followed saw Halfdan succeeded by a line of Viking kings – Guthfrith, Siefred and Cnut – about whom very little is known. What can be seen, however, is that, like Guthrum–Æthelstan in East Anglia, these were men who outwardly embraced the Christian Church and what is more, the Church – so it would seem – had begun to embrace them back.

A sense of ecclesiastical investment in the way this new royal power was framed can be seen in a remarkable description in the *Historia Sancti Cuthberti* (a history of the see of St Cuthbert, dating from the mid-tenth to mid-eleventh century) describing the circumstances of Guthfrith's elevation to the throne in 877. It is not a very reliable source – neither in general nor within the bounds of the specific anecdote that follows – but it does tell us something about how power was being brokered in the north in those days, about the unlikely accommodations that were being reached. Once again, the discorporate form of our old friend St Cuthbert is on hand, still apparently taking an active interest in British politics, this time appearing:

> by night to the holy abbot of Carlisle, whose name was Eadred, [and] firmly enjoining him as follows: 'Go,' he said, 'across the Tyne to the army of the Danes, and say to them that, if they will

obey me, they are to point out to you a certain boy, Guthfrith, Hardacnut's son [...] and at the sixth hour lead him before the whole multitude, that they may elect him king. And at the ninth hour lead him with the whole army on to the hill which is called "Oswiu's down" [Oswigesdune], and there place on his right arm a gold armlet, and thus they all may appoint him as king.'[5]

This, the *Historia* relates, is exactly what Eadred did and, naturally, the Viking army was perfectly happy with this arrangement. Guthfrith was duly made king with 'the great goodwill of the whole multitude'.[6] There are glimpses here, perhaps, of rituals of power being enacted – a glimpse of the royal theatre through which ruler-ship was expressed and validated in the febrile climate of Viking-dominated late ninth-century Northumbria.

Guthfrith ascends the mound, the skies grey and pregnant with rain. A bracing wind is blowing from the west. As the abbot speaks, the syllables of Latin tumble away on the breeze, away from the ears of the uncomprehending multitude who shuffle, cold and confused, their spear-points glinting dully in the leaden light. Dew seeps into woollen cloaks and leather shoes, perfumed with the loamy scent of earth. Some of them know why this place is powerful, but all of them feel it; they know that the dead who sleep under soil have a presence that can touch the living, and this mound is named for a king.[7]

Guthfrith takes the golden ring from the priest. He holds it aloft and a brief shaft of sunlight catches it, burning it for a moment with amber fire. Suddenly a rumble begins, swords on steel rims, ash on linden, a forest thunder. It builds until the hills echo with it, rolling from the fells and dales, crows startled, wheeling from the woods. Guðfrið smiles; he places the ring upon his arm and draws his sword, a silver fish in rapids, dancing in the daylight. A cry of exultation breaks forth, a roar like the falling of trees, rising skyward from a thousand wolfish throats, announcing the birth of a king.

There are fewer reasons to doubt the circumstantial details of the *Historia* than there are reasons to scorn the political and supernatural stories it weaves, and there is the glimmer of truth about the image that the *Historia* obliquely conjures. Taken alongside what we have encountered already of the militarized nature of the body politic – the weapon-waving, the threat and application of violence – we can perhaps see hints of a Viking ceremony of king-making that was a far cry from the democratic fantasies of the Victorian era, where rough but hearty farmers gathered to settle their affairs in straight talk and rough and tumble. Instead, the creation of a new king was probably more like the elevation of a modern tribal warlord, political ascendancy celebrated with the crackle of automatic gunfire, AK-47s discharged recklessly into the sky.

However, the truly revealing part of the *Historia*'s account can be found in Cuthbert's afterthought to Eadred, his injunction that Eadred should also 'say to him [Guthfrith], when he has been made king, that he is to give me the whole territory between the Tyne and Wear'. So, there's the rub: with this line the author of the *Historia* reveals his agenda in telling this (tall) tale – the concern that, right from the outset, the interests of the see of St Cuthbert (that is, the bishopric of Lindisfarne) should be respected and strengthened by future kings of Northumbria. The self-interest, however, was doubtless mutual. Like the unwitting St Edmund, invoked to support the claims of the new East Anglian dynasty, here St Cuthbert – evidently forgetful of the despoliation of his monastery by Guthfrith's putative forebears – was being dragged from his cloud to leave the imprimatur of the Northumbrian Church on a new Northumbrian regime. Church and state had little to lose, and much to gain, by working together to uphold structures of power and privilege.

Guthfrith was buried at York Minster, a very public way to demonstrate the alliance of the new Northumbrian royalty with the Church. Indeed, the kings who followed him – Siefred and Cnut – were, like their East Anglian counterparts, keen to publicize their faith, over-egging the religious iconography of their coinage in a way that has led some to suspect that it was bishops rather than kings who were behind it all.[8] Certain coins of the Northumbrian Cnut, for example, not content with using the patriarchal cross (two crosses for the price of one), also arranged the letters of the king's name at the cardinal points; were they transposed to a human torso, they would be inscribed in the order in which the hand would reach them when marking out the sign of the cross:

Coin of Cnut of Northumbria (*c.* 900–5). The other letters,
read clockwise, spell out the word REX ('king')

In addition, the reverse of these coins bears the legend 'MIRABILIA FECIT' ('he has done/made wondrous things'), a quotation from Psalm 98 with an obvious double meaning: as much as it celebrated the inscrutable doings of the Almighty, it also implied the power of the king over the means of production. Such innovations in coin design betray an active intelligence and a sophisticated grasp of

Christian symbology and scripture, hinting – perhaps – at the hand of the Northumbrian Church in shaping the messages coming from the new Northumbrian court.[9]

These mutual accommodations were driven by primarily political motives. Future Viking kings of Northumbria were manifestly more ambivalent about Christian piety, and markedly more concerned with their own personal power and prestige. In the decades after 900 a new Viking influence came to dominate in Northumbria, one that originated not with the *micel here* but in the colonies of Ireland and the west. The coins they issued deployed an entirely new set of imagery, a deliberate assertion of their distinctive cultural baggage. Hammers, swords, bows and ravens began to mark out a distinctive identity for the Viking kings of Northumbria – a defiant dissemination of martial and mythological symbolism that vied for space with the cross and the name of St Peter. The most striking of these coins, issued in the reign of Sihtric (r. 921–7), feature the hammer of Thor intruding into the inscription itself, the sign of a pagan deity inserted into the very name of St Peter – a pagan graft on to a Christian

A Northumbrian coin of the 920s. The inscription reads SCI (Sancti: 'Saint') PETRI ('Peter') MO (Moneta: 'minted [this coin]'). The 'I' of Petri has been replaced with an upside down hammer

root-stock. It may be that, like the hybrid iconography of the Gosforth and Thorwald crosses, this was a way to bridge a chasm of belief – to encourage a multi-faith population to find common ground (St Peter and Thor were both, after all, famous fishermen) and smooth the path of conversion. But to me it feels like politics: the Viking kings in York needed the support of both the Church and the pagan militarized elite. Coins that combined, however crudely, the symbols of both these camps would have served as a convenient way for kings to demonstrate to the twin pillars of early medieval power that they were both being kept in mind.[10]

In the period immediately after 900, the political situation in Northumbria is plunged into penumbra, a shadow almost as deep as that which cloaks the rest of northern Britain. After Æthelwold's short-lived tenure on the throne (and it is uncertain to what degree he was recognized as 'king of the Danes' in any meaningful sense in Northumbria between 902 and his death in 904), the names of other rulers – Halfdan, Eowils and Ingwær – are known only from the list of 'kings' who died fighting Edward the Elder at Tettenhall in 911. The gloom clears a little, however, with a battle fought at Corbridge (Northumberland) in 918 between an army led by Constantín II of Scotland and a warlord known – in Irish sources – as Ragnall (ON Rögnvaldr; OE Rægnald), the grandson of Ivar.[11]

Ragnall's career, like those of so many other Viking warlords of the tenth century, began in Ireland. In 902, the Viking elite in control of Dublin were driven out by a native Irish coalition led by 'Máel Finnia son of Flannácan, with the men of Brega and by Cerball son of Muiricá, with the Leinstermen; and they abandoned a good number of their ships (and escaped half dead after they had been wounded and broken)'.[12] In the fifteen years that followed, several Viking war-bands seem to have drifted east, looking for new lands and business opportunities. The first to be documented was led by a character called Ingimundr, who was beaten back from

Anglesey by a son of Cadell ap Rhodri, king of Gwynedd (Welsh rulers, unlike almost everyone else in Britain, seem to have been pretty successful at denying the Vikings a significant toehold).[13] After this setback he appeared near Chester where, having first done a deal with King Edward's sister, the redoubtable Æthelflæd of Mercia, he double-crossed the English and attacked the settlement. According to the version written up in the *Fragmentary Annals of Ireland*, Ingimundr's Vikings, thwarted by the town's defences, constructed a roof of hurdles to protect themselves while making a hole in the wall:

> What the Saxons and the Irish who were among them did was to hurl down huge boulders, so that they crushed the hurdles on their heads. What they [the Vikings] did to prevent that was to put great columns under the hurdles. What the Saxons did was to put the ale and water they found in the town into the town's cauldrons, and to boil it and throw it over the people who were under the hurdles, so that their skin peeled off them. The Norwegians' response to that was to spread hides on top of the hurdles. The Saxons then scattered all the beehives there were in the town on top of the besiegers, which prevented them from moving their feet and hands because of the number of bees stinging them.[14]

Perhaps unsurprisingly, having been crushed, scalded and molested by bees, Ingimundr 'gave up the city, and left it'. A good story, certainly. Whether it is true or not is impossible to say, but the town was 'renewed' by Æthelflæd in 907 – probably a reference to the refortification and replanning of the town as a burh.[15]

Ragnall first appears in the written record in 914, where we find him defeating another Viking fleet off the Isle of Man.[16] A few years later he appears again, fighting alongside his kinsman Sihtric (another grandson of Ivar) in Ireland. A year after that, he took men from Waterford and went east, to Britain; there he found himself embroiled in conflict with Constantín II at Corbridge. The battle seems to have been indecisive, but Ragnall had evidently done enough to win trust in Northumbria. He was soon having coins minted in his own name at York, and remained in power in Northumbria until his death in 920, the same year in which the *Anglo-Saxon Chronicle* records him acknowledging the overlordship of Edward the Elder.[17] He was succeeded by Sihtric Cáech, his Irish brother-in-arms, who by this point was recognized as king in Dublin. Sihtric vacated that throne in order to take power in Northumbria, leaving Dublin to a further grandson of Ivar, a kinsman named Guthfrith (not to be muddled up with the Guthfrith we have met before). When Sihtric died in 927, this new Guthfrith also briefly acceded to the Northumbrian throne. It seems confusing, and it is. What emerges from all this intra-familial throne-swapping, however, is evidence of the ties – dynastic, political and economic – that were beginning to bind Viking Britain together, an east–west axis linking Northumbria to the Irish Sea.

That Viking war-bands with connections on both sides of the Pennines were operating in northern Britain in the early tenth century is implied by hoards of silver, of which several have been found across the north.[18] The most famous and substantial of these, the Cuerdale Hoard, is perhaps best explained as the war-chest of a large Viking army, the sort of force that might have been traversing the overland routes between York and the Irish Sea. It was discovered in 1840 by workmen repairing the banks of the River Ribble near Preston, Lancashire. One of the men, Thomas Horrocks, recalled his colleague, James Walne, pushing his spade into 'something like lime' and announcing 'at first it was like Cockle shells but immediately swore it was money'. So it was. Once the authorities had involved themselves and divested the workmen of the coins with which they had stuffed their pockets (they were each allowed to keep a single coin), the rest of the hoard was excavated – revealing, in the words of the Duchy of Lancaster's report to the coroner, 'a very large quantity of silver coins [...] besides some bars or Ingots of Silver, Chains, Armlets and Rings or Ring Money and more of the same sort of corroded metal [lead] which was ultimately supposed to have originally formed a box that had contained them'. The hoard was conveyed by wheelbarrow to Cuerdale Hall where it was taken indoors and laid out on the ground – there was so much of it that it 'covered the floor of one of the sitting rooms'.[19]

The hoard is vast, easily the largest Viking Age treasure ever found in Britain. It weighs some 90 pounds, containing around 7,000 coins plus over a thousand silver ingots and fragments of hack-silver. The coins are varied – Anglo-Saxon, Carolingian, Islamic, coins issued by Viking rulers at York and even a number in the name of 'Alwaldus', probably the doomed West Saxon ætheling Æthelwold – and allow the hoard to be dated to c. 905–10. Most of them were probably funnelled through York. The hack-silver, however, is dominated by jewellery from the Irish Sea region, and the hoard stands as testament to the connections – and the extraordinary wealth – that was being accumulated by Viking groups exploiting the opportunities that lay between Dublin and York.

In 924 Edward the Elder died. It seems likely that his final years were rather less successful than those leading up to 920 – the *Anglo-Saxon Chronicle*, at least, has not much to say about them, and it is possible that the servile postures supposedly adopted by the other kings and potentates of Britain in 920 were swiftly abandoned as the king began sliding towards the grave. We cannot say for certain. What is clear, however, is that the next king of Wessex – Edward's son Athelstan – would present a highly energetic challenge to all of the powers of the north. In 926 Athelstan married his sister to Sihtric Cáech, king of Northumbria, presumably with the hope of establishing a lasting political alliance and a formal bond of kinship with the Viking ruler and any potential offspring. Any such plans were thwarted however by Sihtric's death the following year. The new Viking claimant to the throne, Guthfrith, didn't last long. Presumably infuriated that his plans had come to naught, Athelstan took the direct approach, throwing Guthfrith out on his ear and burning down a stronghold inside York.[20] It was a defining moment in British history. For the first time, a single king had imposed his rule on the vast bulk of the territory that falls within the boundaries of the modern English nation. If Alfred had invented the idea of England, and Edward had begun to hammer it into shape, it was Athelstan who had drawn it whole from the fire – the first true king of England.[21]

His ambitions were not limited to England, however. In 927, Athelstan called an assembly at Eamont Bridge in Cumbria. In attendance were 'Hywel, king of the West Welsh, and Constantine, king of Scots, and Owain, king of Gwent, and Ealdred, Ealdwulf's offspring, from Bamburgh'. (The rulers of Bamburgh and the territory north of the Tyne seem to have retained a lasting autonomy from the 860s onwards.) Its ostensible purpose was to guarantee peace and forbid 'devil-worship', but the *Anglo-Saxon Chronicle* makes it very clear how Athelstan's power was seen from an English perspective: 'he governed all the kings who were in this island'.[22] This was the least of Athelstan's grandiosity: from 928, the kings of Wales began appearing as witnesses to Athelstan's charters, humiliatingly demoted to *sub-reguli* ('under-kinglets'), and Athelstan himself begins to be styled, not only as 'king of the English', but also, on his coinage, as *rex totius Britanniae*:'king of all Britain'.[23]

It was doubtless this swollen sense of *imperium* that compelled Athelstan to war with Scotland in 934. We don't know exactly what prompted it,[24] but we can speculate that the Scottish king wasn't living up to the subservient standards Athelstan had set. It was an elaborate business: Athelstan gathered what seems to have been an enormous force, comprising warriors from England as well as allied contingents from Wales under the kings Hywel, Idwal and Morgan. Then 'going towards Scotia with a great army', Athelstan 'subdued his enemies, laid waste Scotia as far as Dunnottar and the mountains of Fortriu with a land force, and ravaged with a naval force as far as Caithness'.[25] The *Anglo-Saxon Chronicle* has a shorter version ('King Athelstan went to Scotland with both a *here* ['raiding army'] and a *sciphere* ['raiding fleet'] and harried across much of it'), the first time 'Scotland' appears in the historical record as a term to describe northern Britain.[26]

Constantín was beaten and humiliated, his son taken as a hostage, treasure extorted.[27] Later in the year, on 12 September 934, he could be found far from home at Buckingham (Buckinghamshire, England), witnessing a charter on behalf of his new master. He appears as a *sub-regulus* – just another little king.

All of this humiliating was bound to have consequences – Athelstan had all of the rulers of Britain troop out again the following year to undergo the same sort of abasement they had endured at Eamont Bridge, this time at Cirencester (Gloucestershire), where they were joined by Owain, king of Strathclyde (who may also have been at Eamont Bridge).[28] It was probably getting rather too much to bear for many of them. A Welsh poem composed around this time – *Armes Prydein Vawr* ('The Great Prophecy of Britain'), fantasized about a great pan-British alliance – 'the Cymry and the men of Dublin [...] The Irish of Ireland, Anglesey, and Scotland, the Cornish and the men of Strathclyde' – that would rise up to topple the hated English. Even the 'foreigners of Dublin will stand with us' runs the poem, to force the Saxons to 'pay seven times the value for what they have done, with certain death as payment for their wrong [...] Let blood, let death be their companions.'[29]

But it wasn't a fantasy: war was indeed coming. Olaf Guthfrithsson, the son of the man whom Athelstan had turfed out of York in 927, had been busy securing his own empire, fighting and plundering around Ireland throughout the 920s. By 937 – if not long before – he seems to have secured his power in Dublin, and in that year is referred to in Irish chronicles as 'Lord of the Foreigners', having broken the power of his rival – Amlaíb (Olaf) Cenncairech – at Limerick.[30] The victory seems to have given Olaf the freedom to pursue his father's claim to the Northumbrian kingship, and in that year he left Ireland to enter into an alliance with Constantín, king of Scots (who also seems to have roped in Owain of Strathclyde). They must have imagined that together they would be unstoppable, that they would invade England, take back the lands stolen from them, redeem their honour, trample 'the shitheads of Thanet' (as *Armes Prydein Vawr* calls the English) and leave them as 'as food for wild beasts'.[31]

And as the armed men moved through the landscape, the wild beasts – 'corpse sharers, shadow coated' – stalked and followed them, circling overhead, running through woodland, flitting through the dark, expectant of slaughter and the feast to follow: 'the swart raven, horny of beak; the brown eagle of white tail-feather [...] and the silver one, the wolf of the weald'.[32] But it would not be English flesh they feasted on.

No one knows where the battle of Brunanburh was fought, and those who claim to – with any degree of certainty – are overplaying their hand. The problem is that only one place in England – Bromborough in the Wirral – has a place-name that can be definitively shown to derive from the Old English Brunanburh ('Bruna's stronghold'). The Wirral is directly across the water from Dublin, offering secure harbour in the Mersey for a substantial fleet (one source mentions 615 ships). Overland routes from Lancashire across the Pennines (through the Aire Gap) would have led an army assembled there directly to York; alternatively, a camp here – on the borders of Mercia – offered opportunities for raids into Mercia. However, all of this is complicated by the chronicle of John of Worcester. In his account, Olaf's fleet is described as sailing up the Humber, on the east coast of Britain.

Arguments against John's version hinge on the assumption that it would have been ridiculous for Olaf to have taken his fleet all the way around the north of Britain to reach the other side, before landing his army. To attack John's account on this basis, however, is absurd. We have no idea what Olaf did or why he might have done it (perhaps there were reinforcements and mercenaries he hoped to pick up along the way), and, since his objective seems to have been to reassert his claims over the kingship of Northumbria which hinged on control of York, it is perfectly reasonable to suppose that he took a route that brought him as close as possible to his goal. It certainly wasn't beyond the wit of early medieval mariners – only a year earlier, we might recall, Athelstan had dispatched a fleet to harry Caithness, the most north-westerly part of the British mainland. Equally weak is the argument that the reason for John's 'error' in placing Olaf on the Humber is that, because other Viking raids and invasions did indeed come up the Humber, John must have inserted this detail on his own initiative – either because he was confused, or just because it seemed plausible to him (that is, he made it up). It should be obvious that there are methodological problems in disregarding historical records simply because they don't fit a preconceived idea of what 'should' have happened. We just don't know.

What we do know is that the battle, wherever it was fought, shook the nations of Britain. Æthelweard, writing in the late 900s, wrote that 'a huge battle [*pugna immanis*] was fought against the barbarians at Brunandun, wherefore it is still called the "great war" [*bellum magnum*] by the common people'.[33] The *Chronicles of the Kings of Alba* told of the battle of Duin Brunde, 'where the son of Constantine was slain'. The Welsh Annals blankly referred to '*Bellum Brune*' ('the war of Bruin'), almost as if they couldn't bear to repeat the horrid details. The *Annals of Ulster*, however, recalled that 'a great, lamentable and horrible battle was cruelly fought between the Saxons and the Norsemen, in which several thousands of Norsemen, who are uncounted, fell, but their king, Amlaíb [Olaf], escaped with a few followers. A large number of Saxons fell on the other side, but Athelstan, king of the Saxons, enjoyed a great victory.'

It is in the pages of the *Anglo-Saxon Chronicle*, however, that the battle was truly immortalized. In the E manuscript, the scribe simply recorded that 'King Athelstan led an army to Brunanburh.'[34] But it was in the A text that an unknown West Saxon poet went to town. In seventy-four lines of Old English verse, a monument was crafted that celebrated the martial prowess of Athelstan and his brother, the future King Edmund. It invoked the ghosts of the Anglo-Saxon conquerors of old and rubbed defeat in the faces of the other peoples of Britain – a bitter draught they would force down the throats of every idealist who dreamt that, one day, 'the Saxons will sing, "Woe!"'

One day soon the Saxons would indeed sing 'Woe!'; but it would not be this day. Now was the time to sing the triumphal song of a new, self-confident nation. England had been fathered, born and christened – now it had found a voice, and its voice was harsh and crowing. It was, in many ways, a suitable subject for translation by the poet laureate of Victoria's Empire, even if it stands a little at odds with the melancholia that characterizes much else of Alfred Tennyson's poetry:

> Athelstan King,
> Lord among Earls,
> Bracelet-bestower and
> Baron of Barons,
> He with his brother,
> Edmund Atheling,
> Gaining a lifelong
> Glory in battle,
> Slew with the sword-edge
> There by Brunanburh,
> Brake the shield-wall,
> Hew'd the lindenwood,
> Hack'd the battleshield,
> Sons of Edward with hammer'd brands.[35]

Athelstan's victory at Brunanburh ensured that his status was upheld for the rest of his life, and kept a lid on the simmering cauldron of grievance and aspiration that had given rise to the conflict in the first place. In the longer term, its memory inspired a burgeoning sense of English nationalism. When Athelstan died in Gloucester on 27 October 939, his death was not marked with any great fanfare in the *Anglo-Saxon Chronicle*. The *Annals of Ulster*, however, reported that 'Athelstan, king of the Saxons, pillar of the dignity of the western world, died an untroubled death.'[36] His reign, coinciding with that of Constantín II in Scotland, was pivotal for British history, with new identities crystallizing that would shape the history of the island for centuries.

In the short term, however, the immediate political significance of the battle was limited. The hegemony that Athelstan had established over Northumbria died with him, and the following decade and a half bore witness to one of the periods of intense political insecurity to which the Northumbrian kingdom had long been prone. Olaf Guthfrithsson, the Viking king of Dublin who had been defeated and humiliated at Brunanburh, was quick to take advantage.

19

BLOODAXE

[...] that mighty
maker of men
ruled the land from beneath
his helmet of terror;
In York
the king reigned,
rigid of mind,
over rainy shores.

Arinbjarnakviða[1]

Within a year of Athelstan's death, Olaf Guthfrithsson was back in York, claiming power for himself apparently unopposed. He swiftly set about exerting his authority across Northumbria and extending his reach even further south, sacking Tamworth (Staffordshire) and annexing the towns of northern Mercia. This new Viking realm didn't last long, however. Olaf died in 941, possibly during a raid on Tyninghame in Lothian.[2] It was mere months before Athelstan's brother – the new King Edmund – came north to 'liberate' the so-called 'Five Boroughs' (Leicester, Lincoln, Nottingham, Stamford and Derby).

These events are celebrated in a poem in the *Anglo-Saxon Chronicle* which describes the forceful subjection of the 'Danish' population of northern Mercia to the heathen 'Norsemen' – the latter term being used to describe the Dublin-derived Vikings who were now back in power in York.[3] This narrative of unwelcome subjugation may be a fiction of sorts – it seems likely that some, at least, of the folk of northern Mercia would have been perfectly happy (or at least ambivalent) about swapping rule from Wessex with rule from York. But it does point to an interesting perception that was developing in England about the role of 'Danes' in English society. They were still evidently regarded as an ethnically distinct group and retained a distinctive legal status;[4] these 'Danish' English were presumably also distinguishable from the 'English' English by dress or dialect. But, while they were still Danes, they had briefly become – from a certain Anglo-Saxon perspective – '*our* Danes'. This paternal attitude to England's immigrant communities was politically expedient in the 940s, but ultimately it would not last. The way a society treats its ethnic minorities can often reveal a great deal about a nation's political priorities and the challenges it faces, and things were no different in tenth-century England – the young nation was soon to be stress-tested to breaking point.

Those calamities, however, lay in the future. More immediately pressing was the bewildering cast of players who now began to agitate for the Northumbrian throne. The chronology of this period is confused (and confusing). Some of the individuals are indistinct to the point of vanishing altogether, and there is general disagreement among historians about the sequence and veracity of the events recorded. Nevertheless, the following paragraphs offer a summary which, if concise and complex, is not, I hope, misleading.

The claim of the West Saxon dynasty over Northumbria was weak. It had never, before the reign of Athelstan, been subject to southern kings, and its people were naturally mindful of their own distinct customs and cultural heritage. Since 866, this sense of Northumbrian particularism had been overlaid by a stratum of Scandinavian settlement and culture which – while it had changed much in the kingdom – had not fundamentally shaken its independence. Significant elements of the old Northumbrian hierarchy had survived – not least its ecclesiastical magnates, particularly the bishops of Lindisfarne and York – and there is a sense in which the Northumbrian elite were willing to accommodate Viking rulers, provided that they were able to offer a bulwark against the imperial ambitions of Alfred's descendants. Naturally, however, the political aspirations and calculations of factions within Northumbria meant that the individuals and dynasties ascendant at any one time could change rapidly, particularly when the political dynamics were being destabilized by the suddenly inflated power of the English kingdom to the south and – to a lesser extent – by the Scottish kingdom to the north.

In the 940s, the simmering potential for chaos seems finally to have bubbled over, precipitated by the deaths in rapid succession of Athelstan and Olaf Guthfrithsson. The secret deals and back-stabbing that resulted can only be seen obliquely in the sources that survive, but the political meltdown that resulted is all too apparent. Olaf Guthfrithsson was replaced as king in York by his cousin, Olaf Sihtricsson (also known as Olaf Cuarán, or Olaf Sandal). This Olaf was the son of Sihtric Cáech who had ruled in York before the previous Olaf's father, Guthfrith. At the same time, however, another son of Guthfrith – Ragnall (OE Rægnald) Guthfrithsson – also seems to have been in Northumbria pressing his father's (and deceased brother's) claim. At some point in all of this, a man called Sihtric (not the same man as the second Olaf's late father) was causing coins to be minted in Northumbria in his name. (The coins are the only evidence of his existence; he is not otherwise mentioned anywhere in the historical record.) According to the *Anglo-Saxon Chronicle*, however, in 944 King Edmund (like many a bemused student of the Viking Age) had had enough of these shenanigans, and 'brought all Northumbria into his power, and caused two kings to flee, Olaf Sihtricson and Rægnald Guthfrithsson'.[5]

Edmund was an energetic ruler, and swiftly got on with giving the people of Cumbria a hard time, ceding territory (possibly won from the kingdom of Stathclyde) to the new Scottish king Malcolm in a diplomatic move presumably intended to normalize relations on the Anglo-Scottish border. (Malcolm succeeded his father, Constantín II, who abdicated in 943, though he lived for another nine years. Constantín was at least sixty-four when he died, but is likely to have been considerably older, and had reigned for forty-three years; the Old English poem, *The Battle of Brunanburh*, set in 937, describes him as *har hilde-rinc* – 'the hoary (that is, old/silver-grey) warrior'. Silver-haired he may have been, but he had managed to outlive his English nemesis, Athelstan, by fourteen years.) Edmund's firm hand did not, however, bring an end to the turmoil in Northumbria. In 946 Edmund also died (stabbed by a chap called Liofa – described by John of Worcester as 'an atrocious robber'[6] – at Pucklechurch in Gloucestershire) and the new English king, Eadred, a younger brother of Athelstan and Edmund, was obliged to extract pledges of allegiance from the Northumbrian worthies. The north, however, had become ungovernable, and in 948 Eadred was heading there again. He had received the news that the Northumbrians, having renounced their oaths to him in 947, had invited another man to be their king.

His was a name to conjure with: Eric, son of King Harald Finehair of Norway, known to us as Eiríkr Blóðøx – Eric Bloodaxe.

The sources for Eric's earlier life in Norway are all late and are frequently contradictory, but all agree that he was a violent and belligerent man. As the idea of the Viking has percolated through the British psyche, Bloodaxe, over the course of the twentieth century, became emblematic of the domestic Viking; never mind that he was (at least nominally) a Christian and that he lived more of his life as a king than as an outlaw. His (nick)name is enough: it presents with effortless economy, with two short, emphatic syllables, the image of the screaming berserker with the wild beard and the bloodstained battle-axe, eyes rolling and mouth frothing with a lust for battle and a mania for death. The explanation for his nickname, however, was not simply the frequent doing of bloody deeds; those were so commonplace during the Viking Age (and not just on the part of 'Vikings') that it can hardly have raised an eyebrow, let alone inspired an epithet. No, what apparently set Eric apart from his peers were cruelty and kin-slaying. The twelfth-century Norwegian historian Theoderic the Monk described him as *fratris interfector* – 'brother-slayer'. When taken together, the range of sources for Eric's life suggest that Eric, alongside his wife Gunnhild (who, we are told, was a wicked, manipulative and beautiful enchantress – a literary trope for which human society apparently has an inexhaustible patience), was responsible for the deaths of no fewer than five of his brothers: five rival sons of King Harald Finehair bumped off in the pursuit of his own ruthless ambition.[7]

That ambition – to succeed his father and become the undisputed king of Norway – was ultimately fulfilled. Eric ruled as king of Norway for three years during his aged father's dotage and two after his death. But his fratricidal tendencies were to pay dividends of another sort. The end of Eric's reign in Norway was brought about by yet another of Harald's many sons – Haakon the Good, also known as Haakon Aðalsteinsfóstri ('Athelstan's foster-son'). Haakon was, according to the Old Norse saga tradition, raised as an Anglo-Saxon prince in the court of King Athelstan. English sources make no mention of this, but it is perfectly plausible. Fostering of this sort among aristocratic families seems to have been common, an accepted way of forging diplomatic and quasi-familial bonds, and the sagas record that Haakon governed Norway in a fashion far more typical of Anglo-Saxon kings than of their Norwegian counterparts.[8] When Haakon, with his legitimate claim to the Norwegian throne and powerful English connections, arrived in Norway, he provided Eric's many enemies with the perfect banner to rally behind. When the inevitable showdown came, Eric didn't even put up a fight.

Instead, Eric fled to England where, according to Snorri Sturluson's *Heimskringla*, he was accommodated by King Athelstan and deputed to rule in Northumbria; from there, it was said, 'he raided Scotland and the Hebrides, Ireland and Bretland, and so increased his wealth.'[9] Most of the Scandinavian sources broadly agree that Eric was active in Northumbria during the 930s. It is certainly possible that he held some sort of power in Northumbria during Athelstan's reign (we know very little about what exactly was happening in the region during this period), and it is also possible that he was involved in the power politics of the 940s; if this was the case, however, English sources make no mention of it. Whatever the truth, and whatever path he had taken to get there, by 948 Eric emerges into the contemporary historical record for the first time as the man chosen by the Northumbrians to be their king. Unfortunately for him, however, like his previous experiments with executive power, Eric's kingship was not an unqualified success. Immediately after he had been invited to take the throne, in 948 a peeved King Eadred sent an army north to show the Northumbrians who was boss, burning down Ripon Minster before heading back south. The Northumbrians, however, presumably on Eric's orders, 'overtook the king's army from behind at Castleford, and a great slaughter was made there'.[10] This, perhaps not surprisingly, displeased Eadred considerably, and proved to be a spectacular political blunder. 'The king became so enraged', the chronicler of the *Anglo-Saxon Chronicle* A text explains, 'that he wanted to raise an army and utterly destroy. When they heard that,' the chronicler continues, 'they [the Northumbrian bigwigs] abandoned Eric and compensated King Eadred.'[11] It is a revealing comment, one which strongly indicates where the true backbone of Northumbrian independence lay.

A poem, composed in the tenth century (part of which is reproduced as the epigraph to this chapter), pictures Eric at York, brooding and sinister, his barren soul mirrored in the poet's evocation of the Yorkshire countryside: rain-wracked and storm-weathered. One can imagine him, with panic gripping York as word of the king's rage came north, holed up in his royal hall – taciturn, uncompromising, isolated – waiting for the political realities to come crashing down on his head. It is harder to imagine, however, how the city itself appeared in Eric's day. By the tenth century the Roman walls had been buried under an earthen bank with a corresponding ditch on the outer side, probably with a wooden palisade wall on the top and perhaps equipped with timber gate towers and walkways. There may have been stone towers too – the eleventh-century church tower of St Michael at the North Gate in Oxford was originally a free-standing masonry tower incorporated into the defensive circuit of the burh;[12] it is similar to York's oldest standing building, the eleventh-century tower of the Church of St Mary Bishophill Junior.

However, the vast hulking mass of York Minster, the great gothic cathedral that squats at the centre of the city's web of narrow streets and alleyways, was constructed between the thirteenth and fifteenth centuries (obliterating, in the process, much evidence for earlier churches and other buildings on the site). York Castle, or the surviving part of it (Clifford's Tower), is also a product of the late thirteenth century. Likewise, the walls of the city, though the lower courses in many places retain the Roman masonry, were rebuilt and renovated in stone in the thirteenth and fourteenth centuries before their restoration in the nineteenth.

Thus to the untrained eye it appears – despite the picturesque antiquity of the city – as though nothing of Viking Jorvik remains to be seen. But it's there, fundamental, an endoskeleton of words and roads that the intervening centuries have hung their flesh upon. Nearly all of the roads of York that predate the Norman Conquest are (or were) named with the suffix '-gate', from the Old Norse *gata* ('street'). Often the prefixes – which are sometimes Old English, sometimes Old Norse (often impossible to determine given the similarity of the languages), and sometimes Middle English or modern – provide clues to particular trades or notable characteristics of these places over time: Coppergate, for example, means the street of the wood-turners (that is, cup-makers from ON *koppari*);

Micklegate is the big street ('main street' is a better translation); Goodramgate is the street of Guthrum, a fine Scandinavian name. These roads follow what are almost certainly lines that were set in the ninth or tenth centuries, and the width of the houses and shop-fronts on these thoroughfares still preserves the dimensions of the plots of land that, divided by wattle fencing, were once occupied by the Viking Age townsfolk.[13]

Some of these plots have been excavated, most extensively so at Coppergate in digs carried out between 1967 and 1981. What these revealed was a city that, even as Eric Bloodaxe brooded in his hall, was undergoing an economic boom. Leatherwork and textile production, ironwork and copperwork, cup-making and carpentry, bone- and antler-craft, minting, amber-shaping and glass-recycling were all taking place with high intensity in the tenth-century city, many on an apparently industrial scale: moulds and crucibles for the mass production of jewellery and dies for coin production have been found and the sheer quantity of iron slag and wooden cores from cup- and bowl-making indicates production on a scale far beyond the domestic. Raw and manufactured goods were arriving from overseas – amber from the Baltic, silk from Byzantium, pottery from the Rhineland – and local produce was presumably exported via the same trading connections. Scales and large numbers of weights bear testament to the flourishing market that had developed at this commercial-industrial hub on the River Ouse – a major cog in the engine of North Sea trade.

And the population of York was growing too. Plots were becoming increasingly heavily utilized as the century wore on, more and more of the available space given up to timber buildings until the walls of each unit were almost touching its neighbour on either side. Rubbish pits were dug in backyards over and over again, to accommodate the sewage and the food waste, the industrial by-products and the general detritus. In the most waterlogged parts of the city, near the river, decomposition would have been slow and inefficient, parasites breeding in stagnant meres of mud and excrement. Ground level was rising by up to three-quarters of an inch every year (over the course of the tenth century an increase of between 3 and 6½ feet). The monastic writer Byrhtferth of Ramsay, writing at the end of the tenth century, put the population at 30,000. This may be an exaggeration, but the numbers were still high. Extrapolating from the density of settlement and the number of stray finds (principally of coins and pottery), as well as from the number of turds found preserved in the Viking Age soil, has enabled population estimates to be made in the region of 10,000–15,000, a 500 per cent increase on the population of pre-Viking York.[14] Gut worms were endemic and half of women died before they reached thirty-five (without childbirth to contend with, men could hope to hit fifty if they were lucky). In short, this was a society experiencing all of the typical problems of rapid urbanization: overcrowding, filth, disease, infestation.

It was also a city on the make. By 1066 it was easily the second largest in Britain (after London) and the hammers that smashed out thousands of silver coins in the names of Northumbria's Viking kings were working the city's abundant flow of silver into symbols of royal power and civic prestige. Even without evidence of coin production we would know that the coinage was produced in York from the legend that many of the coins bear: 'EBRAICE' (from 'Eboracum', the Latin name for the city). What is less clear is how much of this hustle and bustle was driven by Scandinavian immigrants and how much by native Northumbrians, or even whether such distinctions were noticed or considered important. The archaeology is equivocal – new trading links with Scandinavia certainly opened up, and new styles of object became fashionable. Shoes in a typically Scandinavian style, for example, started to be manufactured in the tenth century. But, crucially, traditional Northumbrian footwear remained in vogue, indicating that not only the expertise but also the market for both styles remained available and viable.[15] Thus the evidence can be argued from multiple perspectives. The only certainty is that tenth-century York was booming, and Scandinavian contacts and culture were playing a leading role.

Not that this made much difference to the political theatre playing out in the early 950s, except perhaps to raise the stakes for the players involved: York had become an attractive prize to kings of any stamp. The Northumbrians themselves, however, were fickle and – from a southern perspective – incorrigible. In 949 they recalled Olaf Sihtricsson to rule over them, but he didn't last long. In 952 Olaf was out, and Eric was back in.[16] This time, however, Eadred seems to have decided to apply pressure where it really mattered in Northumbria, hauling the archbishop of York to the stronghold at Jedburgh because, apparently, 'he was frequently accused to the king'. Nobody knows what threats and promises the king made to the archbishop there, but in 954 Eric was expelled from York for the second and final time; it can be no coincidence that the archbishop, in the same year, was finally restored to his lands by King Eadred. For the third time in his life, Eric Bloodaxe found himself in political exile.

This time, however, there was to be no comeback.

What is the worth of a king, he wonders, who has been driven out by his own subjects, hunted like a wolf's head over the mountains? He needs ships, and men. Perhaps he will go to Ireland. He doesn't know what welcome he might receive there – perhaps he will find kinsmen among the Dubliners, or someone to whom his name still means something, still carries weight. He is tired, mud-splattered, shoulders hunched, his horse slipping on wet stones in the pass. Turning in the saddle, he looks back at the column of dejected men behind him, fewer now he thinks than when they left York.

'*Niþings*,' he murmurs; 'cowards, oath-breakers.'

He is always looking back: listening for sounds of pursuit, watching for the carrion birds that herald the approach of pursuing armies. But he sees only the grim clouds and the grey land, the stones and the heather, the dull mud; a world rinsed of colour. He pulls his cloak, damp and heavy, tightly around himself, turns towards the wind that drives the rain into his face, and carries slowly on.

It is bleak on Stainmore, treeless and rugged, a high wind-scoured upland that reaches 1,370 feet above sea level; there is no protection up here from the Atlantic weather that comes billowing from the west. When I went there it was foul, a cold driving rain forcing me back into the car to sit miserably in a lay-by on the side of the A66, the busy trunk road connecting Carlisle in the north-west to Catterick in the east, by way of Penrith and Barnard Castle, heavy freight thundering past on its way across the Pennines. A few minutes in the elements were quite enough for me, but for Eric in 954, trying to break west for the sea, there would have been no rest and no respite. Perhaps there would have come a moment up here when he saw the land drop away to the west, the blue fells marching on the horizon, the westering sun dazzling him as it dipped below the slate-grey clouds – a beacon of white light offering the promise of salvation. If it did it might have lightened his heart for a moment – held out the hope of a new life and refuge, an opportunity to find the time and space to plan his political renaissance. Perhaps he saw himself coming back this way, at the head of a glorious host, a king of kings. But perhaps he didn't even make it as far as I did.

It is unclear how Eric died, but it was not from internal parasites. He likely had them (as everyone who spent any time in York probably did), and a perennially itchy arsehole can only have contributed to his bad mood. But the sources, though they differ wildly in most respects, are in agreement on one key issue: that Eric Bloodaxe died a violent death. The Norwegian so-called 'synoptic histories' – *Ágrip af Nóregskonungasögum* ('A Synopsis of the Sagas of the Kings of Norway') and *Historia Norwegiæ* – record a tradition that Eric died raiding in Spain, the least plausible explanation of how he met his end.[17] Other sources agree that Eric died in Britain, but the manner of his death, however, remains far less certain. According to the Anglo-Norman historian Roger of Wendover, 'King Eric was treacherously killed by Earl Maccus in a certain lonely place which is called Stainmore, with his son Haeric and his brother Ragnald, betrayed by Earl Oswulf; and then afterwards King Eadred ruled in these districts.'[18] Oswulf was the quasi-autonomous ruler at Bamburgh in the north of Northumbria, and was to become Earl of Northumbria under Eadred when Eric was dead. In this version of events we can see Eric dying with a dagger between his ribs – bleeding out the last of Northumbrian liberty on a lonely moor, friendless and betrayed, his ertswhile companions turning their mounts back to York to tell Oswulf that the dark deed was done, the last impediment to his own ambition now removed.

The sagas, however, tell a different story; a story of how King Játmundr (Edmund) 'mustered an invincible army and went against King Eiríkr, and there was a great battle [...] and at the end of that day King Eiríkr fell and five kings with him'.[19]

In the Norse mythological cycle, the death of the gods at *Ragnarök* represents the tragic, heroic, final stand of a world doomed to die. Of all the deaths and endings it is the death of Odin that is the most poignant, the one that speaks most clearly to the contradiction at the heart of the human condition. Odin may be the darkest of the gods, but he is also the most like us. He has watched the ebb of time across the ages, the rise and fall of kings and nations, the petty hurts and feeble triumphs of humanity. And despite knowing it to be futile, that ultimately he must fight the wolf and fail, he has prepared carefully for that day, selecting and curating the champions who will fight beside him when the last sun rises over the battle-plain. The *einherjar*, they are called, the glorious dead, doomed to die on earth in battle in order that they may fight again, one last time. It is this bloody-mindedness – the obsessive quest for wisdom though it brings no peace, the desire to gain knowledge of a future that cannot be circumvented, the relentless preparation for a doom that cannot be avoided – that reminds us of our own self-defeating consciousness, the knowledge of mortality that defines our humanity.

The capacity to think, to remember, to dream, to prepare against whatever the future holds – all of it leads inevitably to the only certainty that the universe can provide: that all things fade and all things fail. And yet, like Odin, we struggle on heedless of the long defeat, wading against the tide that one day will overwhelm everything. It was acceptance of this harsh reality that permeated Viking warrior culture, shaping its mentality and appetite for adventure – the willingness to stare death and defeat in the eye, knowing that to carry on is futile and that failure is assured, yet determined to fight on regardless, to struggle until the last breath is spent. It is in that struggle – internal, ethical – that true bravery lies; and there, precisely there, eyeball to eyeball with death unflinching, was the place where legends could be born that might outlast the living.

This desire to be remembered – to secure true immortality in the stories told after death – was the force that drove composition of eulogies and praise-poems, the contemporary material on which so much of our knowledge of Viking kings is ultimately founded. When Eric died, his wife was said to have commissioned a poem that commemorated his life and his deeds. The result, *Eiríksmal*, pictures the arrival of the great king in Valhöll, 'the hall of the slain', to take his place among the *einherjar*, the heroes of the past – with Sigmund and his son Sinfjǫtli – and sit by Odin's side. There he would enjoy the pleasures of the hall that are described in the eddic poem *Grímnismál* and by Snorri in *Gylfaginning*: to feast on the hog Saehrimnir who replenishes his flesh every evening; to fight the endless duels with the other *einherjar*, battling without hurt; to drink the mead that flows unending from the udders of the goat Heidrun, brought by valkyries in gilded cups: a warrior's paradise, filled with all the pleasures of a macho life.[20]

The poem, only the beginning of which survives, is cast as a conversation between Odin, the legendary poet Bragi, Sigmund and Eric himself.

O: 'What kind of dream is this, that I thought that a little before daybreak I was preparing Valhǫll for a slain army? I awakened the *einherjar*, I asked them to get up to strew the benches, to rinse the drinking cups, [I asked] valkyries to bring wine, as if a leader should come. I expect certain glorious men from the world [of the living], so my heart is glad.'

B: 'What is making a din there, as if a thousand were in motion, or an exceedingly great throng? All the bench-planks creak, as if Baldr were coming back into Óðinn's residence.'

O: 'The wise Bragi must not talk nonsense, though you know well why: the clangour is made for Eiríkr, who must be coming in here, a prince into Óðinn's residence. Sigmundr and Sinfjǫtli, rise quickly and go to meet the prince. Invite [him] in, if it is Eiríkr; it is he I am expecting now.'

S: 'Why do you expect Eiríkr rather than other kings?'

O: 'Because he has reddened his blade in many a land and borne a bloody sword.'

S/B: 'Why did you deprive him of victory then, when he seemed to you to be valiant?'

O: 'Because it cannot be known for certain when the grey wolf will attack the home of the gods.'

S: 'Good fortune to you now, Eiríkr; you will be welcome here, and go, wise, into the hall. One thing I want to ask you: what princes accompany you from the edge-thunder [battle]?'

E: 'There are five kings; I shall identify for you the names of all;
I am myself the sixth.'[21]

Eiríksmal, unlike the detailed descriptions in *Grímnismál* and *Gylfaginning*, dates to the Viking Age itself. It offers a vivid and immediate depiction of Valhöll and the relationship between Odin, his champions, and his messengers, the *valkyrjur*, the 'choosers of the slain' – the spirits of death and conflict who haunted the battle-fields of the Viking imagination. In the courtly poetry of *Eiríksmal*, valkyries were already undergoing the transformation that would see them become cleaned-up icons of femininity – servile cup-bearers and entertainers for the exclusive clientele at Valhöll, the precursors of the romanticized visions of nineteenth-century painters and the buxom Wagnerian parodies of popular imagination. But for most Vikings these lesser deities would have been possessed of wilder and more savage personae, terrifying war-spirits with names to chill the soul: Tanngniðr ('teeth-grinder'); Svava ('killer'); Skǫgul ('battle'); Randgniðr ('shield-scraper'); Hjalmþrimul ('helmet-clatter'); Geirdríful ('spear-flinger') …[22]

In 954, when the *valkyrjur* came shrieking from the heavens, screaming over the corpse-strewn Stainmore Pass to harvest the souls of the dead and dying, we must picture them coming, not from the clear, crisp skies of Norway or Denmark, nor even from the cold skies above Iceland's ashen peaks, but from the drear, leaden clouds of Yorkshire – come to claim Northumbria's last king.

20

WOLVES

We pay them continually and they humiliate us daily; they ravage
and they burn, plunder and rob and carry to the ship; and lo!
what else is there in all these happenings except God's anger
clear and evident over this nation?

ARCHBISHOP WULFSTAN,
'The Sermon of the Wolf to the English' (1014)[1]

It was 1006 and the Viking army had come from bases in the Isle of Wight, riding unopposed through the heart of Wessex – from Hampshire into Berkshire, from Reading to Wallingford, burning as they went. There they turned on to the Ridgeway, the path that so many armies in the past had taken, and travelled east to Cwichelm's Barrow (a place known today as Skutchmer Knob). There, the *Anglo-Saxon Chronicle* relates, they prepared for the showdown they had been promised and 'awaited the boasted threats, because it had often been said that if they sought out Cwichelm's Barrow they would never get to the sea'.[2]

The barrow, a Bronze Age burial mound, was the shire meeting place of Berkshire. It was a place of power and belonging, an upwelling of the ancient past around which the English organized their lives and, perhaps, a point of access to their own past. Cwichelm was a figure of legend, a West Saxon king who, it was said, had slain 2,045 Britons at a place called Beandun ('Bea's Hill') in 614 – a warrior ancestor whose blade was sorely needed by the English in the dark days of the early eleventh century. Perhaps there was a belief that the dead king was somehow present, that he slumbered under the mound like Arthur, ready to rise up and drive the enemies of the English to their doom.[3] Perhaps this was the story that the Vikings had heard from their victims as the southern shires burned – a defiant threat spat through blood – that if they dared ride too far, if they probed too deeply into the kingdom's heart, Cwichelm would get them. Or perhaps this was where the muster of Berkshire would assemble, a formidable phalanx of West Saxon warriors ready to stand firm in the presence of their ancient king. Perhaps the Vikings who came here felt a creeping dread as they approached from the west, the dark mound casting long shadows in the wan mid-winter light, skeleton trees clutching at the gloomy threatening skies. They knew that the dead shuffled uncomfortably in their chambered tombs, *draugr* who might hunt the living if awoken by the clumsy or the careless.[4]

But no one came; neither the living nor the dead. It was as though everything had deserted the English – even their ancestors.

The Viking army travelled back along the Ridgeway, west towards Avebury where the path turned towards the south, plunging over the edge of the chalk downs into the Pewsey Vale and the low country that rolls away towards the sea. It was here that the Anglo-Saxons chose to mount their defence, a last bid to halt the Viking horde as it made its way back to the Isle of Wight. Word had travelled, watch-fires flickering up from hill to hill, points of angry flame in the grey December twilight, summoning men from Avebury and Marlborough to follow the herepaths – the army-roads – to muster.

They would have seen and heard the carrion birds first, the tattered black shapes wheeling and cascading over the Ridgeway, their hollow, rasping cries announcing the arrival of the Viking army. Larger birds of prey might have joined them, buzzards or even eagles, circling high above the squalling crows. In the woodland that crept up the hillside from the valley floor to the circle of hoary megaliths where the English waited, other shapes might have been seen, moving furtively among the shadows of the ancient trees: a shaggy pelt, a lupine silhouette, a red eye caught in the pale light of the mid-winter sun.

These animals – the crow and raven, wolf and eagle – have a privileged place in early medieval battle literature. Old English verse records a multitude of sightings of these creatures, almost always in connection with death and violence. *The Battle of Brunanburh* describes how the victorious English 'left behind to divide the corpses the dark-coated one, the black raven, the horn-beaked one, and the dusk-coated one: the white-tailed eagle, to enjoy the carrion, that greedy war-hawk, and that grey beast, the wolf of the weald'. Old Norse skalds also tended to use these 'beasts of battle' in triumphal eulogies to successful warlords. 'Great' kings, like Eric Bloodaxe, were routinely praised as bountiful feeders of wolves and fatteners of ravens:

> Battle-cranes swooped
> over heaps of dead,
> wound-birds did not want
> for blood to gulp.
> The wolf gobbled flesh,
> the raven daubed
> the prow of its beak
> in waves of red.
> The troll's wolfish steed
> met a match for its greed.
> Eirik fed flesh
> to the wolf afresh.[5]

The frequency with which these images were deployed is so high that it has come to be thought of as a 'topos', a conventional poetic device thrown in whenever a poet wanted to signal the anticipation or commemoration of violence. Recent zoological research, however, has demonstrated that there is a strange symbiosis between wolves and corvids in the way in which these eaters of the dead track carrion. Wolf packs will follow the movements of airborne scavengers, using their enhanced perspective to identify easy pickings. Perhaps more surprising is anecdotal evidence which suggests that ravens and wolves are able to recognize and follow groups of armed men. In a modern context this has been interpreted as an environmental adaptation to the probability that humans wielding weapons are a likely predictor for the availability of conveniently pre-killed food (through the by-products of hunting). In the early medieval period, however, the presence of large groups of armed men often meant that killing of a different sort was in the offing.[6]

Overton Hill, near Avebury in Wiltshire, is still an eerie and desolate spot. It lies at a crossroads between two ancient paths: one the track of the Ridgeway that cuts its white furrow across the chalk uplands of southern England for 87 miles through Wiltshire and Berkshire, the other the Roman road from Bath to London, now imperfectly followed by parts of the A4. It is an old landscape. The West Saxons knew the place as *seofan beorgas* – the 'seven barrows' – and the mounds of these ancient tumuli still stud the flat high ground where the roads cross, some of them now smothered with beech stands, giving them the appearance of hairy warts standing out across the closely shaved farmland that surrounds them. There are, in fact, more than seven, most of them Roman or Bronze Age in date, though some were reused in the Anglo-Saxon period for secondary burials: a warrior buried with his shield and spear, a woman buried with her child.[7]

From the Seven Barrows the Anglo-Saxons would have been able to see the strange man-made sugar-loaf hill of Silbury and the great long-barrows of East and West Kennet; most prominent of all, however, was the stone circle at their back. Now known as 'the Sanctuary', the circle was once an impressive monument – two concentric circles of standing stones (the outermost with a diameter of about 130 feet) erected in around 2000 BC, once connected by a long avenue to the enormous stone ring that still stands at Avebury, just over a mile to the north-west.[8] The stones of the Sanctuary now are long gone, blown up in the eighteenth century by the local land-owner, but in 1006 it would have stood, ruinous, wind-swept and rime-scoured, an eerie monument to unfathomable antiquity.

It still feels uncanny up on Overton Hill; the landscape is open, exposed, and the wind howls up from the Pewsey Vale, mercilessly driving the clouds overhead. As I walked up the Ridgeway away from the Sanctuary I could see it coming – the brownish veil that smothers the light and blurs the hard edges of things. Rarely have I felt so miserable on a country walk as I did that day, caught in heavy weather at the Seven Barrows. 'There are many pleasanter places', said the one-eyed bagman in Dickens' *Pickwick Papers*, '[...] than the Marlborough Downs when it blows hard; and if you throw in beside, a gloomy winter's evening, a miry and sloppy road, and a pelting fall of heavy rain, and try the effect, by way of experiment, in your own proper person, you will experience the full force of this observation.' It is an ordeal that I have been unwillingly subjected to and can heartily agree that the bagman had the measure of it.

There is no way of knowing what the weather was like on Overton Hill in December 1006, but given the time of year it is unlikely to have been clement. For the English army, waiting in the freezing cold for a Viking host to break the horizon, it would have been a grim place to wait, rain or no. If they still hoped for help from the dead, for some supernatural assistance from the ancient landscape in which they drew their battle-lines, they would once again be disappointed. By the end of the day, the English had been routed from the field, and the Viking host continued its triumphant return to the coast, laden down with plunder.

As they passed the king's capital at Winchester, they jeered at the hapless townsfolk, cowering behind the walls.

*

The events of 1006 were typical of the calamity that befell England between 980 and 1016: a generation of escalating misery during which time Viking armies roamed practically unopposed across the rolling hills of southern England, looting and burning at will. A sense of the scale of the violence can be gauged simply by the number of conflicts recorded, particularly once the eleventh century got under way. Across England, there were (give or take) eighty-eight instances of armed violence recorded in the written record in the thirty-five years up to and including 1016; this compares with fifty-one conflict events recorded over the whole of the preceding eighty years. For the people of southern England, whose experience of Viking incursions had dissipated in the early tenth century, it would have felt as though a forgotten nightmare had dragged itself upright from the mire – a revenant horror, long thought staked and buried, stalking abroad once more.

There are, of course, some issues here about the trustworthiness of the written record – chroniclers sometimes had a vested interest in minimizing or exaggerating the travails of various monarchs – but it is evident that the quarter-century after Eric Bloodaxe's death in 954 had been noteworthy for its stability, its lack of dramatic incident. This seems, in large part, to have been down to the firm grip of one king – a man largely forgotten today, but with a good claim to being one of the most successful and impressive of the Anglo-Saxon kings of England: Edgar *pacificus* – Edgar the Peaceful. It is a name that conjures up images of quiet and contemplation, a just and gentle ruler whose benevolent rule would usher in the golden age of peace and plenty that twelfth-century chroniclers imagined he and his subjects had enjoyed. It was they, however, and not his peers, who conferred the epithet *pacificus* upon him: his contemporaries would take a rather different view.[9]

King Eadred died in 955, one year after seeing his rule extended, formally and finally, to include Northumbria within the English kingdom. He was succeeded by his nephew Eadwig, Edmund's son, but he died in 959 and was succeeded by his brother, Edgar. The most famous achievement of Edgar's reign – and the one incident for which he is chiefly remembered – came towards the end of his life. In 973, he arrived at Chester with – according to the *Anglo-Saxon Chronicle* – his entire naval force, there to meet with the other principal rulers of Britain. Different Norman historians give varying lists of the potentates who were present, but probably among them were Kenneth II of Scotland, Malcolm of Strathclyde, Iago ab Idwal Foel of Gwynedd and Maccus Haraldsson, whom William of Malmesbury called *archipirata* ('arch-pirate') and others referred to as *plurimarum rex insularum* ('king of many islands' – probably Man and the Hebrides).[10] No doubt there were serious and practical issues to discuss – matters of borders and security and the safety of shipping and trade and so on. What Anglo-Norman historians saw fit to record happening there, however, was a most extraordinary spectacle: at least half a dozen of the most powerful men in the islands, cowed into submission by Edgar's majestic presence (or, more likely, the menacing presence of his enormous war-fleet), rowing the English king in a barge down the River Dee. It was a very physical, and very public, demonstration of what it meant to be a 'little kinglet' in Edgar's Britain.

It may be that the way this incident was reported in Anglo-Norman sources was deliberately intended to promote an anachronistic idea of English superiority – issues of insular power dynamics were very much alive in the twelfth and thirteenth centuries and, indeed, have never really gone away. But there is little doubt about who was at the top of the British political food chain in the 970s and, regardless of the details of what took place, it seems likely that the meeting was partly concerned with thrashing out issues of precedence, of putting lands, people and princes into their rightful places; for Edgar seems to have been a king who was obsessed with order. His laws reveal an administration that was determined to regulate and reform – creating nationwide standards of weights and measures and ensuring that coinage was made to uniform standards everywhere it was produced: gone were the idiosyncratic designs of the old Viking kings at York. Edgar's coinage would look and weigh the same, whether it was minted there, or in Exeter,

Chester, Canterbury, Lincoln or Norwich (or anywhere else that coins were made). He was also interested in bringing the whole of his realm into administrative harmony and ensuring that justice was both available and correctly applied. Wessex had long been organized by shires and hundreds, but everywhere else had had different (though perhaps similar) systems of organization. Edgar – perhaps drawing on precedents set by his immediate predecessors – formalized this system, creating new stipulations for the way that courts were held at the hundred (or wapentake in 'Danish' areas) and shire level, making attendance obligatory for the land-holding class.

What really cemented Edgar's legacy, however, was the unprecedented period of peace and stability that England seems to have enjoyed until his death in 975. It was a peace that was achieved to a certain degree at the expense of others: repeated punitive raids into Welsh territory demonstrate that Edgar, despite his nickname, was no pacifist.[11] (Indeed, *pacificus* can be translated as 'Pacifier', just as it can as 'Peaceable' or 'Peaceful'.) It was also a peace paid for through unprecedented investment in the kingdom's naval defences: during his reign the number of English warships, according to later accounts, reached an improbable 4,800,[12] and it is likely that reforms to the manner in which ships and mariners were recruited and obliged to serve the king began during Edgar's reign. It also seems likely that the king's naval power was founded in part on paid fleets of Viking mercenaries. The swelling of English royal authority may have meant that, for some Viking war-bands plying the seas around Britain, the risks of plunder were becoming intolerably high, while at the same time the wealth that the English king commanded may have become an increasingly attractive source of patronage to those prepared to work for him.

All of these achievements added up to what most medieval writers felt constituted a 'Good King': he enforced justice, brought prosperity, upheld the Church and bullied and humiliated all the other (non-English) inhabitants of Britain – especially the Welsh. This was the sort of thing that was guaranteed to ensure a favourable write-up, and indeed his obituary in the D text of the *Anglo-Saxon Chronicle* is largely comprised of effusive praise. And yet, in the eyes of the chronicler – almost certainly Archbishop Wulfstan II of York (d. 1023) – all of his achievements were undermined by the 'one misdeed [...] he practised too widely'. King Edgar, Wulfstan disgustedly reveals, 'loved foul foreign customs and brought heathen habits into this land too firmly, and he enticed outsiders and lured dangerous foreign-folk into this country'.[13]

This censure may have stemmed in part from the pragmatic and conciliatory approach that Edgar adopted. Large parts of his realm had been settled by people of Scandinavian origin for over a century, producing a mixed population whose tastes, trading connections and family ties were as intimately tangled with the wider North Sea world as they were with the populations of Winchester, London or Canterbury. Edgar understood that local interests and national cohesion could be jointly served by recognizing the distinctiveness of local laws and customs in those regions which had become – in Anglo-Saxon parlance – 'Danish'. In his fourth major law code, Edgar promised that 'there should be in force amongst the Danes such good laws as they best decide [...] because of your loyalty, which you have always shown me'.[14] The sudden shift from third to second person feels clumsy when written down, but read out loud at a Northumbrian wapentake or north Mercian *thing*-site, it may have had real dramatic force: that sudden turn to the camera, the steady eye contact that the pronouns imply, delivered a disarmingly direct and personal address from the king exclusively to his Danish subjects.

In some ways, this recognition of a separate and parallel legal tradition stands at odds with Edgar's stated intention (in the same code) to create laws for 'all the nation, whether Englishmen, Danes or Britons, in every province of my dominion'.[15] But, seen more broadly, this limited concession (it does not seem to have overruled all the king's other edicts relating to coinage and administration) can be understood as the product of a keen political intelligence, one that recognized that – in the long term – the cause of national unity was better served by establishing trust and mitigating grievance than by lumbering authoritarianism. The result was the real 'Danelaw', a practical solution intended to bring the most reluctant of his new subjects willingly inside his vision for a coherent and cohesive English state.

Attitudes towards strangers in Anglo-Saxon England had not always been kind, but xenophobia seems to have peaked in the late tenth century, perhaps buoyed by the rising sense of English identity that had been growing since the reign of Athelstan but conditioned over two centuries of Viking depredations of one sort or another. For his own part, the king seems to have been alive to any threat that such sentiments could pose to the peace of his realm (and his revenues). In 969, 'King Edgar ravaged across all of Thanet', apparently because the locals had roughed up some Scandinavian traders. Hostility to foreign nationals on England's estuarine outposts has a distressingly long history, but few have responded so robustly as Edgar. According to the Norman historian Roger of Wendover, the king was 'moved with exceeding rage against the spoilers, deprived them of all their goods, and put some of them to death'.[16]

It was presumably this sort of thing that so offended Archbishop Wulfstan. In 975, however, he would doubtless have been relieved to discover that no longer would he have to endure the 'foul foreign customs' that Edgar had so perversely enjoyed. For in that year the king died. He was thirty-one years old. There followed a disputed succession and the short reign of Edgar's son Edward, known as 'the Martyr' – the last of the long line of 'Ed' kings. When Edward died in March 978, he was replaced by his brother Æthelred. The new king was only a boy of twelve, but he came to the throne already in shadow, his people divided in their loyalties: Edward had died, not of natural causes like their father, but at the hands of men loyal to Æthelred, done to death at Corfe (Dorset). Whether the new king was himself complicit in the killing has generally been doubted by historians, but it can have done little to endear those people to him who had supported his brother's claim. Even as stories of Edward's (improbable) sanctity and martyrdom began to spread, so Æthelred's reputation was stained – like Eric's – with fratricide. Little that occurred over the following forty years would help to restore it.

Thirteen years into Æthelred's reign, in 991, a Viking fleet arrived on the River Blackwater in Essex or, as it was known then, the Pant (OE Pante). These were not the first Vikings to return to England after Edgar's death; raids are recorded from 980 onwards and continued with little pause thereafter. The crown's authoritarian grip seems to have slackened with mortality and inter-familial strife and it is possible that, distracted by a succession crisis, the English administration had become a less reliable paymaster than it had been in Edgar's day, leaving swarms of unemployed marauders plying the coastal waters. Southampton, Thanet and Cheshire were attacked in 980 (the latter menaced *Norwegenensibus piratis*, according to John of Worcester) and Padstow (Cornwall) in 981. Portland, the scene of the first recorded Viking raid in Britain, was raided in 982, two centuries after the first 'Northmen' had spilled Ealdorman Beaduheard's blood on the Portland strand. In the same year London was burned. In 986 Vikings attacked Watchet (Devon), and in 991 a fleet arrived that harried Folkestone and Sandwich (Kent), before sailing north to assault Ipswich (Suffolk). This fleet – of ninety-three ships – was led by a warlord named in the *Anglo-Saxon Chronicle* as Olaf. Most would agree that that individual can be identified as Olaf Tryggvason, a Norwegian aristocrat who would later – as king – be instrumental in the (often brutal) Christianization of Norway.

Olaf's army was met on the Blackwater by an army led by the Essex ealdorman Byrhtnoth at Northey Island, a chunk of land adrift in the estuary, connected by only a narrow tidal causeway. Seen from above – as no one in 991 could have seen it – the frayed edges of the land are an alien wilderness, a madness of trackless patterns and dark pools, spiral rivulets and twisting gulleys, the rising and falling tidal waters cleansing and hollowing banks and channels, depositing the salts and nutrients that sustain a complex ecology of insects and wading birds; it is a dying landscape – swallowed by the rising waters, obliterated by accelerating climate change. A thousand years ago, the land was higher and Northey Island was closer to the mainland. But it would have presented a similar panorama – mud and water, brine and seabirds, the yellowing marsh-grasses and the cushions of dank moss, a flat and broken vista under an endless sky. The English were assembled on the mainland. Out beyond the flooded causeway, the Viking host stood arrayed on the island, their ships moored across the estuary – a hundred masts jutting from the still water like the ruins of a forest, blasted and drowned in the river waters. And there they stood, facing one another, bellowing their insults across the salt-flats as the gulls wheeled overhead.

We would know very little about what happened at the Blackwater were it not for the survival of an extraordinary poetic fragment, *The Battle of Maldon*, which offers in 325 lines of Old English verse a detailed and dramatic account of what transpired. The poem lacks its beginning and its end, a loss that predates the early eighteenth century, but it is remarkable that the poem survives at all. It formed part of the Cotton library (named after its collector, the MP and antiquarian Sir Robert Cotton, 1571–1631), an enterprise of far-sighted bibliophilia undertaken in the wake of the Dissolution of the Monasteries of the 1530s. Cotton's efforts preserved the Lindisfarne Gospels and the vast bulk of surviving Old English poetic literature, among many other priceless works, but all were nearly lost in 1731 when the building in which the library was preserved – the aptly named Ashburnham House – caught fire. Much was saved – including the badly singed *Beowulf* manuscript, but *The Battle of Maldon* was destroyed. Thankfully, however, the poem had been transcribed in 1724 – less than seven years before the fire. It is this version that now provides the basis of all modern versions of the poem.

The poem begins with a Viking spokesman shouting his demands across the water, for rings (*beagas*) and speedily sent tribute (*gafol*) to avert the inevitable killing. The response that the poet places in Byrhtnoth's mouth is the father of all doomed declamations of defiance, words that find their echo in every steadfast utterance delivered throughout England's pugnacious history: the resolve of a proud nation – in the first century of its self-consciousness – to choose death before dishonour. 'Out spoke Byrhtnoth,' the poet proclaims,

> lifted his shield, shook his slim ash spear, held forth with words and, angry and single-minded, gave him answer:
> 'Do you hear, sea-wanderer, what this nation says? They will give you spears as tribute, the poison-tipped javelin and ancient swords, those warlike accoutrements which will profit you nothing in battle. Seamen's spokesman, report back again; tell your people much more distasteful news: that here stands a worthy earl with his troop of men who is willing to defend this his ancestral home, the country of Æthelred, my lord's nation and land. The heathens shall perish in battle.'[17]

There would be blood. And yet, to fight across the causeway was impossible; for a proper battle to take place, the Viking army had to be allowed to cross, and this is precisely what Byrhtnoth, on account of *ofermod*, determined to do. This word – 'over-mood' rendered literally into modern English – has stimulated an enormous amount of speculation and learned wrangling over its precise meaning. Tolkien saw it in almost irredeemably negative terms – as hubris, overweening pride and misplaced confidence, a personal flaw that doomed Byrhtnoth, his men and his nation to destruction.[18] Others, however, have stressed the connotations of exceptional courage, unusual reserves of energy and spirit.[19] The ambiguities are obvious – does 'over' in this context imply 'too much' or an exceptional quantity? What, precisely, does 'mood' mean when it is left unqualified? My personal view is that the ambiguity is deliberate, that the poet has chosen to use a term that is essentially an empty vessel, ready to be filled with our own value judgements; all we see is Byrhtnoth, overflowing with spirit, with gusto, with eagerness to go head on with fate – it is up to us, readers or listeners, to judge his motives and his wisdom.

Across the river 'the slaughter-wolves waded, caring not for the water, the Viking war-band; they came west over Pant, bearing shield-boards over bright water and up onto land, linden-wood braced'.[20]

Some have observed the strategic sense of allowing the Viking army to cross; it was perhaps the only opportunity to bring this Viking horde to battle and prevent them from continuing the coastal rampage that had already struck Folkstone, Sandwich and Ipswich.[21] This may be so, although it is worth remembering that this is a poem – a self-consciously literary product – and may not reflect reality with any great accuracy. Its purpose was to emphasize Byrhtnoth's courage, his stoicism and the resolve of his closest followers to stand and die beside him rather than face the ignominy of surrender or retreat.

Byrhtnoth, for all his valiant leadership, was struck down by a spear and died a prolonged Hollywood death – fending off foes until finally slumping to the earth. Some of the English fled the battlefield, the poet ensuring that their names (Godric, Godwine and Godwig) would live for ever in infamy for what was – in reality – probably the wiser path in the circumstances. But wisdom was not what was at stake here: the animating ethic was one of loyalty, even in death, and of the moral courage that the English shared with their Viking enemies – the idea that to face death unflinching, though it came at them up the salt-flats as inevitably as the tide, and to die in heaps around the body of their slain lord was the greatest end to which a warrior could aspire.

The words that the poet gives to the elderly retainer Byrhtwold, steadfast despite Byrhtnoth's demise, echo down the centuries as the unparalleled expression of heroism in defeat, the determination to go down fighting while all around 'fighting men dropped down dead, exhausted by wounds':

'Will shall be harder, hearts the keener, our mettle shall be more as our strength lessens. Here lies our leader, all hewn down, goodness on the ground. He has cause to mourn whosoever from this fight thinks to flee. I am old in life. I will not leave this place, but I will lie me down by my lord's side, by the man I think so dear.'[22]

Maldon is a better poem than *Brunanburh*, a paean to heroic defeat that transmits pathos and emotional heft through the bitter-sweet song of hard-fought failure – sorrow and glory entwine together, pride and despair. These qualities are nowhere to be found in the crude triumphalism of *Brunanburh*, its poetic force squandered on surface glitter and hollow bluster, an English retort to the skaldic verses prepared for Viking warlords. And for all of the older poem's proto-nationalism, it is *Maldon* that speaks more deeply and with greater truth to sentiments that the British have enduringly valued: that to face one's opponent on a level field and to play the game fairly – to play with heart and courage no matter the outcome, to fight until the bitterest of ends – is where true glory resides, worth a thousand hollow victories or a thousand weaklings sent sprawling in the dirt.

The Battle of Maldon was, however, an anachronism even when it was written, a recapitulation of a heroic ideal that was growing old, couched in language that harked back to the ideals of a vanished past – to the sixth-century world of Beowulf, a legendary lost past. Perhaps this was the poet's intention – to inspire his audience to hold themselves to a higher standard, to raise their spears in the face of unfolding calamity, a call to arms to resist the tidal wave of aggression, whatever the cost: a renewal of the heroic values of Old England. Now, however, the monsters were real, and the heroes were dying. As one scholar remarked, 'the poem looks with longing eyes at a vanished world where heroes could act like heroes' but in the context of 'a world that was rapidly spinning out of English control' – passing, as another Old English poet might have put it, into 'dark beneath the helm of night, as though it had never been'.[23]

*

317

The *Anglo-Saxon Chronicle* account of what happened at the Blackwater is far less expansive. It does, however, record the death of Byrhtnoth at Maldon (the nearest burh to where the fighting took place). Crucially, it also records another event that took place in the aftermath of the battle – one which would have great ramifications over the fifteen years that followed. '[I]n that year,' the *Anglo-Saxon Chronicle* explains, 'it was decided that tribute [*gafol*] be paid to the Danish men for the great terror they had wrought along the sea coast; that was, at first, ten thousand pounds.' Of course, as previous experience and common sense had shown, the only thing this would bring was time, while providing an incentive for further attacks. And, of course, the attacks kept coming, unending, devastating. And as the years of Æthelred's ill-starred reign progressed, the size of the tribute that was paid got ever larger: £16,000 in 994 and £24,000 in 1002. In 1007, at the end of the campaign with which this chapter opened, £36,000 was paid. In 1012, the English crown handed over £48,000 with an undisclosed sum paid out in 1013. The final sum – an astronomical £72,000 – was agreed, in rather different circumstances, in 1016.[24]

These were vast quantities of silver. A pound represented 240 ordinary silver pennies, and the smallest of these sums – the Maldon tribute of £10,000 – was therefore the equivalent of 2,400,000 coins, each one of which had to be hammered out by hand. For context, this would mean having to multiply all of the coins in the Cuerdale Hoard by a factor of 340 to reach this number. The 1016 tribute – if delivered exclusively in coins – would have amounted to a ludicrous 17,280,000 silver pennies. There is no reason, however, to assume that the tribute was all handed over in coins – silver in all sorts of forms, and gold as well, would no doubt have been equally welcome, and the higher value of the latter material would have reduced the volume of material accordingly. But these are still massive sums of material wealth – so much, in fact, that the reliability of the *Anglo-Saxon Chronicle*'s figures has been repeatedly called into question.[25] There seems little reason, however, even if the specific figures are suspiciously rounded, to doubt the overall size of these payments: certainly the late Anglo-Saxon state had the administrative and economic machinery to raise and produce coinage on this scale, and huge numbers of Æthelred's coins – more than the number found in England – have been discovered in Scandinavia. Some of them, like those in the hoard of eighty-two pennies found at Tyskegård on the island of Bornholm (Denmark), appear to have been freshly minted and never to have circulated, as though produced in bulk for the express purpose of raising a tribute payment.[26] The impact all these coins had is clear – the distinctive punky hairstyle with which Æthelred's image is blessed on these coins influenced the royal currency of Danish kings for decades afterwards.[27]

Perhaps this policy would seem wiser in hindsight had Æthelred's military endeavours met with more success; he certainly seems to have tried – refortifying defences that had dropped out of use and throwing up emergency fortifications at places like Old Sarum and South Cadbury; he also reinvested heavily in the English navy, as his father had before him, and it is from Æthelred's reign that we have the first evidence of 'ship-sokes' – a formalized land-based system of militarized naval obligation. But, no matter what he tried, it seemed always to turn out badly: as the *Anglo-Saxon Chronicle* ruefully put it, Æthelred's ship-army 'achieved nothing, except the people's toil, and wasting money, and the invigoration of their enemies',[28] and the situation wasn't helped by the king's reliance on treacherous and inept councillors, a habit that earned him the sobriquet 'the Ill-Advised' (or more familiarly, and inaccurately, 'the Unready') in accounts written after his death (from OE *unræd*, 'bad-counsel', a play on his name Æthel-ræd, 'noble-counsel').

It has been argued, convincingly, that Æthelred has had a bad press.[29] Certainly the primary source for his reign – the version of the *Anglo-Saxon Chronicle* preserved in the C, D and E manuscripts – was written after his reign had come to an ignominious end, and was composed with a degree of bitter hindsight. There were perhaps few kings who could have weathered the storm that broke on him with greater fortitude. But, for one incident at least, Æthelred deserves all of the opprobrium heaped upon him. In 1002 the king had finally decided (on advice) to arrange a payment of £24,000 to a Viking fleet that had, over previous years, 'raided and burned almost everywhere' across the south-west and into the Wessex heartlands.[30] 'It was in every way a heavy time,' the CDE chronicler sums up, 'because they never left off their fierce evil.'[31] There were, therefore, circumstances around the turn of the millennium that perhaps allow us to understand why the king may have felt under siege and susceptible to the temptation of drastic action. The decree that followed, however, was as indiscriminate as it was ill conceived. Later in 1002, Æthelred ordered that 'all the Danish men who were among the English race were to be killed on Brice's Day [13 November], because it was said to the king that they wished to ensnare his life.'[32]

It is obvious that the order cannot have been intended to apply to everyone who had ever been considered 'Danish' in the wider sense; this would have been an absurd idea and impossible to carry out – especially in the north. It is, in fact, entirely unclear to whom Æthelred intended his order to apply, particularly given the multiplying vagaries of Anglo-Danish ethnicity. The tenor of the command, however, was plain enough. Words spoken by power carry weight, legitimizing impulses that might otherwise be suppressed; Æthelred's order was taken seriously in many parts of England, and was most likely interpreted through whatever local animus most energized his subjects. Edgar's policies of multi-cultural authoritarianism had gone, dissolved in the chaos of the renewed Viking menace that had broken on England from 980. Where his father had once punished harshly those who had infringed the rights of foreign traders, Æthelred exhorted the English to murder their neighbours. And murder them they did.

Excavations at St John's College, Oxford, in 2008 discovered the remains of thirty-seven men aged sixteen to twenty-five whose bodies had been dumped in a ditch; study of the bones suggests that they were hacked to death in the years around 1000, many receiving multiple savage blows. There is no evidence that they had attempted to defend themselves – no wounds to hands or forearms that might have come from recent combat; only scorch marks on the bones. They were probably running away. A chilling document survives that spells out the realities of ethnic cleansing in Oxford: a charter, dated to 1004, that explains – in a horribly matter-of-fact tone – the need to rebuild the Church of St Frideswide:

> it will be well known that, since a decree was sent out by me with the counsel of my leading men and magnates, to the effect that all the Danes who had sprung up in this island, sprouting like cockle amongst the wheat, were to be destroyed by a most just extermination, and thus this decree was to be put into effect even as far as death, those Danes who dwelt in the afore-mentioned town [Oxford], striving to escape death, entered this sanctuary of Christ, having broken by force the doors and bolts, and resolved to make refuge and defence for themselves therein against the people of the town and the suburbs; but when all the people in pursuit strove, forced by necessity, to drive them out, and could not, they set fire to the planks and burnt, as it seems, this church with its ornaments and its books. Afterwards, with God's aid, it was renewed by me.[33]

It has been suggested that the age of the victims, and the evidence of healed prior injuries, implies that the men found at St John's College were fighters, not ordinary townsfolk. But in a violent and militarized society the distinction is hardly a useful one. However one chooses to explain or justify the events of 1002, the image that both documents and archaeology present is a grim one: of people driven in terror to seek refuge in the safest place they could find, barricading themselves within what was probably the largest – if not the only – stone building within reach; shut inside, praying desperately that the sanctity of the space might preserve them. There they would have huddled, listening to the sounds outside – the angry shouts, the thud of wooden beams piled against doors and windows. Perhaps, once the burning had begun, once the heat became unbearable and the smoke robbed them of their breath, once they were blinded and choking and wild with panic, the Danes decided to run – to run through the doors and out into the street, into the light and the clean autumn air, there to be hacked apart by the howling mob.[34]

These were not the glorious battles that the Maldon poet had imagined – nor was this the strong and stable nation that Edgar had worked for. That nation would return, but it would take a new dynasty to restore it: a Danish dynasty – a 'Viking' dynasty.

21

MORTAL REMAINS

King Cnut greets in friendship his archbishops and his diocesan
bishops, and Earl Thorkel and all his earls, and all his people [...]
ecclesiastic and lay, in England. And I [Cnut] inform you that I will be
a gracious lord and faithful observer of God's rights and secular law.

'Letter of Cnut to the English' (*c.* 1019–20)[1]

S vein Forkbeard became king of England on Christmas Day
1013. Although his actions seemed to fit the classic Viking
mould of seaborne raiding and extortion, Svein was no mere
chancer. Unlike self-made men such as Guthrum back in the 870s,
Svein Forkbeard was an established figure on the international
stage. The son of Harald Bluetooth, king of Denmark (d. *c.* 985),
Svein had taken the Danish throne from his father in the 980s.
When he conquered England in 1013 he was already a king.

Svein's assaults on England had begun early, in the 990s, and he
had spent two years pillaging the country between 1003 and 1005.
Although he did not lead the assaults that followed throughout the
first decade of the eleventh century – the most devastating of which
fell under the command of a fearsome character known as Thorkell
the Tall – in 1013 he returned with a fleet and, it seems, a clear sense
of purpose. He arrived at Sandwich (Kent), and from there led his
ships northward, prowling the eastern coastline until they reached
the Humber – the gateway to Northumbria. At Gainsborough

(Lincolnshire), the Northumbrians submitted swiftly. Shortly afterwards northern Mercia followed suit and then all the regions north of Watling Street, the old boundary set out in the treaty of Alfred and Guthrum.

When Svein moved south the collapse came quickly, Oxford and Winchester surrendering without a fight. London held firm, its townspeople holding out 'with full battle because King Æthelred was inside'. But it was not enough to avert the disaster hanging over the English king. Briefly thwarted, Svein travelled west, to Bath, where the western nobility submitted to him. This was enough for the remaining English resistance. The Londoners laid down their weapons, pledging themselves to their new lord (because if they did not, the *Anglo-Saxon Chronicle* explains, 'they dreaded that he [Svein] would do them in').² Exhausted by a quarter-century of war, England capitulated with a whimper and 'the whole nation had him as full king'.

Æthelred, with his wife Emma and his sons Edward and Alfred, fled across the Channel to his wife's brother, Duke Richard of Normandy (the beginning of an Anglo-Norman dalliance that would have cataclysmic consequences further down the line). For the first time since the Anglo-Saxons had begun to record their own history, no scion of the house of Wessex – indeed, no ruler of any English royal dynasty – wielded power anywhere in Britain.

The invasions of Britain that came from Denmark and Norway in the eleventh century were important – sometimes shattering – events, but they were not the opportunistic raids of stateless warlords. Instead they were campaigns of conquest, led by powerful Christian kings at the head of well-equipped armies, raised and mobilized at the behest of rulers who were vastly more powerful than the Viking warlords of old. As the High Middle Ages began to dawn in Europe, a unified sense of Christian community and an increasingly homogeneous cultural identity – defined by Roman

Christianity, Cistercian monasticism, Latin literacy and Frankish mounted warfare – was beginning to spread from its heartlands in France and Germany to every corner of Europe: from the Irish Sea to the Elbe, and from the Arctic to the Mediterranean. Kings, supported by a powerful military aristocracy and an all-pervasive Church, were becoming ever more powerful, their administrations more sophisticated and better funded. In the new world that was slowly crystallizing there was diminishing space in which the free-booting marauder could operate. For true Vikings of the old school, the late tenth and early eleventh centuries would be a final flourish: their way of life was dying out.

The northern world had also been changing rapidly, the circumstances in Scandinavia that had given rise to the Viking Age gradually evolving out of existence. Where once Scandinavian society had been dominated by local chieftains and tribal identities, the tenth century increasingly saw assertive dynasties and individuals establishing themselves as the ultimate source of secular power in Denmark, Norway and Sweden. In every case the transformation of Scandinavian society had been a long, slow and tumultuous process, one with its roots in the ninth century (if not earlier). Indeed, the disgruntlement and political upheaval the ambitions of kings generated is considered one of the catalysts for the multifarious seaborne phenomena that defined the Viking Age, a spur to the independent and the dispossessed to seek new lands and livings elsewhere.[3] But, by the late tenth century, a measure of enhanced political stability had been, or was close to being, achieved across Scandinavia – in Denmark under the Jelling dynasty from c. 940, in Norway and Sweden towards the end of the century, and in further-flung outposts of the diaspora as well.[4] The development of these kingdoms was not a linear one, and the shape of the future nations was by no means preordained (though geography played a decisive role), but the trajectory was inexorably towards political consolidation. This did not mean that the temptation for individuals to take to the seas in search of plunder and fame was snuffed out – far from it – but a new path had been set.

The earliest, and most dramatic, evidence of this process can be found in Denmark. Denmark was precocious among its Scandinavian peers – a result of its comparatively close relationship with continental (Frankish) European culture, religion and politics. Its kings were relatively swift to experiment with Christianity and coinage, and keen to adopt the ceremonial trappings of Roman-style kingship. Although we know little of the internal affairs of Denmark during the tenth century, the reigns of King Gorm the Old and particularly his son, Harald, seem to have been pivotal. When Gorm died he was buried in a wooden chamber constructed beneath a vast mound at Jelling (Jutland, Denmark), part of a remarkable ceremonial and religious complex that grew up around the burial in the decades after his death.[5] The most celebrated part

The crucifixion face of the Jelling runestone

of this landscape is Gorm's runestone. Erected, ostensibly, to celebrate Gorm's life – an act of filial piety on the part of Harald, his son and successor – it is, in fact, rather more eloquent on the subject of Harald's own hubris.

'King Haraldr', the inscription runs, 'bade that this monument be made in remembrance of Gormr his father and Thyrvé his mother. That', the rune-carver elaborates, is the 'Haraldr who won for himself the whole of Denmark and Norway and who made the Danes Christian'.

Harald Bluetooth, as he came to be known, was staking out his claim not only as the great unifier, but also as the bringer of salvation to his people. To underline his triumphs, both spiritual and earthly, the runestone is decorated with an image of the crucified Christ – not the suffering god, *christus patiens*, broken and lifeless, but a Christ triumphant, *christus triumphans*, with eyes wide open and body unflinching: resolute, heroic, undefeated. This is Christ as the Anglo-Saxons had imagined him in the decades following their own conversion: 'eager to mount the gallows, unafraid in the sight of many [...] the great King, liege lord of the heavens'.[6] A suitable deity for warrior kings to embrace.

Harald's reign in Denmark, and more generally the journey of Scandinavia towards the mainstream of European culture, is a fascinating subject which would require another book to do it proper justice. His most visible achievements included the construction of massive circular fortifications in Denmark at Fyrkat and Aggersborg (Jutland), Nonnebakken (Funen), Trelleborg (Zealand) and in what is now Sweden at Trelleborg (Skåne). Although the function is uncertain, the symmetrical planning and impressive defences point to a likely military or part-military rationale – at the very least, they speak of the impressive powers of organization and coercion that Harald wielded in the 980s. Similarly, the construction of a monumental timber bridge across the valley of the River Vejle saw the king preside over the expansion of infrastructure at a pitch of ambition and scale worthy of the Roman Empire; 820 yards of oak-timbered road constructed over the impassable marshlands of the river valley, broad enough at 16 feet in width for two horse-drawn vehicles to pass each other, supported on wooden piles up to 20 feet in length.

Neither the ring-forts nor the bridge seem to have much outlasted Harald, but the elevated idea of royal power they represented was much longer lived. Harald's rule demonstrated and ensured that Danish kings had the power, and now the precedent, to mobilize men and resources on an unprecedented scale. And, while the projects that they pursued were still largely driven by their own private ambitions, it was becoming increasingly difficult to distinguish properly between personal and 'national' agenda: the interests of king and nation were becoming ever harder to disentangle.

This is certainly true of Svein Forkbeard's conquest of England in 1013. The question of what motivated the Danish king's desire for dominion in England remains a live one, and no credible account survives to explain his actions. The *Encomium Emmae Reginae* ('in praise of Queen Emma') – a broadly contemporary history commissioned in the 1040s, blatantly biased in favour of the Danish royal family – provides one possible answer. The *Encomium* suggests that Svein's invasion was prompted by Thorkell the Tall's decision, in 1012, to enter King Æthelred's service as a mercenary after several years of terrorizing the English kingdom (earlier in the same year, Thorkell had been in charge of a group who had murdered Ælfheah, the archbishop of Canterbury, at Greenwich – beating him to death with an axe handle after pelting him with 'bones and the heads of cattle').[7] This is possible – Thorkell was cutting an increasingly impressive figure in the early eleventh century, and Svein may well have seen him as a potential rival. But the *Encomium* is not a trustworthy source, and this part reads like a post hoc rationalization. Instead, Svein's invasion was probably driven by opportunism. He was well aware of England's impressive economic potential relative to his own kingdom. He had seen first hand the wealth that English kings were able to rustle up when they needed to – he himself had been a beneficiary. He also knew full well how militarily enfeebled England had become – he had wielded the axe himself on many an occasion. When the time came for Svein's hostile takeover, the Danish king knew that he was pushing on an open door: behind it lay power and riches that dwarfed any returns that his own people could provide.

However, he did not have long to enjoy his new kingdom. Five weeks after becoming king of England, in early February 1014, Svein Forkbeard dropped dead. The cause of death remains a mystery, but by the twelfth century Anglo-Norman writers had hit upon a picturesque legend to account for what – at the time – must have seemed miraculous. As the chronicle of John of Worcester tells it, King Svein was busy carousing with his retinue of Danish warriors when he caught sight of a menacing armed figure approaching – a figure that no one but the king could see. 'When he [Svein] had seen him,' John explains, 'he was terrified and began to shout very noisily, saying "Help, fellow-warriors, help! St Edmund is coming to kill me!" And while he was saying this he was run through fiercely by the saint with a spear, and fell from the stallion on which he sat, and, tormented with great pain until twilight, he ended his life with a wretched death on 3 February.'[8] St Edmund, the East Anglian king martyred by Ivar and Ubbe in 870 (and memorialized in the East Anglian coinage of the early 900s), had appeared like Banquo to wreak his belated revenge.

This, I suppose, was reckoned to be a sort of poetic justice after more than two centuries of Viking harassment. If it is truly what contemporaries believed, however, the comfort it offered was short lived. Æthelred was restored to the throne, it being generally decided by the English magnates that 'no lord was dearer to them than their natural lord', but not before they had extracted a promise from him to 'govern more justly than he did before'.[9] And maybe that would have been the end of it – the English lords even promising to forswear Danish kings once and for all – had it not been for the fact that Svein's son, Cnut, was still in England. And he was showing scant sign of wanting to go home.

*

Cnut's campaign in England began in brutally defiant fashion. He sailed to Sandwich with the hostages provided to his father, put them ashore and had their hands and noses cut off. From that point onward, matters proceeded much as they had in the past. Æthelred once again stumped up tribute (£21,000 according to the *Anglo-Saxon Chronicle*), and once again it failed to deter the attacks. Cnut's armies menaced the coast of England and raided into Wessex, while at the same time exploiting the political divisions that Æthelred's calamitous reign had failed to heal. The situation was, once again, spiralling out of control. Only Æthelred's death would halt the decay and, probably much to the relief of many, he finally died after a short illness on St George's Day (23 April) 1016. As the CDE chronicler unnecessarily reminded his readers, the king ended his days 'after great labour and tribulations in his life'.[10] It was the end of a protracted (and briefly interrupted) reign of thirty-eight years. It had been an uncomfortable time for all of his English subjects: Britons, Anglo-Saxons and Danes alike.

The man who replaced him, his son Edmund who according to the *Anglo-Saxon Chronicle* earned the sobriquet 'Ironside' for 'his bravery',[11] was – from what little is known of him – a rather different proposition. Unlike his father, who hardly ever seems to have taken personal command of English armies, Edmund was a hands-on warlord. He immediately set about raising armies (as he had in fact tried to do, unsuccessfully, during his father's decline) and led them into battle with tireless, relentless, resolve. The year 1016 proved to be a bruising year for everyone. Edmund beat Cnut at Penselwood (Somerset), and a clash at Sherston (Wiltshire) – though bitterly contested – ended inconclusively. Shortly afterwards, Edmund's army drove the Danes away from London and defeated them again at Brentford (Middlesex) and Otford (Kent). It must have seemed that England finally had the champion it needed. But Edmund was to make a mistake in the aftermath of this last victory that would ultimately undo much of his good work. At a gathering at Aylesford (Kent) – perhaps in a fit of *ofermod* – he was reconciled with the Mercian ealdorman Eadric Streona – Eadric the Acquisitor.

Eadric Streona is the principal villain of eleventh-century England. Crowning a multitude of other reported perfidies (which included murder, pillage, appropriation of church lands and property, treachery, oath-breaking and obstruction, as well as a good proportion of the *unræd* whispered into King Æthelred's earhole), Eadric defected to Cnut's army in 1015 – despite his earlier marriage to Æthelred's daughter Edith. He apparently embraced Cnutism with a convert's zeal: according to John of Worcester, during the battle of Sherston, Eadric:

> cut off the head of a certain man called Osmear, very like King
> Edmund in face and hair, and raising it aloft he shouted, saying
> that the English fought in vain: 'You men of Dorset, Devon,
> Wiltshire, flee in haste, for you have lost your leader. Look, I
> hold here in my hands the head of your lord, King Edmund.
> Flee as fast you can.'
> When the English perceived this they were appalled, more by
> the horror at the action than by any trust in the announcer.[12]

If true (and it may well not be), this was pretty appalling stuff. Nevertheless, whatever his crimes, it seems that Edmund decided at Aylesford that it was better to keep Eadric close than leave him outside the tent. It was probably a sound policy – had Eadric been left in the cold he could well have rejoined Cnut or else followed an agenda all of his own; Edmund certainly didn't need a powerful loose cannon threatening his supply chain and his home front. In hindsight, however, it is easy to agree with the E chronicler's verdict that there 'was not a more ill-advised decision [*unræd geræd*] than this was',[13] and ultimately Edmund probably wished that he had acted otherwise. When the decisive battle came – at a place called 'Assandun' (probably Ashingdon in Essex, but possibly Ashdon in the same county), 'Ealdorman Eadric', the *Anglo-Saxon Chronicle* wearily relates, 'did as he had often done before, and was the first to start the flight with the Magonsæte [the people of western Mercia]; thus he betrayed his royal lord and all the English people.'[14] The description of the battle provided in the *Encomium* is more vivid, if rather less reliable. The Encomiast has Eadric announce: 'Let us flee, oh comrades, and snatch our lives from imminent death, or else we shall fall forthwith, for I know the hardihood of the Danes.' The Encomiast also repeats the belief – apparently current at the time, and no less believable now – that 'he did this not out of fear but in guile; and what many assert is that he had promised this secretly to the Danes in return for some favour'.[15]

Despite its pro-Cnut bias, the *Encomium* gave a respectful account of King Edmund's deeds. The words attributed to him are heroic ('Oh Englishmen, to-day you will fight or surrender your-selves all together. Therefore, fight for your liberty and your coun-try, men of understanding') and his actions valiant ('he advanced into the midst of the enemy, cutting down Danes on all sides, and by this example rendering his noble followers more inclined to fight').[16] The fighting, according to the *Encomium*, lasted from morning until after darkness fell. 'And if the shining moon had not shown which was the enemy, every man would have cut down his comrade, thinking he was an adversary resisting him, and no man would have survived on either side, unless he had been saved by flight.'[17] English history now hinged on the outcome of this one battle. A decisive victory for Edmund – particularly one that led to the death of Cnut – would have changed the course of history. But, in the end, 'the English, turning their backs, fled without delay on all sides, ever falling before their foes, and added glory to the honour of Knútr [Cnut] and to his victory'.[18] The exhausted Danish warriors, 'rejoicing in their triumph, passed the remainder of the night amongst the bodies of the dead'. When morning came, they stripped the vanquished of their arms and weapons, but left the bodies where they lay – a carrion feast for the 'beasts and birds'.[19]

Cnut's own poets summed up this victory in a few concise words of praise, the conquest of a nation boiled down to a vision of dark wings fluttering over a field stained black with blood:

'Mighty king, you performed a feat under shield at Assatún(ir); the blood-crane [raven] received dark carrion.' Cnut had won back his father's briefly held throne. The human cost – for the English and the Danes alike – had been terrible.

Runestones stud the Scandinavian countryside, the vast majority in Sweden. Irregular grey monoliths, jutting from the grass like crooked teeth, many still stand in the open air, defying time and weather as the world changes round them. Cut with knotted serpents and angular runes, they frequently carry the sign of the cross, the unmistakable branding of the increasingly ubiquitous faith of the northern world. These are not the exotic remnants of a pagan age, but monuments of the new world that was forming in the early eleventh century, memorials to those who died in the age of Cnut. Of all the stones that are known today, a group of thirty are referred to as the 'England runestones', monuments whose inscriptions make explicit reference to the exploits of these late-period Vikings in England, giving names to the people who helped to shape eleventh-century Britain.[20] Some refer to the payments received by individuals – a record of the wealth that was wrung from the English in those brutal years. Áli, for example, was evidently a forward planner: he 'had his stone raised in memory of himself. He took Knútr's payment in England. May God help his spirit.'[21] Perhaps he invested some of his new-found silver in this shameless act of self-promotion.

Other inscriptions are even more specific, setting in stone particular events that are chronicled in English sources. A stone at Yttergärde in Uppland (Sweden), erected by two men called Karse and Kalbjörn in memory of their father, Ulf, records that 'Ulf has taken three payments in England. That was the first that Tosti paid. Then Thorkell paid. Then Cnut paid.'[22] 'Tosti' was probably a man identified by Snorri as Sköglar-Tosti, father-in-law to both Svein Forkbeard and the Swedish king, Eric the Victorious.[23] 'Thorkell' was Thorkell the Tall, whose exploits deprived the English of £48,000 in 1012. Cnut, of course, needs no explanation.

It was men like Ulf who were the beneficiaries of England's years of pain.

More rarely, runic inscriptions provide a glimpse of the Scandinavians who died in Cnut's England: 'Sveinn and Þorgautr made this monument in memory of Manni and Sveini,' an inscription on a stone in Scania (Sweden) runs. 'May God help their souls well. And they lie in London.'[24] Stunning archaeological evidence for the presence of an eleventh-century migrant community in London was discovered in 1852 in the graveyard of St Paul's Cathedral. A stone, decorated in the Scandinavian Ringerike style with an elaborate backwards-turning beast, once painted in colours of red, white and black, carries a runic inscription down one edge: 'Ginna and Toki had this stone set up.' For whom, we will never know. The gravestone can be seen now in the Museum of London, beside a display of the Viking axes that have been dragged from the stinking mud of the River Thames at low tide – the debris scattered where wave after wave of violence had broken, crashing on the walls of the city that held out until the bitter end.

Most of the Scandinavians who died in England, however, remain nameless, though the manner of their deaths is sometimes laid horribly bare. In 2009, during the initial stages of the construction of the Weymouth Relief Road in Dorset, a grave was discovered on the downs. The skulls were found first, a pile of yellowing husks, forty-seven heads tossed haphazardly into a pit. The bodies were found later, fifty-two headless corpses heaped naked one upon the other – a charnel tangle of ribs and femurs jutting from the earth. Analysis of the remains revealed that the heads had been hacked off with swords. The killing had been hard work – many hands and blades had laboured over it, often it had taken multiple blows to sever the vertebrae, and sometimes the aim of the killers had been poor or hasty, shearing through skulls and faces, blood staining the white chalk in crimson torrents. It would have taken hours. The five heads that were missing from the grave might well have been the only memorial for these men – taken and rammed on to wooden stakes (*heofod stoccan*) and set up to watch sightlessly from the hills.

Analysis of the skeletal remains revealed that all of the people who died here were men, aged mostly between their teens and early adulthood, and that they had died in the years around 1000. Only five of them might have grown up in Britain, the rest came from Scandinavia and the Baltic, from Iceland, Russia and Belarus, from the Arctic and the sub-Arctic, from every corner of the Viking North. They had come to Britain and they had died in England, though what had brought them here, and who did this to them, remains a mystery. The men who died were not professional fighters – their bones show no evidence of wounds gained and healed, of the stresses and strains of a life of battle. Some in fact seem to have suffered from debilitating illness and disability. Perhaps these were people who came to England to seek their fortune, tempted by the silver they had seen flowing north, by stories of adventure and the weakness of the English, lured by the runestones that boasted of payments in the service of famous and mighty lords. All they found was death.[25]

The identities of these people will never be known, but someone, somewhere, must have grieved for them. A sad stone in Norway records that 'Arnsteinn raised this stone in memory of Bjórr his son who died in the retinue when Knútr attacked England.'[26] Perhaps Bjórr was a hardened warrior who came to grief in the thick of battle; or perhaps he was a mere boy, hacked to death before his adventure even began.

Edmund survived the battle of Assandun long enough to negotiate a peace with the victorious Danish king. They may have fought again in the Forest of Dean (depending on how a skaldic reference to a battle at Danaskógar is interpreted),[27] but all sources agree that the parties then met for talks at a place called Olanige ('Ola's Island') near Deerhurst in Gloucestershire. According to a later tradition, the two kings were transported to this island in the River Severn where they engaged in single combat – a royal *hólmgang* to determine the fate of the kingdom. However improbable it may seem, there is no way of knowing whether anything like this really happened. I like to imagine that it did – the two great warriors slugging it out alone, as though two and a quarter centuries of conflict and compromise had been distilled down to this single scene: the young kings of Wessex and of Denmark, the Anglo-Saxon and the Dane, wrestling for the soul of England as the olive-green waters passed slowly by. Whatever the reality, a settlement was ultimately reached. Tribute payment was agreed (the astronomical figure of £72,000 was collected in 1018), oaths were made and hostages were given by both sides. And Edmund was to keep his throne, retaining his familial lands and rule over Wessex; Cnut was to receive Mercia (as well as, presumably, East Anglia and Northumbria). England, so recently assembled, was to be partitioned once more.

That was the idea. As things turned out, however, the details proved academic. Edmund died on 30 November 1016, the third English king (including Svein) to have died in two years. In 1017 'King Cnut succeeded to the whole kingdom of England.'[28] Edmund's sudden and unexplained death has always smelled suspicious. If it wasn't murder, it was certainly convenient for Cnut. A later tradition, first recorded by the Norman historian Henry of Huntingdon in the early twelfth century, had Edmund suffering an unseemly end, shot up the arse with a crossbow while enthroned upon the privy.[29] It is, happily for Edmund's posthumous dignity, unlikely to be true.

Cnut's first actions as king were probably the most radical of his reign. He divided England into four great earldoms that corresponded to the four ancient realms of Wessex (which he governed directly himself, at least to begin with), Mercia (which was given, briefly, to Eadric Streona), East Anglia (given to Thorkell the Tall, who had reconciled with Cnut in 1015) and Northumbria (which was put under the authority of the Norwegian, Eric Hákonarson). The title 'earl' (OE *eorl*) was an Anglicization of the Old Norse title *jarl*, and it was introduced into English at this time, a new rung of power between the existing English nobility and the king. Cnut also took the opportunity to raise the enormous tax agreed at Olanige, crush a number of dissenting English noblemen, and – in what may have been a more popular move – have Eadric Streona killed at London and thrown over the city wall. This was done, according to the *Encomium*, in order that 'retainers should learn from this example to be faithful, not faithless, to their kings'.[30]

Cnut would rule England until his death in 1035, and his sons Harald and Harthacnut until 1042. For the twenty-five years that the Knýtlinga (the house of Cnut) ruled England, the latent Scandinavian influences – already so prominent in the north and east of the country – became a part of mainstream English culture. During those years, England would lie at the heart of a North Sea empire that swelled to include Denmark, Norway and parts of Sweden, and exert claims of lordship over the Norse-speaking communities of the Northern and Western Isles of Britain. Old Norse was spoken at the royal court at Winchester, Scandinavian warlords ruled as earls in what had once been Anglo-Saxon king-doms, and Scandinavians could have runestones raised to them in the graveyard of St Paul's Cathedral. Objects like the gilded bronze brooch found in Pitney in Somerset – hardly an epicentre of Viking settlement – demonstrate the convergence of late Scandinavian and Anglo-Saxon art-styles in places that may have experienced little direct contact with speakers of Old Norse before the reign of Cnut. Likewise, a remarkable monument stone from Bibury in Gloucestershire was carved in the Ringerike style, leonine faces on weird twisting necks sprouting from its base like flowers seeking the sun.

Even after the West Saxon dynasty had been restored in the person of Edward the Confessor, many of these influences remained deeply entrenched. England's last 'Anglo-Saxon' king, Harold Godwineson, had a Norse name (Haraldr) and a Danish mother, as did his brothers Tostig, Svein and Gyrth. Even the great double-handed axes, wielded to devastating effect by so many English warriors in the Bayeux Tapestry's telling of the battle of Hastings, were a Scandinavian import – horse-killing weapons developed in Denmark to stop the Frankish cavalry that was increasingly dominating the continent.

And yet it was at this moment, at the very zenith of Scandinavian influence and power in England, that the Vikings as they had been would begin to fade away.

In some ways, Cnut was the most awesome Viking of them all – a Danish king whose longships bound together a maritime empire through fear and force, and whose skalds composed bloodthirsty eulogies about his victories – just as his ancestors had done. But, in other, perhaps more important ways, Cnut was not a Viking at all. A Danish aristocrat like his father, Cnut was king of England before he was ever a king in Scandinavia (he became king of Denmark in 1018 and of Norway in 1028), and he spent considerable time in Britain. He was emphatically Christian, and in his laws, his coinage, his self-depiction and his generosity to the Church, he presented himself as the quintessential Anglo-Saxon king. He made a point of reconfirming the laws of Edgar and even married the late King Æthelred's queen, Emma – it was at the behest of their son Harthacnut (king of England, 1040–2) that her *Encomium* was later written.[31]

The *Liber Vitae* of New Minster and Hyde Abbey is a book, produced at the beginning of the 1030s, which records donations to the New Minster at Winchester, the church built by Edward the Elder, and which housed the bones of his father, King Alfred. Among its pages is an extraordinary illustration – produced while the king and queen were still alive – of Cnut and Emma presenting an enormous altar cross to the New Minster. Christ and St Peter hover overhead, and an angel places a crown upon Cnut's brow. He stands on the altar steps, at the threshold of the Middle Ages, looking every inch the ideal monarch of a new era. The heathen warlords of the ninth and tenth centuries had gone, and although Scandinavians would continue to bother the British Isles for a century or more, there would be no going back. The world had moved on.

When he died, Cnut was buried at the Old Minster, the venerable church that the New Minster had been constructed to replace. He had earlier, in an expression of a curious affection that Cnut seems to have held for his one-time rival, had the remains of King Edmund Ironside translated there in 1032. Harthacnut, his son by Emma, was buried in the New Minster there in 1042, and his long-lived wife Emma in 1052. In the church next door, separated by a few feet, lay King Alfred and his wife, Ealhswith, their sons Edward (the Elder) and Æthelweard, and Edward's son Ælfweard. For years the house of Wessex and the house of Cnut slumbered on in their separate mausolea – similar but distinct, separated by walls and clear green grass. But as the centuries passed and the old churches tumbled, to be replaced by the great gothic cathedral that still stands in Winchester, the royal tombs were moved – Alfred's family to the monastery at Hyde, and Cnut's family along with a number of others (including Edmund and, perhaps, the tenth-century King Eadred) to the cathedral where they would lie alongside the remains of Anglo-Saxon bishops and Norman princes for hundreds of years.

There they remained until 1642, when soldiers fighting for the Parliamentary army in the English Civil War broke into the cathedral. These men, 'for whom nothing is holy, nothing is Sacred, did not stick to profane, and violate these Cabinets of the dead, and to scatter their bones all over the pavements of the Church'. The stained-glass windows 'they brake to pieces, by throwing at them, the bones of Kings, Queens, Bishops, Confessors and Saints'.[32] In 1661, in an attempt to remedy the chaos, 'the bones of princes and prelates scattered by sacrilegious barbarism' were 'brought together again mixed up' and deposited in the chests that still sit atop the walls of the choir.[33] Subsequent investigations in the late eighteenth and nineteenth centuries revealed total disorder: a hopeless jumble of mortal remains.

New DNA research offers the slender possibility of bringing some sense to it all. But for the time being the puzzle remains unsolved, a physical expression of what England by the end of the eleventh century had become. Anglo-Saxons and Danes, hopelessly muddled together in death, impossible now to tell apart.

EPILOGUE

T he death of the second of Cnut's sons, Harthacnut, in 1041 and the re-establishment of the house of Wessex (in the person of Edward the Confessor) by no means spelled the end of Scandinavian Britain or, indeed, of the Viking Age.

In the north and west, particularly in the island strongholds of Orkney, Shetland, Man and the Hebrides, Viking lordships endured and prospered long into the Middle Ages, exerting a decisive influence on Scottish history for centuries. The Lords of the Isles (Man and the Western Isles) remained independent from Scotland until 1266 (there was a brief period of direct rule from Norway in the late eleventh century that followed the intervention of King Magnus Barefoot). The earldom of Orkney – the polity established in Caithness and the Northern Isles through Scandinavian settlement from the ninth century onwards – was even longer lived; Orkney and Shetland remained a part of the kingdom of Norway until 1467 and 1468 respectively. But, no matter how vitally entangled this northern fringe of Britain was with Scandinavian politics, or how deeply penetrated by Scandinavian culture, language and people, these lordships only emerge into historical view in the late eleventh century, their origins and their development obscure.[1]

The earldom of Orkney, in particular, presents something of a conundrum. The eradication of almost all traces of pre-Scandinavian (Pictish) place-names, language and material culture on the islands has given rise to a suggestion that the settlement of these

341

North Sea outposts was carried on a wave of genocidal migration. Others have stressed the absence of secure chronology, the uncertainties of earlier population size and density, the many centuries of continuing migration and influence from Scandinavia. The evidence is equivocal, though the pride the islanders take in their Viking heritage remains palpable. For these parts of Britain, as for much of England, the Viking Age never really ended. Nobody packed up their battle-axes and Thor's-hammer amulets and went 'home'. These Viking Age immigrants may have imported new ideas and new identities, making accommodations of various kinds with their neighbours, but they were – certainly by the eleventh century – as British as anyone else in these islands.

Scandinavian raids also continued, though they remained the province of kings rather than freebooters. The failed invasion of England in 1066 by the Norwegian king Harald Harðráði ('Hard-ruler') was only one of many. In 1069, in the aftermath of the Norman conquest of England, the Danish king Svein Estridsson (r. 1047–76) captured York in alliance with the last viable member of the West Saxon dynasty (Edgar the Ætheling). William the Conqueror paid him to go away. (In 1075 he came back again for a quick pillage.) Svein's grandson, Cnut IV (r. 1080–6), was keen to keep up this national pastime, and readied a fleet to invade England in 1085. His people were less enthusiastic, however, and refused to serve; when he tried to round them up a second time they chased him into a church and stabbed him to death. Even in the mid-twelfth century, Scandinavian kings sometimes felt the temptation to harass the shores of Britain. The Norwegian king Eystein Haraldsson (r. 1142–57) led a fleet that menaced Orkney, Scotland and northern England in the 1150s during the reign of King Stephen.

Should these be considered Viking raids? Perhaps they should, although – in the end – all attempts to define the limits of the Viking Age dissolve into fruitless semantic arguments. What is perhaps better to acknowledge is that, by the twelfth and thirteenth centuries, the literary idea of the Viking – the image that would shape and colour perception of the Age until the present – was being born, both in Iceland's saga literature and in fanciful Anglo-Norman tales like that of Havelok the Dane. The creation of literary tropes and fantastical tales depended, to some degree, on a critical distance from the world these works sought to describe. It was a past that had become safe to romanticize precisely because it was over.

The Vikings had changed Britain, that is without doubt. But Britain had also changed the Vikings – transforming them until it seemed that they were gone for ever. One of my goals in writing this book has been to try to show them as less monolithic than they are popularly presented as – more susceptible to the influence of their environments and of the people and ideas they encountered. But they were also a vital force: agents of change who transformed the world they moved through, even if they sometimes lost themselves in the process, emerging only as a shadow, a figure of legend to be put back together in new shapes. It has also been my goal to share the stunning legacy of their world, to illuminate to those who may never have encountered it the breadth and depth of the footprint that they have left in Britain, and to allow their story to serve as a reminder that culture, identity and ethnicity are often more complex and contestable than we might imagine.

I have also tried to steer a course that, though it recognizes the debt we owe to Viking culture and the impact of these events and processes on British history, does not diminish the strangeness of the people who fashioned the Viking Age. They were not 'just like us': there is more to being human than using coins or wearing shoes, and mundane things do not readily reveal how people felt, thought and dreamt. But we can still stand where they stood, and feel the grass under our feet and know that they felt it, and taste the sea-breeze on our tongues and know that they tasted it. And when we wait by the shoreline, with the sun dipping like blood into the west and the breakers crashing on the strand, we can still hear their voices singing with the tide, the grinding of keels on the shingle.

ABBREVIATIONS AND PRIMARY SOURCES

Note on the *Anglo-Saxon Chronicle*

Citations from and references to the manuscripts of the *Anglo-Saxon Chronicle* have made use of the editions published under the general supervision of David Dumville and Simon Keynes (see individual volumes below), with reference to the translated editions produced by Dorothy Whitelock and Michael Swanton: D. Whitelock (ed. and trans.), *The Anglo-Saxon Chronicle: A Revised Translation* (1961, Eyre & Spottiswoode); M. Swanton (ed. and trans.), *The Anglo-Saxon Chronicles* (2001, 2nd edition, Phoenix Press). Where a reference to the *Chronicle* is given in the notes simply as *ASC*, the material cited is common to all manuscripts (the 'core' text); otherwise, references specify the manuscript by letter when information is restricted to one or more versions.

Note on Irish Chronicles

Thomas Charles-Edwards has reconstructed and translated the joint stock of a putative 'Chronicle of Ireland' (*CI*) to the year 911 from annals surviving in a variety of manuscripts, principally the *Annals of Ulster* and the Clonmacnoise group (*Annals of Tigernach, Annals of Clonmacnoise, Chronicum Scotorum*), with some additions from the *Annals of Innisfallen, Annals of the Four Masters* and the *Fragmentary Annals*: T. Charles-Edwards (ed. and trans.), *The*

Chronicles of Ireland (2006, Liverpool University Press). I have relied on this edition for translations from these texts until 911. Beyond this date, I have relied on the translations published online by University College Cork: *Corpus of Electronic Texts* (CELT) [http://www.ucc.ie/celt/published/T100001A/]

AC – *Annales Cambriae*; J. Morris (ed.), *Nennius, British History and the Welsh Annals* (1980, Phillimore)

AClon – *Annals of Clonmacnoise* (see 'Note on Irish Chronicles' above)

AFM – *Annals of the Four Masters* (see 'Note on Irish Chronicles' above)

AI – *Annals of Innisfallen* (see 'Note on Irish Chronicles' above)

Alfred-Guthrum – 'The Treaty of Alfred and Guthrum'; S. Keynes and M. Lapidge (eds and trans.), *Alfred the Great: Asser's 'Life of King Alfred' and Other Contemporary Sources* (1983, Penguin)

APV – *Armes Prydein Vawr*; J. K. Bollard (ed. and trans.), in M. Livingston (ed.), *The Battle of Brunanburh: A Casebook* (2011, University of Exeter Press), pp. 155–70, with notes pp. 155–69 and commentary pp. 245–6

ASC – *Anglo-Saxon Chronicle* (see 'Note on the *Anglo-Saxon Chronicle*' above):

    A – J. M. Bately (ed.), *The Anglo-Saxon Chronicle: A Collaborative Edition, vol. 3. MS. A* (1986, Brewer)

    B – S. Taylor (ed.), *The Anglo-Saxon Chronicle: A Collaborative Edition, vol. 4. MS. B* (1983, Brewer)

    C – K. O'Brien O'Keeffe (ed.), *The Anglo-Saxon Chronicle: A Collaborative Edition, vol. 5. MS. C* (2001, Brewer)

    D – G. P. Cubbin (ed.), *The Anglo-Saxon Chronicle: A Collaborative Edition, vol. 6. MS. D* (1996, Brewer)

    E – S. Irvine (ed.), *The Anglo-Saxon Chronicle: A Collaborative Edition, vol. 7. MS. E* (2004, Brewer)

    F – P. S. Baker (ed.), *The Anglo-Saxon Chronicle: A Collaborative Edition, vol. 8: MS. F* (2000, Brewer)

ASN – *Annals of St Neots*; D. N. Dumville and M. Lapidge (eds), *The Anglo-Saxon Chronicle: A Collaborative Edition, vol. 17. The annals of St Neots with Vita prima Sancti Neoti* (1985, Cambridge: Brewer)

ASPR – Anglo-Saxon Poetic Records; G. P. Krapp and E. V. Dobbie (eds), *The Anglo-Saxon Poetic Records: A Collective Edition*, 6 vols (1931–53, New York: Columbia University Press) [ota.ox.ac.uk/desc/1936]

AU – Annals of Ulster (see 'Note on Irish Chronicles' above)

Beowulf – ASPR, volume 4

BM – British Museum registration number

Boethius – Boethius, *Consolatio Philosophiae*; J. J. O'Donnell (ed.), *Boethius: Consolatio Philosophiae* (1984, Bryn Mawr College)

Brunanburh – The Battle of Brunanburh (*ASPR*, volume 6)

BVSC – Bede, *Vita Sancti Cuthberti*; B. Colgrave (ed. and trans.), *Two Lives of Cuthbert* (1940, Cambridge University Press)

c. – circa ('around')

CA – Æthelweard, 'Chronicon' *of Æthelweard*; A. Campbell (ed. and trans.), *The Chronicle of Æthelweard* (1962, Thomas Nelson & Sons)

Canmore ID – Reference number to the Scottish database of archaeological sites, monuments and buildings [https://canmore.org.uk/]

CASSS – Corpus of Anglo-Saxon Stone Sculpture [http://www.ascorpus.ac.uk/index.php]

CC – John of Worcester, *Chronicon ex Chronicis*; R. R. Darlington (ed.), P. McGurk (ed. and trans.) and J. Bray (trans.), *The Chronicle of John of Worcester* (1995, Clarendon Press)

CKA – Chronicle of the Kings of Alba; B. T. Hudson (ed. and trans.), 'Chronicle of the Kings of Alba', *Scottish Historical Review* 77 (1998), pp. 129–61

CS – Chronicon Scottorum (see 'Note on Irish Chronicles' above)

Deor – ASPR, volume 3

DR – Denmark (geographical reference; runestones)

EE – Geffrei Gaimar, *Estoire des Engleis*; I. Short (ed. and trans.), *Gaimar: Estoire des Engleis/History of the English* (2009, Oxford University Press)

Egil's Saga – B. Scudder (ed. and trans.), 'Egil's Saga', in J. Smiley (ed.), *The Sagas of Icelanders* (2000, Penguin), pp. 3–185

EHD – *English Historical Documents*; D. Whitelock, *English Historical Documents 500–1041, Vol. 1* (1979, 2nd edition, Routledge)

Elene – *ASPR*, volume 2

Enc. – *Encomium Emmae Reginae*; A. Campbell (ed. and trans.) with S. Keynes (ed.), *Encomium Emmae Reginae* (1998, Cambridge University Press)

Ex. – Gildas, *De Excidio Britanniae*; M. Winterbottom (ed. and trans.), *Gildas: The Ruin of Britain and Other Works* (1978, Phillimore)

FA – *Fragmentary Annals* (see 'Note on Irish chronicles' above)

FH – Roger of Wendover, *Flores Historiarum*; H. O. Coxe (ed.), *Rogeri de Wendover Chronica; sive, Flores Historiarum* (1841–2, Sumptibus Societatis); translated passages in *EHD*

Finnsburg – *The Fight at Finnsburg* (*ASPR*, volume 6)

GD – Saxo Grammaticus, *Gesta Danorum*; P. Fisher (trans.) and K. Fries-Jensen (ed.), *Saxo Grammaticus: The History of the Danes, Book I–IX. Volume I* (1979, Brewer)

Genesis – *ASPR*, volume 1

GH – Adam of Bremen, *Gesta Hammaburgensis ecclesiae pontificum*; F. J. Tschan (ed. and trans.), *History of the Archbishops of Hamburg-Bremen* (2002, Columbia University Press)

GRA – William of Malmesbury, *Gesta Regum Anglorum*; R. A. B. Mynors, R. M. Thomson and M. Winterbottom (eds and trans.), *William of Malmesbury: Gesta Regum Anglorum* (1998, Oxford University Press)

Grímnismál – A. Orchard, *The Elder Edda: A Book of Viking Lore* (2011, Penguin), pp. 38–41

Gylfaginning – Snorri Sturluson, 'Gylfaginning'; J. L. Byock (ed. and trans.), *The Prose Edda* (2006, Penguin), pp. 9–79

HA – Henry of Huntingdon, *Historia Anglorum*; D. Greenway, *Henry, Archdeacon of Huntingdon: Historia Anglorum/The History of the English People* (1996, Oxford Medieval Texts)

Hávamál – A. Orchard, *The Elder Edda: A Book of Viking Lore* (2011, Penguin), pp. 15–39

HB – *Historia Brittonum*; J. Morris (ed. and trans.), *Nennius, British History and the Welsh Annals* (1980, Phillimore)

HE – Bede, *Historia Ecclesiastica Gentis Anglorum*; D. H. Farmer (ed. and trans.) and L. Sherley-Price (trans.), *Ecclesiastical History of the English People* (1991, Penguin)

Heimskringla I – Snorri Sturluson, *Heimskringla*; A. Finlay and A. Faulkes (eds and trans.), *Heimskringla Volume I: The Beginnings to Óláfr Tryggvason* (2011, Viking Society for Northern Research)

Heimskringla II – Snorri Sturluson, *Heimskringla*; A. Finlay and A. Faulkes (eds and trans.), *Heimskringla Volume II: Óláfr Haraldsson* (The Saint) (2014, Viking Society for Northern Research)

Helgakviða Hundingsbana fyrri – A. Orchard, *The Elder Edda: A Book of Viking Lore* (2011, Penguin), pp. 117–25

HR – Symeon of Durham, *Historia Regum*; T. Arnold (ed.), *Symeonis Monachi Opera Omnia* (2012 [1885], Cambridge University Press); translated passages in *EHD*

HSC – *Historia Sancti Cuthberti*; *EHD* (6)

Krákumál – B. Waggoner (ed. and trans.), *The Sagas of Ragnar Lodbrok* (2009, The Troth)

Lokasenna – A. Orchard, *The Elder Edda: A Book of Viking Lore* (2011, Penguin), pp. 83–96

Maldon – *The Battle of Maldon* (*ASPR*, volume 6)

Maxims II – *ASPR*, volume 6

N – Norway (geographical reference; runestones)

NMR – National Monument Record number (Historic England) [http://pastscape.org.uk]

NMS – National Museum of Scotland registration number

OE *Boethius* – The Old English *Boethius*. S. Irvine and M. Godden (eds), *The Old English Boethius with Verse Prologues and Epilogues Associated with King Alfred* (2012, Harvard University Press)

Orkneyinga saga – H. Palsson and P. Edwards, *Orkneyinga Saga: The History of the Earls of Orkney* (1981, Penguin)

PSE – Abbo of Fleury, *Passio S. Eadmundi*; F. Hervey (ed. and trans.), *Corolla Sancti Eadmundi: The Garland of Saint Eadmun d King and Martyr* (1907, E. P. Dutton)

r. – regnal dates

Ragnarssona þáttr – B. Waggoner (ed. and trans.), *The Sagas of Ragnar Lodbrok* (2009, The Troth)

Ragnars saga Loðbrókar – B. Waggoner (ed. and trans.), *The Sagas of Ragnar Lodbrok* (2009, The Troth)

RFA – *Royal Frankish Annals*; B. W. Scholz (ed. and trans.), *Carolingian Chronicles: Royal Frankish Annals and Nithard's Histories* (1970, Ann Arbor)

Rígsthula – A. Orchard, *The Elder Edda: A Book of Viking Lore* (2011, Penguin), pp. 243–9

Rundata – Scandinavian Runic-text Database [http://www.nordiska. uu.se/forskn/samnord.htm/?languageId=1]

S – Charter number in P. H. Sawyer, *Anglo-Saxon Charters: An Annotated List and Bibliography* (1968, Royal Historical Society) [esawyer.org.uk]

s. a. – *sub. anno* ('under the year')

Sö – Södermanland, Sweden (geographical reference; runestones)

Thrymskvida – A. Orchard, *The Elder Edda: A Book of Viking Lore* (2011, Penguin), pp. 96–101

U – Uppland, Sweden (geographical reference; runestones)

VA – Asser, *Vita Ælfredi Regis Angul Saxonum*; S. Keynes and M. Lapidge (eds and trans.), *Alfred the Great: Asser's 'Life of King Alfred' and Other Contemporary Sources* (1983, Penguin)

Vg – Västergötland, Sweden (geographical reference; runestones)

VKM – Einhard, *Vita Karoli Magni*; S. E. Turner (ed. and trans.), *Einhard: The Life of Charlemagne* (1880, Harper & Brothers)

Völuspá – A. Orchard, *The Elder Edda: A Book of Viking Lore* (2011, Penguin), pp. 5–15

VSG – Felix, *Vita Sancti Guthlaci*; B. Colgrave (ed. and trans.), *Felix's Life of Saint Guthlac* (1956, Cambridge University Press)

Wanderer – *ASPR*, volume 3

NOTES

1. *Wanderer*, lines 101–5

Preface

1. J. Jones, 'Vikings at the British Museum: Great Ship but Where's the Story?', *Guardian* (4 March 2014) [http://www.theguardian.com/artanddesign/2014/mar/04/vikings-british-museum-ship-story]
2. In recent years, spectacular Viking hoards have been discovered in Galloway (2014), at Lenborough, Buckinghamshire (2014) and at Watlington, Oxfordshire (2015)
3. The recently launched 'Viking Phenomenon' project, for example, directed by Professor Neil Price at the University of Uppsala, is a ten-year programme with a budget of approximately six million US dollars. [http://www.arkeologi.uu.se/Research/Projects/vikingafenomenet]

Chapter 1: Outsiders from Across the Water

1. *Beowulf,* trans. S. Heaney, *Beowulf: A New Translation* (1999, Faber), pp. 9–10
2. *ASC* D, *sub anno* 787
3. *ASN*
4. *CA*, p. 27
5. *ASC* D s.a. 787
6. *CC* s.a. 787
7. *EHD*, line 20
8. Although the poem's story is set in a vaguely defined legendary epoch (seemingly the fifth century), it was written in Old English (and presumably in England) at some point between the seventh and the eleventh centuries. The manuscript in which the received form of the poem survives – the Nowell Codex – dates to around the year 1000, and attempts to refine the dating of an earlier archetype remain highly controversial. A recent survey of the issues can be found in L. Neidorf (ed.), *The Dating of Beowulf: A Reassessment* (2014, Boydell & Brewer)
9. *Beowulf*, lines 237–57; trans. Heaney (1999)
10. Gildas, *De Excidio Britanniae (Ex.)*

11. It should be noted that some recent research has proposed dates earlier than Offa's reign for some sections of the dyke. It also remains unclear what should and should not be considered part of the continuous structure. The most detailed review of the evidence can be found in K. Ray and I. Bapty, *Offa's Dyke: Landscape & Hegemony in Eighth-Century Britain* (2016, Oxbow)

12. *ASC* s.a. 796

13. R. Bruce-Mitford, *The Sutton Hoo Ship-Burial, Volumes 1–3* (1975–1983, British Museum Press); M. Carver, *Sutton Hoo: A Seventh-Century Princely Burial Ground and Its Context*, report of the Research Committee of the Society of Antiquaries of London 69 (2005, British Museum Press)

14. The principal source, aside from the *ASC*, is the *Annales Cambriae* ('the Welsh Annals') abbreviated henceforth as *AC*

15. The Ordovices (Gwynedd), Demetae (Dyfed), Silures (Gwent), and Cornovii (Powys); see T. Charles-Edwards, *Wales and the Britons: 350–1064* (2013, Oxford University Press), pp. 14–21

16. R. Bartlett, *The Making of Europe: Conquest, Colonization and Cultural Change 950–1350* (1993, Penguin)

17. M. Carver, *Portmahomack: Monastery of the Picts* (2008, Edinburgh University Press)

18. *Beowulf*, lines 255–7

19. Mercian diplomas S134, 160, 168, 177, 186, 1264 (792–822)

20. C. Downham, '"Hiberno-Norwegians" and "Anglo-Danes": Anachronistic Ethnicities and Viking-Age England', *Mediaeval Scandinavia* 19 (2009), pp. 139–69

Chapter 2: Heart of Darkness

1. *The Holy Bible, King James Version* (1769, Cambridge Edition); [*King James Bible Online*, 2017. http://www.kingjamesbibleonline.org]

2. *Gylfaginning*, ch. 49 (own translation)

3. This, and the subsequent extracts, are taken from the Old English boundary clause of a charter dated to 808 describing a grant of land at North Stoke, Somerset from the West Saxon king, Cynewulf, to the monks of St Peter's Minster (S265)

4. All these creatures, and many others, are mentioned in Old English charter-bounds. A survey of some of the beastly entities that occur in Old English place-names more generally can be found in papers by John Baker ('Entomological Etymologies: Creepy-Crawlies in English Place-Names') and Della Hooke ('Beasts, Birds and Other Creatures in Pre-Conquest Charters and Place-Names in England'), both of which appear in M. D. J. Bintley and T. J. T. Williams (eds), *Representing Beasts in Early Medieval England and Scandinavia* (2015, Boydell & Brewer)

5. There are many examples of parishes in England where this tradition is maintained or has been revived – a notable, and high-profile, beating of the bounds takes place at the Tower of London (http://blog.hrp.org.uk/blog/beating-the-bounds/); it is not possible, however, to determine if any of these traditions have been consistently performed from the early medieval period

6. D. Adams, *The Hitchhiker's Guide to the Galaxy* (1979, Pan Books)

7. Recent books have increasingly addressed the cultural aspects of map-making, including Alastair Bonnett's *Off the Map* (2015, Aurum Press) and Jerry Brotton's *A History of the World in Twelve Maps* (2013, Penguin)

8. P. D. A. Harvey, *Mappa Mundi: The Hereford World Map* (2010, Hereford Cathedral)

9. *Genesis*, lines 103–15

10. *Beowulf*, lines 102–4

11. Ibid., line 710

12. On wolfish imagery in Britain and Scandinavia see A. Pluskowski, *Wolves and the Wilderness in the Middle Ages* (2006, Boydell & Brewer)

13. *Beowulf*, lines 1358–9

14. VSG, pp. 104–5

15. Irmeli Valtonen discusses the cartographical material and the classical tradition of a monstrous north in her *The North in the Old English Orosius: A Geographical Narrative in Context*, Mémoires de la Société Néophilologique de Helsinki LXXIII (2008, Société Néophilologique): 'Thule' was first mentioned by Pytheas (330–320 BC), Hyperborea by Hecateus in the sixth century BC, with some references even earlier

16. VSG, pp. 104–5

17. Visio S. Pauli in Blickling Homily XVI, translated by Andy Orchard in *Pride and Prodigies: Studies in the Monsters of the Beowulf Manuscript* (1995, 2nd edition, University of Toronto), p. 39

18. Jude S. Mackley, *The Legend of St. Brendan: A Comparative Study of the Latin and Anglo-Norman Versions* (2008, Brill), p. 85

19. By the thirteenth century at any rate; *Gylfaginning*, ch. 49

20. E. Christiansen, *The Northern Crusades* (1997, Penguin), p. 76

21. *ASC DE* s.a. 793

22. One of a number of islands around a dozen miles to the south-east of Lindisfarne

23. *BVSC*, ch. 17

24. VSG, ch. XXX

25. Alcuin's letter to Ethelred, *EHD* (193)

26. See, in general, J. Palmer, *The Apocalypse in the Early Middle Ages* (2014, Cambridge University Press)

27. Alcuin's letter to Higbald, *EHD* (194) (Accusing the survivors of an atrocity of having brought it all on themselves through their lifestyle choices, before berating them for defending themselves inadequately, is a form of sanctimony not new to the modern age.)

28. Alcuin's letter to Ethelred, *EHD* (193)

29. See, for example, D. Bates and R. Liddiard (eds), *East Anglia and Its North Sea World in the Middle Ages* (2015, Boydell & Brewer); S. P. Ashby, A. Coutu and S. Sindbæk, 'Urban Networks and Arctic Outlands: Craft Specialists and Reindeer Antler in Viking Towns', *European Journal of Archaeology* 18.4 (2015), pp. 679–704

30. Alex Woolf, 'Sutton Hoo and Sweden Revisited', in A. Gnasso, E. E. Intagliata, T. J. MacMaster and B. N. Morris (eds), *The Long Seventh Century: Continuity and Discontinuity in an Age of Transition* (2015, Peter Lang), pp. 5–18; M. Carver, 'Pre-Viking Traffic in the North Sea', in S.

McGrail (ed.), *Maritime Celts, Frisians and Saxons* (1990, CBA Research Report 71), pp. 117–25

31. *HE* I.15 (Sherley-Price; Farmer)
32. Valtonen, *The North in the Old English Orosius*, Chapter 3
33. For foundational work on the genealogies, see K. Sisam, 'Anglo-Saxon Royal Genealogies', *Proceedings of the British Academy* 39 (1953), pp. 287–348 and D. Dumville, 'Kingship, Genealogies and Regnal Lists', in P. W. Sawyer and I. N. Wood (eds), *Early Medieval Kingship* (1977, Leeds University), pp. 72–104
34. Alcuin's letter to Higbald, *EHD* (194)
35. J. T. Koch, 'Yr Hen Ogledd' in J. T. Koch (ed.), *Celtic Culture: An Historical Encyclopedia*, Vol. III (2006, ABC-CLIO); J. E. Fraser, 'From Ancient Scythia to the Problem of the Picts: Thoughts on the Quest for Pictish Origins' in S. T. Driscoll, J. Geddes and M. A. Hall (eds), *Pictish Progress: New Studies on Northern Britain in the Early Middle Ages* (2011, Brill)

Chapter 3: Mother North

1. R. E. Howard, 'The Dark Man', *Weird Tales* (December 1931)
2. The Gjermundbu helmet is now in the Norwegian Historical Museum in Oslo (http://www.khm.uio.no/english/visit-us/historical-museum/index.html)
3. 'Sermon of the Wolf to the English', *EHD* (240)
4. The best work on this subject has been published by Judith Jesch: for a clear overview of the meaning of the word 'Viking', see *The Viking Diaspora* (2015, Routledge); detailed analysis can be found in *Ships and Men in the Late Viking Age: The Vocabulary of Runic Inscriptions and Skaldic Verse* (2001, Boydell & Brewer)
5. J. J. North, *English Hammered Coinage*, Vol. 1 (1994, Spink), p. 175
6. There are quite a few names of moneyers (individuals responsible for the production of coinage and whose names are frequently recorded on their coins) that fall into this category. Brandr can mean both 'fire' and 'sword' in Old Norse, for instance. (A particularly intriguing example – though not a Norse name – is that of Matathan Balluc. His first name is Gaelic, and he may have been part of the Norse–Irish community that linked York and Dublin in the tenth and eleventh centuries. His second name, however, is the Old English word 'Bollock'. We will never know whether he possessed impressive testicular attributes in the figurative or the literal sense or, indeed, whether the use of the singular was deliberately significant.) However, many of the most famous 'Viking' epithets – 'Skull-splitter', 'Bloodaxe', 'Hard-ruler' and so on – were first recorded in Icelandic literature written down long after the end of the Viking Age
7. Preserved in *Egil's Saga*, and attributed to Egil Skallagrimsson (*c.* 950); translation by J. Jesch in *Viking Poetry of Love and War* (2013, British Museum Press), p. 53
8. Rundata (Vg 61)
9. There is some evidence to suggest that Old Norse speakers also recognized this commonality among themselves – several medieval sources refer to the *Dansk tongu* in terms that indicate that this was a language spoken by Icelanders, Norwegians and Swedes as well as by Danes (Jesch, *Diaspora*)

10. These connections – particularly the link between Jacob Grimm's linguistic revelations and the ethno-archaeological approaches of the early twentieth century are delineated in I. Wood, *The Modern Origins of the Early Middle Ages* (2013, Oxford University Press)

11. The German archaeologist, Gustaf Kossina, is perhaps the central figure of culture-historical theory. His influence on Nazi archaeology and racial theory tainted his legacy in post-war Europe, and more nuanced – and less obviously racist – approaches were pioneered by a new generation of British post-war archaeologists following the lead of pioneers such as Vere Gordon Childe. In many parts of the world, however, these habits of thought have been dying hard and in some cases have sprung back into life, generally where they are underpinned by resurgent nationalist sentiment and/or supported by the state. The former communist republics of Eurasia are notable examples. For an example of the chilling influence of the Russian state in Viking studies, see Leo S. Klejn's paper, 'Normanisn and Anti-Normanism in Russia: An Eyewitness Account', in P. Bauduin and A. Musin (eds), *Vers l'Orient et Vers l'Occident: Regards croisés sur les dynamiques et les transferts culturels des Vikings à la Rous ancienne* (2014, Presses Universitaires de Caen), pp. 407–17

12. P. Geary, *The Myth of Nations: The Medieval Origins of Europe* (2001, Princeton University Press) is a classic debunking of this sort of thing

13. R. M. Ballantyne, *Erling the Bold: A Tale of the Norse Sea-Kings* (1869)

14. J. Parker, *England's Darling: The Victorian Cult of Alfred the Great* (2007, Manchester University Press)

15. C. G. Allen, *The Song of Frithiof, Retold in Modern Verse* (1912, Hodder & Stoughton), with illustrations by T. H. Robinson; R. Wagner [trans. M. Armour], *The Rhinegold & The Valkyrie* (1910, William Heinemann) and *Siegfried & The Twilight of the Gods* (1911, William Heinemann) with illustrations by A. Rackham

16. Adapted from the text of the 2 June 1941 meeting of Nasjonal Samling at Borre, as given by Lise Nordenborg Myhre in 'Fortida som propaganda Arkeologi og nazisme – en faglig okkupasjon', *Frá haug ok heiðni* 1 (1995)

17. Ibid.; see also B. Myhre, *The Significance of Borre* in J. M. Fladmark (ed.), *Heritage and Identity: Shaping the Nations of the North* (2002, Routledge)

18. J. Graham-Campbell, *Viking Art* (2013, Thames & Hudson), pp. 48–81

19. B. Myhre, 'The Significance of Borre' in J. M. Fladmark (ed.), *Heritage and Identity: Shaping the Nations of the North* (2002, Routledge)

20. On the novelty of nationalism see Ernest Gellner, *Nations and Nationalism* (2006, 2nd revised edition, Wiley-Blackwell)

21. In Wodehouse's *The Code of the Woosters* (1938, Herbert Jenkins), Bertie Wooster famously unleashes the following put-down: 'The trouble with you, Spode, is that because you have succeeded in inducing a handful of halfwits to disfigure the London scene by going about in black shorts, you think you're someone […] You hear them shouting "Heil Spode!" and you imagine it is the Voice of the People. That is where you make your bloomer. What the Voice of the People is saying is: "Look at that frightful ass Spode, swanking about in footer bags! Did you ever in your puff see such a perfect perisher!"'

22. J. R. R. Tolkien, letter to his son Michael (45). H. Carpenter (ed.), *The Letters of J. R. R. Tolkien* (2006, 8th edition, HarperCollins), No. 45, pp. 55–6

23. R. Paulas, 'How a Thor-Worshipping Religion Turned Racist', *Vice* (1 May 2015) [https://www.vice.com/en_us/article/how-a-thor-worshipping-religion-turned-racist-456]

24. P. Sawyer, *The Age of the Vikings* (1975, 2nd revised edition, Hodder & Stoughton)

25. Neil Price points the way to this darker, weirder Viking in his introduction ('From Ginnungagap to the Ragnarök: Archaeologies of the Viking Worlds') to M. H. Eriksen, U. Pedersen, B. Rundtberger, I. Axelsen and H. L. Berg (eds), *Viking Worlds: Things, Spaces and Movement*, as well as more generally in his wider oeuvre

26. J. Trigg, *Hitler's Vikings: The History of the Scandinavian Waffen-SS: The Legions, the SS-Wiking and the SS-Nordland* (2012, 2nd edition, The History Press)

Chapter 4: Shores in Flames

1. This Old Irish poem was written into the margins of a manuscript copy of a grammatical treatise (*Institutiones Grammaticae*) by the sixth-century author Priscian of Caesarea (http://www.e-codices.unifr.ch/en/list/one/csg/0904). The manuscript, and the marginalia, date to the middle of the ninth century. Translation from R. Thurneysen, *Old Irish Reader* (1949, Dublin Institute for Advanced Studies), translated from the original German by D. A. Binchy and O. Bergin

2. *AI*; s.a. 795; *ASC* DE s.a. 794; *AU* s.a. 802, 806; *FH* s.a. 800; *HR* s.a. 794

3. *AU* s.a. 795, 798, 807; *AI* s.a. 798

4. BM 1870,0609.1

5. M. Redknapp, *Vikings in Wales: An Archaeological Quest* (2000, National Museum of Wales Books); M. Redknapp, 'Defining Identities in Viking Age North Wales: New Data from Llanbedrgoch' in V. E. Turner, O. A. Owen and D. J. Waugh (eds), *Shetland in the Viking World* (2016, Papers from the Proceedings of the Seventeenth Viking Congress Lerwick), pp. 159–66

6. M. Carver, *Portmahomack: Monastery of the Picts* (2008, Edinburgh University Press), p. 3

7. Ibid.

8. NMS X.IB 189 (http://www.nms.ac.uk/explore/stories/scottish-history-and-archaeology/hilton-of-cadboll-stone/). Where exactly the stone originally stood is unknown but, by the 1660s, it lay somewhere in the immediate vicinity of its replica. See Sian Jones' paper '"That Stone Was Born Here and That's Where It Belongs": Hilton of Cadboll and the Negotiation of Identity, Ownership and Belonging', in S. M. Foster and M. Cross (eds), *Able Minds and Practised Hands: Scotland's Early Medieval Sculpture in the 21st Century* (2005, Society for Medieval Archaeology), pp. 37–54. Martin Carver's paper in the same volume ('Sculpture in Action: Contexts for Stone Carving on the Tarbat Peninsula, Easter Ross', pp.13–36) draws out the wider context

9. The earliest symbol stones may date to the late fourth century. Iain Fraser (ed.), *The Pictish Symbol Stones of Scotland* (2008, RCAHMS) provides a

good introduction. Adrian Maldonado's review of the aforementioned volume in the *Scottish Archaeological Journal*, 30.1–2, pp. 215–17 is a handy guide to the main literature on the subject. The papers in Foster and Cross (eds), *Able Minds and Practised Hands*, provide multiple perspectives

10. A surviving example is the slab that still stands in the churchyard at Eassie near Glamis (Canmore ID 32092). Cf. the fate of the Woodwray cross-slab (Iain Fraser, '"Just an Ald Steen": Reverence, Reuse, Revulsion and Rediscovery' in Foster and Cross (eds), *Able Minds and Practised Hands*, pp. 55–68)

11. Fraser, '"Just an Ald Steen"', p. 62; Carver (*Portmahomack*) gives alternative possibilities, and the true motivations of whoever broke the stones are irrecoverable

12. Carver, *Portmahomack*; the individuals were respectively carbon-dated to 680–900 and 810–1020

13. In fact, there is good evidence that activity at Portmahomack continued for centuries after this incident, a traumatic moment in the life of a settlement, but not its death-knell. What does seem to have changed is the focus of activity on the site (Carver, *Portmahomack*, pp. 136–48)

14. Lord Smith was appointed by the then Prime Minister David Cameron in 2014 to oversee the devolution commitments made by the government during and after the Scottish Referendum of the same year

15. What seems to have been a gaming board was found among the slates (Carver, *Portmahomack*, p. 47)

16. The slate is now housed at Bute Museum (http://www.butemuseum.org.uk/1061-2/). Technically it is two objects: the image is split between two fragments of what was originally one slate

17. C. Lowe, 'Image and Imagination: The Inchmarnock "Hostage Stone"', in B. B. Smith, S. Taylor and G. Williams (eds), *West over Sea: Studies in Scandinavian Sea-Borne Expansion and Settlement Before 1300* (2007, Brill), pp. 53–6

18. M. Blindheim, 'The Ranuaik Reliquary in Copenhagen: A Short Study' in J. B. Knirk (ed.), *Proceedings of the Tenth Viking Congress, Larkollen* (1985, Universitetets Oldsaksamlings Skrifter), pp. 203–18. Egon Wamers gives a sense of the quantity of Irish and British metalwork that made its way to Scandinavia in this period: E. Wamers, 'Insular Finds in Viking Age Scandinavia and the State Formation of Norway' in H. B. Clarke, M. Ní Mhaonaigh and R. Ó Floinn (eds), *Ireland and Scandinavia in the Early Viking Age* (1998, Four Courts Press); also A. M. Heen-Pettersen, 'Insular Artefacts from Viking-Age Burials from Mid-Norway. A Review of Contact between Trøndelag and Britain and Ireland', *Internet Archaeology* 38 (2014) [https://doi.org/10.11141/ia.38.2]

19. As Snorri tells it, at the end of the world 'the ship Naglfar loosens from its moorings. It is made from the nails of dead men, and for this reason it is worth considering the warning that if a person dies with untrimmed nails he contributes crucial material to Naglfar, a ship that both gods and men would prefer not to see built': *Gylfaginning*, 51

20. The word most often used to describe Vikings in Irish chronicles is *gennti* ('gentiles'). Charles-Thomas gives the original word in his translation – I have substituted 'heathen' here and throughout; *AU* s.a. 824

21. J. Jesch, *Women in the Viking Age* (1991, Boydell & Brewer), pp. 45–6
22. Other possibilities include the translation of relics guarded by a warrior retinue, although the composition doesn't seem to support this (one would expect the relics and their bearer to have been the absolute focal point of any such scene); another possibility is that the stone depicts a scene from the life of St Patrick – his abduction by Scottish raiders in the sixth century given an anachronistic treatment *c.* 800. If this is the case, it is probably inspired by or modelled after contemporary events and still therefore reflective of the dangers facing monastic communities at that time. There is no certainty that the warriors depicted are necessarily Vikings, but the broadly known circumstances of its creation and certain details of the ship (the combination of sail and oars) imply that this is the case (see Lowe, 'Image and Imagination')
23. Ibn Rusta, c. 913, translated in P. Lunde and C. Stone, *Ibn Fadlān and the Land of Darkness: Arab Travellers in the Far North* (2012, Penguin), p. 126
24. Ibn Fadlan, describing events of 921–2; Lunde and Stone, *Ibn Fadlān and the Land of Darkness*, p. 53
25. Peter Frankopan, *The Silk Roads: A New History of the World* (2015, Bloomsbury)
26. *AU* s.a. 821; 831; 836
27. Research is under way, and will form part of the research outputs of the Viking Phenomenon project at Uppsala University (http://www.arkeologi. uu.se/Research/Projects/vikingafenomenet/). See also A. Lawler, 'Vikings May Have First Taken to Seas to Find Women, Slaves', *Science* (15 April 2016)
28. S. Brink, 'Slavery in the Viking Age'; S. Brink with N. Price (eds), *The Viking World* (2008, Routledge), pp. 49–56
29. *Rígsthula*, verses 12–13
30. D. A. E. Pelteret, *Slavery in Early Mediaeval England: From the Reign of Alfred Until the Twelfth Century* (2001, Boydell & Brewer)
31. *AU* s.a. 836

Chapter 5: Beyond the North Waves

1. R. Kipling, *Puck of Pook's Hill* (1906, Macmillan)
2. See Chapter 21
3. *Capitulatio de partibus Saxoniae* ('Ordinances concerning Saxony'). See D. C. Munro, *Selections from the Laws of Charles the Great* (2004 [original printing 1900], Kessinger Publishing)
4. Similar fears had been shared by at least some English-speaking peoples, although by the end of the eighth century these had been eroded, forgotten, replaced and transformed by two centuries of Christian mission. See papers in M. Carver (ed.), *The Cross Goes North: Processes of Conversion in Northern Europe, AD 300–1300* (2003, Boydell Press)
5. One of the Saxon tribal leaders – Widukind – had sought sanctuary among the Danes after Charlemagne's early victories, returning in 782 to foment rebellion. The *Royal Frankish Annals* claim that the Danevirke was built new in 808; archaeological investigation has shown, however, that its first stages date to the sixth century and that it was reinforced from the mid-eighth century onward: A. Pedersen, 'Monumental Expression and

Fortification in Denmark in the Time of King Harald Bluetooth', in N. Christie and H. Herold (eds), *Fortified Settlements in Early Medieval Europe: Defended Communities of the 8th–10th Centuries* (2016, Oxbow), Chapter 6

6. *RFA* s.a. 804
7. *RFA* s.a. 808
8. C. B. McClendon, *The Origins of Medieval Architecture: Building in Europe, A.D. 600–900* (2005, Yale University Press), pp. 105–28
9. *Codex Carolinus* 81 (Ibid., p. 112); *VKM*, 26
10. *RFA* s.a. 810
11. For an overview of the Carolingian context see R. Hodges, *Towns and Trade in the Age of Charlemagne* (2000, Bloomsbury Publishing)
12. G. S. Munch, O. S. Johansen and E. Roesdahl (eds), *Borg in Lofoten. A Chieftain's Farm in North Norway* (2003, Tapir Academic Press)
13. S. Ratke and R. Simek, 'Guldgubber: Relics of Pre-Christian Law Rituals?' in A. Andrén, K. Jennbert and C. Raudvere (eds), *Old Norse Religion in Long-Term Perspectives: Origins, Changes, and Interactions* (2006, Nordic Academic Press), pp. 259–64
14. N. Price, 'Belief and Ritual' in G. Williams, P. Pentz and M. Wemhoff (eds), *Vikings: Life and Legend* (2014, British Museum Press), pp.162–95
15. J. Story, *Carolingian Connections: Anglo-Saxon England and Carolingian Francia, c. 750–870* (2003, Ashgate)
16. B. Myhre, 'The Beginning of the Viking Age – Some Current Archaeological Problems', in A. Faulkes and R. Perkins, *Viking Revaluations* (1993, Viking Society for Northern Research), pp. 192–203; Myrhe's arguments are rather more subtle and plausible than they are often presented in the work of others
17. With the exception of the kingdom of Bhutan (which, to the country's inexplicably unique credit, uses a measure of 'gross national happiness' (GNH) to judge the success of its domestic policies)
18. *Gododdin*
19. *Maxims II*, lines 21–8, p. 514
20. 'Kennings' are poetic allusions, used in both ON and OE verse, that provided poets with an endless number of ways to describe things and concepts, often using mythological references or deeply symbolic language. These examples, and their provenances, can be found amongst the eighteen kennings for 'generous ruler' listed in the database of *The Skaldic Project* (http://skaldic.abdn.ac.uk)
21. J. Jesch, 'Eagles, Ravens and Wolves: Beasts of Battle, Symbols of Victory and Death', in J. Jesch (ed.), *The Scandinavians from the Vendel Period to the Tenth Century* (2002, Boydell & Brewer), pp. 251–71
22. T. Earle, *How Chiefs Come to Power: The Political Economy in Prehistory* (1997, Stanford University Press); in some tribal societies – including, possibly, the small kingdoms of early medieval Britain – the potentially apocalyptic outcomes of spiralling violence and rapacity were forestalled by the evolution of ritualized warfare, confined to certain seasons and locations and hedged around with mutually understood norms and rules of engagement. This, of course, only really works if everyone is playing the same game. One of the reasons why Viking attacks in Britain and elsewhere

were reported with such horror and alarm was perhaps in part because they didn't know the rules (or, if they did, chose not to play by them); G. R. W. Halsall, 'Playing by Whose Rules? A Further Look at Viking Atrocity in the Ninth Century', *Medieval History*, 2.2 (1992), pp. 3–12; T. J. T. Williams, *Landscape and Warfare in Early Medieval Britain* (2016, unpublished PhD thesis)

23. This, essentially, was the thrust of the 2014 British Museum exhibition and its accompanying publication, G. Williams et al. (eds), *Vikings: Life and Legend*

Chapter 6: The Gathering Storm

1. *Finnsburg*, lines 5–12
2. We should, however, bear in mind that the record we have of these years is far from being complete – there are, for example, no surviving chronicles produced in Mercia or East Anglia that provide an independent insight into what was going on in these regions, and the West Saxon chronicle only records what its compilers in the late ninth century wanted their readers to remember. There are, in fact, hints that unrecorded coastal raids did occur in Kent (at least), and possibly before the killings in Portland took place. A synod attended by Offa of Mercia in 782 includes provision for an expedition against pagans arriving in ships in Kent and Essex. Susan Kelly (ed.), *The Charters of St Augustine's Abbey, Canterbury, and Minster-in-Thanet*, Anglo-Saxon Charters 4 (1995, Oxford University Press), no. 15
3. It is worth considering that twenty-nine years prior to the publication of this book the Soviet Union was still an apparently permanent feature of the geopolitical scene
4. *ASC* F s.a. 798
5. *ASC* s.a. 813 (F s.a. 815)
6. *ASC* s.a. 823
7. *HA*, iv.29
8. *ASC* s.a. 832; Ships dated to the ninth century and excavated in Norway can be reliably estimated to have had crews of between 40 (the Oseberg ship) and 66 (the Gokstad ship); see T. Sjøvold, *The Viking Ships in Oslo* (1985, Universitetets Oldsaksamling); G. Williams, *The Viking Ship* (2014, British Museum Press). For an introduction to debates regarding the size of ninth-century armies see G. Halsall, *Warfare and Society in the Barbarian West, 450–900* (2003, Routledge)
9. *Elene*, lines 99–123; prose translation of Old English verse by S. A. J. Bradley, *Anglo-Saxon Poetry* (1982, Everyman), p. 168
10. See Halsall, *Warfare and Society*, for the messy reality of early medieval combat; sixty-four shields were excavated with the Gokstad ship, and may have been made specifically for display during the burial rites; they were hung outwards along the gunnels of the ship, thirty-two per side: Sjøvold, *The Viking Ships in Oslo*, p. 58
11. There is a degree of mystery surrounding this object – despite its obvious quality, it seems to have been discarded or hidden, deposited in a pit on a domestic workshop plot in Viking York. The circumstances under which it was disposed of remain obscure; D. Tweddle, *The Anglian Helmet from 16–22 Coppergate* (1992, Council for British Archaeology)

12. J. W. Binns, E. C. Norton, D. M. Palliser, 'The Latin Inscription on the Coppergate Helmet', *Antiquity* 64.242 (1990), pp. 134–9
13. G. Williams, 'Warfare & Military Expansion' in G. Williams et al. (eds), *Vikings: Life and Legend*, pp. 76–115; S. Norr, 'Old Gold – The Helmet in *Hákonarmál* as a Sign of Its Time', in S. Norr (ed.), *Valsgärde Studies: The Place and Its People, Past and Present* (2008, Uppsala), pp. 83–114
14. *ASC* s.a. 833. The literature concerning the nature of military obligation in Anglo-Saxon England is vast. For an introduction to the key themes and literature see R. Lavelle, *Alfred's Wars: Sources and Interpretations of Anglo-Saxon Warfare in the Viking Age* (2010, Boydell & Brewer), and for an influential overview R. P. Abels, *Lordship and Military Obligation in Anglo-Saxon England* (1988, University of California Press)
15. T. J. T. Williams, *Landscape and Warfare in Early Medieval Britain*
16. *ASC* s.a. 835
17. P. C. Herring, *The Archaeology of Kit Hill: Kit Hill Archaeological Survey Project Final Report* (1990, 2nd edition, Cornwall Archaeological Unit)
18. Herring, *The Archaeology of Kit Hill*, p. 141; D. L. Prior, 'Call, Sir John, first baronet (1732–1801)', *Oxford Dictionary of National Biography* (2004, Oxford University Press)
19. M. Peake, *Titus Groan* (1946, Eyre & Spottiswood), p. 1
20. Herring, *The Archaeology of Kit Hill*. It is easy to imagine the voice of David Jason: 'Deep inside this picturesque hill, somewhere in the sleepy countryside of Cornwall, Baron Silas Greenback, the world's most villainous toad, is plotting to detonate a massive nuclear warhead ...'
21. This sort of tautology is a remarkably common occurrence in British place-names. Multiple linguistic layers – Celtic, Latin, Old English, Old Norse, Norman French – have resulted in older word elements (having lost their original sense) being combined with newer words with similar meanings: for example, Eas Fors waterfall on the Isle of Mull ('waterfall' [*eas*, Gaelic] + 'waterfall' [*fors, foss*, ON] + waterfall [ModE]) or Breedon on the Hill, Leicestershire ('hill' [*bre*, Brittonic] + 'hill' [*dun*, OE] + 'on the hill' [ModE]).
22. T. J. T. Williams, '"For the Sake of Bravado in the Wilderness": Confronting the Bestial in Anglo-Saxon Warfare', in Bintley and Williams (eds), *Representing Beasts*, pp. 176–204
23. T. J. T. Williams, 'The Place of Slaughter: The West Saxon Battlescape' in R. Lavelle and S. Roffey (eds), *The Danes in Wessex* (2016, Oxbow), pp. 35–55; T. J. T. Williams, *Landscape and Warfare in Early Medieval Britain*

Chapter 7: Dragon-Slayers

1. A. Lang, *The Red Fairy Book* (1906, Longmans, Green and Co.)
2. *ASC* BCDE s.a. 851; *CA* adds 'on Thanet', *VA* and *CC* suggest Sheppey
3. *FH* s.a. 844
4. *ASC* s.a. 839; 851 (C s.a. 853)
5. All s.a. 837; 838; 839; ADEF s.a. 840 (C s.a. 841); s.a. 851 (C s.a. 853)
6. *ASC* s.a. 848
7. *ASC* s.a. 850 (C s.a. 853); Either the burial mound of a man called Wicga, or a mound infested with 'wiggling things' (Baker, 'Entomological Etymologies')

8. *ASC* s.a. 851 (C s.a. 853). The location of Aclea is unknown, although Ockley in Surrey is a plausible candidate

9. For a sceptical and comprehensive analysis of feuding in Anglo-Saxon England, see J. D. Niles, 'The Myth of the Feud in Anglo-Saxon England', *Journal of English and Germanic Philology* 114 (2015), pp. 163–200

10. G. Williams, 'Viking Camps in England and Ireland' in G. Williams et al. (eds), *Vikings: Life and Legend* (pp. 120–1) is a useful introduction to the subject of Viking camps

11. B. Orme, *Anthropology for Archaeologists* (1981, Cornell University Press), p. 196

12. G. Halsall, 'Anthropology and the Study of Pre-Conquest Warfare and Society', in S. C. Hawkes (ed.), *Weapons and Warfare in Anglo-Saxon England* (1989, Oxford University Committee for Archaeology), pp. 155–78; T. J. T. Williams, 'The Place of Slaughter'

13. Halsall, 'Playing by Whose Rules?'

14. It should be noted, however, that – as I have argued elsewhere – the impression of novelty may be a product of the increased detail present in the source material from the ninth century onward: T. J. T. Williams, 'The Place of Slaughter' and *Landscape and Warfare in Early Medieval Britain*

15. This was normally a reference to Slavic people, but may have referred to any European transported eastward as a slave: Lunde and Stone, *Ibn Fadlān and the Land of Darkness*, p. 222, n. 2

16. Ibn Rusta, *c.* 913, translated in Lunde and Stone, *Ibn Fadlān and the Land of Darkness*, p. 126

17. *EHD* (13.1); R. Abels, 'The Micel Hæðen Here and the Viking Threat', in T. Reuters (ed.), *Alfred the Great: Papers from the Eleventh-Centenary Conferences* (2003, Ashgate), pp. 269–71; T. J. T. Williams, 'The Place of Slaughter'

18. See Chapter 13

19. G. Williams, 'Raiding and Warfare', in Brink with Price (eds), *The Viking World*, pp. 193–203

20. L. Abrams, 'The Conversion of the Danelaw' in J. Graham-Campbell, R. Hall, J. Jesch and D. N. Parsons (eds), *Vikings and the Danelaw: Select Papers from the Proceedings of the Thirteenth Viking Congress* (2001, Oxbow), pp. 31–44; cf. D. M. Hadley, 'Conquest, Colonization and the Church: Ecclesiastical Organization in the Danelaw', *Historical Research* 69, pp. 109–28

21. 'Dore, Whitwell Gap and the River Humber' (*ASC* ABCD s.a. 942); G. Rollason, *Northumbria, 500–1100: Creation and Destruction of a Kingdom* (2003, Cambridge University Press), p. 26

22. *ASC* s.a. 827; S. Keynes, 'Bretwalda or *Brytenwalda*', in M. Lapidge, J. Blair. and S. Keynes (eds), *The Blackwell Encyclopaedia of Anglo-Saxon England* (2008, 8th edition, Wiley-Blackwell), p. 74

23. *ASC* s.a. 867

24. Rollason, *Northumbria*, pp. 192–8

25. All these behaviours are attested to in one way or another in Anglo-Saxon England. Farting in the general direction of the enemy could be one part of the defiant warrior's arsenal; when in 1068 William the Conqueror turned up at Exeter expecting the town's surrender, he was roused to particular

wrath towards the 'irreverent' defenders because 'one of them' – according to the twelfth-century historian William of Malmesbury – 'standing upon the wall, had bared his posteriors, and had broken wind, in contempt of the Normans [*GRA*, b.III]'; in 1006, a Viking army had jeered at the cowering townsfolk of Winchester (*ASC* CDE s.a. 1006), and the display of severed heads seems to have been commonplace in Anglo-Saxon judicial culture: A. Reynolds, *Anglo-Saxon Deviant Burial Customs* (2009, Oxford University Press)

26. *ASC* s.a. 867 (C s.a. 868); *VA*, 27
27. *Ragnarssona þáttr* ('The Tale of Ragnar's Sons'); *Ragnars saga Loðbrókar* ('The Saga of Ragnar Loðbrók'); *Krákumál* ('The Song of Kraka'); *Gesta Danorum* ('Deeds of the Danes') by Saxo Grammaticus (*GD*)
28. *Jarl* is an Old Norse word designating a nobleman – roughly analogous to the OE *ealdorman*
29. Saxo Grammaticus, in perhaps the earliest version of this tale, recounts that there were several serpents given to Þóra, and that they roamed wild over the land, burning and poisoning with their foul breath; *GD*, book IX
30. *Krákumál*, verse 1
31. *Beowulf*, lines 2312–20; trans. Heaney, p. 73
32. *Beowulf*, lines 2275–7; trans. Heaney, p. 72
33. *Maxims II*, lines 26–7
34. *Maxims II*, lines 28–9
35. *Völuspá*, verse 66
36. J. R. R. Tolkien, 'The Monsters and the Critics' [1936], in C. Tolkien (ed.), *The Monsters and the Critics and Other Essays* (1997, HarperCollins), p. 12; *Beowulf*'s dragon is undeniably a model for the depiction of Smaug the Golden in Tolkien's *The Hobbit*, originally published by George Allen & Unwin in 1937
37. The most complete version of the story is told in the late thirteenth-century Old Norse *Völsunga saga*, but it is also told in poetic form in a number of related – so-called 'eddic' – poems compiled together in the Icelandic Codex Regius: J. L. Byock (trans.), *The Saga of the Volsungs: The Norse Epic of Sigurd the Dragon Slayer* (1999, 2nd edition, Penguin); A. Orchard, *The Elder Edda: A Book of Viking Lore* (2011, Penguin)
38. C. E. Doepler, *Der Ring des Nibelungen: Carl Emil Doeplers Kostümbilder für die Erstaufführung des Ring in Bayreuth* (2012 [1889], Reprint-Verlag Leipzig); see also R. Wagner [trans. M. Armour], *The Rhinegold & The Valkyrie* (1910, William Heinemann) and *Siegfried & The Twilight of the Gods* (1911, William Heinemann) with illustrations by A. Rackham
39. J. R. R. Tolkien, 'On Fairy Stories' [1947], in C. Tolkien (ed.), *The Monsters and the Critics and Other Essays*, p. 135
40. E. Magnússon and W. Morris (trans.),*Völsunga Saga: The Story of the Volsungs and Niblungs, with certain Songs from the Elder Edda* (1870, F. S. Ellis)
41. J. R. R. Tolkien, *The Legend of Sigurd and Gudrún* (2009, HarperCollins)
42. G. B. Shaw, 'William Morris as I Knew Him', Introduction to May Morris, *William Morris: Artist, Writer, Socialist*, vol. 2 (1936, Blackwell), p. xxxvii
43. 'Letter 216' in N. Kelvin (ed.), *The Collected Letters of William Morris*, volume 1 (1984, Princeton University Press), p. 205

44. *Beowulf*, in what is clearly intended as a foreshadowing of events to come, refers to the Sigurd legend directly, although the poem substitutes Sigurd's father Sigemund in the role of dragon-slayer; lines 873–99
45. G. Williams et al. (eds), *Vikings: Life and Legend* (pp. 120–1), p. 88; Tatarstan is a Russian republic with its capital at Kazan
46. Rundata (Sö 101; Sö 327); see V. Symons, 'Wreoþenhilt ond wyrmfah: Confronting Serpents in *Beowulf* and Beyond' in Bintley and Williams (eds), *Representing Beasts*, pp. 73–93
47. The Manx stones are as follows: Maughold 122; Andreas 121; Jurby 119; Malew 120; they are identified by the name of the parish in which they were found and the catalogue number assigned in P. M. C. Kermode, *Manx Crosses or The Inscribed and Sculptured Monuments of the Isle of Man From About the End of the Fifth to the Beginning of the Thirteenth Century* (2005 [1907], Elibron Classics). See also S. Margeson, 'On the Iconography of the Manx Crosses' in C. Fell, P. Foote, J. Graham-Campbell and R. Thomson (eds), *The Viking Age in the Isle of Man* (1983, Viking Society for Northern Research). The English stone cross-shaft is designated in *CASSS* as Halton St Wilfrid 1, 2, 9 and 10
48. *Ragnars saga Loðbrókar*
49. R. McTurk, *Studies in Ragnars saga loðbrókar and Its Major Scandinavian Analogues* (1991, Society for the Study of Medieval Languages and Literature)

Chapter 8: Eagles of Blood

1. *Hávamál*, 144
2. One of Ragnar's sons is named as Hvitserk ('Whiteshirt') in *Ragnarssona þáttr*; this may have been an alternative name for the individual named Halfdan and identified as a brother of Ivar and Ubbe in the *Anglo-Saxon Chronicle*: ASC All MSS s.a. 878 (C s.a. 879)
3. *Ragnarssona þáttr*
4. *GD*, book IX; a similar version appears in *Ragnars saga Loðbrókar*
5. M. Townend, 'Knútsdrápa', in D. Whaley (ed.), *Poetry from the Kings' Sagas 1: From Mythical Times to c. 1035* (2012, Brepols), p. 649
6. R. Frank, 'Viking Atrocity and Skaldic Verse: The Rite of the Blood-Eagle', *English Historical Review* XCIX.CCCXCI (1984), pp. 332–43
7. Ibid., p. 337
8. Ibid.
9. Ibid., p. 337
10. *GH* IV.26; The translated passage is taken from A. Orchard, *Dictionary of Norse Myth and Legend* (1997, Cassell), p. 169
11. O. Sundqvist, *An Arena for Higher Powers: Ceremonial Buildings and Religious Strategies in Late Iron Age Scandinavia* (2015, Brill), pp. 110–15
12. Archaeological interventions have discovered evidence for buildings underlying the cathedral church at Gamla Uppsala; these are no longer believed to belong to the temple described by Adam of Bremen; see A. M. Alkarp and N. Price, 'Tempel av guld eller kyrka av trä? : markradarundersökningar vid Gamla Uppsala kyrka', *Fornvännen* 100:4 (2005), pp. 261–72

13. Analysis of the excavated material has cast doubt on whether the human remains should be considered part of the evidence for sacrificial ritual – they seem to have been grouped together and show fewer signs of weathering than the animal bones, implying that they were buried earlier. This research also emphasized the presence of butchery marks on many of the animal bones – including the bones of several brown bears – implying that the animals were killed and cut up before being deposited at the tree (although none of this rules out the possibility that they were suspended from the tree in pieces, or butchered after having been taken down). O. Magnell and E. Iregren, 'Veitstu Hvé Blóta Skal? The Old Norse blót in the light of osteological remains from Frösö Church, Jämtland, Sweden', *Current Swedish Archaeology* 18 (2010), pp. 223–50; see also Price, 'Belief and Ritual' for a wider discussion of the evidence of cult sites

14. Lunde and Stone, *Ibn Fadlān and the Land of Darkness*, p. 48

15. Ibid., p. 162

16. A. E. Christensen and M. Nockert, *Osebergfunnet IV: Tekstilene* (2016, Kulturhistorisk Museum, Universitetet i Oslo)

17. *Orkneyinga saga*, 8; the story is repeated by Snorri in *Heimskringla*, probably drawing on the saga: 'Haralds saga ins Hárfagra', chapter 30 (*Heimskringla I*)

18. N. Price, *The Viking Way: Religion and War in Late Iron Age Scandinavia* (2002, Uppsala University), pp. 100–7

19. *Völuspa*, 28

20. *Hávamál*, 138–9

21. *ASC* s.a. 867

22. 'Ynglinga saga', chapter 8 (*Heimskringla I*)

23. 'Hákonar saga góða', chapters 13–14 (*Heimskringla I*)

24. *CC* s.a. 868, pp. 282–5; also *ASC* All MSS s.a. 868 (C s.a. 869)

25. Halsall, *Warfare and Society*, p. 223

26. It once adorned the walls of the king's palace at Nineveh (in modern Iraq), but can now be seen at the British Museum in London (a fact for which the whole world should be grateful since the remains of Nineveh were systematically obliterated by Islamic extremists in 2015)

27. The Vikings, according to the poem *De bellis Parisiacæ urbis* [or *Bella Parisiacæ urbis*] by the Parisian monk Abbo, may have used some sort of rock-lobber during the siege of Paris in 886, though his account is exaggerated in a number of details (N. Dass (ed. and trans.), *Viking Attacks on Paris: The Bella Parisiacae Urbis of Abbo of Saint-Germain-des-Prés* (2007, Peeters Publishers); Halsall, *Warfare and Society*, p. 225)

28. *ASC* C s.a. 917

29. *CC* s.a. 868, pp. 282–5; *ASC* s.a. 868 (C s.a. 869)

30. We should, however, be slightly cautious about accepting the *ASC* at face value here; Mercia produced no independent chronicle for this period, and the only guide to events is provided by the Wessex-produced *ASC* compiled in the following decades. The reality of West Saxon involvement may have been far more complex and ambiguous than the *ASC*'s version allows

31. *ASC* s.a. 870 (C s.a. 871)

32. Beornwulf (*ASC* s.a. 823; *CC* s.a. 823) and Ludeca (*ASC* s.a. 825; *CC* s.a. 825)

33. *PSE*, V
34. *PSE*, X
35. It is likely, however, that Viking chiefs did indeed play central roles in cult practice. For an introduction to the issues see O. Sundqvist, 'Cult Leaders, Rulers and Religion' in Brink with Price, *The Viking World*, pp. 223–6
36. *PSE*, XIII
37. *PSE*, XIV
38. R. Pinner, *The Cult of St Edmund in Medieval East Anglia* (2015, Boydell & Brewer)
39. The mystery of the Holy Trinity is among the most baffling and incomprehensible aspects of Christian theology. Vatican attempts at clarification cannot always be judged wholly satisfactory (http://www.vatican.va/archive/ccc_css/archive/catechism/p1s2c1p2.htm)

Chapter 9: Wayland's Bones
1. W. Camden, *Britannia*, 'Barkshire', 12: P. Holland (trans.), D. F. Sutton (ed.) (2004 [1607], The University of California): http://www.philological.bham.ac.uk/cambrit/
2. Thomas Hughes, *Tom Brown's School Days* (1857, Macmillan), pp. 11–13
3. The quote is attributed to Vladimir Ilyich Ulyanov (Lenin), but he never seems to have used these precise words. He is, however, recorded saying: 'we […] must probe with bayonets whether the social revolution of the proletariat in Poland had ripened': R. Pipes (ed.), *The Unknown Lenin: From the Secret Archive* (1996, Yale University Press). In 1975, the American columnist Joseph Alsop wrote: 'The Soviets […] merely follow Lenin's advice to probe with bayonets any situation that looks mushy, withdrawing only when the bayonets meet steel' (J. Alsop, 'Post-Vietnam Assessment is Intense and Painful', *Sunday Advocate* (18 May 1975), p. 2-B, col. 2)
4. *VA*, 35–6
5. *VA*, 35–6. No evidence for any major earthworks of this period have yet been discovered at Reading (J. Graham-Campbell, 'The Archaeology of the "Great Army" (865–79)', in E. Roesdahl and J. P. Schjødt (eds), *Beretning fra treogtyvende tværfaglige vikingesymposium* (2004, Aarhus Universitet), pp. 30–46). It is possible that the defences were hastily built, perhaps utilizing buildings and timbers that were already present. If so, this might explain the reluctance of the Viking army to place much faith in the defences
6. *ASC* s.a. 871 (C s.a. 872)
7. *VA*, 35–6, p. 78
8. *EE*, 2953–71; Geoffrey is a little difficult to evaluate as a historian of this period; although his *Estoire des Engleis* (1135–7) contains details that are not preserved anywhere else (and he would have had few reasons to invent them), he also had a habit of including obviously fantastical material and was writing many centuries after the event
9. *ASC* s.a. 871 (C s.a. 872); *VA*, 37–9
10. *VA*, 37–9; Asser is probably mistaken about the death of Sidroc the Old – according to the *ASC* he had been killed at Englefield
11. A number of suggestions have been made. See, for example, P. Marren, *Battles of the Dark Ages* (2006, Pen & Sword Books), pp. 118–21

12. F. Wise, *A Letter to Dr Mead Concerning Some Antiquities in Berkshire: Particularly Shewing that the White Horse, which Gives Name to the Vale, is a Monument of the West-Saxons, Made in Memory of a Great Victory Obtained Over the Danes A.D. 871* (1738, Oxford)

13. Ibid., p. 23

14. Hughes, *Tom Brown's School Days*, p. 13

15. Ibid., p. 7

16. M. Gelling, *The Place-Names of Berkshire*, volumes I and II (1973; 1974, English Place-Name Society, volumes 49/50)

17. It is also possible that battles were not fought at these places at all, that these might simply have been the royal manors closest to where the fighting took place, and therefore useful geographical markers that everyone – especially the king – would have recognized

18. S288

19. S524

20. O. S. Anderson, *The English Hundred Names: The South-Western Counties* (1939, University of Lund), pp. 14–15

21. G. B. Grundy, 'The Ancient Highways and Tracks of Wiltshire, Berkshire, and Hampshire, and the Saxon Battlefields of Wiltshire', *Archaeological Journal* 75 (1918), pp. 69–194

22. NMR: SU 28 NE 4

23. It is also, incidentally, nearer to how it would have appeared to J. R. R. Tolkien when he visited the place with his family in the 1930s – one of a number of sights near Oxford to which the professor drove in his Morris Cowley (named 'Jo'), charging around the countryside in a manner which his biographer Humphrey Carpenter described as 'daring rather than skilful'. H. Carpenter, *J. R. R. Tolkien: A Biography* (2002 [1977], HarperCollins), p. 39

24. The phrase appears in a boundary clause, in a charter of King Eadred (r. 946–55) dated to 955 (S564); the phrases 'Wayland's Smithy' and 'Wayland Smith' may or may not have something to do with the choice of the name 'Waylon Smithers' for the subservient assistant to Springfield power-plant owner Monty Burns. If this is a deliberate joke, the relevance is not altogether clear. It has been suggested that the choice of name may be an ironic inversion of macho stereotypes, the violent, rapey manual labourer becomes, in Mr Smithers, an effete, homosexual personal assistant. I think it's a push, but who knows? The creators of *The Simpsons* have never – so far as I am aware – made any comment on the matter. M. S. Cecire, 'Wayland Smith in Popular Culture' in D. Clarke and N. Perkins, *Anglo-Saxon Culture and the Modern Imagination* (2010, Boydell & Brewer), pp. 201–18

25. Wise, *Letter to Dr Mead*, p. 37

26. Wise also asserted that the tomb was the burial place of the Viking king Bacsecg, a claim for which he offers no supporting evidence whatsoever and which is, needless to say, total bunk. This is not to say, however, that important Vikings were never interred beneath impressive monuments, as the following chapter elaborates

27. *Boethius* II.7; OE *Boethius* XIX. The works traditionally believed to have emanated from Alfred's circle are summarized in S. Keynes and M.

Lapidge, *Alfred the Great: Asser's 'Life of King Alfred' and Other Contemporary Sources* (1983, Penguin), p. 29. Alfred's personal input has, however, been questioned in recent years, especially by Malcolm Godden (M. Godden, 'Did King Alfred Write Anything?', *Medium Ævum* 76 (2007), pp. 1–23). The noun *faber* in Latin means 'smith'; it is uncertain whether Alfred is being playful or erroneously literalistic in his translation of the Latin proper name Fabricius

28. C. R. Peers and R. A. Smith, 'Wayland's Smithy, Berkshire', *The Antiquaries Journal : Journal of the Society of Antiquaries of London* 1 (1921), pp. 183–98

29. N. G. Discenaza, 'Power, Skill and Virtue in the Old English *Boethius*', *Anglo-Saxon England* 26 (1997), pp. 81–108

30. *Beowulf*, line 907; *Deor*, lines 1–13

31. *Völundarkvida*, verse 34

32. Price, 'From Ginnungagap to the Ragnarök: Archaeologies of the Viking Worlds', p. 7

33. Sigmund Freud, 'The Uncanny' (trans. Alix Strachey), in S. L. Gilman (ed.), *Sigmund Freud: Psychological Writings and Letters* (1995, Continuum), pp. 126, 142; see also G. Moshenska, 'The Archaeological Uncanny', *Public Archaeology* 5 (2006), pp. 91–9 and 'M. R. James and the Archaeological Uncanny', *Antiquity* 86.334 (2012), pp. 1192–1201

34. *ASC* s.a. 871 (C s.a. 872)

35. Ibid.

Chapter 10: Real Men

1. *CC* s.a. 850

2. *ASC* s.a. 872 (C s.a. 873)

3. *ASC* s.a. 873 (C s.a. 874)

4. *ASC* s.a. 874 (C s.a. 875)

5. W. J. Moore, *The Saxon Pilgrims to Rome and the Schola Saxonum* (1937, University of Fribourg)

6. St Wystan's churchyard is also notable as the resting place of the extraordinarily multi-talented C. B. Fry (1872–1956). His career took in football, rugby, athletics, acrobatics, politics, writing, publishing, broadcasting, teaching and, above all, cricket. One can't help but think that had Fry been around in 874, the Vikings would have found themselves batting on a very sticky wicket

7. R. I. Page, *Norse Myths* (1990, British Museum Press), p. 35

8. *Gylfaginning*, 21

9. *Thrymskvida*, verse 8; Freya was the goddess of love, sex and fertility: she was frequently an object of desire among gods, giants, elves and dwarves: Orchard, *Dictionary*, p. 48

10. *Thrymskvida*, verses 15–17

11. Ibid., verse 31

12. Page, *Norse Myths*, p. 14

13. P. M. Sørensen, *The Unmanly Man: Concepts of Sexual Defamation in Early Northern Society* (1983, Odense University Press)

14. In general, D. Wyatt, *Slaves and Warriors in Medieval Britain and Ireland, 800–1200* (2009, Brill), pp. 206–14; Sørensen, *The Unmanly Man*, pp. 76, 83

15. Ibid., pp. 17–18, 80, 82, 111; see also, for example, the planned rape of a man and his wife by the hero of *Guðmundar saga dýra* (Wyatt, *Slaves and Warriors*, pp. 211–12)

16. *Helgakviða Hundingsbana fyrri*, verses 37–43

17. *Lokasenna*, verse 24

18. S. W. Nordeide, 'Thor's Hammer in Norway: A Symbol of Reaction against the Christian Cross?', in Andrén et al., *Old Norse Religion in Long-Term Perspectives*. A. S. Gräslund, 'Thor's Hammers, Pendant Crosses and Other Amulets' in E. Roesdahl and D. Wilson (eds), *From Viking to Crusader: The Scandinavians and Europe 800–1200* (1992, Nordic Council of Ministers)

19. J. Staecker, 'The Cross Goes North: Christian Symbols and Scandinavian Women' in M. Carver (ed.), *The Cross Goes North*, pp. 463–82

20. DR 110, DR 209, DR 220, Vg 150; Tentative: Sö 140

21. *Thrymskvida*, verse 30

22. S. Degge, 'An Account of an Humane Skeleton of an Extraordinary Size, Found in a Repository at Repton in Derbyshire …', *Philosophical Transactions* 35 (1727–8), pp. 363–5; M. Biddle and B. Kjølbye-Biddle, 'Repton and the "Great Heathen Army", 873–4', in Graham-Campbell et al. (eds), *Vikings and the Danelaw*, pp. 45–96

23. Degge, 'An Account of an Humane Skeleton'

24. R. Bigsby, *Historical and Topographical Description of Repton* (1854)

25. J. Richards et al., 'Excavations at the Viking Barrow Cemetery at Heath Wood, Ingleby, Derbyshire', *The Antiquaries Journal* 84 (2004), pp. 23–116; cf. Biddle and Kjølbye-Biddle, who suggested – largely on account of the apparent stature of a number of the male skeletons – that many of the later bones were of Scandinavian origin, and were the recovered bones of earlier deceased members of the Viking army

26. According to the thirteenth-century *Chronicon Abbatiae de Evesham*, King Cnut had the relics of Wystan moved to Evesham in the early eleventh century (J. Sayers and L. Watkiss (eds and trans.), *Thomas of Marlborough: History of the Abbey of Evesham* (2003, Clarendon Press)); this is suspicious, however, on a number of levels (How did Wystan's relics survive the Viking takeover? What was the nature of the relics moved by Cnut, and how can we be sure they ever belonged to Wystan? Did Cnut ever move anything to Evesham, or did the monks of Evesham simply need a credible provenance for whatever mouldy old bones they had decided could usefully be attributed to an obscure saint? And so on)

27. If he can be equated with the Imair of the Irish chronicles, Ivar the Boneless had been active in the Irish Sea, on and off, during the 850s, 860s and 870s: C. Downham, *Viking Kings of Britain and Ireland* (2007, Dunedin). The *Annals of Ulster* record his death as 873, the year the *micel here* came to Repton. The tenth-century English chronicler Æthelweard states that he died in 870, but implies that his death came in England. *Ragnars saga Loðbrókar* claims that he was buried in Northumbria under a barrow (see Biddle and Kjølbye-Biddle, 'Repton', pp. 81–4)

28. 'Ynglinga saga', chapter 8 (*Heimskringla I*)

29. Ibn Fadlan; Lunde and Stone, *Ibn Fadlān and the Land of Darkness*, p. 51

30. Ibid., p. 53

31. Although ibn Fadlan recounts that a poor man was also burned in a small boat, and modest boat burials are known from Britain and Scandinavia; ibid., p.4

32. Ibid., p. 54

33. Although it is the diversity of Viking burial practice – as we have already begun to see – that is perhaps its most defining characteristic. N. Price, *Odin's Whisper: Death and the Vikings* (2016, Reaktion Books); also Price, 'Belief and Ritual'

34. *ASC* s.a. 876

Chapter 11: The Return of the King

1. G. K. Chesterton, *Ballad of the White Horse* (2010 [1911], Dover Publications), Book I

2. *VA*, 53

3. *Beowulf*, lines 102–4

4. *VA*, 92; see also the explanatory notes to the text in Keynes and Lapidge, *Alfred the Great*

5. Ibid.

6. *VA*, 55

7. *ASC* s.a. 874; *VA*, verse 48

8. *ASC* A s.a. 877; the events are also mentioned in all other versions of the *ASC* s.a. 877 (C s.a. 878) and *VA*, 49

9. Ibid.

10. *CA*, p. 42

11. *VA*, 52; see also *ASC* s.a. 878 (C s.a. 879)

12. *HSC*, 16

13. L. Simpson, 'The Alfred/St Cuthbert Episode in the Historia de Sancto Cuthberto: Its Significance for mid-Tenth Century English History' in G. Bonner, D. W. Rollason and C. Stancliffe (eds), *St Cuthbert, His Cult and His Community to AD 1200* (2002, Boydell & Brewer), pp. 397–412

14. *HSC*, 12–13

15. *ASC* s.a. 878 (C s.a. 879); *ASN* s.a. 878, p. 78; *VA*, 54, pp. 83–4 ; *CA*, p. 43; *EE*, 3144–56

16. Geoffrey Gaimar later claimed that his body was interred at a place called 'Ubbelawe' ('Ubbe's barrow') in Devon (*EE*, 3144–56)

17. *ASC* s.a. 878 (C s.a. 879)

18. *ASN*, s.a. 878

19. Lavelle, *Alfred's Wars*, pp. 55–106; J. Baker and S. Brookes, *Beyond the Burghal Hidage: Anglo-Saxon Civil Defence in the Viking Age* (2013, Brill), pp. 199–208; Halsall, *Warfare and Society*, pp. 40–133

20. Anglo-Saxon riddles could be surprisingly suggestive. For example, Riddle 44 in the *Exeter Book* is translated into prose by S. A. J. Bradley (*Anglo-Saxon Poetry*, p. 379) as follows: 'A curiosity hangs by the thigh of a man, under its master's cloak. It is pierced through in the front; it is stiff and hard and it has a good standing-place. When the man pulls up his own robe above his knee, he means to poke with the head of his hanging thing that familiar hole of matching length which he has often filled before.' Riddles 25 and 45 are also notoriously rude: all are translated by Bradley; see also K. Crossley-Holland, *The Exeter Book Riddles* (1993, Penguin) [the solution to Riddle 44 is 'Key']

21. The story of Finn and Hengest is told in two Old English poems, *Beowulf* and a fragment known as 'the Fight [or Battle] at Finnsburgh' (*ASPR* 6); it is a tale of divided loyalties, betrayal and revenge. The episode was discussed by Tolkien in a series of lectures, published after his death as 'Finn and Hengest: The Fragment and the Episode' (2006 [1982], HarperCollins)

22. For Anglo-Saxon beacon systems see D. Hill and S. Sharpe, 'An Anglo-Saxon Beacon System', in A. Rumble and D. Mills (eds), *Names, Places & People* (1997, Paul Wathius), pp. 97–108, and extensive discussion in Baker and Brookes, *Beyond the Burghal Hidage*

23. *VA*, 55–6

24. Baker and Brookes, *Beyond the Burghal Hidage*, pp. 186–7; J. Baker, 'Warrior and Watchmen: Place Names and Anglo-Saxon Civil Defence', *Medieval Archaeology* 55 (2011), pp. 258–9

25. Anderson, *The English Hundred Names: The South-Western Counties*, p. 152

26. P. H. Robinson, 'The Excavations of Jeffery Whitaker at Bratton Camp', *Wiltshire Archaeological and Natural History Magazine Bulletin* 25 (1979), pp. 11–13

27. A. L. Meaney, *A Gazetteer of Early Anglo-Saxon Burial Sites* (1964, Allen & Unwin), p. 266

28. *Beowulf*, lines 3137–49

29. T. J. T. Williams, 'The Place of Slaughter'; the place-name Edington (Eðandun) may have been used by the chronicler to suggest a reference to Alfred's grandfather Egbert and his achievements at Ellendun in 825, a victory that prefigured Alfred's own in establishing a greater West Saxon sphere of control (the alliteration, rhyme and equal syllabic count of the two place-names may also have helped to foster the comparison)

30. S290

31. Alfred's Will is translated in Keynes and Lapidge, *Alfred the Great* (pp.173–8); S1508; S765

32. NMR ST 95 SW 38

33. G. K. Chesterton, *Alarms and Discursions* (1910, Methuen)

34. Parker, *England's Darling*

35. Ibid., p. 195, n. 16

36. E. A. Freeman, *The History of the Norman Conquest of England*, 5 vols (1867–79, Clarendon Press), p. 51

37. See especially Parker, *England's Darling*, but also S. Keynes, 'The Cult of King Alfred the Great' in *Anglo-Saxon England* 28 (1999), pp. 225–356 and B. Yorke, *The King Alfred Millenary in Winchester, 1901* (1999, Hampshire County Council)

38. T. Shippey, *The Road to Middle-Earth: How J.R.R. Tolkien Created a New Mythology* (2005, 2nd edition, HarperCollins)

39. Shippey, *Road to Middle-Earth*, pp. 222–31; Tolkien, *On Fairy-Stories*; H. Carpenter, *The Inklings: C.S. Lewis, J.R.R. Tolkien, Charles Williams and their Friends* (2006, 4th edition, Harper Collins], pp. 42–5

40. G. K. Chesterton, 'The Blatchford Controversies' [1904], in D. Dooley (ed.), *The Collected Works of G.K. Chesterton*, vol. 1(1986, Ignatius Press)

41. Chesterton, *Ballad of the White Horse*

42. Parker, *England's Darling*

43. Carpenter (ed.), *The Letters of J.R.R. Tolkien*, No. 80, p. 92

Chapter 12: The Godfather

1. G. K. Chesterton, *Ballad of the White Horse* (2011 [1911], Dover Publications), Book VIII
2. An example of a mid-ninth-century Anglo-Saxon font survives at Deerhurst (Gloucestershire). R. Bryant, *Corpus of Anglo-Saxon Stone Sculpture: Vol. X, The Western Midlands* (2012, Oxford University Press), pp. 161–90
3. *VA*, 46, p. 85
4. E. Dümmler (ed.), *Epistolae Karolini Aevi*, vol. 2 (1895, Berlin), nos 134 and 137; J. H. Lynch, *Christianizing Kinship: Ritual Sponsorship in Anglo-Saxon England* (1998, Cornell University Press)
5. It is possible, however, that Alfred's son Edward was promoted to a 'kingship' – perhaps of Kent – later on; a charter which includes both Edward and Alfred lists him as *rex* on a Kentish charter's witness list (Alfred is designated *rex Saxonum*); Keynes, 'The Control of Kent', *Early Medieval Europe* 2.2 (1993), pp. 111–31
6. *VA*, 56; *ASC* s.a. 878 (C s.a. 879)
7. *ASC* s.a. 880 (C s.a. 881)
8. The evidence is fairly complex, but relates to the naming of moneyers unknown at established southern mints, die links between 'Alfred' coins and others, and the maintenance of a different weight standard. See M. A. S. Blackburn, 'Presidential Address 2004. Currency under the Vikings. Part 1: Guthrum and the Earliest Danelaw Coinages', *British Numismatic Journal* 75 (2005), pp. 18–43
9. G. Williams, 'Kingship, Christianity and Coinage: Monetary and Political Perspectives on Silver Economy in the Viking Age', in J. Graham-Campbell and G. Williams, *Silver Economy in the Viking Age* (2007, Left Coast Press), pp. 177–214
10. Alfred-Guthrum, 1
11. Keynes and Lapidge, *Alfred the Great*, p. 171 (although the dating of the treaty is open to revision: G. Williams, *pers. comm.*)
12. D. Hadley, *The Vikings in England: Settlement, Society and Culture* (2006, Manchester University Press), pp. 31–3; P. Kershaw, 'The Alfred-Guthrum Treaty: Scripting Accommodation and Interaction in Viking Age England', in D. M. Hadley and J. D. Richards (eds), *Cultures in Contact: Scandinavian Settlement in England in the Ninth and Tenth Centuries* (2000, Brepols), pp. 43–64
13. *ASC* s.a. 886 (C s.a. 887)
14. Alfred-Guthrum, 'Prologue'
15. Kershaw, 'The Alfred-Guthrum Treaty'; P. Foote, 'The Making of Angelcynn: English Identity before the Norman Conquest', *Transactions of the Royal Historical Society*, 6th Series, 6 (1996), pp. 25–49
16. Ibid. See also Downham, '"Hiberno-Norwegians" and "Anglo-Danes"'
17. *ASC* s.a. 871 (C s.a. 872); *VA*, 40
18. The large quantities of 'Anglo-Saxon' material culture at a Viking camp like Torksey might even be evidence of this (see following Chapter 13)
19. 'Sermon of the Wolf to the English', *EHD* (240)
20. Ibid.
21. Alfred-Guthrum, 5

22. S362; B. Yorke, 'Edward as Atheling', in N. J. Higham and D. H. Hill (eds), *Edward the Elder, 899–924* (2001, Routledge), pp. 25–39

Chapter 13: Rogue Traders

1. R. E. Howard, 'The Dark Man', *Weird Tales* (December 1931)
2. *VA*, 91
3. *VA*, 91
4. Nor was it any use bothering the king's ear with humiliating apologies, for – as Asser helpfully pointed out – 'what use is their accursed repentance, when it cannot help their slaughtered kinsfolk, nor redeem those captured from a hateful captivity, nor even occasionally be of use to themselves who have escaped, since they no longer have anything by which to sustain their own life?'; *VA*, 91
5. Ibid.
6. *VA*, 8, 11; see also the notes in Keynes and Lapidge, *Alfred the Great*, pp. 232, 234; the issues around Alfred's interactions with the pope are discussed in J. Nelson, 'The Problem of King Alfred's Royal Anointing', *Journal of Ecclesiastical History* 18.2 (1967), pp. 145–63
7. *ASC* A s.a. 853; this was evidently a good lesson in the political advantages that could be gained by turning powerful acquaintances into one's 'sons'
8. S. Irvine, 'The Anglo-Saxon Chronicle and the Idea of Rome in Alfredian Literature', and D. Hill, 'The Origins of Alfred's Urban Policies', in T. Reuter (ed.), *Alfred the Great* (2003, Ashgate), pp. 63–77; pp. 219–33
9. *VA*, 91
10. It only acquired that name in 1897 thanks to the intervention of the great legal scholar Frederic William Maitland: *Domesday Book and Beyond. Three Essays in the Early History of England* (1897, Cambridge University Press); D. Hill, 'The Burghal Hidage – the Establishment of a Text', *Medieval Archaeology* 13 (1969), pp. 84–92
11. The relationship of burhs to the territory that sustained them is drawn out in the greatest detail by Baker and Brookes, *Beyond the Burghal Hidage*; see also papers in D. Hill and A. Rumble (eds), *The Defence of Wessex: The Burghal Hidage and Anglo-Saxon Fortifications* (1996, Manchester University Press)
12. S. Keynes, 'Edward, King of the Anglo-Saxons', in N. J. Higham and D. H. Hill (eds), *Edward the Elder, 899–924* (2001, Routledge)
13. N. Brooks, 'The Unidentified Forts of the Burghal Hidage', *Medieval Archaeology* 8.1 (1964), pp. 74–90
14. J. Haslam (ed.), *Anglo-Saxon Towns in Southern England* (1984, Phillimore)
15. S. R. Bassett, 'The Middle and Late Anglo-Saxon Defences of Western Mercian Towns', *Anglo-Saxon Studies in Archaeology and History* 15 (2008), pp. 180–239
16. G. Williams (ed.), *A Riverine Site Near York: A Possible Viking Camp, and Other Related Papers* (forthcoming); M. A. S. Blackburn, 'The Viking Winter Camp at Torksey, 872–3', in M. A. S. Blackburn (ed.), *Viking Coinage and Currency in the British Isles* (2011, Spink), pp. 221–64; D. Hadley and J. D. Richards, 'The Winter Camp of the Viking Great Army, AD 872–3, Torksey, Lincolnshire', *The Antiquaries Journal* 96 (2016), pp. 23–67

17. P. Wallace, *Viking Dublin: The Wood Quay Excavations* (2015, Irish Academic Press); I. Russell and M. F. Hurley (eds), *Woodstown: A Viking-age Settlement in Co. Waterford* (2014, Four Courts Press)

18. I. Gustin, 'Trade and Trust in the Baltic Sea Area during the Viking Age', in J. H. Barrett and S. J. Gibbon (eds), *Maritime Societies of the Viking and Medieval World* (2016, Oxbow), pp. 25–40

19. Some of the most spectacular finds come from the Danish trading site of Hedeby, near the modern town of Schleswig in Germany; an introduction can be found in V. Hilberg, 'Hedeby: An Outline of Its Research History' in Brink with Price, *The Viking World*, pp. 101–11

20. *VA*, 91

21. Viking skulls from Gotland and Dorset have been found that display evidence of deliberate dental modification – horizontal striations filed into the tooth enamel of the front incisors; the purpose was presumably aesthetic; C. Arcini, 'The Vikings Bare Their Filed Teeth', *American Journal of Physical Anthropology* 128 (2005), pp. 727–33; L. Loe, A. Boyle, H. Webb and D. Score (eds), *'Given to the Ground': A Viking Age Mass Grave on Ridgeway Hill, Weymouth* (2014, Dorset Natural History and Archaeological Society)

22. Deliberately bent coins are a relatively common feature of silver coins in Viking hoards, as are those with evidence of what is known as 'nicking' and 'pecking' (deliberate gouges on the surface of the metal); all are methods of testing the purity of the silver: see, for example, M. Archibald, 'Testing' in J. Graham-Campbell (and contributors), *The Cuerdale Hoard and Related Viking-Age Silver and Gold from Britain and Ireland in the British Museum* (2013, 2nd edition, British Museum Press), pp. 51–63

23. R. Gameson (ed.), *The Codex Aureus: An Eighth-Century Gospel Book: Stockholm, Kungliga Bibliotek, A. 135* (2001, Rosenkilde and Bagger)

24. Trans. University of Southampton [http://www.southampton.ac.uk/~enm/codexau.htm]

25. Certainly, the concept of the trading settlement (emporium) was no novelty: Scandinavia had several, and they would continue to develop throughout the tenth century until the largest of them (Hedeby, Birka etc) took on major significance for North Sea economy and the wealth of Scandinavian monarchies – but this was little different to the situation that had pertained in the Anglo-Saxon kingdoms when the Vikings had arrived (D. Skre, 'The Development of Urbanism in Scandinavia' and sub-papers, in Brink with Price, *The Viking World*, pp. 83–145)

26. G. Williams, 'Towns and Identities in Viking England', in D. M. Hadley and L. Ten Harkel (eds), *Everyday Life in Viking-Age Towns: Social Approaches to Towns in England and Ireland, c.800–1100* (2013, Oxbow), pp. 14–34

Chapter 14: Danelaw

1. *Egil's Saga*, 68

2. 'And Guthrum, the northern king, whose baptismal name was Æthelstan, died; he was King Alfred's godson, and he lived in East Anglia and was the first to settle that land.' *ASC* A s.a. 890

3. See R. Abels, *Alfred the Great: War, Kingship and Culture in Anglo-Saxon England* (1998, Routledge) and Lavelle, *Alfred's Wars*

4. *ASC* s.a. 893–7

5. *ASC* s.a. 897

6. *ASC* A s.a. 901

7. This epithet was coined in the late tenth century by Wulfstan the Cantor to distinguish him from Edward the Martyr; the proliferation of Edwards in royal nomenclature later led to the adoption, from 1215, of a numbering system for Edwards. This, however, started at the number one, with Edward I, disregarding the three – including Edward the Confessor – who had preceded him. The complex science of Edwardology gave medieval historians all sorts of bother: see M. Morris, *A Great and Terrible King: Edward I and the Forging of Britain* (2008, Hutchinson), pp. xv–xvi

8. 'The Will of King Alfred' in Keynes and Lapidge, *Alfred the Great*, pp. 173–8; R. Lavelle, 'The Politics of Rebellion: The Ætheling Æthelwold and West Saxon Royal Succession, 899–902', in P. Skinner (ed.), *Challenging the Boundaries of Medieval History: The Legacy of Timothy Reuter* (2009, Brepols)

9. 'The Will of King Alfred' in Keynes and Lapidge, *Alfred the Great*, pp. 173–8

10. *ASC* s.a. 901

11. Attributed to Ambrosius Aurelianus by Gildas and Bede, but to Arthur in British sources of the ninth century. *Ex.* 26.1; *HE* i.16; *HB*, 56; E. Guest, *Origines Celticae*, Vol. II (1883), pp. 186–93

12. *ASC* A s.a. 901

13. *ASC* D s.a. 901

14. *ASN*

15. Lavelle, 'The Politics of Rebellion'

16. *ASC* A, D s.a. 905

17. *CA*, p. 52

18. The other soft-bearded prince was presumably Beorhtsige, son of Beorhtwulf – whom the *ASC* describes as ætheling (prince). It may be, as some have argued (see Lavelle, 'Politics of Rebellion'), that this Beorhtwulf was a scion of the dispossessed royal house of Mercia, a possibility which puts rather a different complexion on the whole affair; one could quite readily frame the rebellion as armed resistance to a tyrannical and overreaching West Saxon regime: an attempt to restore the pre-878 geopolitics of Britain

19. An initiative that took off in 2001 – the Great Fen project – aims to recreate a much more substantial tract of fen habitat over the next fifty years (http://www.greatfen.org.uk/about/introduction)

20. M. Gelling and A. Cole, *The Landscape of Place-Names* (2014, 3rd edition, Stamford)

21. *Kormáks saga*, chapter 10 (translated by W. G. Collingwood and J. Stefánsson, *The Saga of Cormac the Skald* (Viking Club, or Society for Northern Research), pp. 65–7)

22. Olav Bø, 'Hólmganga and Einvigi: Scandinavian Forms of the Duel', *Medieval Scandinavia* 2 (1969), pp. 132–48

23. T. S. Jonsson, 'Thingvellir as an Early National Cente' in O. Owen (ed.), *Things in the Viking World* (2012, Shetland Amenity Trust), pp. 42–53

24. W. Morris, '1871 and 1873 Journeys to Iceland' in M. Morris (ed.), *The Collected Works of William Morris*, vol. 8, p. 77

25. *Völuspá*, 57, p. 13
26. J. Byock, 'The Icelandic Althing: Dawn of Parliamentary Democracy', in J. M. Fladmark (ed.), *Heritage and Identity: Shaping the Nations of the North* (2002, Donhead), pp. 1–18
27. A. Wawn, *The Vikings and the Victorians* (2000, Boydell), pp. 277–9
28. *Lǫgsǫgumaðr*: the law-speaker was an elected elder/local bigwig whose role was to memorize local law, preside over the *thing* and impose its judgements
29. O. Olwen, 'Things in the Viking World – An Introduction' in Olwen (ed.), *Things*, pp. 4–29; G. Fellows-Jensen, 'Tingwall: The Significance of the Name' in D. Waugh and B. Smith (eds), *Shetland's Northern Links: Language and History* (1996, Scottish Society for Northern Studies), pp. 16–29
30. B. Smith, 'Shetland's Tings', in Olwen (ed.), *Things*, pp. 68–79
31. A. Johnson, 'Tynwald – Ancient Site, Modern Institution – Isle of Man', in Olwen (ed.), *Things*, pp. 104–17 (see also: https://www.thingsites.com/thing-site-profiles/tynwald-hill-isle-of-man)
32. 'Óláfs saga Helga', chapter 80 (*Heimskringla II*)
33. *ASC* A s.a. 909
34. *ASC* A s.a. 911
35. See Baker and Brookes, *Beyond the Burghal Hidage* for the development of Anglo-Saxon civil defence
36. Now a village/suburb on the outskirts of Wolverhampton (West Midlands)
37. *CA*, p. 53
38. Downham, *Viking Kings*
39. Ibid. The sources for this period are woefully inadequate, and the historical arguments surrounding the Uí Ímair are complex
40. D. Horowitz, *Notes and Materials on the Battle of Tettenhall 910 AD, and Other Researches* (2010, self-published)
41. A separate set of annals that provides additional specifics relating to Æthelflæd's remarkable military leadership, later inserted in the C manuscript of the *ASC*
42. *ASC* A s.a. 912
43. J. Haslam, 'The Location of the Burh of Wigingamere – Reappraisal', in A. R. Rumble and A. D. Mills (eds), *Names, People and Places* (1977, Watkins), pp. 114–18
44. *ASC* A s.a. 921
45. *ASC* A s.a. 921
46. *ASC* A s.a. 922
47. *ASC* A s.a. 922
48. *VA*, I, see also Keynes and Lapidge, *Alfred the Great*, p. 225

Chapter 15: Lakeland Sagas

1. W. G. Collingwood, *The Book of Coniston* (1897, Titus Wilson)
2. L. Abrams and D. N. Parsons, 'Place-names and the History of Scandinavian Settlement in England' in J. Hines, A. Lane and M. Redknapp (eds), *Land, Sea and Home: Proceedings of a Conference on Viking-Period Settlement* (2004, Northern Universities Press), p. 380
3. D. Coggins, K. J. Fairless and C. E. Batey, 'Simy Folds: An Early Medieval Settlement Site in Upper Teesdale. Co. Durham', *Medieval Archaeology 27*

(1983), pp. 1–26; D. Coggins, 'Simy Folds: Twenty Years On' in J. Hines et al. (eds), *Land, Sea and Home*, pp. 326–34; A. King, 'Post-Roman Upland Architecture in the Craven Dales and the Dating Evidence' in Hines et al. (eds), *Land, Sea and Home*, pp. 335–44 (see also the broader discussion in Hadley, *The Vikings in England*, pp. 81–144)

4. King, 'Post-Roman Upland Architecture', p. 340
5. Dawn Hadley (*The Vikings in England*, pp. 99–104) provides an excellent overview of the issues and literature
6. See, for example, the names of moneyers working during the reign of Æthelred (R.978–1013, 1014–1016); J. J. North, *English Hammered Coinage*, Vol. 1 (1994, Spink), pp. 162–7
7. K. Leahy and C. Paterson, 'New Light on the Viking Presence in Lincolnshire: The Artefactual Evidence' in Graham-Campbell et al. (eds), *Vikings and the Danelaw*, pp. 181–202
8. J. F. Kershaw, *Viking Identities: Scandinavian Jewellery in England* (2013, Oxford University Press)
9. J. Geipel, *The Viking Legacy: The Scandinavian Influence on the English Language* (1975, David and Charles); see also S. D. Friðriksdóttir, *Old Norse Influence in Modern English: The Effect of the Viking Invasion* (2014, unpublished BA dissertation, University of Iceland) [http://skemman.is/stream/get/1946/17234/40268/1/Old_Norse_Influence_in_Modern_English.pdf]
10. M. Townend, *The Vikings and Victorian Lakeland: The Norse Medievalism of W. G. Collingwood and His Contemporaries* (2009, Cumberland and Westmorland Antiquarian and Archaeological Society), p. 67
11. A. Wawn, 'The Spirit of 1892: Saga-Steads and Victorian Philology', *Saga-Book of the Viking Society* 23 (1992), pp. 213–52; M. O. Townend, 'In Search of the Lakeland Saga: Antiquarian Fiction and the Norse Settlement in Cumbria', in D. Clark and C. Phelpstead (eds), *Old Norse Made New: Essays on the Post-Medieval Reception of Old Norse Literature and Culture* (2007, Viking Society for Northern Research); Wawn, *The Vikings and the Victorians*, pp. 308–9
12. Townend, *The Vikings and Victorian Lakeland*, pp. 33–4
13. For his part, Collingwood seems to have felt no sadness at his eclipse, though it was noted by contemporaries (Townend, *The Vikings and Victorian Lakeland*, pp. 44–5)
14. Ibid., p. 258
15. My own first-edition copy of *Scandinavian Britain*, I recently discovered to my great delight, is *ex libris* Robert Eugen Zachrisson, the famous Swedish philologist and place-name scholar: he signed the flyleaf in 1924 and, at some point, added a personalized bookplate. Zachrisson was responsible for a good deal of pioneering work on, among other things, the etymology of English place-names (including their Norse origins) and the Norman influence on modern English pronunciation; he is chiefly remembered today, however, for an ingenious attempt to overhaul the spelling of English with a system which he called Anglic. Although at the time it received considerable support, with reports (in Anglic) noting that 'leeding eduekaeshonists and reprezentativz of the Pres, who hav been prezent at

korsez givn in Stockholm and Uppsala, hav testified that Anglic is a moest efektiv meenz of teeching English to forinerz', it was – perhaps mercifully – doomed to fail. A sage voice in the *Spectator*, commenting approvingly on these initiatives, observed in 1931 that 'Language can be, and often is, the greatest obstacle to thought, and nowhere is this truer than in thinking about language itself.' There may be something in that, but it was not, thankfully, enough to overcome the 'instinct of every educated man [...] to rise in revolt against any attempt to interfere with a custom sanctified by long usage' (A. Lloyd James, 'Anglic: An International English', *Spectator*, 14 August 1931, p. 7: http://archive.spectator.co.uk/article/15th-august-1931/7/anglic-an-international-english)

16. Townend, *The Vikings and Victorian Lakeland*, p. 157
17. For the tenor of the debate see, e.g., D. Austin, 'The "Proper Study" of Medieval Archaeology', in D. Austin and L. Alcock (eds), *From the Baltic to the Black Sea: Studies in Medieval Archaeology* (1990, Routledge), pp. 9–42; G. R. W. Halsall, *Cemeteries and Society in Merovingian Gaul: Selected Studies in History and Archaeology, 1992–2009* (2010, Brill), pp. 49–88
18. Kitchin exemplifies in many ways the late Victorian churchman and antiquary. His improbable list of accomplishments is a record of his talents, but also serves as an indicator of the excellent connections and oodles of free time that his position in society afforded. He was a fellow of the Society of Antiquaries and a member of the British Archaeological Society, to whom he delivered learned disquisitions on (among other things) the font at Winchester Cathedral and 'The Burial-place of the Slavonians' at North Stoneham Church in Hampshire; he was dean of Winchester Cathedral (from 1883) where he contributed significantly to the restoration of the reredos, and was later dean of Durham Cathedral (from 1894) and chancellor of Durham University (from 1908) until his death in 1912; he wrote the popular hymn 'Raise High the Cross' as well as a three-volume history of France and a biography of Pope Pius II; as a young man in 1863 he was private tutor to Frederik, Crown Prince of Denmark (later crowned King Frederik VIII). He also, and probably this is the least interesting of all his many achievements despite being the one for which he is most remembered, fathered Xie Kitchin, the favourite child-muse of Charles Lutwidge Dodgson, aka Lewis Carroll; indeed, he was himself photographed by Dodgson and the result can be found in the archives of the National Portrait Gallery. A copy of the same likeness hangs on the wall of my study: I am contemplating his magnificent mutton-chops even as I type
19. Wawn, *The Vikings and the Victorians*, p. 128; Townend, *The Vikings and Victorian Lakeland*, p. 52
20. Townend, *The Vikings and Victorian Lakeland*, pp. 189–90; M. Townend, *Language and History in Viking Age England: Linguistic Relations between Speakers of Old Norse and Old English* (2002, Brepols Publishers)
21. G. W. Kitchin, 'The Statesmen of West Cumberland' in *Ruskin in Oxford, and other Studies* (1904, John Murray), p. 56; Isaac Kitchin, my great-great-great-great-grandfather, was born in Cumberland and educated at St Bees Theological College

22. When Kitchin spoke of the 'love of liberty and simple independence, bred in the blood of men of mountain regions' he was also, of course, including himself in this blood-borne character portrait (Ibid.)
23. Quoted in Townend, *The Vikings and Victorian Lakeland*, p. 192
24. D. Griffiths, *Vikings of the Irish Sea* (2010, Oxbow), p. 23
25. W. G. Collingwood, *The Book of Coniston*, pp. 1–7
26. Ibid.
27. Ibid.

Chapter 16: A New Way
1. W. G. Collingwood, *Thorstein of the Mere* (1895, Edward Arnold), p. 1
2. C. Krag, 'The early unification of Norway' in K. Helle, (ed.), *The Cambridge History of Scandinavia, Volume I: Prehistory to 1520* (2003, Cambridge University Press), pp. 184–9
3. e.g. 'Haralds saga ins hárfagra', chapter 19 (*Heimskringla I*)
4. Krag, 'The early unification of Norway'
5. Griffiths, *Vikings of the Irish Sea*, p. 51
6. K. A. Hemer, J. A. Evans, C. A. Chenery, A. L. Lamb, 'No man is an island: Evidence of pre-Viking Age migration to the Isle of Man', *Journal of Archaeological Science* 52 (2014), pp. 242–9; Charles-Edwards, *Wales and the Britons*, pp. 14, 148–52
7. *AU* s.a. 878
8. *AU* s.a. 839
9. A. Woolf, *From Pictland to Alba, 789–1070* (2007, Edinburgh University Press), pp. 9–10
10. Ibid., p. 66
11. Ibid.
12. Ibid., pp. 93–8
13. *CKA*
14. *The Annals of St-Bertin*, s.a. 847; J. Nelson (ed. and trans.), *The Annals of St-Bertin* (1991, Manchester University Press)
15. *CKA*; *AU* s.a 866
16. *AC* s.a. 870
17. *AU* s.a. 870
18. *AU* s.a. 871
19. *CKA*; Woolf, *From Pictland to Alba*, p. 109
20. *AU* s.a. 873
21. Downham, *Viking Kings*
22. Glasgow Community Planning Partnership, *Govan Area Partnership Profile 2016* (2016, Glasgow City Council) [https://www.glasgow.gov.uk/councillorsandcommittees/viewSelectedDocument.asp?c=P62AFQDNT1Z3DN0GUT]
23. K. Goodwin, 'The Glasgow Effect', *Guardian* (10 June 2016) [https://www.theguardian.com/cities/2016/jun/10/glasgow-effect-die-young-high-risk-premature-death]
24. 'No City for Old Men', *The Economist* (25 August 2012) [http://www.economist.com/node/21560888]
25. A. Campsie, 'Everything You Need to Know About Clyde Shipbuilding', *Scotsman* (30 March 2016) [http://www.scotsman.com/heritage/

people-places/everything-you-need-to-know-about-clyde-shipbuilding-1-4086097]

26. I say probably, because, as others have observed, none have survived in their original settings: H. Williams, 'Hogbacks: The Materiality of Solid Spaces' in H. Williams, J. Kirton and M. Gondek (eds), *Early Medieval Stone Monuments: Materiality, Biography, Landscape* (2015, Boydell & Brewer)

27. J. T. Lang, 'Hogback Monuments in Scotland', *Proceedings of the Society of Antiquaries of Scotland* 105 (1976), pp. 206–35

28. See, for example, the largest of the brooches, BM 1909,0624.2; Graham-Campbell, *The Cuerdale Hoard*, contains considerable detail on the contents of the hoard and its protracted recovery

29. NMS X.FC 8 [http://www.nms.ac.uk/explore/stories/scottish-history-and-archaeology/hunterston-brooch/]

30. The Irish of the tenth century had their own word for this phenomenon: *Gallgoídil* ('foreigner Gaels'); see Downham, '"Hiberno-Norwegians" and "Anglo-Danes"'

31. *CKA*

32. *AU* s.a. 900; *CS* s.a. 900

33. The development of the Scottish nation is a complex subject to which this book cannot hope to do justice; for the fullest narrative treatment, see Woolf, *From Pictland to Alba*

Chapter 17: The Pagan Winter

1. *Völuspá*, v. 45 (author's translation)

2. There's no point searching for it – it was flattened after excavation in 1946 to facilitate the progress of farm traffic

3. For discussion of the burial see: http://skaldic.abdn.ac.uk/db.php?table=mss&id=22110&if=myth; see also Wilson, *Vikings in the Isle of Man*

4. These are often, mistakenly, assumed to have been used as the figureheads of ships. Five such pillars accompanied the occupants of the Oseberg burial into the grave-mound, and we can presume therefore that they had some purpose in the most elaborate Viking death theatre. Handles at the base of the posts would have allowed these objects to be attached to another object – what, why or precisely how is unknown

5. Lunde and Stone, *Land of Darkness*, pp. 47–8

6. H. E. Davidson, 'Human Sacrifice in the Late Pagan Period of North-Western Europe' in M. O. H. Carver (ed.), *The Age of Sutton Hoo: The Seventh Century in North-Western Europe* (1992, Boydell Press), pp. 331–40

7. Griffiths, *Vikings of the Irish Sea*, pp. 81–3

8. Reynolds, *Anglo-Saxon Deviant Burial*

9. Ibid.

10. Price, 'Belief and Ritual'

11. Price, *The Viking Way*

12. The list of objects is adapted from that published by the Norwegian Museum of Cultural History [http://www.khm.uio.no/english/visit-us/viking-ship-museum/exhibitions/oseberg/in-the-grave.pdf]

13. [http://www.khm.uio.no/english/visit-us/viking-ship-museum/exhibitions/oseberg/in-the-grave.pdf]

14. Canmore ID 9383
15. Sjøvold, *The Viking Ships in Oslo*
16. The story of the discovery of the grave is dramatic in itself, involving a race against time by archaeologists, bracing themselves against the dire Orkney storms that sweep off the Atlantic in the autumn; Graham-Campbell, *Vikings in Scotland: An Archaeological Survey* (1998, Edinburgh University Press), pp. 138–40; see also http://www.orkneyjar.com/history/scarboat/
17. Broadly speaking: as ever, the details are contradictory and late
18. C. Abram, *Myths of the Pagan North: The Gods of the Norsemen* (2011, Bloomsbury), pp. 157–68
19. Maughold (I) [202A]; Kirk Michael (III) [215]; individual Manx runestones are identified by the parish in whch the stone was found, followed by the individually assigned number of the stone within that parish. The Rundata reference is provided in square brackets
20. This is not to say that Scandinavian runestones never feature carved crosses – they frequently do – but the style and form of these monuments is usually very different
21. Braddan (IV) [193A]
22. Andreas (II) [184]
23. Ballaugh [189]
24. Andreas (I) [183]
25. Braddan (III) [191B]
26. Braddan (II) [191A]
27. The twin ravens Huginn ('thought') and Muninn ('memory') were key attributes of Odin; see, esp., *Gylfaginning* 38
28. W. S. Calverley and W. G. Collingwood, *Notes on the Early Sculptured Crosses, Shrines and Monuments in the Present Diocese of Carlisle* (1899, Titus Wilson); C. A. Parker, *The Ancient Crosses at Gosforth and Cumberland* (1896, Elliot Stock)
29. *Gylfaginning* 51
30. *Völuspá* 59, p. 13
31. *Völuspá* 65, p. 14
32. Abram, *Myths of the Pagan North*, p. 165
33. Price, 'Belief and Ritual'
34. Abram, *Myths of the Pagan North*

Chapter 18: The Great War

1. *APV*, lines 14–17, 115–20
2. Halfdan didn't last long according to the *HSC*. In punishment for his depredations 'he began to rave and stink so badly that his whole army drove him from its midst'
3. *ASC* s.a. 875; see also *CKA* and Woolf, pp. 111–12
4. *ASC* s.a. 875
5. *HSC*, ch. 13
6. Ibid.
7. Oswiu of Northumbria (r. 640–70) was the king whose reign can be said to have ushered in that kingdom's Golden Age. It was Oswiu who had killed (against all expectations) the notorious pagan king of Mercia, Penda, in the battle of the Winwæd in 655 – an act which had made him the most

powerful man in Britain and overturned the last bastion of non-Christian belief on the island. During his reign he had also presided over the Synod of Whitby (664), a meeting which formally brought religious observance into line with Roman practice, and Northumbria firmly into the orbit of the mainstream religious–political–intellectual circles of post-Roman Europe. For any king to be proclaimed at a place named Oswiu's Hill would have been to make an unmistakable political statement and, indeed, we may well wonder if this place had a long association with the public acknowledgement of kingship in Northumbria; see also discussion and references in Hadley, *The Vikings in England*, pp. 37–41

8. Hadley, *The Vikings in England*, pp. 44–54
9. Ibid.; Blackburn, *Viking Coinage*; G. Williams, 'Kingship, Christianity and Coinage'
10. G. Williams, 'Kingship, Christianity and Coinage'
11. This identification has at times been contested, see Downham, *Viking Kings*, pp. 94–6
12. *AU* s.a. 902
13. *AC*; *FA*
14. *FA* s.a. 907; see also Lavelle, *Alfred's Wars*, pp. 230–3
15. Hadley, *The Vikings in England*, p. 177
16. *AU* s.a. 913
17. *AU* s.a. 917; *ASC* s.a. 924
18. J. Graham-Campbell, *The Viking-Age Gold and Silver of Scotland*, AD *850–1100* (1995, National Museums of Scotland); Graham-Campbell, *Cuerdale*
19. T. Hugo, 'On the Field of Cuerdale', *Journal of the British Archaeological Association* 8 (1853), pp. 330–5; Graham-Campbell, *Cuerdale*, pp. 21–37
20. *ASC* D, s.a 926, *ASC* E s.a 927; *GRA* 1.3
21. Woolf, *From Pictland to Alba*, p. 158; *EHD* (104)
22. *ASC* D s.a. 926
23. North, *English Hammered Coinage*
24. Woolf, *From Pictland to Alba*, pp. 164–6
25. *HR*
26. *ASC* D s.a. 934; Woolf, *From Pictland to Alba*, p. 161, n. 73
27. *CC* s.a. 934
28. *GRA* 1.3
29. *APV*, lines 132, 143, 162
30. *AFM* s.a. 937
31. *APV*, lines 40, 60
32. *Brunanburh*, lines 61–5; M. Alexander (trans.), *The Earliest English Poems* (1991, Penguin), p. 97
33. According to Æthelweard, writing in the late tenth century; *CA*, p. 54
34. *ASC* E, s.a. 937
35. A. Tennyson, 'The Battle of Brunanburh', lines 1–14 in C. Ricks (ed.), *The Poems of Tennyson* III (1987, Longman), pp. 18–23
36. *AU* s.a. 939

Chapter 19: Bloodaxe
1. *Egil's Saga*, 80, v.4 (p. 159)

2. *The Chronicle of Melrose*, s.a. 941; J. Stevenson (ed. and trans.), *A Mediaeval Chronicle of Scotland: The Chronicle of Melrose* (1991 [reprint of 1850s edition], Llanerch)
3. *ASC* A s.a. 942
4. See Chapter 20
5. *ASC* A s.a. 944
6. *CC* s.a. 946
7. G. Williams, *Eirik Bloodaxe*
8. Ibid.
9. 'Hakonar saga góða', chapter 3 (*Heimskringla I*)
10. *ASC* D s.a. 948
11. *ASC* A s.a. 948
12. M. Shapland, *Buildings of Secular and Religious Lordship: Anglo-Saxon Tower-nave Churches* (2012, unpublished PhD thesis, UCL)
13. R. Hall, *Viking Age England* (2004, The History Press), p. 283; R. Hall, 'York', in Brink with Price (eds), *The Viking World*, pp. 379–84; Hadley, *The Vikings in England*, pp. 147–54; the full Coppergate excavations are published in twenty-one volumes by York Archaeological Trust
14. Hall, 'York', p. 376
15. Q. Mould, I. Carlisle and E. Cameron, *Leather and Leatherworking in Anglo-Scandinavian and Medieval York* (2003, CBA/York Archaeological Trust)
16. Olaf ended his days as a monk on Iona, not the retirement one might imagine for a Viking king – it shows how much the cultural compass had shifted since the Viking Age began
17. G. Williams, *Eirik Bloodaxe*
18. *FH* I
19. 'Hakonar saga góða', chapter 4 (*Heimskringla I*)
20. *Grímnismál*, verse 36
21. Slightly adapted from R. D. Fulk, '(Introduction to) Anonymous, Eiríksmál' in D. Whaley (ed.), *Poetry from the Kings' Sagas 1: From Mythical Times to c. 1035* (2012, Brepols), p. 1003
22. Price, *The Viking Way*

Chapter 20: Wolves

1. 'Sermon of the Wolf to the English', *EHD* (240)
2. *ASC* CDE s.a. 1006
3. No Anglo-Saxon remains have been found, although the former use of the mound as a Bronze Age burial mound has been confirmed: A. Sanmark and S. J. Semple, 'Places of Assembly: New Discoveries in Sweden and England', *Fornvännen* 103. 4 (2008), pp. 245–59
4. The walking dead appear frequently in Old Norse literature, most famously in *Grettis saga*: see G. A. High (trans.) and P. Foote (ed.), *The Saga of Grettir the Strong* (1965, Dent)
5. *Egil's Saga*, 61, v.11 (p. 116)
6. T. J. T. Williams, 'For the Sake of Bravado in the Wilderness'; E. M. Lacey, *Birds and Bird-lore in the Literature of Anglo-Saxon England* (2013, unpublished PhD thesis, UCL), pp. 114–19
7. T. J. T. Williams, 'Landscape and Warfare in Anglo-Saxon England and the Viking Campaign of 1006', *Early Medieval Europe* 23 (2015), pp. 329–59

8. The stones replaced an even older timber monument; J. Pollard, 'The Sanctuary, Overton Hill, Wiltshire: A Re-examination', *Proceedings of the Prehistoric Society* 58 (1992), pp. 213–26. J. Pollard and A. Reynolds, *Avebury: The Biography of a Landscape* (2002, Tempus)

9. *CC*

10. This Maccus may conceivably have been the man who ended King Eric's life in 954: there is no way to be certain. More importantly, this reference represents the first time that a kingdom of the isles is mentioned in contemporary records. A political entity that brought together the Scandinavian-settled territories of north-western Britain and the Irish Sea was coming into view for the first time

11. Lavelle, *Alfred's Wars*

12. *CC*; *FH*

13. *ASC* D s.a. 959; in the twelfth century, William of Malmesbury helpfully elaborated on Wulfstan's sentiments by explaining how the English had picked up the despicable foreign habits of drunkenness from the Danes, effeminacy from the Dutch and ferocity from the Germans (*GRA*)

14. *EHD* (41)

15. Ibid.

16. *FH*

17. *Maldon*, lines 46–56; trans. Bradley, *Anglo-Saxon Poetry*

18. J. R. R. Tolkien, 'The Homecoming of Beorhtnoth Beorhthelm's Son' in *The Tolkien Reader* (1966, Ballantine)

19. Neil Price, in a personal communication to me, suggested the old-fashioned word 'vim' – a particularly apposite approximation

20. *Maldon*, lines 96–100

21. Halsall, *Warfare and Society*, p. 183

22. *Maldon*, lines 312–19

23. J. D. Niles, 'Maldon and Mythopoesis', *Mediaevalia* 17 (1994), pp. 89–121; *Wanderer*

24. Other, smaller sums were dished out on an ad hoc basis; S. Keynes, 'The Historical Context' in D. Scragg (ed.), *The Battle of Maldon AD 991* (1991, Blackwell), p. 100

25. See J. Gillingham, '"The Most Precious Jewel in the English Crown": Levels of Danegeld and Heregeld in the Early Eleventh Century', *English Historical Review* 104 (1989), pp. 373–84 and 'Chronicles and Coins as Evidence for Levels of Tributes and Taxation in Late Tenth and Eleventh Century England', *English Historical Review* 105 (1990), pp. 939–50

26. J. C. Moesgaard, 'The Import of English Coins to the Northern Lands: Some Remarks on Coin Circulation in the Viking Age based on New Evidence from Denmark', in B. J. Cook, G. Williams and M. Archibald (eds), *Coinage and History in the North Sea World, c. AD 500–1250: Essays in Honour of Marion Archibald* (2006, Brill)

27. E.g. coins of Svein Estridsen (r. 1047–76)

28. *ASC* CDE s.a. 999

29. S. Keynes, 'The Declining Reputation of King Æthelred the Unready' in D. Hill (ed.), *Ethelred the Unready: Papers from the Millenary Conference* (1978, BAR), pp. 227–53; L. Roach, *Æthelred* (2016, Yale University Press)

30. *ASC* A s.a. 1001

31. *ASC* CDE s.a. 1001
32. *ASC* CDE s.a. 1002; A. Williams, '"Cockles amongst the Wheat": Danes and English in the Western Midlands in the First Half of the Eleventh Century', *Midland History* 11 (1986), pp. 1–22
33. *EHD* (127); S909
34. A. M. Pollard, P. Ditchfield, E. Piva, S. Wallis, C. Falys and S. Ford, '"Sprouting like Cockle amongst the Wheat": The St Brice's Day Massacre and the Isotopic Analysis of Human Bones from St John's College, Oxford', *Oxford Journal of Archaeology* 31 (2012), pp. 83–102

Chapter 21: Mortal Remains
1. *EHD*, 48
2. *ASC* CDE s.a. 1013
3. T. Lindkvist, 'Early Political Organisation: Introductory Survey' in K. Helle (ed.), *The Cambridge History of Scandinavia, Volume 1: Prehistory to 1520* (2003, Cambridge University Press)
4. See chapters by I. Skovgaard Petersen ('The Making of the Danish Kingdom'), C. Krag ('The Early Unification of Norway'), M. Stefánsson ('The Norse Island Communities of the Western Ocean'), T. Lindkvist ('Kings and Provinces in Sweden') in Helle (ed.), *The Cambridge History of Scandinavia*
5. A. Pedersen, 'The Royal Monuments at Jelling' in G. Williams et al., *Vikings: Life and Legend*, pp. 158–60
6. *The Dream of the Rood* (*ASPR* 2); Alexander, *Earliest English Poems*, p. 87
7. *ASC* CDE s.a. 1012
8. *CC* s.a. 1013, p. 477
9. *ASC* CDE s.a. 1014
10. *ASC* CDE s.a. 1016
11. *ASC* D s.a. 1057
12. *CC* s.a. 1016, pp. 487–9
13. *ASC* E s.a. 1016
14. *ASC* D s.a, p. 152
15. *Enc.* 10; pp. 24–7
16. Ibid.; pp. 26–7
17. Ibid.
18. Ibid.
19. *Enc.* 11; pp. 28–9
20. They carry, in fact, some of the earliest uses of the term 'England' to be found anywhere, proof that the concept of England had become sufficiently concrete by the eleventh century to be common currency outside Britain (Jesch, *Ships and Men*, pp. 70–7)
21. U194
22. U344; see discussion in S. B. F. Jansson, *Swedish Vikings in England: The Evidence of the Rune Stones* (1966, UCL)
23. Jansson, *Swedish Vikings in England*, pp. 12–13
24. DR337
25. Loe et al., *Given to the Ground*
26. N 184

27. M. O. Townend, *English Place-Names in Skaldic Verse* (1998, English Place-Name Society), p. 31
28. *ASC* CDE s.a. 1017
29. *HA*, vi. 13, pp. 360–1
30. *Enc.* ii.15; *CC* s.a. 1017
31. In addition to a previous wife, an English noblewoman named Ælfgifu
32. M. Biddle and B. Kjølbye-Biddle, 'Danish Royal Burials in Winchester: Cnut and his Family' in Lavelle and Roffey (eds), *The Danes in Wessex*, pp. 231–2
33. Ibid., p. 232

Epilogue
1. B. E. Crawford, *The Northern Earldoms: Orkney and Caithness from AD 870 to 1470* (2013, Birlinn); Woolf, *From Pictland to Alba*, pp. 275–311

FURTHER READING

The Vikings and Viking Age Scandinavia

S. Brink with N. Price (eds), *The Viking World* (2008, Routledge)

J. Graham-Campbell and G. Williams, *Silver Economy in the Viking Age* (2007, Left Coast Press)

K. Helle (ed.), *The Cambridge History of Scandinavia, Vol. 1: Prehistory to 1520* (2003, Cambridge University Press)

J. Hines, A. Lane and M. Redknapp (eds), *Land, Sea and Home: Proceedings of a Conference on Viking-Period Settlement* (2004, Northern Universities Press)

J. Jesch, *Ships and Men in the Late Viking Age: The Vocabulary of Runic Inscriptions* (2001, Boydell & Brewer)

J. Jesch, *The Viking Diaspora* (2015, Routledge)

N. Price, *The Vikings* (2017, Routledge)

P. Sawyer (ed.), *Oxford Illustrated History of the Vikings* (1997, Oxford University Press)

B. B. Smith, S. Taylor and G. Williams (eds), *West over Sea: Studies in Scandinavian Sea-Borne Expansion and Settlement Before 1300* (2007, Brill)

G. Williams, P. Pentz and M. Wemhoff (eds), *Vikings: Life and Legend* (2014, British Museum Press)

Myths and Beliefs

C. Abram, *Myths of the Pagan North: The Gods of the Norsemen* (2011, Bloomsbury)

A. Andrén, K. Jennbert and C. Raudvere (eds), *Old Norse Religion in Long-term Perspectives: Origins, Changes, and Interactions* (2006, Nordic Academic Press)

N. Price, *The Viking Way* (2017, 2nd edition, Oxbow)

Vikings in Britain and Ireland

J. Carroll, S. H. Harrison and G. Williams, *The Vikings in Britain and Ireland* (2014, British Museum Press)

C. Downham, *Viking Kings of Britain and Ireland* (2007, Dunedin)

J. Graham-Campbell (and contributors), *The Cuerdale Hoard and Related Viking-Age Silver and Gold from Britain and Ireland in the British Museum* (2013, 2nd edition, British Museum Press)

K. Holman, *The Northern Conquest: Vikings in Britain and Ireland* (2007, Signal Books)

England

J. Graham-Campbell, R. Hall, J. Jesch and D. N. Parsons (eds), *Vikings and the Danelaw: Select Papers from the Proceedings of the Thirteenth Viking Congress* (2001, Oxbow)

D. M. Hadley, *The Vikings in England: Settlement, Society and Culture* (2006, Manchester University Press)

D. M. Hadley and J. D. Richards (eds), *Cultures in Contact: Scandinavian Settlement in England in the Ninth and Tenth Centuries* (2000, Brepols)

R. Hall, *Viking Age England* (2004, The History Press)

R. Lavelle and S. Roffey (eds), *The Danes in Wessex* (2016, Oxbow)

Scotland

B. Crawford, *Scandinavian Scotland* (1987, Leicester University Press)

J. Graham-Campbell, *Vikings in Scotland: An Archaeological Survey* (1998, Edinburgh University Press)

A. Woolf, *From Pictland to Alba, 789–1070* (2007, Edinburgh University Press)

Western Britain and the Irish Sea

D. Griffiths, *Vikings of the Irish Sea* (2010, Oxbow)

M. Redknapp, *Vikings in Wales: An Archaeological Quest* (2000, National Museum of Wales Books)

D. Wilson, *Vikings in the Isle of Man* (2008, Aarhus University Press)

The Viking Revival

D. Clark and C. Phelpstead (eds), *Old Norse Made New: Essays on the Post-Medieval Reception of Old Norse Literature and Culture* (2007, Viking Society for Northern Research)

M. Townend, *The Vikings and Victorian Lakeland: The Norse Medievalism of W. G. Collingwood and His Contemporaries* (2009, Cumberland and Westmorland Antiquarian and Archaeological Society)

A. Wawn, *The Vikings and the Victorians* (2000, Boydell)

ILLUSTRATION CREDITS

Integrated

p. 50 Norwegian propaganda for the SS by Harald Damsleth, 1940–5

p. 55 Engraving of the Hilton at Cadboll stone by Charles Carter Petley, 1812 (*Wikimedia Commons*)

p. 118 Snorri Sturluson, as imagined by the artist Christian Krohg, 1899 (*Wikimedia Commons*)

p. 177 Alfred the hero, as envisioned by Morris Meredith Williams, 1913 (*Photo © Historical Picture Archive/Corbis/Corbis via Getty Images*)

p. 219 A thing in progress, Halfdan Egedius, 1899 (*Wikimedia Commons*)

p. 221 Þorgnýr the law-speaker holds forth; Christian Krohg, 1899 (*Wikimedia Commons*)

p. 234 Frontispiece to *Thorstein of the Mere*, drawn by W. G. Collingwood, 1895

p. 251 Hogbacks at St Thomas', Brompton, drawn by W. G. Collingwood, 1927

p. 269 Vidar and Fenrir on the Gosforth Cross; Julius Magnus Petersen, 1913 (*Wikimedia Commons*)

p. 276 Coin of Cnut of Northumbria, *c*.900–5 (*© Gilli Allan, 2017*)

p. 277 A Northumbrian coin of the 920s (*© Gilli Allan, 2017*)

p. 326 The crucifixion face of the Jelling runestone; Julius Magnus
   Petersen, 1869–71 (*from Peder Goth Thorsen, De danske
   runemindesmærker, 1879, National Museum of Denmark*)

Plate sections

A ninth-century gravestone from the monastery at Lindisfarne
   (*Photo by CM Dixon/Print Collector/Getty Images*)
The late-tenth-century Gjermundbu helmet (*© 2017 Kulturhistorisk
   museum, UiO/CC BY-SA 4.0*)
A lead weight, adapted from a piece of ecclesiastical metalwork
   (*© The Trustees of the British Museum*)
The Inchmarnock 'hostage stone' (*© Headland Archaeology (UK)
   Ltd*)
The reconstructed Viking Age long-house at Borg, Lofoten (*Hemis/
   Alamy Stock Photo*)
The Gokstad Ship, built *c*.890, now housed in Oslo (*© Thomas
   J. T. Williams*)
The Coppergate Helmet, a Northumbrian helmet forged between 750
   and 775 (*courtesy of York Museums Trust: http://
   yorkmuseumstrust.org.uk/CCBY-SA4.0*)
Sigurd pierces the body of the dragon Fáfnir from beneath on a
   runestone from Ramsund, Södermanland (Sweden)
   (*robertharding/Alamy Stock Photo*)
Ivar and Ubbe setting sail for England (*Photo by Fine Art Images/
   Heritage Images/Getty Images*)
Wayland's Smithy in *c*.1900 (*Photo by Henry Taunt/English Heritage/
   Arcaid/Corbis via Getty Images*)
The village of East Lyng, attached to the Isle of Athelney (*© Historic
   England Archive*)
A reconstruction of the Viking camp at Repton (*© Compost Creative*)
An Anglo-Saxon font at Deerhurst in Gloucestershire (*Colin
   Underhill/Alamy Stock Photo*)
The early medieval crypt of St Wystan's Church at Repton (*Heritage
   Image Partnership Ltd/Alamy Stock Photo*)

A reconstruction of the Viking camp at Torksey (© *Compost Creative*)

The eighth-century *Stockholm Codex Aureus* (*Art Collection 3/Alamy Stock Photo*)

Tingwall: an assembly site on Mainland, Shetland (© *Thomas J. T. Williams*)

A hogback stone from Govan Old Church, Glasgow (*Glasgow University Library, Special Collections*)

The whalebone plaque from the tenth-century boat burial at Scar, Orkney (*World History Archive/Alamy Stock Photo*)

Thorwald's Cross, at Andreas Parish on the Isle of Man, depicts – on one side – Odin swallowed by the wolf Fenrir at *Ragnarök*. The other side displays an apparently Christian scene (*Photographs by CM Dixon/Print Collector/Getty Images*)

The Cuerdale Hoard (© *The Trustees of the British Museum*)

Coins of Viking rulers in England (© *The Trustees of the British Museum*)

Reconstruction of tenth-century dwellings at Coppergate, York (© *York Archaeological Trust*)

Northey Island, Essex (© *Terry Joyce; Creative Commons Attribution Share-alike license 2.0*)

The Sanctuary monument at Overton Hill, Wiltshire, erected around 2000 BC, as drawn by William Stukeley in 1723 (*Chronicle/Alamy Stock Photo*)

The inscription on a runestone in Väsby, Uppland (Sweden) (*Berig, Wikimedia Commons*)

Stone found in 1852 in the graveyard of St Paul's Cathedral, London (*Granger Historical Picture Archive/Alamy Stock Photo*)

A mass grave of over fifty decapitated men, most of them originally from Scandinavia, found near Weymouth in Dorset in 2011 (© *Oxford Archaeology*)

Cnut and his queen, Emma (Ælfgifu), depicted in the pages of the eleventh-century *Winchester Liber Vitae* (*Photo by Photo12/UIG/ Getty Images*)

INDEX

Gevninge, Zealand, 85
Gildas (British monk), 7
Gjermundbu helmet, 38, 84
Glasgow, 249–50, 251, 252
Glastonbury, Somerset, 36
Gloucester, 166, 226, 286
Godfred, Danish king, 69–70, 71, 72, 78
Gododdin, 7
Gokstad ship, near Oslo, 96, 261
Gorm the Old, King of Denmark, 326–7
Gosforth, Cumbria, 267–8, 269, 278
Govan, Glasgow, 249–50, 251, 252
Greek world, maps in, 21
Grimsby, Lincolnshire, 230
Grove, Barry, 55
Gunnhild, wife of Eric, 292
Guthfrith, Viking king of Northumbria, 273–6
Guthfrith, Viking king of Northumbria (grandson of Ivar), 280, 281–2, 283, 290
Guthrum, Viking chieftain, 158, 161, 165, 176, 192; accord with Alfred, 182–4, 185, 188–9, 190, 193, 231; baptism of, 180–1, 182–4; death of (890), 210; as king of East Anglia, 185–7, 189
Gwent, 10
Gwynedd, 10, 279

Haakon the Good, King of Norway, 292
Hadrian I, Pope, 70
Hæsten, Viking warlord, 210–11
Hafrsfjord battle-site, Norway, 46–7
Hägar the Horrible (comic strip), 37
Hákon, King of Norway, 117
Halfdan Long-leg, 115
Halfdan (son of Ragnar Loðbrók), 110, 118, 143, 158, 161, 273
Halfdan the Black, 46, 50
Halton, Lancashire, 108
Harald Bluetooth, King of Denmark, 323, 326–8
Harald Finehair, King of Norway, 46, 115, 242–3, 291, 292
Harald Hard-ruler, King of Norway, 44, 342
Harald, King of England (son of Cnut), 337

Haraldsson, Maccus, 309
Harold Godwineson, King of England, 337
Harthacnut, King of England (son of Cnut), 337, 338, 339
Harun al-Rashid, 71
Hastings, Battle of (1066), 337–8
Heahmund, bishop of Sherborne, 143
Heath Wood cemetery, Derbyshire, 158–9, 160, 262
Hebrides, 241, 244, 245, 253, 261
Hedeby, Schleswig, 32, 69, 72, 79, 114
'hell', origins of word, 25
Hengestdun (Kit Hill), Cornwall, 86–9, 90, 91
Henry II, King, 232
Hereford, 199, 226
Hertford, 226
Higbald, Bishop, of Lindisfarne, 30–1
High Middle Ages, 324
Hilton of Cadboll stone, 54–6
historical record, xx, xxii; absence of Viking written sources, 13; *Annals of St-Bertin*, Frankish, 247, 253; *Annals of St Neots*, 212; *Annals of Ulster*, 246, 248, 285, 286; and battle of Brunanburh, 284–5; British written sources, 13; *Chronicles of the Kings of Alba*, 285; early vernacular written records, 7; *Fragmentary Annals of Ireland*, 279; *Frankish Royal Annals*, 69, 71; geographical origins of Vikings, 14–15, 66–7; lack of detail in Scotland, 245–6; Scotland in, 282–3; *see also Anglo-Saxon Chronicle*; Asser, bishop of Sherborne
hogbacks, 250–1, *251*, 252, 254, 262
hólmgang (ritual duel), 215–16, 217, 222–3
Holy Roman Empire, 67–72, 75–6
homosexuality, 153–4
horned helmet myth, 37–8, 44
Howard, Robert E., 'The Dark Man' (1931), 36
Hrothgar, legendary Danish king, 4, 22, 34
Hughes, Thomas, *Tom Brown's School Days*, 127, 134
Hunterston Brooch, 253–4
Huntingdon, Cambridgeshire, 227
Hywel, king of the West Welsh, 282

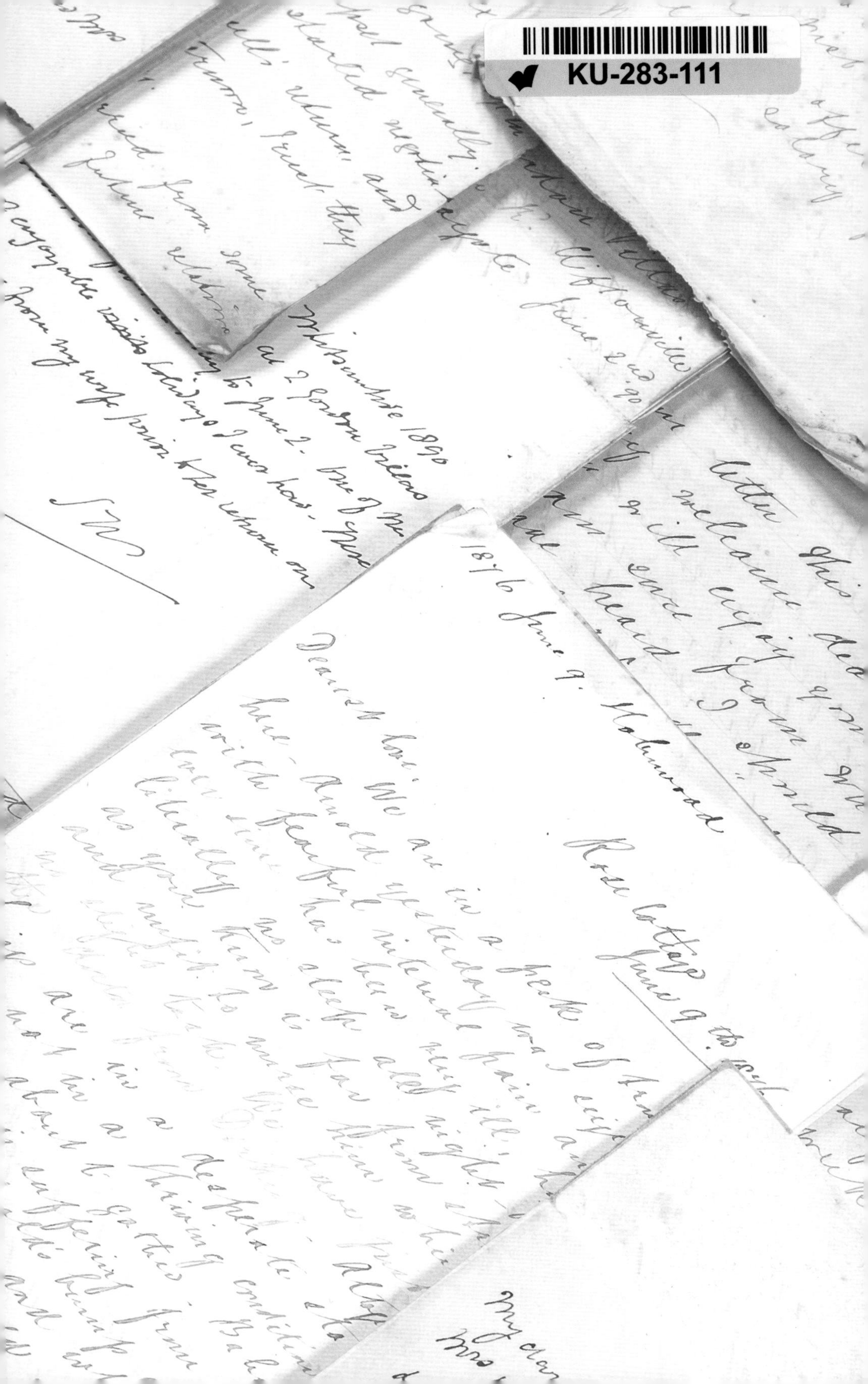

1876 June 9. Holmwood

Rose Cottage
June 9th

Dearest Rose,

We are in a peck of troubles...

Warrior Queens & Quiet Revolutionaries

KATE MOSSE

WARRIOR QUEENS & QUIET REVOLUTIONARIES

How Women (Also)
Built The World

MANTLE

First published 2022 by Mantle
an imprint of Pan Macmillan
The Smithson, 6 Briset Street, London EC1M 5NR
EU representative: Macmillan Publishers Ireland Ltd, 1st Floor,
The Liffey Trust Centre, 117–126 Sheriff Street Upper,
Dublin 1, D01 YC43
Associated companies throughout the world
www.panmacmillan.com

ISBN 978-1-5290-9219-6

1 3 5 7 9 8 6 4 2

A CIP catalogue record for this book is available from the British Library.

Typeset by Palimpsest Book Production Ltd, Falkirk, Stirlingshire
Printed and bound by CPI Group (UK) Ltd, Croydon, CR0 4YY

Visit **www.panmacmillan.com** to read more about all our books
and to buy them. You will also find features, author interviews and
news of any author events, and you can sign up for e-newsletters
so that you're always first to hear about our new releases.

To my beloved Greg and Martha and Felix, as always

for my dear friend and publisher
Maria Rejt

and for my great-grandmother
Lily Watson (1849–1932)

Contents

Martha Louisa 'Lily' Green with her mother Elizabeth, c. 1855

Author's Note

IT BEGAN WITH MY first edition of *Lady into Woman: A History of Women from Victoria to Elizabeth II* by **Vera Brittain** (1893–1970), stumbled upon in a second-hand bookshop. Published in 1953, it was billed as the 'first comprehensive history of women to appear for twenty years'. The jacket is torn and the pages musty from living too long in attics and rooms left abandoned but, in its pages, my younger self was introduced to women I'd never heard of: the Japanese businesswoman **Yone Suzuki** (1852–1938), said in 1918 to be the richest woman in the world; or **Vijaya Lakshmi Pandit** (1900–1990), the Indian ambassador to Moscow and Washington, and President of the United Nations General Assembly; or **Frances Power Cobbe** (1822–1904), the Irish suffragist, founder of animal advocacy and anti-vivisection organizations, and lifelong partner of the Welsh sculptor **Mary Lloyd** (1819–1896).

The more I read this, and books like it, the more I was swept up into all the magnificent under-heard stories. Finally, at the age of sixty, I was ready to contribute my own collection of missing names to this library of extraordinary women.

There are very many women who could have been included in the pages that follow. The Population Reference Bureau (PRB) estimates that, since 190,000 BCE, some 117 billion people have been born on earth, so that's a lot of women jostling to be heard . . . but celebrating some names is better than celebrating none.

Any book of this kind is, by its very nature, selective. Although

Britain and North America are particularly well represented, I've worked to include as diverse a mixture of women from as many cultures as I could manage, from almost every epoch, women outstanding in every field. My aim was to paint a global and broad-brush picture of what history could look like if women's achievements had been documented as thoroughly as men's accomplishments. The book is also personal – including women from antiquity who've captured my imagination or kept me company through my life – and although some of the women are little known or now barely visible, others will be familiar. It's not a question of either/or, but rather my attempt to expand the existing historical record.

My choices were guided, in the first instance, by the thousands of women worldwide who were nominated for our global #WomanInHistory campaign. I was publishing *The City of Tears* in the third and, in some ways, most challenging lockdown in the UK in January 2021. There seemed no end in sight – a rising death toll, fear, such loss and grief, incompetent and dishonest political leadership – and in those grim winter days, I wanted to do something positive to mark the launch of the novel. Because I couldn't be out meeting readers, I reached out to them on social media with a simple question – who is the one woman from history you would like to celebrate or you think should be better known?

Within days, we had thousands of nominations, from women and men from all over the world, celebrating women of every period of history, known and less known: an email nominating the third-century ruler **Zenobia**, queen of the Palmyrene Empire in Syria, who ruled as regent for her son after her husband's assassination; a nomination from a young woman in China introducing me to the writer **Ding Ling**; a passionate message from a Russian contributor sharing her admiration for the work of poet **Marina Tsvetaeva**; a nomination from a Belfast student who'd read a biography of **Mary Elmes**, the Irish woman who saved Jewish children from Nazi concentration camps.

They were each and all admiring, positive, vibrant stories of amazing women. The campaign took on a life of its own and was a wonderful, much-needed reminder that most people want to build up, not pull down, to find connections with others and be part of something larger. That remembrance of the past and of those in whose footsteps we walk is essential for thriving in the present.

As the lockdown deepened in February, the list continued to grow. We published the first one thousand names on International Women's Day, 8 March 2021, but the names kept flooding in from all over the world – the nineteenth-century Jewish-Italian writer **Rachel Luzzatto Morpurgo**, the first woman to publish poetry in Hebrew in over two thousand years; the Black-Trinidadian dancer, choreographer and anthropologist **Pearl Primus**; the freedom rider **Pauli Murray**, who'd taken a stand against the racist Jim Crow laws of the segregated American South in the 1940s, over a decade before **Rosa Parks**. I was learning so much and I didn't want to stop quite yet. I started to believe there was a book to be written. Not fiction, but rather a celebration of these extraordinary women who'd entered my life. I began to dig deeper, supplementing that original list of thousands of names through my own reading, support from researchers, biographers, historians and social anthropologists, biographies, histories, online sources and university archives, campaigning organizations, novels, films and plays. The guiding principle was simple – to shine a spotlight on exceptional women and to light the touch paper for readers to seek out others; to marvel at amazing lives from all over the world and from every era.

So, this book is a celebration, yes, but it's also a detective story. The final piece of the puzzle was deciding to discover more about my own missing woman from history – my great-grandmother **Lily Watson** (1849–1932). As I dug deeper into family history, I realized that her life, and lost reputation – she was a well-known novelist in her day – was the glue I needed. I turned sleuth, spending the summer and autumn of 2021 making phone calls, tracking down diaries, letters, photographs, out-of-print works until, little by little, I started to get a sense of who Lily had been and how she, too, had disappeared from the record.

Warrior Queens & Quiet Revolutionaries is not intended to be read straight through like a novel but, rather, each chapter dipped into. It's a dictionary of names, a starting point. Chapters are divided by category – warriors, writers, inventors – rather than by alphabet. Within each chapter, which are broadly chronological, I've highlighted a handful of trailblazers, amplified by shorter pen portraits – sometimes only a line or two – of many, many more. Sometimes, there are no connections between the women featured other than the fact they were women and achieved extraordinary things, and the number of names might be overwhelming. But I've deliberately included as many as possible – there are nearly a thousand in all – precisely so readers' curiosity will be stimulated to seek out more comprehensive biographies, autobiographies and works of scholarship beyond the pages of this book. Each woman is described on her own terms (rather than through her relationships with others), but I hope each story will create a ripple effect, giving a sense of eras and movements, of connections, influences and trends. In this way, I've tried to paint a broader picture of innumerable women's lives at any given time, in any given place. The first time a woman is mentioned, her name is followed with her dates of birth and death if known.

Wherever possible, I have referred to those who appear in the way they chose to identify themselves. I have used accepted honorifics or born names the first time a woman appears, but after that refer to them by their commonly used name or nickname. In accordance with contemporary dating methods, I have used BCE (Before Common Era) and CE (Common Era) rather than BC (Before Christ) and AD (Anno Domini).

Reluctantly, I took the decision to include only a very tiny number of the amazing women and girls who are making history right now, and to whom we owe so much. That book – we might call it *Living Legends* – is an even bigger project, and ever changing, so for another volume.

The further back in history one goes, the harder it is to find consistent spellings and verifiable biographies – particularly of women who are routinely left out of the official record. I've worked to find balance – of background, culture, period of history, country of origin, age – but inevitably English-language sources are dominant. I'm very grateful to translators and historians who've shared their work. In the twenty-first century, with the endless visible tabulating of our lives, there will be more easily accessible biographical information to investigate (though it won't all be honest!), but only provided technology finds a way to store and catalogue the information available online and on social media. When researching further back in time, we're dependent on documents being curated and saved. So much has been lost.

Kate.

Kate Mosse
October 2022

The deed box, discovered in December 2021, containing nearly five hundred letters between Lily and Sam

Foreword

**'a book of myths
in which
our names do not appear'**

'Diving into the Wreck',
Adrienne Rich, 1973

THIS BOOK HAS BEEN a long time coming, though I didn't realize it.

It was there, in the child I was in dusty classrooms, motes of chalk floating in the still afternoon air, the corridors hushed and empty, waiting for the bell to ring. It was there in double English, as I spent lessons in the company of Alexander Pope, Thomas Hardy, William Shakespeare and Charles Dickens, not quite understanding why **Jane Austen** (1775–1817) was the odd one out. It was also there in music history – Debussy and Beethoven, Schubert and Shostakovich. Most of all, it was there in history: kings and generals, engineers and inventors, Fleming and Bell, Gladstone and Palmerston, Caesar and Napoleon.

God bless Good Queen Bess.

I went to a two-thousand-strong girls' comprehensive school in Sussex in the 1970s, the result of a recent merger between the old grammar and secondary modern schools. I remember leaking taps, the smell of Bunsen burners in the chemistry lab, long corridors, a well-stocked library. There were some male teachers, but the majority were women who were passionate about education for girls. Women who believed in the importance of girls having their own space to learn and to have the chance to become the selves they wanted to be: Miss Lowther, who'd taught in a missionary school in South East Asia in the 1930s; Miss King, our head teacher; Miss Dickinson and Mrs Hooper, who both inspired my love of history; Miss Herd, who taught me the violin in her freezing terraced house near the Catholic church with only a single bar heater for warmth during long December afternoons.

The corresponding boys' school was on the other side of the hedge on the playing fields, the frontier patrolled each lunchtime by teachers. Though we did joint school concerts from time to time, it was a predominantly female world. The curriculum was varied and ambitious, but also traditional and old-fashioned. The book plates in our textbooks and library books, the names and date stamps of the girls who'd held these same primers, studied these same words, followed the same rubrics going back years, the scribbled notes in pencil in margins, all glimpses of how a girl was educated. Generations of pupils at Chi High learned about photosynthesis, atoms and elements, the laws of thermodynamics and sonata form.

And yet . . .

It's hard to notice absence. It's an undercurrent, an awareness that something's skew-whiff, like a splinter beneath the skin, trying to put one's finger on what's wrong, what's a little off. And all this was in the 1970s, a decade of change. The Equal Pay Act had come into force the year before I first put on that green blazer, when the world was trying to change, but it took me years to see what had been niggling at me for all that time at school. Though I was sometimes lonely – and arrived early and left late to avoid being picked on by the groups of older girls who hung around the bus station smoking, with their skirts rolled up and boyfriends loitering – they were, for the most part, happy years. I loved school.

Those languid slow days of the 1970s are still vivid to me. The red-brick Victorian angles of the old grammar-school building, the cast-iron windows propped open at the top with a long wooden pole; the temporary Nissen huts with slippery narrow steps; the swimming pool with slime on the surface of the unheated water; the smell of waxed floors in the hall and the sly hint of cabbage in the maths classroom after lunch. As I look back, all the images coalesce and settle themselves into a coherent story. We make sense of things, we speed time up, we forget the boredom of those days, the isolation. We turn it all into our own history.

And then my world got bigger. When I left school in 1980, I knew more or less nothing. I'd learned how to regurgitate facts successfully. I'd studied history books and classic novels, poetry and musical scores. I'd shambled through Latin translation with more enthusiasm than rigour, but I was an innocent in the real world and had been nowhere much: camping holidays in Normandy and the New Forest, a hotel in the Channel Islands, an orchestra trip to Chartres and a Girl Guides trip to Ostend, several times to Newlands Valley in the Lake District. And I was loved, encouraged to think that the person I wanted to become – whoever she might be – was worthwhile.

It wasn't until I arrived at university that I met girls who, from the cradle, had been made to feel second best, or who had been treated differently from their brothers. And it wasn't until I started to read more widely, and think more critically, that I realized that my world, which felt equal and in no way restricted, was not the world everyone inhabited. I was introduced to new writers, among them **Maya Angelou, Marilyn French, Nawal El Saadawi, Flannery O'Connor, Betty Friedan, Dale Spender, Germaine Greer, Simone de Beauvoir, Andrea Dworkin, Mary Daly, Casey Miller** and **Kate Swift, Angela Y. Davis, Toni Morrison, Robin Morgan, Gloria Steinem, Mary Wollstonecraft, Audre Lorde** and **Adrienne Rich**. The kaleidoscope shifted, the fractal images realigned.

Was it that simple?

It's not, of course, how things happen. It is usually a gradual opening of one's eyes to realize we're being shown a partial view of the world. Or rather, women and men alike were only being told one half of the story.

Once you've noticed the absence, it's obvious. So blindingly obvious that you can't believe you didn't notice it before. How did I not see, quite simply, that the world I lived in, my day-to-day experience, didn't match the one about which we were being taught in our history books, English curriculum, science papers?

There were exceptions, of course – a kind of pervasive myth of a unique and extraordinary woman to balance the platoons of men. I came to understand later that this is another part of the misleading narrative. Think back to your classroom, to the roll call of inventors and politicians, military leaders and scientists, philosophers and composers, thinkers and mystics, and ask yourself this question:

Where were the women?

From textbooks and reference books in libraries, from the documents we seek out in archives and museums, it's evident how easily women's achievements vanish from the official record. It's a cliché to say that history is written by the victors, though nonetheless true for all that. But it's also written by those with access to pen and paper, to the opportunity to write or publish, to prioritize. As a writer of historical fiction, who spends a fair bit of time in archives and libraries, I'd add that history is often written with an agenda – to prove just cause, to prove superiority on the grounds of gender, age, race, physical ability, faith, tradition. To shore up power.

But beyond that, we have to ask why are women's contributions and experiences so routinely overlooked or misattributed or undervalued? Is it accident, design, politics, careless neglect? Is it because recorded history has, for the most part, been traditionally vested within institutions of learning – monasteries, male-only colleges and universities – where women were not allowed?

As time went by, I began to wonder what it was about women that made the authors of written history so reluctant to celebrate their achievements. Is it a question of rewriting history to suit the customs of the time so that a woman who behaves differently is not recorded? Is it the lack of opportunity, of a family wanting to safeguard her legacy? All of these reasons, or none?

In the modern era, with the range of technologies available, one would hope that it would be easier to redress the imbalance of representation. Sadly, the same bias persists. There is still an undervaluing of women's contributions and achievements. On Wikipedia, the world's most successful online encyclopaedia (which I greatly admire), a 2018 survey found that – across all language platforms – some 90 per cent of editors were men, only 8.8 per cent women and 1 per cent identifying as other. (In English-language Wikipedia, the figure rose to 13.6 per cent female editors.) A 2021 study found that, in April 2017, 41 per cent of biographies nominated for deletion were about women, despite the fact that only 19 per cent of the 1.5 million biographies on the site were about women. Wikipedia is trying to address some of the issues, but as an organization they are far from untypical: in the *Oxford Dictionary of National Biography*, in September 2021, there were 64,451 biographical articles about men and only 9,315 about women . . .

'No person is your friend who demands your silence, nor denies your right to grow.'

Alice Walker

At the heart of the beautiful and fierce poem quoted at the beginning of this chapter by **Adrienne Rich** (1929–2012) is this question: who decides whose names get to be written in the 'book of myths' and who is left out? In other words, 'what is history?' Who makes it, who chooses what matters and what does not? How is it recorded or lost or distorted? When the collection *Diving into the Wreck* won the National Book Award for Poetry in 1974, Rich shared it with her fellow nominees **Audre Lorde** (1934–1992) and **Alice Walker** (b. 1944). The three poets had written a joint statement and agreed that whoever won would accept the award on behalf of 'all the women whose voices have gone and still go unheard in a patriarchal world . . .'

So how do we begin to put back all the missing stories, all the overlooked and under-heard stories? How do we acknowledge and honour them fairly and with respect for endeavour, stamina and perseverance? And how do we put back those whose achievements have been misattributed or misappropriated? In science, it's known as the 'Matilda Effect', the bias against acknowledging the achievements of female scientists whose work has been – or is – misattributed to their male colleagues. First described by American suffragist, science writer and abolitionist **Matilda Joslyn Gage** (1826–1898) in 1870, the term was coined in 1993 by Professor **Margaret W. Rossiter** (b. 1944). It's a phenomenon that holds true in other areas of women's endeavour, too . . .

This book you hold in your hands is an attempt to answer some of these questions. I am not an historian and this is not a book of history, but rather a personal collection of the names of women who inspire or intrigue (or sometimes horrify!) me. The intention is not to write something definitive – that's impossible and, besides, there's a mighty selection of wonderful books out there, as well as social media campaigns and podcasts doing just that. It's also not about ignoring the amazing men who also have done extraordinary things. But I am curious about those women in whose footsteps we walk – which is why I've included as many names as I could squeeze in – to make this a genuine celebration of women's unsung achievements through the ages. This book is a celebration, not a history.

It's also a family memoir, a personal voyage of discovery inspired by the life of my great-grandmother **Lily Watson**.

Growing up, I'd heard stories – little more than rumours, really – that there had been a writer in the family before me. But my gentle father was never one for reminiscing and it was many years after my grandmother died that I became a novelist. By the time I wanted to know more, anyone who had known Lily was many years dead. My sketched ideas for *Warrior Queens & Quiet Revolutionaries* started to find their shape around this very personal quest to find out more about the great-grandmother I'd never known, and excavating her life was to become the spine of the book. I wanted to walk in her footsteps, to find out what kind of woman she'd been, what she thought and how she lived, what she had experienced over the course of her long life, stepping from one century into the next.

Lily was, I discovered, not only a novelist, but also an essayist, a columnist, a woman of faith and writer of children's stories. She sat on committees for education and welfare, and was well known and well respected in her day. Yet despite her contemporary visibility, it was nigh on impossible to find out anything about her. Lily, like so many women, has all but vanished from the official record. Step by step, I gathered material – borrowed photographs taken down from a cousin's wall, mentions in a visitors' book in the Lake District or notes of a committee meeting in London. I trawled online booksellers for copies of her books and journalism, hunted down diaries, applied for birth and death certificates – and, most of all, tracked down her letters – until I was ready to start putting her on the page.

My hope is that *Warrior Queens & Quiet Revolutionaries* will, in its turn, inspire as I have been inspired. It's a love letter to the importance of history and about how without knowing where we come from – truthfully and entirely – we cannot know who we are.

It's about advocating for women of the past, so as to make a more honest space for all the women and men of the present and future. It's about honouring those to whom we owe so much: trailblazers and quiet revolutionaries, women of conviction and faith, warrior queens and women of courage, mothers of invention, sisters, friends, lovers, mothers, aunts, carers, daughters, grandmothers, role models, fierce opponents and gentle strangers. So that, together, we can celebrate some of the extraordinary women who also built our world.

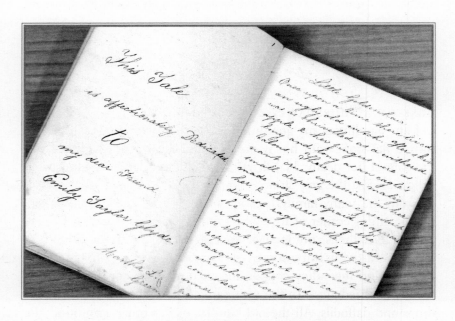

Lily's first novelette, Little Goldenhair: A Fairy Tale, *July 1861*

Lily

DUSK ON A THURSDAY evening in mid-July, 2021.

I am standing at my grandmother's grave at Newlands Church. A simple flat stone with her name – Beatrice Elizabeth Mosse – and the date of her death: 11 May 1981. A single celandine stands vivid yellow against the grey stone.

From the many family holidays in the 1970s and early 1980s to this beautiful corner of the Lake District, in the shadow of Causey Pike and Catbells, my teenage memories are mostly of cloud and drizzle. But, at this soft summer's end of day, the setting sun is painting the fells and the valley copper and gold. The shadows are long on the wild-daisied grass. In the springtime, there'll be a carpet of snow-drops and daffodils. All the old families of this quiet community lie here, their graves marked by a plain wooden cross or headstones of flint or stone. Tall sycamore trees covered in lichen, and a glorious copper beech, the colour of claret, stand among the yew and the ash. A drystone wall separates the churchyard from the fields. This evening, there is a light breeze, and the only sound is of cattle and my feet on the gravel path. No traffic, no voices.

The sixteenth-century church itself is very plain: a tiny white-washed roughcast building with a green-slate roof, simple and narrow arched windows – two with stained glass, the others plain – and a porch. A single bell. Inside, a wooden gallery, a reading desk, dark oak pews and a pulpit dated 1610. The substantial Bible on the lectern was given by my grandmother, Betty, in the early 1960s. It's inscribed: IN THANKS-GIVING FOR THE PRIVILEGE OF WORSHIPPING HERE DURING

MANY HOLIDAYS 1901–1961. Attached to the church is a square side room. From 1877 until 1967, it was the village school built by the parishioners of Newlands Valley, now it's a meeting room dedicated to parochial business and used as a place of quiet and reflection.

I am far from the first writer to have halted here awhile. It's only a short walk over the beck to the tiny hamlet of Littletown, where Mrs Tiggy-Winkle lived, created by Cumbrian writer and conservationist **Beatrix Potter** (1866–1943). And the great Lakeland poet, William Wordsworth, out walking with his daughter in 1826, glimpsed Newlands Church through the leaves:

> *How delicate the leafy veil,*
> *Through which yon house of God*
> *Gleams, 'mid the peace of this deep dale*
> *By few but shepherds trod!*

'To May', William Wordsworth, 1826

Then, as now. It is enchanting, it feels timeless.

I am here, for the first time in thirty years, to walk in the footsteps of my grandmother – a woman I knew and loved – and my great-grandmother, a woman I never met. The author of fourteen novels, volumes of poetry, devotional works, criticism and numerous articles, my great-grandmother Lily has left barely a footprint. All of her books are now out of print, she doesn't appear in anthologies of Victorian literature, the online references to her are few and hard to find. Yet she was celebrated and well known in her day, her novels eagerly anticipated. For more than fifty years she was a correspondent for *The Girl's Own Paper* (now *Woman Magazine*) and her most famous novel, *The Vicar of Langthwaite*, was reprinted in 1897 with a foreword by former prime minister William Gladstone. Her absence from the official record, from history, tells the story of so many women.

Lily was born Martha Louisa Green at East Reach, Taunton, in Somerset on 11 October 1849, the eldest of seven children of the Reverend Samuel Gosnell Green, a Baptist minister, and his wife Elizabeth Leader Collier. Her grandmother, Eliza Lepard, was descended from French Huguenots, who fled persecution and came to England in the seventeenth century. The earliest photograph I have, grainy and slightly blurred, shows Lily standing beside her mother. There is no date, but I think she must be six or seven, so taken in the mid-1850s. It shows a thin, pale girl with a direct stare, her hair pulled back from her face – or perhaps a page-boy cut, it's hard to tell – and a high forehead. Standing beside her mother, she's wearing a shift dress with a ruched panel and looks serious and determined. Her mother Elizabeth's expression is hard to read.

Lily's father was a well-known and well-respected preacher and teacher, the author of eighteen books of theology and biblical studies. He served in Somerset and Yorkshire, then Greater London. He was editorial secretary of the Religious Tract Society in London and a member of many philanthropic organizations. A scrapbook-cum-memoir written by my godmother Sister Katherine Maryel – my grandmother's niece – claims Lily was also descended from the Welsh privateer, plantation owner and notorious Lieutenant Governor of Jamaica in the 1670s, Henry Morgan. I can find no evidence for this beyond the fact that Lily often told pirate stories to her grandchildren. It's something else to bear in mind – that you might just as easily discover, or expose, appalling pieces of family history you'd rather not know.

As I began the steady work of piecing together Lily's life, it quickly became clear how difficult it could be to track down accurate dates, even for a middle-class Englishwoman whose family history might be comparatively well documented. It's what historians call the 'silence in the archives'. It's not just a matter of women's lives being overlooked or ignored, but often whether any documents were deposited in archives in the first place. If no one has chosen to preserve or protect documents – the verifiable details about a woman's experience – then the material simply won't be there for historians to find. As my detective work continued, I was to come up against this problem time and again – tantalizing references to diaries, to journals, to letters written to – and by – Lily that could no longer be found.

It was as if their voices simply faded into the darkness.

In a family tree I've inherited – handwritten on brittle and faded paper taped together – the boys are listed before the girls, regardless of the order in which they were born. The girls' dates are often missing and women, if they married, almost always changed their names, making them harder to keep in sight. Names are often misspelt, or spelt differently on different documents; and since a great deal of what is available online has been put there by family members, it is not always accurate. Hearsay, family myth, guesswork – all play their part. There was also a devastating piece of medical history I had known nothing about.

The only way to verify the precise date of Lily's birth was to apply for her birth certificate and, with the help of an archivist friend, map her history and those of her children through the census. I was oddly pleased to discover we were both born in October. Daft, I know, but Lily was already haunting me. For years, as I've said, I'd thought I was treading new ground as a novelist – the first to live by my pen in a family of teachers, solicitors and vicars. But now, it seemed, there had been a different story hiding in plain sight all along. Far from being the only author, I was one among several. This, too, I liked.

Lily always wrote. I have a small blue notebook dated 26 July 1861, and signed Martha L. Green, Lily's given name. It's a fairy story filled with her distinctive pen-and-ink line drawings and dedicated to a friend. On the title page of *Little Goldenhair: A Fairy Tale*, she describes herself as the authoress of *Tulip, May & Rosa, The Fairies, Rose's Pilgrimage, The Schoolboys* and *The Forbidden River*. The notebook contains illustrations of girls in ball gowns and flounced skirts, old women bent like a question mark in woods, a handsome hero with curled hair. The ink is faded and so, although Lily's handwriting is beautiful, it's hard to read. What's interesting is that it is more than a hundred pages, a short episodic novel rather than a long short story. The ambition and stamina of a writer is already there at the age of eleven.

Part of a fiercely Nonconformist family whose lives revolved around preaching and Chapel, Lily was well educated, familiar with Latin, Greek, Italian, French and German, knowledgeable about music and painting. Her experiences growing up in Yorkshire, attending school in Edinburgh, on walking holidays in Austria and Switzerland, would go on to form the framework for much of her adult fiction in the years to come. That, and her profound sense of faith and the importance of girls' education. Despite her conservative political views, Lily understood how much it mattered that women had the liberty and opportunity to speak for themselves.

But all this was still some way off.

∞

Top left: Ding Ling (1904–1986)
Top right: Nadezhda Mandelstam (1899–1980)
Bottom left: Ann Petry (1908–1997)
Bottom right: Rabia Balkhi (*c*. tenth century)

1

The Pen Is Mightier

'I would venture to guess that Anon, who
wrote so many poems without signing them,
was often a woman.'

A Room of One's Own
Virginia Woolf, 1929

IF MUCH OF WOMEN'S absence from history is down to the lack of
record, it's also due to the fact that women have not always been free
to express their truths and realities. If women cannot write, or are
not allowed to write, or are dependent on someone else speaking on
their behalf, then many of our experiences will be lost. So where else
to begin our celebration of incredible women than with writers? The
poets and playwrights, novelists, biographers, historians and dreamers
whose voices sing to us down the generations.

When I began researching Lily's history, I was conscious of the fact
that, as a middle-class woman, she'd always had access to pen and
paper, to books and libraries. This was nineteenth-century England, so
it's tempting to think that there were no barriers to women writing at
all. And, no doubt, there were many fewer, though the frequency with
which women still felt obliged, for many and various reasons, to publish
under male pseudonyms – for example, **Mary Ann Evans** (1819–1880)
writing as **George Eliot,** or **Sidonie-Gabrielle Colette** (1874–1954),
known as **Colette**, who was convinced to publish her first four 'Claudine'
novels under the nom de plume 'Willy', attributed to her husband –
illustrates the difference between something being forbidden and
something being seen as appropriate or accepted.

Lily was born in 1849, just two years after the publications of *Jane
Eyre, Wuthering Heights* and *Agnes Grey*. In the Editor's Preface to
a new edition of *Wuthering Heights* published in 1850, **Charlotte
Brontë** (1815–1855) explained why she and her sisters initially had
chosen to disguise their identities as Currer, Ellis and Acton Bell:

'. . . we did not like to declare ourselves women, because –
without at that time suspecting that our mode of writing and
thinking was not what is called "feminine" – we had a vague
impression that authoresses are liable to be looked on with
prejudice.'

The possibility of women writing their own lives begins not only at
home, but with the nature of broader society, by archaic custom or
newly enforced laws, by parents and by rulers both. Do they grant
girls the same rights as boys, to learn to read, to have access to learning,
to attend schools or institutes of education? In other words, are women
empowered to have control over their own narratives, to be visible?
And the fewer women who can write, the harder it is for another
woman to take up her pen. Out of context, our stories are less likely
to be considered relevant. They are less likely, in other words, to be
considered 'history'.

> 'I am Black and lesbian, and what you hear
> in my voice is fury, not suffering.'
>
> **Audre Lorde**

Each writer here – and there might have been thousands more –
speaks for herself as an artist, as a woman, and from the point of view
of her own very particular set of circumstances. With skill, brilliance,
imagination, they each also look beyond race, class, sexuality and
nationality to a shared humanity – what Adrienne Rich calls 'the dream
of a common language'. And it's what Audre Lorde fought for in the
1960s and 1970s, not least in her powerful essay 'The Master's Tools
Will Never Dismantle the Master's House', published in 1984 in *Sister
Outsider*. It's a rallying cry analysing her experiences as a Black lesbian
feminist at a New York University Humanities conference. In it, Lorde
notes how her contribution was being curtailed to her own lived experience, whereas others were invited to speak, to talk, to lecture on
anything. Lorde's essays salute the power of anger, as well as promoting
what would now be termed intersectionality, and her words are as
pertinent today as they were forty years ago.

∞

LET'S BEGIN AT the beginning with once upon a time . . .

The first named writer in world history is a woman. **Enheduanna** (2285–2250 BCE) was the High Priestess to Inanna – one of the most powerful of ancient Mesopotamian goddesses, associated with love, war, sex and political power – and she lived in the twenty-third century BCE in the Sumerian city state of Ur, southern Mesopotamia (modern-day Iraq). A breathtaking landscape of plains and desert, Sumer is one of the earliest known civilizations – alongside Ancient Egypt, the Indus Valley civilization, the Minoan civilization and ancient China.

From excavations in the nineteenth and early twentieth centuries, we know Ur was once a coastal city, near the mouth of the Euphrates on the Persian Gulf. The town itself was, so far as archaeologists can tell, divided into neighbourhoods, with merchants in one quarter, artisans in another. Wide streets, narrow alleyways, open spaces for gatherings. Houses were constructed from mud bricks and mud plaster, with civic buildings strengthened with bitumen and reeds. It was here that Enheduanna lived and wrote. An alabaster carved disc found during the excavations at Ur between 1922 and 1934 confirms her importance, as does the later discovery of a handful of Babylonian clay tiles with words attributed to her. The excavations were led by Leonard and Katharine Woolley. Katharine is thought to have been the inspiration for Louise Leidner in *Murder in Mesopotamia* by **Agatha Christie** (1890–1976). Christie's second husband, Max Mallowan, was Woolley's assistant, and Christie knew and loved that part of the world. Her 1951 novel *They Came to Baghdad* is dedicated to 'my many archaeological friends in Iraq and Syria'.

Enheduanna's catalogue includes a collection of forty-two temple hymns – *The Sumerian Temple Hymns*, three long poems to Inanna and three poems to the moon god, Nanna. If nothing else, it confirms that noblewomen in Mesopotamia, at least, could be educated, literate artists.

'You may forget but
let me tell you
this: someone in
some future time
will think of us'

Sappho

THE ISSUE OF the preservation of work is crucial. Unsurprisingly, the further back one goes, the fewer extant documents remain. The poet **Sappho** (*c.* 630–*c.* 570 BCE) is celebrated both for her elegiac and her lyric poetry which was written to be sung – many images show her with her lyre. Sappho was known as the 'Tenth Muse' or 'The Poetess' (Homer was 'The Poet'). Her poetry is exquisite, delicate celebrations of family and love, memory and legacy, though obsession with her sexuality has tended to overshadow the wider range of her writing. Legends talk about her love for a ferryman, though some experts believe this was an attempt to heterosexualize her reputation. And there's no doubt that part of Sappho's enduring fame lies in the battleground around her sexuality – we get the words sapphic and lesbian from her name and her home island.

In truth, we know little of Sappho's life. She appears in the *Suda* – the extensive tenth-century Byzantine encyclopaedia and grammatical dictionary of the ancient Mediterranean world, which has some thirty thousand entries. The caveat is that not all entries were contemporaneous and many are retrospective rewritings by Christian compilers. Errors, deliberate or lazy, slip in. But we do know Sappho was exiled to Sicily around 600 BCE and may have continued to work until 570 or so. We also know she wrote more than a staggering 10,000 lines of poetry, though only about 650 lines have survived. But those beautiful fragments tell a huge story. Her poetry is usually referred to by its fragment number – 'Ode to Aphrodite' is fragment 1, for example – and, in recent years, more fragments have been found, including in 2014 'The Brothers Poem' or 'Brothers Song'. Echoes from history.

Like Sappho, **Pamphila of Epidaurus** (first century CE) is also described in the *Suda*. Her thirty-three-volume history of Greece – *Historical Commentaries* – has sadly not survived intact, but enough has been quoted by other ancient historians to give us at least a sense of her work. 'Outing' herself as a woman, Pamphila claims that she gathered her material from eavesdropping on conversations between her husband and his male friends. The *Suda* also credits her with summarizing other contemporary historians' work, and some literary historians think she might be the author of the unattributed *Treatise on Women Famous in War*, fourteen biographies of celebrated women. Can you imagine that ancient roar of warrior queens and female commanders? It's a book I would love to read.

It's been inspiring trying to hear the voices of women from so far back in time. There's an awareness, too, of how it's likely that the women we do know today are only a tiny fraction of those who might have written about their lives and times. So many lost words.

> 'What you have learned is a mere handful; what you haven't learned is the size of the whole world.'
>
> *Avvaiyar*

THE MOST FAMOUS of all Tamil poets is **Avvaiyar**.

In fact, it's a generic title – meaning 'respectable woman' – and Avvaiyar is not actually one single woman, but at least three. A symbol of Tamil culture and wisdom, the first Avvaiyar lived during the third century BCE and wrote at least fifty-nine poems. The second was writing during the tenth century. It's the third who is most widely known, for *Vinayagar Agaval* – a devotional hymn to Ganesh – and *Aathichoodi*, a collection of inspirational aphorisms on how to live, one of which (quoted above) is inscribed on the wall at NASA in English translation. There is a statue to Avvaiyar in Tamil Nadu, an elderly and wise woman holding a staff in her right hand and a scroll in her left, strong and steady with wisdom, looking out over the Bay of Bengal. The importance of statues of women – of women of achievement being visible and publicly honoured – will come up time and again in the pages that follow.

Four hundred years later and some seven hundred kilometres to the north on the banks of the Musi River in India, **Atukuri Molla** (1440–1530) was one of the most important Telugu poets, known for translating the *Ramayana* from Sanskrit into Telugu. Her statue in Hyderabad became a rallying point for women's rights protests in 2006.

One of the most celebrated Sufi poets and ascetics was the sixteenth-century poet Queen **Habba Khatoon** (1554–1609). Known as the 'Nightingale of Kashmir', details of her life are thin on the ground. She is thought to have been born in Chandhara in Kashmir, and was known as Zoon. Legend holds that, famous both for her beauty and her glorious voice, she attracted the attention of Yousuf Shah Chak who, in 1579, would go on to be the last Muslim ruler of Kashmir and rule until 1586. Zoon is thought to have entered the court somewhere around 1570, possibly as his queen consort. When Yousuf Shah Chak was exiled after the Mughal conquest of Kashmir, Khatoon became a wandering poet. Her tomb outside Athwajan is rather untended, but a mountain in Gurez is named after her, as is a ship in the fleet of the Indian Coast Guard, and her songs remain popular and are still widely performed today.

> 'I am caught in Love's web so deceitful.'
>
> *Rabia Balkhi*

FROM INDIA TO Afghanistan, and back six hundred years, one meets the iconic tenth-century poet-princess of the royal court, **Rabia Balkhi**. Born in Balkh, an ancient city in northern Afghanistan known as the 'mother of cities', she is one of very few female writers of medieval Persian to be recorded by name (she also wrote in Arabic). In what is a familiar pattern, confirmed details of her life are hard to come by. Her legend is that she fell in love with her brother's Turkish slave. Disapproving of her choice, her brother incarcerated Rabia in the *hamam* and ordered her wrists to be slit. Her last poems to her lover are said to have been written on the walls of her tomb in her own blood.

Rabia's tomb was a much-visited site in Balkh and many hospitals and universities are named in her honour. The portrait of her wearing a blue khimar with a book, inkwell and quill are everywhere in Afghanistan. A long-term symbol of independence for Afghan women, as of August 2021 her legacy is under threat. A female student, who'd fled as the Taliban swept into Kabul, wrote in an American newspaper of how when her university was summarily closed to female students and tutors, she witnessed a painting of Rabia Balkhi being erased from the wall. This is not 'silence in the archives', but rather a deliberate eradication of a female poet from Afghanistan's history. It is far from the only occasion when a woman's achievements have been erased from the records of the past in order to limit women's endeavours in the present.

AT MUCH THE same time, the extraordinary **Hrotsvitha** (*c.* 935/973–*c.* 1002) was making her mark in northern Europe. Born in Lower Saxony, she entered the abbey in Gandersheim as a canoness. Gandersheim is a town of half-timbered buildings in the valley of the River Gande, set within a region of deep forest and mists and mineral springs.

I first heard of Hrotsvitha in 1985, when I went to see the travelling exhibition of *The Dinner Party*, the inspirational and monumental 1979 feminist art installation by American artist **Judy Chicago** (b. 1939). I still have the exhibition guide, a faded claret-coloured A3 brochure explaining how the work was made and how the banners that hang in the doorway are intended to 'express the belief and hope that once reverence for the feminine is re-established on Earth, a balance will be restored to human existence and "Everywhere will be Eden once again".' In the pages that follow is the list of the thirty-nine women who have place settings and the 998 historical and mythical women's names (and one man, included in error) painted on the handmade white heritage tiles that appear on the floor.

Hrotsvitha has her own place setting and could find a home in most of the chapters of this book. Though she wrote in Latin, she is considered the first female writer and poet from Germany, one of the first female historians and one of the first northern Europeans to write about Islam. She was also the first playwright in the modern era to write dramatic pieces, often weaving in information about her life and those of other women. She dedicated *The Book of Legends* to her teacher **Abbess Gerberga II** (*c.* 940–1001). Her most celebrated piece, *The Book of Drama*, is a Christian reinterpretation of the work of the Roman playwright Terence, a story of strong women triumphing over adversity.

Her works were lost for some time after her death, until they were rediscovered by a German scholar in the Emmeram monastery in Regensberg in 1493. They were published in the original Latin in 1501 and translated into English in the 1600s. Though I have no idea whether or not my great-grandmother might have heard of Hrotsvitha, I think her reimagining of the myths of antiquity through the lens of medieval Christianity would have appealed to Lily, whose novels and devotional essays were written with the sense of Christian morality being the foundation of a 'good' life. During my family research, I would discover book reviews written by Lily for magazines which gave me some idea of the contemporary authors she read and admired. But Hrotsvitha? I just don't know, but her importance endures.

> 'Autumn is no time to lie alone.'
>
> **Murasaki Shikibu**

AT ABOUT THE time Hrotsvitha is believed to have died, the Japanese author **Murasaki Shikibu** (*c.* 973/978–*c.* 1014/1031) was born in what is present-day Kyoto.

A daughter in a high-born family of male minor nobility and poets, Murasaki learned to write Chinese, the language of the Japanese court and government, by eavesdropping on her brother's lessons. Unusually, she remained living within her father's household after puberty – possibly until her mid-twenties – and married late. Sometime around 1005, five or six years after her husband had died after only two years of marriage, Shikibu was summoned to court as a lady-in-waiting. Already a respected poet – there are some 128 poems in her *Poetic Memoirs* – she began to keep a diary of her life at court, the rivalries, spite and day-to-day experiences. But Shikibu became a literary sensation with the epic *The Tale of Genji*, which runs to over a thousand pages. Considered to be the world's first novel – and performed in episodes at court – it's written in Japanese, probably over many years, and is hugely significant for being written in *kana* rather than in transliterated Chinese characters. Boasting an eye-watering cast of characters, the story of a prince and his lovers, it sings with a love of the beauty of nature, the exquisite power of poetry, music and calligraphy, though the tone darkens in later chapters (some historians have suggested the final fourteen chapters might have been written by someone else). The first English translation appeared in 1935 and Lady Shikibu's diary is included in *Diaries of Court Ladies of Old Japan*, which was published in the same year. Images of Shikibu often show her dressed in a violet kimono, the colour associated with her name. A trailblazing woman and writer.

> 'Things remain, but all is lost.
> Now he is no more.'
>
> **Li Qingzhao**

SOME FIFTY YEARS after Shikibu's death, the Chinese poet, author and collector **Li Qingzhao** (1084–1155) was born in what is now Jinan, eastern China. Only fragments of Li's poems have survived, but they give a glorious sense of her eventful life in imperial China of the late eleventh and early twelfth centuries.

Her earlier poems have the colour, the cadence, the delicacy of love poetry. After the northern Song capital fell in 1127, Li and her husband fled south to safety and her poetry became shot through with expressions of patriotism and hatred of war. There is a life-sized statue to her in Baotu Spring Garden in Jinan. Fashioned in white marble, wearing a full-length dress and a long kimono with wide sleeves fastened on the left, she is holding a scroll in her right hand. Her gaze is direct and clear. Li even has two planetary craters – one on Mercury, one on Venus – named after her.

> 'God knows I never sought anything in you
> except yourself. I wanted simply you,
> nothing of yours.'
>
> **Héloise d'Argenteuil**

A CLOSE CONTEMPORARY of Li Qingzhao was the medieval scholar, mystic and nun **Héloise d'Argenteuil** (*c.* 1098 or 1100/1101–

c. 1163/1164), who was born in Paris at the very beginning of the twelfth century. I first came across her as a teenager in the classroom, learning about her doomed love affair with her one-time teacher, Peter Abelard, and its violent consequences – a story recorded through a lifetime of letters written between them. Their story has captured generations of writers and film-makers, from Alexander Pope's poem 'Eloisa to Abelard' in 1717 to the great Ulster-Scots writer **Helen Waddell** (1889–1965) in the twentieth century.

Steeped in history and atmosphere, with a sense of unavoidable heartbreak and tragedy, Waddell's *Peter Abelard* is one of the reasons I fell in love with historical fiction as a reader and, later, one of the reasons I became the kind of writer I am. Many of us fall in love with history because of the plays we have seen, the books we have read, the paintings that stirred our curiosity.

Waddell was a near contemporary of my great-grandmother and they have a great deal in common. Both lived inspired by the Church and theology, with Christianity at the heart of their daily lives. Both were middle-class women who wrote fiction, poetry and theological works. Lily was a wife and mother, Waddell a fond sister and aunt, and they were both successful and respected writers in their day. But although Waddell is commemorated in Belfast's Writer's Square – an open space of grey stone and sharp angles where quotations from twenty-seven of Northern Ireland's most celebrated authors are etched upon the ground – otherwise her name has mostly vanished from the record, and her books, like those of Lily, are today out of print.

Waddell was a literary celebrity in her day. Born in Tokyo and brought up in Northern Ireland, Waddell was a classical scholar, translator, publisher and poet, author of *The Wandering Scholars* and her one dazzling novel, *Peter Abelard*, which was a runaway bestseller in 1933.

The real Héloïse, as opposed to the creation of novelists and poets, was a renowned woman of letters, a philosopher, a celebrated scholar and a nun who became one of the highest-ranking abbesses in the Catholic Church. D'Argenteuil's influence on French and European literature and culture was immense – not least in establishing the ideals of courtly love, a literary form that would be taken up by Chrétien de Troyes among others in years to come. Her letters to her lost love are erudite, clever, moving, scholarly and beautiful.

'As for those who state that it is thanks to a woman, the lady Eve, that man was expelled from paradise, my answer to them would be that man has gained far more through Mary than he ever lost through Eve.'

Christine de Pizan

LIVING SOME TWO hundred years after Héloise, **Christine de Pizan** (c. 1364–c. 1430) is also one of the thirty-nine women celebrated at Chicago's *The Dinner Party*.

Pizan was perhaps the first woman in France – maybe in all of Europe – to earn her living solely by writing and teaching. She began writing professionally at the age of twenty-five, when her husband died leaving her with young children to support – time and again we'll see women taking up their pen when challenging domestic circumstances force it. An early feminist – though this term wasn't to come into usage for another four hundred years – Pizan had hard-hitting views on the ways in which men tried to curtail women, blame them, diminish them, deny them opportunities. Written in part in response to the misogyny of much courtly literature, *The Book of the City of Ladies* (1405) is a medieval precursor to the play *Top Girls* by **Caryl Churchill** (b. 1938). In it, de Pizan brings together famous women from history to build her allegorical city – using books as building blocks supporting her argument of how important a contribution women make to society and the value of education for all.

Beyond the text itself – and that of *The Treasure of the City of Ladies* which followed – the books are glorious because of their illustrations. Bright, vivid, eye-catching, they give a wonderful insight into court fashions of the period – de Pizan herself appears in some images dressed in a blue cotehardie and white wired 'horned' headdress. She was prolific, impressively hard-working, producing poetry, epistles, treatises about the morality of war and education. She also wrote *The Song of Joan of Arc* in 1429, celebrating the end of the siege of Orléans. Apart from the records of the French saint's trial in 1431, it is the only surviving contemporary record of **Joan of Arc** (c. 1412–1431).

Women keeping other women's stories alive.

∽

RESEARCHING AND WRITING The Joubert Family Chronicles, I've been immersed in the sixteenth and seventeenth centuries. I'd hazard a guess that one of the reasons women were attracted to various forms of Protestantism during those years of bloody and violent religious upheaval in Europe was that the new faith seemed to offer them a chance not only to write and translate, but also to be published and read beyond their immediate circle. Devotional texts only, of course, but it was a significant new freedom all the same . . . And for women who could not read or write in Latin, they were suddenly being invited in by a Church speaking to them in their own language. It offered a more direct relationship with God.

In 1560, **Anne Locke** (*c.* 1533–after 1590) published 'A Meditation of a Penitent Sinner' as an appendix to four sermons by John Calvin, translated by Locke from the French. It was the first sonnet cycle to be written in English. A staunch Protestant, Locke was exiled during the five-year reign of **Mary I** (1516–1558), but returned to England when **Elizabeth I** (1533–1603) took the throne, and she became one of the most important translators and commentators of Calvinist writings. Because she signed her work only with her initials – A. L. – her identity was hidden until relatively recently. Was it to protect herself as a Protestant, or because she was a woman? We'll never be sure.

It is also worth noting that in sixteenth-century England women were not allowed in law to run their own businesses, except if they were widowed. There are many examples of women taking over their late husbands' work, not least in the area of printing and publishing. Notable names include **Elizabet Allde** (d. 1640), **Mercy Meighen** (d. 1654), **Susan Islip** (d. 1661) and bookseller **Anne Moseley** (d. 1675).

> 'I live, I die, I burn, I drown'
>
> *Louise Labé*

ON THE OTHER side of the Channel and the religious divide, the Catholic poet **Louise Labé** (*c.* 1524–1566) was celebrated by her peers – like Sappho before her – as 'The Tenth Muse'. Writing frankly of female desire and lust, of the contradictions of love, Labé established a salon in Lyon and encouraged other women to write. Her *Oeuvres*, published in 1555, contained not only sonnets composed by her – she wrote in both French and Italian – but also those of other writers. As well as being a patron of the arts and a writer, Labé was an accomplished archer and horsewoman – nicknamed both 'La Belle Amazone' and 'La Belle Cordière', the latter because her husband and father were rope makers. She served in the Dauphin's army (the future Henri II) at the siege of Perpignan in 1542, and is said to have worn male clothing and fought in jousts, though these are stories that may have been circulated after her death. The historian **Alice E. Smith** (b. 1983) has cautioned that often reports, or allegations, of women wearing male clothing were intended to denigrate, rather than being an illustration of female independence or power.

Yet despite her contemporary fame, Labé also fell victim to the 'Matilda Effect'. Her works were regularly attributed to male authors and her character was attacked to undermine her reputation – the austere French Protestant theologian Jean Calvin, no admirer of women or Catholics, called her a 'common whore'. Others have suggested that the poet Labé has been confused with a famous courtesan of the time, also known as 'La Belle Cordière', or that she might not have existed at all. Times have changed. Whether or not some aspects of Labé's biography can be verified, her poetry speaks for itself and she's rightly considered one of the finest and first French female poets.

In 1642, Cromwell's men shut all the theatres in England and Ireland. For eighteen years, the stages were empty, abandoned to the rats and damp, to dust and memory.

After the years of turmoil of the Civil War and following Cromwell's Protectorate and his brutal conquest of Ireland, the Restoration of the Monarchy in 1660 saw Charles II take the throne, and a golden era for women in the theatre began. Although there had been the occasional female performer – according to the Court Records of 1612 Mary Frith, on whom the role of Moll Cutpurse in *The Roaring Girl* by Middleton and Dekker was based, 'sat upon the stage in the public view' – now, for the first time, actresses with leading and speaking roles appeared on English stages, **Nell Gwyn** (1650–1687) the most famous among them. London was alive with first nights, the swish of the red-and-gold curtains – it was a new era of celebrity. Playwrights were working around the clock to satisfy the huge public appetite for comedy and drama, and one of the most important of them was the peerless and astonishing **Aphra Behn** (*c.* 1640–1689).

> 'A thousand Martyrs I have made,
> All sacrific'd to my desire;'
>
> *Aphra Behn*

Behn was perhaps the first female British author to make a living as a writer and, like Labé before her, wrote frankly about her life as a woman, about desire and sexuality, and about politics in the wider world.

Much of her younger life remains a mystery and it's possible she deliberately obscured her origins: she may have been born in Kent, or she may not; she may have spent time in Suriname, or she may not; she might have been a Catholic and she may have worked as a spy for Charles II in the 1660s – though some contemporary historians think this might be little more than coffee-house gossip and misogynist malice. Behn probably spent time in a debtors' prison in the late 1660s. But I'm not sure any of this matters in terms of the importance of her writing.

Behn was a versatile and wonderfully colourful writer, ambitious and clever, publishing poetry, novels and dramas. Her rumbustious play *The Rover*, which premiered at the Duke's Theatre in London in 1677, is a riotous Restoration comedy featuring a band of English women and men on the loose in Naples during Carnival. Her poem 'The Disappointment' is about the attempted rape of Cloris by Lysander, resulting in his impotence . . . And her celebrated 1688 novel *Oroonoko*, with its themes of racial injustice and the place of women in the world, has good claim to be seen as the first abolitionist novel. Behn wasn't the first British woman to publish a play – **Elizabeth Cary** (*c.* 1584/1586–1639) wrote and published *The Tragedy of Mariam* in 1613 and the philosopher, science fiction author and playwright **Margaret Cavendish** (1623–1673) published two volumes of plays in the 1650s. But, of the three, Behn was the most prolific, writing some nineteen plays and collaborating on many more, and had none of their advantages (Cavendish was a duchess and Cary a viscountess).

Celebrated, notorious, often vilified and admired in turn – there are many paintings and etchings of Behn still in existence – her reputation was traduced after her death. Her unashamed representation of female sexuality and inequality between the sexes – not to mention her joyful exploration of women's love for women, and men's love for men – saw her work branded as immoral and, for three hundred years and more, her contribution to the development of English literature was deliberately down-played or dismissed as blowsy, overblown. It's interesting to speculate if it was, in part, Victorian double standards and prudishness that found Behn's frank treatment of sex and sexuality inappropriate in a female writer, when her work was very much in step with the male writers of her time. Again, it is thanks to feminist scholars and fellow female authors starting to look at her work with fresh eyes that her reputation began to be restored. Here's **Virginia Woolf** (1882–1941) in A *Room of One's Own*:

> 'All women together ought to let flowers fall upon the grave of Aphra Behn . . . for it was she who earned them the right to speak their minds . . . Behn proved that money could be made by writing at the sacrifice, perhaps, of certain agreeable qualities; and so, by degrees writing became not merely a sign of folly and a distracted mind but was of practical importance.'

In 1707, the Acts of Union between England and Scotland were passed during the reign of **Anne Stuart** (1665–1714), formally creating the new combined nation state of Great Britain. At her death, Queen Anne was succeeded by her second cousin, George I, and the Hanoverian era and the Age of Enlightenment began.

The eighteenth century would see huge strides made in science and medicine, but also in music and theatre. It was a century of revolution, from France to America to Haiti and, all over the world, more women than ever began to pick up their pens to make their voices heard.

We might start with Anglo-Irish novelist and playwright **Frances Sheridan** (1724–1766), who gave her scribbler son and daughters the best possible start in their literary lives. Though her father opposed women's education, she was hugely successful as both a novelist and a playwright, with novels including *Memoirs of Miss Sidney Bidulph* and plays such as *The Discovery*, which enjoyed a long run in London on Drury Lane. **Charlotte Lennox** (*c.* 1730–1804) was a Scottish actor turned novelist, poet and playwright. Her 1752 novel *The Female Quixote* parodied some of the misogynistic ideas in Cervantes's celebrated and popular epic. It's a pattern we saw with de Pizan two centuries earlier – and we'll see again – a woman reacting to dismissive male authors' critical views of women's characters with devastating wit.

'I had rather be in a state of misery, and envied for my supposed happiness, than in a state of happiness, and pitied for my supposed misery.'

Elizabeth Inchbald

Elizabeth Inchbald (1753–1821) was a novelist, a playwright and adaptor, a theatre entrepreneur and an actress capable of playing both Shakespearean and 'breeches roles', all the more impressive because she had to cope with a childhood stutter. One of the first female theatre critics, her plays were so successful that she wrote herself into financial security and independence. She was erudite, but brim-full of gossip and anecdote, pointed and sharp, and it's a great loss to discover she burnt her memoirs rather than publishing them. But in the preface of her novel *A Simple Story*, she stated how her career as a writer had been driven by financial instability and how she had been forced 'to devote a tedious seven years to the unremitting labour of literary productions'. Although Inchbald wrote about contemporary mores and social issues, to shine a light on the world in which she lived, she was primarily writing to entertain rather than to transform societal norms.

Other women were turning to polemic and essay writing to effect change.

'A woman has the right to be guillotined; she should also have the right to debate.'

Olympe de Gouges

In 1791, a year before **Mary Wollstonecraft** (1759–1797) published her ground-breaking 'A Vindication of the Rights of Woman', the French playwright, feminist and abolitionist **Olympe de Gouges** (1748–1793), born Marie Gouze, wrote 'Declaration of the Rights of Woman and of the Female Citizen' in response to the omission of women from the French Revolution's Bill of Rights. Though she was derided by male critics – Horace Walpole called her 'a hyena in petticoats' – de Gouges was principled, gifted, determined and a fearless campaigner for equality of citizenship. As an illustration on the murky and shifting politics of the French Revolution, de Gouges was hated on all sides. She was perceived as too radical by the moderates and as a Royalist by the extreme left, possibly because she'd dedicated the 'Declaration of the Rights of Woman' to Marie Antoinette. Charged with treason, she was sent to the guillotine by Robespierre in 1793. As a playwright, too, her work has often been ridiculed and maligned. Using the archives of the Comédie Française – where female playwrights were almost always recorded alongside a man – to prove his case, Rousseau denounced the idea of women writing in their own right.

> 'I do not wish [women] to have power over men; but over themselves.'
>
> **Mary Wollstonecraft**

DURING THE YEARS of the American War of Independence, **Phillis Wheatley Peters** (1753–1784) became the first published African American poet. The best-known image of her – reproduced as a frontispiece in her 1773 edition of *Poems on Various Subjects, Religious and Moral* – suggests a poised and thoughtful young woman, in a white ruffled cap and apron and a ribbon around her neck. She's holding a quill in her right hand and there is an inkwell, paper and a book on the desk.

An enslaved woman originally from West Africa – possibly Gambia or Senegal – Wheatley was stolen as a child, taken to North America on a slave ship and bought by the Wheatley family in Boston. They recognized her talent – though, of course, any success she achieved would benefit them – and helped her writing to find an audience.

Bigotry and racism in America obliged them to travel to Britain, where the influential Methodist evangelist and abolitionist **Selina Hastings** (1707–1791), the Countess of Huntingdon, helped Wheatley to secure a publisher in London. There were more obstacles. She had to appear before eighteen men to prove that she had written her poems – shades of Joan of Arc at her trial – but her first poem was published in 1767 and, by 1771, her work was circulating in London. Her best-known poem – 'On Being Brought from Africa to America' – is a searing protest against slavery.

There are thirty-nine poems in the 1773 collection – more than 145 other poems are thought to be lost. Wheatley was not only the first African American woman to be published, but also the first African American poet, female or male, though she didn't benefit from her writing. She never lived to see slavery abolished and died in straitened circumstances. It wouldn't be until the nineteenth century that **Hannah Bond** (b. *c.* 1832), writing under the pen name **Hannah Crafts**, would follow in her footsteps and become the first enslaved, fugitive African American woman to publish a novel.

> 'The world is a severe schoolmaster, for its frowns are less dangerous than its smiles and flatteries . . .'
>
> **Phillis Wheatley**

The additional challenge of battling racism as well as sexism was also endured by **Rachel Luzzatto Morpurgo** (1790–1871). Born into an influential Jewish family in Trieste, northern Italy, she was (so far as we know) the first Jewish woman to write poetry in Hebrew under her own name in two thousand years. Attacked by male critics, who refused to believe a woman capable of writing in Hebrew at all, Morpurgo was an accomplished poet and scholar, despite having little time to write. Her work is an intriguing mixture of lyric reflection and everyday domesticity, often painfully capturing the confinement of women's lives and the inequalities they suffered. And this signature, at the end of the poem 'On Hearing She Had Been Praised in the Journals', published in 1847, breaks the heart:

I've looked to the north, south, east, and west:
a woman's word in each is lighter than dust.
Years hence, will anyone really remember
her name . . .

Wife of Jacob Morpurgo, stillborn

IF THE EIGHTEENTH century belonged to playwrights and poets, the nineteenth belongs to the novel.

On the cusp of the new century, Gothic fiction was hugely popular and **Ann Radcliffe** (1764–1823) was its queen. The highest-paid writer, male or female, of the time, Radcliffe wrote five novels, the fourth of which – *The Mysteries of Udolpho* – was published in four volumes in 1794, becoming an instant, influential and enduring bestseller. It was the first of her novels to appear in its debut edition with her name on the title page, her first three novels having been published anonymously. Jane Austen, who admitted she'd devoured the book, parodies it in her debut novel *Northanger Abbey*; it is mentioned in William Makepeace Thackeray's *Vanity Fair* and Fyodor Dostoevsky's *The Brothers Karamazov*, and *Udolpho* is used as a shorthand to reference a certain type of fiction by Edgar Allan Poe, Anthony Trollope, Henry James and even **Lucy Maud Montgomery** (1874–1942) of *Anne of Green Gables* fame. The novel itself is set in south-west France and Italy, places Radcliffe never visited. But what makes the writing stand out is the equality given to its female and male characters. Radcliffe's women have agency and are portrayed as capable, far from the wailing and terrified creatures of much Gothic fiction of the time. I can't imagine that my great-grandmother approved of Mrs Radcliffe's 'romances', as she always termed them, but Lily's descriptions of the mountains and landscapes of Italy, Germany and Switzerland have a great deal in common with Radcliffe's epic novelscapes.

'I have love in me the likes of which you can scarcely imagine and rage the likes of which you would not believe. If I cannot satisfy the one, I will indulge the other.'

Mary Shelley

Perhaps the greatest of all Gothic novels is *Frankenstein*, a work that's remained in print ever since its first publication in 1818. The daughter of the great social reformer, philosopher and women's rights campaigner Mary Wollstonecraft, **Mary Shelley** (1797–1851) began her masterpiece when she was only eighteen years old. Staying on the banks of Lake Geneva in 1816, a summer of endless rain and black skies, with her lover Percy Bysshe Shelley, her stepsister-in-law Claire Clairmont, John Polidori and Lord Byron, they challenged one another to make up a horror story to keep the beleaguered household entertained. *Frankenstein; or, The Modern Prometheus* was published anonymously on New Year's Day two years later, when Mary Shelley was twenty, her name only appearing on the second edition printed in Paris in 1821. It is a masterpiece, yes, but the breadth and range of the rest of Shelley's work is often overlooked, even though she wrote many other novels, books of travelogue and biography, and edited her late husband's letters. Her novella *Matilda*, written between 1819 and 1820, when she was grieving for the loss of two more of her children, was finally published posthumously – more than a century after her death – in 1959.

Like Mary Shelley, **Emily Dickinson** (1830–1886) cannot be said to be an author who has disappeared from literary history, but I'm including her because the story of her publication and reputation is worth revisiting. It plays to issues of legacy and how women's writing is curated, or secured, kept in print or censored.

Dickinson, whose exquisite poems interrogate themes of grief and death and faith, immortality and invisibility, was prolific. But, like Rachel Morpurgo, she was barely published in her lifetime – only 10 of nearly 1,800 poems and one letter were published while she was alive, possibly without attribution. I still have my old Faber edition of *The Complete Poems*, bought in the late 1970s, its blue cover faded, the margins filled with a blizzard of annotations in blue biro. There are 1,775 poems, all untitled. The likely date of composition for some is there, but most float free on the page. The capitalization and punctuation are distinctive, and original. Though they were living at much the same time, I doubt if my great-grandmother knew of this reclusive American poet, but I think her verses would have spoken to Lily. The stillness of them. Dickinson's life has been studied by countless scholars and her poems, her letters, her motivation and ambitions for her writing analysed and turned inside out. She often dressed in white – though the only authenticated portrait of Dickinson as an adult is a daguerreo-type taken in 1846 or early 1847 showing her in a dark dress with a velvet necklace – and lived a solitary life in the family home in Amherst, conducting her friendships through letters. So many letters. She made her younger sister Lavinia promise to burn them after her death and, devastatingly, Lavinia did. But since Dickinson did not mention her poems, they survived the bonfire. A heavily edited first collection was published in 1890, but it was not until 1955 that a complete, and mostly unaltered, collection of Dickinson's poetry was published.

So, even when an author's reputation seems secure, investigate the history that made it so. And, of course, it's far from the only time that editors or family members have sought to manage, or obscure, or manipulate an author's intentions – think of the first edition of *The Diary of a Young Girl* by **Anne Frank** (1929–1945), heavily edited by her father for publication.

MY GREAT-GRANDMOTHER CAME of age during a golden age of female novelists writing in English. What distinguished many of these great nineteenth-century novels was that they put ordinary life on the page, and life outside of London, from Yorkshire and Manchester, Kentucky to Massachusetts. Social history, domestic lives, a new generation of authors was putting the inner lives of women on the page and holding up a mirror to the lives of countless female readers.

Leading nineteenth-century novelists include: **Elizabeth Gaskell** (1810–1865); **Harriet Beecher Stowe** (1811–1896); **Ellen Price** (1814–1887); **Charlotte Brontë** (1816–1855); **Emily Brontë** (1818–1848); **Anne Brontë** (1820–1849); **Mrs Oliphant** (1828–1897); **Louisa May Alcott** (1832–1888); **Mary Elizabeth Braddon** (1835–1915); **Violet Paget/Vernon Lee** (1856–1935); **Alice Dunbar Nelson/Monroe Wright** (1875–1935); and **Radclyffe Hall** (1880–1943).

> 'Perhaps it is just as well to be rash and foolish for a while. If writers were too wise, perhaps no books would get written at all.'
>
> **Zora Neale Hurston**

There was a similar energy and urgency in Europe too. In France, the radical and inspiring **Amantine Dupin** (1804–1876) wrote under the pen name **George Sand**, and **Victoire Léodile Béra** (1824–1900), the feminist journalist and novelist, published under the combined name of her twin sons **André Léo**. In Germany, **Louise Otto-Peters** (1819–1895), a novelist, poet and librettist, was known as the 'songbird of the German woman's movement'. In Spain, the radical thinker and campaigner **Rosario de Acuña** (1851–1923) was publishing plays, essays, short stories and poetry under the male pen name **Remigio Andrés Delafón**. Examining themes of marriage and divorce, women's rights and injustice, atheism and illegitimacy, Delafón's work often scandalized the authorities. In Romania, the award-winning children's author and poet **Elena Farago** (1878–1954) was one of the most celebrated translators on the continent. And in Norway, **Elise Aubert** (1837–1909) was publishing short stories and newspaper serials – just like my great-grandmother – under the pseudonyms 'Tante Dorthe' and 'E-e'.

In South America, one of the most important Latin American authors of the nineteenth century was born in Argentina in 1818. A novelist, short-story writer, essayist, revolutionary, memoirist – and, for seven years, First Lady of Bolivia – **Juana Manuela Gorriti** (*c.* 1818–1892) spent her time writing, speaking and travelling between Argentina, Peru and Bolivia. Like Louise Labé three hundred years earlier, Gorriti established a salon, in Lima, which brought together other writers, held musical recitals, poetry evenings and lectures, often about women's lives.

In North America, **Frances Anne Rollin Whipper** (1845–1901) wrote a biography of the African American activist, physician, soldier and writer Martin Delany under the male pseudonym **Frank A. Rollin**. Published in 1883, *The Life and Public Services of Martin R. Delany* is the first full-length biography written by an African American writer. A political activist, abolitionist, women's rights activist and teacher, in later life Rollin Whipper also became one of the first Black female physicians in the United States. Another multi-talented woman, who kept moving forward all of her life.

And in the same year as Rollin Whipper published her biography of Delany, the writer and formerly enslaved woman **Mary Prince** (*c.* 1788–1833) died. Born in Bermuda, she attempted to escape abuse at the hands of her 'owner' when she arrived in England in 1828.

Her case was taken up by the Anti-Slavery Society and, in 1831, Prince published *The History of Mary Prince: A West African Slave*, the substantial record of an enslaved woman's life, making her the first recorded Black British woman to write an autobiography. It was a huge success in its day and sold out its first three printings.

> 'Strange, when you ask anyone's advice you see yourself what is right.'
>
> **Selma Lagerlöf**

IN THE LATE nineteenth and early twentieth centuries, women all over the world were breaking the literary glass ceiling for the first time. In Sweden, the first woman to win the Nobel Prize in Literature, in 1909, was **Selma Lagerlöf** (1858–1940). In 1894, she met the Swedish-Jewish writer **Sophie Elkan** (1853–1921), who became her collaborator, her friend, lover and companion. Lagerlöf's letters to Elkan were published in the early 1990s, as was her correspondence to her assistant, literary advisor and secretary – and later politician – **Valborg Olander** (1861–1943).

In Lebanon, **Zaynab Fawwāz** (*c.* 1850/1860–1914) was a Shiite novelist, playwright, poet and feminist historian. Her 1893 play *Love and Faithfulness* (also sometimes translated as *Passion and Fidelity*) is considered the first play written in Arabic by a woman and her 1899 novel *The Happy Ending* was the first Arabic novel written by a woman.

In America in 1921, **Edith Wharton** (1862–1937) was the first woman to win the Pulitzer Prize in Literature for *The Age of Innocence*. Despite not publishing her first novel until she was forty, she wrote twenty-two novels and novellas, including *The House of Mirth*, as well as some eighty-five short stories, poetry, books on design, travel, literary and cultural criticism, her memoir *A Backward Glance*, and ghost stories – Wharton was the queen of what she called the 'thrill of the shudder'. She was also passionate about dogs and had a pet cemetery at her home in Lenox, Massachusetts, headstones marking the graves of some of the dogs she owned over her lifetime. Many photographs of Wharton show her with dogs, my favourite being one where a chihuahua is balanced on each of Wharton's shoulders, nestled beneath the brim of her boater.

In Japan, novelist, diarist and short-story author **Natsu Higuchi** (1872–1896) – known by her pen name **Ichiyō Higuchi** – became the country's first professional female writer of modern literature. A year before her death, she became a household name with the publication of her novella *Takekurabe* – first translated into English as *Comparing Heights* in 1930 – which tells the story of a group of young people over a four-month period living in the red-light district of Yoshiwara, in Edo (modern-day Tokyo). A novel about women's roles and male expectations, the clash between the values of old Japan and the new, it scandalized some critics on first publication, but became a cult classic. Higuchi herself is still a much-revered writer in Japan.

> 'To him we cannot answer "Tomorrow,"
> his name is today.'
>
> **Gabriela Mistral**

In Chile, **Gabriela Mistral** (1889–1957) was the first Latin American writer to win a Nobel Prize in Literature in 1945. A poet, teacher, writer, diplomat and philosopher, Mistral moved to France in 1926 to work for the newly formed Institute for Intellectual Cooperation of the League of Nations. Writing poetry infused with suffering, with grief, with her love for children, Mistral published hundreds of articles, lectured in the United States, toured the Caribbean, Brazil, Uruguay and Argentina. She also held professor-ships at several universities, before settling finally in Long Island in 1953 with her friend and partner, the American translator **Doris Dana** (1920–2006). Dana, who inherited her estate, published the first English-language translation of Mistral's poetry. Mistral's face appears on the 5,000 Chilean peso note.

In neighbouring Argentina, fellow poet **Alfonsina Storni** (1892–1938) was a friend of Mistral's. A prominent figure in the Argentinian women's movement, she also wrote essays, journalism and drama, often about female oppression and male perfidy. Her sonnet cycle *Ocre* was published in 1925 and made her a household name in the literary community of Buenos Aires. The song *'Alfonsina y el mar'* is inspired by Storni's death by suicide at La Perla beach outside Buenos Aires.

In Wales, **Dorothy Noel 'Dorf' Bonarjee** (1894–1983) was another trailblazer. Born in India, she was the first woman to be awarded a law degree by University College London, in 1917, having earlier studied French in Aberystwyth. In 1914, Bonarjee took part in the Eisteddfod at the University College of Wales and was awarded the Bardic chair, the first foreign student and first woman to have done so. She is the only Indian listed in the Welsh National Biography among some five thousand entries . . .

Finally, in Russia, female poets were risking their lives to have their voices heard, recording the great suffering and shifting allegiances in the period covering the end of Tsarist Russia, the era of Bolshevik Revolution and into the Soviet era.

Mirra Lokhvitskaya (1869–1905) was regarded by her contemporaries as the 'Russian Sappho', the first Russian woman to win the Pushkin Prize for Poetry, which she also won for her fifth and last volume of poetry. She was written out of the history books in Soviet times, but is now acknowledged as one of the most original and influential voices of the Silver Age of Russian Poetry.

> 'You will hear thunder and remember me
> and think: she wanted storms.'
>
> *Anna Akhmatova*

Born twenty years later, **Anna Akhmatova** (1889–1966), the pen name of **Anna Andreevna Gorenko**, was one of the most significant Russian poets of the twentieth century. Her work includes the dazzling *Requiem*, a beautiful elegy to the suffering of the Soviet people during the Great Terror (or Great Purge). Written over a period of time – possibly as much as three decades – Akhmatova redrafted and redrafted *Requiem*, kept it safe, holding words in her head until she could record them, carried the manuscript with her as she lived and worked. It's unimaginable that such an important work of literature could so easily have been lost, since Akhmatova was often out of favour with the Soviet authorities and much of her writing and information about her was destroyed. *Requiem* did not appear in book form in Russian until 1963 (published in Munich), and the complete poem was not published in the USSR until 1987.

> 'There are books so alive that you're always
> afraid that while you weren't reading, the
> book has gone and changed, has shifted like
> a river . . .'
>
> **Marina Tsvetaeva**

Akhmatova's friend **Marina Tsvetaeva** (1892–1941) was born in Moscow. The daughter of a concert pianist and a father who was the founder of the Museum of Fine Arts, she published her first collection of poetry when she was eighteen. Her poetry was technically and emotionally ground-breaking, influenced by Russian folk song, with a distinctive syntax like Emily Dickinson's work. Her writing is alive with the hardship and suffering of her life – her younger daughter died of hunger in an orphanage in 1919 during the Moscow famine. She emigrated with her husband and elder daughter first to Berlin, then Prague, before settling in Paris in 1925. Shunned by the expat community and living in poverty – her husband had worked for the secret police – it was her correspondence with fellow poets that sustained her during the years of exile. Tsvetaeva dedicated work to Akhmatova, who had remained in the Soviet Union.

Reluctantly she returned home from exile in 1939, and it was a tragic mistake. Her husband was executed and her surviving daughter was sent to a gulag. Tsvetaeva died by suicide in August 1941, a few weeks after the Nazi invasion of the USSR.

> 'I decided it was better to scream. Silence is
> the real crime against humanity.'
>
> **Nadezhda Mandelstam**

Two of the most extraordinary memoirs of those terrible years are by **Nadezhda Mandelstam** (1899–1980). *Hope Against Hope* and *Hope Abandoned* – the titles are a pun on her name, as *'nadezhda'* means 'hope' in Russian – lay bare the terror and the impossibility of a writer's life under Stalin. In her books, she describes how she memorized, transcribed and kept safe her husband Osip Mandelstam's writing. Without her, most of his extraordinary poetry would never have survived. She details his persecution under Stalin, his first and second arrests, their internal exile and finally his death in 1938, just before his forty-seventh birthday, in a transit camp en route to the Siberian gulag. Nadezhda Mandelstam was given the news of his death, sometime after it had happened, by a clerk in a post office, returning to her a package she had sent: 'It would be easy enough to establish the date on which the parcel was returned to me – it was the same day on which the newspapers published the long list of Government awards – the first ever – to Soviet writers.'

Yet, she survived. Mandelstam spent much of the Second World War living in exile in Tashkent with Anna Akhmatova, only being given permission to return to Moscow in 1964. There, finally, she began writing the story of their lives – *Hope Against Hope* and *Hope Abandoned*. She died in Moscow on 29 December 1980 at the age of eighty-one, and is buried in the Kuntsevo Cemetery on the banks of the Setun River. Her husband is buried in an unmarked mass grave.

> 'Literature ought to join minds together . . .
> turning ignorance into mutual
> understanding.'
>
> ***Ding Ling***

In China, **Ding Ling** (1904–1986) – the pen name of the author **Jiang Bingzhi** – would grow up to face similar painful and impossible challenges as Akhmatova and Tsvetaeva in having to live and work under an all-seeing, all-controlling Communist regime.

Her earliest writing was explicitly feminist in tone. In an article, 'Thoughts on March 8', written for a party newspaper, Ding condemned male double standards – especially those of male cadres – which led to accusations of her being too 'rightist'. She was forced to retract her views and to undergo a public self-confession. Her 1948 novel *The Sun Shines Over Sanggan River* – which won the Stalin Prize for Literature in 1951 – is about land reform and peasant life and steers clear of commentary on women's lives. Her compliance with party values made no difference. Denounced and purged from the party in 1957, accused of being pro-Western, Ding's fiction and essays were again banned. Imprisoned and sentenced to manual hard labour, she was not 'rehabilitated' for nearly twenty years – she was freed in 1975 and restored to the Communist Party in 1979. But she never lost her faith in the power of literature to join people together. In an introduction to *Miss Sophia's Diary and Other Stories* – the story was originally published in 1927 – Ding paid tribute to the importance of literature in other languages and from other cultures.

> 'This has always been a man's world, and none of the reasons that have been offered in explanation have seemed adequate.'
>
> **Simone de Beauvoir**

ALL OVER EUROPE, things were changing and women were at the forefront.

Simone de Beauvoir (1908–1986), one of French literature's most significant figures, was born in Paris in the early years of the twentieth century. A writer, social theorist, philosopher, novelist and thinker, de Beauvoir's reputation is also secure thanks to her ground-breaking 1949 treatise *The Second Sex*, one of the building-block texts of Western contemporary feminism. But she also wrote novels, biographies, autobiographies, essays on philosophy, politics and social issues. She wasn't the first woman to be awarded the Prix Goncourt – Russian-French writer **Elsa Triolet** (1896–1970) won in 1944, the Belgian-born author **Béatrix Beck** (1914–2008) won in 1952 – but de Beauvoir was the third for her novel *The Mandarins* in 1954.

Publisher, bookseller and poet **Adrienne Monnier** (1892–1955) was also born in Paris. One of the first women in France to open a bookshop and lending library, her 'La Maison des Amis des Livres' became a place where poets and writers of the day came to give readings. The famous 1921 painting of her by Paul-Émile Bécat shows a formidable woman in a felt cloche hat with a brim, wearing her trademark long dress and cape, standing in front of bookshelves. There are also many photographs of her with her friend, and sometime lover, **Sylvia Beach** (1887–1962), who set up the even more famous bookshop Shakespeare and Company around the corner. In 1925, they founded a literary magazine *Le Navire d'Argent* (*The Silver Ship*), translating into French some of the greatest

English-language authors of the day – James Joyce, Ernest Hemingway, **Gertrude Stein** (1874–1946), T. S. Eliot. Though Beach closed her doors during the Second World War, Monnier managed to keep 'La Maison des Amis des Livres' open during the German occupation of Paris. Diagnosed with Ménières disease in 1954, Monnier died by suicide in 1955. Beach survived her, dying in 1962.

Another queen of French literary society was the award-winning Belgian-French author **Marguerite Yourcenar** (1903–1987). She published around fifty works – essays, short stories and novels including *The Garden of Illusions* in 1921 and *Memoirs of Hadrian* in 1951. She won the Prix Femina in 1968, she won the *Grand Prix de l'Académie Française* in 1977 and, in 1980, became its first female member – one of only nine female 'immortels' to date. It's said that the signs for the toilets in the Académie were altered to read 'Messieurs' and 'Marguerite Yourcenar'. Portraying gay and bisexual lives in her work as both honourable and, for want of a better word, practical, the dedication in her memoir to her lifelong partner, American English professor and translator **Grace Frick** (1903–1979), in *Memoirs of Hadrian*, is beautiful:

> 'Even the longest dedication is too short and too commonplace to honour a friendship so uncommon . . . in the entire life of some fortunate writers, there must have been someone who . . . bolsters our courage . . . approves, or sometimes disputes, our ideas . . . who shares with us, and with equal fervour, the joys of art and living . . .'

The Swedish-speaking Finnish novelist, children's author, artist and short-story writer **Tove Jansson** (1914–2001) was born in Helsinki, then part of the Russian Empire, a few weeks after the beginning of the First World War. Jansson was originally an artist. She held her first solo exhibition in 1943, at the same time as designing graphics for book covers and writing short stories and articles for publication. Beloved for her children's novels about the Moomins, she worked with her lover and partner, the American-born Finnish artist **Tuulikki Pietilä** (1917–2009), who was known as 'Tooti' and was probably the inspiration for the Moomin character 'Too-ticki'. They collaborated on many projects, including the Moomin illustrations which are now exhibited at the Moomin Museum in Tampere, southern Finland. Jansson won the Hans Christian Andersen Medal in 1966.

In Poland, their contemporary **Seweryna Szmaglewska** (1916–1992) was to become one of the most important Polish writers of the twentieth century. One of very few Polish prisoners to survive incarceration at Auschwitz-Birkenau to testify at the Nuremberg Trials, after the Second World War she became celebrated for writing novels for young people and adults, including her memoir *Smoke over Birkenau* and her novel *Black Feet,* published in 1960.

ALL OVER THE world, as the twentieth century shifted shape after the First World War, and then shifted and shifted again, women writers were recording change, committing their widely different experiences to paper.

In India, the novelist, short-story writer, film-maker and campaigner **Ismat Chughtai** (1915–1991) was one of the most significant voices in Urdu literature of the twentieth century. She was put on trial in 1945 in Lahore – two years before the Partition of India and creation of Pakistan – and charged with obscenity for her short story 'Lihaaf', which the authorities felt promoted female homosexuality. She was acquitted. Her near contemporary, the prize-winning Bengali novelist, short-story writer, journalist and teacher **Mahasweta Devi** (1926–2016) was born in Dacca (present-day Bangladesh). The author of more than one hundred novels and over twenty collections of short stories, her first novel, inspired by the life of the **Lakshmibai, Rani of Jhansi** (*c.* 1828–1858), was published in 1956. Putting the lives of marginalized communities and women centre stage, Devi shone a light on the often brutal suppression of tribal communities and untouchables in West Bengal by powerful upper-caste landlords, moneylenders and corrupt government officials.

> 'I speak out of the deep of night
> out of the deep of darkness
> and out of the deep of night I speak.
>
> **Forough Farrokhzad**

Turkish novelist and thinker **Elif Shafak** (b. 1971) introduced me to the work of the inspirational Iranian poet and documentary film-maker **Forough Farrokhzad** (1934–1967). Brave, a writer of protest and principle, she wrote about women's hidden lives, expectations and desires. Farrokhzad died in a car crash in Tehran in 1967 and her poetry was banned for more than a decade after the Islamic Revolution. Since then, her reputation as one of Iran's greatest writers has been steadily growing.

> 'There is no greater agony than
> bearing an untold story inside you.'
>
> *Maya Angelou*

In North America, too, new voices were coming to the fore in all kinds of genres. **Ann Petry** (1908–1997) originally published her first short story, 'Marie of the Cabin Club', under a male pseudonym of Arnold Petri. Petry trained as a pharmacist and was intended to go into the family business, but moving to Harlem in New York just before the outbreak of the Second World War – and witnessing the poverty, segregation and hardship in Black urban communities at first hand – she began writing journalism, articles and fiction instead. Petry volunteered for the National Association for the Advancement of Colored People (NAACP), joined the American Negro Theatre in Harlem and, in 1946, published her debut novel, *The Street*. The story of a young Black single mother struggling against discrimination, sexual harassment and class divisions in New York during the war, it was a barn-storming bestseller and the first novel by an African American woman to sell more than a million copies. Photographs show her in a black suit with white collar and tie, and her trademark three strings of pearls. In 1947, Petry returned to Connecticut, where she began writing for children and published a biography of the great abolitionist **Harriet Tubman** (1822–1913).

Zora Neale Hurston (1891–1960) was another key figure in the Harlem Renaissance. A novelist, anthropologist and film-maker, Hurston depicted life in the early 1900s in the racially divided American South and her best-known novel, *Their Eyes Were Watching God*, was published in 1937. She also wrote more than fifty short stories, plays and essays, and had a fierce interest in African American and Caribbean folklore. Hurston's fiction went unacknowledged for years, and she died without receiving the money she'd earned from her writings. Then, in 1973, **Alice Walker** went in search of her unmarked grave, found it and, two years later, published an article in the March 1975 edition of *Ms.* magazine entitled 'In Search of Zora Neale Hurston'. Finally, fifteen years after Hurston's death, interest in this incredible writer was revived. As a postscript, a collection of folktales gathered during the 1920s – *Every Tongue Got to Confess* – was published in 2001 after the manuscript was discovered in the Smithsonian archives.

> 'Create dangerously, for people who read dangerously . . . [Write] knowing in part that no matter how trivial your words may seem, someday, somewhere, someone may risk his or her life to read them.'
>
> **Edwidge Danticat**

In 1950, **Gwendolyn Brooks** (1917–2000) won the Pulitzer Prize for Poetry, making her the first African American writer to win a Pulitzer. Appointed Poet Laureate of Illinois in 1968, she was the first African American woman to be inducted into the American Academy of Arts and Letters in 1976.

The American-born Irish writer **Anne McCaffrey** (1926–2011) was the first woman to win a Hugo Award for fiction – winning in 1968 for her novella *Weyr Search* – and the first to win a Nebula Award. Fellow American, the legendary **Ursula K. Le Guin** (1929–2018) – who published a translation of Gabriela Mistral's poetry – was the first woman to win a Hugo for a full-length novel in 1970, *The Left Hand of Darkness*, and the first woman to win for a short story in 1974.

> 'If there's a book that you want to read, but it hasn't been written yet, then you must write it.'
>
> **Toni Morrison**

THERE ARE MANY thousands of writers whose names could be in this chapter, and even more whose names have been forgotten or marginalized – especially those whose work has never been translated into other languages, so has stayed primarily within the borders of their country.

Censorship still flexes its muscles all over the world and, by these lights, any woman picking up a pen is still, in some ways, being transgressive. It matters now, as much as it ever did, that women's writing is kept on the shelf and that women, whoever they are, feel they have the right to make their voices heard.

As we've seen, prizes are one of the most effective ways of keeping works of quality in print and on the shelf for future generations of readers. The Women's Prize for Fiction is the largest annual celebration of international women's writing in the world. Open to women of any nationality writing in English, it was first awarded in 1996 to **Helen Dunmore** (1952–2017). Winners include **Carol Shields** (1935–2003) and the British writer **Andrea Levy** (1956–2019), as well as those still burning bright such as **Ali Smith** (b. 1962), **Kamila Shamsie** (b. 1973) and **Chimamanda Ngozi Adichie** (b. 1977).

Each year, the winner is presented with a small bronze statue known as 'The Bessie', the original cast of which was donated by the sculptor **Grizel Niven** (1906–2007). I have a resin copy, a gift from 1996 when we launched the prize. About ten centimetres high, my Bessie sits on my desk watching over me as I write.

> 'A word after a word after a word is power.'
>
> ***Margaret Atwood***

NORTHERN BAPTIST COLLEGE, RAWDEN.— Mr. H. J. Paull, Architect.

Rawdon Baptist College, Yorkshire

Lily

My GREAT-GRANDMOTHER'S PARENTS, Samuel Gosnell Green and Elizabeth Leader Collier, were married in October 1848. Lily was born a year later. Her father continued his ministry in Taunton until 1851. A few months after the birth of Lily's eldest brother, Frederick, the family moved to West Riding in Yorkshire where Samuel was to teach classics and mathematics at the Horton Baptist Academy.

Founded by the Yorkshire and Lancashire Baptists in 1804 in Little Horton, the academy's first principal aimed to identify and train preachers committed to evangelism. Lily was very young, and it's impossible to know if she registered the family's changed circumstances. But the environment and prosperous industrial landscape must have been very different from the soft green hills of Somerset.

The soil around Bradford was too poor for arable crops, so manufacturing and trade had flourished. It had always been a multicultural area – Angles, Norse, Danish, Norman French, as well as people of Celtic origin had settled there – but in the early nineteenth century, German cloth merchants and immigrants from Ireland were drawn to Bradford to work in the growing textile industries. These were the boom years, leading to Bradford being nicknamed the 'Wool Capital of the World', but massive expansion also led to huge problems of overcrowding and pollution. Grey stone and slate, the rattle of cotton mills and back-to-back slum housing, fifteen-hour days and the endless grind and belch of machinery all took an immense toll. Social campaigners were trying to raise the living standards of the many people who lived and worked in the mills. Horton Baptist Academy itself was housed in a converted weaver's shed and had outgrown itself. By the time the Green family arrived, there were plans to move to a new academy in a village some nine miles away to the north-west of Leeds.

Rawdon Baptist College was a purpose-built residential teaching college in woodlands overlooking the River Aire. The architecture was ornate, a kind of Tudor Gothic, with a library, classrooms and principal's residence in the main building, and apartments on either side. It was grand, it was modern, it was comfortable. The opening ceremony was held on 4 September 1859 and, though I assume Samuel was there, I don't know if Elizabeth and their children were with him: Lily was now nearly ten, Frederick was eight, Samuel (Junior) had been born in 1853, Edwin in 1858. What we do know is that Samuel took over as principal in 1863 and remained there until 1876. Lily's remaining siblings – Arnold, Helen (known as Nellie) and Alfred – were all born there, and possibly two other brothers whose brief lives have not been recorded. We also know that Lily's experiences at Rawdon were significant and would, more than thirty years later, be the inspiration for her most successful novel, *The Vicar of Langthwaite*. It was a place that mattered to her.

We all leave clues to our lives, to the people we are, sometimes without meaning to. By reading everything I could get my hands on – letters, diary entries, her novels, essays and poems – I have been able to get some sense of the woman Lily was in her middle and old age. But it's been harder to find Martha Louisa Green, the girl she was before she became Mrs Lily Watson. It's not solely the lack of sources, although I haven't yet found anything written by her in childhood apart from her 1861 novelette. It's more that I can get only glimpses of her from photographs and from the observations of other people. It's a matter of interpreting the silences and the absences, the things not said, as much as the few hard facts.

When beginning to research any life, the first decision must be how far back should you go? Where does a biography begin and end? Historians, like biographers, must be detectives. The business of writing is one of collecting clues and interpreting them, about 'reading against the grain' as E. H. Carr wrote, about separating the things that matter from those that, in the end, are merely background noise.

Spending time in archives, libraries and museums, you learn that the more you discover, the more there is to discover. Like links on a silver chain, one piece of knowledge leads to another and then to another, until you find yourself perhaps several generations away from those whom you'd set out to research. At the same time, you must pay attention to the context, the environment in which a person was raised or lived, the attitudes of family and community. These things will make a difference: support or resistance, unfairness or privilege, opportunity or repression, a world small or vast. Everything contributes.

Walking in Lily's footsteps, I had to be strict. I didn't want to dilute her presence at the heart of things, or disappear down too many rabbit holes, but I had very little information about her in her younger years. Instead, I tried to find what contemporaneous records I could. That included the 'Autobiography and Notes' of Samuel Watson, a young man who, in the summer of 1866, would see Lily's photograph in an album and fall completely in love. I hoped, by seeing her through young Sam's eyes, I might get closer to knowing her.

I don't have the photograph that caused Sam's heart to sing. But I do have another of Lily propped up against the screen of my computer. It shows a slight girl of about fourteen, thoughtful and serious and determined, her hair in ringlets and a pendant around her neck.

Top: Huda Sha'arawi (1879–1947)
Bottom: Helen Keller (1880–1968)

2

Blackboards & Bluestockings

'I celebrate teaching that celebrates transgressions –
a movement against and beyond boundaries.
It is that movement which makes education
the practice of freedom.'

Teaching to Transgress,
bell hooks, 1994

LILY GREW UP IN a school. Years later, she was to use her childhood as the inspiration for the heroine in her bestselling novel *The Vicar of Langthwaite*. The daughter of a respected teacher at Rawdon Baptist Academy, later the principal, Lily would often have been in the company of professors and male students. She valued the acquisition of knowledge, and had access to books via the school library. She admired the teachers themselves, and those who dedicated themselves to learning. Compared to her brothers, her educational opportunities were limited – and, in years to come, she would prioritize her sons' education over that of her three daughters – but set beside the vast majority of girls at the time, Lily was lucky.

For most of human history, education has been in the hands of the few – the wealthy and the powerful at court, within ivy-drenched university walls and religious institutions. Women were almost always excluded – many still are – or tolerated as an exception to the rule. They might have been the daughters of kings or viziers, wives of rulers or sisters coat-tailing on their brothers' lessons. But women and girls have fought across the centuries for the right to an education, so in this chapter, we'll celebrate some of the inspirational women – scholars, teachers, professors, librarians, lecturers – who made all the difference.

'One child, one teacher, one book, one
pen can change the world.'

Malala Yousafzai

Even in 2022, the fight for equality of education for women and girls with their male counterparts is far from over. The battles fought by the inspirational educational campaigner **Malala Yousafzai** (b. 1997) – who was shot by the Taliban in Pakistan in 2012 for the 'crime' of going to school – are still raging. Yousafzai jointly won the 2014 Nobel Peace Prize at the age of only seventeen, the youngest ever Nobel laureate, but her fight goes on. Since August 2021, girls cannot attend school beyond the age of thirteen in Afghanistan. We can imagine and know all sorts of reasons for this inequality – misogyny, ideology, fear, a male desire for power or control – but perhaps Christine de Pizan's centuries-old analysis is most true . . .

'Not all men (and especially the wisest) share the opinion that it is bad for women to be educated. But it is very true that many foolish men have claimed this because it displeased them that women knew more than they did.'

The situation in Afghanistan is a tragic step backwards. Fathers and brothers are campaigning alongside their sisters, mothers and daughters to reverse this new edict, one of many to curtail and restrict the lives of girls and women. But it's far from the only country in the world where boys are given more educational opportunities than girls. So, I want to go back in history and seek out some of the early pioneers making their voices heard in the battle for equal education.

LET'S START IN Egypt, as one of the oldest recorded civilizations. Egyptologists and historians give different dates for the divisions of Ancient Egypt into the Old, Middle and New Kingdoms – and they're not distinctions Egyptians themselves would have recognized – but it's the New Kingdom (*c.* 1550–*c.* 1070 BCE) that interests us in our quest for evidence of female teachers. Under Egyptian law of the time, high-born women enjoyed the same rights as men, their standing dependent on social class, not sex. All landed property descended in the female line, a woman could sell, buy and administer her own property, make legal contracts, act as an executor of a will, witness legal documents, bring an action at court. It's on such parity that equality is founded.

Deir el-Medina was a village on the west bank of the Nile, opposite the opulent city of Luxor, a village created for the artisans and craftsmen of Thebes working on the tombs in the Valley of the Queens and the Valley of the Kings. From excavated documents, preserved for so many years in the parched sands, we have evidence of women both writing and teaching, though not on an equal footing with their male counterparts. Nonetheless, there were female scribes, religious leaders within certain cults, all teachers if you will.

But it's to Ancient India and Greece we must turn to find some of the first female teachers and thinkers whose individual identities have been recorded. **Gargi Vachaknavi** (*c.* ninth to the seventh century BCE) was an Indian natural philosopher. Often known simply as Gargi, it's hard to date her precisely. Some contemporaneous documents mention her as one of the two wives of a Vedic sage who lived around the eighth century BCE. In the Hindu epic *Mahabharata*, Gargi is described as a philosopher who never married. Or it's possible that this refers to **Sulabha Maitreyi** – referred to simply as Maitreyi – who was also a philosopher and mentioned in the *Upanishads*. In ancient Sanskrit literature, Gargi is known as a *brahmavadini*, a commentator of the Veda. Is it possible that, like Avvaiyar, she was more than one woman but with a single name?

The same is true of **Pythia** (*c.* seventh century BCE to the fourth century CE), certainly a title not an individual woman. In Delphi, below the south-western slopes of Mount Parnassus in Greece, Pythia, also known as the Oracle of Delphi, was the high priestess of the Temple of Apollo. Mentioned by Aeschylus, Aristotle and Thucydides among others, Pythia was the most prestigious and best-documented of the Greek oracles. Named high priestesses of Delphi include **Themistoclea** (534–459 BCE), who was considered a philosopher and recorded as Pythagoras's teacher.

> 'Or how Aspasia's parties shone,
> The first Bas-bleu at Athens known'
>
> **Hannah More**

From Delphi to Athens to meet the legendary teacher and rhetorician **Aspasia** (*c.* 470–*c.* 400 BCE). Born in Meletus, in present-day

Turkey, little is known of her life nor how she came to be settled in Athens – she was known as a 'metic' woman, that's to say a foreign resident without the full rights of a citizen. A teacher and rhetorician, what today we might call a philosopher, and highly acknowledged thinker, her reputation was denigrated by some contemporaries – Aristophanes, Cratinus and Eupolis all referred to her as a prostitute or madam – but Plutarch wrote of her and Socrates described Aspasia as his teacher. So, in common with many women of achievement, you could say she was well documented rather than well regarded. It wasn't until the eighteenth century that Aspasia's reputation as a writer and thinker began to be restored. The British abolitionist, wit, religious thinker and philanthropist **Hannah More** (1745–1833) includes Aspasia in her famous poem 'The Bas Bleu: or, Conversation' as an example of a brilliant orator and teacher. A 'bas-bleu' is a bluestocking . . .

Living in the high, semi-arid region of Cappadocia, in central Turkey, **Macrina the Younger** (*c*. 327–379 CE) was an early Christian thinker and teacher. She transformed her family's estates into a community of female and male philosophers and ascetics. A biography written by her brother, *Life of Macrina*, makes clear she was respected and influential, that she was a woman whose advice was highly sought after and valued. The biography states she rejected classical learning in favour of scripture, and sought a life of piety and virginity, though it's a pity we do not have her own account of her life to compare to her brother's biography.

> 'Reserve your right to think, for even to think wrongly is better than not to think at all.'
>
> *Hypatia*

A contemporary of Macrina, **Hypatia** (*c*. 355–415/416 CE) is best-remembered for the tragedy of her death rather than the importance of her life. In her time, she was one of the most celebrated teachers of philosophy, mathematics and astronomy in the world. She lived and taught in Alexandria, on the delta of the Nile, publishing treatises on mathematical texts (though none has survived), constructing scientific equipment and being skilled in the use of the astrolabe for ship navigation – she is recorded as having taught Synesius how to use one – and inventing a device for measuring fluid density.

These were complicated times. The old Pagan world was collapsing and the Jewish community was in conflict with the upstart Christian religion, which was riven with infighting. Hypatia was caught in the crossfire. In attempting not to be partisan, she allowed Christians as well as Pagans to attend her lectures, which pleased nobody. Driving through Alexandria in either 415 or 416, Hypatia was ambushed, dragged from her carriage by a murderous Christian mob, stripped and beaten to death, her body burned. Was the brutality of her murder due to her being a woman in what was traditionally a male space, a woman literally being cut down to size? It would be far from the only time. The astrologer and poet **Khana**, who lived sometime between the ninth and the twelfth centuries, is said to have had her tongue cut out to prevent her from teaching, on the orders of either her husband or, in some versions, her father, who resented being overshadowed by her brilliance.

Four hundred years after Hypatia's murder, the world's first university was founded by a woman in Morocco. **Fatima bint Muhammad Al-Fihriya** (*c.* 800–880 CE) is credited with establishing the al-Qarawiyyin mosque in Fez in 859, as a place both of worship and of learning. There are some who have tried to question her role – in part because the evidence of her work was only recorded by Ibn Abi Zar' in the fourteenth century – but majority opinion is that she was instrumental in the mosque's creation. With its green-tiled prayer hall and white minaret, it's a familiar landmark on the Fez skyline even today. Al-Qarawiyyin collected an extraordinary range of manuscripts for its library, including a document dating from 1207 said to be the world's oldest surviving medical degree. Although students were male, there was a gallery overlooking the scholar's circle where women might sit to listen to their discussions. The educational wing started to accept female students in the 1940s and became a state university in 1963, making it the oldest continuous establishment of higher education anywhere in the world.

In 1475 in Korea, **Queen Insu** (1437–1504) published an instruction manual for women, *Naehun*. The oldest surviving work by a Korean woman, it gives a fabulous glimpse both into the Korean court of the time and to fifteenth-century attitudes to gender and sexuality based on Confucian ideals. It would be two hundred years before **Im Yunjidang** (1721–1793) became the first acknowledged female Confucian philosopher in Korea, although probably she was not accepted as such during her lifetime. Nobly born, she argued for a woman's right to become a sage. Thirty-five pieces of her work have survived, all published after her death.

> 'Though I am a woman, the nature I originally received is no different from that of a man.'
>
> **Im Yunjidang**

IN THE MEDIEVAL era in Europe, formal education and scholarship for girls and women was mostly vested within Christian religious institutions, as we've already seen with Hrotsvitha or Héloise d'Argenteuil.

Agnes d'Harcourt (d. *c.* 1291) was a nun at the Abbey of Longchamp, a convent of Poor Clares established to the west of Paris by the younger sister of the king, Saint Louis. Taking her vows in 1260, d'Harcourt served alongside the abbey's founder, **Isabelle of France** (1225–1270), and became abbess in 1279. Her biography of her friend and mentor, *The Life of Isabelle*, is thought to be the first biography in French of a woman written by another woman. D'Harcourt is one of the 998 historical and mythical women's names painted on the handmade white tiles of Judy Chicago's 'Heritage Floor' surrounding *The Dinner Party*.

> 'Do not lose heart, even if you should discover that you lack qualities necessary for the work to which you are called.'
>
> **Angela Merici**

In Lombardy, two centuries later, **Angela Merici** (1474–1540) went a step further in formalizing education for women and girls within a religious framework, by founding the Company of St Ursula in 1535.

With twelve teaching companions, she dedicated her life to providing a religious education for girls to prepare them to be better Christian wives and mothers. Within four years, Merici's original group had more than doubled. Members took no vows, nor had a habit specific to their order, but Merici – who went on to open orphanages and girls' schools – did write a 'Rule of Life' for the group, which included a commitment to celibacy, poverty and obedience.

What was exceptional about Merici's mission was that it took education out of the home. Most girls, if they received an education at all, received it from their parents, often eavesdropping on their brothers' lessons, a pattern we'll see in the pages that follow. Beatified in 1768, and later canonized in 1807, Merici deserves to be celebrated as an early pioneer in girls' education.

A little later, the Spanish Dominican nun and scholar **Juliana Morell** (1594–1653) travelled with her father to France as a child and studied Greek, Latin and Hebrew, as well as mathematics, rhetoric, ethics, astronomy, music, law and physics. Born in Barcelona, by the age of twelve, in 1606 or 1607, she had written a thesis on ethics and morality, and in 1608, defended her law thesis in Avignon and may have been awarded a doctorate. If so, that would make her the first woman ever to receive a doctoral degree. That same year, Morell joined the Dominican convent of San Práxedes in Avignon. She took her final vows in the summer of 1610 and, three years later, became abbess, a position she held until her death. During her years within the convent, she published poetry in Latin and French, translated religious texts and wrote a manual entitled 'Spiritual Exercises for Eternity and a Small Preparatory Exercise for the Holy Profession'. However, the first woman to receive a doctorate, for which the evidence is certain and undisputed, is the Venetian scholar **Elena Lucrezia Cornaro Piscopia** (1646–1684). She received a doctorate in philosophy from the University of Padua in 1678. Either way, Morell, like Piscopia a century later, was an extraordinary woman.

In England, there had been choir schools attached to cathedrals from the early Middle Ages – the King's School, Canterbury, was founded in 597 and the King's School, Rochester, in 604. With the foundation of universities from the twelfth century, schools independent of the Church started to be established – Winchester in Hampshire in 1382, Oswestry School in Shropshire in 1407 and Eton in Windsor in 1440 being the three first 'free' schools. Only boys were accepted.

The extension of a network of grammar schools in England started in the mid-sixteenth century during the brief reign of Edward VI, providing an education to the sons of the middle classes all over the country. The Reformation throughout Europe and the availability of new vernacular editions of the Bible were transformational – Jacques Lefèvre d'Étaples published the first Bible in French in Antwerp in

1530, Luther's translation from the original Hebrew and Greek was finished in 1534, and the King James Bible was published in English in 1611, having been proposed at the 1604 Hampton Court Conference. All had a huge effect on literacy, since women and men could now read Holy Scripture for themselves. Many women were taught to read by parish priests, if there was no one at home able to do so.

Following the Act of Uniformity in 1662, religious dissenters set up academies to educate students of Nonconformist families who weren't prepared to subscribe to the articles of the Church of England. Some of these 'dissenting academies' still survive, the oldest being Bristol Baptist College. Mostly intended to train boys for ministry, Manchester College and Regent's Park College within the University of Oxford were also part of this tradition as, of course, was Rawdon Baptist Academy in Yorkshire, where my great-grandmother spent her childhood.

By the seventeenth century, there were strong voices advocating for girls' education, specifically for schools for girls. Philanthropists endowed schools in their home towns and dame schools, run by women, grew in popularity as ideas about education changed.

> 'Women are from their very infancy
> debarred those Advantages with the want of
> which they are afterwards reproached.'
>
> *Mary Astell*

A key pioneering campaigning voice was the writer and philosopher **Mary Astell** (1666–1731). Born in the year of the Fire of London, she has good claim to be termed the first British feminist, some 170 years before the word came into general circulation.

A passionate advocate for fairer education for girls and educational opportunities for women, in 1694 she anonymously published 'A Serious Proposal to the Ladies for the Advancement of their True and Greatest Interest Part I'. It's interesting that instead of using the words 'by Anon.' or something similar, Astell described the work as being written 'By a Lover of her Sex', thereby not only refusing to deny the author was female but also emphasizing her purpose. Clear-sighted, laying bare the hypocrisy and nonsenses by which critics tried to justify limiting women's education, Astell made a strong case for all-female colleges. She followed it three years later with proposals for female-designed education. In 1709, she was appointed head of a charity school for girls in Chelsea, London. Astell designed the curriculum and it was probably the first school in England to have had an elected all-female board of governors.

MY GREAT-GRANDMOTHER WAS a woman of her time and class. Lily believed in girls' education and purposeful scholarship, though as much as a way of producing obedient wives and good mothers as for any grander ambition. In the later years of her life, she served on committees for the Surrey Education Board and wrote articles about education for girls. Lily was a keen reader, spoke French, Italian and German, had a passable knowledge of Latin and Ancient Greek, and was a successful novelist and poet. Yet, all the same, I suspect she would have hated to be thought intellectual or called a 'bluestocking'.

The expression actually dates from the mid-eighteenth century and is usually attributed to the Irish intellectual **Elizabeth Vesey** (1715–1791) – 'Sylph' to her friends. She invited a distinguished foreign gentleman to speak at one of her literary parties in Bath. He declined, on the grounds that he wasn't dressed appropriately. Vesey is said to have dismissed his excuse and ordered him to come in his 'blue stockings', that's to say his everyday clothes. The anecdote was recounted by **Madame d'Arblay** (1752–1840), the diarist and novelist better known as **Fanny Burney**, and gained traction. But the first significant literary explanation of what it meant to be a 'bluestocking' was the wonderful long-form poem citing Aspasia, as we saw earlier, written by Hannah More in 1783 and published in 1787, 'The Bas Bleu: or, Conversation'. It's a superb history of the art of conversation, which namechecks Vesey and **Elizabeth Montagu** (1718–1800), 'Queen of the Bluestockings' – who had a rival salon in London – as well as famous figures from contemporary literary London to classical antiquity. More's introduction is gently mocking of male critics whose own earlier gatherings were waylaid by more trivial pursuits.

By the late nineteenth century, the term 'bluestocking' was almost always intended to be derogatory, sneering at women who were intellectual, who read and debated, who campaigned for women's access to higher education. But, by the twentieth century, women campaigning for higher education had made the term their own. Harriet Vane, heroine of four novels by **Dorothy L. Sayers** (1893–1957), returns to her alma mater in *Gaudy Night*, the 1935 detective story set in a fictional Oxford women's college inspired by Somerville College. A terrific puzzle, it's also an excellent digest of discussions around women's education and what it means to be a bluestocking. The real Somerville College was named after the Scottish scientist and polymath **Mary Somerville** (1780–1872) in 1879. The word 'scientist' was coined to describe her – before Somerville, they talked only of 'men of science'. An astronomer, a meteorologist, physicist and science writer, her book, *Physical Geography*, published in 1848, was the first ever geography textbook written in English.

> 'Women, like men, must be educated with a view to action, or their studies cannot be called education.'
>
> **Harriet Martineau**

In many parts of the world during the nineteenth century, the idea that all children should be educated, regardless of sex or class – and that education would lead to a more successful and prosperous society – was gaining in popularity.

The great social thinker, abolitionist and reformer **Harriet Martineau** (1802–1876) – like my great-grandmother, of French Huguenot descent – was one of many campaigning in the UK for more ordered provision of education for girls. It's a century that saw an influx of women working outside the home as governesses or teachers in dame schools and private boarding schools. Some were excellent. Others, like Cowan Bridge School in Lancashire where the Brontë sisters were pupils, abused and humiliated the girls in their care. Cowan Bridge was put on the page as Lowood school in *Jane Eyre*.

According to Vera Brittain in *Lady Into Woman*, there were some 24,700 governesses in the UK in 1851, receiving an average salary of only £25 a year. Fifty years later, according to the Census of 1901, some 120,000 women had chosen to enter the teaching profession. Along with domestic work, teaching was one of the few areas – perhaps because it was, in some ways, seen as caring for children, so therefore women's work – where women could earn their own money.

Women who taught were not always respected, however. Nineteenth-century literature is awash with governesses and teachers, often presented as creatures to be pitied or despised. And their position was precarious – neither part of the family, nor part of the household staff.

Other governesses appearing in novels include: *Emma* by **Jane Austen**; *The Governess* by **Marguerite Blessington** (1789–1849); *Agnes Grey* by **Anne Brontë** (1820–1849); *Jane Eyre* by **Charlotte Brontë**; *The Good French Governess* by **Maria Edgeworth** (1768–1849); *Caroline Mordaunt, or, The Governess* by **Mary Martha Sherwood** (1775–1851); and *East Lynne* by **Mrs Henry Wood** (1814–1887).

The 1880 Education Act made education compulsory for all children until the age of ten. In 1893, under the Elementary Education (School Attendance) Act, it was raised to the age of eleven and the right to education extended to children who were deaf and blind. In 1899, the school-leaving age was increased again to thirteen. It was the same for girls as for boys, suggesting that to the authorities at least, the importance of a basic education for girls was becoming more widely accepted.

The world was changing at last, and not just in Britain, of course.

WE PROBABLY ALL have teachers who changed how we saw the world or inspired us to fall in love with learning. The daughter of a teacher, the wife of a teacher, the daughter-in-law of a teacher, I've seen at first hand how students never forget someone who believed in them when no one else did.

Honor Drayton, the sixteen-year-old protagonist of my great-grandmother's 1896 novel *A Fortunate Exile*, is seen as a 'troublesome' child, a girl who is boisterous and doesn't fit in. Sent away to boarding school in the Jura Mountains, she is rescued from her teenage misery by the guidance of the headmistress, Miss Arundel. Though the novel itself has very old-fashioned views about what constitutes appropriate female behaviour, it's also vehement in its admiration for teachers and women in education, fostering confidence and self-respect in their charges. So here are a few more pioneering women contemporaneous with Lily, whom she might have read about or admired.

'We shall overcome and success will be ours
in the future. The future belongs to us.'

Savitribai Phule

One of the most significant voices in India of the nineteenth century
was **Savitribai Phule** (1831–1897). A poet, and educational and social
campaigner, Phule is considered the first professional female teacher
in India as well as one of the founding mothers of Indian feminism.
Despite huge opposition, she and her husband set up one of the first
schools for girls in India – at Pune in Maharashtra – in 1848, and
went on to open a further seventeen. A campaigner for social justice,
the dispossessed and unsupported, Phule also opened a care centre
for pregnant rape victims and campaigned for the rights of widows.
As bubonic plague swept through Maharashtra in 1897, she opened
a clinic for victims. Phule died, as she had lived, after contracting
the illness from one of those she was trying to save.

'Special children must have special schools,
with well-trained teachers who use
materials adapted to those children's
capabilities.'

Margaret Bancroft

Born in Philadelphia, **Margaret Bancroft** (1854–1912) was a pioneer
in education for children with disabilities, in a time when children
with different needs were often confined to an asylum. **Anne Sullivan**
(1866–1936) was another outstanding teacher, best known for her work
with the author and disability activist **Helen Keller** (1880–1968), who
lost her sight and hearing when she was eighteen months old. Sullivan
taught her to read by tracing words on the palm of her hand.

'What do I consider a teacher should be? One
who breathes life into knowledge so that it
takes new form in progress and civilization.'

Helen Keller

Italian doctor **Maria Montessori** (1870–1952) founded a new form of education for pre-school children that still bears her name today, persevering with her system of play-based learning despite huge opposition from male students and professors who objected to a woman being allowed to study medicine at all. Born five years after Montessori in Florida, **Mary McLeod Bethune** (1875–1955) was an African American civil rights activist and presidential advisor who founded a private school for African American girls in Daytona, Florida, at the turn of the last century. There is an amazing photograph from around 1905 of her standing with her students in line on a dusty road – the youngest girls are in white dresses, the intermediate class wearing white shirts and knee-length skirts, the oldest students in white shirts and long skirts, black stockings and boots, with straw boater school hats.

> 'I'm writing to free myself and free women from this prison. My writing is dedicated to all women over the world.'
>
> *Huda Sha'arawi*

By this time, the fight for education for girls was happening all over the world, often as part of the broader campaign for women's rights. Known as Egypt's 'first feminist', advocate for female suffrage, nationalist, poet and educational campaigner **Huda Sha'arawi** (1879–1947) removed her veil at Cairo railway station when returning from the International Women's Suffrage Alliance Conference in Rome in March 1923, causing uproar. **Ceza Nabarawi** (1897–1985) and **Nabaweyya Moussa** (1886–1951) also removed their veils that day. Sha'arawi was the leader of the first women's street protest in 1919 and founded the Egyptian Feminist Union in 1923 which, among other things, campaigned for increased educational opportunities for girls and women. She led an all-female picket at the opening of the Egyptian Parliament in 1924, successfully fought for the marriage age of girls to be raised to sixteen and opened a girls' school. As the Founding President of the Arab Feminist Union, she published several magazines, a memoir, *The Harem Years*, and *Women Between Submission and Freedom*, one of the cornerstone texts of Egyptian feminism.

Following in her footsteps five years later, the Lebanese feminist, educational reformer and translator **Anbara Salam Khalidi** (1897–1986) also made history. In 1927, invited by the American University of Beirut to speak about her time studying in England in the 1920s, she removed her veil in the lecture hall, the first Muslim woman in Lebanon to do so publicly. She translated Homer's *Odyssey* and Virgil's *Aeneid* into Arabic, the first to do so, and campaigned tirelessly for girls' right to an education.

> '[Becoming a professor was] my contribution to the battle for fair dealing for women in public and professional life'.
>
> *Edith Morley*

One of the absurdities of higher education in the nineteenth century was that, even when women were gradually allowed to attend university and to sit examinations, they were not awarded degrees. It wasn't until 1920 – a year after Britain's Sex Disqualification (Removal) Bill was passed, which transformed women's professional and educational opportunities – that female students at Oxford were finally awarded degrees. The University of Cambridge made their female students wait until 1947, two years after the end of the Second World War . . .

Edith Morley (1875–1964) always knew what she wanted. Part of a large family, with a significant age gap between her oldest and youngest siblings, she insisted on being sent away to boarding school like her brothers, rather than being educated at home with a governess as her father had wanted. (Morley's childhood has many things in common with that of my great-grandmother's fictional heroine in A *Fortunate Exile*.) Morley excelled and, in 1899, achieved first-class honours as an external student at Oxford – although, of course, she wasn't awarded her degree, but she didn't let that hold her back. In 1903, she became an assistant lecturer in English at University College in Reading and in 1907, when the college was preparing for university status and therefore decided to award professorships to all heads of departments, they passed Morley over as the only woman. She protested, fought her case and won. In 1908, she was appointed professor in English language, making her the first female professor in England, though it was given begrudgingly – she didn't have an assistant, because it wasn't seen as appropriate for a man to be asked to work under a woman, and after her retirement, the chair was not filled.

Morley was a suffragette. She had her goods seized for refusing to pay her taxes on the grounds that, if she couldn't vote, then she shouldn't be taxed. She spent the night of the 1911 Census walking up and down Aldeburgh High Street with **Elizabeth Garrett Anderson** (1836–1917) – the first woman to be awarded a medical degree in the UK – as part of a similar protest about representation under the law. Morley's publications include *Women Workers in Seven Professions*. The University of Reading holds her correspondence and her lecture notebooks among other papers. A memoir, *Looking Before and After*, was published posthumously. Morley was awarded an OBE – not for her work in education, but for her work with Belgian-Jewish refugees during the Second World War.

Morley wasn't the first female professor in the United Kingdom, though. In 1892, Austrian-born **Emma Ritter-Bondy** (1838–1894) was appointed professor of piano at the Glasgow Athenaeum School of Music, now the Royal Conservatoire of Scotland. It would be another forty-eight years before a second woman was named professor in Scotland. Physician **Margaret Fairlie** (1891–1963) was appointed professor of obstetrics and gynaecology at University College, Dundee, which was part of the University of St Andrews, in 1940.

> 'Every true mathematician sees mathematics everywhere – in a child's swing or a pendulum, in the outline shape of a tree and that of its leaves, in the clouds.'
>
> *Kathleen Ollerenshaw*

We'll meet more women of science, medicine and law in the chapters that follow, many of them trailblazers within universities or institutes of learning, too. But here's one last professor to celebrate, the remarkable **Kathleen Ollerenshaw** (1912–2014).

A shining star in her field, Ollerenshaw was almost completely deaf from the age of eight – she did not receive her first effective hearing aid until 1949, when she was thirty-seven years old – so learned to lip read, refusing to let what was then seen as a disability to be used as an excuse by others to reduce her opportunities. At her entrance interview for Somerville College, Oxford, to read mathematics, she didn't inform the college she was deaf until she had been offered a place. Though it was for her work in education that she received her damehood, she was a woman who forged several careers: she was a part-time lecturer in mathematics at the University of Manchester, an honorary member and vice-president of the Manchester Astronomical Society, a Conservative councillor for Rusholme from 1956 until 1981, was Lord Mayor of Manchester, High Sheriff of Greater Manchester, and was one of the key movers in the creation of the Royal Northern College of Music. Ollerenshaw was also an extraordinary sportswoman – lacrosse, cricket and hockey, a keen skier and mountain climber, a figure skater and an ice dancer. Her autobiography – gloriously called *To Talk of Many Things* – was published when she was ninety-three.

A final teacher, the pioneering and extraordinary **Beryl Gilroy** (1924– 2001), award-winning author, children's writer, educator and the first recorded Black British head teacher in Britain. Born in Guyana (then British Guiana) in 1924, she went to teacher training college in Georgetown, then came to England in 1952. Initially, she found it hard to find employment as a teacher, but studied for a diploma in child development and then for a BSc in psychology, and was able to start her London career. In 1968, Gilroy was appointed as a deputy head teacher and, the following year, became the first Black woman head teacher in the London borough of Camden. Her autobiographical account of her experiences, *Black Teacher*, was published in 1976. In the early 1970s she wrote for the pioneering series *Nippers*, edited by children's author and journalist **Leila Berg** (1917–2012), addressing issues such as racism and interracial marriage. Gilroy published her first novel, *Frangipani House*, in 1986, followed by other novels and a collection of poems. Her final novel was published posthumously in 2001. A true trailblazer.

'With a library you are free, not confined by temporary political climates. It is the most democratic of institutions because no one – but no one at all – can tell you what to read and when and how.'

Doris Lessing

THE FINAL AND joyous part of the story of broadening educational opportunities for girls lies in the development of the public library service and free – or almost free – access to books.

Libraries, now, are the most democratic of public spaces. Built of brick and glass, marble or wood, in the heart of towns and cities worldwide, all readers enter on an equal footing. Inside, there will be books to change a life, to inspire, to encourage, to take us on a journey through time and place and space, to any country imagined or real, to hold a mirror up to nature and help us to stand in other people's shoes.

For so long as there have been words inscribed and traced, written down, there have been those who've sought to gather them together. The oldest known library in the world dates from the seventh century BCE in Nineveh, present-day Iraq. Built for the Assyrian ruler Ashurbanipal, nineteenth-century excavations revealed a cache of some thirty thousand cuneiform tablets.

The most famous library of antiquity is probably the Great Library of Alexandria. Built sometime during the reign of Ptolemy the Great in the fourth century BCE following his father's design, estimates vary widely as to how many scrolls might have been stored there – possibly as many as five hundred thousand. A Wonder of the Ancient World, feted by scholars and historians, the library was part of a larger institution dedicated to the Nine Muses. Although folklore has the library being destroyed by fire by Julius Caesar during the Siege of Alexandria in 48 BCE, in truth it's likely that it was mostly storage facilities that were burnt and that the library itself declined over centuries due to lack of funding and support.

Then, as now.

Long after the Western Roman Empire had fallen, Constantinople, the capital of the Byzantine Empire, was thriving. During the fourth century BCE, Constantine established the first Imperial Library, which grew slowly over the next century until there were some one hundred and twenty thousand scrolls and codices held. Disastrously, most of its treasures were lost in 1204, during the Christian sacking of the city.

Though it's known there were many private libraries in ancient China, particularly in the east of the country – the earliest known private library in China was built during the time of the Northern Wei Dynasty (386–534 CE) – the oldest surviving library was founded in 1561 by a government official, in Ningbo, Zhejian Province, and held more than seventy thousand volumes.

Worldwide, dynastic rulers, wealthy individuals, religious institutions, have always sought to acquire and collect precious and rare books, women as well as men. In the sixteenth century, **Jeanne d'Albret** (1528–1572), the Protestant queen of Navarre, and **Catherine de' Medici** (1519–1589), queen consort of France from 1547 to 1559, then queen regent from 1560 to 1563, both built extensive personal libraries. In England, **Mildred Cecil** (1526–1589), Baroness Burghley, is known to have curated one of the largest private libraries in the land, though most of her collection has been lost.

Regarding those libraries attached to museums and to places of study, to cathedrals and synagogues and temples, to palaces and private homes, the collections are sometimes made more widely available to scholars, other times access is tightly controlled. The issue for women is, of course, evident. For much of history, women were barred from these spaces. And if the majority of curators were men, then it is likely there will be fewer works by women placed on the shelves or kept in the archives.

The Malatestiana Library in Cesena in Italy is considered to be the first public library in Europe – that's to say, the first library not owned by the Church, and it was opened to the public in 1454. France's Bibliothèque Nationale in Paris opened its doors to the public in 1692. In Madrid, the Palace Public Library was founded by Philip V in 1712, though not opened to the public as the Biblioteca Nacional until 1896. The Library within the Royal Palace of Mafra in Portugal dates from the early eighteenth century, intended originally as a Franciscan Friary. And in St Petersburg, the extraordinary warrior queen **Catherine the Great** (1729–1796) – who ruled Russia for more than thirty years – approved the project to build the Imperial Public Library in 1795, eighteen months before her death. As well as her own extensive private collection, much of the foundation collection had been looted from the Załuski Library, seized by Russian forces after the Partition of Poland in 1794. Built in Warsaw between 1747 and 1795 by the Załuski brothers, both Roman Catholic bishops, it was the first Polish public library and one of the earliest public libraries in Europe, welcoming women as well as men. Catherine was also instrumental in changing women's education in Russia, establishing the Smoly Institute in 1764 to teach daughters of the nobility, and the Novodevichii Institute for middle-class girls the following year.

> 'I have found the most valuable thing in my wallet is my library card.'
>
> **Laura Bush**

In terms of building nationwide networks, America was ahead of the game. There were parochial libraries attached to Anglican churches throughout the American colonies from the earliest days of the eighteenth century. New York City got its first public library in 1729, launched with a donation of books from the Society for the Propagation of the Gospel. The first free public library supported by taxation in the world was the Peterborough, New Hampshire Town Library, founded in April 1833. Between 1881 and 1919, Andrew Carnegie's fortune helped fund more than 1,700 public libraries throughout the United States.

> 'To my thinking, a great librarian must have a clear head, a strong hand, and, above all, a great heart. And when I look into the future, I am inclined to think that most of the men who achieve this greatness will be women.'
>
> **Melvil Dewey**

In London, a library was founded as part of the British Museum in 1753, based on the collections of Sir Hans Sloane, among others. The key piece of civic legislation in the UK was the Public Libraries Act of 1850, which gave boroughs power to set up free public libraries. The first opened at the Salford Museum and Art Gallery in November that same year. Two years later, the Campfield Library in Manchester was the first to operate a free lending service without subscription.

Enriqueta Rylands (1843–1908) was a British philanthropist and curator, the founder of the John Rylands Library in Manchester in memory of her husband. Secretly negotiating the purchase of the second Earl Spencer's complete library as the foundation collection, she hired the leading Manchester historian and curator **Alice Cooke** (1867–1940) to manage it. The library was inaugurated in October 1899, on the same day that Rylands became the first woman to be granted the Freedom of the City of Manchester. A life-sized white marble statue of Rylands stands in the Reading Room of the library on Deansgate, watching over the collections she helped build.

Researching *Warrior Queens & Quiet Revolutionaries* in June 2021, to my delight I discovered that one of Rylands's advisors was Lily's father, Reverend Samuel Green, and both he and her brother, Arnold, had helped with the collections prior to the opening. Reverend Green also published a memoir of John Rylands. Later on, when more of Lily's letters came into my possession, I learned that the connection was stronger still. Lily and Enriqueta Rylands were personal friends of long standing. There's a letter dated Easter Morning 1890 when Lily writes that she's about to visit Mrs Rylands at Longford Hall. In February 1899, the two women are on holiday together and it is to Mrs Rylands that Lily takes her mother to recuperate after an operation in 1901.

Our second library pioneer is **Dorothy B. Porter** (1905–1995), a quiet revolutionary and five-foot-high dynamo. The first African American woman to complete a degree in library science at Columbia University, she was appointed Librarian at Howard University in Washington in 1930. Over the next forty-three years she built up a comprehensive collection of Black history and culture, as well as celebrating African American scholars, African history, and building Black special collections. She also reorganized the classification system to prevent Black authors from being automatically pigeon-holed under either 'colonization' or 'slavery' rather than being valued as writers in their own and any field – before her intervention, the Dewey Decimal System only had those two categories for any work on Black culture or history:

'I went around the (Howard) library and pulled out every relevant book I could find – the history of slavery, Black poets – for the collection. Over the years the main thing I had to do was beg – from publishers, authors, families. Sometimes it meant being there just after the funeral director took out the bodies and saying, "you want all this junk in the basement?"'

Our final game-changer is the mighty **Florence Boot** (1863–1952). The daughter of a bookseller from St Helier in the Channel Islands, she assisted her husband in founding one of the world's most successful chains of pharmacies – Boots and Co. Ltd – that still has a presence on British high streets today. Boot founded the first all-female hall of residence at the University of Nottingham – known affectionately these days as 'FloBo House' – and it was she who had the brainwave of 'selling beauty' and selling it in the middle of each store. Then, in 1898, she launched the Boots Book-Lovers Library, an affordable subscription service. For Florence, the reading revolution – as part of the education revolution – was as much about giving girls and women independence and financial security as it was about knowledge for knowledge's sake.

> 'The healthy-minded, attractive, alert and intelligent college girl would, in a number of cases, not need more than three months' training as a shop assistant to enable her to earn her own living: six months ought to see her getting more than merely her bread and butter, and in a twelvemonth she could be absolutely independent.'
>
> *Florence Boot*

Boot, who was an almost exact contemporary of my great-grandmother Lily, curated the first selection of books herself and published her first catalogue in 1904. Pretty soon, every branch had a lending library, with dedicated and skilled staff. Books – bearing the distinctive 'green shield' logo on the front and an eyelet on the spine – were displayed on open shelves so readers could browse. Her lending libraries were a huge success. By 1938, some 35 million books a year were being lent out. A revolution indeed.

Martha 'Lily' Green, c. 1863

Lily

IN HIS 'AUTOBIOGRAPHY AND NOTES' – which he began writing in the autumn of 1891 – Lily's future husband Samuel Watson was, by his own admission, a timid boy, a boy who suffered terribly with a stammer and ill health, a boy who never felt confident or sure.

One of fourteen children, few of whom survived to adulthood, Sam was born at 12 Bouverie Street in London on 26 October 1839, into a family who had risen quickly. His paternal great-great-grandfather was a farm labourer and his great-grandfather a soldier, but his grandfather 'by sheer industry' had become a solicitor and founded the firm of Watson & Sons in 1809.

It was a Nonconformist household and life revolved around work and Chapel. His father William – whom he describes as a man of 'strict uprightness, but very little emotion' – was a deacon of the Lion Street Chapel, in Walworth, where Lily's grandfather was the minister. Of his mother Ann, who was a daughter of an ironmonger, Mr Deane, of Old London Bridge, Sam writes how she never spoke 'an unkind or uncharitable word'.

The modest pages of his 'Autobiography' are full of faith and piety, days lived in strict observation. Of crossing the fields home from chapel with a lantern, going to school in the countryside of Brixton Hill, playing around the windmill on New Park Road in Clapham, being bullied and despairing of ever curing his stammer. He mentions seeing the great Chartist March setting out from Kennington Common on 10 April 1848 and, later, being articled to his father against his will. We understand his mortification at not being able to speak in front of other people. The problem became so bad that in 1859, Sam wrote to the author of *The Water Babies*, the Reverend Charles Kingsley – himself a stammerer – for advice. It was the beginning, as Sam writes, of his 'emancipation'.

Then, in July 1866, came the moment at which Samuel's life changed. He was visiting his sister and her husband in Lancashire. In an album of family photographs, Sam saw a photograph of a young woman and asked who it was. Martha Louisa Green, he was told, the eldest daughter of Reverend S. G. Green, President of Rawdon College. Samuel writes that he 'was profoundly struck and much excited'. So much so, he persuaded his brother-in-law to take him to Bradford that afternoon.

At the Zion Chapel, he saw Lily for the first time – he remembers she had a 'red ribbon over her hair' and writes that it was 'love at first sight'. It is tantalizing not to have any record of this first meeting from Lily's point of view, only to have Sam's memories of the encounter. She was only sixteen, but I'd love to know if Lily noticed the shy, awkward solicitor from London, ten years her senior, or if he was simply another face in the congregation, a distant relative.

Samuel was bowled over. On returning to London, he hired an elocution master, determined to become able to express himself. By 1867, he was again pressing his brother-in-law to arrange a meeting between him and Miss Green. A plan was arranged that they would go on holiday to Dunoon in Scotland, where the Green family went every year. They met on the station at Penrith and, when Sam saw Lily on the train, he wrote: 'Here by God's grace is the one voice for me . . . From that moment, my heart was fixed on her and has never swerved for a moment. All I am in life I owe to her.'

What is frustrating, as I try to catch sight of my great-grandmother, is that Sam claims Lily wrote a 'most vivid account' of the Dunoon holiday. Is it still out there somewhere, in a box in an attic? So often, in research, one comes across references to documents or books or letters that have vanished, or have not been thought of significance or interest. But we do know – whether it's the fragments of classical poetry by Sappho or the discovery in 1945 of the Nag Hammadi Codices, Gnostic early Christian texts dated to the fourth and fifth centuries – that documents that were lost may, sometimes, be found. Perhaps I will be lucky . . . I was with much else.

I've not been able to discover why Lily's mother was so opposed to the match. Sam writes: 'if I had not been so bound and chained with my love, I never should have stood her insults . . .' Was it a matter of class, or Sam's prospects or concern for her child? Did Mrs Green feel her daughter was too young? And what did Lily herself think of her mother's opposition? She remained close to her mother, and spent time with her family through her married life, so relations seemed to have remained affectionate.

But given Lily and Sam were engaged by early 1868, it's not unreasonable to assume that they stood firm against Mrs Green's objections and that Lily – whether for reasons of love, for reasons of escape, for reasons of companionship – felt a commitment to Sam. Since she was under twenty-one, she would have needed to have her parents' blessing and consent, so Reverend and Mrs Green must have relented. Sam writes sweetly that he took Lily to meet his father, who: 'quite approved of what I had done'.

The wedding took place on 23 September 1870, a few weeks before Lily's twenty-first birthday. Since the Marriage Act in 1836, Nonconformists had been free to marry at their own place of worship rather than an Anglican church, so the service was held at the Baptist Chapel at Rawdon College. I have a copy of the marriage licence but, so far, have unearthed no photographs of the wedding, nor any record of who was there. For the time being, Lily is still Martha Watson née Green, and her voice little more than a whisper.

When I was writing the first draft of this book, I didn't feel I was getting much of a sense of Lily and Sam's early married life. Did they suit one another? Were they good companions? Did Lily like living in London, having grown up in Yorkshire? They always lived in what was then Streatham, first in Sam's old lodgings, then in a house called 'Eversley' on Clapham Park Road. Later they would move to 'Poplars' at 179 New Park Road, a large Victorian house built by Cubitt on Brixton Hill. It's this house my father, my aunt and my godmother and their first cousin once removed, Sister Katherine, remembered. Set back on a wide avenue with other similar substantial family homes, a pig farm across the fields beyond the bottom of the garden. I knew Sam travelled to the office by tram. And Lily? Well, that's the question. She was a wife, she was a mother, they went twice to Chapel on Sundays. But how did she spend her days? I didn't feel I knew her.

Then, that moment. It was early December 2021, wet and blustery, the world full of COVID uncertainty still. But I had finished a draft of this book, done the editing and rewriting and supplementary research, and was about to send the typescript to my publisher when I received a phone call from my second cousin, Vanessa Watson. We had become friends through Sister Katherine, who was her beloved aunt. Vanessa had already been more than generous with sharing family documents with me – Lily had been her great-grandmother too – and she was good company.

Now it seemed Vanessa had discovered another heavy black deed box, the kind lawyers have, biding its time at the back of her attic. She hadn't had the chance to go through it before, but it contained more letters from Lily to Sam. Would I like to see them?

'How many letters?' I asked.

'At least three hundred, maybe more . . .'

This is the kind of treasure every researcher dreams of finding. The book was due to be delivered in a week's time, but how could I pass up this chance? The handful of letters and journals Vanessa had already shared with me – and documents and photographs my cousin and close friend Anne Renshaw had shown me – were wonderful. I had sketched out a serviceable biography. But now I could do more. I asked my publisher for a two-week extension.

On Monday 20 December 2021, a few days before Christmas, a van arrived with the metal box. About eighteen inches wide by eleven inches deep, the black paint was worn and specked with rust. An old distempered label with the words 'Watson Family Relics' printed on it. I lifted the lid, releasing the intoxicating smell of mustiness and old documents and secrets. The box was full – thin pink tracing paper, black-bordered notelets, fragile writing paper and postcards, tiny envelopes with red penny stamps. At least three hundred letters written by Lily, possibly twice as many.

Pretty soon I accepted it would take much longer than a couple of weeks to decipher and read all of the letters in the deed box. Mice had done their worst, so lots of the letters were frilled and shredded around the edges. Though I had become used to it, Lily's handwriting was difficult to decipher and so many of the letters were faded and written on delicate and transparent paper, with bleached ink; Lily often added postscript sentences up the middle or at the edge of the page, cutting across the main text. And she always wrote on both sides of the paper, so there was often a shadow of words bleeding through, making it hard to read. Finally, although most letters had an address and a date at the top, often the year was missing, and the letters were stacked in no real order.

I realized I'd need professional help to transcribe everything properly and that would take time, time I didn't have if the book was to be delivered to the publisher by my deadline. But the letters were glorious. I felt – finally – I was in Lily's company. I learned that, over their long marriage, she and Sam wrote to each other almost every day, sometimes several times in one day, for a period of about thirty years.

Warm and affectionate, sometimes chiding, supportive, domestic, occasionally gossipy, Lily's letters to Sam tell the story of their family and a life built together. I don't have many of his letters to her – though he has annotated some of Lily's letters and kept occasional diary entries. But it was possible, all the same, to piece together many of the key moments in their shared history.

The earliest letter I found in the box is dated 9 July 1874, four years into their marriage. Sent from Rawdon College, Lily had gone to stay with her parents for the summer, taking their two children – Ethel, who'd been born in 1871, and Reggie, born in 1873 – with her.

'My now darling,' the letter begins, then details her journey from their home in London in a horse-and-fly to King's Cross, then the train up to Leeds. A letter the following day is written on pink almost-tissue paper, so light and delicate, a response to having found a letter from Sam waiting for her at Rawdon College.

'I heard yesterday,' she writes, 'from my dear old husband asking me to keep a diary like Pamela . . . I feel much happier and brighter today and am altogether now settled in this lovely place, though I miss my darling.'

Reading a letter like this, of course, brings its own challenge of interpretation. There is no way of knowing whether Lily was simply unhappy at being separated from her husband, or at having to stay with her parents for the summer – she's still at Rawdon in August – or if there was some bigger issue. This pattern – of Lily taking the children away for the summer and Sam joining them intermittently – is one that will continue for much of their life, and was not uncommon for a middle-class Victorian family.

Lily might well have been pregnant – Harold would be born in the spring of 1875 – or she might have been out of sorts. Depressed, or suffering some medical complication she doesn't talk about. She is never explicit about her own health, never mentions pregnancy or childbirth. Instead, she writes about celebrating her brother Alfred's ninth birthday and taking her sister Nellie to the dentist, and remembering the horror of 'the gas' when she was a child.

On 13 August, she writes: 'I am afraid my yesterday's letter was rather depressing and doleful. I am brighter today, however, and better able to see the cheerful side of things.'

Was Lily worried about upsetting him, so far away in London? Or about him being worried about her? A pattern emerges through their correspondence of how sweetly thoughtful they were of one another. He seems more often in need of reassurance than does she, and Lily often tries to amuse him with pen portraits and sketches. He relied on her. In a note sent, it seems, on the spur of the moment from his chambers in Fleet Street on 22 March 1901, Sam writes: 'My own darling, just a line as I know you like to have letters. I love you, and long to see you. The older I grow, the more I love you . . . and depend on you more . . . Always most lovingly, Sam.'

For her part, in 1874 the twenty-four-year-old Lily calls him 'my old boy', 'my dearest old Indian', and signs off as 'your loving wife' or 'your devoted Lily'. It's hard to say but, reading letter after letter, it feels like the expression of genuine affection and companionship.

Or maybe that's just the story I want it to be.

Top: Cornelia Sorabji (1866–1954)
Bottom left: Ethel Benjamin (1875–1943)
Bottom right: Helena Normanton (1882–1957)

3

A Woman's Place Is at the Bar

'The tongue is the female weapon.'

Still Harping on Daughters
Lisa Jardine, 1983

LILY WAS THE WIFE of a solicitor. Sam had been given little choice in the matter. It was the career intended for him. In 1854, Sam had started to accompany his father to the office of Watson & Sons in Bouverie Street, though we know from his 'Autobiography and Notes' that it was against his will. In 1857, he was articled to his father and he remained a solicitor for his entire working life:

'I protested against it, vehemently desiring to be a farmer . . . My father, however, insisted and very glad I am he got his way. He said and rightly that as I was his only son it would not do to let the business pass out of my hands. I have lived to see the wisdom of this.'

From everything I've read, I can't help wondering if Lily might have been the more natural lawyer of the two: she was logical, analytical, steady. Their two older sons, Reggie and Harry, will follow Sam into the family firm, but it doesn't seem to have occurred to either of them that their daughters might have any aptitude for the law or that they, too, could carry on the family business. The girls were destined for marriage. Two generations later, though, Harold's grand-daughter, Vanessa Watson, will become a lawyer.

Times do change.

But during the second half of the nineteenth century, women were still trying to find a way into the very male bastion of the law, against huge opposition, knowing that women's lives would be immeasurably improved if women were allowed to advocate for themselves. The law is not justice. And if the law is unjust or biased, then women must campaign to change it.

So, let's raise a flag for those who campaigned for women's equality under the law and for those who challenged the idea that justice should remain a matter of luck for women within a system designed by men, for men.

WE'LL START IN Italy in the Middle Ages, in Bologna where the teaching of law as a modern discipline began. **Matilda of Canossa** (*c.* 1046–1115) – also known as **Matilda of Tuscany** – was key to the foundation in 1088 of what is essentially Europe's first law school at the University of Bologna. Born in Lucca in Tuscany, she became known as 'La Gran Contessa' and was one of the most powerful women of the Middle Ages. A skilled horsewoman and strategist, she is fabled for brokering peace between the papacy and the Holy Roman Emperor and bringing warring factions to the table. More than five centuries after her death, her remains were transferred to St Peter's Basilica in Rome in 1630, making her the first woman ever to be laid to rest there.

Bologna soon became the powerhouse of the development of legal training during the Middle Ages. In 1237, **Bettisia Gozzadini** (1209–1261) made history by being awarded a degree in law, one of the first women to obtain a university degree. She went on to become a teacher, working at first from her own home, then at the university itself, making her, in 1239, the first woman to lecture at a university. Legends about Gozzadini are legion: that she dressed as a man to obtain an education; that she taught from behind a screen so as not to distract her students with her beauty; that her skills as an orator were so exceptional that no room within the university was large enough to contain all those who wanted to listen.

The Museum of the History of Bologna has a seventeenth-century terracotta bust of Gozzadini, one of a series of sculptures honouring celebrated Bolognese women from the worlds of academia and the arts from the 1200s to the 1600s. Her name is also inscribed on the white floor tiles surrounding Chicago's artwork *The Dinner Party*.

'. . . Though justice be thy plea, consider this:
That in the course of justice none of us
Should see salvation.'

Portia

From teacher to practitioner and **Giustina Rocca** (d. 1502), who is often considered the world's first female lawyer. Born in Trani in the second half of the fifteenth century, she was an advocate, particularly in cases involving diplomatic relations between Trani and Venice. She's thought to have been the inspiration for the character of Portia di Belmonte in Shakespeare's *The Merchant of Venice*. Shakespeare often turned to history for inspiration, so it's possible Rocca's story had reached English shores.

The power of the Italian schools notwithstanding, mercy and justice for women under the law was very much slower to arrive in the United Kingdom.

'Why is England the only country obliged to
confess that she cannot contrive to
administer justice to women?'

Caroline Norton

Every woman going through a divorce in the UK owes a debt to the English poet, pamphleteer and justice campaigner **Caroline Norton** (1808–1877). Norton's husband accused her of adultery. He lost the case, but not only did he still refuse to grant her a divorce, he also denied her access to her three young sons and even continued to claim her earnings from her own writings as his own. Norton used her personal experiences, her victimization, to campaign to change the law.

Norton refused to accept the injustice of her situation. At this time in England, married women were essentially their husband's property: any money they'd brought into the marriage belonged to him, any children belonged to him, and wives – even if the wronged party – had very few rights. Challenging the legal status quo and the lack of women's rights – at the time, only a man could petition for divorce –

Norton battled against what she described as state-supported domestic violence, coercive control and injustice against women. In 1855, frustrated by repeated delays to the Marriage and Divorce Bill being brought before Parliament, Norton published a brilliantly argued open letter to **Queen Victoria** (1819–1901), who had been monarch since 1837:

> 'The vague romance of "carrying my wrongs to the foot of the throne," forms no part of my intention: for I know the throne is powerless to redress them . . .
>
> 'I connect your Majesty's name with these pages from a different motive; for two reasons: of which one, indeed, is a sequence to the other. First, because I desire to point out the grotesque anomaly which ordains that married women shall be "non-existent" in a country governed by a female Sovereign; and secondly, because, whatever measure for the reform of these statutes may be proposed, it cannot become "the law of the land" without your Majesty's assent . . .'

Norton's dogged and meticulous campaigning would lead to the Custody of Infants Act 1839, the Matrimonial Causes Act 1857 and the Married Women's Property Act 1870, three pieces of legislation of enormous significance to women's lives. My great-grandmother Lily, too, would have cause to be grateful when Sam's chambers, Watson & Sons, almost collapsed in an embezzlement crisis in 1880.

Widely seen as a victim of injustice, Norton modelled for the Irish painter Daniel Maclise for his fresco of *Justice* in the House of Lords, unveiled in 1849. Norton published nine novels, two plays, eleven poetry collections and seven political pamphlets. In April 2021, her biographer, the historian **Antonia Fraser** (b. 1932), unveiled an English Heritage blue plaque at Norton's former house in Mayfair, London.

> 'A married woman, in short, had no legal existence.'
>
> ***Antonia Fraser***

Norton's campaigning notwithstanding, discrimination against married women in the UK would continue well into the twentieth century. In 1922, the Law of Property Act enabled a husband and wife to inherit each other's property and, from 1926, women were allowed to hold and dispose of property on the same terms as men. But the marriage bar still operated – whereby a woman would have to give up her job on marriage. The bar was removed for female teachers in 1944, in 1946 for women working in home civil service jobs, but not until 1973 for women in the foreign service.

> 'Four words keep coming back to me: resist, insist, persist, enlist.'
>
> **Hillary Rodham Clinton**

By now, all over the world, women were coming to the same conclusion as Caroline Norton. Namely that, unless women's voices were heard, the law would always be stacked against them. Increasingly, women wanted not only to campaign for change outside the corridors of justice, but also to operate within them. Let's celebrate a few more legal firsts.

The first female justice of the peace in the United States was **Esther Morris** (1812–1902). First appointed in South Pass City, Wyoming, in February 1870, she unexpectedly found herself appointed in Sweetwater County. There was a vacancy only because the male justice had resigned in protest at the territory's support of the women's suffrage amendment, a satisfying example of someone cutting off their nose to spite their face.

> 'If nations could only depend upon fair and impartial judgments in a world court of law, they would abandon the senseless, savage practice of war.'
>
> **Belva Lockwood**

One of the first female lawyers in the United States, **Belva Ann Lockwood** (1830–1917) was also the first woman to run for president.

In 1879, she successfully petitioned Congress to be allowed to practise before the Supreme Court, the first woman attorney given this privilege. Lockwood ran for president in 1884 and 1888 on the ticket of the National Equal Rights Party, and was the first woman to appear on official ballots.

It takes great strength to struggle not only against sexist attitudes but also against racism too, and to prevail. **Charlotte E. Ray** (1850–1911) had that determination and became the first African American female lawyer in the United States. Graduating from Howard University School of Law in 1872, Ray was the first woman admitted to the District of Columbia Bar and the first woman admitted to practise before the Supreme Court of the District of Columbia.

> 'Something which we think is impossible
> now is not impossible in another decade.'
>
> ***Constance Baker Motley***

IT WOULD BE a long wait before an African American woman would become a federal judge. After graduating from law school in 1946, **Constance Baker Motley** (1921–2005) worked for the NAACP as a civil rights lawyer. The fund's first female attorney, she was a key figure in the desegregation of schools in the South – Motley was part of the landmark Brown v Board of Education of Topeka trial in 1954, in which the Supreme Court overruled a previous ruling and agreed that state laws allowing racial segregation in state schools was unconstitutional – and also succeeded in having 1,100 Black children reinstated to school in Birmingham, Alabama, who had been expelled for taking part in street demonstrations in the spring of 1963. Part of the legal team representing the Freedom Riders and Martin Luther King, she was also a campaigner for women's rights. In 1962, Motley became the first African American woman to argue a case before the Supreme Court – she'd go on to win nine of her ten cases – and, two years later, she was the first African American woman elected to the New York Senate.

'I do not like to recall my first lecture; but the men behaved well. One rather dreaded contest was all I have to record, and a little sarcasm cured the men. I found them docile and very appreciative.'

Cornelia Sorabji

Cornelia Sorabji (1866–1954) was the first woman graduate from Bombay University, the first to study law at Oxford University, one of the first women called to the Bar in 1923, when the law barring women from practising was repealed, and the first female lawyer in India. Later photographs show her in her horsehair wig and white jabot, but photographs of her as a student at Somerville College show her in a veil and sari. Just imagine how she must have felt in that examination hall – the only woman allowed to be there, thanks to a special dispensation – surrounded by male students and male invigilators, many of whom disapproved of her presence. What fortitude it must have taken to ignore their comments, their derision, and concentrate only on the matter in hand, though she took it in her stride.

At every step of the way, Sorabji had to battle to be allowed to fulfil her vocation. A brilliant advocate and campaigner, in 1902 she petitioned the India office to provide female legal advisors to represent women and minors in provincial courts. Like Norton before her, she knew that without women's voices in the room, women were less likely to receive a fair hearing. Two years later, she was appointed 'Lady Assistant' to the Court of Wards of Bengal. Over the next twenty years, Sorabji would help more than six hundred women and orphans fight legal battles. She wrote about her struggles – in *Between the Twilights, India Calling: The Memories of Cornelia Sorabji* and *India Recalled*. In 2013, a bust of Sorabji was unveiled at Lincoln's Inn. In the same year, a play written by **Jocelyn Watson** called *Cornelia Calling* was staged in London by Kali Theatre Company. In a blog for the British Library, Watson explained how she used documents about, and by, Sorabji held in the archives. It's another crucial reminder of how, if we want the women of the past to speak to the women of today, we must value, protect and preserve their authentic voices.

'I must admit I was not free from trepidation when I first stepped up to the Bench. However, what was foremost in my mind was a fierce determination to make a success of this experiment. I knew I was a test case. If I faltered or failed, I would not just be damaging my own career, but would be doing a great disservice to the cause of women.'

Anna Chandy

The first female judge in India was **Anna Chandy** (1905–1996). Born into an Anglican Syrian Christian family, she was the first woman in Kerala to take a law degree and, in 1937, became the first female judge in India. In 1948, she was appointed a District Judge and, in 1959, was appointed to the Kerala High Court, making her the first female High Court judge in India.

The third of our pioneering legal women in India was **Durgabai Deshmukh** (1909–1981), who founded the Andhra Women's Conference in 1937. The only female member of the Constituent Assembly of India, Deshmukh worked to establish a Central Social Welfare Board in 1953 and became its first chair. Building on the work of Sorabji and Chandy, she was instrumental in setting up separate Family Courts, to ensure justice for women and children – particularly those with disabilities – and in 1958 was the first chair of the National Council on Women's Education. Deshmukh was imprisoned three times for her opposition to British rule and described by **Indira Gandhi** (1917–1984) as the 'Mother of Social Work in India'.

Finally, born a generation after Deshmukh, **Leila Seth** (1930–2017) would go on to become the first woman judge to serve on the Delhi High Court. In 1991, Seth became the first female chief justice of a state High Court and was also the first female lawyer designated as a senior counsel by India's Supreme Court. She was also part of the Justice Verma Committee established to overhaul India's rape laws in the aftermath of the horrifying 2012 Delhi gang-rape case of **Jyoti Singh** (1990–2012). She also become vocal in her support of her son, novelist Vikram Seth, when he came out as gay, writing extensively in the Indian media in favour of LGBT rights.

> '[We] will not hold ourselves bound by any laws in which we have no voice, no representation.'
>
> *Abigail Adams*

In New Zealand on 17 September 1897, **Ethel Benjamin** (1875–1943) became the first woman, in what was still the British Empire, to appear as counsel in court and the second to be admitted as a barrister and solicitor, a couple of months after Canadian lawyer **Clara Martin** (1874–1923). Benjamin had to fight every step of the way. The Otago District Law Society restricted her access to their library and the New Zealand Law Society omitted to invite her to official functions and tried to enforce a dress code. But in experiences common to trailblazing women everywhere, there were practical obstacles put in her way too – for example, like there being no bathroom or a private space where she could change.

Tiny acts of petty sabotage.

Benjamin opened her own private legal practice, mostly acting for clients from the Jewish community and women with financial interests, as well as publicans and hoteliers – in a wine-producing nation, she was a rare nineteenth-century women's rights advocate who didn't support temperance. In 1899, she was also a founding member of the Dunedin branch of the Society for the Protection of Women and Children.

> 'The radicalism of a baby – of a well-born little Chinese girl who would not behave as she was supposed to – became the radicalism of what, in the West, would be a debutante turned anarchist.'
>
> *Tcheng Yu-hsiu*

Tcheng Yu-hsiu (1891–1959) was the first female lawyer and the first female judge in Chinese history. Having studied first in Tokyo, then in Paris, in 1931 she became President of the University of Shanghai School of Law. She advocated for women having choices in marriage and was a skilled orator. All the same, when her autobiography *My Revolutionary Years* was published in 1944 – under her married name of **Madame Wei Tao-ming** – it was promoted as having been written by the wife of the Chinese Ambassador to Washington, despite her own extraordinary accomplishments. The memoir begins with her description of how much she admired the sixth-century warrior princess Mulan and explaining how, from the earliest age, inspired by her mother and against her grandmother's opposition, she had always been a rebel . . .

Until 1933, the definition of a lawyer in Japan stood as 'a male Japanese national' of at least twenty years of age. Three years after the law changed, the first three women were admitted to the Bar: **Masako Nakata** (1910–2002), **Ai Kume** (1911–1976) and **Yoshiko Mibuchi** (1914–1984). Mibuchi became the first woman judge in the Nagoya District Court and, thirty years later, was the first female chief judge of the Niigata Prefecture Family Court.

Ascensión Chirivella Marín (1894–1980) became the first female lawyer in Spain. A powerful advocate for women's rights, she campaigned for women's right to vote, the right to run for political office and the right to divorce. Marín was forced into exile in Mexico in 1939 at the end of the Spanish Civil War.

One of the founding mothers of the feminist movement in Romania, **Ella Negruzzi** (1876–1948) was also the first female lawyer in Romania. She co-founded the Association for the Civil and Political Emancipation of Romanian Women in 1917, followed by the Group of Democratic Lawyers in 1935 and the Women's Front in 1936.

Stella Thomas (1906–1974) was the first female magistrate in Nigeria. Born in Lagos – of Yoruba and Sierra Leonean descent – in 1933, she became the first woman of African descent to qualify as a lawyer. She's also considered to be the first Black British woman to qualify as a lawyer, having studied at Oxford. She was a member of both the League of Coloured Peoples and the West African Student Union, working alongside Jamaican playwright, poet and activist **Una Marson** (1905–1965). Thomas actually appeared in Marson's 1933 play *At What a Price*, one of the very few plays of the period to have an all-Black cast. Marson herself was the first Black woman to be employed by the BBC during the Second World War and became the producer of the radio series *Calling the West Indies*, which would later become *Caribbean Voices*.

Born sixteen years after Thomas, fellow Nigerian lawyer **Modupe Omo-Eboh** (1922–2002) was called to the Bar at Lincoln's Inn in 1953. Returning home to Lagos, she worked as a lawyer, magistrate, chief magistrate, administrator-general, director of public prosecutions and acting solicitor-general before she was appointed a judge in Benin City in 1969, becoming Nigeria's first female judge.

Mehrangiz Manouchehrian (1906–2000) became Iran's first female lawyer in 1947 and, in 1963, was one of two women appointed as the first female senators in Iran. A feminist and musician, she was a member of the Women's Organization of Iran and instrumental in drafting the Family Protection Act, a set of laws extending women's rights within marriage.

> 'Protests against the mandatory hijab are here to stay. The only way to deal with them is to pay attention.'
>
> **Nasrin Sotoudeh**

With the emergence of a strict Islamic ruling party in Iran, many of the gains for women have been rescinded. The Iranian human rights lawyer **Nasrin Sotoudeh** (b. 1963) has repeatedly been imprisoned, has been on hunger strike during the last decade, and has been prevented from practising. Sotoudeh has represented imprisoned Iranian opposition activists and politicians, as well as prisoners sentenced to death for crimes committed when they were children and women arrested for appearing in public without a hijab. Clients have included Nobel Peace Prize laureate, lawyer and former judge, activist **Shirin Ebadi** (b. 1947), founder of the Defenders of Human Rights Centre in Iran. In 2004, Sotoudeh was listed by *Forbes* magazine as one of the '100 Most Powerful Women in the World'.

First female lawyers/judges include: **Adolphine Kok** (1879–1928) in the Netherlands; **Maria Angélica Barreda** (1887–1963) in Argentina; **Helena Wiewiórska** (1888–1967) in Poland; **Juliette Smaja Zerah** (1891–1974) in Tunisia; **Laure Pillay** (1917–2017) in

Mauritius; **Frances Claudia Wright** (1919–2010) in Sierra Leone; and **Marie 'Mame' Bassine Niang** (1951–2013) in Senegal.

Esilda Villa (1909–1947) was the first woman lawyer in Bolivia and a key figure in the Bolivian women's movement in the early twentieth century. She passed her Bar examinations in 1928, but was refused a licence to practise because women were not at that time considered citizens under the Bolivian constitution. International pressure forced a change of heart and Villa was granted her licence the following year. In the *Bulletin of the Pan American Union* for 1929, there's a charming paragraph: 'Senorita Esilda Villa has passed her examination as attorney in the Supreme Court in Oruro. Senorita Villa, who is the first woman lawyer in Bolivia, has received many congratulations.'

Ten years later, when Villa passed the examination to become a trial lawyer, the Supreme Court again refused to issue her a licence. Yet again, she protested. Yet again, she won. As Hillary Clinton said: 'Insist, persist.'

> 'Even in my own time and in my own life, I have witnessed a revolution.'
>
> **Sarah Day O'Connor**

NOWHERE IN ANY of my great-grandmother's letters to Sam is there any indication of her thoughts about the emerging revolution in the legal profession. Given her anti-suffrage views, I suspect Lily might have considered the business of the law was men's work. The prevailing attitude in the press, and law schools, to women lawyers was predominantly antagonistic.

I found myself wondering if it was something Lily and Sam discussed. In the latter years of the nineteenth century, there were regular columns in newspapers about women entering the professions – medicine as well as law – and a great deal of mostly negative publicity about women who were making their mark. Did they see it as a threat to Sam's livelihood, or to their son Harold's opportunities? By the time the Sex Disqualification (Removal) Act was finally passed, Sam would be gone.

They had strong family links to Scotland. Lily had been at school in Edinburgh for a time and, of course, Sam had followed the Green family on holiday to Dunoon in the summer of 1867, with the express purpose of wooing Lily. Now, a powerhouse of female legal talent was establishing itself on both sides of the Scottish border, including **Madge Anderson** (1896–1982). She was the first woman to graduate from the University of Glasgow in law and the first woman admitted to practise both in Scotland and England. Anderson set up her own legal practice in Glasgow in 1927, then decamped to London to join forces with **Edith Berthen** (1877–1951) and **Beatrice Honour Davy** (1885–1966) at the UK's first all-female-led law firm. In 1937, Anderson passed the English Law School exam to become qualified in England and became a partner – the business was renamed the 'Firm of Messrs Berthen, Davy and Anderson'.

In 1888, **Eliza Orme** (1848–1937) became the first woman to achieve a law degree in England. She began working in legal practice in 1872, but because she wasn't allowed to practise on her own behalf, Orme established an office on Chancery Lane drafting conveyancing documents and patents. From the mid-1880s, Orme worked with **Reina Lawrence** (*c*. 1860–1940), an American lawyer and borough councillor, to whom she left everything at her death.

In England, **Carrie Morrison** (1888–1950) was the first woman who qualified as a solicitor in 1922 and **Maud Crofts** (1889–1965) was the first woman to be articled and to hold a practising certificate in 1923, after a ten-year campaign. **Ivy Williams** (1877–1966) was the first to be called to the Bar in 1922, though she never practised.

> 'I still do not like to see women getting the worst end of any deal for lack of a little elementary legal knowledge which is the most common form among men.'
>
> *Helena Normanton*

That accolade falls to the extraordinary **Helena Normanton** (1882–1957), who had been admitted to the Middle Temple as a student on Christmas Eve 1919, just twenty-four hours after the Sex Disqualification (Removal) Act had been passed. That same day, seven women were appointed as magistrates.

Normanton has a whole heap of other firsts to her name: the first woman to obtain a divorce for a client; the first woman to appear before the High Court and Old Bailey; the first woman to act for the prosecution in a murder trial; the first woman to conduct a case in the US for a woman's right to keep her name on marriage; the first married British woman to hold a passport under her unmarried name. She was the founder of the Magna Carta Society and a member of CND. There are many wonderful black-and-white photographs of Normanton, including one taken in 1950 showing her with black round-rimmed glasses, wearing her barrister's wig and white ruched jabot and cuffs, looking directly into the camera. In October 2021, **Brenda Hale** (b. 1945), who was the first woman to head the UK Supreme Court, unveiled a plaque at what was Normanton's home in Bloomsbury from 1919 to 1931.

> 'She [Normanton] had to overcome a great deal of prejudice and discrimination. A blue plaque is a fitting tribute to her courage and her example to women barristers everywhere.'
>
> *Brenda Hale*

Blue plaques mark sites of historical or cultural importance, honouring those who've made a significant contribution in their field, and have been running since 1866. Yet there continues a clear imbalance in the numbers of women honoured. The first woman to be celebrated was the Welsh actress **Sarah Siddons** (1755–1831), although the original plaque no longer exists. By the early years of the twentieth century, there were still only five women with plaques dedicated to them – including one of my great-grandmother's favourite authors, **George Eliot** – and, in 2020, it was estimated that still only 14 per cent of the 950-plus plaques celebrate women. Only 4 per cent of plaques commemorated people from a Black, Asian or minority ethnic background.

Visibility matters.

∞

To FINISH, LET'S raise a glass to a final magnificent seven from the UK, France, Tunisia and the United States.

Rose Heilbron (1914–2005) also has a list of dazzling firsts to her name. Born into a Jewish family in Liverpool at the beginning of the First World War, everything about her life and career shows her determination. She was the first woman to achieve a first-class honours degree in law at the University of Liverpool; the first woman to win a scholarship to Gray's Inn; one of the first two women to be appointed King's Counsel in England; the first woman to lead in a murder case in 1950; the first woman recorder; the first female judge to sit at the Old Bailey; and the first female treasurer of Gray's Inn. She was also the second woman to be appointed a High Court judge, after **Elizabeth Lane** (1905–1988). Heilbron also advocated strongly for women continuing to work regardless of their marital status. On 27 March 1952, after speaking at Manchester University about the importance of women not wasting their training and keeping their careers after marriage and motherhood, the headline of the *Daily Mirror* read: 'Rose . . . the woman who would not be wasted'.

> 'Pain is the root of knowledge.'
>
> *Simone Veil*

Simone Veil (1927–2017) – activist for women's rights, magistrate and campaigning politician – transformed the lives of women in France. She served as Health Minister in several governments and is celebrated for her support of the 1974 act giving French women safe access to contraception and for the 1975 law that bears her name, legalizing abortion in France. Veil was President of the European Parliament from 1979 to 1982, the first woman to hold the office, her passion in part coming from the fact that she was a Holocaust survivor of both Auschwitz-Birkenau and Bergen-Belsen. Veil served as President of the *Fondation pour la Mémoire de la Shoah* for seven years from 2000 and was dedicated to European cooperation as a bastion against unrest. Elected to the *Académie Française* in 2008, she received the grand cross of the *Légion d'Honneur* in 2012.

The French Tunisian-Jewish lawyer **Gisèle Halimi** (1927–2020) is another familiar name in France, thanks to her work as counsel for the Algerian National Liberation Front, most notably with **Djamila Boupacha** (b. 1938), whose forced confession to having planted a bomb at a café in September 1959 was the result of rape and torture by French soldiers. Boupacha refused to accept what had happened to her and brought a legal case against her torturers. It was reported on by Simone de Beauvoir for *Le Monde*, and Halimi subsequently wrote a book about the case in 1961 (with an introduction by de Beauvoir), which became a rallying cry in France. Ten years later, Halimi founded the feminist group *Choisir* ('To Choose') to protect women who admitted to having illegal abortions, working closely with Simone Veil. In 2022, a campaign was launched to have Halimi admitted into the Panthéon in Paris, where the 'great men' of France are entombed by a 'grateful nation' – the inscription on the façade reads: AUX GRANDS HOMMES LA PATRIE RECONNAISANTE. Perhaps it's no surprise that the first woman was not entombed here until 1995 and there have still been only six. In November 2021, the American-born performer, Resistance agent, civil rights campaigner and icon **Josephine Baker** (1906–1975) was the first woman of colour to be laid to rest beneath its dome.

> 'Women belong in all places where decisions are being made. It shouldn't be that women are the exception.'
>
> **Ruth Bader Ginsburg**

Finally, it's fitting to end this chapter on trailblazing women lawyers with the tiny-but-mighty powerhouse **Ruth Bader Ginsburg** (1933–2020). Known as the 'Notorious RBG', she was an associate justice of the Supreme Court of the United States from 1993 until her death in September 2020. Ginsburg was the first Jewish woman and only the second woman to serve on the Court, after **Sandra Day O'Connor** (b. 1930). At the time of writing, the impartiality of the Supreme Court of Justice is being challenged, and the landmark ruling for women's abortion rights in the United States of America, *Roe v. Wade*, was revoked in June 2022, now that Bader-Ginsburg was no longer there to defend it. The pendulum swings. No progress can be taken for granted. Women have to fight for their rights, then fight to keep them.

Elegant and inquisitive to the last, with her trademark glasses and magnificent collars, let's leave the last word to RBG: 'Real change, enduring change, happens one step at a time.'

A woman's place is at the Bar.

> 'There never will be complete equality until women themselves help to make laws and elect lawmakers.'
>
> **Susan B. Anthony**

'Poplars', New Park Road, Brixton Hill

Lily

IN HER SCRAPBOOK, MY godmother Sister Katherine noted that Lily's father, Samuel Green, was distantly related to the notorious Henry Morgan – Morgan the Pirate – the violent and rapacious scourge of the Spanish Main and Lieutenant-Governor of Jamaica in the 1670s. It certainly doesn't fit with Lily's Huguenot antecedents, and it's impossible this far after the event to know how a rumour like that took hold, or if there's any grain of truth in the story at all.

What's undeniable, though, is that Lily loved to write and tell pirate stories to her grandchildren. I have letters written to my father, sent when he was confined to bed for a year in 1930 with tuberculosis. They are filled with pictograms, sketches of pirates with eye-patches and cutlasses, stories where the pirate is always more of a Robin Hood figure – outside of the law but on the side of justice – rather than an opponent to be feared.

I don't think this suggests Lily had a hankering for adventure on the high seas. I don't believe she wanted to sail the world or live a wild life. Rather, her pirate stories are fairy tales, like her 1867 novella, *Little Goldenhair*, that begins with a 'once upon a time', and ends with 'I shall remember the lesson life has taught me.'

Lily and Sam lived in a protected world, and were happy there: a comfortable house in Streatham, Sam's daily journey to his office in Bouverie Street and home again; his club and her sojourns with her family. Long summer holidays in Europe, and frequent visits to hotels and friends in England. In a century of wars, none of their sons was destined to be a soldier, even though for most of Lily's married life,

Britain was involved in conflicts somewhere in the world – Burma, India, China, Afghanistan, Crimea, the Eastern Cape of South Africa, Bhutan, New Zealand, Canada . . .

It's always been a truism in the writing of history – and historical fiction – that mostly people don't know they're living through it. Only hindsight gives perspective and significance. In the past few years, though, that's changed. The fracturing of the closer European alignment, the rise of populism and the worldwide COVID pandemic, war in Ukraine, the rolling back of women's rights – we know we are living through history. This is what history feels like.

Working on the second draft of *Warrior Queens & Quiet Revolutionaries* in January 2022, I went back to Lily's correspondence, frustrated that nothing of the wider world seemed ever to make it onto the page. Attempting to catalogue the letters in order – many are dated only with the day and month, not the year – I scoured them for references to current affairs, but found nothing: no politics, domestic or international, no comments about Crown or State, nothing about women making history in her lifetime.

In more than five hundred letters and notes, the only newspaper clipping I found is a small paragraph from spring 1900, the date written – 7 April – in Sam's meticulous handwriting on the corner. The headline was 'Mistress and Maid' and reported how an old lady, Florence Lockwood – a widow of Westbourne Park Villas, Bayswater – had been sentenced to four months' imprisonment for neglect, cruelty and violent abuse of her maid, Emily Gibbs. Enslavement, we'd call it now. Apart from the date written in Sam's handwriting, there was nothing to show why it had been kept. Did they know Mrs Lockwood? Or was there some family connection with Emily Gibbs?

Although Lily lived during the reign of **Queen Victoria**, I have no idea what she thought about the fact that there was a woman on the throne. Caroline Norton's open letter in 1855 made the point that it *should* make a difference to ordinary women's lives that the head of state was a woman, but did it? On 23 January 1901, the day after Victoria died on the Isle of Wight and the newspapers were full of nothing else, Lily's letter to Sam gives no indication that something momentous is happening.

'Just a few words, dear . . .' she begins, 'to say I will be arriving home tomorrow at 5 p.m.'

Victoria Regina et Imperatrix – Queen and Empress – was not a warrior queen, but she was arguably the most famous and powerful woman of her time. There are more statues of Victoria in the UK than any other person. Her name is still scattered across the globe – cities, states, lakes, railway stations and waterfalls are named after her. She was the longest-serving British monarch until **Elizabeth II** (b. 1926), who, in 2017, became the first British monarch to reach a Sapphire Jubilee, and a Platinum in 2022. Not a warrior queen either, but a woman of great fortitude, stamina and service.

Queen Elizabeth is part of my family history too. My father invited my mother to watch Elizabeth II's coronation from a balcony in Pall Mall in London on 2 June 1953. He had been a captain in the Welsh Guards, and still had visiting privileges. Encouraged by the atmosphere, the sense of occasion and hope, he screwed his courage to the sticking place, and proposed. They married a year later on 29 May 1954, the day before my father's thirtieth birthday, at St Mary's Church, Ewell, and remained together until his death on 18 May 2011. My mother died three years later, on 21 December 2014, the shortest and darkest day of the year. A day she had always hated.

They were beloved, and are very much missed.

Laskarina Bouboulina (1771–1825)

4

Warrior Queens & Pirate Commanders

'I will not resign myself to the lot of women who bow their heads and become concubines. I wish to ride the tempest, tame the waves, kill the sharks.'

Triệu Thị Trinh, third century CE

WHETHER OR NOT LILY admired Victoria, whether she mourned her, she must surely have felt that her death marked the end of an era.

Within history the most visible women have, of course, always been queens and leaders. The quiet revolutionaries have mostly been overlooked. Since history has traditionally been the story of conquest, of battles, of faith, then it stands to reason that those men – and women – occupying the highest positions of power, most firmly in the public gaze, are likely to be the better known. Even if not every detail of their lives is recorded, set down for posterity – misinterpreted or manipulated – their presence roars from the archives.

It's wise to remember, though, that sometimes the only source of a woman's life – particularly in the distant past – could well be a chronicler who might or might not approve of her power. A common complaint in the archives is of a wife or lover exerting 'undue influence'. Raising the spectre of a woman's sexuality and 'virtue' as a way to discredit her opinions or undermine her reputation has often been a strategic move.

As well as contemporaneous documents and records, another reason we know these warrior queens and pirate commanders so well is that their lives, unlike those of ordinary people, have often inspired plays, songs, operas, novels, films, paintings, sculpture or music. They live on in the popular imagination of successive generations, not only as biographies on the pages of a history book.

Many of the women celebrated in this chapter are well known, others, less so. I wish I had space to include more, but it's important to have the historical context too, the influences that one generation might have on the next, or the one after. Every woman included is not here as a heroine, an 'angel in the house' to be admired or venerated, but rather because her presence in the world made a difference. Putting women back into history and keeping them there requires repetition, not just one mention in one book, until they, too, become household names.

I'M STARTING IN Egypt again, because I fell head over heels in love with history because of it when I was nine years old.

London 1972, a cold and damp July afternoon, the Tutankhamun exhibition at the British Museum. I would be just one of 1.6 million visitors who would queue over the next nine months to see treasures looted from the boy-king's tomb.

I have an illustrated hardback book on my shelves entitled *All Colour Book of Egyptian Mythology*, bought for me by my mother from the museum gift shop that day. I can still picture myself in the railway carriage on the journey home, silent and fascinated by the vivid golden images, the stories behind the artefacts, the sense of the ancient world come to life.

We also have a tenuous family connection with Egypt. My maternal great-grandfather was a Coptic Christian, adopted from Cairo as a child and brought to London, where he married an Englishwoman and had four very English children – Ethel, Fred, George and my granny, Alice. It wasn't until I was in my late teens that I learned my granny's maiden name had been Hassan.

Although my mother had never been to Egypt, she felt – like me – some kind of affinity and, nine years later, a few weeks shy of my twentieth birthday in 1981, we went on an Egyptian adventure together. We saw the sights: the pyramids at Giza, the chaotic street markets of Cairo, the Aswan dam and Abu Simbel, the Valley of the Kings, the white stucco buildings and faded grandeur of old Luxor. Palm trees and the Nile and the desert. But back in the 1970s, all I had were images in my precious copy of the *All Colour Book of Egyptian Mythology*, the beginnings of a passion for the stories of the past, in particular for extraordinary female leaders.

In the Old Kingdom, there had been suggestions that there might have been female Pharoahs – for example **Merneith** (*c.* 2970 BCE) is named in the list of Egyptian rulers on the Palermo Stone. Another, **Khentkawes** (*c.* 2550/2520–*c.* 2510/2490 BCE) is represented as a ruler on her tomb, showing her enthroned, holding a sceptre and wearing both a tie-on beard, which signals kingship, and the royal 'uraeus' cobra on her brow. Some historians consider her title was as the 'Mother of Kings' rather than the ruler in her own right. But it is at the end of the Middle Kingdom (*c.* 2040–1782 BCE) that the first universally accepted female Pharoah, **Sobekneferu** (d. 1802 BCE), ruled for nearly four years. She is evidenced to have taken the five royal names of a king, along with the epithet 'Son of Ra' amended to 'Daughter of Ra'. In portraits, she is shown with both male and female signifiers, wearing the male-style kilt over female dress. She's also shown with a coronation cloak.

Nearly three hundred years later, **Hatshepsut** (1507–1458 BCE) was widowed and usurped her son to become Egypt's second – and fearless – female Pharoah. She commissioned hundreds of buildings, temples and statues, and her own mausoleum was the first built in the Valley of the Kings. During her twenty-one-year rule, her public portrayal was often as a man. Historian Alice E. Smith suggests that although there is significant evidence of her female predecessors – such as Khentkawes – having done the same, the reason that Hatshepsut is so often described as cross-dressing is perhaps because her portrayal was about power, pure and simple, rather than 'feminine' power or beauty as displayed by **Nefertiti** (*c.* 1370–1330 BCE).

The glorious stucco-coated limestone bust of Nefertiti was found in Armana by the German archaeologist Ludwig Borchardt in 1912 and, in contravention of international agreements, smuggled out of the country to Berlin in 1913. Hugely influential, Nefertiti ruled alongside her husband from 1353 to 1336 BCE, and may have ruled the New Kingdom outright after his death. Though her tomb has never been found, there are several surviving wall paintings, including a beautiful portrait where she's playing a game of senet, a kind of chequers.

> 'I will not be triumphed over.'
>
> ***Cleopatra***

More than a thousand years later, we come to the acknowledged last female pharaoh of Egypt, **Cleopatra VII** (69–30 BCE), and there is no doubt of her authority. By the age of twenty, she had been crowned, deposed, reinstated, married two of her half-brothers and ordered the execution of a half-sister. She famously had affairs with both Julius Caesar and Mark Antony, leading to Antony's rival, Octavian, attacking their combined forces at Actium in 31 BCE. Taken captive in Alexandria, and knowing she would be publicly paraded and executed, Cleopatra poisoned herself – possibly by snake venom – rather than allow herself to be humiliated. Cleopatra has been immortalized in statuary, poetry, films and plays – not least by Shakespeare, whose depiction is still as fresh today as when *Antony and Cleopatra* was first performed in 1607 – making her one of the most famous women in history.

> 'If you weigh well the strengths of our armies you will see that in this battle we must conquer or die. This is a woman's resolve. As for the men, they may live or be slaves.'
>
> ***Boudica***

ANOTHER CELEBRATED WARRIOR queen from history is **Boudica** (*c.* 30–61 CE), often still referred to as Boadicea, the leader of the Iceni tribe in the east of Britain in the first century CE. After the death of her husband, Boudica's estates were illegally seized by order of the Roman governor. When she protested the decision, Boudica was flogged and her daughters – still children – were publicly raped. This shocking act of violence united the Iceni with the neighbouring Trinovantes tribe and, in 60–61, Boudica led the combined forces – some one hundred thousand warriors – in revolt against the Roman occupiers. She overwhelmed the Roman Ninth Legion, destroyed Camulodunum, present-day Colchester, then led her troops to St Albans and London, slaughtering between seventy thousand and eighty thousand people before she was finally defeated. History is not sure what happened next. The Roman historian Tacitus claims Boudica died by suicide rather than fall into her enemy's hands; others suggest she died of wounds sustained in battle.

In 1902, a bronze statue called 'Boadicea and Her Daughters' was erected by Westminster Bridge in London. The front plinth reads: BOADICEA (BOUDICCA), QUEEN OF THE ICENI WHO DIED AD 61 AFTER LEADING HER PEOPLE AGAINST THE ROMAN INVADER. The statue had been nearly half a century in the making – it was not erected until some seventeen years after the artist's death, the year after the death of Queen Victoria. The parallels drawn between the late monarch and Boudica – whose name also means 'victory' or 'she who brings victory' – were deliberate. Two exceptional female leaders.

THE QUESTION OF where and to whom statues are erected is a huge contemporary issue, particularly when the people honoured have been demonstrably active or complicit in slavery or conquest and oppression. Are statues only to commemorate and celebrate, or can they be trusted to serve as a reminder of the uglier and darker times of history? Can they do both?

As part of this debate, increasingly urgent questions are being asked about the lack of women's representation. The statistics are even worse when statues of mythical or symbolic figures are not included. A survey conducted in 2019 reported that in the UK 86.3 per cent of statues of historical figures were male, and the figure for women plummets when royal statues are removed. Until 2021, there were more statues to men named John than all the women put together and, in Edinburgh, at the time of writing, there are more statues of animals than of women. It's worse in the US, where some 92.4 per cent of statues of historical figures are male. In France in the nineteenth century, twenty statues of celebrated women – '*Reines de France et Femmes illustres*' – were commissioned for the Jardin du Luxembourg in Paris, including those representing Jeanne d'Albret and **Blanche of Castile** (1188–1252). It is one of the most visited areas of the gardens. But such displays are the exception that proves the rule. Worldwide, the proportion of statues of women to men is very low.

This absence matters. Because by leaving out the vast majority of the women who also built our world – and for Black women and other women of colour the absence is even more acute – we are being told a partial, very misleading story. For many people, the daily walk past a statue is part of living history, a reminder of those in whose footsteps we walk. Which is why campaigns to erect statues to great women is so important, a very visible way of putting women back into the history books.

History was made in the UK in October 2021 when the first statue of a Black woman, **Henrietta Lacks** (1920–1951), created by a Black woman – the Bristolian sculptor **Helen Wilson-Roe** (b. 1964) – was erected at the University of Bristol. Lacks's cells were taken in the 1950s, and used without her consent, to create the HeLa cell line, which has been crucial in medical research, not least of all in the development of *in vitro* fertilization. Her name was publicly used too after her death without consent and her private medical records were made available to the media, a shocking lack of respect for Lacks as a person.

> 'A landscape full of places named after women and statues of women might have encouraged me and other girls in profound ways.'
>
> **Rebecca Solnit**

BOUDICA WAS NOT the only warrior queen in Roman-occupied Britain. **Cartimandua** (d. after 69 CE) was queen of the Brigantes, a Celtic tribe in the north of England. She was, for the most part, ruling under Roman protection rather than fighting against them. What little we know of her life also comes from Tacitus and he is ambivalent, despite her supposed loyalty to Rome. Cartimandua has been fictionalized in several novels and films, most notably **Barbara Erskine**'s (b. 1944) novel *Daughters of Fire*.

Septimia Zenobia (*c.* 240–*c.* 274 CE) was queen of the Palmyrene Empire, in what is now Syria. She became ruler after the assassination of her husband and stepson in 267 CE, expanding her kingdom into Roman-occupied Egypt and Anatolia. The Romans responded by besieging her treasury and although she and her son escaped the siege, they were then captured and taken hostage. It's said she was led through the streets of Rome bound in golden chains as part of a military victory, the humiliation Cleopatra sought to escape. Zenobia's legacy is one of intellectual strength, of creating a court of scholarly pursuit, as well as governing a stable multiethnic and multicultural state.

'For my own part, I adhere to the maxim of antiquity, that the throne is a glorious sepulchre.'

Theodora

Theodora of Byzantium (c. 500–548 CE) began life as a dancer, mime-artist – and possibly courtesan. She travelled to North Africa, before settling outside Alexandria and converting to Christianity. It is then that she made her way to Constantinople, where she met Justinian. In 525 CE, he changed the law to marry her and, when he was crowned emperor two years later, Theodora was crowned empress at his side. They ruled together until her death at the age of forty-eight. Justinian never remarried.

Theodora is far from missing from history – and there are many excellent biographies and novels – but I'm including her because her representation is an object lesson of how we should beware of believing everything we are told by historians who might have their own agenda.

Because here's the thing. Most of what we know about Theodora's life, and statements attributed to her, comes from the work of Procopius, who offered three wildly differing portrayals. The first, *The Wars of Justinian*, completed in 545 CE, just three years before her death, paints a picture of a principled and courageous wife who saved her husband's throne. In *Secret History*, Theodora is depicted as vulgar, sexually voracious, calculating, shrill – textbook epithets for traducing a woman's reputation, where accusations of immorality are used to undermine integrity and honesty. Finally, in Procopius's third portrayal, *Buildings of Justinian*, she is again a paragon of sober, wise leadership. The same woman, the same historian. Which should we believe?

What we do know is that, during Justinian's rule, laws were passed expanding the rights of women in divorce and property ownership. Her name appears in some legislation passed at the time, again supporting the idea that Theodora was actively involved. The death penalty was introduced for rape, the exposure of unwanted children – that's to say, leaving them outside to die of hypothermia and hunger – was forbidden, and mothers were granted some rights of guardianship. We can't be certain, but it strongly suggests Theodora used her influence and her power to effect improvements to women's lives. A saint in the Eastern Orthodox Church, her feast day falls on 14 November.

An extraordinary story, an extraordinary woman.

Wu Zhao (624–705 CE) was the first and only female emperor of China. Commonly known as **Wu Zetian**, she was a woman of extraordinary political ability who ruled as the 'Holy and Divine Emperor' of the Second Zhou Dynasty for fifteen years. Having poisoned the crown prince and exiled other claimants, she first established her elder son on the throne after her husband's death, then deposed him six weeks later and replaced him with his younger brother. She established a network of spies, undertook a root-and-branch reform of government, tax and education, and expanded her empire by invading Korea in 688 CE. She was finally overthrown in 704, when she was eighty years of age. A warrior to the last.

JUMPING FORWARD IN history, we come to an era that inspired the first of my historical novels, and the most inspirational and least known of the Crusader queens, **Melisende, Queen of Jerusalem** (1105–1161).

One has to guard against eulogizing any aspect of Crusader history – they were bloody religious wars of conquest and devastation – but Melisende is a woman I admire. She was athletic, a keen horsewoman and diplomat, and I first came across her when I was shown the exquisite Melisende Psalter held in the vaults of the British Library in London. With its ivory covers inlaid with turquoise and garnet, and its illuminations of gold and lapis lazuli, it's one of the few treasures known to have belonged to Melisende.

Entranced by the psalter, I became fascinated by her almost complete absence from history, given her extraordinary life and achievements, and began researching her life. Again, much of what we know comes from a male historian. The difference here is that William of Tyre hugely supported Melisende.

> '. . . the rule of the kingdom remained in
> the power of the lady queen Melisende, a
> queen beloved by God, to whom it passed
> by hereditary right.'
>
> **William of Tyre**

The eldest of the four daughters of Baldwin II in Outremer – meaning 'beyond the sea', the Crusader name for the Holy Land – Melisende was raised to succeed her father. From an early age, her name appeared alongside his on official documents and in diplomatic correspondence. Although she was married to a wealthy crusader, Fulk of Anjou, her father held a coronation ceremony investing the kingship of Jerusalem three ways – between Melisende, her husband Fulk and his grandson, the future Baldwin III, who'd been born in 1130 – and, in an extraordinary move, he made Melisende her son's sole guardian.

Baldwin II died in 1131 and, as he'd clearly feared, Fulk refused to accept his wife as his equal. Melisende went to war against her husband to secure her rights and – again, extraordinarily for those times – the clergy and nobility of Outremer supported her. They were reconciled by 1136 and she appears genuinely to have mourned him when he was killed in a hunting accident in 1143. Fulk is thought to have sought his wife's forgiveness by commissioning the beautiful psalter I saw in the British Museum.

Melisende ruled as queen from 1131 to 1153, and again as regent for her son Baldwin III. She refused to move aside when he came of age in 1145 and held on to power until 1152, when she was compelled to step back by the young king's supporters. She endowed many convents and religious institutions, including the most important site in Christendom: the location of Christ's tomb, the Church of the Holy Sepulchre. She also founded the Convent of Bethany in 1143. (The fact that my godmother Sister Katherine's order was the Society of the Sisters of Bethany was another connection that drew me to Melisende.) A generous patron of the arts, she commissioned many works of art, books and buildings throughout Jerusalem, creating a thriving and flourishing cultural city. The sister to three extraordinary women, and grandmother to the last great Crusader queen of Outremer, **Sybilla** (1159–1190), Melisende deserves to be a household name. She was buried in the Abbey of Jehoshaphat, at the foot of the Mount of Olives, just a few steps above the Tomb of Mary, the mother of God. But perhaps her best epitaph is these words written by William of Tyre:

'She was a very wise woman, fully experienced in almost all affairs of state business, who completely triumphed over the handicap of her sex so that she could take charge of important affairs . . .'

'Grief is not very different from illness: in the impetus of its fire, it does not recognize lords, it does not fear colleagues, it does not respect or spare anyone, not even itself.'

Eleanor of Aquitaine

FROM ONE OF the least known to perhaps the most famous of medieval queens, **Eleanor of Aquitaine** (*c.* 1122–1204). A patron of the arts, a leader of armies, a skilled negotiator and strategist, Eleanor was one of the most powerful women in Western Europe. Queen consort of France from 1137 to 1154 through her marriage to Louis VII and queen consort of England from 1154 to 1189, she survived and thrived, faced set-backs and calumnies, to live into her eighties. Forced to endure a kind of semi-imprisonment for sixteen years by her estranged husband Henry II of England, she became even more active in public life after he died in 1189, and ruled as regent for her son, Richard I of England, while he was away on Crusade. The mother of five daughters and five sons, Eleanor was, like Melisende, remarkable for her ability to acquire and hold power, and to successfully keep the support of churchmen and military advisors in a century rife with shifting allegiances. She died at Fontevraud Abbey, in the Loire Valley in France, where her tomb can be found. She lies between the stone effigies of Richard and Henry, who are sleeping in death. Eleanor, however, has a book in her hands, as if she still might wake and start to read . . .

ALONGSIDE THESE HUGE figures in history, there were, of course, countless other women leaders, crown or no crown, who stood up for their communities and their land. Alaïs – the hero of *Labyrinth*, which is set in Languedoc during the Albigensian Crusade of 1209 and its aftermath in 1244 – was inspired, in part, by the spirit of such courageous women.

In Wales, for example, **Gwenllian ferch Gruyffydd** (*c.* 1100–1136) took up arms against Norman rule, launching several raids in the 1120s and 1130s. During the period of disruption known as the 'Anarchy', Gwenllian raised a force aiming to cut off supplies to the Norman stronghold of Cydweli Castle. Betrayed, she was beheaded on the battlefield. For some, her spirit endures as a symbol of Welsh independence.

A generation later in England, **Nicola de la Haye** (*c.* 1150–1230), sometimes described as the 'woman who saved England', successfully defended Lincoln Castle twice against prolonged sieges. De la Haye had inherited the position of Constable of Lincoln Castle from her father and, throughout her life, continually had to fight to keep her title. In 1216, despite being a woman and in her sixties, she was appointed by King John as Sheriff of Lincolnshire. Her success in holding the castle in May 1217, during the first Barons' War – defeating Louis of France – was a turning point in English history. Diplomat, politician, a woman strong of heart and character, she lived to be nearly eighty, an extraordinary age in the thirteenth century.

We see, then, how warrior women can become symbols beyond their own history and reputation, beyond time and place. Their names are not forgotten, though sometimes the flesh-and-blood woman behind the legend becomes obscured.

In Japan, **Tomoe Gozen** (twelfth century) was a legendary *onna-musha* or *onna-bugeisha* (*gozen* is a title of respect bestowed by a shogun teacher), a female warrior and heroine of the Genpei War. In 1182, Tomoe is reputed to have led three hundred samurai in battle against two thousand warriors of a rival clan. In the fourteenth-century epic, *The Tale of Heike*, she is described as: 'a warrior worth a thousand, ready to confront a demon or a god, mounted or on foot'. Fearless and described always as beautiful, capable of riding wild horses on impossibly steep terrain, Tomoe retired, unlike many warriors, to enjoy a long life.

Evidence from the Battle of Senbon Matsubarau in 1580 shows the tradition of female warriors fighting alongside samurai continued.

DNA sequencing has proved that of the 105 people killed in the conflict, thirty-five were women.

Five hundred years after Tomoe, another legendary *onna-bugeisha*, **Nakano Takeko** (1847–1868), fought in the Battle of Aizu in the autumn of 1868. Although she, and other female fighters, were not recognized as an official part of the army, Takeko led a unit that was later described as *Jōshitai* – the 'Women's Army'. Her weapon was the *naginata*, a long stave with a blade at one end. Can you imagine the sound, a forest of wood and the metal tips glinting, the snap of pennants in the wind, as the women rode out?

Shot in the chest while leading a charge against the Imperial Japanese Army – and not wanting her body to be paraded as a gruesome war trophy – Takeko asked her sister to cut off her head and bury it. Later, it was interred beneath a pine tree at the Hōkai-ji Temple in modern-day Fukushima. Her statue there shows her with her *naginata* in her hand, and even today, more than 150 years after her death, girls come to the monument during the Aizu Autumn Festival each year to commemorate Takeko and her valiant Women's Army.

Another legendary fighter, **Khutulun** (*c.* 1260–*c.* 1300) was the great-great-granddaughter of Genghis Khan, whose Mongol Empire was starting to splinter. By 1260, her father Kaidu Khan was in dispute with his uncle Kublai Khan, provoking an armed conflict that would last for thirty years. Kaidu's most trusted military advisor and general was not one of his fourteen sons, but his beloved daughter. Both the Venetian explorer Marco Polo and Persian statesman and historian Rashid al-Din wrote accounts of meeting her, Polo describing her as a 'hawk'.

Khutulun was also a famous wrestler, and this is where the lines between fiction and fact become blurred. Under pressure to marry, legend has it, she said she would only accept someone who could beat her in a wrestling competition. If she won, they had to present her with one hundred horses – some versions of the story say one thousand – and it is said that is how she built up her own herd of ten thousand horses. Kaidu failed to secure his daughter's succession as Grand Khan and little is known of her after his death, though it's believed she chose her husband herself and had several children.

Khutulun's story is yet another example of how even a woman famous and celebrated in her day can vanish from the record. For centuries she was forgotten, until the early eighteenth-century French orientalist and traveller Francois Pétis de la Croix wrote a story inspired by her life story – 'Turandot', or the 'Turkish Princess' – though rather than wrestling her suitors, his princess sets them riddles. That story inspired the commedia dell'arte piece *Turandot* by Italian playwright Carlo Gozzi in 1762 which, in its turn, inspired many more pieces of theatre and music including Puccini's famous 1924 opera.

> 'I am not afraid; I was born to do this.'
>
> **Jeanne d'Arc**

Perhaps the most enduring symbol of stoical female resistance is **Joan of Arc** (1412–1431). Jeanne d'Arc was also known as La Pucelle, or the Maid of Orléans, and was little more than a child when she joined the army of the French king at Orléans in April 1429, which had been besieged by English forces for seven months. A devout Catholic, Jeanne claimed to have seen visions of the Archangel Michael among other saints. The English forces were superior in terms of both numbers and resources, so when the siege was lifted a mere nine days after her arrival, the legend of La Pucelle was born.

The following year, Jeanne was captured by the English and, after a show trial, she was convicted as a heretic and burnt at the stake on 30 May 1431. She was only nineteen years old.

Having written novels set against the backdrop of religious conflict – from *Labyrinth* to *The Burning Chambers* and *The City of Tears* – I'm haunted by the idea of what it must have been like for a young woman alone, surrounded by male inquisitors determined to condemn her. The black-and-white photograph of **Joan Plowright** (b. 1929) – child-like, powerless, strong – taken in 1963 on the stage of Chichester Festival Theatre in Bernard Shaw's *Saint Joan* sums up, for me, more than anything the courage of these warrior women. Declared a martyr in 1456 and beatified in 1909, Jeanne was canonized in 1920.

While guarding against seeing global history through a very partial Western Christian lens, it's also true that Joan's name has become a byword for any courageous, principled warrior woman taking a stand against overwhelming odds. So even though each of these women have their independent history and should be seen in their own right, as a shorthand, here, across many centuries and different lands, are one or two other so-called Joans . . .

We'll start in the third century CE with **Triệu Thị Trinh** (*c.* 226–248). Sometimes known as the Vietnamese Joan of Arc – although since she predates La Pucelle by some twelve hundred years, we should, rather, be calling Jeanne the 'French Lady Triệu' – she fought against Chinese rule and refused to accept the limitations placed on her by traditions of the time. She is said to have died by suicide rather than fall into the hands of her enemies.

Like La Pucelle, the so-called Russian Joan of Arc came from a humble background. **Alyona Arzamasskaia** (*c.* 1640s–1670) was born into a peasant family, was married and widowed young, then lived as a nun at Nikoleavskii monastery. Though she learned to read and study medicine there, she hated the confinement and, in 1669, she fled, cut her hair and began dressing as a man. In 1670, she joined the Peasants' Revolt in southern Russia, gathering a regiment of some three hundred to four hundred men from around her home town, none of whom had any idea their commander was a woman. Initially, Arzamasskaia and her troops were successful, until the Tsar launched a campaign to crush the rebels. She was captured in December and sentenced to be burnt at the stake. Witnesses reported that she did not make a single sound as she died in agony, a warrior to the last.

> 'Monsieur, you are indeed welcome.
> I surrender arms to you.'
>
> *Madeleine de Verchères*

Born eight years after Arzamasskaia's execution, the Canadian Joan of Arc was **Marie-Madeleine Jarret** (1678–1747). Known also as **Madeleine de Verchères**, she is credited with repelling a raid by the First Nation Iroquois on Fort Verchères in Quebec (then known as New France) when she was fourteen years old. Madeleine had been left alone with one elderly man and only two soldiers but, by rushing from place to place, firing cannons and muskets to give the impression the fort was better defended than it was, she won the day. After eight days, when reinforcements arrived, she gave over command of the fort. However, the governor of New France, Louis de Buade, Comte de Frontenac, did not mention Madeleine in his report of conflicts with the Iroquois that year and she did not seek recognition until 1699, when she wrote to the wife of the French Minister of the Marine, describing her role in the defence of Fort Verchères and petitioning for a pension.

Like many of our women lost to history, de Verchères's life and achievements received little attention in the century following her death. But following the 1837 Rebellion in Lower Canada, she started to become seen as a heroine of French-Canadian history. During the First and Second World Wars, the story and image of Madeleine de Verchères were used to encourage Canadian women's participation in the war effort, especially in Quebec.

'What matters to God is your intention.
Your intention is what God accepts.'

Kimpa Vita

Another extraordinary woman in her own right, the Congolese Joan of Arc, **Kimpa Vita** (c. 1684–1706), had a certain amount in common with her French namesake. As a young woman, Dona Beatriz Kimpa Vita had visions and attempted to reconcile Catholic doctrine with traditional African beliefs in order to unite the country, which had suffered from Portuguese aggression. When only in her teens, she launched a non-violent campaign for the liberation of the Realm of the Kongo, opposing all forms of slavery, both local and those linked to European colonization, leading thousands of people in the recon- struction of Mbanza Kongo. After a near-death experience in 1704, Vita believed she spoke with the voice of St Anthony, the patron saint of Kongo, and launched her own religion, Antonianism, the first Black Christian movement in sub-Saharan Africa. Hailed as a prophet and leader, she was captured at the instigation of Capuchin missionaries and, like Jeanne two hundred and fifty years before her, she was burnt at the stake as a heretic on 2 July 1706. She was twenty-one years old.

The Filipina Resistance leader **Gabriela Silang** (1731–1763) used sometimes to be known as the Joan of Arc of Ilocandia. She and her independence fighters besieged the city of Vigan, held by the colonial Spanish forces, on 10 September 1763. They failed. Silang was captured and executed ten days later. Her legacy endures – the Gabriela Women's Party, established in 1984, was named after her.

The Spanish Joan of Arc is **Agustina of Aragón** (1786–1857), who defended Zaragoza against the French, first as a civilian and later as a professional officer in the Spanish Army. Agustina is the only identifiable figure in Goya's *The Disasters of War* and Byron wrote several stanzas about her in *Childe Harold*. It's said that on 15 June 1808, during the battle for Zaragoza, Agustina loaded a cannon and fired on the French attackers, giving the fleeing Spanish inhabitants the courage to return to their city to defend it. She was one of the rare fighting women who survived to retire, marry and live until the grand old age of seventy-one.

> 'The young intellectuals are all chanting, "Revolution, Revolution", but I say the revolution will have to start in our homes, by achieving equal rights for women . . .'
>
> **Qiū Jǐn**

The so-called Chinese Joan of Arc was **Qiū Jǐn** (1875–1907). A swordswoman and fighter, a pioneering feminist, a poet and essayist, she was the first woman to lead an armed uprising against the Qing Dynasty. She was also a women's rights activist, fighting for equal rights and education, and against the practice of foot binding. Arrested by imperial forces in 1907, and charged with conspiracy to overthrow the government, she was beheaded in her home village at the age of thirty-one.

Aurora Mardiganian (1901–1994) survived the Armenian genocide during the First World War, where as many as one million Armenian women and men died at the hands of Ottoman Turks. They were executed, or died from starvation or disease, during the mass deportation death marches from eastern Anatolia to the Syrian desert. Although the figures are disputed, independent journalists and advisors bore witness to the atrocities and the forced conversion to Islam of Armenian women and girls. Kidnapped on the death march, and sold into slavery in Anatolia, Mardiganian managed to escape into Georgia, then to St Petersburg and finally, with the help of an aid agency, to New York. In collaboration with a screenwriter, she published a memoir, *Ravished Armenia: the Story of Aurora*

Mardiganian, the Christian Girl, Who Survived the Great Massacres.
It was filmed as a silent movie, *Auction of Souls*, with Aurora playing
herself, and predictably she became known in the British and
American press as the Armenian Joan of Arc.

> 'With my country threatened and my family
> in danger, I set about making preparations
> for war. From that time forward, my life was
> never the same.'
>
> **Ani Pachen**

Finally, the woman the media referred to as the Tibetan Joan of
Arc. Warrior nun **Ani Pachen** (1933–2002) led a force of around six
hundred fighters against the Chinese invasion of neighbouring
Buddhist Tibet in 1958, resisting the resulting genocide during which
some six hundred monasteries are believed to have been destroyed.
Though there are several versions to the story of Pachen's early life,
it appears she was in training to be a Buddhist nun. After her father's
death, she saw it as her duty to join the Resistance instead to defend
her country and their way of life. She took part in the Tibetan Uprising
in the capital city of Lhasa in March 1959, and after months of
evading the Chinese, Pachen was finally captured. Brutalized and
tortured over the next twenty years, she was kept in some of the
harshest prisons in China – for nine months, she was shackled and
kept in solitary confinement – but she never lost her Buddhist faith.

When she was released in 1981, during a slight thawing of relations
between China and Tibet, Pachen continued to protest against the
genocide and Chinese occupation. In danger of being re-arrested,
she fled on foot through the Himalayas to Nepal in 1988. Her memoir,
Sorrow Mountain: The Journey of a Tibetan Warrior Nun was published
in 2000, two years before Pachen died in exile in India:

> 'Life is impermanent, like lightning in the sky, like dewdrops on
> the grass. Our loved ones and our wealth last only a fleeting
> moment. The only changeless truths are the teachings of Buddha.'

∞

> 'Our histories cling to us. We are shaped by
> where we come from.'
>
> **Chimamanda Ngozi Adichie**

MY GREAT-GRANDMOTHER LILY was born in 1849, at the height
of a period of huge colonial expansion and conquest. All over the
world women – as well as men – were taking up arms to resist the
European invaders. Although, to my knowledge, Lily never wrote
about politics or foreign affairs, I suspect her sympathies would have
been with the British Empire, rather than with those fighting to guard
or regain their independence and traditions, or those fighting against
the enslavement of their people and the theft of their sovereign land.

So, let's meet more of the courageous female leaders who resisted,
persisted, insisted and, finally, enlisted.

Settling in the tropics of north-eastern Brazil, within a community
of Afro-Brazilian people who'd freed themselves from slavery, **Dandara**
(d. 1694) lived at the end of the seventeenth century. Palmares was
a place of white sandy beaches, clear lagoons and coral reefs, but it
was under attack from European invaders. Skilled in the Brazilian
martial art of *capoeira*, Dandara fought fiercely, especially as tensions
between the Portuguese and the Dutch escalated. A peace treaty
signed in 1678 did not commit to an end to slavery, so Dandara
refused to surrender and kept fighting for another sixteen years. Finally
caught in February 1694, Dandara died by suicide rather than submit.

> 'I am a warrior in a time of women warriors;
> the longing for justice is the sword I carry.'
>
> **Sonia Johnson**

A century later in South America, **Manuela Sáenz** (1797–1856)
was a prominent Ecuadorian revolutionary and women's rights activist.
Originally married to a wealthy English merchant, and living a
socialite existence in Lima, Peru, Sáenz became involved in political
and military affairs. Leaving her husband, she began an eight-year
collaboration and relationship with Simón Bolívar that lasted until
his death in 1830. After she prevented an 1828 assassination attempt

against him, Bolívar began to call her *'Libertadora del Libertador'* (the 'Liberator of the Liberator'). Though in 1821 she had been awarded the highest distinction in Peru, the *Caballeresa del Sol* (the Order of the Sun), after her death Sáenz's role was generally overlooked until the late twentieth century. Today she is recognized as both a feminist symbol of the nineteenth-century wars of independence and a key figure in her own right.

From South America to the West Indies, and one of the most famous women in Jamaican history, **Nanny of the Maroons** (c. 1686–c. 1733). Celebrated in poems, portraits and on the 500-dollar note, Queen Nanny was born in Ghana in 1686. Little is recorded about her early life, but we do know that she and other previously enslaved people sought refuge in the Blue Mountains region of Jamaica where they established a settlement, Nanny Town. The Maroons were descendants of enslaved people living independently and Nanny trained her warriors in the art of guerrilla warfare. She also was rumoured to use *obeah* – a form of spiritual and supernatural practice – to protect them from the British.

The fighting continued for six years, until Nanny Town was destroyed in 1734. It's not clear if she survived and went into exile, or if she died in the fighting, but her legacy was secure. In 1739, another Maroon leader signed a peace treaty with the British and was granted five hundred acres of land, the settlement becoming known as New Nanny Town. Nanny was declared a National Hero – 'the Order of National Hero' – by the Jamaican government, the only woman to have been commemorated in this way and one of only seven recipients overall.

In West Africa in Dahomey, modern-day Benin, **Seh-Dong-Hong-Beh** (c. 1815/1835–after 1851) was a leader of the Dahomey Amazons. In 1851, she led an all-female army consisting of six thousand warriors against the Egba fortress of Abeokuta. In 1851, British naval commander Frederick Forbes drew Seh-Dong-Hong-Beh – which means 'God Speaks True' – in her uniform, armed with a musket and holding a captive's severed head. A passionate abolitionist, Forbes had travelled to the Dahomey kingdom in 1849 – an empire that existed between 1625 and 1894 – determined to convince the king to stop the internal African slave trade. He described the female Dahomeyan army in detail, commenting on their lifestyle and behaviour. Many Amazons were enlisted as small girls of between eight and ten years of age, but his portrait shows a woman perhaps in her early twenties. Seh-Dong-Hong-Beh was not mentioned in the French army account during the Dahomey–French wars in 1890, so she might have died in battle or retired. The army was known for its fearlessness – in one of the final battles against the French, before Dahomey became a French colony in 1892, it's said that only seventeen of the 434 Amazons came back alive. There are descendants of these warrior queens living in present-day Benin today.

> 'If you, the men of Asante, will not go forward, then we will. We, the women, will. I shall call upon my fellow women. We will fight. We will fight till the last of us falls in the battlefields.'
>
> **Yaa Asantewaa**

Showing the same kind of determination, **Yaa Asantewaa** (c. 1840–1921) was born in the Ashanti Empire, present-day Ghana, homeland of Nanny of the Maroons and a country rich in gold. The British attempted to take it by force in the 1890s. In 1900, they captured and exiled the king, but failed to recognize the importance of the queen mother, Yaa Asantewaa, who was ruling as regent. When the British governor-general attempted to occupy the throne, Yaa Asantewaa led a military operation in an engagement known as the War of the Golden Stool, or the Yaa Asantewaa War, besieging the British for three months. By September, although sixty of the Ashanti leaders had surrendered or been taken in battle, Yaa Asantewaa continued her campaign with her army of women warriors. She was finally captured; her lands became part of the British Gold Coast and she died in exile in the Seychelles in 1921.

The great Tamil warrior **Velu Nachiyar** (1730–1796) was the first Indian queen to wage war against the mighty British East India Company in 1780. Born in Tamil Nadu, Nachiyar was trained in martial arts, horse riding and archery. She was proficient in several languages including Urdu, French and English. In the mid-eighteenth century, she married the king of Sivagangai and ruled alongside him for twenty years. When he was killed in battle in 1772, Nachiyar escaped with their daughter and raised a 5,000-strong army with the help of the former Sultan of Mysore and several local feudal lords and merchants. One of her leading commanders was **Kuyili** (1700s–1780), who may or may not have been Nachiyar's adopted daughter. Kuyili covered herself in ghee and set herself alight to destroy the British store of ammunition, so is considered the first suicide bomber and first woman martyr in Indian history. After Nachiyar had reclaimed her kingdom, she established her own women's army, the Udaiyall, and ruled until her death in 1796. In 2014, a six-foot-high bronze statue of Nachiyar, her sword in hand, was erected in Sivagangai.

> 'If defeated and killed on the field of battle, we shall surely earn eternal glory and salvation.'
>
> ### *Lakshmibai*

Probably the most famous of the warrior queens fighting against British occupation in India is **Lakshmibai, Rani of Jhansi** (1828–1858). Born a century after Nachiyar, in the northern city of Varanasi – one of the seven sacred cities of Hinduism – she was raised in the company of boys and received an education usually denied to girls. As a result, Lakshmibai was a skilled horsewoman, often taking the reins rather than riding in a litter like most noblewomen of the time. Adept in martial arts, she married the Maharajah of Jhansi in 1842 at the age of fourteen. She had a son, who died four months after birth, so two years later they adopted a cousin's boy to be their heir. When her husband died, the British governor-general annexed Jhansi, contravening a pre-existing agreement. The twenty-two-year-old queen refused to yield. She joined the Indian Rebellion against the British East India Company in 1857 and, possibly dressed as a man, led her troops into battle. She died in action.

In the early years of the nineteenth century in the northern United States, Indigenous peoples were also resisting the annexation of their lands by white settlers. **Bíawacheeitchish** (c. 1806–1858) – a name which means 'woman chief' – was a warrior of the Crow Nation and 'two-spirit', what today we might call non-binary. Bíawacheeitchish lived within the male culture of her tribe rather than the female – though she never adopted male clothing – took over the household of her adoptive father after his death and rose to be the third most important in the 160-strong council of chiefs. She had a reputation as a courageous fighter, leading raiding parties, and took four wives. Other women warrior chiefs of the Crow Nation include **Akkeekaahuush** (*c.* 1810–1880) – which means 'Comes Towards the Near Bank' – and **Biliíche Héeleelash** (*c.* 1837–1912), 'Among the Willows'.

ALTHOUGH MY GREAT-GRANDMOTHER wrote children's stories about pirates, her adult fiction was very much set within historical or contemporary worlds that she knew. Yet nineteenth-century literature was awash with pirate stories: R. M. Ballantyne's *The Coral Island: A Tale of the Pacific Ocean* came out in 1857; Walter Scott's *The Pirate* was published in 1822; and *Treasure Island* by Robert Louis Stevenson, a third Scottish bestselling writer, was serialized between 1881 and 1882 in the children's magazine *Young Folks* and published in book form in 1883. All of these pirate stories were firmly promoted as boys' reading, so I think it's likely that Lily's sons, Reggie, Harry and Leader, might well have had the volumes on their bookshelves.

Many other pirate novels, like Emilio Salgari's *The Black Corsair* and Rafael Sabatini's *Captain Blood*, claimed to have been inspired by real buccaneers and pirates. But what about the women? We know that there were a few women who, out of necessity or a desire for adventure or revenge, also took to the seas and became 'she-captains'.

In the fourteenth century, **Jeanne de Clisson** (1300–1359) was known as the 'Lioness of Brittany'. Vowing to avenge her husband's execution for treason in 1343, she acquired three warships with the assistance of the king of England, painted them black and fitted them out with red sails, then launched a campaign of terror against the French king and French ships in the English Channel. Her flagship was known as *My Revenge* and, for thirteen years, de Clisson ruled the Channel, running down ships and slaughtering their crew. All but one. She always left one man alive to carry her message of defiance.

A century later, **Sayyida al Hurra** (1485–1561), the queen of Tétoun in northern Morocco, was also a pirate commander, controlling the west side of the Mediterranean Sea in an alliance with the Turkish corsair Barbarossa of Algiers, who held the eastern waters. The title 'al Hurra' means the 'free one', suggesting that, from 1515 to 1542, she ruled as queen in her own right after the death of her first husband, and is most likely the last Islamic woman to legitimately have held such a title. She was a key protagonist in the sixteenth-century struggles between the Ottoman and Christian empires in Spain and Portugal.

Despite her liking for pirate stories, I doubt if Lily would have heard of Sayyida. But I'm sure she'd have been familiar with **Gráinne O'Malley** (*c*. 1530–*c*. 1603). A towering figure in sixteenth-century Irish history, Gráinne was head of the O'Malley clan who, for more than three hundred years, ruled the southern shore of Clew Bay and most of the barony of Murrisk. One of her many legends has it that when she asked to accompany her father on a trading trip to Spain, and was refused on the grounds that her long hair would catch in the ship's ropes, she chopped off her hair rather than accept her father's decision. The act earned her the first of her nicknames, Gráinne 'Mhaol', *maol* meaning bald or cropped hair. Later in life, when her lover was killed, she took revenge by storming his murderers' castle at Doona and acquired a second nickname, the 'Dark Lady of Doona'.

At her father's death, Gráinne took the helm as captain of the fleet. In 1593, after her sons and her half-brother were taken captive, O'Malley sailed to England to petition **Elizabeth I** for their release.

Extraordinarily, given how she lived, Gráinne survived into her early seventies, and died of natural causes in 1603. Buried in the Cistercian abbey on Clare Island, she became a national folk hero, fictionalized in novels, films and plays. She is sometimes used as the personification of Ireland. A mighty seven-foot four-inch statue of O'Malley was unveiled at Westport House, in County Mayo, in 2003. Strong, determined, the statue of the pirate queen is again looking out over the western seaboard where, once, she ruled the waves.

The largest pirate fleet commanded by a woman that I've discovered was amassed by **Zheng Yi Sao** (1775–1844), the pirate queen of the South China Seas, who inherited her dead husband's informal command over the entire pirate federation and led a fleet of possibly as many as sixty thousand pirates. When she was forced to surrender in 1810, she was in personal command of twenty-four ships and more than one thousand pirates.

But despite Zheng Yi Sao's extraordinary achievements, in popular culture eighteenth-century female pirate history really belongs to two women, **Anne Bonny** (1697–1721) and **Mary Read** (1685–1721). Their lives read like a nautical sensation novel – embracing notoriety, courage, disguise, romance, impossible adventures, danger and glory. Read, who was born in England, began dressing as a boy when she was a child, first as a way to secure an inheritance, then as a way to enlist in the Navy, fighting with British and Dutch forces against the French. Once peace was declared, and so now with no hope of advancement, Mary joined a ship bound for the West Indies. She was kidnapped by pirates, and aligned herself with their interests. Then, in 1720, she joined Anne Bonny and her partner, the notorious pirate 'Calico Jack' Rackham.

The Bonny and Read legend began.

> 'If you had fought like a man, you needn't be hanged like a dog.'
>
> **Anne Bonny**

Anne Bonny was born in Ireland, though she moved to Carolina in North America when she was ten. She may have 'married' a female pirate, then did marry James Bonny, a sailor and pirate, but at some time after 1714, she and James moved to the Bahamas, which is where Calico Jack saw her and fell in love. When Bonny's husband refused to divorce her, they fled the island, with Bonny disguised as a man, to crew Calico Jack's ship.

With both Anne Bonny and Mary Read disguised, the trio spent years at sea in the Caribbean, with a price on their heads until finally, in October 1720, their ship was seized. Contemporary reports talk of how Read and Bonny were the only two left fighting, as the men cowered below deck. Arrested and condemned, Calico Jack was executed, but the women were both granted a stay of execution by 'pleading the belly' – that's to say, claiming they were pregnant. And this is where the story ends. Read died in prison in April 1720, probably from postpartum fever. But Bonny? There is no record either of her release, or of her execution. A ledger in a church in Jamaica lists an Anne Bonny dying in December 1733. Other stories have her escaping to America and settling there. Who's to say . . . The legend of Bonny and Read – and some of these other astonishing 'she-captains' – inspired the next novel in The Joubert Family Chronicles, *The Ghost Ship*.

Finally, one of the most extraordinary naval military commanders in history was also a woman. Known as the *kapetanissa*, **Laskarina Bouboulina** (1771–1825) was the heroine of the Greek War of Independence of 1821 and, it seems, the first woman to attain the rank of admiral.

Bouboulina was born in prison, but grew up hearing stories of sailing and the sea. Much of her life story is well known. She was widowed twice and left with seven children from two marriages, and a large fortune. She built up her own fleet of ships, including an eighteen-cannon warship, *Agamemnon*. On 13 March 1821, Bouboulina raised the Greek flag and began a naval blockade against the Turkish fleet, playing a key role in their defeat.

The later years of her life remain murky, and she was killed in a domestic dispute rather than in battle, but her legacy as a fearless and courageous woman lives on. The museum dedicated to her in Spetses has several items on display, including her favoured weapon. A gift from Tsar Alexander I, it's a Mandinka sword of north-west African origin, fashioned to contain poison at its tip. The museum also displays her silk headscarf, beautifully embroidered with real gold and silver thread, and a bronze statue stands at the harbour entrance. Bouboulina's hair is covered by a headscarf, her right hand resting on her sword. Her left shields her eyes as she looks out to sea, like Gráinne O'Malley.

A saint? One woman's freedom fighter is another woman's mortal enemy; it depends where on the divide you stand. The impulse to sanitize the past, to glamorize it and gloss over the violence or the cruelty, is to do history a disservice. All the same, we can still salute the determination of these warrior queens and pirate commanders who survived, as women, in a desperate and dangerous man's world.

Dearest,
Alfred died peacefully this morning.
I feel very broken hearted but shall come home soon.
Your Lily

Received this from my wife
8 July 1882

Note from Lily to Sam about the death of her brother,
July 1882

Lily

THERE ARE, SOMETIMES, BURIED within documents, stories of such tragedy and loss that one wonders how they remained hidden. Within the Green and Watson families, was one such devastating secret.

While rummaging through a plain cardboard folder trying to verify another slippery date, I found a different kind of family tree. A partial document, in which not everyone is listed. In the bottom right-hand corner, there's a white sticker with the name and an address in Sussex – Hadley Dean. In ink below, a date: February 1977.

The document is typewritten and, next to each name, either the letter 'H' is written in red biro or a capital 'C' is written in green. The heading is stark: 'Haemophilia sufferers or believed sufferers and carriers or possible carriers only'.

The first recorded mention of haemophilia dates from the Talmud, when a ruling by Rabbi Judah decreed that a baby boy should not be circumcised if two of their older brothers had bled to death following the procedure. Other rabbinical rulings followed. In the tenth century, a Muslim doctor described cases of male members of the same family dying from excessive bleeding after a trauma. Some early treatments to try to induce blood clotting included injecting lime, bone marrow, oxygen, hydrogen peroxide and gelatin.

In 1803, Dr John Conrad Otto published a paper about a familial bleeding disorder that only affected males. Though the term 'haemophilia' dates from 1828, mostly it was known as the 'bleeding disease' and seen as a royal affliction of Europe. Queen Victoria was a carrier of haemophilia B, or factor IX deficiency, and passed the trait on to three of her nine children. Her beloved son Leopold, always a delicate child, was to die of a haemorrhage after a fall on 28 March 1884. He was thirty years old.

In the first years of their marriage, Lily was pregnant every other year. The family was living in Streatham and all six children were born there – Ethel in 1871, Reginald in 1873, Harold in 1875 and Winifred in 1879 at 'Eversley', then Arnold – known by his middle name, Leader – in late 1885, and my grandmother, Betty, on 12 December 1891 at 'Poplars'.

Holding this family tree in my hand, I saw how all three of Lily's sons were sufferers. In the letters I've read, I found no references to Reggie's health and only once does she mention Harry was ill. In a diary entry from November 1900, Sam wrote: 'Harry has quite broken down in health.' But that crisis clearly passed.

Leader, on the other hand, was more seriously ill. Like his brothers he was sent away to school – first to Margate, then to Eastbourne – but he was often sent home. In a letter from 'Poplars' on 10 April 1895, Lily wrote: 'Leader is a fearful handful. He has been in mischief and causing a great commotion all the morning and my nerves are all on edge. I don't know what to do for I cannot bear a further three weeks of it.' The letter is conversational, as if she is speaking to Sam, and it's one of the very rare occasions when she mentions her writing: 'Have been writing, but under difficulties. Only five more chapters, hurrah!' I think this must be *A Fortunate Exile*, which was published in 1896. Lily finishes with her customary 'I shall not write on now. You are not forgotten by your loving wife.'

Leader's letters from school are sweet. He writes to Ethel to make sure she is looking after his goldfish, and to Winnie about her attempts at catching butterflies, and signs off: 'Your loving brother Leader Watson always needing stamps!' His letters to his mother are more formal, reporting diligently on fishing expeditions and how he is learning new dance steps. But I assume his health was deteriorating because, by May 1898, Leader had been brought closer to home and was attending a day school in Streatham. His report says he 'is intelligent and promising', but that he has been 'seriously handicapped by absence from school'.

Lily seems to have spent the August of 1898 with Leader in St

Leonard's on the East Sussex coast, no doubt hoping that the sea air would do him good. But her son was dying. In the deed box, I found a letter to Sam dated 1 September detailing what the doctor had said and reassuring him that Leader is a 'shade better'. Did Lily believe this, or was she simply trying to comfort her husband?

The following day, there's a telegram written in pencil: 'Leader passed peacefully away about 3pm – funeral cannot be here – home by eleven-thirty today – break it gently.'

Reading Leader's death certificate, I discovered he had died after three days of haemorrhaging from his mouth and gums. Three days. Just the thought of those terrible and endless hours at his bedside, with Lily unable to help her son as she watched him die, is heart-breaking.

Haemophilia was incurable. For Lily, the horror of this illness would not have been new. Of her four brothers, three were haemophiliac – only Edwin escaped – and there's mention in family documents of two other brothers who did not survive long enough to be registered, suggesting that perhaps those ghost children were sufferers too.

Sixteen years earlier, Lily had been at another death-bed in her parents' house. There's a scribbled note I found to Sam in the deed box: 'Dearest, Alfred died peacefully this morning'. At the bottom of the page, Sam has added in his precise, tight handwriting: 'Received this morning from my wife 8 July 1882'.

Their eldest daughter Ethel never had children, but Winifred would turn out to be a carrier. It's the only reference to the 'family weakness' I've been able to find in Lily's letters. On 19 July 1904, Lily would write two letters on one day from the Lake District, the first with the happy news that Winnie's suitor had proposed. 'Well, my darling – this is one more great event in our pleasing lives together. Mr Scott is writing to you.' Lily continues: 'haemophilia must be spoken of, in justice to him'. In a second letter, written hours later and marked '2nd update', she repeats it: 'I presume you will leave all details e.g. the family weakness till that interview'.

One of Winnie's sons would be a sufferer and, in 1910, her daughter would die after only a few weeks of life. My grandmother, Betty, was tested too and proved negative, as did my aunt Margaret and my cousin Anne. On our side of the family, the illness seems to have died out within three generations.

I wonder if Lily saw her son's death as God's will and accepted it, or raged against the unfairness? I could find no letters talking about what she felt after Leader had gone – perhaps because she and Sam were together at 'Poplars'? Or maybe it was simply too difficult to express. I wonder, too, if her faith made the loss easier to bear? Sam was in no doubt – in his diary, he writes: 'We are all terribly distressed but feel it is for the best. We shall see him again.' Was Lily as sure?

Lily never wrote explicitly about haemophilia in articles that I've been able to find, nor does the condition appear in any of her books. But her third novel, *In the Days of Mozart*, published in 1891, has a relationship between an older sister and a delicate brother at the heart of the story. Set in Austria in the late eighteenth century, Rudolph, a musician and composer, is suffering from tuberculosis. Elsa, older and stronger, sacrifices her chance of happiness in order to care for him. It's a story about duty, about female responsibility, about the transcendent power of music and faith, about endurance in the face of hardship and injustice. The novel ends with Rudolph dying in Elsa's arms, taking him 'far, far beyond the reach of her sympathy or tender care'. An experience Lily had already been through twice before.

There is also, always, the erroneous idea that those in the past mourned less than we would do at the loss of someone beloved. It's true to say expectations were different then. Life expectancy in the 1870s was only 42.1 years for women and 39.6 years for men. In 1893, there were 159 perinatal deaths for every 100 live births. Until the early 1900s, the life expectancy for boys with haemophilia was only thirteen years. Would Lily have been aware of these harsh odds? Even if she were, would knowing the odds make the grief and the fear of loss any less fierce?

On the page, death can be beautiful to write, dramatic even. A moment of resolution or closure. That is not how it feels in real life.

Top left: Susan La Flesche Picotte (1865–1915)
Top right: Sophia Jex-Blake (1840–1912)
Bottom: Dorothy Hodgkin Crowfoot (1910–1994)

5

Mothers of Invention

'The idea of winning a doctor's degree gradually assumed the quality of a great moral struggle, and the moral fight possessed immense attraction for me.'

Pioneer Work in Opening the Medical Profession to Women
Elizabeth Blackwell, 1895

HAEMOPHILIA IS STILL INCURABLE, but today there are effective treatments to encourage clotting. And much more is known about the condition.

In 1925, Von Willebrand's disease – which has similar markers to haemophilia – was first recognized by the Finnish physician Erik von Willebrand. In 1937, doctors discovered clotting problems could be corrected by adding platelet-free plasma, called anti-haemophilic globulin. And in 1944, Argentine physician Alfredo Pavlovsky identified haemophilia A and haemophilia B as two distinct diseases. We also now know that women can suffer from haemophilia too, though very rarely it's linked to the X-chromosome that only women carry.

In the 1930s, snake venom was still being used to help blood clotting. Hospital-based plasma transfusions continued until the 1950s. By 1960, the life expectancy for a boy or man with severe haemophilia was still only about twenty years of age. Then, in 1965, the American physician **Judith Pool** (1919–1975) discovered cryo-precipitation, a process for creating concentrated blood clotting factors, which significantly improved the quality of life for haemophiliacs.

None of this would be in time to save Lily's brothers or her son, but it's an example of how the women (and men) of science and medicine can transform lives. So, here are women physicians and physicists, chemists, biologists, mathematicians, engineers and computer scientists, whose quest for knowledge changed the world.

> 'It is important to note early that women's
> historically subordinate "place" in science
> (and thus their invisibility to even
> experienced historians of science) was not a
> coincidence and was not due to any lack of
> merit on their part . . . It was due to the
> camouflage intentionally placed over their
> presence in science.'
>
> **Margaret Rossiter**

As we have seen, it was the American science historian Margaret W. Rossiter who coined the phrase the 'Matilda Effect' to refer to the deliberate suppression of the contributions of female scientists within research, as well as the frequent crediting of their work to male counterparts. Rossiter believes that because few male historians were willing to write about female scientists, or their achievements, it meant that even if a woman was visible within her lifetime, her work quickly became invisible after her death. It's all about the recording – who records what and who values it. The further back in time one goes, the harder it is to discover the names of any individual physicians or healers. And, even when women's names were recorded, those who wish to erase women's contributions can either ignore them or suggest they were somehow symbolic, rather than real. That's the case with one of the two earliest recorded women healers in Ancient Egypt.

It's not certain if **Merit Ptah** (*c.* 2700–*c.* 2200 BCE) was a real person. Originally thought to be a physician at the Pharaoh's court during the Second Dynasty, it's now suggested that she was a twentieth-century invention of Canadian feminist, medical historian and obstetrician **Kate Campbell Hurd-Mead** (1867–1941). But **Peseshet** (*c.* 2613–2494 BCE), who probably lived under the Fourth Dynasty, did exist and is considered by historians to be the first verified female physician. An inscription found at the tomb of Akhet-Hetep at Giza suggests Peseshet's title was 'lady overseer of the female physicians' and she might also have trained midwives at Sais, a town on the western Nile Delta. Like many Egyptian temples, the Temple of Sais had an associated medical school with female students as well as teachers, particularly in gynae-cology and obstetrics. A surviving inscription found at Sais reads: I

HAVE COME FROM THE SCHOOL OF MEDICINE AT HELIOPOLIS, AND HAVE STUDIED AT THE WOMEN'S SCHOOL AT SAIS, WHERE THE DIVINE MOTHERS HAVE TAUGHT ME HOW TO CURE DISEASES.

In Classical Greece, women could train as doctors – though they were very much in the minority thanks, in part, to Aristotelian ideas of the humours and supposed differences between women and men. In *Politics*, Aristotle wrote: 'the male is by nature superior and the female inferior, the male ruler and the female subject'. Much of his reasoning was based on the idea that women – impulsive, deceitful, jealous – were mentally as well as physically different from men. His unfortunate attitudes greatly influenced ideas of what women were considered capable of doing. But there were opportunities for midwives to receive medical training and to become *iatromea*, a doctor-midwife.

Though some question whether or not she was a real person, **Agnodice** (fourth century BCE) is usually credited as the first female physician and midwife in ancient Athens. The Roman historian Gaius Julius Hyginus wrote in his *Fabulae* that she studied medicine and practised in Athens disguised as a man, because women were forbidden to work as physicians on male patients. As her popularity with female patients grew, rivals accused her of inappropriate behaviour. She was tried and was forced to reveal her own sex by lifting her tunic. The charge was changed from immorality to illegally practising medicine – a no-win situation – but her patients defended her and she was acquitted. The law against female physicians in Athens was subsequently revoked.

Though there were many barriers to women practising as physicians, it wasn't uncommon for the daughters and wives of celebrated doctors to follow in the family tradition. **Antiochis of Tlos** (first century BCE) was a Roman physician who began working alongside her father in the ancient hilltop citadel of Tlos, now on the southern coast of Turkey. Unusually, Antiochis did not concentrate primarily on pregnancy and childbirth, but treated illnesses that afflicted both men and women. In 1892, an Austrian expedition found a pedestal to her there, the inscription of which read: ANTIOCHIS OF TLOS, DAUGHTER OF DIODOTUS, COMMENDED BY THE COUNCIL AND THE PEOPLE OF TLOS FOR HER EXPERIENCE IN THE DOCTOR'S ART, HAS SET UP THIS STATUE OF HERSELF.

One of her successors, **Metrodora** (*c*. 200–400 CE), was the Greek physician and the author of *On the Diseases and Cures of Women*, the world's oldest medical textbook written by a woman. The work was often referenced by other female physicians and medical writers in ancient Greece and Rome. Covering many areas of medicine (though, oddly, not obstetrics), it was later translated and published in medieval Europe.

> 'We cannot live in a world that is not our own, in a world that is interpreted for us by others. An interpreted world is not a home.'
>
> *Hildegard of Bingen*

THE IDEA OF a polymath, someone who is skilled in many different areas, dates from fifteenth-century Italy, and the phrase 'Renaissance man' – or 'Universal Man', *Uomo Universale* – is still in current usage. But, here's the thing, the original Renaissance Man might actually have been a woman who lived four centuries earlier.

Hildegard of Bingen (*c*. 1098–1179), also known as **Sibyl of the Rhine**, could feature in many chapters of this book. A renowned composer, a poet, a Christian missionary and a prolific writer on natural and scientific subjects including botany and medicine, she entered the Benedictine convent at Disibodenberg at the age of fourteen and became a great religious leader, founding communities throughout Germany and conducting preaching tours. Her writings – which include some four hundred letters, a morality play and musical compositions – make up one of the largest surviving bodies of medieval work. She's included in this chapter because Hildegard is also considered Germany's first female physician.

A respected advocate for scientific research, Hildegard was an early promoter of the use of herbal medicine to treat ailments, often using herbs from the physic garden of her convent. Around 1150, in her book *Physica*, she catalogued the use of herbs in medicinal treatment, though she diagnosed and gave treatment using both classical and contemporary texts too.

In the European Middle Ages, many women worked as herbalists, midwives, surgeons and healers. Hildegard was an exceptional person, but she was far from the only one. We have the names of twenty-four women described as surgeons in Naples, in Italy, between 1273 and 1410, and references have been found to some fifteen female physicians, many of them Jewish, in Frankfurt between 1389 and 1497. Hildegard is another of the thirty-nine women celebrated at the table of Judy Chicago's *The Dinner Party*. Her place setting is inspired by a Gothic cathedral, her plate painted as a rose window.

> 'A medical man likes to make psychological observations, and sometimes in the pursuit of such studies is too easily tempted into momentous prophecy which life and death easily set at naught.'
>
> **George Eliot**

Trota of Salerno (early twelfth century) is also present at *The Dinner Party* table, described as a 'physician and gynaecologist'. Now, it's generally accepted that 'Trotula' refers to a group of three texts on women's medicine – and other medical issues – that were composed by more than one author in the twelfth century. There was, however, a woman identified as Trota, the most celebrated of the so-called 'Ladies of Salerno', the first and most important medical school of its time founded in the ninth century. By the twelfth century, the Trotula were some of the most celebrated sources of medical knowledge in Western Europe. *Conditions of Women, Treatments for Women* and *Women's Cosmetics* were written in Latin and circulated, anonymously at first, throughout medieval Europe, from Spain to Ireland, Poland to Sicily. In opposition to Christian belief of the time – namely, that women should suffer during childbirth as punishment for Eve's sin – the texts advocated for the use of opiates during labour and challenged medical orthodoxy by suggesting men might also be infertile. Some 130 copies have survived, as well as more than 60 copies of medieval vernacular translations, testament to how widely they were read and how much they were valued. They remained key texts on women's diseases for some five hundred years. Her place at *The Dinner Party* has an image of the tree of life. As of 2022, the Brooklyn Museum, where the original artwork is exhibited, has not updated the information on either Trota's name nor the supposed date of her death.

Other female physicians associated with Salerno include **Rebecca Guarna** (*c.* 1200) who published treatises on fevers, embryos and urine, and **Constance Calenda** (fifteenth century), who lectured on medicine and became a professor at the University of Naples.

It seems Italy was far ahead of the curve in terms of allowing women to train and practise as physicians. There are few extant records of female physicians in medieval England in the thirteenth century. Two sisters, named **Solicita** and **Matilda**, were recorded working in Hertfordshire. We know, of course, that women were midwives and *sage-femmes* – literally, wise women – and every village and small town would have someone who was trusted in the traumatic, often fatal, but everyday drama of childbirth.

It was at the University of Bologna, the birthplace of modern anatomical study, that the first woman recorded as practising pathology and anatomy, **Alessandra Giliani** (1307–1326), was a student. Giliani is a good example of the 'Matilda Effect', as male commentators later challenged whether or not she had existed at all – some even claiming she was an invention by Machiavelli, others admitting she existed but thinking she was written out of history because the idea of a woman practising anatomy was seen as too challenging. And, though it's true that all evidence of her work was either lost or destroyed, a plaque at the Church of San Pietro e Marcellino in Rome describes her achievements. Contemporary historical documents record that Giliani was a brilliant *prosector*, a preparer of corpses for anatomical dissection, and confirms that she carried out her own experiments.

Only a generation later, **Dorotea Bucca** (1360–1436) was to hold a chair of medicine and philosophy at the University of Bologna for over forty years.

> 'It is better and more becoming that a woman clever and expert in the art should visit a sick woman . . . a woman would allow herself to die before she would reveal the secrets of her illness to a man . . . Thus it is that the laws say that lesser evils should be permitted, so that greater ones may be avoided.'
>
> ***Jacobina Felice de Almania***

In Paris in 1322, the Florentine physician **Jacobina Felice de Almania** (fourteenth century) was put on trial for unlawful medical practice. Known for treating men as well as women, she conducted physical examinations and prescribed potions and herbs – in other words, she used traditional female skills alongside more contemporary medical techniques. Despite eight witnesses testifying to her excellence, she was found guilty – in part on the grounds that since a woman could not be a lawyer, she could also not be a doctor – and together with her fellow accused, she was excommunicated. After that, her name disappears from the records. This cuts to the heart of the challenge facing women in the medieval period: they could not practise without a licence, yet were not admitted to schools of learning in order to gain a licence. De Almania's court case is considered one of the pretexts for women being banned from academic study in France until the nineteenth century.

A century later in China, **Tan Yunxian** (1461–1554) was a herbalist and physician during the Ming Dynasty in China. Descended from a family of physicians, Tan learned her skills from her grandparents and her father. Her medical practice was restricted to treating women and so-called 'women's complaints', such as problems with menstruation, miscarriage, infertility and postpartum fatigue. Tan Yunxian also practised the burning of moxa, or dried Artemisia, on specified parts of the body. Since this required the physician to touch the patient, male doctors were not allowed to perform this treatment on women. In 1511, she published *Miscellaneous Records of a Female Doctor*, thirty-one case studies, making it the earliest known printed record of a female physician's work. The studies also included accounts of treating illnesses not specific to women, such as nausea and skin rashes.

'It is my deliberate opinion that the one essential requisite of human welfare in all ways is scientific knowledge of human nature.'

Harriet Martineau

THE BIGGEST CHALLENGE with gathering evidence of named female physicians is, as we've seen, that women worked in the shadows because they were often not allowed to practise legally in most countries. The Royal College of Physicians in London admitted that it used the silence on women in its founding documents as an excuse for excluding women from membership until the early twentieth century, taking its lead from a 1511 Act of Parliament that called women doctors 'the great multitude of ignorant persons' carrying out 'the Science and Cunning of Physick and Surgery'.

When women do appear in the records, it's usually because they are being prosecuted for practising medicine – in other words, when their disguise has been discovered. Now and then, we catch a glimpse of what must have been reality for many. Trying to do good, always fearful of being betrayed or caught, working to the flickering light of candles. The first woman so far discovered to be recorded as practising medicine in Elizabethan England was **Alice Leevers** (sixteenth century). She was prosecuted in 1586, the legal document describing her as an 'unskilled woman, and a demented old wife'. Henry Carey, 1st Baron Hunsdon and cousin to Queen Elizabeth, intervened and Leevers was – exceptionally – allowed to continue her vocation.

We've also noted women following in their parents' footsteps. Many wives worked with husbands. Having been widowed, **Susan Reeve Lyon** (seventeenth century) appears in the records of both the Royal College of Physicians and the Society of Apothecaries. As we've seen with printing and publishing, widows were allowed to inherit their husband's trade and continue working, so the guild allowed Lyon to maintain the business and supervise an apprentice. However, marrying again put her foul of the law. She was summoned before the college censors in February 1631 and banned from making any more medicines, despite the college acknowledging her skill. And although Nicholas Culpeper is well known, it was actually his wife **Alice Culpeper** (1625–1659) who was responsible for the publication of many of his works after his death, securing his reputation – and her unwarranted anonymity. Another woman working with her husband was **Anna Manzolini** (1714–1774), a fabled anatomist, anatomical wax modeller and lecturer on anatomical design at the exceptional University of Bologna. Together with her husband, she founded an anatomy school and worked dissecting bodies, setting the standard for generations of anatomists to follow. Extraordinarily, after the death of her husband, she was given a dispensation by the Pope – after a rigorous examination – to continue working as a demonstrator of anatomy to medical students at the university.

Born nearly a decade later, **Elizabeth Nihell** (1723–1776) trained as a midwife at the Hôtel-Dieu in Paris, since there was no equivalent school in Britain. She spent her career working in London, when female midwives were in competition with male doctors. She campaigned against male midwives and, in 1760, having attended over nine hundred births, wrote A *Treatise on the Art of Midwifery Setting Forth Various Abuses Therein, Especially as to the Practice with Instruments*. She wrote that women who used male midwives had 'sunk to so low a degree of cheapness [to] a sort of prostitution'. Harsh words, indeed.

> 'Unless I am allowed to tell the story of my life in my own way, I cannot tell it at all.'
>
> *Mary Seacole*

In contrast, our next medical pioneer, you might feel, needs no introduction. Today, she is a superstar and one of the most written about women of the nineteenth century. But the story of the rise and fall of her reputation is a sobering reminder of how easy it is for even the most famous women in their day to disappear from history, and how much celebrating the achievements of women of the past really matters.

Mary Seacole (1805–1881) was a nursing pioneer, healer and businesswoman. Tireless, dogged, brilliant and determined, she was born in Jamaica to a white Scottish father and a Black mother, from whom she learned many of her healing skills. In the 1820s, Seacole travelled to London, then to Cuba, Haiti and the Bahamas. She nursed victims of the 1850 cholera epidemic in Kingston and in Panama the following year, before returning to Kingston during the yellow fever outbreak of 1853.

But it is for her work in Crimea that she is best known. Unsupported by the authorities, Seacole decided to fund her own passage to what is now Ukraine and set up her own 'British Hotel', offering care for wounded and convalescent soldiers. She quickly became a legend, so much so that when she returned to Britain with little money after the conflict ended in 1856, a four-day fundraising gala took place on the banks of the Thames for her in 1857 to support 'Mother Seacole'. Her autobiography, *Wonderful Adventures of Mrs Seacole in Many Lands*, came out the same year and was a huge bestseller.

Fame, though, failed to protect her legacy. Class and racism, too, played their part, not least in that many historians of the nineteenth and twentieth centuries chose not to consider Seacole's achievements part of British history, even though she was a British citizen. After her death in 1881, she largely vanished from the record for almost a century and was only brought back to prominence by the tireless efforts of campaigners including the Mary Seacole Trust. Now there is a blue plaque at her former home in Soho Square and, in 2016, a statue to her was erected in the grounds of St Thomas's Hospital on London's South Bank. Her grave is at St Mary's Catholic Cemetery in Kensal Green, a carved stone palm tree on the headstone, with her name and dates picked out in gold. In 2004, she was voted the greatest Black Briton in a poll of more than ten thousand people.

> 'I attribute my success to this – I never gave or took any excuse.'
>
> *Florence Nightingale*

Born fifteen years after Seacole, **Florence Nightingale** (1820–1910) also founded a Crimean field hospital, in Scutari just outside Istanbul. Her achievements were lauded at the time: Nightingale implemented a system of hygiene and ventilation, massively reducing the death rate for wounded soldiers, although the figures were still high. On returning to England, she devoted her life to social and public health reform and, in 1858, was admitted to the Royal Statistical Society. Like Seacole, 'the lady with the lamp' worked to professionalize nursing, founding a training school and sending nurses to care for the poor and disadvantaged in workhouses. They both achieved extraordinary things, but Seacole's reputation was allowed to dwindle whereas Nightingale's was protected. She was a middle-class woman, well connected in British society, she published more than 150 articles and was a celebrated statistician too. But both pioneers deserve to be remembered, not set against one another as competitors but rather celebrated as contemporaries living lives of extraordinary public service. Inspired by Seacole and Nightingale, the 1901 Census recorded that there were some 68,000 nurses working in the UK.

Known as the 'Florence Nightingale of America' and the 'Angel of the Battlefield', **Clara Barton** (1821–1912) was the founder of the American Red Cross. A teacher and feminist pioneer, she served as a nurse during the American Civil War. Her name appears on the tiled floor of Chicago's *The Dinner Party*.

> 'We had seen great suffering but greater courage. We had learned to take responsibility and to act on our own when required. We had learned to be patient.'
>
> *Emma Duffin*

In the twentieth century, the Northern Irish nurse, diarist and welfare worker **Emma Duffin** (1883–1979) would write about her experiences, first during the First World War and then during the Second World War. Despite having no professional training or nursing experience, together with three of her sisters Duffin enlisted as a nurse in the Voluntary Aid Detachment (VAD), working first in Alexandria in Egypt, then in Le Havre in France.

She kept a diary and, though much less known than *Testament of Youth* by feminist and pacifist Vera Brittain, Duffin's record of active service is just as important an account of women at the Front. Between the wars, she worked for the Belfast Council of Social Welfare, campaigning for subsidized housing and giving free legal advice. She took up her pen again after the outbreak of the Second World War and, like other former VADs, began nursing, particularly during the Wehrmacht's Blitz bombing of Belfast in 1941. Duffin donated her writings, including her diaries, to the Public Record Office of Northern Ireland. On International Women's Day 2017, a blue plaque was erected at her former home on University Square, Belfast.

'It may be that the issues I have raised
today as the lone woman here, have been
defeated. But one day there shall be many
of us standing here and you will listen to
our voices then!'

Senedu Gebru

Also active during the Second World War, **Senedu Gebru** (1916–2019) was the founder of the Ethiopian Red Cross. An educational campaigner, freedom fighter, feminist, playwright and poet, she was educated in Switzerland and Paris. Senedu returned to Addis Ababa in 1933 to teach, while also working as an interpreter for foreign journalists. During the Second World War, she joined the Resistance. She was captured by Mussolini's forces, but survived.

In 1957, she was the first woman to be elected to the Ethiopian Parliament and, in 1960, became the vice-president of the Senate. She wrote in Amharic and in 1950 published her only book, a collection of poems, short stories and songs, under the title *YaLebbe Meshaf* (*Book of My Heart*).

'My whole life is devoted unreservedly to
the service of my sex. The study and
practice of medicine is in my thought but
one means to a great end . . . the true
ennoblement of woman.'

Elizabeth Blackwell

WE COME, NOW, to the first of our founding mothers of modern medicine, **Elizabeth Blackwell** (1821–1910). A woman driven to make other women's lives better, her story marks the beginning of a sea-change in medicine in the English-speaking world. Like Seacole and Nightingale, though Blackwell's legacy is secure, we shouldn't ever forget how hard she worked to make it so.

Born in Bristol in 1821, her family emigrated and settled in Ohio ten years later. Blackwell was a talented musician and raised funds to pay for her medical training by working as a music teacher in North Carolina. Rejecting a professor's suggestion that she should disguise herself as a man in order to trick her way in, she was refused by more than ten medical schools. She persisted and, on 23 January 1849, became the first woman in the United States to take a medical degree. Blinded in one eye in that same year – the year my great-grandmother Lily was born – Blackwell was unable to become a surgeon as she'd hoped, so instead focused on general medicine.

She co-founded the New York Infirmary for Indigent Women and Children, the Woman's Medical College of the New York Infirmary and a medical college for women which pioneered a four-year course with extensive clinical training. On New Year's Day 1859, she was the first woman in the UK to have her name entered in the General Medical Council's medical register. In 1871, she co-founded the National Health Society, and she supported the founding of the London School of Medicine for Women. Her autobiography *Pioneer Work in Opening the Medical Profession to Women* was published in 1895.

At her place setting of *The Dinner Party*, the 'E' on the front of the runner beneath her plate is embroidered with a stethoscope.

> 'Nowhere in Europe was the woman who wished to study medicine so stubbornly opposed as in Britain.'
>
> ***Elizabeth Garrett Anderson***

The second of our mothers of medicine, who had to endure huge opposition from within her own family as well as from the wider medical establishment, was born fifteen years after Blackwell. Another with many firsts to her name, **Elizabeth Garrett Anderson** (1836–1917) was the first woman to gain a medical qualification in Britain. Her many achievements include joining the British Medical Association in 1873 – no other women would be invited to join for another nineteen years – and, in 1874, co-founding the London School of Medicine for Women, the first hospital in the UK to be staffed wholly by women and the only teaching hospital in Britain to offer medical courses for women. In 1883, she became the dean, the first female dean of any medical school in Britain. She was also the first female doctor of medicine in France. A political campaigner and suffragette, in 1909 she became the first elected female mayor for the town of Aldeburgh in Suffolk. There is a blue plaque at her former home in Upper Berkeley Street, London.

> '. . . but that very many women have wished that they could be medically attended by those of their own sex I am very sure, and I know of more than one case where ladies have habitually gone through one confinement after another without proper attendance, because the idea of employing a man was so extremely repugnant to them.'
>
> **Sophia Jex-Blake**

The third of our founding mothers of nineteenth-century medicine is **Sophia Jex-Blake** (1840–1912), physician, teacher and suffragist and the best-known of the Edinburgh Seven.

Jex-Blake began studying medicine at the University of Edinburgh in 1869, though the university charged women higher fees and insisted they attend separate classes. There was significant opposition from some male students and lecturers, and the female students endured a campaign of bullying and physical intimidation. The flashpoint was an anatomy exam on 18 November 1870, a notorious engagement that would become known as the Surgeons' Hall Riot. When the seven women arrived, they were confronted in the street by two hundred or so male students, who abused them, pelted them with mud, and the college's pet sheep was driven into the exam hall to disrupt the examinations.

It was a mis-step on the part of their male opponents. Though none of the women were allowed to graduate, the Surgeons' Hall Riot turned out to be a turning point. There was a public outcry and headlines in the Edinburgh newspaper, *The Courant*, and public opinion turned in their favour. Jex-Blake led the Edinburgh Seven to file a lawsuit against the university for failing to allow them to complete their medical education. They passed their exams and won the lawsuit, but lost on appeal, so were forced to take their fight to Parliament. Jex-Blake completed her medical education in Switzerland and, in 1877, she and four other women passed their medical exams at the College of Physicians in Dublin, Ireland. Jex-Blake went on to become the first practising female doctor in Scotland and co-founded the London School of Medicine for Women with Garrett Anderson.

Thanks to their efforts, a new Medical Act was passed in 1876, but change would come slowly and incrementally. Thirty years later, only twelve women doctors were recorded in the 1901 Census, though there were some 1,740,800 domestic servants, representing half of all women in paid employment.

Women's work . . .

In 2019, on the 150th anniversary of their matriculation, the Edinburgh Seven were awarded posthumous degrees. A plaque was unveiled at the University of Edinburgh by **Anne, Princess Royal** (b. 1950) and seven current female students at Edinburgh accepted the degrees on their behalf.

The Edinburgh Seven were: **Isabel Thorne** (1834–1910); **Mary Anderson Marshall** (1837–1910); **Sophia Jex-Blake**; **Emily Bovell** (1841–1885); **Edith Pechey** (1845–1908); **Matilda Chaplin** (1846–1883); and **Helen Evans** (1883/1884–1903).

THE 'GLASS CEILING' – a phrase to describe the often-invisible barriers women come up against in their careers – was coined by the American management consultant **Marilyn Loden** (b. 1932) at a conference in May 1978. Every one of the female doctors trying to acquire a medical education and permission to practise or research would understand what this meant.

One of the few ways in which the glass ceiling can be cracked, broken and shattered is by sheer force of numbers. Once something's been done once, it's then easier for it to happen a second time, then a third – even if each subsequent victory is slow in coming. And, of course, it's worth repeating there may have been other 'firsts' who were not recorded. But, still, let's celebrate more women who were first in their country or their field, helping to chip away at that glass ceiling for the women following after them.

Kusumoto Ine (1827–1903) was, so far as we know, the first woman to practise Western medicine in Japan. She was the daughter of a Japanese mother and a German father, a doctor who worked on the island of Dejima, previously a Portuguese and then a Dutch trading colony. During the Edo period it was the only place of direct trade and exchange between Japan and the outside world, where foreigners might work. Kusumoto's reputation soared after she qualified as a doctor of Western medicine. Something of a folk heroine, her life has been celebrated in novels, plays, comics and musicals.

Her contemporary **Rebecca Crumpler** (1831–1895) was the first recorded African American woman in the United States to earn a medical degree. Crumpler worked for eight years as a nurse before being accepted at the New England Female Medical College in Boston. She completed her training in 1864, becoming the first Black graduate in the school's history.

Jane Waterston (1843–1932) was the first female doctor in South Africa. Arriving from Scotland in 1867, she was appointed super-intendent of a new girls' section at the Lovedale Missionary Institute. She trained at the London School of Medicine for Women in 1880, before working in a private practice in Cape Town where she established a 'Ladies Branch of the Free Dispensary', an organization that cared for mothers and trained midwives. Given the South African title *Noqataka*, 'the mother of activity', for her work in disadvantaged communities, Waterson became the second woman to be made a fellow of the Royal College of Physicians of Ireland in 1925 and, in 1929, was made a doctor of laws by the University of Cape Town.

Constance Stone (1856–1902) was forced to leave her native Melbourne to study because the university would not accept women. She trained first in Pennsylvania, received her MD in Toronto and, inspired by the New Hospital for Women in London, returned to establish a sister organization in Australia. Stone was the first woman to be registered with the Medical Board of Victoria and worked in private practice with her sister **Clara Stone** (1860–1957). In 1899, she was one of eleven female doctors in Melbourne who founded the Queen Victoria Hospital for Women run 'by women, for women'.

The obstetrician and surgeon **Matilde Montoya** (1859–1939) was the first woman to practise medicine in Mexico. A campaign was waged against her by male doctors, but she applied to the National

School of Medicine in Mexico City and was accepted on her second attempt. Once there, male students and other surgeons again tried to intimidate her but, fearless and determined, she graduated in 1887. In 2019, Google celebrated her 160th birthday with a doodle of Montoya with her stethoscope around her neck.

Her counterpart in India was **Kadambini Ganguly** (1861–1923), the first Indian woman to practise Western medicine in India and one of the first Indian women awarded with a degree in modern medicine. **Rukhmabai** (1864–1955) was another of the trailblazing women to practise in British-controlled India. She was also involved in a landmark case in the 1880s involving her own marriage as a child bride – the marriage was eventually dissolved, sometimes it's suggested on the order of Queen Victoria herself, to whom Rukhmabai made a direct appeal. Her campaigning ultimately contributed to the Age of Consent Act in 1891.

Susan La Flesche Picotte (1865–1915) was the first Indigenous woman in the United States to take a medical degree. The daughter of an Omaha chief in north-east Nebraska, Picotte taught at a Quaker school on the Omaha reservation before being accepted to medical school. Returning home after graduating at the top of her class, Picotte looked after a population of more than one thousand three hundred people and helped drive political reform. Battling years of racism and sexism, and unequal healthcare for Indigenous people, in 1913 she finally opened a hospital in the reservation town of Waterhill.

Eloísa Díaz (1866–1950) was the first woman to become a doctor of medicine not just in Chile but in all of South America. In 1898, she was appointed director of Santiago's School Medical Service and went on to found nurseries and healthcare centres for the poor, school camps and school breakfast services, and waged campaigns against tuberculosis and alcoholism.

Díaz was a contemporary of Irishwoman **Emily Dickson** (1866–1944), who was not only the first female fellow of the Royal College of Surgeons in Ireland, but also the first female fellow of any of the royal colleges of surgery in Great Britain and Ireland.

Emily Siedeberg (1873–1968) was New Zealand's first female medical graduate. The daughter of an Irish Quaker and a German-Jewish architect, Siedeberg grew up in Dunedin. Appointed Medical Superintendent at St Helen's Hospital, Dunedin, in 1905, she was a founding member of the Dunedin branch of the New Zealand Society for the Protection of Women and Children and became Honorary Life President in 1949.

The first female radiologist in the UK was the Irish physician **Florence Stoney** (1870–1932). Like many of her fellow travellers, Stoney attended the London School of Medicine for Women, before going on to establish an X-ray department at the Elizabeth Garrett Anderson Hospital for Women in 1902. During the First World War, Stoney helped to organize a unit of women volunteers alongside the Women's Imperial Service League and the Belgian Red Cross, then worked as head of the X-ray and electrical department at Fulham Military Hospital from 1915 to 1918, one of the first female physicians employed there full time.

Margaret Cruickshank (1873–1918) was only the second woman in New Zealand to complete a medical course in 1897 and was New Zealand's first registered female doctor. She spent her entire career in Waimate in the South Island, visiting patients on horseback, by gig, or bicycle. She worked tirelessly during the flu epidemic of 1918, before it claimed her life. Five years later, the town's grateful residents erected a statue in her honour inscribed to: THE BELOVED PHYS-ICIAN FAITHFUL UNTO DEATH. It is one of New Zealand's few memorials to a woman other than Queen Victoria.

Czech physician **Anna Honzáková** (1875–1940) was the first woman doctor to graduate from the Charles-Ferdinand University in Prague in 1902. She ran a private gynaecological surgery in Prague for thirty-five years and created a fund to support poor and sick women. Working to honour other women in her field, she wrote a biography of **Anna Bayerová** (1853–1924), the second Czech female doctor after the Bohemian medic **Bohuslava Kecková** (1854–1911). Neither was allowed to practise in their home country, because their degrees were from Swiss universities and so not recognized.

Petronella van Heerden (1887–1975) was a pioneering gynaecolo-gist and the first Afrikaner woman to qualify as a doctor. Her PhD thesis on endometriosis, awarded in 1923 in Amsterdam, was the first doctoral thesis written in Afrikaans. Van Heerden settled in Cape Town, served on the committee of the Cape National Party in 1924, and published two memoirs – *Candle Snuffings* (1962) and *The Sixteenth Cup* (1965) – as well as articles on feminism, lesbianism and sexual identity, and critiques of gender inequality. She was also a keen archaeologist. There's a fabulous photograph of her, lying face down in the dirt with her tools around her, excavating the Natufian graveyard at Wady El-Mughara at Mount Carmel in Palestine in 1931, taken by her friend and leading Palaeolithic archaeologist **Dorothy Garrod** (1892–1968). Garrod, who was director of the excavation, became the first woman to be awarded a professorship at the University of Cambridge, in 1939.

María Teresa Ferrari (1887–1956) was the first female university professor in any discipline in Latin America and one of the first permitted to teach, though, like her European sisters, Ferrari had to fight to be awarded her professorship. An Argentine educator, physician and women's rights activist, she was a pioneering researcher in women's health, using radiation therapy rather than surgery for treating uterine tumours and developing a scope that revolutionized vaginal examination.

Hilana Sedarous (1904–1998) was the first female Coptic doctor in modern Egypt. Having trained and qualified in London in 1930, she returned to Cairo and opened a private clinic specializing in obstetrics and gynaecology. After retiring, she became an author and translator of children's books.

Meanwhile, **Irene Ighodaro** (1916–1995) was a Creole physician and social reformer, the first woman from Sierra Leone to qualify as a medical doctor, and **Susan Ofori-Atta** (1917–1985) was the first Ghanaian woman to earn a university degree and the first female doctor in Ghana. She helped establish the Women's Society for Public Affairs and was one of the founding fellows of the Ghana Academy of Arts and Sciences.

Elizabeth Awoliyi (1910–1971) was the first woman to practise as a surgeon in Nigeria. The first West African woman to earn the licence of Royal Surgeon in Dublin, in 1938 she became only the second West African woman to qualify in orthodox medicine, after **Agnes Yewande Savage** (1906–1964), who'd graduated in medicine from the University of Edinburgh in 1929. A member of the Royal College of Physicians in the UK and the Royal College of Obstetricians and Gynaecology, Awoliyi also held a diploma from the Royal College of Paediatrics and Child Health. She began her career at the Massey Street Hospital in Lagos, becoming medical director in 1960. An advisor to the Federal Ministry of Health, she was also President of the National Council of Women's Societies of Nigeria from 1946 until her death in 1971.

Finally, **Dorothy Brown** (1919–2004) was the first African American female surgeon in the South of the United States and, in 1959, was the first African American woman to be made a fellow of the American College of Surgeons.

This list of pioneering women to celebrate attests to the fact that the driving force for many women wanting to work in medicine in the nineteenth century, as it had been in the distant past, was to be able to give women the specific care they needed and deserved, appropriate to female needs. Not just pregnancy and childbirth, but every other condition or ailment that might affect women from cradle to grave.

> 'As for private practice, I sometimes wonder whether it was not easier to make a start in the old days, when a woman doctor could count on the loyalty of a group of devoted feminists who would choose a woman because she was a woman.'
>
> **Alice Hamilton**

THERE IS LITTLE in Lily's letters about her own health. Every now and again, there are comments that suggest she might be suffering from some kind of depression or fatigue, but she is never explicit. She makes no reference to her health during her pregnancies, nor her experiences during childbirth, but that is no more than one might expect from a woman of her time writing to her husband. It's possible she might have been less guarded with her daughters or her own mother, though I doubt it. Lily's primary definition of herself was as a wife, a mother, a Christian – not a woman.

> 'A modern and humane civilization must control conception or sink into barbaric cruelty to individuals.'
>
> **Marie Stopes**

A complete history of the struggles of women with fertility and childbirth is beyond the scope of this book. But there are two names that stand out in the context of contraception. Both **Margaret Sanger** (1879–1966) in America and **Marie Stopes** (1880–1958) in the UK were pioneers in the campaign for women's reproductive rights. Stopes was a palaeobotanist and the first female academic at the University of Manchester. The publication of her sex manual *Married Love*, in 1918, shone a spotlight on the subject of birth control for the first time. She founded the first birth control clinic in Great Britain in 1921, and gradually built up a network across the UK, run by midwives and supported by visiting doctors. Free and open to all married women, the clinic gave advice on birth control including the cervical cap, *coitus interruptus* and spermicides based on soap and oil, as well as the use of olive oil-soaked sponges – a technique dating back to Agnodice and Antiochis in Greek and Roman times. For all the good they did, both also supported troubling and racist ideologies – Sanger opposed a woman's right to choose and was a eugenicist, as was Stopes, who opposed mixed-race marriage.

In every period of history, and almost every culture, male control over women's reproductive rights has been a key way in which women's choices are limited – battles that are still raging today, from North America to Honduras to Poland. There are currently fifteen countries in the world that prohibit abortion altogether, even if the mother's life is at risk, and many more with severe restrictions. In March 2022, a proposed bill in Missouri in the United States attempted to make it illegal for a woman to get an abortion even in the case of an ectopic pregnancy – quite literally, a death sentence. In June 2022, just fifteen words from the Supreme Court was all it took to overturn nearly fifty years of precedent and remove the constitutional right to access abortion for 40 million US women. The fight for *Roe v. Wade* to be reinstated is only just beginning. Women's rights over their own bodies are being eroded in an unprecedented way in the twenty-first century.

∞

THERE WERE, OF course, women working in research as well as on the front line as medical practitioners. Developments in the treatment of haemophilia would come too late for Lily's son, Leader, but she would not have been unaware that, in hospitals and laboratories throughout the world, scientists were striving to create vaccines and treatments for illnesses that had previously proved fatal. In 1924, the year my father was born, children in France would start to be vaccinated with BCG, named after the two French bacteriologists who invented it – Albert Camette and Camille Guérin.

In America, biologist **Mary Jacobi** (1842–1906) was researching menstruation, partly in order to challenge many of the fallacies used to justify discrimination against women. The first woman to study medicine at the University of Paris and the first to be accepted into the New York Academy of Medicine, Jacobi also created the Association for the Advancement of the Medical Education of Women to address inequalities in the training of female students.

Fellow American **Nettie Stevens** (1861–1912) originally trained as a teacher to fund her studies, so it wasn't until she was in her thirties that she moved to Stanford and began her research in earnest. She was, in fact, the biologist and geneticist who discovered sex chromosomes, following on from the work of Gregor Mendel in the late nineteenth century – though her work was misattributed to male scientists and went unacknowledged for some years. In 1906, her male colleagues appeared at a conference to present their theories on sex determination, but Stevens was not invited to speak . . .

The pioneering chemist **Alice Augusta Ball** (1892–1916) developed the 'Ball Method', a ground-changing treatment of Hansen's Disease – leprosy – by delivering a water-soluble injection of chaulmoogra oil, a substance derived from the seeds of the tropical evergreen tree. Ball was the first woman and first African American to receive a master's degree from the University of Hawaii. She was also the university's first female professor and first African American professor of chemistry. Ball didn't get to see the results of her work. She died at the age of only twenty-four in 1916 from chlorine poisoning. The college president continued her work and it quickly became a worldwide treatment used until the 1940s, but he failed to credit her initial discovery. It was only thanks to a brief mention in a 1922 medical journal, where it was stated how Ball had created the chaulmoogra solution, that her name wasn't lost to history. In 2000, the University of Hawaii placed a dedication plaque to Ball underneath its only chaulmoogra tree and, seven years later, posthumously presented her with its Medal of Distinction.

> 'And so this is the satisfactory thing about science, you see, that sometimes the answer is the answer that you get.'
>
> *Janet Vaughan*

In contrast to Alice Ball, a scientist whose name needs little introduction is the extraordinary **Janet Vaughan** (1899–1993). Vaughan was a friend of Virginia Woolf and, in part, the inspiration for the characters of Chloe and Olivia in *A Room of One's Own*. Working at University College London in the early 1930s, Vaughan secretly gave anaemic patients liver, rather than dosing them with arsenic, having used herself as an early guinea pig. A British physiologist, academic, and academic administrator, this ground-breaking research into haematology and blood transfusions would lead to the creation of London's first blood banks during the Second World War. She was one of the first civilians to enter the concentration camp Bergen-Belsen at the end of the war, served as Principal of Somerville College, Oxford, from 1945 to 1967, received her damehood in 1957, became a fellow of the Royal Society in 1979 and continued her research into radiation well into her nineties.

The most celebrated female chemist of all time is, without doubt, the Polish-French scientist **Marie Skłodowska Curie** (1867–1934). Honoured not just for her work, but for the difference she made to the opportunities of so many women coming after her, she is the towering scientist of her generation.

Because the University of Warsaw did not accept women in the 1880s, Curie studied mathematics and physics in Paris. Working with her husband, she discovered that uranium emitted rays and, in 1898, coined the term 'radioactivity'. In November 1903, they shared the Nobel Prize in Physics with Henri Becquerel, although the committee had to be persuaded that Marie was an equal partner. She won the Nobel Prize again in 1911, this time in Chemistry – and without sharing the honour – for her discovery of two elements, polonium and radium. In addition to her Nobels, her list of 'firsts' is dazzling –

the first female physics professor at the Sorbonne, the first woman to win any Nobel Prize, the first person and only woman to win a Nobel twice, and the only person to win in two different fields, and, in 1995, Curie became the first woman to be entombed for her individual achievements in the Panthéon in Paris.

Adrienne Rich's poem 'Power', written in 1974, paid tribute to Curie and the physical suffering she endured in the name of research:

> *She died a famous woman denying*
> *her wounds*
> *denying*
> *her wounds came from the same source as her power.*

Her daughter **Irène Joliot-Curie** (1897–1956) won a Nobel Prize in Chemistry in 1935, the year after her mother's death. They are the only mother and daughter to both have been celebrated by the Nobel Committee. Like her mother, Irène died of leukaemia caused by excessive exposure to radiation.

Until the twenty-first century, the Nobel Committee had a poor track record in honouring the work of women in science. Too often, it was assumed that the woman was merely an assistant to her male colleagues rather than an equal partner – the 'Matilda Effect' in action. Since 1901, there have been fifty-eight female Nobel laureates across all disciplines, but fewer than 3 per cent of Nobel science winners are women: four in physics; seven in chemistry; and twelve in physiology or medicine. To date, no Black women or other women of colour have received a Nobel Prize in these categories.

Lise Meitner (1878–1968) is one of the most notorious examples of the 'Matilda Effect'. In 1944, she was denied a share of the Nobel Prize in Chemistry, which was awarded exclusively to Otto Hahn for their joint work. Sometimes referred to as the 'German Marie Curie' (though Meitner was actually Austrian), she was part of the team that discovered the radioactive isotope protactinium-231 in 1917. She was the first woman to graduate from the University of Vienna and the first woman to become a full professor of physics in Germany, though she lost her position in the 1930s because of the discrimination and mounting violence against Jewish people. In 1938, she fled to Sweden where she lived for many years, ultimately becoming a Swedish citizen.

Meitner was nominated nineteen times for a Nobel Prize in Chemistry between 1924 and 1948, and twenty-nine times for a Nobel Prize in Physics between 1937 and 1965. Perhaps the most important scientist never honoured by the Nobel Committee, the chemical element 109 meitnerium was named after her in 1997.

Asima Chatterjee (1917–2006) was an Indian organic chemist. Her research included ground-breaking anti-epileptic and anti-malarial drugs. Chatterjee was the first woman to receive a doctorate of science from an Indian university and become a fellow of the Indian National Science Academy in 1960, the first woman to win the Shanti Swarup Bhatnagar Award in chemical science in 1961 and the first female scientist elected General President of the Indian Science Congress Association. To this list of pioneering women to be celebrated we should add **Sarah Gilbert** (b. 1962), who designed the Oxford/ AstraZeneca COVID-19 vaccine, and Hungarian biochemist **Katalin Karikó** (b. 1955), who was pivotal to the creation of the Pfizer COVID-19 vaccine.

> 'I was captured for life by chemistry and by crystals.'
>
> *Dorothy Hodgkin Crowfoot*

The first British woman to win a Nobel Prize in Chemistry – and only the third woman overall – was **Dorothy Hodgkin Crowfoot** (1910–1994). However, the *Daily Mail* headline on 30 October 1964 read: 'Oxford housewife wins Nobel Prize'. Other newspapers followed suit, the *Daily Telegraph* pointing out she was a 'mother of three'. Many of the interviews asked how she coped with juggling her domestic responsibilities and scientific work . . .

A 'married mother of three' she might have been, but Hodgkin Crowfoot was absolutely one of the greatest scientists of the twentieth century, whose research revolutionized the lives of millions. She proved it was possible to have both a family and a career. Her first major discovery came in May 1945, when she decoded the molecular structure of penicillin by the use of X-rays. In 1954, she published the structure of vitamin B12, which would prove essential for the treatment of anaemia. In 1969, she discovered the structure of insulin, which significantly improved treatment for diabetes. She is one of very few women in science besides Curie – another being the American geneticist **Barbara McClintock** (1902–1992) – to have won a solo award.

Rosalind Franklin (1920–1958) is sometimes known as the 'wronged heroine' or the 'Dark Lady of DNA', another Nobel laureate that never was. An English chemist and X-ray crystallographer, her work was central to the understanding of the molecular structures of DNA. Yet her colleague Maurice Wilkins not only shared her work with fellow biologists without her permission, but also allowed the 'double helix' theory to be published in *Nature* magazine in 1953 without even acknowledging her. Watson, Crick and Wilkins won the Nobel Prize in 1962 for their work, four years after Franklin's death at the age of only thirty-seven. Watson did state that Franklin should have been awarded a Nobel in Chemistry too, but the Nobel Committee claimed they could not nominate posthumously.

Three final, life-changing Nobel laureates. **Trudy Elion** (1918–1999), the American biochemist and pharmacologist, shared the 1988 Nobel Prize in Physiology or Medicine for the development of new drugs including the game-changing AIDS anti-viral drug AZT. The German-born theoretical physicist **Maria Goeppert-Mayer** (1906–1972) jointly won the 1963 Nobel Prize in Physics, only the second woman to do so after Marie Curie, for her revolutionary work in discovering how the nucleus was structured. In 1986, the Maria Goeppert-Mayer Award for early-career female physicists was established in her honour. It would not be until 2018 that Canadian optical physicist **Donna Strickland** (b. 1959) would be the third woman to be honoured in this category.

And two more who got away. Austrian scientist **Marietta Blau** (1894–1970) was a particle physicist. Credited with developing photographic nuclear emulsions, Blau was also nominated several times during the period 1950–1957 for the Nobel Prize in Physics and once for the Nobel Prize in Chemistry. She never won, and the Chinese-American particle and experimental physicist **Chien-Shiung Wu** (1912–1997) was denied her share of Nobel recognition too. Shiung Wu worked on the Manhattan Project to develop nuclear fission and the nuclear bomb, helping to develop a process for separating uranium into uranium-235 and uranium-238. She conducted the eponymous Wu Experiment, a discovery which resulted in her two male colleagues winning the 1957 Nobel Prize in Physics. Wu's nicknames include the 'Queen of Nuclear Research', the 'First Lady of Physics' and, predictably, the 'Chinese Madame Curie'.

> 'My wish is that through the use of atomic energy, cancer treatment will be within the reach of the masses, just as aspirin is'.
>
> *Sameera Moussa*

Egypt's first female nuclear researcher was **Sameera Moussa** (1917–1952). She studied at Fuad I University in Cairo and became its first female faculty member. She specialized in gas thermal convection and later received her PhD in atomic radiation. Moussa believed in the concept of 'Atoms for Peace'. She might have achieved this, except during a research trip to the University of California in America in 1952, her car was forced off the road. Though the driver jumped free, Moussa was killed immediately. The case remains unsolved, though there have been many suggestions that it was the work of the Israeli Intelligence and Secret Service organization, Mossad.

Katharine Burr Blodgett (1898–1979) might need little introduction, but we should celebrate her achievements all the same. The first woman awarded a doctorate in physics from the University of Cambridge and the first female scientist at General Electric, she invented 'invisible glass', hugely important not only for spectacles and lenses, but also for film cameras and periscopes. On 13 June 1951, 'Katharine Blodgett Day' was celebrated in her home town of Schenectady, New York, where she lived with her partner Gertrude Brown.

> 'The unforgotten moments of my life are those rare ones which come after years of plodding work, when the veil over nature's secret seems suddenly to lift, and when what was dark and chaotic appears in a clear and beautiful light and pattern.'
>
> *Gerty Cori*

Gerty Cori (1896–1957) was born into a Jewish family in Prague. In 1922, she and her husband left Europe for the comparative safety of the United States. Despite attempts to discriminate against her employment in favour of her husband's, they continued to work as a team. In 1947, she was the first woman to be awarded the Nobel Prize in Physiology or Medicine, awarded jointly with her husband, for their discovery of the catalytic conversion of glycogen, which revolutionized treatment for diabetes.

> 'Above all, don't fear difficult moments.
> The best comes from them.'
>
> **_Rita Montalcini_**

Another Nobel laureate, the magnificent Italian neurobiologist **Rita Levi-Montalcini** (1909–2012), was a pioneer in the field of the treatment of cerebral palsy and other neurological diseases. Her life is the stuff of legend. Born in Turin to Italian-Jewish parents at the beginning of the twentieth century, she had to fight fiercely to be allowed to train as a doctor at all, beginning her training at the University of Turin. Her academic career was cut short by Mussolini's introduction of anti-Semitic laws barring Jewish people from academic and professional careers. Refusing to be defeated, Montalcini set up her own makeshift laboratory in her bedroom and kept working in secret – an experience brought to the small screen some fifty years later as part of the science documentary *The Life and Times of Life and Times*.

In 1945, Montalcini was invited to Washington University in St Louis to attempt to replicate some of her ground-breaking home laboratory experiments. She succeeded and was offered a research associate position, a post she held for thirty years. She was made a full professor in 1958 and, in 1963, became the first woman to receive the Max Weinstein Award, given by the United Cerebral Palsy Association. In 1986, she was jointly awarded a Nobel Prize in Physiology for research into the nerve-growth factor NGF and, in 2009, became the first centenarian Nobel laureate. There are plenty of photographs, including several with Montalcini sipping a glass of champagne. But my favourite is her standing at a lectern in a black suit, with crisp white blouse, delivering a lecture at the age of a hundred. A tiny woman, with a cloud of white hair and a mischievous smile, she was still changing the world in her second century.

> 'We rise to the knowledge of truth, like those giants who climbed up to the sky by standing on the shoulders of one another.'
>
> *Emilie du Châtelet*

EACH OF THESE extraordinary scientists was, in part, building on the work of women who had gone before them, working in the fields of physics, mathematics and astronomy.

Over a hundred years before Curie was born, the French natural philosopher and mathematician **Emilie du Châtelet** (1706–1749) published the ground-breaking *Foundations of Physics* in 1740. Tackling three of the major issues facing natural philosophers in the early eighteenth century: the problem of bodies, the problem of force, and the question of appropriate methodology, the book was circulated widely, republished and translated into other languages, and turned much of accepted thinking on its head. She also translated Newton's *Principia Mathematica* from Latin into French. Published posthumously in 1756 – and heavily referenced in Diderot's *Encyclopédie*, one of the most significant works of the French Enlightenment – du Châtelet's remains the standard translation, even today.

Marie-Sophie Germain (1776–1831) was a brilliant German mathematician who wrote under the male pseudonym of Monsieur LeBlanc. Learning from books and lecture notes begged, borrowed or stolen from the newly established École Polytechnique in Paris, Germain engaged leading mathematicians in dazzling, written mathematical debate, only later revealing she was a woman. Nearly a hundred years before the Nobel Prizes were launched, Germain was the first woman to win a prize from the Paris Academy of Sciences in 1816.

Working a century later, **Amalie Noether** (1882–1935) was a leading German-Jewish mathematician, particularly in the field of algebra. She developed theories of rings and fields, and discovered the connection between symmetry and conservation laws, known as Noether's theorem.

'Last night, when sweeping over a part of
the heavens with my 5-feet reflector, I met
with a telescopic comet.'

Caroline Herschel

German astronomer **Maria Kirch** (1679–1720) was the first woman
to discover a comet, though her discovery was initially attributed to
her husband. But the most celebrated female comet hunter of the
eighteenth century was fellow countrywoman **Caroline Herschel**
(1750–1848).

Having contracted typhus as a child, Herschel grew to only just
over four feet tall, and lived a confined life with very little formal
education until she was twenty-two. Exchanging Hanover for Bath,
where her brother William was teaching music and staging concerts,
Herschel was sent to join him with the intention of pursuing a career
as a singer. It's the kind of European story my great-grandmother Lily
would have loved – the relationship between Germany and England,
with music at the heart of it. But the Herschel siblings' joint passion
for astronomy soon eclipsed their commitment to music and, soon
after William's discovery of the planet Uranus in 1781, they moved
to Windsor and Caroline's career in astronomy began.

Herschel discovered eight comets and has many other firsts to her
name: she was the first woman in England to receive a salary as a
scientist; the first to publish scientific findings in the *Philosophical
Transactions* of the Royal Society; the first awarded a Gold Medal of
the Royal Astronomical Society in 1828; and, in 1835, the first woman
to be named an honorary member of the Royal Astronomical Society,
along with Mary Somerville. Herschel is another of the thirty-nine
stars honoured at the table in Chicago's *The Dinner Party*. Her runner
is iridescent with the gold stars of the night sky and a telescope is
entwined within the capital 'C' of her name.

'Are you not convinced daughters
can also be heroic?'

Wang Zhenyi

The Chinese astronomer **Wang Zhenyi** (1768–1797) was born eighteen years after Herschel. She refused to accept the limitations placed on her because of her sex, and educated herself in astronomy, mathematics, geography and medicine. Publishing articles entitled 'Dispute of the Procession of the Equinoxes', 'Dispute of Longitude and Stars' and 'The Explanation of a Lunar Eclipse' among others, Wang put forward ideas that would become the foundation for astronomy in the nineteenth and twentieth centuries. Her rallying cry for girls to be given the same opportunities as boys has become an anthem for women in science all over the world.

> 'Teaching man his relatively small sphere in the creation, it also encourages him by its lessons of the unity of Nature and shows him that his power of comprehension allies him with the great intelligence over-reaching all.'
>
> **Annie Jump Cannon**

Fifteen years after Herschel's death, one of the brightest lights of American astronomy was born. **Annie Jump Cannon** (1863–1941) was a data scientist, one of the so-called 'Harvard Computers', an all-female group working with Edward Pickering to map and define every star in the visible universe. Cannon had lost almost all of her hearing as a child, so had been taught at home by her mother who instilled in her a love of the stars.

Nicknamed the 'census taker of the sky', Cannon had to fight to be acknowledged for her contributions – there are many who think the Harvard Classification Scheme of Stars should be known as the Cannon Classification Scheme. Cannon joined the 'Harvard Computers' in 1896, after **Williamina Fleming** (1857–1911), who originally had been Pickering's maid, and **Antonia Maury** (1866–1952), who came from a family of astronomers and insisted on her work being attributed if Pickering wanted to retain her services. Cannon published her first catalogue in 1901, and was made Curator of Astronomical Photographs at Harvard in 1911, after years of being overlooked and underpaid. On the eve of the First

World War, she was admitted as an honorary member of the Royal Astronomical Society.

Another of the 'Harvard Computers' was **Henrietta Swan Leavitt** (1868–1921) who, like Annie Cannon, was also deaf. Leavitt changed how we saw the world when she published a paper in 1912 showing how the distance of a star from the Earth could be measured. The tools she developed for measuring the size and rate of the expansion of the universe are still used in 2022.

> 'Young people, especially young women, often ask me for advice. Here it is, *valeat quantum.* Do not undertake a scientific career in quest of fame or money. There are easier and better ways to reach them. Undertake it only if nothing else will satisfy you; for nothing else is probably what you will receive. Your reward will be the widening of the horizon as you climb. And if you achieve that reward you will ask no other.'
>
> **Cecilia Payne**

Born in the twentieth century, **Cecilia Payne** (1900–1979) was a British-born astronomer and astrophysicist. Having completed her studies at Cambridge (though not allowed to take her degree), she moved to Harvard in the United States where she was the first woman to be promoted to full professor from within the university. The first person ever to earn a PhD in astronomy from Radcliffe College, Payne essentially established what the universe is made of by discovering that stars were composed primarily of hydrogen and helium. Her groundbreaking conclusion, published in her 1925 doctoral thesis, was initially rejected because it contradicted the scientific wisdom of the time, but independent observations eventually proved her discoveries were correct. In 1926, at the age of twenty-six, she became the youngest scientist to be listed in American Men of Science, and refused to give up working when she married and had children.

The bias against female scientists didn't vanish in the twentieth century, but things became a little easier in the UK after the Sex Disqualification (Removal) Act was passed in 1919. Some of the women named here are better known than others, but listing their achievements alongside those who came before them is important in helping to give a fuller picture of all the discoveries in medicine, virology, engineering and science that have made our world what it is today. Mothers of invention, all.

WOMEN WERE MAKING their mark in the field of engineering too. American engineer **Edith Clarke** (1883–1959) was the first woman to be professionally employed as an electrical engineer in the United States, the first female professor of electrical engineering, the first woman to deliver a paper at the American Institute of Electrical Engineers and the first woman named by them as a fellow. A bright spark . . .

Dorothée Pullinger (1894–1986) was a British engineer. Originally denied membership of the Institution of Automobile Engineers – on the grounds that 'a person' in their constitution meant 'a man' – Pullinger nonetheless worked as a 'lady superintendent manager' for seven thousand female munitions workers making shells. In 1919, she became a founder member of the Women's Engineering Society and helped establish an engineering college for women. Returning to munitions work during the Second World War, she was the only woman appointed to the Ministry of Production's industrial panel. In 2012, she became the first woman to be inducted (albeit post-humously) into the Scottish Engineering Hall of Fame.

> 'Way is being made by electricity for a higher order of women – women set free from drudgery, who have time for reflection; for self-respect.'
>
> **Caroline Haslett**

Caroline Haslett (1895–1957) was an English electrical engineer and administrator. One of the founding members and first secretary of the Women's Engineering Society, as well as editor of its journal,

The Woman Engineer, she was the first female member of the Federation of House Builders. Haslett became the first director of the Electrical Association for Women in 1925, her chief motivation being to harness the benefits of electrical power to emancipate women from household chores.

THANKS, IN PART, to Margot Lee Shetterly's 2016 book *Hidden Figures: The Untold Story of the African American Women Who Helped Win the Space Race*, the names of other pioneering women of space are becoming better known. Picking up Annie Jump Cannon's mantle, **Dorothy Vaughan** (1910–2008) was an African American mathematician and 'human computer' who worked for the National Advisory Committee for Aeronautics (NACA) and NASA. Having been passed over for promotion for many years, in 1949 she became acting supervisor of the West Area Computers, the first African American woman supervisor. Vaughan later headed the programming section of the Analysis and Computation Division (ACD) at Langley, famously the headquarters of the CIA.

Katherine Johnson (1918–2020) was another of the trailblazing African American mathematicians working at NASA in the period after the Second World War. Johnson's calculations were essential to the beginning of the Space Shuttle programme. In 2015, she was presented with the Presidential Medal of Freedom by Barack Obama. In 2019, she was awarded the Congressional Gold Medal and, in 2021, Johnson was inducted into the National Women's Hall of Fame.

The third of our 'hidden figures' is **Mary Jackson** (1921–2005), who worked at NACA and NASA with Johnson and Vaughan. Jackson started at the segregated West Area Computers in 1951, but took advanced engineering classes and, in 1959, became NASA's first female African American engineer. In 2019, she was posthumously awarded a Congressional Gold Medal and in 2021, the Washington DC headquarters of NASA was renamed the Mary W. Jackson NASA Headquarters.

During the same period, the 'Mother of Computer Science in China', **Xia Peisu** (1923–2014), was the leading developer of China's first indigenously designed general-purpose electronic computer. **Hu Qiheng** (b. 1934) led the National Computing and Networking Facility of China, overseeing China's connection to the internet in 1994. In the Soviet Union, mathematician and computer scientist **Rozetta Zhilina** (1933–2003) developed algorithms and computer programmes for solving problems in physics, mechanics and nuclear weapons. In India, **Sanghamitra Mohanty** (1953–2021) worked in the fields of artificial intelligence, image and speech processing, as well as weather prediction.

And last but by no means least, the British computer scientist and a near contemporary of Jackson, Johnson, Vaughan and their fellow 'human computers', **Mary Berners-Lee** (1924–2017). A mathematician and early computer scientist, she was based at the University of Manchester working on Mark 1, Ferranti Mark 1 and Mark 1 Star computers. Berners-Lee also helped develop a programme for the RAF to track weather balloons and interpret their readings. She was clearly an inspiration and role model to her son, Tim, inventor of the world wide web.

> 'Think big. That's what I have always been encouraged to do and it works. Throughout my life, I've been taught that anything is possible.'
>
> *Martha Lane Fox*

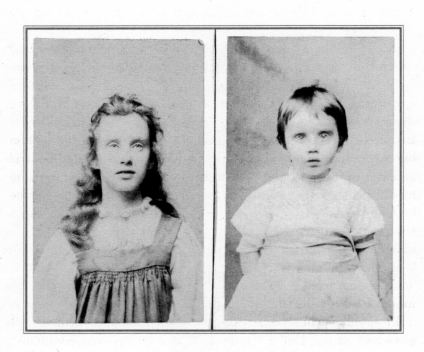

Winnie and my grandmother, Betty, 1894

Lily

LILY MIGHT HAVE BEEN very much a Victorian wife and mother, but she was not afraid to speak her mind. In one letter, dated 1 March at 'Eversley'– so probably written in the late 1870s – she takes her husband to task for sending the 'usual' telegram saying he will not be home to dinner. The letter points out that the household is organized around his needs, that other 'professional men' do manage to include dinner 'in their day's programme', and essentially asks him to do better. Equally interesting is that she encloses two cheques – 'one for bank, other to be cashed' – which confirms that it is her money, at this point, that is keeping the household afloat.

In another, when Sam is clearly worried about something, Lily gives him advice. Dated 5 June 1879, it is lovingly but essentially a 'buck-up' letter:

> 'First – does not past experience show that your forebodings are invariably unfulfilled? Second – that worrying never does the least good? Third – have you not acted in the best interests so there is no cause for self-reproach? . . . Cheer up and take courage. Even if things seem dark, they will brighten, as in the past. Your loving wife, Lily'

Unless other letters come to light, there's no way of knowing what prompted this. But it's possible that Sam was – on this occasion – right. A crisis was brewing.

In 1880, a scandal put their comfortable life under threat. Robert

Watson, a cousin and one of Sam's partners at Bouverie Street, out of the blue disclosed 'his falsifications and forgeries'. It was revealed he had been defrauding the firm for some time and siphoning the other partners' savings, leaving Sam and the other partners with heavy liabilities. By this time, Lily and Sam had two sons and two daughters and though there was never any question of them losing their house – surely Lily's parents would have stepped in – the spectre of ruin must have been devastating. In 1876, Lily's father, Reverend Samuel Green, had resigned as Principal of Rawdon College and moved to London to take up a post as an editor at the Religious Tract Society, so they were close neighbours and would have been aware of what was happening.

Sam wrote of their debt to his friend Leopold Salomons, who lent them money and financial advice. 'But for him,' Sam wrote in his diary, 'I should this day be a beggar.' Salomons remained a close friend. His is one of the first letters of condolence received after Leader's death, preserved in Sam's file of correspondence: 'My dear old friend, this is as hard a letter to write as it will be to receive . . .'

Ten years before this crisis, the Married Women's Property Act had been passed in 1870, thanks to the work of legal campaigners including **Barbara Bodichon** (1827–1891). It would be significantly extended in 1882, and across other British territories, effectively ending the practice of *couverture* whereby husband and wife were considered a single person in law (with the woman having few, if any, rights). This was a crucial reform because it meant that, up to a point, Lily's own money was protected.

I've not yet found any letters from Lily to Sam about the crisis, so I don't know how long it took for them to feel secure again. In a later letter, Sam will claim that both he and Lily are extravagant. However, at a partners' meeting in December 1893 – interestingly, Lily was present – there is discussion about Sam's inability to live within his means. Was it her money and prudence that eventually put the marriage back on an even keel?

I wonder, too, if this was perhaps the reason for a longer gap between children? Winnie had been born in the spring of 1879, just before Lily's 'buck-up' letter to Sam, but Leader was not born until the end of 1885.

The financial crisis was significant for another reason. In her scrapbook, Lily's granddaughter, my godmother Sister Katherine, claims that Lily began to write for a public readership because she needed to contribute to the household finances after Robert Watson's embezzlement. This, again, is one of the challenges of research. It might well have been something Sister Katherine heard her grandmother say but, since she was only a child at the time, this as many of her reminiscences of Lily can't be first-hand.

In this case, it is possible that Lily's precarious family financial situation did encourage her to take up her pen. For Mrs Samuel Watson would, under the name of Lily Watson, begin to write for *The Girl's Own Paper*.

Launched on 3 January 1880, the paper was published by the Religious Tract Society, costing one penny. Lily's father was one of the editors who put together the sixteen three-column pages, with steel engravings and the first serial of two long stories, as well as a short story, three poems and articles – on the 'Girlhood of Queen Victoria' and 'Fashionable Costumes of Long Ago'. There were also pieces on needlework and a competition inviting girls to write 'an essay on the life of any one famous English woman, born in the present century'.

Exactly the kind of writing competition that might have caught my eye, as it happens . . .

The chief editor of *The Girl's Own Paper* was Charles Peters, who worked there for twenty-eight years and died in harness. He had clear ambitions for the paper that it should be used to: 'foster and develop that which was highest and noblest in the girlhood and womanhood of England . . . putting the best things first, and banishing the worthless from its pages.'

As the paper grew in reputation and circulation, the range of improving articles became wider. Making pincushions and tips on folding linen now sat alongside pieces on girls' education, reviews and pen portraits, and the popular 'Answers to Correspondents'. It became, if you like, a one-stop shop for a certain kind of woman, leading a very particular type of aspirational middle-class Victorian life.

In its sixty-six-year history, contributors included **Noel Streatfeild** (1885–1986) of *Ballet Shoes* fame, 'Just William' creator **Richmal Crompton** (1890–1969), **Angela Brazil** (1868–1947), the creator of the 'Scarlet Pimpernel' **Baroness Orczy** (1865–1947), and the British missionary, explorer, nurse and author **Kate Marsden** (1859–1931). In the 1890s, the paper helped fund Marsden's expedition to Siberia and serialized her writings about it.

To this list of celebrated contributors, we should add Lily Watson. In the course of her writing life, Lily wrote nearly one hundred articles and pieces for *The Girl's Own Paper* – Sister Katherine claims Lily was, in fact, writing an article for the publication (now *Woman's Magazine*) on the day she died.

But family folklore that Lily took up her pen as an immediate response to their straitened circumstances doesn't quite fit the dates. The first contribution by Lily – the serialization of her debut novel *The Mountain Path* – was published in 1885, five years after the family's financial crisis. That said, from then on, all of Lily's novels – with the apparent exception of *The Vicar of Langthwaite* – were first serialized in the newspaper before subsequent publication in book format. The majority of Lily's journalism – articles such as 'What Can the Middle-Aged Woman Do When Her Work for the War Is Over' (1918), 'Getting the Women Together' (1924) and 'Getting on Each Other's Nerves' (1925) – was published in the early twentieth century and in the years after the First World War under the new editor, **Flora Klickmann** (1867–1958).

Klickmann – who would later become a passionate environmentalist and campaigner against chemicals in farming and gardening – had more serious ambitions. As well as including articles about missionary work, she set about offering advice on how to apply for higher education. Interestingly, *The Girl's Own Paper* moved from Paternoster Road to Bouverie Street in 1902, just along from the offices of Watson & Sons. This could mean something, or nothing.

LILY'S LETTERS TO Sam – and the few written to her children and grandchildren – give little away as to her innermost thoughts. They are brim-full of everyday life, of domestic concerns, with love for her husband and family. But she plays her cards close to her chest. It was only through reading Lily's articles that I started to get a deeper sense of what most mattered to her. She was an interesting mixture, though not untypical of her time. She was traditional in her views of girls'

and women's roles as wives and mothers, 'helpmeets' to the men in their lives. Yet, at the same time, she was committed to education for girls and the importance of having purpose. Her attitudes were very much what we might call 'Victorian': home and hearth, self-improvement, Christian charity, political with a small 'p', a sense of an ordered England where everyone knew their place.

Lily filed book reviews, essays on the religious writings of Browning and Ruskin, biographies of Joan of Arc and Flora Macdonald, a critical analysis of George Eliot's Maggie Tulliver in *The Mill on the Floss*. Her breadth of reading and writing is evident. She is also often judgemental and uncompromising, clear in her opinions and her right to express them. In 'Girls as Daughters', printed in Volume 21 (1900), she tackles the issue of individualism and how relationships between girls and their mothers were changing to the detriment of society.

'Now the whole subject of what is usually called "Women's Rights", political, social, and so on, is too vast to be discussed here, and one can only just touch the fringe of it, as it were. I should be a traitor to my sex did I not rejoice in the increasing facilities for development, for a full, free, and noble life offered to women. Every year sees some advance in the opportunities for mental and physical culture placed before them. The spectacle so often seen in the past, of a number of young women shut up in one family, spending the day in fancy-work, or occupations simply invented to kill time, is happily becoming rare.'

So far, so good. But, as the article continues, Lily is critical about the silliness of modern girls and it's clear she disapproves of some of the other consequences of emancipation in terms of disrupting the natural order of the home:

'For a houseful of daughters to be dutiful and good in the truest sense, it is not necessary for them to beset their mother, possibly still in the prime of life, in a worrying phalanx, nor for half-a-dozen people to do the work of two. Let each have her own career or occupation – not necessarily wage-earning – leaving one at least as the "home daughter".'

This attitude was not untypical: that a daughter – never a son – should give up her own personal ambitions and expectations if required to do so. Literature is full of such women. Lily's novels all have this moral – that although a woman should be educated and fulfilled, her most significant role will be to support and cherish her father, her brothers and, in time, her husband and children.

Later letters between Lily and Sam suggest Lily was opposed to women's suffrage – on the grounds that women would lose the privileged position they had in society (though this speaks to the experience of a very narrow band of women). This made me wonder about Lily's relationship with her own daughters. Though my grandmother, Betty, would have only been eight when Lily wrote 'Girls as Daughters', Winnie was twenty-one and Ethel, recently married, was twenty-nine. Did they read the piece as veiled criticism, or as a validation of choices they had made? There is no one left to ask. All I can say is that Lily the polemicist seems slightly at odds with the warm and loving woman she seems in her letters.

The more I researched, the more I wondered if I would have liked Lily. Then, I stopped. It shouldn't matter whether I like her or not. My task is to find a way to put her – honestly, truthfully with the material I have – onto the page. Women's inclusion in the historical record cannot be dictated by likeability. After all, it's not the judgement for the most part put on men. My responsibility is to do my best to represent Lily as she was, not impose my own politics or twenty-first-century attitudes on her.

All the same, I *want* to like this great-grandmother of mine and it was disappointing to learn Lily attended anti-suffrage meetings. I would have wanted her to be storming the barricades, not supporting the patriarchal *status quo ante*. But that is to miss the point. Would I try to persuade her to support the right of women to vote if she was campaigning against it? Absolutely. Would I respect her right to think differently? Again, absolutely.

Many organizations and books putting women back into history have been obliged to defend their inclusion of certain women: those who colluded with enslavement in nineteenth-century America or Jamaica, say, or who were Nazi sympathizers or supporters, or who stood against rights of other women to have agency over their own bodies, their lives, their votes – from fictional Aunt Lydias in Margaret

Atwood's *The Handmaid's Tale* to conservative campaigners such as **Phyllis Schlafly** (1924–2016) in America, opposing **Shirley Chisholm** (1924–2005) and others fighting for the Equal Rights Amendment in the 1970s. Or those women at the forefront of overturning *Roe v. Wade* in 2022.

But unpalatable as it might seem, in the matter of recording history it's wrong to only include women who we now consider worthy, who were – in a phrase Lily might have used – 'on the side of the angels'. Because that, ironically, takes us very close to those divide-and-rule Victorian values of the 'Angel in the House' as the sole representative of female ambition.

Women contain contradictions, as do men. Promotion is one thing, inclusion is another. For history to be valid and valuable, to reflect the genuine state of things at any given time, in any given place, then all women who made a contribution, for good or for ill, need to be included, regardless of their views or their loyalties. Otherwise, we too, regardless of our intentions, are colluding in a strategy that sets women against one another. We do not expect all men to agree with one another simply because they are men, so why expect women to do so? We don't have to agree, or think the same, or 'approve' of other people's choices in order to listen to them or defend their right to speak. We must strive to put all the sources we find back into the record because it's only by doing so that we will succeed in creating the authentic past. Excluding views with which we don't agree is one of the many reasons why in addition to women, so many people of colour, indigenous voices, working-class voices, disabled voices, LGBTQIA+ voices are missing. It's our duty to include the whole glorious, complex, contradictory mixture of human actions and emotions, attitudes, choices and opinions. We must learn to embrace the inconsistencies.

Of course, it's nevertheless demoralizing when women one admires have opposing views to our own. In *Lady into Woman*, Vera Brittain puts it beautifully. Acknowledging the intelligence of some of the anti-suffrage women – such as novelist **Mrs Humphrey Ward** (1851–1920), who was the Founding President of the Women's Anti-Suffrage League, or the distinguished unofficial diplomat, archaeologist and explorer **Gertrude Bell** (1868–1926) – she wrote: 'it's as though a close friend were discovered in an ungenerous act of betrayal'.

I like the Lily I'm getting to know through her letters. I like her optimism and her hope, her determination, her loyalty to her family. I admire her courage, her stoicism and her industry. I applaud her joy in travel and nature, trips to Switzerland and to Cannes, Yorkshire and Derbyshire, the watering holes of the South Coast to the Scottish Highlands.

While I was researching, it always gave me great pleasure to find any personal link between us. For example, on 7 August 1897, Lily writes from Earnley Rectory outside Chichester, a few miles from where I sit now and write. A flying visit to stay with her sister Nellie, and Lily talks about visiting Chichester Cathedral and the 'dry and dusty' country roads. Insignificant in the scale of things, but another connection all the same.

Reading Lily's journalism, I suspect we would not have seen eye to eye on many political issues. She had firm and determined opinions and I don't imagine she invited dissent. Everything I'm discovering reinforces the fact that she was a woman of significance in her community and beyond – Gladstone and the literary press certainly thought so. In the end, perhaps only the 'Matilda Effect' can fully explain why she has all but disappeared from the historical record.

∞

Shirley Chisholm (1924–2005)

6

A Woman's Place Is in the House

'I am standing as a woman, not because I believe there is any antagonism between men's and women's interests but because I believe there is need in the House of Commons for more women who can represent directly the special experience and point of view of women.'

Eleanor Rathbone, 1922

HISTORY IS A PENDULUM. It swings back and forth, rather than always onwards. The world isn't constantly improving for women: things improve, then they go backwards. We know this, we see this. Just consider the revoking of *Roe v. Wade* and the battles over women's right to choose raging all over the world.

Looking at suffrage and representation, we can find ancient societies where things seemed more equitable. We can look at the more modern world and log the progress: civil rights, abolitionism, Chartism, socialism, religious emancipation, anti-colonialism, Fabianism, indigenous land rights, trade unionism. We understand how these movements often intersect as part of a broader picture of revolution, of liberation, of freedom from discrimination. And many of the women we've already celebrated for their writing, their leadership, their scientific and medical skill, their legal practice – well, many were also active in the feminist and civil rights movements too.

This chapter is not about matrilineal societies, where descent is followed through the female not the male lines. Today, the largest matrilineal society is the Minangkabau in Indonesia. Others include the Khasi in India, the Mosuo in China, the Bribri in Costa Rica and the Akan in Ghana. There's ample evidence that in most matrilineal societies women's standing is equal or better.

Marie Guyart (1599–1672) was a French nun who worked with the First Nations people of Canada during the seventeenth century. She observed in 1654 that Iroquois women had equal standing and a deciding vote in councils. Property and descent were passed through the female line, crucial because a key issue in women's rights is often tied up with property and wealth. We'll see more examples from Māori, Aboriginal and indigenous peoples in later chapters. But this chapter is not about the ways in which women's position within communities during different eras changed and evolved. Rather, it is specifically about those who fought to have a voice – fought for the right to vote, to be enfranchised, for the right to be full and independent citizens.

> 'Any great change must expect opposition, because it shakes the very foundation of privilege.'
>
> **Lucretia Mott**

Thanks to twenty-four-hour media, we're aware at every moment of much of what is happening in any corner of the globe. For most of human history, of course, countries and cultures worked more independently. But one movement for change feeds another. At certain points in history, a domino effect was in evidence as women in many cultures started to challenge the status quo that kept them without voice, without authority. Sisters fought against traditions giving their brothers preferential treatment, asked why they had less control of their money, their opportunities, their property and their status.

Beginning in the early eighteenth century, the suffrage movement was global. As monarchies tumbled and countries large and small started to want to shape their own societies, there was a clear shift in Europe, North America and Oceania from an era of queens and kings ruling by divine right to acceptance of ideas of justice for all.

In Sweden, conditional women's suffrage was in effect during the Age of Liberty (1718–1772), and the Corsican Republic granted women the vote in 1775. In many countries, local states passed legislation significantly earlier than national governments. New Jersey awarded women the vote in 1776, though that was rescinded in 1807 so that only white men had voting rights. An amendment in Kansas in 1867 to enfranchise the newly liberated Black Americans was accompanied by a parallel amendment to give votes to women too. In the UK, the Municipal Franchise Act in 1869 gave some women rate-payers the vote in local elections and the 1888 County Council Act gave women the vote at county and borough council elections.

The first province to grant women the vote – and not rescind it – was the Pitcairn Islands in 1838, inhabited by descendants of the 'Bounty' mutineers. They were followed by the Isle of Man in 1881, and Franceville in 1889–1890, though some of these were only briefly independent states. The Kingdom of Hawaii introduced universal suffrage in 1840, but a second constitution in 1852 specified it should be limited to males over twenty years old.

The pendulum swings back.

In the years after 1869, a number of provinces held by the British and Russian empires conferred women's suffrage. Some of these, such as Finland, later became sovereign nations. In 1893, New Zealand became the first self-governing country in the world in which all women had the right to vote in parliamentary elections, though women could not stand for election until 1919.

> 'The young women of today, free to study, to speak, to write, to choose their occupation, should remember that every inch of this freedom was bought for them at a great price . . . The debt that each generation owes to the past it must pay to the future.'
>
> **Abigail Scott Duniway**

SO LET'S FOCUS here on individuals rather than countries, starting with **Lydia Taft** (1712–1778). She may have been the first woman to vote legally in colonial America. The facts are disputed, but it's claimed that, at a town meeting in Massachusetts Colony in October 1756, the men of Uxbridge allowed 'the widow Josiah Taft' to vote on the principle of 'no vote, no taxation'. This was important because Josiah's estate was substantial. But it would be 164 years before the constitution would be amended at federal level.

Lucretia Mott (1793–1880) was an American Quaker, abolitionist and social reformer. Like many women involved in suffrage movements, her active involvement dates from a flashpoint moment. In

1840, she was one of several women excluded from the World Anti-Slavery Convention in London. Furious, she protested. When slavery was later outlawed in 1865, Mott advocated giving former slaves, both male and female, the right to vote. The way women were prevented from doing anything worthwhile is the same frustration recorded by Florence Nightingale's youthful bitter pen.

> 'A nourishing life – that is the happiness, whatever it be. A starving life, that is the real trial.'
>
> **Florence Nightingale**

In 1848, Mott was invited by **Jane Hunt** (1812–1889) to the meeting that led to one of the most significant moments in the women's rights movement in the United States, the Seneca Falls Convention. There is a wonderful painted metal blue-and-yellow sign, with a map of New York State at the top and the date the sign was erected by the State Education Department in 1932 – TO MARK THE SPOT: FIRST CONVENTION FOR WOMEN'S RIGHTS WAS HELD ON THIS CORNER 1848. And brooches have survived, circular with a sunflower bearing the date in the centre and the words NATIONAL AMERICAN WOMAN SUFFRAGE ASSOCIATION round the edge.

> 'The best protection a woman can have . . . is courage.'
>
> **Elizabeth Cady Stanton**

The driving force behind the convention was **Elizabeth Cady Stanton** (1815–1902). A writer, abolitionist and activist, she was also the lead author, with Mott, of its 'Declaration of Sentiments'. The mother of seven children, she was less able to travel and campaign, so became the primary writer for the cause. **Susan B. Anthony** (1820–1906), another Quaker and abolitionist, met Cady Stanton in 1851. Together, they founded the New York Women's State Temperance Society – after Anthony had been barred from speaking at a Temperance conference – and, in 1866, they founded the American Equal Rights Association to campaign for equal rights for both women and African Americans.

> 'It was we, the people, not we, the white male citizens; nor yet we, the male citizens; but we, the whole people, who formed the Union . . . Men, their rights and nothing more; women, their rights and nothing less.'
>
> **Susan B. Anthony**

In 1876, Anthony and Stanton began working with the science historian Matilda Joslyn Gage on what would become the six-volume *History of Woman's Suffrage*. Gage advocated dress reform and cut her hair short, remaining a campaigner until the last. Anthony didn't live to see women receive the vote – she died in 1906 – but the Nineteenth Amendment, passed in August 1920, became known as the 'Susan B. Anthony Amendment' to honour her work. Anthony's place setting at *The Dinner Party* reflects Chicago's view of her as the 'queen of the table'. On her runner, the names of some of the other women in the movement are there, and the three capital letters of her name are each illustrated, the letter 'A' entwined with the American flag.

Although the Nineteenth Amendment technically gave the vote to all women, in reality many Black women and other women of colour remained disenfranchised until state laws designed to keep Black voters from the polls via taxes and literacy tests were removed in the Voting Rights Act of 1965. There were no African American women at the Seneca Falls Convention, which was actually a very small gathering. Many Black women, at the same time, were fighting for suffrage within their churches and other communities, as well as joining the fight against racism.

Sarah Parker Remond (1824–1894), speaker, campaigner and abolitionist, is believed to have been the only Black woman out of 1,500 women who signed the 1866 petition. The daughter of the most prominent African American family in Salem, Massachusetts, Remond sailed for England in 1858 to undertake a speaking tour of the UK. Over the next three years, she delivered forty-five lectures on abolition and civil rights in seventeen cities and towns in England, three in Scotland, and four in Ireland, all to considerable acclaim and extensive press coverage on both sides of the Atlantic.

Carrie Chapman Catt (1859–1947) was a key figure in helping to get the Nineteenth Amendment over the line in 1920. Three years later, she wrote a history of women's suffrage in America. A committed pacifist and anti-segregationist, she campaigned against white supremacy and racial segregation. In 1924, she was voted leader of the National Committee on the Cause and Cure of War (NCCCW) and worked to raise awareness of the acts of violence and discriminatory legislation against German Jews. She was also instrumental in the decision of the US government to ease immigration laws in order to allow more European Jews to be offered refuge in America.

Catt appeared on the front cover of *Time* magazine in June 1926, one of the few women so honoured. With her distinctive feathered hat, her expression is wry – perhaps because the caption reads: '*An Iowa Farmer's Daughter*'.

Although Catt formed the League of Women Voters in 1920, in order to encourage women to vote, most of the campaigning suffrage organizations were disbanded after the Nineteenth Amendment had been passed. African American women were left to continue their fight for their voting rights, fighting segregation and racist laws as well.

> 'If white American women, with all their natural and acquired advantages, need the ballot,' she said, 'how much more do Black Americans, male and female, need the strong defense of a vote to help secure their right to life, liberty and the pursuit of happiness?'
>
> *Adella Hunt Logan*

Adella Hunt Logan (1863–1915) was one of the key African American suffragists working to make the movement more inclusive. The 1895 National American Woman Suffrage Association (NAWSA) convention was held in Atlanta, looking for support from southern states for their constitutional amendment on women's suffrage. Yet Jim Crow segregation laws meant African American women and men were turned away from the convention. Mississippi had already passed a new constitution to disenfranchise Black male voters, and other southern states followed suit. Hunt Logan herself, however, managed to get inside and hear

Susan B. Anthony speak, and became a member of NAWSA. This lack of inclusivity would remain an issue for the women's movements in America and the UK well into the twentieth century and beyond.

> 'We are tired of having a "sphere" doled out to us, and of being told that anything outside that "sphere" is unwomanly. We want to be natural for a change.'
>
> **Kate Sheppard**

Born in the year of the Seneca Falls Convention, **Kate Sheppard** (1848–1934) is one of the mothers of the women's movement in New Zealand. Emigrating with her family from Liverpool when she was twenty, she joined several religious and social organizations, including the Women's Christian Temperance Union. Relentlessly organizing petitions and public meetings, writing to the press and developing relationships with politicians, Sheppard was the editor of *The White Ribbon*, the country's first woman-run newspaper, and published pamphlets including *Ten Reasons Why the Women of New Zealand Should Vote* and *Should Women Vote?* Her tireless hard work paid off and a thirty-thousand-signature-strong petition was presented to Parliament which helped usher in New Zealand as the first self-governing country in the world to establish universal suffrage in 1893. In 1991, Sheppard's image replaced that of Queen Elizabeth II on the New Zealand ten-dollar note.

South Australia gave women the vote in 1894 and the Scottish-born author, teacher and journalist **Catherine Spence** (1825–1910) became Australia's first female political candidate in 1897. Called the 'Greatest Australian Woman' by author and feminist **Miles Franklin** (1879–1954), Spence was commemorated on the Australian 2001 Federation five-dollar note. However, laws specifically intended to deny the vote to Aboriginal and Torres Strait Islander people were enacted by Queensland (1885), Western Australia (1893) and the Northern Territory (1922). Meanwhile, the Commonwealth Franchise Act of 1902 granted voting rights to men and women of all Australian states, except it wasn't all people. Indigenous people were excluded unless they'd already had a prior right to vote before 1901. It would not be until the Commonwealth Electoral Act of 1962 that all Aboriginal and Torres Strait Islander people had the option to enrol and vote in Australian federal elections.

Edith Dircksey Cowan (1861–1932) would be the first Australian woman to serve as a member of Parliament in the Legislative Assembly of Western Australia from 1921. Since 1995, Cowan's picture has been on Australia's fifty-dollar note. **Vida Jane Mary Goldstein** (1869–1949) was one of four female candidates to stand at the 1903 federal election in Victoria – alongside trade unionist **Selina Anderson** (1878–1964), **Nellie Martel** (1855–1940) and **Mary Moore-Bentley** (1865–1953) – the first such election where women were eligible to stand. Despite their efforts, Victoria was the last Australian state to implement equal voting rights, with women not granted the right to vote until 1908.

In Canada, **Thérèse Casgrain** (1896–1981) would help to found the Provincial Franchise Committee for Women's Suffrage in 1921. Later, she hosted the influential programme *Fémina* for Radio-Canada and, in the 1940s, became the first female leader of a Canadian political party, the Co-Operative Commonwealth Federation (CCF). A campaigner to the last, in the 1960s Casgrain founded the Quebecois chapter of Voice of Women for Peace to mobilize against the Cold War nuclear threat.

> 'Because these girls are like creatures kept in a box. They may have hands and feet and a voice – but all to no avail, because their freedom is restricted. Unable to move, their hands and feet are useless. Unable to speak, their voice has no purpose. Hence the expression.'
>
> *Toshiko Kishida*

In Japan, **Toshiko Kishida** (1863–1901) – who wrote under the pen name **Shōen** – was one of Japan's first-wave feminists, growing up during the Meiji Taisho period, where the country was beginning to open up to new ideas and reforms. Embarking on a national lecture tour, in April 1882 Kishida gave a speech titled 'The Way of Women' at the inauguration of the Osaka Provisional Political Speech Event, urging women to become educated as a basis for equality. But it's her famous 1883 'Daughters in Boxes' speech for which she is most remembered. Criticizing the family system, and the inequalities of girls and women within it, it was more challenging and radical than the authorities were prepared to accept. Kishida was arrested, tried and fined. Four years later, the Peace Preservation Law was passed prohibiting women from engaging in political activity, effectively ending Kishida's public-speaking career.

So, WOMEN'S SUFFRAGE in the nineteenth century became a kind of fragmented global movement, but the campaigns and battles varied in different countries depending on history and tradition.

Some of the earliest European countries to give women the vote were the Grand Duchy of Finland in 1906, as we've seen, Norway in 1913, Iceland in 1914, Denmark in 1915 and the USSR in 1917. France, home of the Enlightenment, would be one of the last. In Switzerland, women did not have the right to vote until 1971 . . .

We've already met one of the earliest French campaigners, Olympe de Gouges. In 1791, she responded to the French Constituent Assembly's *Declaration of the Rights of Man and of the Citizen* with her answering *Declaration of the Rights of Women and of the Female Citizen*. She was outspoken in her condemnation of the slave trade in the French colonies, she wrote more than forty plays, most of them political, advocated women's and children's rights and for better conditions in prisons.

> 'Both sexes must be equal before the ballot box – and before the guillotine.'
>
> **Hubertine Auclert**

Nearly fifty years later, in a year of revolutions, one of the most important figures of the next generation of French feminists, **Hubertine Auclert** (1848–1914), was born. Though little known outside academic circles, she is credited with bringing the word 'feminism' into more common usage in the 1890s. (The word itself first appeared in 1837 when the French philosopher and utopian socialist Charles Fourier used *'féminisme'* specifically to mean advocacy of women's rights.)

Born in Allier, a region of deep forests and plains, ancient castles and Bourbon history, Auclert was intended for a life of seclusion within the convent. When her brand of egalitarian Christianity proved too challenging for the sisters of Allier, she went instead to Paris. In 1876, she founded the Société le droit des femmes (Society for the Rights of Women, which became the Société le suffrage des femmes – Women's Suffrage Society – in 1883). When the International Congress on Women's Rights was held in Paris in 1878, and failed to support women's suffrage, Auclert stepped up her campaign.

Following in the footsteps of Lydia Taff in Massachusetts a century before, Auclert launched a tax revolt in 1880, arguing that if women were not allowed to vote, then they should not be taxed. Like de Gouges, she demanded equality in all things. If anything, Auclert became more radical with age. In 1908, she smashed a ballot box to pieces during a Paris municipal election and, in 1910, she and fellow activist and author **Marguerite Durand** (1864–1936) presented themselves as candidates in the elections for the legislative assembly. Auclert died in 1914, the day after France declared war on Germany, and was interred in the Père Lachaise Cemetery in Paris, her inscription reading simply: SUFFRAGE DES FEMMES. It wouldn't be until 1944 that women in France finally received the vote.

The third of these early French powerhouse feminists was **Marguerite de Witt-Schlumberger** (1853–1924). A key figure in the temperance and social purity movements, which campaigned to end prostitution and opposed sexual double standards between women and men, she served as the president of Union française pour le suffrage des femmes (the French Union for Women's Suffrage) in 1913 and, during the First World War, encouraged women into the workplace. The following year, Witt-Schlumberger met with women from the International Women's Suffrage Alliance (IWSA), of which she became vice-president in 1917.

Frustrated that women's voices were not being heard in peace negotiations – women were denied the chance to take part in official proceedings – de Witt-Schlumberger was a key mover in setting up the Inter-Allied Women's Conference in Paris in February 1919. Running parallel to the Paris Peace Conference, their aim was to ensure women's issues were not forgotten and that promises made about women's suffrage were not reneged upon. It was not until April that the delegates were allowed to present a resolution to the League of Nations Commission. As well as political and social equality, the resolution covered the trafficking and sale of women and children. The delegates achieved some – though by no means all – of their aims, including measures to prevent trafficking, gaining the right for women to serve in the League of Nations in all capacities, and adoption of their provisions for humane labour conditions. There exists a wonderful posed photograph of all fifteen delegates standing on a Parisian stone staircase with a black wrought-iron balustrade, wearing fur hats, gloves and coats against the February cold.

Delegates in Paris 1919 included: **Jane Brigode** (Belgium); **Marie Parent** (Belgium); **Louise van den Plas** (Belgium); **Cécile Brunschvicg** (France); **Marguerite Pichon-Landry** (France); **Marguerite de Witt-Schlumberger** (France); **Graziella Sonnino Carpi** (Italy); **Eva Mitzhouma** (Poland); **Nina Boyle** (South Africa); **Millicent Garrett Fawcett** (UK); **Rosamond Smith** (UK); **Ray Strachey** (UK); **Katharine Bement Davis** (US); **Florence Jaffray Harriman** (US); and **Juliet Barrett Rublee** (US).

The Italian feminist and peace activist **Graziella Sonnino Carpi** (1884–after 1956) was the Italian delegate to the 1919 Inter-Allied Women's Conference. However, women's rights in Italy were dealt a blow when Mussolini came to power in 1922, with a focus on women's roles as wives and mothers and a determination to return women to the home. In addition, by December 1938 the Women's Union had replaced all its Jewish delegates. Capri spent the war in Switzerland.

The politician, lawyer and writer **Clara Campoamor Rodríguez** (1888–1972) is considered by many to be the mother of the feminist movement in Spain. And **Marie Stritt** (1855–1928) was a leading force in the German women's suffrage movement. She campaigned for women's education and against state-regulated prostitution, and also fought to reform divorce laws and women's right to birth control and abortion.

Moving east, **Elena Văcărescu** (1864–1947) was a Romanian-French writer, twice a laureate of the Académie Française, who benefited from the concessions won for women at the 1919 conference. First a substitute delegate, then a full delegate to the League of Nations between 1921 and 1958, she was one of the few women to serve with the rank of ambassador in the history of the League of Nations.

Văcărescu's near contemporary was **Rosika Schwimmer** (1877–1948). A Hungarian-Jewish-born pacifist and feminist, she co-founded the Campaign for World Government with **Lola Maverick Lloyd** (1875–1944), an organization which would play a key role in the creation of the International Criminal Court. Schwimmer also co-founded the Hungarian Feminist Association, helped organize the IWSA conference in Budapest in 1913 and, like Văcărescu, became one of the world's first female ambassadors. Despite her extraordinary service, when she applied for naturalization in America, she was rejected because of her pacifist views. Though her case was overturned on appeal in 1928, that appeal was then overturned by the US Supreme Court in 1929 and, for the rest of her life, Schwimmer was stateless. Nominated for the Nobel Peace Prize in 1948, Schwimmer died before the committee could make its decision. It wasn't until 1952 that US naturalization laws were changed to allow conscientious objectors to be considered for citizenship.

Born two years after Schwimmer, **Yevgenia Bosch** (1879–1925) was a Bolshevik activist and politician in Soviet-controlled Ukraine and is sometimes described as the first modern female leader of a national government. She served first as Minister of Interior and then Acting Leader of the provisional Soviet government of Ukraine in 1917. **Berta Pīpina** (1883–1942) was the first woman elected to the Latvian Parliament. She argued for state support for mothers and families and against legislation that demanded married women give up paid employment. During the Second World War, after the Soviet invasion, she was deported to Siberia, having been condemned as an enemy of Soviet-controlled Latvia. She died in a gulag and, like many other Latvian men and women, was erased from the history books.

Perchuhi Partizpanyan-Barseghyan (1886–1940) was an Armenian teacher, writer and humanitarian worker, one of the first three women – with **Katarine Zalyan-Manukyan** (d. 1965) and **Varvara Sahakyan** (d. 1934) – elected to serve as members of the eighty-strong Parliament with the formation of the First Republic of Armenia in 1919. Her son translated her memoirs into French and published them in Marseille in 2016. In neighbouring Azerbaijan, the freedom fighter and politician **Ayna Mahmud gizi Sultanova** (1895–1938) became the first Azerbaijani female cabinet minister in 1938. Poet and editor **Doria Shafik** (1908–1975) was one of the leaders of the women's liberation movement in Egypt, playing a key role in gaining Egyptian women the right to vote in 1956. Once described in the press as 'the only man in Egypt', Shafik set up the Daughters of the Nile Union in 1948. On 19 February 1951, she led a 1,500-woman demonstration and stormed through the gates of the Egyptian Parliament while it was in session. In 1954, she declared a hunger strike until Egyptian women were granted equal constitutional rights to men. In 1956, the council granted Egyptian women the right to vote and run for political office. In 2016, Google celebrated her birthdate with a doodle.

Each of these extraordinary women broke new ground, making something that had never been done possible, rather than impossible.

> 'So long as law and custom treat women as one race and men as another there will remain a women question, and not until men and women, equal and united side by side, work together free and untrammelled, will the women's movement be a thing of the past.'
>
> **Equal Rights International pamphlet, 1938**

IN EVERY COUNTRY of the world, women and the men who love them will always admire those who led the way to change. Those who, often at a cost to both their emotional and physical well-being, fought to make their society more equal.

The UK was part of the global suffrage movement, but its struggle also has its own distinct character. Thanks in part to the many commemorations that took place in 2018 to mark the hundredth anniversary of some women in the United Kingdom gaining the vote, many of the names of the British suffrage movement are very well known. Some, less so.

Let's start with the gloriously named **Muriel Matters** (1877–1969), whose story shows how close the links were between campaigners in North America, the Antipodes and the United Kingdom. Born in Adelaide in southern Australia, Matters came to Britain in 1905 and was the 'organizer in charge' of the first 'Votes for Women' caravan that toured south-east England: Surrey, Sussex, East Anglia and Kent in 1908. As a Sussex girl born and bred, I looked in vain in the local archives for evidence that the caravan had passed through my home town of Chichester, but found nothing.

Matters's aim was simple – to take the message of women's suffrage beyond the streets of London, Manchester, Edinburgh and Belfast to smaller towns and rural communities. It was an attempt to build grass-roots support and encourage new branches of the Women's Freedom League, a breakaway organization to the Pankhurst-led Women's Social and Political Union. The following year, Matters pulled off one of the most notorious publicity stunts of the suffragette movement. On 16 February 1909, the day of the State Opening of Parliament, Matters hired a small dirigible airship, intending to shower the Palace of Westminster with pamphlets. Decorated in purple and green, with 'Votes for Women' on one side and 'Women's Freedom League' displayed on the other, bad weather meant that she barely made it out of the suburbs of south-west London. There is a fabulous sepia photograph that appeared in the newspapers with the caption: 'The Successful Start for Westminster Which Ended in Failure to Reach Their Destination'. Another shows her in the tiny wicker basket, her hat held firm on her head by a white scarf, and holding a megaphone. Her stunt might not have disrupted Parliament, but thousands of handbills were scattered and her flight – and smiling face – made headlines around the world. At the house where Matters lived in Hastings for the last twenty years of her life, the blue plaque reads: ADELAIDE BORN ACTIVIST – FIRST WOMAN TO 'SPEAK' IN THE HOUSE OF COMMONS.

> 'Courage calls to courage everywhere, and its voice cannot be denied.'
>
> **Millicent Garrett Fawcett**

One of the very best-known names in the British suffrage movement is that of politician, writer and feminist campaigner **Millicent Garrett Fawcett** (1847–1929) who, from 1897 until 1919, led Britain's largest women's rights association, the National Union of Women's Suffrage Societies. In 2018, she was the first woman honoured with a statue in Parliament Square. It was crafted by sculptor **Gillian Wearing** (b. 1963), after a campaign led by **Caroline Criado Perez** (b. 1984). Fawcett is wearing her tweed walking suit and holding a banner on which words taken from her famous 1920 speech (quoted above) are engraved.

> 'Deeds, not words, was to be our permanent motto.'
>
> **Emmeline Pankhurst**

At the heart of the campaign for women's suffrage in the UK was the extraordinary Pankhurst family – mother **Emmeline Pankhurst** (1858–1928) and her daughters **Christabel Pankhurst** (1880–1958), **Sylvia Pankhurst** (1882–1960) and **Adela Pankhurst** (1885–1961). They, perhaps more than any other of the British suffragettes, have been held up as the figureheads for the fight for votes for women in the UK. In the early years of the twentieth century, after years of trying to bring about change through moderate means, Emmeline Pankhurst was one of several who believed things had to change. Suffrage bills taken before Parliament in 1870, 1886 and 1897 had looked promising, yet each had been defeated, and Emmeline was frustrated with the inability of the Independent Labour Party to move things forward. It was time for more militant action.

In October 1903, Pankhurst and her daughters founded the Women's Social and Political Union (WSPU) with other colleagues, a women-only group focused on direct action in order to win women the vote. An activist, she led by example, fearless in her strategies to draw attention to their cause, which put the WSPU at odds with some of the more moderate campaigners who were still trying to work with the established political parties. In 1906, a journalist at the *Daily Mail* used the diminutive term 'suffragette' rather than the usual 'suffragist', intending it to be derogatory. As had happened with the term 'bluestocking', Pankhurst and her allies embraced the term. Pankhurst's writings about their experiences – not least of all the horrors of Holloway Prison and the violence of force feeding – were critical in helping, eventually, to sway public opinion in their favour.

The lives of the Pankhursts, severally and individually – from cradle to grave – have been very well represented in literature, biography, film, theatre and television. But there were many others who deserve to be household names too.

Mary Jane Clarke (1862–1910), a younger sister of Emmeline Pankhurst, was arrested on Black Friday, 18 November 1910 – when some three hundred women marched on Parliament demanding voting rights, and were beaten and some sexually assaulted. Arrested for breaking a window, she was taken to Holloway, where she was force fed. Released on 23 December, she died of a brain haemorrhage two days later. **Emmeline Pethick-Lawrence** (1867–1954) said Clarke was 'the first woman martyr who has gone to death for this cause'.

Born ten years later, **Edith Rigby** (1872–1950) founded the Preston branch of the WSPU in 1907. She was particularly focused on the differences between the lives of middle-class and working-class girls and women. An activist and hunger striker, subjected to force feeding, she was jailed seven times, on one occasion in 1913 for having planted a bomb in the Liverpool Corn Exchange. With her cropped hair and men's clothing, legend has it that Rigby was the first woman in Preston to own a bicycle. The most famous photograph is of her being arrested by a policeman, her face pressed up against black wrought-iron railings.

The first full-time employee of the British suffrage movement was **Elizabeth Wolstenholme-Elmy** (1833–1918). Her job? To lobby Parliament about laws that harmed women. She was also one of the key figures in a red-letter day of the suffragette calendar: Sunday, 21 June 1908, the day of the mass rally organized by the WSPU, following a successful march organized the previous week by the less militant National Union of Women's Suffrage Societies. Seven processions marched from different points in London. Wolstenholme-Elmy led the procession from Euston Road with Emmeline Pankhurst; Oldham's **Annie Kenney** (1879–1953) headed the march from Paddington; and Christabel Pankhurst and Bristolian Emmeline Pethick-Lawrence led the protestors from the Victoria Embankment. Women had been asked to wear white dresses (though photographs of the day show Emmeline Pankhurst in purple), which must have been an extraordinary sight. Some five hundred thousand people gathered in Hyde Park, with banners and flags, to be part of what was said to be the largest ever mass rally held in Britain. A sea of purple and white and green beneath a blue summer sky. On that day in June, the pendulum was swinging in the right direction.

I would love to know if, six miles to the south in Streatham, my great-grandmother Lily knew the march was happening and, if so, what she thought of it. Did she talk about it with her daughters, with her sons and husband, with people at her church? She had been opposed to women's suffrage, but might such a show of mass support have changed her mind?

Let's finish with some of the other suffragettes who might have been there on 'Women's Sunday': **Rosa May Billinghurst** (1875–1953), a polio sufferer who campaigned on a tricycle; **Annie Kenney**, who was jailed for assault after heckling Sir Edward Grey at a rally in Manchester and who co-founded the first WSPU branch in London with **Minnie Baldock** (1864–1954); **Helen Crawfurd Anderson** (1877–1954), who was a rent strike organizer, communist activist and Glaswegian politician; Leeds suffragette **Mary Gawthorpe** (1881–1973), described by writer and journalist **Rebecca West** (1892–1983) as a 'merry militant saint'; **Sophia Duleep Singh** (1876–1948), a god-daughter of Queen Victoria and a leading member of the Women's Tax Resistance League together with Southend's **Rosina Sky** (1877–1922).

Around the plinth of the statue of Millicent Fawcett in Parliament Square are inscribed the names of fifty-one courageous women and four men who played their part in the fight for votes for women. Of the women listed above, only Sky and Crawfurd-Anderson are missing.

FROM 1919, THE campaigning focus shifted. First, to extend the franchise to all women – it wouldn't be until 1928 that the Equal Franchise Act would give all women in the UK aged twenty-one and over the right to vote on the same terms as men. Second, to see women elected into Parliament. Throughout the UK, women had been serving on district and county councils for many years, but to see women sitting in the House of Commons – that was the next goal.

The first woman to be elected to Westminster in 1918 – representing Dublin St Patrick's – was the Polish-born Irish politician, revolutionary and socialist **Constance Markievicz** (1868–1927), though she never took up her seat. An active participant in the Easter Rising in 1916, she was sentenced to death; though later the sentence was commuted to life imprisonment because she was a woman. When Markievicz discovered she wasn't going to be executed, she was reported to have said: 'I do wish your lot had the decency to shoot me.' She was released in 1917 as part of a general amnesty for the protestors. A statue of Markievicz with her cocker spaniel, Poppet, stands on Townsend Street in Dublin. Her advice to campaigning and activist women was to 'dress suitably in short skirts and strong boots, leave your jewels in the bank and buy a revolver'.

The 1918 general election fielded seventeen female candidates, including Christabel Pankhurst. Only Markievicz was successful.

> 'If you want an MP who will be a repetition of the 600 other MPs don't vote for me. If you want a lawyer or if you want a pacifist don't elect me. If you can't get a fighting man, take a fighting woman. If you want a Bolshevist or a follower of Mr Asquith, don't elect me. If you want a party hack don't elect me. Surely we have outgrown party ties, I have. The war has taught us that there is a greater thing than parties and that is the State.'
>
> **Nancy Astor**

The first woman to take her seat in Parliament was **Nancy Astor** (1879–1964), who contested her husband's constituency of Sutton Plymouth in a by-election in 1919. She served from then until 1945 and, though she had previously taken little part in the suffragette movement, became a vocal supporter of the extension of the franchise.

> 'I doubt whether there is any subject in the world of equal importance that has received so little serious and articulate consideration as the economic status of the family – of its members in relation to each other and of the whole unit in relation to the other units of which the community is made up.'
>
> **Eleanor Rathbone**

When **Eleanor Rathbone** (1872–1946) first stood for Parliament, she campaigned as a feminist. Rathbone had been one of the 720 'steamboat ladies' – they'd travelled to Dublin by boat – female students of Oxford and Cambridge who were awarded *ad eundem* degrees by Trinity College Dublin when their own universities refused to confer degrees on women. A lifelong campaigner for women's welfare and a family allowance being paid directly to women, in 1897 Rathbone became the honorary secretary of the Liverpool Women's Suffrage Society Executive Committee. She worked her way into national politics. In 1909, she was elected as an independent member of Liverpool City Council. She opposed violent repression in Ireland, campaigned for women's rights in India, and one of her first speeches in the House of Commons was against female genital mutilation. Rathbone contested the 1922 general election as an Independent candidate at Liverpool East Toxteth. She lost, but was finally elected as an independent MP for Combined English Universities in 1929. She was also instrumental in the enacting of the 1945 Family Allowances Act, the first law in the UK to provide child benefit.

FOR MUCH OF the twentieth century, the battlegrounds for women in many parts of the world shifted from suffrage – once that battle had been won – to issues of national independence, civil liberties and land rights. We'll focus on some of those women of conviction in Chapter 9. For now, let's just pick out one or two female politicians who, for good or ill, made a difference, then finish with a few pen portrait firsts.

The 'Lioness of Labour' was the mighty Scottish politician **Jennie Lee** (1904–1988). Adopted as the ILP candidate for a by-election for Lanarkshire North in 1929, she won, making her the youngest female member of Parliament. She was re-elected in the general election a few months later and held the seat until 1931, then finally won election again as a Labour Party MP from 1945 to 1970 for the Staffordshire constituency of Cannock. She was appointed as the first Minister for the Arts in Harold Wilson's government of 1964, playing a crucial role in the founding of both the Open University and the Arts Council.

> 'I will fight for what I believe in until I drop dead. And that's what keeps you alive.'
>
> **Barbara Castle**

Barbara Castle (1910–2002) was a Labour member of Parliament from 1945 to 1979, and one of the longest-serving female MPs in British history. Born into a politically engaged family, and having served on St Pancras Metropolitan Borough Council in London from 1937, she was elected as the MP for Blackburn in the historic Labour landslide 1945 general election. Castle had won her place on the shortlist when the women of the Blackburn Labour Party threatened to resign if there were only male candidates. Tireless and always true to her principles, she served as Minister for Transport, First Minister of State, Secretary of State for Employment, and Secretary of State for Health and Social Services. Castle was finally defeated in the 1979 general election that saw the Conservative **Margaret Thatcher** (1925–2013) elected as the first female prime minister of the United Kingdom. Thatcher served from 1979 to 1990, making her not only the first woman to hold that office but also the longest-serving British prime minister of the twentieth century.

Months after losing her seat in 1979, Castle was elected to the European Parliament, representing first Greater Manchester North, then from 1984 to 1989 Greater Manchester West, and led the Labour delegation in the European Parliament. Her diaries – *The Castle Diaries* – chronicled her time in office and form an extraordinary record, not just into the workings of government but also of what it was like to be a woman in the very male world of the House of Commons.

> 'A country's greatness lies in its undying ideals of love and sacrifice that inspire the mothers of the race.'
>
> **Sarojini Naidu**

In India, the poet, activist, suffragist and politician **Sarojini Naidu** (1879–1949) was known as the 'Nightingale of India'. Appointed President of the Indian National Congress in 1925, she became the first female governor of an Indian state after Independence. Her birthday on 13 February is celebrated as Women's Day in India.

> 'People tend to forget their duties but remember their rights.'
>
> **Indira Gandhi**

Indira Gandhi was the first and, to date, only female prime minister of India, serving from January 1966 to March 1977 and again from January 1980 until her assassination in October 1984. In 2020, Gandhi was named by *Time* magazine as one of the 100 most influential women who defined the last century.

Fatima Jinnah (1893–1967), widely known as the *Māder-e Millat* (Mother of the Nation), was one of the founders of Pakistan. A dentist by profession – one of the first female dentists in the country – she was a fierce critic of the British Raj and a leading member of the All-India Muslim League. After independence, Jinnah co-founded the Pakistan Women's Association and remained a key supporter and advisor to her brother, the first Governor-General of Pakistan.

The world's first elected female prime minister was **Sirimavo Bandaranaike** (1916–2000), who was appointed prime minister of Sri Lanka (then the Dominion of Ceylon) in 1960. A Buddhist, though educated in Catholic schools, she was a social worker and educator by vocation and only went into politics after her husband's assassination in 1959. A controversial figure, she survived an attempted coup d'état in 1962 and was stripped of her civil rights in 1980 for abuses of power. **Khertek Anchimaa-Toka** (1912–2008) was a Tuvan/Soviet politician. Appointed chair of the Little Khural of the Tuvan People's Republic from 1940 to 1944, she was the first non-royal female head of state.

Eugenia Charles (1919–2005) was prime minister of Dominica from 1980 until 1995, the first and only woman to have held the position. She was also the first woman lawyer in Dominica and second female prime minister in the Caribbean, after **Lucina da Costa** (1929–2017) of the Netherlands Antilles. Sometimes described as the 'Iron Lady of the Caribbean', Charles was the first woman in the Americas to be elected in her own right as head of government and was the world's third-longest serving female prime minister, after Gandhi and Bandaranaike.

Lidia Gueiler Tejada (1921–2011) was the first female president of Bolivia from 1979 to 1980, and the second female head of state in the Americas. And **Agatha Barbara** (1923–2002) was the first female president of Malta, having served as a Labour member of Parliament and a minister. She remains the longest-serving woman MP in Maltese political history.

> 'If they don't give you a seat at the table,
> bring a folding chair.'
>
> **Shirley Chisholm**

The American politician, educator and author **Shirley Chisholm** fought both racism and sexism. In 1964, she was elected to the New York State Assembly and, four years later, became the first Black woman to be elected to Congress. In 1972, Chisholm became the first Black candidate to run for a major party nomination, and the first woman to run for the Democratic Party's presidential nomination. She was also a key figure in the Equal Rights Amendment campaign. In 2015, she was posthumously awarded the Presidential Medal of Freedom.

Elisabeth Domitien (1925–2005) was prime minister of the Central African Republic from 1975 to 1976, the first and only woman to hold the position. **Maria de Lourdes Pintasilgo** (1930–2004), a chemical engineer, was the first and only woman so far to serve as prime minister of Portugal. Born two years later, **Kubra Noorzai** (1932–1986) was the first woman to become a government minister in Afghanistan, serving as Minister of Public Health for four years from 1965, and was one of the first women to stop wearing a veil in public. Noorzai was part of the advisory committee that reviewed the draft 1964 constitution, which granted women the right to vote and stand for election. An extraordinary woman; one can only imagine what she would have felt seeing those advances being rolled back by the Taliban after they recaptured power in Afghanistan in 2021.

> 'Freedom of expression – in particular,
> freedom of the press – guarantees popular
> participation in the decisions and actions of
> government, and popular participation is
> the essence of our democracy.'
>
> **Corazon Aquino**

Corazon Aquino (1933–2009), known as Cory, was the first woman to be elected president of the Philippines, holding the position from 1986 until 1992 after the fall of President Marcos. **Golda Meir**

(1898–1978) was the first and only woman to hold the office of prime minister of Israel in 1969, and the first in any country in the Middle East.

> 'I found that a whole series of people opposed me simply on the grounds that I was a woman. The clerics took to the mosque saying that Pakistan had thrown itself outside the Muslim world and the Muslim ummah by voting for a woman, that a woman had usurped a man's place in the Islamic society.'
>
> **Benazir Bhutto**

Benazir Bhutto (1953–2007), who served as prime minister of Pakistan from 1988 to 1990 and from 1993 to 1996, was the first woman to head a democratic government in a Muslim country. Although allegations of corruption cast a shadow over some of her achievements – in 2003, she was found guilty with her husband of money laundering – her pro-democracy agenda and support for women's rights made her a feminist icon in Pakistan. It also made her a target. Bhutto was assassinated after a political rally in Rawalpindi in 2007.

As I write this book in 2022, there are currently more elected female world leaders than ever before, though the pattern of history shows that nothing can be taken for granted. So, let's raise our glasses to a few of the living legends who are still changing the world for the better . . .

Vigdís Finnbogadóttir (b. 1930) was the world's first woman democratically elected president, a position she held from 1980 to 1996, and Iceland's first and only female president. She remains the longest-serving elected female head of state.

> 'In terms of being able to renew my nation, to be able to bring back a devastated country, to restore hope to our people, to

> lift women and to give them a new horizon,
> a new ambition and new dreams, in respect
> of all of that, I think we've accomplished it,
> and I feel very good about that.'
>
> *Ellen Johnson Sirleaf*

Nobel laureate **Ellen Johnson Sirleaf** (b. October 1938) served as president of Liberia from 2006 to 2018, the first elected female head of state in Africa. Arrested as a result of her open criticism of the military government in 1985, she was sentenced to ten years' imprisonment. Sirleaf won the Nobel Peace Prize in 2011, in recognition of her efforts to bring women into the peacekeeping process and, in 2016, she was elected chair of the Economic Community of West African States, the first woman to hold the position.

> 'It is absolutely imperative that every human
> being's freedom and human rights are
> respected, all over the world. Freedom and
> human rights – that is what the world needs
> most, that is what everyone longs for, and
> should be entitled to, in order to be able to
> live with dignity.'
>
> *Jóhanna Sigurðardóttir*

Jóhanna Sigurðardóttir (b. 1942) was Iceland's first female prime minister, serving from 2009 to 2013. When she lost a bid to head the Social Democratic Party in 1994, she raised her fist and declared 'My time will come!', which became a popular rallying cry. When she became prime minister in February 2009, she was the world's first openly lesbian head of government.

Mary Robinson (b. 1944) was the first female president of Ireland, serving from December 1990 to September 1997. She also served as United Nations High Commissioner for Human Rights from 1997 to 2002. **Gertrude Ibengwe Mongella** (b. 1945) is a Tanzanian politician and first president of the Pan-African Parliament. **Sheikh Hasina Wazed** (b. 1947) served as prime minister of Bangladesh from 1996 until 2001, then since January 2009. She is the longest-serving prime minister in the history of the country. **Kamla Persad-Bissessar** (b. 1952), currently leader of the opposition in Trinidad and Tobago, was the first female prime minister, serving for five years from 2010. She was also the country's first female attorney general and the first woman to chair the Commonwealth of Nations.

> 'When it comes to human dignity, we cannot make compromises.'
>
> *Angela Merkel*

Angela Merkel (b. 1954) was the first female chancellor of Germany, serving from 2005 to 2021, having been leader of the opposition from 2002. Holding a doctorate in quantum chemistry, and working as a research scientist as well as leading Germany, she was a key voice in international cooperation, both in terms of the EU and NATO. Merkel served as President of the European Council in 2008, played a central role in the negotiation of the Treaty of Lisbon and the Berlin Declaration, and was a key voice in the global financial crisis of 2007–8 and the European debt crisis. An extraordinary woman.

Lateefa Al Gaood (b. 1956) became the first female candidate to be elected to the Council of Representatives of Bahrain in 2006. She is currently the only female member of the council and is also the first woman in the Gulf region to win in a legislative general election. **Ursula von der Leyen** (b. 1958) is a German politician and physician, the first female president of the European Commission. **Nicola Sturgeon** (b. 1970) is the First Minister of Scotland and Leader of the Scottish National Party, the first woman to hold either position. **Sanna Marin** (b. 1985), who has been prime minister of Finland since December 2019, is the world's youngest female head of state. And in 2021, Estonia, Sweden, Samoa and Tunisia elected female prime ministers for the first time in their history, while in January 2022, **Xiomara Castro** (b. 1959) was sworn in as the first female president of Honduras.

Women of all ages, of all ethnicities, of all political persuasions, fighting for the right to be heard and considered. Fighting for all of our rights to be heard.

A woman's place is in the House.

Sam, Lily, Betty and Winnie's son, Patrick,
Causey Pike, Lake District, August 1915

Lily

IN AUGUST 1901, THE Watson family stayed for the first time at Stair Mill in Newlands Valley. There would be many visits to this green corner of Cumbria in the years that followed and it was a place very dear to my grandmother. The Bible on the lectern of the tiny church in the green shadow of Catbells is inscribed by her, signing her name as Betty Mosse (née Watson).

When I started my research, I assumed that trip in 1901 was Lily's introduction to the Lake District. But once the deed box with its cache of letters came into my hands, I saw I'd been wrong. Three years earlier, in October 1898, Lily had gone to Keswick with Ethel, Winnie and her 'darling Betty' to stay at Belle Vue, Lake Road. It was clearly a change of scene intended to help after the sorrow of Leader's death. Her first letter to Sam from Keswick is written on paper edged with black and begins: 'Here I am, darling.' It's filled with descriptions of the fells and Lily's delicate ink sketchings. As usual, she wrote every day. Sam put all the letters together in a paper wrapper with a note that said: 'it did her great good'. Was it possible the Lake District became their new family holiday destination because there were no memories there of her lost son? No memories of her brother Alfred, no ghosts at all?

From other letters sent in 1901, it seems Lily might not have been well that summer. A few weeks after returning from Stair Mill, Lily was writing from Room 264 of the Strathearn House Hydropathic Establishment in Crieff on headed notepaper: 'Sept 20th 1901 Another wet day, dear! But I do not mind. I feel happy and as content as possible.' Three days later, there's a passing mention of a 'very distressing experience', though Lily doesn't say what it was. A couple of weeks after that in October, Lily is writing from a private hotel in Tunbridge Wells and saying she feels 'much better'.

Here, Lily's silence is tantalizing. For all her letter writing, she almost never committed her emotions to the page. She writes about where she is, and what is happening, things that need to be done and domestic arrangements, but rarely about how she feels.

The first entry in the visitors' book for Stair Mill comes from the following year. In September 1902, Lily wrote: 'We have spent a most delightful time under the roof of Mrs Robinson, whose kind attention, excellent cooking, and good management have been much appreciated.'

Stair Mill was a tall white building with a black wrought-iron balustrade around a first-floor terrace, set on a switchback corner of a bend. The attached two-storey house, pleasingly symmetrical with sash windows and latticed porch, was owned by Mrs Robinson with her two daughters, Florrie and Eva, and her son, Nathan. It also doubled as the village post office, serving just a few dozen homes in a radius of a couple of miles of narrow, valley roads.

Behind the whitewashed buildings, a garden sloped steeply uphill with Newlands Beck running alongside. Always the sound of water singing, calling, racing over the slabs of slate-grey flat rock, up and under Stoneycroft Bridge. On bright days in summer, the purple and greens of heather and bracken look almost gaudy on the lower slopes of Causey Pike. An ascent of 1,750 feet, some one and a half miles, it's not for the faint-hearted. The summit has no cairn, just a small platform of naked rock, light brown and seamed with the hollows of many years' erosion. The shimmering of Derwentwater in the distance and a panorama down to Maiden Moor, Borrowdale to the west and the old mine road. It's one of the principal fells of the north-west Lakes. On wet days, the peak vanishes beneath mist and fog and low cloud.

Lily was back the following year, in July 1903. Sam had taken the older boys fishing in Kent. Lily writes her first holiday letter on the Northern Express itself, telling him how Betty is 'wild with excitement'. They arrive at Stair on 4 August. Her brother Arnold and sister Nellie join them – and she tells Sam they are arguing. Tucked in among the letters are postcards – one of the Bowder Stone sent on 12 August.

Another, of Wordsworth's grave in Grasmere, is from my grandmother Betty to her father. And on another, this time of Derwentwater, Lily scribbles: 'Here is a day, love, of sublime beauty.' They are going to the Old Farm at Grange and for a walk to Keswick. On 20 August, her letter says how much she is looking forward to seeing him: 'I need not write a long letter, as I hope we shall meet a few hours after you read it.'

In 1904, Lily went to Stair Mill in early July: 'The fact this is our third visit in consecutive years,' she wrote in the visitors' book, 'speaks for itself. We are always happy here, and sorry to depart.'

On 10 July, she writes to Sam about how she'd escaped the heat of the day by walking at dusk 'alone to Newlands Church, the great mountain being above it in the beautiful candlelight'. Two days later, another letter:

> 'I am sitting, dearest, in the woods behind the Guest House by the Newlands Beck. Reginald, Winifred and Betty are fishing further on. It is a heavenly day and the cool rush of the stream is divine. Close by is a pool, some eight feet deep, where the guests dive.'

Twenty-five years later, my father and his sister and brother would swim in those same clean, cold waters. In the 1970s, my sisters and I did the same.

THE VISITORS' BOOK is a wonderful source of information. Sam didn't manage to join them at all in 1904, the year of Winnie's engagement. Lily not only lists the exact dates of each holiday, but also the names of those staying with them at the Mill. Cousins, children, friends, the children's nanny and close household staff from London. Sometimes, Ethel and her husband Rex Earle are there. There's no visit in 1905 – I think this might be because Lily's mother died in May and her father was seriously ill, dying just four months later in September. In 1906, it appears to be just Lily and fifteen-year-old Betty, with three family servants. By this time, Winnie is with her new husband in India. In the entry in the book for 4 July–1 August 1911, Lily writes rather archly in the third person: 'This is

Mrs Watson's seventh visit and she thinks it has been the most delightful of all. Glorious weather, lovely scenery and the utmost care and attention from the kind hostess and her family.'

Landscape plays a key role in Lily's fiction – as it does in mine – the sense that, perhaps, the natural world echoes and mirrors human emotions. Her love of the mountains of Switzerland and Austria, of wild and unforgiving terrain, sings from the pages of *Within Sight of the Snow, The Mountain Path* and *In the Days of Mozart*. Landscape becomes a healing and curative environment in *A Fortunate Exile*. Her last published novel, *A Child of Genius*, begins with the sixteen-year-old Katharine Lovell trying to commit to paper the beauty of the view she sees from her window on Lake Geneva.

As I researched, I realized that Lily published all of her novels within a ten-year period between 1888 and 1898. As a white woman in a middle-class professional household, Lily had help with her home and children, so her writing time was not circumscribed as it was – as it is – for so many other women. The 'pram in the hall', as Cyril Connolly put it, was not a practical issue for her. All the same, it's intriguing that her most intense period of writing coincided with being a mother to six young children, three of whom were suffering from an incurable illness of the blood.

Until I read her letters, I was surprised that Lily never put the Lake District on the pages of a novel, since it was so important during the latter years of her life. Her descriptions of the mythical Northminster in Yorkshire in *The Vicar of Langthwaite*, and her protagonist Estelle Hawthorne's joy in nature, are some of the strongest passages of that novel: 'the wood was blue underfoot' with wild hyacinths, 'sweeps of hillside, fringed by the dim purple of distant moor'.

But now I think I understand. There are some places that speak to us as writers, others that remain silent or whisper only to our private selves. Perhaps Stair Mill was too domestic, a place where she was very much Mrs Samuel Watson, wife and mother, sister and aunt, rather than 'Lily Watson, Authoress'. But why, after ten years of extraordinary productivity, did she stop? Did her sharp sense of social injustice and concern simply mean she felt she came to believe there was more important work to be done than 'storytelling'?

In the early years of the twentieth century, Lily mostly turned away from fiction and appears to have refocused her writing energies on

essays, polemics, poetry and devotional texts. Her last publication –
Three Voices & Other Poems – came out at Christmas 1931, a few
weeks before she died in the cold new year of 1932. In it, we find
the only mentions of this place in the Lakes that was so important
to her outside of her personal correspondence, including the poems
'Wet Weather in the Lake District' and 'Vision', which she wrote after
an early walk to Newlands Church during the First World War:

> *The lights and shadows on the fells were*
> *Changing*
> *As up the vale I pressed.*

I want to imagine Lily sitting at a desk by a window on the first
floor, looking out over a green and misty world. I want to imagine
her hearing the sound of the sheep and the single tolling of the bell
calling the men home from the fields.

I have a photograph of Lily and Sam sitting on rocks out on Causey
Pike, smart in long coats and hats, with my grandmother Betty and
one of Winnie's children, Patrick, behind. There are other photographs of Betty in her walking clothes, long cardigans, heavy twill
skirts and sturdy boots; or with her friends, Florrie and Eva. Florrie
and my grandmother stayed in touch until Granny's death in 1981.

In 1978, seventy-eight years after my grandmother first went to
Newlands Valley, I climbed Causey Pike with my father. Granny was
ill and being cared for in a nursing home so, for the first and only
time in my life, I kept a diary to share the two weeks of our holiday
with her.

That diary, which my mother kept all this time, is a green-lined
exercise book. Painfully old-fashioned and pedestrian, I filled it with
many tedious descriptions of the weather, an obsessive amount of
information about our journey from Sussex to Newlands, a roll call
of the nine counties through which we passed. It is numbingly dull.
But, reading it now, I see so many connections linking my childhood
to that of my grandmother and my great-grandmother before her.

And there are some vivid fragments: visiting Spiderwells, the rock
pool Granny had always loved; walking along the panoramic ridge
to the neighbouring village of Grange; going to Little Town to see
where Granny met Beatrix Potter; looking at the Devil's hand and

knee prints on Barrow; the gravity-defying Bowder Stone, the almost exact picture postcard that Lily had sent to Sam in August 1903; the Stone Circle at High Briery; listening to my father reading the lesson in Newlands Church on Sunday from my grandmother's Bible. Heavy photograph albums of tissue paper and glue, a black-and-white passing of the years, a record of life lived. An August wet and cold enough to have a fire in the evenings. My childhood, the lives of my father, Richard, his mother, his grandmother.

Lily's visits continued, though I've had to patch the timeline together from a variety of other sources. There are fewer letters between Lily and Sam after 1906 and this could mean anything. Possibly because they were more often together in the same place, so had less need to write. Or, perhaps, there is another deed box still waiting to be found.

In July 1918, there is a single entry from my grandmother in the visitors' book, signing herself for the first time as Betty Mosse of Homefield Road, Wimbledon. Though it was her honeymoon, it reads simply: 'My twelfth visit!'

For Lily and her family, the exploration of the north-western Lakes and fells – later mapped out by Wainwright in his famous series of love letters to the Lake District – was a hugely important part of their family life. Wainwright's *A Pictorial Guide to the Lakeland Fells* is a series of seven books written over a period of thirteen years from 1952, consisting entirely of reproductions of his original manuscripts, hand-produced and handwritten in pen and ink. I have my father's copy of book six, *The North Western Fells* – soft yellow board with his scrawled signature, all but illegible, inside the front cover. When I began this journey of discovery into Lily's life, it's the book I took with me to connect me to the past. Above all, she knew Borrowdale and Derwentwater, the villages of Newlands Valley, the towns of Keswick and Grange.

In 1930, my six-year-old father would contract TB from drinking unpasteurized milk from local cattle. He wrote about it – his beloved sister Margaret running pell-mell down through the valley to fetch a doctor. My father was confined to bed, then used a wheeled chair for the next year. The Mosse family would not return to Newlands Valley for twelve months, but I have albums of heavy grey paper, filled with Box-Brownie photographs clipped into place in the corners, that show many more years of climbing and walking and watching the sun going down on Catbells.

And it would be there, in 1939, that my grandparents, my aunt and my father sat around the wireless on 3 September to hear Prime Minister Chamberlain declare that Britain was now at war with Germany.

These are quiet and personal details, insignificant in the broader scheme of things. But this, too, is history.

Top: Wangari Maathai (1940–2011)
Bottom left: Sacagawea statue (*c.* 1788–1812)
Bottom right: Rachel Carson (1907–1964)

7

Women Nurturing Nature

'Those who contemplate the beauty of the Earth find reserves of strength that will endure as long as life lasts. There is something infinitely healing in the repeated refrains of nature – the assurance that dawn comes after night, and spring after winter.'

Silent Spring
Rachel Carson, 1962

MOST PEOPLE HAVE HEARD of the Hanging Gardens of Babylon. Situated in what is now Iraq, they were one of the seven wonders of the Ancient World and the only one whose actual site has never been found. Whether they were real, mythical, perhaps named for other magnificent gardens in the classical world, we'll probably never know.

But we do know that humanity's use of the enclosure of outdoor spaces began about 10,000 BCE, probably to protect the land from animals or destructive invaders. In every culture and in every period of history, women and men have used the plants, flora and fauna that surrounded them to treat illness and provide food, but also to make their environment beautiful and pleasant. Egyptian tomb paintings during the Middle Kingdom depict ornamental gardens, and Darius the Great of Persia is reported to have enjoyed a 'paradise garden'. In the fourth century BCE, there were gardens at the Academy of Athens and there's evidence that trees were routinely planted at sites of civic and religious significance – plane trees, the arbutus or strawberry tree, black poplar and cypress.

The study of plants in the eastern Mediterranean from this era would form the basis of botanical knowledge for the next two thousand years or so. And there's plenty of archaeological evidence of ornamental gardens throughout the Roman Empire too – from Hadrian's Villa built in Tivoli around 120 CE, to Fishbourne Roman Palace in

West Sussex, dating from around 75 CE. These traditions continued after the fifth-century Roman decline in Byzantine and Moorish Spain. At the same time, different horticultural traditions were developing in China, and then in Japan.

But to discover one of the first named female gardeners – and one of the first female explorers – we'll need to go to Aotearoa. There are some one thousand islands in the Pacific Ocean, of which New Zealand is the largest. Some were created by volcanic eruption, severe and green; others are low-lying atolls, or sandbanks with white sands and sapphire seas, aquamarine and coral reefs. According to Māori oral history, the first Polynesian explorers reached the southern oceans somewhere around the year 640 CE, voyaging in double-hulled canoes with sails, and navigating by the stars. Six hundred years later, sometime between 1200 and 1300 CE, the first Polynesian seafarers arrived to settle Aotearoa (North Island) and Te Waipounamu (South Island).

Among these courageous explorers was a pioneering female gardener **Whakaotirangi**, who might be the world's first known domestic gardener. She described the techniques she used to plant, grow and store seeds, making it possible for her people to settle in one place rather than having to keep moving when the natural food sources ran out.

Around the same time, in medieval Europe, gardening as a discipline or occupation was very much the province of religious institutions, most famously physic gardens of convents and monasteries. The practice was particularly strong in Languedoc during the period I've written about in *Labyrinth*, where Catharism and the active leadership of female priests – *parfaites* – led to a focus on developing natural remedies. One of the greatest of those Cathar leaders and wise women was **Esclarmonde of Foix** (after 1151–1215), who became a Cathar after she was widowed in 1200. Her name, in Occitan, might be translated as 'light of the world'.

But in terms of pioneering women – explorers, botanists, palaeontologists, anthropologists, interpreters of the natural world – our knowledge was to be transformed in the seventeenth century, an era of exploration and curiosity, of collectors and taxonomy – the naming of things. Two centuries later, women botanists and gardeners would face similar battles to their sisters in medicine, law and academia, in not being allowed to formally train or be accepted as equals with their male counterparts. But during the Enlightenment, and perhaps partly due to the Romantic movement's close connection with the natural world, gardening and travel were seen as suitable and appropriate occupations for a 'lady'.

Maria Sibylla Merian (1647–1717) was a German naturalist, illustrator and explorer. One of the first naturalists to study insects, she travelled to Surinam on the north-east coast of South America in 1699 and published her findings. One of the most significant contributors to the field of etymology, during her lifetime Merian recorded and illustrated the life cycles of some 186 species.

> 'My Journeys were begun to regain
> my health by variety and change of aire
> and exercise . . .'
>
> **Celia Fiennes**

Closer to home, **Celia Fiennes** (1662–1741) is one of the earliest travel writers. In 1684, she set off to explore England on horseback, continuing her peregrinations, on and off, until 1712. The aim of her journeys was for the sake of her health but also to celebrate her native landscape and 'cure the evil Itch of overvalueing fforeign parts'. She was a natural travel writer, enthusiastic about each of the places she visited and describing everything that took her fancy – from Newcastle to Bath, Harrogate to Cornwall. Fiennes wrote up her adventures for private family reading but, in 1812, the poet Robert Southey published extracts, and a complete edition of her writings, *Through England on a Side Saddle*, appeared in 1888. Proof that some of the greatest treasures can be on our own doorsteps, there is a stone memorial to her in Noman's Heath in Cheshire.

> 'True knowledge consists in knowing things,
> not words.'
>
> **Mary Wortley Montagu**

One of the UK's most famous travellers and explorers is **Mary Wortley Montagu** (1689–1762). A poet and writer – also extraordinary for having advocated smallpox inoculation, helping to prepare the ground for Edward Jenner's smallpox vaccine in 1795 – Wortley Montagu wrote about her life with her husband, the British ambassador to Turkey, living in Istanbul and travelling in the Ottoman Empire in the early years of the eighteenth century. Her letters are still a classic of travel writing of the period. Nearly a century later, another aristocrat, the biblical archaeologist **Hester Stanhope** (1776–1839), would follow in Montagu's adventurous footsteps, travelling extensively in the Near and Middle East.

> 'I like travelling of all things; it is a constant change of ideas.'
>
> **Hester Stanhope**

Jeanne Baret (1740–1807) is the first recorded woman to have circumnavigated the globe on a ship. Disguised as a man and calling herself Jean, Baret enlisted as a valet and assistant to Philibert Commerçon, who was the naturalist on board Louis-Antoine de Bougainville's two expedition ships. She was an expert botanist herself. They headed first to Montevideo in Uruguay, rounding the Cape, before arriving in Tahiti in 1768 when it seems – though this part of the story is sketchy – that Baret was unmasked as a woman. They journeyed on to Papua New Guinea, Indonesia, Madagascar and Mauritius. Her life – and their voyages – is the stuff of legend. After Commerçon's death, Baret ran a tavern in the Mauritian capital Port Louis (she was fined for selling alcohol on a Sunday) then returned to France in 1774 or 1775, after a decade of adventures. In 1785, she was given a pension by the Marine Ministry, suggesting her reputation was at least secure in her lifetime. Despite this, although seventy species are named for Commerçon, only one – a variety of nightshade, *solanum baretiae* – honours Baret's extraordinary work.

> 'There, too, in many a sheltered chink
> The foxglove's broad leaves flourished fair,
> And silver birch whose purple twigs
> Bend to the softest breathing air.'
>
> **Dorothy Wordsworth**

MY OWN LITERARY love affair with the Lake District and Newlands Valley began, thanks to my grandmother, with **Dorothy Wordsworth** (1771–1855). My grandmother gave me my first volume of *The Grasmere and Alfoxden Journals* before our Mosse family holiday in 1978. It's here with me now, more than forty years later, on my desk in Sussex, a little battered and weary from travel, but holding so many memories.

Dorothy was born on Christmas Day in 1771 and had a huge influence on her brother's poetry. Virginia Woolf wrote how: 'Dorothy stored the mood in prose, and later William came and bathed in it and made it into poetry.' Though she doesn't seem to have had any ambitions to be a published writer in the same way as her brother, Dorothy left a huge body of work. She was an exquisite nature writer, with a tenderness when describing plants and trees, the light of the moon or the shadows at dusk, that gives character to the living world. An early environmentalist, she was also a radical figure in the growing tradition of women walking – she often walked as much as twenty miles a day. Her *Grasmere and Alfoxden Journals* detail, with an expert eye, her travels in the Lake District, Scotland and, later, in Europe, the colour and song of the birds, the flowers and the light, the heather and the quality of the land underfoot. She is one of our greatest, if unacknowledged, interpreters of nature.

> 'In my youth I dreamed of travelling. In my old age, I find amusement in reflecting on what I have beheld.'
>
> *Ida Pfeiffer*

Born more than twenty-five years after Wordsworth, the Austrian traveller and collector **Ida Pfeiffer** (1797–1858) was also passionate about recording and cataloguing the natural world. Unlike Wordsworth, who wrote mostly about landscapes she knew well from her childhood and adulthood living with her brother, Pfeiffer circumnavigated the world not once, but twice. She's a wonderful example of life beginning at forty – or, in Pfeiffer's case, forty-five. Once her sons were old enough, she left her husband and, in 1842, set off globe-trotting. Her first journey was down the Danube from Vienna to Istanbul, then on to Jerusalem and Egypt. The publication of her memoir of that journey –

A Viennese Woman's Trip to the Holy Land – funded her next expedition. Vienna's Natural History Museum bought more than 700 specimens from her final trip to Madagascar, including 10 species of spiders and 185 species of insects. She died of malaria and was the first woman to be buried in the rows of honoured dead in Vienna Central Cemetery.

One of the most significant women in the history of the United States was the naturalist, explorer and tracker **Sacagawea** (*c*. 1788–1812). A bilingual Shoshone woman, enslaved as a child, she acted as a guide and interpreter to the Lewis and Clark expedition, the US military expedition commissioned by President Thomas Jefferson to explore the Louisiana Purchase and the Pacific Northwest and find a practical route across the western half of the continent. The campaign's secondary objectives were to study the area's plant and animal life, and to establish trade. Despite being pregnant, Sacagawea travelled thousands of miles from North Dakota to the Pacific Ocean, liaising with Indigenous populations. She was the only woman in the expedition and, unlike the male guides, she was not paid . . .

The National American Woman Suffrage Association adopted Sacagawea as a symbol of female independence and fortitude. With sixteen statues to her name, she is one of the most represented women in the US, but there are many troubling aspects to the way her story has been told – not least her misrepresentation and appropriation by successive generations of historians – and a statue of her with Lewis and Clark, depicting her as subservient to the men, was taken down in Charlottesville in 2021. Sacagawea has a place setting at Judy Chicago's *The Dinner Party*.

THERE IS NO collective noun for a group of gardeners or plant hunters, but perhaps we could borrow one that's used for seaweed, reeds and mosses – a clump.

The first of our plant hunters, a near contemporary of Sacagawea, was the field botanist and plant hunter **Ellen Hutchins** (1785–1815). Living in Bantry Bay in Ireland, Hutchins discovered at least seven new species and made a huge contribution to our understanding of seaweeds, lichens, mosses, liverworts and other cryptogams (non-flowering plants), identifying over a thousand plants. She also collected and identified shells. Cursed by ill health, Hutchins corresponded with fellow botanists and it's only thanks to her surviving letters that the extent of her contribution to botany is known. She died at the young age of twenty-nine, after a long illness, and was buried in an unmarked grave in Bantry. Thanks to campaigners, a plaque was erected to her in 2015, two hundred years after her death. Some eight plants are named after her.

From Bantry to County Kerry on Ireland's west coast. More than a hundred years after Hutchins' pioneering work, fellow Irishwoman **Maude Delap** (1866–1953) was the first person to breed jellyfish in captivity. She was also involved in extensive study of plankton off the coast of Valentia Island. Delap had a sea anemone named after her and was made an associate of the Linnean Society of London in 1936.

In 1815, a genus of red seaweed was named after English botanist **Amelia Griffiths** (1768–1858), who identified some 250 species of seaweed along the coasts of Devon, Cornwall and Dorset. She is little known today compared to her West Country neighbour, **Mary Anning** (1799–1847), but it wasn't always so. Anning, who was born in Lyme Regis in 1799, has become a more familiar name in the past few years after enduring hundreds of years of neglect. She was a trailblazing palaeontologist, fossil hunter, dealer and collector, and her work was misattributed to the male collectors to whom she sold her fossils. In 1865, nearly twenty years after her death, an anonymous article appeared about her in *All the Year Round*, the periodical set up by Charles Dickens. In the twenty-first century, after decades of campaigning – and novels, films (though the 2020 film *Ammonite* is heavily fictionalized) and plays celebrating her life and achievements – Anning's reputation has been secured. In 2010, the Royal Society included Anning in a list of ten British women who've most influenced the history of science. The famous oil painting of Anning, with straw bonnet and basket, her fossil-hunting hammer in her hand and her black-and-white dog Tray curled on the ground at her feet, was painted before 1842 and hangs in the Natural History Museum in London. In May 2022, a statue was installed in Lyme Regis after a four-year effort by the Mary Anning Rocks campaign.

Of course, what is also important is not only the collection and classification of plants, but also the way in which they were painted and recorded. The Bristolian watercolourist and artist **Sarah Anne Bright** (1793–1866) was one of our earliest photographers, though it was not until 2015, when her initials were discovered on a photogram, that she received credit for her work. She produced an image 'The Quillan Leaf' in 1839, one of the first ever photograms. Born six years later, the illustrator and botanist **Anna Atkins** (1799–1871) self-published some of her photograms in *Photographs of British Algae: Cyanotype Impressions* in 1843, and contributed to the very first book to have printed photographic images. A skilled artist, she produced detailed engravings of shells for her father's translation of *Genera of Shell*. She also collected and catalogued dried plants and was elected a member of the London Botanical Society in 1839.

By the middle of the nineteenth century, several women were following in the footsteps of Amelia Griffiths and Mary Anning. The British geologist, botanist and mineralogist **Catherine Raisin** (1855–1945) was the first female head of a geology department, and the first woman to be awarded the Geological Society's Lyell Fund. But because women were banned from attending Society meetings, the professor under whom she had studied geology was obliged to accept it on her behalf. In 1889, Raisin became the second woman to be awarded a doctorate by University College London. She spent her entire academic career at Bedford College in London, rising to vice-principal. Passionate about women's opportunities in higher education, Raisin founded the women's discussion group the Somerville Club, became a fellow of the Linnean Society in 1906 and was one of the first female members of the Geological Society – together with **Gertrude Elles** (1872–1960).

The first woman to be awarded a doctorate from University College London was the Scottish palaeontologist and geologist **Maria Ogilvie Gordon** (1864–1939). At the age of eighteen, she left Aberdeenshire to study music in London, before deciding her heart lay in science. Her studies took her to Munich and, in 1891, she was invited to accompany an eminent geologist on a field trip to the Dolomites. Like a character in one of my great-grandmother's novels, Gordon spent her summers climbing and hiking, collecting and studying fossils. In 1893, she published an article in the quarterly journal of the Geological Society, detailing some 354 species of molluscs and corals. She was the first woman to receive a PhD from the University of Munich. Her original manuscript of her findings was lost during the First World War, and when she returned to Munich in 1920, she had to rewrite it from scratch. It was finally published in 1927. She also wrote more than three hundred articles and two guidebooks to the Dolomites and South Tyrol. She was buried in Allenvale Cemetery, Aberdeen. A new fossil fern genus, discovered in the Dolomites, was named after her in 2020, *Gordonopteris lorigae*. As if this was not enough, she was also a campaigner for the rights of women and children, and was involved in the post-First World War negotiations at the Council for the Representation of Women in the League of Nations.

> 'I look upon a year lived as a year earned; and each year earned means a greater treasury of experience and power laid up against time of need.'
>
> ***Anna Botsford Comstock***

In New York State, Gordon's near contemporary **Anna Botsford Comstock** (1854–1930) was concentrating on studying insects rather than plants. One of the world's earliest conservationists, she began by illustrating her husband's books. Having completed a degree in natural history, Comstock began writing herself, including *The Handbook of Nature Study*. She was the first female professor appointed at Cornell University and the mother of what, today, we would call nature studies, taking science lessons out of the classroom and into the field.

On the other side of the United States, horticulturist **Kate Sessions** (1857–1940) was the first woman to graduate from the University of California with a science degree; she then moved to San Diego in 1885 to open a nursery. Known as the 'Mother of Balboa Park', Sessions arranged to lease thirty acres of land from the city council, in exchange for planting one hundred trees a year there and some three hundred more in the rest of San Diego. Single-handedly, she transformed a dry cityscape with almost no plant life into an urban landscape with flourishing green spaces. There is a geranium named for her, as well as schools, a botanical garden, a canyon and a room at a local inn! In 1998, a bronze sculpture by San Diego artist, philanthropist and engineer **Ruth Hayward** (b. 1934) was installed in Balboa Park.

> 'I hope when children see the statue, they get the message that one person can really make a difference.'
>
> *Ruth Hayward*

Meanwhile, in September 1898, an enterprising nineteen-year-old Welsh woman, **Dorothea Bate** (1878–1951), presented herself at the Natural History Museum in London and talked her way into a job. She had no formal qualifications and there were no female scientists working there, yet the curator of birds admired her spirit and gave her a chance. Bate repaid his confidence, working at the museum for the next fifty years and becoming one of the most significant scientists studying ornithology, palaeontology and archaeozoology. The extent of her achievement, succeeding in such a male environment, can be seen in the black-and-white photograph of the geology department of the Natural History Museum taken in 1938. Bate is sitting in the front row, a flower in her buttonhole, one of only three women in the picture. During her long career at the National History Museum, she published some eighty reports and reviews, as well as writing maybe a hundred unpublished papers. On the sixtieth anniversary of her death in December 2017, a blue plaque to Bates's life and work was unveiled at Napier House in Carmarthen, south-west Wales, where she was born.

Born the year after Bate, botanist and historian **Agnes Arber** (1879–1960) was the first woman to receive the Gold Medal of the Linnean Society and the first female botanist elected as a fellow of the Royal Society. Her scientific research focused on flowering plants and, during her long career, she published extensively on both philosophy and botany. Her almost exact contemporary was the Dutch botanist and plant pathologist **Johanna Westerdijk** (1883–1961). Known as 'Hans' to her friends, in 1917 she became the first female professor in the Netherlands at the University of Utrecht. A pioneer in mycology and plant pathology, she also promoted women's opportunities in science. It was Westerdijk who identified the fungus causing Dutch elm disease. It's said that the sign above the door to her laboratory read: FOR FINE MINDS, THE ART IS TO MIX WORK AND PARTIES.

The gloriously named **Thistle Harris** (1902–1990) was an Australian botanist, educator, author and conservationist. For many years, she worked with her husband, naturalist and zoologist David Stead, and after his death in 1957 she bought Wirrimbirra, an estate at Bargo, south-west of Sydney, in order to create a wildlife sanctuary as a memorial to his life and work. She was also active in environmental protests, most notably the campaign to save Lake Pedder in south-west Tasmania. While the campaign failed in its objective to prevent the flooding of the land and lake in 1972, the high-handed destruction of this wilderness had far-reaching consequences. It triggered the foundation of the Tasmanian Wilderness World Heritage Area and helped bring about a major change in public perception. Her step-daughter, David's eldest daughter, was the award-winning novelist **Christina Stead** (1902–1983).

> 'I most carefully confined myself to facts and arranged those facts on as thin a line of connecting opinion as possible.'
>
> *Mary Kingsley*

THE NINETEENTH CENTURY was home to many extraordinary British explorers. **Mary Kingsley** (1862–1900) was an ethnographer and scientific writer who travelled extensively in West Africa. Her near contemporary was the extraordinary **Gertrude Bell**. A diplomat without portfolio, passionate about art and archaeology, Bell's writings about her travels in Mesopotamia, Syria, Palestine and Arabia brought the deserts of the Middle East to life both for British readers and for the government. A hugely influential figure in the story of the foundation of modern-day Iraq, she died in Baghdad in 1926. As mentioned earlier, I was disappointed to learn she was also a founding member of the Women's National Anti-Suffrage League, and its first honorary secretary.

> To wake in that desert dawn was like
> waking in the heart of an opal . . . See
> the desert on a fine morning and die –
> if you can!'
>
> *Gertrude Bell*

Following in Bell's footsteps, a generation later, the Italian-English writer and photographer **Freya Stark** (1893–1993) was an explorer and Arabist, who wrote extensively on her travels in the Middle East and Afghanistan as well as several autobiographical works and essays including *Baghdad Sketches* and *A Winter in Arabia*. She worked for the British Ministry of Information during the Second World War. Stark's final trip was to Afghanistan when she was seventy-five years old. She died in Asolo, northern Italy, a few months after her one hundredth birthday. There is a glorious photograph of her taken by Robert Mapplethorpe in 1975, where Stark is reclining on a sun lounger in a patterned dress and a hat, holding a book in her left hand and a cocktail in her right!

> 'I have no reason to go, except that I have
> never been, and knowledge is better than
> ignorance. What better reason could there
> be for travelling?'
>
> *Freya Stark*

Perhaps a little less well known these days than either Stark or Bell, the naturalist, explorer and writer **Isabella Bird** (1831–1904) was the first woman elected a fellow of the British Royal Geographical Society. Bird climbed mountains in Hawaii, rode over eight hundred miles of the Rocky Mountains in the US on horseback, and travelled through China, Japan and Malaysia taking extraordinary photographs. Her letters to her sister during her American expedition formed the basis of perhaps her most famous book, *A Lady's Life in the Rocky Mountains*. Then, as if she had not achieved enough, she studied medicine so that she could work as a missionary.

Bird arrived in India in February 1889, in her late fifties, still full of enthusiasm and curiosity. She visited missions and founded a hospital, travelled to the border with Tibet, then on through Persia, Kurdistan, Armenia and Turkey. In 1897, now in her sixties, she sailed the Yangtze River in China and the Han River in Korea, then saw in the new century during a last trip to Morocco, where she became ill. Bird returned home and died in Edinburgh in October 1904, having lived life on her own terms. Bird is one of the real-life characters in Caryl Churchill's play *Top Girls*, with much of her dialogue being taken verbatim from Bird's own writings.

> 'I still vote civilization a nuisance, society a humbug and all conventionality a crime.'
>
> **Isabella Bird**

In other parts of the world, women with an independent income were also shedding their domestic responsibilities and setting out to discover the world. After her husband died in 1874, the wealthy Parisian philanthropist **Louise Bourbonnaud** (*c.* 1847–1915) decided to shake off her widow's weeds and travel. She, too, kept copious notes and took many photographs. She began by exploring North America, followed by the Caribbean and then South America, but it's for her writings about Vietnam and its capital city, Saigon, that she is best remembered. Determined to prove how women were capable and independent, she endowed the Louise Bourbonnaud Prize in 1891 in association with the Société de Géographie in Paris, the world's first and oldest geographical society, to honour travellers of French origin.

Belgian rather than French, **Berthe Cabra** (1864–1947) travelled with her husband, a commander in the Belgian Army, and, in 1905, became the first European woman (that we know of) to travel across the whole of central Africa from east to west. A keen collector, she gave items acquired on her journey to the Royal Museum of Central Africa in Flanders. Cabra was given several awards, including the Congo commemorative medal in 1929, and endowed a generous scholarship at the Colonial University of Antwerp.

> 'Nothing in life is to be feared, it is only
> to be understood. Now is the time to
> understand more, so that we may fear less.'
>
> **Marie Curie**

WHEN I WAS a child, I was obsessed by Scott's doomed *Terra Nova* expedition to the Antarctic in 1910. I clearly remember watching a re-run of the 1948 film starring John Mills as Scott with my parents in the 1970s, the curtains drawn on a Sunday afternoon and the soaring, beautiful score by Ralph Vaughan Williams filling the room. I've never been to Antarctica or the Arctic, but have always felt that to travel to these most extreme landscapes of ice and snow must take a very special kind of courage.

The Russian explorer **Maria Pronchishcheva** (1710–1736), who only lived to be twenty-six, is considered the first female polar explorer. Also known as **Tatiana Fyodorovna Pronchishcheva**, she sailed down the Lena River with her husband, from Yakutsk, the coldest major city on earth, which lies about 240 miles south of the Arctic Circle. A bay in the Laptev Sea is named after her. Thirty-three years later, anthropologist and explorer **Aleksandra Potanina** (1843–1893) accompanied her husband on a number of expeditions through Siberia, as well as central Asia and China. Her focus was the regions' indigenous peoples and when *The Buryats* was published in 1887, she was awarded a gold medal from the Russian Geographical Society and was the first woman to be invited to join. A crater on the planet Venus is named after her, as is a glacier in Mongolia.

Ingrid Christensen (1891–1976) was a Norwegian polar explorer who made four trips to the Antarctic with her husband. She was the first woman to see Antarctica, the first to fly over it and one of the first to set foot on the mainland, together with her daughter and two fellow female explorers – **Lillemor Rachlew** (1902–1983) and **Solveig Widerøe** (1914–1989). In 1937, the Four Ladies Bank in Prydz Bay, in eastern Antarctica, was named in honour of this quartet of female explorers.

> 'To aim for the highest point is not the only
> way to climb a mountain.'
>
> **Nan Shepherd**

In the very male world of climbing and mountaineering, three names stand out. The first is the Scottish climber, poet and novelist **Anna 'Nan' Shepherd** (1893–1981). Her beautiful *The Living Mountain*, which came out in 1977, blends ecology and spirituality and puts it at the heart of our relationship with nature.

The second is the extraordinary Japanese mountaineer **Junko Tabei** (1939–2016), who was the first woman to reach the summit of Mount Everest in 1975. Though she studied literature at university, mountaineering was her passion. Battling sexism, Tabei founded the Ladies' Mountaineering Club in 1969 because so many men refused to climb with her. Sixteen years after her triumph on Everest, she became the first woman to complete the Seven Summits – an ascent of each of the highest mountains on every continent. An asteroid, 6897 Tabei, and a mountain range on Pluto, Tabei Montes, are named after her.

The third is the amazing **Hulda Crooks** (1896–1997), who on 24 July 1987 – at the age of ninety-one – reached the summit of Mount Fuji. The 4,326-metre-high Crooks Point is named after her.

FROM THE HIGHEST summits, we now reach up into the air itself with the earliest female aviators.

> 'I've always had the feeling that nothing is impossible if one applies a certain amount of energy in the right direction. If you want to do it, you can do it.'
>
> ***Nellie Bly***

Nearly fifty years after **Ida Pfeiffer**'s double circumnavigation of the world, the American daredevil, investigative journalist and inventor **Nellie Bly** (1864–1922) made her own record-breaking trip around the world in tribute to Jules Verne's 1873 novel *Around the World in Eighty Days*. Commissioned by New York's *The World* newspaper, she beat the fictional Phileas Fogg by eight days. The paper dedicated the whole of its front page on 26 January 1890 to her: 'Nellie Bly Makes the News', screamed the headline, with a cartoon showing Bly in her tweed travelling clothes surrounded by male travellers from history. Another column was headed: 'Father Time Outdone – Even Imagination's Record Pales Before the Performance of the "World's Traveller"'. An extraordinary and intrepid journalist, as well as an explorer, Bly got her major break by pretending to be mad to get herself committed to Blackwell's Island Insane Asylum in 1887 so that she could write an investigative report on conditions there. Bly also reported for the *New York Evening Journal* on the third Suffrage March, where **Alice Paul** (1885–1977) and **Inez Milholland** (1886–1916) led ten thousand women through Washington DC on 3 March 1913:

> 'Picture if you can an endless chain of butterflies, divided into sections according to color fluttering along and it will give a little impression of the parade which made history . . . I was never so proud of women; I never was so impressed by their ability; I never so realized their determination and sincerity. I am glad I am one.'

Most people have heard the name of aviator and pilot **Amelia Earhart** (1897–*c*. 1937), the first woman to fly solo across the Atlantic Ocean and the founder of The Ninety-Nines, an organization for female pilots. Most people also know that she disappeared with her navigator, Fred Noonan, in July 1937, somewhere over the Pacific Ocean near Howland Island and was declared dead eighteen months later. But the New Zealand aviator **Jean Batten** (1909–1982) deserves to be just as much of a household name. She was the first woman to fly solo from England to Australia and back again. Then, in November 1935, she set a new record for flying from England to Brazil. She was also the first woman to fly from England to South America and, in October 1936, flew from New Zealand to England in just over eleven days, a record that remained unbroken for forty-four years. In my favourite photograph of her, Batten is dressed in her fur-lined flying jacket and goggles, holding a bouquet and her black cat Buddy!

> 'Flying does not rely so much on strength, as on physical and mental co-ordination.'
> **Raymonde de Laroche**

Other female firsts in the sky include: **Hélène Dutrieu** (1877–1961) in Belgium; **Raymonde de Laroche** (1882–1919) in France; **Lydia Zvereva** (1890–1916) in Russia; **Bessie Coleman** (1892–1926) in America; **Park Kyung-won** (1901–1933) in Korea; **Kwon Ki-ok** (1901–1988) in Korea; **Amy Johnson** (1903–disappeared 1941) in UK; **Lotfia al-Nadi** (1907–2002) in Egypt; **Hanna Reitsch** (1912–1979) in Germany; **Sarla Thukral** (1914–2008) in India; and **Melody Danquah** (1937–2016) from Ghana.

Pilot, stunt-driver, adventurer, film-maker, the wonderfully named Canadian-American explorer **Aloha Wanderwell** (1906–1996) was the first woman to circumnavigate the globe by car. Between 1922 and 1927, when she was only sixteen, she travelled nearly five hundred thousand miles across eighty countries in a Ford 1918 Model T, beginning and ending her journey in Nice in France. For the next five years she performed on stage, gave travel lectures and, with her husband Walter 'Cap' Wanderwell, made films of their travels. In 1932, her husband was shot and killed on their yacht *Carma* in Long Beach, California. Wanderwell later remarried and continued her travels. A true performer, a true adventurer.

> 'A nomad I will remain for life, in love with
> distant and uncharted places.'
>
> **Isabelle Eberhardt**

TO ACQUIRE KNOWLEDGE, to learn about other cultures and traditions, to broaden one's horizons, the desire to live an unrestrained life – there are myriad reasons why women travelled, why they challenged themselves to go higher, faster, further. Some settled in their new lands, others brought what they had seen and learned home to the country of their origins.

Pioneering landowner and garden designer **Ella Christie** (1861–1949) brought a corner of Japan home to her family estate, Cowden Castle, in Scotland. Much like characters in my great-grandmother Lily's novels, she and her sister were educated at home and made several trips to Europe with their father.

In 1904, Christie headed to India, then in 1905 on to Kashmir,

Tibet, Sri Lanka, Malaya and Borneo – she was the first Western woman to meet the Dalai Lama – writing in her diaries about her adventures and in detailed letters to her sister. In 1907, she went to China, Korea and Japan, where she fell in love with the precision, imagination and formality of Japanese gardens. Three years later, and again in 1912, she travelled in the Russian Empire. The first British woman to visit Khiva in Uzbekistan, she wrote about her trips in *Through Khiva to Golden Samarkand*. She also wrote a cookbook with her sister and a joint autobiography, *A Long Look at Life by Two Victorians*. Christie was one of the first women to be elected to the Royal Scottish Geographical Society in 1913. During the First World War, she ran canteens for the Red Cross on the Western Front and, in 1939, at the outbreak of the Second World War, she published *Ration Recipes* in aid of the Scottish Red Cross.

But Christie is perhaps best remembered for commissioning the great Japanese designer and horticulturist **Taki Handa** (1871–1956) to create a seven-acre Japanese garden at Cowden Castle in 1908. Handa imported plants from her homeland and, when she returned to Japan, Christie employed Japanese gardeners to care for the space. Considered the best Japanese garden in the West – and named *Sha Raku En*, or 'a place of pleasure and delight', by Christie – it was featured in magazines and newspapers throughout the world. After Christie's death in 1949, it was maintained by gardener Shinzaburo Matsuo, who lived and worked at Cowden from 1925 until his death in 1937. After that, the gardens fell into disrepair and were vandalized, before finally being closed to the public. In the last few years, a major fundraising campaign restored the gardens, which opened again in 2019, once again a corner of Japan in the Scottish Highlands.

> 'A garden is a grand teacher. It teaches patience and careful watchfulness; it teaches industry and thrift; above all it teaches entire trust.'
>
> **Gertrude Jekyll**

At the other end of the country, one of the greatest horticulturists and inspirational landscape gardeners of all time was already creating extraordinary spaces. **Gertrude Jekyll** (1843–1932) was a painter, a musician, an embroiderer, a photographer, someone who could work in both wood and metal. Most of all, she was one of our most prolific and mesmerizing garden designers. Over her long life, she created nearly four hundred gardens in Europe, America and the UK, from Lindisfarne to Connecticut, Hestercombe in Taunton to her own house at Munstead Wood, outside Godalming in Surrey. Jekyll bred many new plants, and kept copious notebooks and drawings, published some twenty books and contributed more than a thousand articles to magazines including *Country Life*. She was a talented artist and photographer too, inspired by the Arts and Crafts Movement, and she carried this into her designs, often working with leading architects of the day such as Edwin Lutyens.

There are many photographs of Jekyll, particularly in her later years, with her distinctive walking stick or umbrella in her right hand. But my favourite pictures are two oil paintings by William Nicholson. The first, her official portrait, hangs in the National Portrait Gallery in London and depicts a serious woman, with wire-rim glasses. There is something of the cloister about it. The second is more playful. Painted in 1920, *Miss Jekyll's Gardening Boots* shows only a pair of black, shabby boots, the sole of the left boot coming away from the leather. Dedicated 'For EL', it was a gift to Lutyens.

> 'It sometimes happens that the town child is more alive to the fresh beauty of the country than a child who is country born. My brother and I were born in London . . . but our descent, our interest and our joy were in the north country . . .'
>
> ***Beatrix Potter***

BEATRIX POTTER, OF course, is where this book began. In Newlands Valley with my great-grandmother, and their shared love for Little Town, Catbells and Mrs Tiggy-Winkle. But Potter is included in this chapter because even though she is world-famous for writing thirty books – twenty-three of them for children – she was also a natural scientist, an illustrator, an expert in mycology and a conservationist.

Although Potter grew up in London, she spent childhood holidays in Scotland and the Lake District. Thanks to a legacy from her aunt, and her success as a writer, she was able to buy Hill Top Farm in Near Sawrey, between Hawkshead and Lake Windermere, in 1905. My grandmother remembered meeting her on family holidays and, on the bookshelves in my study, I have some of the original editions of her 'Tales' – *Squirrel Nutkin, Mrs. Tiggy-Winkle, Jeremy Fisher, Jemima Puddle-Duck* and *Pigling Bland* – all hand sewn and with pale hardboard covers, the heavy, shiny white paper marked here and there with children's fingerprints. In 2015, the manuscript for an unpublished book was discovered by a children's publisher in the archives of the Victoria and Albert Museum in London. This newly discovered story – *The Tale of Kitty-in-Boots*, with illustrations by Quentin Blake – was published the following year to mark the 150th anniversary of Potter's birth.

When Potter died in 1943, she left almost everything to the National Trust – four thousand acres of land, herds of cattle and Herdwick sheep, sixteen farms and cottages. This extraordinary gift enabled the land to be preserved and forms a huge part of what is now the Lake District National Park. Her husband continued to run the business until his death in 1945, then bequeathed the remainder of the estate to the National Trust.

Potter's passion for conservation – and for protecting animals and birds – was becoming increasingly common in the late nineteenth century. As so many photographs of those days show, there was a huge fashion for feathers in millinery. Motivated by this, three women – one from Lancaster, one from Manchester and one from Hythe in Kent – co-founded what would go on to become the Royal Society for the Protection of Birds, now the largest conservation organization in the UK.

Appalled by the number of birds killed for their plumage, **Emily Williamson** (1855–1936) asked her friends to sign a pledge that they would not wear feathers, and began campaigning on the issue. In the first three months of 1884 alone, some 350,000 birds from East India, 400,000 from Brazil and West India, and at least 7,000 birds of paradise were brought to the UK for the purposes of fashion. In 1889, Williamson founded the all-female Plumage League from her home in Didsbury, in the southern suburbs of Manchester, in part out of frustration that the all-male British Ornithologists' Union were not doing enough. In 1891, Williamson's group merged with Croydon-based Fur, Fin and Feather Folk, set up by the Belfast-born businesswoman, humanitarian and social reformer **Eliza Phillips** (1823–1916), evangelical Christian **Margaretta 'Etta' Lemon** (1860–1953) and others, including **Winifred Cavendish-Bentinck** (1863–1954), the Duchess of Portland, to form the Society for the Protection of Birds. At its inception, all its members were women.

In 1921, after years of campaigning, the Plumage Act was passed. Despite this triumph of seeing the Act come into law, the names of these three women disappeared from the history books. A successful campaign to honour Williamson led to a bronze statue being commissioned from Sheffield artist **Eve Shepherd** (b. 1976). The statue – which shows Williamson with a copy of the 1921 Act in her hand – will be unveiled at Didsbury's Fletcher Moss Park on 17 April 2023, the anniversary of her birth. As of 2020, the Royal Society for the Protection of Birds (RSPB) looks after two hundred nature reserves in the UK, has an income of £112 million per annum, has twelve thousand volunteers, two thousand employees and 1.1 million members, of which I am one.

It was only thanks to the campaign to erect a statue to Williamson that her great-great niece, Newcastle University's professor of ethology **Melissa Bateson** (b. 1968), discovered they were related: 'It feels like an extraordinary coincidence that both my father and I made our careers studying the behavioural biology of birds without knowing about Emily and her achievements . . . We clearly have birds in our blood.'

Putting women back into history, one statue at a time . . .

> 'The more clearly we can focus our attention on the wonders and realities of the universe about us the less taste we shall have for the destruction of our race. Wonder and humility are wholesome emotions, and they do not exist side by side with a lust for destruction.'
>
> **Rachel Carson**

Working to protect birds in the United States was **Rosalie Edge** (1877–1962), who founded the Emergency Conservation Committee after learning how some seventy thousand bald eagles were being slaughtered in Alaska. Dedicated to protecting all species of birds and animals, both those at risk and those not under threat, Edge ended years of eagle and hawk hunting in a particular section of the Appalachian Mountains by buying the property in 1934 and founding the world's first refuge for birds of prey, the Hawk Mountain Sanctuary. In 1948, she was described in *The New Yorker* magazine as: 'the only honest, unselfish, indomitable hellcat in the history of conservation.' In 1960, the sanctuary gave scientific data to fellow American conservationist and marine biologist **Rachel Carson** (1907–1964), providing crucial evidence of the link between the decline in the raptor population and the unregulated spraying of DDT.

Carson is one of the mothers of the modern environmental movement. She began her career as an aquatic biologist in the US Bureau of Fisheries, but the success of her trilogy of books telling the life story of our oceans enabled her to become a full-time writer: *The Sea Around Us* won a US National Book Award in 1951, followed by *The Edge of the Sea* in 1955 and a reissue of *Under the Sea Wind*, which had first been published in 1941. Her gift was in making science accessible and gripping for the general reader, writing articles under the gender-neutral byline R. L. Carson to get her pro-environment message across. Poetic and inspirational, her writing shimmers with awe and wonder for the natural world.

Carson's most important book was yet to come. In the late 1950s, she turned her attention to the close study of conservation and pollution, especially that caused by indiscriminate use of synthetic pesticides. Raising the spectre of an eerily quiet emergence from winter in a natural world ravaged by humankind, *Silent Spring* was published in 1962 and took the world by storm. One of the foundation texts of conservation, it brought environmental concerns to the attention of a much broader general public and, despite fierce opposition from the chemical companies, as well as repeated attacks both about her health and her sexuality, ordinary people responded. Carson's courage and her refusal to back down helped bring about a reversal in national pesticide policy in the US. In turn, this led to a nationwide ban on DDT and other pesticides, as well as inspiring a grassroots environmental movement that has grown into the global campaign.

All of Carson's books remain in print and, in 1995, her surviving letters to her close friend **Dorothy Freeman** (1898–1978) – *Always, Rachel: The Letters of Rachel Carson and Dorothy Freeman, 1952–1964: An Intimate Portrait of a Remarkable Friendship* – were edited and published by Freeman's granddaughter. Her achievements are all the more extraordinary when set against the terrible struggles she had with her personal life and her health. By 1963, she was suffering with breast cancer and, weakened by radiation treatment, she was unable to accept in person many of the awards bestowed on her, not least the Cullum Geographical Medal from the American Geographical Society. In February 1964, Carson died of a heart attack and complications from her cancer treatment. In 1980, she was posthumously awarded a Presidential Medal of Freedom.

'In every outthrust headland, in every curving beach, in every grain of sand there is the story of the earth.'

Rachel Carson

Critical to our understanding of the oceans was **Marie Tharp** (1920–2006), the oceanographic cartographer who co-created the first scientific map of the ocean floor of the Atlantic. And **Anna Mani** (1918–2001) was an Indian meteorologist, responsible for standardizing drawings for more than one hundred weather instruments. Appointed Deputy Director General of the Indian Meteorological Department, Mani also set up a network of weather stations to measure solar radiation.

The American conservationist **Margaret Murie** (1902–2003), known as Mardy, is seen by many as the grandmother of the conservation movement. Born five years before Rachel Carson, the adventurer and naturalist spent nearly forty years studying wildlife in Alaska and Wyoming. In 1956, she started campaigning to protect Alaska's natural territory, persuading President Eisenhower to allocate eight million acres to create the Arctic National Wildlife Refuge. It is still the largest protected area in the country, providing habitat for a vast range of animals, including polar, grizzly and black bears, wolves, eagles, lynx, moose, caribou, marten and beaver, as well as countless migratory birds. Murie was instrumental in helping to pass the Wilderness Act, which today protects more than one hundred million acres of the United States.

> 'When you realize the value of all life, you dwell less on what is past and concentrate more on the preservation of the future.'
>
> *Dian Fossey*

IN THE TWENTIETH and twenty-first centuries, the conflict between environmental sustainability, land rights, corporate greed, deforestation and poaching has made conservation an ever more dangerous business. **Dian Fossey** (1932–1985), the ground-breaking primatologist and biologist, spent nearly twenty years studying the mountain gorillas of Rwanda. She identified and catalogued aspects of gorilla behaviour, but also witnessed the violence and brutality of poaching, and was perhaps forced to retaliate in kind. She founded the Digit Fund to counteract poaching, destroying traps, encouraging local authorities to enforce anti-poaching laws, identifying perpetrators. Fossey was found murdered in her cabin in the Virguna Mountains in December 1985. The case remains open because the perpetrators have not yet been brought to justice.

Another woman who gave her life for what she believed was the Honduran activist and botanist **Blanca Kawas Fernández** (1946–1995). In the early 1990s, she began working at the Honduran Ecology Association, where she was involved in preserving more than four hundred plant species, flora and fauna, and attempting to protect natural habitats such as coastal lagoons, mangroves and rainforest. In February 1995, she was murdered at her house in Tela, on the north Caribbean coast. Her death led to a change in the law. Because the Honduran authorities were making inadequate efforts to solve the crime, the Centre for International Justice sent a request to the Inter-American Commission on Human Rights, in which they declared the state of Honduras responsible for her murder, and that of two male colleagues. A court ruling in 2009 set international legal precedent that governments must protect environmental activists.

Twenty-one years after Kawas's murder, fellow Honduran activist and indigenous leader **Berta Cáceres Flores** (1971–2016), who ran a successful grassroots campaign to force the world's biggest builder of dams to pull out of building at the Rio Gualcarque, was assassinated in her home by armed intruders. Despite the *Kawas v. Honduras* ruling, twelve land defenders were killed in Honduras in 2014, making it the world's most dangerous country, relative to its size, for those seeking to protect rivers and forests.

Javiera Rojas (*c.* 1979–2021) was a Chilean environmental activist and land defender. Known for taking part in protests against the Prime Thermoelectric project and in the successful campaign to prevent the Tranca dam being built in 2016, she was found murdered in December 2021.

> 'There is still so much in the world worth fighting for. So much that is beautiful, so many people working to reverse the harm, to help alleviate the suffering. And so many young people dedicated to making this a better world. All conspiring to inspire us and to give us hope that it is not too late to turn things around, if we all do our part.'
>
> *Jane Goodall*

British primatologist **Jane Goodall** (b. 1934) is the world's foremost expert on the behaviour and lives of chimpanzees. Equipped with little more than a notebook, binoculars and her fascination with wildlife, Jane Goodall first travelled by boat to Kenya in 1957 and her love affair with the continent of Africa began. In more than sixty years of ground-breaking work, Goodall has campaigned to protect chimpanzees from extinction, and has redefined species conservation to embrace environmental needs.

'We have a responsibility to protect the
rights of generations, of all species, that
cannot speak for themselves today. The
global challenge of climate change requires
that we ask no less of our leaders, or
ourselves.'

Wangari Maathai

Kenyan biologist **Wangari Maathai** (1940–2011) was the first
woman from Africa to win a Nobel Peace Prize, the first female
professor in Kenya and the first woman in all of east and central
Africa to receive a doctorate in biology. She started a movement in
1977 to try to prevent the deforestation that was threatening the
livelihoods of the rural population by encouraging women to plant
trees in their communities. The Green Belt movement spread,
resulting in the planting of more than thirty million trees throughout
Africa.

'Some people say that the climate crisis is
something we have all created. But that is
just another convenient lie. Because if
everyone is guilty then no one is to blame.'

Greta Thunberg

MANY OF THE current leaders of the global environmental movements are courageous and principled women, speaking out despite
the dangers.

They include: **Sônia Guajajara** (b. 1974), leader of the Articulation
of the Indigenous Peoples of Brazil; **Hindou Oumarou Ibrahim**
(b. 1984), a member of the indigenous Mbororo people; **Amelia
Telford** (b. *c.* 1994), an Aboriginal and South Sea Islander activist
who founded the first climate network for indigenous youth; Ugandan
climate justice activist **Vanessa Nakate** (b. 1996); **Luisa-Marie
Neubauer** (b. 1996), who was one of the main organizers of the
Friday school climate strike movement; **Disha Ravi** (b. *c.* 1998), a

founder of Fridays for Future in India; indigenous Brazilian campaigner **Artemisa Xakriaba** (b. *c.* 2000); **Quannah Rose Chasinghorse** (b. 2002), who leads protests against drilling in Alaska; Swedish environmental activist **Greta Thunberg** (b. 2003); Canadian indigenous campaigner **Autumn Peltier** (b. 2004); and India's **Ridhima Pandey** (b. 2008), among many, many more.

Walking in the footsteps of the great activists and adventurers of the past, the fight for the future of our planet is in their hands.

The Watson Family: Harold, Winnie, Sam, Lily, Reggie, Betty (seated on grass),
Ethel and Rex Earle, c. 1903

Lily

In 1909, Lily did an extraordinary thing. She turned away from the Baptist Chapel and joined the Church of England. Though she rarely confided her innermost emotions to paper, you would have thought that something as significant as this would appear in her daily correspondence. But there's nothing. At this moment, when I would again so much like to be inside Lily's head, she is silent. I couldn't find a single letter, sent to Sam or anyone else, about what lay behind this late change of path.

Lily's entire life had been lived as a Nonconformist, a member of a leading Baptist family who chose, almost exclusively, to marry within the faith. Her father was a highly respected and decorated theologian and scholar. In 1870, he published his *The Revised Grammar of the Greek Testament*, served as President of the Baptist Union of Great Britain and Ireland for 1885–6 and, in 1903, his *A Handbook of Church History* appeared. Lily came from Baptist royalty, as if that wasn't a contradiction in this fundamentally egalitarian faith. At the heart of things is a sense of an individual's direct relationship with God, unmediated by a priest speaking Latin, an unshakeable belief that salvation rests in a person's own belief in Jesus and God. Baptists trust in the supreme authority of the Bible and, as a denomination, it is much less hierarchical than either the Catholic or High Anglican Church.

And yet . . .

At the age of sixty, after a lifetime at chapel, Lily became a member of the congregation of the new Church of St Margaret the Queen,

Streatham, and worshipped there for the remainder of her life. Deconsecrated now, it's a magnificent red-brick Grade II-listed Victorian building which must have dominated the landscape before the fields of Streatham Hill were gradually absorbed into the sprawl of London.

It seems astonishing to me that Lily – whose life had been so shaped by Nonconformism – should have changed her theological allegiance. I went back to the letters, rooting out any with a dateline of 1904 or 1905, but still found nothing. A clue to the timing of this might be that both of her parents died in 1905 – her mother Elizabeth in May and her father four months later. I wonder if it was this that gave her the courage – or the freedom – to start thinking about a change? On the other hand, four years seems a long time to wait. Her eldest daughter Ethel had married a Church of England priest in 1898 – and my grandmother, Betty, would follow suit in the wartime summer of 1918 and marry an army chaplain – so I wondered if conversations with her eldest son-in-law might have influenced her, though he rarely appears in letters. A final question: did she try to persuade Sam to join her in Anglican worship? If not, did he support her or did her 'conversion' cause tensions in their marriage?

Considering all this more than a hundred years later, it occurs to me that perhaps the reason is more prosaic. Maybe it was a practical decision rather than one of doctrine? Simply, that this impressive new church had been built on her doorstep and Lily wanted to be part of her local community. To sit side by side with her neighbours in the pews on Sunday. There is no doubt, from the voluntary positions she held and the articles she was writing for *The Girl's Own Paper*, that public service and practical Christianity were fundamental to Lily's life. She had strong beliefs, yes, but she was not by nature sectarian.

There are clues, of course, in her most famous and celebrated novel, published in 1893. I inherited an 1897 edition of *The Vicar of Langthwaite* from my grandmother, Betty. It comes with a Foreword in the form of a letter from Gladstone, several pages of glowing (if often patronizing) reviews and a Preface from Lily herself, once more in that odd third-person voice:

'This story was not written with any intention of embodying a religious polemic in fiction. Such an attempt would be open to at least three objections: it would certainly be inartistic, and it would probably be both dull and unconvincing. The author's first and last desire has been to tell her tale rather than to point a moral. She has, therefore, simply tried to sketch, with fidelity, some aspects of English life which have, as a rule, been ignored by novelists, or deemed only worthy of caricature, and which may yet be found to possess an imaginative charm and pathos of their own.'

This is an excellent justification of fiction – that, through the pages of a novel, we can stand in other people's shoes, we can enliven issues that are complicated or difficult, we can put the lives of those who are under-heard or unheard on the page. It is a fine novel, full of affection for Yorkshire and the mythical Northminster Theological College (modelled on Rawdon College), full of sympathy for the attitudes churchmen hold with regard to 'Dissenters' but alive to their lack of Christian values of tolerance. The rigid puritan Dr Yorke, who is handing over care of his school to a more scholarly successor, is a superb counterpoint to the more emollient Hawthorne. The politics and the petty annoyances of life in a small and secluded community are beautifully drawn. As are the lives of the sisters, aunts and daughters whose opportunities for love and life are curtailed by the toils and enmities of their overbearing male guardians, relatives and tutors. It's a compelling read, with the courage not to contrive an implausible or unconvincing happy ending.

There is drama, there are superbly visual action scenes, there is an underlying sense of the sacrifices to be made for principle and for belief. There is also a strong sense of the values of Yorkshire and a disdain for the glittering society of London and the South. There are passages to rival Arnold Bennett or George Eliot, a writer Lily admired and often quotes.

But, most of all, particularly in the mesmerizing character of Estelle Hawthorne herself – the novel was originally to be called *The Professor's Daughter* – there is a message that true faith lies in the natural world, in creation, not in the fundamentalist theologies of men.

It is a novel, of course, not an autobiography. The characters' actions and opinions belong to them, not to Lily. Even if we do take *The Vicar of Langthwaite* as a plea for faith over the rigidity of doctrine, it doesn't really explain why Lily joined the Church of England so late in her life. But shimmering beneath the surface of the novel is that plea for tolerance, for understanding. I would go so far as to say that Lily believed that all Christians, chapel or church, would surely be reunited at the last.

It was fun, but also strange, for me to read. So much of my historical fiction has, at its heart, faith and the sometimes terrible consequences of faith – usually manipulated by the rich and powerful at the expense of the poor and the voiceless. I've written about Cathar Christian lives in thirteenth-century Languedoc, Huguenot and Catholic lives in fifteenth- and sixteenth-century France and the Netherlands in The Joubert Family Chronicles. I have always imagined myself there, seeing the many ways in which peaceful societies are destroyed, ruled and re-shaped, shipwrecked, by organized religion, on the pretext of religion. Estelle's naive and pure simplicity of faith in *The Vicar of Langthwaite* has much in common with Arinius in *Citadel*, the third in my Languedoc Trilogy, though I wrote the novel many years before I had read any of Lily's fiction. Here, for what it's worth, is the greatest connection between my great-grandmother's work and my own writing. The DNA of family history, perhaps.

I was brought up in the Church of England, in a quiet, unassuming way. Walking across the fields to Fishbourne Church in the summer, the long way round in winter. I was one of the first girls to serve as an acolyte and thurifer in Chichester Cathedral in the 1970s, until suddenly I could no longer say the words and mean them.

Lily's realignment of faith – or, perhaps realignment of worship – was to be a significant moment in the lives of many women in the Watson family. In the mid-1920s, my godmother would first meet Sister Josephine from the Society of the Sisters of Bethany at 'Poplars'. Many years later, having served as a cook in the Honourable Artillery Company and the Civil Nursing Reserve during the Second World War, she would join the order as a novice in 1951, be professed in January 1953 and become Sister Katherine Maryel SSB. A generation later, another of Lily's granddaughters, my aunt, would be one of the first women ordained into the Church of England at Chelmsford Cathedral on 30 April 1994.

Would Lily have been proud of her granddaughter, Margaret? Lily's journalism suggests she believed women's roles within both home and chapel should be nurturing and supportive, rather than taking to the pulpit or the soapbox. But, in her letters, she's affectionate about her daughters and clearly wants them to be happy, so who's to say? Maybe Estelle Hawthorne, whose faith is purest, the least complicated, knows best: 'I have always been taught to believe that our knowledge of religious truth grows from age to age, and that if it is put into creeds, it is like imprisoning something which is growing and alive within a sealed casket.'

Faith is living and evolving, Lily has her heroine assert. Attitudes change, formal structures and traditions can be rewritten. Of many generations of believers and potential priests in the Green, the Watson and the Mosse families, among all of Lily's children and grandchildren, only my Aunt Margaret had a calling.

So FAR AS I can tell, these early years of the twentieth century were settled in the Watson household. The marriage of Lily and Sam had weathered the loss of their youngest son – or, at least, they had learned to live with grief. There were no further financial concerns, there was order and routine. Their other children had all survived to adulthood and some had children of their own – Reggie had four, Harold had three. Winnie married William Schroder Scott in Bombay (now Mumbai) in November 1905, having met her husband by chance on a train in England. As custom dictated, she sailed out to join him.

Scott was working as a manager of the Great Indian Peninsular Railway. I can find no evidence that either Lily or Sam, or both, were at the wedding in India. Winnie's three children – Patrick, Wyndham and Sholto – would be born there, as well as a daughter, Rosemary, who is recorded on the family tree as being born and dying in 1910. And, in the last months of the Great War, Lily's beloved youngest daughter, Betty, would be married according to the rites of the Anglican Church at St Margaret the Queen in July 1918.

In the deed box containing the cache of letters was a heavy cream document with the title: 'Memorandum regarding my daughter Beatrice Elizabeth Watson, July 1893'. A meticulous archivist, Sam had put together folders for Harold, for Winnie, for Leader and for my grandmother, containing letters and notes from them – I assume that the folders for Reggie and Ethel went missing. There are twelve diary entries for my grandmother, the earliest being 2 February 1893 and the last 2 August 1902. In March 1893, Sam wrote: 'It is impossible to say how great a delight this child is to us.' In May 1894, he wrote: 'Lily and I live in the light of her presence . . . really, I sometimes think that no child has ever given us more joy than this darling.' In August 1902, he says that she is 'as sweet as ever'.

I don't know why the entries stopped then, or if there are pages missing. I don't know if my grandmother was aware of how precious she was to her parents – she was born twenty years after their first child and, perhaps, all the more cherished after the death of Leader, especially after everyone else had left home. All the photographs I have of Lily, Sam and Betty in the Lake District bear out that there was an ease in her relationship with her parents. I also have three postcard-sized drawings – each with the heading 'Drawn by Lily Watson to amuse Beatrice 18th July 1894' – with something of the style of *Struwwelpeter*. Also, a scrap of paper with Betty's rather rough seven-year-old's handwritten instruction to 'Keep Your Desk Tidy Please'. Lily has written at the top: 'Left on my desk 27th March 1899'. Clearly, she treasured it enough to keep it.

Thanks to Sister Katherine's scrapbook – and photographs in family albums – there is a glimpse of Betty's wartime wedding, though I have nothing directly from either Lily or my grandmother. Sister Katherine writes how disappointed she and her older sister, Judith, were not to be bridesmaids because of wartime constraints (only Reggie's oldest daughter, Laetitia, was a bridesmaid). But she writes of her excitement of being at 'Poplars' when ladies from St Margaret's came to admire Betty's trousseau: 'There were several people from the Parish also viewing. It was all laid out on beds, and I can remember the embroidery and bunches of violets which Granny had done on some winter nightgowns.'

I have two photographs of the wedding on 4 July 1918, a Thursday afternoon. Holding the brittle photographs in my hands, it's extraordinary how strong that sense of a languid Edwardian summer is. The clothes and the hats, the formal smiles. Meanwhile, on the other side of the Channel, the Australian Corps and US Army infantry, supported by British tanks, were in the process of attacking and taking the town of Le Hammel in northern France. And two weeks later, while my grandparents were at Stair Mill on their honeymoon, climbing Catbells and walking in the footsteps of Dorothy Wordsworth, the last major German attack of the war would begin – the Marne–Reims Offensive – marking the beginning of the end of the war.

Looking at the sepia images of the wedding party taken in the garden of 'Poplars' in July 1918, this all seems very distant. My grandmother's thoughtful and careful expression, my grandfather standing full-square in the garden – on leave from his position as an army chaplain – they appear to me almost like characters in a play. Something like Shaw's *Heartbreak House*, a little exaggerated and not quite real, but full of meaning. This privileged middle-class world is so very removed from the blood and the gas and the mud of the Trenches, the visceral and heartbreaking experiences written about by Vera Brittain, Emma Duffin and **Edith Cavell** (1865–1915). And, as I go back to the album time and again, looking for clues, I also find myself wondering if this is the only positive consequence of the family illness, haemophilia.

Unlike almost every other mother of her acquaintance, Lily did not have to watch her sons put on army uniforms and be sent to the Front. Reggie's and Harold's condition kept them safer than their friends, alongside whom they'd sat in the schoolroom, fingers inked and their primers open. Broken spines of old books, the roll call of that generation of lost boys. Where are they now? Names remembered only as letters and engravings on memorial boards and stone monuments:

Known unto God.

Top: Dhammananda Bhikkhuni (b. 1944)
Bottom: Rose Hudson-Wilkin (b. 1961)

8

Women of Faith

'All shall be well, and all shall be well, and
all manner of thing shall be well.'

Revelations of Divine Love
Julian of Norwich, *c.* 1373

THROUGHOUT HISTORY, RELIGION HAS been both a force for
good and the cause of terrible persecution and destruction. We've
seen how some women were liberated from the strictures of their
times in the quiet of the cloister or mosque or temple, while others
were imprisoned and stifled. We've seen how polytheistic cultures
afforded both women and men leading roles and authority as teachers,
whereas monotheistic cultures very often sidelined women. And we've
seen how male-dominated religious orthodoxies can be used – and
have been used – to oppress women and girls. Finally, of course,
there's the problem of unintended consequences. So many terrible
things have happened because well-intentioned people were unable
to read the future.

My great-grandmother had no doubt. Faith, for her, was Protestant
Christianity – at first, as a Baptist, later as an Anglican, so this chapter
is inevitably particularly concerned with the changing position of
women within Christianity and what that might have meant to Lily.

But what if we think more broadly? What if we separate faith from
organized religion and think instead in terms of mission or vocation,
rather than rigid adherence to one particular creed – Judaism,
Shintoism, Christianity, Hinduism, Islam, Buddhism or Taoism? What
about African Traditional religions or the Baha'i faith? Or Atheism
or Stoicism or Humanism? Any structured philosophical, or perhaps
even psychotherapeutic, framework intended to help humankind
come to terms with the big questions of life and death, and what
happens next? What, then, does faith look like?

'The sad truth is that most evil is done by
people who never make up their minds to
be good or evil.'

Hannah Arendt

IN THE FOUNDING centuries of Christianity – when there were
fierce battles not only between the older religions and the new, but
also within Christianity itself – there are records of women throughout
the Roman Empire being martyred for their faith. The word 'martyr'
derives from the Greek word for 'witness', and we find these women
in Thessaloniki in Greece, Tebessa in North Africa, Mérida in Spain,
in Rome itself.

In second-century Lyon in Gaul, three women were among those
martyred, including a slave, **Blandina** (d. *c.* 162–177 CE), who is said
to have converted many to Christianity. In 180 CE in Carthage, then
part of the Roman Empire in what is now Tunisia, the Scillitan
Martyrs were a group of twelve women and men beheaded after
refusing to recant and deny their faith. And some twenty years later
in the same city, **Vibia Perpetua** (*c.* 182–*c.* 203 CE), a well-educated
and high-born Roman woman, was executed with an enslaved woman,
Felicitas (d. *c.* 203 CE). Perpetua had just given birth and she kept
a diary of her imprisonment, detailing the physical hardships, not
least because she was prevented from breastfeeding her baby. Her
account – *The Passion of Perpetua and Felicity* – represents one of
the earliest Christian testimonies. A few years later in Alexandria, on
the delta of the Nile, we know of the execution of **Potamiaena**
(d. *c.* 205 CE) from the writings of Eusebius. She was martyred, having
endured imprisonment, torture and sexual assault, alongside the
soldier who tried to shield her.

One of the best known of the early Christian female martyrs is
Catherine of Alexandria (*c.* 286–305 CE), better known as **St
Catherine**. Tradition holds that she was a scholar in an influential
family, who became a Christian at the age of fourteen and converted
hundreds to the faith before she was condemned by the Roman
emperor Maxentius to be executed on a spiked wheel, from which
the Catherine wheel firework gets its name (though she actually died

from decapitation when the wheel broke). Catherine is one of the Fourteen Holy Helpers in Catholicism and one of the saints who appeared to Joan of Arc to counsel her.

In the shadow of three mountains in the Sinai desert stands the oldest continuous working monastery in the world, dedicated to St Catherine. The monastery coalesced around a chapel built at the site of the Burning Bush, seen by Moses, and the Well of Jethro. The pilgrimage site was fortified on the orders of Justinian I in 527 to preserve it. On 30 December ten years ago, I joined a coach excursion to visit the monastery.

Driving for hours through the arid landscape, oppressed by the silence and the granite face of Mount Sinai and Mount Horeb, the sweep of the sand dunes touched with occasional patches of vegetation, it felt as if I was slipping back through time. Once we arrived, I felt even more disassociated from the modern world. The monastery complex is filled with colour and contrast – icons and sunlight through stained glass, shaded corridors lit by heavy hanging lamps, with a basilica and a mosque. A site revered by Christianity, Islam and Judaism, it houses the world's oldest-surviving operating library, with priceless books in many ancient languages – Hebrew, Greek, Arabic, Syriac, Christian Palestinian Aramaic, Georgian, Ge'ez, Latin, Armenian – including a fragment of the *Codex Sinaiticus* and a letter from the Prophet Muhammad to the monks of the monastery dated 628, written just four years before he died.

One of the earliest records we have of the monastery is written by **Egeria** or **Etheria** (fourth century CE). An early Christian writer and traveller, originally from Galicia or Gaul (Spain or France), she wrote a detailed account of a pilgrimage to the Holy Land in around 381–386 for her 'sisters' back home: 'Ladies, light of my eyes, deign to remember me, whether I am in the body or out of the body.' It's a moment in history I've written about in my 2012 novel *Citadel*, when the idea of pilgrimage, of building a global Christian community, was becoming popular for those with the resources to fund such journeys.

Written in Latin, *The Travels of Egeria* is the earliest surviving account of a Christian pilgrimage and she writes about visiting Sinai and seeing the 'Burning Bush' in the year 382. Only one incomplete eleventh-century manuscript has survived, transcribed into the eleventh-century Codex Aretinus 405, and it begins in the middle of a sentence. Eleven short quotations were also found in a ninth-century manuscript from Toledo. But these fragments do give a flavour of her voice. Egeria is a wonderful narrator, detailed and curious. She stayed in Jerusalem for three years, visiting Jericho, travelling to the tomb of Job in modern-day Syria, to Mount Nebo, to the Sea of Galilee. Just imagine her courage – a woman travelling alone to Constantinople, Jerusalem and Mesopotamia, and home again.

> '. . . meanwhile, as we journeyed, we arrived at a certain place where the mountains through which we were going opened up and made an immense valley, huge, very flat, and quite beautiful, and across the valley appeared the holy mountain of God, Sinai.'
>
> *from* **The Travels of Egeria**

WHILE I WAS researching this chapter, I was still trying to make sense of Lily's decision to exchange chapel for church. I realize, of course, my own experiences have led me to include more women from Christianity than other world religions. As someone who was brought up in a Church of England background, some of my earliest strong female role models were women from the Old Testament – for example, Deborah from the Book of Judges, a prophetess, military leader and the only female judge. It was years before I discovered how women's writings had been deliberately left out of the collection of books that became the Christian Bible – in other words, realizing that it was a selection of writing, actively chosen for a reason and with an agenda, rather than a single, unified text. It was later still that I understood that other texts – such as the Book of Esther – were, in fact, keystone texts appropriated from the Jewish Bible, the *Tanakh*.

In earlier chapters, we've met women from beyond the Christian world – the polytheistic religions of Ancient Egypt, Greece and the Indian subcontinent, from Islamic, Jewish, Hindu and Sikh as well as Christian traditions. Women writers, leaders, travellers, doctors, teachers, suffragists, conservationists for whom the framework of faith provided strength and courage to achieve whatever they wanted to achieve. In most instances, in pretty much all faith systems, the organized or state religion favours men significantly over women. In patriarchal societies, women are at best tolerated or, at worst, are second-class citizens, and little evidence of women's lives will have survived. But, as with every other area of female endeavour, women of faith have always sought to fulfil their mission.

> 'All you need to know is that the future is wide open and you are about to create it by what you do.'
>
> ### Ani Pema Chödrön

In Nepal, the aunt and foster mother of the Buddha, **Mahaāpajāpati Gotamī** (sixth century BCE), was the first woman to receive Buddhist ordination, becoming a bhikkhuni. In Sri Lanka, **Saṅghamitrā** (third century BCE) was a royal princess who became a nun when she was eighteen years old and Sanghamitrā Day is celebrated as a national holiday. In Tibet, Tibetan Buddhist leader **Machig Labdrön** (1055–1149) was said to have been a leader in the eleventh century. American nun **Ani Pema Chödrön** (b. 1936), born **Deirdre Blomfield-Brow**, was ordained as a bhikkhuni within Tibetan Buddhism in 1981. In Thailand, women had been forced to go to India or Sri Lanka to be ordained since a 1928 law was passed banning women's full ordination. In the twenty-first century, though, women have been challenging the ruling. In December 2018, Thai businesswoman **Boodsabann Chanthawong** (b. 1970) was one of twenty-one women to swap her white prayer robes for the distinctive saffron robes of a Buddhist monk. Defying generations of Thai Buddhist tradition, she was ordained as a novice monk at the Songdhammakalyani monastery, an unrecognized all-female monastery outside Bangkok. The abbess of the monastery, **Dhammananda Bhikkhuni** (b. 1944), was ordained in Sri Lanka in 2011, making her Thailand's first woman to receive full monastic ordination. The first female monk ordained in Thailand was **Varanggana Vanacivhayen** (b. 1947) in 2002.

'I'm just a small crack in the wall; the wall
of patriarchy; on the wall of the hierarchy;
on the wall of injustice. Soon there will be
more cracks and someday the wall will fall.'

Dhammananda Bhikkhuni

THE PROBLEM WITH gathering information about early female religious leaders is, in part, our old friend archival silence. If women were leading religious communities, often it was in secret and there were no records. Or else, even if there were records, many have been lost or even destroyed. But in every religious tradition some names survive. For example, in India there is a school of thought that claims that **Prajnātārā** (fifth century CE), the twenty-seventh Indian Patriarch of Zen Buddhism, might have been a woman. Perhaps the main reason for this suggestion is that the ordination name combines the names of two female Buddhist deities. Two centuries later or more, **Andal** (seventh or eighth century CE) was the only woman among the twelve Alvar saints of south India. In thirteenth-century Japan, the first female Zen master was one of the first Japanese abbesses, **Mugai Nyodai** (1223–1298). Was each of these woman a 'black swan', unique and inexplicable? Or, if there was one, might there also have been more?

'And so it was twenty years and more from
the time that this creature first had feelings
and revelations before she had any written.
Afterwards, when it pleased our Lord, he
commanded and charged her that she should
have written down her feelings and
revelations, and her form of living, so that his
goodness might be known to all the world.'

Margery Kempe

I KNOW FROM her letters that Lily hugely admired **Margery Kempe** (*c.* 1373–after 1438), as did my grandmother, Betty.

An English Christian mystic, Kempe was unusual in that she was married – she had at least fourteen children – rather than being a nun or abbess. I've inherited a battered old edition of *The Book of Margery Kempe*, handed down to me from my grandmother who, in turn, had been given it by Lily. Possibly the first autobiography in the English language, it chronicles Kempe's domestic life – pregnancies, births, business in her native Lynn (now King's Lynn), but also pilgrimages to holy sites in Europe and the Holy Land. Kempe was arrested many times for the heresy of Lollardy – the Lollards were followers of John Wycliffe who tried to live a life of contemplation and poverty inspired by Christ – and might well have suffered from postpartum depression. She could not read or write, so dictated her visions to be transcribed, often speaking of herself in the third person. Kempe was a contemporary of the mystic and anchorite **Julian of Norwich** (1343–after 1416) and is known to have received counsel from her.

> 'Truth sees God, and wisdom contemplates
> God, and from these two comes a third,
> a holy and wonderful delight in God,
> who is love.'
>
> **Julian of Norwich**

Sometimes also known as Juliana, she lived most of her life in seclusion as an anchoress – a kind of hermit within sight – in a cell attached to the Church of St Julian of Norwich. She, too, experienced visions after a life-threatening illness when she was thirty and wrote two versions of *Revelations of Divine Love*, the second – the Long Text – some twenty years after the first. A profound work of Christian theology, covering all manner of religious and mystic experiences, to the existence of evil and the nature of God, it is one of the earliest surviving documents authored by a medieval woman and the only surviving document of the period by an anchoress.

> 'God has given me the bread of adversity
> and the water of trouble.'
>
> **Anne Askew**

Born nearly a century later, the Protestant martyr **Anne Askew** (1521–1546) was a woman of deep conviction who would ultimately die for her faith. Condemned as a heretic at the end of the reign of Henry VIII, Askew is the only woman on record known to have been both tortured in the Tower of London and burnt at the stake. She's also one of the earliest known female poets to compose in vernacular English – and, by the by, the first Englishwoman to demand a divorce using scripture to justify her case.

Askew is one of the most significant writers of the English Reformation yet most often overlooked. In part, this might be because of the legacy of her martyrdom, which erased everything else about her life. Her case was featured prominently by John Foxe in his extremely biased *Actes and Monuments*, usually known as *Foxe's Book of Martyrs*. Also, there is evidence that the publisher of her memoir *Examinations*, John Bale, interposed many of his own, often misogynistic views into the text. *Examinations* chronicles Askew's relentless persecution and gives an unparalleled insight into the lives of women in the sixteenth century in England. Though it's a book of great honesty and fortitude – and her courage shines from every page as she details her confrontations with male authority figures who picked over every aspect of her life, looking for pretexts to condemn her, from her progressive divorce, to her unorthodox religious beliefs – it's clear that her words have been edited and adapted.

A generation later in York, a Roman Catholic martyr, **Margaret Clitherow** (1556–1586), was pressed to death in 1586, despite being pregnant, after she transformed her home into one of the most important hiding places for Catholic priests in the north of England. Known as the 'Pearl of York', her house on the Shambles has since been turned into a shrine and it holds her preserved hand as a relic. She was canonized in 1970.

Some six years after Clitherow's execution, **Walatta Petros** (1592–1642) was born into a high-ranking family in the ancient Christian kingdom of Ethiopia, one of the first countries in the world to officially adopt Christianity as the state religion. Legend has it that the Ark of the Covenant – the chest described in the Book of Exodus that is supposed to have contained the tablets of stone holding the Ten Commandments given by God to Moses – is held in a treasury beside the Church of Our Lady Mary of Zion in Aksum, at the heart of the ancient first-century Aksumite kingdom. The Ark was believed to have been stolen from Jerusalem in the tenth century BCE by Menelik, the son of Solomon and the Queen of Sheba.

Walatta Petros was married to one of the emperor's counsellors, but became a nun after her three children died in infancy. Later, she led a non-violent protest against the Jesuits, who were trying to impose their brand of Catholicism over Ethiopia's older traditions. What little we know comes from *The Life and Struggles of Our Mother Walatta Petros*, which was written in Ge'ez in 1672 by one of her disciples, and is one of the earliest surviving biographies of an African woman.

WHEN I WAS researching grail legends for my 2005 novel *Labyrinth*, I became fascinated by many of these interconnected origin stories. The line between history and mythology is very blurred, but we do know that there was an ancient and isolated Jewish community living between modern-day Tigray and Amhara, which almost certainly pre-dated the arrival of Christianity. Previously known by the derogatory term Falasha Jews, they are now known as Beta Israel.

As with all major religions, things change and evolve over time. Groups that were united divide into separate communities. Within Judaism, the world's oldest enduring monotheistic religion, there has been a steady change in the role and position of women as faith leaders, particularly during the twentieth and twenty-first centuries. But this evolution has deep roots.

In the sixteenth century, in what is now Kurdistan, **Asenath Barzani** (1590–1670) was a Jewish-Kurdish poet and theologian. One of the first women acknowledged as a rabbinical scholar, she is buried beside her father in Amadivah in northern Iraq. Their grave became a pilgrimage site for many Jewish travellers. Three centuries later, **Hannah Rachel Verbermacher** (1805–1888) was born in a shtetl in Ludmir, in what is now north-western Ukraine. Sometimes known as the 'Maiden of Ludomir', she is considered the only independent female rebbe, spiritual leader, in the history of the Hasidic Jewish movement.

'History takes time. History takes memory.'

Gertrude Stein

THE PIONEERING WOMAN considered to be the forerunner of the first woman rabbi in the United States is **Rachel 'Ray' Frank** (1861–1948). The daughter of Polish immigrants who settled in California, Frank taught at Oakland's Sabbath school – one of her students was the writer Gertrude Stein – while working as a newspaper correspondent. A skilled public speaker, Frank delivered a sermon on the eve of Yom Kippur, the Jewish Day of Atonement, when visiting Spokane in September 1890, thereby launching her career as 'the Girl Rabbi of the Golden West'. Frank spent much of the next decade travelling, speaking in both Reform and Orthodox synagogues, giving sermons, officiating at services and reading scripture. Although the newspaper headlines referred to her as a rabbi – an article on 19 October 1898 in the *San Francisco Chronicle* was headlined: 'First Female Rabbi – A California Girl to be so Ordained' – Frank always denied she had any desire for ordination. It's possible that the lack of an established Jewish community and leadership on the West Coast contributed to Frank's opportunities to take to the pulpit, but it's no doubt she opened the door for those women coming after her.

The world's first acknowledged female rabbi was **Regina Jonas** (1902–1944), who was ordained in Germany in 1935. Yet her extraordinary achievement was all but lost to history until the 1970s.

In her bid to be ordained in 1930, Jonas wrote a thesis: 'Can a Woman Be a Rabbi According to Halachic Sources?' Her conclusion, based on biblical, Talmudic and rabbinical sources, was that she could. After five years of teaching religious studies and giving 'unofficial' sermons, many about the importance of women within Judaism, a liberal rabbi decided to go against opposition and ordain Jonas. Despite this, Berlin's Jewish community were unwilling to accept a woman rabbi and there's evidence that she was considering emigrating to Palestine, some years before the foundation of the state of Israel.

In November 1942, Jonas was arrested by the Gestapo and deported to Theresienstadt Ghetto, where she worked as a rabbi for two years and was part of the Jewish Council, until she was deported with the majority of the Council to Auschwitz in June 1944 and put to death at the age of forty-two. For some reason, none of the hundreds of people who lectured and spoke in Theresienstadt mentioned Jonas's name or work, and her contribution was erased until a throwaway comment in *The American Israelite* in 1973, following the ordination of rabbi **Sally Priesand** (b. 1946). Priesand was America's first rabbi in the Reform movement and the article mentioned that the only other known Jewish woman to receive ordination had been 'Regina Jonas of Berlin'.

Even so, it wasn't until nearly twenty years later, once the archives were opened after the fall of the Berlin Wall in 1991, that a brilliant piece of academic detective work led **Katharina von Kellenbach** (b. 1960) to discover Jonas's writings. A German-born researcher and lecturer in the department of philosophy and theology at St Mary's College of Maryland, von Kellenbach had travelled to Berlin to research attitudes of both the Protestant and Jewish religious establishments to women seeking ordination in the 1930s. In the newly available archives, she found two existing photos of Jonas, as well as her rabbinical diploma and seminary dissertation. It's another reminder of the importance of preservation and excavation. Women bringing other women's stories back to life.

> 'We all, I think, believe in compassion. If you look at all the world religions, all the main world religions, you'll find within them some teaching concerning compassion.'
>
> ***Jackie Tabick***

To finish this section, a few more rabbinical firsts. **Sandy Eisenberg Sasso** (b. 1947) was the first female rabbi in Reconstructionist Judaism. **Amy Eilberg** (b. 1954) was the first female rabbi ordained in Conservative Judaism and **Sara Hurwitz** (b. 1977) is considered to be the first female Orthodox rabbi. **Naamah Kelman-Ezrachi** (b. 1955) was the first woman in Israel to become a rabbi and **Shira Marili Mirvis** (b. 1980) became the first woman to hold the sole position of leader of an Orthodox community in Israel in 2021. **Jackie Tabick** (b. 1948) became Britain's first female rabbi in 1975.

∞

IN ALL RELIGIONS, there are schisms and breakaway groups. There are those who wish to preserve the traditions of the past, as if set in stone – literally, in some cases – and others who think faith and thought are always evolving as the world itself ages and transforms. In Hindu temples and Islamic mosques, women are making their voices heard and fighting for their vocation to be accepted and valued on the same terms as their male counterparts.

Within Hinduism, in many corners of the world a quiet revolution is underway to allow women to become priests, particularly in regions such as Pune in Maharashtra, where **Savitribai Phule** founded her first girls' school, and the south-western state of Kerala. Meanwhile, in 2010, Leicester's **Chanda Vyas** (*c.* 1952) was appointed the UK's first female Hindu priest. In contrast, the Catholic Church still does not permit women to be ordained. Within women-only mosques – from America to China to the UK – women are now leading prayers. Organizations such as the Inclusive Mosque Initiative established in London in 2012 and its current director **Naima Khan** (b. 1972) offer a space for worship without gender segregation. The African American Muslim theologian **Amina Wadud** (b. 1952) made headlines around the world in 2005 when she first led gender-mixed Friday prayers in New York. She continues to campaign for gender equality within Islam throughout the world.

> 'So while I am Muslim and now feminist, I only became a feminist when I could help to construct the understanding of Islamic feminism as both an affirmation of my faith and of my humanity and a movement towards the equality for all.'
>
> **Amina Wadud**

OBSTACLES PUT IN front of women of faith is nothing new. The pendulum swings . . . Different countries, different interpretations of religious texts, different times, but the same story prevails.

After the Reformation and bloody wars of religion that raged throughout Europe in the fifteenth and sixteenth centuries, there were many male priests who actively preached against women's leadership within the Christian Church. In Scotland in 1558, the founder of the Scottish Presbyterian Church, John Knox, published his notorious pamphlet *First Blast of the Trumpet Against the Monstrous Regiment of Women*. He wrote:

> 'To promote a woman to bear rule, superiority, dominion, or empire above any realm, nation, or city, is repugnant to nature; contumely to God, a thing most contrary to his revealed will and approved ordinance; and finally, it is the subversion of good order, of all equity and justice.'

Knox's extraordinary attack – betraying, surely, a fundamental insecurity, might have been triggered by the reign of **Mary I** and the restoration of Catholicism in England, coupled with his antagonism to **Mary Queen of Scots** (1542–1587), also known as **Mary Stuart**, and the knowledge that **Elizabeth** was next in line for the English throne. But his misogynist ideas about the ability of women were far from new. In early Christian thought, there were important women writing and teaching. But, as the Church structures and hierarchy became formalized, opposition to women intensified. Perhaps it's no wonder that during the seventeenth century, several women formed new sects or religious movements rather than submit to the status quo.

> 'What matters to God is your intention.
> Your intention is what God accepts.
> Marriage is useless, for your intention is
> what God accepts. Baptism is useless, for
> your intention is what God accepts.
> Confessions are useless, for your intention
> is what God accepts.'
>
> **Kimpa Vita**

In central Africa, **Kimpa Vita** (1684–1706) was the founder of her own Christian sect, Antonianism, based on the teachings of St Anthony. She preached that Christ, and other early Christian leaders, originated from the Kingdom of Kongo – a flourishing economy based on trading in ivory, copper, salt, cattle and slavery. The country was a battleground between indigenous rival tribes, then Portuguese and Dutch colonizers. Brought up in the Jesuit Catholic tradition, Vita is considered by many to be an early anti-slavery campaigner. She challenged the male priests and governors of the time and has often been described as the 'Congolese Joan of Arc' – not least because she claimed her authority came from visions. She was sentenced to be burnt at the stake as a heretic by an ecclesiastical tribunal, in July 1706.

IN MY FICTION, I've written a great deal about heresy and how allegations of heresy were used to control, undermine and destroy. Often, the infraction seems so very small. The differences between various Protestant denominations can sometimes seem very slight to outsiders too, from being a Baptist to becoming an Anglican, say, as in Lily's case. But they are often considered to be fundamental, deal-breakers. And often, the newer denominations focus more on the individual and less on religious hierarchies.

Quakerism is a good example of this. The Society of Friends was founded in England in 1652, based on principles of simplicity, peace, integrity, community, equality and stewardship, coupled with a sense that human beings are inherently good. The Quaker name came from the nature of their worship at that time, distinguished by violent tremblings and quaking caused by the intensity of their religious experience. Quakers were persecuted by the Puritan majority, who believed – essentially – that they were heretics. Jews, Muslims and Hindus, as well as any Christian who was not an Anglican – Catholics, Lutherans, Anabaptists, Ranters – were all, to their mind, heretics. As with almost all religious dissent, it was a matter of power, of loyalty to the state, rather than a matter of personal faith.

Nottingham preacher **Elizabeth Hooton** (1600–1672) was the first female Quaker minister. Imprisoned and tortured for her beliefs, she was one of the group of travelling preachers in the north of England known as the Valiant Sixty. She later crossed the Atlantic to New England, where Quaker communities were also under attack from the settler Puritans. The death penalty for blasphemers had been revoked, but the 'Cart and Tail Law' was a common punishment – those condemned were stripped to the waist, tied behind a cart and dragged from town to town, where they were whipped with a knotted rope.

> 'We are all thieves;
> We are all thieves;
> We have taken the scripture in words, but
> know nothing of them in ourselves.'
>
> ***Margaret Fell***

In Westmoreland, **Margaret Fell** (1614–1702) was imprisoned in Lancaster Castle, possibly along with her six daughters, for preaching and organizing Quaker prayer meetings. In her 1666 tract *Womens Speaking Justified*, she argued that although St Paul had spoken out against women preaching, he had said nothing about the Holy Spirit speaking 'through' women. It's thought that Fell's success and popularity gave rise to one of Samuel Johnson's more regrettable comments, as reported by his biographer, James Boswell: 'I told him I had been that morning at a meeting of the people called Quakers, where I had heard a woman preach. Johnson: "Sir, a woman's preaching is like a dog's walking on his hind legs. It is not done well; but you are surprised to find it done at all."'

Bathsheba Bowers (1671–1718) was born into a Quaker family in Massachusetts, later living in Pennsylvania and South Carolina. A vegetarian and a gardener, she became a preacher only reluctantly, partly in the face of the growing Puritan persecution of Quakers. Her only surviving work is *An Alarm Sounded to Prepare the Inhabitants of the World to Meet the Lord in the Way of His Judgments* (1709). It was part autobiography and part statement of faith, and Bowers was considered an eccentric.

> 'Do all your work as if you had a thousand
> years to live; and as you would if you knew
> you must die tomorrow.'
>
> ***Mother Ann Lee***

By the mid-eighteenth century, Quakerism in the UK had moved away from physical manifestations of worship, except for one group in Manchester. They split from the mainstream in 1747 and became known as the 'Shaking Quakers'. **Ann Lee** (1736–1784) and her parents were members of this congregation. In 1770, having given birth to four children, all of whom died, Lee had 'a special manifestation of Divine light', and became leader of the Shakers. Four years after that, Mother Ann Lee, as she became known, had another revelation directing her to establish a Shaker Church in America. She and her followers set sail for New York in May 1774, where she went on to found a new community in Albany County and preached there until her death.

Born fourteen years after Lee's death, **Nakayama Miki** (1798–1887) also founded a new religion, Tenrikyo, in Japan in 1838. Miki's followers believed she was a living goddess with powers to heal. Tenrikyo's aim is the promotion of a 'joyous life' based on charity and what today we'd call mindfulness. Despite this, Miki was persecuted and arrested for establishing a religious group without authorization.

The first major religion founded by an American woman was the Church of Christ, Scientist, established by **Mary Baker Eddy** (1821–1910) in New England in 1879, with a focus on healing through Bible study and the sharing of testimony.

In nineteenth-century Australia, there were women also leading church communities in established branches of Christianity. **Sarah Jane Lancaster** (1858–1934) was the leader of Australia's first Pentecostal congregation. Pentecostalism is a form of Christianity that emphasizes the work of the Holy Spirit over ritual, and Pentecostals believe in speaking in tongues and the power of direct and physical worship. They have some similarities to the Shakers. An evangelical preacher, Lancaster printed tracts and pamphlets, published a magazine, and led the movement to have Pentecostalism recognized as a religious denomination in law.

Meanwhile, in 1873, **Martha Turner** (1839–1915) became the first female minister in Australia in the Unitarian Church. Unitarians do not believe in the Holy Trinity, but worship God alone as a single entity. Like the Quakers, they do not accept the concept of original sin – that is, Eve's taking of the fruit from the tree in the Garden of Eden – or of eternal punishment for sins committed on earth.

∞

WHILE I'M SURE Lily would believe in the concept of sin, would she also have subscribed to the doctrine of original sin? Possibly. Baptists consider the Bible the sole authority for how to live a good Christian life. They were missionaries, taking the word of God all over the world. The concept of a family is important, too. Like the Cathars in thirteenth-century Lombardy and Languedoc, the Church is not so much represented by a particular place or building, but rather a family of believers, committed to Christ, to one another and to the service of God in the world.

> 'Nobody pointed out to me that the ministry was taboo for women!'
>
> *Violet Hedger*

All the same, things were changing within the Baptist Church in step with wider society. Having left Rawdon in 1876, Reverend Green had continued to build his reputation as a preacher. In 1883, he became the first Ridley lecturer at Regent's Park College in London. Lily's eldest brother, Samuel Green, also taught at Regent's Park College between 1878 and 1925. It was there, in September 1919, that **Violet Hedger** (1900–1992) would begin her studies, making her the first woman to enter a Baptist college to be trained for ministry.

Did Lily's brother know Hedger, or teach her? Did he welcome her? In an interview in the *Baptist Times* to mark her ninetieth birthday, Hedger talked about the opposition she faced from tutors, fellow students and even her own family. All the same, Hedger graduated in 1923, was ordained and inducted in 1926 at Littleover in Derbyshire and, from 1934 to 1937, was minister of North Parade, in Halifax, making her the first sole pastor in charge of a church. She was the first woman to conduct a broadcast service in Britain in March 1937, then served in Chatham in Kent throughout the Second World War, preaching alongside Anglican priests in pubs and clubs, and in the open air.

Outside of the Baptist Church, other Protestant denominations, during the course of the 1930s and 1940s, began to ordain female ministers for pragmatic reasons, not least to compensate for the lack of male priests to minister to congregations during the Second World War.

THINGS MOVED MORE slowly within the Anglican Church. The Movement for the Ordination of Women (MOW) – which followed in the footsteps of the 1930s Church League for Women's Suffrage – was founded in the UK in the late 1970s, following the decision in 1978 by the Church of England General Synod – yet again – to refuse women's ordination. At the same time, a similar group was being formed in Australia by doctor and campaigner **Patricia Brennan** (1944–2011). Their persistence and commitment to their calling paid off. Finally, in 1992, the General Synod in the UK voted in favour. Two years later, the first thirty-two women were ordained priests in the Church of England at Bristol Cathedral on 12 March 1994. The oldest was sixty-nine, the youngest was thirty. A plaque was erected to mark the historic occasion, but there was a problem. In 2022, the plaque was removed and a wry notice put up to explain why . . .

> 'The reason that the original plaque is being replaced is that it did not mention any of the women who were ordained. Instead it mentioned the men that ordained them. The new plaque has the names of all those ordained on it . . . The new plaque will be slightly bigger than the old plaque.'

Artist and Church of England ordinand **Robyn Golden-Hann** (b. *c.* 1965), a traditionally trained stonemason and former head carver at Salisbury Cathedral, carved the new plaque from Welsh slate. It was unveiled by the Bishop of Bristol, **Vivienne Faull** (b. 1955), in March 2022, perhaps with a twinkle in her eye at the irony of it, to mark the twenty-eighth anniversary of the historic event.

> 'I refuse to believe in a God that doesn't care about the diminishing state of my race.'
>
> ***Eve Pitts***

Eve Pitts (b. 1952), the first Black female vicar in the United Kingdom, was also ordained in 1994. Born in Jamaica, Pitts moved to England to join her parents when she was twelve. Her first church was in Bartley Green, Birmingham, a notorious pocket of National Front activity at the time. A fearless and fierce campaigner against racism within the Church and the legacy of slavery, since 2015 Pitts has been campaigning for the Church of England to recognize 1 August as Emancipation Day, marking the day in 1834 that the Slavery Abolition Act came into force in British overseas colonies. She is currently vicar of Holy Trinity Church in Birchfield.

> 'I am very conscious of all those who have gone before me, women and men, who for decades have looked forward to this moment.'
>
> **_Libby Lane_**

The first female bishop, **Libby Lane** (b. 1966), who was elected to the House of Bishops in 2015 and appointed Bishop of Stockport, was also ordained a priest in 1994. **Rose Hudson-Wilkin** (b. 1961) was appointed Bishop of Dover in 2019, the first Black female bishop in the UK, a full thirty years after **Barbara Harris** (1930–2020) was appointed bishop of the Diocese of Massachusetts in the US. The first Black female bishop in Africa was **Ellinah Wamukoya** (1951–2021), appointed to the Diocese of Swaziland in 2012.

More names to be engraved on the wall and recorded in our books.

ON 30 APRIL 1994, a few weeks after that first women's ordination service in Bristol, I was one of a huge congregation of family and friends who gathered in Chelmsford Cathedral to see my aunt **Margaret Booker** (1920–2012) and fifty-two other women ordained. The first woman licensed as a lay reader in Ely Diocese, in 1971, my aunt had been ordained as Deaconess in 1983 and Deacon the following year. Finally, in 1994, and approaching her seventy-fourth birthday, she was to be a priest in her own right. For her entire life,

she'd had a calling and faith. My cousin Anne Renshaw later said, at her funeral service, that: 'she was a priest long before she was ordained, it was just in her'.

It was a day of great joy and celebration. The bishop talked of the hundreds of years of service that the women had already given to the Church. A lone male voice temporarily disrupted the service by objecting – a man who went to every one of the women's ordination services – and my father Richard was furious. He was a committed Christian who believed absolutely in women's ministry, and was very proud of his big sister. We all were. And though my own knowledge is limited by the framework of my own life and times, I do know that there are countless other quiet pioneers like my aunt, across history and across the world, who have proclaimed to any who will listen that there is something greater in existence than the world we can see.

> 'Every perfect life is a parable invented by God.'
>
> **Simone Weil**

∞

Lily, c. 1910

Lily

IT'S 1918 AND THE First World War is over. Beyond the walls of 'Poplars' on New Park Road, Streatham, the world is changing. Especially for women.

Not, of course, for all women, and not in all countries or political systems – but the campaigning work of suffragists and suffragettes had led to Lloyd George's coalition UK government passing the Representation of the People Act in February 1918, enfranchising all men over twenty-one, as well as women over the age of thirty who met minimum property requirements – namely, if they were householders, the wives of householders, occupiers of property with an annual rent of £5 or graduates of British universities. This led to some 8.4 million new voters. In November 1918, the Parliament (Qualification of Women) Act was passed, allowing women to be elected to the House of Commons.

Did Lily vote in the general election of 1918, despite her opposition to women's suffrage? If so, for whom? Did she discuss it with her husband or her sons, with her daughters? Or did she pretend it wasn't happening? Did that younger generation see it as something that would improve their lives, give them more agency, or were the battles of Westminster a far cry from Ethel's life in a vicarage, Winnie's in India as the wife of a railway manager, my grandmother Betty as a newly-wed in Wimbledon? Were they simply glad the war was over? I wish I knew.

I have a black-and-white photograph of Lily from this time. Her grey hair is swept up, she is wearing a pale formal lace dress and a heavy fur coat. On the back, my grandmother has written: *My Mother 1921*, followed by her own initials, so Lily must have been in her early seventies. But it's the same expression, the same determined and direct gaze as in the portrait of the girl, Martha Louisa Green, which I keep on my desk propped up against my computer screen.

It's the Roaring Twenties and the codified Victorian society within which Lily grew up has been resolutely swept away. Automobiles and omnibuses have replaced carriages and flys, aeroplanes are replacing steamer ships. I've found no letters between Lily and Sam from 1920, but, in her articles for *The Girl's Own Paper*, I detect an undercurrent of Lily struggling to find order and familiarity in a world that is changing too fast.

The following year, 1921, is a year of conflict. In part as a consequence of the Russian Revolution of 1917, Communist parties and Communist youth parties are being formed in countries across the globe, including China, Italy, Czechoslovakia and Portugal. Also, in 1921, the Russian Red Army invades Georgia and the White Army occupies Mongolia; the Jaffa Riots in Palestine result in ninety-five deaths of Jewish and Arab people; the Irish War of Independence is still raging.

It's late summer and the heatwave that's gripped Europe for several months shows no sign of abating. London is hot and airless. The carts and bicycles in New Park Road churn up the dust. That year, the family is not at Stair Mill. Betty's daughter Margaret is about to celebrate her first birthday, and perhaps a small party was planned.

There was no indication that 21 August 1921 was going to be a significant day. No warning signs, no portentous diary entries, nothing to make that particular Saturday in that punishing hot and dry summer stand out.

There are few references to Sam's health in their surviving letters. The vast majority of correspondence I've read was written between the 1870s and the early 1900s. In recent years, Sam and Lily have travelled less and been more often together in London. Apart from his childhood stammer, the only reference to any medical condition was in a letter dated 2 August 1903 about how his hearing was causing him trouble. Lily's reply surprised me: 'There is nothing to which faith healing would be better applied than to your hearing.'

But that was nearly twenty years ago and he is eighty-two now.

At midday, Sam returned home for lunch saying he felt unwell. Did Lily call a doctor or has this happened before? Did she put it down to the heat or to indigestion? Was she alone in the house or were her housekeeper, Mrs Creed, and her daughter there?

So many questions unanswered.

Sister Katherine – who would only have been ten at the time – claimed family folklore had it that Sam turned to Lily and said: 'Today, I shall be with the Lord.' Lily began to recite his favourite psalm – Psalm 23, 'The Lord is my shepherd' – but, before she had finished, Sam was dead. Dead in a matter of minutes. A heart attack.

They had been married for more than fifty years, Lily's whole adult life. They had brought up six children, and lost one. Sam's parents and Lily's parents were dead, as were three of her brothers and her sister Nellie. Now, Sam. There are no letters, no death notices and no letters of condolence carefully preserved in a folder. Sam was the one who made notes, who saved things. He was the keeper of records, not Lily.

I have spent a year in her company, researching and reading and trying to hear her voice whispering down the years. But, at this life-altering moment of Sam's death, I have no idea of how Lily felt on that stifling August day, the sounds of the afternoon going on outside the house they had lived in together for almost all of their married life. Did she weep, did she pray? Was she grief-stricken or accepting? Was she relieved for him that his passing was painless and quick?

In her fortitude, Lily has much in common with all those women of courage and conviction to come in the next chapter – women who, whatever the situation, however personally dangerous or challenging, simply 'got on with it'. No fuss, no self-pity, just a firm belief that if this was how things were, one had to do one's best.

The only clues to Lily's state of mind are in her writing. In later poems – written in what she calls her 'days of Autumn' – Lily's confidence in the life to come remains unshakeable. She and Sam had been only momentarily separated, not for ever. She believed that, one day, they would be reunited:

> *The way of the soul to the dwelling of Light*
> *Is by One, and by One alone.*

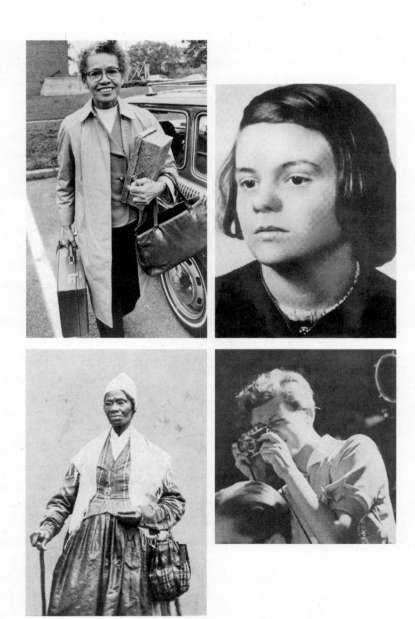

Top left: Pauli Murray (1910–1985)
Top right: Sophie Scholl (1921–1943)
Bottom left: Sojourner Truth (1797–1883)
Bottom right: Gerda Taro (1910–1937)

9

Women of Courage & Conviction

'I have lived to see my lost causes found.'

Proud Shoes
Pauli Murray, 1956

COURAGE COMES IN ALL shapes and sizes. The courage to move mountains or, sometimes, just the courage to carry on. As I edit this chapter, I'm watching the faces of women in Ukraine fighting to protect their homeland. And ten months after the storming of Kabul by the Taliban, women in Afghanistan are still resisting a regime that seeks to control and limit every part of their lives. In my fiction, I write about 'ordinary' women and men living through extraordinary moments of history. From warrior queens to quiet revolutionaries, it's the quality of conviction that gives someone the strength to keep fighting for what she believes in – the right to be a priest, a writer, a doctor, a teacher, a scientist, a politician – in the face of seemingly intractable opposition. The courage to lead a nation, to travel the world, to dive to the bottom of the ocean or reach for the stars. To save the planet. The courage to put oneself in harm's way.

In this chapter, we'll meet abolitionists, land activists and indigenous activists, women who served or resisted during two world wars, feminists and civil rights campaigners, each and every one driven by a personal sense of conviction, and all motivated by a universal courage.

I'M GOING TO begin this chapter in the eighteenth century. There is a case to be made that during times of extreme conflict or when there are huge and significant changes in society, women's opportunities to step outside of the domestic sphere and play an active role are sometimes greater than in times of stability. When the status quo appears to be functioning, there can be less enthusiasm for change.

The eighteenth century was the Age of Revolution – uprisings and revolts in Haiti and Serbia and China, wars of independence in Greece and India, in America and France, of course. When the French Revolution began in 1789, French women were largely confined to the private sphere, their worlds limited by domestic duty and family obligation. However, the ideas of equality and fraternity that sparked the French Revolution engaged women from all backgrounds. The *salonnières* – educated and influential women such as **Madame de Staël** (1766–1817) running literary salons much like those of Elizabeth Vesey and Elizabeth Montagu in London – were debating property rights and universal suffrage. Working-class women were taking to the streets with the radical *sans-culottes* – literally those 'without breeches', to distinguish them from the moneyed classes – demanding affordable bread so they could feed their families. In theory, the demands of the French revolutionaries were equality for all – and that included women and enslaved people in French colonial territories overseas. In practice, women had to fight even harder for their voices to be heard.

One of the most courageous of the revolutionary women who drew support from all classes of society was **Théroigne de Méricourt** (1762–1817). A woman from a small town in Belgium, she endured a great deal of hardship in her life and fled to Paris to be part of the Revolution. She wore the blood-red or white riding outfit of a man, carried a weapon – though the famous steel engraving of her by Auguste Raffet in uniform carrying a sabre comes from 1847, so might not be accurate – and was as comfortable at the 'tribune' (speakers' podium) in the National Assembly as she was talking with the *poissardes*, the street women who worked in the market of Les Halles. De Méricourt was among those who had a warrant issued for her arrest for her part in one of the earliest and most significant events of the Revolution, the Women's March on Versailles. Also known as the October March, it began among women in the marketplaces of Paris on 5 October 1789. Like Olympe de Gouges before her, de Méricourt was ruthlessly attacked and slandered by the Royalist press as a 'patriot's whore'. It's not so different from the way that the gutter press and media attempt to denigrate and destroy female celebrities in the twenty-first century. She suffered badly when imprisoned in Austria under false charges. Though she, unlike de Gouges, ultimately survived the Revolution, she spent the remainder of her life institutionalized. Though she was a towering figure, and has a small part in the novel *A Place of Greater Safety* by **Hilary Mantel** (b. 1952), she is largely missing from popular culture and from history books.

> 'I can offer you nothing but my life, and I thank heaven that I am free to dispose of it; I desire only that . . . my head, carried through Paris, may be a rallying standard for all the friends of law.'
>
> **Charlotte Corday**

Charlotte Corday (1768–1793) is infamous for stabbing the revolutionary Jacobin leader and journalist Jean-Paul Marat in his bath in Paris in 1793. A Royalist sympathizer, she was convinced that Marat was responsible for the chaos and bloodshed as France spiralled, once again, into bloody civil war. Corday travelled to Paris to kill Marat and made no attempt to flee. She was guillotined four days later. Unlike de Méricourt, Corday has often been represented in paintings, plays and poems and was nicknamed *'l'ange de l'assassinat'* (the 'angel of assassination') by the author and poet Alphonse de Lamartine.

Lucile Desmoulins (1770–1794) was a diarist and revolutionary combatant during the shifting allegiances of the French Revolution. A major character in Mantel's 1992 novel, she is the leading female protagonist in Georg Büchner's 1835 play *Danton's Death*. Arrested on suspicion of having conspired to help her husband, the journalist and politician Camille Desmoulins, escape from prison, she was guillotined in April 1794 during the 'Terror'. But the most extraordinary of the *filles sans-culottes*, as they became known, was **Pauline Léon** (1768–1838), the founder of the Society of Revolutionary Republican Women. She worked to form a female militia and played a major role in turning opinion against the 'incorruptible' Robespierre in the later years of the Revolution. Her organization was short-lived, facing opposition not only from men, but also from some women –

and, in truth, even many of those within the organization believed that women should come second to men – and it was revolutionary fervour that drove Léon and others, not a desire for women's rights per se. In October 1793, despite women having played a key role in the Revolution and the overthrow of the monarchy, societies for women were banned by the National Convention. Once again, women's rights were to take second place to the rights of men . . .

'If particular care and attention is not paid to the ladies, we are determined to foment a rebellion, and will not hold ourselves bound by any laws in which we have no voice or representation.'

Abigail Adams

IN EIGHTEENTH-CENTURY AMERICA, women were also fighting to make sure that their demands and requests were not forgotten in the former colony's War of Independence. Here, women's rights were to become even more tied up with abolition and ideas for equality for all citizens, regardless of the colour of their skin or their sex. And here, too, women and enslaved people were fundamental to the success of the Revolution and yet were still being told that the changes they wanted to see would have to wait until 'more important' issues were resolved . . .

Abigail Adams (1744–1818) was the second 'First Lady' of the new emergent United States, after **Martha Washington** (1731–1802). Adams was a prolific correspondent – more than a thousand letters have survived between her and her husband, John Adams, one of which includes the now famous phrase that the new government should 'remember the ladies'.

There are, however, few letters from Martha Washington that reveal her views on enslavement – and she kept away from political intrigues and negotiations – but since she and her husband lived on a plantation, Mount Vernon, in Virginia, I think it can be assumed that she was not personally engaged in the abolition movement. She helped run and manage her husband's estates, raised their children and grandchildren, nieces and nephews, and was for forty years Washington's 'worthy partner'. This dividing line between the northern and southern states over abolition would be a fault line running through the administration of the new republic and would lead, ultimately, to the American Civil War in 1861.

Abigail Adams, on the other hand, was a vocal and committed abolitionist, dedicated to securing representation for all citizens in the new United States of America. She played an active part in politics and supported her husband, managing their assets and promoting his reputation. At the relocation of the capital to Washington DC in 1800, Adams became the first 'First Lady' to live in the White House, then known as the President's House, but returned to their home 'Peacefield' in Quincy, Massachusetts, after his presidential election defeat later that year. The house is now part of the Adams National Historical Park. She died of typhoid fever in 1818, having outlived all of her six children. She was a Unitarian and, like Lily with her Sam, believed absolutely that she and John would be reunited after death. Adams was the only woman until **Barbara Bush** (1925–2018) to have been both the wife and the mother of an American president.

> 'The rights of the individual should be the primary object of all governments.'
>
> *Mercy Otis Warren*

Mercy Otis Warren (1728–1814) also came from Massachusetts. Passionately committed to the cause of independence, she was in regular contact with both Abigail Adams and Martha Washington. She was a poet, a pamphleteer and a playwright and, in 1805, she published her *History of the Rise, Progress, and Termination of the American Revolution*, one of the earliest eyewitness accounts of the progress of the Revolution.

So, to one of the most celebrated women of the era, **Elizabeth Griscom Ross** (1752–1836), known as **Betsy Ross**, though her story is not perhaps quite as it's been told. Ross is credited with sewing the first American flag in 1776 – a field of blue, with its thirteen red and white stripes and thirteen stars representing the founding states. It's true Ross was an upholsterer and a seamstress, and it's also true that there were many women making regimental flags, standards beneath which men could march and sail and fight. But, since Congress did not actually pass the Flag Act until June 1777, a year after Ross was supposed to have sewn 'Old Glory' – and the story about her having created the flag seems to have surfaced a century later in 1876, promoted by her grandson – it's possible it emerged as a story needed to reinforce the history that the founding fathers wanted to be told.

Another entry in Adrienne Rich's 'book of myths'.

∞

THROUGHOUT HISTORY, WE'VE known women who campaigned for the abolition of slavery, alongside other important issues of the day: the principles are the same, from Ancient Egypt to the modern day. There is no moral justification for the powerful to enslave others, to treat another human being as less than human. The names of many of the abolitionists, particularly in Britain and America, are well known. Opposition to slavery was at the heart of the Quaker movement and, everywhere, women were at the heart of these campaigns.

> 'Laws and customs may be creative of vice; and should be therefore perpetually under process of observation and correction.'
>
> **Harriet Martineau**

Irish abolitionist **Mary Ann McCracken** (1770–1866) was still protesting and handing out leaflets well into her eighties to keep slave ships out of Belfast Harbour. **Lucy Townsend** (1781–1847) started the Ladies' Anti-Slavery Society in Birmingham. **Harriet Martineau** was one of the founding mothers of sociology and, like Abigail Adams, was a Unitarian. An economic journalist and social scientist, Martineau wrote extensively about abolition in the context of economic and social systems, as well as discrimination against women. Dogged by ill health for most of her life – she was profoundly deaf and suffered from heart disease – she nonetheless travelled around America for two years from 1834, to see for herself the strength of feeling for abolition. Martineau publicly announced her support for the cause in *The Martyr Age of the United States*, but like many other abolitionists, she received death threats and was attacked at meetings.

In the UK, the slave trade had been abolished in 1807 – making it illegal for any British ship or British subject to trade in enslaved people. The Act declared that the trade in enslaved people from Africa was to be 'utterly abolished, prohibited and declared to be unlawful'.

In remaining British colonies, the Bill for the abolition of slavery became effective on 1 August 1834, in part thanks to the women and men working on the plantations themselves. Known as the Baptist War, or Christmas Rebellion because it started after 25 December 1831, it was an eleven-day uprising of perhaps as many as sixty thousand of Jamaica's three hundred thousand enslaved people, the largest ever slave rebellion in the British Caribbean.

In America, things were moving at a different pace. Thomas Jefferson had also passed a law in 1807, banning the importation of enslaved people from Africa, but the Thirteenth Amendment ending slavery on American soil wouldn't be passed by the Senate until December 1864 and not ratified until after the end of the Civil War in 1865. More than ten thousand enslaved people were immediately freed, though their situation remained precarious.

There are, of course, many women who were significant in the fight against slavery in American history whose stories have been lost to history or were never recorded. However, two of the key names that have come down to us through history are **Sojourner Truth** (1797–1883) and **Harriet Tubman**.

> 'If the first woman God ever made was strong enough to turn the world upside down all alone, these women together ought to be able to turn it back, and get it right side up again! And now they is asking to do it, the men better let them.'
>
> ***Sojourner Truth***

Born as **Isabella Baumfree** in New York State, Truth was first sold as a child at the age of nine. In 1826, she 'walked' to freedom with her infant daughter, having to leave her other children behind. The New York Anti-Slavery Law emancipating all enslaved people took effect in 1827 so, the following year, she sued her former owner for custody of her son and won – the first Black woman to win such a case against a white man. In 1843, believing she had received a calling from God, she changed her name to Sojourner Truth and became a preacher, campaigning for equal rights for women as well as men, Black people as well as white.

It was at the 1851 Women's Rights Convention in Ohio that Truth delivered her 'Ain't I a Woman?' speech, one of the most famous in history. Recently, historians have reassessed what we thought we knew. Truth's first language was actually Dutch, but her words were transliterated into the dialect of the Southern states. That myth-making notwithstanding, the sentiments are powerful and strike to the heart of the campaign for women's rights as fundamental, not an after-thought.

Truth never learned to read or write, but with the help of a friend and neighbour, in 1851 she published the *Narrative of Sojourner Truth*, recounting both her life as an enslaved woman and her transformation into an activist. More than 120 years after her death, the National Congress of Black Women commissioned the Canadian sculptor and painter **Artis Lane** (b. 1927) to create a bronze bust of Truth. Unveiled by **Michelle Obama** (b. 1964) in April 2009, it's on permanent display in Emancipation Hall in the Capitol Visitor Center. Truth is the first African American woman to have a statue in the Capitol building and one of the thirty-nine place settings of Judy Chicago's *The Dinner Party*, the only Black woman at the table.

> 'If you hear the dogs, keep going. If you see the torches in the woods, keep going. If there's shouting after you, keep going. Don't ever stop. Keep going. If you want a taste of freedom, keep going.'
>
> **Harriet Tubman**

A generation after Truth, the conductor of the 'Underground Railway', **Harriet Tubman** (1822–1913), was also born enslaved, in Dorchester County, Maryland. Suffering abuse and beatings, a traumatic head wound when she was only twelve left her with lifelong injuries and, perhaps, contributed to her religious visions. In 1849,

Tubman escaped to Philadelphia, but returned to Maryland to start rescuing her family, one by one.

Codenamed 'Moses', Tubman created a network of safe houses with anti-slavery activists, saving the lives of more than seventy enslaved people and she 'never lost a passenger' on the underground railway. When the American Civil War began in 1861, Tubman worked as a nurse and a cook for the Union Army, then as a spy and scout. She was the first American woman we know of to lead an armed expedition, and guided the raid at Combahee Ferry which liberated more than seven hundred enslaved people in June 1863, two years before the Thirteenth Amendment was passed. Celebrated in her lifetime, Tubman became a national icon after her death. There are several surviving photographs of her, the most striking one taken in the 1870s. Tubman is wearing a black-buttoned jacket and long skirt, with a white necktie, standing with her hands resting on the back of an upholstered chair and looking directly into the camera. Her gaze has something to say to us still.

> 'The way to right wrongs is to turn the light of truth upon them.'
>
> **Ida B. Wells**

The extraordinary **Ida B. Wells** (1862–1931) is another magnificent woman who could have been included in many different chapters. An American investigative journalist, campaigner, teacher and civil rights leader, she was one of the founders of the NAACP. Born into slavery in Mississippi, Wells was freed by the Emancipation Proclamation on New Year's Day 1861, issued by President Abraham Lincoln during the Civil War. She first worked as a teacher in Memphis, Tennessee, but soon was writing for the *Memphis Free Speech and Headlight* newspaper covering incidents of racial segregation and inequality, and became a co-owner. She was one of the loudest, and fiercest, voices against lynching – and the lies and racism used to justify it. In the 1890s, Wells published pamphlets such as *Southern Horrors: Lynch Law in all its Phases* and *The Red Record*. A white mob destroyed her newspaper offices, but Wells continued to write and speak out. Courageous and principled, she travelled across the United States and overseas, speaking also for women's suffrage and civil rights. In 2020, Wells was posthumously awarded a Pulitzer Prize special citation honouring 'her outstanding and courageous reporting on the horrific and vicious violence against African Americans during the era of lynching'.

> 'I want to be remembered as someone who used herself and anything she could touch to work for justice and freedom . . . I want to be remembered as one who tried.'
>
> ### Dorothy Height

The 'godmother of the Civil Rights movement' is considered by many to be **Dorothy Height** (1912–2010), another of the significant voices campaigning to end the lynching of African Americans. In 1957 Height became the fourth president of the National Council of Negro Women, a position she held for forty years. Under her leadership, the NCNW supported voter registration in the South as well as financially aiding civil rights activists throughout the country. Height was one of the organizers of the March on Washington for Jobs and Freedom in August 1963, though she was not invited to speak. Originally, no women were included as speakers on the programme at all, but Height helped persuade the organizers to think again.

Over the next few years, she travelled widely, working as a visiting professor at the University of Delhi, India, and with the Black Women's Federation of South Africa. In 2004, she was awarded the Congressional Gold Medal and inducted into the Democracy Hall of Fame International. Height is the only African American woman to have a federal building named after her in Washington DC.

> 'People always say that I didn't give up my seat because I was tired, but that isn't true. I was not tired physically, or no more tired than I usually was at the end of a working day . . . No, the only tired I was, was tired of giving in.'
>
> ### Rosa Parks

In 1900, the former Confederate states passed new constitutions which effectively disenfranchised Black voters. The Jim Crow laws legalized segregation in public buildings, shops and restaurants, and on the public transport system. On 1 December 1955, **Rosa Parks** (1913–2005) refused to give up her seat in the 'colored' section of the bus for a white passenger. She was arrested for civil disobedience and violating Alabama's segregation laws.

Parks was by no means the first Black woman to resist – fifteen-year-old **Claudette Colvin** (b. 1939) had been arrested nine months earlier, as had **Irene Morgan** (1917–2007) in Virginia back in 1944, and **Lillie Bradford** (1928–2017) in 1951, for refusing to give up their seats to white passengers – and there had been court challenges of the racist Jim Crow policy before. But the National Association for the Advancement of Colored People thought that Parks's case had a higher chance of success (though some African American and Black British historians have also suggested that colourism might also have played a role in the selection of Parks). She was forty-two at the time, and was a successful and admired local citizen, worked for the NAACP and was politically astute. Her act of resistance, coupled with all those that had gone before, changed history.

One of my favourite photographs of Parks is her standing with sculptor **Artis Lane** at the unveiling of her bronze bust and painting. Parks is glorious in orange, Lane is wearing blue jeans and a denim shirt. Behind them is Lane's exquisite oil painting of Parks sitting on that bus in Montgomery, Alabama. It's not actually 'the' bus, but rather an image of the day just over a year later, 21 December 1956, when Montgomery capitulated and desegregated the public transport service.

> 'When my brothers try to draw a circle to exclude me, I shall draw a larger circle to include them. Where they speak out for the privileges of a puny group, I shall shout for the rights of all mankind.'
>
> **Pauli Murray**

Another early 'freedom rider' was the inspirational **Pauli Murray** (1910–1985), who was arrested with a friend in Virginia in early 1940 and charged with disorderly conduct. That experience was the beginning of her activism. Murray went to law school and, in 1946, became the first Black deputy attorney general licensed by the California Bar. An outspoken and learned civil rights activist, the NCNW named her woman of the year. In 1947, *Mademoiselle* magazine did the same. Murray was also an award-winning author and poet. Her *Song in a Weary Throat*, published posthumously in 1987, won both the Robert F. Kennedy book award and the Lilian Smith book award. A teacher of law at the Ghana School of Law, Murray was the first African American to receive a doctorate in juridical science from Yale in 1965.

Murray became a professor at Brandeis in Massachusetts where, as well as teaching law, she was responsible for introducing the first African American studies course and women's studies course. Throughout her life, Murray struggled with what she called her 'in-betweenness' – what today we might call non-binary – and campaigned vigorously against all forms of gender discrimination. It was Murray who coined the phrase 'Jane Crow', succinctly making the comparison between discrimination against women and discrimination on the grounds of race.

When Murray was in her sixties, she went from being an icon of progressive activism to take a different path. In a new departure, Murray went to theological college and, in 1977, became the first African American woman ordained as an Episcopal minister. Simply, Murray never gave up trying to make the world a better place, writing: 'One person plus one typewriter constitutes a movement.' Murray is also one of the women commemorated in the calendar of saints of the Episcopal Church, alongside Elizabeth Cady Stanton, Sojourner Truth, Harriet Tubman and **Amelia Bloomer** (1818–1894).

DURING THE NINETEENTH century, women throughout the world were also at the forefront of campaigns against child labour and the desperate living conditions of many working women and girls. As Harriet Martineau wrote in her pamphlets – enslavement, fights for civil rights and enfranchisement, economic dependency, lack of water and food, temperance societies, poverty and lack of education, faith – they were all interconnected.

Mary Anne Rawson (1801–1887) argued against child labour and all forms of slavery, and was part of a successful campaign persuading people to boycott sugar from the West Indies. In the Victorian novels my great-grandmother read – and wrote, in the case of *The Vicar of Langthwaite* – the living conditions of working people, the malnourishment of children and soldiers sent to fight in the Afghan and Boer wars were subjects of gross injustice that appeared time and again.

> 'It is when the community is shaken to its foundations . . . that a deeper unity of humanity evinces itself.'
>
> ***Emily Hobhouse***

Without **Emily Hobhouse** (1860–1926), the appalling conditions inside British concentration camps in South Africa would not have come to the attention of the general public. A pacifist and feminist, known as the 'Angel of Love', Hobhouse was born in Cornwall and spent her first thirty-five years living with her father in his vicarage. After his death, she worked with temperance societies in America then, on the outbreak of the second Boer War in 1899 – and having heard how Boer women and children were being incarcerated in camps – Hobhouse travelled to South Africa to see the conditions for herself. She was horrified and her dispatches helped force an amelioration in British policy. In 2020, it was announced that a museum celebrating her life would open at her former home in St Ive, near Liskeard.

> 'It is a fact, that numbers even of moral and religious people have permitted themselves to accept and condone in man what is fiercely condemned in woman.'
>
> ***Josephine Butler***

LIKE MY GREAT-GRANDMOTHER, faith was at the heart of the campaigning life of **Josephine Butler** (1828–1906). Another woman of conviction, who could feature in many chapters of this book, she was a social reformer, an early suffrage campaigner, an abolitionist, the author of more than ninety books and pamphlets, a Christian feminist, a campaigner for education and the rights of women, an opponent of the trafficking of women and girls into prostitution, and a leader of attempts to end the legal practice of *couverture* in British law – something that had proved critical for Lily when Sam's business partner defrauded his practice. From 1869, she campaigned for the abolition of legislation that put the blame and disgrace solely onto the women involved in sex work, rather than criticizing the men and the social conditions that made prostitution so widespread. Butler travelled internationally and her campaigning led, in 1883, to the repeal of the Contagious Diseases Act. Married to an Anglican priest, she wrote a biography of St Catherine of Sienna. There is no mention of Josephine Butler in either Lily's letters or articles for *The Girl's Own Paper*, but I feel sure Lily would have known of her work and admired it. When Butler died, she was described by suffragist leader Millicent Fawcett as the 'most distinguished Englishwoman of the nineteenth century'.

ONCE DUBBED THE 'most dangerous woman in America', **Mary G. Harris Jones** (1837–1930), known as 'Mother Jones', was an activist and union organizer. Originally from Ireland, she was a dressmaker and teacher who co-founded the Industrial Workers of the World in 1905. Having lost her four children and husband to yellow fever in 1867, and witnessing her dress shop destroyed in the great fire of Chicago in 1871 – which killed three hundred people and left a hundred thousand homeless – Jones became a shop steward for the United Mine Workers union, perhaps thinking she had nothing left to lose. In 1903, she organized a children's march from Philadelphia to President Theodore Roosevelt's home town of New York to highlight the evils of child labour and long working hours. Things would not change until 1938, when President Roosevelt signed the Fair Labor Standards Act into law, but it's no doubt that Mother Jones's children's crusade brought the issue to widespread public attention.

At about the same time in Glasgow, **Mary Barbour** (1875–1958) was fighting widespread poverty in the city. The heroine of the Glasgow

Rent Strike of 1915, she fought tirelessly for the welfare of women and children in Govan, was one of the founders of the Women's Peace Crusade, and the first female bailie in Glasgow. In 1920, she became one of five women elected as councillors to Glasgow Town Council – together with **Eleanor Stewart** (1899–1965), **Mary Bell** (1885–1943), **Jessica Baird-Smith** (1883–1962) and 'mother of the flock' of female councillors, **Mary Anderson Snodgrass** (1862–1945). In 2011, Glasgow Women's Library commissioned twenty-one artworks as part of their twenty-first anniversary celebrations, which led to a resurgence of interest. In 2013, the Remember Mary Barbour Association was founded to campaign for a statue, which was finally unveiled at Govan Cross in March 2018. Showing Barbour hatted and booted, with her right arm raised, she is leading 'Mrs Barbour's Army'.

Born in Newcastle-upon-Tyne thirteen years after Barbour, **Francesca Wilson** (1888–1981) began her humanitarian work helping French evacuee children in the Haute-Savoie. She then joined the Serbian Relief Fund. Her first book, *Portraits and Sketches of Serbia*, was published in 1920 and helped shine a spotlight on the grim conditions there after the First World War. Between 1919 and 1922, Wilson worked with the Quaker Relief Mission in Vienna set up by fellow Quaker humanitarian **Hilda Clark** (1881–1955) and her friend **Edith Pye** (1876–1965).

They were extraordinary women. Clark was a 'birth-right' Quaker from Somerset; Londoner Pye became a Quaker by choice. Clark was a doctor; Pye a nurse and midwife. Before working in Vienna, they'd founded a maternity hospital at Châlons-sur-Marne. They spent their lives, quite simply, doing good, going where they were most needed. There is a wonderful photograph of Clark taken around 1915. She is smiling, standing beside a car wearing a trench coat and the Quaker star armband on her left sleeve. As the clouds of war began to gather once again, Clark became co-ordinator of the German Emergency Committee, using her connections to create documents to help smuggle Jewish people out of Austria after the 1938 Anschluss. She returned to England at the beginning of the war, but continued her humanitarian work in London and Kent until her Parkinson's disease became too severe.

Clark died in Somerset in 1955. When Pye died ten years later, she was buried beneath the same headstone.

'We have shown that workers like us, new to these shores, will never accept being treated without dignity or respect'.

Jayaben Desai

JAYABEN DESAI (1933–2010) led a walkout of workers at the Grunwick film processing plant in north-west London in 1976, protesting against working conditions and the lack of respect shown to newly arrived immigrant workers, many of them Asian women. Her courage and stamina triggered the support of other workers for the Grunwick strikers and, for the next two years, Mrs Desai (as she was always known) led the pickets in their battle. Although the protest was not ultimately successful – this was the beginning of the Thatcherite era of curtailment of trade union rights – Desai remains an inspirational role model.

Leader of the 'headscarf' revolutionaries, **Lillian Bilocca** (1929–1988) improved safety in the fishing industry after the 1968 Hull triple trawler tragedy where fifty-eight people lost their lives. She gathered ten thousand signatures for her petition, the Fisherman's Charter, and presented it to the government. The government later implemented all the proposals in the charter.

The guiding principle of all these women of conviction and courage was a determination to change the day-to-day world for the better for everyone. Campaigning for equality, an end to discrimination and unfairness.

AT THE HEART of my historical fiction is a question: what would I, as a woman, have done had I been there? In *Labyrinth* in 1209, as the Catholic crusaders laid waste to cities from Béziers to Bram; in Amsterdam, in *The City of Tears*, during the Alteration of 1578; most especially in *Citadel* in Carcassonne during the Second World War, when the streets of La Cité were filled with the *vert-de-gris* of the Gestapo. Would I have been courageous enough to take a stand?

There are two distinct women's narratives during the Second World War. Some women were part of official networks, such as the Special

Operations Executive (SOE) in Britain or the American Office of Strategic Services (OSS). Others attempted to keep things going on the 'home front', wherever home might be, or resisted the invaders to protect their families and defend their countries.

> 'If you had to calculate whether you would do any good by protesting, you wouldn't have gone. But we acted from the heart. We wanted to show that we weren't willing to let them go.'
>
> *Elsa Holzer*

Elsa Holzer (1904–*c*. 1989) was one of the women who, in the bitterly cold Berlin of February 1943, took part in the Rosenstrasse Protest. Just before dawn on 27 February, the Gestapo started to round up the Jewish men remaining in Berlin, sometimes separating them from their non-Jewish wives. Holzer was one of them. As news spread, relatives started to gather outside the Jewish welfare office in Rosenstrasse where the men were being held. At first just a few women, then hundreds and then thousands, refusing to disperse despite being threatened with being shot. The protest hit the national news, then the international news, until, on 6 March, Goebbels ordered the men's release. The monument *Block der Frauen* (Block of Women) by German sculptor **Ingeborg Hunzinger** (1915–2009) stands in memorial to that protest.

Historians of the Second World War differ in their interpretations of the protest – some see it as a significant moment, others that it made no material difference to the progress of the war. But it does appear to be the only significant mass public demonstration by Germans against the deportation of their Jewish relatives, friends and neighbours.

Mary Elmes (1908–2002) is sometimes known as the Irish Oscar Schindler. One of her earliest memories of the First World War was the sinking of the British passenger ship, the *Lusitania*, by a German U-boat off the coast of Cork in 1915. She was only seven years old and she never forgot what she saw that day. Elmes later worked for the ambulance service during the Spanish Civil War, fleeing north over the border into south-west France as Franco's forces advanced. She helped set up makeshift camps and headed the Quaker delegation in Perpignan. When Jewish prisoners started to arrive at Rivesaltes, one of the holding camps on the Roussillon coast where prisoners were kept before being deported, Elmes and her colleagues did what they could to save as many children as possible. In August 1942, she 'spirited away' seven children bound for Auschwitz and, over the next eight weeks, saved many more. Like many women involved in Resistance work during the Second World War, Elmes seldom talked about her experiences and refused all honours. But eleven years after her death, she was given Israel's highest honour – Righteous Among Nations – the only Irish woman to have been so acknowledged.

In the Netherlands, **Corrie ten Boom** (1892–1983) was a watchmaker and member of the Dutch Reformed Church who, with her father and sister, protected many Jewish families by hiding them in her home in Amsterdam. They were all arrested and sent to prison camps, where they died. However Corrie – she later discovered only because of a clerical error – was moved to a women's labour camp, and eventually released. After the end of the war, she set up a rehabilitation clinic for survivors of the camps. She told her story in an autobiographical novel, *The Hiding Place*, which came out in 1971. **Frieda Belinfante** (1904–1995), a cellist and conductor, was a part of the Dutch Resistance. After the war, Belinfante emigrated to America and was the founding artistic director and conductor of the Orange County Philharmonic.

> 'Stand up for what you believe in even if you are standing alone.'
>
> *Sophie Scholl*

In Germany, **Sophie Scholl** (1921–1943) was born into a middle-class Christian family in the south of the country. After Germany invaded Poland on 1 September 1939, and her older brothers were sent to the Eastern Front, Scholl's opposition to National Socialism began. In 1942, she enrolled at the University of Munich to study biology and philosophy – another brother, Hans, was also enrolled there studying medicine – and, over the next year, with three fellow students, the five friends began a campaign against Nazism called the White Rose. The group published six pamphlets in all until – in what has become an iconic moment in every film or documentary about Scholl's life – she was seen with a stack of pamphlets by a janitor, a staunch supporter of the Nazi regime, who reported her to the Gestapo. Her brother was also arrested with a draft of the seventh pamphlet in his bag. She and Hans tried to take responsibility for the White Rose, to save their colleagues, though it didn't work. Scholl was convicted of high treason and executed by guillotine, at the age of only twenty-one, along with her brother and friends.

When researching *Citadel*, I was inspired by many extraordinary women of both the SOE and the OSS, but particularly the often-overlooked stories of local Resistance units. I discovered that the Carcassonne Resistance was betrayed, its members caught and executed at Baudrigues on 19 August 1944, the day before the Nazis withdrew from the south-west. There was, so far as I know, no wholly female unit, but all sorts of women were active in the Resistance and the Maquis, particularly in the final eighteen months of the occupation. There is a monument in the heart of the Bastide, the lower town of Carcassonne, listing the names of all the men who died that day. At the bottom of the plinth, there's inscribed a heartbreaking sentence: AND TWO UNKNOWN WOMEN. That was the inspiration for *Citadel*.

Virginia Hall (1906–1982) was the first female agent sent into Vichy France in August 1941, using codenames 'Marie' and 'Diane'. Nicknamed 'Artemis' by the Nazis, she worked for both the SOE and OSS and created the Heckler network in Lyon. An expert in organizing support and safe houses, supplying agents with weapons and helping downed airmen to escape, by 1944 she was working with the Maquis in Haute-Loire prior to the arrival of the American army in September. She joined the newly formed CIA in 1947, though she found desk work less to her satisfaction than being in the field.

Krystyna Skarbek (1908–1952) – also known as **Christine Granville** – was a Polish agent of Jewish descent who became a spy behind enemy lines. Working in Nazi-occupied Poland, and described by journalist Alistair Horne as the 'bravest of the brave', she was the longest serving of all British female agents. She survived the war, but was stabbed to death in London by an obsessive stalker in 1952.

> 'One needs to feel that one's life has
> meaning, that one is needed in this world.'
>
> ### *Hannah Szenes*

Poet **Hannah Szenes** (1921–1944) was one of thirty-seven Jewish SOE recruits from British Mandate Palestine, parachuted into Yugoslavia to rescue Hungarian Jews about to be deported to Auschwitz. She was caught at the border, arrested and tortured, but refused to speak. Executed by firing squad, she is largely forgotten in Hungary, but is a national heroine in Israel, where several streets have been named after her.

> 'If they kill me they kill me physically and
> that's all, they won't win anything . . . they'll
> have a dead body, useless to them, but they
> will not have me, because I will not let
> them have me.'
>
> ### *Odette Sansom*

Odette Sansom (1912–1995) – codenamed 'Lise' – was born in Amiens, France. A courier for the Spindle network, she was arrested near Annecy in the Alps in April 1943 and deported to Ravensbrück, the all-female concentration camp some fifty miles north of Berlin. Despite enduring repeated and horrifying torture, she refused to betray any of her fellow agents, and survived to write of her experiences. The first woman to be awarded the George Cross, she was also awarded the Légion d'Honneur by the French government.

One of my favourite photographs of a *résistante* is that of **Simone Segouin** (b. 1925) posing for photographers with soldiers during the liberation of her home town, Chartres, on 23 August 1944. Dressed in shorts and a beret, Segouin is holding her machine gun and being watched by an American GI, a French police officer, local civilians and two rather bored-looking boys. Taught to shoot by her father, a decorated veteran of the First World War, Segouin joined the FTP, a communist Resistance group fighting Fascism and, in 1944, was given the codename 'Nicole Minet'. An active fighter, fearless and unsentimental, she was present at the liberation of Paris on 24 August, two days after being photographed by Robert Capa in Chartres.

> 'Two and a half million Indians volunteered for the war effort and it was the largest single volunteer army . . . we must not forget their contribution. Noor was part of this.'
>
> **Shrabani Basu**

Noor Inayat Khan (1914–1944) – codenamed 'Madeleine' – was the first female wireless operator to be sent into occupied France. A pacifist turned war heroine, she was betrayed, captured and executed in Dachau concentration camp. Her final word, uttered as the German firing squad raised their weapons, was simply '*liberté*'. Although the most famous photograph of Khan is one of her in an RAF uniform, my favourite is an image from her younger days in the family's pre-war Paris apartment. She is wearing a white sari, sitting cross-legged on cushions, and holding a veena, one of the oldest of classical Indian stringed instruments, as if just about to play. Khan was posthumously awarded the George Cross and a Croix de Guerre and, in 2012, a statue was unveiled of her in London's Gordon Square. The campaign was led by Khan's biographer **Shrabani Basu** (b. 1962), who founded the Noor Inayat Khan Memorial Trust.

> 'She [Lindell] was an impossible character and disliked by everyone in normal circumstances. But in the camp, you needed someone like that.'
>
> **Yvonne Baseden**

Yvonne Baseden (1922–2017) – codenamed 'Odette' – was, like Sansom, born in France. She was bilingual, and fluent in several other languages, including Spanish, Italian and Polish. Having trained in the UK, she was the youngest SOE operative to be parachuted into France. She was captured in June 1944, imprisoned in

Saarbrücken and then transferred to Ravensbrück in September 1944. One of about five hundred women released from Ravensbrück to the Swedish Red Cross in April 1945 in the closing days of the war, she was driven in one of the 'White Buses' across Germany and Denmark to Sweden. Baseden famously spent her first night of freedom sleeping beneath the skeletons of dinosaurs on the floor of the Malmö Museum of Prehistory. She was one of the first guests on the iconic British television show *This is Your Life* in 1955.

Mary Lindell (1895–1987) was also imprisoned in Ravensbrück. A front-line nurse during the First World War, first for the Voluntary Aid Detachments and then the Red Cross, Lindell was awarded a Croix de Guerre for service in both world wars. She founded the 'Marie-Claire' escape network, was imprisoned twice, but emerged as a controversial figure – there were allegations of her being a double agent and many of her fellow prisoners later talked of her stubbornness and intractability. Lindell was arrested in Pau in November 1943 and shot while trying to escape, before being transported to Ravensbrück in September 1944.

Like Baseden, Lindell survived Ravensbrück, and she died in Germany in 1987. **Violette Szabo** (1921–1945) – codenamed 'Louise' – did not. Another British-French SOE operative awarded the George Cross posthumously for her work gathering intelligence and supporting networks rescuing Allied airmen, Szabo was captured during her second mission, interrogated and tortured. She was executed in Ravensbrück in February 1945.

Vera Atkins (1908–2000) was a Romanian-born intelligence officer, who worked in the France section of the SOE from 1941 until 1945. She was part of the team who saved the Enigma code-breakers in Poland.

Fighter pilot and squadron commander **Raisa Surnachevskaya** (1922–2005) was one of the members of an all-female unit formed after the German invasion of the Soviet Union in 1941. She's one of the few women known to have flown in combat while pregnant.

> 'France made me who I am. Parisians gave me everything . . . I am prepared to give them my life.'
>
> **Josephine Baker**

How best to describe the American-born, French-by-adoption agent **Josephine Baker (1906–1975)**? An actress, music hall star, cabaret artist – the highest-paid performer of her day – she was also a pilot, a lieutenant in the French Air Force's Female Auxiliary Corps during the Second World War and, later, a civil rights activist. She was the only woman who spoke at the 1963 March on Washington before Martin Luther King's famous speech. She was the sixth woman – and first woman of colour – to be placed in the Panthéon, her coffin filled with earth from four places where she had lived.

Lucie Aubrac (1912–2007), a Communist and former teacher, formed the Resistance group La Dernière Colonne, later known as Libération-sud, with her husband. Aubrac carried out two sabotage attacks at train stations in Perpignan and Cannes in 1941, organized the distribution of ten thousand propaganda flyers and worked on the underground newspaper *Libération*. In 1943, Aubrac famously negotiated directly with Klaus Barbie, the notorious and vicious Gestapo chief in Vichy France, for the release of her husband. She later freed him and fifteen fellow prisoners by attacking the convoy he was being transported in.

In 1944, Charles de Gaulle appointed her a Resistance representative to the new consultative assembly, making her the first woman to sit in a French parliamentary assembly.

Marie-Madeline Fourcade (1909–1989), codenamed *'Hérisson'* ('Hedgehog'), was the leader of the Alliance network. Over her time as a *résistante*, she took care of some 3,000 agents and survivors, and published *Mémorial de l'Alliance*, dedicated to the Resistance group's 429 dead. Despite her known achievements and courage, Fourcade was never honoured by de Gaulle. However, by the time of her death, things had changed. She was celebrated by fellow Resistance fighters and the French government at a memorial service at l'Église Saint-Louis des Invalides in Paris, the first woman to have been so honoured, before being buried at Père Lachaise Cemetery.

Agnès de la Barre de Nanteuil (1922–1944) – known as 'Agent Claude' – joined the Resistance with her mother, having worked for the Red Cross. Part of her responsibilities were placing landing lights for Allied parachuters. Returning home after one such operation in March 1944, she was arrested by the Gestapo. Despite being tortured in prison, she revealed nothing, and was being deported to Germany in August 1944, together with her sister, other Resistance workers and Allied prisoners, when the train was attacked. She died ten days later, at the railway station of Paray-le-Monial, in eastern France.

The Médaille de la Résistance was established by General Charles de Gaulle on 9 February 1943. Awarded to approximately 38,000 living people and nearly 25,000 posthumously – including **Agnès de la Barre de Nanteuil** – proportionately few were presented to women. Of those that were given to women, many were to those from outside France, including the exceptional New Zealander **Nancy Wake** (1912–2011). Codenamed 'Hélène' by the SOE, 'Andrée' by the Resistance and the 'White Mouse' by the Gestapo, she was a courier and a vital part of the network smuggling Allied airmen out of France and into Spain. As well as the Médaille de la Résistance, she received the Medal of Freedom from the United States, the Légion d'Honneur and the Croix de Guerre, the Companion of the Order of Australia and the Badge in Gold from New Zealand.

All the same, there are many, many women whose heroism goes unrecorded and unacknowledged. And of the 1,061 Croix de la Libération awarded by de Gaulle for exceptional acts of bravery, only six were given to women . . .

Recipients of the Croix de la Libération include: **Berty Albrecht** (1893–1943); **Laure Diebold** (1915–1965); **Marie Hackin** (1905–1941); **Marcelle Henry** (1895–1945); **Simone Michel-Lévy** (1906–1945); and **Émilienne Moreau-Evrard** (1898–1971).

Amsterdammer **Jos Gemmeke** (1922–2010) was a member of the Dutch Resistance in the occupied Netherlands. She helped distribute the illegal underground newspaper *Je Maintiendrai* – 'I Will Stand Firm' – in The Hague, and undertook several missions to deliver radio equipment and microfilms intended for the headquarters of the Dutch Secret Service in London, cycling across enemy lines from Holland into Belgium. Gemmeke was one of only two women to be appointed Knight in the Military William Order. She was also awarded the King's Medal for Courage in the Cause of Freedom by the British government. The Norwegian teacher **Frieda Dalen** (1895–1995) was the first woman to address the United Nations at its inaugural General Assembly in January 1946, having led the civil resistance against the Nazi occupation of Norway in 1940.

'Not for me the glad tidings of forthcoming salvation; everything is lost and I so want to live.'

Ester Wajcblum

Ester Wajcblum (*c.* 1924/1927–1945) was a Jewish Resistance fighter in one of the Sonderkommando units in Auschwitz, prisoners forced to work for the regime, notably in disposing of the corpses of those murdered in the gas chambers. She took part in the Sonderkommando rebellion at Auschwitz II-Birkenau on 7 October 1944, attacking the SS guards, killing three and wounding a dozen or so more. The plan had been to destroy the gas chambers and crematoria using gunpowder smuggled in over a period of months by the young Jewish women forced to work in the munitions area. A few escaped, but most were recaptured, tortured and executed, Wajcblum being one of them. It was the last public execution to be held there. Two weeks later, the Germans abandoned the camp.

'You hang me now, but I'm not alone. There are two hundred million of us. You can't hang us all. They will avenge me.'

Zoya Kosmodemyanskaya

In the Soviet Union, as in France, much of the resistance to Nazi occupation was led by young partisans. **Zoya Kosmodemyanskaya** (1923–1941) was eighteen when she joined a partisan unit and, in November 1941, was sent to burn the village of Petrishchevo in Vologda Oblast, in north-western Russia, where a German regiment was stationed. Caught, beaten and interrogated, she was hanged in the village square with a sign saying 'houseburner' round her neck. Stories of how she never stopped resisting and shouting at her captors, even as they were killing her, began to circulate and she was posthumously declared a Hero of the Soviet Union.

> 'The Soviets are coming soon, and your days
> are numbered. Our blood will not be shed
> in vain . . . Soviet power cannot be killed!'
>
> **Tatiana Solomakha**

One of Kosmodemyanskaya's heroines had been **Tatiana Solomakha** (1892–1918), a Bolshevik revolutionary and one of the victims of the White Terror. She took part in the first Russian Civil War in 1917 when she was only seventeen, then joined the Red Army. Captured by the White Guards, she was executed along with nineteen others in November 1918. Her mother and two brothers were also victims of the White Terror.

DURING THE SECOND World War in the Pacific, there were women in Hawaii, Myanmar and Manila resisting Japanese occupation. In the 1850s, America had pushed Japan into disadvantageous trade agreements and, although Japan fought on the side of the Western Allies in the First World War, the country was forced to sign humiliating treaties that restricted its power in the Far East. Increasingly, Japan became more aligned with fascist ideology and, in the 1930s, embarked on a campaign to seize Chinese territory. When the Second World War began, Japan allied with Italy and Germany.

> 'War is war. It's not the people who are
> wicked . . . I never expected to come out
> alive from that Japanese cell. So I've learned
> that happiness comes only from within. You
> do good to others, it will come back to you.'
>
> **Elizabeth Choy**

Elizabeth Choy (1910–2006) was born in British North Borneo, now the Malaysian state of Sabah. She travelled to Singapore to study, intending to become a teacher. At the time of the Japanese invasion of Singapore in 1942 she was working in a hospital canteen. Despite witnessing the violence with which Japanese forces treated civilians who did not cooperate, she smuggled letters and food to British prisoners, supplied medicine, money and carried messages to the POWs in Changi prison. Arrested and tortured over a period of a hundred days, Choy refused to confess to sabotage and was eventually released. After the war, Choy was the only woman elected to the 1951 Legislative Council. She also became the first principal of the Singapore School for the Blind in 1956.

'If your pictures aren't good enough, you're not close enough.'

Gerda Taro

As WELL AS these active participants in combatant roles, there were also several women of courage working in war zones as journalists and photographers. Their work provides an essential record of those who were part of history as it happened. They include the German-Jewish war photographer **Gerda Taro** (1910–1937). Born **Gerta Pohorylle** into a Galician Jewish family in Germany, she escaped the Nazis by moving to Paris in 1933, where she met the Hungarian photojournalist Endre Friedmann. They began working together under the pseudonym 'Robert Capa', pretending to be an American photographer and his agent. When they began to publish separately, she took the pseudonym Gerda Taro, though it's acknowledged Taro took many of the early images subsequently attributed to him. They covered the Spanish Civil War, working on the front line. Taro was fatally wounded at the Brunette Front near Madrid when, travelling with wounded Republican soldiers, their car collided with a tank. She was buried in Père Lachaise Cemetery in north-eastern Paris, but her name was soon forgotten, and their photographs were published under the name of Robert Capa. It wasn't until the beginning of the twenty-first century that Taro's contribution to war photography was properly recognized.

'Nothing attracts me like a closed door. I cannot let my camera rest until I have pried it open.'

Margaret Bourke-White

The American correspondent and photojournalist **Margaret Bourke-White** (1904–1971) was the first foreign correspondent allowed into the Soviet Union in the 1930s, and the first female photojournalist for *Life* magazine. She not only exposed the realities of war but also the hardships of home. The first woman to be allowed to work in combat zones during the Second World War, she was the only foreign photographer in Moscow when the Nazis invaded Russia in June 1941. She was at Buchenwald concentration camp in 1945, then in India in 1947 for the Partition of India and formation of Pakistan – a bloody, devastating and life-altering period of history – and covered the Korean War in the 1950s. A woman of great courage who had the knack of always seeming to be right there at the heart of history with her camera, Bourke-White interviewed and photographed Mahatma Gandhi just hours before his assassination in January 1948.

> 'Women war photographers had to fight on two fronts: the bombs, and the men.'
>
> *Lee Miller*

Lee Miller (1907–1977) was an American photographer, surrealist muse and photojournalist who began life as a fashion model in New York City in the 1920s, before going to Paris to become a fashion and fine art photographer. During the Second World War, she was a war correspondent for *Vogue* – one of several female American journalists covering the war in Europe – photographing key moments including the London Blitz, the liberation of Paris and the liberation of the concentration camps at Buchenwald and Dachau. One of the most famous photographs of Miller is of her taking a bath in the bathroom of Hitler's Munich apartment in April 1945 – the shot was taken by fellow *Life* magazine photographer David Scherman. On the floor are her boots, still covered with the filth of Dachau.

Virginia Cowles (1910–1983) – described by journalist **Christina Lamb** (b. 1965) as the 'Forrest Gump of journalism' – was a third female American war correspondent who had the knack of being in the right and most dangerous place at the right time. Cowles was in Berlin on 1 September 1939 as the Germans invaded Poland; in London on 7 September 1940 to witness the first day of the Blitz; and in Paris on 14 June 1940 as the French capital fell to the Nazis. Her dispatches from the front line were extraordinary.

Other extraordinary and brave women recording the reality of life in a war zone in the twentieth and twenty-first centuries include: the French photojournalists **Catherine Leroy** (1944–2006) and **Françoise Demulder** (1947–2008) in Vietnam; **Christine Spengler** (b. 1945) who followed the Troubles in Northern Ireland and the conflict in Afghanistan; American photographers **Susan Meiselas** (b. 1948), president and co-founder of the Magnum Foundation and known for her images of the conflict in Nicaragua in the 1980s; and **Carolyn Cole** (b. 1961), who is associated with Liberia. The German-born photographer **Anja Niedringhaus** (1965–2014), the only woman on a team of eleven Associated Press photographers that won the 2005 Pulitzer Prize for Breaking News Photography for coverage of the Iraq War, died in the line of duty. Niedringhaus was shot dead by an Afghan policeman in Kabul in April 2014 whilst covering the presidential elections.

'In the end, all the struggles have the same objective: the defense of life.'

Ana Sandoval

IN SOME WAYS – and many women and men speak of this – there was, at least, a clarity during the two world wars. When one's country, or community, is actively under attack and the choice is to defend, to contribute to the war effort, or do nothing, the choice is simple. But it requires a very different kind of courage and sense of conviction when you are a lone voice against the state.

Truganini (c. 1812–1876) was one of the most significant figures in First Nation Aboriginal culture. A Nuenonne woman, an activist, leader and daughter of a chief, she was born on what became known as Bruny Island, south of Hobart, the capital of Van Diemen's Land, later Tasmania. Much of her history has been distorted. The indigenous people who refused to work for the British colonizers, or resisted, were hunted down and put in camps, or executed. Truganini, with others, became an outlaw, but was caught by the British and imprisoned, before forcibly being resettled at Oyster Cove. But she was a clever negotiator, a powerful figure within her community, and a towering figure in the history of Australia. Today, Truganini is commemorated in many songs, pieces of theatre, plays and works of literature. She should be celebrated for the whole of her long, resilient and extraordinary life.

Two years after her death, Truganini's skeleton was exhumed by the Royal Society of Tasmania and later placed on display, despite having previously pleaded with the colonial authorities for a respectful burial. It wasn't until April 1976 that her remains were finally cremated and scattered according to her wishes. In 2002, some of her hair and skin were found in the collection of the Royal College of Surgeons of England and returned to Tasmania for burial.

> 'For many years the men, the chiefs, the members of Parliament, the Kingitanga, have been searching for answers to our issues regarding land and the betterment of our people . . . All of this was done without us; the women . . . and no benefit has come back to our people . . . we women have not yet tried!'
>
> *Ākenehi Tōmoana*

Born twenty-two years after Truganini, **Ākenehi Tōmoana** (c. 1834–1908) was a prominent Māori leader. Women of chiefly status – *wāhine rangatira* – had been used to wielding decision-making power, but the imperialist system forced them to find new ways to assert their authority. A landowner, Ākenehi was a vocal advocate for the Māori women's movement, determined to fight restrictions imposed by European laws on Māori women's rights to own land. In 1893, she accompanied **Meri Te Tai Mangakāhia** (1868–1920) to the Kotahitanga Māori Parliament to call for Māori women to be able to vote and stand for parliamentary seats, arguing that, as landowners, they were entitled to political representation.

As we saw in Chapter 6, New Zealand led the world in terms of women's suffrage. At least three Māori women were included in the signing of the Treaty of Waitangi in 1840, at a time when women in general terms had little power. Māori men first voted in 1868 and both Māori and Pākehā women could vote in 1893, the same year that **Elizabeth Yates** (*c.* 1845–1918) was elected Mayor of Onehunga, now part of Auckland, the first time such a post had been held by a woman anywhere in the British Empire. **Elizabeth McCombs** (1873–1935) was New Zealand's first female member of Parliament in 1933 and **Matiu Rātana** (1905–1981) was the first woman to represent Māori interests in Parliament in 1949.

One of the most important women's voices of the twentieth century was the legendary Māori elder and activist **Whina Cooper** (1895–1994). Born **Hōhepine Te Wake**, she was a former teacher and campaigner who became part of the protest against an area of leased mudflats at Whakarapa on New Zealand's North Island. Though Cooper and her fellow protestors were charged with trespassing, they managed to prevent the project from going ahead. In 1951, Cooper was elected the first president of *Te Rōpū Māori Toko I te Ora* (the Māori Women's Welfare League). When she stepped down six years later, she was given the title *Te Whaea o te Motu* – 'Mother of the Nation'. In 1975, at the age of seventy-nine, Cooper led a march from the northern tip of the North Island to the New Zealand Parliament in Wellington to protest the loss of Māori land and to demand acknowledgement of their property rights under the Treaty of Waitangi. There is a wonderful photograph of Cooper addressing the crowds in Hamilton in her *kahu huruhuru* – feather cloak – and a magnificent pink headscarf.

Born thirty years after Cooper, **Tuaiwa Hautai 'Eva' Rickard** (1925–1997) was an activist for Māori and women's rights. She is particularly celebrated for her ten-year campaign to have ancestral lands by Raglan Harbour returned to local indigenous ownership. In 1978, she was filmed being arrested with nineteen fellow Māori protestors on the ninth hole of the Raglan golf course. Their court appearances resulted in a surge of public interest and, in the end, the land was returned.

In Australia, **Oodgeroo Noonuccal** (1920–1993) – originally **Kathleen Ruska**, then **Kath Walker** – was an inspirational woman in many different ways. An award-winning actress, an army officer during the Second World War, the first Aboriginal woman to publish a volume of poetry, she was also secretary of the Federal Council for the Advancement of Aborigines and Torres Strait Islanders for Queensland during the 1960s and was a key figure in the campaign to allow Aboriginal people full citizenship. Named Aboriginal of the Year in 1985, her commemorative plaque was one of the first installed on Sydney Writers Walk in 1991.

> 'It's time for us to remember that rights are
> not handed on a platter by governments,
> they have to be won.'
>
> **Faith Bandler**

Noonuccal's near contemporary was **Faith Bandler** (1918–2015), a civil rights activist of Scottish-Indian and South Sea Islander heritage. She came to public attention during the 1967 referendum to change the constitution to ensure that indigenous people were included in future national censuses. She was the co-founder of the Aboriginal Australia Fellowship with **Pearl Gibbs** (1901–1983), a member of the Aboriginals Progressive Association. In 1938, Gibbs was involved in organizing Day of Mourning protests – a protest at the 150th anniversary of the First Fleet, which came about in part due to the lack of recognition of the Aboriginal boycott of the centenary 'celebrations' – and, two years later, became the first Aboriginal woman to make a broadcast on Australian radio. Between 1954 and 1957, Gibbs was the only Aboriginal member of the New South Wales Aborigines Welfare Board and the only woman ever to serve on the board.

MOVING BACK IN time and to North America, **Ga'axstal'as** (1870–1951) – also known as **Jane Constance Cook** – was a cultural mediator and activist born on Vancouver Island, Canada. Raised by a missionary couple, the daughter of a Kwakwaka'wakw woman and a white fur trader, she campaigned for First Nation peoples to retain rights of access to land and resources. She testified to the Royal Commission of 1914 and, in 1922, was the only woman on the executive of the Allied Indian Tribes of British Columbia.

'Asking you to give me equal rights implies
that they are yours to give.
Instead, I must demand that you stop trying
to deny me the rights all people deserve.'

Elizabeth Peratrovich

Elizabeth Peratrovich (1911–1958) of the Tlingit nation was Grand
President of the Alaska Native Sisterhood and instrumental in the
passing of Alaska's Anti-Discrimination Act of 1945, the first legislation
of its kind in the United States. In 2021, the celebration was moved
from April to 16 February, the day the Act had been passed some
seventy-five years earlier. The Peratrovich family papers, including
correspondence, personal papers and news clippings related to her
civil rights work, are held at the Smithsonian National Museum of
the American Indian.

In 1988, 21 April was named as Elizabeth Peratrovich Day in
Alaska for: 'her courageous, unceasing efforts to eliminate discrimination and bring about equal rights . . .'

'We, the women of South Africa, wives and
mothers, working women and housewives,
African, Indians, European and Coloured,
hereby declare our aim of striving for the
removal of all laws, regulations, conventions
and customs that discriminate against us as
women, and that deprive us in any way of
our inherent right to the advantages,
responsibilities and opportunities that
society offers to any one section of the
population.'

South African Women's Charter

IN SOUTH AFRICA, another part of the world still marked by its past
in the British Empire, **Lillian Ngoyi** (1911–1980) – known as 'Mama
Ngoyi' – was a seamstress, a nurse and an anti-apartheid activist, and

became the first woman elected to the executive committee of the African National Congress. In August 1956, Ngoyi spearheaded a march of twenty thousand women, organized by the Federation of South African Women, to the Union Buildings of Pretoria in protest against the apartheid government's laws requiring women to carry passbooks. A petition with fourteen thousand signatures was handed over by these courageous women, who stood in silence for half an hour before singing the protest song 'Wathint'abafazi Wathint'imbokodo' – 'You strike women, you strike a rock'.

> 'Men are born into the system, and it is as if it has been a life tradition that they carry passes. We as women have seen the treatment our men have – when they leave home in the morning you are not sure they will come back. We are taking it very seriously. If the husband is to be arrested and the mother, what about the child?'
>
> *Lillian Ngoyi*

The Women's March Pretoria protestors included: **Reverend Motlalepula Chabaku** (1933–2012); **Bertha Gxowa** (1943–2010); **Helen Joseph** (1905–1992); **Fatima Meer** (1928–2010); **Rahima Moosa** (1922–1993); **Lillian Ngoyi** (1911–1980); **Albertina Sisulu** (1918–2011); and **Sophia Williams-De Bruyn** (b. 1938).

One of the many iconic photographs of that day shows Ngoyi with Rahima Moosa, Helen Joseph and Sophia Williams-De Bruyn outside the Union Building with stacks of petitions in their hands. Arrested several times, Ngoyi was kept under house arrest at home in Soweto for fifteen years.

> 'Regardless of how many years we have spent in this life, we must get up and shout.'
>
> *Fatima Meer*

Fatima Meer, who was born and died in Durban, was also at the Women's March on that day in August 1956. An author, anti-apartheid and human rights activist, she was one of the founding members of the Federation of South African Women.

> 'Women are the people who are going to relieve us from all this oppression and depression. The rent boycott that is happening in Soweto now is alive because of the women. It is the women who are on the street committees educating the people to stand up and protect each other.'
>
> **Nontsikelelo Albertina Sisulu**

So, too, was 'Mother of the Nation' **Nontsikelelo Albertina Sisulu**. A nurse, social and anti-apartheid campaigner, she was known as 'Mama Sisulu'. The only woman at the inaugural conference of the African National Congress Youth League in 1944, she was one of the first women to be arrested under the General Laws Amendment Act of 1963. For fifty years, she gave her energies to the Albertina Sisulu Foundation, caring for children, young people with disabilities and older citizens, and providing nurses in Tanzania after independence. In 1986, she was awarded honorary citizenship of Reggio nell'Emilia in Italy and served as the president of the World Peace Council in Switzerland between 1993 and 1996. In 1994, she became one of the first members of the new democratic government in South Africa and served for four years. When she died on 2 June 2011, Sisulu was given a state funeral and flags were ordered to be flown at half mast.

> 'I stand for simple justice, equal opportunity and human rights. The indispensable elements in a democratic society – and well worth fighting for.'
>
> **Helen Suzman**

For thirteen of her thirty-six years in the whites-only House of Assembly in South Africa, **Helen Suzman** (1917–2009) sat alone, representing a range of opposition parties after all other reforming politicians lost their seats in the 1961 election. I often try to imagine what it must have been like, day after solitary day, as an English-speaking Jewish woman facing an army of Calvinist Afrikaner men, enduring not only misogynistic abuse from Nationalist MPs, but anti-Semitic abuse, too. But Suzman never backed down. Accused by a minister of asking questions deliberately intended to make South Africa look bad overseas, she replied: 'It is not my questions that embarrass South Africa, it is your answers.'

Nominated twice for the Nobel Peace Prize, her image appears on stamps in Liberia and South Africa. When she died in Johannesburg on New Year's Day 2009, as with Mama Sisulu, flags were ordered to be flown at half mast.

After years of campaigning, harassment and exile, **Ruth First** (1925–1982) was murdered by the South African police in Mozambique. First's parents were Jewish, they had emigrated from Latvia in 1906 and were founding members of the Communist Party of South Africa. An investigative journalist, married to fellow Communist and anti-apartheid activist Jo Slovo, First was one of the 156 defendants in the Treason Trial of 1956–1961. Though acquitted, she was listed and banned from attending meetings and from publishing. Two years later, she was arrested and held in isolation under the Ninety-Day Detention Law, the first white woman to be detained. In response, she wrote an account of her experiences of interrogation and confinement, *117 Days*, which was reissued in 2010 with an introduction by her daughter, the novelist and writer **Gillian Slovo** (b. 1952). Forced into exile in 1964, she lived in London, was a research fellow at the University of Manchester, lectured in development studies at Durham University, then returned to Mozambique in 1978 to take up a position as director of research at the Centre of African Studies at Eduardo Mondlane University in the capital, Maputo. It was there, on 17 August 1982, that First was assassinated, opening a parcel bomb sent to the university on the orders of the South African police. In 2005, the South African Ministry of the Environment launched three environmental patrol ships – one named for **Lillian Ngoyi**, one for **Victoria Mxenge** (1942–1985) and one for **Ruth First**.

Women of great courage and conviction, who never gave up campaigning for what they knew to be right. A fairer, more equitable world.

IT WAS IN the mid-1970s when, growing up in a small cathedral city in southern England, I started to become aware of a world much broader than the one outside my window. Phrases such as 'women's libbers' were always delivered with disdain on the television news or in headlines in the newspapers. I didn't know that this was second-wave feminism, but I could see that women all over the world were marching: France, Germany, America, Italy, Spain, many of them following in the footsteps of early civil rights marches or the student anti-war marches of the 1960s. On 24 October 1975, some 90 per cent of women in Iceland went on strike to protest the gender pay gap and 'demonstrate the indispensable work of women for Iceland's economy and society'. It was the beginning of the UN Decade for Women . . .

> 'Men weren't really the enemy – they were fellow victims suffering from an outmoded masculine mystique that made them feel unnecessarily inadequate when there were no bears to kill.'
>
> ***Betty Friedan***

One of the foundation texts of second-wave feminism is *The Feminine Mystique* by American activist and writer **Betty Friedan** (1921–2006). Hers was one of the first feminist names I remember hearing and, as a teenager, I read her work. Tireless and uncompromising, Friedan co-founded the National Organization for Women in 1966 and was elected its first president. NOW intended to bring women 'into the mainstream of American society now [in] fully equal partnership with men'. In 1970, she organized the nationwide Women's Strike for Equality on the fiftieth anniversary of the Nineteenth Amendment to the United States Constitution, which granted women the right to vote. The march led by Friedan in New York City alone attracted over fifty thousand people, wildly exceeding everyone's expectations. The following year, Friedan joined with other leading feminists and civil rights activists to establish the National Women's Political Caucus.

Other members included: **Bella Abzug** (1920–1998); **Shirley Chisholm** (1924–2005); **Fannie Lou Hamer** (1917–1977); **Aileen Hernandez** (1926–2017); **Florynce Rae Kennedy** (1916–2000); and **Gloria Steinem** (b. 1934).

The focus of much of the mobilization in America during the 1970s was the battle to pass the Equal Rights Amendment – an amendment to the Constitution intended to guarantee equal legal rights for all American citizens regardless of sex. The intention was to end legal distinctions between men and women in matters of divorce, property and employment.

Though the first attempt was introduced to Congress in 1923 – by Alice Paul and **Crystal Eastman** (1881–1928) – it was the rise of the Women's Movement in the 1960s that turned the spotlight again on the ERA. It was approved by the House of Representatives on 12 October 1971 and by the Senate on 22 March 1972, both major political parties were in favour and all looked set for individual state ratification until lawyer and conservative activist **Phyllis Schlafly** mobilized conservative women in opposition, arguing that the ERA would disadvantage housewives, cause women to be drafted into the military and to lose protections such as alimony. Anti-abortion, anti-LGBT rights and pro-traditional gender distinctions, her arguments had a lot in common with the opposition of middle-class British women to women's suffrage a century before. Her campaign to derail the ERA was successful. Despite many attempts in the 1970s and beyond to move the ERA forward, as of 2022, it has still not been passed in every state . . . and so still cannot be included as an Amendment to the Constitution.

> 'The housewife is an unpaid employee in her husband's house in return for the security of being a permanent employee.'
>
> *Germaine Greer*

ONE OF THE most celebrated Australian feminist writers is **Germaine Greer** (b. 1939). Her first book text, *The Female Eunuch*, came out in 1970 and is seen as another foundation text of second-wave feminism. As in New Zealand, during the 1970s and 1980s, much of the focus of the Australian feminist movement was on indigenous rights and social policy. Forty years after *The Female Eunuch* was published, Australia's first female prime minister, **Julia Gillard** (b. 1961), was elected. Her 'misogyny speech' – delivered off the cuff after being accused by the leader of the opposition, Tony Abbott, of sexism, is one of the most watched speeches on social media of all time.

> 'I will not be lectured about sexism and misogyny by this man; I will not . . . If he [Abbott] wants to know what misogyny looks like in modern Australia, he doesn't need a motion in the House of Representatives, he needs a mirror.'
>
> **Julia Gillard**

Meanwhile, in the UK, the first national Women's Liberation Movement conference was held at Ruskin College, Oxford, at the end of February 1970. Four resolutions were passed, demanding equal pay, equal educational and job opportunities, free contraception and abortion on demand, and free twenty-four-hour nurseries. The organizers included socialist feminist historian and theorist **Sheila Rowbotham** (b. 1943), author of the influential 1969 pamphlet *Women's Liberation and the New Politics*; inspirational historian **Sally Alexander** (b. 1943), author of the ground-breaking *Becoming a Woman*; and research professor and psychoanalyst **Juliet Mitchell** (b. 1940). It was originally intended as a women's history conference – both Alexander and Rowbotham were aware of how little history was written by, or about, women – but some six hundred activists attended the three days of conference and the movement was born.

That same year, another foundation text of 1970s feminism – *Sexual Politics* by American writer **Kate Millett** (1934–2017) – was published. I still have my old battered copies of this and *The Female Eunuch*, the paper slightly yellowed and the spines broken, remembrance of my political awakening. Four years later saw the publication of *Women, Race and Class* by **Angela Y. Davis** (b. 1944).

> 'I am no longer accepting the things I cannot change. I am changing the things I cannot accept.'
>
> ***Angela Y. Davis***

Angela Y. Davis is an American political activist, philosopher, academic, scholar and author. A Marxist and long-time member of the Communist Party USA, she was a founding member of the Committees of Correspondence for Democracy and Socialism (CCDS). She is the author of more than ten books on class, feminism, race and the US prison system. Inducted into the National Women's Hall of Fame in 2019, in 2020 she was included in *Time* magazine's list of the 100 most influential people in the world. When she came to London in 2022 for the publication of her autobiography, she headlined the Women of the World (WOW) festival at the Southbank Centre.

Born a few years after Davis, **Olive Morris** (1952–1979) was a key figure in the Black Women's Movement in the UK. She co-founded the Organization of Women of African and Asian Descent and was an influential community leader, particularly within the squatters' rights campaign in London.

Trailblazers, all.

> 'A political struggle that does not have women at the heart of it, above it, below it, and within it is no struggle at all.'
>
> ***Arundhati Roy***

WOMEN ARE MARCHING still. As **Hillary Rodham Clinton** (b. 1947) said in Beijing on 5 September 1995 at her speech to the UN Fourth World Conference on Women: 'human rights are women's rights and women's rights are human rights . . .'

On 21 January 2017, millions of women in Washington and throughout America marched – to advocate legislation and policies regarding reproductive rights, immigration and climate change. In Iran, in December that same year, **Vida Movahed** (b. 1986) removed her white headscarf in Enghelab Street in Tehran, tied it to a stick and waved it as a protest against the compulsory wearing of the hijab. She was arrested that day and held in prison for a month, but other women re-enacted her protest and posted photos of themselves on social media, becoming known as the 'Girls of Enghelab Street'.

On New Year's Day in 2019, women in Kerala formed a 385-mile 'wall of protest' to fight for gender equality. In January 2021, thousands of women marched in Poland against new restrictive abortion laws; in August 2021, there were street protests in Kabul at the Taliban-imposed restrictions on women's and girls' lives; in September 2021, women marched for abortion rights in Chile and El Salvador. In Mexico in November 2021, hundreds of women carrying crosses bearing the names of murdered women marched in Mexico City to draw attention to rising cases of femicide on the 'Day of Dead Women' protest. In March 2022, women marched in Russia, for peace in Ukraine. In Lahore, Multan and Karachi, and in other cities in Pakistan, thousands of women marched for an end to violence against women and for equal wages. And in June 2022, after the repeal of *Roe v. Wade*, women marched throughout America to protest over the curtailment of a woman's right to choose.

> 'When the men are silent, it is our duty to raise our voices on behalf of our ideals.'
>
> *Clara Zetkin*

International Women's Day, now celebrated all over the world, was first celebrated in 1911. It came out of the labour movement and the global suffrage and civil rights movements. In New York in 1908, some fifteen thousand women marched through the streets demanding shorter working hours, better pay and the right to vote. German socialist activist and labour leader **Clara Zetkin** (1857–1933) first suggested the idea of an international women's day and proposed the idea to an International Conference of Working Women in Copenhagen in 1910. The one hundred women there – representing some seventeen countries – agreed unanimously. In 1917, Russian women demanded 'bread and peace', and the right to vote. A few generations later, in 1975, the United Nations began celebrating International Women's Day, as a way of marking how far things have come for women, and also as a reminder of how things can still go backwards. Women need to keep fighting for – and securing – their rights to play as large or as small a role in their society as they want to. Not every woman wants a seat at the boardroom table, or to take up arms or to become prime minister, but she who does should not be prevented by laws that discriminate against her.

> 'If the women of the world had not been excluded from world affairs, things today may have been different.'
>
> **Alice Paul**

OF COURSE, THERE are countless thousands of women of conviction and courage who could be celebrated in this chapter. It seems to me there's more publishing, more diversity in writing, more honest debate than in recent years about what needs to be done to achieve true gender equality, and about how to make any discussions genuinely inclusive. According to the World Economic Forum's Global Gender Gap Report 2021, the time needed to change the global gender gap has increased, in the last generation, from 99.5 years to 135.6 years.

The pendulum keeps swinging.

I'd like to give the final word in this chapter to the great Egyptian feminist, novelist, polemicist, doctor and campaigner against female genital mutilation, **Nawal El Saadawi** (1931–2021). The author of more than fifty books, including ground-breaking works such as *The Hidden Face of Eve*, El Saadawi was several times imprisoned for her beliefs and wrote *Memoirs from the Women's Prison* on toilet paper with a smuggled eyebrow pencil. Founder of several campaigning organizations, including the Egyptian chapter of the Arab Women's

Solidarity Association, she was a fierce, brilliantly independent teacher and campaigner who grew more – rather than less – radical with age. In 2020, *Time* magazine named her among the one hundred most influential women of the twentieth century.

> 'Women are half the society. You cannot have a revolution without women. You cannot have democracy without women. You cannot have equality without women. You can't have anything without women.'
>
> ***Nawal El Saadawi***

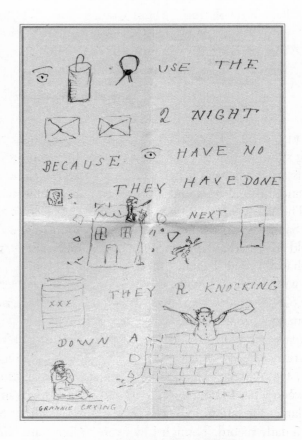

Pictogram sent by Lily to her granddaughter,
Margaret, c. 1926

Lily

SEPTEMBER 1921. THE HEATWAVE and the drought of a long, scorching summer that gripped the whole of the country continued. The fields and gardens and parks of London were yellow and dusty, the trees and shrubs dead from lack of water. T. S. Eliot was in Margate, writing 'The Wasteland', sitting in a Victorian shelter looking out over Margate Sands: 'I can connect nothing with nothing.' I do not think Lily would have had any patience for Eliot's modernist despair.

But what of life at 'Poplars', now that Sam is dead?

In his will, Sam left Lily their house and £12,371 – worth approximately £625,000 today – to 'one whose love, devotion and courage during our long, married life has been unceasing'.

Fifty years of letters, of affection, of shared history, now gone.

As I write a version of Lily's life, surrounded by photographs and letters, by family trees and document wallets, it's frustrating that the gaps between what I know for certain and what I might imagine are growing larger the later into her life I have gone. Without Sam, there is less of a daily record. Though Lily wrote to her grandchildren and children, fewer of those letters have come down to me. Like a photograph fading slowly in the sun, Lily is becoming less clear. And I keep thinking about whose life is seen as valuable, and which lives are recorded with assiduity, truth and integrity. The fact that someone like my great-grandmother – with all her advantages, her contemporary visibility, her access to writing materials and the means to preserve her words – could so easily disappear from the record highlights how quickly, and how easily, history can be made and unmade.

Lily lived for another eleven years after Sam's death. I have several letters from this time, all with her characteristic pictograms and drawings, still full of humorous and exciting stories. She sent them to her grandchildren, my father and my aunt. It's clear Lily loved children and knew how to engage with them. A picture emerges of a beloved grandmother at the heart of her extended family, firm of opinion but indulgent and fun. Every year, she held a Christmas party. Each grandchild would be presented in their Sunday best and given a gift, before sitting down to a huge tea laid out on the dining-room table decorated with snow houses and candles. A little later, everyone could look forward to an entertainment performed by the adults. One year, it was *Aladdin*, the next a pirate story . . .

Sister Katherine's scrapbook is wonderful about this period of Lily's life *'entre les deux guerres'*. A woman who held tea parties for the ladies of the parish and opened her house so that the Sunday-school children could play in the garden. Sister Katherine writes of how the children from St Phillips 'travelled in a brewer's wagon filled with wooden benches drawn by two carthorses . . .' From her descriptions, too, a sense of 'Poplars' emerges, its rhythms and character: large rooms overlooking the lawn; a dining room with a huge painting of mountains in cloud held 'firm to the ceiling with chains'; a harmonium in the nursery; and a large Persian cat called Pompeii, with long grey fur, who ruled the drawing room. There was a knot garden, a maze of clipped hedges made out of aromatic herbs, out of sight of the main house where the family used to sit. Beyond that still there were fields, as dry and yellow as London's parks.

I know she continued to fill her days with good works. She was a member of the Mothers' Union and on many committees, including the education board of Surrey Education Authority, and she continued to be part of the community of St Margaret the Queen. The articles she writes during this period are serious and Lily is prolific. Op-ed pieces about protecting the nation's food, about citizenship and faith, about daughters and marriage, about girls' education, about caring for children. She's something in the way of the regular columnist in *The Girl's Own Paper* on matters of faith, a kind of religious agony *aunt*. In terms of long-form writing, she publishes a couple of books for children and devotional verses for women and girls, but sadly no more full-length fiction. Maybe she no longer had the appetite for it, or the stamina to juggle so many made-up characters in her head.

There are family challenges, too. Winnie decides to divorce her husband and returns from India for good. I imagine Lily was distressed by this. She would have expected Winnie to see things through, but there are photographs of them together, so clearly Lily welcomed her back even if she didn't approve. Sister Katherine remembers Lily telephoning her father, Harold, and asking him to come round to discuss the 'crisis'. The divorce does not go through until after Lily's death in 1932.

At this point in my research, I discovered another intriguing thing, another extraordinary point of reference. Winnie, without it ever being mentioned by her mother, has also taken to writing.

In 1923, two years after Sam's death, she publishes her first novel, *Ann's an Idiot*. Writing under the pen name **Pamela Wynne** (1879–1959), Winnie will go on to publish more than sixty romantic novels, many inspired by her years living in India, and two of them – *Dangerous Innocence* (1925) and *Devotion* (1931) – were turned into major motion pictures. Winnie's novels were considered 'steamy' in the language of the time and, of course, I can't help but wonder if Lily was scandalized by her daughter or proud of her success.

Or, possibly, a bit of both.

Winnie, unlike Lily, does have her own page on Wikipedia . . .

Top: Amrita Sher-Gil (1913–1941)
Bottom left: Amelia Bloomer (1818–1894)
Bottom right: Edmonia 'Wildfire' Lewis (1844–1907)

10

Razzle Dazzle

'History is no longer just a chronicle of kings and statesmen, of people who wielded power, but of ordinary women and men engaged in manifold tasks. Women's history is an assertion that women have a history.'

'Daughters in Boxes',
Kishida Toshiko, 1883

WARRIOR QUEENS AND QUIET revolutionaries, women of faith and courage, mothers of invention and legal pioneers, writers, humanitarian workers and intrepid explorers, we've already celebrated nearly a thousand extraordinary women and lit the touchpaper, I hope, for readers to discover many more.

What we've also seen is how one of the most effective ways women's achievements are kept in the public eye – or put back centre stage – is through their representation in fiction, art, sculpture, theatre, film, opera, photography, even on postage stamps and bank notes. From a statue at Govan Cross in Glasgow to a blue plaque on a house in Belfast, these visible signs of a woman's life remain so important.

So, now it's time to raise our hats to women whose creative skill, inventiveness, or physical prowess have made a mark. All those who ran faster, jumped higher, swam further, who razzled and dazzled and entertained, who allowed their imaginations to change what we thought was possible.

TECHNOLOGICAL INVENTION IS often presented as a male preserve, but a significant number of the innovations we take for granted today were, in fact, invented and first patented by women. It's particularly difficult for women to be recognized in this area because finance and sponsorship are also male-dominated areas. You have to have the idea, test the idea, make the prototype and then find someone with deep pockets to help bring it to market . . . Each step is a possible hurdle at which an inventor could fall.

'. . . and if as some suppose, at one period of [Earth's] history the air had mixed with it a larger proportion than at present, an increased temperature from its own action as well as from increased weight must have necessarily resulted.'

Eunice Newton Foote

We've met some of our medical mothers of invention, so let's shine a spotlight on their 'hardware sisters', starting with **Eunice Newton Foote** (1819–1888). Growing up in Bloomfield, New York, she was an American scientist and inventor. After her marriage, Newton Foote lived briefly in Seneca Falls and attended the famous Women's Rights Convention of July 1848. Both she and her husband signed the Declaration of Sentiments, the document protesting women's disenfranchisement. As far back as 1856, Newton Foote had discovered that too much carbon dioxide in the atmosphere could cause the Earth to warm – what we now call 'greenhouse gases'. Her experiment was simple: she placed two identical thermometers in identical glass cylinders, removed air from one and added air into the other. Once the temperatures equalized, she placed the cylinders in the sunshine and recorded the resulting temperature every two to three minutes. She repeated the experiment in the shade, and with moist and dry air, thereby discovering that damp air became significantly hotter than dry air.

And yet . . . In August 1856, she had to sit in the audience at an American Association for the Advancement of Science (AAAS) meeting and listen as Joseph Henry, secretary of the Smithsonian Institution, presented her research – but failed to recognize its implications – that increased carbon dioxide in the atmosphere would cause global warming.

Newton Foote is yet another victim of the 'Matilda Effect'. Because her experiment didn't explain exactly how the greenhouse effect worked, when a male scientist figured out that piece of the puzzle three years later, the entire discovery was attributed to him. It was not until 2011, when the geologist Raymond Sorenson came across a report written by Joseph Henry of Newton Foote's experiment, that her role started to be acknowledged. Her other inventions include, satisfyingly, a patent in 1860 for a 'filling for soles of boots and shoes' to stop them squeaking and a new paper-making machine. She's linked in my mind to fellow American **Margaret Knight** (1883–1914), who founded the Eastern Paper Bag Company in 1870 and created flat-bottomed bags for carrying groceries. Practical, helpful and ecologically friendly.

> 'If nobody else is going to invent a dish washing machine, I'll do it myself!'
>
> *Josephine Cochrane*

One of my favourite stories is about the invention of the first automatic dishwasher by **Josephine Cochrane** (1839–1913), presumably after a particularly large dinner party with no one helping her to wash up! Cochrane designed the machine in a shed behind her home in Chicago, with the help of mechanic George Butters, who became one of her first employees in the Garis-Cochrane Manufacturing Company (Garis was her unmarried name). Cochrane's patent was issued on 28 December 1886, and she was posthumously inducted into the American National Inventors Hall of Fame in 2006.

Lizzie Magie (1866–1948) was a feminist and writer from Illinois – and a games designer. She supported the single tax movement – an economic theory proposing that all government taxes should be replaced by a single tax based on land, rather than buildings occupying the space. Does that sound familiar? Magie went on to invent 'The Landlord's Game' as a kind of economics tutorial. It's a sort of unknown older sister to the world-famous game 'Monopoly'.

> 'If necessity is the mother of invention, then resourcefulness is the father.'
>
> *Beulah Henry*

A generation later, one of America's most dazzling and prolific inventors I've included was born in Raleigh, North Carolina. **Beulah Henry** (1887–1973), often known as 'Lady Edison', registered 49 patents and worked on over 110 inventions, most of which were designed to make ordinary, everyday life easier. Her first invention, a vacuum-sealed ice-cream freezer, was patented in 1912. She went on to invent the 'protograph', a typographical device that produced an original and four typewritten copies without carbon paper; an umbrella with interchangeable covers to match a person's outfit; a lockstitch bobbin-less sewing machine; the 'Kiddie Clock', to help children learn to tell the time; and the 'Miss Illusion' doll, with eyes that changed colour. She was inducted into the American National Inventors Hall of Fame in 2006, more than thirty years after her death. Fellow inventor **Mary Pennington** (1872–1952) was also inducted posthumously in 2018. Pennington was a bacteriological chemist, refrigeration engineer and food scientist, who was a pioneer in the safe preservation, handling, storage and transportation of perishable foods.

Mary Anderson (1866–1953) was an American rancher, developer, viticulturist and the inventor of the windscreen wiper! On 10 November 1903, Anderson was granted her first patent for an automatic car window cleaning device controlled from inside the car. And **Ruth Benerito** (1916–2013) was an American chemist and inventor who held fifty-five patents, her most famous being for the development of a treatment for cotton, making it a hugely practical wash-and-wear fabric. Another invention, during the Korean War, was for delivering fat intravenously to severely wounded soldiers who couldn't eat in any other way.

IN EUROPE, TOO, women inventors were making their mark. More than a century earlier, **Jeanne Villepreux-Power** (1794–1871) was born in the Limousin in central France. The daughter of a shoemaker and a seamstress, she was originally a dressmaker in Paris and was very successful, creating wedding gowns, notably for the **Duchess of Berry** (1798–1870). But, as time went by, she became fascinated by marine biology. Her research and experiments led her to invent the aquarium. Meanwhile, in Germany, a Dresden woman called **Melitta**

Bentz (1873–1950) invented the paper coffee filter. Using the blotting paper from her son's school book, she rolled it into a funnel, balanced it inside a tin and poured hot water over the coffee grounds. She patented her filter in 1908 and, at Christmas of that year, started a company to market her invention. More than a hundred years later, the Melitta company is still going strong.

> 'Hope and curiosity about the future seemed better than guarantees. The unknown was always so attractive to me . . . and still is.'
>
> ***Hedy Lamarr***

Perhaps the most extraordinary female inventor is the Austrian-born American film actress and engineer **Hedy Lamarr** (1914–2000). Celebrated as an amazing actress, she made some thirty films between 1930 and 1958, including *Samson and Delilah* in 1949. But, while she was taking the box office by storm, Lamarr also invented a radio guidance system for Allied torpedoes with composer George Antheil. Although the technology was not adopted until the 1960s, her discovery formed the basis for Bluetooth, GPS and WiFi technology. Married and divorced six times, Lamarr is the only person, woman or man, both to have a star on the Hollywood Walk of Fame *and* to have been inducted into the National Inventors Hall of Fame.

> '. . . I played with Meccano. I spent my pocket money on penknives, an adjustable spanner, a glue pot and other simple hand tools.'
>
> ***Tilly Shilling***

From tiny inventions can come life-changing results, in this case a brass washer in the shape of a thimble. **Beatrice 'Tilly' Shilling** (1909–1990) studied electrical and mechanical engineering at university. In 1940, she discovered how to prevent the planes flown by Battle of Britain fighter pilots in the Second World War from stalling, an invention that became known as 'Miss Shilling's Orifice'. After the war, she continued working for the Royal Aircraft Establishment, studying supersonic aircraft and rocket propulsion, and worked on the British bobsled team's sled ahead of the 1968 Winter Olympics. She was also a record-breaking motorcyclist, one of very few women to be awarded the Brooklands race-track gold star.

> 'The costume of women should be suited to her wants and necessities. It should conduce at once to her health, comfort, and usefulness; and, while it should not fail also to conduce to her personal adornment, it should make that end of secondary importance.'
>
> *Amelia Bloomer*

A CENTURY EARLIER, on both sides of the Atlantic, women were beginning to challenge traditional clothing that restricted their freedom to move, even sometimes to breathe. Possibly the best known of the 'free-clothing' women's rights campaigners was **Amelia Bloomer** (1818–1894). She founded and edited the first US newspaper for women, *The Lily* – the first woman ever to own and edit any newspaper for women – and advocated women rejecting the restrictive corsets and bustles of the day in favour of 'Turkish pantaloons', which became known as bloomers in her honour . . .

The fashion for clothing that did not inhibit women was linked with women's broader emancipation in education and in sport. Bicycling was becoming popular. There is a much-shared, sinister photograph taken in 1897 of male students in Market Square in Cambridge protesting against women being admitted to the university. It shows an effigy of a 'new woman' on a bicycle, wearing a pair of bloomers, being dangled out of a second-floor window.

Another mother of vestimentary invention was **Mary 'Polly' Jacob** (1892–1970), who was later known as **Caresse Crosby**. Refusing to wear her corset as being too restrictive and uncomfortable, she instead sewed two handkerchiefs together, and the first modern bra was born.

There had been versions as early as the 1860s, the most famous being the 'breast supporter' created by couturier **Herminie Cadolle** (1845–1926), the founder of the Cadolle Lingerie House, which was displayed at the Great Exhibition in 1890. Cadolle should be seen as the inventor of the bra, but Crosby was first to be granted a patent in 1914 and set up a company to manufacture them, before selling on to the Warner Brothers Corset Company in 1922. In later life, Jacob founded Women Against War and Citizens of the World. An uplifting tale of invention . . .

CLOTHING REFORM WAS to play a crucial part in the history of women's sport. Here, perhaps more than almost any everyday activity, women have had to fight to be included on the same terms as their male counterparts – or sometimes to be allowed to compete at all. Issues of propriety, of clothing, of what was deemed appropriate or possible all played their part. But, despite the obstacles, individual women broke records and made it possible for others to follow.

In September 1875, fourteen-year-old Londoner **Agnes Beckwith** (1861–1951) made history by diving from a boat at London Bridge and swimming to Greenwich in one hour and seven minutes. As well as breaking many other records, Beckwith travelled the world with her troupe, performing a kind of Victorian version of synchronized swimming. There is a wonderful poster of her 1885 show at the Royal Aquarium Westminster, with an image of Beckwith in her swimming costume, billed as the 'greatest lady swimmer in the world'. Her costume looks more like the corsetry that a can-can dancer at the Folies-Bergère might wear, all ruffs and frills.

The first modern Olympic Games were held in Athens in 1896. There were 280 athletes, representing twelve countries, and all of the athletes were men. Four years later in Paris, women were allowed to compete individually in tennis and golf, and in women's teams in sailing, equestrianism and croquet. The American sailor **Hélène de Pourtalès** (1868–1945) became the first ever female-team Olympic champion, representing Switzerland, and British tennis player **Charlotte Cooper** (1870–1966) was the first ever female tennis champion, making her the first individual female Olympic champion.

There were 22 female athletes in all, that's to say 2.2 per cent of competitors. By 1908, there were 37 women. Small steps . . .

The 1912 Summer Olympics in Stockholm were the first games to include women's swimming. Among the first women who took part was the great Australian swimmer **Fanny Durack** (1889–1956). She won her first title in 1906 and, from 1912 to 1920, held the women's freestyle swimming world record for 100 metres, and the 200-metre freestyle record from 1915 to 1921. At first, Durack and her close friend and swimming rival **Mina Wylie** (1891–1984) were refused permission to attend the 1912 Olympics. Then they were allowed to go but only provided they funded themselves and raised enough to pay for their own chaperones. It was worth it. Durack won a gold medal for the 100-metre freestyle, becoming the first Australian woman to win a medal, and Wylie won silver. Durack was so famous that, when a statue of the Madonna and Child was shelled in Brebières in January 1915, leaving it in a near-horizontal position as if diving off the blocks, Australian soldiers nicknamed the statue 'Fanny'.

The Winter Olympics were first held in 1924, though women could only compete in figure skating. Austrian figure skater **Herma Szabo** (1902–1986) became the first ever female Winter Olympic champion. Later, the return of the Summer Olympics to Paris saw a record 135 female athletes compete. Women's fencing made its debut, with the Danish foil fencer **Ellen Ossier** (1890–1962) winning gold. Other female medal winners included British poet **Dorothy Stuart** (1889–1963), who was the first woman to win a medal in the Arts for Mixed Literature.

I enjoy watching big global sporting competitions on television, particularly the Olympic Games, but until I began research for *Warrior Queens & Quiet Revolutionaries*, I had no idea that they used to include an arts component. It turns out that, in keeping with Olympic Committee founder Pierre de Coubertin's mission to marry the athletic with the aesthetic, creative competitions were an integral part of the games from 1912 to 1948. There were five categories of individual competition open to women and men, honouring their achievements over the previous four years in the disciplines of architecture, literature, music, painting and sculpture. Each artwork was also required to 'bear a definite relationship to the Olympic concept'. Dorothy Stuart's silver-medal-winning poetry entry in 1924 was 'Sword

Songs', inspired by fencing, but there were many difficulties around the judging, in particular in relation to subjectivity. The host country very often tended to reward its own artists more significantly, as in Germany in 1936. After 1948, the Arts medals were discontinued.

> 'All I've done is run fast. I don't see why people should make much fuss about that.'
>
> **Fanny Blankers-Koen**

The 1948 'Austerity' games were held in London in August, the first since the notorious 'Nazi' games of Berlin in 1936 where German-Jewish athletes had been prevented from taking part. My father, having fenced in army clubs during the Second World War, was one of the reserves for the épée class. The star of 1948 was the Dutch athlete **Fanny Blankers-Koen** (1918–2004), who won four gold medals and set world records in long jump, high jump, hurdles and sprint. Thirty years old and pregnant with her third child, her nickname was 'The Flying Housewife' . . .

> 'This ability to conquer oneself is no doubt the most precious of all things sport bestows.'
>
> **Olga Korbut**

I can remember watching **Olga Korbut** (b. 1955) at the 1972 Munich games on the television, a tiny girl with bunches, wearing a white leotard and a dazzling smile. Known as the 'Sparrow from Minsk', she won four gold medals and two silver medals at the Summer Olympic Games of 1972 and 1976, competing individually and as part of the Soviet team. In 1988, she was the first person to be inducted into the International Gymnastics Hall of Fame. Korbut emigrated to America in 1991, and later revealed that she and fellow gymnasts had been subjected to physical and sexual abuse at the hands of their coach. Fifty years later, the exploitation of young women and girls in sport has not gone away.

'I don't run away from a challenge because I
am afraid. Instead, I run towards it because
the only way to escape fear is to trample it
beneath your foot.'

Nadia Comăneci

At the Montreal Summer Olympics in 1976, a fourteen-year-old
gymnast from Romania, **Nadia Comăneci** (b. 1961) achieved a perfect
10 for her routine on the uneven bars. The UK was in the grip of a
heatwave, Elton John and Kiki Dee were No. 1 in the UK pop charts
with 'Don't Go Breaking My Heart' and, as I watched Comăneci on
the television in her white leotard, I remember realizing we were
almost exactly the same age.

She went on to score another six 10s and won the overall gold
medal, as well as gold on the beam and the uneven bars. Comăneci
also holds the record as the youngest ever gymnastics all-round champion. Since the age-eligibility rules have been revised, that's a record
that cannot be broken. With six other gymnasts, she defected from
Romania in November 1989, walking over the border into Hungary,
then to Austria and the United States embassy, who put her on a
flight to New York. She became an American citizen in 2001.

'It's about standing up and being counted
and saying you're proud of who you are.'

Megan Rapinoe

A final piece of Olympic history. Football was a demonstration sport
in the 1896 Olympics – in other words, a sport played to showcase the
sport itself rather than as part of the medal competition. With the exception of the Los Angeles games in 1932, male football has been in every
Games since then. But women's football was not added until 1996 in
Atlanta, far too late for one of the greatest British footballers of all time.

Lily Parr (1905–1978) was born in St Helens on Merseyside. She
grew up kicking a ball about with her brothers and made her debut
at the age of fourteen for her local team. Scouted by the manager of
the most successful team of the time, the 'Dick, Kerr Ladies', Parr

was offered a job at the Preston Munitions Factory where most of the women on the team worked. There had been huge interest in women's football during the First World War and the Preston team, which played its first game on Christmas Day 1917, regularly drew huge crowds. The record-breaking match between Dick, Kerr Ladies and St Helens on Boxing Day in 1920 at Goodison Park is estimated to have been watched by a crowd of 46,000 people. The success of the women's game was resented by some and, the following December, the Football Association declared the game 'unsuitable' for women. By banning its members from hosting women's teams, they essentially shut down the women's game. The ban was not lifted until 1971.

Despite the ban, Parr and her teammates played on. The exact tally varies, but it's estimated she scored nearly one thousand goals between 1919 and 1951. When she finally retired from professional football, Parr worked as a nurse at Whittingham Mental Hospital near Preston. It was there Parr met her life partner, Mary. They lived together in the village of Goosnargh in Lancashire until Parr's death in 1978. She was the first woman to be inducted into the National Football Museum's Hall of Fame in 2002 and, in 2019, the museum unveiled a statue, all five-foot-ten of her. Created by Sussex sculptor **Hannah Stewart** (b. *c.* 1976), it's the first statue of a female footballer in the UK.

On 31 July 2022, a record-breaking crowd of 87,192 watched the English Lionesses beat Germany 2-1 in the final of the 2022 Euros at Wembley. More than 17.5 million more watched on television, the biggest audience for any European final. After fifty-six years of hurt, football came home . . .

THE PARALYMPICS HAS grown from being a small gathering of former Second World War veterans in 1948, to a major part of the Olympic programme. A German neurologist, Ludwig Guttman, was looking for a way to help his paraplegic patients at Stoke Mandeville hospital outside of London. Sixteen veterans in wheelchairs faced off in archery and netball competitions. The first International Stoke Mandeville Games were held four years later, when a team of veterans from the Netherlands competed alongside the British teams, and, from then on, the Games were held every year.

The ninth Games are now considered the first Paralympic Games and took place in Rome in September 1960, six days after the closing ceremony of the Olympic Games. Twenty-three nations took part, sending four hundred athletes – all in wheelchairs – who competed in eight sports.

> 'The Chicago Special Olympics prove a very
> fundamental fact, the fact that exceptional
> children . . . can be exceptional athletes,
> the fact that through sports they can realize
> their potential for growth.'
>
> *Eunice Kennedy Shriver*

In America, two years after the Rome Olympics, **Eunice Kennedy Shriver** (1921–2009) founded a camp for children with disabilities and special needs at her Maryland farm. Camp Shriver later evolved into the Special Olympics in 1968 in Chicago, expanding into international territories during the 1970s and 1980s, and now holds more than a hundred thousand events a year throughout the world. A pioneer working with children with special and additional needs, Shriver was awarded the Presidential Medal of Freedom in 1984 and, in 1990, was granted the Eagle Award from the United States Sports Academy. She was the second American – and the first woman – to appear on a US coin while she was still alive.

> 'To my surprise, I was soon in the middle of
> the podium!'
>
> *Margaret Maughan*

Britain's first Paralympian gold medallist was **Margaret Maughan** (1928–2020). Paralysed from the waist down in a road accident in Malawi in 1959, she was flown home to Stoke Mandeville for treatment. She took up archery there, hoping it would help maintain her balance in her wheelchair, and discovered she had an aptitude for it. Selected to represent Britain in those first Paralympic Games in Rome in 1960, she not only won a gold medal in archery but also won the fifty-metres women's backstroke. She won another gold in dartchery, the pairs archery competition, at Heidelberg in 1972, plus two silvers in Toronto in 1976. Her final gold came in lawn bowls in the women's pair at her fifth Paralympics in Arnhem in 1980.

Ten years ago, at the age of eighty-five and resplendent in the British team's white- and sky-blue tracksuit, Maughan lit the Paralympic flame at the opening of the London 2012 Summer Paralympics. Simply magnificent.

> 'A photograph is a secret about a secret.
> The more it tells you the less you know.'
>
> **Diane Arbus**

LILY'S PHOTOGRAPH HAS kept me company through the writing, the rewriting, the editing of this book, and the table in my study was always covered with family photographs. Although we know that photographs can be retouched, there is nonetheless a promise that you are seeing something of the real person behind the fixed smile or unwavering stare.

In addition to those we've already met, there have been many extraordinary female photographers of every nationality. As some women had more freedom to travel, they took advantage of a level of independence and the ability to go anywhere and see everything, taking photographs of what they saw.

Here are three more game-changers.

> 'I longed to arrest all the beauty that came
> before me and at length the longing has
> been satisfied . . . My aspirations are to
> ennoble Photography and to secure for it
> the character and uses of High Art by
> combining the real and ideal and sacrificing
> nothing of the Truth by all possible devotion
> to poetry and beauty.'
>
> **Julia Margaret Cameron**

Though she had been interested in photography since the late 1850s, **Julia Margaret Cameron** (1815–1879) became a professional photographer relatively late in her life, when one of her daughters gave her a sliding-box camera for a Christmas present in 1863.

In January 1864, she photographed nine-year-old Annie Philpot – an image she described as her 'first success' – and, the same year, registered her work and prepared it for exhibition and sale. She was elected to the Photographic Society of London and, in 1886, became a member of the Photographic Society of Scotland.

In 1865, Cameron held her first solo exhibition and her prints were in great demand. Over the course of her career, she made some nine hundred photographs – images of distinguished men of the day, from Charles Darwin, Sir John Herschel and Henry Longfellow, to their neighbour on the Isle of Wight, Alfred, Lord Tennyson. Her images of women and girls are distinguished by a pre-Raphaelite kind of dreaminess, the interplay of light and shade; and her *tableaux vivants* were inspired by literature – she illustrated Tennyson's *Idylls of the King* – as well as ideals of beauty and Christianity. Though her style did not appeal to everyone – many contemporary critics disliked her soft-focus approach, and criticized her use of children – since the twentieth century, Julia Margaret Cameron has been acknowledged as a ground-breaking artist. In 1873, she retired with her husband to Ceylon, where he had bought a small coffee planta-tion years before. They raised eleven children, five of their own, five children of relatives who'd been orphaned, and a destitute Irish girl they had taken in. An extraordinary woman whose work transformed the art of photography, her work is still as modern and fresh today as it was in the mid-nineteenth century.

> 'That the familiar world is often unsatisfactory cannot be denied, but it is not, for all that, one that we need abandon . . . Bad as it is, the world is potentially full of good photographs. But to be good, photographs have to be full of the world.'
>
> **Dorothea Lange**

Unlike Cameron, the American documentary photographer **Dorothea Lange** (1895–1965) had little interest in classifying her photographs as art. Her concern was to record and document, honestly and with integrity, those people whose lives she witnessed. She saw photography as a way to effect social change. Her most iconic photograph – of thirty-two-year-old Florence Owens Thompson and her children, taken in March 1936 in Nipomo, California – became a symbol of the desperate hardship of the Great Depression. Lange was working as a photographer for the Resettlement Administration, a government agency working to raise public awareness of the plight of farmers. On 10 March, two of Lange's photographs of the Nipomo pea pickers' camp were published in *The San Francisco News* under the headline 'Ragged, Hungry, Broke, Harvest Workers Live in Squallor' [sic] and the photograph of Thompson, which later became known as *Migrant Mother,* was published in the paper on 11 March to accompany an editorial 'What Does the "New Deal"' Mean To This Mother and Her Children?' That same day, the *Los Angeles Times* reported that the State Relief Administration would deliver food rations to two thousand itinerant fruit pickers.

Lange's commitment to social justice and her faith in the power of photography to effect change never faltered. In 1942, when the government's War Relocation Authority assigned her to document the wartime internment of Japanese Americans – a policy Lange fiercely opposed – she took critical images, which the government suppressed.

> 'I tend to think of the act of photographing, generally speaking, as an adventure. My favorite thing is to go where I've never been.'
>
> *Diane Arbus*

The third of our trailblazing women is fellow American **Diane Arbus** (1923–1971), who perhaps did more than any other photographer of the time to represent marginalized groups – carnival performers, people with dwarfism, strippers, cross-dressers, nudists, movie fans, what she called 'freaks' – believing that all people were worthy of beautiful representation. Arbus photographed her subjects in their homes, on the street, in the workplace, in the park, again changing ideas of what was a 'suitable' location for a photograph. By the early 1960s, her reputation was growing. Her work appeared in magazines such as *Esquire* and *Harper's Bazaar*, and in 1963, the Guggenheim Foundation awarded Arbus a fellowship for her proposal entitled: 'American Rites, Manners and Customs'.

In 1972, a year after her death by suicide at Westbeth Artists Community in New York City, Arbus became the first photographer to be included in the Venice Biennale. Arbus has had more than twenty-five major solo exhibitions, eight authorized publications, television documentaries and countless articles about the importance and power of her work.

Other legendary photographers include: **Laylah Amatullah Barrayn** (b. *c.* 1992); **Ilse Bing** (1899–1998); **Hou Bo** (1924–2017); **Claude Cahun** (1894–1954); **Marti Friedlander** (1928–2016); **Eunice 'Una' Garlick** (1883–1951); **Gertrude Käsebier** (1852–1934); **Rinko Kawauchi** (b. 1972); **Galina Kmit** (1931–2019); **Ekaterina Kruchkova** (b. 1974); **Jungjin Lee** (b. 1961); **Annie Leibovitz** (b. 1949); and **Tina Modotti** (1896–1942).

> 'Every time I have had a problem, I have confronted it with the axe of art.'
>
> *Yayoi Kusama*

GOING BACK BEFORE the advent of the daguerreotype and silver nitrate, female artists and painters had to struggle not only to win a commission but also to be allowed to show their work in salons or galleries. It was a strange contradiction. Painting as a hobby or pastime for women was acceptable, but being a professional painter was not. In terms of reputation, there was an equivalent issue. Women were often not allowed to attend art school and their work was rarely afforded the respect or the celebration of their male counterparts. We will never know how many works have been lost to us because of these prejudices, but here are a few artists whose work has survived for us to celebrate.

The Antwerp-born **Caterina van Hemessen** (1528–after 1565) is one of the earliest women credited with producing a self-portrait. In fact, so far as records show, it's the first ever self-portrait showing an artist at an easel. Painted in 1548, it shows her sitting at her easel wearing a black over-partlet with red velvet undersleeves, her hair covered by a white linen hood. She holds a single paintbrush in her right hand and, in her left, a palette and fan of five more brushes. The Latin inscription reads: I CATERINA VAN HEMESSEN HAVE PAINTED MYSELF / 1548 / HER AGE 20. A very similar painting to survive – the clothes are all but identical – shows a young woman playing the virginal. Some historians think it could be a companion 'selfie', others that it is more probably a portrayal of her sister, Christina. Van Hemessen is the earliest female Flemish painter whose attributed body of work survives.

> 'My illustrious lordship, I'll show you what a woman can do.'
>
> **_Artemisia Gentileschi_**

One of the most famous artists of the Italian Baroque is **Artemisia Gentileschi** (1593–c. 1656). For a long time, the story of Gentileschi's rape as a young woman overshadowed her achievements as an artist. But there's no doubt that her appalling experience – and the horror of the trial to bring her rapist to justice – fuelled her work. Working as an artist professionally from the age of fifteen, she was the first woman to become a member of the Accademia delle Arti del Disegno in Florence. She depicted strong and courageous women from the Bible, from myth and legend, and didn't shy away from depicting violence – say, in *Judith Slaying Holofernes* or *Jael and Sisera*. In *Susanna and the Elders*, two men are whispering and looming over an almost naked young woman. She 'painted' herself into history too, including *Self-Portrait as Catherine of Alexandria*. Her date of death is not certain – it's been proved she was still accepting commissions in 1654 – but it's possible she died in the plague that devastated Naples in 1656. Gentileschi is one of the thirty-nine women celebrated at the table in Judy Chicago's *The Dinner Party*.

A beautiful example of an artist speaking to a fellow artist . . .

'I was practically driven to Rome in order to
obtain the opportunities for art culture and
to find a social atmosphere where I was not
constantly reminded of my color. The land
of liberty had no room for a colored
sculptor.'

Edmonia Lewis

Born over two hundred and fifty years after Gentileschi, **Edmonia**
'Wildfire' Lewis (1844–1907) is one of the earliest female African
American artists to gain both national and international acclaim. Born
free in upstate New York of Native American and African American
heritage, Lewis began to create work that told the untold stories of
her own heritage through a female lens. Her inspirations were drawn
from leading figures in history, including abolitionists and heroes of
the Civil War, people Lewis knew. In 1867, she created *Forever Free*,
a white marble sculpture to commemorate the ending of enslavement,
her title taken from President Lincoln's Emancipation Proclamation.
By the 1870s, her work was selling for vast sums and, in 1876, she
was invited to take part in the Centennial Exposition in Philadelphia.
Her painting *The Death of Cleopatra* drew huge crowds. She moved
to Europe, living in Rome and then in Paris for five years from 1896,
before relocating to London. Lewis is buried in St Mary's Catholic
Cemetery in Kensal Green, where Mary Seacole and Krystyna Skarbek
also both lie.

'It is my duty to voice the suffering of men,
the never-ending sufferings heaped
mountain-high.'

Käthe Kollwitz

Born in Prussia, **Käthe Kollwitz** (1867–1945) is perhaps the
foremost artist of social protest of the twentieth century. An extraordinary sculptor, printmaker, lithographer and woodcut etcher,
Kollwitz used her skills to depict brutality and conflict in sequences
such as *The Weavers* and *The Peasant War*. At the heart of her work

is rage against the devastation of war. Her younger son was killed during the First World War and inspired sculptures such as *Grieving Parents* and *Mother with Her Dead Son*. In the Neue Wache building in Berlin, designed as a memorial to the Victims of War and Tyranny, there is an enlarged version of the statue.

Though she remained a pacifist and socialist throughout her life, during the Second World War Kollwitz stood firm against Nazi intimidation. She was evacuated from Berlin in 1943 and much of her work was lost. She died in Saxony a few weeks before victory in Europe. The first woman to be elected to the Prussian Academy of Arts, there are four museums dedicated solely to her work and one of the most prestigious art prizes in Germany is the Käthe Kollwitz Prize, awarded annually by the Academy of the Arts in Berlin.

> '. . . pain, pleasure and death are no more than a process for existence. The revolutionary struggle in this process is a doorway open to intelligence.'
>
> **Frida Kahlo**

Personal suffering also imbues the vivid, searingly honest, visceral paintings of the magnificent **Frida Kahlo** (1907–1954). Kahlo suffered from polio as a child, then a serious bus accident when she was eighteen left her in chronic pain, with multiple medical problems that would last for her entire life. Taking inspiration from Mexican popular culture and folk art, Kahlo's work explores gender, sex, class, race and identity, mixing autobiographical with fantastical elements. Kahlo's first solo exhibition in Mexico was in 1953, shortly before her death at the age of forty-seven. Her work remained relatively undiscovered until the 1970s, when a new generation of art historians and feminist historians started to celebrate and discuss her influence. Now, she is even more celebrated than her husband, the artist Diego Rivera (she was the third of his five wives).

> 'Through my earth/body sculptures, I
> become one with the earth . . . I become an
> extension of nature and nature becomes an
> extension of my body.'
>
> *Ana Mendieta*

In this period of huge variety and richness in Latin American art, Kahlo's near contemporary **María Izquierdo** (1902–1955) was the first Mexican woman to be exhibited in the United States; the artist and draughtswoman **Tarsila de Aguiar do Amaral** (1886–1973) – who, along with **Anita Catarina Malfatti** (1889–1964) and others, was instrumental in bringing European Modernism to Brazil – was to become one of Brazil's most important modernist artists; and the reputation of innovative 'earth/body' Cuban artist **Ana Mendieta** (1948–1985) grew after her sudden, tragic death.

Like Kahlo, Mendieta used her own body as both inspiration and canvas, drawing on her feelings of displacement from her native Cuba and focusing on a feminist interpretation of themes such as violence, life, death, identity, place and belonging. In 1973 she performed 'Rape Scene', created out of the rape and murder of a fellow student on the Iowa University campus by another student. Issues of sexual violence against women and the failure of university authorities to prosecute attackers remain live issues in 2022, just as fifty years ago. Mendieta died in 1985, falling from a window at the apartment in Greenwich Village where she was living with her husband of eight months. Despite the fact that they had been heard arguing, and despite the fact that Carl Andre had scratches on his face, he was acquitted of her murder . . .

> 'Men are afraid women will laugh at them.
> Women are afraid men will kill them.'
>
> *Margaret Atwood*

In November 2020, the United Nations released figures demonstrating that six women around the world are killed every hour by men, most by men in their own family or their partners. In the UK, a woman is killed by a man every three days. According to the UN, figures for femicide throughout the world make terrifying reading – in South Africa, Russia, Brazil, Afghanistan, Morocco, Thailand and India. Femicide is a global epidemic.

Like Frida Kahlo, **Emily Kame Kngwarreye** (1910–1996) had to wait a very long time for public recognition. An Aboriginal Australian from the Utopia community in the Northern Territory, Kngwarreye originally painted for ceremonial and traditional reasons, working with tie-dying and block painting, before moving on to acrylic. Her style was what became known as 'dot painting' with bold, expressive lines or 'yam tracks'.

Awarded an Australian Artist's Creative Fellowship by the Australia Council in 1992, Kngwarreye was one of three female artists chosen to represent Australia at the Venice Biennale in 1995. *Earth's Creation* is a magnificent set of four floor-to-ceiling panels, acrylic on canvas, representing her home lands of Alhalkere after the rains. Eleven years after her death, the painting was sold at auction for A\$1,056,000, setting a record for a work by an Aboriginal artist at that time.

> 'I can only paint in India. Europe belongs to Picasso, Matisse, Braque – India belongs only to me.'
>
> **Amrita Sher-Gil**

Sometimes known as the Indian Frida Kahlo, **Amrita Sher-Gil** (1913–1941) was an avant-garde Hungarian-Indian painter and a pioneer in modern Indian art. In her brief and brilliant career, she burned bright.

Born in Budapest, the daughter of a Punjabi Sikh scholar and aristocrat and a Hungarian-Jewish opera singer, Sher-Gil began formal art lessons when she was eight, once the family had moved to India. She studied in France and Italy, speaking her mind and having love affairs with women and with men. (Her painting *Two Women* is thought to be a self-portrait of Sher-Gil and her lover of the time.) Her paintings are glorious, richly coloured, usually of strong women captured in moments of intimacy. There are two self-portraits painted when she was only seventeen and eighteen, but it was her 1932 oil painting *Young Girls* that brought her to wider public attention.

A few days before the opening of her first solo show in Lahore in 1941, Sher-Gil fell into a coma and died, just before midnight on 5 December. Her mother accused her husband of having murdered her – he was a half-cousin – though it's possible that it was the result of complications from a botched abortion. Her work and dazzling short life have inspired generations of artists and novelists.

Like Sher-Gil, British artist and actress **Pauline Boty** (1938–1966) burned bright and died young. Known as the 'Wimbledon Bardot' at art college in the 1950s, her glamorous good looks were often used as a way to undermine her significance as an artist. One of the founders of the British Pop Art movement, she was the only 'girl in the gang'. Her first group show was in London in 1961 and her first solo show, in 1963, established her as a significant artist in her own right. Her work – which was often joyously sexual and liberating – challenged the everyday sexism of the world around her, making her an icon of the feminist movement. After her death at the age of twenty-eight, her paintings were stored away in a barn and largely forgotten for thirty years. I first saw pieces by Boty at Pallant House Gallery in my home town of Chichester in 2013 and was bowled over. Novelist Ali Smith put Boty's life and work on the page in her 2016 novel, *Autumn*.

As a rather depressing footnote, as of 2019, the National Gallery in London only had twenty female artists in its permanent collection, including Gentileschi's *Self-Portrait as Catherine of Alexandria*. The Metropolitan Museum of Art in New York lags further behind. Only seven female artists are included in its permanent collection, one of whom is the French-American artist **Louise Bourgeois** (1911–2010), a dazzling woman whose artistic practice spans a century.

> 'To be an artist, you need to exist in a world of silence.'
>
> **Louise Bourgeois**

Bourgeois was born on Christmas Day in 1911. Her work explores trauma, femaleness, fear, loss of control and displacement. Though she was a printmaker as well as a painter, it is for her often monumental sculptures that she is best known, including *Maman*. Created in 1999, the thirty-three-foot-wide, thirty-foot-high stainless steel, bronze and marble spider is one of the world's largest sculptures. Bourgeois said of the piece: 'The Spider is an ode to my mother. She was my best friend. Like a spider, my mother was a weaver . . . Like spiders, my mother was very clever . . . spiders are helpful and protective, just like my mother.'

THE VISIBILITY AND success of female actors often masks the fact that, behind the scenes, there have been far fewer women playwrights commissioned – especially for the bigger stages – and fewer female directors.

At the same time as I was writing *Warrior Queens & Quiet Revolutionaries*, I was beginning a new career at the age of sixty, by adapting one of my own novels, *The Taxidermist's Daughter*, for the sixtieth anniversary season of Chichester Festival Theatre in April 2022. It was also the first play by a living woman on the main stage in the theatre's history.

> 'I was proud that the subject matter was the suffragettes. I was proud that the story was coming to the fore because I felt incredibly passionate about it.'
>
> **Rebecca Lenkiewicz**

The first woman to have a play performed at the Olivier, the main stage at the National Theatre, was **Rebecca Lenkiewicz** (b. 1968), with her 2008 piece *Her Naked Skin*.

In the past decade, things have begun to shift. In 2018, the Royal Shakespeare Company announced that, for the first time in its history, all the plays in its season in its two main theatres would be directed by women. In the UK, at least there are now more female artistic directors running buildings (as opposed to companies) than ever before. They include: **Charlotte Bennett** and **Katie Posner**, Paines Plough; **Róisín McBrinn**, Gate Theatre (Dublin); **Nadia Fall**, Theatre Royal

Stratford East; **Vicky Featherstone**, Royal Court Theatre; **Tamara Harvey**, Theatr Clwyd; **Lynette Linton**, Bush Theatre; interim AD **Stef O'Driscoll**, Gate Theatre (London); **Catriona McLaughlin**, Abbey Theatre; **Rachel O'Riordan**, Lyric Hammersmith; **Indhu Rubasingham**, Kiln Theatre; **Roxana Silbert**, Hampstead Theatre; **Michelle Terry**, The Globe; **Jackie Wylie**, National Theatre of Scotland; and **Erica Wyman**, Acting AD at the RSC.

The Abbey Theatre in Dublin was one of the first to have a female artistic director. **Lelia Doolan** (b. 1934) ran the Abbey from 1971 to 1973, a theatre with an impressive legacy that opened in 1904 with premieres including *Spreading the News* by **Isabella Augusta, Lady Gregory** (1852–1932) among others, a folklorist, dramatist, benefactor and co-founder of both the Irish Literary Theatre and the Abbey Theatre.

Of course, the 'establishment' route is not the only way to change the world. Across the globe, from **Adong Judith** (b. 1977) in Uganda, co-founder of the all-female theatre company 'Silent Voices Uganda', to **Jaila Baccar** (b. 1952) in Tunisia, co-founder of the New Theatre in 1976 with her husband Fadhel Jaïbi, women are setting up their own theatre companies to produce work that more appropriately reflects their passions, lives, heritage languages and cultural inspirations.

So, change is happening.

There's a whole book to be written about the extraordinary artists both front of house and behind the curtains in the world of theatre – but here are just a last few razzle dazzlers to celebrate.

Martha Morton (1865–1925) was the first woman to direct a play on Broadway and the first American female playwright to enjoy a sustained and successful career. When she was nineteen, she wrote her first play and directed her first Broadway production two years later. Success after success followed but, when she tried to join the American Dramatists Club, she was turned down. So she started her own organization, the Society of Dramatic Authors, with fellow female writers, and was hugely important in opening the doors to other women in theatre, including **Lillian Trimble Bradley** (1875–1959), a playwright equally determined to make her mark. When a producer expressed interest in producing her 1891 play *The Woman on the Index*, Bradley agreed, provided she could be his assistant director. She'd got her foot in the door. Later that same year, she was appointed as general stage director of the Broadhurst Theatre and went on to direct a total of eight Broadway productions.

> 'Though it is a thrilling and marvelous thing
> to be merely young and gifted in such
> times, it is doubly so, doubly dynamic –
> to be young, gifted and black.'
>
> **Lorraine Hansberry**

Another American trailblazer was the extraordinary **Lorraine Hansberry** (1930–1965), the first African American female writer to have a play staged on Broadway. Hansberry moved to Harlem in 1951 and worked for the Black newspaper *Freedom*, writing not only about the civil rights movement, but also on issues of feminism and sexuality. She wrote of her attraction to women, and in 1953 she married Robert Nemiroff, a Jewish publisher, songwriter and activist. They were together for four years, and continued to work together after their divorce in 1964. After her death, Nemiroff donated all her unpublished scripts and notebooks to the New York Public Library, but blocked all references to her lesbianism, despite Hansberry herself having said towards the end of her life that she was 'committed [to] this homosexuality thing'.

Hansberry's first play A *Raisin in the Sun*, about the lives of African Americans struggling to survive in racially segregated Chicago, opened on Broadway in 1959. Hansberry won the New York Drama Critics' Circle Award, making her the youngest playwright and the first African American writer to do so. For the next few years she was in great demand. Her famous phrase about being 'young, gifted and black' came from a speech she gave at a creative writing conference in 1964, and Hansberry later used the title for an autobiographical play. It also inspired the song by **Nina Simone** (1933–2003). Hansberry died of pancreatic cancer when she was only thirty-four years old and, though many of her writings were published in her lifetime, the only other play performed was *The Sign in Sidney Brustein's Window*. It ran on Broadway for 101 performances and closed the night she died.

At much the same time in London, the 'mother of modern

theatre', the director and innovator **Joan Littlewood** (1914–2002), was building her Theatre Workshop. After years of searching for a permanent base, in 1953 she took up residence at the Theatre Royal in Stratford, East London, living and sleeping in the theatre with her company while the building was restored. She quickly gained an international reputation, performing throughout Europe and the Soviet Union. In 1955, she directed and starred in the British première of Bertolt Brecht's *Mother Courage and Her Children*. Other ground-breaking productions included A *Taste of Honey* in 1958 by **Shelagh Delaney** (1938–2011) and the satirical musical *Oh, What a Lovely War!* in 1963.

'I appeared in many school productions, but I had to play my parts in white face, including Lady Bracknell and Lady Macbeth! I went along with it because I was very anxious to learn my craft, and to be taken seriously as a dramatic actress. You see, I couldn't sing or dance, and dramatic roles were non-existent for black actresses, so I had to "white up" to gain experience.'

Pauline Henriques

Pauline Henriques (1914–1998) – known as **Paul** – moved to England with her family from Jamaica in 1919. In 1932, she enrolled in the London Academy of Music and Dramatic Arts to study drama. She was a regular presenter on the radio programme *Caribbean Voices* and, in 1946, made history by becoming the first Black female actress on British television, appearing as Hattie Harris in a BBC television version of Eugene O'Neill's *All God's Chillun Got Wings*. In later life, under her married name Pauline Crabbe, she worked with unmarried mothers and pregnancy counselling services for teenagers, and was secretary to the Brook Advisory Centres, then vice-chair until her retirement in 1986. She was also the first female Black British Justice of the Peace, a true Renaissance woman.

∞

MY GREAT-GRANDMOTHER LILY loved music. It appears in several of her novels and is at the heart of her historical novel *In the Days of Mozart*, though it's clear that she considers it the woman's role to support the male genius rather than put her own talents first.

Of all the areas of the arts, classical women composers are considered to be as rare as hen's teeth. Often, even those who love music struggle to name a single female composer. This is, in part, because of how music venues have been programmed, with established composers favoured, but historically also because of the issue of women having access to musicians – particularly orchestras – to perform their work. Symphonies, concerti, operas, song cycles all became popular because they were heard. With much classical music in the Western world coming from court composers – who were almost always men – it was a closed shop that kept women out. But, of course, there were women writing music, as well as performing and conducting, and they deserve to be celebrated too.

In February 1625, **Francesca Caccini** (1587–after 1641) saw her opera *La liberazione di Ruggiero dall'isola d'Alcina* performed in Florence. A poet, lute player, music teacher and singer, Caccini's work is considered to be the first opera composed by a woman, in a century in which Italian religious institutions were fertile ground for female composers. Some dozen or so nuns published music, including organist and singer **Claudia Rusca** (1593–1676) with a collection of *Sacri Concerti* in 1630. Ten years later, also in Milan, **Chiara Margarita Cozzolani** (1602–1676/1678) published *Primavera di fiori musicali*. And in 1665, **Isabella Leonarda** (1620–1704) published a book of motets, while the singer **Barbara Strozzi** (1619–1677) was one of the most prolific composers of the Baroque period, male or female, publishing eight volumes of her own music.

In Germany and France, too, women were making their mark. Harpsichordist **Elisabeth Jacquet de la Guerre** (1665–1729) composed in a number of different forms, including the ballet *Les jeux à l'honneur de la Victoire*, which has been lost. **Princess Amalie of Saxony** (1794–1870) wrote chamber music, opera, sacred music and comedies. She was a renowned harpsichord player, too.

Two of the best-known female composers and pianists in nineteenth-century Germany are **Fanny Mendelssohn** (1805–1847) and

Clara Schumann (1819–1896). Mendelssohn grew up in Berlin and received a musical education with her younger brother, Felix. Fanny Mendelssohn's works include an orchestral overture, a piano trio and quartet, more than a hundred pieces for piano, four cantatas and some 250 lieder, which were mostly unpublished in her lifetime. Because of family and societal pressures, several of her works were published under her brother's name, including her *Easter Sonata*. She died in Berlin in 1847. Felix followed her to the grave six months later.

From Berlin to Paris. **Pauline Viardot** (1821–1910) was not only one of the most important mezzo-sopranos of the nineteenth century, but also a highly respected and popular composer. Her five 'salon' operas include *Cendrillon* – a version of *Cinderella* – which she wrote at the age of eighty-three.

> 'Because I have conducted my own operas and love sheep-dogs; because I generally dress in tweeds, and sometimes, at winter afternoon concerts, have even conducted in them; because I was a militant suffragette and seized a chance of beating time to 'The March of the Women' from the window of my cell in Holloway Prison with a toothbrush; because I have written books, spoken speeches, broadcast, and don't always make sure that my hat is on straight; for these and other equally pertinent reasons, in a certain sense I am well known.'
>
> *Ethel Smyth*

One of the greatest British composers, **Ethel Smyth** (1858–1944) should be a household name. A suffragette, she studied composition at the Leipzig Conservatory in the 1870s. Versatile and ambitious, she composed chamber pieces, orchestral pieces, symphonies and choral arrangements including her *Mass in D*, and six operas, though she often had trouble finding musicians to perform her work. A friend of Emmeline Pankhurst, Smyth composed 'The March of the Women' in 1910 to words by fellow suffragist and actress **Cecily Hamilton** (1872–1952), who did briefly join the WSPU. It became the anthem of the Women's Social and Political Union. When Smyth was arrested in London in 1912, together with one hundred others, she was sent to Holloway Prison in London. There, she famously conducted fellow suffragettes singing in a rousing chorus . . . with her toothbrush.

Smyth's opera *The Wreckers* is extraordinary – rousing, ambitious, epic – but Smyth had to battle to see it performed. Attempts to stage it in France came to nothing. It finally received its premiere in Leipzig in 1906, but was not heard in English until 1909 with a libretto by Henry Bennett Brewster, with whom she had a long-term friendship and probable love affair, despite the majority of her romantic attachments being with women. During the First World War, Smyth worked in a French military hospital, but by then she was losing her hearing. She concentrated her creative energies on prose, writing eight volumes of autobiography. Much honoured in her lifetime, she became Dame Ethel Smyth in 1922 – still the only female composer to have been awarded the honour – and, four years later, was the first woman to receive an honorary doctorate in music from Oxford University. Because she was also a passionate golfer, her ashes were scattered in woods close to Woking Golf Club.

The plate at Smyth's place setting at Judy Chicago's *The Dinner Party* depicts a grand piano with raised lid, painted keys and a stand with notations from her opera *The Boatswain's Mate*. The runner has a musical stave with the capital 'E' in Ethel twisted into the image of a treble clef.

> 'As far as women conductors are concerned, yes you can get on, but you don't get the same chances as men because the people hiring don't think of you. And a lot of women conductors won't say that because they're afraid.'
>
> **Odaline de la Martinez**

ALTHOUGH IT'S AT a slow pace, change is gradually happening in the world of Western classical music. In 1984, the Cuban-American conductor and Ethel Smyth specialist **Odaline de la Martinez** (b. 1949) was the first woman to conduct at the BBC Proms since its inception in 1895; the Australian conductor **Simone Young** (b. 1961) became the first woman to conduct the Vienna Philharmonic in 2005. Young is currently the chief conductor for the Sydney Symphony Orchestra.

And there are the same battles going on in other areas of music. **Zenzile Miriam Makeba** (1932–2008) was a South African singer, actress and songwriter, fundamental to the late twentieth-century explosion of interest in Afropop; born in the same year, the jazz harpist and composer **Dorothy Ashby** (1932–1986) revolutionized what had always been seen as a purely classical or folk instrument; and Cape Verdean singer **Cesária Évora** (1941–2011) was known as the 'Barefoot Diva', since she performed her beautiful songs without wearing shoes.

Finally, who better to finish this constellation of shining stars than someone who weaves magic out of thin air. Magician **Ellen E. Armstrong** (1914–1979) is the only African American woman to have had her own US touring magic show. She worked first with her father, then took over when he died in 1939, keeping his motto 'Going Fine Since 1889'. She adopted the stage name 'Mistress of Modern Magic' and, with sleight of hand and tricks such as 'Hippity-Hop Rabbits' and the 'Mysterious Jars of Egypt', she travelled all over America for another thirty-one years.

A Mistress of Modern Magic indeed.

> 'Practice means to perform, over and over again in the face of all obstacles, some act of vision, of faith, of desire. Practice is a means of inviting the perfection desired.'
>
> *Martha Graham*

THE MORE I looked, the more I found. The traces of their razzle dazzle remain – innovative, dynamic, boundary-stretching, entertaining women. Each made something special of her life and it was so sad to have to shut my biographies and encyclopaedias, to abandon the reference libraries and accept that I was going to have to leave so many women out, at least for now. I don't feel I've done justice to whole areas of creative endeavour – dance, architecture, ceramics, textiles.

But I still hold fast to the idea that it is better to try, and fail, than not to try at all.

Stoneycroft Bridge, above Stair Mill, Newlands Valley

Lily

WHAT MORE IS THERE to say?

It's 1930, the beginning of a new decade and the world is changing. In India, in China, in Turkey, in Germany, in Ethiopia, new regimes and rulers are sweeping away the old guard. It is twelve years since the Armistice, supposedly 'the war to end all wars', but the Great Depression has cast a shadow and few believe these are days of hope.

Lily's eldest son, Reggie, died in June 1927. But Ethel, Winnie and Harold – now a partner at Watson & Sons in Bouverie Street – are close at hand. My grandmother Betty is only a phone call away. Most Sundays, Lily would go to lunch with Harold and his family around the corner in Streatham. They would sit and do the *Times* crossword together.

Betty and my grandfather were preparing to move from Horsham down to the south coast. He was vicar designate for the new parish of Aldwick in West Sussex – it was hoped the sea air would help my father's recovery from TB. One of the last of Lily's letters I've seen was sent to my father who was confined to bed. Dated 26 September 1930, it begins 'Darling Richard' and attaches a colourful postcard of three children, which she says reminds her of him, his brother John and his sister Margaret. Lily asks if he likes properly written letters or if he'd prefer to receive a pictogram instead. She enquires after his tortoise and talks of the conkers on the ground at 'Poplars'. She finishes: 'Goodbye my darling, your very loving London Grannie, Lily Watson.'

Much of her writing now is about faith and her absolute security in the knowledge that she would, when her time came, be called home. There is no equivocation, no uncertainty.

I have a copy of Lily's will, dated 18 June 1925. In it she details certain legacies – to her Streatham housekeeper Mrs Creed and her daughter, her former maid and 'dear friend' Alice Lovett, and the Reverend Lucius Palmer Smith (the first vicar of St Margaret the Queen). Otherwise, she divides her estate equally between her five surviving children. (After Reggie's death in June 1927, there is a codicil redistributing his share equally to his four children.) She refers to personal letters and papers giving 'certain private directions' which, to my knowledge, have not survived. She has stocks in various companies including the Port of London, the Canadian Pacific Railway, British East India, London Assurance and Phoenix Assurance, as well as Post Office savings.

What moved me most – and surprised me – were the very specific instructions given as to her burial and cremation:

(1) To see that my body is burnt and that my ashes are thrown to the winds . . .
(2) To see that until actual cremation my body is placed in an open or unfastened coffin . . .
(3) To make absolutely certain by some small operation such as the opening of a vein by my medical attendant that I am actually dead before being placed in my coffin . . .

The fear of being put 'living into the tomb' was a staple of Victorian sensationalist fiction and a common trope in horror stories. But for it to be so vivid a terror for Lily that she mentions it in her will seems out of character for the sensible, practical, stoic woman I imagine her to have been.

Lily Watson died at home on 17 January 1932 at the age of eighty-two. On the death certificate, breast cancer is given as the cause of death. Had Lily been prepared and said her goodbyes, or had she soldiered on in silence? At this moment, I find the lack of her voice so achingly sad.

A measure of a good life, perhaps, is how we leave it. Life and death are two sides of the same story. So, I'd like to imagine her comfortable in her bed, in the house she had lived in for so many years. Though it was midwinter, I'd like to imagine it was just light and that she heard the first blackbird singing in the white January air. I'd like to imagine she was aware of the Sunday church bells ringing for the eight o'clock service, that she was peaceful, and without fear. I'd like to hope that she'd had time to take her leave of those she loved. And I wonder if she thought of the Yorkshire landscape she loved so much, of the mountains of Switzerland and the lakes, of the garden of 'Poplars' leading down to the disappearing fields. Of Newlands Valley. Did she think of Sam and Leader and Reggie? Of her parents and siblings?

It is 1932, but this is a Victorian house still. The curtains will be drawn, the inhabitants will wear black and armbands until after the funeral. Four days later, Lily will be laid to rest at her beloved St Margaret the Queen.

In a family of vicars and priests, who reads the lesson? Who leads the service? Which prayers are chosen? Which hymns are sung? What is said of her life as an author, of her success as a columnist and poet and novelist? For those advanced in years and with long memories, is Lily there as the girl she was, the girl who wrote fairy tales and loved the mountains? Is she there as a reader who spoke Italian and German, a little Greek and Latin, a smattering of French? Is she present as the young wife, married in the chapel at Rawdon College before being transplanted to London? Is she there as a mother who has buried two sons? Is she there as the woman who climbed Causey Pike and picnicked on Catbells? Is she there as the grandmother who sent pictograms and presents and laid on entertainments at Christmas? All of the experiences that made her the woman she was, cradle to grave.

More than anything, this is history.

In researching Lily's life, I learned more about my grandmother too. My cousin Anne shared an essay written by Betty, found some-where in a box of photographs, that talks about her lifelong love for Newlands Valley, for Stair Mill and the Lake District. How, on her honeymoon in July 1918, she and her new husband walked to the church on Sunday only to find it closed. How, when they were staying there with Lily three years later, grandfather was invited to take the service and she realized, when 'kneeling at the altar rail', that she was expecting a second baby. Being there with her mother and her sister, Winnie. Later, her own children. How she gave the church a green-and-white burse and veil. On the sixtieth anniversary of her first visit, a Bible. The same Bible that I have touched and listened to my father read from in the 1970s. The essay, written in blue biro on lined paper, finishes:

> 'Although my beloved husband wishes to lie with his family in a Sussex country churchyard, he absolutely understood why I wished to end my days as one with the land I loved so much.'

It was the extraordinary gift her mother had given her. A sense of belonging, a sense of a place.

Newlands Church, Keswick, summer 2022

Afterword

MID-MORNING ON A SATURDAY in late October 2021, a few days after my sixtieth birthday.

Newlands Valley is solden now, copper and claret and shimmering greens. A light mist hangs over Causey Pike and the ground is damp underfoot. Leaves cover the ground and terracotta pathways, but the air is fresh and the clouds race and jostle against a briefly blue sky. It's not cold, but there's a chance of rain later.

I have come full circle. It's autumn and I'm back in this tiny churchyard with the benign ghosts of my great-grandmother and grandmother. The yellow celandine – so vivid against the grey stone in summer – has gone but the valley is full of colour. I have a photograph of Lily in my pocket, the one I've kept propped against my computer screen while I've been writing this book. There's no reason to have it with me, except the sense that I am bringing her home.

In the peace and tranquillity of this gentle churchyard that holds so many of my family's memories within the perimeter of its drystone walls, I think of the closing paragraph of *Wuthering Heights*. The narrator Lockwood, a wiser and more thoughtful man after the violence of the stories he's witnessed, finds the three plain headstones – Catherine Earnshaw, Heathcliff and Edgar Linton – high on the moors:

'I lingered round them, under that benign sky; watched the moths fluttering among the heath and hare-bells; listened to the soft wind breathing through the grass; and wondered how anyone could ever imagine unquiet slumbers for the sleepers in that quiet earth.'

This, then, is it. The truth of a life, the quality of it, the value of it. Out of all these individual lives – some dazzling and brilliant, burning bright, others quiet and principled – is history made. The contradictions and the achievements, the unintended consequences and the deliberate attempts to stamp one's vision, one's ambition, one's purpose on the world.

I've learned so much compiling this book and spent a year in the company of inspirational and extraordinary women. So, what about the question of women's history – and women's absence from it? It's both complicated and, at the same time, very simple. On the one hand, we've seen how throughout history, all over the world, tradition, religion, social mores or the law itself actively discriminate against women, making it hard or even impossible for women to fulfil their potential. In every era, there have been – and are still – men who seek to silence or to control women. There are also men who have been determined to make things equitable – brothers, husbands, friends, fathers who've advocated for their sisters, their wives, their colleagues and their daughters.

In terms of the official record and how history is made, that's a little more complicated. It's crucial that documents are kept, that letters are treasured, that physical evidence of a woman's presence is preserved so as to prove that women were there too. Digital information records everything and technically should preserve everything. But how can we find out what is important, and what is not? How can we shift through the countless dates and facts? How can we tell what is true? And how can we confront our own unconscious bias to 'see' some women more than others?

But for all the flaws of any book like this – the shadows of all those women not included or known about – it's better to try to celebrate some than not to celebrate anyone at all. The central issue remains the same. We must value women's work, rather than dismiss it or misattribute it, so that archives, museums and libraries, places of learning and popular culture, are expanded to be more inclusive.

Women were there too. We were there too. History, completed.

There's also the crucial question of legacy. Many of the women in this book are known only because family members, or historians, or enthusiasts, have worked to bring their names into the light. They have kept the flame burning. This is where the arts play such a huge part in making the women of the past visible to the women and men of the present. And it's why this book and others like it are important too. A dictionary of names, yes. But the more of us who share these names, write books about them, shout about them, the more we can weave women back into the fabric of history. I worry for those coming after us, trying to stitch together a story. I've relied on letters and postcards. I have boxes of letters my mother sent to me, and have kept cards and drawings by my children. But if so much communication is now electronic – WhatsApp and email – how, then, do we preserve those stories? Old photographs? Physical books handed down or won as prizes, with inscriptions, dates and scribbles in the margins? Pen on paper? Letters hold the scent of the past in a way that a text message does not.

Many of the women in this book changed the world around them – the warrior queens, the mothers of invention, the women of conviction and of science, the women of courage – but so did many millions of quiet revolutionaries whose lives had their own individual importance. Those who tried to make women's lives better one street, one village, one town at a time. They, too, belong in the history books, because it is from all the other Lilies that the true colour of the real world as it was lived – with women's stories put back at its centre – can be found.

What of Lily herself? As a detective, I have been only partly successful in reassembling her life. I'd like to find the time to read and catalogue all the family letters and fill in any gaps. Perhaps there are more documents still to be found. I'd like to write her a fuller biography and see her novels back in print. Because it still vexes me that, for all her achievements, I found only one reference to Lily in the wider world – a short mention in the Victorian Circulating Library lists of nineteenth-century women authors. I've excavated more reading between the lines of her fiction and journalism. Everything else has come from family documents and letters that I've traced, borrowed and studied. But maybe that's enough? That our words, our deeds, speak for us.

For all that, to my mind Lily deserves her place in some *Dictionary of National Biography* or digital encyclopaedia. It might read something like this:

'Lily Watson was the pen name of Martha Louisa Watson, née Green (11 October 1849–17 January 1932). She was an English novelist, journalist, prolific letter writer, a children's writer, author of devotional tracts, poet, author of fourteen novels, several collections of poetry, literary criticism and more than a hundred articles for *The Girl's Own Paper* between 1885 and 1932.'

Lily was a woman of principle and hard work, a woman whose Christian faith was the bedrock of her long life. She was a daughter and a sister, a wife, a mother and an aunt, a grandmother. I'm very proud she was my great-grandmother. And I will always remember her.

> *I pause in life's declining day,*
> *Look through the sunset glow, and wait*
> *While memory traces all my way.*

'The Record of a Happy Life'
Three Voices and Other Poems
Lily Watson, 1909–1930

Acknowledgements

IN A BOOK OF this nature, researched over several years – and during the COVID pandemic – there are many people whose help I appreciated. First, the thousands who contributed to the global #WomanInHistory social media campaign, and especially friends who got the campaign started in January 2021, including: JoJo Moyes, Lee Child, Bettany Hughes, Ken Follett, Damian Barr, Paula Hawkins, Anita Anand, Sara Collins, Professor Kate Williams, Julia Spencer-Fleming, Madeline Miller. The full list of nominations and those who joined the campaign is available at www. panmacmillan.com/blogs/fiction/kate-mosse-woman-in-history.

As well as the many excellent books celebrating women from history listed in the Bibliography and the organizations dedicated to amplifying the voices of women in particular fields, do visit @OnThisDayShe @she_made_history @the_female_lead @womeninspire @FinnClodagh @WomenRead @WhatsHerNamePC and the ground-breaking www. younghistoriansproject.org to discover even more extraordinary women whose names and achievements should be better known.

In researching my own family history, I am indebted to the previous owners of Stair Mill in Newlands Valley, Peter and Jackie Williams, and the current owners Susan and Martin Duke; to Katherine Slay, who guided me through archival research; my cousin David Booker for links to Stair Mill; and my wonderful cousins Anne Renshaw and Vanessa Sharman (née Watson), who shared my passion for this family detective story and generously put letters, photographs, diaries and reminiscences into my hands.

I was lucky to have several expert and academic readers helping me make sure that different communities were properly represented, including Sarah Shaffi, Dee Hudson, Kay Eldridge, Sue Nyathi, Olivia Wyatt and Alice E. Smith, whose additional research and fact-checking was invaluable. Thanks, too, to the historians who helped point me in the right direction, including Suzannah Lipscomb, Janina Ramirez, Jonathan Phillips and Greg Jenner. Any errors that have slipped through are mine, and mine alone.

As always, thanks to everyone at The Soho Agency, especially my old friend Mark Lucas, and Niamh O'Grady, Alice Saunders and Sophie Laurimore, and George Lucas at InkWell Management in New York. Huge thanks to my brilliant publisher/editor Maria Rejt, and the wonderful team at Pan Macmillan UK, including Kate Tolley, Alice Gray, Kate Green, Sara Lloyd, Stuart Dwyer, Lara Borlenghi, Lucy Hale, Claire Evans, Charlotte Williams, Jamie Forrest, Connie Roff, Richard Green, Rory O'Brien, Simon Rhodes, Lindsay Nash, Holly Sheldrake, Siân Chilvers, Katie Tooke, Jonathan Atkins, Leanne Williams and Sam Fletcher. Thanks, too, for contributions from sister publishing offices, especially Veronica Napier and Terry Morris at Pan Macmillan South Africa, Teesta Guha Sarkar at Pan Macmillan India, John Girvan and Ingrid Olhsson at Pan Macmillan NZ/Australia.

As ever, thank you to those friends, neighbours and family who, despite everything happening in their lives, were always there and supportive, especially Jonathan Evans, Saira Keevill, Clare Parsons, Tony Langham, Anthony Horowitz, Jill Green, Haydn Gwynne, Issy van Randwyck, Sally Clay and Linda and Roger Heald. My love to my fabulous sisters Caroline Matthews and Beth Huxley, for all the 'walking-and-talking', my terrific brothers-in-law Mark Huxley and photographer extraordinaire Benjamin Graham, my nieces and nephews – in particular Ellen Huxley and Thea Huxley, who helped wrestle the #WomanInHistory spreadsheets into shape – and my love to Oliver Halladay, the tree whisperer, and my legendary mother-in-law, Rosie Turner – aka Granny Rosie.

Finally, as always, all of everything to the bedrocks of my life: my inspirational and brilliant daughter Martha Mosse, my incredible and inspiring son Felix Mosse and my beloved husband Greg Mosse, my first reader, first editor and first and forever love. Without you, none of this would matter a jot.

Kate Mosse
October 2022

Picture Acknowledgements

All come from the author's or author's family collection, with the exception of:

Page 14 top left © Alamy Stock Photo
Page 14 top right © Alamy Stock Photo
Page 14 bottom left © Carl Van Vechten Papers Relating to African American Arts and Letters. James Weldon Johnson Collection in the Yale Collection of American Literature, Beinecke Rare Book and Manuscript Library
Page 14 bottom right © Hemesh Alles
Page 50 © Wikimedia Commons
Page 54 top © Wikimedia Commons
Page 54 bottom © PhotoQuest/Getty Images
Page 86 top © Hulton Archive/Stringer/Getty Images
Page 86 bottom left © Alamy Stock Photo
Page 86 bottom right © Alamy Stock Photo
Page 110 © Alamy Stock Photo
Page 144 top left © Alamy Stock Photo
Page 144 top right © Alamy Stock Photo
Page 144 bottom © Harold Clements/Stringer/Getty Images
Page 192 © PhotoQuest/Getty Images
Page 228 top © Wendy Stone/Getty Images
Page 228 bottom left © Alamy Stock Photo
Page 228 bottom right © CBS Photo Archive/Getty Images
Page 266 top © Lalit/AP/REX/Shutterstock
Page 266 bottom © Alamy Stock Photo
Page 294 top left © C Curtin/AP/REX/Shutterstock
Page 294 top right © ullstein bild Dtl./Getty Images

Bibliography

This is a personal list of further reading. Some of the titles I have read, others I have not, but I wanted to create a library of significant work by other female authors.

I've tried to include at least one publication by or about every woman mentioned in *Warrior Queens & Quiet Revolutionaries*, though that has not always been possible. Authors are listed alphabetically by surname or, if a biography, under the surname of the subject. Publication dates are – wherever possible – for current editions rather than date of first publication.

Battling Bella: The Protest Politics of Bella Abzug by Leandra Ruth Zarnow (Harvard University Press, 2019)

First: 100 Years of Women in Law by Lucinda Acland and Katie Broomfield (Scala Arts & Heritage Publishers, 2019)

My Dearest Friend: Letters of Abigail and John Adams (Harvard University Press, 2007)

Dearest Friend: A Life of Abigail Adams by Lynne Withey (Simon & Schuster, 2001)

We Should All Be Feminists by Chimamanda Ngozi Adichie (Fourth Estate, 2014)

Selected Poems by Anna Akhmatova, translated by D. M. Thomas (Vintage, 2009)

Invisible Agents: Women and Espionage in Seventeenth-Century Britain by Nadine Akkerman (Oxford University Press, 2018)

Becoming A Woman: And Other Essays in 19th and 20th Century Feminist History by Sally Alexander (Virago, 1994)

The Virago Book of Spirituality: Of Women and Angels by Sarah Anderson (Virago, 1997)

A History of Women in 100 Objects by Professor Maggie Andrews and Dr Janis Lomas (The History Press, 2018)

Jurassic Mary: Mary Anning and the Primeval Monsters by Patricia Pierce (The History Press, 2014)

Susan B. Anthony: A Biography by Kathleen Barry (NYU Press, 2020)

Cory: Corazon Aquino & the Philippines by Beatrice Siegel (Penguin, 1988)

Diane Arbus: An Aperture Monograph: Fortieth-Anniversary Edition by Diane Arbus (Aperture, 2011)

The Letters of Heloise and Abelard: A Translation of Their Collected Correspondence and Related Writings by Héloïse d'Argenteuil, edited by Bonnie Wheeler with Mary Martin McLaughlin (Palgrave Macmillan, 2009)

The Examinations of Anne Askew by Anne Askew (Oxford University Press, 1996)

My Story: An Autobiography by Mary Astor (Windham Press, 2013)

A Life in Secrets: Vera Atkins and the Lost Agents of SOE by Sarah Helm (Abacus, 2006)

Rise Up Women!: The Remarkable Lives of the Suffragettes by Diane Atkinson (Bloomsbury, 2018)

Women Heroes of World War II – The Pacific Theater: 15 Stories of Resistance, Rescue, Sabotage, and Survival by Kathryn J. Atwood (Chicago Review Press, 2016)

Negotiating with the Dead: A Writer on Writing by Margaret Atwood (Virago, 2003)

Outwitting the Gestapo by Lucie Aubrac, translated by Konrad Bievber (Nebraska University Press, 1993)

Jane Austen's Letters, selected by Deirdre Le Fay (Oxford University Press, 2011)

Josephine Baker: The Hungry Heart by Jean-Claude Baker and Chris Chase (Cooper Square Publishing, 2001)

Faith: Faith Bandler, Gentle Activist by Marilyn Lake (Allen & Unwin, 2002)

Mrs Barbour's Daughters by AJ Taudevin (Oberon Books, 2015)

Labour Women in Power: Cabinet Ministers in the Twentieth Century by Paula Bartley (Palgrave Macmillan, 2019)

The Light of Days: The Untold Story of Women Resistance Fighters in Hitler's Ghettos by Judy Batalion (Morrow, 2021)

Discovering Dorothea: The Life of the Pioneering Fossil-Hunter Dorothea Bate by Karolyn Shindler (Natural History Museum, 2017)

The Second Sex by Simone de Beauvoir, translated by Constance Border (Vintage, 2015)

A Woman in Arabia: The Writings of the Queen of the Desert by Gertrude Bell (Penguin Classics, 2015)

On this Day She: Putting Women Back Into History, One Day at a Time by Jo Bell, Tania Hershman and Ailsa Holland (Metro Publishing, 2021)

A Black Women's History of the United States by Daina Ramey Berry and Kali Nicole Gross (Beacon Press, 2020)

Daughter of the East: An Autobiography by Benazir Bhutto (Simon & Schuster, 2008)

A Lady's Life in the Rocky Mountains by Isabella Bird (John Beaufoy, 2017)

The Life and Travels of Isabella Bird: The Fearless Victorian Adventurer by Jacki Hill-Murphy (Pen & Sword, 2021)

The Beginning of Women's Ministry: The Revival of the Deaconess in the Nineteenth-Century Church of England, edited by Henrietta Blackmore (Boydell Press, 2007)

The Hiding Place by Corrie ten Boom, with Elizabeth and John Sherill (Hodder & Stoughton, 2004)

The Excellent Doctor Blackwell: The Life of the First Woman Physician by Julia Boyd (The History Press, 2005)

Around the World in Seventy-Two Days And Other Writings by Nellie Bly (Penguin Classics, 2014)

Following Nellie Bly: Her Record-Breaking Race Around the World by Rosemary J. Brown (Pen & Sword, 2021)

Portrait of Myself by Margaret Bourke-White (Franklin Classics, 2018)

Lady into Woman: A History of Women from Victoria to Elizabeth II by Vera Brittain (Hassell Street Press, United States, 2021; Andrew Dakers Ltd. 1953 hardback)

The Brontës by Juliet Barker (Abacus, 2010)

The Heart of the Race: Black Women's Lives in Britain by Beverley Bryan, Stella Dadzie and Suzanne Scafe (Verso, 2018)

The Complete Works of Fanny Burney (Delphi Classics, 2015)

Daughters of Africa: An International Anthology of Words and Writing by Women of African Descent from the Ancient Egyptians to the Present, edited by Margaret Busby (Jonathan Cape, 1992)

New Daughters of Africa: An International Anthology of Writing by Women of African Descent, edited by Margaret Busby (Myriad Editions, 2020)

Barbara Bush: A Memoir (Simon & Schuster, 1994)

Josephine Butler: Patron Saint of Prostitutes by Helen Mathers (The History Press, 2021)

Josephine Butler: A Very Brief History by Jane Robinson (SPCK Publishing, 2020)

In Focus: Julia Margaret Cameron – Photographs from the J. Paul Getty Museum (Getty, 2006)

Always, Rachel: The Letters of Rachel Carson and Dorothy Freeman, 1952–1964: An Intimate Portrait of a Remarkable Friendship, edited by Martha Freeman (Beacon Press, 1996)

Silent Spring by Rachel Carson (Penguin Books, 2020)

Women Heroes of the American Revolution: 20 Stories of Espionage, Sabotage, Defiance, and Rescue by Susan Casey (Chicago Review Press, 2015)

Politics & Power: Barbara Castle: A Biography by Lisa Martineau (Welbeck Publishing, 2011)

She Wolves: The Women Who Ruled England Before Elizabeth by Helen Castor (Faber & Faber, 2010)

Edith Cavell: Nurse, Martyr, Heroine by Diana Souhami (Riverrun, 2015)

The Blazing World and Other Writings by Margaret Cavendish, edited by Kate Lilley (Penguin Classics, 1994)

Women Scientists in India: Lives, Struggles, Achievements by Anjana Chattopadhyay (National Book Trust India, 2018)

Shirley Chisholm: The Last Interview and Other Conversations (Melville House, 2021)

Come, Tell Me How You Live: Autobiography by Agatha Christie (HarperCollins, 1999)

Agatha Christie: A Mysterious Life by Laura Thompson (Headline, 2020)

Khiva to Samarkand – The Remarkable Story of a Woman's Adventurous Journey Alone Through the Deserts of Central Asia to the Heart of Turkestan by Ella R. Christie (Trotamundas Press, 2009)

Lifting the Veil by Ismat Chughtai (Penguin, 2018)

Unwell Women: A Journey Through Medicine and Myth in a Man-Made World by Elinor Cleghorn (Weidenfeld & Nicolson, 2021)

The Book of Gutsy Women: Favourite Stories of Courage and Resilience by Hillary Rodham Clinton and Chelsea Clinton (Simon & Schuster, 2020)

Hard Choices: A Memoir by Hillary Rodham Clinton (Simon & Schuster, 2015)

Sisters in the Struggle: African American Women in the Civil Rights–Black Power Movement, edited by Bettye Collier-Thomas and V. P. Franklin (NYU Press, 2001)

Claudette Colvin: Civil Rights Activist by Cathleen Small (Cavendish Square Publishing, 2020)

When Women Ruled the World: Six Queens of Egypt by Kara Cooney (National Geographic, 2018)

She Speaks: Women's Speeches That Changed the World by Yvette Cooper (Atlantic Books, 2020)

Charlotte Corday by Bernardine Melchior-Bonnet (Perrin, 2000)

Looking for Trouble by Virginia Cowles (Faber & Faber, 2021)

Invisible Women: Exposing Data Bias in a World Designed for Men by Caroline Criado Perez (Vintage, 2020)

The British Christian Women's Movement: A Rehabilitation of Eve by Jenny Daggers (Routledge, 2017)

Beyond God the Father: Toward a Philosophy of Women's Liberation by Mary Daly (Beacon Press, 1992)

Women, Race & Class by Angela Y. Davies (Penguin, 2019)

Truth and Dare: Stories About Women Who Shaped Ireland by Martina Devlin (Poolbeg Press, 2018)

The Complete Poems by Emily Dickinson (Faber, 2016)

I Myself Am a Woman: Selected Writings of Ding Ling, edited by Tani E. Barlow with Gary J. Bjorge (Beacon Press, 1990)

She Captains: Heroines and Hellions of the Sea by Joan Druett (Simon & Schuster, 2001)

Pirate Women: The Princesses, Prostitutes, and Privateers Who Ruled the Seven Seas by Laura Sook Duncome (Chicago Review Press, 2019)

The Female Lead: Women Who Shape Our World by Edwina Dunn (Ebury, 2017)

The Female Lead Volume 2: We Rise By Lifting Others by Edwina Dunn (Ebury, 2021)

The Huguenot Experience of Persecution and Exile: Three Women's Stories by Charlotte Arbaleste Duplessis-Mornay, Anne de Chaufepié and Anne Marguerite Petit Du Noyer, edited by Colette H. Winn, translated by Colette H. Winn and Lauren King (Iter Press, 2019)

Amelia Earhart: The Sound of Wings by Mary S. Lovell (Little, Brown, 2009)

Elizabeth, the Queen by Alison Weir (Vintage, 2009)

Elizabeth's Women: The Hidden Story of the Virgin Queen by Tracy Borman (Vintage, 2010)

A Time to Risk All: The Incredible Untold Story of Mary Elmes, the Irish Woman who Saved Children from Nazi Concentration Camps by Clodagh Finn (Gill Books, 2017)

Manifesto: On Never Giving Up by Bernardine Evaristo (Penguin, 2021)

Forough Farrokhzad: Another Birth and Other Poems by Forough Farrokhzad, translated by Hasan Javadi and Susan Sallee (Mage Publishing, 2010)

Women's Suffrage: A Short History of a Great Movement by Millicent Garrett Fawcett (Alpha Editions, 2020)

Through England on a Side-Saddle by Celia Fiennes (Penguin English Journeys, 2009)

Through Her Eyes: A New History of Ireland in 21 Women by Clodagh Finn (Gill, 2019)

117 Days by Ruth First, Introduction by Gillian Slovo (Virago, 2010)

Women in the War: The Last Heroines of Britain's Greatest Generation by Lucy Fisher (Harper Element, 2021)

Escape Through the Pyrenees by Lisa Fitko, translated by David Koblick (Northwestern University Press, 1991)

Gorillas in the Mist by Dian Fossey (Weidenfeld & Nicolson, 1983; reissued Orion, 2011)

Madame Fourcade's Secret War: The Daring Young Woman Who Led France's Largest Spy Network Against Hitler by Lynne Olson (Random House, 2020)

The Feminine Mystique by Betty Friedan (Penguin Classics, 2010)

Elizabeth Garrett Anderson by Jo Manton (Methuen, 1987)

The Book of Hope by Jane Goodall (Viking, 2022)

Outsiders: Five Women Writers Who Changed the World by Lyndall Gordon (Virago, 2018)

Ingenious Trade: Women and Work in Seventeenth-Century London by Laura Gowing (Cambridge University Press, 2021)

The Female Eunuch by Germaine Greer (Harper Perennial Modern Classics, 2006)

The Anna Karenina Fix: Life Lessons from Russian Literature by Viv Groskop (Penguin, 2018)

The Well of Loneliness by Radclyffe Hall (Penguin Classics, 2018)

A Woman of No Importance: The Untold Story of Virginia Hall, WWII's Most Dangerous Spy by Sonia Purnell (Virago, 2019)

Fannie Lou Hamer: America's Freedom Fighting Woman by Maegan Parker Brooks (Rowman & Littlefield Publishers, 2020)

Women in Conservation by Carol Hand (Core Library, 2016)

Writings of Agnes of Harcourt: The Life of Isabelle of France and the Letter on Louis IX and Longchamp (University of Notre Dame Press, 2003)

Open Wide the Freedom Gates: A Memoir by Dorothy Height (Public Affairs US, 2003)

Rose Heilbron: Legal Pioneer of the 20th Century by Hilary Heilbron (Hart Publishing, 2012)

Rose Heilbron: The Story of England's First Woman Queen's Counsel and Judge by Hilary Heilbron (Hart Publishing, 2012)

Helen of Troy: Goddess, Princess, Whore by Bettany Hughes (Pimlico, 2013)

The Comet Sweeper: Caroline Herschel's Astronomical Ambition by Claire Brock (Icon Books, 2017)

The Quiet Revolution of Caroline Herschel: The Lost Heroine of Astronomy by Dr Emily Winterburn (The History Press, 2017)

She-Merchants, Buccaneers and Gentlewomen: British Women in India by Katie Hickman (Virago, 2020)

In the Shade of Spring Leaves: The Life of Higuchi Ichiyo, With Nine of Her Best Stories by Ichiyō Higuchi, translated by Robert Lyons Danly (W. W. Norton and Company, Inc., 1992)

Selected Writings by Hildegard of Bingen (Penguin Classics, 2001)

Hildegard of Bingen: The Woman of Her Age by Fiona Maddocks (Faber & Faber, 2013)

Agent of Peace: Emily Hobhouse and Her Courageous Attempt to End the First World War by Jennifer Hobhouse Balme (The History Press, 2015)

Rebel Englishwoman: The Remarkable Life of Emily Hobhouse by Elsabé Brits (Robinson, 2019)

Dorothy Hodgkin: A Life by Georgina Ferry (Granta Books, 1999)

South Riding by Winifred Holtby (Virago, 2010)

Teaching to Transgress by bell hooks (Routledge, 1994)

Elizabeth Hooton: First Quaker Woman Preacher (1600–1672) by Emily Manners (Forgotten Books, 2018)

Gardening Women: Their Stories from 1600 to the Present by Catherine Horwood (Virago, 2010)

The Plays of Hrotsvitha of Gandersheim, edited by Robert Chipok, translated by Lanissa Bonfante (Bolchazy Carducci Publishing, 2013)

Hypatia: The Life and Legend of an Ancient Philosopher by Edward J. Watts (Oxford University Press USA, 2019)

Women in Science: 50 Fearless Pioneers Who Changed the World by Rachel Ignotofsky (Wren & Rook, 2017)

Women in Sport: Fifty Fearless Athletes Who Played to Win by Rachel Ignotofsky (Wren & Rook, 2018)

31 Fantastic Adventures in Science: Women Scientists in India by Nandita Jayaraj and Aashima Freidog (Penguin Random House India, 2019)

100 Nasty Women of History: Brilliant, Badass and Completely Fearless Women Everyone Should Know by Hannah Jewell (Hodder & Stoughton, 2017)

Sophia Jex-Blake: A Woman Pioneer in Nineteenth-Century Medical Reform by Shirley Roberts (Routledge, 1993)

Fatima Jinnah: Mother of the Nation by M. Reza Pirbhai (Cambridge University Press, 2017)

Joan of Arc: A History by Helen Castor (Harper Collins, 2015)

Autobiography of Mother Jones by Mary Harris Jones (Dover Press Publications, 2004)

Vanguard: How Black Women Broke Barriers, Won the Vote, and Insisted on Equality for All by Martha S. Jones (Basic Books, 2020)

Wild Swans: Three Daughters of China by Jung Chang (HarperCollins, 2012)

Bikes and Bloomers: Victorian Women Inventors and their Extraordinary Cycle Wear by Kat Jungnickel (MIT Press, 2020)

Revelations of Divine Love by Julian of Norwich (Penguin Classics, 1998)

The Life of Saint Katherine of Alexandria by John Capgrave and Karen A. Winstead (University of Notre Dame Press, 2011)

The Virago Book of Women Gardeners by Deborah Kellaway (Virago, 2016)

The Book of Margery Kempe, translated by B. A. Windeatt (Penguin Classics, 2000)

Margery Kempe's Spiritual Medicine: Suffering, Transformation and the Life-Course by Laura Kalas (Boydell & Brewer, 2020)

Eve Was Framed: Women and British Justice by Helena Kennedy (Vintage, 1993)

Working-Class Suffragette: The Life of Annie Kenney by C. M. Talbot (Oldham Writing Café, 2018)

Memoirs of an Early Arab Feminist by Anbara Salam Khalidi, translated by Tarif Khalidi (Pluto Books, 2013)

Spy Princess: The Life of Noor Inayat Khan by Shrabani Basu (The History Press, 2008)

Travels in West Africa by Mary Kingsley (Penguin Classics, 2015)

The Immortal Life of Henrietta Lacks by Rebecca Skloot (Crown Publishing, 2009)

Dorothea Lange: A Life Beyond Limits by Linda Gordon (W. W. Norton and Company, Inc., 2009)

Dorothea Lange: Aperture Masters of Photography (Aperture, 2014)

Daughters of Light: Quaker Women Preaching and Prophesying in the Colonies and Abroad, 1700–1775 by Rebecca Larson (University of North Carolina Press, 2000)

Ann Lee (The Founder of the Shakers): A Biography, with Memoirs of William Lee, James Whittaker, J. Hocknall, J. Meacham, and Lucy Wright by Frederick William Evans (HardPress Publishing, 2020)

Jennie Lee: A Life by Patricia Hollis (Oxford University Press, 1998)

Etta Lemon: The Woman Who Saved the Birds by Tessa Boase (Aurum Press, 2021)

Difficult Women: A History of Feminism in 11 Fights by Helen Lewis (Vintage, 2021)

Licoricia of Winchester: Power and Prejudice in Medieval England by Rebecca Abrams (Unicorn Publishing Group, 2022)

Lindell's List: Saving British and American Women at Ravensbrück by Peter Hore (The History Press, 2016)

What Is History, Now? by Suzannah Lipscomb and Helen Carr (Weidenfeld & Nicolson, 2021)

The Voices of Nîmes: Women, Sex, and Marriage in Reformation Languedoc by Suzannah Lipscomb (Oxford University Press, 2022)

The Master's Tools Will Never Dismantle the Master's House by Audre Lorde (Penguin Classics, 2018)

Sister Outsider by Audre Lorde (Penguin Modern Classics, 2019)

A History of the World with the Women Put Back In by Kerstin Lucker and Ute Daenschel (The History Press, 2019)

The World We Once Lived In by Wangari Maathai (Penguin, 2021)

Strong Female Lead: Lessons from Women in Power by Arwa Mahdawi (Hodder Studio, 2021)

Hope Against Hope by Nadezhda Mandelstam (Vintage, 1999)

Hope Abandoned by Nadezhda Mandelstam (Vintage, 2011)

Rising: 30 Women Who Changed India by Kiran Manral (Cloudtail India, 2022)

A Place of Greater Safety by Hilary Mantel (Fourth Estate, 1992)

The Rebel Countess: The Life and Times of Constance Markievicz by Anne Marreco (Phoenix, 2002)

On a Sledge and Horseback: To the Outcast Siberian Lepers by Kate Marsden (Forgotten Books, 2016)

Eleanor Marx: A Life by Rachel Holmes (Bloomsbury, 2015)

Mary Queen of Scots by Antonia Fraser (Weidenfeld & Nicolson, 2018)

Women in the Picture: Women, Art and the Power of Looking by Catherine McCormack (Icon Books, 2021)

The Life and Times of Mary Ann McCracken, 1770–1866 by Mary McNeill (Irish Academic Press, 2019)

Catherine de Medici: A Biography by Leonie Frieda (Weidenfeld & Nicolson, 2005)

The Rival Queens: Catherine de' Medici, her daughter Marguerite de Valois, and the Betrayal That Ignited a Kingdom by Nancy Goldstone (Weidenfeld & Nicolson, 2016)

Lioness: Golda Meir and the Nation of Israel by Francine Klagsbrun (Schocken Books, 1990)

Golda Meir: A Reference Guide to Her Life and Works by Meron Medzini (Rowman & Littlefield Publishers, 2020)

You Have Struck a Rock: Women Fighting for Their Power in South Africa by Gugulethu Mhlungu (Kwela, 2021)

Give Us Freedom: The Women Who Revolutionised the Modern World by Rosalind Miles (Little, Brown, 2021)

Sexual Politics Paperback by Kate Millett (Virago, 1977)

The Selected Poems of Gabriela Mistral, translated by Ursula K. Le Guin (University of New Mexico Press, 2011)

What is Feminism? by Juliet Mitchell and Ann Oakley (Wiley-Blackwell, 1986)

The Letters of Mrs Elizabeth Montagu, With Some of the Letters of Her Correspondents (Cambridge University Press, 2015)

Women of Invention: Life-Changing Ideas by Remarkable Women by Charlotte Montague (Chartwell, 2018)

Fierce Convictions: The Extraordinary Life of Hannah More by Karen Swallow Prior (Thomas Nelson, 2014)

Sisterhood Is Global: The International Women's Movement Anthology by Robin Morgan (Penguin, 1985)

Before and After: Reminiscence of a Working Life by Edith Morley (Two Rivers Press, 2016)

The Virago Book of Women Travellers by Mary Morris (Virago, 2020)

Mouth Full of Blood: Essays, Speeches, Meditations by Toni Morrison (Vintage, 2020)

Two in the Far North, Revised Edition: A Conservation Champion's Story of Life, Love, and Adventure in the Wilderness by Margaret E. Murie (Graphic Art Books, 2020)

Song in a Weary Throat: An American Pilgrimage by Pauli Murray (Liveright, 2018)

Speeches and Writings of Sarojini Naidu (Franklin Press, 2018)

The Mother of Us All: A History of Queen Nanny, Leader of the Windward Jamaican Maroons by Karla Gottlieb (Africa World Press, 2000)

The Heptameron by Marguerite de Navarre (Penguin Classics, 1994)

Bloody Brilliant Women: The Pioneers, Revolutionaries and Geniuses Your History Teacher Forgot to Mention by Cathy Newman (HarperCollins, 2019)

Florence Nightingale: The Woman and Her Legend by Mark Bostridge (Penguin, 2020)

Rebels at the Bar: The Fascinating, Forgotten Stories of America's First Women Lawyers by Jill Norgren (NYU Press, 2016)

Helena Normanton and the Opening of the Bar to Women by Judith Bourne (Waterside Press, 2016)

The Case of the Married Woman: Caroline Norton: A 19th Century Heroine Who Wanted Justice for Women by Antonia Fraser (Weidenfeld & Nicolson, 2021)

The Hidden Lives of Tudor Women: A Social History by Elizabeth Norton (Pegasus Books, 2018)

Becoming by Michelle Obama (Penguin, 2021)

To Talk of Many Things: An Autobiography by Dame Kathleen Ollerenshaw (Manchester University Press, 2004)

Upanisads, translated by Patrick Olivelle (Oxford World's Classics, 2008)

My People by Noonuccal Oodgeroo (Wiley, 2011)

Grace O'Malley: The Biography of Ireland's Pirate Queen 1530–1603 by Anne Chambers (Gill Books, 2019)

African Europeans: An Untold History by Olivette Otele (Hurst, 2020)

Sorrow Mountain: The Journey of a Tibetan Warrior Nun by Ani Pachen with Adelaide Donnelley (Transworld, 2000)

Prison Days by Vijaya Lakshmi Pandit (Speaking Tiger Books, 2018)

Queens of Jerusalem: The Women Who Dared to Rule by Katherine Pangonis (Orion, 2021)

Suffragette: My Own Story by Emmeline Pankhurst (Hesperus Press Classics, 2016)

Deeds Not Words: The Story of Women's Rights – Then and Now by Helen Pankhurst (Sceptre, 2018)

Sylvia Pankhurst: Natural Born Rebel by Rachel Holmes (Bloomsbury, 2021)

Blood, Fire and Gold: The Story of Elizabeth I and Catherine de Medici by Estelle Paranque (Ebury, 2022)

The Rebellious Life of Mrs Rosa Parks by Jeanne Theoharis (Beacon Press, 2015)

Reflections by Rosa Parks: The Quiet Strength and Faith of a Woman Who Changed a Nation by Rosa Parks with Gregory J. Reed (Zondervan, 2018)

He Reo Wahine: Māori Women's Voices from the Nineteenth Century by Lachy Paterson and Angela Wanhalla (Auckland University Press, 2017)

What Stars Are Made Of: The Life of Cecilia Payne-Gaposchkin by Donovan Moore (Harvard University Press, 2020)

Perpetua's Passion: The Death and Memory of a Young Roman Woman by Joyce E. Salisbury (Routledge, 1997)

The Life of Walatta-Petros: A Seventeenth-Century Biography of an African Woman by Galawdewos, edited and translated by Wendy Laura Belcher and Michael Kleiner (Princeton University Press, 2018)

Great Women Artists by Phaidon Editors (Phaidon, 2019)

Litigating Women: Gender and Justice in Europe, c.1300–c.1800, edited by Teresa Phipps and Deborah Younge (Routledge, 2022)

The Book of the City of Ladies by Christine de Pizan (Penguin Classics, 1999)

Pocahontas and Sacagawea – Interwoven Legacies in American History by Cyndi Spindell Berck (Commonwealth Books, 2015)

The Tale of Beatrix Potter: A Biography by Margaret Lane (Penguin, 1986)

The History of Mary Prince: A West Indian Slave by Mary Prince (Penguin Classics, 2000)

Across Boundaries: The Journey from a South African Woman Leader by Mamphela Ramphele (Feminist Press, 1999)

Lady Doctors: The Untold Stories of India's First Women Doctors by Kavitha Rao (Westland, 2021)

Women of Westminster: The MPs Who Changed Politics by Rachel Reeves (Bloomsbury, 2020)

Trailblazing Women of the Georgian Era: The Eighteenth-Century Struggle for Female Success in a Man's World by Mike Rendell (Pen & Sword History, 2018)

On Lies, Secrets, and Silence: Selected Prose 1966–1978 by Adrienne Rich (W. W. Norton and Company, Inc., 1989)

Feet in Chains by Kate Roberts, translated by Katie Gramich (Parthian, 2012)

Mary Robinson: The Authorised Biography by Olivia O'Leary and Helen Burke (Hodder & Stoughton, 1998)

Betsy Ross by Peter Roop and Connie Roop (Scholastic, 2022)

A Century of Women: The History of Women in Britain and the United States by Sheila Rowbotham (Viking, 1997)

Dreamers of a New Day: Women Who Invented the Twentieth Century by Sheila Rowbotham (Verso, 2010)

Revolutions: How Women Changed the World on Two Wheels by Hannah Ross (Weidenfeld & Nicolson, 2021)

Women in the Resistance by Margaret Rossiter (Praeger Publishers, 1986)

Woman at Point Zero by Nawal el Saadawi (Zed Books, 2015)

Walking through Fire: The Later Years of Nawal El Saadawi, In Her Own Words by Nawal El Saadawi and Sherif Hetata (Zed Books, 2018)

The Autobiography of Margaret Sanger (Dover Books, 2004)

Code Name: Lise: The True Story of Odette Sansom, WWII's Most Highly Decorated Spy by Larry Loftis (Mirror Books, 2020)

Women and Gender in Medieval Europe: An Encyclopedia, edited by Margaret C. Schaus (Routledge, 2007)

At the Heart of the White Rose: Letters and Diaries of Hans and Sophie Scholl, edited by Inge Jens, translated by J. Maxwell Brownjohn (Plough Publishing House, 2017)

A Great Task of Happiness: The Life of Kathleen Scott by Louisa Young (Macmillan, 1995)

Les Parisiennes: How the Women of Paris Lived, Loved and Died in the 1940s by Anne Sebba (Weidenfeld & Nicolson, 2016)

The Wonderful Adventures of Mrs Seacole in Many Lands by Mary Seacole (Penguin Classics, 2005)

In Search of Mary Seacole: The Making of a Cultural Icon by Helen Rappaport (Simon & Schuster, 2022)

On Balance: An Autobiography by Leila Seth (Penguin Books India, 2008)

Harem Years: The Memoirs of an Egyptian Feminist, 1879–1924 by Huda Sha'awari (Feminist Press, 1987)

Doria Shafik, Egyptian Feminist: A Woman Apart by Cynthia Nelson (The American University in Cairo Press, 1996)

Frankenstein: The 1818 Text by Mary Shelley (Penguin Classics, 2018)

Kate Sheppard, a Biography: The Fight for Women's Votes in New Zealand – The Life of the Woman Who Led the Struggle by Judith Devaliant (Penguin, 1992)

The Living Mountain: A Celebration of the Cairngorm Mountains of Scotland by Nan Shepherd (Canongate, 2019)

Hidden Figures: The Untold Story of the African American Women Who Helped Win the Space Race by Margot Lee Shetterly (Morrow, 2016)

The Tale of Genji by Murasaki Shikibu, translated by Arthur Waley (Tuttle Shokai, 1935); translated by Edward Seidensticker (Everyman, 1992)

The Authority Gap by Mary Ann Sieghart (Doubleday, 2021)

Albertina Sisulu by Sindiwe Magona and Elinor Sisulu (David Philip Publishers, 2018)

This Child Will Be Great: Memoir of a Remarkable Life by Africa's First Woman President by Ellen Johnson Sirleaf (Harper Perennial, 2010)

Impressions That Remained: Memoirs of Ethel Smyth (Brousson Press, 2005)

Sophia: Princess, Suffragette, Revolutionary by Anita Anand (Bloomsbury, 2015)

India Calling: The Memories of Cornelia Sorabji, India's First Woman Barrister (Oxford University Press, USA, 2001)

Cornelia Sorabji: India's Pioneer Woman Lawyer: A Biography by Suparna Gooptu (Oxford University Press, India, 2010)

An Indian Portia: Selected Writings of Cornelia Sorabji, 1866–1954 by Cornelia Sorabji, compiled and edited by Kusoom Vadgama (Blacker, 2011)

Women of Ideas – and What Men Have Done to Them: From Aphra Behn to Adrienne Rich by Dale Spender (Thorsons, 1983)

Star of the Morning: The Extraordinary Life of Lady Hester Stanhope by Kirsten Ellis (Harper Press, 2008)

Elizabeth Cady Stanton: An American Life by Lori D. Ginzberg (Hill & Wang, 2009)

Baghdad Sketches: Journeys through Iraq by Freya Stark (Tauris Parke, 2011)

Freya Stark by Caroline Moorehead (Allison & Busby, 2014)

The Valleys of the Assassins by Freya Stark (John Murray, 2021)

The Autobiography of Alice B. Toklas by Gertrude Stein (Penguin Modern Classics, 2001)

Outrageous Acts and Everyday Rebellions by Gloria Steinem (Picador, 2019)

Redeemed Bodies: Women Martyrs in Early Christianity by Gail P. C. Streete (Westminster/John Knox Press, 2009)

Elizabeth Stuart: Queen of Hearts by Nadine Akkerman (Oxford University Press, 2021)

In No Uncertain Terms: Memoirs by Helen Suzman (Mandarin, 1994)

Women, Astronomy and Greenwich by Kelley Swain (Royal Observatory, 2011)

Violette: The Missions of SOE Agent Violette Szabó GC by Tania Szabó (The History Press, 2018)

Gerda Taro: Inventing Robert Capa by Jane Rogoyska (Jonathan Cape, 2013)

Women's Football: The Secret History of Women's Football by Tim Tate (John Blake, 2016)

Margaret Thatcher: The Authorized Biography, Volume One: Not For Turning by Charles Moore (Penguin, 2014)

Margaret Thatcher: The Authorized Biography, Volume Two: Everything She Wants by Charles Moore (Penguin, 2016)

Margaret Thatcher: The Authorized Biography, Volume Three: Herself Alone by Charles Moore (Penguin, 2020)

No One Is Too Small to Make a Difference by Greta Thunberg (Penguin, 2019)

Toksvig's Almanac 2021: An Eclectic Meander Through the Historical Year by Sandi Toksvig (Orion, 2021)

Truganini: Journey through the Apocalypse by Cassandra Pybus (Allen & Unwin, 2020)

The Narrative of Sojourner Truth (Penguin, 1998)

Ain't I A Woman? by Sojourner Truth (Penguin, 2020)

Forgotten Women: The Scientists by Zing Tsjeng (Cassell, 2018)

Selected Poems of Marina Tsvetaeva, translated by Elaine Feinstein (Hutchinson, 1971, 1994)

No Love Without Poetry: The Memoirs of Marina Tsvetaeva's Daughter by Ariadna Efron, translated by Diane Nemec Ignashev (Northwestern University Press, 2009)

Harriet Tubman: The Road to Freedom by Catherine Clinton (Back Bay, 2005)

Bound for the Promised Land: Harriet Tubman: Portrait of an American Hero by Kate Clifford Larson (One World, 2004)

A Life: The Autobiography of Simone Veil (Haus Publishing, 2009)

Mission France: The True History of the Women of SOE by Kate Vigurs (Yale University Press, 2021)

In Search of Our Mother's Gardens: Womanist Prose by Alice Walker (Weidenfeld & Nicolson, 2005)

Mercy Otis Warren: Selected Letters (University of Georgia Press, 2009)

Martha Washington: First Lady of Liberty by Helen Bryan (John Wiley, 2002)

Women, Writing and Religion in England and Beyond, 650–1100 by Diane Watt (Bloomsbury, 2019)

Queens of the Conquest: The Extraordinary Women Who Changed the Course of English History 1066–1167 by Alison Weir (Vintage, 2008)

Queens of the Crusades: Eleanor of Aquitaine and her Successors (England's Medieval Queens) by Alison Weir (Vintage, 2021)

The Woman's Hour: The Great Fight to Win the Vote by Elaine Weiss (Penguin, 2019)

Sisters in the Resistance: How Women Fought to Free France by Margaret Collins Weitz (Wiley, 1995)

The Road to Seneca Falls: Elizabeth Cady Stanton and the First Woman's Rights Convention by Judith Wellman (University of Illinois Press, 2004)

The Light of Truth: Writings of an Anti-Lynching Crusader by Ida B. Wells (Penguin Classics, 2014)

Phillis Wheatley: Complete Writings (Penguin Classics, 2002)

Ten Women Who Changed Science, and the World by Catherine Whitlock and Rhodri Evans (Little, Brown, 2007)

Rival Queens: The Betrayal of Mary, Queen of Scots by Kate Williams (Hutchinson, 2019)

Power in Numbers: The Rebel Women of Mathematics by Talithia Williams (Race Point Publishing, 2018)

A Vindication of the Rights of Woman; An Historical and Moral View of the French Revolution by Mary Wollstonecraft (Oxford University Press, 2008)

The Grasmere and Alfoxden Journals by Dorothy Wordsworth (Oxford World's Classics, 2002)

Recovering Dorothy: The Hidden Life of Dorothy Wordsworth by Polly Atkin (Saraband, 2021)

The Pioneering Life of Mary Wortley Montagu: Scientist and Feminist by Jo Willett (Pen & Sword Books, 2021)

Selected Letters by Mary Wortley Montagu, edited by Isobel Grundy (Penguin Classics, 1997)

Miscellaneous Records of a Female Doctor by Tan Yunxian, translated by Lorraine Wilcox with Yue Lu (The Chinese Medicine Database, 2015)

Index

Britannia:
Great Stories from British History

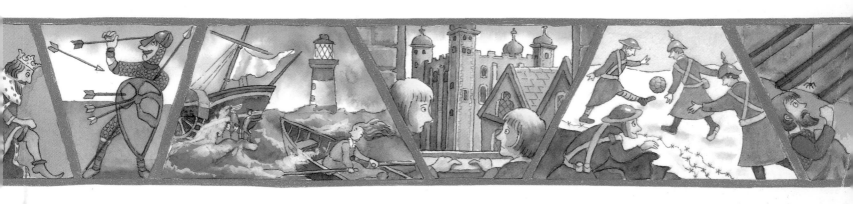

For almost two thousand years, the mythical figure of Britannia,
seated on the globe, has represented an island proud of itself
and its achievements. She has waved her trident over
the pages of history and turned a chaotic jumble of events into
a grand pageant of heroes, adventurers, villains and comedians.
She is the storyteller who rewrote the past into
the kind of stories a nation wants to tell about itself.

Britannia:

Great Stories from British History

Geraldine McCaughrean
and Richard Brassey

Orion
Children's Books

for Neil and Iwona
G. McC.

for George
R.B.

Also by Geraldine McCaughrean:

Cowboy Jess
Cowboy Jess Saddles Up
Robin Hood and the Golden Arrow and a World of Other Stories
King Arthur and a World of Other Stories
George and the Dragon and a World of Other Stories
Stories from Shakespeare

First published in Great Britain in 1999 by Orion Children's Books
This new edition first published 2014 by Orion Children's Books
a division of the Orion Publishing Group Ltd
Orion House
5 Upper St Martin's Lane
London WC2H 9EA
An Hachette UK Company

1 3 5 7 9 10 8 6 4 2

Text copyright © Geraldine McCaughrean 1999, 2011
Illustrations copyright © Richard Brassey 1999, 2011

The rights of Geraldine McCaughrean and Richard Brassey to be identified
as the author and illustrator respectively of this work has been asserted.

A catalogue record for this book is available from the British Library

Printed and bound in China by C&C Offset Printing Co Ltd

ISBN 978 1 4440 1390 0

Contents

Since When Was History True?

THERE WAS A TIME WHEN PEOPLE FIRMLY BELIEVED THAT A FEW YEARS EARLIER – in, say, their great-grandfather's time – dragons and giants roamed the neighbourhood. Their past was told to them by storytellers, but they knew the stories were true, because the village down the road told a similar tale. Folklore was history.

That is why this book begins with events which no twentieth-century historian would even trouble to write down, and goes on to recount things which twentieth-century historians have long since debunked.

Over the centuries, history has been "adjusted" countless times to suit the ends of scheming statesmen. It has been "tidied up" to make for a better story. It has been "improved on" so as to paint a grand and flattering picture of Britain as "Britannia's realm", ordained and governed by God Himself.

Nowadays, thankfully, we look at ourselves more shrewdly, knowing that in every period of history our ancestors were probably just like us: good, bad and accident-prone. History has become an exact science, concentrating on known facts.

Certain stories are no longer told, because there may be only a grain of truth in them.

But wouldn't it be a terrible pity if, as a result, those stories were to wither and die? These grand adventures have forged our national identity as a race of heroes, saints and underdogs destined for greatness. In my book, that makes them history.

So watch out, as you read, for myth, propaganda, embroidery and downright lies, but remember: these stories are, in themselves, a part of British history . . . as well as our national heritage.

Geraldine McCaughrean

Gogmagog and the Exiles of Troy

about 1100 BC

As the city of Troy burned, the conquering Greeks spilled Trojan blood and laid waste to the marvels of the city. But as well as looting and destroying, they took prisoners – hundreds of prisoners – and carried them back to Greece to work as slaves.

Those hundreds became, in time, thousands – generations of slaves toiling away their days in the villas and harbours and vineyards of Greek kings. Gradually, they began to forget their Trojan heritage, the glory which had once been theirs. Not Brutus. Though born a slave and the son of slaves, Brutus felt Trojan nobility boiling in his veins, and by telling the great old stories, he stirred up his fellow slaves to remember, too, and to rebel. They fought their Greek masters, broke free and ran.

That army of freed men would have followed Brutus anywhere. All their lives they had known nothing but work and whip, whip and work. Now they were drunk on liberty and looking for a homeland to call their own.

Over mountains and plains and wintry wastes of sea, Brutus led his "Trojans", until they came to the Isle of Albion, walled with white cliffs, and they set their hearts on owning it. Sailing past the cliffs, and keeping offshore of the pebbly southern beaches, Brutus landed his fleet in an inviting river estuary, saying:

"Here I am and here I rest,
And this town shall be called Totnes"
(which perhaps sounded better in his native tongue).

So what if this place were peopled by giants with heads like haystacks and fists like club hammers? Nothing but slavery held any fear for Brutus's men. They were warriors, with warrior blood in their veins, whereas the giants were merely big, with fewer brains, for all the size of their heads.

By cunning and by military might, the Trojans drove back the giants, until, like bees trapped in a bottle, the last and fiercest were congregated all in

one narrow isthmus of the island – in Cornwall. Largest and most ferocious of them all was Gogmagog. His temper was as hot as lava, and his belch as loud as erupting volcanoes, and he stamped so hard that the Cornish rocks under him were compressed to shiny tin.

Though they had been felling giants like so many trees, even the fearless Trojans swallowed hard at the sight of Gogmagog dancing on the Cornish hills, wielding his blunt stone hammer, singing out blood-thirsty recipes for Trojan pie.

Now in those days, battles were not a scrimmaging scrum of punches and blows and the victory going to the only men left standing. Lone champions did battle on behalf of their armies. But who could wrestle Gogmagog and live?

Only Corineus was willing to try. "I am ready!" he cried, stripping off his armour and rolling up his sleeves. "I will fight him!"

Brutus's army gave a low groan at the thought of their finest general, hero of many a battle, dying in his second-best tunic, neck broken by a grinning gargoyle of a giant. But the message went out – shouted in at every cave door and down every rabbit hole: "Corineus will fight Gogmagog, if he dares to show himself!"

As the sun rose next day, high on a headland, like a lighthouse signalling danger, a dark shape loomed up against the brightness of the sky: Gogmagog. The giant picked up a cow and ate it, throwing the bones into the wind, so that they scattered among the ranks of the Trojans. "Send out your man!" he said, "or leave this island to me and mine!" He made Corineus look like a seedling beside an oak.

But Corineus was quick and nimble. By the time Gogmagog had raised his fist to crush him, Corineus was shinning up the thongs of the giant's sandals, clambering up his tunic, swinging from his beard. And Corineus was strong, too. He could twist the hairs in a giant's ear so that tears sprang from his eyes, and when he butted his head against the bridge of the giant's nose, Gogmagog's purple eyes spun.

Geoffrey of Monmouth, a cleric from Wales (or possibly Brittany) was a lecturer at Oxford between 1129 and 1151. In 1136 he produced *A History of the Kings of Britain*, merging folklore, legend and half-remembered facts into a sequence of events masquerading as history. Just when the country was trying to establish a sense of national identity, Geoffrey's book demonstrated that a kind of noble destiny was at work in the unfolding of history. It was accepted without quibble. In the Middle Ages, the story of Brutus the Trojan was firmly believed to be true (possibly even by Geoffrey), but it is actually the work of some lover of the classics who wanted to make Britain as grand as Rome and Greece. Gog and Magog are monstrous figures in the Old Testament. Every locality had its folk memories of local giants, so Geoffrey probably lent one of these a name suggestive of pagan evil and menace.

Corineus was light on his feet, and knew how to throw an opponent off balance or trip him from behind. Corineus swarmed over Gogmagog, wearying him with bruises, rattling him with laughter. All day they wrestled, while the bright sea winked and the seagulls screamed with excitement, and the grass wore thin on the headland. All Cornwall shook so that its smooth coastlines were made jagged by cliff-falls into the sunny sea.

But as the sun itself grew weary and dropped down the westerly sky. Gogmagog caught hold of Corineus and whirled him around in the air. "Fall into the sea and be lost, you bird-dropping, you pebble, you rain-drop!" he bellowed, and threw Corineus towards the sea.

Only by clinging to the grass with the tips of his fingers did Corineus save himself from plunging over the cliff-edge, and as he hung there, over the deadly drop, Gogmagog put his fists on his hips and laughed. Pausing only to shout a string of curses at the watching Trojans, the giant lifted a foot to stamp on Corineus's fingers . . .

But at the last moment Corineus swung sideways, snatching hold of a thorn bush, and Gogmagog's foot broke off the cliff's edge, so that he pitched, bellowing and tumbling, heels over howling head, down into the sea below.

Thus Corineus won for himself the little dominion of Cornwall, and Brutus's Trojans the whole realm of Albion. The smaller, female giants, creeping out from their homes in caves and potholes and the mouldy boles of ancient trees, pleaded piteously for their lives. And the Trojans, lonely for wives, married them and bred a race of hard-working, deep-digging, tall-tale-telling sons.

King Leir

about 8 0 0 B C

THERE WAS ONCE A KING WITH THREE daughters. Weary of responsibility, he decided to lay aside his crown and divide his kingdom between his daughters.

"Tell me," he said, calling them before him. "How much do you love me?"

"More than emeralds or pearls or rubies," said Gonerilla.

"More than any man on earth!" said Regan.

"And you, Cordeilla?" asked Leir of his third and favourite daughter. "What have you to say?"

"Nothing," said Cordeilla.

"Nothing?"

"I love you as much as a daughter should," said the princess, declining to flatter the old man, "and I think you will find, Father, that the world respects a king because of his title. Give that up and the world may treat you more unkindly than it does now."

Leir was cut to the quick by her coldness, but he hid his hurt behind towering rage. "I had meant to give you the best and greenest part of my kingdom. But now I shall give you nothing, you unfeeling child – no, not even so much as a dowry or a place in my home!"

So the youngest princess, for speaking the truth, was banished over the sea to Gaul, and King Leir laid aside his crown, intending to spend the rest of his life enjoying himself with his friends. (He had a great many friends – 140 knights, in fact.) "I shall come to stay with each of you in turn," he told his two dutiful daughters.

But as Leir grew older and more frail, he discovered that Gonerilla and Regan did not love him quite as much as they had vowed. They turned his friends out of doors, told him they had house-room for only twenty-five, then only ten, then just one. Their husbands seized his last remaining lands, ignoring his ranting protests.

Realizing the truth of Cordeilla's words, Leir set off, through storm and hardship, for Gaul, to ask for help. He must recover his crown and depose the villains who were devouring his country. On board the ship, dishevelled and frail, he was treated no better than a common vagrant by the crew. It was true, then, what Cordeilla had said: that it was the crown people respected and not the man wearing it. What kind of welcome would he receive from the daughter he had so wronged?

If this story reads like a fairy tale, it is no surprise. Geoffrey of Monmouth, who included it in his *History of the Kings of Britain* (about 1136) probably derived it from a folk tale – maybe not even a British one at that. His King Leir supposedly came to the throne very young, owing to the sudden death of his father Bladud in a flying accident using magical wings. Raphael Holinshed, in his *Chronicles* of 1577, retold Geoffrey of Monmouth's story but altered minor details. Gonerilla became Goneril, Cordeilla Cordelia, Leir became Lear. Shakespeare used the Holinshed versions for his great tragedy. But the play's comments on old age, madness and power are all Shakespeare's own.

The place-name Leicester does not really have a connection with any King Leir.

Cordeilla, however, had found real happiness. Aganippus, King of the Franks, had taken her for his wife, despite her lack of dowry, despite her banishment. He valued her for what she was, an honest, brave and virtuous woman. As Leir found, she had always loved him more than had either of the hypocrites Gonerilla or Regan. At a word, she and Aganippus mustered an army to wreak vengeance on the heartless sisters.

Gonerilla and Regan, too intent on squabbling with each other, could not hold out against the avenging wrath of the invading army, and died, along with their husbands. Leir was reinstated King of Britain, and for three happy years he reigned, a wiser and more humane king for his one disastrous mistake. When he died, Cordeilla buried him in a vault under the bed of the River Soar, and founded a city nearby – Leicester or Leir-under-the-Soar. She ruled in his place, tempered by hardship and injustice into the most tender and just of queens.

The Three Plagues of Lud's Town

about 300 BC

DID YOU EVER HEAR IT SAID THAT TROUBLES come in threes? They did for the people of New Troy.

Several generations after the coming of Brutus, a king was crowned whose name was Lud. His one ambition in life was to make New Troy the most beautiful city in the world. He built houses and towers, wharves and storehouses, streets and council halls, and he strengthened the walls against attack by any marauding foe. But the foes who came could not be kept out by mere stones and timber. Three plagues fell on the people of New Troy.

First came the Coranieid – out of the bottomless lakes and over the shale shores, all the way from Otherworld. They were shifting, whispering shadows, picking the mud from the walls with their long fingernails, picking the nails out of ship's hulls with their sharp little teeth. They lurked in every alleyway and hollow tree, every empty ale cask and cattle trough, armed with needle-sharp swords and butterfly nets. And no matter what plans were made to drive them out, the Coranieid always knew ahead of time, always escaped.

"If only my clever little brother Llefelys were here and not living far away," Lud said, as the Coranieid whispered like starlings in the city dusk. "He would know what to do."

The next plague was of thefts – not the odd bushel of corn gone missing, but whole warehouses of wine and grain and salted beef. Lud set guards outside every storehouse, then doubled the guard, but the thieving went on, night after night, until half their winter provisions were gone. There were no more banquets, no more fairs: only hunger and worry and aggravation at never catching the thief.

"If only Llefelys were here," Lud would say. "He would know who was doing this."

Then came the shrieks. They were terrible, chilling, ear-splitting brays which pierced the ear-drum

13

and shivered the brain to dust. Every May Day Eve, the shrieks sounded in the sky over New Troy. Men and women fell dead, and the expressions on their faces did not bear looking at. "If only Llefelys were here," Lud said. "I must speak to him before next May Day."

The two brothers met in the middle of the sea, their ships banging rail to rail. Lud clasped his brother close. "You are good to come: I need your help."

Llefelys listened to Lud describing the three plagues. "I can tell you how to defeat the Coranieid," he said. "I have met their kind in Brittany. But we must take precautions. They sieve the words from the wind, you know, and not a whisper escapes them." He took out a long copper tube which he placed against Lud's ear. Putting his mouth to the other end, he spoke in a whisper: "Kudjj eitho wihfldnn unt er sunbumflicekr wolembluch."

Lud looked at him blankly. Llefelys took the speaking tube to the edge of the ship and poured a flagon of wine down it. With spluttered curses, out of the tube slid a sodden Coranieid. It sank out of sight in the sea. Now Lud was able to hear every word his brother said down the tube, and the fairies could not eavesdrop.

"And as for the thefts of food and drink," said Llefelys, laying aside the hearing trumpet, "that's the work of a giant. I know him well: we studied under the same apothecary. He has obviously mixed himself a potion which sends your guards to

sleep, and while they sleep, he helps himself. Here's what you must do . . ."

"And as for the shriek," said Llefelys a while later, "that will cost you a pot of honey and a sail of your largest ship . . ."

Lud embraced his brother, thanked him and waved him farewell. He had the three solutions now to his three problems. "I should have liked Llefelys by my side, even so," he said to himself, and the Coranieid sieved the words out of the air and crunched them between their yellow teeth.

First Lud ordered his men to catch insects –

crane-fly, mosquitoes and wasps – out of the summer air. These he crushed into a fine powder and mixed with brine. Then, when a high wind was blowing, Lud ordered the potion to be sprayed from the ramparts of New Troy, so that the air glittered with rainbow droplets. Harmless to ordinary people the infusion worked like strychnine on the Coranieid, and they could be seen shrivelling up like fallen leaves. The first plague was over.

Next Lud dismissed the guard outside the storehouses and granaries of New Troy and took their place himself. Alongside him stood a bath of cold water and his two-edged sword. At around three in the morning, a smell came to him on the breeze. At once he leapt – splash! – into the bath. The cold bit him to the bone, but it jarred him wide awake. The giant, thinking his magic perfume must have sent everyone to sleep, came whistling down the road, dragging several empty sacks. He had not even troubled to carry a weapon. At the sight of a man sitting in a bath of water, fully clothed and wide awake, the giant stopped short.

"No more of your thieving, you villainous oaf!" declared Lud, springing to his feet. The sword trembled in his chilly grasp, but the thought of his hungry people heated his temper red hot.

"All right. I shall come no more," said the giant, feeling the tip of Lud's sword against his navel, "and if you don't kill me, I'll even make good what I've taken."

"Swear it on your mother's life!" insisted Lud through chattering teeth.

"Oh, I do, I do," the giant assured him affably. "Now please let me go. It's May Day Eve tomorrow and I want to be many a mile away when that accursed shriek sounds!"

"Before you go, you can do a job of work for me," said Lud. "I want you to dig me a hole outside the city walls – a very big hole indeed."

So the giant dug a hole – at extraordinary speed, because he was so anxious to be gone – and Lud spread the largest sail of his largest ship over the hole to conceal it. A bowl of honey was placed on the centre of the sailcloth, and then Lud issued wax earplugs to his soldiers and plugged up his own ears.

At about midday on the May Day Eve, the shrieks sounded, far away to the north. Even so, several men and women fell dead and a water tower crashed to the ground. But instead of covering their heads with their arms, Lud and his soldiers were able, for the first time, to watch the sky. Winging towards them came two great dragons.

The King Lud mentioned by Henry of Huntingdon in his *Historia Anglorum* (1154) had existed in many forms earlier in history. He began life as Nodens, a British god adopted by the Irish then the Welsh who told stories of Lludd-of-the-Silver-Hand. Centuries later, Lludd or Lud had become a legendary king, featuring in the great *Mabinogion* cycle of medieval Welsh stories. During the Middle Ages, a gate really did stand on Ludgate Hill, decorated with images of English kings, including Lud. Defaced, restored, improved upon, it was finally destroyed in the Great Fire. A reconstruction survived until 1760. Though London may have derived its name from one man or a local tribe, that name was probably Londinos, or something similar. It was certainly not named after Lud.

One was red as blood, the other white as a glacier. And as they flew they lunged at one another, clashing wings, engulfing each other in gouts of fire and smoke. Above all they shrieked – that ear-splitting, brain-shattering shriek which had killed so many of Lud's subjects. Scales the size of shields rained down on the city. The fight was terrible to watch, and yet it was plain neither beast would win; they were doomed to fight every May Day Eve until the end of time.

At the sight of the honey, something astonishing happened. For the shrieking dragons broke off fighting, and hovered directly over the square of sailcloth. The smell seemed irresistible to them, for they circled lower and lower and came slowly in to land.

The sailcloth sank under their weight and spilled them into the pit, but the dragons barely noticed; they were too busy gorging on the honey. No sooner had they licked up the last dregs, than they fell deeply asleep, coiled round and about each other. Out from hiding raced Lud and his army of men. They folded the sailcloth over the dragons, and stitched it into a parcel. Then they carried the parcel as far as they could to the west, where they buried it in a stone-lined hole at the top of the highest mountain they could find, and filled it in with boulders and loose earth.

New Troy was restored to the peace of earlier, happier times, and such was the gratitude of the people that they renamed the town after their hero. City of Lud, they called it – Caer Luddein. And in time, blown on by wind and rain, that name was worn down into London. Lud was buried there, by Lud Gate. And if you walk to the top of Ludgate Hill, you may still see, spread before you, the city which Lud rescued from its three plagues.

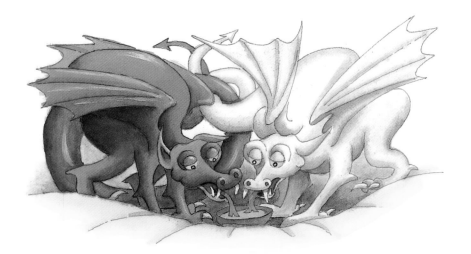

The Tin Islands

about 100 BC

YELLOW AMBER AND PURPLE CLOTH, pottery and jewellery, spices, sponges and glass: the merchants of Phoenicia had wonders to tempt the most wary. Long before the Romans came to Britain, they knew of its existence, for Phoenician merchants were bringing tin and skins and slaves from some northern island realm they referred to as "Cassiterides": the Tin Islands.

Now tin, as a constituent of bronze, was of vital importance to the Romans. They did not want to be dependent on the Phoenicians – to have to pay Phoenician prices for this valuable commodity. So they ached to find these "Cassiterides", to tap their bottomless resource of tin.

Battening on to the wake of a Phoenician trader, one Roman captain determined to follow him to his secret source. He would not let the ship out of his sight until he had found out where the Phoenician went ashore to barter for the so-called "white lead". Day and night he matched the Phoenician's speed, though the merchant was as eager to *keep* his trade secrets as the Roman was to have them. The merchant tried altering course, veering wildly about on the open ocean to give his pursuer the slip. But the Roman clung on grimly, following every tack and gybe. It terrified him, for Roman ships were coastal vessels, not built for open sea, and the Phoenician took him into grey, heaving waters very different from the sunny Mediterranean.

"So. You dog my heels, do you?" muttered the Phoenician under his breath. "Very well, I shall lead you where you have no wish to go." And he set course for shallow water.

Inhabitants of the region now called Syria, the Phoenicians were intrepid explorers, venturing farther and farther afield in search of new markets, new commodities to sell. They were middle-men creating contact between continents and empires. Their trading visits undoubtedly enriched the lives of the Ancient Britons. But the fact that merchants found a ready market here for luxury goods dispels the picture of Ancient Britons as primitive savages.

Phoenician trading accounts for some amazing archaeological finds within the British Isles: Roman coins predating the Roman invasion, Scandinavian amber, Egyptian glass beads . . . The above story was recorded by Phoenician chroniclers in the first century BC. It is not recorded what became of the Roman ship or its crew.

Reserves of tin are largely exhausted now, but 2,000 years ago Britain was sole supplier to a Europe clamouring for bronze tools and weaponry. It was inevitable that the Roman Empire would not rest until it had found and conquered the "Islands of Tin".

Perhaps he thought he knew the coastal waters well enough to pick his way through deep-water channels. Perhaps he realized that his nation's secret had to be protected at whatever cost. With a sickening, grinding judder, his vessel ran aground. Too intent on following to put about in time, the Roman vessel too lumbered on to the hidden shoals. Within sight of one another, the two ships were quickly dismantled by pounding waves – reduced to flotsam and the cries of drowning men.

The Phoenician captain clung to a spar and kicked out for land, knees scraping on the rocks which had sunk him. The sea washed him up, limp and cold as seaweed, on a lonely beach, ship gone, cargo lost, but his life still clenched in his chattering teeth.

Months later, weary hundreds of miles away, he found his way home. Recounting his story, he was able to report to his fellow merchants, to the governors and ministers of his home town, that the whereabouts of the Tin Islands had been kept out of Roman hands. They were not slow to show their appreciation. "You shall have the value of your cargo!" they declared. "The state awards it you for the service you have done us all!"

"I Came, I Saw, I Conquered"

55 BC

FOR A LAND-LOVING MAN LIKE ME FROM A warm, sunny city, the crossing was a nightmare. The cavalry had not even managed to set sail from Gaul because of a contrary wind. Then, just as the white cliffs of Albion came into sight, a storm blew up which split the fleet and drove half of us one way, half the other. The landing site was unsuitable, the tide was against us, and the Britons were ready and waiting for us, armed to their blue-painted nostrils.

They came screaming down the beach. The keels of our big ships were so deep that Caesar could not get in close to the shore. Do you know what a Roman soldier's armour weighs? This chain mail tabard, the bronze helmet, the leather body armour? Even in August the British sea is not clear like the Mediterranean. Looking over the side, we could not see how deep the water was or where it was safe to step. If we fell over in all that weight of armour . . .

The Britons had no such problems. Their arms and legs were bare. They waded out towards us to fight us in the surf where we were at our most helpless. They were even driving their chariots in and out of the water, raising glassy fantails of spray higher than our heads: an awesome sight.

Then the standard-bearer leapt overboard, brandishing the Eagle of the Tenth Legion. To lose that to the enemy! Unthinkable! "Leap down, soldiers!" he yelled. "Unless you want to betray the Eagle to the enemy!"

There was no more hesitating then. Men from the other ships jumped in with both feet, wallowing about like seacows, staggering towards the shore, sandals slipping on the slimy seabed.

But I was one of Caesar's reserve. He was sending us in by the boatload to wherever the line looked weakest. I and four others jumped into a little boat and rowed for an outcrop of rocks about halfway to the shore. We climbed on to it and began throwing rocks and pebbles – as good a weapon as any against half-naked men. I tell you, we pelted them like shepherd boys scaring off wolves.

Unfortunately we got isolated from the main force, and to my – er – discomfort, I realized that the tide was going out. The stretch of water separating us from the beach was growing narrower and narrower; dry sand was appearing nearer and nearer to our rock. The Britons came at us with everything: rocks and chariots, spears and darts and arrows . . . The four men with me, seeing it was

hopeless, jumped back into the boat and pulled away. "Come on, Scaeva!" they called. "Leave it, Scaeva!" But I had the madness of battle on me. That Eagle-bearer had inspired me, I suppose. We were within clear sight of Caesar's ship, and I did not want him to see me turn tail. So the four pushed off without me – left me standing on this pile of rocks, soaked by the waves breaking behind me, being pelted like a target at a fair. When I raised up my shield now, I could see daylight through it from the spear-holes, the axe-slashes, the tears made by their rocks and arrows.

Those chariots of theirs were terrifying: we have nothing like it. They circled me at full tilt, their wheel-hubs striking sparks from the rocks, the spray blinding me. An axe smashed my helmet, a rock hit me in the face and broke my nose: the world turned red in front of me. I used my spear first, but that was soon wrenched out of my hands. Then I used my sword. By Mars! I thought, I'll take a dozen of you down with me to the Underworld!

A sudden sharp pain in my thigh! An arrow. My sword broke like glass against a battle axe. They battered my shield out of my hand. Time to go, Scaeva, I said to myself, and I dived off the rock before the tide left me there, utterly high and dry.

Jove, that water was cold! The frigidarium at the public baths was never as cold as that sea. I could see my comrades leaning over the side of a ship, beckoning, whistling, calling my name. The sea seemed to be inside me and out, flowing through my wounds, washing the strength out of me. Arrows kept falling all round me. But at last – I hardly remember it – hands were pulling me over the rail, my blood running down into the scuppers. "My shield!" It was all I could say. "My shield!"

Once the legions were ashore, things took a different turn, of course. The men closed ranks, locked shields, formed squares, gave those barbarians a lesson in Roman warfare. Discipline. It is discipline that makes the difference, you see: discipline and years of professional training. The enemy fled. But without cavalry, how could we give chase? Hopeless. We had just to watch them run.

"My shield!" It was all I could think of. "My shield! I lost it at the rock!" It is the ultimate disgrace for a Roman soldier (except perhaps for losing his legion's Eagle) to lose his shield. When I saw Caesar coming towards me I thought it was to reprimand me. I racked my brains for an excuse, but all words seemed to have bled away down my nose.

"What is your name?" He was speaking to me. Julius Caesar, greatest of the Romans. Better I should have drowned than come back without my shield!

"Scaeva, Caesar. Forgive me, Caesar, my shield . . ."

"Scaeva, you fought today as a Roman should. You set an example for all soldiers to follow. Such courage merits promotion, *Centurion* Scaeva."

Centurion! There is no higher honour a soldier can win than to be made a centurion for his valour. One day grandchildren, as yet unborn, will talk of it as they run their little fingers over my battered nose. My wife will write it on my memorial stone: "Scaeva: he was made centurion by Julius Caesar the day Rome conquered Albion."

But Mars deliver me from actually having to *live* in this bleak, miserable country. We are going home tomorrow, thanks be to the gods.

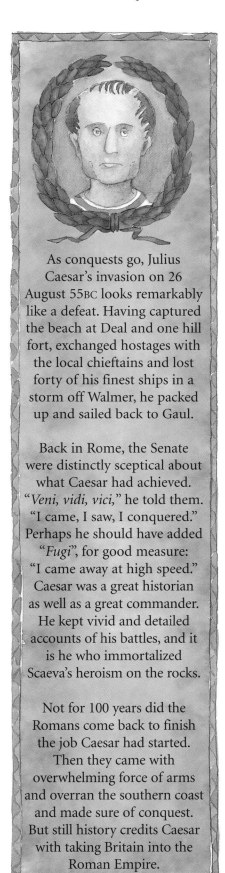

As conquests go, Julius Caesar's invasion on 26 August 55BC looks remarkably like a defeat. Having captured the beach at Deal and one hill fort, exchanged hostages with the local chieftains and lost forty of his finest ships in a storm off Walmer, he packed up and sailed back to Gaul.

Back in Rome, the Senate were distinctly sceptical about what Caesar had achieved. "*Veni, vidi, vici,*" he told them. "I came, I saw, I conquered." Perhaps he should have added "*Fugi*", for good measure: "I came away at high speed." Caesar was a great historian as well as a great commander. He kept vivid and detailed accounts of his battles, and it is he who immortalized Scaeva's heroism on the rocks.

Not for 100 years did the Romans come back to finish the job Caesar had started. Then they came with overwhelming force of arms and overran the southern coast and made sure of conquest. But still history credits Caesar with taking Britain into the Roman Empire.

The Resting Place

AD 50

THERE WAS ONCE A HILL SO CLAD IN MAGIC that it attracted legends to it like roosting birds. The Celts called it the Island of Glass and in winter it was ringed with floodwater, so that it stood rooted in its own reflection. All around it were lesser hills, like children round their mother.

But this story begins on another hill, thousands of miles away. Joseph of Arimathea, as he stood on Golgotha Hill watching Jesus die on a wooden cross, was moved to offer his own tomb to Jesus's family so that they would have somewhere to lay His body. True, Joseph was a rich man and could afford to buy another grave, but a man does not lightly give up the resting place he has chosen for his mortal remains.

Within days, Joseph's tomb was restored to him, empty, vacated. Jesus had risen from the dead. But Joseph did not choose to reclaim his resting place. He was a disciple, now, a true believer, wandering the world, passing on to people the teachings of Jesus and the news that He had risen from the dead.

With a small band of friends, Joseph sailed for Albion. His ship navigated the Severn River, from where he travelled inland to the county called

Summer Land and the cluster of hills round about the Island of Glass. The friends were all weary. Climbing a small hill for a better view, Joseph leaned heavily on his thorn-wood staff and christened the place Weary-All Hill. From the crest, the Island of Glass was clearly visible. What a long way he had come from Golgotha to reach this green place. Joseph drove his staff into the soft, damp, autumn ground, curled up in his cloak and went to sleep.

He dreamed of wings and of light, of music and voices and ladders between the sky and the hill. "Rest *here*, Joseph," said the Angel Gabriel, hovering on kestrel wings. "Build *here*, Joseph."

On waking, Joseph told his followers, "Here is where we shall live and work."

They were not looking at him. They were staring at his staff. While they had slept, its smooth shaft had grown a dozen twiggy shoots, and small green nodules were starting to form. By Christmas it would be in blossom.

Weary-All Hill (though of God's making) actually belonged to a local nobleman. He was a busy man; he had no interest in stories of miracle-workers in far-off lands, who died and came back

from the dead. Frankly, he did not believe a word of it. But the hill was too steep to farm, so he gave Joseph and his friends permission to build.

Joseph built a church out of wattle and daub – a crude, draughty place, with few comforts. But the view was second only to Paradise, and the birdsong sweeter than the singing of angels. A little religious community grew up, converts to Christianity arriving one by two by three. Joseph was content. He had found his second resting place: a good place to pass eternity. He was buried somewhere on the hill: the exact spot was soon forgotten. The wattle-and-daub church fell into ruins. But one thing lasted, as fresh and new as on the day of its coming. Each Christmas time, Joseph's thorn-wood staff would erupt into blossom – a miraculous sight. Soon people were making pilgrimage just to see the Holy Thorn. Some said it reminded them of Jesus's crown of thorns. Some said it put them in mind of life springing up new out of stark, thorny death.

Some also liked to think that Joseph had brought with him a treasure far more precious than a walking stick. It was rumoured that he had owned the room where Christ and His disciples ate their Last Supper together before the crucifixion. As the owner of the room, Joseph must, of course, have owned the crockery they used. And *that* meant he must have owned the cup from which Jesus drank, saying "Take, eat. This is my blood which is shed for you and for all Mankind."

What if Joseph had brought that cup with him to Weary-All Hill? What if he had hidden it somewhere near the wattle-and-daub church? So began the greatest treasure hunt in the history of Britain – the quest for the Holy Grail: prize beyond price, wonder beyond magic, visible only to the pure of heart.

Five centuries later, in the days of King Arthur, legend claims that the Holy Grail was found by the best of Arthur's knights.

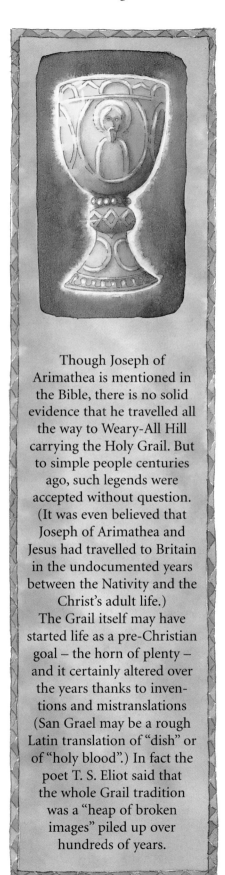

Though Joseph of Arimathea is mentioned in the Bible, there is no solid evidence that he travelled all the way to Weary-All Hill carrying the Holy Grail. But to simple people centuries ago, such legends were accepted without question. (It was even believed that Joseph of Arimathea and Jesus had travelled to Britain in the undocumented years between the Nativity and the Christ's adult life.)

The Grail itself may have started life as a pre-Christian goal – the horn of plenty – and it certainly altered over the years thanks to inventions and mistranslations (San Grael may be a rough Latin translation of "dish" or of "holy blood".) In fact the poet T. S. Eliot said that the whole Grail tradition was a "heap of broken images" piled up over hundreds of years.

Boudicca the Firebrand

60

HER NAME MEANT "VICTORY". EVEN IN the good days, she looked like a firebrand, that fiery red hair tumbling down past her waist. Boudicca was married to Prasutagus, chief of the Iceni tribe on the flat lands of Norfolk. Though the Romans had conquered and colonized the entire country, they allowed many of the revered local kings to keep their thrones. So Boudicca was a queen and her three daughters were princesses. Then Prasutagus, her husband, died, and his greedy and arrogant Roman landlord decided to help himself to Prasutagus's silver plate and armoury, his chariots and cattle, his lands and power. He had Boudicca lashed to a cart and flogged till her red hair was redder still with blood. And all the while, she could hear the screams of her daughters, as laughing Roman soldiers mauled them.

What were they now? A widow and three girls, dispossessed and homeless. But Boudicca was a queen, and her daughters were princesses, and the Iceni were a warrior tribe. Boudicca spoke to her people, her voice loud and harsh.

"Do you see what meekness and tolerance bought us? Will you stand by and see your gods cast down? Your priests murdered? Your old way of life swept away? *Your queen flogged?* Don't our holy Druids prophesy that the Romans will be swept out of this land of ours?" She lifted her face to the sky. "O Adraste, goddess of war! Tell us what you would have us do! Shall Boudicca run north and hide her children and weep? Or shall the Queen of the Iceni and her warriors march south *and take our revenge?*"

She pulled from under her cloak something large and live and struggling. The watching crowd thought at first it was a baby, but then they saw that she had hold of it by its long silken ears.

"The hare! The hare! Let the hare run!" cried the Iceni, knowing what powers of prophecy were in a running hare. Boudicca threw the animal down.

It froze, terrified, blinded by the sudden light. Then it saw a space where the crowd had parted, and bolted for freedom. "*To the south! To the south!*" cried the Iceni. The omen had been given. The war was under way.

All the humiliation and resentment against their Roman conquerors was focused on Boudicca now, and not only the Iceni but the Trinovantes too, and all those whipped up along the way. Rebellion kindled like a grassfire, and a great army rallied to the chariot of Queen Boudicca.

Sharp blades projected from both wheels of that chariot. It cut through a rank of foot soldiers like a scythe through ripe corn. The Romans, lulled by peaceful years of supremacy, suddenly found their villas in flames around them, their shops looted and destroyed.

Colchester was razed to the ground, and the head of Emperor Claudius' statue lopped off and thrown into the river. Hundreds died – not just Romans but anyone who had crept under their protection and begun to live in the Roman way. Murderous with hate, Boudicca was always a furlong ahead of her army, chariot blades clearing their path, her blood-curdling war cry freezing the blood.

Suetonius Paulinus, Roman governor of Britain, was far away, on the other side of the country, attempting to stamp out the subversive influence of the Druid priests. By the time news reached him of Boudicca's uprising, she had driven a wedge through the legions of Rome and rampaged south to London. He could do nothing to turn her back. The vast rambling sprawl of London could not withstand her savagery.

Over mud lanes and marble pavements Boudicca's chariot wheels rolled, and the air was so full of ash from burning buildings that her skin was spotted like a leopard's, her red hair just one more tongue of flame. Ships blazed and sank alongside the Thames wharves. And everywhere the sooty air rang with the cry:

"*Boudicca! Boudicca!* Victory! Victory!"

Suetonius Paulinus made his stand in the Midlands, his 10,000 men to Boudicca's 50,000. He chose a spot where three hills protected his army's back and rear flanks, and his cohorts formed squares, the sun snagging on their regimental eagles, on their standards, on their spear-points.

Such stillness they presented, in comparison with the torrent of men and women who teemed down on them. The cry of "*Boudicca!*" rang back off the faces of the hills. But the Roman cohorts were silent, except for the jingling of a horse's bridle, the beating of a single drum like a steady heartbeat.

They seemed barely human, those squares of armoured military might, every head helmeted, every face obscured. Some of the red crests of the centurions were as long as Boudicca's hair. Every long rectangular shield was locked against the shield alongside. It was like hurling water on to a box of bronze, and though Boudicca charged once, twice, a third time, she could not break those disciplined squares.

Then the cohorts began to beat on their shields with their short swords and to push forward, slicing, stabbing, routing, re-forming into squares. They came on with such ruthless certainty that the Britons turned tail and ran.

Boudicca's shrill, grating voice summoned her daughters to her chariot. She pulled them in over the tailboard. They crouched, bleeding, against her legs as she whipped up her horses to a last frenzied gallop. This time her bladed wheels cut down her own people as she fled capture.

She drove as far as the great forest of Epping – in those days a tossing, immeasurable sea of dense green trees older than either Romans or the tribes of Britain. Out of the sunlight she flashed, into its ominous shade. The Romans could not fail to follow. The trail of a battle chariot carrying four women is not hard to trace. Escape only bought Boudicca a little time: a brief respite to be alone with her daughters and to shed the bloody madness of battle.

They came to rest in a clearing where the trees stood too close and the undergrowth too dense for the chariot to pass. White and purple bell-flowers swung from twining stems among the saplings and fallen boughs.

"Remember Caractacus who fought the Romans for ten years in Wales?" said Boudicca. "First they captured his wife and children, then they took him to parade in the streets of Rome. That must never happen to us." The three girls shuddered and lowered their heads. "What do you say, children? Let's gather flowers and make a drink to refresh our flagging souls." So they picked the purple flowers and stewed them into a purple liquor. "Let us drink to Adraste, who shall give us the last victory. And as you drink, remember the prophecies of the Druids. One day these Romans will be gone, swept away and forgotten." Then she kissed her three daughters tenderly, and they all drank. Poison to make them sleep. Poison to put them beyond reach of Roman revenge.

Their bodies were never found.

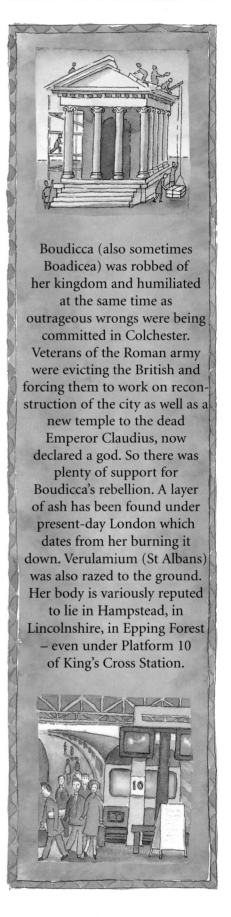

Boudicca (also sometimes Boadicea) was robbed of her kingdom and humiliated at the same time as outrageous wrongs were being committed in Colchester. Veterans of the Roman army were evicting the British and forcing them to work on reconstruction of the city as well as a new temple to the dead Emperor Claudius, now declared a god. So there was plenty of support for Boudicca's rebellion. A layer of ash has been found under present-day London which dates from her burning it down. Verulamium (St Albans) was also razed to the ground. Her body is variously reputed to lie in Hampstead, in Lincolnshire, in Epping Forest – even under Platform 10 of King's Cross Station.

Running Towards Paradise

300

HIS SANDALLED FEET TROD THE MOSAIC floors depicting all the Roman immortals, but Alban's mind was filled by only one god – a god so immense and magnificent that He overflowed Alban's mind and spilled out of him in a torrent of joy. But these were times when the Roman army, in which Alban was a soldier, was still dutiful to the gods of Rome. Though Alban and his fellow legionaries were born in Britain, they occupied and policed it on behalf of Rome, and were obliged to worship Roman gods –

Neptune and Jupiter, Janus and Juno and Diana. Loyal Romans purged Christians like the lice in their uniforms.

When the search party came to the house of Amphibalus, a Christian priest fleeing persecution, they immediately arrested the man they found there. It was not until he was brought for judgement that they realized it was not Amphibalus at all, but it was a Roman in disguise. Alban of Verulamium had taken the priest's place to allow him time to escape.

The judge was incensed that Alban, who served under the Roman eagle, symbol of Jupiter, should so deny the Roman gods. "Make sacrifice to the true gods of Rome!" he demanded, but Alban refused. "I worship only the living and true God." Neither torture nor threats could break his resolve.

"Take him out and put an end to him!" raged the judge, and Alban was led away to die. A large crowd had gathered at the place of execution, on a hilltop beyond the river. They stood speculating on what Alban had done and why. Alban was so eager to keep his appointment with immortality that, instead of walking to the bridge, he hurried straight down to the riverbank. The tumbling water slid to a halt, evaporated, and was gone, leaving him a dry path to cross over. Minutes later he crested the hill and crossed as easily from life to death, his head slashed from his shoulders by a Roman sword.

"Let that set an example to any other Roman who thinks to abandon the gods of Olympus!" said the judge, watching from his window.

It did set one, too. For Alban was happy to die. Roman soldiers had always been ready to die for the Roman eagle, for Caesar, for their honour, but they had never loved their gods enough to die like that: fearless, happy, eager to set out on the road to paradise. Alban was Roman Britain's first martyr. And martyrs make for converts.

During the fourth century, Christianity swept Roman Britain, until it was the predominant religion. When the Roman Empire crumbled and the Roman armies withdrew from Britain, they left behind them a Christian country.

Then the Danes came, under their raven-banner. The Vikings and the Danes arrived in longships, burned down the monasteries, slaughtered the monks, stole the crucifixes and tore up the Gospels. They brought with them their own gods: Thor and Odin, Wotan and Freya – gods who admired bloodshed and awarded paradise only to warriors. The few Christians who survived the rout fled west into Wales and Ireland, leaving the stones of their churches to be re-used for pagan temples or swallowed up once more by primeval forest. Their villages were lived in now by the pagan, blond-haired, blue-eyed Angles.

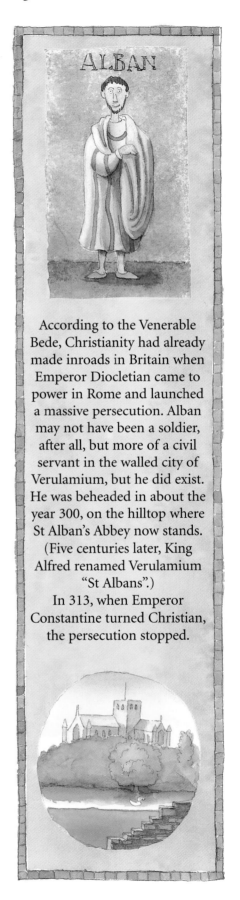

ALBAN

According to the Venerable Bede, Christianity had already made inroads in Britain when Emperor Diocletian came to power in Rome and launched a massive persecution. Alban may not have been a soldier, after all, but more of a civil servant in the walled city of Verulamium, but he did exist. He was beheaded in about the year 300, on the hilltop where St Alban's Abbey now stands. (Five centuries later, King Alfred renamed Verulamium "St Albans".)

In 313, when Emperor Constantine turned Christian, the persecution stopped.

The Hallelujah Victory

429

"HELP US! HELP US!" THEY BEGGED. "SAVE US! You know the mind of God, Father! When will He help us?"

Bishop Germanus thought they were talking about their immortal souls, but they were not at all. The Britons he had come to visit were talking of their homes, their wives, their children. "We write to Rome, but they send no troops to help us, and we – God forgive us – we have forgotten all the arts of war we ever knew!"

The Roman legions had been withdrawn from England, as the Roman Empire shrank and disintegrated. For centuries the occupying forces had defended the land, fortified its borders, kept at bay all inter-lopers and barbarians. But now the Romans were gone, leaving the door to Britain banging open in the wind.

Scenting rich pickings, the Picts and Scots seized their chance – hardy, unconquered peo-ple who could fight with all the skill which the southern Britons had forgotten. They launched more and more audacious raids, burned villages, took cattle, killed anyone who stood in their path. "Now they are coming in hundreds – and with Saxons among them – and how shall we stand against them?" they begged the visiting bishop.

"Do as I say, and all may be well," Germanus told the Britons, though secretly his heart quailed when he thought what the future might bring the people of the southern kingdoms.

The people did as Germanus instructed. They took their stand on high ground, on three sides of a valley – well strung out – a laughably small number in the face of the advancing army of Picts and Scots and Saxons.

On came the raiders, shaggy as beasts, silvered over with the glint of axeheads, spearheads, arrowheads, swords. They filled up the valley like a summer brook swelling into a winter river. The noise of their feet, their baggage, their ugly nasal languages rose up unmuffled by distance. Then, at a signal – the slow silent arc of a single arrow – the Britons did as they had been told to do. They opened their mouths and shouted:

"Hallelujah!"

An avalanche of sound tumbled into the hollow, bounded and resounded around, redoubled by the kettle-hollow basin of the place, echoing, re-echoing, as if the Day of Reckoning had come and a million angels were all shouting:

"Hallelujah!"

The second cry met with the first and swelled it, ricocheted around the reverberating rocks till there was more sound in the valley than air, and all of it the one word:

"Hallelujah!"

The men below turned and fled. They thought that all their enemies must have united as never before, congregated around this one valley to ambush and destroy them. And they fled. Not a stroke was struck, never an axe fell, but the Scots and Picts were routed as totally as if God had taken up arms against them.

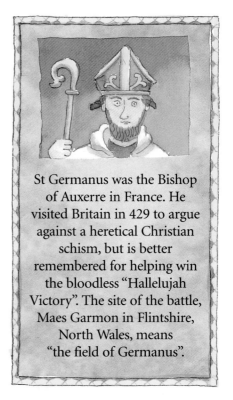

St Germanus was the Bishop of Auxerre in France. He visited Britain in 429 to argue against a heretical Christian schism, but is better remembered for helping win the bloodless "Hallelujah Victory". The site of the battle, Maes Garmon in Flintshire, North Wales, means "the field of Germanus".

Hengist, Horsa and the Lovely Rowena

449

AFTER THE SCOTS AND THE PICTS CAME THE Jutes, sweeping in like the sea. There was no stopping the relentless push westwards of these Germanic hordes urgent for land, greedy for the rich orchards and fields and vineyards of Kent.

King Vortigern, already plagued by attacks from northerners, saw the forces of Hengist and Horsa closing on his coastline and knew that the Jutes were too strong for him. He did not fall on his knees and pray. He did not reach for his sword either. He saw another way of surviving. Why should he not *ally their power* to his?

Perhaps it was cowardice, perhaps it was cunning, but Vortigern went down to the shore and greeted the brothers, chieftains of the Jutes: "Ah! Just the men I need!"

He pitted Hengist and Horsa against the Picts and Scots, saying he would pay them if they were victorious. (He was secretly hoping they would kill each other and leave Kent in peace.) But the Jutes easily defeated the northerners. And as soon as they had, they returned, palms outstretched for their pay. And on top of money they wanted land. What they could not get by threats, they took by force, and far from sailing away over the horizon, more of their kith and kin began to arrive.

On board one Jute ship was Hengist's daughter, Rowena. One sight of her, and Vortigern's soul was in thrall. For those blue eyes, for that yellow hair, for that tall, willowy form, he would have sold the sun out of the sky, the salt out of the sea, anything that was his or not his to give. In exchange for Rowena's hand in marriage, he gave Hengist the throne of Kent.

Perhaps he knew it was lost already, that it was Hengist's for the taking. But there were those who thought him a traitor. Not least his sons.

Dispossessed of their inheritance, shamed by their father's marriage, Vortimer and his half-brother took up the fight which Vortigern had let fall. They rallied the men of Kent fleeced and scattered by the Jutes, and at the Ford of the Eagles clashed with such a clamour that the river water shivered like broken glass.

Horsa, the brother of Hengist, fell at the hands of Vortimer, and Vortimer's brother fell at the hands of Hengist.

Rowena's blue eyes swam with tears when the news came from Aylesford. "I weep that your dear son is dead," she told her British husband. But in truth, her Jute heart howled for vengeance at the death of her uncle, Horsa, and with misery that the Jutish fleet was even now sailing away in defeat.

Biting her tongue, Rowena awaited her chance. She paid a servant to poison young Vortimer's food and, when he died, wept crocodile tears over his grave.

"Invite my father to come back," she crooned as she consoled her grieving husband. "The time is past for wars. The land has drunk blood enough. Let us make peace, the men of Kent and the men of Jute. Do, I beg you."

So a great feast was arranged between the chieftains of Britain and Hengist's warriors.

"Let there be no weapons brought," said Hengist, "for we shall sit down as friends and hospitality forbids that those who eat together should bear arms."

"Naturally," said Vortigern. "The laws of hospitality are the same the world over."

It was a feast to stretch the powers of the chroniclers who wrote of it. The fire spits bent under the weight of roasting meat. After such a meal, there were many oaths sworn of undying friendship and never-ending peace. "Is not Britain large enough for all of us?" cried Vortigern, face flushed, unsteady on his feet, fingers clumsy in his wife's yellow hair. "Shall we not put the killing behind us?"

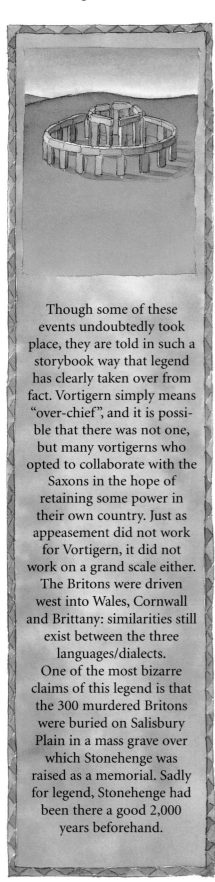

Hengist too pulled himself to his feet. He did not seem to have drunk so deep. "Now, men," he said, without raising his voice. And from under their cloaks, from out of their boots, from hidden sheaths and false pockets, the Jutes drew their daggers.

Rowena looked on, unmoved, unafraid. She stretched wide her sea-blue eyes, so as not to miss a single death. No tears fell from her blue eyes.

No dagger was turned on Vortigern, for he was beneath contempt, already shackled to his enemies by love of a woman. Overturning his chair, clutching his misery to him in trembling hands, he fled, calling to Rowena to follow. But she did not. When 300 Britons lay dead on the floor, Rowena raised her glass to the ghost of Horsa and wished him peace in his warrior heaven.

Though some of these events undoubtedly took place, they are told in such a storybook way that legend has clearly taken over from fact. Vortigern simply means "over-chief", and it is possible that there was not one, but many vortigerns who opted to collaborate with the Saxons in the hope of retaining some power in their own country. Just as appeasement did not work for Vortigern, it did not work on a grand scale either. The Britons were driven west into Wales, Cornwall and Brittany: similarities still exist between the three languages/dialects.

One of the most bizarre claims of this legend is that the 300 murdered Britons were buried on Salisbury Plain in a mass grave over which Stonehenge was raised as a memorial. Sadly for legend, Stonehenge had been there a good 2,000 years beforehand.

The Castle Which Could Not Stand

about 4 5 0

VORTIGERN WAS DESPERATE, HUNTED LIKE A FOX across the length and breadth of his own kingdom by the enemy he had thought to befriend. Holding his life in his teeth, holding his power in sweating hands, he finally found himself with his back to the Welsh mountains. There he made his stand. Planting his foot on the crest of Dinas Emrys, he commanded, "Build me a castle! You men, quarry. You men, heave. Build me a fortress!" He thought that if he built the walls high enough, both his crown and his life would be safe inside.

But though every day Vortigern's castle grew, by night it crumbled into a pile of rubble.

The wind blew dusty mortar into Vortigern's open mouth. "Find me a prophet! Find me out what evil magic is eating away at my castle!" he demanded.

Superstitious advice poured from his wise men. "Your castle will not stand, my lord, until the noble blood of a fatherless boy is spilled on the foundations."

"Find one, then, and split him!"

The countryside was scoured, but though there were many children whose fathers had died, or gone away to war, there was not one who had *never had a father*.

"Who's this?" sneered Vortigern when a brown-eyed boy was at last brought before him.

"His mother entered a nunnery the day her child was born," his advisors told him. "The child was brought up by his grandfather – a magician."

"But who was his *father*?" Vortigern wanted to know.

The child did not answer, but his mother did. "Something between a dream and a nightmare," she said, unashamed. "One night I dreamt of a man wearing a golden crown. He fathered my child, then melted away with the daylight."

The little boy stared at the woman wearing the nun's habit. This was the first time he had seen his mother, and the first he had heard tell of his dream-father. Now, in this moment of discovery, he was to die.

"Bind him and slit him and let his blood flow!" cried Vortigern. "Tonight my castle will not fall down!"

"It will and it shall, while you build it there!" The boy's voice was high, but clear and loud. It captured every ear. "Don't you know what lies beneath this ground?"

The King snorted. "Nothing. Who knows? The ruin of something Roman." (Indeed, there were signs of ancient building, mossy with mould.) The wise men were asked, but the wise men did not know.

"Then I shall tell you," said the boy. "I have dreamed this place, and the future will come of it. Below here lies a pool of water, and at the bottom of the pool, two stone tanks. Unless you drain the pool, you may as well build on quicksand."

A muscle in Vortigern's cheek twitched. Silence hung over his army of builders until at last he spoke: "Look and see. We can kill him after."

They broke up the ground with picks. It fell away into a hollow place beneath, splashing into water. They laid bare a vast man-made basin, a sink of black water, and pumped it out down the mountainside. As the water drained away, two stone vaults the shape of coffins were uncovered.

"Inside each is a dragon," said the boy. "I have dreamed them, and the future will come of it. Wake the dragons if you dare, King Vortigern; they will tell you your fate."

"If anything were ever living in there, it is certainly dead by now," sneered Vortigern, and had his men set to with cold hammers.

The coffins broke like eggs hatching. Out of the first came a red dragon, writhing, the colour of blood. Out of the second came a white dragon, the colour of frost. Their tails intertwined, then they turned on each other and fought. The white dragon was low and slinking: it overturned the red and scuttled for its throat. But the red dragon was leaping lively. It threw off the white one, blinding it with scarves of scarlet smoke. Then, with a lunge, the red jaws fastened on the white throat till its fire was out.

As the vanquished dragon dragged itself back into the crater to die, the red victor leapt skywards. It passed so close to Vortigern that its claws tore his cloak and its hot breath singed his beard. The horror of it rooted him to the spot.

"I have dreamed this fight, and the future will come of it," said the fatherless boy. "The red dragon represents the Britons, Vortigern: the men you betrayed to Hengist and Horsa. The white dragon is the invading horde you have brought down on us. For a time they will triumph over us, but the Britons will drive them out, as you yourself have been driven out. Uther Pendragon will rule after you are dead. The Jutes and Saxons are coming after you, Vortigern, but beyond them, behind them comes an Age of Gold!"

Vortigern's whole army turned and looked across the plain. The sun flashed off some distant metal – a spearhead? a helmet? an army?

"The pit is drained. The dragons are gone. Fill in the hole and start building, you idle dogs!" The King would have liked to cut the boy's throat and silence his prophesying. But there was not a man there who would have been ready to do it. There was magic in the lines of his small hands and in every word he spoke. "What is your name, you with the Devil for a father?"

But this time the boy's mother spoke for him. "My son's name is Merlin."

Vortigern's castle was never finished. Though its foundations were sure, so too was the future. The Jutes killed him, and buried him in a pit. And the Britons rallied under Uther Pendragon. Dragon-headed Uther, they called him, because there was fire in his blood and magic in his eyes. His best friend was Merlin the Druid, Merlin the Magician, and it was to him that Uther entrusted the safety and education of his son: the Once-and-Future-King, Arthur.

A blood sacrifice, such as the "wise men" recommended, was common practice when building in pre-Christian times and in the early centuries AD. The remains of human sacrifices have been found among the foundations of Cadbury Castle in Somerset. In some versions of this legend, the boy is not Merlin but Ambrosius or Emrys Gwledig, and Vortigern, shaken by the affair of the dragons, makes Emrys king of western Britain. Emrys later executes Vortigern for his unpatriotic deeds.

Fragments of all kinds of earlier folklore are in evidence here. The dragons are, of course, the dragons buried by Lud (see page 16). Merlin is a Celtic bard or Druid – a prophet figure who was only incorporated into the Arthurian legends later. In truth, the Britons were ultimately driven west off their lands, dispossessed utterly by Jute and Saxon invaders.

St David and the Naked Ladies

519-589

ARRIVING IN THE VALE OF ROSES IN THE WEST OF Wales, St Patrick looked round him and thought, "I shall settle here." But an angel, stooping hawk-like out of a cloudless sky, urged him on his way. "This place is meant for David," said the angel, "and David is not yet born!" So St Patrick pressed on to Ireland and won it for Christ. For fifty years the Vale of Roses stood waiting.

By the time David arrived there, though, to found a monastery, the area lay at the mercy of a brutish man called Boia and his equally brutish wife. David and his monks wanted only to farm the land and to pray, but Boia wanted them gone. He set out from home, blustering and boorish, telling his wife he meant to run them off his land.

When he came back, he was meek and mild, speaking of 'joy', saying he was sorry for his sinful life. He had met David, and he was a changed man.
　　　　　　　and tell that blanket-tossed
　　　　　　o shift his bag of bones off
　　　　　ed his wife, but Boia only
　　　　away eyes and a wistful smile.
　　　　s-in-Christ, wife," he said.
　　　　rs and took matters into her
　　　　1g her serving maids she told

them, "Over there yonder stands a barn of a place full of lonely men, all priding themselves that they can live without wives and sweethearts, all sworn to shun women till their dying day. Get up there in your nothing-at-alls. When those monks see what they are missing, they will break their vows, and give up religion!"

The maids went – big buxom girls, with blushing cheeks and curvy bodies which they flaunted outside David's window. "Come out, saintly David, and see what you be missing by living the single life! There's kisses a-plenty out here!" They perched themselves on gates. They lounged against door posts. They rang the monastery bell and peeped in at the alms window. "Oh, *do* come out and look us over, boys! There are arms out here just waiting to hold you close!"

David saw them, and his mouth set in a hard, straight line. He kept on at his work. He behaved as if the naked ladies were no more of a nuisance than the sheep which roamed about the monastery buildings pushing their noses in at the doors. He outstared their brazen winks. He resisted their beckoning fingers. "The joys of this world, brothers, are no match for the joys of heaven," he told his monks.

And because he resisted the ladies, the other monks were able to do the same. For all the hardship of their solitary life, they loved God and their abbot enough to shun the pink maid-servants of Boia. Why, they had seen sights far more wonderful! They had seen flat ground heave itself upwards into a hill when David spoke, so that the crowds might hear him better. They had seen springs burst out of the ground at his command. They had seen the waters at Bath bubble hot with healing grace after David's blessing. They had seen the sick healed, and barbarians like Boia transformed into gentle lambs. His maid-servants could offer them nothing so miraculous. The girls shivered in the cold, put on their clothes and went home.

In time, Boia and his neighbours had cause to be glad they had not driven David out of the Vale of Roses. Famous for his wisdom and goodness, David made his little, sleepy corner of the world famous. He made it wise with his saintly wisdom, and peaceful by his saintly example. But not till after his death did David do them the greatest favour of all. Even from beyond the grave, he brought them victory over the Saxons.

In huge marauding hordes the Saxons came, and in skirmish after fray they fought the Britons. Though David was a man of peace, and would never have raised up a sword in anger, he gave his neighbours the best advice. "Wear a leek in your caps," he said.

"A leek?"

"A leek. There is nothing so Welsh as a leek, and the Saxons have no understanding of the magnificent nature of a leek."

It would be a badge – a mark by which a Briton, in the whirling madness of battle, could instantly recognize a fellow Briton. A man half-crazed with battle fever, half expecting at every second the slash of a blade to catch him unaware, lashes out at everyone who comes near. But in the great battle of 640, the Britons stuffed leeks in their caps, just as St David had taught them to do, and knew each other instantly on the battlefield. The Saxons (perhaps because they wore no distinguishing badge, perhaps because the prayers of St David confounded them) inflicted terrible wounds on each other and were defeated.

After the battle, the Welsh offered up thanks to St David (though he had been sleeping peacefully in his grave in the Vale of Roses for fifty years), named the day for him and declared David the patron saint of Wales.

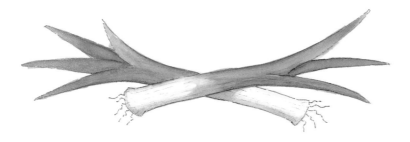

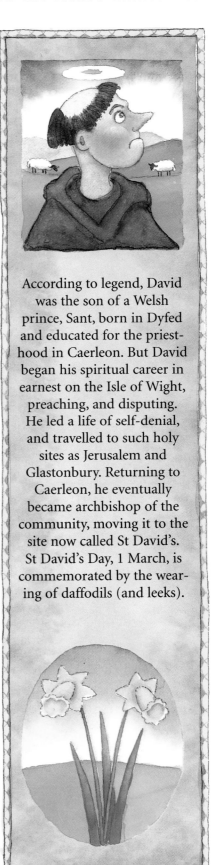

According to legend, David was the son of a Welsh prince, Sant, born in Dyfed and educated for the priesthood in Caerleon. But David began his spiritual career in earnest on the Isle of Wight, preaching, and disputing. He led a life of self-denial, and travelled to such holy sites as Jerusalem and Glastonbury. Returning to Caerleon, he eventually became archbishop of the community, moving it to the site now called St David's. St David's Day, 1 March, is commemorated by the wearing of daffodils (and leeks).

"Not Angles but Angels"

597

WITHIN THE MARKET PLACE IN ROME, SLAVES were just another commodity. Listless and afraid, chained and herded, they were on a par with the penned pigs or the chickens hung up by their feet. They were on sale. They were thirsty, too, under the hot Italian sun, and the flies pestered them. Among them today were foreign slaves whose blond hair glistened and glinted in the strong sunlight – an unusual sight among the swarthy, brown- and red-haired Romans.

Brother Gregory, walking through the market, commented to his companion on the beauty of the blond-haired slave children. "What is their nation?" he asked.

"They are Angles, Brother, from Britain."

"Not Angles but angels," joked Gregory. "They have angelic faces. Are they Christians?"

"No, Brother."

"What is the name of their king?"

"King Ella," came the reply.

"Then Ella-lujah shall be sung in their land!" quipped Gregory and his companion laughed indulgently. Gregory liked to pun. Fortunately, his sense of humour was not the best thing about him.

Gregory was renowned throughout Rome, not for his jokes but for his goodness and charity; he had the ear of the Pope himself. So taken was he with the angelic appearance of those Angle slaves that he went to the Pope now and asked to be sent as a missionary to convert their pagan island to Christianity. The Pope could not spare him – knew that Gregory was loved too much within the city for him to risk martyrdom in God-forsaken Angle-Land. His request was refused.

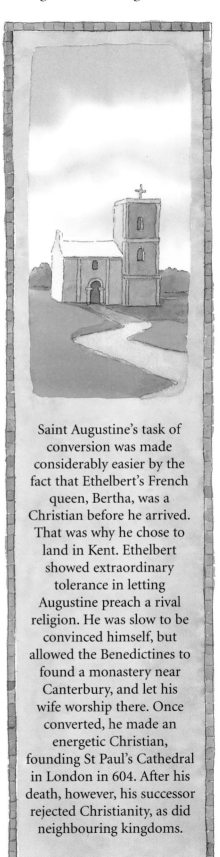

But Gregory remembered those blond-haired, blue-eyed children – nursed the memory even after the Pope was dead, even after Rome had elected *him* to the highest office in the world. Pope Gregory the Great summoned a Benedictine monk called Augustine and told him, "Take forty monks and travel to England with the good news of Christ!"

Halfway there, the forty lost their nerve. They wrote asking to come home, but Gregory answered them with a letter of such eloquence and fiery inspiration that they forged onward. Armed with a silver cross and a picture of Christ crucified, Augustine landed near Ramsgate, and invited King Ethelbert of Kent to hear him preach.

The King agreed to meet them, but only in the open air, wary of the evil magic that might be practised on him indoors.

Augustine used no evil magic. Even so, within months Kentishmen and women were flocking to hear the Benedictines preach and to be baptized. Soon after Ethelbert himself knelt at Augustine's feet for baptism, one thousand of his subjects were baptized in a single day. In pairs they waded out into the River Swale, one sinking the other beneath the water as Augustine bellowed his blessing from the bank. Whole families walked into the Swale that day and waded out again Christians.

Saint Augustine's task of conversion was made considerably easier by the fact that Ethelbert's French queen, Bertha, was a Christian before he arrived. That was why he chose to land in Kent. Ethelbert showed extraordinary tolerance in letting Augustine preach a rival religion. He was slow to be convinced himself, but allowed the Benedictines to found a monastery near Canterbury, and let his wife worship there. Once converted, he made an energetic Christian, founding St Paul's Cathedral in London in 604. After his death, however, his successor rejected Christianity, as did neighbouring kingdoms.

King Arthur and his Questing Knights

6th century

KING ARTHUR'S FABLED COURT AT CAMELOT stood on the fringes of the Summer Land, not far from the Island of Glass. Raised and educated by the prophet-magician Merlin, and armed with a magical sword Excalibur, Arthur set about freeing his kingdom from evil and the forces of darkness. To that end, he assembled the finest knights in the land. So that they would not quarrel about which of them was the grandest or highest ranking, he seated them at a great round table.

Giants and dragons were slaughtered, maidens were rescued and quests were mounted. But the greatest quest of all was to find the Holy Grail.

An image of that cup, which Christ had used at the Last Supper, which Joseph of Arimathea had brought to the Summer Land and hidden in a secret place, which none but the pure of heart would be allowed to find – showed itself one feast-day to the knights of the Round Table. Immediately the knights took it for a sign that they should go questing in search of the real thing.

Sir Gawain searched, but gave up. Sir Lancelot searched, but could not find it because his heart was not pure enough. But Galahad his son, along with Sir Bors and Sir Perceval, came at last to the mysterious castle of Corbenic, where, in a radiance of light, Jesus Christ Himself appeared to them. Amid the sound of English birdsong, Christ gave them bread and wine, then entrusted them with the very cup from which they had just drunk: the Holy Grail.

The happiness of that moment broke Galahad's heart like a loaf of bread; Perceval devoted himself to a life of prayer, and Bors returned to recount the story to his fellow knights.

But the Golden Age of King Arthur was over within a few short years. In gathering together all the good knights, Arthur had driven the forces of evil to unite in a single, menacing army. The fate of Albion had to be settled by one last battle.

In the water-threaded Summer Lands, man by man, the knights of the Round Table fought and died. The black-armoured knights of treachery and sin and greed were all killed, but at terrible cost. Only the good Sir Bedivere was left standing and, lying wounded at his feet, Arthur, clenching the last minutes of his life like sand in his fist.

"Carry me to those woods," he told Bedivere. "There is something I must do before I die." A stretch of water glinted through the trees. Arthur was desperate to reach it, but his wounds were too deep. "Take my sword," he told Bedivere. "Take Excalibur, and throw it into the water."

"*Excalibur?*" Bedivere was appalled.

He stood by the waterside, his feet in the soft, oozing black mud, and the sword in his hands. But the sheer beauty of that shining blade, that elaborate jewelled hilt, seemed far too marvellous to sink in fathomless muddy water.

He hid the sword and went back.

"What did you see when you threw it?" asked Arthur.

"I saw the moorhens run and the ripples spread," said Bedivere with a shrug.

"Then go back and take the sword from where you hid it and *do as I commanded you!*" raged the King, his eyes bloodshot with fury.

Bedivere meant to do it, he really did. He ran to the reeds and pulled out Excalibur. But the sword had such memories for him – such happy memories! Soon Arthur would be dead. Was there to be nothing left to show for the court of Camelot, the Golden Age? Again he hid the sword, and hurried back, fearful the King would die alone.

"What did you see?" whispered Arthur.

"I saw the fish scatter and the reeds shake."

"*Villain! Traitor! Liar! Must I do the job myself?*" Arthur tried to get up, but fell back in agony. Bedivere took to his heels and ran – back to the waterside, scrabbling in among the reeds. Swinging the sword round his head, he flung it, letting fall a sob of effort and misery.

But just before the expected splash, a woman's hand rose from the heart of the lake and caught Excalibur by the hilt. Three times it brandished the blade, slicing the moonbeams. Then Arthur's sword sank, drawn down out of sight.

A Romano-British war-lord named Arturus, living in the west of England, is mentioned in Welsh chronicles, a fighter of notable courage against invading Saxons.

Most Arthurian legends originate, however, from the Age of Chivalry in the eleventh and twelfth centuries, when various "literary" writers recreated him in a complex cycle of stories, none of which is likely to be true. They required a Christian figure of courtly character, pitting himself against evil. There had to be a romantic element – romantic love was just being invented – and a code of knighthood (which did not even exist in the era when Arthur supposedly lived). A body of ancient Celtic myths has become interwoven with the Arthurian legend. In it Merlin is an important figure.

Extensive efforts have been made to site Camelot, but these are driven more by romantic wishful thinking than archaeological probability.

Arthur saw from Bedivere's face that his order had been carried out, his loan repaid to the Lady of the Lake. He sank into semi-consciousness, and Bedivere knelt over him, listening for the King's last breath.

Then the sound of oars behind him made him start to his feet. Through the trees came three women, veiled and with their hands drawn up inside their broad sleeves.

"So. It is time," they said to Bedivere. "He has earned his rest." They carried the King, with the greatest ease, aboard a low black craft moored among the reeds.

"Where are you taking him?" cried Bedivere distractedly. "Have some pity, won't you? Let him die in peace!"

"Die?" said the women. "He is sleeping. After such a life, is he not entitled to sleep? When Albion needs him, he will come back, never fear." Then each woman took hold of an oar and they rowed away, into the veiling vapours which evening had drawn up from the sodden landscape.

And where did they take him? To Avalon. A land of magic.

But where is Avalon? Why, it is the Island of Glass, of course. Or if not that island, some place very like it.

When Bedivere retraced his steps, the battlefield still lay strewn with dead. But the Knights of Arthur were all gone – all gone to Avalon to sleep alongside their king, heads pillowed on blossom petals from the Holy Thorn, sipping, in their dreams, from the Holy Grail, until their next summons to arms.

These days, the waters have drained away from the Island of Glass. But the hill is the same hill, the earth of the hill the same earth, the secrets of the hill the same well-kept secrets. Kestrels still hover, and the magic still clings.

Fleeting Glory

726

"A SHIP! A SHIP HAS struck the rocks, Father!" cried the fisherman's daughter above the howling wind. Dafyd leapt up and ran outdoors. The wind which met him was full of sea spray and cries, and fragments of rigging like twigs blown off a tree.

The ship in the bay lay on its side, surf crashing down on it like fists. "Help me, with the rowing boat!" Dafyd told his daughter, "or many a good man will drown tonight!"

Twenty men they dragged from the water by the scruff of the neck. Each frozen face spluttered thanks in some strange, un-Welsh tongue. At last the hulk settled and disintegrated under the strengthening daylight. Dafyd sent his daughter over the hill to fetch a monk to speak words over the dead.

Back at the hut, huddled by the fire, one of the survivors in particular seemed to command the respect of the others. All eyes were on him when he spoke.

"Reckon he's the captain," said Dafyd to his wife, "for all he doesn't look much."

The monk laughed at the simplicity of the fisherman. "O ignorant man! Do you not know English when you hear it spoken?" he said, and went to ask this "captain" who he was. A moment later he came reeling back and sat down on a crab pot. "By the saints!" he gasped (in Welsh). "D'you know what you've done, Dafyd? You've only saved the King of Wessex, that's all! You've only rescued King Ine of Wessex!"

"Oh yes?" responded the fisherman dubiously. "And where's Wessex, then?"

King Ine, spared from an early death, spent a great deal of time at his prayers after that. He founded a church on that bleak Cardiganshire coast, in thanksgiving, and he was an altogether devout and Christian king. His queen was equally saintly, and looked forward to the time when (as was the practice in those days) King Ine would resign his crown to a younger man and live out his life in prayer and contemplation.

She was to be disappointed. Ine might be a good king, but he was also a persistent one. Having grown used to power, he did not welcome the idea of giving it up. "Another month or two," he told his wife. "Just until I am content they can manage without me." But the months passed and still Ine held the reins of power, forever travelling from castle to castle, forever checking that his orders were being carried out.

After one particularly lavish night of feasting, he once again set out for yet another corner of the kingdom. He grumbled when the Queen asked them all to turn back. "There is something I forgot," she said.

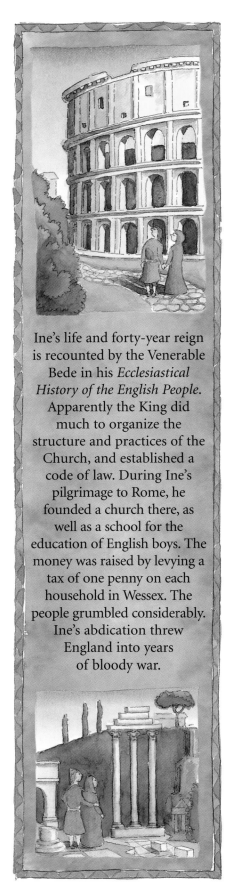

Ine's life and forty-year reign is recounted by the Venerable Bede in his *Ecclesiastical History of the English People*. Apparently the King did much to organize the structure and practices of the Church, and established a code of law. During Ine's pilgrimage to Rome, he founded a church there, as well as a school for the education of English boys. The money was raised by levying a tax of one penny on each household in Wessex. The people grumbled considerably. Ine's abdication threw England into years of bloody war.

"I have things to do. Affairs of state! You really must not delay like this, wife," Ine complained, but the Queen insisted. They retraced their steps to the castle.

The banners and pennants had gone from the walls. The minstrels had been paid off and gone. Litter from the feast lay strewn around the yard and the great hall, and dogs were chewing on bones amid the dirty strewings. Chickens pecked up and down the long table where, the night before, roast swans had stood amid custards and sweetmeats. Worst of all, on the couch where King Ine and his Queen had reclined to eat, a gigantic sow was lying on her side with a dozen piglets suckling.

"Someone will pay for this!" raged Ine. "Is this the esteem I am held in? Who is responsible for this disgrace?" He glanced around him at the carls and serfs, but they only looked at the Queen.

"What's the matter, my lord?" she asked innocently. "Did you expect to leave a trail of lasting glamour behind you, after you were gone? Did you think one night's pomp and splendour would fend off dirt and decay for ever? Our feast last night was like the rule of a good king – one brief span of glory. But everything passes. Everything decays. Every king will one day be reduced to a pile of forgotten bones. Life is so fleeting."

Many men, when lectured by their wives like this, would have called it nagging. But standing there in that squalid hall, Ine suddenly glimpsed the scale of eternity, and the absurdity of kingly pomp. His lifetime was nothing but one grain of sand in a sand dune of lives, and he had already wasted too much of it fretting about detail.

So although Ine realized that his queen had deliberately staged the pigs, the dogs, the litter, he took her lesson to heart. Soon afterwards, he resigned his crown to a younger man. He made a pilgrimage to Rome, then cut off his hair, and lived like a poor peasant for the rest of his life, working with his hands, thinking, praying and, of course, talking to his wife about the things which really matter.

Offa's Shame

794

IT IS ONLY NATURAL THAT A BRIDEGROOM SHOULD be nervous. But as King Ethelbert stepped out-of-doors and walked towards his horse, his legs shook, he staggered and almost fell. The waiting horses bolted, sending wedding gifts and bundles of clothing tumbling to the ground. Thatching slumped from the roofs. It was not Ethelbert who was trembling, but the earth itself. Dust rose so thickly that, for an hour, night returned.

"It is a bad omen, son," said his mother. "Do not go to Mercia!"

The King of East Anglia laughed. "It would be bad luck indeed not to marry the fairest maid in Christendom! When I take the Princess Alfleda for a wife, Anglia shall be united with Mercia and I shall be the happiest of men. If this is an omen, Mother, it is sent to some greater man than me."

Meanwhile, in the next-door kingdom, another woman wept and turned her face to the wall. "I tell you my poor heart will break! I shall never know another moment's happiness if this wedding takes place!"

King Offa slapped his forehead. "But what would you have me do, lady? My word is given! The betrothal is made. My daughter Alfleda is promised to Ethelbert. He is on his way here to marry her, even now! Why should they not wed?"

Pale and anguished, Queen Drida dabbed away tears. "It should be enough that I ask it," she said, and bit her beautiful blood-red lip.

A hundred miles away, sleeping on the cold ground under a snow shower of stars, King Ethelbert screamed in his sleep. He dreamed that his mother stood at the foot of a big double bed, weeping tears of blood. The tears splashed on to the sheets of the bed, while an armed man swung an axe over and over again, splintering the canopy, the legs, the footboard, splitting the mattress till the air was snowy with feathers. He knew it was his bed, too: his bridal bed.

Never before had the spoiled Queen Drida striven so hard to get her way. It made her sulky that Offa begrudged her what she asked. "Alfleda is too good for this yokel king!" said Drida. "There are far greater men over the ocean for her to marry. I will not have her wasted on a fenland peasant!"

"Silence, Drida," said Offa. "I have accepted the man's gifts and promised him my daughter's hand. Say no more about it. My mind is made up."

Queen Drida did hold her tongue – bit into it with sharp little teeth and kept silent. But the ambition did not die within her, nor her determination to stop the marriage.

White-faced for want of sleep, grimy and dishevelled from his journey, King Ethelbert of Anglia smiled broadly at the sight of Offa's castle. Here was the home of his beautiful bride. Tomorrow he would marry Alfleda. He was a truly lucky man.

As he stepped in at the door of Offa's throne room, he hesitated. There was an uneasy atmosphere.

The Queen was looking steadfastly at the floor. But Offa opened his arms in welcome, beaming with delight: "Come in, son-in-law! Come in and welcome!" Two long tables groaned under joints of meat, custards, sweetmeats and cakes. Ethelbert took his place at the feast, and Alfleda sat down beside him, birdlike and delicate. The double doors closed against the weather, and a bolt shot home.

Hours later, flushed with wine and laughing with joy, Ethelbert was shown to his room by the Queen. It was luxurious, with a curtained bed, tapestries on the wall and, at the centre of the room, a vast chair piled with down-filled cushions. Ethelbert thanked the Queen over and over again: "Such a welcome . . . such a feast . . . such a fine, comfortable room." This was the last night he would retire to bed alone: tomorrow he would be sharing his dreams with the lovely Alfleda. Weary and overfed, he flung himself down in the great chair.

Lurching backwards and sideways, the chair twisted and buckled. Then it plunged through a jagged hole in the thin planks which had been supporting it. Down it fell into darkness, into the musty, hollow darkness of a hidden well. Ethelbert saw the room's light recede to a smaller and smaller circle, then the chair struck the bottom of the well and splintered under him. The fall broke his bones, knocked all the wind out of him. But finding himself alive, Ethelbert began to yell for help.

He was heard, too. Queen Drida's hired men came out of hiding and ran to the brink of the pit. They brandished triumphant fists, like hunters who have snared a bear. Then as he went on shouting – "Get me out! Pull me up! For pity's sake, help me!" – they began to throw things down on to him – the bedspread, the sheets, the pillows. They ripped apart the bed and threw it down, bit by bit, on to Ethelbert. Soon no more sound came from the well.

"Haul up the body, cut off his head, and bury him somewhere out of the way," said Queen Drida.

Offa no sooner learned what his wife had done, than the servants came running to him in terror, speaking of lights shining in the dark – lights which hovered over a piece of newly turned earth, lights marking a murdered man's grave. Offa went to see for himself, and sure enough, lights hung like altar candles over the place where the body and head of King Ethelbert had been hurriedly crammed underground. In a guilty panic, Offa told the servants to bury the remains somewhere else, before the lights attracted attention. But within hours the men were back, banging on his door, shouting in hoarse whispers that the lights were shining now over the new burial place.

That was when the real terror began – the guilt which troubled Offa's sleeping and waking hours. "Drida, you have made a murderer of me!" he said. "You and your scheming and ambition! How will we ever be clean of this good man's blood?"

The Queen gave a petulant shrug.

Offa covered his head with his hands. "But Drida! Alfleda loved him! She *wanted* to marry him. And now he is dead!"

In the course of his long reign (almost forty years), Offa expanded his kingdom from Mercia to encompass Kent, Sussex, Wessex and East Anglia, making him the most powerful monarch prior to AD 1000. He called himself *rex Anglorum*: the King of the English. Versions of the story of Ethelbert and Alfleda (or Alfrida) vary so widely that there is probably little truth in the details. In another telling, a nobleman called Winebert beheads Ethelbert the moment he steps through Offa's door. But quite possibly Offa did assassinate this rival monarch for political reasons. The murdered King was certainly declared a saint. The achievement for which Offa is best remembered is the building of a 100-kilometre-long earthwork – Offa's Dyke – as a defence against Welsh raiders with whom he spent his whole time at war. After his death, his kingdom fragmented again.

Again that pettish shrug. "She's not my daughter, she's yours. I never liked her. Why should that simpering girl get what she wants? Do I? What has she ever done to deserve a beautiful young man like that? She's always been a thorn in my side, with her sheep's eyes and praying hands and hair like a yard of weak ale. I cannot abide her. Better she should be married to someone far away. On the other side of the . . ."

Offa did not stay to hear more. He ran from the room, sickened by the jealousy of his spoiled wife. He ran to his Bible, but found no comfort there. He ran to his confessor, but his confessor blanched white as a ghost. Offa's conscience was as bad as if he had done the deed himself. His dreams ran red with blood. The eerie, hovering lights beckoned him back time and time again to the place where Ethelbert lay; they even escorted the body as Offa removed it to a place of honour in Hereford Cathedral.

So ignoring his wife's shrill complaints, Offa set off on a journey far longer than Ethelbert's. He set off for Rome, to do penance for the death of an innocent man and to beg forgiveness from the Pope. And when he returned, he could be found, on many and many a day, crouched beside the dead King's tomb, recounting all that he had seen and done in the Eternal City.

The bronze likeness of the young dead King listened, holding his severed head in his lap, erect and serene, though with an expression of wistful sadness, perhaps at all pleasures of life which he had died too soon to enjoy.

The Kingly Martyr

869

INSTEAD OF WHITE GULLS, BLACK RAVENS WERE flying that summer over the eastern coast: the raven banners of Vikings. They swooped in across the ocean and gorged on Christian blood. Monasteries were sacked for the sake of their holy treasures, and villages burned for the sheer pleasure of destruction. Only King Edmund of East Anglia stood between his people and the Vikings. But Edmund's faith burned within him like the candle in the sanctuary which, by day or night, never goes out. He did not believe for a moment that God would suffer the true religion of Christ to be snuffed out by pagans.

So, as the Viking cleavers sliced through the November air, and the banner of the cross fell to an unkindness of ravens, what thoughts passed through the King's mind? He was defeated. His knights lay dead around him. His own life was at the mercy of a Viking warlord.

The Viking leader eyed his prisoner like a bird of prey. His eyes were paler than water. He had a certain respect for the King of this flat, damp, fertile kingdom. "You fought well. You are not dishonoured by defeat, King Edmund. I may yet spare your life."

No change of expression crossed Edmund's battle-weary face, but a flicker of hope must have kindled painfully in his heart.

"Yes, you shall go free – why not?" said his captor, spreading his hands in a gesture of generosity. "Just forswear that milksop religion of yours and honour the Norse warrior gods who overthrew you today."

Edmund's head dropped forward. "I will never renounce my faith in Christ Jesus."

The pale yellow moustache rucked into a sneer, and the Viking slouched sideways in his chair. "Take him out and let the archers put him to some use."

Edmund was dragged roughly away, the guards snatching off his cuirass and shirt as they went. They tied him to a tree, and he saw the Viking archers restringing their longbows. It was late November: his bare limbs jumped with cold.

"There is still time to change banners!" called the man with pale blue eyes. "What has he ever done for you, this Christ? This Jesus Christ?"

"He has blessed my soul with bliss, as I pray He will one day bless yours," said Edmund. "I forgive you this spilling of my blood."

The Viking leader turned away with disgust and vexation. As he went, he could hear the whisk of arrows through the leaves, the thud of arrowheads sinking into the tree's trunk. Then the archers found their distance, and began to hit their mark. It gave him no satisfaction.

The name of Bury St Edmunds bears witness to the final place of the martyred king. His bones were moved there after a miracle cult grew up around his memory. He was probably about twenty-nine years old when he died.

Tradition has it that King Offa, who had no son of his own, adopted Edmund, the son of a Frankish king, to be his heir. Little else is known about him.

When the arrows had finally killed Edmund, his head was cut off, and the Vikings moved on to lay waste to more kingdoms. The King's followers, reeling with horror, despair and fatigue, emerged from hiding. But though they were able to cut down the body bristling with arrows, they could not find his head. For days they searched, but without success.

As they combed Eglesdane Wood one last time, a voice called out: "*Over here!*" Everyone asked everyone else. "Was that you?"

Then the voice came again. "*I am here! This way! Over here!*" Their hair stood on end.

Following the voice, they came to a clearing. Then a dozen men gasped and froze, their hands on their sword hilts. There stood a huge wolf, grey as winter, its front paws straddling the bloody head, its lower jaw resting on the pale forehead of the martyr-King. They waited for it to spring, but the wolf backed grudgingly away from its prize, as though it had merely been waiting for them to come. A page darted forward and grabbed up the head, but the wolf did not move to recapture it, nor to run away. Hastily the King's party beat back through the woods. Walking, they broke into a run as they realized the wolf was dogging their footsteps, keeping the scent of them in its nostrils, watching them with its yellow eyes. But they got back safely to the body of the dead King. Now he could be laid to rest.

They took him to Hoxne. And every time they looked back, the wolf was still following, loping along after the horses, melting into the trees if they reined in.

Word of Edmund's death was spreading – not of his defeat, but of his marvellous courage, his saintly faith. Edmund their king had gone to join the saints. Now there was one more saint in heaven to watch over the people of Anglia.

As the sorry remains, body and head, were lowered into the grave, an uninvited guest stood watching from the church lych-gate. With watchful eyes, the wolf observed the laying to rest of the dead King. Only then did it turn and lope back into the forest whose trees, in the rising wind, whispered a thousand prayers for the soul of St Edmund.

Alfred and the Cakes

878

LFRED THE GREAT OF WESSEX HAD FOR HIS ancestors three of the ancient Saxon gods: Woden, Sceaf and Geat. So when Saxon Britain began to fall, field by town, to the invading Danes, Alfred and his brother Aethelred went out to fight them. In 871, at the battle of Ashdown, the marauders were routed for the first time.

It was a hard won victory. Though their muscles should have ached with exhaustion, success lent the Saxon troops new energy. They set about hewing and gouging the hillside nearby as they had hewn and gouged the Danes, carving out the shape of a gigantic white horse in the chalkstone, for future generations to see and remember.

But the Danes came back again and again. They killed Aethelred and cowed the Saxons to such an extent that they abandoned their king. Along with a few loyal men, Alfred alone held out against them, a mysterious figure living a shifting, ghostly life, haunting the countryside, emerging from hiding to attack the Danes.

By 878, things were going so badly that Alfred's pocket army was confined to the Isle of Athelney in the middle of the Summer Land. Their shelter was in turf cottages and their food was bread made

from acorns grubbed from under the spreading oak trees.

Alfred sought shelter from a local man – a cowherd – and asked whether he might sleep a night or two at his house.

"By all that's holy, my little place ain no fit shelter for a king, sire! But you'z honour me and the wife past all speaking, if you'z see fit to sleep under our roof!"

Denewulf was not exaggerating: his little turf-roofed house was mean and small and bare. But Alfred was simply glad to be out of the rain. He had no fear for his safety among these good people: they were all ready to lay down their lives for the Saxon cause. This cowherd, for instance. He would return the man's loyalty if ever it were within his power to do so.

With much bowing and blushing – "My wife – where is the silly woman? – she'll make you some food – prepare you up a bed" – Denewulf seated Alfred on a rush stool in front of the fire and dashed away again to try to find his wife and tell her the wonderful honour which had befallen them. Alfred spread out his great swordsman's hands to warm them at the grate.

"What you'm doing in here soaking up th'heat?" asked an imperious voice behind him.

Alfred turned round and caught his first sight of the cowherd's wife. "Your husband said I might stay here for a while."

"Oh yes, that be typical of 'im, the lummock." The woman had never seen a king before. She did not see a king now – only some mud-stained, unkempt ragamuffin with leaves in his hair, sitting on her best rush stool. "Well, you'm best make yourself useful. Can you do that?" she snapped. "Shake the blankets? Sweep out the straw?"

The King had never been asked such a thing before. "I expect so."

Alfred was dog-tired, but he was also a gentle-man. So he did as he was told, and thanked the lady when she brought him a bite of food. Her manners were not quite those of a royal valet, nor was bread and cheese exactly a banquet, but Alfred was used to less. He realized that the woman had no idea who he was.

He marvelled at the bareness of her existence – the few sticks of furniture, the empty store cup-board, the single cooking pot. But he marvelled, too, at the way she could whip up an egg, a spoon of flour and honey into a cake-mix, and set the lit-tle scones to bake on a griddle over a twig fire.

"Now you'm watch them cakes and don't you'm take youz eyes off 'em, or I'll have words to say!" barked the woman. "I have to milk the cows. Someone has to . . . And *no nibbling*, you hear?" were her parting words.

Alfred smiled to himself, then settled down in front of the hearth, legs stretched out, and watched the cakes. Little bubbles rose up to the surface of each scone and popped with a sigh. They swelled, as if with Saxon pride . . .

As he sat, Alfred sank into thinking, remember-ing the bad times, remembering the good.

One day, in the forests, he had come across a lady in blue standing very still in a downshaft of sunlight. "Are you lost, lady?" he had asked. But when she turned towards him, he had known in an instant, with absolute certainty, that he was looking at Mary, mother of Jesus, at the Holy

Madonna herself. Speechless with awe, Alfred had done the only thing his wits would allow, and cast at her feet the most precious object he was carrying – his jewelled cloak pin. Before disappearing like a summer mirage, the lady had opened her lips and said . . .

"You goon! You great lazy, idle, good-for-nothing lummock! You let my cakes burn!" Alfred slipped off his stool in waking and peered around him: the hut was oddly dark. It seemed to be full of smoke. "You great hulking fool of a wet Wednesday! What you got for brains, frogspawn or mud?" Six smouldering little cakes reproached him from the griddle, as black and brittle as charcoal.

"I'm –"

"I know what *you* be," the woman went on. "Anyone can see what *you* be! You be your mother's greatest shame and your father's worst mistake! You be a wet cloud looking for someone like me to rain on! What *you* be is –"

"The King of Wessex," said a voice behind her. Her husband, the cowherd, stood in the doorway, paler than the pail of milk he was carrying. But it was not he who had spoken. It was one of the officers behind him, cloaks thrown back off their mail shirts, swords drawn. The woman's mouth froze in mid-word. "Son of Aethelwulf," the officer went on. "Kin to the gods Woden, Sceaf and Geat; Lord of Wessex. What shall I do with her, sire?"

The woman's mouth still spoke its small, silent "O". Her eyes filled with tears. Now she would be hanged, and her hut burned down, and her husband's cattle forfeit to the army. Now she would be cursed by her neighbours, remembered as the shrew who had bad-mouthed the greatest man in England. She fell to her knees and curled her body into a crouching bow. She could find no words to excuse her offence.

Alfred picked up a cake and burnt his fingers doing it. He smiled to himself and then at the others. "Why, help her to her feet, man! She's perfectly right! This good woman left me to mind her cakes, and I let them burn. She's quite right – I am a fool! Shall I hang her for telling me the simple truth? Here, madam." He pulled out his purse. "Here's recompense for the cakes, and a little something for your . . . honest and fearless nature. Now gentlemen! Let's sit and discuss what can be done to pull England from the fire before she burns, shall we?"

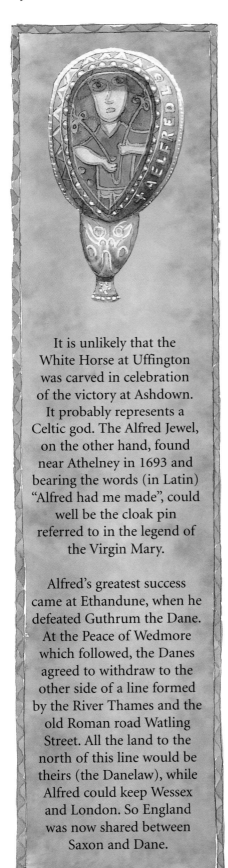

It is unlikely that the White Horse at Uffington was carved in celebration of the victory at Ashdown. It probably represents a Celtic god. The Alfred Jewel, on the other hand, found near Athelney in 1693 and bearing the words (in Latin) "Alfred had me made", could well be the cloak pin referred to in the legend of the Virgin Mary.

Alfred's greatest success came at Ethandune, when he defeated Guthrum the Dane. At the Peace of Wedmore which followed, the Danes agreed to withdraw to the other side of a line formed by the River Thames and the old Roman road Watling Street. All the land to the north of this line would be theirs (the Danelaw), while Alfred could keep Wessex and London. So England was now shared between Saxon and Dane.

Dunstan and the Devil

about 980

THERE WAS A MAN WHO LIVED through the reigns of eight kings, and lent his advice to six of them. Small wonder that kings and nobles held no dread for him. St Dunstan was of the opinion that God was on his side, and that made him a dangerous man to cross. His enemies said he dabbled in the black arts – and that made him more dangerous still.

As a young man, he was by trade a blacksmith – or perhaps it was merely a hobby of his, for later, when King Edmund made him Abbot of Glastonbury, he set up a forge in a little stone cell projecting from the outer wall of the abbey and would go there, by way of relaxation, to forge horseshoes and pokers and scythes. Local people would call on him and ask him, "Make me this, Father Abbot," or "Make me that."

One day an uncommonly pretty woman came and fluttered her lashes at Dunstan, asking if he would make her a toasting fork. While he worked, she moved about the room – a flick of the hips, a flash of the eyes, a smile. But Dunstan kept his eyes firmly on his work. The hammer clanged down. Sparks exploded: there was a smell of sulphur. The woman became still more daring, brushing up against him, fingering his tonsure. It was only as she stepped over a hammer on the floor that her skirts lifted, and Dunstan glimpsed her feet.

Lifting his blacksmith's tongs red-hot from the furnace, he reached out with them – and seized the woman by the nose!

How she shrieked and screamed. But Dunstan did not let go. How she altered into a mottled, bent old crone gripped in the lips of the red-hot pincers. But still Dunstan did not let go. Now she was not even female, but a sooty writhing fellow roaring and trumpeting in the grip of the tongs. But Dunstan still did not let go – no, not even when the Devil himself was dancing in front of Dunstan on his two cloven hooves.

"You should not have let me see your feet," said Dunstan smiling grimly. Then he threw the Devil out of the window, just as the bells rang for vespers.

The Devil was a fool, really, to approach Dunstan in the shape of a woman. For women were not a breed St Dunstan much cared for. In those days, it was the custom for certain orders of priests to marry and have families. But Dunstan thought the whole priesthood should stay unmarried. The arguments had been dragging on, bitter and unresolved, for many years when, one day, a meeting took place in an upstairs room at Calne in Wiltshire.

Opinions were equally split. It was hard to see how a final decision could be reached. Dunstan closed the proceedings. "We shall never agree, so I say, let the decision rest with Christ Jesus Himself!"

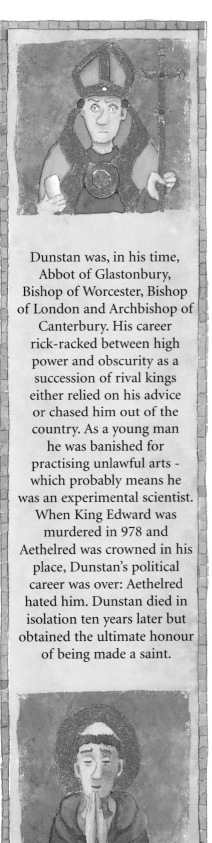

There was an ominous groaning of timbers. Then a large portion of the floor suddenly fell away, and the long central table listed and slid through the hole like a sinking ship, carrying with it everyone on one side of the room.

It was a long drop. In the room below, some lay trapped under the table or under fallen roofbeams. Some staggered ghostly white from the ruins, showered with plaster. Dunstan and his followers, however, were left in the upper room, like angels looking down on the chaos below.

Dunstan's enemies said he had sabotaged the floor. Dunstan said that God had taken a hand. And even if dry rot were really to blame, still Dunstan carried the day. Marriage was forbidden to the clergy.

Not that some monks cared what Dunstan said. Some monks did not give a fig for the holy life or their vows of poverty and virtue. The monks of Middle Fen, for instance. Their lives were as easy and pleasant as they could make them, and they never gave God or religion a thought from one day's end to the next. Their wives and children, sweethearts and friends all lived together in the abbey which stood on an island in the midst of Middle Fen – a rowdy, lawless rabble with wine-stains on their habits and money on their minds.

But Dunstan came down on them like the wrath of God. No sermons or penances. No fines or trials. He simply turned them into eels, every one, and emptied them into the rivers and dikes and ponds and marshes of the fenland. That's why the place is called Ely – the place of eels – and why Dunstan is better remembered than any of the kings he served.

Dunstan was, in his time, Abbot of Glastonbury, Bishop of Worcester, Bishop of London and Archbishop of Canterbury. His career rick-racked between high power and obscurity as a succession of rival kings either relied on his advice or chased him out of the country. As a young man he was banished for practising unlawful arts - which probably means he was an experimental scientist. When King Edward was murdered in 978 and Aethelred was crowned in his place, Dunstan's political career was over: Aethelred hated him. Dunstan died in isolation ten years later but obtained the ultimate honour of being made a saint.

London Bridge is Falling Down

1013 and 1016

"THE VIKINGS ARE COMING! THE VIKINGS are coming!"

The cry had echoed so often up the river reaches, and yet it never failed to terrify. London was the great prize in the game, and London was being captured and recaptured now like a carcass of meat wrangled over by lions.

In 1013, King Swayne the Dane had taken the city from King Ethelred, but Ethelred was determined to take it back. He enlisted the help of King Olaf of Norway, and sailed up the Thames estuary – more dragon-headed ships lunging upstream, more cries of "The Vikings are coming!"

Swayne was ready for them. His men were massed on London Bridge, at their feet lay huge cairns of rock for pelting the attacking ships. There were archers, too, and spear-wielders.

But Ethelred knew the river: it was *his* river. He had foreseen the blockade, and equipped Olaf's ships accordingly, each with a high platform rising from the foredeck.

"He thinks to shield his rowers from the rocks," thought Swayne, peering against the brightness of the river. "It is protection for the rowers."

But as the dragon-prows nosed closer, Ethelred's and Olaf's men swarmed up on to the platforms so as to stand almost on a level with their opponents on the bridge. They stood in pairs, one holding a coil of rope tipped with a grappling hook, the other holding a shield with which to fend off the arrows, the stones, the spears.

Insanely, it seemed as if they would really moor up to the bridge, for they pitched their grappling irons at the bridge's wooden pilings.

Their faces were on a level with the bridge parapet: like sailors in two closing warships, both sides looked each other in the eye. There was a moment's silence, like a pause to draw breath. Then the men on the bridge were hurling, shouting, bloodying their hands on the large rocks in their haste to heave them over on to the ships beneath.

Six, a dozen, twenty of the men on the platforms were dislodged by stones and plunged into the river. Some fell stunned to the decking. But then the rowers swung their legs over the benches and faced the other way. The dragon-headed ships dropped back downstream, but between them and the bridge now ran a dozen stout ropes.

"Heave!" cried Ethelred.

"Heave!" cried Olaf. And the rowers heaved till the muscles stood proud of their shoulders. The ropes twanged taut, spraying silver droplets into the air.

The grappling irons chewed on the wood of the bridge; two broke free and splashed into the river, but the rest held. The strain stirred the wooden pilings of the bridge in their muddy sockets in the river bed.

What with the great weight of stones amassed on the wooden planking and the great press of defenders, the bridge was already overladen. Now, as its pilings were dragged out from under it, London Bridge broke its wooden back.

For a moment it staggered drunkenly on its unsteady legs. Then down into the Thames fell stones and shields, timber and helmets and men. The dragon-headed longships rolled on the huge wave which washed downstream from the splash, and the rowers rested on their oars as silence fell over the wide, grey river.

Within three years another king held London – Edmund Ironside – and London Bridge had been built up again, too strongly for whole galleys of rowers to pull it down. But King Canute was a man who did not pit brawn against brawn. He brought the power of cunning to the problem of capturing London.

Arming his men with picks and shovels in place of swords, he had them dig. He had them dig a channel just a hand-span wider than the beam of his ships. It ran south from the Thames. Then west. It bypassed London, looping to the south, and, when flooded with Thames water from either end, it filled to a depth just a hand-span deeper than the draw of Canute's ships. Long chains of men, heaving like barge horses on cables of rope, hauled the entire navy of Canute round Edmund Ironside's London, and attacked from the west – from inland! – unexpected, unresisted, irresistible.

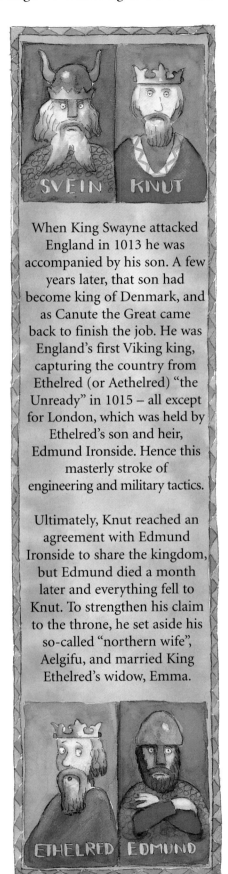

When King Swayne attacked England in 1013 he was accompanied by his son. A few years later, that son had become king of Denmark, and as Canute the Great came back to finish the job. He was England's first Viking king, capturing the country from Ethelred (or Aethelred) "the Unready" in 1015 – all except for London, which was held by Ethelred's son and heir, Edmund Ironside. Hence this masterly stroke of engineering and military tactics.

Ultimately, Knut reached an agreement with Edmund Ironside to share the kingdom, but Edmund died a month later and everything fell to Knut. To strengthen his claim to the throne, he set aside his so-called "northern wife", Aelgifu, and married King Ethelred's widow, Emma.

Canute Defies the Sea

about 1 0 2 0

GOOD OR BAD, A KING DRAWS FLATTERERS like a horse draws flies, and King Canute, in his fenland kingdom, had accumulated a veritable swarm.

"The sun is shining today, my lord, because it is glad to see you so well!"

"The kings of all Europe are trembling this morning, your honour, at the thought of your might and wisdom!"

"The Pope himself is surely envious of your saintliness, my lord!"

Canute stood up suddenly. "I dare say I could cross swords with the moon and win," he suggested.

"Oh, no doubt! No question, my lord King!"

"And command the sea itself to do my bidding."

"The seas, my lord King, would be honoured to serve you," said the toadies.

"Then take hold of my throne – you – you – and you! – and be so good as to carry it down to the beach," said Canute, to the court's surprise.

The sea lay vast and grey, breathing shallowly, lapping at shells on the wet sand. Canute had his throne placed a few steps from the water's edge and sat in it. His courtiers stood about, hands clasped on their stomachs, smiles set hard. The tide was rising.

"Hold off, Sea!" commanded Canute, holding up one royal hand. "I, Canute, say you shall not rise today!" His courtiers looked at each other, but went on smiling. "Stay back, thou great wet thing!" commanded Canute, holding up both royal hands. "I, Canute, command it!"

But, of course, the sea continued to lap the shore, and every seventh wave ran higher up the beach, wetting dry sand, turning dry stones. Soon the legs of the throne were awash. The royal feet were distinctly wet. The courtiers, hopping about dismally, kept on smiling.

"O unruly and uppish monster! Do you defy me? Do you dare to invade my kingdom?" protested Canute. A large grey wave wetted everyone to the knees and the backwash dragged sand from under their sodden velvet shoes.

"I really think, your Majesty," began the chancellor, "it's not quite safe to . . ."

"But you told me I was more powerful than the sea!" Canute retorted, and he sat fast, until the throne itself was being rocked by large cold waves, and his courtiers were up to their waists in brine.

"Scurvy ocean!" Canute declaimed. "I see that you have not heard of King Canute the All-Powerful! I see we must wrestle hand-to-hand!"

"No! No, my lord!" cried several of his courtiers, wading through the swell. "Please!"

"You mean to say I am *not* all-powerful?" said Canute with exaggerated amazement. "You mean to say that the winds and waves do *not* obey God's anointed king?"

"I –"

"We –"

"Ah –"

"No? Then in future, I'll thank you not to tell me such monumental untruths, gentlemen. I look to you for your help and advice and measured opinions. I do *not* look to you for flattery, lies and servility. Do I make myself clear?"

"Perfectly!" howled the court in unison as a great wave broke and left them flailing ashore, tripping and gasping, and dipping for their hats in the unheeding sea.

At one time, King Canute ruled three kingdoms – England, Norway and Denmark – and spent long periods overseas. But his twenty-year rule in England was a time of relative stability. After his death, his empire fell apart as his sons fought for supremacy. His first heir died. His second heir, Hardaknut, was hated, unlike Knut who was revered as a wise, religious man.

The story of Knut and the sea was and is frequently mis-told, as if Canute believes the sea will obey him, but only because listeners like to hear of the proud being humbled.

"Macbeth Does Murder Sleep"

1040
(Shakespeare, *Macbeth*)

MACBETH WAS EXULTANT AS HE RODE homeward from the coast. He had fought a whole fleet of Danish invaders and won. At his side rode his friend Banquo, Thane of Lochaber. Suddenly, out of the dank, wreathing mist, three old women appeared. "Hail Macbeth, Thane of Glamis. Hail Macbeth, Thane of Cawdor. All hail Macbeth, soon to be King of Scotland!"

"None of these titles is mine," said Macbeth. "You mistake me for my father even to call me Thane of Glamis." But perhaps these old crones were witches. Perhaps they were blessed with the magic powers and could see events in the future as other people saw fish in a pond.

"Have you nothing to say to me?" asked Banquo, eager for a prophecy of his own.

"No king thou, but a father of kings!" chanted the gnarled, weather-blasted crones. Then they were gone, swallowed up by the mist . . . and approaching, each from a different direction, were two messengers. Macbeth's father was dead: the title "Thane of Glamis" had passed to him. And King Duncan, in acknowledgement of his victory over

the Danes, had awarded valiant Macbeth the estates of Cawdor.

Two prophecies come true in as many minutes! The news shook Macbeth more than any battle. For if two prophecies could come true, why not the third? Might Macbeth one day be king? The thought warmed him like a great dog leaning against his belly.

If Macbeth were ambitious, his wife Gruoch was eaten up with ambition. There was royal blood in her veins and it cried out for power. When she heard tell of the three witches, heard of her husband's new titles and saw the hunger in him to be king, she swept aside all his qualms, drowned out the whispers of his conscience, telling him, "Yes! Murder Duncan and be king!"

Duncan and his son, Prince Malcolm, were invited to stay at the castle of the Macbeths, near Inverness. After the old man had gone to bed, Gruoch drugged his bodyguards and, when they were slumped snoring by the King's bed, Macbeth took their daggers and stabbed Duncan through the heart. In the morning, when the body was found, he feigned horror and outrage – and, blaming the guards, killed them outright.

Duncan's son, Malcolm, was not fooled for one moment. He fled – over the border into England, rightly supposing that he was the only person who stood between Macbeth and the crown which he and Gruoch so insanely craved.

The great prize was won, just as the witches had said it would be. The metal crown weighed heavy on his temples . . . but the second prophecy dragged like a sea-anchor on his heart. Banquo's sons would be kings? How? Why not Macbeth's?

He would kill Banquo. No! He would pay for Banquo to be killed: a king does not need to sully his hands. It was done: another obstacle removed, another bloody notch cut in Macbeth's conscience.

But he could not rest easy until he had visited the three old hags again.

He was not disappointed; the three old women were still there on the heath. Their mumbling toothless heads emerged from the rocky dark like tortoises emerging from their shells. "Show me the future!" he demanded. "Is my crown secure? Am I safe from my enemies?"

They looked at him with eyes as yellow as cesspits. "Macbeth shall not be conquered till Birnam Wood comes to Dunsinane."

Macbeth gave a shrill, gasping laugh. Safe, then! Birnam Wood stood several miles from his castle at Dunsinane, and how could a *forest* move? He told his wife. He told his men-at-arms: "I am invincible. Nothing can defeat me till Birnam Wood comes to Dunsinane!"

Meanwhile, in England, Malcolm threw himself on the mercy of Edward the Confessor and scuffed his heels around the English court. He won over to his cause the Earl of Northumberland and a thane called Macduff, wronged and driven out of Scotland by King Macbeth. They raised an army and marched on Dunsinane: Macbeth's spies quickly brought him word of it, but Macbeth only laughed. Cloaked round in his magical prophecy, he was smugly complacent.

A servant came stumbling into the room, eyes bulging, mouth a-jabber. "The wood, sire! The wood . . . !" He almost died, Macbeth's fingers around his throat, for the news he brought: that Dunsinane Wood appeared to be *moving towards the castle*.

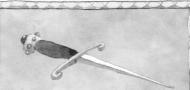

The source of this story is Raphael Holinshed's *Chronicles* of 1577, and it was this book which Shakespeare would have used when he wrote his tragedy, *Macbeth*. It is known that Macbeth seized the throne by murdering Duncan, and that he suffered defeat at the hands of Prince Malcolm. But Holinshed made free with the facts and Shakespeare adjusted them even more.

In fact Macbeth ruled Scotland for seventeen years, and his reign was thought of as a time of prosperity. He gave large sums to charity (possibly to salve a bad conscience) and went on pilgrimage to Rome. And although he lost the battle at Dunsinane, he escaped and survived three further years before he was killed by Malcolm. Shakespeare depicted Lady Macbeth as a woman driven to madness then suicide by her guilt, but Gruoch's true fate is unknown. She simply disappeared.

In the context of eleventh-century Scotland, there is nothing remarkable about the violence of Macbeth's rise and fall. It was the masterpiece Shakespeare wove around the events which immortalized this obscure chapter of Scottish history.

Macbeth flung him aside and ran to the battlements. The raw wind stung his eyes to tears as he stared. The prophecy clamoured in his head, indistinguishable from the alarm bell.

In marching through Birnam Wood, Macduff had told every soldier to strip a branch from the trees and to carry it, and so mask the size and nature of the force coming against Macbeth. It would keep him guessing.

But as far as Macbeth was concerned, the battle was already lost. His heart crumpled within him. He looked around and saw that his men, too, remembered the prophecy. It hamstrung them; it set their sword-hands shaking. With one last effort of will, he rallied them to the attack. The portcullis lifted, and they forayed out to meet the enemy they knew would destroy them . . .

Lady Godiva's Shameless Ride

about 1050

PEOPLE DID NOT KNOW HOW GODIVA COULD BEAR TO LIVE WITH Leofric: his meanness, his little acts of spite, his nasty temper. And she so kind and beautiful! People said what a shame it was that the best wives sometimes marry the worst men.

But Lady Godiva loved her husband. Even though he was not handsome or gentle or even very pleasant, she genuinely loved him. It saddened her that he was so unpopular with the people. Leofric was Earl of Chester, which gave him, for his income, the revenue of the city of Coventry. Tithes, rent, fines, fees and levies, Leofric took them all. If anyone could not pay, he evicted them. Sometimes Lady Godiva would try to help the hardest pressed, with a coin from her own purse, but she had to do it in secret: Leofric looked on charity as throwing good money after bad.

"The Bible tells us we should help the poor," Godiva pointed out gently.

"The Bible tells us to work hard and pay our taxes," said Leofric disagreeably. "They have plenty of money, you take my word. You shouldn't believe their hard-luck stories."

He raised the taxes, until the people complained aloud. Then he punished them with higher taxes.

"Don't do this, husband," said Lady Godiva one day, as he sat composing a new proclamation. "I have never contradicted you before, but this new tax of yours is wrong. It will cause such suffering."

"Keep your place, woman," snapped Leofric. "What do you know of such things?"

"But the people will hate you for this tax. Don't do it, I beg you."

Leofric laughed. "What do I care if they hate me, so long as they pay?"

Lady Godiva breathed deeply. "If you really need this money, I will give it you out of my own inheritance."

That silenced his laughing. "I'll have you know, madam, that your money is already mine to do with as I please. And I do not please to use my *own money* to pay what the people of Coventry owe me."

Lady Godiva was quiet for so long that Leofric thought he had won the argument. But then his wife drew herself up to her full height. "My money may be yours, Leofric, but I think you will agree, my body is my own. If you will not be ashamed, I must be ashamed for you. Withdraw this latest tax . . . or I shall ride naked through the streets of Coventry in token of the people you have left naked to wind and rain."

Leofric snorted with scorn. "*You?* The virtuous Lady Godiva? You would die of shame, and I would die of laughing." His quill nib scratched on the parchment like a rat on a granary wall.

Next Sunday, in every church in Coventry, there was an astonishing announcement made. "Tomorrow, Lady Godiva, wife of the Earl of Chester, will ride naked through the streets of the city. Let her shame fall on Leofric for his greed."

Some priests whispered it, some choked on the word "naked", some never even reached the end before uproar broke out. Soon everyone had grasped the news, including Leofric, dozing sleepily in his scarlet padded pew.

His first thought was to put his wife under lock and key, but Godiva was too quick for him; she had already gone into hiding. "She will never do it," he comforted himself, but he did not sleep well that night, in his big Coventry house.

Next morning, he woke to the sound of hooves on the cobbles below. They rang through the silent city streets. He threw open the shutters and shouted along the whole length of Broadgate: "Don't do this, Godiva! Don't do this to me!"

The rising sun shone on her long, loose hair falling over her bare shoulders, breaking over the horse's rump. She rode bareback, astride her grey mare. From the crown of her head to the soles of her feet, she was stark naked.

Godiva did not feel the cold; her skin burned with shame and anger. This was not the act of some brazen woman carrying out a shocking dare. Godiva was humiliating herself in the hope of humbling her husband. She did not round her shoulders nor cower down over the horse's neck, but inwardly she knew what agonies she would suffer when exposed to the whistles and stares of a market-day crowd.

Was this not a market day?

On market days, the city was busy even before sun-up, crowded with people setting up stalls, opening the front windows of their houses to trade with passers-by; countryfolk walking in from the outlying villages with eggs, vegetables and wicker-work. On market days carts vied for right of way; tinkers bawled and shouted.

So was this *not* a market day?

The streets were so quiet! No carts rattled over the cobbles. No one was setting up their wares in the market place. Godiva raised her eyes. Every house shutter was closed, every door shut. Somewhere a dog barked. Water gurgled down the drain in the middle of the road. But no one shouted, no one pushed a handcart through the alleyways. No one stared.

Leofric came running, Godiva's cloak bundled up in his arms. He tried to throw it over her, but she shrugged it off and it fell into the drain. "Godiva, please! Look at you! You'll die of cold. I'll die of shame! What are you doing to me?"

"You have stripped the people bare with your taxes and your levies," said Godiva looking steadfastly ahead. "The people of Coventry will think no less of me for this. But *your* name will go down in history as the man who swindled Coventry." Her bare heels thudded into the horse's withers, and it broke into a trot.

Leofric looked around him, cringing, anticipating the laughter, the hoots, the crude jokes that would shower down on his lovely wife and on him. These people were nothing but despicable peasants, after all.

He saw the closed windows, the shut doors, the empty alleyways and the silent market place. Every citizen had turned his face to the wall and shut his eyes, sooner than shame Lady Godiva.

Not quite *every* one shut their eyes. Tom Henny rubbed his sweaty hands in glee and knelt down by the keyhole. Tom often went out late at night and peeped through shutters in the hope of seeing a pretty girl undressing. The sight of Lady Godiva naked was going to be sweet as honey! Let the other prudes shut their eyes: Tom would look his fill. He licked his lips as the clip-clop of hooves came closer. He pressed his eye to the keyhole . . .

A sudden unseasonable swirl of wind gusted down the street, lifting an eddy of dust. Tom Henny gave a scream of pain. A piece of grit had embedded itself in his eye. As the hooves clopped by outside, he had no thought of seeing Lady Godiva, dressed or naked. All he could think about was getting the grit out of his eye.

Leofric waited in Cathedral Square for his wife to ride back the way she had gone. "I give in!" he called, as she came into view. He spoke in a loud voice, knowing the town stood listening behind its closed shutters. "You have your wish! I shall not impose the new tax. If that earns me the respect of these decent people, I shall be rich enough."

The town remembered that day – wrote of it in the annals of the county, with a sigh of admiration for Lady Godiva. They saved their scorn for Tom Henny – Peeping Tom, as they called him. He had to endure the silent contempt of his neighbours as, collar up, hat pulled down, he went about, day by lonely day, trying to conceal his one blind eye.

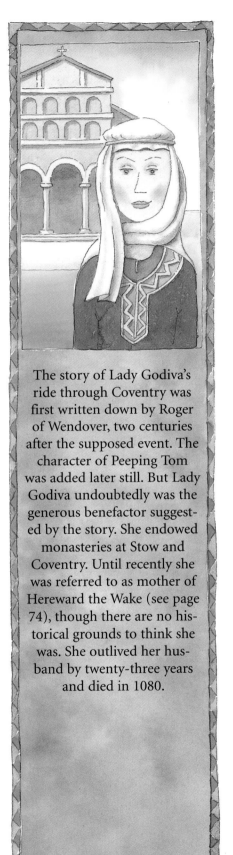

The story of Lady Godiva's ride through Coventry was first written down by Roger of Wendover, two centuries after the supposed event. The character of Peeping Tom was added later still. But Lady Godiva undoubtedly was the generous benefactor suggested by the story. She endowed monasteries at Stow and Coventry. Until recently she was referred to as mother of Hereward the Wake (see page 74), though there are no historical grounds to think she was. She outlived her husband by twenty-three years and died in 1080.

Swearing on the Bones

1064

Before the death of Edward the Confessor, promises were flying about more plentiful than starlings around the spires of Westminster Abbey. King Edward favoured Harold, Earl of Wessex, as his successor, but William, Duke of Normandy, had a powerful claim as well. There was bound to be a struggle for power when the old King died. Already the rival candidates were trying to extract promises of support from anyone and everyone.

Then Harold was shipwrecked on the shores of France, and taken prisoner. Duke William was informed, and arranged for Harold to be set free. Indeed, Harold was very glad to escape a stone dungeon floor and sharing his food with rats.

So when the two men met, there was no unpleasantness between them Harold said how grateful he was. William said it was nothing: all that he asked in exchange was that Harold should swear to forfeit his claim and help William to his rightful place on the throne of England. "Here. Your word on it!"

The table was spread with cloth of gold. Wine stains and fragments of chicken speckled it, but William cleared space to set down the Gospels.

Did Harold wet his lips or look shiftily about? Did he hide one hand under his tabard and cross his fingers? No. Harold had lied to better men than this before now. He would lie with gusto, knowing that the throne rightfully belonged to him, knowing that God would turn a deaf ear. Solemnly, he laid his hand on the Gospels – William covered it with his own, sword-hardened palm and Harold swore: "to help William, Duke of Normandy, to win the crown of England".

The hand lifted off his. He felt his freedom already. He could not wait to get back across the Channel. With the flourish of a magician, William of Normandy drew off the cloth of gold; it cracked like a banner on a windy day. His eyes were still on Harold, still fixing him, as a cat fixes a cornered mouse. Two armed men sprang forward, and Harold thought, they are going to stab me.

But the two soldiers only lifted the table top off its trestle legs to reveal, underneath, a big carved,

darkwood chest. That too was opened. Inside it lay something which stood Harold's hair on end.

"Bones?" he said.

"The relics of a dozen saints," said William. "Can there be any oath so solemn as the oath sworn on the relics of a saint?"

Harold went pale and shuddered. Not for an instant did he consider keeping his promise, laying aside his claim to the throne. But it was as if, in that moment, the windows of heaven closed and the angels deserted him.

Edward the Confessor did name Harold his heir; the Witan Council of wise men elected him, too, and Harold said nothing in defence of Duke William's claim. In short, he broke his promise, in order to be crowned King of England.

William wrote reminding Harold "of the oath which thou hast sworn with thy hand upon good and holy relics". But Harold wrote back that he had promised what did not belong to him, "a promise which I could not in any way perform". War was just a matter of time.

That year Halley's comet swung low through the sky like a burning tear. What could it mean? Did it foretell disaster?

William mustered his invasion forces, but for a long time the wind blew against him. Indeed, hurricanes smashed his ships and drowned his crews. Perhaps the saints were not on his side after all. Overhead the comet hurtled on through space, bearing the colours of neither side, instead unfurling a blank white banner.

Then the Norwegian King invaded England from the north. Harold had to hurry north to Stamford Bridge and counter the invasion. He fought a masterly battle – defeated the Norwegians, and rode south again, flushed with victory. Perhaps the comet plunging past the earth meant disaster for the Northmen, after all. Or perhaps it acclaimed the coming of Harold the Victor, a king destined to win many such victories.

His fleet was still sailing up and down the Channel, guarding the south coast against William's threatened invasion. Still an adverse wind kept William from setting sail. Harold, rushing south as fast as his battle-weary army could go, smiled every time he saw a weathercock on a church roof.

But then the English navy ran out of provisions and had to put back to port for more. *That* was when the wind came about, when William set sail. Four days after the battle of Stamford Bridge, William of Normandy landed his invasion force at Pevensey Bay.

First ashore were the archers, shaven-headed, in short tunics. Then came the horsemen, in coats of mail, with polished conical helmets, lances and heavy broadswords. Next came the workmen: sappers and armourers, smiths and fletchers. And last of all came William himself.

Tripping, he promptly pitched on his face in the sand and cut himself. Superstitious dread seized on a thousand men. Was this an omen? Had the comet in the sky signalled disaster for the Normans and not, after all, for Harold the Oath-breaker?

With remarkable presence of mind (considering the pain in his knees), Duke William closed his fist around a lump of sandy soil and held it aloft. "Now I have taken possession of England and will defend it with my blood!" he bellowed, and a thousand men let go their pent-up breath in a gasp of relief.

Harold was in no mood to negotiate. Besides, he had already parcelled out England to his own choice of friends, knights and barons: they would never let him abdicate. So the English troops, only returned in the nick of time and exhausted from the high-speed journey, made their stand near Hastings, mustered on top of a hill, behind a wooden palisade. It gave the Normans marshy ground to cover and a steep climb before they could even cross swords with the English.

With horrid fascination the English watched a single rider break ranks and ride forward up the hill: a troubadour-knight known as Taillefer or "the Iron Cleaver". He began to sing – a ballad of heroism and self-sacrifice – and as he sang, he tossed his sword in the air and caught it, again and again, so that its arcing, somersaulting blade sliced the sunlight into spinning shards. It mesmerized the eye – such juggling, such foolhardy panache. With suicidal daring, Taillefer hurled himself on the first two Englishmen in his path, and cut them down, before he himself was pulled down and lost from sight amid the confusion of the first charge.

The Normans were galvanized into action. Time and again they made sallies up the hill, shouting, "God strengthen us!" but were thwarted by the wooden palisade and javelins thrown back with the cry, "God Almighty!" Duke William, leading a charge uphill, felt the horse under him shudder then plunge to its knees, a spear in its chest. But he no sooner hit the ground than he was on his feet again, leading the assault on the palisade. They captured the hill, but not the English standard. That stood at King Harold's side, surrounded by his finest knights, and evening was coming on.

"Shoot your arrows into the sky!" called William to his archers. "Let them fall on the English faces!"

The archers arched their backs, squinted into the evening clouds. They fired their arrows upwards as if they would shoot the very evening star out of the sky. And their arrows fell like rain.

Harold looked up at the sound of whistling in the skies, and saw a hail of death falling on him. It was the last thing he saw. An arrow entered his eye, filled his brain with light and then with darkness. Like a comet plummeting away into unfathomable space, Harold fell: from noise to silence, from glory to oblivion. All around him the English still cried, with futile desperation, "God Almighty!"

But all Harold could hear was the rattling of bones underground.

The full story of Harold's sworn oath, the Norman invasion and the battle of Hastings is told in the Bayeux Tapestry, a long strip of linen embroidered in wool, probably by English needlewomen. The embroidery was commissioned by Bishop Odo, half-brother of William the Conqueror, to commemorate the victory. It naturally presents William in a good light and Harold as an oath-breaker who deserved to lose the crown. The comet is there, foretelling Harold's downfall.

Unfortunately, it is now thought that the figure seen pulling an arrow from his eye may not be Harold at all. So the best "known" fact about Harold (i.e. that he died of an arrow in the eye) may not even be true. No other record exists describing his death.

Hereward the Wake

1070

He was always a wild boy. From the start, Hereward was so wild that they say his own father declared him an outlaw and drove him out to live in the forests and fens. Hereward was a young man full of rage and fire. But when the Normans came and the country was taken out of Saxon hands, Hereward's rage suddenly found a fitting target. He vowed to drive the Normans out of England or make them wish they had never come.

The good Saxon abbot of St Peter's Abbey had been replaced with a Norman one. So Hereward felt free to storm the Abbey and pillage it of every candlestick and cross and chalice. A military campaign needs funds, after all.

But afterwards, a dream rose into Hereward's sleep like mist rising off the fens. He saw St Peter, angry and woebegone, searching, searching under every bush and in the hollow of every tree. He was searching for his treasure. "Oh Hereward, Hereward, what have I ever done to you?" glared the eyes of St Peter.

At first light, Hereward packed up the treasure of St Peter's Abbey and sent it back – every last chalice, plate and candlestick. "My quarrel is with the Normans, not with the saints,"

he told his bewildered men. Armed with his sword Brainbiter, Hereward the Wakeful harried the Normans as a fox harries a chicken coop. Suddenly, stealthily, out of darkness or mist, his band of loyal Saxons would fall on barracks or encampments, on castles or shipments of coin, till the Normans were run ragged with chasing him. Elsewhere King William's Norman Conquest was quick, easy, unopposed. But in the fenlands, thanks to Brainbiter and the Saxon who wielded it, the rivers often ran red with Norman blood.

The landscape itself defied conquest. Hidden within its wet wilderness, Hereward and his men were as elusive as fish underwater. At long last, William found out that Hereward's stronghold was on the remote and moated Island of Ely. He determined, difficult as it would be, to put Hereward the "Wakeful" to sleep once and for all.

He would throw a bridge or causeway across the water, so that his army could storm the island. Of course, he needed labourers to build such a bridge, but it never occurred to him that the enemy would volunteer to help build it . . . Hereward covered his long blond hair with a hessian hood, shouldered a bag of tools and set off to build bridges for the Normans. Day after day, he sank pilings, raised levees, knocked in nails, dug drainage trenches. He even helped build the tower at one end of the bridge, though he was not sure what it was for.

"Ah! So you are the woman I sent for," said King William, suppressing a shudder of revulsion. "Do you know your task?"

The woman in front of him ran her fingers through tangled masses of greasy, grey plaits. "I must curse the Saxons and blast their souls to ashes." Her voice was so loud that the King involuntarily put his hands over his ears.

"Not that I believe in your magic," he said, paying her in French gold, "but these Saxons are as superstitious as fishwives. They have a horror of witches like you – and you, madam, have made an art of horror, so I hear."

The witch looked at him with contempt and fingered the mummified shrew strung round her neck. "You do your part, and I will do mine," she said.

As the causeway neared completion, William massed his forces, ready to swarm across the water into Hereward's stronghold. Shortly before dawn, the workmen were withdrawn. The French witch mounted the tower like a great black spider climbing into its web, and her ugly voice rasped out:

"A curse on you, Hereward's men! Your luck is held in a sieve! Your blood is curdling in your veins! The hairs fallen from your head are in my cauldron! I have spoken with the spirits. I have warned the worms of your coming! My toads have walked on your faces while you slept: I know your

dreams! My cat has scratched a hole for your skulls to lie in!"

Under the causeway, though no one knew it, one workman had remained behind. Hereward clung to the underside of the bridge like a crab in an upturned boat, and between his teeth was a burning fuse. He stuffed kindling into a crevice and lit it. Then he dropped down and waded, chin-deep, back to his island stronghold. The noise of the witch's insane laughter disturbed him. His men were as bold as greyhounds, but he knew what terror the black arts could strike in them. He saw their eyes glimmer in the dark, staring out at that crazy crone. Then he realized that the glimmer in their eyes was firelight. His fire had taken. The causeway was burning.

Two hundred Normans had already started across the bridge before they realized that it was alight. The witch was chanting incantations now, curses in rhyme. She worked herself to such a frenzy of abuse that she was unaware of the panic below, the splash of men jumping for their lives, the groaning of timbers breaking, the roar of fire. Gradually, an orange glare suffused the whole scene. throwing every figure into silhouette, showing the gaunt latticework of her flimsy tower.

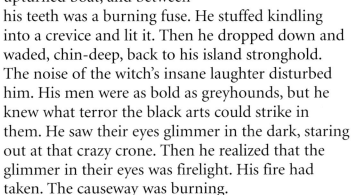

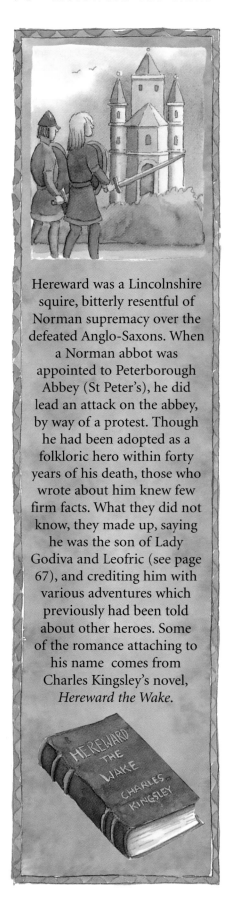

Hereward was a Lincolnshire squire, bitterly resentful of Norman supremacy over the defeated Anglo-Saxons. When a Norman abbot was appointed to Peterborough Abbey (St Peter's), he did lead an attack on the abbey, by way of a protest. Though he had been adopted as a folkloric hero within forty years of his death, those who wrote about him knew few firm facts. What they did not know, they made up, saying he was the son of Lady Godiva and Leofric (see page 67), and crediting him with various adventures which previously had been told about other heroes. Some of the romance attaching to his name comes from Charles Kingsley's novel, *Hereward the Wake*.

No one gave a thought to saving the witch – William's men were too busy saving themselves. When the fire reached her, she screamed curses against Norman and Saxon alike, dancing puppet-like on an orange platform. Then, with a soughing rush of wind and ash, the burning tower listed and toppled into the river. The witch was silenced. The marsh soaked up her black magic. A constellation of burning cinders settled with a hiss on the sodden landscape.

Of course sometimes the wild places of England can be as confusing and dangerous to a Saxon as to a Norman, and more than once Hereward himself went astray. After a daring raid on Stamford, as his band made their way through Rockingham Forest, cloud blotted out the moon and left them blunderingly, helplessly lost.

All of a sudden, a gentle light began to shine ahead of him, and he glimpsed another out of the corner of his eye. Soon, individual flames – disembodied balls of light – were settling like birds on the branch of each tree. A soldier gasped and dropped his shield, but Hereward picked it up and gave it back to him. "Don't be afraid," he said. "It's just St Peter returning a favour." And no mistake, there were candles of phosphorescence glowing on every tree and shield rim – enough to see by, enough to reach a dry bed by an Anglo-Saxon hearth.

Margaret's Prayer

1070-1071

K ING MALCOLM WAS NOT A MAN EASILY moved to pity. But when he saw Margaret, her sister and her mother, storm-soaked and exhausted, he was very moved indeed, and the feeling in his heart was nothing like pity.

A ship, bound for Hungary but driven ashore on the Scottish coast, had brought to his doorstep Edgar Aetheling, a claimant to the throne of England. The Norman conquest, rebellion and civil war had erased young Edgar's hopes of ever wearing the crown, and now he was fleeing for his life with his mother and two sisters, Christina and Margaret. Malcolm Canmore, King of Scotland, opened his door to the runaways – gave them food and shelter and warm whisky. But his eyes were always and only on Margaret, the stillness of her hands, the long-lashed lids of her downcast eyes.

Everything about Princess Margaret delighted him, from her soft psalm-singing to the Hungarian lilt of her accent. He was nearly forty and she was twenty-four. He quickly made up his mind to marry her. There was only one obstacle to overcome: Margaret was already promised in marriage: to God.

She had long since made up her mind to be a nun, and all her education had prepared her for a cloistered life. She was altogether out of place at the court of King Malcolm, a barbarous, uncultured man who swore and drank and whose chief joy in life was to ride over the border and kill Englishmen. So her mother and sister were startled when, without explanation, Margaret the pious, Margaret the pure, suddenly abandoned her vocation and agreed to marry Malcolm Canmore.

Pleased as he was, Malcolm was baffled by his new bride. She left his bed at unearthly hours of the night; she ate like a sparrow. She no sooner had money in her purse than it was gone and she was asking for more. She even stole from him! He saw her scribble hasty notes and dispatch them furtively by rider or runner. Even in broad daylight she would often disappear – he had no idea where – creeping out of the house alone, without a word, and not returning for hours.

Malcolm began to suspect the worst. Was she meeting a lover? Was she lavishing her money on some sweetheart? Could this lady, who had been unwilling to marry and stain her purity, really be deceiving him? He vowed to find out. The very next time she slipped away down the back stairs, he followed her, at a distance, to see where she went. He followed her northwards along the winding streets of Dunfermline town. How eagerly she moved, head down, hurrying through the alleyways! At last she ducked in at the dark doorway of a low building.

Hand on knife, Malcolm followed, swearing to kill her then and there if his suspicions proved right. Already he could hear that soft sweet voice of hers whispering tenderly . . .

The place was more of a cave than a room: a gloomy, secret place. Peeping inside, Malcolm crossed himself and dodged hastily backwards, cracking his head on the arch. Smiling now, he bent for a second look.

There knelt his wife in front of a simple altar, her lips moving in fervent prayer.

"Lord God, protect and bless my beloved husband, and grant me the power to work some good upon his nature. He does not mean to be so fierce and brutal. He has a good heart underneath his shouting and cursing. Be good to him! Perhaps he has his reasons. Perhaps he does not enjoy the same happiness as I am blessed with."

Tears of remorse sprang to Malcolm's eyes. How he had misjudged his beautiful queen! Well, he would make things up to her! Perhaps with her help he could even make things up with God! Following his wife home again, he saw what became of his stolen money, too. She gave it liberally to the beggars and maimed old soldiers who haunted the lanes of Dunfermline town.

After that, the court of Malcolm Canmore was a different place. Not that the Scottish lords there were any-the-less wild or warlike, but their days followed a different course. Every morning, nine little orphans were brought to the Queen's private room so that she could sit them on her

lap and feed them with her own spoon. Before every one of her own meals, the Queen would serve twenty-four poor people with food. The chamberlain had the nightly task of finding six poor people, fetching them to the castle, and making them presentable: because somewhere between a triple dose of prayers in the middle of the night and going briefly back to bed, the King and Queen liked to wash the feet of the poor, in keeping with what the Bible taught. During Lent as many as 300 needy citizens would file daily into the great hall, the doors would close, and the King and Queen in person would serve them a meal.

Monasteries and churches were built; religious men came to advise Malcolm on how to breathe new life into Scottish worship. And those hastily scribbled letters? They were indeed to spies. Margaret kept spies all over Scotland, so as to know about the English captives being held to ransom on Scottish soil. As well as ensuring that they were not cruelly treated during their captivity, she frequently paid their ransom herself.

She went on stealing gold from Malcolm's coffers; he often saw her do it. But now it made him laugh, rather than rage. His saintly little queen never ceased to amaze and astound Malcolm. Though she ate less than any of the chickens in the yard, she was tireless in her work. Furthermore, she gave birth to eight strong, healthy babies one after another, and they all lived to adulthood – a miracle indeed in those days.

One thing did not change about Malcolm's life; oddly, Margaret made no attempt to change it. She never said to Malcolm, "For the love of God or for love of me, don't go to war. Don't go raiding over the borders. Don't kill and plunder and burn . . ." Raids and wars were as much a part of her husband's life as the cut of his beard or the shoes he wore. But every day he was away, she prayed for his safe and speedy return. Even when she was ill. Even when the pain cramped her stomach like a sword thrust, she prayed for him and for his people rather than for herself.

She was ill when he set off the last time, with their oldest son, Edward. She was dying when they brought her the news that they were both dead.

If her waiting women expected Margaret to turn her face to the wall in despair – if they expected her to reproach God for rejecting her prayers, she surprised them one last time.

"All praise be to Thee Almighty God, who has been pleased that I should endure such deep sorrow at my departing, and I trust that by means of this suffering it is Thy pleasure that I should be cleansed from some of the stains of my sins." Then in the middle of reciting the Communion prayer, she simply stopped breathing.

Queen Margaret made a radical impact on eleventh-century Scotland. She was quickly declared a saint - Scotland's only royal saint - and though the account of her life by Turgot, her confessor, may exaggerate somewhat, her life patently merited sainthood. Turgot, a monk, was commissioned by Margaret's daughter (later Queen Matilda of England) to write *The Life of St Margaret*. Several miracles were reported soon after her death.

Who Killed Red Rufus?

1100

WHEN HE WAS ILL, THERE was no one more religious than William Rufus. But when he was well, he was the Devil made flesh. He plundered Church coffers and jeered and sneered at its faith. Each time a church post became vacant, Rufus postponed appointing a new man – left the position empty, and took all the revenue himself. Or else he sold the post to the highest bidder. There was not one sincere religious conviction in his whole blasphemous soul. The only music which moved him was the jingle of money and the cry of the hunt.

From the people, he took the great primaeval forests, declaring all the wild life in them his to hunt. And he guarded this royal prerogative with grotesque cruelty, maiming and hanging poachers, razing villages to the ground which were in his way. It is said that the Saxon oaks groaned under slavery to this Norman tyrant. Consequently, this ruddy-faced Rufus was not a man blessed with good friends . . . nor a man short of enemies.

One summer morning in 1100, William-called-Rufus was staying in Winchester, for the hunting. After a huge breakfast, he was preparing to hunt when a fletcher, or arrow-maker, presented him with six new arrows. He admired them, passed two to his closest companion, Walter Tirel, and went outdoors to the waiting horses. As he mounted up, a letter arrived post-haste from a monastery in Gloucestershire: a letter of warning.

One of the monks had dreamed a dream: a woman kneeling in front of the throne of Christ, begging Him to free England from the yoke of King William. The warning rolled harmless off the King's back. He just laughed, screwed up the letter, and spurred his horse to a gallop. Once inside the forest, the huntsmen split up. William and Tirel set up on either side of a clearing, while the beaters startled a roe deer out of the undergrowth. It sprang between the two men. The King raised his crossbow to shoot, but the arrow glanced off the deer's hide. "Shoot, Walter! Shoot!" shouted the King, and Tirel fired.

With a whistle, a thud, a bolt struck William Rufus in the chest. He was dead before he hit the ground. From everywhere, men came running forward to stare at the body on the ground. Tirel knelt over it. "It wasn't me!" he said.

"The arrow's like the ones he gave you this morning," the royal huntsman pointed out. The stares were all turned on Tirel now – fixed, accusing stares. Without a word, Tirel remounted his horse and galloped south, towards Southampton. He could see that he was going to get blamed, guilty or not.

Hours later, a pair of charcoal-burners were scuffing their way through the woods collecting brushwood and dead twigs when they came across the body of the King, the triple feathers of a crossbow bolt emerging from his chest like a seedling. Of his courtiers and huntsmen and friends – of his brother Henry – there was not a sign.

The charcoal burners bundled Rufus on to their handcart and trundled him out of the green forest gloom, jolting him over tree roots and leaving behind a trail of blood like scarlet periwinkles growing in his wake. "Him bled all the way," they told the priests at Winchester Cathedral, tipping the King out on to the stone slabs.

But no one was interested. Duke Henry was already there, at the cathedral, arguing with the bishop, trying to lay hands on the royal treasure which was kept there. *He* was now King, he said, the crown had passed to *him*. The argument grew noisy and undignified. The bishop maintained that William's *other* brother, Duke Robert, was the rightful heir. But Robert was away crusading – not there to defend his interests.

William Rufus, his face smeared redder than red now with his own heart's blood, lay on the flags of Winchester Cathedral and said nothing at all.

When it came to burying Rufus, the Church had its revenge. They called him an unbeliever, a heretic, a blasphemer. They called him an enemy of the Church and a sacrilegious villain. They deigned to sink him in the ground – under the floor of Winchester Cathedral, no less – but no one spoke a word of prayer over him. No one sanctified his burial or prayed for his soul.

Seven years later the cathedral tower crashed down, shattering sepulchres and statues, fonts and pulpits. Devout folk locally blamed the presence of evil Rufus.

But the people who lived by the forest saw things differently. They said that the forest, older than Christianity, had exacted a blood sacrifice, so that its crowns of green might continue to flourish. In that case, just whose hand fired the crossbow hardly matters.

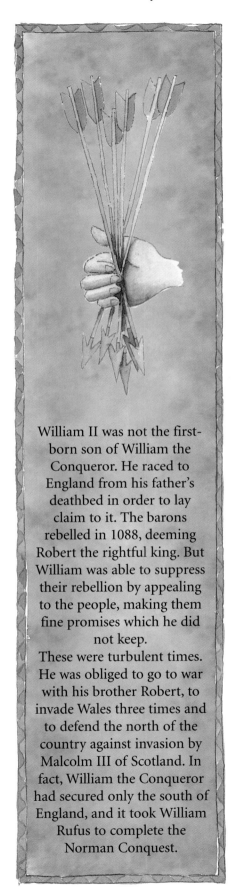

William II was not the first-born son of William the Conqueror. He raced to England from his father's deathbed in order to lay claim to it. The barons rebelled in 1088, deeming Robert the rightful king. But William was able to suppress their rebellion by appealing to the people, making them fine promises which he did not keep.

These were turbulent times. He was obliged to go to war with his brother Robert, to invade Wales three times and to defend the north of the country against invasion by Malcolm III of Scotland. In fact, William the Conqueror had secured only the south of England, and it took William Rufus to complete the Norman Conquest.

The White Ship

1120

AT LAST THERE WAS PEACE. After years of war between England and France, a peace had been struck, and the future blossomed with promise. King Henry I's heart was crammed with cheerful memories and optimistic plans as he boarded his ship at Barfleur, bound for England. The ship rubbed flanks with another in the harbour – *La Blanche Nef* – the *White Ship* – whose captain had begged for the honour of conveying the King's party home. But Henry's ship was ready, laden and rigged. So, sooner than snub the good captain, Henry had entrusted his children to the *White Ship*, along with the royal treasure. They could follow on the next tide, Prince William and the rest.

Of course, as far as Henry was concerned his children *were* the royal treasure. He was a harsh, demanding father, not above dragging one daughter through a frozen moat to teach her a lesson; but he adored his children. His oldest son, his heir, Prince William, had grown into as fine a young man as any father could hope for. In France he had won his spurs, remembered his manners, charmed the French court. And Maud! How lovely little Maud had looked as she wished him *bon voyage*. Fortunate England that it should enjoy both peace and the promise of such princes and princesses. Fortunate Henry. The sea was calm, the sky generous and big. The King watched Barfleur slip below the horizon, then walked to the prow to watch for the Dover coast.

The tide ebbed and flowed once more. The young people of the royal party, no longer required to be on their best behaviour, drank a little too much and became noisy and excitable. When French priests came down to the waterfront to bless *La Blanche Nef*, the English crew and passengers told them in blunt, colourful English: "Take yourselves off, you sheep-faced bunch of old women!" Even so, long after the *White Ship* had set sail, one of those priests stayed on, looking out to sea, moving his lips in silent prayer. He stood there till the grey of evening turned to night.

On board the King's ship, the look-out cocked his ear and looked back southwards. Everyone heard it: a strange shrill cry carrying over the water. Gulls, they thought. Gulls, thought the King.

The *White Ship*'s eager captain, Thomas Fitz-Stephen, had set himself the task of overtaking the royal ship, proving the excellence of both ship and crew. The prow cut smartly through the waves, unslowed by cross-winds or swell. But the steersman, either drunk or ignorant of the rocky Raz de Catteville, was taking the *White Ship* to her death.

When she struck rocks submerged by high tide, the people aboard loosed a cry – a single scream of horror which travelled like cannonfire across the sea. Within minutes the vessel lay with her keel ripped open, the sea gushing in.

"Hold her to the rocks with grappling hooks!" Captain Fitz-Stephen commanded. "The rocks will hold her up till help comes!" But the rocks only chewed the ship apart, board by board.

"Get the prince away safe!" commanded the captain, and even amid the panic and confusion, one jolly-boat was got off, with Prince William kneeling up, white-faced on the rear thwart.

It was not a sight for a boy to see – his friends, his brothers, his sisters being washed one by one off the tilting deck. The noise was terrible – the howled prayers, the curses, the cries, the submerged rocks grinding on the keel. If the tide had been lower, the rocks themselves would have stuck up out of the water: somewhere to cling. But the rocks were only a darkness now below the water. Swimmers trod nothing but numbing, icy water.

"My sister! I hear my sister!" cried Prince William. "Row back! We must save Maud!" His beloved sister's screams drew him like a magnet.

The rowers did turn back. They were able to snatch Maud from where she clung to the stringy rigging sluiced by icy sea. But the water round about her was alive with swimmers. Like sharks they snatched at the oars. Hands shark-blue with cold came over the side of the boat, the drowning trying to pull themselves aboard. Desperately, the rowers tried to prise the fingers loose, but the boat rolled lower and lower . . . until the sea simply washed in over the back and sucked everything down in the foundering swirl of the *White Ship*.

Captain Fitz-Stephen, surfacing from an eternity of airless cold, grasped a broken spar to keep himself afloat. Two men erupted through the surface nearby and heaved themselves over a piece of flotsam. One was a scrawny young courtier, Geoffrey Daigle, wearing thin, torn silks, one a fat Barfleur butcher in a sheepskin jacket.

"What of the King's son? Are the King's children safe?" called the captain.

"All gone! Drowned and gone!" came the reply, and the captain, his honour already drowned in the Raz de Catteville, let go the spar and slid back down into the dark. Better to die than to live with the shame of what he had done.

Before morning the butcher of Barfleur found himself alone on the ocean, sole survivor of the wreck of the *White Ship*.

It is said that the royal treasure washed up intact on a French beach. Not so the heir to the English throne.

When the news reached England, no one knew how to tell the King. No one wanted to be the man who broke the King's heart. So they found a young boy and taught him to say the words parrot-fashion. "The *White Ship* is gone down, sire. Your children are lost."

When the King heard the words, he rose to his feet and stood silent for a few moments. Then his knees gave way, and he crashed to the ground, unconscious. It is said that King Henry I never smiled again.

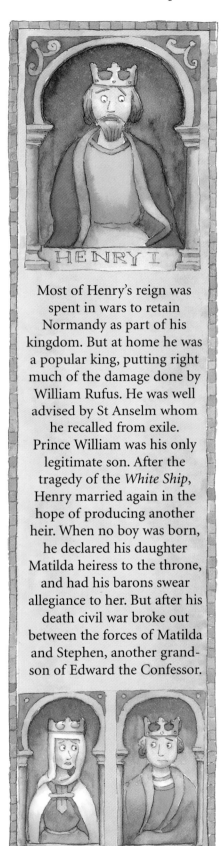

HENRY I

Most of Henry's reign was spent in wars to retain Normandy as part of his kingdom. But at home he was a popular king, putting right much of the damage done by William Rufus. He was well advised by St Anselm whom he recalled from exile. Prince William was his only legitimate son. After the tragedy of the *White Ship*, Henry married again in the hope of producing another heir. When no boy was born, he declared his daughter Matilda heiress to the throne, and had his barons swear allegiance to her. But after his death civil war broke out between the forces of Matilda and Stephen, another grandson of Edward the Confessor.

MATILDA   STEPHEN

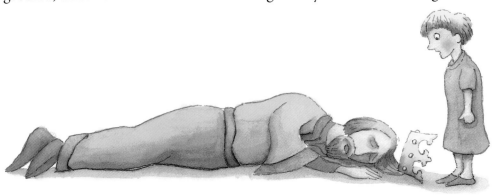

"This Turbulent Priest"

1170

As young men, Thomas à Becket and King Henry II were the best of friends. They were forever horsing about, vying with each other as to who wore the most splendid clothes or made the most witty remark. Once, the King had pulled off Thomas's cloak for a joke, and given it to a poor old man, telling Becket that "charity demanded it".

Thomas was only a low-born commoner, but he showed such genius at any and every job that he rose from soldier to ambassador to chancellor! Henry was happy to work hand-in-glove with clever, witty, tactful, *loyal* Thomas. He even entrusted his son's education to him.

The Church, on the other hand, was regularly troublesome to Henry. The Church felt less need to obey the King than it did God and the Pope. Henry's solution was to put someone he could trust in authority over the Church. And who better than Becket?

"I do not want the office," said Thomas. "You will take your favour from me, and our love will then become hatred."

Henry should have listened; Becket's advice had always been sound. But he brushed the warning aside. In 1162, Thomas à Becket was consecrated Archbishop of Canterbury.

He changed then. As if Henry had accidentally spoken some magic word, Becket began to alter. He resigned as chancellor, laid aside the rich clothes, the vanity and splendour of court life, and dressed like a monk, with a hair shirt against his skin. Each night, after supper, he had himself flogged, in penance for his sins. He gave away his belongings – and he gave over his loyalty – the loyalty which, till that time had belonged entirely to Henry II – to God and to the Church.

Suddenly he was the champion of the clergy, defending the Church against any and every attack. Henry found to his dismay that, far from gaining influence over the Church, he was being thwarted at every turn by Archbishop Becket. Henry felt betrayed. Becket's former friends and colleagues felt betrayed.

The two men clashed most fiercely when Henry tried to make the clergy answerable to the law. At that time, a priest could rob or murder or burn down a house and still escape arrest. Extraordinarily, Becket refused to give up this much-abused privilege. Henry retaliated by confiscating castles and fining Becket for leaving his post as chancellor. He took his son out of Becket's care.

On the day the King's pages threw mud at him and called him "Traitor!", Becket realized the danger he was in, and took a ship for France. For two years the cold Channel flowed between the two friends, and a still colder hostility.

Then the quarrel was patched up and Becket came home. The nobility still resented him, but not the common people. He was one of them! He was a saintly man who daily washed the feet of the poor! They had tasted his charity, his goodness, his sanctity! They welcomed him home like a conquering hero, thronging Canterbury in the hope of glimpsing the great man.

Becket had not mellowed in the least. He was as pious and as unyielding as ever. Now he began to wield a power even Henry did not possess. He began to excommunicate his enemies.

A king can cut off a man's head, but the man's soul is free to fly up to heaven. An archbishop – by snuffing out a candle, ringing a bell, closing a book – can condemn a man's soul to burn in everlasting fire. How could Henry compete with that kind of power?

Far away, in his French territories, Henry raged at Becket's insolence, pride and thanklessness. "A fellow that has eaten my bread! A fellow that came to court on a lame horse with a cloak for a saddle!" He fumed and fulminated. His chair turned over, and he began to pace the room, throwing his hands about in melodramatic gestures, smacking at his forehead, groaning and gasping with exasperation. "What cowards have I brought up in my court, who care nothing for their duty to their master! Will no one rid me of this turbulent priest?"

Four knights – Sir Reginald Fitzurse, Sir Richard le Breton, Sir Hugh de Merville and Sir William Tracy – looked at one another, got up and left the room. They sailed to England that night.

They rode to Canterbury Cathedral with a band of horsemen, but went inside alone, unarmed. Naturally. It is a sacrilege to wear a sword inside a church.

Becket kept them waiting. When he finally deigned to see them, there were heated words behind closed doors, and then an argument which spilled out into public.

"We bring you the commands of the King . . . Will you come with us to the King and account for yourself?"

"I will not."

"Absolve the bishops you excommunicated!"

"I will not!"

Their voices rang up and down the echoing cloisters of the huge building. "In that case, the King's final demand is that you depart out of this realm and never return!"

"I do not choose to go. Nothing but death shall part me from my Church!"

At that moment, the bell began to ring for vespers. The great cathedral stirred itself for divine service. The nave would be filling with townspeople. The sounds of holy ritual chased the knights outside into the late afternoon. There they threw off their white cloaks – and began buckling on swords.

A friend of Becket's, who had witnessed the argument, shook his head anxiously. "My lord Archbishop, it is a pity you will never be advised. You would have done far better to have kept quiet and answered them mildly."

But Becket was in no mood for advice or soft words. He set out along the cloisters, towards the cathedral, to conduct vespers – found he had left his cross behind – would not go on till it was fetched. Monks flitted past in alarmed disorder. "They are arming!"

"Let them arm. Who cares?" Those were Becket's exact words.

The monks wanted to lock the cathedral doors – they had already locked the hall door.

"I will not have the church turned into a castle," said Becket irritably.

Meanwhile, finding the hall doors locked against them, the four knights could have gone round to the main entrance and got in easily, but they dragged a ladder over to a window and broke in that way, hurrying through the building, hard on the heels of Becket.

Daylight was all but gone. The only light in the nave came from banks of tallow candles: lozenges of gold floating in the cavernous dark. Some monks had run and hidden. Others were determined to protect their archbishop, even if it cost them their lives. "What are you afraid of?" asked Becket, annoyed by their busy comings and goings.

"Where is the traitor? Where is Thomas Becket?" *Becket-ket-ket*. It echoed round the nave. No one answered.

"Where is the archbishop . . . *ishop . . . ishop*?"

That title Becket was ready to acknowledge. "I am here."

Fitzurse had never meant this to happen. He owed so much to Becket. In a low quick whisper he said: "Flee, or you are a dead man."

"I am ready to die. And may the Church, through my death, obtain peace and liberty. I charge you in the name of God that you hurt no one here but me."

There was a noise of running feet: townspeople had heard there was something amiss and began flocking up the nave now, only to find a man with a sword barring their way to the choir. The darkness added to the confusion.

Fitzurse suddenly grabbed Becket and tried to drag him away. Perhaps he still thought to take the archbishop prisoner and avoid bloodshed. But Becket tore loose: "Off, Reginald. Touch me not!"

Then Tracy and le Breton were on him. But Thomas was tall and strong: he threw Tracy to the ground. He called Fitzurse a Judas. Again Fitzurse told him to run. Again Becket refused. In a clumsy muddle of movements, Fitzurse waved his sword and knocked off Becket's mitre; perhaps he was still trying to frighten him. A monk tried to fend off the second, heavy, downward blow, but fell to his knees as the blade broke his arm, and cut deep into Becket's head. A third stroke felled Thomas to his knees, hands raised as if in prayer.

For a moment all was stillness: a candlelit silence. Then Becket keeled over on to his face, with no more noise than a cloak makes in falling from a man's shoulders.

A fourth blow scalped him. The most vicious wound of all was made last, through the open wound. They made very sure the "turbulent priest" was dead.

When Europe heard the news, it quaked like a drumskin. The primate of England murdered in his own cathedral on the orders of his King?

When Henry heard the news, he gasped and wept inconsolably. What a terrible mistake, he cried. His words had been misunderstood! He had never meant his old friend to be murdered!

When he got back to England, he took off his royal clothes and walked barefoot to Canterbury Cathedral in a hair shirt and pilgrim's cloak, to kiss the flagstones where his friend had died. Beside the tomb, he fell weeping on his face and allowed each one of the eighty bishops and monks to lash him with whips: five lashes each.

The watching thousands crowding the streets of Canterbury were impressed. Nothing less would have satisfied them, but they were impressed.

Quite soon there came news of miracles bestowed by the dead archbishop. Pilgrims began to converge on Canterbury from all over the country. After all, Becket the martyr was an easier man to love than Becket the cantankerous archbishop. And the common people had a new voice to speak for them in heaven: a man low-born like themselves, their very own saint.

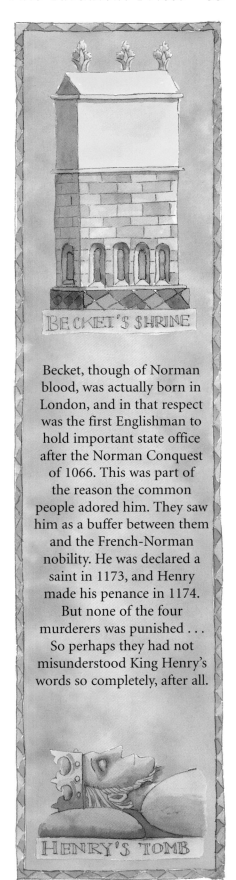

BECKET'S SHRINE

Becket, though of Norman blood, was actually born in London, and in that respect was the first Englishman to hold important state office after the Norman Conquest of 1066. This was part of the reason the common people adored him. They saw him as a buffer between them and the French-Norman nobility. He was declared a saint in 1173, and Henry made his penance in 1174. But none of the four murderers was punished . . . So perhaps they had not misunderstood King Henry's words so completely, after all.

HENRY'S TOMB

The Fair Rosamond

about 1175

ELEANOR OF AQUITAINE WAS A WOMAN WHO HAD GONE TO THE Crusades, worn eastern robes in the palaces of Constantinople, captured the hearts of a hundred troubadours and broken them all by marrying a second husband, this time for love.

But Henry II was ten years younger than she, and a man of such immoderate passions that, in his tempers, he bit men's shoulders or fell on his face and chewed the straw. It was unlikely, from the very outset, that he would ever give his love to Eleanor alone.

He had a whole gaggle of lovers, but none took so firm a hold on his heart as Rosamond Clifford, known as the Fair Rosamond.

Some said that they had been sweethearts since childhood days, and that Henry had secretly married Rosamond before he ever met Queen Eleanor. But whatever the truth, Henry determined to keep Rosamond both secret from the Queen and hidden from any eyes but his. So he shut her up – a willing captive – somewhere he was sure the Queen would never find her, and he visited her as often as he was in Oxfordshire. Perhaps the Queen suspected. Perhaps she kept watch. Or perhaps it was by chance that she saw Henry striding out one day across his estates at Woodstock Park, and spotted something trailing from his heel. His spur had snagged a thread of silk, and as he walked towards the house, it pulled taut behind him. Where had he been, to have embroidery thread caught around his spur?

He did not see Eleanor standing in the shade of a tree, and when he had passed by, she stepped out and picked up the thread, following it back in the direction the King had come. Through the vegetable garden it ran, around a bush, across a grassy lawn to the maze.

It was notoriously huge and complex, the maze Henry had designed to ornament his park; a knot of paths circling and doubling back on themselves. Eleanor had never entered it, for she was a busy woman and could not spare time on such idle amusements. But she entered it now.

The paths wound to and fro until, without the thread to guide her, Eleanor would have been hopelessly lost. But the strand of blood-red silk led her unerringly to the centre, and at the centre she found a door. Through the door she went, down stairs into a subterranean passage-way which twisted as intricately below ground as the maze had done above. She was not bewildered by the dark and twisting corridors, for she had the thread in her hand. She had long since guessed what she would find at her journey's end.

Soon a glimmer of light showed ahead of her, and the passage opened into a large, well-lit room hung with tapestries. A beautiful young woman with yellow hair leaned intently over her embroidery; at her feet a basket of silks, the red skein half pulled out and unravelled almost to its end. The sewer looked up, thinking that Henry had forgotten something and returned. Her lovely face registered first shock, then fear, then a slightly proud defiance.

"Tell me your name," demanded the Queen.

"I am Rosamond Clifford, ma'am."

"Are you held prisoner here against your will?"

"Oh no, ma'am! It is my joy and duty to –"

But Eleanor had turned her back – gone. Within half an hour she had returned. In the meantime, Rosamond's courage had risen. "Did you ask him? Did Henry tell you? We were married these many years since, and have a son true-born and –"

"I will ask you again," Eleanor interrupted. "Are you held prisoner here against your will?"

"I told you before," said Rosamond. "I am not."

Rosamond Clifford may well have married Henry when he was a boy; he once swore that their son was legitimate. But whether and however Eleanor discovered her husband's secret love, the part about the poison and the dagger never happened. Rosamond died much later at Godstow Abbey near Oxford, where she had been living for many years. Perhaps Eleanor obliged her to enter the convent.

Eleanor of Aquitaine continued to be a sore trial to her husband in all kinds of ways. She tended to support his enemies and favour her sons before her husband. But given their natures, it must have been an extraordinary marriage.

The mazes built in those days would have been elaborate, raised-turf patterns, not the obscuring kind with high hedges, so the story of the thread is also probably a fiction.

"In that case, you are free to go," said the Queen. She took out from a pouch at her belt a little Turkish dagger, souvenir of the Crusades, also a small bottle of some blue-green liquid. "Shall you die by the dagger or by the poisoned cup? For die you shall, Fair Rosamond, and with you your shame and the shame of my husband, King of England."

There was no crying out, no appealing to Henry to overrule his wife; they were far from the house and deep underground. "Nothing you can do will alter the fact that Henry loves me best!" said Rosamond through her tears. "Nothing in any of your apothecary's bottles will ever serve to make you young again, nor blot out the truth – that you were married first to King Louis and abandoned him so as to be Queen of England! I *love* Henry! I have always loved Henry – not his country, not his title! And Henry loves me. So which of us do you think is his *true* wife?"

But it was fruitless to argue with Eleanor about love. Eleanor knew all about love. Leaving the house, she locked the door behind her. Leaving the maze, she sheathed the little Turkish dagger. For Rosamond had chosen the poison in preference to the blade. Even now she lay amid her tapestries and silks with an empty cup in her hand and a thread of spilled wine amid her yellow hair.

The Troubadour Rescues His King

1193

"HAIL, KING OF ENGLAND, IN VAIN YOU disguise yourself. Your face betrays you." As Richard awoke, it was a moment before he could remember where he was, or what had brought him to be captured at sword point in this dirty, ill-lit room which smelled of ale. Then it came back to him – his eventful homeward voyage from the Holy Land, his landfall on unfriendly shores, his attempt to reach home, disguised as a peasant. Now, in this flea-ridden inn, alone and friendless in exceedingly dangerous times, he had fallen into the hands of Duke Leopold of Austria.

Richard had made enemies of half the crowned heads of Europe. They tussled over him like dogs over a bone. Duke Leopold waited to see who would offer most for his prestigious prisoner. His enemies either wanted to ransom Richard for cash, or to kill him. His brother, Prince John, was longing to hear that Richard had died on his way home so that he could seize the crown of England. If news could be kept quiet of Richard's capture, there was a chance he would moulder away in some obscure dungeon and never reappear.

Fortunately, the truth got free. Rumours of the King's capture spread far and wide: somewhere the King of England, Richard the Lion-Hearted, lay in chains, his only hope the persistence of his friends in seeking him out.

Blondel was a troubadour – a writer of ballads, a singer of roundelays. Richard was partial to music and verse and to handsome young men. He had encouraged and rewarded Blondel, and Blondel was, in return, devoted to his king. As soon as he heard Richard was missing, he vowed he would travel the world until he had found him.

Day after week after month the troubadour roamed Europe, earning his bread with a song, sleeping under the stars. A musician could go anywhere. So long as Blondel was careful whom he questioned and how many questions he asked, he would not arouse suspicion. And if he kept his eyes open and listened carefully in the alehouses and market squares, he was sure he could track Richard down.

Eighteen months later, having found no trace or whisper of an imprisoned king, he was less sure.

At last, just when he was on the point of despair, he struck up conversation with an innkeeper's wife. She said: yes, there was a rumour – it might only be gossip – you know how people talk – but up at the castle – that gloomy place, aye, up yonder by the river – she had heard tell there was a prisoner locked up in the tower who was of such importance that the duke guarded him day and night.

Tall, people said he was, with the kind of clothes the angels in heaven would wear if they could afford them. Blondel feigned a mild interest and bent his head low over his lute, tuning its strings . . .

As soon as he could get away without attracting attention, he climbed the road to the castle, meandered through the open gates. Taking up a position at the foot of the tower, he began to sing, loudly and brightly.

Pigmen at the sties, squires at the tilt, ladies embroidering at their windows all glanced curiously in his direction. It was not unusual for troubadours to travel about the countryside singing for their supper, and it made a pleasant interlude in the forbidding silence of brooding Castle Dürrenstein. Blondel's sweet voice echoed off the wall and came back at him, mocking. He shifted his ground to the other side of the tower, and sang again.

Slumped in his cell, his wrists shackled by long chains, assailed by the smell of the slop pail and his warders' feet, Richard Coeur de Lion fumbled his way out of a dream. He had dreamed he was in England again, singing a duet with dear Blondel. The pain of finding himself still imprisoned in his cell was as sharp as ever. The singing had stopped.

Blondel's singing had caught the attention of the castle keeper, a young knight with a large retinue of musicians and entertainers. The troubadour's voice and appearance were most agreeable, and time hangs heavy for a knight in times of peace. There was great prestige to be had from entertaining an accomplished troubadour, so he invited Blondel to join his retinue. Blondel accepted at once. It would give him time to delve deeper into the castle's secrets.

For several weeks Blondel sang and wrote verse and indulged in witty conversation with the castle staff, though to no effect. They gave nothing away. Perhaps they knew nothing. Perhaps he was wasting his time in the wrong place, while Richard lay rotting somewhere else entirely . . .

Richard, who paced his cell endlessly to exercise his legs, looked out of the window, tormented to see other men walking free. The roses in the keeper's garden were just coming into bloom. He watched them, recalling the dog-roses in the English hedgerows. The knight was out enjoying his rose garden, too. With him were all his foolish, fashionable hangers-on – pretty boys every one of them. Suddenly Richard gripped the bars and his cheeks scraped against their rusty metal. Could it be? Could it possibly be?

Richard knew he must not call out, must not draw attention to Blondel if he were there incognito. But oh! They were turning away – moving out of the garden! How to signal Blondel without endangering

his life? Richard cleared his throat. He had had no cause to sing for a year and a half, but now he began a song – a song he and Blondel had sung together a dozen times, a song he had no difficulty in remembering.

> *"If everything were as I wish it,*
> *We would not divided be;*
> *He in the east and I in the west*
> *And in between, the sea."*

Smiling despite himself, he fixed his eyes on his troubadour's face and willed him to hear.

A spasm passed through Blondel, which he hid with a sneeze. Unwrapping his lute from its cloth bag, he began to strum it. Supplying the chords at first, then joining in the descant of the song floating down from the tower, he moved away little by little from the group of squires and jongleurs. He was singing louder now, joining in split harmony with the singer in the tower, just as he had done a dozen times sitting at Richard's feet.

> *"The time until his ship comes home,*
> *Is time most pitiful to me;*
> *He in the east and I in the west,*
> *And in between, the sea."*

When the song ended, Blondel calmly wrapped up his lute again and sauntered back to the others. Tomorrow he would tell the knight that he was leaving – on a pilgrimage or a Crusade. Then he would quit Castle Dürrenstein and head for England.

He knew now where the King was being held. Prince John might try to persuade the people his brother had died, but Blondel knew differently. He could tell the churchmen and barons and ministers and diplomats where to find their true king. All the way home, that knowledge gave rise to new songs which the troubadour sang to the seagulls from the deck of the cross-Channel packet.

Although it is true the Duke of Austria captured Richard and imprisoned him at Dürrenstein, the King was soon moved to Castle Triefels in Germany where he was tried and offered freedom in exchange for an astronomical ransom. Great doubt has to be cast on the truth of the Blondel legend, though the troubadour probably was part of Richard's retinue. £100,000 was raised in ransom – a sum which beggared England after years already spent financing Richard's crusading. The Lion Heart, spoiled, reckless, full of vices and never home, was hardly his country's best friend.

The Three Outlaws

about 1 2 0 0

THE MEN OF THE NORTH COUNTRY could not come to terms at all with King John's claim to own the Forest of Englewood. It is one thing to say that the cows in a field belong to the farmer who raised them. It is quite another to say that the deer, the partridge, the wild pig and rabbits belong to one man, simply because he says so. The men of the borderlands continued to hunt there as their fathers and grandfathers had always done.

But the sheriff and justice of Carlisle were eager to prove themselves loyal officers of the King, so they hanged one man after another for killing the King's deer.

Sooner than hang, accused men slipped away into the forest and lived as outlaws, never able to visit their homes or families again. And the three bravest who ever took shelter under the greenwood trees were Adam Bell, Clym of the Cleugh, and William Cloudeslee.

One night, by the campfire, William said, "It's half a year since I saw my wife and children. Tomorrow I think I'll take a walk into Carlisle Town and pay them a visit."

"Don't be a fool, Will!" exclaimed Adam. "The sheriff has your house watched! It's too dangerous. Doesn't the little pig-boy bring you messages from home? Be content!"

But Will's mind was made up. He mingled among the last travellers of the day and arrived just before the city gates shut for the night, making his way from shadow to shadow, to rap on the shutters of his house. His wife's pale face appeared at the window.

"Will! Are you mad? What a risk to come here!" But she slipped the latch, and Will Cloudeslee was once again in his wife's arms, his children dangling from his belt and wrists and jerkin. He could hardly credit how much and how little things had changed. Alice was as beautiful as ever. His children had grown so big! Old Meg still sat by the fire.

"She's *still* here?" Will whispered.

"Of course! You said she could stay, when she had nowhere else to go. She took you at your word!" Alice whispered, laughing. "She's part of the furniture now."

Will greeted the old lady by the fire, asked after her health, then turned his attention to his family.

Everyone thought Old Meg was bed-ridden; a harmless, helpless old woman. So they never thought she could slip out of her shadowy corner, out of the house and away down the alley. Never for a moment did it occur to them that a guest treated with such kindness might betray them for a quick profit. Old Meg went straight to the sheriff. "If I give into your hands that outlaw William Cloudeslee, what will you give me?"

Old Meg sold Will to his enemies for a piece of scarlet cloth, then creeping back to her place by the fire, she sat with the parcel crammed under her dress, warming her wicked knees.

At around midnight, Alice glanced out of the window, and saw the glimmer of chain mail. Armed men. "You are betrayed, Will," she said. "Run!"

But it was too late. The sheriff's men surrounded the building and there was nothing for it but to stay and fight, or surrender and be taken. "Get into the bedroom," said Alice picking up an axe. "I'll guard the door while you use your bow."

Will looked at her across the heads of their children. "I do not deserve you," he said.

The sheriff sneered when he saw his best men running to shelter from Will's flying arrows. "Burn the place down! That will put an end to his archery."

The town's people, brought from their beds by the commotion, gave a roar of protest as they saw burning faggots stacked against the house. "What about the man's children? What about his wife? For shame!"

The sheriff simply narrowed his eyes against the smoke, covered his nose against the stench of burning.

Will fought on till the sound of his children's crying blinded his own eyes with tears. "I won't have your lives on my conscience!" he called to Alice. "Pull the sheets off the bed and tear them in strips . . ."

Alice would have chosen to stay with her husband, but for the sake of her children she allowed Will to lower them all to safety down ropes of knotted sheets. The people in the street rushed forward in such numbers to help them down that the sheriff's archers were knocked off their feet. The burning house overhung them like a breaking wave of fire.

Remembering Old Meg, Will ran to save her, too. But the old crone only boggled at him, with mad, soot-rimmed eyes, and clutched a parcel to her stomach. She would not let it go – not even to put her arms around his neck. Back he ran to the window, firing arrows till the flames singed and broke the bowstring. Then he stepped out on to the sill. So much chain mail was gathered in the street below that it looked like silver sea into which he leapt . . .

"Who is the gallows for?" the little pig-boy asked the morning watchman.

"For William Cloudeslee, the outlaw," came the response.

The boy ran with the news all the way to the greenwood. "Adam Bell! Clym of the Cleugh! Where are you?" Then, crouched by the camp fire, he told them their friend was condemned to hang at noon.

"That doesn't give us long," said Adam thoughtfully. "Can you get us into Carlisle, boy?"

"Not till the gates open again! The sheriff has ordered them kept shut till Will is dead!"

"Ah, but they will open for a *King's messenger*, I know," said Clym, whose plan was already taking shape. "You and I, Adam, shall pretend to be messengers bearing a letter for the sheriff. There's only one small difficulty . . ."

"What? The guard? The gatekeeper?" Adam was eager to help.

"No. The fact that I'm not a *writing* kind of man."

Fortunately, Adam Bell could both read and write. With a tree stump for his table, he penned an impressive-looking letter which they rolled up and sealed with candle-tallow. Forest bark served in place of the royal seal. "A fitting seal for a king who thinks he owns the forest," said Adam Bell.

"No one enters until the outlaw is dead," said the gatekeeper for the third time.

"Then you'd best tell the hangman to prepare for a second hanging!" roared Adam Bell, "for by this hand, the King will have you hanged if you delay his messengers another minute!"

The gatekeeper blenched. He looked at the letter they wagged in his face, but he was not a reading sort of man, and he could not have told the royal seal from a lump of candle-tallow. So he opened up, and the two men strode in.

As he went to hang the keys back inside the gatehouse, an arm circled his throat and a hand relieved him of the keys. The "King's messenger" he had just admitted said, "I think *I* shall be gatekeeper of Carlisle today, and you shall be Clym of the Cleugh. Bind him, Adam, and see that he doesn't escape."

William was carried to the gallows bound hand and foot, lying face down in the execution cart. The streets were full of angry murmurings. "What has the man done but shoot a deer? Shame on the sheriff for his spite! Shame on the justice for his heartlessness!"

William was lifted to his feet, and a noose placed around his neck. The ropes round his ankles were freed so that he could climb the ladder to the gallows. The sheriff of Carlisle stood at his window rubbing his hands with glee. Beside him stood the justice, saying, "One fewer outlaw to trouble the King's deer . . ."

Those were the last words he spoke. Two arrows flew across the town square and plunged into the hearts of both sheriff and justice.

Then chaos. Adam cut Will's bonds, and Clym cleared a path across the square with his sword. The guards, slow to realize what was happening, had to push the crowds aside to give chase through the narrow streets. Under their feet they found the city pigs, let loose from their sties to trip them up. The three outlaws had plenty of time to unlock, open, close and relock the city gate. They stood on the outside breathless and laughing.

Clym slung the keys over the top of the gate. "I resign as gatekeeper!" he called. "I think I'll go back to an honest profession as outlaw!"

When they reached Englewood they found a visitor in their camp. She stood amid the green-clothed men, children clinging to her skirts, weeping as if her heart were broken. "And all for my sake!" they heard her say.

"Alice?" said Will Cloudeslee.

She stared at him as if he might be a ghost. "But I thought . . . I thought you must be dead!"

"Who, me? Never!" Then he drew his wife aside, kissed her and made her this promise. "Go home, my love. Wait for me seven years, and I shall return to you a pardoned man. Adam and Clym and I shall go to London and win the King's forgiveness. Until then, Alice, keep me alive in your thoughts and prayers, and I shall keep to the greenwood like the nightingale keeps to the tree – out-of-sight but singing, my dear, out-of-sight but singing."

Clym of the Cleugh is the borderland Robin Hood. Many of the adventures of the three outlaws overlap with those told about Robin, and Will Cloudeslee, in shooting an apple off his son's head, manages to absorb the William Tell story too. The three may well have been based on real local men, however. Outlawry was common enough in King John's reign. John's seizure of the great forests as his own personal hunting grounds caused untold suffering to the peasantry.

Cuckoos

about 1 2 1 2

THE KING'S OWN MESSENGERS WERE ACCUSTOMED to causing a stir. Usually, when they rode into a town or village, people rushed out of doors to stare, local dignitaries hurried to fawn and flatter them, the inn prepared a splendid supper. But when King John's messengers rode into Gotham, nobody paid the smallest notice.

Four men came quarrelling down the road carrying between them a great length of picket fence. "It's your fault," said one.

"Well, how was I to know?"

At a shout from the royal messengers, the men with the fence all bumped into each other and stumbled to a halt. "We been trying to catch the cuckoo up yonder," explained one. "Sings in that bush on the hill. Pretty as a picklejar."

The man behind him joined in: "We knocked in this fence right around it! Got that bush so surrounded there was no getting out . . ."

"We had him, didn't we? We had him surrounded!" said a third eagerly.

"Then the cuckoo up and flew off," said the fourth sorrowfully dabbing his eyes.

King John's messengers looked at one another. One tapped his forehead with one finger. "You, sirs, are cuckoos yourselves if you didn't think of that . . ." began the chief messenger. But he was left talking to himself as the four cuckoo-catchers bumbled away down the road.

A man without trousers and wearing a jacket with wet coat-tails came sprinting down the street holding a big eel at arm's length. Dashing straight past without so much as a glance at the King's messengers, he ran to the village pond and threw the eel into it with a triumphant shout of, "There now! Drown and good riddance to you!"

Intrigued, the messengers asked what had happened. The villager looked at them with a slightly crazed grin and said, "I'm sorry you had to see that, but the vile beastie ate all the fish in our lake. So we held a trial and found it guilty and condemned it to death-by-drowning. That there was the execution."

"But eels can" – The royal messenger did not finish. Clearly the man was a lunatic if he thought he could drown eels – just as his neighbours were lunatics if they thought . . .

A woman carrying a bag of oatmeal came bustling out of the inn, calling back over her shoulder: "I'm just off down to the river to cook your porridge, Jack!" She curtsied as she passed the troupe of royal messengers. "River's bubbling nicely this morning!" she observed (as someone might comment cheerily on the weather). "Must be right hot to bubble like that! Porridge will be cooked in no time." They could not help noticing that her ears were painted green.

"They're all mad!" whispered the banner-bearer. "Are they dangerous, do you think?"

"You, sir! Come hither!" called the chief messenger imperiously. "You, farmer!"

"Oo? Me, sirrah?" A farmer leading a sway-backed old horse out of town, with two bags of grain slung across the saddle, shot them a hunted, guilty look and started talking before they could stop him. "I know what you're going to say! I know, and it's all true! This old horse shouldn't have to carry those heavy sacks, should she? Not after the lifetime of service she's given me! Well, neither shall she, sirs! Neither shall she! I'll spare her! You have showed me I am a cruel and unfeeling man!" So saying, he tugged the sacks off the old horse and tucked one under each arm. "I'll carry them myself, so I will!" Then he clambered awkwardly astride the animal's back, still clutching the sacks, and clicked his tongue for her to walk on.

"Let us hurry back and tell the King. This is no fit place for him! The village is full of half-wits! I swear there's not a soul living here but he's mad!" And so the royal messengers left at a gallop, sleeping in the forest sooner than stay in Gotham overnight.

When they had gone, the good gentlemen of Gotham converged on the Cuckoo Bush Inn for a pint or two of ale. "Reckon that put paid to them," said Farmer Giles.

"Reckon it did," said the carpenter.

"No hunting lodge hereabouts for King John, then," said the innkeeper's wife, brushing oatmeal off her dress. Everyone spat on the floor in unison.

"No Gothamites banned from their own forest, just so some king can enjoy his sport in sole splendour," said the man busy wiping the smell of eel off his hands.

"There's wisdom in what you say," said the innkeeper's wife with a wink. "But then Gotham was always blessed with a wealth of wise men."

The so-called "wise men" of Gotham first appeared in Andrew Boorde's sixteenth-century book, *Merrie Tales of the Mad Men of Gotham*, but were the stuff of folk legend before then. It has been suggested that the original wise men only feigned madness to dissuade King John from building a hunting lodge locally and annexing the surrounding forest for his own private hunting. This would have caused them very real hardship.

There are about twenty different, comic lunacies attributed to them, including trying to rescue the moon from a pond – a story the Moonrakers (see page 174) would almost certainly have known.

Lost in the Wash

1216

PERHAPS IF HE HAD BEEN MORE HANDSOME, MORE successful, more popular, King John would have minded less about clothes and jewellery. As it was, he carried his wealth of showy possessions with him everywhere he went. Even when the King of Scotland invaded and John set out to fight him, he took with him a baggage train of personal belongings, including the Crown Jewels.

Pushing too far south, into the Cambridgeshire fens, the Scottish invaders overreached themselves; John was easily able to turn them back, without heavy loss of men. But it left him in inhospitable fenland – a damp, shivering landscape which he hated. He had been feeling unwell lately, which made him even more irritable and impatient to get home. The sooner he and his men marched north and inland to Nottingham, the happier he would be.

And there at his feet, invitingly flat and golden, lay the vast sands of the Wash, a bite-shaped indent in the eastern coast of England. John studied the map. "If we cut across here," he said, drawing a jewelled finger across the Wash, we can take fifty miles off our journey and be out of this pestilential county by nightfall."

So out on to the hard-packed sand threaded a long line of horses and carts, banners, dogs and wagons. John slouched in his saddle: this salt air would be ruining the vellum of his books and the silver-gilt embroidery on his robes. A vast mackerel sky gave an impression of rippling water overhead. There was spray in the air, such as marks the turn of the tide. The tide.

Some of the wagons were having difficulties – sinking into the wet sand, bogging down. The sandy, featureless plain grew more beautiful by the minute, with little twisted cords of silver, and a bluey tinge reflected from the sky. It was no longer clear where the beach ended and the sky began. The horses' hoof prints were filling with water, making a line of silver stitches across the brocade tan of the sands.

Then the mist came down – a white pall of water droplets which hung on the men's eyelashes and beards and wetted them to the skin. The distant cottages on which they had taken a bearing dissolved like lumps of sugar in milk, and the gulls fell suddenly silent.

A horse floundered and fell to its knees. Its back arched as though it were leaping invisible fences, but its feet did not move – could not move. Soon only its head was straining and tossing, while the quicksand swallowed it up. A cart turned over with a crash of breaking crockery.

The tide did not roll in. It seemed to well up from below ground. The orderly line of troops and baggage carts broke up in panic. More horses pitched nose-down, their riders flying, hands-out, into the soft, receiving sand. Suddenly they could barely hear one another above the noise of the sea. "Look to the Crown Jewels!" shouted King John. "Look to my royal treasure!"

But men were running for dry land now (though they could not see it), jumping from island to island of damp sand, while the channels in between became wider and deeper. Soon there were no more dry patches, and the soldiers were all knee-deep and floundering, the sea pushing against their thighs, dragging the sand from under their boots. Here and there, groups of men trapped by quicksand bawled for help, but the sea piled up behind them, filling up the bottom segment of the sky.

The carts were afloat now, mostly on their sides. They banged against the horses, and mounted knights cursed and abandoned them. The sea came looting its way through the bags and baggage of the royal party, snatching here a coronet, there a jewelled glove. It leafed through the pages of the King's library. Chests too heavy with gold to float bubbled pearls of air, then sank underwater and into the sand. Gold chains looped and knotted themselves to the seaweed, and gem stones glistened in one last brilliant cascade before joining all the other, unremarkable pebbles on the seabed.

The loss gripped at John's chest so hard that he thought his heart was failing. Every time he thought of his ermine and scarlet wool, he groaned with physical pain. Dozens of good men had disappeared without reaching the shore, and the survivors sat about, shocked and shivering. But John thought of each piece of beautiful treasure, the buying of it, the price he had paid, the exquisite craftsmanship, the pleasure it had given him – and misery made him clutch his stomach and howl like a dog.

They pushed on to Nottingham, where John consoled himself by gorging on preserved peaches and cider. Within a fortnight, he was dead of dysentery, unmissed and unmourned, with an epitaph which damned him as "the worst King in English history".

King John's disastrous shortcut across the Wash took place only a year after his unwilling signing of the Magna Carta. The accident was recorded many years later, by one Matthew Paris, who undoubtedly exaggerated. But since much of the royal treasure catalogued before 1216 cannot be traced, there may well be some truth in the story.

Despite his reputation for greed, cruelty and cowardice, King John was a hard-working king in England, unlike his brother Richard, who saw the territory simply as a source of revenue for his crusading. Despite the popular image of John as an oafish brute who could neither read nor write, he was a fastidiously clean, cultured, intelligent man who possessed a large library of books. He travelled the country checking on the honesty of his officials.

"Wrap Me Up In A Cloak of Gold"

1255

TWO DOZEN BOYS WERE playing football with a pig's bladder. Someone skied the ball. It flew high over a wall, then they heard it bounce ringingly on the paved courtyard inside. Both teams scattered.

"What about my ball?" called little Sir Hugh. "I want it back!"

"Not going in there!" his friends shouted as they ran.

"Mother said to keep away!"

"A fairy lives there, says mine!"

Hugh, too, was afraid of the beetling stone walls and the big dark mansion beyond. But he stayed rooted to the spot, thinking about his ball. A gate creaked. A lady came out. She was dark-haired and beautiful, with a fine aquiline nose and dark eyes. He noticed that her gown was green – the colour fairies wear: an unlucky colour – but she smiled pleasantly enough. "Come in, little Sir Hugh. Come in and fetch your ball."

"I can't! I won't!" he blurted. "I mustn't! Not without my friends." His own rudeness embarrassed him, but the lady took no offence. She simply reached out, took Hugh by the hand and led him indoors. The gate banged shut behind them.

She smiled while he fetched his ball, smiled while he apologized for his rudeness. "Would you like some sherbet, Hughie?" she asked.

She led the way along stone corridors, through wood-panelled rooms hung with tapestries. At last they came to a windowless chamber lit by candles. "Sit down, Hughie. See, there is a golden chair for you to sit on."

"I should be going."

"Ah, but have some sweets before you go. Boys like sweets." She held out to him a plate of sugar bonbons, and he sat in the ornate golden chair, his feet swinging clear of the ground. The sweets were good . . . but they made him sleepy – they, or the incense burning in the room, or the soft glimmer of the candles. He only screamed when he saw the knife.

"No use screaming," said the lady in the same soft voice. "The walls here are a yard thick. No one will hear you." She scooped him up out of the chair as easily as if he were a baby, and laid him face-up on her dressing-table. Sleep, like a dozen strong hands, stopped him struggling.

"Let me say my prayers, at least!" he whispered.

But she stabbed him, then and there, in the throat, so that the blood ran down. The football, rolling out of his hands, bounced – *tch tch tch* – down a flight of stone steps. Sinking her fingers in his golden hair, gripping both ankles in one large hand, she carried him to the well by the high wall, and dropped him down it.

When little Sir Hugh did not return home, his mother went looking for him. His friends told her about the football and helped her search, sorry now that they had run off and left their friend alone. The town watch called at the big dark mansion behind its high perimeter wall, but the lady there only smiled pleasantly: no, she had not seen the boy.

His mother became more and more distracted. The river was dragged; the huntsmen checked their traps in the greenwood. But there was no trace of the boy. Then a servant lad, passing by the well, heard singing without knowing where it came from:

"Mother, mother, make my bed.
Make for me a winding sheet.
Wrap me up in a cloak of gold.
See if I can sleep."

The lad stopped passers-by: "Listen: can you hear that?"

Hugh's mother came and listened, white-faced, by the well, her hands clasped over her mouth to contain her terror.

"Mother, mother, make my bed.
Make for me a winding sheet.
Wrap me up in a cloak of gold.
See if I can sleep."

The body was grappled up from the bottom of the well and given a Christian burial wearing a cloak of gold. The well fell silent then, though no one dared drink from it. Many more ball games were played up against the high stone wall, but never again was a lost ball retrieved. Never again did the lady in green open her gate and invite a child in – for she had been tried for murder and burned to dust in the market place, along with all her kith and kin.

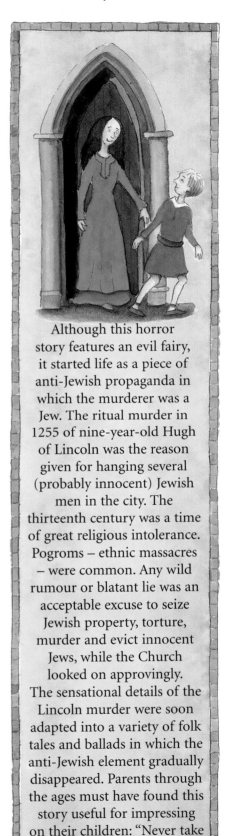

Although this horror story features an evil fairy, it started life as a piece of anti-Jewish propaganda in which the murderer was a Jew. The ritual murder in 1255 of nine-year-old Hugh of Lincoln was the reason given for hanging several (probably innocent) Jewish men in the city. The thirteenth century was a time of great religious intolerance. Pogroms – ethnic massacres – were common. Any wild rumour or blatant lie was an acceptable excuse to seize Jewish property, torture, murder and evict innocent Jews, while the Church looked on approvingly. The sensational details of the Lincoln murder were soon adapted into a variety of folk tales and ballads in which the anti-Jewish element gradually disappeared. Parents through the ages must have found this story useful for impressing on their children: "Never take sweets from a stranger".

"A Prince Who Speaks No Word of English"

1284

When English money shall become round
Then the Prince of Wales shall be crowned
in London.

Thus ran the ancient prophecy of the bard Merlin. So when King Edward I issued new coins worth a halfpenny and a farthing, the Welsh stirred like a field of daffodils in a rising wind. Their leader, the mighty Llewellyn, led an insurrection against the newly-crowned King of England. Wild Welsh mountain men raided the western counties of England, and the bards swore to conquer London.

Edward had spent time in Wales and knew the terrain. He imported mountaineers from the Pyrenees, expert in mountain warfare. He armed a thousand pioneers with hatchets to hack their way through Welsh defences, and sent a fleet to attack Anglesey. To his dismay, Prince Llewellyn found himself alone and hunted.

To baffle his pursuers, he had a blacksmith re-shoe his horse with the horseshoes back-to-front, so as to leave misleading hoofprints. But the blacksmith ran squealing to the English, and they were soon on his trail again.

Crossing the River Wye, Llewellyn set the bridge alight behind him, leaving the English milling helplessly about on the opposite bank, unable to cross. But they simply trekked downstream until they found a place shallow enough to ford.

Still, Llewellyn did not have far to go to join the Welsh forces massing nearby, and lead them into one last, decisive battle. So hiding in a barn, he waited for his pursuers to give up and return to prepare for the battle. When everything fell silent, he ran outside, only to come face-to-face with a single rider, lance levelled . . .

Adam de Frankton wiped the tip of his lance on the grass and rode on to join his regiment. The battle went against the Welsh, who seemed confused and disorganized: only afterwards did the English discover why. Frankton rode back to the farmyard where he had stuck the running Welshman like a boar and left him bleeding to death. He found the man dead but, discovering the signet ring on his finger and the letters in his pocket, realized he had killed Prince Llewellyn! The Welsh had fought without a leader. It was no wonder they had lost.

"How does the prophecy go?" said Edward toying with the bloodstained letters which Frankton had brought him. "'Then shall the Prince of Wales be crowned in London?' Well, then. Cut off Llewellyn's head and carry it to London. Impale it on the walls of the Tower — and crown it as befits a traitor."

What did those blood-soaked letters recovered from Llewellyn's body say? Would they tell him which chieftains were loyal and which were not? With calm deliberation, Edward tossed the letters unopened into the fireplace and watched them burn. "They would only make me suspicious of men I would rather trust," he said.

It took more than one battle to subdue Wales. While Llewellyn's head, crowned with a wreath of ivy, glared out across London, Edward spent months in Wales, building fortresses, holding talks with surly chieftains. His wife Eleanor, to be close by her husband, lived first at Rhuddlan, then at newly completed Caernarvon Castle.

One day in April 1284, Edward was again in conference with Welsh chieftains — some restive and resentful, some resigned to defeat, some undecided what to make of this conciliatory Englishman who beat them in battle but still wanted their friendship. Today the King's thoughts were plainly elsewhere. When a messenger arrived, Edward pushed back his chair and hurried from the room.

He returned grinning, his face flushed with pleasure and with an announcement to make: "Meet me in one week at Caernarvon, my lords," he said, "and I will present you with a prince born in Wales who can speak no word of English nor ever did any wrong to man, woman or child!"

Until Edward I's "prophetic" issue of half-penny and farthing coins, the practice had been to cut pennies into halves and quarters. This encouraged the crime of "clipping" whereby people shaved slivers of silver off every piece of money which came their way. Introducing small-denomination coins and so doing away with the excuse to cut coins was one of Edward's first acts of reform in a long, intelligent reign.

The baby's mother, Queen Eleanor of Castile, bore Edward eleven children and shared his work for thirty-six years; the couple were devoted to each other. When she died in Nottinghamshire, Edward transported her body back to London, raising a stone cross wherever her body rested on the journey. Three of these nine Eleanor crosses still exist. Unfortunately, the "Welsh-speaking" Prince Edward, in whose birth everyone took such delight, proved a grave disappointment as King Edward II. Forced to abdicate, he died in prison, probably murdered.

The Welsh were taken aback – delighted. What could it mean? A Welsh-speaking prince? The conference broke up excitedly and in a new mood of optimism.

It was a hushed, expectant gathering of shaggy, battle-scarred, weather-beaten, warriors, wrapped in Welsh-wool cloaks who crowded into the courtyard of Caernarvon Castle in the May sunshine to meet their new prince. Edward emerged to meet them, his queen at his shoulder. Cradled in his arms was a new-born baby. "According to my promise, I give you a prince born in Wales, who can speak no word of English!" and he lifted the baby high, for everyone to see.

The Welsh might have taken it for an insult – a joke at their expense. They did not. Edward was not deriding them. The baby Prince Edward was to have a Welsh nurse and Welsh servants, guaranteeing that his first words would be Welsh. Wales was no longer an independent country; it was a mere principality within Edward's kingdom. But conquerors have treated their vanquished foe far worse. One by one, the warlords came forward and, taking the baby's tiny hand between huge, gnarled fingers, kissing it through bushy beards, they swore an oath of loyalty to the English King.

A year later, Edward's first-born son, Alfonso, died, and the infant Edward became heir to the throne. At twenty-four he was crowned in Westminster Abbey.

So what of Merlin's prophecy?

When English money shall become round
Then the Prince of Wales shall be crowned in London.

Robert the Bruce and the Spider

1306-1314

"ROBERT THE BRUCE, LOST, STOLEN OR STRAYED!" read the English proclamation jeeringly, for the so-called King of Scotland had been gone all year and those trying to hunt him down could find no trace.

Dispossessed of his country by the English and driven to live as an outlaw, he and his companions were on the run, propping up branches for shelter, sleeping on animal skins, eating rabbits, berries and fish. With winter coming on, Robert the Bruce deemed it better the ladies should go to Kildrummie Castle, into the care of his young brother Nigel, while he and his few companions headed further north.

The news that reached them was all bad. Though Bruce kept his comrades entertained with stories of questing knights and poems about the heroes of Scotland, his spirits sank lower and lower. Every day, relations and friends were being captured, imprisoned, put to death. Perhaps he should abandon any dreams of driving the English out of Scotland. Six battles he had fought with the enemy, and six times his fortunes had fallen still lower.

One night, sheltering in a dilapidated hut on the island of Rathlin, he lay looking up at the roof. A spider hung there from a single thread, trying to swing from one rafter to the next so as to establish a web. Again and again it tried, though surely the distance was too great. Four, five, six times it tried. What perseverance! Did it never know when to give up? Why did it not scuttle away into a corner and weave there? Bruce found himself oddly caught up in the efforts of the spider. His eyes hurt with watching it so intently. I too, have made six attempts, he thought. If this creature tries again – if it succeeds – then, by all that's holy *so will I!*

The little gossamer thread was barely visible, and yet from it now hung the rest of Bruce's life. He forgot to swallow. He forgot to blink. The spider gathered its legs into a single black pellet. Swinging across the dark chasm of the roof, the little trapeze artist reached its goal and began, without respite, to construct a gossamer kingdom between the rafters.

In that moment, a surge of determination swept through Robert the Bruce which drove out all his weariness and despair. He would live to see the English driven out, and to be acknowledged King of Scotland! "And when I do, I shall make a pilgrimage to Jerusalem to give thanks. This I swear, Lord!"

The spider brought no sudden change in Bruce's luck. He learned that Kildrummie Castle had been taken, and the ladies there – his sister and wife – had been shut up like wild beasts in wooden cages, and hung over the battlements. Another sister had been placed in a nunnery. And his young brother Nigel – no more than a boy – had been hanged. But now, instead of increasing his despair, such news only fuelled Bruce's zeal for revenge. Even though the people were too terrified to answer his call to arms, and two more of his brothers were captured and hanged, Robert the Bruce would not give up hope.

He gained the friendship of Black Douglas, terror of the Borders, and at last highland and lowland lairds began rallying to his cause. More and more castles were captured by his growing army.

At Stirling, King Edward sent against him the greatest army ever led by an English king. When it came into sight, Black Douglas reported back to Bruce that it was the "most beautiful and most terrible sight". Sixty thousand men, better mounted and better armed than the Scots, came on like cloud shadow over the landscape.

Bruce said, "If any man of you is not ready for either victory or death, let him leave now!" But not one man quit the field. The odds were against them two to one, but everyone knew that on this battle the future of Scotland rested: its independence, its nationhood, its pride. The lines were drawn up for the battle called Bannockburn.

"They are kneeling to beg forgiveness!" cried King Edward, thinking the Scots were going down on their knees in hope of mercy.

"Yes, but they are asking it from God, not from us," said an English baron. "They are praying. These men will conquer or die."

The English cavalry moved off, formidable in their fine armour, on their huge horses, speeding from a walk to a trot, from a trot to a canter. Helmet crests and pennons flickered as if a grass fire were devouring the plain . . . And then all of a sudden they were stumbling and pitching, their horses tripping and going down. Knights fell from their ornate saddles and lay pinned to the ground by their weight of armour. Bruce had had his men dig 10,000 holes to the depth of a man's knee –

10,000 artificial rabbit holes in which a galloping horse could step and break a leg. Many of the horses and many of the knights did not stir, for Bruce had also strewn the plain with spiky calthrops which lie always with one lethal point upward.

Bruce's cavalry rushed the English archers: after that the English military advantage had gone. King Edward fled. The attendant who escorted him safely off the field (valuing his honour more than Edward did) turned back and threw himself into the mêlée to die fighting. But as the royal banner retreated, so the English ranks broke and ran, all the heart gone out of them.

The battle of Bannockburn established Robert the Bruce as King of Scotland. But the Pope said he would only acknowledge Bruce if he went on Crusade to the Holy Land.

No penance could have pleased Bruce more, remembering the vow he had made on Rathlin. He longed to see Jerusalem. But illness had dogged him down the years, and now it caught up with him. Leprosy prevented Bruce from keeping his promise to the Pope. So he sent for his best friend and bravest fighter, Black Douglas, and asked him, "Keep my promise. When I am dead, go to the Holy Land in my place. Carry my heart with you, and bury it in the Holy Sepulchre where Christ lay down and rose again to life."

Black Douglas did as he was asked. Though Robert the Bruce was buried, wrapped in cloth-of-gold, in Dunfermline Abbey, his heart, sealed in a lead casket, was worn around Douglas's neck the day he joined battle with the Infidel.

He had travelled only as far as Spain (then occupied by Moorish Moslems). Cut off from his troops, Douglas saw no escape. So he wrenched the casket from round his neck and hurled it forward, over-arm, crying, "Pass onward . . . ! I follow or die!"

The descendants of Douglas emblazon their shields with a bleeding heart surmounted by a golden crown to commemorate this last great act of loyalty and devotion.

King Edward II took with him to Scotland a Carmelite priest called Baston, renowned for his skill as a poet. The intention was that Baston should record in verse the King's glorious victory over the Scots. In the event, Baston was taken prisoner, and Robert the Bruce persuaded him to celebrate the Scottish triumph instead. His poem still exists.

After the battle of Bannockburn, the "wild men" of Scotland grew more and more audacious, annually raiding Durham and Northumbria. Peace was only struck when Bruce's young son, David, became betrothed to an English princess.

The Brawling Scottish Wench

1338

WITH A USURPER ON THE THRONE OF Scotland, hammered in place by English armies, the Scottish people seethed with indignation and resentment. Their loyalty was to the child king, David II, and despite a catastrophic defeat at Halidon Hill, when 10,000 Scots fell under a sleet of English arrows, individual strongholds still held out against the English invaders.

Away on the coast, its feet in the ocean, its face turned to the land, Dunbar Castle came under siege by the English. The lord of the castle was away, fighting in the cause of the young King David, leaving his wife in sole charge. But his wife was more formidable than many a knight; his wife was Agnes, daughter of Randolph. With her swarthy skin and the hairband worn low across her eyebrows, she had the look of a war stallion champing at the bit. And they called her Black Agnes.

William Montacute, Earl of Salisbury, pitched camp so as to isolate Dunbar on its rocky promontory. Then he brought up his great machines of war – his trebuchets. These gigantic catapults lobbed boulders in great arcs of destruction, demolishing whole sections of battlement, crumbling masonry like Scottish shortbread.

"Watch for the white flag," said Salisbury, confidently expecting Black Agnes to appear pleading for her life.

And indeed, shreds of fluttering cloth did appear on the battlements. A group of women moved slowly along the parapet flicking napkins. But not as flags of surrender. They were *dusting* the castle walls, flicking away grime and chippings, as though Salisbury's trebuchets had simply spoiled their housekeeping! Even some of the English troops gave a gasping laugh of admiration at such cool audacity.

Salisbury was not amused. "*Bring up the sow!*" he bellowed.

Now the "sow" was a siege engine with a sloping, arrow-proof roof which enabled workmen to get close up to a castle wall and work in safety, digging to undermine the wall. The roof protected them from archers on the battlements. Up trundled the sow now, concealing dozens of English solders beneath its roof of timber and hide.

Black Agnes peered over the wall.

"Beware, Montacute, your sow is about to have piglets!" she called down.

Again a gasp from the English camp. For a gigantic heap of debris – masonry, boulders from the beach and sundry castle rubbish suddenly lurched forwards into view, toppled from behind by crow bars. Tons of rock cascaded over the battlements on to the sow below. Agnes had predicted the exact spot at which Salisbury would attempt to break through. She had arranged the perfect answer to Montacute's sow. The hide roof smashed and splintered under the falling rock. The men beneath it screamed and went down, or ran for their lives squealing like demented piglets. "Oh look!" said Agnes, two hands clasped at her breast. "See the English piggies run!"

Earl Salisbury was spitting with rage.

Consequently, when a traitor came to his tent by night – a servant from the castle – the earl rubbed his hands with malicious delight. *Now* I have you, Black Agnes, he thought. "You say you can give the castle into my hands, man?"

"For gold enough," said the servant, "I can do King Edward that service. Come to the gate at midnight, and I'll tell you how."

With only his squire for company, William Montacute went at midnight – and, to his amazement, found the portcullis of Dunbar Castle raised just as high as a man's head! At this time of night, Agnes would be in her night-gown, sleeping. There was not even a sentry on watch! What could be easier? "Go on, go on in," he urged his squire.

With a rattle and a clank, the portcullis fell, its mesh of bars jarring the drawbridge on which Earl Salisbury was standing. On one side stood his squire, round-eyed with terror, fingers poking through the cullis, whimpering. On the other stood Salisbury. He had been within one pace of stepping into Agnes's trap, and though the trap had been sprung too early, he took to his heels now and ran, pursued all the way back to his tent by the ringing, rasping laughter of Black Agnes watching from the battlements.

Scottish minstrels were soon writing ballads about Black Agnes. One verse ran:

That brawling, boisterous, Scottish wench
Kept such a stir in tower and trench,
That came I early, came I late,
I found Black Agnes at the gate.

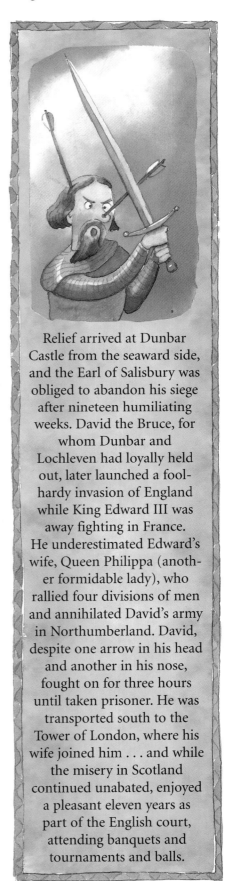

Relief arrived at Dunbar Castle from the seaward side, and the Earl of Salisbury was obliged to abandon his siege after nineteen humiliating weeks. David the Bruce, for whom Dunbar and Lochleven had loyally held out, later launched a foolhardy invasion of England while King Edward III was away fighting in France. He underestimated Edward's wife, Queen Philippa (another formidable lady), who rallied four divisions of men and annihilated David's army in Northumberland. David, despite one arrow in his head and another in his nose, fought on for three hours until taken prisoner. He was transported south to the Tower of London, where his wife joined him . . . and while the misery in Scotland continued unabated, enjoyed a pleasant eleven years as part of the English court, attending banquets and tournaments and balls.

The Black Prince Wins His Spurs

1346

Hᴇ ᴡᴀs ᴏɴʟʏ sɪxᴛᴇᴇɴ, and barely able to contain his pride, as his father, the King, dubbed him a knight. For almost as long as Prince Edward could remember, England had been at war with France,
but this was to be his first military expedition and the biggest of the war – a foray into northern France, with the chance of rich pickings.

Then, somehow the King overreached himself and suddenly he was in retreat, chased by the full might of French nobility and half of Europe with them. Sixteen-year-old Prince Edward did not regret the turn of events, but it looked as if his first campaign was going to end not quite according to plan.

King Philip of France and 68,000 men were marching to confront a mere 7,800 English and Welsh. But Prince Edward's worst fear was not of dying. It was of being sent away to a place of safety: heir to the throne, too precious to lose, too young to be trusted with his own life. To his great relief, it did not happen. Instead, his father invited him and the other knights and earls to dine in his tent on the eve of battle, and to offer up prayers. No mention was made of preserving his life.

The Prince determined to observe and learn. There would never be a bigger or better lesson in kingship and military command. So he watched everything. He saw how his father, armed with only a white wand, surveyed his troops, encouraging them, making jokes, telling them to eat well and take a glass of wine. He saw how the archers – the great bowmen of England – settled down to sleep under their blankets, in the teeming rain, helmets by their feet. He ran his unpractised eye over Crécy Hill, struggling to interpret his father's strategy.

He swelled with pride at being given command of 3,800 men; he bridled a little at being given the Earl of Warwick and Sir Godfrey de Harcourt to help command them. But he was glad enough of their wisdom and advice when, out of the morning rain, the French army came lumbering into view – a solid mass of armour and silks and saddleclothes, of bannerets, nodding horses and slogging footsoldiers, all bearing down on Crécy Hill.

His thoughts then were a wild confusion of prayers, fears and hopes, dense as the flock of ravens and crows which circled over the battlefield. And yet some part of his brain went on seeing with icy clarity.

He saw the French advancing – then the French heralds darting to and fro trying to tell them to halt: King Philip had not yet formed his battle plan. The army would not or could not halt: its numbers were too vast to absorb the command.

He saw the Genoese crossbowmen in the front – 1,800 of them – fumbling with their weapons in the downpour, the strings too wet to be strung. He noted, by contrast, the steely composure of the English bowmen as they rose to their feet, undaunted by their night on the muddy hill. From under their helmets they drew dry bowstrings, calmly and deliberately strung their longbows – and fired.

As in a dream, Edward saw that sleet of arrows, that whistling storm within a storm. For lightning was crackling between sky and earth and the air was smoky with rain. At noon the sun went out: darkness ate it away bit by bit: a dread omen for one side or the other. Then the Genoese were running from the storm of arrows, running and being hacked down by their own side for getting in the way, clogging up the road.

Now the French knights were within range of the arrows. Riderless horses capered and reared in terror, though those behind kept pushing forward, unaware of what was happening at the front. Forward went the Prince's Welshmen – the Cornishmen too – with their gruesome long knives – *snicker-snack*! – dealing out death in the midst of the milling confusion.

The clouds drew back to reveal the sun, restored after its eclipse, shining full in the face of the French, blinding them. *There* was the strategy of Crécy Hill! Prince Edward flushed full of hot pride in his father who rode now helmetless through the field.

One tiny scene of heroism fixed itself in the boy's mind: the old blind King of Bohemia riding into battle between two French knights, their bridles tied together so as to steer the old man's horse. Flank against flank they rode, Bohemia's white plumes nodding proudly as he rode to certain destruction, fighting the noisy darkness until it overwhelmed him. Edward rose in his saddle to see what became of the three . . .

Then suddenly, as if from nowhere, two French regiments were closing on his own flank. They had skirted round the chaos in mid-field to attack the Prince of Wales.

After that, Edward felt nothing except the hot churning hysteria of battle – lashing out, kill-or-be-killed. All those strokes and parries practised for tedious hours in the tilt yard came back to him now. But for every Frenchman he killed, two more seemed to materialize. Out of the corner of his eye, he saw the Earl of Warwick dispatch a herald to fetch help.

But help did not come. The King refused to send it. "Is my son dead, then? Or unhorsed, or so badly wounded that he cannot defend himself?"

"No, thank God, but he is in great need of your help!" panted the herald.

"Then go back to those who sent you and tell them not to send again nor expect me to come. Let my boy win his spurs, for I am determined that the glory and honour of this day shall be given to him!" Some who heard him asked themselves: what manner of man refuses help to his son?

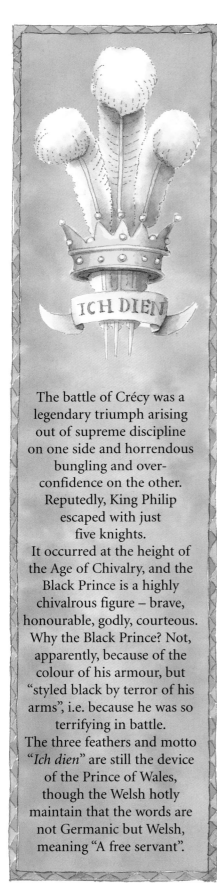

The battle of Crécy was a legendary triumph arising out of supreme discipline on one side and horrendous bungling and over-confidence on the other. Reputedly, King Philip escaped with just five knights.

It occurred at the height of the Age of Chivalry, and the Black Prince is a highly chivalrous figure – brave, honourable, godly, courteous. Why the Black Prince? Not, apparently, because of the colour of his armour, but "styled black by terror of his arms", i.e. because he was so terrifying in battle.

The three feathers and motto "*Ich dien*" are still the device of the Prince of Wales, though the Welsh hotly maintain that the words are not Germanic but Welsh, meaning "A free servant".

The troops arrayed on Crécy Hill did not break rank, or chase after the French when the French scattered, or rush down to plunder the dead. Disciplined to the last, the bowmen stood longest, until night was resting on their bowtips, and hymns of thanksgiving were flocking into the darkening sky along with the ravens and crows. Bonfires were lit; an army of torches were lit from the bonfires.

Those who had seen the prince fight were full of admiration, calling him his father's son, dubbing him "the Black Prince". The King came looking for his son, his hood of mail pushed back. Those nearby said that there were tears in his eyes. "Sweet son," he said, rushing to embrace the boy, searching every inch of his face. "You are indeed my son, for you have acquitted yourself most loyally this day and you are worthy to be a king!"

"The victory was all yours, Father."

"Nay, yours, son, yours!" There was a wild relief in the King's face which hinted how hard it had been for him not to send help.

From the prince's hand drooped three ostrich feathers, specked with blood. He had recovered them from the helmet of the fallen King of Bohemia, along with the old man's device: "*Ich dien*". "I serve".

"It shall be my device now," he said, "and the coat of arms of every Prince of Wales to come."

Then the battle-fever drained out of him and he was left white-faced and weary, with trembling limbs: sixteen again, for all his glittering spurs.

"Oss! Oss!" "Wee Oss!"

1347

THE FRENCH INVADERS CAME, THINKING IT would be easy to help themselves to the wealth of Padstow.

Across the Channel, Calais was under siege, and the fishermen and shopkeepers, the craftsmen and farmers of the little Cornish port had built two ships by their own efforts and set sail to help King Edward capture the city. No sooner were they gone than a fleet of French ships, knowing Padstow lay unprotected, sailed the other way, thinking to take over the town.

But they had not reckoned with Ursula Birdhood.

"Fetch out your red cloaks and your scarlet petticoats!" Ursula told the women of the town, "and meet me at Stepper Point!"

If Ursula was a witch, she was a wholesome witch, and if there was magic in her, it was of a very ancient kind. And her magic was small alongside that of the 'Obby 'Oss, dancer-in of the May!

Every May Day, from before daybreak till long after dark, the Padstow Hobbyhorse dances through the streets, twirling and leaping on its twin thin legs, its black cloth body flapping, its black conical body as pointed and jaunty as a witch's hat. And all the while it dances, it drives out winter and fetches in spring.

Now the French were invading, with swords sharp as winter and faces cruel as February, and nothing but a handful of women to keep them out. By the time Ursula Birdhood and the women of Padstow reached the headland at Stepper Point, a crescent of French warships was dropping anchor in the bay.

If those women were frightened, they sang the fear out of their throats. If their legs were shaking, they danced the fright out of their legs. In a deep, gruff voice, Ursula Birdhood began to sing and everyone joined in the familiar words:

"Unite and unite and let us unite
For summer is acome unto day . . ."

A drum took up the beat – a jogging, syncopated beat, like a horse trotting over broken ground:

"And whither we are going we will all unite
In the merry morning of May!"

They sang the Night Song and after that the Day Song, even richer with magic:

"O where is St George
O where is he O?
He is out in his long-boat all on the salt sea O.
Up flies the kite and down falls the lark O . . ."

This same story – of dancing women in red scaring off a French invasion – is told in at least one other place, across the Severn Estuary, in Wales. So it is unlikely both versions are true, but all the more likely that something of the sort did happen *somewhere*.

Age-old songs can become altered over the years into gobbledegook. One Padstow verse which runs:
Aunt Ursula Birdhood she had an old ewe
And she died in her own Park O'

But until 1850 the 'Obby 'Oss dancer *was* accompanied through the streets of Padstow on May Day by a character representing "an old woman in a red cloak". Was she Aunt Ursula? The horse itself has its origins in a Celtic religion older than Christianity, and brings fertility and renewal. It used to be thought that if the 'Oss threw its skirts over a young wife, she would give birth within the year.

The Padstow celebration is one of the most exciting and genuine folk rituals still observed in England. Most were suppressed or "adopted" by Christianity, or frozen out by disapproving Victorians.

Out at sea, the Frenchies saw the flicker of red cloth on the top of Stepper Point, though the singing was too far off to be heard.

"Il y a quelqu'un!"
"Là! En haut!"
"Les soldats anglais?"

They pointed, shouting.

Then, indistinct among the red glimmer of moving figures, they saw another shape – one which struck far more fear into their superstitious souls: a big flapping creature, black and headless, conical as a witch's hat and madly leaping on tireless legs – a creature they could make no sense of, unless . . . unless it was . . .

"Le Diable! Le Diable hors d'Infer!"

Had the English won the Devil over to their side, and were they even now whipping up magic on Stepper Point headland to sink the French, to crack their hulls like eggshells, to whisk their souls away like spray off the white wave tops? From time to time a single unheard voice exhorted, "Oss! Oss!" – but the dancers shouted their answer loud enough for the cry to cross the water: *"Wee Oss!"*

The French weighed anchor and sailed away. Ursula Birdhood watched them go, standing on the headland, red cloak streaming out behind her, one hand knotted in the tail of the nodding, skittering Hobbyhorse of Padstow.

The Garter

1348

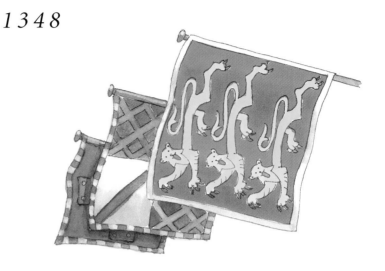

THE DANCERS PROMENADED UP AND DOWN, forming circles, forming lines, interweaving like the threads of the silken banners overhead. Surrounded by the heraldry of fifty ancient families and the crested helmets of warrior knights, the dancers themselves formed a kind of heraldry, bright with colours and chivalric splendour.

Then the Countess of Salisbury's garter slipped, slid down and came off altogether, to lie on the marble floor. Nobody could miss it. A page tittered. A gossip pointed. And the music ended just as King Edward saw it too.

Splendid in a quartered doublet of silk-lined velvet, he made a low sweep of his hand, a flourishing bow to his dancing partner, and his fingers scooped up the offending garter.

The countess flushed a vivid red. The silk stocking, which the garter had been holding up, wrinkled unceremoniously round her ankle. Was the King going to make some coarse joke? Humiliate her in front of her friends and inferiors? Would this model prince really do such a thing?

Edward pointed a toe and slipped his own foot through the garter, sliding it up as far as it would go round his manly calf. The crowd did not know if it was a joke. Two or three nervous giggles erupted from the courtiers. King Edward, turning his leg this way and that, heel in, heel out, looked up sharply. "Shame on him whose thoughts are shameful!" he said.

"*Honi soit qui mal y pense.*"

The order of the Garter is the oldest surviving order of Chivalry in Europe and was invented in the wake of an English victory in the Hundred Years War with France. Chivalry was reshaping the very nature of bravery, virtue and love. The story is cast into doubt by another in which Edward gave the signal for a victorious battle charge by waving his own blue garter. But whatever the origin of the award, it is now worn by only twenty-four honoured recipients (plus royal and overseas VIPs) at any one time, and only when one dies is another appointed to this most prestigious circle of all.

It was the kind of slogan noble houses were adopting the length and breadth of Europe, in the great race to invent a new, more civilized nobility: devices, mottoes, heraldic beasts, liveries, crests and honours. Some flattering duke jotted down the King's words in a commonplace book. The music struck up again and the countess, still pink with a mixture of embarrassment and pleasure, joined fingertips with the King once more. The slow, prancing geometry of the next dance began.

The lady's garter flashed and flickered on the King's calf – elevated now to the status of colours on the lance-point of a jousting chevalier. By the end of the dance the King had pursued his chivalrous thought still further. Again he thrust forward his leg and declared: "Only the greatest in the land shall wear such a garter! Let it be awarded only to my most favoured subjects! Only the most esteemed and chivalrous men in the kingdom will share with me this honour, this privilege of wearing . . . *the Garter!*"

And so the Order of the Garter began – at a time when English pride was at its height, when it lay in the power of a king to grant everlasting glory.

Dick Whittington

1358 - 1423

NCE UPON A TIME, A POOR boy called Dick lived in a village in the middle of nowhere. He had no mother or father to feed or clothe him, no future, so it seemed. "You should go to London!" said a neighbour. "They say the streets there are paved with gold!"

So Dick set off to walk, thinking London must be just over the hill. A hundred hills later, he found himself in narrow streets, among high houses and the shouts and bustle of London. His poor sore feet found no golden pavements to walk on – not so much as a golden pebble. And his stomach was empty.

He got work scraping pots in the kitchen of Captain Fitz-Warren, a rich merchant. Though Dick could eat the scrapings, the cook was a cruel bully. Dick slept in an attic so overrun with mice that with his first sixpence he bought a cat. That cat was a good friend to Dick, and he came to love it . . . almost as much as he came to love Captain Fitz-Warren's daughter, Alice. Sweet, kind, beautiful Alice. "If I weren't me and you weren't you, I would marry you one day!" he used to say.

"Who knows what you might be one day," Alice would say in reply.

But the cook's cruelties were too much for Dick to bear, and one very early morning he and his cat ran away. He might have walked all the way home, had he not stopped to rest on a milestone at Holloway. Across the fields came the distant ringing of Bow Bells in Cheapside – a familiar enough sound – except that today he seemed to hear words among the clamour: "Turn again, Whittington, thrice Lord Mayor of London!"

At once, Dick ran back the way he had come, and was busy scrubbing the kitchen floor before the cook even woke.

That day the house was all at sixes and sevens. Captain Fitz-Warren was setting sail. All kinds of people had invested in his voyage, hoping for huge profits when the merchant sold his cargo in distant parts. "Why not invest something yourself, Dick?" asked the merchant.

"Me? But I have nothing, sir," said Dick.

"You have that cat of yours! I need a cat to keep down the rats on board my ship."

Dick did not want to be parted from his friend, but at the last moment, he agreed.

Disaster! Captain Fitz-Warren's ship ran aground on the shores of a country where no one wanted or needed his valuable cargo. The caliph there had everything a man could desire: gems and silk, sherbet and oysters, palace walls clad in beaten gold.

One thing more the caliph had. Rats. His realm, his palace, even his throne-room swarmed with rats, because there were no cats in the whole land. When Puss saw the rats, he slew them by the dozen, by the tens of dozen, while the caliph watched in wonder. "For this cat I will pay three sacks of diamonds!" he declared.

Dick's fortune was made. With the proceeds, he became a respected London merchant and before long he was elected Lord Mayor of London – not once but three times. Bow Bells rang once again for Dick Whittington – on the day he married Alice Fitz-Warren.

The True Story

Sir William Whittington of Gloucestershire had three sons but, when the youngest was still a baby, he was out-lawed. The two older brothers sent Dick to London to be apprenticed to a distant relation, Sir Ivo Fitzwaryn. Sir Ivo was a mercer – a dealer in fabrics – and Dick's first job, at thirteen, was to stand outside his master's shop shouting, to attract customers. "What d'ye lack? What d'ye lack?"

From early morning till Bow Bells rang at eight, Dick learned his trade. They were eventful times. He saw John Wycliffe tried for heresy, saw Wat Tyler's rebels come flooding over London Bridge, saw the plague carry off 30,000 people in a single year.

They were fashionable times, too – times when the rich spent lavishly on clothes. There was no better time to be a mercer. The London mercers had money to spare, so became the bankers of the day as well, growing even richer from lending money.

By the age of twenty-nine Richard Whittington had £10 of his own to invest. At thirty-five he was an alderman and sheriff. King Richard II appointed him Mayor of London (there was no Lord Mayor then). His fellow Londoners re-elected him time after time.

Mayor Whittington invented street lighting, commanding every citizen to hang a lantern out-side his door at night. He invented the public drinking fountain, too. He was the terror of dis-honest tradesmen, prosecuting those who gave short measure, watered beer, overcharged or sold shoddy goods. He rebuilt his parish church, built almshouses for the poor, began a vast library . . . and lent King Henry V £60,000 towards the cost of fight-ing a war in France.

He entertained Henry and his new bride, Princess Catherine of France, to a feast more splendid than any ever seen before, warm-ing the banqueting hall with three blazing fires of costly cedarwood and cinnamon. Queen Catherine clapped her hands in delight at such sweet-smelling, extravagant fires.

"Ah, but I shall feed them with something more costly still than cedarwood!" declared Sir Richard, and promptly tossed into the fire all record of moneys he had lent King Henry. "Thus do I acquit your Highness of a debt of £60,000" he said.

Henry was staggered. "Never had a prince such a subject!" he cried.

"Never had a subject such a prince," said Whittington with a gracious bow.

Whittington *did* marry his employer's daughter, Alice. But they had no children. So when the great man died a widower, his immense wealth was bequeathed to London – to rebuild Newgate Prison, to restore St Bart's Hospital, to put windows in the Guildhall, to found a college . . . and his library of books was given to the Greyfriars. He had many "cats" (for the word means a cargo-carrying sailing boat); but as to the furry kind – well, they leave no pawprints on the pages of history.

Say "Bread and Cheese"

1381

"WHEN ADAM DELVED AND EVE span, who was then the gentleman?" John Ball asked the question in market squares all over Kent, and no one could answer him. Everybody is descended from Adam and Eve. So how come some people have become knights and barons, the rest starving serfs, taxed and oppressed by their so-called "betters"? Ball was a "Lollard". He wanted to end the feudal system. The people of Kent were eager to help him.

At Dartford, the cry was taken up by Walter the Tiler (or Wat Tyler).

Unlike Ball (an educated priest with strong religious beliefs), Tyler was a hooligan and a murderer. But the people followed him, like children following the Pied Piper. Joining forces with John Ball and a thatcher named Jack Straw, Tyler began to march towards London trailing behind him a growing army of protesters. Some just wanted to tell the young King their grievances; some wanted to bring down the old order, some simply a chance to pillage the city and cut a few throats.

Out of other counties came other columns of marchers. The citizens of London, faced with this flood of angry rebels, slammed the gates of London Bridge, to keep them out.

"Tell them to gather on the Thames shore at Rotherhithe on Thursday, and I will speak to them," said King Richard.

He was only fifteen, but appeared calm as he and a company of barons sailed down-river to meet the rebels. At the sight of him, the huge crowd on the bank raised a noise "like all the devils in hell", and surged towards the river. It was impossible to judge their mood. "Don't go ashore, your Majesty!" the barons begged. "It's too dangerous!"

So the boy-king stood up in the prow of the barge. "What do you wish?" he shouted.

"Come ashore, and we'll tell you!" the mob shouted back.

The Earl of Salisbury stood up, rocking the boat. "Gentlemen, you are not properly dressed for conversation with a king!" As the barge pulled out again into mid-stream, the crowd muttered angrily, and headed for London. Finding the gates of London Bridge shut, they threatened to burn down the suburbs and take the city by storm.

Could they be fought off? The Lord Mayor was doubtful. The City itself was full of rebel sympathizers – maybe as many as 30,000 living *inside* the gates might rise up, too, if it came to a battle. Slowly, creakingly, the gates were swung open, and the mob surged across – hundreds of hungry men. Sooner than be plundered of everything, grocers and bakers hurried into the street to distribute food.

A mob is a mindless, savage beast. This one went through the city looting, setting fire to the homes of lawyers, courtiers and churchmen. They burned down the Savoy Palace, the house of the Knights Hospitallers and the Marshalsea Prison. It was a night for settling old scores. Wat Tyler searched out an old employer who had crossed him once, and hacked off his head.

His power-crazed army grabbed people in the street, shaking them by the throat and screaming: "Say 'bread and cheese!'" When times are hard, the poor and the ignorant always blame foreigners for their troubles. Any trace of a foreign accent and they killed their victim. "Say 'bread and cheese!'"

"Brod unt cheess."

"Kill him! Kill the foreigner!"

Sixty-two innocent Flemish citizens were murdered that night for the crime of speaking with an accent. Meanwhile, inside the Tower of London, Richard II and his Council discussed the best way to deal with the revolt.

"When they're all drunk or asleep, we can go out and kill them like flies!" it was suggested. "Not one in ten has a weapon, and we can muster – what? – 800 armed men!"

But the Earl of Salisbury shook his head. The mob must be appeased, soothed with kind words. "If we should begin to kill them, and not go through with it, it will be all over with us and our heirs. England will become a desert."

So Richard sent word telling the rebels to meet him at Mile End meadow where he would discuss their demands.

Only half the mob believed him. The rest were too busy cutting throats. Waiting till the gates of the Tower were opened and the King's party gone, Ball and Tyler and Straw sped across the drawbridge, scouring the maze of apartments and staircases for the people they hated most. They slashed the bed of the Princess of Wales. They beheaded the Archbishop of Canterbury, killed a prior, a friar and a sergeant-at-arms, and mounted their heads on poles to decorate London Bridge. Then on to Mile End meadow.

Tens of thousands of peasants from every county in England confronted Richard as he rode out to speak with the leaders of the Peasants' Revolt. Some of his pages and courtiers were so scared that they turned their horses and galloped away, abandoning the young King. But his nerve held.

"My good people. What is it you want and what do you wish to say to me?"

"We want you to make us free for ever," said a man nearby.

"I grant your wish," said Richard.

Just like that. An end to serfdom. An end to one man "owning" another.

It took the wind out of their sails. It defused the moment. It turned the mob back into a dignified assembly of loyal subjects. "Go home now," said Richard. "Leave two men behind from every village, and I will have letters written, sealed with my seal, for them to carry home. I shall send my banners, too, as proof that you have my authority."

Thirty secretaries were summoned to write those precious letters, and as each one was sealed and delivered, large numbers of protesters turned for home, saying, "All's well. We have what we wanted."

Not Wat Tyler. Not Jack Straw. Not John Ball, nor thousands of others. They had the City of London at their mercy, and were not going to leave till it was stripped bare. Still more peasants were converging on London, and the looters had no wish to share their plunder with newcomers.

Almost by chance, King Richard and sixty out-riders came face-to-face with the vast, drunken mob at Smithfield. Fresh in Richard's mind were the horrors he had found at the Tower – those four headless bodies, the blood, the trail of destruction leading from room to room. And yet the words of the Earl of Salisbury were still ringing in his ears: ". . . England will become a desert."

When he recognized the King, Tyler gave a terse laugh and fumbled for his stirrup, to mount. He was keyed-up, drunk on stolen wine and lack of sleep. "Stay here. Don't stir until I give you a signal. When I make this sign, come forward and kill everyone except the King. He's young and we can do with him what we please."

Then he rode forward – so impetuously that his horse ran its nose into Richard's. "King," he blurted out, "do you see all those men there? They are all under my command and have sworn to do whatever I shall order." He wanted the King's letters, he said – would not leave London without them in his hand.

"That is what has been ordered. They will be delivered as fast as they can be written." The fifteen-year-old King answered calmly.

But Tyler was hysterical, overwrought, wanting to prove what power he wielded. "Give me your dagger!" he told the King's squire. The squire refused, but Richard told him to give it up. "Now your sword!" demanded Tyler. The squire refused.

The Mayor blustered: "How dare you behave thus in the presence of the King!"

Richard remembered those four headless bodies, all that blood. "Lay hands on him!"

A sword struck Tyler so hard on the head that he fell. The royal party milled around, their horses blocking the crowd's view. A squire dismounted and finished Wat Tyler where he lay. Messengers rode off to the city for reinforcements.

Then the body was spotted. "They have killed our captain! Let's kill the whole pack of them!" The mob drew a single breath. Arrows were laid to ash-wood bows, and the crowd began to move, like volcanic lava, bubbling, seething. What happened in the next few seconds would decide the fate of everyone there.

"No one follow me!" said King Richard, and urged his horse towards the furious crowd. Rising in his stirrups, he yelled: "Gentlemen! What are you about? You shall have no other captain but me. I am your King!"

It was a startling gesture from a boy of his age. Thousands drew back from the brink. Some hotheads wanted to cut down the King, but hesitated, uncertain.

That hesitation gave time for several thousand armed men to ride, pell-mell, out of London, and reinforce King and court.

John Ball and Jack Straw crept away, hoping to hide.

"Let's charge, and kill them where they stand!" urged one of Richard's knights, but the King would not hear of it. There was no need. The balance of power had changed. King Richard was demanding the return of his banners, the handing back of his letters. And the people were passing them forward – banners and letters – giving up their passports to freedom.

In front of their eyes, Richard tore up the letters, crushed the waxy seals, and they stood and watched him do it – docile, cowed, leaderless. Like sheep they scattered. Like sheepdogs at their heels, new proclamations chased them out of town. Anyone not resident in London one year or more was to be gone by Sunday or lose his head.

As they streamed over London Bridge, three severed heads grinned down at them from the top of poles: not the archbishop nor the prior nor the sergeant-at-arms, but Wat Tyler, Jack Straw and John Ball. On the various roads to London, thousands of peasants still thronging to join in the Peasant's Revolt heard that it was over – and turned back.

Who was in the wrong? Wat Tyler and his murderous louts? The King and Parliament, with their broken promises? After the peasants returned home, every letter was revoked, every charter withdrawn. Even more hardships were heaped on the peasants. Large crowds were forbidden to gather. Richard II imposed his authority by marching around the country with an army of 40,000 men. The nobles were no more ready to set serfs free than to give away their own knives and forks. Property is property, after all.

In some regions, the Peasants' Revolt was not so easily snuffed out. There were risings all over the country, and nobles shut themselves up in their castles and trembled. But order was gradually restored by the usual means: battles, trials, beheadings; in Essex, 500 peasants were killed.

"A Little Touch of Harry in the Night"

(Shakespeare, *Henry V*)
1415

FROM THE FRENCH CAMP FLOATED THE NOISE OF blacksmiths hammering home rivets, a minstrel singing, men laughing; banners of red-and-yellow light. But within the English camp there was hardly a sound, hardly a light showing. Six thousand exhausted men had walked through teeming rain 260 miles from Harfleur, with too little to eat and disease dogging them every step of the way. In the morning they would have to confront the army barring their road to Calais and escape. And the well-equipped French outnumbered them four-to-one. There did not seem much to sing about, as the rain teemed and the dark pressed suffocatingly close.

"Who goes there?" The sentries were jumpy.

"Friend."

"Whose regiment?"

"Sir Thomas Erpingham's." The cloaked figure moved closer, hood pulled forward against the filthy weather. The sentry let him pass and join a group of men sitting round a damp little fire.

"It's all right for the King," one was saying. "He wants to win the throne of France, so we have to come here and die."

"Is that how you see it?" said the hooded stranger equally. He took a sip of ale, before passing his tankard on round the group. "I would have thought the King had a heavy burden to carry. He's the father of his men. He has to provide for them, pray for them, look after them . . . All those wives and children depending on him to bring home their menfolk – that's a terrible responsibility for any man."

"Yeah, but tomorrow he'll be up there on his big horse on top of a hill somewhere, watching us get trampled by the French cavalry."

"Oh, why? Was Harfleur like that?"

Another answered instead. "No! No, at Harfleur, Harry was right there at our elbow, fighting like a demon!"

"Yeah, you can say that for the saucy rogue," admitted a sergeant grudgingly.

"Harry's not afraid to get his hands dirty."

They turned to speak more, but the stranger was moving away. For a second the firelight caught his face and the sergeant's hand shot out and gripped the man alongside him. "Oh no! You know who that was, don't you? You know what I just done? I only went and called the King of England a saucy rogue to his face!"

Henry walked on, moving between the dim red circles of dying campfires like a meteor through the dimness of space, calling out greetings to those he knew by name. Some recognized him, even bareheaded and without his surcoat of leopards and lilies. The King was a tall, erect figure, with a long, straight nose and strong jawline. His voice was sometimes soft and soothing, sometimes bright and laughing, depending on the nature and needs of his men. He played dice with some, exchanged memories with others, broke bread with them, listened to their jokes. He did not sleep that night, but the following morning his men were less weary because of it.

Only then did he begin to speak of glory.

His sword was drawn as he spoke, rallying them, encouraging them, praising their valour and skill as warriors. The men farthest off craned to catch every last word. Henry invited all those who wanted to leave, to go with his blessing – but warned them that they would miss out on the glory, miss out on being part of the greatest battle ever fought. No one got up to leave. When he had finished, there was no more talk of dying under French hooves, no more lolling in the mud nursing belly aches and fear. Henry had his men mustered and ready while the French were still quarrelling about who would lead the charge.

So sure of victory were the swaggering French knights, that they bragged to one another: "I shall capture the English banner!"

"I shall take a thousand prisoners!"

"They haven't above 900 men-at arms! The rest are nothing but poxy archers!"

Their horses pranced and capered under them, so unruly that their commander could not apply his battle plan. They even managed to trap 3,000 of their own crossbowmen behind them, leaving them unable to fire on the enemy for fear of hitting French knights.

At mid-morning, with a shout from Henry of, "Banners advance! In the name of Jesus, Mary and St George!" and with a blare of trumpets, the

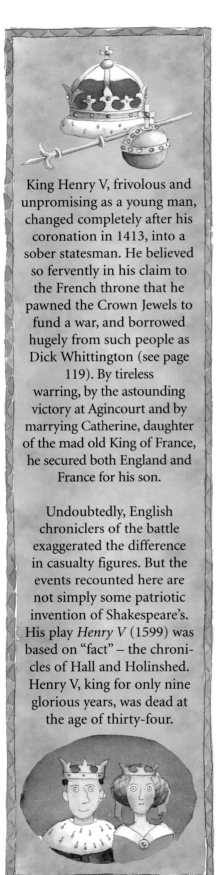

King Henry V, frivolous and unpromising as a young man, changed completely after his coronation in 1413, into a sober statesman. He believed so fervently in his claim to the French throne that he pawned the Crown Jewels to fund a war, and borrowed hugely from such people as Dick Whittington (see page 119). By tireless warring, by the astounding victory at Agincourt and by marrying Catherine, daughter of the mad old King of France, he secured both England and France for his son.

Undoubtedly, English chroniclers of the battle exaggerated the difference in casualty figures. But the events recounted here are not simply some patriotic invention of Shakespeare's. His play *Henry V* (1599) was based on "fact" – the chronicles of Hall and Holinshed. Henry V, king for only nine glorious years, was dead at the age of thirty-four.

English trudged a half mile towards the enemy. When the French banners were just within range of the archers' arrows, the English halted and sank long, sharpened stakes into the sodden ground, points outward.

With a single unearthly note, the bowstrings of the English longbowmen loosed a swarm of arrows, blackening the sky. Death fell on the French like a plague of locusts.

Enraged by such unexpected casualties, 1,000 knights spurred their lumbering great horses into a charge. But the ground in front of them was boggy, and the English archers could fire off twelve arrows a minute – metre-long arrows whose tips could pierce armour. By the time the French cavalry reached the longbowmen, 850 out of 1,000 were dead. The survivors rode on to the wooden stakes, or were pulled from their saddles and done to death by the archers. Riderless horses and fleeing French knights turned and galloped back the way they had come – trampling their own foot-soldiers.

The first line of French infantry finally surged up. But they were so tightly massed that they had no room to swing their weapons. They could only mill about, gasping for breath. The English archers threw down their bows and fell on them with swords and axes. Unaware of the disaster at the front, more French men-at-arms came marching up from behind. The first line, now trapped, could neither advance nor retreat. More Frenchmen died of being crushed, than of wounds inflicted by the English.

The aristocratic knights, in their heavy, ornate armour lay in the mud, helpless to get to their feet, trampled by horses and running feet, drowning in mud. In three hours, 10,000 Frenchmen died – half of all the noblemen in France were either killed or captured.

The cost to the English was a mere one hundred men.

"Hang on the Bell, Nelly!"

1460

"AND THIS BE THE sentence OF this court; that you be taken from this place and, at the sounding of the curfew bell, hanged by the neck until you are dead. And may God have mercy on your soul."

The young man standing between his guards sagged a little at the knees, and a young women in the court cried out, "*No!*" But the judge did not so much as look up. He had passed the death sentence so often before. In these days of war, death was commonplace.

This was the time of the Wars of the Roses. The young man – Neville Audeley – was a Lancastrian. In attempting to visit his sweetheart, Nell, he had been unlucky enough to fall into the hands of Yorkist troops. His only crime was to be on the wrong side in the wrong place, during an endlessly bloody civil war which had torn apart families, and pitted neighbours and towns against one another. Once, Neville had given Nell roses, but all she had left now were the thorns embedded deep in her heart.

There was hope, even so. Neville was the nephew of the Earl of Warwick, and his uncle had influence. A word at court, a favour owing, and the earl might just win a reprieve for his nephew. But court was far off in London, and there was so little time! To Neville, gripping the bars of his prison cell, it seemed that the sun was crossing the sky with the speed of a cannonball, bringing his death hurtling towards him.

"Time to go," said his gaoler, jangling the keys in the lock.

"But my reprieve! What of a reprieve?"

"What of it? If it comes after curfew, they may paste it on your tombstone." He tied Neville's hands and led him down a dank stone passageway.

The day outside was already grey with age. There were a few townspeople still on the streets, despite the closeness of curfew. They would have to hurry home to put out their fires while the bell tolled . . . while Neville kicked out his life to the sound of St Peter's church bell. I shall never hear the last stroke of that curfew bell, he thought to himself, as he set his foot on the bottom rung of the gallows ladder.

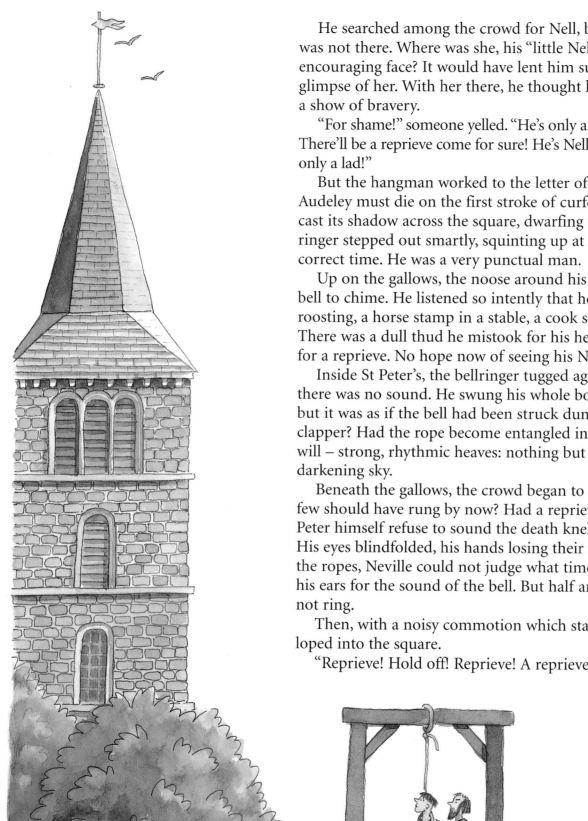

He searched among the crowd for Nell, but to his utter dismay she was not there. Where was she, his "little Nell"? Where was her sweet, encouraging face? It would have lent him such courage to catch one last glimpse of her. With her there, he thought he might at least have put on a show of bravery.

"For shame!" someone yelled. "He's only a boy! Hold off, hangman. There'll be a reprieve come for sure! He's Nelly Heriot's sweetheart! He's only a lad!"

But the hangman worked to the letter of the law, and the law said that Audeley must die on the first stroke of curfew. The belltower of St Peter's cast its shadow across the square, dwarfing the town gibbet. The bell-ringer stepped out smartly, squinting up at a corner of sky to judge the correct time. He was a very punctual man.

Up on the gallows, the noose around his neck, Neville waited for the bell to chime. He listened so intently that he could hear the starlings roosting, a horse stamp in a stable, a cook scrape a spoon around a pot. There was a dull thud he mistook for his heart breaking. Too late now for a reprieve. No hope now of seeing his Nelly again.

Inside St Peter's, the bellringer tugged again on the rope, but again there was no sound. He swung his whole body weight on the rope's end, but it was as if the bell had been struck dumb. Had frost broken off the clapper? Had the rope become entangled in the rafters? He pulled with a will – strong, rhythmic heaves: nothing but silence throbbed out into the darkening sky.

Beneath the gallows, the crowd began to stir restlessly. Surely the curfew should have rung by now? Had a reprieve already come? Or did St Peter himself refuse to sound the death knell of this poor young man? His eyes blindfolded, his hands losing their feeling with the tightness of the ropes, Neville could not judge what time had passed. Still he strained his ears for the sound of the bell. But half an hour went by, and it did not ring.

Then, with a noisy commotion which startled everyone, a rider galloped into the square.

"Reprieve! Hold off! Reprieve! A reprieve from the King!"

At the foot of the ladder, the crowd swept Neville Audeley along with them in a mad stampede for the church. The streets were dark: it was way past curfew, and yet curfew had not rung! Now they were free to satisfy their curiosity as to why.

As they got there, the bellringer had just finished climbing the long succession of ladders to the top of the belltower. He peered ahead of him in the shadowy belfry, mobbed by bats. At first he mistook the pale figure for a ghost. Then he saw it for what it was.

Nell had climbed up the tower and, despite the dizzying drop below her, leapt out to clasp the bell's huge clapper, wrapping her arms and legs around it like a lover, cloaking and muffling it with her clothing and hair. A hundred times and more the bell rope had swung her against the great brass wall of the bell, and yet she had not let go. Sickened by the motion, battered and bruised by the crushing impact, she had still refused to let the bell sound, refused to lose her grip, refused to die.

Half insensible, she refused even now to let go until the people called up to her through the wooden platforms of the tower: "He's safe! Your sweetheart is safe!" Only then did she allow her hands to be prised from its clapper, and permit the bellringer to carry her down the tower across his shoulder. ". . . must not ring . . ." she repeated, over and over, without opening her eyes, ". . . must not ring tonight . . ." until, at the church door, Neville's kisses finally silenced her.

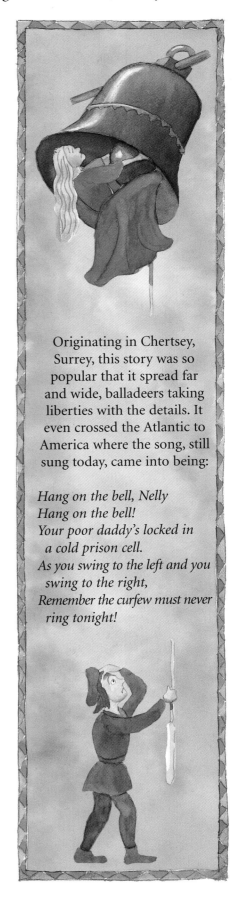

Originating in Chertsey, Surrey, this story was so popular that it spread far and wide, balladeers taking liberties with the details. It even crossed the Atlantic to America where the song, still sung today, came into being:

Hang on the bell, Nelly
Hang on the bell!
Your poor daddy's locked in
a cold prison cell.
As you swing to the left and you
swing to the right,
Remember the curfew must never
ring tonight!

The Princes in the Tower

1483

"MOTHER, MOTHER, WHO ARE THE BOYS IN the velvet coats who came to the Tower today with all those servants and fine baggage?"

"That is Prince Edward, my dear – king as shall be – and his brother Richard. Their father is newly dead of a fever, and soon Edward will be crowned. Think of that!"

"Poor souls," said Mary.

"Why do you say that? The Tower of London isn't all dungeons and guardrooms, you know. The state apartments are very fine."

"No, no. Poor boys to have lost their father, I mean," said Mary.

"Mother, mother, *when* is Prince Edward going to be crowned? I see him and his brother playing in the gardens and on the battlements, but the coronation never comes . . . They look sadder than they did. Only today I heard a servant call out: 'My Lord Bastard!'"

"Ah, child. There'll be no coronation now. It is held that Edward was born illegitimate. He cannot

be king. Their uncle is crowned instead: King Richard III."

"Poor boys," said Mary.

"Mmm, but to be king at twelve, and to carry the whole weight of government on those narrow shoulders. It would have been a hard life for the boy."

"No, not to lose the crown, I mean," said Mary. "Poor boys, to be called such names by their own servants."

"Mother, Mother, why do the princes never play in the Tower gardens any more? I see them at the windows, looking out, and they look so sad and pale."

"I think, child, that their palace has become a prison, and they are kept locked up tight, for fear some politicking nobleman argues that Edward is true King. So many factions. So many ambitious men. The world is a wicked place these days, my dear."

"Poor souls," said Mary.

"To be squabbled over like a hand of cards? Yes, my dear."

"No, no. Not to be able to play out-of-doors, I mean," said Mary.

"Mother, Mother, where are the princes? I never see their faces at the window any more."

"Sshsh, my dear. No more questions. Best to keep silent in these wicked times."

"Tell me. I want to know. What has become of the princes?"

"Very well. I shall tell you what is said. They say that the King – King Richard, that is – gave the orders. He chose the most ambitious man at court, and told him, 'Do it.' James Tyrrell was eager to 'oblige' the King in anything. So he summoned two men, his keeper of horse, John Dighton and Miles Forest who looks after – looked after the princes."

"The boys were asleep together in the one bed, their arms tight round each other. Forest took hold of a feather pillow, Dighton another . . ."

"Oh Mother, no!"

". . . and they pressed the pillows over the boys' faces. The sleepers woke, of course, and struggled, but what could two little boys do against two grown men? After a while they stopped struggling. Forest and Dighton hid the bodies, and it was as if those little princes had never lived."

"King Richard did that? But why?" asked Mary. "He already had the crown! Why did he need to kill them?"

"Hush, child, speak lower. If he did order it done, then it did him no good. Richard himself is dead – killed in battle – and there's a new king crowned. A Tudor king. King Henry VII. He says that Richard killed the princes in the Tower. So keep quiet, little child, and say no more. These are not times to question what we are told."

"Poor souls," said Mary.

"Yes. They were only children. No older than you, after all."

"I did not mean the princes, Mother. I meant us. To live like pawns in a chess game and never know enough to tell black from white."

The Wars of the Roses (1455-87) was a time of turmoil, with factions forming alliances, then betraying each other. The crown kept changing hands. That is why it is so difficult to arrive at the truth of what happened to the princes in the Tower.

Some 200 years after their disappearance a box was unearthed by builders. It contained the skeletons of two children aged about ten and twelve – probably, but not certainly, the princes. The bones were interred in Westminster Abbey.

After defeating Richard III at the battle of Bosworth, Henry Tudor set about systematically blackening Richard's name. All at once Richard was a hunchback, a child killer, a psychopath. (Shakespeare, living under a Tudor monarch, helped greatly in this reshaping of history, casting Richard as the arch villain.) Historians think Henry (whose own claim to the throne was not strong) might equally have ordered the killings. So might Henry Stafford, Duke of Buckingham, who may have been waiting his chance to usurp both Henry and Richard.

A Recipe for Simnel Cake

1487

TAKE ONE COUNTRY, NERVOUS AND UNSETTLED.
Take one king, newly crowned and with a shaky claim to the throne.
Add ambition. Take a gamble.
Take one fifteen-year-old:
Lambert Simnel.
Spread thickly the rumour that *he* is the rightful heir to the throne.
Whip up the Irish and a few English lords.
Raise an army.

Lambert Simnel was pretending to be the Earl of Warwick.

The priest called Father Symonds had tutored Lambert well. By the time he turned up in Ireland, he carried himself like an earl, could speak intelligently about affairs of state, and seemed to be acquainted with all the lords and ministers of court. He was handsome and pleasant, and people instantly warmed to him. They listened with bated breath to the thrilling account of his escape from the Tower of London, where wicked King Henry VII had locked him up.

The Irish sank to their knees and paid homage. They also swore to put this wronged boy back in his rightful place: the throne of England.

In fact, Father Symonds was banking on the fact that the Earl of Warwick had been murdered by King Henry. Secretly. Unwitnessed. What could the King say, then, when this "escaped Earl of Warwick" suddenly appeared to claim his rightful crown? "You are an impostor; I have already murdered the real Earl of Warwick"? Hardly.

And Father Symonds' obedient, talented protégé had managed to convince the Irish. Lambert Simnel knelt at the altar rail of St Patrick's Cathedral, Dublin. The crown was placed on his shining blond hair, and a fanfare acclaimed him Edward VI, *rightful* King of England.

There were only two drawbacks Father Symonds had not foreseen. In point of fact, Henry VII had *not* murdered Edward, Earl of Warwick: he was still alive! Secondly, Edward, Earl of Warwick, was *not* a handsome, intelligent, well-informed young man. He was a gormless ninny, as everyone knew who had ever met him.

King Henry fetched out the real earl, and paraded him through the streets of London, saying, "Speak to him! Anyone may speak with him! Ask him who he is!" It seemed a simple way to prove that the rumours from Ireland were all nonsense.

"Ah, well yes, he *would* produce an impostor," argued Father Symonds, "and pass him off as the real earl. But we know the real one, do we not? We have met the true Edward Plantagenet!"

Some believed him in all sincerity. Some simply *chose* to believe him since, to them, any usurper was preferable to the upstart Henry VII.

Francis the First Viscount Lovell, for instance, was ready to throw in his lot with the young "King Edward VI". So, too, was the Earl of Lincoln.

But Lincoln had met the real Edward Plantagenet many times in the past. So what expression crossed Lincoln's face when he met the boy impersonating him? Surprise? Amusement? Whatever thoughts went through his mind, he bent and kissed the hand of Lambert Simnel, and his face betrayed not a qualm, not a doubt.

Perhaps Father Symonds miscalculated. Perhaps, by the time he found out the Earl of Warwick was still alive, he was in too deep to turn back. Perhaps he staked too much on the unpopularity of Henry VII. The English lords who rose up in support of "King Edward VI" brought with them a few household armies; the Irish brought daggers and short swords. Altogether, they were no match for the army which came against them at Stoke. King Henry fought his rival for the throne, and won.

Lincoln was killed and Lovell fled, their hopes and fortunes dashed. Lovell made for his house at Minster Lovell, and hid in an underground room. "Lock the door and make it secret," he told a servant. "I have not been here, you understand? You have not seen me – or the King will have my head before the week's out!"

Father Symonds and Lambert Simnel did not slip so easily through the King's fingers. They were caught at once, and people winced to think what hideous punishment awaited them.

To everyone's astonishment, Henry VII, far from loosing the full might of royal justice on his enemies, seemed mildly amused by the whole affair. He invited the rebel lords to dine with him, and as they sat there, a serving boy came to serve them each with meat.

They looked once, they looked twice. An earl choked on his bread and grabbed for a cup of wine. It was! It had to be! The last time they had seen this boy, they had bent their knees and bowed their heads and sworn everlasting fealty to him and his descendants. It was Lambert Simnel. Henry had cut off neither his head nor his hands. "I have put him to work in the scullery," said Henry brightly. "He turned the spit where your meat was cooked tonight, so if it is underdone, you can blame – well, you may blame the King, I suppose!"

Lambert Simnel must have given satisfaction in the King's kitchen, for within a few years he had risen to the post of royal falconer.

There is a tradition that Lambert, while working in the King's kitchen, invented the Simnel cake one Eastertime. A spicy fruit cake, flavoured with almonds, he topped it with eleven marzipan balls, in token of the eleven faithful disciples. The twelfth was missed off, of course, because Judas, the twelfth disciple, betrayed Jesus. And nobody likes a traitor.

The Lambert Simnel episode is most remarkable for the way Henry VII handled it. Instead of applying the tyrannical cruelty of earlier ages, he used a lightness of touch which amazed and amused everyone. Afterwards, he was called "the Solomon of English kings".

In 1708, during building work at Minster Lovell mansion, a locked subterranean room came to light. Inside, the skeleton of a man sat with his head resting on a table, as if asleep. As the door opened, both clothes and bones crumbled to dust. Could this have been Francis, First Viscount Lovell? Did his servant run away, fearing arrest? Or was he simply too stupid to realize that a young man entombed below his own house needs food and water to survive?

The Faery Flag

1490

THE WIFE OF THE FOURTH LAIRD of the MacLeods led him by the hand to a bridge near Dunvegan, and kissed him on the cheek. "Twenty years I have been a wife to you, MacLeod," she said, "and twenty years I have kept secret my birth and parentage."

"What do I care where you come from or who your parents were?" he said bluffly. "You've been a good wife to me. Better than most."

"That's because I am different from most. I am a fairy," she said, "and being a fairy, I came only for a while. I must go back now to my land. But before I do, I have a present to give you, in token of the love that has been between us." And she gave him Britach Sith: "the Faery Flag". "If ever the clan of the MacLeods is in mortal danger, unfurl this banner, and the tide of fortune will turn. Three times its magic will come to your family's aid." Then she stepped away from him, over the parapet of the bridge, and disappeared like the spray of the water beneath.

Now the bold MacLeods are not people to ask help of anyone, especially the fairies. And though the fourth laird treasured the banner, at Castle Dunvegan – a memento of his faery wife – he never unfurled it. Nor did his children.

But a hundred years later, when a future laird was born, a slight, diaphanous figure was glimpsed within the castle walls one day, descending the stairs from the room which held Britach Sith. The baby's nurse saw the wraith cross to the cradle and (though she feared the child would be stolen away to the Land of Faery or replaced with a changeling) she could neither move nor cry out. Singing a strange, lamenting tune, the fairy tenderly wrapped the baby in the flag and began to rock him in her arms. Then she laid him back in the cradle.

After she had gone, her tune stayed lodged in the nurse's brain like a splinter in a finger. Singing it, she found she had the power to soothe the loudest crying. Never again was a nurse employed to care for any heir to the MacLeod estates unless she had learned the faery lullaby from her predecessor. And yet still no human hand had unfurled the banner for its real purpose – to summon aid. The MacLeods were Scotsmen, and Scotland is a land of granite.

In battle, the Faery Flag was guarded by twelve of the finest men, each one holding a rope tied to the flagstaff, so that Britach Sith might never fall to the enemy. But what enemy could stand, anyway, in the face of the ferocious MacLeods, beards piled on their chest, red hair flying? None but the MacDonalds.

At Glendale, MacDonalds as numberless as the thistles on the braes, came clamouring down to the noise of drum and fife, and hemmed in the MacLeods.

"The Faery Flag! Unfurl the Faery Flag!" came the cry, and the Twelve Finest unfurled the banner from its pole-head with a century of creases kinking its silken design.

Perhaps the sun came out to shine in the MacDonalds' eyes. Perhaps magic threads entwined themselves in the hearts of the MacLeods. Either way, before sunset, the glen was strewn with dead MacDonalds, and the day belonged to the MacLeods.

Back and back came the MacDonalds intent on revenge, numberless as the tics on the heather. At the battle of Waternish, thirty years later, the MacLeods of Clanranald once more faced destruction at the hands of their age-old enemy.

"The Faery Flag! Britach Sith or we die!" came the cry, and the little silken bundle at the head of the flagstaff licked out like a dragon's tongue over the heads of the Twelve Finest.

Suddenly, the MacDonalds' charge faltered and stumbled to a halt, the men behind cannoning into those leading. Claymores dropped from hands weak with fright, and the hardest men of the glens turned tail and fled. For marching down on them they saw an army of 10,000 men, bright with raised weapons, russet with jutting beards and wild red hair. Whether the light had tricked them or whether magic fibres of the flag had strangled their courage, the battle was a rout, and victory went to the MacLeods.

Many wars have washed over the purple hills of Scotland and stained the glens with blood. And many more MacLeods have travelled to dangers farther afield. But the Faery Flag has yet to be unfurled a third time. It lies folded within Castle Dunvegan, awaiting the third and last cry of "The Faery Flag! The Faery Flag! Unfurl the Faery Flag!"

Some believe the Faery Flag to have come to Scotland with the Norwegian king, Harald Hardraade, when he set out to conquer England in 1066. He flew a flag which he called Land-Ravager, a magic flag which, once unfurled, supposedly brought destruction to any enemy. On his journey south to fight King Harold, he lost Land-Ravager somewhere among the lochs and glens of Scotland. Even in this century, during the First and Second World Wars and on battlefields far away from the braes, men of the MacLeod clan carried photographs of Britach Sith over their hearts. Some of them even came home again, their photographs as creased and tattered as the flag itself.

Tyndale's Crime

1536

LET ME TELL YOU ABOUT TYNDALE. WHO AM I? Nobody much. In fact, I won't tell you my name, or I'll be in trouble with the authorities again. But to my mind, William Tyndale was one of the great men of all time. And now they've burned him. Like a log of wood, they've burned him.

He studied at Oxford and Cambridge; he was a brilliant scholar – could speak five languages! His colleagues had nothing but good to say about the man. But when he set about translating the New Testament from Latin into English, for the common people to read, suddenly he was a criminal. He had to go abroad to get it done.

"If God spares my life, ere many years I will cause the ploughboy to know more of the Scriptures than you do," he told his learned colleagues before he went.

Even abroad they hounded him. Some villain overheard the printers talking about the new book they were working on: Tyndale's New Testament. "What a revolution this will stir up in England!" the printers said, and this eavesdropper thought, Revolution? Here's news the authorities will want to know about.

When they raided the printers, only the first ten sheets had been run off. But William was too quick for them. He had those ten sheets rolled up in his pack, and he was away to another city before they could lay hands on him.

He was in danger the whole time, every day of every year, but he pressed on with his work. Two editions were printed finally – one large, for reading aloud in public, one small enough to fit in a man's pocket. Anyone's pocket. Yours and mine.

He needed help, naturally, to distribute them. An association of European merchants, regularly travelling to and fro across the Channel in the course of their business, hid Tyndale's little printed Bibles among their goods. The books sold for two shillings, in shady corners and at back doors – black-market Bibles, selling like smuggled rum. There were 6,000 in the country before the bishops even knew what was happening. Everyone wanted one. *I* wanted one. I don't ever remember wanting a thing so much, or prizing anything so dearly as that parcel slipped into my hand one rainy day on Sheep Street.

All the clever men, the scholars and bishops bleated that it was an "ignorant piece of work", riddled with errors. What did a few errors matter to the likes of us who had always been shut out from understanding, because nobody taught us Latin? We knew it was an excuse. We knew they wanted to keep God to themselves – not share Him about. "Pearls trampled under the feet of swine," was how they put it. We didn't care. We had the Word of God in our own hands at last, in our own language. My old mother learned to read, specially to be able to read Tyndale's Bible.

When they couldn't track down the printing presses, they bought up thousands of finished copies and burned them in great bonfires. But the more they burned, the more people wanted to know what it was they were missing.

So the King made it illegal to own a Tyndale Bible.

Troopers searched high and low, in bread ovens and mangers and haylofts. Anyone found owning a Bible or reading one was put in prison for a month. I was one.

It was Shrove Tuesday, 1527. There were six of us. They dressed us up in penitential robes and gave us candles to carry, and faggots of wood. And there was this great parade through the streets – a public humiliation. We had to kneel on the ground and beg forgiveness from the people for our "crime". Then we were led three times round a bonfire – had to fuel it with those faggots of wood – and they made us throw our Bibles into the flames.

It was like throwing my very heart, I can tell you. It's hard to put into words, but I hated myself for doing it. Tyndale had given us this great book and here I was, destroying his years of work, *apologizing* for the joy he had given me. Of course I never meant a word of what I said that day. But I said it, even so. Like the apostle Peter denying Christ three times, to save his skin.

And now they've thrown Tyndale himself into the flames. Do you want to know his last words, before they strangled him at the stake and set him alight? "Oh Lord, open thou the King of England's eyes." That's what he said.

Well, you can burn a man and you can burn his books. But the truth won't burn, no more than water or milk. Fifty thousand copies of Tyndale's Bible have come into this country since the presses started up in Belgium. They might as well try to gather up the stars as to keep all those out of the hands of the people. It can't be done. Look here, hidden behind this panel in the wall: here's proof. Hold it. Open it. Read it. They will never stop up God's mouth – not now He's able to speak to us face to face, in Tyndale's English.

Tyndale's translations were not the first. As far back as John Wycliffe in the reign of Richard II, the Bible had been available in English. But copies of that had been hand-written and cost the great sum of £30 apiece, so they were scarcely meant for ordinary people.

Though Tyndale's translations were suppressed (of the first 15,000 volumes imported to England only three or four are left in existence) King Henry VIII was forced to acknowledge a need for a Bible in English. He therefore authorized a new translation – and the Great Bible came into existence.

These beautiful, large-format volumes were chained to church pulpits and read out at weekly services. People flocked to hear them in such vast numbers that the nobility and clergy must have taken fright. Within a couple of years Henry passed a law forbidding anyone to own or read or listen to readings from an English-language Bible unless they were of noble birth or a member of the clergy. Ordinary people were once again shut out. Two more reigns came and went before they were allowed access to the Word of God.

The Ghost of Anne Boleyn

1536

When the old queen died, Anne Boleyn and her train of ladies wore yellow dresses, in celebration. "Now am I a queen indeed!" she said gleefully.

She had already won the heart of King Henry VIII away from his wife of eighteen years; in order to marry Anne, he had divorced Catherine. But now everyone would regard Anne as the true queen – even those who had questioned Henry's right to set aside his first wife. All that remained was for Anne to give Henry a child – a male heir – and their happiness would be complete.

She gave him a daughter – Elizabeth – but then Catherine had achieved *that* much. No, no. What Henry really wanted was a son, and Anne would give him that, too. Already she was pregnant again.

Turning the handle of the door, Anne entered, already shuffling the handful of pretty phrases which she would deal the King if she found him there. Henry was there, but to her surprise, not alone. One of the ladies-in-waiting was sitting on his knee, giggling at some witty remark of his, her fingers sunk lovingly in his beard.

At the sight of Anne, Jane Seymour flinched; her cheeks flushed red. But Henry's big, fat-chopped face looked oddly calm, oddly undisturbed. He made no hasty move to slide the wench off his lap. "Be at peace, sweetheart," he said to Anne, "and all shall go well with thee."

Anne Boleyn stirred herself from frozen aston-ishment to shrill hysterics. One hand went to her round belly, the other to her forehead. She was hot. She was cold. Tears pricked behind her eyes. She felt sick. The roaring in her ears told her she was about to faint.

The shock of finding her husband with another lady sent Anne into labour much too soon. The baby she was expecting – a boy – was born dead. Afterwards, Henry shouted at her for allowing "the loss of his boy". Anne reproached him for being the cause. But Anne had seen him wear that expression before – when people had counselled him against divorce, when people had spoken up for the ex-queen. Henry might just as well have shut the visor of a helmet: his face was all steel.

His love for Anne went out like a snuffed candle. All the fun had been in the chase and the wooing. Now he had seen another pretty face and he wanted to have it. Anne Boleyn was headstrong and gave herself airs. Saucy little Jane Seymour was far more agreeable, far more accommodating. No one had been able to stop him changing wives before – indeed his toadying ministers had smoothed the way to it. And if he could do it once, what was to stop him doing it again? The toadies would arrange it.

So he cut Anne Boleyn adrift.

There are always a ready supply of people who will say anything for money, or because they have been told to. A good lawyer can whip up a whisper of gossip – the smallest, spiteful rumour – into a mountain of damning evidence. Before long Anne was accused of being unfaithful to Henry with a whole host of men – even her brother. Accusations were flung like clods of mud, until the truth disappeared altogether. Henry had no interest in the truth – only the outcome. The Queen must die, so that he could marry Jane Seymour.

He un-married Anne. He un-queened Anne. He sent for a swordsman to cut off her head.

Getting up at two in the morning, she said prayers till dawn. Later, she sent for Sir William Kingston and said, "I hear I shall not die afore noon, and I am very sorry therefore, for I thought to be dead by this time and past my pain."

"The pain will be little," he said, his eyes fixed awkwardly on the carpet at her feet.

Anne nodded. "I have heard say the executioner is very good," she said, putting both hands round her throat, "and I have a little neck."

In the morning of 19 May 1536, Henry VIII went hunting in Richmond Park. He was restless and excitable as he stood beneath the shade of a large oak tree and the eager hounds turned and leapt and yelped on their leashes. Across the park came a dull roar – the signal gun being fired at the Tower of London.

"Aha! The deed is done!" cried Henry jubilantly punching the air with both fists. "Uncouple the hounds and away!" Next day, when he became betrothed to Jane Seymour, he wore a white silk suit – a sort of fancy-dress intended for gala days.

But Anne Boleyn's spirit was not so easily done down. Her headless ghost leads a nightly procession of phantom knights and ladies through the Tower, down to the chapel of St Peter-ad-Vincula within the Tower's precinct, where her body was interred. And every 19 May, a ghostly coach drawn by four headless black horses drives up to the gates of Blickling Hall where Anne was born. In it sits a ghost, her severed head resting in her lap. Meanwhile her father's accursed spirit is chased by a pack of shrieking demons over forty Norfolk bridges from midnight till dawn: an everlasting penance for giving his daughter into the hands of a murderer.

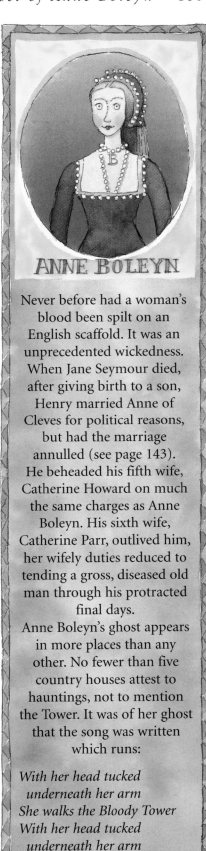

ANNE BOLEYN

Never before had a woman's blood been spilt on an English scaffold. It was an unprecedented wickedness. When Jane Seymour died, after giving birth to a son, Henry married Anne of Cleves for political reasons, but had the marriage annulled (see page 143). He beheaded his fifth wife, Catherine Howard on much the same charges as Anne Boleyn. His sixth wife, Catherine Parr, outlived him, her wifely duties reduced to tending a gross, diseased old man through his protracted final days.

Anne Boleyn's ghost appears in more places than any other. No fewer than five country houses attest to hauntings, not to mention the Tower. It was of her ghost that the song was written which runs:

With her head tucked
underneath her arm
She walks the Bloody Tower
With her head tucked
underneath her arm
At the midnight hour . . .

"Little Jack Horner Sat in a Corner"

about 1 5 3 7

LITTLE JACK HORNER sat in the corner of the inn, the Christmas pie on the table in front of him. He was deeply depressed. What would become of the animals, he wondered; of the fish in the ponds, of the crops in the fields, of the books on the shelves, of the wines in the cellar? What would become of the tenants who rented their land from the monasteries, of the church plate and the saintly relics? And what would become of him, if the abbey ceased to exist?

He knew the answer to all but the last. Everything would go to the King – that insatiable, Godless villain, Henry VIII, who had set about disbanding holy communities a thousand years old. Perhaps during Jack's service the odd teaspoon or bottle had found its way into his pocket, but on the whole he considered himself an honest, loyal, hardworking servant. But where would loyalty and hard work get him if the monastery were dissolved? He would lose his position, his livelihood, his home. Would his master still employ him when that master became plain "Richard Whiting, Gent", rather than Abbot of Glastonbury?

Horner eyed the pie. Well, perhaps the bribe would work after all, and Glastonbury would be spared. Jack did not hold out much hope. He had heard what happened to other monasteries – their treasures confiscated, their statues smashed, their monks turned out of doors. Jack failed to see how one Christmas pie was going to persuade the King of England to spare Glastonbury. Even this one.

Jack had helped to "bake" it. He had fetched the deeds from the abbot's great oak chest, rolled them tight and bent them round until all twelve fitted inside the pie dish. Then he had watched as the baked pastry lid went on. It was like the old nursery rhyme: "four-and-twenty blackbirds baked in a pie" . . . Only this pie had twelve surprises inside it: the deeds to twelve manorial estates owned by Glastonbury Abbey. The bribe was supposed to persuade King Henry not to close down the abbey.

"That's a fair pie you have there," the inn-keeper said, startling Jack Horner who was lost in thought. "You'll not be wanting supper, then?"

"Yes, yes!" said Horner. "The pie's not mine. It is a present for the King. Bring me something hot, please, and a mug of porter."

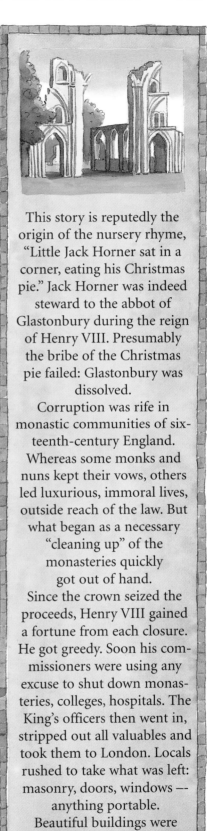

After the first, Jack drank several more mugs, and the more he drank, the deeper he sank into brooding melancholy. What did the King of England want with twelve Somerset estates? What had he ever done to deserve them? Loyalty and hard work ought to count for something! Jack Horner clumped an angry fist down on the table. The pie jumped. Its pastry lid came loose.

The fingers of Jack's other hand went up to his mouth. What had he done? One corner of a deed showed white like a piece of tripe. Little Jack Horner glanced around the dimly lit inn. No one was looking. The document slipped out of the pie easy as winking. The pastry slipped back into place. Then, with trembling fingers, Jack broke the wax seal, pulled the ribbon . . .

Mells in Somerset.

It was the best estate of all the twelve. The plum. Horner knew its spreading beech trees, its stew ponds and hayricks, its skylines and rambling manor house. He closed both hands around the document and kissed it.

Well? Weren't eleven manors bribe enough for anyone? King Henry would never know there had been twelve to start off with. If the abbey were dissolved, then better that Mells should be kept back. If Henry spared it – well, then, Jack would always return the deed to Abbot Whiting, and be thanked for saving it.

A log settled in the grate and Jack guiltily crammed the parchment under his jacket. It lay over his heart, muffling the quick beat. He tried to summon the landlord, but the voice cracked in his throat. He breathed deep and tried again. "Landlord! A drink for everyone here, and have one yourself!"

Drinkers looked around, smiling. Horner felt a glow of pleasure.

"Thank you kindly, sir, and who shall I tell folks is treating them?"

"Tell them: 'a man of property'. Tell them: 'the Master of Mells', my good man. Jack Horner of Mells in the county of Somerset."

This story is reputedly the origin of the nursery rhyme, "Little Jack Horner sat in a corner, eating his Christmas pie." Jack Horner was indeed steward to the abbot of Glastonbury during the reign of Henry VIII. Presumably the bribe of the Christmas pie failed: Glastonbury was dissolved.

Corruption was rife in monastic communities of sixteenth-century England. Whereas some monks and nuns kept their vows, others led luxurious, immoral lives, outside reach of the law. But what began as a necessary "cleaning up" of the monasteries quickly got out of hand.

Since the crown seized the proceeds, Henry VIII gained a fortune from each closure. He got greedy. Soon his commissioners were using any excuse to shut down monasteries, colleges, hospitals. The King's officers then went in, stripped out all valuables and took them to London. Locals rushed to take what was left: masonry, doors, windows — anything portable. Beautiful buildings were reduced to ruins. It has been called the Great Pillage.

The Flanders Mare

1540

HENRY RESTED HIS HANDS ON HIS BELLY, AND contemplated the two paintings. What a masterly painter Holbein was! And what a statesman Cromwell had been to track down two such handsome girls! Lutherans, too! A marriage to one of these princesses would endear him to half Europe, as well as filling that cold space in his life left by the death of his third wife.

Poor little Jane. He mourned her even now – even though he detested wearing black. At the cost of her own life, she had given him a boy child, a male heir, and for that he would always thank her. But a man cannot be expected to do without a wife; not a man of such royal appetites as Henry VIII. One more glance at the portraits, and Henry made

his choice: the older girl, Anne. What though she could play no music? There are more important attributes in a wife.

Anne was wooed, and Anne was won, though not by Henry in person: he left all that to his diplomats. Anne was sent for and Anne came, crossing the Channel in the depths of winter. The closer she came, the more impatient he grew to see her. So, summoning seven gentlemen of about his own age, he told them to put on grey overcoats and saddle up: they were all riding to Rochester. Behind their obliging smiles, he glimpsed a certain unwillingness, given the filthy weather, but he just could not wait another moment to see his future bride! Henry, too, called for his horse to be saddled and for a grey overcoat to wear.

Eight anonymous gentlemen, all in grey, rode to Rochester, where Anne of Cleves had paused on her journey to London. What a surprise she would have, that beauty from Flanders, when her betrothed suddenly appeared and presented her with a New Year present of tippet and muff, and along with them his undying devotion!

The surprise was mutual.

What did the princess think, still queasy from the crossing, when she first saw her bridegroom? A mountain of bejewelled lard, sweating cheeks bulging through a square beard, eyes piggy with outrage. When she reverently fell to her knees

before him, she could smell a whiff of disease from his lap and legs and feet.

What did Henry think when he first saw his bride? Nothing that could be put into words. He simply stared at that pock-marked face, that stocky body, that nose. The hands she thrust into his were dry as pigskin. When she spoke to him in some ugly, guttural language he did not understand, he could not get away quickly enough.

Thomas Cromwell would pay for this.

"Alas! Whom shall men trust? She looks like nothing so much as a great Flanders mare!" blared the King.

The official meeting of bride and groom at Blackheath scarcely went any better. Admittedly, inside a brocaded tent, with music and quantities of warmed wine within reach, Henry found it easier to be civil. But no one had the right to be as ugly as that! He felt duped. He had been sold a pup. Thomas Cromwell must get him out of this marriage or face the consequences.

The lawyers picked over the princess's life as if checking for nits. But though she had been betrothed as a child to someone else, the law said it was not enough of an impediment. Furthermore, the King's allies would be seriously offended if the wedding were called off. "Is there then no other remedy but I must put my neck into the yoke?" bayed the King.

Cromwell would pay with his: one neck for another. Even as Henry placed the wedding ring on Anne's finger, he was thinking how to be rid of her. She was, after all, his fourth wife, and a man who takes four wives can always take a fifth . . .

The wedding over, the bride was quickly dispatched to Richmond "for the good of her health". Her ugliness was a crime, pure and simple: a kind of treason. He owed it to his people to be rid of her. Besides, Henry had seen a face he much preferred.

Archbishop Cranmer, having just performed the marriage, dutifully listed all the reasons why it should be dissolved. Convocation declared it null and void. Parliament stifled its groans and passed a Bill to the same effect. All eyes turned on Cromwell, who had masterminded the marriage: yet another over-ambitious man brought down by trying too hard to please: yet another casualty of the King-who-liked-marrying.

Meanwhile, Anne of Cleves was approached in private, by flattering, diplomatic men, and offered the chance to retire peacefully from her position as Queen and wife. They promised that her position at court would be that of the King's sister; no one would have precedence over her, except for the

Discussing remarriage, after Jane Seymour's death in childbirth, Henry asked Francis I of France to assemble a selection of pretty candidates for him to choose from. "It is impossible to bring ladies of noble blood to market, as horses are trotted out at a fair," retorted Francis. That is how Hans Holbein came to paint two pictures – of Anne and of her sister Amelia – so Henry could "view" them without committing himself.

Unfortunately, Holbein omitted the smallpox scars which pitted Anne's face, and painted a flattering portrait. Cromwell's agents abroad, anxious to bring about the alliance, also reported nothing but good. Thomas Cromwell, when he saw the King's reaction, tried to duck the blame, but when he could not extricate Henry from the marriage, went to the Tower and was beheaded in July 1540. This is the man who had helped Henry become supreme head of the Church.

King's daughters and his future queen. And she should have £4,000 a year to live on.

Anne of Cleves sat in the window of Richmond Palace, one hand spread across her throat as she listened. She did not reply at once. Perhaps she was trying to choke back tears of disappointment. "You may tell the King I live only to please His Majesty, and will act according to his wishes – though I hope I may be allowed sometimes to see the Princess Elizabeth who has become most dear to me."

The French ambassador caught her eye. The smile was so fleeting that he thought he must have imagined it, and yet so dazzlingly happy that, for a moment, the ex-Queen of England had appeared truly beautiful.

Six months later, the King was paying a visit to his ex-wife. The servants listening at the door heard laughter all afternoon. The Lady Anne had acquired a good grasp of the English language, and the King was as relaxed as anyone had ever seen him. Plainly, Henry and Anne were finding each other the best of company. She was witty and clever, well read and well bred. Best of all she was a good listener. While she sewed, the King talked, describing events at court, scandals uncovered, visitors up from the country, the word from overseas.

"Do you suppose they might be reunited?" whispered a lady-in-waiting sentimentally.

"He must lack company – a sick old man like that, surrounded by toadies."

"Do you suppose he has come to claim her?" whispered an equerry.

But the King swept out again and left, he in excellent good humour, she waving brightly from the window till he was out of sight. The Lady Anne seemed greatly cheered by the visit. Perhaps Henry had let slip that he was secretly married already to Catherine Howard.

The Staircase

1560

THE QUEEN, HER HEAD ON ONE SIDE, contemplated the portrait being held up by two equerries. The man in the picture was handsome – dashing, even. "Hang it at the foot of my bed, where I can see it when I wake!" she said.

Elizabeth I was going through the motions – pretending to be contemplating marriage to yet another eligible suitor. This time it was an archduke – the man in the portrait. Before him there had been King Philip of Spain, the eldest Prince of Sweden, the Earl of Arran . . .

But those well acquainted with Elizabeth knew she cared nothing for any of them. She was not stirred by the archduke in the portrait, nor by any Spaniard, Swede or Scotsman. Elizabeth was in love with Robert Dudley, her master of the horse.

His relatively lowly station did not matter (a commoner can soon be made a baron or an earl), nor did his father's execution for treason. No, there was only one small impediment to Elizabeth marrying her true love: Robert Dudley already had a wife.

"The Queen is only waiting for her to die," wrote the Spanish ambassador in his letters home.

But why should Dudley's wife, Amy Robsart, die? A young woman in the prime of life? It was said by some that she was ill. Others said that she was all too healthy for Dudley's liking and that he was wondering how to change that.

Amy Robsart sat in the big dark house on Cumnor Hill. The servants had all gone out to the fair in nearby Oxford: she had insisted on them going, despite her pain and low spirits. Every night she rubbed the apothecary's lotion into her breast, but it seemed to do no good. Perhaps the pain came simply of a broken heart. For she was a woman whose husband did not love her – a woman who, just by continuing to breathe, blocked her husband's path to success and happiness. That was why she had not refused the wine at dinner, even though she feared it might be poisoned.

Not that Robert would do such a thing. Oh no, surely not her Robert who, in marrying her, had promised to cherish her. But the Queen – ah, the Queen's wishes could creep like ivy into every last crevice of her kingdom. Amy could feel those wishes entwining her, dragging on her, sapping her strength. A loyal subject ought to help the Queen to happiness, rather than hinder her.

The big dark house creaked and rustled around her, its corridors, landings and stairs unlit. It was not her own house. It belonged to a friend of Robert's. And Robert was away at court, as usual, dancing, paying compliments, exchanging witty remarks with the Virgin Queen. The pain in Amy's chest grew worse. The trees on Cumnor Hill put their heads together and whispered – gossip and rumour, rumour and gossip.

Robert Dudley was out riding with the Queen when the messenger arrived from Cumnor. Terrible news, a tragic accident. "What has happened?" asked Dudley.

"It's your wife, sir. Found yesterday, sir. A tragic fall, sir. The stairs . . ."

Amy Robsart lay spread-eagled at the foot of the staircase in the house at Cumnor Hill, her neck broken, her feet bare, her skin as pale as her night-dress. The coroner's jury brought in a verdict of accidental death. In the dark, unfamiliar house, she had tripped and fallen. The other possibility – that she had committed suicide – could not be put into words, for that would have meant a suicide's burial in unconsecrated ground.

The public, however, were in no doubt as to what had happened. Dudley had wished his wife dead and now she was. In the public imagination, Robert Dudley was a murderer, and people hated him for it. The rumour-mongers whispered:

"Have you heard? The Queen is secretly married to Dudley!"

"She is making him Earl of Leicester."

"She means him to rule England with her!"

"A murderer in the arms of our Queen!"

But they were all wrong. The truth was that Amy Robsart's suspicious death had made such a marriage impossible. Dudley was so unpopular now that Elizabeth would antagonize the whole country, her ministers and her allies by marrying him.

Concealed behind the red curls, the porcelain-white skin, the coquettish flirting, the bright, bird-like eyes, was a steely, calculating brain. If Elizabeth had ever considered marriage to the beautiful Robert Dudley, she shut her mind to it now. Love was sweet, but politics were crucial. Marriage to her, she proclaimed, "was a matter of the weal (well-being) of the kingdom". She would only marry if it were in the country's best interests.

She did indeed make Robert Dudley Earl of Leicester, and as he knelt before her to receive the accolade, she tickled his neck playfully and giggled. The courtiers turned to one another with raised eyebrows and meaningful looks. But they were entirely wrong. The earldom was intended to make Robert Dudley a fit suitor for a queen, but not Queen Elizabeth. She had suggested he should woo the troublesome Mary Stuart, Queen of Scots.

Elizabeth was Queen first, woman afterwards. She did not marry the man in the portrait, nor the Duke of Anjou, nor Emperor Charles IX, nor the Duke of Alençon, nor the Earl of Essex, nor any of the other suitors who wooed her. She was in her mid-twenties and yet she had no illusions left. She was a queen, and whoever smiled or bowed or sent her gifts or poetry or portraits was thinking chiefly of her crown, not her beauty.

She was a kind of staircase ambitious men wanted to climb.

Elizabeth never married, although Parliament and the country urged her to, and she assured them she would. She liked to keep suitors dangling for as long as possible, for while a suit continued, she was in a very strong position to negotiate.

Did Amy Robsart kill herself? Was she murdered on her husband's orders? Or by Sir William Cecil, the Queen's Secretary, who frowned on the romance and knew the scandal would force Elizabeth to shun Dudley? Or did Amy just trip in the dark and fall, her spine breaking easily because of the breast cancer which some say was already killing her? The truth will never be unearthed now.

Robert Dudley took a second wife in 1573 and married again, bigamously, in 1578. Elizabeth was fleetingly furious with him, but relented and, despite his poor military record, appointed him commander of forces against the Spanish Armada in 1588. That same year, however, he suddenly died: poisoned. Rumour had it that poison meant for his wife had somehow found its way into his own food.

Walter Raleigh Salutes the Queen

1580

IT WAS NO WEATHER FOR FINERY. BUT QUEEN Elizabeth shone like the sun wherever she went (as she never tired of being told). So Walter Raleigh pulled on his finest shirt, with its wide, stiff ruff of pleated cotton at the throat. His manservant helped him into the stiff, bombasted brocade doublet and short-hose, then pulled the laces tight. (The bright lining showed through the slashed panels of the plump hose like segments of Seville orange.) He drew on his own pale, silvery, silk stockings and secured them with tasselled garter-ribbons above his knee. Then he slid his arms into the painted leather over-doublet and his feet into his new low-heeled, calfskin shoes which he fastened with ribbon bows. He buckled on his embossed swordbelt, then, last of all, swung round him his brand new cloak – a masterpiece of panned, piped, interlined, gilt-clasped, silver-corded velvet. Raleigh was about to meet the Queen of England for the very first time.

Magnificent as Raleigh looked, his outfit paled into shabbiness beside the Queen's finery. As she descended from her coach, the small boys who had chased three miles in its wake caught their breath and gasped. She was as marvellous as a galleon new-rigged, as an angel among shepherds. Her pale kid shoes might as well have belonged to a fairy-tale princess.

But this was not London. It was a country town. This was countryside overshadowed by forest, overhung with cloud, overrun with mud. Elizabeth hesitated and looked around her, with obvious unease, skirts bunched within her two fists, to lift them clear of the dirt. Across her path lay . . . a large, brown puddle.

A cold, spitting rain fell on Walter's hair as he took off his hat and bowed low. A cold, reproachful blast of wind ruffled his cuffs as he unfastened his splendid cloak. Then, with a bull-fighter's flourish (but the careless expression of one who does such things every day) Walter Raleigh laid down his cloak. He laid it down over the puddle – it made a soft, velvety squelch – inviting the Queen to walk over it rather than dirty her shoes.

The sight of that handsome velvet cloak lying in the mud made even Elizabeth catch her breath. She stared for a moment as the cloth grew sodden and settled, then she turned a dazzling smile at the owner. The glance lengthened as she took in his dashing good looks, his exquisite tailoring. Then she stepped on to the cloak, as carefully as a skater stepping on to the ice of a pond. Momentarily, the crowd glimpsed the pale prettiness of her shoe.

The cloak lay ruined, soaked. But as Walter said, with a shrug, to any who mentioned it, that was a small sacrifice to please a queen. Even the beaux and coxcombs strutting in the Queen's wake held handkerchiefs to their noses and whispered among themselves that it was "cleverly done", even they admired the panache of it – the grand, chivalric flourish of it. Raleigh was a made man.

It is not known with any certainty whether the incident of the cloak actually took place – several towns lay claim to it – and whether it was this which first endeared Walter Raleigh to Queen Elizabeth I. Certainly he became a great favourite of hers after joining court at the age of thirty. She heaped gifts of land on him and sent him on various missions of exploration and conquest. But she never seems to have found him reliable enough to entrust with high office. He could not intrigue as well as those around him and eventually lost his head for treason. The cult of Elizabeth's beauty gave rise to music, literature and art, even after Elizabeth herself, vain to the last, had decayed into a sad, painted old lady with rotten teeth and a flame-coloured wig. At the end, she sat up in a chair for three days and nights for fear, if she went to bed, death would lay hands on her.

Francis Drake and a Game of Bowls

1580-1588

THE SUN ROSE BRIGHT AND CHEERFUL, BUT THE bride did not. Lizzie Sydenham put on her wedding finery with a heavy heart. Her mother and father greeted her with little cries of admiration and happiness – "Fancy! Our little Lizzie a bride!" – but she could not smile.

Even so, she knew better than to say, "I don't want to marry. I do not love this man." So she took the nosegay of flowers from her mother and stepped out of doors for the short walk to church. What good would be served by defying her parents' wishes?

Her one true love was oceans away, attempting the impossible, trying to sail around the world. If he were not already dead, it would take several miracles to bring him safe home. Her parents said Francis Drake was a nobody, a rough, coarse, low-born pirate, for all the gold, silver and pearls he had stolen in the Spanish Main. Lizzie did not believe it, but when, after years of waiting, Francis still had not come home to claim her, what else could she do but accept the respectable, unremarkable gentleman waiting for her now at Stogumber Church? Suddenly, something made her look up.

It happened so fast: there was no dodging aside, no ducking down or turning to run. She stopped stock still, and with a massive thud which shook the ground and raised a spew of dust, a great round stone ball landed at her feet. It struck so hard that it half sank itself in the dirt. The little wedding party stared.

Lizzie's father said that it must be masonry from the church roof. Her mother said someone was trying to kill them. But Lizzie simply handed back her bouquet and said, "I shan't marry today. Francis has fired a cannon ball across the world to forbid it. He wants me to wait for him, so I shall."

And she did. Nothing would persuade her to break her vow. When Francis Drake sailed into Plymouth harbour, and all the church bells in the West Country welcomed him home, Lizzie Sydenham stood waiting.

The rock was not a cannonball at all, of course. Nothing so ordinary. It was a meteorite. While Drake's little vessel the *Golden Hind* sailed round the world, a fragment of debris from an exploding star had been voyaging through the vastness of space, to land at Elizabeth Sydenham's feet. The Spanish said Sir Francis Drake had a drum with which he could summon up the wind. They said he had a mirror in which he saw the future. They said that he had sold his soul to the Devil for mastery of the seven seas. But then the Spanish were superstitious, and their captains preferred not to admit that any Englishman could get the better of them. Ever since Drake had sailed up the River Tagus to Cadiz, and burned the King of Spain's warships, they had called him "El Draco" – "The Dragon" – a beast of fire and destruction.

With Spain's fleet – its "Invincible Armada" – massing for war on the other side of the Channel, the English themselves liked to think that Drake possessed magic powers. They told how he had *made* the entire English fleet, sitting on a cliff one day, whittling a twig. Every splinter had turned by magic into a ship on the sea below.

The Spanish, on the other hand, had felled an entire forest, to build their fleet.

When the Armada finally attacked, the English admirals – Drake, Hawkins, Frobisher and Lord Howard of Effingham – were playing a game of bowls on Plymouth Hoe, a grassy flatness overlooking the sea. The pleasant knock of wood against wood was interspersed with talk of strategy, and jokes about Spanish beards.

Suddenly there was a shout, and a look-out came pelting along the Hoe: "They're coming! They're coming! The Spanish fleet is sighted! They're coming!"

Snatching up gloves and sword belts, peering out to sea, the various commanders started for their ships at a run. There were crews to turn out, gangplanks to raise, ropes to cast off, anchors to weigh, drums to be sounded, wives to kiss goodbye . . . The fate of the country was about to be decided.

"Hold hard, friends, hold hard!"

They turned back. Drake stood just as before, a cluster of bowls at his feet. "Plenty of time to win the game and beat the Spaniards too!" he said, in his slow, Devonshire drawl. And he bowled – slow and steady and true.

The other men walked back, laid aside their gloves, took their turns. Over the horizon a hundred topsails, like puffy white clouds, moved into sight. Crowds gathered along every quay and jetty and cliff, standing on tiptoe, craning their necks to see. But the English commanders finished their game before strolling sedately to their ships and giving battle-orders, for all the world as if they were ordering dinner.

The English ships were smaller, quicker and more manoeuvrable than the lumbering Spanish galleys and galleons. They could dart in close, loosing cannonfire and arrows. Drake used fire-ships, too – filled with kindling or gunpowder, helms lashed on collision course, while down below, the fuses burned . . . Fire ships wrought havoc among the Spanish fleet, blasting them out of the water or burning them down to their keels. El Draco could indeed breathe fire.

Even so, the Spanish sea captains believed that their honour depended on victory, and their honour was worth more to them than their lives. They fought with frenzied heroism, until blood ran in

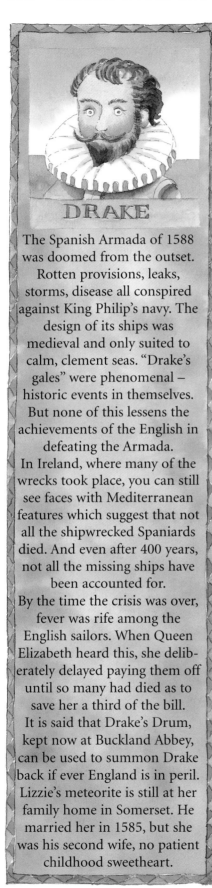

DRAKE

The Spanish Armada of 1588 was doomed from the outset. Rotten provisions, leaks, storms, disease all conspired against King Philip's navy. The design of its ships was medieval and only suited to calm, clement seas. "Drake's gales" were phenomenal – historic events in themselves. But none of this lessens the achievements of the English in defeating the Armada.

In Ireland, where many of the wrecks took place, you can still see faces with Mediterranean features which suggest that not all the shipwrecked Spaniards died. And even after 400 years, not all the missing ships have been accounted for.

By the time the crisis was over, fever was rife among the English sailors. When Queen Elizabeth heard this, she deliberately delayed paying them off until so many had died as to save her a third of the bill.

It is said that Drake's Drum, kept now at Buckland Abbey, can be used to summon Drake back if ever England is in peril.

Lizzie's meteorite is still at her family home in Somerset. He married her in 1585, but she was his second wife, no patient childhood sweetheart.

streams from their gunports and their ships foundered under them. Their commander-in-chief, the Duke of Medina Sidonia, was an incompetent, but they fought on despite him, till ammunition ran out on both sides, and the noise of battle fizzled into silence.

Then the Spanish beat north up the English Channel, planning to skirt the north coast of Scotland and sail home. That is the day, legend says, when Francis Drake went ashore, and danced with the witches and demons on a windswept clifftop, summoning up a storm.

Gales came in from the west. Damaged, leaking ships, manned by injured, hungry crews, wallowed lower and lower in the water. The storms, which raged for a fortnight, drove ships on to rocks, on to sandbars, into unfriendly harbours, or simply swamped them in deep water, leaving not a trace. Of 130 ships which set sail, just over half reached home, and of 27,000 men only some 9,000 survived to feel the Spanish sun on their faces. Then they lay in their mangled ships and died of fever, as though fate had damned every last man.

On his journey home overland, the Duke of Medina Sidonia was pelted with stones by small boys for his disgraceful failure.

Drake went home to Lizzie. But ambition for gold and glory soon sent him back to plundering the Spanish Main. He died there, and was lowered to his eternal rest in the vaults of the sea.

The Long-Expected End

1587

MARY SPRINKLED sand over her letter, to stop the ink running, then shook off the surplus. It made a noise like voices whispering.

She had pondered long and hard whether to answer the letter from Anthony Babington. He was a dear, devoted, devout young man, but rash and passionate. He said he was planning to assassinate Queen Elizabeth and put Mary in her place.

So long as she did not actually *acknowledge* his suggestion, she could not be accused of conspiring with him. But surely a letter would be safe enough hidden inside the empty casks which left Chartley House?

Letters from her friends and supporters arrived in the full casks, and her own left in the empty ones. It was a fine, convenient arrangement and a great comfort to a woman kept under house arrest for the best part of twenty years. Mary folded the letter, and allowed her hand to rest on it, trembling. She had just given her consent to his assassination plot.

Mary Queen of Scots was Elizabeth's second cousin, a Catholic and a serious nuisance. She threatened the nation's stability. Every Catholic would have liked to see Elizabeth dead and Mary crowned in her place. Elizabeth, for her part, would have liked to see Mary dead and out of the way.

And yet they were cousins. Elizabeth must not seem unnaturally cruel to her own flesh and blood. It was a problem. Best if Mary should be discovered committing some gross act of treason, plotting some coup. So Elizabeth put her secret service to work, spying on Mary, keeping a watch on her and her friends, vetting all her visitors – intercepting all her mail.

So when Babington wrote to Mary of killing the Queen, and Mary wrote back, encouragingly, Sir Francis Walsingham, head of the Queen's secret service, read both letters. After all, it was he who had organized the business of the wine casks.

Mary was damned by that letter to Babington. Babington and his fellow conspirators were doomed men. Their plot gave Elizabeth just the excuse she had lacked all these years. Now she could put Mary to death.

In September, Babington and thirteen other conspirators were dragged through the streets of London on hurdles, face-up to the sky, to a scaffold of dizzying height where they were hanged, drawn and quartered.

Elizabeth's Council clamoured for Mary to be imprisoned at once in the Tower of London, but Elizabeth sent her to Fotheringay Castle instead – yet another secure house in the long line of comfortable prisons. At Fotheringay she was in the charge of Sir Amyas Paulet.

Tearfully Elizabeth received loyal deputations from her people calling for the death of the treacherous Mary. With great shows of unwillingness, she finally allowed herself to be persuaded. Mary was guilty of treason. Wild delight met the announcement, with church bells ringing all day and bonfires lit in the streets. Elizabeth's adoring public bayed for Mary's blood. All Elizabeth had to do was agree.

Mary's son James pleaded for her life – but not very hard. He was in line to become King of England, and nothing must jeopardize that. He would be a fool, he wrote to a friend, "if I should prefer my mother to the title".

Elizabeth signed the death warrant . . . but would not give instructions for it to be sent. "What a great relief it would be to me," she murmured aloud, "if some loyal subject were now to kill Mary . . ."

Amyas Paulet, Mary's prison warder, refused to take this heavy hint. He wrote back that he would not "make shipwreck of his conscience without law or warrant".

And so the warrant was sent – oh, quite against Elizabeth's will – an abuse of trust (she said), a wicked flouting of her will! She had never intended it to be sent! The man responsible would pay!

Even so, on Tuesday, 7 February, a hand knocked gently on the door of Mary's apartments and a gentleman informed her, with great civility and courtesy, that, "Tomorrow morning, ma'am, you must die."

Mary spent the night praying, then in the morning dressed entirely in black with a veil of white lawn over her auburn hair. At forty-four, her former beauty had faded. Years of enforced idleness, sitting over books or embroidery or letters had made her portly, with a fat face and double chin. Her shoulders stooped. And yet it was a dignified, fearless figure who was led into the great hall of Fotheringay Castle to be confronted by a scaffold draped in black, two executioners, a huge axe.

Her servants were beside themselves with grief, trembling, sobbing, swooning. Though Mary wept at being parted from them, her sole companions for so many years, she told them to be glad, not sorry. "For now thou shalt see Mary Stuart's troubles receive their long-expected end."

JAMES I

The executioners tugged inexpertly at her clothing. She smiled: "I was not wont to have my clothes plucked off by such grooms." Then she knelt at the block and prayed in Latin: "Into your hands, O Lord . . ."

The axe fell; the room flinched with a single spasm at the noise of it. There was a ghastly moment of unforeseen horror. The head was not off! The axe man took a second stroke.

He lifted the severed head up for all to see . . . and the auburn wig and the blood-stained white lawn came away in his hand, letting fall a head of close-cropped grey hair with two ringlets over the ears.

"God save the Queen!" said the headsman.

"Amen!"

"This be the end of all the enemies of Her Majesty!" said the Earl of Kent. But the communal cry of "Amen" broke off, as the skirts of the dead woman began to stir.

Out at the hem nosed a little dog, whimpering and afraid. One of Mary's dogs. It trotted into the pool of blood between head and shoulders, and lay down, whining, inconsolable. Nothing could erase that image from the minds of those who saw it.

No more could Elizabeth's raging and protests and loud public regrets erase the impression that she had got her wish at last: Mary Queen of Scots was extinguished and Queen Elizabeth could sleep easy in her bed.

William Davison, Elizabeth's secretary (and innocent scapegoat) was accused of sending the death warrant to Fotheringay against Elizabeth's wishes. He was tried, fined and imprisoned in the Tower. No one seriously expected the sentence to be carried out, but Elizabeth insisted on it. Mary's perfidious son, on his mother's death, became King James VI of Scotland. When Elizabeth died childless (even though James was widely believed to be a secret Catholic), he became King James I of England, too.

The City of Raleigh

1587

THE FIRST ENGLISH COLONISTS TO CROSS THE Atlantic landed on Newfoundland, squabbled, fought, fell ill and gave up. Setting sail again for England, their ship went down with everyone aboard. So much for conquering the New World.

Roanoke Island, at first sight, seemed a far more promising place to begin. It rose out of the curved horizon, green and clad in trees. There were rumours of gold and pearls.

One hundred and seven settlers built a fort there. But instead of planting crops, they went hunting for gold. They quarrelled with the local people and ran desperately short of supplies. When a hurricane struck, they were so terrified that they begged a visiting ship to take them home. Sir Richard Grenville, calling at Roanoke, found no one there. He did his best to revive the settlement by landing fifteen men with enough provisions for two years.

In due course, Sir Walter Raleigh arrived with another group (this time including women and children). It was their task to found the "City of Raleigh" in this land called "Virginia" after the Virgin Queen Elizabeth. But where were Grenville's fifteen sailors? There was not a trace – except for one skeleton of a murdered man!

Undaunted, the settlers took over the deserted fort, built timber cabins, cleared land and planted it. A baby girl was born – she too was called Virginia. With just a few more supplies from England, the community would be able to survive the whole year round!

"I'll go myself and get them!" said John White, elected leader of the little community.

But when he reached home, he found that England had troubles of her own. War with Spain was brewing. The novelty of the New World had worn off, and nobody was interested in the troubles of a handful of settlers. It was two frustrating years before he could lead a relief expedition.

It was an anxious voyage for White. How many more children would have been born? Would tornadoes have struck? Or hostile natives? As the ship sighted land, the cheerful sight of rising smoke was a great relief to him.

Then he realized that the smoke was a forest fire, nothing more. The ship fired its guns to attract attention. John White leaned eagerly over the rail, to see which of his friends would come running down to the beach: Mary, Ananias or even Virginia.

No one came.

It was getting late and there was a heavy sea running. Not until the next morning did the captain send two boats ashore. One overturned in the surf

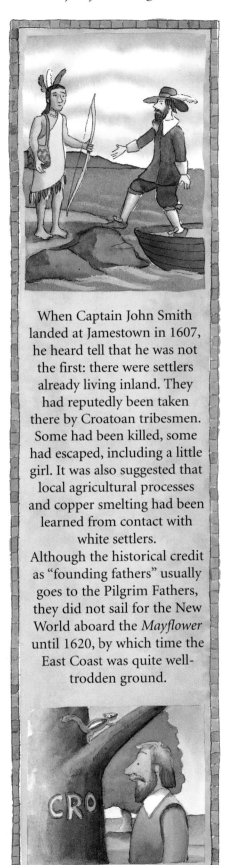

and seven people were drowned. But the survivors scrambled ashore. A trumpeter blew several blasts on his damp trumpet, and the rest broke raggedly into song.

There was no reply to their singing. Though they sang till their voices cracked, no one came. There was no one left to come.

Not a trace remained of the settlement. Not only had the people disappeared, but the cabins, too! Books lay around like dead birds, fluttered by the wind. But there was no Mary, no Ananias, no little Virginia Dare.

There were no graves, either, no skeletons or bloodstains. John White took heart from that. "They have moved on. It was agreed among us: if a move was decided upon, they would leave word: a message carved on a tree – a cross beneath it if danger had driven them to it. Look for a sign. Look for a message!" And he ran from tree to tree, searching. "Over here! Make haste, there's something here!"

There carved in a tree were just three letters: C R O. What did it mean? There was no cross underneath, but then perhaps the person who carved them had been prevented from finishing. Anyway, what sense could be made from three letters: C R O?

John White said, "Croatoan. They have gone to Croatoan Island. The Croatoans are friendly. I am greatly joyed. It means my friends are safe!"

And with quite extraordinary confidence in those three crude letters, he set sail again for England. Incredibly, he did not make for Croatoan Island or enquire any further. It was as if the people with whom he had been entrusted had simply gone on ahead of him to somewhere he could not follow.

The next time English ships happened to anchor off Croatoan Island, they found no trace of any English prisoners or settlers. Six expeditions Sir Walter Raleigh sent in search of the citizens of the City of Raleigh: they found nothing.

And yet 100 years later, Croatoans sided with the English in the War of Independence, saying that they had taken all their laws and religion from English settlers. Some had blue eyes, fair hair and beards. They told a legend at their firesides, too, of a little white maid who grew up into a beautiful woman, and then changed by magic one day into a white deer. Was that child Virginia Dare, born in hope, christened in thanksgiving, lost while the world was looking the other way?

When Captain John Smith landed at Jamestown in 1607, he heard tell that he was not the first: there were settlers already living inland. They had reputedly been taken there by Croatoan tribesmen. Some had been killed, some had escaped, including a little girl. It was also suggested that local agricultural processes and copper smelting had been learned from contact with white settlers.

Although the historical credit as "founding fathers" usually goes to the Pilgrim Fathers, they did not sail for the New World aboard the *Mayflower* until 1620, by which time the East Coast was quite well-trodden ground.

The Spanish Galleon of Tobermory

1588

NOT FOR THE FIRST TIME AND NOT FOR the last, love came in a dream. Viola, the King of Spain's daughter, dreamed of a man, and his face was so fine and his whole bearing so kingly that she swore to find him, even if it meant sailing the world round. Past Scotland she came, to the island of Mull.

Her galleon, the *Florencia*, dropped anchor in Tobermory Bay, for the cliffs had the same ragged edges as in her dream. There indeed she found the man she had dreamed: MacLean of Duart. Viola thought her happiness would never end, that MacLean would marry her and make all her dreams come true. The man himself was hugely flattered. There was only one snag: MacLean of Duart already had a wife – a fiery Scottish wife who did not mean to lose her husband to the lady in the bay.

Wife MacLean took matters into her own hands, took a keg of gunpowder, too, and went aboard the *Florencia*. "Leave my man be, ye black-eyed hussy!" she told Viola. "Have ye not men enough in your country that you must come stealing ours?"

"I must go where my heart leads," said Princess Viola. "I was meant to marry MacLean: my dream told me so."

Wife MacLean left the ship – left, too, her keg of gunpowder and a slow-burning fuse. Not all the Northern Lights on Midsummer Eve ever lit up the Hebridean skies like the explosion which rocked the galleon *Florencia* that day and scattered her to the four winds. The mast was shot like a harpoon at the whaley moon. Pieces of plank skimmed over the water. Only one soul escaped . . . the ship's cook, who was blown, by the force of the explosion, all the way from ship to shore.

Had the cook died in his galley, perhaps the fate of the *Florencia* might have remained a Hebridean secret. Instead, word reached the King of Spain, who was filled with such spitting wrath that men fled him like a keg of gunpowder.

"Get you to Mull!" he told his trusted sea-captain. "Kill the man MacLean, his wife and all his children! Kill his dogs and cats and the birds in his chimneys! Kill his servants and kinsmen and neighbours! Break down his walls and burn every blade of grass on Mull, for he has robbed me of my daughter, lovely as any dream!"

When MacLean of Duart saw the Spanish man o' war drop anchor in Tobermory Bay, his big stomach quaked and his heart beat so wildly that all thought of Princess Viola fell out of it. "See what ye have done, ye foolish wife!" he whispered.

But his wife squared her square shoulders and stuck out her several chins. She summoned all of the eighteen witches of Mull, and pointed to the ship in the bay. Like frogs all hopping into the one pond, the eighteen witches of Mull pooled their eighteen magics, pooled their curses, pooled their worst of wicked spells. Above the bay, they spread their arms, their feather-white shawls. Eighteen seagulls flew out to sea, circling and soaring, screaming fit to chill the blood of any fiery Spaniard.

The wind too began to scream, like a million gulls, and the waters of the bay swirled. The ship's mast turned like the spoon in a mixing bowl. Then down went the ship, confusing sea foam with rich Spanish lace.

When the storm was spent, not a trace remained of the captain or his ship. Within a matter of years, only the ghost of a memory survived, faint as any dream.

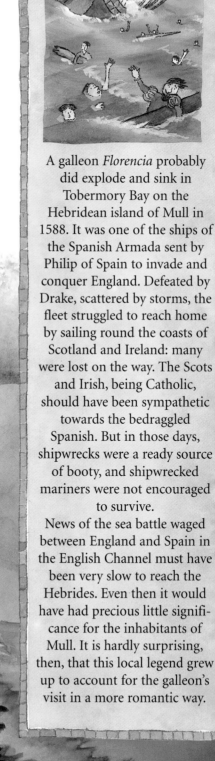

A galleon *Florencia* probably did explode and sink in Tobermory Bay on the Hebridean island of Mull in 1588. It was one of the ships of the Spanish Armada sent by Philip of Spain to invade and conquer England. Defeated by Drake, scattered by storms, the fleet struggled to reach home by sailing round the coasts of Scotland and Ireland: many were lost on the way. The Scots and Irish, being Catholic, should have been sympathetic towards the bedraggled Spanish. But in those days, shipwrecks were a ready source of booty, and shipwrecked mariners were not encouraged to survive.

News of the sea battle waged between England and Spain in the English Channel must have been very slow to reach the Hebrides. Even then it would have had precious little significance for the inhabitants of Mull. It is hardly surprising, then, that this local legend grew up to account for the galleon's visit in a more romantic way.

The Theatre that Disappeared

1598

RICHARD BURBAGE TRIED EVERY LINE OF argument he knew. He began good humouredly, in comic vein: "Where will the groundlings throw their apple cores if not at us actors?"

He pulled himself up to his full height (which was not great): "Is this not the Age of Poesie? And are we not the finest of a fine profession, speaking verse of genius, holding up to humanity the bright likeness of its image?"

He tried again: "My father built this theatre! It is the oldest and most visited in London – yeah, in the kingdom!"

He even tried darkest tragedy, and he was famous for his tragic roles. "And wilt thou see us cast upon the mercy of the rude winds? Hoist up upon the shoulders of misfortune for want of a house over our untousled heads?"

But the landlord only crossed his arms, pursed his lips and scowled. "I say the lease is up and that's an end. You actors can take your theatricals, Richard Burbage, and shift yourselves off my ground. The Theatre is closed, and there's an end!"

Burbage threw an arm across his eyes and struck the pose of a man betrayed by fate. But when he took his arm away, the landlord had gone. He was standing alone in the street. Tugging down his doublet, he replaced his hat at a rakish angle and squared his stocky shoulders. "Very well, you wish the Theatre gone, do you? Then go it shall!" he said under his breath.

He went in search of his elder brother, Cuthbert, and told him to hire a cart. "A big cart. Better still, five carts. Then find John and Francis and Will – everyone who's sober. We have work to do." And as the light faded and the streets emptied, a caravan of carts negotiated the narrow lanes of London, southwards towards the river.

Lying in bed the next morning, the owner of the land, north of the city walls, where the Chamberlain's Company had acted night after night, mused on the value of the Theatre, now that its lease had expired. There was not much to be done with a circular building open to the elements in the centre. Cock fighting, perhaps, or a bear pit. Boxing, even. But all those were lewd and Godless pastimes and attracted lewd and Godless people . . .

His wife threw open the window and emptied out the night-soil. She stayed there, pot upraised, her head outside, beyond the sill.

"Close the window, woman. I am in a draught. Did you hear that traffic last night? Horses and carts all night long."

His wife drew her head back inside, but still stood holding the pot at shoulder height. "It's gone," she said.

"What's gone?"

"The Theatre. It has . . . walked in the night."

"Fallen down, you mean?" He ran to the window, the noises of early-morning London rising up like starlings to circle his head. But there in a cityscape he knew as well as his wife's bumpy profile, was a hole. Where, the day before, the Theatre had stood lay a heap of thatching, a snow of plaster, and wattle enough to fence a field. All the timber uprights, and joists and beams and benches, all the barge boards and staging and duck boards and doors had gone, loaded aboard the Burbages' carts and trundled away in the night, southwards over the river.

The landlord's mouth opened and shut, opened and shut, but he knew no poetry with which to express his feelings. He was, after all, neither a theatrical man nor a poet.

SHAKESPEARE

The Theatre, London's first purpose-built permanent theatre was built by Richard Burbage's father James, in 1576. When the lease expired, Richard, Cuthbert, and the rest of the "Chamberlain's Company" of actors, took its timbers to Southwark (maybe not in just the onr night) and used them to build a new theatre. Several of them, including William Shakespeare, went into business together, sharing the profits. The building they put up was much the same octagonal shape as the Theatre had been – a wooden O. This was the Globe Theatre, up and running. It made Shakespeare and his fellow shareholders rich men. Richard Burbage played all the great Shakespearean roles – Hamlet, Othello, Lear, Macbeth, Richard III. But perhaps his greatest role was in creating the Globe Theatre, during the Golden Age of dramatic art. In 1613 the Globe burned down during a performance of *Henry VIII*. It was rebuilt, but closed thirty years later when the Puritans suppressed the theatres as sinful. In 1997 it opened again, reconstructed in all its Elizabethan glory.

Gunpowder, Treason and Plot

1604-1605

GUY FAWKES LIT THE fuse of the gunpowder and doubled back the way he had come. With an enormous thud, the charge went off, shattering the great slabs of the city wall into flying flint. Guido Fawkes had done it! His fellow troopers cheered, and the officers puffed out their cheeks in admiration at his cool, reckless courage.

That was at Calais. They made him a captain for his bravery at Calais. Everyone said there was no better explosives man in the Spanish army than Guido Fawkes of England.

He was still abroad eight years later when his old friend, Thomas Winter, came looking for him. He had a job for Guido – a job for a good explosives man. This time, however, Guido would be striking a blow for his religion – a blow for Catholicism, which England had suppressed with fire and sword for half a century. This time the target was Parliament.

The plot had already been hatched before Captain Fawkes joined it. In April conspirators met at the house of Robert Catesby, a tall, fair-haired man seething with indignation at the plight of English Catholics. King James (that worthless Scots popinjay) would gather, with all his lords and ministers, in the Lords' Chamber of the Palace of Westminster for the State Opening of Parliament. One explosion would put paid to the whole pack of them!

This was no rash, spur-of-the-moment piece of mischief. The conspirators gave themselves nine months to prepare. Thomas Percy, a white-haired, respected gentleman with influential friends, managed to secure a small house right alongside the palace. The cellar lay hard up against the cellars of the Lords' Chamber. All they had to do was tunnel through and lay the charge.

From May to December no one lived in that house but Guido Fawkes – or rather "John Johnson", for that was what he called himself.

December

All those days of waiting, doing nothing: for a man of action like Guido it was a torment. Then one December night, eleven men came to the door, darkly dressed, hats pulled down, spades and adzes and picks hidden under their clothes; also food and ale enough for a fortnight.

Down in the cellar they began to dig – not with great ringing, noisy blows, but with quiet gouging and grubbing and boring. They dug till their hands bled and their backs refused to straighten, but the tunnel progressed with ridiculous slowness.

"At this rate we shan't be through in time for the opening of Parliament!" Catesby fretted.

On 7 February it was announced by the town criers that the parliamentary session had been postponed indefinitely. The men in the cellars fell on each other's aching shoulders and laughed with relief. Time for a rest! Extra time for the tunnel to be finished! God must be on their side . . . but then they had known that all along.

That night, Guido Fawkes and Robert Keyes went across the river to a lock-up in Lambeth. It was dark, and no one saw the two men furtively transferring barrels to a nearby rowing boat. They had chosen a moonless night to row their gun-powder across the Thames to Westminster.

They dug by lantern light, those eleven desperate men, thinking to scratch their way through yards of solid rock. Then all of a sudden, in the middle of the day, came a rushing sound like water or an avalanche.

The diggers in the tunnel fell on their faces. Those nearest the cellar turned to run. What was it? Running feet? Were they found out? Or was the tunnel caving in on their heads?

It was neither. The rushing noise continued. "John Johnson" ran outside into the street. There stood a wagon being filled with coal. The noise was of coal being shovelled out of a room *above* their tunnel – a room they had never even known existed! The coal merchant's vault must lie *directly below* the Lords' Chamber. They had never needed to dig a tunnel – only to secure that vault and pile their gunpowder there!

The tunnel was abandoned. God must truly be on their side – but then they had never doubted it.

Percy managed to rent the place. Spring and summer drifted by, with "John Johnson" caretaker now of a coal-dusty vault. One by one, thirty-six kegs of gunpowder were transferred from their hiding place to the alcoves of the cellar.

October

In one week the hall above would be plush with ermine robes, glittering with coronets, crowded with Protestant statesmen.

Of course there would be Catholics, too. In among the elder statesmen would be good Catholic men, like Lord Monteagle. It upset the conspirators, of course it did. Catholics kill Catholics? Still, it could not be helped.

Perhaps someone thought it could. For Lord Monteagle received a letter – unsigned – advising him not to attend Parliament on 5 November, if he wanted to avoid an "unseen blow". Monteagle read and re-read the letter, then sat tapping it against his lips, wondering what it could mean, what to do with it, who should see it . . .

4 November

It was time for Guido Fawkes, their explosives expert, to stack the kegs, lay the fuses and lie in wait to light them. The other conspirators dispersed – some were already in the Midlands, ready to raise up the revolution in the wake of the bomb-

ing. Fawkes was cock-a-hoop. Sir Robert Cecil, Secretary of State, had ordered a search of the cellars, but his incompetent men had found nothing! The way was clear. The time was ripe.

Coal dust glittered like jet in the light from his candle. Guido made himself as comfortable as he could in the cold and clammy dark. His breathing was shallow, his heartbeat steady. This for Guido was a simple act of war. Below ground, he could not hear the church clocks striking midnight.

Tramp tramp tramp. There was the scrape of pikes against stone, a jangle of keys; dancing yellow lantern light sprang into the vault. So sure was Robert Cecil about the letter Monteagle had showed him that he had ordered a *second* search. This time his troopers saw the kegs at once. Then they saw, standing against the far wall, the dark figure of a tall man. He did not struggle as they bound his wrists.

They manhandled him all the way to the King's bedchamber, shouting questions in his face, punching and kicking him. But the man from the cellar gave only his name: "John Johnson".

November

Though the others fled, Sir Robert Cecil seemed to know exactly where to find them. Fawkes refused to name them, but they were tracked down anyway, within three days. They rushed out of doors, swords in hand, and three were gunned down: Catesby and Percy killed by a single bullet.

The gaolers broke Fawkes on the rack. It startled them how long he held out, but in the end, a man can be made to confess to anything on the rack.

He was the last to die. His fellow conspirators had all died traitors' deaths when Fawkes was led out to execution. But the crowd were still in good voice, taunting and jeering. "Traitor! Coward! Murderer! Villain! Devil!" Their hatred and disgust knew no bounds. They would savour his agonizing death: hanged, cut down alive, disembowelled, quartered, and only then beheaded. Guido could barely climb the ladder; the rack had crippled him. But shakily he reached the top, the hangman, the noose.

Whispering a prayer, he jumped from the ladder. His neck snapped. The crowd groaned. The villain had cheated them! He was already dead, and they had been robbed of an afternoon's entertainment.

Guido Fawkes, now referred to as Guy, was born Protestant, but converted to Catholicism after his widowed mother married a Catholic country gentleman. Full of religious zeal and a love of adventure, he left England in 1593 and went to fight in Catholic causes in Europe. He was thirty-five when he died. In 1606 Parliament decreed that 5 November should be kept as a day of thanksgiving for their deliverance. But the burning of a guy on Bonfire Night is a later, Victorian addition to the festivities.

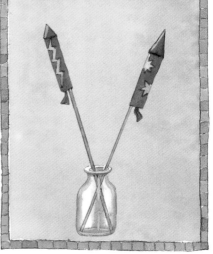

Chicken and Bacon

1626

"KNOWLEDGE IS POWER," SAID FRANCIS BACON, and being an eloquent and sought-after lawyer, he knew the taste of both. Unfortunately, Bacon spent money as he spent words – in extravagant torrents. In order to pay his bills, he was quite prepared to prosecute former friends, marry for money, and accept bribes. It has to be said that though Bacon wrote volumes about virtue, he did not possess much himself.

His glittering legal career came to an end in the Tower of London, imprisoned for dishonesty, and though King James I generously set him free, the last five years of his life were spent writing, studying and pleading for reinstatement.

Everything interested him – from law to poetry, science to politics. And when it came to science, he did not stop short at dry theory: he believed in experimentation and irrefutable proof. Knowledge, he said, came as the fruit of experience.

Riding in a coach one bitter March day, with Dr Witherborne, the King's doctor, the two got talking about the rotting process in food.

"I have observed that the cooler the pantry, the fresher the food," mused Witherborne.

Bacon was not feeling well that day, but a sudden idea so intrigued him that he quite forgot his aches and pains, and leapt down from the carriage. Beating on the door of a cottage at the bottom of Highgate Hill, he fetched out a timid, startled woman. "I want to buy a chicken!" demanded Bacon.

"Yes, sir! Of course, sir! Got a nice little hen-bird out back . . ." She wrung the hen's neck and brought it to him, swinging it limply by its head.

"Could you pluck it, my good woman?"

The woman plucked it, while Bacon stamped about in the garden gathering up fistfuls of snow and cramming them into the pockets of his frock coat. "And draw it?" he called. The woman pulled out the chicken's giblets and washed the carcass at the pump.

Then Bacon sat down on a stool in her cottage and began to ram handfuls of snow into the chicken.

"Are you gone entirely mad, Bacon?" enquired the King's doctor politely.

"I find myself asking," replied Bacon, grunting and red in the face with exertion, "whether *snow* cannot be used to preserve meat, as well as salt. What would you say?"

Excitement carried him through; he completed the stuffing. But when it was done, and the chicken sat pinkly lopsided on the table, leaking snow, Bacon found he did not feel at all well. Staring at hands blue with cold, he murmured, "I must lie down a while, Witherborne."

The doctor offered to take him home – it was only a few miles – but Bacon could not face the journey. "Take me to Arundel's house. It is only a step down the road."

The Earl of Arundel agreed, yes, of course Bacon must be put to bed in his house, and told his maid to run warming pans over the sheet in the guest room. But it had been a long while since the guest bed was slept in. The warming pan raised a gentle steam off the damp sheets, and while Bacon lay clutching his chilled stomach, the bed cooled around him.

Within a couple of days, his cold had turned to bronchitis, his bronchitis to pneumonia. He was running a temperature, alarming the maids with feverish talk of knowledge and power, chickens and immortality.

The last piece of knowledge to be grasped by the great genuis of Francis Bacon was brought to him minutes before his death. It did not concern the nature of God, the afterlife or any of the usual things which prey on the minds of the dying. It concerned the well-being of a frozen chicken sitting on a plate in a pantry downstairs.

"It is not decayed one jot," Dr Witherborne whispered in his ear, and a serene smile spread across Bacon's face. He died in the powerful knowledge that refrigeration does indeed preserve food.

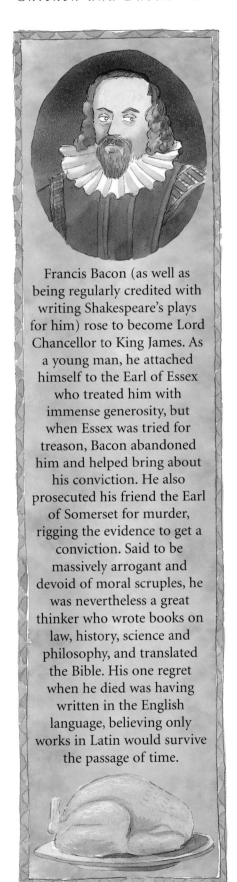

Francis Bacon (as well as being regularly credited with writing Shakespeare's plays for him) rose to become Lord Chancellor to King James. As a young man, he attached himself to the Earl of Essex who treated him with immense generosity, but when Essex was tried for treason, Bacon abandoned him and helped bring about his conviction. He also prosecuted his friend the Earl of Somerset for murder, rigging the evidence to get a conviction. Said to be massively arrogant and devoid of moral scruples, he was nevertheless a great thinker who wrote books on law, history, science and philosophy, and translated the Bible. His one regret when he died was having written in the English language, believing only works in Latin would survive the passage of time.

Jenny Geddes Strikes a Blow

1637

KING CHARLES I BELIEVED THAT HE HAD BEEN placed on earth by God to rule His people. He knew he was in the right. In fact Charles did not even feel the need of a Parliament in order to rule.

John Knox believed that Jesus Christ was the only intermediary between an individual and his God. In church even a king had no higher role than his fellow men: he certainly did not have the right to set bishops in authority over the people. Knox had studied under the great preacher Calvin, and he knew he was in the right. What is more, he had utterly convinced the people of Scotland.

So, when nearly a century later, Charles I ordained that Scottish worship should fall into line with the Church of England, acknowledge him as head of the Church and submit to his bishops, Presbyterian Scotland seethed. *Bishops* dictate to Presbyterian ministers? *Bishops* lord it over Scottish congregations, wearing their

fancy garb and offering up prayers for an English king? *Bishops* stand up in the pulpit of the High Kirk of St Giles', where John Knox had stood and preached Reformation? It seemed they must. One Sunday, the music began and the procession of ministers headed by a bishop glided serenely into position between the altar and the people. The whole nave of St Giles' rumbled with resentful murmurings.

Jenny Geddes was just a poor market-stall holder, not a trouble-maker. But the sight of those rich, white robes encrusted with precious wire and gemstones, and the bishop's droning, patronizing sermon, put her into such a towering rage that she leapt to her feet. Snatching up the three-legged stool she had brought to sit on, she hurled it at the bishop in the pulpit – a wild, inaccurate throw – shrieking, "Ye'll nae say your mass in my lug!" The stool bounced and clattered and broke.

But nobody ever saw where it landed. For by then the kirk was in uproar. The congregation surged to its feet with a kind of angry cheer. The bishop, mouth ajar, struggling for words to condemn such blasphemy, saw a tide of angry faces, saw that the tide was rising – moving forward – coming after him! Clutching his robes in both fists, he turned to run down the pulpit steps, but already he was surrounded. Half carried, half chased, he and his fellow ministers were thrown out of the High Kirk of St Giles' like cats out of a fish shop. The Scots valued their religion above their king, and if Charles wanted to send any more bishops into Scottish kirks, then he would have to send an army first!

Soon after that, a document was drawn up entitled the "Solemn League and Covenant", plainly stating the way in which the Scottish Church should be governed. Scots flocked from far and wide to sign it – to declare themselves "Covenanters", willing to lay down their lives in defence of their religion.

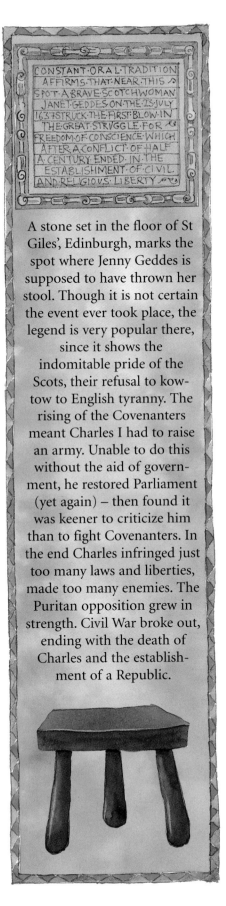

CONSTANT·ORAL·TRADITION AFFIRMS·THAT·NEAR·THIS SPOT·A·BRAVE·SCOTCHWOMAN JANET·GEDDES·ON·THE·23·JULY 1637·STRUCK·THE·FIRST·BLOW·IN THE·GREAT·STRUGGLE·FOR FREEDOM·OF·CONSCIENCE·WHICH AFTER·A·CONFLICT·OF·HALF A·CENTURY·ENDED·IN·THE ESTABLISHMENT·OF·CIVIL AND·RELIGIOUS·LIBERTY

A stone set in the floor of St Giles', Edinburgh, marks the spot where Jenny Geddes is supposed to have thrown her stool. Though it is not certain the event ever took place, the legend is very popular there, since it shows the indomitable pride of the Scots, their refusal to kow-tow to English tyranny. The rising of the Covenanters meant Charles I had to raise an army. Unable to do this without the aid of govern-ment, he restored Parliament (yet again) – then found it was keener to criticize him than to fight Covenanters. In the end Charles infringed just too many laws and liberties, made too many enemies. The Puritan opposition grew in strength. Civil War broke out, ending with the death of Charles and the establish-ment of a Republic.

The Witch-Finder General

1646

MATTHEW HOPKINS COULD BARELY believe his good fortune as the names poured from Elizabeth Clarke's lips. Names and confessions and a fascinating glimpse of things forbidden. Elizabeth Clarke was a witch; he had never doubted it. Was she not bent and deformed – a yammering old woman whose very face scared small children? Wringing a confession from her, he had felt the hot, mouth-drying thrill of prising open a human soul like a shellfish and exposing all the vileness inside. What a pleasure it had been to hear her damn herself with talk of "familiars" and "spells" and satanic rites! Thirty-two names she had given him. Thirty-two witches – imagine! Thirty-two fewer servants of the Devil, thanks to his energetic, brilliant interrogation of this wicked old crone.

Before she and her friends were even swinging from the gallows, Matthew Hopkins was riding north from Chelmsford to rid Norfolk and Suffolk of witches too.

The pious Protestant people of East Anglia greeted "Witch-Finder General", Matthew Hopkins, much as they would a rat-catcher. They were prepared to pay good money to be rid of the evil in their midst. Yes, they knew of an old woman who lived alone with a black cat or two and said her prayers in Latin. Yes, they had known carts stick in mud, a cow fall in the river, a child die who had been well only days before. They gave him names by the score.

Matthew Hopkins accepted £6 from the people of Aldeburgh for cleansing the town of witches. They cheerfully pointed the accusing finger. It was not for them to enquire *who*, exactly, had designated Matthew Hopkins Witch-Finder General. It was not for them to question his motives or methods. He was doing God's work, wasn't he, rooting out servants of the Devil?

He said he carried "the Devil's list of all English witches". And besides, he had the needle. Hopkins was a pricker, and a pricker is a valuable man to have around when there are witches. No easy matter, sometimes, to find the "witch's mark" – that red, sunken place on the body which, when pricked, feels no pain. Hopkins knew where to look – the soles of the feet or the scalp of the head. Then out would come the needle – three inches of spike on a handle, like a bradawl. And in it would go, without a cry of pain from the accused.

The actual torture of a prisoner might be forbidden . . . but that was no drawback to a man gifted in the art of *persuasion.* Starvation. Solitary confinement. Forcing someone to sit cross-legged for days at a time . . . there are many ways of making a person confess. In Kings Lynn they paid him £15 for the work he did.

Why, in Brandeston village, the *entire village* denounced their vicar as a witch, so how could there be any doubt? It was just a matter of obtaining a confession. So John Lowes was locked up and kept awake day and night for a week, forced hourly to run up and down his cell until he agreed to say anything. Anything. Everything. How he had bewitched cattle. How he had sunk that ship in calm weather . . . So what, if he did retract it all afterwards? These witches will say anything to save their necks . . . How those parishioners wagged their heads as Lowes was led to the gallows. *They* knew him for what he was; *they* were not going to shed any tears at the man having to read his own burial service to himself because, as a witch, he was denied a clergyman.

By the time Matthew Hopkins got to Stowmarket, his fee had gone up to £23.

In Bury St Edmunds, all told, he had sixty-eight people put to death.

His real triumph came when he hanged nineteen women in a single day.

What things they confessed to! What sensational pictures they drew – of dancing demons, Satan dressed as a bridegroom, cows jumping over stiles, men flying over weathervanes on the backs of black dogs. What a spectacle they made for the crowds to watch as they struggled with the hangman, swearing their innocence! The people of East Anglia were kept in a state of glassy-eyed hysteria, as Matthew Hopkins prowled among them, pointing the finger, jabbing with his needle.

After he retired – after that jealous wretch, John Gaule, slandered him, and his health broke down – did Hopkins lie awake at night and wonder about the pains in his chest, the blood in his lungs, about the cold sweat and colder nightmares that crawled over him? Did he wonder whose curse was gnawing on him; of those 400, which witch had done for him?

Matthew Hopkins was a self-appointed witch-finder. He and his assistants John Stearne and Goody Philips quickly got rich, preying on superstitious, vindictive people. They were helped by widespread membership of a rabid Protestant cult which prized the line in the Bible, "Thou shalt not suffer a witch to live" and thought the Devil was infiltrating the countryside with armies of witches. Civil War was raging. The Rev John Lowes had Royalist sympathies; his parishioners/accusers were mostly Puritans who hated his politics. For fourteen months, Hopkins had free rein. Then John Gaule, a vicar, wrote a pamphlet exposing him – his lack of credentials, the spring-loaded, retractable "pricker", the ease of extracting confessions from tormented prisoners. There was no scandal. Hopkins retired quietly to Essex, his fortune made, and died of TB. Another, less reliable story says that he was tried as a witch himself, put to ordeal by water, and drowned. Similar witch-hunts happened all over Europe and Russia. It has been estimated that one million innocent women died.

Cromwell and the Goosefeathers

1649

OLIVER CROMWELL WAS A MAN OF THE FENS. HE knew the lores and traditions of those flat, wet, wilderness lands, and he knew their uses. When he needed men to fight King Charles I, he had only to show a goosefeather to the men of the fens and they were obliged to join him – obliged by age-old tradition to offer help and protection to anyone carrying a split goosefeather.

Little by little, battle by battle, Cromwell and his Roundheads got the better of the King and his Cavaliers in a Civil War which saw the country hacked into bloody factions.

Once or twice the trick with the feather recoiled on him. At Snow Hall in Norfolk, it seemed that Cromwell had King Charles cornered, but the King's party escaped through the fens, showing a split goosefeather to the Norfolk Roundheads who barred their way. What could the sentries do? They were fenland

men. They honoured the ancient symbol, and let the King slip by, though it left them in fear and trembling of their lives. What would Cromwell say when they admitted to letting the King go?

He said little. Though victory had been snatched from him, and the war prolonged by wearisome months, he listened to the sentries' explanation, took the split goosefeather from their trembling fingers and said, "Better that the King should go free than that old customs should be broken."

Of course his religious zeal gave Cromwell perfect confidence in the ultimate outcome of the war. He knew it was only a matter of time before he defeated Charles. Victory came at the battle of Naseby, and within the year the defeated Charles was brought to trial for his life.

The trial was never going to be fair, but it was no more unfair than the times decreed. Besides, only one outcome was possible in the circumstances. Charles Stewart, one-time King of England, was found guilty and condemned to death by beheading.

The night before the execution, Cromwell sat eating supper when there was a knock at the door. It was a messenger from the King.

"His Majesty scorns to ask mercy," said the messenger, "but demands the right and privileges owing to one who presents this!" And he threw down a split goosefeather on to the table.

Even after supper had been cleared, Cromwell went on sitting at the table. All night long he sat there, twirling the broken feather between his fingers, his eyes looking unseeing into the darkness.

It snowed during the night – soft, white flakes, as though the sky were moulting, and a multitude of downy feathers fell on Whitehall, blurring the outline of the scaffold. Charles put on two shirts that morning, so that any trembling from the cold might not be mistaken for fear.

"I go from a corruptible crown to an incorruptible, where no disturbance can take place," he said, mounting the scaffold. Then he told the executioner the signal he would make when he was ready for the axe to fall, and knelt down at the block.

Afterwards, the King's remains were coffined on the spot and carried away. Cromwell went to see the body – stood for a long time holding the lid raised, gazing at his dead adversary. There was no trace of triumph in his eyes, no hatred or gloating satisfaction. There was no guilt, either. "His body was made for long life," was all he said. Then he laid a single, split, white goosefeather on the King's breast and closed the lid. His conscience was clear. After all, he had granted the King a kind of safe passage: he had set his soul free.

Cromwell and his New Model Army defeated Charles I in the Civil War of 1642-9 and established a Commonwealth, with him as Lord Protector. He was a clever statesman and military leader, but as much a dictator as any king and a dyed-in-the-wool Puritan, abolishing such jolly pastimes as dancing, the theatre and Christmas. When Charles's son, Charles II, was restored to the throne, and the Commonwealth was over and gone, Cromwell's body was made to pay for what he had done. It was dug up from Westminster Abbey and hanged from the gallows at Tyburn. The head was cut off and impaled on a pike, on the roof at Westminster Hall. Twenty years later, in a storm, it rolled down the roof and landed at the feet of a guard who took it home and hid it up his chimney. Passing from hand to hand, bought and sold like stolen goods for 250 years, it was at last presented to Cromwell's old Cambridge college and given a decent burial.

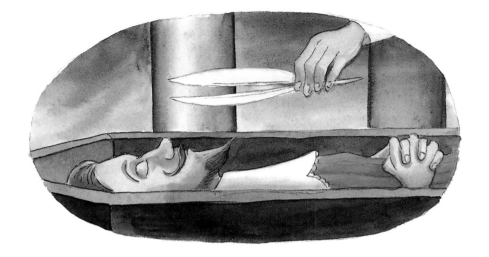

The Moonrakers

1650s

WHEN WILTSHIRE WOOL WAS THE FINEST IN the world, some of the richest men in England were the wool merchants who set up business in Swindon. But they were foreigners – men from Holland and Flanders – and on spring days, when lambs were gambolling in the field, the woollenmen would sit sipping Wiltshire wine and sighing. Come autumn nights, too, when the fleeces were baled, the woollenmen still sat sadly, staring into empty glasses and sighing. They longed for a taste of home, for proper Hollands gin – but they were not prepared to pay the crippling tax that the British Government added to the price of imported liquor. A cask of "Hollands", with import duty, cost a week's profits.

And so, these men of business, and merchants and movers of goods, set about quenching their thirst. They diversified. That is to say, they opened up a new line of business. From the moonlit decks of little ships sailing up the Solent came shadowy figures to the weed-slippery coves of the Hampshire coast. They carried mysterious bundles which they hid under the stooks on haywains, and from there the cargo bumped inshore to church crypts and village lock-ups, to pigeon lofts and dry wells and disused outbuildings. Along hollow hedges and down old lead mine-shafts came casks of Hollands gin, travelling north in a series of overnight stages, to the thirsty woollenmen of Swindon.

Don't picture a handful of dubious-looking characters with eye-patches and a beltful of pistols. These smugglers were not recruited from among rogues and vagabonds. Hundreds of ordinary people were soon employed, year in, year out, in fetching home the Hollands. For a quid of tobacco or a little brandy cask (duty-free, of course), a vicar might allow the use of his crypt or turn a deaf ear to the sound of carts at midnight. For a bunch of lace, the innkeeper's wife might lay out supper after hours, and watch the wall while the "Wiltshire gentlemen" refreshed themselves on their journey. And the excisemen, though they might ride patrol, and offer rewards, and lie in ambush on moonlit nights, rarely made an arrest. Smuggling was no crime in the eyes of true-born Englishmen. This was easing the springs of contentment. This was the occupation of gentlemen and right-thinking citizens.

Consequently, when the dewponds and duckponds of England greened over with summer algae, their depths often concealed a cask or two of Hollands bound for Swindon – casks which lay there for one night, then moved on northwards. One night, the smugglers of Cannings village grew over-bold, and went out when the moon was full, to the village pond, armed with rakes and an easy conscience.

"Where is it, Sam?"

"Over left of centre, Will. There, just where the moon is . . ."

Out of nowhere, the excisemen were on them, galloping up with muskets and dark lanterns and barking commands: "Stand still! His Majesty's Excise! Show your faces! Name your business!" There was an incriminating silence. "Just as I thought! Smugglers!" said the captain.

Then Jack Brown jerked his rake at the pool and began lurching from foot to foot as if he were two-parts drunk and three-parts simple. "S'a moon, maisters, that's what. Moon's falled in the pond, see maisters? Gonna rake it out an' be rich frever'n'ever!"

"Amen!" said Sam Baker, rolling his eyes and letting his hands dangle like a fool.

"Rich! Rich! Yeah! Wanna share, maisters?" asked Will recklessly. "Ye help us get her out, an' ye can 'ave a share, right enough. Must be worth plenty, woun't you say? Peece o' the moon?"

The excisemen looked at the moon's reflection in the pond. They looked at the fools on the bank splashing away with their rakes, trying to rake the moon out of the pond. "More brains in a duck egg," said the captain of the patrol. "Sergeant, let's leave these buffoons to drown themselves. Raking for the moon, indeed! They're stark mad!" And they rode off, laughing at the stupidity of Wiltshire yokels.

They should have known better. There is no such thing as a stupid Wiltshireman. Within half an hour, another three barrels of best Hollands had been dragged out of the pond and were on their way north.

For 200 years the Wiltshiremen ran Hollands gin, French brandy and tobacco, duty-free, to grateful customers. Somewhere along the way, the smugglers came by the name of Moonrakers. It was a title no right-thinking Englishman disdained to wear, a name whispered with pride and relish.

The villages of All Cannings and Bishops Cannings both lay claim to the story of the Moonrakers, but plenty of other Wiltshire villagers consider it theirs. In fact "Moonraker" has become a term to describe any Wiltshireman. In other versions, the villagers pretend to think the moon's reflection is a cheese which they want to drag out and eat. And since the story turns up in other forms and other countries – *Brer Rabbit*, for instance – it may well be a story-teller's invention. Rudyard Kipling immortalized the work of the Wiltshiremen in his poem "A Smuggler's Song" and the famous lines:

Five and twenty ponies
Trotting through the dark –
Brandy for the Parson,
'Baccy for the Clerk;
Laces for a lady, letters for a spy,
Watch the wall, my darling,
while the Gentlemen go by!

The Royal Oak

1650s

CHARLES I'S SON HAD HIMSELF CROWNED IN Scotland, and rode south to be avenged on Cromwell for killing his father, and to take up his father's place on the English throne.

It was a misguided idea. Cromwell was ready for him. At the battle of Worcester, 4,000 died and over 7,000 more were captured within five hours. Charles Stuart was forced to flee for his life. At three in the morning, after the battle, he and a handful of supporters reached a Catholic house where they could finally snatch a bite to eat and take stock of their dire situation. Cromwell would be scouring the country for Charles – to put an end once and for all to the Stuart royal line. The King must disguise himself and get away to France.

So they buried his fine clothes in the garden and cut his long, ringleted hair short. The would-be King of England was rechristened Will Jones the woodcutter.

"Don't walk so upright and dignified," they told him, "and try to talk like a peasant."

The rain poured down all day. Charles stood dismally in a wood, with a billhook in his hand, getting drenched to the skin, while bands of Roundhead cavalrymen beat at the door of every royalist house in the Midlands.

At nine o'clock, under cover of darkness, Charles Stuart and a man called Penderel set off for Wales on foot.

The old patched shoes they had given "Will Jones" were too small and the King's feet hurt. The coarse woollen stockings chafed the King's feet raw. Penderel chivvied him on to the next safe address – only to be informed that the countryside was rife with Roundheads: they must turn back. But at least the King was able to beg a pair of soft green stockings.

In wading across a stream, those green stockings filled up with sand. The King sat down, refusing to go on. Tactfully, respectfully, Penderel insisted, until the hunted King reached Boscobel House in Shropshire, and was given into the care of one Colonel Carlos with instructions to get him to the sea.

"There are Roundheads everywhere," Carlos told him. "Any minute they will come here to Boscobel, searching. It's best we hide somewhere outside."

So, provided with a ladder, a cushion and some bread and cheese, King Charles II and Colonel Carlos climbed into an oak tree. Roped with ivy, dense with leaves and peppered with acorns, the oak took the King to its noble heart. He was so exhausted that he fell asleep almost at once, his head cradled on Carlos's arm. The colonel's arm went numb; his legs roared with cramp, but he dared not move: if the King stirred in his sleep, he might easily fall off the branch and plummet to his death.

Down below, the clop of horses, the rattle of weapons announced a party of Roundheads searching the forest. Carlos prayed. The King woke and prayed, too.

"Did you see a tall man, richly arrayed – a man running for his life, perchance?" asked a voice directly beneath the tree.

"I did so, sir!" said a girl's voice, eager and bright. "Going that way, two hours since."

The horses galloped away into the distance: the Roundheads had been sent on a false trail.

A reward of £1,000 was offered for the capture of Charles Stuart. And yet he passed safely from one household to the next and no one betrayed him. When the King expressed a longing for roast mutton, his host and hostess went out and stole a sheep so as to grant the King his wish: Charles cut and cooked the chops himself, finding the novelty of it hilarious. On the road south, an innkeeper called out: "God bless your Majesty wherever you go!"

During Oliver Cromwell's Commonwealth, most of the rural festivals and semi-pagan rites were banned – along with such harmless pleasures as dancing, theatre and Christmas. All the old May-Day celebrations were axed, many of which involved a pre-Christian reverence for oak trees. The story of the Royal Oak gave the perfect excuse to revive some of these customs. Oak-Apple Day (29 May and Charles Stuart's birthday) is known, in different parts, as Arbor Tree Day, Shit-Sack Day, Pinch-Bum Day, Oak and Nettle Day ... and not all have much or anything to do with Charles's lucky escape. Wearing a sprig of oak leaves on Oak-Apple Day is seen, however, as a declaration in favour of monarchy.

Later on, "Will Jones the woodcutter" was transformed into "Will Jackson the servant" and had to share a horse with a maid. Awe-struck at having to wrap her arms around the King's royal person, Mistress Lane frequently forgot to treat him like a scullion. Once, they rode directly into the middle of a troop of Roundheads . . . but passed unnoticed.

Once on the journey, "Will Jackson" was told to wind the spit over the kitchen fire, to brown the meat. In his ignorance, he wound the handle the wrong way. "What manner of man are you that you don't know how to wind up a jack?" demanded the cook.

Charles thought quickly. "Where I come from we can't afford to eat roast meat," he said piteously. "And when we do, there's no jack to cook it on."

When the horse cast a shoe, they had to stop at a forge and listen meekly while the blacksmith talked on and on about "that rogue Charles Stuart". In fact Charles Stuart even joined in, agreeing with the smith.

A ship lay at Shoreham bound for France. As Charles, exhausted and careworn, climbed gingerly into a sailor's canvas hammock, the ship's captain rushed below decks. "I know very well who you are!" he said. The King, too weary to rise, boggled over the side of the hammock at the captain, who fell on his knees. "And I would lay down my life to set your Majesty safe in France!"

Lying in that hammock, listening to the creak of the ship's timbers, his cabin rocking gently around him, Charles pondered how to reward such people – all those brave, loyal souls who had been willing to risk their lives and lands to help a defeated man escape his enemies. One day he would return to England and occupy his rightful place as king. No more need for hiding like an acorn buried in the ground. He would flourish like a mighty oak, giving shelter to his people.

When the story of Charles's escape became known, the acorns of the oak tree at Boscobel were planted far and wide. From the acorns grew oaks, and by every oak an alehouse or inn. On Oak-Apple Day, the King's health was drunk at those inns. Long after Cromwell and his Commonwealth were gone and forgotten, the Royal Oaks flourished. And even after the oaks perished, the story survived.

The Tyburn Dancer

1660s

THE DRIVER BANGED ON THE COACH ROOF. "You ladies may want to draw the blinds! We are coming to Hounslow Heath, and the gibbets are not a pretty sight to look on!"

Even with the blinds closed, the passengers on the post-coach could hear the creak of ropes, the jingling of chains, as hanged men swung in the breeze. Hounslow Heath was forested with gibbets, for any highwayman hanged at Tyburn had his body returned to the scene of his crime and hung up in chains . . . and the heath was a favourite haunt of such men.

"Foul beasts," said Lady Cynthia, fanning herself furiously.

Lord Babbacombe patted her hand. "Destroy 'em like the vermin they are, I say!"

"Isn't there something rather romantic about them?" said Lady Dorothea. "Living by moonlight, on the brink of disaster?"

"Not when they strangle a defenceless woman for the crucifix round her neck," said her husband. "That's what happened last week, close by here."

Lady Cynthia whimpered.

"Let 'em all dance at a rope's end, I say!" declared Lord Babbacombe.

As if in answer, a voice just beyond the closed blinds cried, "Stand and deliver!"

The coach lurched to a halt. The driver swore. Lady Cynthia swooned clean away, and Lord Babbacombe tried to hide underneath her spreading skirts. Dorothea's husband – a man of considerable wealth – hurried to prime his pistol, but the priming pin fell into the dark bottom of the coach and rattled out of sight.

The door opened, and there stood a man, prodigiously tall in his tricorn hat, one foot up on the running board and a pistol in each hand.

"Permit me to introduce myself. Claude Duval, native of France and gentleman of the English countryside. Your money, if you please, sirs!" Then he saw Dorothea. "If your hand is already spoken for, lady, I must settle for your jewels," he said, and somehow succeeded in bowing, without his pistols so much as wavering.

"Sir, my heart belongs to my husband here, but your manners commend you," said Dorothea looking him boldly in the eye. "I have heard your name spoken in the most exulted circles, Monsieur, though I had hoped never to meet you myself."

The eyebrows above the mask rose a little, and the mouth below it smiled. "Madam, pray do not fear for your safety. Your beauty is such that I could ask nothing more precious from you than the honour of a dance."

Dorothea did not turn to her husband for advice: her eyes remained fixed fast on Duval. "But where is your music, Monsieur?" she asked.

He made a flamboyant gesture with one pistol. "We have the music of the spheres, do we not, Lady?"

"In that case, I shall pay your toll, Monsieur Duval."

There was no moon: highwaymen do not work by moonlight. But the stars shone on that stately pavane. The men by the coach watched open-mouthed as the two figures paced out a dance in time to Duval's humming.

"They say a woman was murdered last week, by one of you 'gentlemen', for the sake of the crucifix around her throat," said Dorothea pertly.

"Do not bless him with the name of 'gentleman'," said Duval. "The dogs who do such things are beneath contempt, and I will shoot him myself if he ever crosses my path! May the lady's ghost hang round his neck till doomsday."

"And where, pray, will your ghost be seen after you are dead, Monsieur Duval?"

"Why, dancing on Hounslow Heath, God willing, with a woman of grace and spirit!"

"Just so long as you never dance on Tyburn Tree," she said, and for the first time that night a shiver of clammy fright went through her.

When the dance ended, Claude Duval took the gems from around Lady Cynthia's neck, a watch and purse from the man hiding under her skirts. He asked of Dorothea's husband just £100 – a tenth of what he might have demanded. But from his dancing partner he took nothing. "I consider myself in your debt, Lady," he said, thrusting the pistols back into his waistband and bowing with a flourish of his tricorn. "My life is far sweeter for meeting you tonight!" Then he whistled for his horse, mounted and rode away.

Afterwards, Dorothea thought of him often and wistfully, though her husband never mentioned the incident, or allowed her to speak of it. When she opened the newspaper one morning and read that Duval was betrayed, arrested, condemned to hang, her own words clanged in her head like a funeral bell: "Just so long as you never dance on Tyburn Tree."

Screwing up her courage, Dorothea hired a chaise to take her to Tyburn. But as she approached the place of public execution, she tapped on the coach roof and called for it to stop. All around the gallows washed a sea of satin and lace, a raft of elegant hats, the susurration of a hundred sighs. Half the ladies in London seemed to have come to make their farewells to the French gallant.

Later, when the notorious Claude Duval had kicked out his last dance at the end of the hangman's rope, been hung up in chains, cut down and buried, a headstone appeared mysteriously to mark the place. It read, "Here lies Claude Duval. If you are a man, beware your purse, if a woman, your heart. He has made havoc of both."

Unknown to Dorothea, her husband had repaid his own debt of honour for the gentlemanly fashion in which Duval had treated both his wife and his wallet.

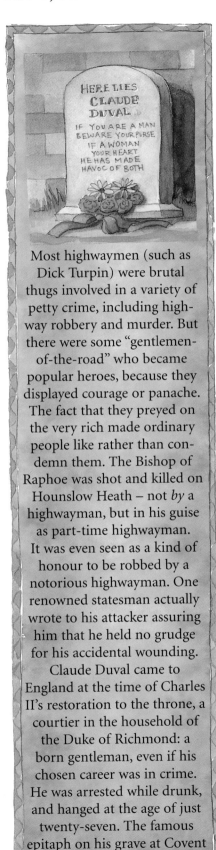

Most highwaymen (such as Dick Turpin) were brutal thugs involved in a variety of petty crime, including highway robbery and murder. But there were some "gentlemen-of-the-road" who became popular heroes, because they displayed courage or panache. The fact that they preyed on the very rich made ordinary people like rather than condemn them. The Bishop of Raphoe was shot and killed on Hounslow Heath – not *by* a highwayman, but in his guise as part-time highwayman. It was even seen as a kind of honour to be robbed by a notorious highwayman. One renowned statesman actually wrote to his attacker assuring him that he held no grudge for his accidental wounding. Claude Duval came to England at the time of Charles II's restoration to the throne, a courtier in the household of the Duke of Richmond: a born gentleman, even if his chosen career was in crime. He was arrested while drunk, and hanged at the age of just twenty-seven. The famous epitaph on his grave at Covent Garden no longer exists.

The Village that Chose to Die

1665

THE FIRST INSTINCT was to run: to pack up bags and bedding and children into a cart and to get away. And when the first cases of plague hit Eyam Village, some did go. There were a few deaths in the autumn, then a season of happiness, when the village seemed to have been spared. In the spring, it came back: the Black Death – moving through Eyam like a stray cat scratching at every door to be let in.

The people went along to the church that day with their minds full of plans and fears. Where should they go? To which relative? Not the plague-stricken London, that was sure. They had only half an ear to lend William Mompesson, their priest. But then they realized what he was saying.

"The plague travels about the country in the blood of those fleeing it. In trying to get away, folk take a death sentence to another community of souls, condemning them too, to die. When a fire breaks out, we protect the houses round about by making a firebreak and starving the fire of new timber. That's what we must do here. As we are Christians, we must be prepared to die in order that others may

live. For Christ says, 'Greater love hath no man than this . . .'"

Stunned, the people of Eyam gaped at him. He made it sound so simple. Isolate the disease so that the disease might die out. He was asking them to stay in Eyam, to make no move to get away; to cut themselves off and let the plague burn itself out within the available people – within their children, their loved ones, themselves. Three hundred and fifty people, waiting for an inevitable and terrible death. And yet the man had such an air of certainty. Amid all the confusion and terror, he *knew what to do*. They must simply stop struggling – deliver themselves into the hands of God and the plague.

Of course they did everything within their power to avoid infection. Some smoked pipes all day long, some wore charms and bunches of herbs, some carried nosegays to keep off the stench of death. But the people of Eyam followed the instructions of their priest. As travellers neared the village a sentry would call out, "Go back! We have the plague in Eyam. Go round us, and remember us in your prayers!"

Supplies of food and quicklime and tobacco and so forth were brought to the boundary stone or the well and left where the payment lay, in vinegar-washed, sterile coins. The curious came for a while, to shout questions across the river. But soon no one came. For all Eyam knew, the rest of the world had died.

If William Mompesson thought that God would spare the people because of their selflessness, he was mistaken. One by one they fell ill, each one suffering days of tormenting pain and wretchedness while neighbours watched from a distance, much as people might watch a rabid dog die in the street. The lucky ones died suddenly, after a few hours of raging fever. Sooner than move bodies through the streets, families dug graves in their gardens, ready for when they were too ill to dig them. Mrs Hancock buried her husband, three sons and three daughters in the field beside her house, within the space of eight days.

The church was locked – too good a breeding ground for the disease – but William Mompesson kept on holding services, out in the open air, under a scorching summer sky endlessly smutted with flies and the ash of fumigating fires. He had raised this dwindling little congregation of patient saints halfway to heaven. William Mompesson had done that much for them, and that was more than any surgeon or apothecary could have done.

On 7 September 1665, George Viccars, a tailor in Eyam, in the Peak District, received a parcel of cloth from London, and in it a cloud of fleas, thought to be the source of the epidemic. He was first to die. Three-quarters of the population of Eyam died of bubonic plague within a year. Unlike other "plague villages" which were totally abandoned during the Black Death of the fourteenth century, Eyam survives to the present day. Meanwhile, in London, nearly 70,000 deaths were attributed to the Great Plague.

The Great Fire of London

1666

IT WAS NOBODY'S DOING, NOBODY'S FAULT. Suddenly, at two in the morning of Sunday, 2 September, a pile of firewood stacked against the wall of the baker's shop in Pudding Lane burst into flames. (It was the back wall of the oven, and so of course the bricks grew hot.) Mr Faryner the baker woke to find the room full of smoke and, when he reached the head of the stairs, could see at once there was no escaping that way. The whole of the ground floor was alight.

"Wife! Wife! Wake up unless you want to burn in your bed!"

They climbed out of a dormer window in the roof and spread-eagled themselves against the roof tiles, feeling for the gutter with their feet. The air was full of smuts and smoke. At the window the maid sobbed: "I can't! I can't do it, Mr Faryner! I'll fall! It's too high!"

There was no turning back for her – no reasoning with her as she grew more and more hysterical. The baker pressed on, balancing his way along the guttering, while down in the street a crowd of neighbours gathered, stupid with sleep. They watched till the screaming figure of the maid fell back from the window, replaced by leaping spectres of flame.

For an hour the baker's shop alone burned – a bad blaze but not the first in a city of wooden and wattle houses. Neighbours fearing for their own property fetched out buckets of water, but there was no organized attempt to isolate the fire. A brisk wind was blowing. Above the heads of those watching, burning straws and cinders and ash floated in search of kindling.

By morning, the whole street was ablaze.

Lord Mayor Thomas Bludworth was a dithering, indecisive man. He would not order the pulling down of undamaged shops and houses to make a firebreak. "Who will pay for the rebuilding?" he asked querulously. For hours he hesitated, while the fire leapt from roof to rooftop and strung the narrow streets with yellow buntings of flame.

Cellars packed with fuel, barrels of pitch, winter supplies of tallow exploded, throwing burning clods of wattle high into the air and showering the streets with tiles. Families in the path of the fire began to bundle their belongings together into chests and bags and to move their children out of doors. Here and there, gangs of men banded together to fight the fire, but all they had were buckets of water and hand-held squirts. They might as well have spat on the flames. King Charles II, looking out over London, saw the daylight choked by a rising mass of black smoke. "Tell the Lord Mayor he may have all the soldiers he needs!"

"How did it begin?" was all the Lord Mayor wanted to know. "Who's to blame?"

"Foreigners!" people told him. "Fire raisers! Revolutionaries!"

Mr Faryner the baker was summoned to tell what he knew of the fire. Anxious that no one should blame him, he remembered mysterious, suspicious circumstances – the fire starting far from the bread oven, for no good reason. And it had spread so fast and so far! There must have been arsonists operating all over the city!

People powerless to stop the fire turned their energies to finding the culprits. A Frenchman was knocked down with an iron bar for the crime of being foreign. A woman holding her apron gathered up in front of her was set upon by a mob screaming, "Look! Look! She has fireballs hidden in her apron! She's carrying fireballs! Arsonist!" The woman sprawled senseless in the open drain, and a dozen fluffy yellow chicks scattered out of her apron and ran cheeping hither and thither.

At last, the Lord Mayor gave permission for a firebreak to be made, and soldiers with billhooks began pulling apart whole streets of houses, while the householders screamed prayers and abuse and clutched their children close or dragged their furniture clear of the tumbling masonry. But it was too late. The fire leapt their firebreak, a surf of sparks spilling onwards to set alight wash-lines, hay-carts and more thatches.

Down at the river, the watermen had mustered every watertight boat and barge in the city and were busy evacuating families and goods downriver. The river was a red glare, the smoke an artificial night, but the watermen were pitiless in demanding their fee. As the hours passed, and they found they had more trade than they could handle, they demanded higher and higher sums. Huge purses of money changed hands so that a dresser and a harpsichord should float with their owners downstream, out of danger. Already there were tables and benches afloat on the tide, safer in the water than out of it.

Crowds jostled at the waterside for a chance to board, children up to their knees in mud, women balancing on jetties and landing stages, men haggling and swearing. In among them, pickpockets were lifting a fortune in watches and silk handkerchiefs, an unattended valise here, there an unguarded roll of cutlery.

The goldsmiths and silversmiths of the city converged on the Tower of London, to deposit their valuables in the stone vaults and impregnable dungeons of the ancient fortress. But would even the Tower keep out the fire now shredding to rags the London skyline? Church spires were toppling like trees, stone buildings crazing, crumbling, crumpling, their stones bursting like bombs.

The booksellers of London chose St Paul's Cathedral as a safe place for their stock, for it was built in stone and lead and bronze – not kindling like the houses which jostled round it.

Many people also looked for sanctuary in the various churches, only to be harangued by preachers wild-eyed with zeal. "This is the judgement of the Lord! Yea, He hath poured out brimstone on the heads of the unrighteous!" They were out on the streets, too, the evangelists, bellowing in the ears of the milling crowds, their spittle gleaming in the firelight: "God sendeth down destruction on this City of Sin, on this generation of sinners!"

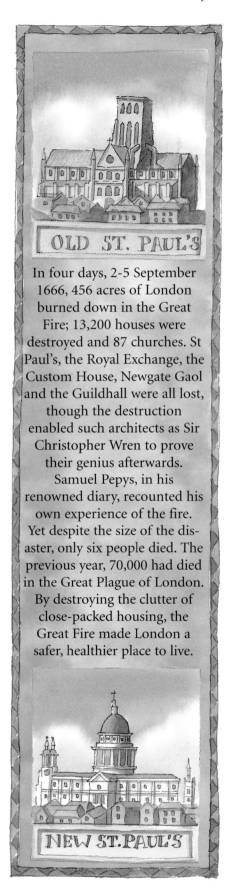

OLD ST. PAUL'S

In four days, 2-5 September 1666, 456 acres of London burned down in the Great Fire; 13,200 houses were destroyed and 87 churches. St Paul's, the Royal Exchange, the Custom House, Newgate Gaol and the Guildhall were all lost, though the destruction enabled such architects as Sir Christopher Wren to prove their genius afterwards.

Samuel Pepys, in his renowned diary, recounted his own experience of the fire. Yet despite the size of the disaster, only six people died. The previous year, 70,000 had died in the Great Plague of London. By destroying the clutter of close-packed housing, the Great Fire made London a safer, healthier place to live.

NEW ST. PAUL'S

Certainly hell did seem to have risen close to the surface of the world that day. In places the ground was too hot to walk on, and the air seared nose and throat and lungs. Rats and mice driven from the burning buildings squealed like demons along the streets. At one time, an area two miles long and one mile wide was alight and burning. The army was blowing up buildings with gunpowder now, adding to the din.

At eight o'clock on Tuesday night, a cry went up which turned the booksellers' hearts to printer's pulp. St Paul's was burning. Lead streamed molten out of its roof, pouring down in cataracts of incandescent silver, splashing on to the faces of the saints and madonnas, obliterating the bronzes on the floor: "Here lies the body of . . ." Into the vaults it poured, making a bonfire of the books and pamphlets and maps and Bibles in a blaze which leapt back up to the carved angels on the hammer beams. The great bells, set swinging and ringing by the hot updraught, began to lose their shape, to soften and bow, to sag, to melt in brilliant torrents.

In the Inner Temple, the beautiful, ancient buildings wavered in the heat-warped air – a golden rain of sparks falling on their roofs. A sailor called Richard Rowe, accustomed to going aloft in rigging, clambered on to the roof of the great hall, as lawyers in wigs and gowns gaped up at him, clutching precious documents. All he had was a pillow, and as he straddled the roof ridge, he beat at flames which scuttled like rats across the tiles.

The great fire had reached the limit of its strength. The explosions had finally starved it of new food. Now, here, at the Inner Temple, it lost the fight against a single man and a pillow. Richard Rowe saved the great hall, to the choking cheers of lawyers and judges, clerks and secretaries. As he sat there astride the roof, all he could see as far as the levelled horizon was smoking devastation.

Outside London, in the parks, 100,000 people huddled bewildered and homeless amid the few worldly goods they had managed to save – a cradle, a wheelbarrow, a sedan chair. The King organized relief supplies of food to be fetched in from the countryside, and personally administered the billeting of the homeless in pubs, inns and churches. Before long, he was commissioning brave new buildings, planning a more open, elegant city than the one which had grown up hugger-mugger, in squalor and overcrowded filth, over 1,000 years. But those who had lost their homes simply roamed about the ruins, picking over the ashes of their houses, counting the cost.

Colonel Blood Steals the Crown Jewels

1671

ONE DAY, WHILE MR TALBOT EDWARDS, THE deputy keeper, and his wife were taking tea, a clergyman and his wife called at the Tower and asked if they might view the Crown Jewels.

It was not an unusual request. Old Mr Edwards was accustomed to giving his little informative talk as he displayed the royal sceptre, the sword of state, the jewelled gauntlets and coronets and, of course, the coronation crown. He had been doing it for years.

Such an agreeable couple, Mr and Mrs Edwards agreed afterwards – especially when the gentleman called a week later with a pair of gloves for Mrs Edwards "in gratitude for her great kindness". Seeing the pair of pistols hanging on the wall of the apartment, the clergyman admired them so much that he begged to buy them, then and there!

The friendship flourished. So it seemed the most natural thing in the world that their clergyman friend should bring along two acquaintances – visitors to London – to view the Royal Regalia. That was the morning of 9 May.

Beginning his well-worn talk, Mr Edwards laid out the gems and collars, diadems and weapons on the table in the Jewel Room. "And this, gentlemen, is the coronet worn by . . ."

Suddenly, Talbot Edwards – who was past eighty – found himself enveloped in darkness – a cloak over his head, a wooden bung pushed into his mouth to gag him.

"Give us the crown, the orb and the sceptre and no one will get hurt!" the clergyman hissed in the old man's ear.

But Edwards took his responsibilities to heart. The shame of losing the treasures in his charge to a band of tricksters and brigands was more than he could bear. He began to struggle and moan and kick and wrench himself to and fro in their grasp. They struck him once with a wooden mallet, then when he still struggled, struck him again and again.

"Keep him quiet, can't you?" Colonel Blood snarled.

They stabbed Edwards to silence him.

Colonel Blood beat the crown of England out of shape and crammed it under his cloak. Another man dropped the orb down the front of his baggy breeches. But the sceptre of state was too long to fit up a sleeve or down a trouser leg. They flung it on the table and began to file it in two.

Then a sharp whistle from their look-out on the floor below warned of danger: visitors for the Edwardses! The keeper's son and son-in-law were coming up the stairs! Edwards' visitors opened the door of the apartment to be met by a stampede of masked men, a volley of shouts and swearwords. They were shoved aside, but quickly realized what was happening, crying, "Stop the thieves!"

There was a warder on the drawbridge. Running towards the commotion, he was confronted by the small black circle of Blood's pistol barrel pointing in his face. He saw the hammer lift, the spark flash, then fear swallowed him up in a black unconsciousness he mistook for death. The shot had missed, but Blood and his cronies were through the iron gate and running for the tethered horses.

Talbot Edwards' son put on such a sprint that he crashed into Blood and bowled him off his feet. The crown clattered to the ground, gems and pearls

jarred from their settings and rolled away like so many pebbles.

The news was shouted from street to street clear across London: "Have you heard? Someone's tried to steal the Crown Jewels! . . . A band of brigands! . . . They broke the sceptre! . . . They murdered the guards! . . . But they've been caught! . . . And now Blood is refusing to speak to anyone but the King of England himself!"

To everyone's surprise, King Charles II granted Blood an audience.

But did the colonel throw himself on the King's mercy? Did he plead insanity or swear that he had been forced to commit the crime against his will? Far from it.

"Yes, I did it!" said Blood. "I would never deny it to save my life. It was my plan and it was only by the greatest bad luck that it failed. I'm no more sorry than I was when I kidnapped the Duke of Ormonde! No more sorry than when I lay in hiding at Battersea and aimed a gun at you, Charles Stuart, as you went down to bathe in the river."

The audacity of the man, the knowledge he had come so close to being assassinated all but silenced the King. "What stopped you shooting me?" he asked at last.

"My heart was checked by an awe of majesty which caused me to spare the King's life," said Blood. "I shall never name my accomplices. If any of us die, the rest are sworn to be avenged for that death. But if your Majesty were to spare us, the pardoned men would doubtless be ready to do the King great service. We have already proved our daring, you'll agree."

"Take them back to the Tower," said the King, and his court waited, with horrid glee, to see what terrible retribution would overtake the villainous, the shameless, the arrogant Colonel Blood. As if the King could be intimidated by empty threats! As if the King would use the services of such unmitigated rogues!

Within days, Blood was free. Not only free, but his estates were restored to him along with an income of £500 a year. Talbot Edwards lived, but received almost nothing for his loyal service – a pittance in comparison with the rewards Blood received from the King.

So did the King so much admire daring and audacity that he was ready to let an unrepentant criminal go free? Or was he scared of revenge attacks following Blood's death? Or did Blood and the King share some secret which placed the lout beyond reach of the law? Rumour spread that he had done the King some huge favour so murderous and wicked that he held the King in the palm of his hand, free to say what he liked, do what he pleased, rather than swinging at the end of a hangman's rope.

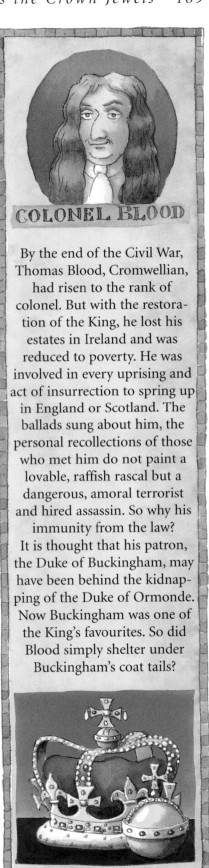

COLONEL BLOOD

By the end of the Civil War, Thomas Blood, Cromwellian, had risen to the rank of colonel. But with the restoration of the King, he lost his estates in Ireland and was reduced to poverty. He was involved in every uprising and act of insurrection to spring up in England or Scotland. The ballads sung about him, the personal recollections of those who met him do not paint a lovable, raffish rascal but a dangerous, amoral terrorist and hired assassin. So why his immunity from the law?
It is thought that his patron, the Duke of Buckingham, may have been behind the kidnapping of the Duke of Ormonde. Now Buckingham was one of the King's favourites. So did Blood simply shelter under Buckingham's coat tails?

Run for Your Life!

1685

WHEN KING JAMES II PUT DOWN REBELLION in the West Country, he wanted to make sure that no one ever dared to question his kingship again. So he employed Judge Jeffreys to make an example of the rebels, and the judge went to it with a will. He hanged men by the hundred.

Young Hughie was famous. Throughout Somerset he was renowned for the speed and distance he could run. Champion of a hundred races, Hughie of Westonzoyland was both sprinter and marathon runner and could outpace running dogs and outstay an army horse.

"They say you can run, boy," said Judge Jeffreys, supercilious under his black cap.

"I can."

"And I say you can't. A wager on it. What do you say?"

"I have nothing to wager," said Hughie, wary of the gleam in the judge's eye.

"Wouldn't you wager your *life*, boy, that you could outrun a runner of mine?"

"That I would!" Hughie was over-quick to accept the bet. There among the numberless nooses, the trees dangling with hanged men, the muttered prayers of Catholic priests over Protestant prisoners, he grabbed at the chance to live. He knew he could outrun any man in the county. To win his life

he was ready to run as he had never run before.

"Then fetch out a horse and tie him to the stirrup!" commanded the judge. "If he tires before the horse, he shall hang. If the horse tires first, I shall rethink my verdict." And before Hughie could draw a good, deep breath, someone slapped the horse across the rump and it sprang forward.

The animal was unnerved by seeing movement in the corner of his eye, by the noise in his swivelling ear of a man's laboured breathing. At first the two of them jostled one another – man and horse, horse and man. The jeering spectators fully expected to see Hughie dragged to his death.

But Hughie timed his strides by the hoofbeats, stretched his gait to match the sway and thrust of the big fetlocks, and soon the pair were running side by side, leaving their captors staring after them. In a panic, soldiers mounted up to give chase and keep the prisoner in sight.

Across the green curves of Somerset, Hughie and the stallion ran; across the green swelling hills, across pillaged farms, past burned buildings and the wreckage of gun carriages. Horse ran and man ran, and if once the pace slowed, there were plenty of shouts from behind to spur on the frightened beast.

In time the horse became accustomed to his running-mate, and Hughie, far from hating the beast, found more in common with its pounding, pungent bulk than with the men hooting and whooping behind. He made of himself a machine, his legs the mill-paddles, the ground the water driving them. "I will run for my life or die running," he told himself.

He thought of Anne, his sweetheart, her sadness at thinking him dead, her joy in finding him alive, his life won back like a trophy. *She* was the trophy at the end of the race. *She* was the goal which kept him running when his legs burned like twin fuses and his lungs were two tattered flags, when his head rolled on his shoulder heavy as a cannonball.

The stallion had no such goal. That is why, in the end, he tired. After three hours of running, his breath broke in his windpipe and his sweating flanks heaved. He slowed to a canter, to a trot, to a walk, then pitched down so that Hughie fell on top of him.

To Hughie's surprise the noise, swelling louder and louder as his pursuers caught up, was of breathless cheering. Miles earlier, the jeering had given way to admiration – wonder, even – at the strength and courage of a young man who could outrun a horse. They took off their hats in salute to him. They carried him back to the judge eagerly, with the news loud in their mouths: "He did it, sir! He did it! The horse tired first! He did it!"

The news of the rebels' defeat by the King's army reached Westonzoyland fast. So did the story of the race: man against horse, horse against man, and how their Hughie had won it. At the village inn they drank a toast to their champion runner: the man who could win any race in the county and who had given them back their pride as West Countrymen, even in defeat. They rattled at Anne's shutters and crowned her with may, because until Hughie came home, his sweetheart was the next best person to crown. She came down to them and danced, in celebration.

Then the news arrived that Hughie was hanged.

The judge had never meant to keep his side of the bet. The race had been, for him, no more than a moment's entertainment in a long tedious day. In Westonzoyland, joy turned to outrage, then to gnawing, blistering despair. While village thoughts turned again to killing and rebellion and revenge, Anne slipped quietly away.

A ghost runs now across the Summer Land: not a boy's athletic ghost timing its paces to the beat of ghostly hoofbeats, but a little pattering ghost wearing a crown of may. Because Anne drowned herself at the news of her sweetheart's death. Now her ghost gasps and sobs and stumbles breathlessly on, everlastingly trying to outrun her grief.

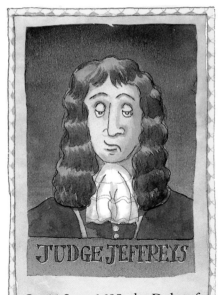

JUDGE JEFFREYS

On 11 June 1685, the Duke of Monmouth, illegitimate son of Charles II, landed at Lyme Regis, hopeful of wresting the crown from his uncle, King James II. Over 4,000 West Countrymen mustered to his Protestant cause. For a month – the so-called "Duking Days" – these rebels held Somerset, and Monmouth was proclaimed King in Taunton market-place. But when James brought his full wrath to bear, his army easily defeated the rebels at the battle of Sedgemoor. Monmouth was captured, and cravenly and unsuccessfully begged for his life, even at the cost of turning Catholic. Meanwhile the notoriously harsh Judge Jeffreys was sent to Taunton to try captured rebels. His "Bloody Assize", estimated to have hanged 200 men, transported 800 more to the West Indies and whipped and fined countless others. His barbarism inflicted wounds on the West Country for which neither he nor James, his paymaster, were ever forgiven.

Glencoe

1692

THE THING WAS TO GET IT OVER AND DONE WITH, then put it out of mind. The thing was to say: these are not people, these are MacDonalds. War hardens a man, and after a few years in the army, he can stomach almost anything. It is a lot to ask of a man, even so, to eat another man's food, to sleep under his roof, to accept his hospitality, then to murder him.

Still, King William was determined to be rid of the "Auld Fox" MacIan and the rest of the MacDonald clan once and for all.

So we were billeted on them, with the excuse that the garrison at Fort William was too overcrowded to hold us. As we marched into the glen – 120 men of the Earl of Argyll's Highland Regiment – McIan's sons appeared and asked if we came as friends or foe. "As friends," said Glenlyon. "As friends".

For fifteen days we lived in their poor wee houses, in that great valley called Glencoe, where a river of wind flows always cold, and where the snow fortifies the mountains into castles high as the sky.

The Master of Stair had said it must be done in winter, because it was the one time the Highlanders could not elude us and carry their wives, children and cattle to the mountains.

They did not suspect anything. After all, the "Auld Fox" had pledged his allegiance to King William, so he thought he had nothing to fear, even though we were Campbells. (The Campbells and MacDonalds have hated each other for as long as I can remember; that's why Stair chose us for the job.) Also, we had accepted MacIan's hospitality, and that should have guaranteed our goodwill. That's the unwritten law of the Highlands.

So we played cards with the MacDonalds, we drank with them, exchanged stories with them. We sat down to suppers cooked by the women, and our knuckles knocked against their knuckles as we reached into the same bowl for our food. The children tugged at our uniforms, wanting to be sung a song. Their mothers hushed them to bed: "Do nae fash the officer: he needs his sleep."

But there wasn't to be any sleep. At nightfall we were summoned outside and given our orders by Glenlyon. We did not go back in to our beds. When they saw us checking our muskets, the MacIan boys asked: "What's happening?" But Glenlyon only laughed and told them we were going out next day to tackle a local band of robbers.

The time was set for five in the morning, when the clansmen would be asleep or just stirring. So we waited, watching the moon move over the glen through tangles of snow-cloud, a thistledown of snow blowing.

Come five o'clock we went to it. Bayonets fixed. No shot to be fired, that was the order. But some of us were jumpy – or squeamish – and we used our guns. The MacDonalds would have woken anyway, I know. The screaming would have woken them soon enough.

We killed more than thirty. You wouldn't think that would take long. And yet the screaming seemed to go on for an eternity. Sometimes I hear it still in my sleep. Men, women, children. Everyone under seventy years, the order said, and don't trouble the Governor with prisoners. If they locked the doors against us, we set the house alight and burned it down, with the people inside. Women. Children. Fourteen in one house.

In the confusion, some got away, out of the vil-lage. It didn't matter. It's so cold up there, the snow lay so deep, and them in their shirts for sleeping, barefoot, without cloak or blanket: we knew they would freeze to death on the mountainsides.

In the house where I had stayed, nine clansmen were gathered round the morning fire when we went in shooting. Four died where they sat. We split up and went after the women, the bairns, the old folk. I came face-to-face with the owner of the house, the one whose knuckles had brushed mine as I reached for bread at supper. Odd how, in all the din – the smashing of furniture, the screaming, the shooting, the curses – there seemed nothing between us but silence. A blanket of silence. Then the man said, "Let me die in the open air, man, no under ma ain roof."

I had steeled myself against the usual things: "Let me live. Spare my wife. Pity the bairns." This seemed such a small thing to ask: "Let me die in the open air."

"For your bread which I have eaten," I said, "I will." So we pushed him out of doors with our musket butts, and he stood there in the dark, his face underlit by the snow. We levelled our muskets.

Then he up with his plaid – that piece of tartan they all wear for a cloak – and threw it in our faces and ran. We fired after him, but the snow swallowed him up. Maybe he lived. Maybe he froze to death, being without his plaid. Part of me hopes he got clear.

CAPTAIN CAMPBELL

The Glencoe massacre was an atrocity brought about by one man's obsessive loathing of the MacDonald clan: Secretary of State for Scotland, Sir John Dalrymple, Master of Stair. Stair had already persuaded King William to put to the sword anyone who would not pledge allegiance to the crown. But MacIan *had* signed. Even so, Stair succeeded in sending 120 Campbells, commanded by Captain Campbell Glenlyon, to massacre the clan. More than thirty were killed, another 300 fled into the blizzard. Chieftain MacIan was shot in bed by a man he had invited to dine; his wife died of her injuries. His sons escaped. The legend of the woman and child was added later — echo of Snow White. Another legend tells of the Campbells led astray by mountain spirits on the way home.

The British public were so shocked by the massacre that Stair was shunned for a time . . . but was ultimately made an earl. Politically, the massacre was a disastrous move, unifying Highlanders and Lowlanders in bitter hatred of the English.

But Glenlyon saw it happen and came down on us raging. "There's two more run into the forest yonder!" he bellowed at me. "Get after them and finish them both!"

From the edge of the wood I could hear them crashing through the deadwood; clods of snow slumped down from the trees, showing the way they had gone. Besides, I could see their footsteps in the snow – one set deep, one set so small and light that it scarcely dented the snow. Pretty soon the snowy trees swallowed up the roar of burning buildings behind me, the crack of muskets. It was silent where I found them: a silent, grey, hollow world pillared with bare tree trunks. A woman and a child, too exhausted to go any further, clung to one another gasping, their breath curling into the air like musket smoke. I fired once, reloaded, fired a second time.

Twigs and snow tumbled down on to me from where the musket balls had holed the leaf canopy overhead. The woman looked at me, her hand clamped over the child's mouth to keep him from screaming. We neither of us said one word.

Then I pulled the shawl from round her shoulders, turned on my heel and headed back. On the way, Providence set a wolf in my path, and I killed it and daubed the shawl with blood. I had to have something to show Glenlyon.

All in all it's not a night's work I'm proud of. If you ask me, I'd say the killing was folly as well as a sin. When word spread, even the sassenachs* pitied the MacDonalds, whereas up till then Highlander and Lowlander had scorned one another. We Campbells were shamed by it. That's my opinion.

I don't tell people I was there. I don't say, "I was at Glencoe." You only have to mention the word and men shudder. I shudder: almost as if the snow blew inside me that night, and lodged where it's never going to thaw. At five in the morning, I lie awake and shiver.

*Sassenach (literally Saxon) is an abusive term for a Lowlander or non-Scot.

The Lighthouse and the Storm

1703

HENRY WINSTANLEY DESIGNED PLAYING CARDS and lived in the depths of the country, miles from the sea. So he was not the most obvious contender for the task of building a lighthouse. But whereas others tried and gave up, Winstanley maintained it was perfectly possible and that he was the man to do it. In 1696 he mustered carpenters and engineers and, with his meticulous plans rolled up under his arm, sailed out to the Eddystone Rock to start work.

Ever since vessels first set sail from the English coast, the Eddystone Rock had been a menace to sailors. On a calm sunny day, it looked like nothing – a jag of rock jutting high enough out of the sea for gulls to perch. But in a fog, or when the waves ran so high as to hide it altogether, the Eddystone Rock could rip the keel out of sloop or merchantman or fishing smack. Countless sailors had drowned in the waters around it, and their sunken ships were now crewed by conger eels and shoals of ghost-white cod.

The task would have been hard enough, even under ideal conditions trying to work on a weed-slippery, spray-wet rock while battered by wind and sea, trying to sink foundations sufficiently deep to raise up an indestructible tower twenty-five metres tall. As it was, Winstanley had to contend with dangers of a different sort.

Press gangs roaming the inns and kitchens of the south coast in search of able-bodied men saw work begin on the Eddystone Rock and rubbed their hands with glee. When a press-gang paid a visit there, the builders would have nowhere to run. Winstanley's workmen were coshed and bound and carried off to serve as seamen in the Royal Navy – pressed men – leaving nothing but a scattering of tools and timber. Winstanley recruited fresh men, but there was an understandable shortage of volunteers.

During construction, Winstanley often chose to sleep on site rather than waste time coming ashore. One night, he and his builders were woken by the rhythmic splash of oars, the thud of a rowing boat pulling alongside the rock. French troops, in cockaded hats and with muskets primed, came scrambling over the moonlit reef, barking unintelligible commands at the sleepy, bewildered English. For a few minutes it seemed as if the entire construction team would be murdered where they huddled.

Winstanley tried to reason with them: "Look, I know we're at war, your country and mine. But you French *need* this lighthouse just as much as the English! Does the rock sink only British ships? Does it drown only English seamen?"

Despite his protests, Winstanley's builders were stripped naked and cast adrift in a rowing boat. But at least *they* stood on English soil next day, whereas Winstanley found himself in a French prison. The Admiralty were incensed. They arranged for a mutual exchange of prisoners – and put Winstanley back to work building the Eddystone Light.

At last a core of stone was grafted on to the rock, and on to that a wooden tower, with a windowed chamber at the summit where hung a kind of three-tiered chandelier, crammed with tallow candles. The night those candles were first lit, Winstanley's face glowed almost as bright with pride in a job well done.

"It'll never stand up!" people said.

Praise for Winstanley's handsome lighthouse was guarded. A great many people said it would fall down within days. "I only wish," Winstanley answered them, "that I may be in the lighthouse in circumstances that will test its strength to the utmost."

November 1703 ended amid filthy weather. Then, on the twenty-sixth, a gale struck the south of England more ferocious than any recorded before or since. People woke with the impression that the world was coming to an end, and when they looked out of their windows, they were certain of it.

In London 700 boats and barges were ripped off their moorings and piled up in matchwood mountains against the bridges. The roofs were ripped off houses like so many fish-scales, whirling the contents into the sky, pelting those outdoors with furniture, masonry and tiles, cats and food and roofbeams. Churches collapsed as though built of biscuit crumbs. A flood tide, inflated by the wind, swept up the river and swamped the City, washing over the venerable stone floors of Westminster Hall, setting afloat the bodies of those killed in the maelstrom. Off the coast, three warships foundered with 1,500 men aboard, and 200 sailors were glimpsed, stranded and drowning on the Goodwin Sands.

The face of the English countryside was scarred by those two days of the Great Storm. Whole villages foundered, whole copses were uprooted, barns folded flat. At least 8,000 people died, though the chaos and horror were so great that no true count was ever made. Tens of thousands were injured.

In the depths of the Essex countryside, in the parish of Littlebury, one house stood pretty much unscathed. Hardly any damage befell the home of Henry Winstanley, engraver, inventor, designer of playing cards and lighthouses. A small silver replica of the Eddystone Lighthouse fell from a table: that is all.

Winstanley was not home to see it, however. He was out on the Eddystone Rock, visiting his lighthouse which had recently been increased in height to thirty-seven metres.

On the morning of 28 November, the Great Storm subsided. When the people of Plymouth looked out to sea, they could see the horizon once more, though the sea was still white with rollers. They looked towards the Eddystone Light, fully expecting to see it wrecked, its pulleys and winches snapped off like tree branches, its lattice windows smashed. But they saw none of this. In fact, they saw nothing. Not a trace. Every stone and plank and nail and candle of the Eddystone Lighthouse had disappeared, as surely as if it had never existed. And with it had gone its creator.

A new light was built five years later, and stood for almost fifty years before catching fire. The lead roof, in melting, poured down in a glittering torrent – directly into the gaping mouth of the lighthouse keeper. His slow, agonizing death is commemorated in the local museum by the lead ingot which solidified inside his stomach. But of Winstanley, nothing remains but rumours mouthed by silent conger eels and ghost-white cod.

The Great Storm of 1703 was a hurricane which originated in North America, crossed the Atlantic and carved a path across Europe before spending itself in the Siberian wastes. In Britain it caused an estimated £4 million worth of damage – the equivalent of billions nowadays; 400 windmills were destroyed and hundreds and thousands of cattle and sheep drowned in the floods. The writer, Daniel Defoe, wrote of the scene in London: "no pen can describe it, no tongue can express it, no thought conceive it, unless some of those who were in the extremity of it."

The present Eddystone Lighthouse, built in 1882, is the fourth construction on the rock.

The Bubble Bursts

1720

STRANGE AND FAR-OFF LANDS have always held most magic for those who will never go there. In the early days of the eighteenth century, South America was imagined as a faery mound shot through with precious ore. It had gold, and everyone dreams of laying hands on gold.

The South Sea Company *did* exist: it was not imaginary, nor was it set up with a view to defrauding anyone. Real ships *did* sail, from time to time, between England and South America. There *was* some money to be made. But that has nothing to do with what happened in the City of London during the winter of 1719.

Rumours spread that British cargoes landing in South America would be exchanged for outlandish quantities of gold and silver. Investors in the South Sea Company stood to increase their money a hundredfold. Here was no shady, crooked enterprise: the Government itself held South Sea Company stock! Here was an opportunity for people of all kinds to get rich fast. Even when war broke out, ending trade agreements, people went on believing the South Sea Company would somehow continue to bring home vessels wallowing under tons of gold.

There was a stampede to invest. The value of shares soared: money was pouring in – not from South America but from eager investors all over England. A kind of investment fever broke out, which saw all manner of people thrusting their savings at the company's brokers, begging to be allowed to share in the bonanza. A few cautious voices warned against it: no company could or would pay profits of the kind talked of.

But the directors of the South Sea Company realized just how deep they could dip into the pockets of the gullible. When the share price began to drop, and uneasy crowds gathered outside the offices, well-dressed men strolled among them still beaming with confidence. They had *been* in Peru and Chile. They had *seen* the gold ingots piled up in the streets like bricks. Any fool could see how much those shares would soon be worth!

Fools there were in plenty. The share prices soared again. New shares were released – at a price. Hurry, hurry, hurry. Only the quick will get rich . . .

'Change Alley in the City of London was a scrum of people, from dawn till dusk, buying shares from trestle tables. A blizzard of application forms! Quill pens were at a premium; so was ink and somewhere flat to write. A man bent double by disease was charging a penny for the use of his back as a table. He went home with a big bag of pennies – solid, round, brown pennies – and kept them under his bed. A frenzy of greed had gripped the country – a kind of trance which no amount of shouting or cool reason could penetrate.

Those with wit enough saw the game for exactly what it was – a hysterical dash to buy worthless pieces of paper for absurd sums of money. Those with no conscience set up joint stock companies of their own, and issued shares, selling them in 'Change Alley. Why invest in South American gold when you can invest in a process to make sea water drinkable? Or in a perpetual motion machine? Or in re-floating treasure ships wrecked off the coast of Ireland? Why not put your money into making planks from sawdust or importing donkeys from Spain? Fortunes were to be made overnight: did it not say so on the handbills? One day a notice went up offering shares in the ultimate deceit:

A Company for Carrying on an
Undertaking of Great Advantage,
But Nobody to Know What It Is.

The shares sold. Share-fever was such that people could hardly help themselves any more.

To those who did not have £100 to invest right away, came a new temptation: £100-shares in return for a down-payment of £2. Only £2 down and you could be holding a share document worth £100, then and there! Who could fail to be tempted? In the course of a day, 1,000 of these shares were issued, in a room crammed from door to window with pushing, impatient people, all chinking their golden guineas. At the end of the day, the office was locked. The broker washed the ink from his fingers, emptied the day's takings into a carpet bag, and caught the boat for France. He had invested one day of his time and earned £2,000.

Very soon afterwards, Mr Knight, treasurer of the South Sea Company, packed a bag, disguised himself, and also made his way to the Thames. A vessel was waiting to take him to Calais. The value of South Sea shares was dropping. Nothing could hide the truth this time. An airy idea had been inflated to impossible size, and now the South Sea Bubble had burst. There was nothing in it – nothing but hot air and greedy hopes.

Thousands were ruined, their savings gone, their dreams sunk in the South Sea. It almost brought down the Government. It threatened to topple the King from his throne. Public despair was so great that the sighs must have been heard as far away as South America.

It was Dean Swift, author of *Gulliver's Travels*, who coined the name "bubble" for the kind of shady business which thrives by attracting absurd amounts of investment. It still happens today. Sir Robert Walpole, foreseeing the grief to come, had actually begun moves to ban bubble companies before the South Sea Bubble burst, but had been powerless to enforce the ban. The entire national mood was soured by the affair. A period followed of bitter cynicism in all aspects of public life.

Makers and Breakers

1730s

IN THE BRIGHT, LARGE-WINDOWED COTTAGE IN Bury, the weavers worked away on their looms, passing the woof through the weft, tapping each strand into place, their cloth growing inch by laborious inch. And as they worked, they talked of John Kay and his invention.

"Looms twice the width of these . . ."

"Double the quantity in a working day!"

"And better quality, they say!"

But their tone was not full of admiration. The flying shuttle made a weaver's task easier and produced better, broader woollen cloth, but they did not want to handle one, to master the magic of threading and throwing the ingenious shuttle.

"Should not be allowed."

"Canna be left to go on."

"Must be stopped."

"Putting skilled men out of work!"

And the mood of seething resentment came bubbling to the boil. Then, when all the useful daylight was gone and all that remained were warps and wefts of moonbeams, the weavers and their neighbours converged on Kay's house and attacked. They broke all his windows.

He was baffled, bruised and bewildered. "Why can they not see? This is their future! This is for their good!"

But the weavers hated him. They looked around them and saw all the old ways dying out, the woollen trade becoming an empire in the hands of a few wealthy industrialists, its workers forced to work harder, longer, for less. That shuttle would take food out of their children's mouths. That was how they saw it.

It was just the same when Kay moved away to Colchester – then to Leeds. Oh, his flying shuttle caught on (it was too good an invention not to) but the manufacturers who used it did not pay him anything, behaving as if they had invented it themselves.

When he started up an engineering business, the mobs again gathered to throw bricks through the windows, smash his looms. Lonely and dejected, he went back to his home town of Bury, where he lay awake nights wondering what he had ever done for these people to hate him so much. "Because a thing is new must it be bad?"

One day, the mob surrounded his house. He could hear them jeering and swearing, racketing about, their women cursing, the children bright-eyed at the prospect of destruction, excitement, violence. John Kay apologized to the friends who were visiting him. "I hope nothing unpleasant will spoil our . . ."

A shoulder thudded against the door. A window caved in, in an explosion of breaking glass. The mob poured in, like the sea into a foundering ship. John tried to save his latest models, his books, his few possessions, but saw them sunk beneath a flood of flying fists, kicking clogs, jostling shawls and wooden clubs. The satisfying sound of splintering wood made these people deaf to reason. A mob has no ears.

He fled upstairs, where his friends had already had the good sense to hide. But the mob's leader broke off and looked around. "Let us find Kay. Where is Kay?"

Kay's guests flapped open a folded woollen sheet and threw it over their friend. Then before John could protest, they bundled him up into a shuttle-shape parcel and, lifting him between them, galloped down the stairs. Passing for looters robbing the house, they got Kay away unharmed – though not undamaged.

He was a bitter man. Desperate to earn a living, he left England for France, but did no better there. Just once, he came back, to seek justice against those mill owners who had stolen his invention. He got none. Those opportunists soured him far more than the ignorant louts who had almost killed him. For the manufacturers had known just what they were doing when they tricked him out of his percentage. Besides, the wreckers – those frightened vandals who had wanted to dam the tide of progress – would quickly be swept away by it. Within a few generations, they would be living huddled in urban slums, working on deafening machines for twelve hours a day, their children crawling up and down beneath the looms, their lives reduced to figures in a ledger: profit and loss. Theirs was the loss; theirs and John Kay's. He died destitute in France.

JOHN KAY

James Hargreaves met the same reaction with his spinning jenny, Samuel Crompton with his spinning mule. When Richard Arkwright was developing his machine, superstitious neighbours complained they heard the noise of "the Devil tuning his bagpipes, and Arkwright dancing to the music". But from such inventions sprang the Industrial Revolution, transforming England's landscape, its economy, its whole social structure for ever. For a century, Progress did battle with those it was putting out of work. In 1811, a group calling themselves "Luddites" attacked stocking-making machines, power looms and shearing machines. In the countryside, "Captain Swing's" men broke up the threshing machines which deprived them of vital winter work. These were times of bread riots, enclosures, dispossessions, protest, suffering. The Government's only solution was to send in the troops.

"Charlie Is My Darling"

1746

PRINCE CHARLES EDWARD, SON OF THE EXILED James Stuart III, landed at Eriskay determined to raise a rebellion and restore his father to his rightful position: King of England and Scotland. His Scottish supporters – Jacobites – came to greet him. But they watched appalled as the prince's troops came ashore. Where were the French armies that had been promised? How were they supposed to topple King George II from the throne with this pocket army? "You must go home, your Highness," they said.

"Home? I am come home!" declared the prince.

His youth, his energy won over the hard men of the glens. As the song runs:

> *They've left their bonnie Hieland hills,*
> *Their wives and bairnies dear,*
> *To draw a sword for Scotland's Lord,*
> *   the young chevalier.*
> *Oh! Charlie is my darling, the young chevalier!*

At first they carried the day entirely, captured Edinburgh and took control of the borderlands. They had forced their way as far south as Derby before they fully grasped how incompetent their "Bonnie Prince Charlie" was. Did he really think he could take and hold London with an army of 5,000 men? They insisted he turn back. Pettish and sulking, Charles grudgingly agreed. In the meantime, the Duke of Cumberland was marching to intercept the rebels.

On 16 April 1746 he cut them off at Culloden Moor, and shot the heart out of the Jacobites. Afterwards he slaughtered their women and children too, winning himself the name "Butcher Cumberland". But the Culloden massacre lit such a fire of hatred that the Highlanders' love for their bonnie prince burned all the brighter. He was all they had left, and they guarded him like a treasure. King George offered £30,000 for the capture of the "Young Pretender", and yet no one informed on him. It was as if mists and heather had swallowed him up.

For five months, the fleeing Prince Charlie was passed from hiding place to hiding place, from caves to cellars, fed on the meagre supplies of his supporters. Told of the reward on his head, Charles grinned. "Then I offer £30 for the head of George II!"

The Kennedy brothers, wild and shaggy as Aberdeen bullocks, robbed a Hanoverian general of his baggage – all to provide the bonnie prince with a fresh suit of clothes.

When the redcoats swarmed in like red ants from all sides and not a rat could have crept away unnoticed, one of his bodyguards said, "Lend me your wig and cloak, sire. I will lead them off." Roderick MacKenzie went out into the open, showed himself and ran. He fetched after him horsemen, foot-soldiers, and such a hue and cry as the Highlands had rarely seen. They shot him down in Glen Moriston, and as he fell he shouted, "You have killed your prince!" The head was dispatched to London and put on public display – to show what became of ambitious usurpers. A one-time servant of Charles's went along – whether to grieve or simply to stare, no one knows. But in his astonishment he exclaimed aloud: 'That's no Charlie!' It was four days before the English troops discovered their mistake – and by that time Charlie himself was heading for the safety of the Hebrides.

No sooner had he put to sea than a storm hammered on the little boat and drove it sixty miles in ten pitch-black hours. Every moment, the men aboard thought to be hurled against rocks, shipwrecked on one of the islands invisible in the dark. But when dawn crawled in under the pall of black cloud, they spotted Benbecula, and were able to pull ashore. While the storm raged on, the prince took up "royal residence" in a doorless cow-house, with a rag of sailcloth for a blanket and nothing to eat but oatmeal and stolen beef.

From Benbecula, he set sail for Stornaway, but was driven ashore on Glass Island, where the people were hostile: he had to pretend to be a shipwrecked merchant. In Stornaway, one of the servants in the party got drunk and boasted wildly that he knew how the prince was going to get to France: that called for a change of plan. Putting in once more at Glass, the party was attacked and had to row on, without food or fresh water, for two days.

Spotted by an English man-of-war, the rowers bent their backs over the oars, rowing till the breath foamed through their gritted teeth. "I'll be sunk sooner than be taken," vowed the prince. Then the wind dropped, the warship was becalmed, and the oarsmen sculled out of sight of English telescopes. "It's clear," said Charles Edward, "I was not designed to die by weapon or water."

But when his friend Clanranald found him on the island of South Uist, the fugitive prince had been reduced to living in a hovel, on a diet of crabs, haggard by sickness and hunger, dressed in filthy rags. It was decided he must be got away to Skye.

So it was that the bonnie prince met Flora of the clan MacDonald, who lived by the Uist seashore. Her mother, Lady MacDonald, lived on Skye, which gave Flora the perfect excuse for making the voyage there.

When Flora entered the hut where the prince was hiding, she carried under her arm a bundle of clothes which she told him to put on: a flowery linen dress and a deep-hooded bonnet. Bonnie Charlie became "Betty Burke", and "a very old, muckle ill-shaken-up wife", by all accounts, striding out with his skirt in his fists, towards the rowing boat on the beach.

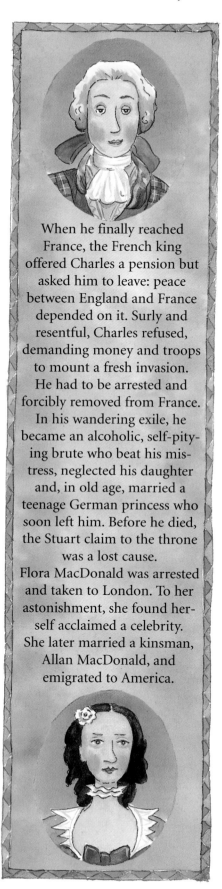

When he finally reached France, the French king offered Charles a pension but asked him to leave: peace between England and France depended on it. Surly and resentful, Charles refused, demanding money and troops to mount a fresh invasion. He had to be arrested and forcibly removed from France.

In his wandering exile, he became an alcoholic, self-pitying brute who beat his mistress, neglected his daughter and, in old age, married a teenage German princess who soon left him. Before he died, the Stuart claim to the throne was a lost cause.

Flora MacDonald was arrested and taken to London. To her astonishment, she found herself acclaimed a celebrity. She later married a kinsman, Allan MacDonald, and emigrated to America.

As the little boat, carrying Flora, "Betty Burke" and three kinsmen, rolled ashore over the Skye surf, a detachment of militiamen came pelting down the beach to seize them. "Put out again! Pull away!" cried Neil MacDonald.

Flash. Flash. The flash of the muskets reached them before the noise. *Crack. Crack.* Musket balls dug tussocks of spray out of the water. "I beg you, Miss Flora, lie down in the bottom of the boat or you may be hit!" said the prince.

"I shall not, unless you do so yourself, sir," replied Flora.

"Me? I was not designed to die, either by . . ."

"Then I shall not, sir." They argued briefly, while the musket balls kicked splinters out of the boat's side. In the end, the prince had to agree to lie alongside her, while the oarsmen heaved away, and the waves rose up between guns and boat.

At long last they succeeded in landing Bonnie Prince Charlie on Skye – though truly it was no safer a place than any of the others; his life was still in hourly danger. He made a very poor woman, by all accounts. "Your enemies call you the 'Pretender,'" joked one friend, "but you are the worst I ever saw!" "Betty" lifted her skirts too high when they forded one stream, and let her petticoats trail in the water at the next one. Passers-by stared at her, house-maids fled her. It was finally decided that "she" would be safer dressed as a man.

And so it was to a Scotsman, dressed in traditional tartan coat and waist-coat, kilt, wig and bonnet that Flora MacDonald said farewell. The militia were closing in; cordons were thrown across the countryside like nets to catch salmon. And yet the prince was still smiling when she parted from him, still confident that he would reach France and come back one day as king. It was that certainty which made his supporters believe in him when all hope seemed gone. But it was their selfless bravery which saved Charles's skin and wrapped him round in the myth of the "bold young chevalier".

"Give Us Back Our Eleven Days!"

1751

EVERYONE KNOWS THAT there are 365 days in a year. By 1752, nearly everyone knew why: because it takes 365 days for the earth to circle the sun once.

But astronomy, though it deals with such vastnesses as space and time, is an exact science. The cleverest of astronomers had already worked out that it took precisely 365 days 5 hours 48 minutes and 49 seconds – which is exact, but harder to remember. Also, calendars are incapable of dealing in hours and minutes and seconds.

If left uncorrected, century by century, a gap would develop between the seasonal year and the calendar – summer would fall in spring, winter in the autumn.

The Romans had found the solution centuries before – the leap year – and in 1582 the Pope had adjusted his calendar to match that of the Caesars. England, however, had not. In 1752 Parliament decided to accept the New Style Calendar. It almost solved the problem. Only eleven days were left – the accumulation of 1,500 years of sloppy time-keeping. The only tiny adjustment which still remained was to change 3 September to 14 September, and England and Europe could start again, level.

Say, "Time" to an astronomer, and he sees planets swinging through aeons of silent space.

Say "Time" to a mathematician and he sees a column of figures.

But say "Time" to ordinary, uneducated people who can neither read nor add up and have no interest in astronomy, and they see a collection of minutes with birth at one end and death at the other. The Bible speaks of three score years and ten allotted by God to Man. But precious few people lived to seventy in 1751, and death lurked in ambush round every corner. Suddenly it was announced that 3 September had become 14 September, and all they could see was that they were eleven days closer to their deaths.

LORD CHESTERFIELD

The Julian Calendar, adopted by Julius Caesar in 46 BC, was reformed in 1582 by Pope Gregory XIII: 5 October became 15 October. Italy, France, Spain and Portugal accepted this, but England and Russia (disinclined to do anything at the suggestion of a pope) did not. Two hundred years later, Europe and England were operating eleven days apart, and the 4th Earl of Chesterfield took it upon himself to put matters right. He published articles, then drew up a bill to put it through Parliament. Not only was 3 September to become 14 September, New Year's Day – formerly 25 March - was now to be 1 January. Chesterfield never foresaw what a furore he would cause.

You would expect the hundredth year of every century to be a leap year. But, to keep the New Style Calendar accurate, only one century in four follows this rule.

Eleven sweet days had been sliced out of their lives; eleven days in which to earn money to feed their children, eleven days to share with their families before they died. It was as if they had gone to sleep and woken up eleven days later. They were convinced they had been robbed: the Great Time Robbery. No matter what the clever, educated people said – "All right for them; they live longer than us!" – the poor, unlettered, uninformed common people did not listen. Panic made them deaf. They poured on to the streets, rioting and yelling, "Give us back our eleven days! Give us back our eleven days!"

The Church might have soothed them. But churchmen (who tend to deplore change) dug in their heels and complained that the religious festivals were fixed by God and that Parliament could not slide them about like so many pieces on a chessboard. "We shall abide by the old ways!" they said, and clung doggedly and unhelpfully to their old calendars. Anything sooner than conform to a popish one. There was only one thing for the Government to do: wait for the outrage to burn itself out, for the protests to fizzle out, and for the eleven days to be forgotten.

Time, after all, is a great healer.

Slave in a Free Country

1763-1765

"SHIPPED BY THE grace of God in good order and well conditioned, 200 slaves marked and numbered . . . God send the good ship to her desired port safely. Amen."

So read the bill of lading on the day 200 (or 300 or 500) men, women and children were herded aboard a ship, branded with hot irons, manacled and kept in order with whips and boiling water. This was the slave trade, and until 200 years ago, it was thought of as any other trade. The Africans carried off by force from their homelands to work as slaves on the cotton and sugar plantations of America and the Caribbean were, in law, "goods and chattels" to be bought and sold like livestock. Such big profits came from the plantations and from the slave trade itself that few questioned the cruelty, the downright sin of enslaving fellow human beings.

Black faces were a common sight in London in the eighteenth century. West Indian merchants would bring with them their household servants. The London newspapers often carried advertisements for runaway slaves, offering a reward for their return. So it was not the novelty of seeing a Negro which stopped Granville Sharp in his tracks that day. It was the desperate state of the young man.

He had a bloody rag tied round his head and was feeling his way along the railings of Mincing Lane, knees bent, back rounded, jaw sagging with misery. The curly black hair above the bandage was crisply matted with blood.

"Who are you, sir? You need help. What has happened to you? I was on my way to visit my brother – he's a doctor. Won't you let me take you to him?"

The man's head rolled on his shoulders. He was close to unconsciousness. "Jonathan Strong, sir . . . my name. My master . . . my master . . ."

Granville's brother took one look and said, "He must be got to St Bartholomew's or he won't last."

On the way to the hospital, they listened, in incoherent snatches, to Strong's story. He was the slave of a Barbados lawyer called David Lisle who had returned to live in London. Lisle had, in a fit of rage, smashed his pistol down repeatedly over Strong's head. Then, finding he had as good as blinded the man, he had pushed him out of doors as being of no further use.

For days Jonathan Strong, his skull fractured, hung between life and death. It was four months before he was able to leave hospital. All this while, the Sharp brothers visited him, and afterwards found him a proper, paying job. He was very happy and undyingly grateful.

But two years later, Jonathan was walking down a London street when a shout made him turn. There, like a scene from his worst dream, stood Lisle, red-faced with fury, pointing his finger at Strong and shouting, "Stop that man! Escaped slave!" A brief scuffle, and Strong was seized; people turned aside to avoid the unpleasantness.

Not so Granville Sharp. When Strong got word to him, Sharp went in high dudgeon to the Lord Mayor's office, and took out a summons against Lisle for detaining Jonathan without a warrant.

It was not that Lisle wanted his slave back for his own use. Seeing his slave was fit to work again – his "damaged property" mended – Lisle promptly "sold" Strong to a Jamaican planter. He shook hands on the deal, at least, though the planter would not part with hard cash until his purchase was aboard ship.

That is why it was the captain of the ship who arrived at court on the day of the Lord Mayor's decision. He had come to collect his cargo.

"It seems to me," said the Lord Mayor querulously, "that the lad has not stolen anything, and is not guilty of any offence. He is therefore at liberty to go where he pleases."

Granville Sharp raised both fists in triumph and his face broke into a grin. But not Strong's. "What's the matter, Jonathan? You're free! Didn't you hear?"

Strong shook his head sadly. "If you think that, sir, you know little of my master."

And he was right. No sooner did he step outside into the street than the sea captain grabbed him by the arm: "You're coming with me, piccaninny."

"Sir! I charge you for an assault!" Sharp's cheeks were flushed and his white lace stock rose and fell as he struggled to master his anger. The captain's hand slid off Jonathan's arm. "I want no trouble, me," he muttered.

Hotly indignant, Sharp strode home, Jonathan following after him with a hasty skip and a jump. While he was in Sharp's company, he was safe; no one dared touch him. And that was almost as good a feeling as being a free man!

The lawyers all told Granville Sharp that, in law, Jonathan was not a man but a "chattel". They said there was no chance of winning any court case. Granville was outraged. Where was the justice in that? So he set about studying the law himself, to find if it were really true. And he published what he discovered:

"There is no law to justify . . . the servitude of any man in England."

Soon everyone was discussing it. At dinner tables up and down the land, families argued and took sides:

"I'll tell you what freedom means – the freedom of an Englishman to trade in slaves, without these meddling do-gooders interfering!"

"Oh, but tolerance and liberty, my dear! They've always been at the backbone of England's greatness! How can there be slaves *in England*? Surely, in England . . ."

Meanwhile, the wheels of law slowly turned. Lisle brought a lawsuit against Granville Sharp. Being a lawyer, he won, too. Triple damages were awarded against Granville. Law, it seemed, had decided that Jonathan Strong was *not* a free man. He was a slave. And that made him the property of Lisle to do with as he liked.

The judgement caused a stir. Granville Sharp was the grandson of a bishop, not to mention a true Good Samaritan. What he had done, he had done out of kindness and Christian charity. And did English law favour *Lisle*? Lisle the brute? Lisle the lawyer? Surely that could not be right?

When, soon after, an almost identical case arose (concerning an escaped slave, James Somersett, wrestled off the London streets and sold back into slavery), the case of Jonathan Strong had so changed public opinion that this time the judge was ready to create legal history.

"As soon as a Negro comes into England, he becomes free," he declared as he gave judgement. The escaped slave left the court a free man.

But it was a judgement made too late to save Jonathan Strong. He was "property" once more: a chattel to be shipped in chains, flogged, forced to work for nothing for the rest of his natural life. Every crusade leaves behind its casualties. Jonathan was not the first, nor the last. He was simply the one whose face haunted Granville's dreams after he saw his friend herded aboard ship for Jamaica and clapped in the hold with the rest of the cargo.

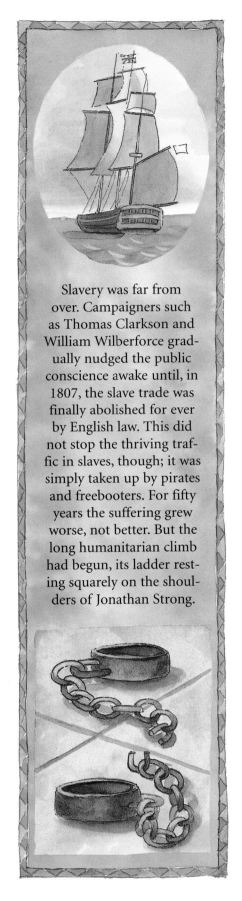

Slavery was far from over. Campaigners such as Thomas Clarkson and William Wilberforce gradually nudged the public conscience awake until, in 1807, the slave trade was finally abolished for ever by English law. This did not stop the thriving traffic in slaves, though; it was simply taken up by pirates and freebooters. For fifty years the suffering grew worse, not better. But the long humanitarian climb had begun, its ladder resting squarely on the shoulders of Jonathan Strong.

Mary's Bible

1804

THERE WAS A KNOCK, AND Mr Edwards went to the door. It was late for callers, and he was surprised to find a young girl on his doorstep. Her clothes were covered in grass and her hems were black. She looked exhausted. Mr Edwards thought she might be going to ask for money as she thrust a money-box at him.

"Mr Edwards, sir? My name is Mary Jones and I've come from Abergynolwyn. Your friend Mr Hughes sent me. I've been saving up, you see. Are there any left? He said they might all be gone!"

Mr Edwards looked up and down the street for signs of a cart. "You have come all the way from Abergynolwyn today? How did you get here?"

"I walked. I'm good at walking. I walk to school every day and home again."

"But it must be twenty-five miles, child! You must be worn out – famished! Come in, come in!"

As she ate supper, the girl explained in breathless, excitable Welsh, how she had come to buy a Bible with the pennies she had saved.

"Oh, but Mary, do you read English well enough to read the Bible?"

"Oh, not an *English* Bible," Mary said. "I've come to buy a Welsh one."

"Oh, but Mary! Did Mr Hughes not explain? The Bible in English you might just afford, but in Welsh? Welsh editions are fearfully costly."

"That's why it has taken me so long to save up," said Mary patiently. "I knitted socks to sell at market. I helped with the harvest. I did gardening and washing for the neighbours . . . The village helped, too, of course: they gave the last shilling. So it only took me six years."

Mr Edwards was astounded. He gazed at this small, solemn, brown-eyed girl. "And do you mean to say you have worked for six years and come all this way to Bala, just to have a Welsh Bible of your own?"

"It's all I have ever wanted," she said simply. "Ever since the village got a school and I learned to read . . . Do you think there *will* be one left?"

The supplies of Welsh Bibles were indeed strictly limited. They arrived a few at a time, at the house of a local minister, the Reverend Thomas Charles, and quickly sold out – to wealthy householders and clergymen and schools. There was just one left when Mary and Mr Edwards reached the minister's house. The two men watched Mary Jones run her fingers over the tooled binding, the marbled end pages, the maze of Welsh words, then fold it to her chest in blissful delight. A moment later she said, "I must be going. I've twenty-five miles to go by nightfall. It will be easier going back," she explained. "I don't have all that money to carry, and I can always stop along the way and read my Bible."

The Reverend Charles could not get it out of his mind – that young girl's heroic endeavour, her single-minded determination. It thrilled and delighted him . . . and at the same time it enraged him. No one should have to scrimp and save and work and wait six years then walk twenty-five miles to own a Bible in their own language!

At the next conference he went to in London, he stood up and told Mary's story.

"Inspiring!" said the people who heard it. "Marvellous! Charming!"

"Yes, but *wrong*," said the Reverend Charles. "A Bible should not be a luxury, whatever your language. It should be affordable to everyone, rich or poor, Welsh or English."

"No matter what language they speak!" cried a fervent voice from the back of the hall. "So let's do something about it! God has shown us our duty through this child!"

A clamour of boots hammered on the hall floor like a roll of divine thunder.

Out of that evening, the British and Foreign Bible Society was formed – a society which still exists today to make sure the Bible is affordable and available to no matter who, no matter where. And Mary Jones was the cause of it all. It was as if her determination and perseverance had been large enough to inspire a thousand others to do as she had done and to make the impossible happen.

The British and Foreign Bible Society was founded in 1804, with the Reverend Thomas Charles of Bala a founder member. It is now a member of the United Bible Societies which has made the Bible accessible to people in over 200 countries. The Bible has been translated into more than 2,100 languages and dialects.

No one has ever been able to trace Mary Jones. Poor rural families left little documentary record, and the girl concerned may well have been renamed for the sake of simplicity and Welshness. It does not seem likely that a Welsh minister would have made up the whole story, just to sway feelings at a public meeting. Someone somewhere may, all unknowing, own the very Bible Mary saved up and walked so far to buy.

England Expects

1805

THE SNIPER AMONG THE CREW OF THE *REDOUBTABLE* WAS SENT aloft into the rigging as soon as the fleet took up battle formation. The French and Spanish ships of the combined fleet were a magnificent sight, stringing out into a huge crescent – the cupped hand which would seize England for Emperor Napoleon Bonaparte. Nothing stood in Napoleon's way but this last great sea battle. Trafalgar, it would be called, after the nearby Spanish headland.

Through his spyglass, the French sniper saw the flagship, *Victory*, and a tingling shiver ran through him. Nelson's ship! Heart of the English fleet. Within its soaring wooden walls rode the commander-in-chief on whom the English pinned all their hopes: the famous admiral who suffered seasickness when he put to sea!

Soon the British fleet would also be stringing out into a crescent opposite the combined fleet, and the two lines of ships would blast relentlessly away at each other with cannon fire until one side or other could take no more. The sniper breathed a prayer for his ship's safe deliverance.

But the British fleet did not string out. It came steadily on – two clusters of warships sailing head-on into the crescent. It was madness! Without turning broadside to the enemy, they could not fire their guns! With a roar like a dragon waking, the French and Spanish cannon opened fire. For twenty minutes they spat venom at the *Victory* and the huddle of ships beyond her, and yet the British fleet did not turn to fire a single shot in return! The signal flags with which Nelson had addressed his sailors – "England expects that every man will do his duty" – soon hung in smoke-soiled rags and tatters, the rigging in knotty festoons.

But at the end of that twenty minutes, the *Victory* was passing close by the stern of Villeneuve's flagship, the *Bucentaure*, gun doors open, cannon primed. When at last she fired such a broadside into the *Bucentaure*, 400 men fell instantly to the deck, dead or wounded.

Suddenly the English ships were rubbing sides with the French and Spanish ones, firing into them from such close range that great gaping holes were blasted in the wood walls, and buckled cannon rolled over into the sea. Villeneuve had never encountered these tactics, and by the time he realized that Nelson had rewritten the manual of sea-going warfare, it was too late to think up counter measures. The English ships grappled with the combined fleet, and English sailors swarmed over on to French and Spanish decks. The battle of Trafalgar was to begin with a surprise and end in hand-to-hand combat.

Up on his masthead perch, the French sniper watched in horror the rack of the combined fleet. He saw twelve good ships sunk or disabled, saw his own ship grappled and pulled close to the *Victory*. *Redoubtable* heeled and lurched over. The top of the mizzen mast was caught in the broken and flying rigging of the *Victory* and, for a while, the two ships clung to each other like wrestlers in a fight to the death.

And there he was on the quarter-deck: Nelson! It had to be him! His uniform did not give him away, for he was not wearing all the gold braid and epaulettes of dress uniform, but he was wearing the four medals of knighthood which his adoring country had awarded him. And it was on those medals that the sniper took aim.

Such a tiny man – small as Napoleon himself! Skinny, too. Only one arm, one eye and built like a sickly stray kitten. How had this man cast such a vast shadow over the destiny of his country? The sniper's hands shook with excitement, but he aimed true. He could at least make Horatio Nelson pay for thwarting Bonaparte. The flash of the musket blinded him for a moment, then the smoke cleared, and he saw Nelson on his knees – a frozen tableau of officers watching their commander fall. Nelson slumped over on to his side.

Someone shouted, "There he is!"

The Frenchman in the rigging of the *Redoubtable* put a hand to his chest in wonderment. Could he be feeling the little Englishman's pain! Was this the penance for taking a hero's life? To feel his death pangs? Then the sniper looked down and understood. He saw the English sharpshooter, musket smoking. As he fell out of the rigging, he thought: "*Enfin. Je l'ai tué.*" At least I killed him.

Nelson was carried gently below decks. Officers clamoured and crowded round, calling for the ship's surgeon, telling themselves that he was not badly hurt . . . But Horatio Nelson knew he was dying. Inside his head images of his past life were flooding in like the sea into a holed ship: the coldness of the surgeon's knife that day his arm was amputated; the glitter of flying stone fragments before his right eye was blinded. The polar bear loomed up again over him which, at sixteen, he had fought on the Arctic pack-ice. The parsonage where he was born. The face of Lady Hamilton, passion of his life. One kiss from her soft lips and the pain in his side would surely cease . . .

"Kiss me, Hardy," said Nelson, to the officer crouching beside him. They puzzled over it a long while after. Had he perhaps said, "Kismet – (Fate) – Hardy"? They scribbled them down, these last, strange words of a famous man. "Have them take care of Lady Hamilton. Without my protection, I fear . . ." Hardy soothed his commander with assurances, promises, a kiss of farewell. Word came that the battle was won; England had carried the day. "Thank God – I have done my duty," whispered Nelson.

Not far off, an explosion seemed to rupture the ocean: a French battleship burnt down to its store of gunpowder. Before the splinters of timber had finished rattling down on to the littered sea, Horatio Nelson was dead.

The other casualties were buried at sea, but Nelson was the hero of the hour; he must receive a funeral befitting a saviour of his country. So his little battered and maimed body was put into a barrel, steeped in brandy to preserve it, and guarded night and day by a sailor with a drawn sabre. HMS *Victory* limped home, as mangled by war as Nelson had been, slow to reach harbour and the waiting crowds.

As well as the grand officials, the knights and earls and statesmen who walked behind the flag-draped coffin to St Paul's Cathedral were forty-eight common sailors who had served under Nelson. Weeping openly, those forty-eight were allowed to tear fragments from the flag as keepsakes of their dead commander.

But Emma Hamilton, great love of Nelson's life, was shunned, abandoned to poverty and loneliness. It was as if the nation's tears had blinded them to her very existence.

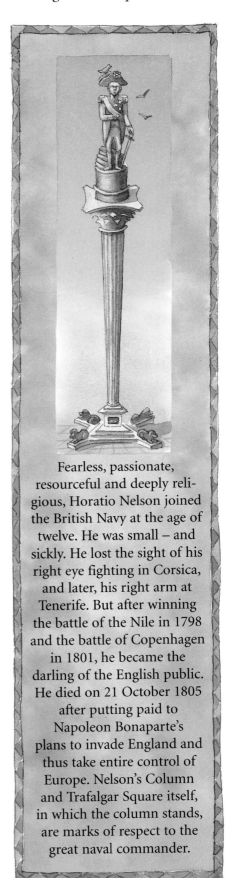

Fearless, passionate, resourceful and deeply religious, Horatio Nelson joined the British Navy at the age of twelve. He was small – and sickly. He lost the sight of his right eye fighting in Corsica, and later, his right arm at Tenerife. But after winning the battle of the Nile in 1798 and the battle of Copenhagen in 1801, he became the darling of the English public. He died on 21 October 1805 after putting paid to Napoleon Bonaparte's plans to invade England and thus take entire control of Europe. Nelson's Column and Trafalgar Square itself, in which the column stands, are marks of respect to the great naval commander.

The *Rocket* Speeds to Victory

1829

"Now lads, I venture to tell you that I think you will live to see the day when railways will supersede almost all other methods of conveyance in this country, when mail coaches will go by railway and railroads will become the great highways for the King and all his subjects." In the heady excitement of the opening, George Stephenson's words swept his employees up on a tide of enthusiasm. They cheered and stamped their heavy boots. But could it really be true? Could railways really be the transport of the future? Here, at Stockton, they were busy assembling a 90-ton train the like of which had never been seen before: six freight wagons, a covered coach for VIPs, twenty-one coal wagons kitted out to carry 450 passengers, and six more full of coal! And *Locomotion* was supposed to pull it – an engine barely taller than a man, Stephenson's brainchild. In front rode a horseman holding a green flag – almost as if they were going into battle.

But as the train gathered speed, Stephenson had to shout for the flag-man to get out of the way. Other riders galloping alongside for the sport of racing the train were left far behind, as *Locomotion* accelerated to the fabulous speed of 15 miles an hour (24 kph)!

There was a hero's welcome waiting in Darlington – and 150 more passengers and a brass band wanting to join the return journey to Stockton.

The Stockton–Darlington line, though, was just a freight line – a means of shifting large quantities of coal very cheaply along a shuttle line. When it came to building the first passenger line, from Liverpool to Manchester, the investors employed George Stephenson as chief engineer, laying the tracks, but announced a competition to find the best locomotive for the route. The deadline was 6 October 1829, the prize £500.

This time George worked with his son Robert to develop his entry for the competition. They incorpo-

rated a tubular boiler, which allowed large quantities of water to be heated up at any one time. There were two other locomotives entered: Braithwaite and Ericsson's *Novelty,* and the *Sans Pareil* built by Hackworth. Between 6 and 14 October, there was a gala atmosphere at Rainhill, Liverpool, with huge crowds attending every day, bands playing and a great grandstand seating such dignitaries as the Duke of Wellington, then Prime Minister.

The referees looked over the *Sans Pareil* and declared it did not comply with the rules . . . but she would be allowed to compete anyway. The course was a stretch of track rather more than two kilometres in length, which had to be completed, there-and-back, ten times over. On the eighth trip the pump broke and the *Sans Pareil* puttered to a halt.

The crowd had taken a fancy to the *Novelty*: it was small and spry, with only the vestige of a chimney, and a jolly red flag flying. But with an alarming bang, the boiler blew after just two trips. "And they say these things will take the place of horses?" people snorted to one another.

Up and down, up and down, up and down went the *Rocket*. Tireless as a donkey giving rides on a beach, the *Rocket* lumbered to and fro. Pulling a load of 17 tons, she travelled the 30 miles stipulated – then she travelled them again to please the crowds. At one point she touched 30 mph (48 kph) – faster than any stagecoach could go. The crowd was a roaring sea of cheers, thousands of day trippers witnessing this dawn of a new age. The Duke of Wellington stood up in the bandstand and waved his hat as Stephenson's *Rocket* trundled by yet again, steam flaring from the crown-shaped tip of its sturdy flue.

One year later, a similar locomotive was coupled up to thirty-three carriages, all packed with notables: the Duke of Wellington, Sir Robert Peel, the Rt Hon William Huskisson MP for Liverpool . . . and steamed out of Liverpool to the music of an onboard band. Despite the flying smuts which blackened their faces and clothes, despite the noise, and the juddering of the hard seats, the passengers were cock-a-hoop. They were in at the beginning of something momentous. Here was history in the making!

At Parkside, the train wheezed to a halt to take on water. Some of the gentlemen passengers, including Mr Huskisson, got off to stretch their legs. They strolled down the track . . . ignorant of the fact that another string of carriages was moving down the adjacent track. As they saw the danger, the knot of men scattered, all jumping clear of the tracks, except for Mr Huskisson, who tried to reboard the train.

He got the carriage door open, but it swung back on him and barged him off his feet – knocked him on to the rails, in fact, where one of the great slicing, steel wheels rolled over him.

Suddenly there was no more music, no more singing, no more cheering. As the litter bearers carried the man away and the locomotive gathered speed, its steam cast a pall over thirty-three silent carriages. Women dabbing cinders from their eyes, dabbed away tears as well. It was no longer a day of triumphant celebration. William Huskisson had died of his injuries. The festivities planned in Manchester were cancelled. George put his arm around his son's shoulders. "There's no undoing what's done," he said. "No going back."

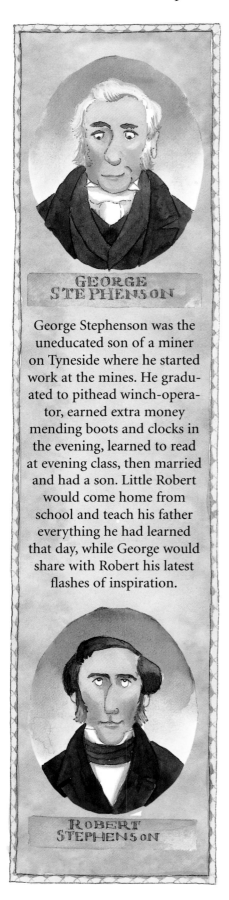

GEORGE STEPHENSON

George Stephenson was the uneducated son of a miner on Tyneside where he started work at the mines. He graduated to pithead winch-operator, earned extra money mending boots and clocks in the evening, learned to read at evening class, then married and had a son. Little Robert would come home from school and teach his father everything he had learned that day, while George would share with Robert his latest flashes of inspiration.

ROBERT STEPHENSON

The Resurrection Men

1829

"ANOTHER ONE FOR THE GRAVEROBBERS, EH, William?" said Burke.

"Disgraceful trade. Fancy a man engaging in a Godless business like that, William," replied Hare with a snigger. "Sacrilege, I call it."

Many of the graves in the cemetery had recently been surrounded with great iron railings – as though the dead had been penned into their plots. But then, understandably, mourners did not want grave robbers digging up their nearest and dearest within hours of them being laid to rest. And there was a thriving market for bodies dug up on dark nights among the lowering yew trees. The medical profession needed its cadavers and would pay good money for one, without asking where it came from. The police were cracking down, patrolling cemeteries, making arrests, but even so, today's grave would have a grille of iron around it before nightfall.

The crunch, crunch of the constable's boots on the pavement behind them held no fear for Hare and Burke. Their conciences were clear. As far as they were concerned, the crack-down on grave-robbing could only serve to boost business; they were not in that line of work.

"Our meat is *fresher*, eh William?" whispered Hare, and lifted his hat to the constable.

Burke and Hare went home to their wives, and their wives agreed: there were easier ways to lay hands on supplies than wrestling iron bars in the graveyard and dodging watchful policemen. They all went out to an inn for supper, and struck up a friendship there with a young man.

"Won't you come home for a nightcap?" asked Mrs Hare. "William and I do so welcome company…"

Burke set down a sack in the ill-lit basement yard, and money changed hands. Their customer was bursting to tell them of a comical story he had just read in his newspaper. "Did you hear tell of the old woman who sneezed?" he snickered. "I read they opened the coffin – and up she sat and sneezed! Ha! ha! ha!"

"There's no fear you'll be troubled in that way," muttered Hare. "This one died of natural causes

Ever since medicine became a clinical science, there has been a need for cadavers or dead bodies. Students of medicine need to dissect bodies to understand the nature and workings of human anatomy. In nineteenth-century Edinburgh (as elsewhere) they were kept supplied by body-snatchers who stole newly-buried corpses from graveyards. In Edinburgh, Doddingston Village churchyard was frequently pillaged by these so-called "Resurrection Men". Fortifying the graves, and a police crackdown in the 1820s helped to stamp out the practice. But some body-snatchers simply resorted to a worse way of acquiring bodies. William Hare and William Burke may never even have bothered to rob graves. They were arrested in 1829 for murdering fifteen people for the sake of their cadavers. Their wives had helped them lure victims to their deaths. Hare offered to co-operate in return for supplying evidence which sent Burke to the gallows; in fact he was probably the worse villain of the two.

three days back." There was a brief glimmer of light as the sack was taken in at a basement door, then renewed darkness.

Next day, as the student doctors crowded about the scrubbed dissecting table of Edinburgh University, the corpse upon it was the finest yet. It showed no sign of decay. It had surely never lain underground, in the damp Edinburgh clay. In fact the young man lying dead on the table looked very much as he had looked in life, apart from a certain blueness in the face.

"Good God! I know him!" exclaimed one of the students, turning deathly white.

"Didn't you know he was dead? Didn't anyone tell you he died?" his colleagues asked, each wondering how he would feel if the body in front of him proved not to be a nameless stranger.

"And how would they? I was *drinking* with him last night!" spluttered the student.

"I fear our friends have overstepped the mark this time," remarked Dr Knox.

But he continued his lecture. For it was hardly *his* fault if Burke and Hare had graduated from grave-robbing to cold-blooded murder. And there was no point in wasting such an excellent cadaver.

Victoria's Room

1837

"I CRIED MUCH," WROTE ALEXANDRINA VICTORIA in her diary that night. She was eleven years old, and she had just been told the secret her mother had been keeping from her: one day she would be queen.

Why did she cry? Perhaps she was afraid. Perhaps she could see ahead of her a life of unrelenting hard work, never free to do as she liked. Maybe she thought that the loneliness of her childhood would now go on for ever.

At least now she could make sense of all the studying her mother made her do, all the huffy unkindness of her English relations who looked upon her as a little German interloper, all the loneliness.

Once a week, a child was invited to play – a child chosen by her mother. Not the same child every week, so that they could become firm friends. Never anyone silly or mischievous who might make her laugh – just a succession of miscellaneous strangers, once a week. "I may call you Jane, but you must not call me Victoria," she would tell them, not knowing why, only knowing that life was governed by her mother's rules. She had her dolls – her host of elegant china-headed dolls. But somehow they were not the same as having a true friend.

For all she was a princess, no one showered her with toys or treats or sweets. No, it was bread and milk out of a little silver bowl for Victoria. She was not allowed to read stories: after all, what *use* were stories except for frivolous entertainment?

Lonely but never alone, Victoria could not even escape to the solitude of her own bedroom. Every night she had to bed down in the great hollow emptiness of her mother's bedroom, and every time she woke, it was to the sound of her mother's soft breathing. Sixteen, seventeen, eighteen, and still she was sharing a bedroom! How she longed for a room of her own.

Victoria woke one morning sensing that something momentous had happened. Her mother was whispering to her in German: to get up, to put on her wrapper; there was an important visitor to see her. Fuddled with sleep, her heart jumpy with odd foreboding, Alexandrina Victoria fumbled her feet into her satin slippers and made herself presentable.

As soon as she saw the Archbishop of Canterbury, po-faced, holding himself as he did at state occasions, she knew that someone had died. It was her Uncle William, he told her. The King of England was dead.

With a rustling flurry, like a theatre curtain falling, the ladies in the room sank down. For a moment Victoria thought they had fainted with shock, but no. They were curtseying to their new monarch – to her – to eighteen-year-old Queen Victoria.

A million thoughts and images tumbled through her head in those first few moments: the hot, distant countries she had never seen and over which she now held absolute sway. Those dark, frightful valleys she had visited with her mother, where coal dust had turned all the

After moving to Buckingham Palace, Victoria arranged for her mother's suite of apartments to be a long way from her own. By 1840, she was no longer lonely: she had married her cousin Albert – a suitable candidate found for her by her family, but a love-match as far as Victoria was concerned. They were to have nine children.

The English monarchy was in a bad state when Victoria came to the throne. A string of kings, mad, bad or just plain despised had brought royalty into disrepute. She changed all that. She ruled for longer than any other monarch in the history of England. Albert fired her with enthusiasm and energy for all kinds of projects, including the Great Exhibition of 1851. She was a devoted mother, had a will of steel and ruled at a time when the economy was, in any case, thriving. In 1876, she became Empress of India. The British people, the British Empire, adored their little Queen, and when Albert died and she retired into perpetual mourning, they resented her absence from public life. She died aged eighty-one and gave her name to an entire era.

people and houses and grass coal-black. All those huge cathedrals and little parish churches where every day from now on prayers would be offered up for "Victoria our Queen". The Houses of Parliament which smelled of leather and passed the laws to which she must now set her signature. The marriage which would now be arranged for her – how she hoped it could be to cousin Albert! She thought of the pageant of kings and queens which had already filed past into history, of the soldiers in red who would die for her in foreign wars. All these thoughts and more fell like an avalanche on Victoria, on this tiny, slender girl in her night clothes.

But her first command, as Queen of England, was for a room to be prepared: a room of her own.

"I will try to fulfil my duty towards my country and to do what is fit and right," she wrote that night. And when she closed her diary, the room around her listened in respectful silence. Though a thousand choices were closed to her, she felt a new sense of freedom. It was up to her now, how she lived the lonely life of a queen.

Her china-headed dolls sat quietly round, watching her, outnumbered now by millions of other loyal subjects.

Fire Down Below

1838

Dr Dionysius Lardner said it couldn't be done. No steamship could carry enough fuel, he said, to voyage more than 2,000 miles, and America was 3,000 miles away; it was totally impractical to talk of sailing steamships between England and New York.

The shipping companies prayed he was wrong. To win the race across the Atlantic was everything. The rewards would be huge to whichever steamship company could first prove Dionysius Lardner mistaken!

Whichever ship was first across the Atlantic was certain to make headline news. Already the *Sirius* was preparing to set sail from Cork in Ireland – the furthermost westerly point. But a rival ship was out to beat her – and to beat her in style, sailing not from Ireland but from England, a day farther east.

On Saturday, 31 March, the SS *Great Western*, dream-child of Isambard Kingdom Brunel, set sail from Blackwall Docks in London. Down the Thames, round the south coast and she would be in Bristol, bound for New York. There were passengers in plenty ready to sail on her: after all, her designer was an acknowledged genius. Brunel had built bridges and viaducts, railways and tunnels. He had spanned gorges and linked cities . . . and now he had turned his attentions to the Atlantic.

But at the mouth of the Thames, disaster struck.

The brand-new felt cladding the brand-new boilers caught fire, filling the engine room with dense, choking smoke. Captain Claxton ran the *Great Western* ashore on the mudflats and everyone tackled the fire.

Claxton himself went down into the noxious fumes and the heat. Overhead, flames were licking the underside of the decking. The boiler was singing with heat. The great pillars of steel, like the columns of a Greek temple, were ringing with a discordant music all their own. Claxton called for the fire-hose to be turned on and directed it at the fire which hissed steam, in addition to the smoke and fumes. Soon he was ankle-deep in water, and the fire reduced to sullen red embers glimmering in the corners of the boiler room like the eyes of a hundred rats.

All of a sudden, a weight like a sack of grain fell on him from above, knocking all the wind out of him. He cursed choicely and picked himself up. What had hit him? Who was dropping things on to him from the open hatchway? None too gently, he felt for the thing with his foot: it was soft and sodden. A man! And, lying face-down in dirty water, he was either dead already or about to drown! Instantly Claxton snatched hold of him. Then he cursed again. "Hoi! Up there! Fetch ropes! Hurry! It's Brunel! He's fallen!"

I.K. Brunel began his career working for his engineer father. He went on to become chief engineer of the Great Western Railway, designing lines, trains, sheds and stations, then set his sights on grander, interlinked networks of travel. After the *Great Western* came the *Great Britain*, at that time the biggest ship in the world, the first with an iron-hull, the first to be driven by a screw-propeller rather than paddle-wheels. Next came the monumental *Great Eastern*, four times larger, capable of carrying a year's exports to India in one trip. In no other age could Brunel have achieved what he did. The Victorian passion for techno-logy put him to work and, in return, he added hugely to Victorian prosperity. Bridges, railways, buildings, ships, tunnels, viaducts still exist today as monuments to his genius.

In climbing down to help Claxton, Brunel had rested his foot on a burned rung which gave way. If Claxton had not been standing underneath, he would have crashed on to metal from a dizzying height.

Claxton tied a rope under his friend's armpits, and somehow they manhandled Brunel up through the funnelling smoke and steam towards the blue square of the forehatch. Even laid out on deck, with a sail for a bed, he remained unable to speak. But until the fire was under control there was no time to care for him any more tenderly.

They set him ashore at Canvey Island, and sailed on without him. They were in Bristol within forty-eight hours. It astounded the crowds who had heard tell of the fire and quite thought the *Great Western* a burned-out hulk in the Thames estuary. Here she was, with nothing to show for the fire but a few scorchmarks.

They would not sail on her, though. Only seven passengers were ready to put their faith in the *Great Western*; the rest had been scared off by the fire. For those seven it was a memorable voyage. One wrote in his journal that New York harbour was crowded with welcoming boats, "Flags were flying, guns were firing, and cheering rose from the shore, the boats and all around loudly and gloriously . . . It was a moment of triumph."

Not that they had won the race: *Sirius* had arrived just hours before, despite departing earlier and farther west. But *her* coal had been all used up, and her crew had had to burn everything combustible on board – including passengers' luggage – just to make harbour. The *Great Western*, on the other hand, had used only three-quarters of her fuel. Dr Lardner had been proved wrong: steamships *could* link England and America.

Sixty-eight passengers made the return voyage to England, and for twenty years the SS *Great Western* plied the oceans of the world, a handsome tribute to her designer. When she was broken up in 1857, Isambard Kingdom Brunel was there to bid her farewell.

Saving Grace

1838

IT WAS FOUR IN THE MORNING WHEN GRACE PULLED ON HER CLOTHES AND climbed the stairs to the light. It was her turn to check the lighthouse lamp then sit up, so that her father could get to bed. All around her the storm raged: torrential rain and the everlasting thunder of the sea rolling against England's north-east coast, breaking against the Longstone Rock, throwing its spray as high as her bedroom just below the lamp. The noise of it drowned out even the click of the lighthouse engine as she sat in her room watching for first light when she must douse the light. Her window was cloudy with condensation from her wet stockings and petticoat. She and Father had got soaked through the previous afternoon, lashing down the coble-boat.

It was not until she went back up the steep steps to put out the light that she looked across towards Brownsman Island to glimpse her old home and saw not the abandoned buildings of Brownsman Island but the huge, dark looming prow of a ship.

"Father! Father! Father! A wreck! A wreck, Father!" she shouted, running backwards down the spiral stairs. "A ship is wrecked on Big Harcar!"

"Now God help us, and your brother not here!"

From five till seven they stood there in the lamp room, William Darling holding a telescope, Grace a pair of field glasses. The storm-clouds kept the scene almost as dark as night, and all they could make out was that the vessel was a steam paddle-ship – the *Forfarshire*, perhaps. And if it were the *Forfarshire*, William knew there were probably sixty people on board.

It was not until the eye of the storm passed over the reef that a shaft of light, like God's own sword-blade, lit Big Harcar and showed the huddle of people clinging to the rock itself.

"Can it be done, Father?" asked Grace.

"Maybe, if Brooks were here."

It was true, that if Grace's brother, Brooks, had been at home that night, instead of on the mainland, he would have gone with his father in the coble – gone to try to lift those people off before the sea did. "Then I must take Brooks's part!" said Grace.

Her mother was dead set against it. She had heard the bang of the maroons – the signal which summoned out the lifeboat – and she knew the coble needed three strong men to row it in rough weather.

But William Darling knew the lifeboat would never arrive in time. The sea's huge swell heaved up like a great grey tongue to lap at the survivors. He must mount a rescue mission or stand and watch those people washed away, one by one.

Instead of a tender goodbye, Grace got nothing but reproach from her mother, who said she would hold Grace to blame if William drowned. Grabbing up a shawl, a blanket and a bonnet, and slipping off her flannel petticoat to save it getting soaked, Grace helped her father unlash the rowing boat. Spray

covered her like thick, white sheets. The oars rattled like bones in their rowlocks. But Grace rowed. Sometimes the water tried to wrench the oar out of her hand, at others she found herself scooping at empty air, but she went on rowing. She rowed alongside her father, her shoulder against his, as though through a tunnel of sea. She rowed until her hands were full of blisters. All she could think of were those other cold, white hands clinging and clawing, slipping and losing their grip on the treacherous rocks. Big Harcar was no more than a perch for puffins, a basking place for seals; its rocks disappeared with every breaking wave.

They could not row there direct, but had to let the wind drive the little boat south, into the lee of the reef and then row in from there. And *if* there was someone there, among the survivors on the rock – some strong, uninjured man not yet perished with cold or mad with fright – they might just be able to make the rescue and get back to the lighthouse. If not, there was no chance. Grace and her father would join the casualties lost in the sinking of the steamer.

Back in the lighthouse, Mrs Darling watched for a sight of them. Despite a lifelong horror of heights, she dragged herself up one flight of stairs after another, hoping each one would raise her high enough to see over the towering waves. But the little coble had utterly disappeared, as if the sea had swallowed it whole. Fainting with horror, it was not until she came round that she glimpsed it – pitching like a shuttlecock over the mountainous swell.

There were nine on the rocks, including one woman, clasping her two dead children, not realizing the cold had stolen them from her. And there *was* a seaman still calm, still strong enough to pull on an oar. For a few horrific minutes, William Darling leapt across to the rock, and Grace was left trying to hold the boat steady, all alone, with oars set so far apart that her arms were at full stretch just to grip them.

Five people were taken off. The other four had to wait for the coble to make a return trip. Two of the men agreed to go with William on that second voyage. So while Mrs Darling and Grace wrapped the survivors in blankets and plied them with black tea, the lighthouse keeper went out again into the storm, which was working itself into a frenzy. Grace and her mother hardly expected to see him again. But finally, finally, he and the other six staggered in, dumb with weariness, numb with cold, their faces caked into masks by the sea's salt.

Like the pillar of stillness at the centre of a tornado, the Longstone Lighthouse cocooned those twelve people until the sea slackened, the clouds cleared and the rain ceased to fall. While they waited, William Darling wrote up his report on the wreck, mentioning only in passing that nine lives had been "saved by the Darlings". Little did he know what a storm of praise, congratulation, publicity and admiration would break over their heads when the rescue was reported. When people read in their papers of the lighthouse keeper and his brave daughter, Grace's adventure had only just begun.

Grace and her father were both awarded gold medals from the Royal Humane Society and silver medals for bravery by the "Shipwreck Institution", a forerunner of today's Royal National Lifeboat Institution. (In fact Grace has been cited as an inspiration behind the founding of the RNLI.) She also received £100 reward, and Queen Victoria wrote to her in person, praising her bravery. But as she battled her way through the storm of publicity and was acclaimed a national heroine, some local Northumbrians grew bitter and insulting, suggesting she had done it for the money. She was the butt of hate mail and malicious lies. The money, in any case, would have bought her little in the way of happiness: four years after the wreck of the *Forfarshire*, Grace Darling died in her father's arms, of tuberculosis.

Rebecca and Her Daughters

1840s

"AND THEY BLESSED REBEKAH AND said unto her, Let thy seed possess the gate of those which hate them." That was the verse which began it. That was where the Bible fell open, those were the words which sprang off the page. Just when every Welsh heart was brooding bitterly about having to pay tolls to the Government – just to be allowed to pass along a road! – there was the Good Book speaking out on the matter. And the Welsh have always taken their Bible seriously.

Dafyd, the Turnpike, keeper of the toll-gate on the London road, woke to the sound of horns and whistles and gunfire, and tumbled out of bed. Along the road came a crowd of people led by five or six women – at least they were *dressed* like women. They wore bonnets and dresses and aprons, though to judge by the size of their boots, they were six feet tall and shaved once a week. The people in the procession behind them were locals – poor hill-farmers, dyers and tradesmen. Dafyd knew it, though it was hard to make out particular faces in the dark.

"Now I don't want no trouble," said Dafyd, trying to sound commanding (though that is difficult for a man in his nightshirt). "Why don't you all go off home now?"

The biggest of the "women" simply turned to the crowd and said, in a ringing Welsh bass, "My children, this gate has no business here, has it?"

The crowd roared, "No, Mother, it has not!"

"Then what is to be done with it, children?"

"Mother, it must be levelled to the ground!"

Then the axes came out. Rebecca and her Daughters were destroying yet another toll-gate, hacking the bars from their cross-trees, the hinges from their posts.

Dafyd ran a few steps forwards. After all, he was paid to man the gate; he ought to defend it. But the Daughters restrained him with huge, calloused hands. "We mean you no harm, man. Best just pack up your things."

Knowing that already half the toll-gates in Carmarthen were down, Dafyd hurried indoors and began to carry his few possessions – bed and chair, breadbin and toolbag – out of doors. Then the toll-booth too was destroyed – set alight with Dafyd's own lantern.

The horns and whistles blew, the guns sent Dafyd's cat haring into the wood, then "Rebecca and her Daughters" were gone. The local people disbanded silently and the darkness swallowed them up.

Within the hour, a detachment of special constables came trotting along the road to where Dafyd sat in his fireside chair on the grass verge of the road. "You're too late, as usual," he said. "Far too late."

In Carmarthen that June, thousands of protesters carrying placards, scythes and pitchforks marched into the town and began pulling down the workhouse. Beds were tumbled out of windows; pots and pans rained on to the cobbles. To poor, working people, the workhouse represented everything wrong with society: a prison for the poor, where the only crime of the inmates was to be penniless. That's why they tore it down. For long enough the rich landowners and businessmen had grown fat on the toil and tolls of the poor. Now that was all about to change.

The magistrates went out to remonstrate with the mob, reading them the Riot Act: "You are hereby charged to disperse peaceably . . ."

The mob washed over them like the sea over sandcastles.

Then the dragoons arrived from Cardiff – a sixty-mile gallop from barracks. Two of their horses dropped dead as they entered the city, but for the first time the rioters were obliged to break off from their vandalism and run.

The dragoons used the flat of their swords, not the sharp edges. After all, they were Welshmen themselves, from poor Welsh homes, and knew injustice when they saw it. They scattered the mob and took a hundred prisoners, but they did it gently, almost sympathetically.

Before long, Rebecca and her Daughters regrouped stronger and more determined. There was no *one* Rebecca, you see. No *one* ringleader. The men in bonnets and aprons began to meet in secret and to list their demands, instructing the magistrates, the landowners, the Church to dismantle their toll-gates or to expect a bullet through the window or a fire in their stables.

Righteous anger had given way to thuggery and terrorism. One night, an old woman on the Glamorgan-Carmarthen border was shot dead in cold blood, just for manning a toll-gate. The law had become so weak that the inquest jury declared she had died from a "suffusion of blood . . . cause unknown". The coroner did not even dare condemn the crime of murder.

But when the toll-gate in Gower Street, in the heart of London, was filed off its hinges overnight the Government felt the Welsh problem had come too near to home. It stirred itself like a sleeping dog. The movement was destroyed, hacked apart as ruthlessly as any toll-gate or turnpike booth. It imprisoned the ringleaders or sent them to a life of hard labour in Australia.

But while, with one hand, the authorities meted out prison sentences and transportations, with the other hand it wrote legislation for the abolition of toll-gates from the nation's public roads. So the sound of those horns and whistles and pistols, the swish of petticoats and the tramp of worn boots *had* been heard, even from the other end of the long London Road.

The early years of Queen Victoria's reign were marked by huge social unrest. Poverty and hardship caused by an economic depression gave rise, in 1838, to the Chartist Movement, which agitated for every man to have the vote and for reform of Parliament. The Charter petition was signed by so many that when rolled along the lanes to London, it was the size of a cartwheel. Parliament ignored it. A "Chartist" rebellion at Newport, Wales, in 1839 was put down with great ferocity. This is the setting into which Rebecca and her Daughters were born. The many anonymous Rebeccas would have been Chartists to a man.

Father of Nobody's Children

1869

AT SIX O'CLOCK THE CHILDREN SAID A PRAYER THEN clattered towards the door. Some were more eager than others: it was cold outside. One boy dawdled at his desk, wiping his slate, and dropping his chalk. "Run off home, boy," said the teacher.

"Please, sir. Let me stop."

"Nonsense. It's time to go. Your mother will wonder what is keeping you."

"I ain't got no mother." The lad scuffed a bare foot on the plank floor.

"Where do you live, then?"

"Don't live nowhere."

The teacher sighed. After ten hours teaching he was weary and wanting his supper. He did not know the boy by sight – every day new pupils found their way to the charity school; he hoped this was not going to be some hard-luck story. Barnardo knew home life was hard – downright miserable – for most of the children attending his ragged school. But he had never set much store by melodramatic tales of children living rough on the streets, parentless and homeless. That was just

romantic exaggeration. Surely. "Where did you sleep last night?" he asked.

"Down Whitechapel, sir, along o' the Haymarket, in one of them carts as is filled with 'ay. Then I met a chap as told me to come up 'ere to school and you'd maybe let me lie near the fire all night. I won't do no harm, sir, if you let me stop."

A coldness blew through Barnardo which had nothing to do with the bitter weather. "Is it possible?" he asked himself. Then he asked Jim Jarvis: "Are there other boys who do that – sleep where they can – out in the open?"

"Oh yes, sir, lots. Heaps on em! More'n I could count!"

Barnardo took Jim Jarvis home and gave him hot coffee. He was a perky lad, witty and cheerful – except for his eyes where some drowning-depth of sorrow contradicted the saucy grin. Over supper Jim told his life story. From the age of five he had been on his own, fending for himself, an orphan. He got work with a man called "Swearing Dick" on the barges who beat him regularly, and threatened to set his dog on Jim if he tried to run away. A job on a market stall was no better. It was the police he feared most, because they would either kick him or arrest him and send him to the workhouse.

At about midnight, Barnardo set off with Jim Jarvis to see the boy's "lay", as he called it. Jim led the way to Petticoat Lane, to an old-clothes market, where he scrambled up on to the iron roof of a shed. Reaching down a stick, he helped Barnardo up too. Alongside was a hayloft and, though it was padlocked shut, some of the hay had trickled out through the slats. Eleven boys had grubbed together these wisps and were lying stretched out on them now, on the tilt of the roof, feet in the guttering. They lay close-huddled for warmth, like hamsters in a nest. No blanket over them, no clothes capable of keeping out the cold. Their sleeping faces were white and thin as skulls.

"The foxes have their holes, the birds their nests, but the Son of Man has nowhere to lay his head."

Thomas Barnardo had thought God was calling him to go to China, to be a missionary. For years he had cherished the idea – only really filling time in London, until his posting came through. Now, all of a sudden, he realized: God had not been whispering "China" in his ear. God had been bellowing in his face: "Help these children. Save these children. They have no one but you. They are nobody's children but yours and Mine!"

Barnardo could not bear it. To wake the boys would have been like fetching the dead from their graves. They would clamour at him for food, turn those hollow, reproachful eyes on him. The horror of their loveless, hopeless lives gripped him as he climbed down, legs trembling. Jim Jarvis watched him, bird-like, head cocked on one side, but the doctor could say nothing, do nothing but walk away, striding out faster and faster, until he was almost running.

Thomas J. Barnardo founded a home for homeless boys and soon afterwards another for girls. He was tireless in his efforts, not only to help the children but to enlighten the comfortable middle classes who genuinely did not know what was happening in the streets of their Victorian cities. He tackled all the social evils, turning drinking halls into evangelical tea-halls, turning drunkards and criminals into evangelists. He taught and preached, raised money, wrote articles and addressed public meetings. He told the story of Jim Jarvis many times, embroidering it considerably over the years but always to good effect.

A complex man, Barnardo gave himself the title "doctor" though he never qualified as one. He was criticized for "staging" the photographs he sold to raise funds: before-and-after photographs of his forlorn street children. Hugely slandered, hugely admired, he drove himself repeatedly into a state of nervous collapse. But his homes multiplied, his message got through. Barnardo Homes became an institution of British life for which thousands and thousands of children, right up to the present day, have had cause to be thankful.

The Last Train Ride

1879

EVERYONE WAS IN A HURRY TO GET HOME – Scotsmen returning to Scotland for the holidays, families who had been south for Christmas, workers anxious to get back to the warmth of a fireside and a good supper . . . Though Christmas was over, the New Year was still to come.

It was a filthy night, but the lights of Dundee burned all the brighter for that. And crossing over the Tay would be part of the fun. The new bridge was still a wonder to those contemplating a trip over it – a stone and metal monument to progress and prosperity.

By seven in the evening, the wind was howling, hurling itself against the signal boxes as if it would swallow them whole; unfurling dense, silver banners of rain across the starless sky. With each new gust, the carriages juddered and the luggage jumped about in the luggage van. Children with their noses pressed to the steamy windows would recoil against their mothers, then be drawn back to cloud the windows even more with their excited breathing. The noisy rhythm of the wheels on the track – "nearly-there-nearly-there-nearly-there" – was all but drowned out by the storm.

Then, all of a sudden, the countryside of lashing trees and huddled buildings gave way to rainy darkness: the train was crossing the Firth of Tay (though the river far below was not even visible through the rain). The locomotive gave a baleful whistle which the wind tore in shreds.

Two signalmen stood discussing the safety of their signal box – whether it might blow down, whether the storm would blow itself out by morning or racket on into Hogmanay. The London–Dundee train went by them wrapped in its cloak of sooty steam, slowing down for the bridge. Out over the Tay it thundered, a snake of lights, a wisp of white steam. Then a plume of sparks rose up – golden rain amid the silver. There was a tremendous flash.

Too far off for sound to carry. But as the signalmen watched, the snake of lighted carriages disappeared abruptly from sight.

Passengers on board, tumbled together by sudden braking, felt nothing now – nothing but an absence of sound. Oddly, for a second or two, the rain outside the windows rained upwards, because they were falling so fast. No time for anything more than a joining of hands, then the Tay was boiling over the wreckage and the storm was hooting.

Running down to the foreshore, the two signalmen shouted out at every tight-closed front door they passed: "*The bridge! The bridge! The train!*" But when they reached the mudflats (where the waves were breaking big as the open sea) there was nothing to do but stare into blackness. With a triumphant flourish, the storm uncovered the moon, briefly casting a ghastly, ghostly pallor over the river. The whole centre section of the Tay Bridge was gone, like a smile with its teeth smashed away. The train must have driven out on to thin air, then plunged into the deep, icy water of the Tay.

Next day, divers were needed to find the sunken train, rolled and scoured by the river's current. Of the seventy-nine people aboard, not one lived to see in the New Year of 1880.

The bridge, 3¼ kilometres (nearly 2 miles) long, had only been open for nineteen months when on 28 December 1879 half a dozen of its central spans collapsed into the river. 1880 claimed the eightieth victim of the disaster. Architect Sir Thomas Bouch (who had designed the bridge with insufficient strength to withstand even low winds) died, vilified and reproached for his incompetence. A second, unfinished bridge of his had been found to be as dangerous as the first. Fortunately or unfortunately, the disaster was immortalized by the so-called poet William McGonagall in a work of such awfulness that it is performed today as a comic turn. He followed it up with an ode to the beautiful *new* Tay Railway Bridge, which was completed in 1890.

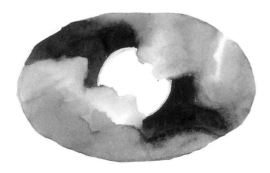

Dr Crippen on the Waves

1910

NOT FOR THE FIRST TIME, Captain Henry Kendall wiped the glass of the bridge-house and peered at the couple on the deck below: Mr Robinson and son. In his many years at sea, Kendall had developed an eye for oddities among his passengers, and there was something distinctly odd about Mr Robinson and son.

Why, for instance, did they stay so muffled up in this fine July weather? And why, when they thought no one was looking, were they *holding hands*?

Before setting sail, he had read newspaper descriptions of a couple wanted for murder. Old newspapers were probably still lying around the ship detailing the sensational crime. As far as he remembered, a dentist's wife had been done to death, her body cut up and hidden under the floorboards. Her husband, mysteriously gone missing with a lady friend called Ethel, was number one suspect. Captain Kendall's thoughts returned time and time again to the description of the man called Crippen.

And yet this ship had set sail from Antwerp in Belgium, not from Britain. Could Crippen have escaped to Belgium

before the body of his wife was found? Could this be him now, trying to reach Canada and a new life with his accomplice? Was "Master Robinson" the reason Hawley Crippen had murdered his lawful wedded wife?

Captain Kendall left the bridge and strolled down to the sundeck. Casually he struck up conversation with Mr Robinson and son, though the two seemed in no mood to talk. Robinson's lids were slightly closed and there were pad marks on the bridge of his nose, though he had not worn glasses since boarding.

Dr Crippen had worn glasses.

Robinson's top lip was paler than the rest of his face. He had recently shaved off a moustache.

And Dr Crippen had worn a moustache.

The son wore a trilby hat several sizes too big, and an awkward, hesitant smile. His hands were very small and pale, and his coat too broad for his shoulders.

Kendall was certain. But what to do about it? The SS *Montrose* was outside British waters now, and, when it docked in Canada, Crippen would be on foreign soil. He might get clean away.

At least he might have got clean away, had he taken passage on a less modern ship.

Kendall hurried along to his brand-new radio room and told his brand-new radio operator, "Here's a job for you. Radio London and tell them we have Dr Hawley Crippen and his lady friend Ethel aboard."

When Chief Inspector Walter Dew received the telegraph from Captain Kendall, he left at once for the docks. He took passage aboard the SS *Laurentic*, a faster ship than the *Montrose*. In a matter of days, he could overhaul Kendall's ship and be in Canada ahead of Crippen. But the arrest must be made aboard the British ship, and that meant boarding her before she docked. Nothing must be left to chance.

"Mr Robinson!" said Captain Kendall, and the little man gave a visible start. His top lip was no longer white, thanks to the sea air, but his expression was still nervy and anxious. "Soon be there now," said Kendall, bluff and jovial. "I have just taken aboard the local pilot to see us safely into the mouth of the St Lawrence River. I wondered, would you and your son care to meet him?"

Mr Robinson and his son exchanged glances. He smiled weakly. "Delighted, I'm sure." The shores of Canada were within sight. A new life was so close that Hawley and Ethel could almost smell it. Where was the harm in accepting the captain's invitation? They could not very well refuse.

As they entered the captain's cabin, a man stood up. He was not their idea of a shipping pilot: a tall man in a bowler hat and overcoat.

"Hawley Harvey Crippen . . . Ethel Le Neve – I arrest you for the murder of Belle Crippen on or before 9 July 1910."

The little man trembled violently from head to foot; the woman beside him clutched the sleeve of his coat. "Thank God it's over," said Crippen. "The suspense has been too great. I couldn't stand it any longer." And meek as a lamb, he allowed Chief Inspector Dew to hand-cuff him and lead him away.

US-born Dr Hawley Crippen was the first criminal to be captured through the invention of ship-to-shore radio. He disappeared from his home in Camden Town on 9 July, shortly before police discovered his wife's dismembered body under the floorboards. The mild-mannered dentist had escaped from England with his lover, Ethel Le Neve, and reached Belgium undetected. But on 20 July, they boarded the SS *Montrose* bound for Quebec. The arrest took place on 31 July. He was promptly returned to London and charged at Bow Street court one month later. He was hanged on 23 November the same year.

The First and Last Voyage of the *Titanic*

1912

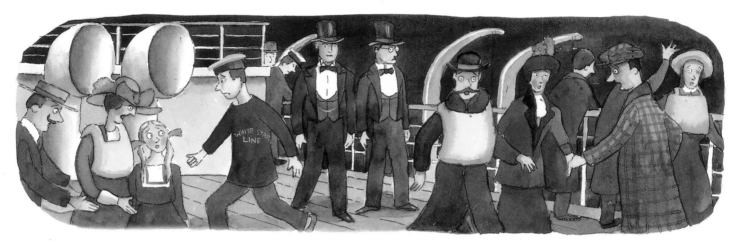

BEN GUGGENHEIM SLIPPED HIS ARMS INTO THE silk-lined sleeves of his evening jacket and turned to his cabin mirror to fasten his tie. "What say we take a turn around the deck and listen to the band?" he said to his secretary.

Outside, on deck, it was a beautiful, frosty, starlit night – only a chilly breath of a breeze and a calm, smooth sea. The ship was ablaze with lights. The band played a lively little dance number from its huge repertoire. An altogether perfect evening . . . were it not for the screaming.

All round, people were praying and running, sobbing and swearing, hugging or struggling to climb up high. Steerage passengers were still streaming up from the lower decks, and the ship groaned in agony as its back prepared to break.

"Unsinkable" they had said in the advertisements: "the ship that cannot sink". The newspapers had made much of her size and safety, her luxury and collision-proof double hull. Pride of the White Star Line, the *Titanic* was the last word in elegance and technology. People had flocked to buy tickets for her first voyage – the rich and glamorous, quite at home beneath the chandeliers of her immense ballroom, poor Irish emigrants who could only afford the smallest, cheapest cabins on their trip to

a new life in America. The ship was a little world in miniature: rich on top, poor on the bottom, but all heading in the same direction. And she was so *big* – the length of London's Shaftesbury Avenue, and just as brightly lit!

The iceberg, by contrast, moved like a dirty brown slab, hidden for the most part underwater. It had broken away from the polar pack ice to float aimlessly south across the shipping lanes. And it too was titanic.

The look-out Fred Fleet saw it at the last moment and shouted a warning, clanged the alarm bell three times. The ship seemed only to graze against the great ice hulk, then sail by, a rattle of ice skittering across the decks. "That was a close shave," said Fleet to himself.

But there was a ninety-metre gash below the waterline, a gash which had pierced both layers of the double hull and buckled the whole structure. Icy water was already pouring in. The "unsinkable" *Titanic* had two hours to live.

The bow and wheel-house were already underwater, but the stern was still afloat and reasonably level. One of the huge funnels disintegrated and toppled into the water amid the swimmers and rafts and life-boats.

There had not been enough lifeboats – not enough for even half the people aboard. A strange oversight. Perhaps on an unsinkable ship, lifeboats had not seemed important. Some boats had capsized on launching. As a result, the lifeboats, floating now within the glow of the ship's lights, were crammed with precious cargoes of silks, satins, furs and diamonds. Women and children first. That is the rule at sea.

Of course some men had been too panic-stricken to care about the etiquette of the sea. Some had tried to disguise themselves as women. Some had jumped into the water and been pulled aboard. And there were the sailors who had had to get the boats away. But for the most part, true gentlemen had stayed behind: Jack Phillips the wireless operator, for instance, tapping away at his Morse key over and over and over again: "Come at once. We have struck an iceberg. It's CQD, old man. Position 41º 40'N, 50º 14'W. Come at once. We have struck –" Gentlemen.

Like the ones in the water who had found the rafts too crowded to take another soul, and swum away again, with a cry of "Good luck – God bless you!" Gentlemen.

Like the engineers still labouring to provide power, so that all the lights in the ship could blaze during the evacuation, be seen by rescue ships, raise the spirits of those caught up in the death of the *Titanic*. True gentlemen.

Like the musicians playing even now a jaunty little tune, while the deck beneath them tilted more and more steeply. True gentlemen.

There were wives, too, who chose to stay behind with their husbands.

And men like Ben and Victor, who seeing how some must live and some must die, had thrown off their life-jackets and turned away from the lifeboats. "Tell my wife I played the game out straight to the end," Ben had called to those in the boat. "No women shall be left aboard this ship because Ben Guggenheim is a coward."

The band struck up "Abide with me." The lights were flickering now in some of the portholes. It was two in the morning of 15 April, and the ship was going down. The entire front half disappeared. The stern section stood on end, then, like a still photograph, hesitated for a full five minutes before slipping out of sight.

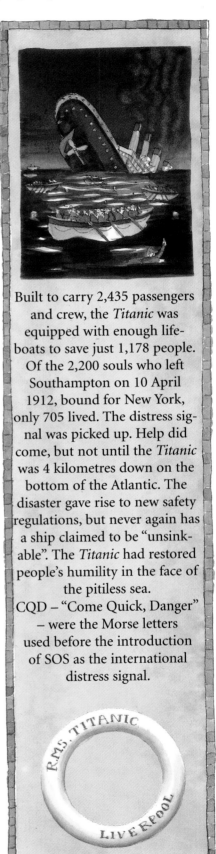

Built to carry 2,435 passengers and crew, the *Titanic* was equipped with enough lifeboats to save just 1,178 people. Of the 2,200 souls who left Southampton on 10 April 1912, bound for New York, only 705 lived. The distress signal was picked up. Help did come, but not until the *Titanic* was 4 kilometres down on the bottom of the Atlantic. The disaster gave rise to new safety regulations, but never again has a ship claimed to be "unsinkable". The *Titanic* had restored people's humility in the face of the pitiless sea.

CQD – "Come Quick, Danger" – were the Morse letters used before the introduction of SOS as the international distress signal.

"Just Going Outside"

1912

THERE WAS NOTHING TO BE GAINED BY SUCH A JOURNEY, except honour and adventure. And yet honour is everything to such men. They wished for the honour of being first to set foot at the South Pole.

So the worst thing that could happen to them, it seemed at the outset, was that the Norwegians would get there first. The competition was so fierce between Captain Scott's team and Roald Amundsen's that the desperate cold, the grit-sharp flying snow, the blinding brightness of the polar plains did not seem the real enemies at all. Scott and Wilson, Evans, Bowers and Oates left their last depot with nine days' supplies, expecting that two long marches would make them the first men in history to visit the South Pole. The excitement lent them an energy they could never otherwise have mustered.

Then they saw it – a black speck in the distance, something which did not belong in the white, untrodden snow of virgin territory. When they got closer, their worst fears were confirmed: it was a flag. There were sledge tracks, too, and paw prints. The desolate Antarctic, last unconquered territory on the planet, was no longer theirs, no longer the prize they had expected after months of agonizing effort. Amundsen was ahead of them.

In a way, it would have been less terrible to turn back then and there, not to have to march on, dragging the cripplingly heavy sledge, eating up more of their dwindling provisions. Then they would not have had to stand at the South Pole and taste the bitterness of defeat. Their achievement was immense, and yet they accounted it "a horrible day"

that 17 January when they stood at the bottom of the world amid the footprints of another expedition. The Norwegians had beaten them by just thirty-five days. "All the daydreams must go," wrote Scott in his diary, "it will be a wearisome return."

And so it was. The calm weather which had made it possible to trek so far from help or shelter began to break up. A change of wind blew snow through the fabric of their clothes and filled up their mittens. The weather was deteriorating unexpectedly early, the temperature dropping unimaginably low, the wind stiffening. The cold was unspeakable – unspeakable chiefly because these men were English officers and gentlemen; to have complained or inconvenienced their friends would have been dishonourable. And honour was everything.

Then Edgar Evans died.

Laurence Oates got frostbite in his foot. It had been troubling him even at the Pole; ten weeks later, he could go no further. He knew that he too was going to die, but took comfort from the thought that his regiment might be proud of him. On the night of 6 March, he bedded down, fervently hoping to die in his sleep. Once again luck was against him. He woke to the knowledge that his failure to die promptly would delay his friends – perhaps even prevent them reaching safety themselves. As undemonstrative as ever, he crawled out of his sleeping-bag and got painfully to his feet. A blizzard was blaring outside: a white madness.

"I am just going outside and may be some time," he said.

The others sat up. "No!"

"We can still make it, old boy!"

"You said yourself . . ."

But the tent flap dropped back into place, and Oates was gone: no grand scene, no heroic declamation – "just going outside".

"We knew that poor Oates was walking to his death," wrote Scott, ". . . it was the act of a brave man and an English gentleman."

His self-sacrifice would be wasted if the others did not push on, try to reach the depot. Twenty miles to go. But they knew inwardly, beneath their endlessly cheerful banter, that they would probably not make it. They were down to their last primus-filling of oil and next to no food: a smear of cocoa and lump of pemmican. Scott succumbed to frostbite, but there was such a short way left to go – only fifteen and a half miles! He knew he would lose his foot, but would he lose his life too? Eleven miles.

Wilson and Bowers were planning to go ahead to the depot, for more fuel. But the blizzard shut down, as if the flapping tent of frozen sky had fallen on them. Discussing how they should best finish their doomed expedition, they resolved to go out and meet death face-to-face, to walk, with or without baggage, until they dropped in their tracks. But the blizzard thwarted them. The blizzard had picked up the outside world and shaken it out of existence. Besides, a tent and sledge might be found, whereas three men, falling separately, along an unmarked path would soon be obliterated by the snow, never to be found. So they settled themselves as comfortably as they could and waited. It would not be a long wait.

On 20 March, they had enough tea for two more cups, enough food for two meagre days. On the twenty-ninth the blizzard was still raging, and Scott wrote the last words in his diary: "For God's sake, look after our people."

The snow did all it could to bury the tent, but its flue and a bamboo upright on the sledge still showed above the drifts when a search party found Scott's last camp, eight months later. The three had come to within eleven – about sixteen kilometres – miles of safety.

They lay in their sleeping-bags, letters and diaries intact. Even the worst luck, the worst weather, the worst wilderness in the world could not succeed in erasing the indelible mark left by such courageous men.

As well as his diary, Robert Falcon Scott left a number of letters. "We are pegging out in a very comfortless spot," he wrote to his best friend, J. M. Barrie, author of *Peter Pan* and godfather of his son. "We are showing that Englishmen can still die with a bold spirit, fighting it out to the end." Great as Amundsen's achievement was, the sheer tragedy of Scott's trip, the cheery, stiff-upper-lip composure of that diary inspired more awe than any success story. Everyone wanted to think that they too, could go out to face death like Oates.

Votes for Women!

1913

ABOARD THE TRAIN THERE WAS A HOLIDAY atmosphere. Everyone was travelling to the same destination: Epsom Downs. It was Derby Day, and people who never thought of going to the horse-races flocked to Epsom for the grandest race of the year. Families with picnic baskets and six sticky children, clerks and factory workers, young couples smiling shyly at each other, brash men in loud sports coats. No one paid much attention to the young woman sitting in a corner of the carriage, her handkerchief held to her mouth.

"Now, George, I don't want you gambling your money away."

"Just a flutter, dear. Just a flutter."

"Perhaps just a shilling on the King's horse. It's only patriotic to bet on His Majesty's horse . . ."

The young woman's teeth tore a small hole in the corner of her handkerchief. Emily Davison stepped down from the train, and the cheerful crowd swept her along. The green of Epsom Downs was submerged beneath the colourful holiday clothes of the race-goers. The amplified voices of stewards speaking through megaphones sounded like dogs barking. Bookmakers stood on boxes shouting the betting odds they were offering. Bookies' runners gesticulated like lunatics, using their secret sign language. Emily too, had a secret. Someone had daubed "Votes for Women" on the fence. Her fingers brushed the words as the crowd carried her along.

She did not place any bets. She did not sip tea at the cafeteria or look over the horses in the saddling enclosure for a likely winner. Not until the big event – the Derby Sweepstake itself – was about to begin did she worm her way through the crowds to a place by the white rails of the race course. From there she would have a perfect view of the runners thundering down the straight. The crowd gave a single excited cry of "They're off!" and the 1913 Derby had begun.

240

The King's horse did not take the lead. It was halfway down the field as the runners entered the straight. The crowd to either side of Emily leaned forwards, shouting for the horse they had backed. Perhaps they thought Emily was doing the same.

"Votes for Women!" Her voice came out small and piping. How fast they moved. She had not realized how fast a galloping horse moved. Slipping under the rail, she felt the ground tremble under her feet.

Someone made a grab to pull her back, but she ducked forwards – a small, pale figure in hat and gloves, purse hanging from her wrist. The front-runners tried to avoid her, but the ones behind had no time. She flung herself under the hooves of the King's horse – it was done in a flash – and many in the crowd saw the muddle of hooves and clothes and thought a jockey had come unseated. Then a strange, delayed gasp of revulsion went up, half drowned by the shouts of the spectators down by the winning post, still cheering their horses on.

"... sheer suicide ..."

"... madwoman!"

"... what possessed her ..."

"... anything to draw attention to themselves ... Is she dead?"

"... these suffragettes."

The voices reached Emily as if down the dark shaft of a well. The stewards and first-aiders who came to her side were sharp-voiced with disgust. She had spoiled the day for so many people.

Before Emily Wilding Davison died, she was a leading militant in the Women's Social and Political Union founded by Emmeline Pankhurst. Though the campaigners had resorted to arson, slashing paintings, smashing windows, invading Parliament, even street fighting with the police, neither these efforts nor public outrage at the ill-treatment of suffragettes brought about a change. With the outbreak of the First World War, the WSPU ceased its campaigns to help with the war effort. Women made themselves so indispensable while the men were away fighting that afterwards society acknowledged there was no going back. In 1918, women over thirty who were married, householders or university graduates were given the vote. Not until 1928 did all women over twenty-one obtain the vote.

No Man's Land

1914

IT WAS CHRISTMAS DAY, BUT NOTHING TO SHOW for it being Christmas. There was no snow, no laughter, no celebration. Nothing to celebrate. The guns had fallen silent, but before long they would be pounding again, shaking the mortar out of the sky, shaking the rats out of their holes, making the dead tremble out on no-man's-land. Rags of torn clothing hung on the barbed wire out there, like bunting, but they hung there every day, gradually losing their colour. It was not Christmas which had put the bunting there. It was the war.

"It will be all over by Christmas," they had said at the beginning. But they had not said *which* Christmas or whether, when it finally ended, there would be anyone left alive to see it.

*"Stille Nacht, heilige Nacht
Alles schlaft, einsam wacht . . ."*

The soldiers sitting slumped in their swampy trenches, remembering past Christmases, thought at first that the carol was in their imaginations. Then they realized that the singing was real, that it was drifting over from the German trenches on the other side of no-man's-land. The enemy were remembering Christmas, too.

Of course they were. Christmas is universal. And what were they – those German infantrymen over there – but young men far from home, wishing they were somewhere else this vile, wartime Christmas Day in France. Only weeks before, the British Tommies might have believed all that propaganda about Germans murdering babies and burning churches. But they knew better now. The enemy they knew as "Jerry" was just as frightened, just as homesick. He, too, had a wife back somewhere – children maybe – sitting through Christmas Day clutching his mud-spattered letters home and remembering . . .

*"Silent night, holy night
All is calm, all is bright . . ."*

The Welsh Fusiliers over in the next trench were joining in now. Forever singing, those Taffies. Some of them were singing in Welsh, others in English. Same carol, just different words. Same meaning. Same Christmas.

Suddenly *everyone* burst out singing.

Then a German called out: something about schnapps: something about sharing a drink. He rose up into view, and the singing petered to a halt. Would he be shot down by a sniper? What sniper? How can you shoot a man when you've just been singing along with him? Other heads rose above the muddy parapets, dirty, fatigued faces looking at one another across the grassless, treeless, lifeless no-man's-land which separated the German trenches from the English ones.

Something round and brown dropped out of the slab-grey sky, and all the heads ducked. Hands flew up to shield vulnerable eyes and ears. Was it a shell? A mortar? The brown globe bounced two or three times, then rolled to a standstill. It was a football.

A football in no-man's-land? Was it English or Welsh or German? It was neutral. No-man's-land is neutral. It belongs to nobody, except perhaps the dead who die out there, hanging on the barbed wire.

First one, then five, then a dozen men scrambled out of their trenches, each one exhorting the men behind to follow. A few hung back – suspicious of an ambush. But enough jogged out on to the barren wasteland, greatcoats dangling stiffly down to their ankles, cigarette smoke curling from the cupped palms of their hands. Enough for a game of football.

Jerry and Tommy exchanged cigarettes, swigs of liquor. Someone marked out goal-mouths with bundled up coats. There were shouts and cheers, and little puffs of smoky breath as the players panted in the cold air. For half an hour or more that game lasted.

Then somewhere far off – far up the line – artillery started up: a gentle *whoomp, whoomp*, like a heartbeat. The smokers dragged deep on their cigarettes and threw them down. The players shook hands, gathered up their greatcoats, pointed to the faint red glare in the distant sky. The sound of gunfire came closer.

Without anyone giving a direct command, the men returned to their respective trenches. They did not hurry. Machine-gunners checked their ammunition. Riflemen eased the springs of their carbines. The Welsh were the last to stop singing.

Nothing had changed. The end of the war had come no closer. There would be no spontaneous laying down of arms in defiance of the commanding officers, no mutinous refusal to fight any more. But something had happened, out there in no-man's-land; something every man there would remember until he died – whether he died next morning out on the wire or lived to see other, peacetime Christmas Days.

The mortars began to thud, crazing the slab-grey sky, making the muddy earth trickle in slurries down into the trenches. Cowering soldiers hunched their shoulders against it and buttoned up their greatcoats. Out on no-man's-land the football lay forgotten, like a Christmas hazelnut after a splendid meal.

The sculptor-artist Henri Gaudier-Brzeska, as well as several other eye-witnesses, wrote of the Christmas Day football match in his letters home. He was killed, aged twenty-four, in 1915, fighting in a war which, between 1914 and 1918, would see nine million die.

Derailing the Country

1926

TIME WAS, IT WAS EVERY BOY'S DREAM TO DRIVE A railway engine, and one engine in particular: the *Flying Scotsman*. Bob Sheddon, however, saw it as his patriotic duty – to keep the railways running. The strikers had vowed to bring the country to a standstill, but Bob was determined to drive the *Flying Scotsman* from Edinburgh to London on Monday, 10 May.

The view from her twelve carriages that day was of quiet streets, smokeless factory chimneys, silent stockyards. It was like Sunday in the mid-week. The country was holding its breath, waiting to see whether the Government or the trade unions would be the first to back down in their argument over the miners' dispute.

Bob's volunteer fireman was a student from Edinburgh University, Robert Aitken. Some of his friends were working at the docks or driving lorries, helping to defeat the strike. Not that his friends would ever do that kind of work once they had their degrees. Indeed, they might never dirty their hands again with machine oil or crates of fish,

but it was a lark – or else their patriotic duty: every volunteer had his own motives for trying to break the General Strike. Some thought the striking miners and transport workers and dockers and factory hands were bloody-minded Communists trying to bring down the Government and sow the seeds of anarchy. Some thought that the suffering caused to ordinary people – if London, say, ran out of food – was simply not justified. For some it was just a game: to break the strike.

The *Flying Scotsman* rattled along, trailing steam-clouds of glory. "What speed did you say she could do?" said Robert.

"Sixty mile an hour," said Bob. "Not through Dam Dyke, naturally."

The huge, sleek engine sighed steam as she slowed to a mere six miles an hour for the level crossing near Cramlington. That was when they saw it – a gap in the rails ahead.

Robert hung half out of the cab, peering through the steam. "Piece of rail – gone!" he gasped. "We'll never stop in time!"

Bob slammed on the brakes. The gigantic metal wheels spun on the tracks, and sparks flew. But a steam engine needs time to slow down and stop, even from six mph. She trundled on, wheels skidding, the carriages jolted by the sharp braking. On and on she rolled, until in ponderous slow motion one wheel found no rail under it, and she slumped over sideways. The *Flying Scotsman* jumped the tracks and ploughed into a disused signal box at the side of the line. The first carriage jack-knifed. The guard's van was thrown on to its side. All along the length of the train passengers slithered to the floor. There was a smell of burning and cries of "Fire!"

Police and firemen and ambulances were quick to arrive. So, too, were crowds of onlookers . . . only they did not rush forward to offer help or comfort. They held off at a distance, flapping their caps and grinning. As passengers staggered away, dishevelled and shaken, some in tears, some dazed and expressionless, the crowd began to jeer and whistle. Strikers from nearby Cramlington. Perhaps they were only jeering the driver and volunteer fireman. Or perhaps they deemed the passengers strike-breakers, too, for trying to travel despite the strike.

Sabotage, the police said, carrying away two iron bars and a sledge hammer from near the scene of the crash. Still, no serious harm was done. Only one person was injured. The boilers of the *Flying Scotsman* were doused and she was not much damaged. Copies of the *British Gazette* blew about on the lines and were turned back to pulp by the rain. Tomorrow's edition would say how the *Flying Scotsman* had been derailed by strikers.

But there would be other train crashes to report as well. That same Monday, at Bishop's Stortford, a goods train ran into a passenger train and one man was killed. Between Berwick and Edinburgh three people died in a collision.

Were they casualties of the strike or of the strike breakers? It depends on your point of view. Either way, they were just as dead.

The General Strike of 1926 lasted from one minute to midnight on 3 May until twenty past noon on 12 May. A million miners had been told their pay was to be cut to save money. When they refused to accept the pay-cut, they were locked out. Nearly two million workers downed tools in support of them, but the Conservative Government under Prime Minister, Stanley Baldwin, instead of negotiating, set out to break the General Strike. The *British Gazette*, published by the Government, was full of anti-strike propaganda. The Trade Unions published a rival publication: the *British Worker* full of pro-strike propaganda. After nine days of chaos, which split public opinion right down the middle, the General Strike caved in. The miners stayed on strike all summer but in the end poverty defeated them.

Memories of a Jarrow Marcher

1936

WHEN THE BIG CRANES CAME DOWN, I FINALLY grasped the truth. The shipyard was gone, closed, finished, and every man who worked there was out of work for good. Including me.

Grandpa refused to believe it. He kept going down there, oiling things, keeping things serviceable for when it opened up again. Me, I knew better. I was out grubbing up coal dust for fuel. It was risky: I could have been caught and fined, but I couldn't have Mam and the bairns shivering. The lad next door stayed in bed a lot – just to keep warm. You can't feel hungry if you're asleep.

The streets were always ringing empty. Me, I went walking. All the way to Newcastle and back was nothing. We were always good walkers, we Jarrow lads, and it passed the time.

We couldn't move away to seek work. Dad had spent his savings buying the house, but he couldn't have sold it for a ten-shilling note. Who'd want to live in Jarrow where three men in four were out of work?

Mothers didn't eat; they gave what food there was to their menfolk and bairns. This is the twentieth century I'm talking about, and women and babies were so weak with hunger that they died of the least little thing. My sisters Jean and Annie got out. They went south and got work in London as waitresses. Some days, I thought I'd never see them again.

A year went by and nobody at Westminster even troubled to come and see what the shipyard closure had done to us.

Then up gets Joe Symonds – I'll never forget it. "I am prepared to march 7,000 men to London and demand justice!" says Joe. "The working-class people of this town must rise in strength and demand that something be done!"

Well, everyone liked the idea; we all wanted to go. There *could* have been 7,000. But the organizers said thousands would be hard to feed and shelter, so they settled on 200. We drew lots in our house. I won. But our Jack gave me his waterproof, Dad gave me his suit, our Tom gave me his cap. Mam gave me a kiss. So in a way we all went on the Jarrow Crusade.

Red Ellen led us – our MP, Ellen Wilkinson. They called her Red Ellen because of her hair, not because she were a Communist. This had nothing to do with politics, see? This was about starvation.

We didn't want charity; we wanted work. We wanted people down south to know what we were suffering up in Jarrow. So we would walk all the way to London and present a petition to Parliament, and along the way we could tell people how we came to be in such a plight.

It put heart into us, just to be *doing* something for a change. We were going to call it the Jarrow Hunger March, but then one of the marshals said "Crusade" would be nicer. So Jarrow Crusade it was. We carried a banner with those two words, ahead of 200 men all in their Sunday best, and the Mayor of Jarrow and Red Ellen – not forgetting Paddy the dog, of course. He was our mascot. He trotted along with us, chipper as you like, all those miles to London.

We walked for fifty minutes, rested for ten, and kept going ten hours a day. Every town we reached, we rushed to the post office to collect letters from our families. That helped with the homesickness. After a while we were all best-muckers – friends to the end! We looked out for each other. Tynesiders might be rough, tough men, but they can be tender as lassies when there's a need.

Jarrow, Chester le Street, Darlington, Ripon, Harrogate, Leeds, Wakefield, Sheffield, Chesterfield, Nottingham . . . Everywhere we stopped, people welcomed us. That "Crusade" idea caught their imagination. Also, we didn't make political speeches. We just told how it was: how many were out of work, how many babies died before their first birthday. People who, up till then, had been calling us a bunch of bolshevik trouble-makers, found themselves cheering Miss Ellen and writing letters to the papers saying, "Something must be done!"

Leicester, Northampton, Bedford, St Albans . . . And folk were so *good* to us! They laid on hot dinners, campsites, sandwiches. A cinema manager let us in free to see a moving picture. A theatre owner sent the artistes round by taxi to give us a show. The Leicester Co-op workers stopped up all night mending our boots. Medical students turned out all along the way to cure our ills, and never charged a penny piece. And we got fit and we got fed and we were treated decent – which is more than we had been back home. We missed our wives and bairns, of course we did, and the walking was hard on the feet, but it was a fine time – a grand time.

Then we reached London.

The police were suspicious of us, but they couldn't stand in our way. We weren't the Peasants' Revolt. We were a bunch of men all spruced up, carrying a message from 11,572 people to their elected government. And any Englishman has a perfect right to petition his government about an injustice.

We had a rally in Hyde Park. That was the best day for me: holiday crowds and music. Someone called my name – and there was Jean and Annie! – along with hundreds of other Jarrow-born lassies and lads who'd gone after the work in London. A few tears flowed, I can tell you!

Then there was that meeting in Farringdon. That put the cap on things. Maybe Sir John thought he was helping; maybe he fancied the cheers. But up stands Sir John Jarvis, MP, and says he's opening a new tube works at Jarrow. The journalists grabbed the news and ran.

Next day the papers were full of it: "Jarrow To Have New Works", it said. So that was all right, wasn't it? The happy ending everyone wanted. The great British public breathed a sigh of relief – and put us clean out of mind.

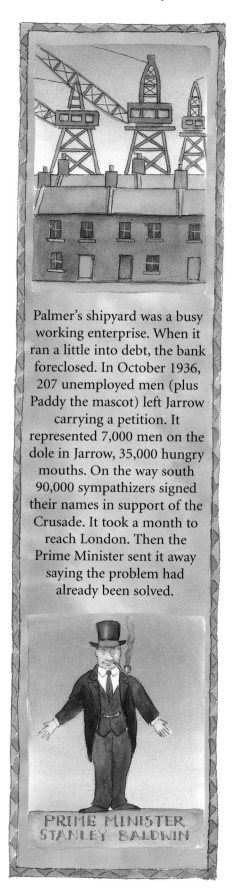

Palmer's shipyard was a busy working enterprise. When it ran a little into debt, the bank foreclosed. In October 1936, 207 unemployed men (plus Paddy the mascot) left Jarrow carrying a petition. It represented 7,000 men on the dole in Jarrow, 35,000 hungry mouths. On the way south 90,000 sympathizers signed their names in support of the Crusade. It took a month to reach London. Then the Prime Minister sent it away saying the problem had already been solved.

PRIME MINISTER
STANLEY BALDWIN

Next day we were offered a jolly trip on the Thames. We didn't know it was a trick to get us out of the way. When we got back, the petition was already handed in. The politicians had said, "Yes, but look: the Navy will be ordering new ships soon, from some place or other, and Sir John is opening these tube works . . . What more is there to say?"

Billy Thompson – our Mayor – was grand. He showed them his chain-of-office – a chain of little gold hawsers and anchors to represent the thousand ships built in Jarrow. "If you're not going to help us, this means nothing," he said, and dropped it – *clunk* – on the table. Grand gesture. Then we all shuffled off.

Do I sound ungrateful to the great Sir John Jarvis, MP? Well, Sir John's tube works, if they ever opened, would employ 150 men: 150 out of 7,000. And just by talking about it, he had lost us everything. So we took out the ten-shilling notes we had saved for the train fare, smoothed them flat, and bought our tickets home.

Of course, when the orders for new Navy ships came along, they did not go to Jarrow. Palmer's shipyard had been sold off, hadn't it? All its machinery sold for scrap to the Belgians. The Belgians put in a bid and got the work. Well, they had the machinery, didn't they?

It did no good at all, the Jarrow Crusade. It was a grand effort – got the whole country stirred up – but it did no good. When we got home, the cranes were still gone. The streets of Jarrow were always ringing empty. It was a ghost town. A dead town. Red Ellen said it had been murdered.

The Brave Little Boats of Dunkirk

1940

WE KNEW THINGS WERE GOING BADLY WHEN the command came to retreat. Tanks were breaking through our lines, we were passing whole convoys of lorries on fire, and there was shellfire all around. We knew things had gone wrong altogether when they told us to destroy all our kit. But I could barely believe it when I realized that the whole British Expeditionary Force was on the retreat across France.

Each man was supposed to keep one blanket and a full pack: everything else had to be destroyed to keep it out of German hands. Wireless sets lay about with their valves smashed and their insides hanging out. Gun-sights had to be broken and the breeches of the big guns blocked with concrete or rocks. I remember Harry and I had nicked a case of wine along the way. We had to smash even that. It drained away into the ground like blood. All the time, droves of miserable, muddy men were streaming by on foot.

The Germans had us pretty much surrounded on three sides. Then it rained again. It rained hard.

Trouble was, the vehicles abandoned by one platoon blocked the roads for the rest of us trying to get west to the coast. It was chaos – mud and confusion. Finally, about twenty-five miles from Dunkirk, the road ahead was clogged solid and we had to pick our way on foot, single-file. Down every road came these single-file streams of men, all converging on Dunkirk like rivers giving into the sea. The beaches, when we got there, were a mass of men. I never saw a crowd like it. My stomach turned to water at the sight. We were sitting ducks! The German army was closing in on us and the German air force could fly over to bomb and machine-gun us whenever they liked. Soon we would all either be dead or taken prisoner. I remember saying to Harry, "This is the end of the war for us, mate."

There were a handful of destroyers off shore, sent to take off as many as possible of us. But there were just so many to be taken off! Already the destroyers were being dive-bombed and sunk.

Harry and I took shelter in the cellar of a house near the beach, waiting for our turn to go aboard the rescue ships. How can I describe it? It was the biggest queue in the world: men waiting to go home, to stay alive. The queue moved forward twenty metres each hour. But it was quite well organized. Food was being shared out and there were pickets on duty to make sure no one jumped the queue.

Oddly, the Germans did not come when we expected. Our air force had lots of planes in the air, trying to protect us from the bombing and machine-gunning. Harry and I broke into a shop and took some deckchairs and food and drink; then we sat and got rather woozy, I have to admit, trying not to think about our chances. Surely, Hitler had won. It's not a wide stretch of water, the English Channel, but it's quite wide enough. You can't walk home across it. So what escape did we have, realistically?

I was out there three days. Others were there eight or nine. We were like mice trapped in the corner of a room, just waiting for the cat's paw to drop. Still the Germans did not arrive. It was uncanny, inexplicable. Harry said, "Maybe they don't like sand in their boots." Day and night, day and night. The beaches stank of death, noxious smoke, sewage, blood, iodine and wet wool.

Then, do you know what? Other boats started to appear off-shore – not naval ships but private boats – ferries, yachts, tugs, barges, launches. It was like a regatta! Practically every English boat capable of crossing the Channel seemed to have come to help pick up men! All day they kept coming. All day and all night.

Soldiers were wading out into the water to climb aboard: some, more organized, were waiting their turn at the harbour. They waited for the signal, then ran zig-zagging at full tilt along the harbour wall to some grey navy ship or millionaire's sleek motor yacht.

When that low-flying bomber came over, the vibration of its engine made my teeth chatter. It dropped a bomb ten metres away and I was drenched in sand. Harry was killed outright. That's when my nerve broke. I ran into the water, heading out for a motor-boat put-putting towards the beach.

It was the kind of boat you might take for a trip round the bay. A big sea would have swamped it. And here it was, my one tiny chance to get away. Up to my waist. Up to my shoulders. Trying to keep my feet. The water was cold: it climbed inside my clothes, layer by heavy layer. A helmet floated past. I think I trod on a man's kitbag.

There was an old man aboard the motor-boat. He left the helm and came to pull me aboard – me and six or seven others. We were so eager to climb in, and so clumsy, that we nearly overturned him. As he leaned towards me, his face was grey and drawn with fright, cold, uncertainty. I suppose mine was much the same, though, and I was less than half his age.

The beach was a seething mass of men and noise: shouting, explosions. But out on the water, I don't believe we spoke one word all the while the boat was picking its way through the other craft and out to sea. Then the Frenchman beside me started repeating over and over and over again: "*Merci. Merci, merci, merci.*"

Sometimes the old man acknowledged another boat-owner with a nod or a brief wave: sailing people all know each other. There were bankers and factory hands and doctors and teachers and fishermen, sea scouts and taxi-drivers; boys too young for the army and old men who had fought in the last war. There were fireboats and fishing smacks and lifeboats. A lovely old paddle-steamer chugged and splattered past us, like something from an older, sweeter world. Some vessels had been across the Channel several times already, and picked up soldiers and taken them home, then come back for more. The risks were horrific, what with German planes overhead and the shelling. I saw a pleasure boat blown out of the water, a yacht turned over. I saw a destroyer burning on the horizon under a pall of smoke. This was no trip around the bay. I cowered down in the bottom of the boat, my head up against a slopping petrol can. It's not a wide stretch of water, the Channel, but it's wide enough to die in.

The old man told us how he had been listening to the wireless when the call had gone out: "The Admiralty has made an order to all owners of pleasure crafts, fishing boats, or freighters between thirty and one hundred feet in length to report to the Admiralty at Dover."

This was his fourth trip.

I never saw a sight so stirring as the white cliffs of Dover parting the sky from the sea, and the winking of the harbour lights. There was hot food waiting, and first-aid for the wounded as well as blankets and smiles. As I climbed the steps up the harbour wall, I realized that I did not even know the name of the man who had rescued me. I turned to ask, but he was already pushing off again, putting out to sea, heading for the Dunkirk beaches to snatch up a few more lives.

That was four years ago – May 1940. Now I'm going back, too. It is 6 June, and we are all set for the big one – the Allied Invasion of Europe. Back then, the papers called it the miracle of Dunkirk – a victory! That was no victory. As Winston Churchill said, "You don't win wars by evacuations." No, Dunkirk was a hellish, humiliating defeat for us. Now the same men are going back over there to take Europe from the Nazis. You want to see what victory looks like? Watch us.

At this point in the Second World War, the advancing Germans were pushing back the British Expeditionary Force thirty to forty miles a day. When Prime Minister Winston Churchill realized he would have to evacuate the troops off Dunkirk beach, he expected to be able to rescue about 45,000 men before the Germans arrived and captured or killed the rest.

To the utter disgust of his generals, Hitler ordered his troops to halt their advance. To this day, no one knows why.

Instead of two days, Operation Dynamo (as the evacuation was called) went on for nine tireless days and brought out 338,226 British soldiers. Eventually the Germans did arrive: 45,000 men were captured. But enough had got away to make a real difference to the course of the war. It is just possible that his strategic blunder at Dunkirk lost Hitler the Second World War. Operation Dynamo cost its heroes dear; approximately 2,000 civilians and British Navy men were killed fetching troops off the beaches; 235 of the 600 brave little boats which set sail were sunk by enemy fire.

Improving on History

(50,000 BC, 1907, 1953)

AN EXPECTANT hush fell over the lecture hall as Charles Dawson rose to speak. The newspapers had hinted at what he would say, and no one in the world of archaeology wanted to miss it. He peered down at them from the lectern – a man known for his painstaking archaeology, for his thoroughness and attention to detail. He spoke of a gentle afternoon walk in the Sussex countryside. Not the stuff of headlines, surely?

"Two workmen were digging gravel . . . I asked if they had found bones or other fossils there . . . urged them to preserve anything they might find . . . One of the men handed to me a small portion of an unusually thick human parietal bone . . . Some years later, in the autumn of 1911, I picked up another and larger piece . . ."

Science called the find "Dawson's Dawn Man" of Piltdown – *Eoanthropus dawsoni* – a creature neither ape nor man but part-way between the two. Here was the living proof (fossilized proof, anyway) which archaeology had been longing for. Darwin's theory of evolution had been proved, and by a find in the English Sussex countryside!

Nearly one hundred years before, Charles Darwin had put forward the theory that mankind did not spring into existence perfectly formed, out of clay, by the finger of God, but had developed over millions of years, by random accident, from ape into man. Darwin had stirred up a hornet's nest; there were many people, even in 1912, who rejected Darwinianism as a wicked heresy against God. But now Dawson had found the *proof* – an example of a Dawn Man, part ape, part man. Piltdown Man was the missing link in a chain of conclusive evidence: mankind truly was descended from the apes.

The top of the Piltdown skull was shaped like early man's, the jaw like that of an ape. Immediately opinion was split between those who said jaw and skull had washed by chance into the same gravel bed, and those who accepted that jaw and skull belonged together. For a couple of years the controversy raged . . . until Dawson produced a *second* Piltdown skull, and there was no further talk of him having made a mistake. In fact he was the hero of the hour. He had found the missing link!

But shortly, the cataclysm of the First World War pushed Dawson's discovery out of everyone's mind. What did it matter how mankind had originated: the question was, did mankind have a future?

Charles Dawson, briefly feted and famous, fell ill in 1915 and by the following year himself lay buried in the English countryside. Now it was up to his friend and colleague, Arthur Smith Woodward, to defend Piltdown Man from doubting Thomases, to field the questions of palaeontologists wanting to research further. His life's work, whether he chose it or not, became Piltdown Man.

Time passed. In China, Java and Africa other ape-men were found: Darwin's theories were proved time and again. Oddly, though, these new finds had jaws like early man and crania like apes. Well, perhaps primates had evolved by two *different* routes into modern man: one jaw-first, one cranium-first.

Then carbon-dating – a method of testing bone – was developed which could prove, past doubt, whether Dawson's jaw and cranium were of the same age and therefore parts of the same skull. The test was made. To everyone's astonishment, all the bone proved much *younger* than expected.

Those who had always had their doubts began to mutter "hoax". Science steeled itself to study the two Piltdown skulls for signs of forgery. Once they started looking, the signs were easy to find.

The teeth had been filed down with a metal implement. The bones had been stained artificially to a similar colour. The jaw came from an orang-utan; the cranium was no older than the thirteenth century.

In 1953, the myth of Piltdown Man was exploded as a fake, an invention, a hoax. All those papers, all those debates and learned articles and digs had been for nothing.

But why? Why would anyone embark on such a hoax? To discredit a hated rival? As a student prank which got out of hand? Was it a plot by fundamentalist Christians wishing to discredit the whole theory of evolution? Or did someone want so *much* for the proof to be there that he felt driven to plant it himself? Did someone crave the glory of finding it – want his name associated with the most important find in the history of history? Could he not wait for the proof to surface of its own accord? Was it impatience with the slow unravelling of history?

History knit itself up over millions of years; it only unravels at its own measured pace. It will not be hurried, not for the glory of any one historian or to satisfy the curiosity of those most thirsty to know.

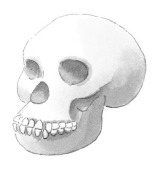

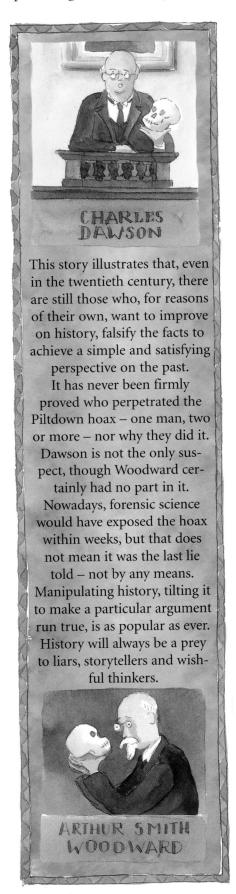

CHARLES DAWSON

This story illustrates that, even in the twentieth century, there are still those who, for reasons of their own, want to improve on history, falsify the facts to achieve a simple and satisfying perspective on the past.

It has never been firmly proved who perpetrated the Piltdown hoax – one man, two or more – nor why they did it. Dawson is not the only suspect, though Woodward certainly had no part in it. Nowadays, forensic science would have exposed the hoax within weeks, but that does not mean it was the last lie told – not by any means. Manipulating history, tilting it to make a particular argument run true, is as popular as ever. History will always be a prey to liars, storytellers and wishful thinkers.

ARTHUR SMITH WOODWARD

Breaking the Time Barrier

1954

ROGER BANNISTER SHARPENED HIS RUNNING spikes on a grindstone in the hospital laboratory. The weather was all wrong for running. This would not be the day when he ran his fastest race. But he went on sharpening his spikes . . . just in case the weather changed.

He was a medical student. His final exams were coming up. Soon the gruelling duties of being a young hospital doctor would leave no time for sport. So this might be his last summer's running. It would have been good to prove himself – to perform the impossible.

Bannister sighed and laid the spikes aside. What difference would sharp spikes make, when there was a gale blowing?

At the running track in Oxford, the wind tugged violently at the flag on the church roof. Bannister tried on his new, super-light running shoes, but his mind was pretty much made up: too windy for a record-attempt. At 5.15 p.m. it rained.

Watching the competitors limber up, the crowd was restless, keyed up. They had come there to see Bannister break the record for the mile. This was where he had run his first races as an Oxford student, so they were willing him on. They wanted him to perform the impossible tonight, in Oxford, in front of their very eyes.

If only they understood what they were asking! Only once would Bannister be able to pour all his nervous energy, his physical strength, his terror into making this run. If he tried and failed, it would not be in him to try again.

The flag on the church was wavering, the wind gusting more gently now. Bannister made his decision. He would try to run the mile in less than four minutes: a feat which had never been done, in the whole history of running.

The runners lined up. Perfect silence. *Bang!* . . . *Bang!* Two pistol cracks. A false start. A surge of fury went through Bannister.

The runners lined up again. This time there was no mistake. His friend Chris Brasher took the lead, setting the pace. "Faster!" hissed Bannister in his ear, but Brasher would not speed up, knowing that if Bannister sprinted too soon, his stamina would not last the mile. "Relax!" called a friend from the crowd.

The Oxford crowd was willing him on. Even the wind held its breath. But Bannister was barely aware of his surroundings. At the half-mile mark he knew he was in with a chance. His legs seemed to be working independently; the ground had no hold on them. His mind was detached. In a kind of trance he took over the lead, put in his final burst of speed.

The winning tape seemed to recede with every step. He must not slow, must not falter. His lungs had to go on feeding his blood; his heart had to go on pumping the oxygen round. This was his one chance in life to do a thing supremely well. If he failed, the world would turn a cold shoulder against him. The winning line taunted him . . .

He snapped the tape with his chest, snapped that invisible barrier everyone had said could not be broken. He had broken the four-minute mile.

It was then he realized – while pain wrung his muscles, and his lungs raged for air – while he collapsed into semi-consciousness – why he had been driving himself for eight years, why he had expended so much effort on achieving this moment. Suddenly he was free of the need to prove anything, free of the need to test himself, free of wanting something so very much. He was utterly, perfectly happy. Even though the crowd saw someone in a state of desperate, agonizing exhaustion, Roger Bannister was happier than he had ever been in his life. The tannoy announced: "Results of the one mile. In first place, Bannister with the time of three minutes . . ." The crowd's cheering drowned out the rest. Split seconds did not matter. For the first time a man had run one mile in less than four minutes.

Roger Bannister was part of a remarkable flowering of English running talent during the 'fifties. The previous year he had failed to win a medal at the Olympic Games – a disappointment made worse by carping public criticism of his go-it-alone attitude. But after the four-minute mile he needed a suitcase to carry all the fan mail. One specially minted, costly trophy had to be given back, because in those days the maximum value of any prize won by an amateur was just £12.

His running mates that night also became household names. Chris Brasher organized the London Marathons, Chris Chataway, another pace setter, became a Cabinet Minister. The 3 minute 59.4 second record was soon broken again, once the psychological four-minute barrier had fallen, but it is Bannister who is remembered best from that era of sporting excellence. He went on to become a neurologist.

Teaching the World to Sing

1984

IT WAS OCTOBER. THE first Christmas goods were appearing in the shops. Soon everybody would be out there again, spending too much money.

Bob Geldof sat in his London flat watching the television news. It was not Christmassy, the news. Famine and war. In Ethiopia and the Sudan several million people were about to starve to death. On the screen, withered, skeletal babies lay on the ground, fly-blown, grotesque, too weak to cry. Their mothers, old women in their twenties, looked at the camera expressionless; they had long since despaired of anyone helping them. They simply sat and watched their children die.

Viewers everywhere reached for their cheque books, knowing anything they could do would be too little too late: a futile gesture. Geldof reached for the telephone instead. He booked himself a flight to Ethiopia, and went there to see for himself. All the way there, all the way back, all the time he walked among the stench of death, he thought what everyone else was thinking: something ought to be done.

The difference was, Geldof did it.

When he got home, he called up his friends – his famous, glamorous, glitzy, talented, show-business, star-rated friends. He did not ask them for money. He asked them for their time. "There's this number I want to record," he said.

They called the group, "Band Aid". The song was titled, "Do they know it's Christmas?" It was in honour of those people for whom there can be no such thing as a happy Christmas.

It was performed by a larger number of famous recording artists than had ever gathered on one stage before. And the public loved it. It sold more copies than any other recording that year. And every penny of the £10 million profit went to Africa for famine relief.

What is more, it was fun to do! It was like one great party, where everybody arrives in party mood. Even Geldof had not foreseen how much fun it would be or how much money it would raise. He had to form a trust just to handle the proceeds. Somehow he had tapped into the conscience of the entire Western world.

But the world's poor swallowed it down like one drop of rain falling on a desert. So how could he say Band Aid was over, draw a line under it, call it a day?

Out of Band Aid grew Live Aid. One year later Geldof organized a sixteen-hour concert to be played live and screened all over the world. No one said no to Bob. People gave, free-of-charge, satellite time, studio time, technical support, transport, secretarial services . . . In a matter of weeks the idea took shape: not one, but two concerts – one in Wembley Stadium, London, the other in JFK Stadium, Philadelphia. Phil Collins sat down at a piano and sang in Wembley. Then he got on a plane and flew to Philadelphia, walked on to the stage in the JFK and sang the same song. The watching millions could not believe their eyes.

The truth was, the world had shrunk to such an extent that the people of a hundred nations were sitting together on one couch to watch TV and join in the singing. Forty per cent of the world's population were invited to that party, were asked by their favourite pop idols, heroes and statesmen to give money and to save lives.

It did not just "happen", of course. Celebrities did not simply roll out of bed and decide to go along. For ten weeks, hundreds of technicians, lawyers, politicians, secretaries, singers worked non-stop to make it happen. Not all of them were rock fans. ("I didn't even know who Geldof was," said the American producer of Live Aid. "My son did, but I didn't.") But the goodwill was there, because people knew it was going to work. It had the energy of youth behind it. And no one said no to Bob.

Well, perhaps there was one. During the concert, a light aircraft would persist in cruising over the JFK stadium towing advertising banners. The pilot refused to go away. So Bob Geldof asked Ronald Reagan, President of the United States, to telephone the airfield. He did. Within minutes, the light aeroplane was gone.

It was fun to do and it was fun to watch. It was the biggest party the world had ever known. And every pound, dollar and rouble, every shekel, lira and krona of the £48 million raised was going to put food in the mouths of starving children.

"Where do I go and what do I do?" asked superstar Dionne Warwick stepping out of a taxi. Everyone wants to help, if only someone is there to tell them how.

BOB GELDOF

Out of Live Aid and Band Aid came Sport Aid – another £21 million – raised by running ten-kilometre races in nearly 300 cities throughout the world. These were phenomenal fund-raising efforts, galvanizing all the great names of the moment – far too many to list. They did not put an end to world poverty, but they did save thousands of lives. It was possible to invest in communities for the future, as well as saving them from destruction. They also made a whole generation confront the problem of world hunger, its root causes, and how much the developed world can do to ease it.

Set in a Silver Sea

1993

IT WAS AS THOUGH THE *BRAER*'S HEART FAILED HER in the face of the storm. Her engines fell silent and left only the miscellaneous clanking of a big metal ship adrift in a mountainous sea. For six hours she drifted, while those aboard and those on shore struggled to stave off disaster. Could a tug be got out to her? Could a tow line be attached? Could the engines be restarted?

But every minute, the sea was shouldering the *Braer* inexorably towards land, shoving and bullying her into the shallows. With a noise of rending metal, it ran her aground on the rocks of Garths Ness, stoving in her watertight sides. She bled black blood.

Oil, in thick clots, haemorrhaged out of her. Every wave carried some of the *Braer*'s cargo ashore and daubed it on the rocks, on the weeds, on the sand. Hour by hour, the *Braer* broke up.

Though the sea was rough, a black ring of calm lay around the stranded ship like an evil spell. The coastline, wild, beautiful and little visited till now, withered. The oil crawled in at the noses of seals and the gills of fish, larded the sea birds which landed on the flattened, oily waves, scalded all the fronded sea-plants, fish eggs and shrimps. Crustaceans let go their grip on the oily rocks and rattled away like black pennies on to the sea bed.

Disaster. An ecological tragedy. Those who went to the coast after the stranding of the tanker waded through an oily slick which pulsed with small animals in the last throes of death. They bewailed the devastation – done in a day, but never, surely, to be undone. At best, Garths Ness would take decades to recover: no wildlife, no livelihood for the fishermen, no delight to the senses – just the stench of oil and dead things.

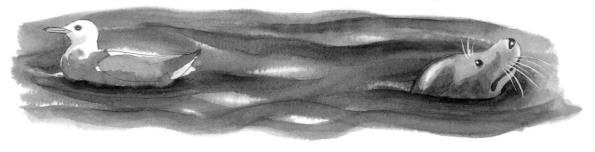

Five years later, an independent survey team went looking for the long-term effects of the *Braer* oil-spill. With more and more oil tankers plying the world's seas, such accidents are bound to happen increasingly often. So it is essential to know what other stretches of cliffs, inlets, bird colonies and fishing communities can look forward to. The worst had to be looked in the face.

The survey found . . . nothing.

Not a trace of oil remained. The sea's surf had scoured clean each pebble and shell. Its tides had dragged the black slime deep into its digestion, and its tide rips had shredded the slick into infinitesimal smallness. Fish shoals had come back. Birds had nested on the cliffs. A profusion of shellfish were busy muscling each other off the shining rocks.

The oil, prehistoric product of a million acres of primaeval forest, had become once again harmless vegetable matter – harmless as dead leaves in autumn crumbling into mulch.

The sea had proved so full of life, that though it had drunk poison, it had failed to die.

The *Braer* oil tanker was stranded at Garths Ness in the Shetlands on 5 January 1993. Science fully expected the oil-spill to do lasting damage, but all the gloomy predictions were proved wrong by the phenomenon of the self-cleansing sea. The story told here does not mean that the sea can digest any amount of pollution. (Every metre of the Atlantic sea lanes between England and America is now polluted, and inshore fishing has been seriously affected.) What it does prove is that nature has powers of regeneration which surpass our wildest imaginings.

Beginning at the End

2010

AS A BOY, PETER HIGGS'S HEROES were scientists. Written up on the wall at school were the names of just such heroes, and Peter wanted his name up there too. One problem: when it came to practical experiments, he had to admit he was hopeless. No, if he was to be a scientist, his work would have to be the kind you do in your head – formulating theories …

Long ago, scientists deduced that the earth travels round the sun. Later, they explained how atmosphere and gravity wrap the planet round. Only a century ago, they discovered the atom – the tiny building block of life – and within it the smallest particles in existence. They observed the Universe through telescopes and worked out how it began.

Fourteen billion years ago, there was a vast BANG! and there, in an instant, were the makings of space itself, time, matter, anti-matter, light, heat, mass, movement, gravity. Life … But the more that scientists learned, the more questions arose. Are there other worlds out there? Other dimensions? What gives mass to atoms? Why does 96% of the universe appear to be … missing?

Peter Higgs came up with an astonishing idea. Just suppose another atomic particle exists, as well as the ones we know about already; another particle that affects the way all the rest behave. That might explain a mystery or two. Colleagues were reaching the same conclusion. But it was still only a theory. How to prove it? As Professor Higgs says, 'It has to be put to the test, or it's just a game.' And his was just one of countless ideas simmering in the heads of theoretical physicians, untested, unproven except on paper. In the past, to test an idea, a scientist did experiments, took samples, used microscopes … How do you go looking for an invisible particle, which might or might not exist, for fleeting moments, in a place the size of the universe?

So began the greatest physics experiment in the history of the world: to find out what the universe is made of and how it works.

The laboratory is vast: at its heart a ring-shaped tunnel 27 kilometres round, 100 metres below ground at CERN in Switzerland. It is called the Large Hadron Collider. Dozens of British scientists helped design it … But then so did the rest of the world. The greatest experiment of all time cannot be performed by one man, or even one country. Anyway, when you are exploring a time before this planet existed, what do national borders matter?

Alongside the Large Hadron Collider, in smaller tunnel loops, atomic particles – protons – whirl faster and faster: not singly but in 'bunches' of a hundred billion. Batches of 6000 'bunches' are loosed into the 27km corridor, half circling one way, half the other. Steered by magnetism, accelerated still more, to almost the speed of light, they finally collide, sending fragments ricocheting and spiralling, converting energy into mass, forming new particles. A few of these collisions are captured by banks of high-speed cameras. And the photos show what might have been happening one hundredth of a billionth of a second after the Big Bang. That's how long it took for space, time, matter, anti-matter, light, heat, mass, gravity, movement – everything – to begin.

Will CERN find out where all that 'missing' anti-matter has gone? Will they discover 'other' particles? New dimensions? Or will physicists have to think things out all over again? They may. The achievement comes in finally finding out something that is true, here and everywhere and for ever. The LHC will make thousands of such discoveries.

So now forget that little outcrop of rocks called Britain, formed only a blink ago. Think bigger. Look beyond even the planet earth – a grain of sand in the cosmos. Out there in space are countless unsolved puzzles. It will take scientists the world over, working together, to solve them.

The Large Hadron Collider is the biggest machine ever built. It contains the world's largest magnet weighing more than the Eiffel Tower. Over 1800 physicists from 85 countries work on the project. Every second their work produces 40 million megabytes of information.

You can join in the 'Hunt for Higgs' online at: www.sciencemuseum. org.uk/antenna/bigbang/ huntforhiggs/index.asp

There are 100 billion suns in our galaxy, 100 billion galaxies – just within range of our telescopes! To travel even this far – and at the speed of light – would take you six billion years. And yet one second before the Big Bang, all this, and more, took up less space than a single atom.

All the ingredients of plants, planets, stars, galaxies and your body were created within minutes of the Big Bang.

This may not be the first – or last – Universe. Still expanding outwards from the Bang, this one may slow down, stop and collapse inwards, triggering another Big Bang, another universe … over and over, for ever.

Index